1 MONTH OF
FREE
READING

at
www.ForgottenBooks.com

By purchasing this book you are eligible for one month membership to ForgottenBooks.com, giving you unlimited access to our entire collection of over 1,000,000 titles via our web site and mobile apps.

To claim your free month visit:
www.forgottenbooks.com/free100004

ISBN 978-1-5281-7384-1
PIBN 10100004

AN

ABRIDGMENT

OF THE

LAW OF NISI PRIUS.

VOL. II.

18. EJECTMENT.
19. EXECUTORS AND ADMINIS-
    TRATORS.
20. FACTOR.
21. FISHERY.
22. FRAUDS, STATUTE OF.
23. GAME.
24. IMPRISONMENT.
25. INSURANCE.
26. LIBEL.
27. MALICIOUS PROSECUTION.
28. MANDAMUS.
29. MASTER AND SERVANT.

30. NUSANCE.
31. PARTNERS.
32. QUO WARRANTO.
33. REPLEVIN.
34. RESCOUS.
35. SHIPPING.
36. SLANDER.
37. STOPPAGE IN TRANSITU.
38. TITHES.
39. TRESPASS.
40. TROVER.
41. USE AND OCCUPATION.
42. WAGER.

◆

BY WILLIAM SELWYN, Esq.

OF LINCOLN'S INN, ONE OF HER MAJESTY'S COUNSEL,
LATE RECORDER OF PORTSMOUTH.

◆

Quilibet scriptor adeo anxiè sit solicitus, ut ad veritatem dicat, perinde ac si totius
operis fides uniuscujusque periodi fide niteretur.   PRÆF. 6 REP.

Tenth Edition,
WITH ALTERATIONS AND ADDITIONS.

LONDON:

V. AND R. STEVENS AND G. S. NORTON,

(*Successors to the late J. & W. T. CLARKE, of Portugal Street,*)
Law Booksellers and Publishers,
26 AND 39, BELL YARD, LINCOLN'S INN.

MDCCCXLII.

LONDON:
WILLIAM STEVENS, PRINTER, BELL YARD,
TEMPLE BAR.

CONTENTS OF VOL. II.

—◆—

CHAPTER XVIII.

EJECTMENT.

		PAGE
I.	Of the Nature of the Action of Ejectment	684
II.	By whom an Ejectment may be brought	689
III.	For what Things an Ejectment will lie	694
IV.	In what Cases previous Steps must be taken before Ejectment brought	696
V.	In what Cases a Notice to Quit must be given before Ejectment brought, 698. Requisites of Notice, 701. Waiver of Notice, 705. Where Notice is not required, 710. Stat. 1 Geo. IV. c. 87, for Recovery of Lands unlawfully held over	712
VI.	Of the Mode of proceeding in Ejectment, and herein of the Declaration	714
VII.	Of the Service of Declaration	718
VIII.	Of the subsequent Proceedings, Judgment against casual Ejector, 720. Appearance of Defendant, 721. Consent Rule, 721. Stat. 11 Geo. II. c. 19, s. 13, enabling Landlord to defend	722
IX.	Of the Proceedings in Ejectment, directed by Stat. 4 Geo. II. c. 28, s. 2, in order to obviate the Difficulties attending Re-entries at Common Law, for Non-payment of Rent Arrear, 723. Of the Proceedings where the Possession is vacant	725
X.	Of the Pleadings and Defence, 728. Entry barred by Fine and Non-claim, 728. Entry barred by Statute of Limitations, 21 Jac. I. c. 16; 3 & 4 Will. IV. c. 27	732
XI.	Evidence	743
XII.	Verdict, 759. Judgment, 760. Execution, 761. Costs	762

		PAGE
XIII.	Writ of Error	763
XIV.	In what Cases a Court of Equity will restrain the Party from bringing further Ejectments, by granting a perpetual Injunction	763
XV.	Of the Action of Trespass for Mesne Profits .	765

CHAPTER XIX.

EXECUTORS AND ADMINISTRATORS.

I.	Of Bona Notabilia	769
II.	Of the Nature of the Interest of an Executor or Administrator in the Estate of the Deceased, 774. In what Cases it is transmissible, 777; and where an Administration de bonis non is necessary . . .	778
III.	Of limited or temporary Administrations	779
IV.	Of an Executor de son Tort . . .	781
V.	Of the Disposition of the Estate of the Deceased, and of the Order in which such Disposition ought to be made .	784
VI.	Admission of Assets . . .	788
VII.	Of Actions by Executors and Administrators .	791
VIII.	Of Actions against Executors and Administrators .	796
IX.	Of the Pleadings, 801; and herein of the Right of Retainer, 805. Evidence, 806. Judgment, 808. Costs .	808

CHAPTER XX.

FACTOR.

Of the Nature of the Employment of a Factor, 810. Power and Authority, 811. Lien, 817. Liability of Principal, 820. Stat. 4 Geo. IV. c. 83; 6 Geo. IV. c. 94, 820. Evidence 825

CHAPTER XXI.

FISHERY.

I.	Of the Right of Fishery in the Sea, and in the Creeks and Arms thereof, and in fresh Rivers . .	827
II.	Of the different Kinds of Fishery, 829. Several Fishery, 829. Free Fishery, 830. Common of Fishery .	832

CONTENTS.

CHAPTER XXII.

FRAUDS, STATUTE OF.

Statute 29 Car. II. c. 3, entitled " An Act for Prevention of Frauds and Perjuries."

PAGE

I. Introduction. The first, second, and third Sections, relating to Parol Demises, Assignments, and Surrenders . 833

II. The fourth and seventeenth Sections, relating to Agreements, 838. On the Effect of Parol Evidence of a Variation or Waiver of a written Agreement . . 867

III. The fifth and sixth Sections, relating to the Execution and Revocation of Wills, 870; and Stat. 7 Will. IV. & 1 Vict. 26, for the Amendment of the Laws with respect to Wills 889

CHAPTER XXIII.

GAME.

I. Of the Right of taking and destroying the Game at Common Law, and of the Stat. 1 & 2 Will. IV. c. 32 . 895

II. Of the Appointment and Authority of Gamekeepers . 902

III. Of the Destruction of the Game at improper Seasons of the Year 904

IV. Of the Duties made payable in respect of Game Certificates . . . . . *ib.*

CHAPTER XXIV.

IMPRISONMENT.

I. Of the Nature of the Action for False Imprisonment, and in what Cases it may maintained . . 907

II. Statutes relating to the Action for False Imprisonment, 21 Jac. I. c. 12, 913; 24 Geo. II. c. 44 . . 914

III. Of the Pleadings . . . 920

CHAPTER XXV.

INSURANCE.

		PAGE
I.	Of Insurance in general	929
II.	Of Marine Insurance, 930. The Policy, 930. Different Kinds, 931. Requisites, 932. Rule of Construction	947
III.	What Persons may be insured, 948. Who may be Insurers, 948. What may be insured	950
IV.	Of Losses—	
	1. By Perils of the Sea	953
	2. By Capture	955
	3. By Arrests, &c.	957
	4. By Barratry	959
	5. By Fire	963
	6. By other Losses	ib.
V.	Of total Losses and of Abandonment	965
VI.	Of partial Losses	976
VII.	Of Adjustment	979
VIII.	Of the Remedy by Action for Breach of the Contract of Insurance, and herein of the Declaration, 980. Pleadings, 983. Consolidation Rule	984
IX.	Of the several Grounds of Defence on which the Insurer may insist—	
	1. Alien Enemy	985
	2. Illegal Voyage or Illegal Commerce	ib.
	3. Misrepresentation—Concealment—Suppression	989
	4. Breach of Warranty	994
	Express 1. Time of Sailing	ib.
	Express 2. Safety of Ship at a Particular Time	996
	Express 3. To depart with Convoy	997
	Express 4. Neutral Property	999
	Implied 1. Not to deviate	1004
	Implied 2. Seaworthiness	1010
	5. Re-assurance	1013
	6. Wager Policy	ib.
X.	Evidence, 1016. Damages	1022
XI.	Premium, Return of	ib.
XII.	Of Bottomry and Respondentia	1028
XIII.	Insurance upon Lives	1030
XIV.	Insurance against Fire	1033

CHAPTER XXVI.

LIBEL.

PAGE

I. Of the Nature of a Libel, and in what Cases an Action may
be maintained for this Injury . . . 1038
II. Of the Declaration and Pleadings . 1043
III. Of the Evidence . . . 1046

CHAPTER XXVII.

MALICIOUS PROSECUTION.

I. Of the Action on the Case for a Malicious Prosecution, and
in what Cases such Action may be maintained . 1054
II. Of the Declaration, 1062. Defence, 1063. Evidence . 1064

CHAPTER XXVIII.

MANDAMUS.

I. Nature of the Writ of Mandamus, 1069. Mandamus to re-
store or admit Persons to Corporate Offices . . 1070
II. In what other Cases the Court will grant a Mandamus . 1075
III. Where not 1078
IV. Form of the Writ . 1081
V. Of the Return 1083
VI. Of the Remedy where the Party to whom the Writ of Man-
damus is directed does not make any Return, or where
he makes an insufficient or false Return . 1086

CHAPTER XXIX.

MASTER AND SERVANT.

I. Of Actions by Servants against their Masters for the Recovery of their Wages 1091
II. Of the Liability of the Master in respect of Contracts made by
the Servant 1094
III. Of the Liability of the Master in respect of a tortious Act
done by the Servant 1097

PAGE

IV. Of Actions brought by Masters for enticing away Apprentices and Servants, and for Injuries done to their Servants, 1102; and herein of the Action for Seduction, 1103. Witness, 1104. Damages . . . 1106

CHAPTER XXX.

NUSANCE.

I. In what Cases an Action for a Nusance may be maintained, 1108; and herein of the Right to Use of Light, 1109; Water, 1110; Way, 1112; and Pew . . 1113

II. By whom and against whom an Action for a Nusance may be maintained . . . 1117

III. Pleadings .. . 1119

IV. Evidence, &c. 1120

V. Costs . . 1121

CHAPTER XXXI.

PARTNERS.

I. What is necessary to constitute a Partnership 1122

II. How far the Acts of one Partner are binding on his Co-partners 1128

III. Of Actions by and against Partners, 1134. What Remedy one Partner has against another . . 1137

IV. Evidence 1140

CHAPTER XXXII.

QUO WARRANTO.

I. Of the Origin and Nature of Quo Warranto Informations, and Statutes relating thereto, viz. Stat. 4 & 5 Will. & Ma. c. 18, and 9 Ann. c. 20, 1143. Proceedings against the City of London, in the Time of Charles the 2nd . 1148

II. In what Cases the Court will grant an Information in Nature of Quo Warranto . . . 1149

III. Of the Limitation of Time for granting an Information . 1155

IV. Of the Construction of Charters, and of the Operation and Effect of a new Charter . . . . ib.

PAGE

V. Bye-Laws 1158
VI. Of the Inspection of the Records of the Corporation . 1163
VII. Of the Pleadings . . . . . . *ib.*
VIII. Evidence . 1165
IX. Judgment . . 1168

CHAPTER XXXIII.

REPLEVIN.

I. In what Cases a Replevin may be maintained . 1172
II. Of the Proceedings in Replevin at Common Law, and the
Alterations made therein by Statute . . 1174
III. Of the Duty of the Sheriff in the Execution of the Replevin,
1176. Of the Pledges, 1176. Bond from the Party
replevying, 1176. Sureties under the Stat. 11 Geo. II.
c. 19, s. 23 1177
IV. Of Claiming Property, and of the Writ de Proprietate pro-
bandâ 1182
V. Of the Process for removing the Cause out of the Inferior
Court, 1183; and herein of the Writs of Pone, Recordari
facias loquelam, and Accedas ad Curiam . 1183, 4
VI. By whom a Replevin may be maintained . . 1185
VII. Of the Declaration 1186
VIII. Of the Pleadings :
  1. Of Pleas in Abatement; and herein of the Plea
     of Cepit in alio loco . . . 1188
  2. General Issue . . . 1190
  3. Of the Avowry and Cognizance :
     1. General Rules, &c. relating to the Avowry,
        and herein of the New Rules . 1190
     2. Of the Avowry for Damage feasant, 1192.
        Pleas in Bar, 1193. Escape through
        Defect of Fences, 1193. Right of Com-
        mon, 1194. Tender of Amends . 1196
     3. Of the Avowry for Rent Arrear, 1197.
        Pleas in Bar, 1198. Eviction, 1198.
        Non dimisit, Non tenuit, 1199. Riens
        in Arrear, 1200. Tender of Arrears . 1201
  4. Property . . . . *ib.*

CONTENTS.

PAGE

5. Statutes:
    1. Of Limitations 1201
    2. Of Set-off 1202
IX. Of the Judgment:
    1. For the Plaintiff 1203
    2. For the Defendant . . . . ib.
X. Of the Costs, and herein of the Costs in Error . 1207

CHAPTER XXXIV.

RESCOUS.

Rescous 1209

CHAPTER XXXV.

SHIPPING.

I. Of the Ship Registry Statute, 3 & 4 Will. IV. c. 55 . 1213
II. Of Seamen's Wages, and the Statutes relating thereto,
    viz. 5 & 6 Will. IV. c. 19, 1231 ; 8 Geo. I. c. 24 . 1234
III. Of the Liability of Ship-owners for the Repairs, &c. , 1239

CHAPTER XXXVI.

SLANDER.

I. Scandalum Magnatum 1241
II. Of the Action for Slander; and in what Cases it may be main-
    tained 1243
III. Of the Declaration, and herein of the Nature and Office of
    the Innuendo 1250
IV. Of the Pleadings, 1254. Evidence, 1256. Costs . 1258

CHAPTER XXXVII.

STOPPAGE IN TRANSITU.

Nature of this Right, 1260. Who shall be considered as capable
    of exercising it, 1261. Where the Transitus may be
    said to be continuing, 1263. Where determined, 1272.
    How far the Negociation of the Bill of Lading may tend
    to defeat the Right 1278

CHAPTER XXXVIII.

TITHES.

PAGE

I. Definition, 1281. Of the Remedies in the Common Law Courts for the Recovery of Tithes or the Value thereof . 1282

II. Debt on Stat. 2 & 3 Edw. VI. c. 13, for not setting out Tithes, 1284. Of the Provisions of the Statute, and the Construction thereof, 1284. Of the Persons to whom Tithes are due, 1300. Of the Persons by whom and against whom an Action on the Statute may be brought, 1301. Of the Declaration, 1302. Pleadings, and herein of the Statutes of Limitation, 1303. Evidence, 1304. Verdict, 1307. Costs, 1308. Judgment . . 1308

III. Of the Stat. 6 & 7 Will. IV. c. 71, for the Commutation of Tithes in England and Wales, amended by Stat. 7 Will. IV. & 1 Vict. c. 69, 1309; Stat. 1 & 2 Vict. c. 64, for facilitating Merger of Tithes ; Stat. 2 & 3 Vict. c. 62, for explaining the Acts for the Commutation of Tithes 1311

CHAPTER XXXIX.

TRESPASS.

I. In what Cases an Action of Trespass may be maintained . 1312
II. Where Trespass cannot be maintained . . 1318
III. Of the Declaration . . . 1321
IV. Of the Pleadings, and herein of the New Rules . 1325
    1. Of the Plea of Not Guilty . . . ib.
    2. Accord and Satisfaction . 1326
    3. Liberum Tenementum . . 1327
    4. Estoppel . . 1328
    5. License . . 1329
    6. Process . 1332
    7. Right of Common . 1333
    8. Right of Way . 1334
    9. Tender of Amends . 1340
V. Evidence . . ib.
VI. Damages, 1342. Costs . . 1342

CHAPTER XL.

TROVER.

PAGE

I. Of the Nature and Foundation of the Action of Trover, and
   in what Cases such Action may be maintained   .   1343
II. By whom and against whom Trover may be maintained   . 1364
III. The Declaration, 1366.   Plea, and herein of the New Rules,
   1368.   Defence, and herein of the Doctrine of Liens,
   1370.   Evidence, 1378.   Of staying the Proceedings,
   1383.   Damages, 1383.   Costs, 1384.   Judgment   . 1384

CHAPTER XLI.

USE AND OCCUPATION.

Use and Occupation   . 1385

CHAPTER XLII.

WAGER.

I. Introduction, 1398.   Of Legal Wagers, 1398.   Form of
   Action   1400
II. Of Illegal Wagers   ,   ib.

INDEX TO PRINCIPAL MATTERS   .   1407

AN ABRIDGMENT

OF

THE LAW OF NISI PRIUS.

CHAPTER XVIII.

EJECTMENT.

I. *Of the Nature of the Action of Ejectment, p.* 684.

II. *By whom an Ejectment may be brought, p.* 689.

III. *For what Things an Ejectment will lie, p.* 694.

IV. *In what Cases previous Steps must be taken, before Eject-ment brought, p.* 696.

V. *In what Cases a Notice to Quit must be given before Eject-ment brought, p.* 698 ; *Requisites of Notice, p.* 701 ; *Waiver of Notice, p.* 705 ; *Where Notice is not required, p.* 710 ; *Stat.* 1 *Geo. IV. c.* 87, *for Recovery of Lands, &c. unlawfully held over, p.* 712.

VI. *Of the Mode of Proceeding in Ejectment, and herein of the Declaration, p.* 714.

VII. *Of the Service of Declaration, p.* 718.

VIII. *Of the Subsequent Proceedings, Judgment against Casual Ejector, p.* 720 ; *Appearance of Defendant, p.* 721 ; *Consent Rule, p.* 721 ; *Stat.* 11 *Geo. II. c.* 19, *s.* 13, *enabling Landlord to defend, p.* 722.

IX. *Of the Proceedings in Ejectment, directed by Stat.* 4 *Geo. II. c.* 28, *s.* 2, *in order to obviate the Difficulties attend-ing Re-entries at Common Law, for Non-Payment of Rent Arrear, p.* 723 ; *Of the Proceedings where the Pos-session is vacant, p.* 725.

X. *Of the Pleadings and Defence,* p. 728 ; *Entry barred by Fine and Non-claim,* p. 728 ; *Entry barred by Statute of Limitations,* 21 Jac. I. c. 16, 3 & 4 Will. IV. c. 27, p. 732.

XI. *Evidence,* p. 743.

XII. *Verdict,* p. 759 ; *Judgment,* p. 760 ; *Execution,* p. 761 ; *Costs,* p. 762.

XIII. *Writ of Error,* p. 763.

XIV. *In what Cases a Court of Equity will restrain the Party from bringing further Ejectments, by granting a perpetual Injunction,* p. 763.

XV. *Of the Action of Trespass for Mesne Profits,* p. 765.

I. *Of the Nature of the Action of Ejectment.*

AN ejectment is a possessory action, wherein the title to lands and tenements may be tried, and the possession recovered in all cases where the party claiming title has a right of entry ; whether such title be to an estate in fee, fee tail, for life, or for years. From this description it should seem, that, in strictness, this action could be maintained for the recovery of that species of property only, whereon an entry can be made. But it will be found that, in a few instances, which will be more particularly mentioned hereafter, this action has been extended beyond these limits. After the disuse of real actions (1), questions of title to land were usually tried in actions of replevin or trespass *quare clausum fregit ;* and this practice continued, until the method of trying titles by the action of *ejectio firmæ,* was introduced (2). But in the *ejectio firmæ,* damages only could be recovered until some time between the 6th Ric. II. and 7th Edw. IV. ; about which time it appears, from the Year-book of 7 Edw. IV. fol. 6, that it had been resolved by the judges, that the term, as well as damages, might be recovered (3). The action

---

(1) By stat. 3 & 4 Will. IV. c. 27, s. 36, all real and mixed actions, (except a writ of right of dower, or writ of dower *unde nil habet,* or a *quare impedit,* or an ejectment,) and plaints in the nature of any such writ or action, (except a plaint for free-bench or dower,) were abolished after the 31st December, 1834.

(2) In the conclusion of *Alden's* case, 43 Eliz., 5 Rep. 105, b., Sir E. Coke has remarked, that titles of land were *at that day* for the most part tried in actions of *ejectio firmæ.*

(3) " Until the end of Edw. IV. the possession was not recovered in an *ejectio firmæ,* but *only damages.*" Hale's H. C. L. by Runnington, Serjt.

of ejectment now in use is formed on the plan of the *ejectio firmæ*, in its improved state, after it had been decided that the term might be recovered. In the action of ejectment, as was before observed, not only the title to the lands in question may be tried, but the possession also may be recovered, which circumstance renders it the most eligible mode of proceeding; inasmuch as in trespass, although the right may be ascertained, damages alone can be recovered. In the action of ejectment, indeed, the damages which are given are merely nominal; but the law has provided another remedy for the injury sustained by the party claiming title, in being kept out of possession from the time when his title accrued, to the time of recovering possession in the ejectment, *viz.* by an action of trespass for mesne profits; for a further account of which, see *post*, Sect. XV.

Of the Requisites to support an Ejectment.—In order to maintain ejectment, the party at whose suit it is brought, must have been in possession, or at least clothed with the right of possession, at the time of the actual or supposed ouster (a). Hence, this action is termed a possessory action. The party who has the legal estate in the lands in question, must prevail: hence, a party who claims under an elegit (b), subsequent to a lease granted to a tenant in possession, cannot recover: although he give notice to the tenant, that he does not intend to disturb the possession, and only means to get into the receipt of the rents and profits of the estate. In the case of *Lade* v. *Holford*, Bull. N. P. 110, Lord *Mansfield*, C. J., declared, " that he and many of the judges had resolved never to suffer a plaintiff, in ejectment, to be nonsuited by a term standing out in his own trustee, or a satisfied term set up by a mortgagor against a mortgagee; but that they would direct the jury to presume it surrendered." From this doctrine a conclusion has been drawn, which the case by no means warrants, *viz.* that a plaintiff in ejectment may recover on an equitable title.—The true meaning of the resolution delivered by Lord *Mansfield* is, that where trustees ought to convey to the beneficial owner, it shall be left to the jury to presume that they have conveyed accordingly: or where the beneficial occupation of an estate by the possessor (c), (under an equitable title,) induces a probability that there has been a conveyance of the legal estate to the person who is equitably entitled to it, a jury may be directed to presume a conveyance of the legal estate. An estate was devised to trustees in trust for I. S., an

(a) Keilw. 130, a.
(b) *Doe d. Da Costa* v. *Wharton*, 8 T. R. 2.
(c) Per *Kenyon*, C. J., 7 T. R. 3, and 8 T. R. 122.

---

ed. 1820, p. 201. See further, on this subject, a very learned and elaborate note by the reporters in *Doe d. Poole* v. *Errington*, 1 Ad. & Ell. 756, n. I am not aware of any judgment for the recovery of the term prior to that in East. T. 14 Hen. VII. Rot. 303, a copy of the record of which will be found in Rastal's Entries, fol. 252, b., 253, a., ed. 1670.

infant, with directions to convey the same to him on his attaining twenty-one (*d*). In an action of ejectment, brought four years after I. S. attained twenty-one, it was holden, that a jury might be directed to presume a conveyance to I. S. in pursuance of the trust. In these cases, when a conveyance is presumed, there is an end of the legal estate, created by the term. But where the facts of the case preclude such presumption, or if there are not any premises (*e*), from which a surrender of the term can be presumed (4); or, if it appear in a special verdict (*f*), or special case (*g*), that the legal estate is outstanding in another person, the party who is not clothed with the legal estate cannot prevail in a court of law (5). In 1772, a term of 1000 years was created by deed for the purpose of securing a sum of 5000*l*.; and in 1787, the principal and interest having been paid, the residue of the term was assigned in trust for the devisees of the person who created the term. In 1789, the premises were conveyed to a purchaser by deed, and the residue of the term was assigned in trust for the purchaser, her heirs, and assigns, or as she should appoint, and in the meantime *to attend the inheritance*. The purchaser entered into the possession of the premises, and continued so possessed till her death. In 1808, she executed a marriage settlement, reserving to herself a power of appointment by deed or will, and after the marriage, she, in 1815, devised all her real estate. Neither in the marriage settlement, nor in the will, was any mention made of the term of 1000 years. She and her husband having both died, it was holden (*h*), on ejectment brought by her heir at law, that there was no ground whatever for presuming that this term, *which was assigned to attend the inheritance*, was ever surrendered (6). It

(*d*) *England d. Syburn* v. *Slade*, 4 T. R. 682.

(*e*) *Doe d. Blacknell* v. *Plowman*, 2 B. & Ad. 573.

(*f*) *Goodtitle d. Jones* v. *Jones*, 7 T. R. 49.

(*g*) *Roe d. Reade* v. *Reade*, 8 T. R. 122.

(*h*) *Doe d. Blacknell* v. *Plowman*, 2 B. & Ad. 573.

(4) " Upon principle, a term of years assigned to attend the inheritance, ought not to be presumed to be surrendered, unless there has been an enjoyment *inconsistent with the existence of the term, or some act done in order to disavow the tenure under the termor, and to bar it as a continuing interest*." 3 Sugden, V. & P. 28, 10th edition.

(5) " As to the doctrine, that the legal estate cannot be set up at law by a trustee against his *cestui que* trust, that has been long repudiated." Per *Ellenborough*, C. J., in *Doe d. Shewen* v. *Wroot*, E. 44 Geo. III. B. R., 5 East, 138. See further on this point *Lessee of Massey* v. *Touchstone*, reported in a note to *Shannon* v. *Bradstreet*, 1 Sch. & Lefr. p. 67.

(6) In this case, the Court of K. B. denied the authority of the cases of *Doe d. Burdett* v. *Wrighte*, 2 B. & A. 710, and *Doe d. Putland* v. *Hilder*, 2 B. & A. 782, which went to establish the presumption of the surrender of a satisfied term, on the mere ground that the term had been left undisturbed for a long period. In *Doe d. Putland* v. *Hilder*, a

will be observed also, that in the foregoing cases, in which a surrender was presumed, the presumption was made in favour of the party who had proved a right to the beneficial ownership; the possession was consistent with the existence of the surrender required to be presumed, and made it not unreasonable to believe that the surrender should have been made in fact. But where the court were called upon to declare that the presumption ought to have been made in favour of a person who had proved no right to the possession, no title, no conveyance, and one who stood on mere naked possession, without any evidence how or when he acquired it, and who laid before the jury only a partial statement of the ground of presumption, the court refused (i) to make it.

A. devised an estate to trustees for a term of years, in trust to pay annuities, and for other purposes mentioned in the will, with remainder to B.; B., eighteen years after the death of A., leased the premises for lives. In an action by the lessee of B., the jury were told by the judge that they could not presume a surrender of the term; and upon motion this direction was holden to be right (k).

The plaintiff in ejectment must recover on the strength of his own title, and not on the weakness of that of the defendant (l). Possession gives the defendant a right against every person who cannot show a good title (m). But a lessee will not be permitted to defend an ejectment against his own landlord, from whom he has received possession, on a supposed defect in the title of the landlord (n); nor if B., claiming under A., let lands for a year and die, and A., after the expiration of the term brings an ejectment

(i) *Doe d. Hammond* v. *Cooke*, 6 Bingh. 174.

(k) *Day* v. *Williams*, 2 Cr. & J. 460.

(l) Per *Lee*, C. J., delivering the opinion of the court, in *Martin* v. *Strachan*, 5 T. R. 110, n.

(m) Per Lord *Mansfield*, C. J., 4 Burr. 2487.

(n) See *Driver d. Oxendon* v. *Laurence*, 2 Bl. R. 1259.

---

term of years was created in 1762, and assigned over to a trustee, in 1779, *to attend the inheritance.* In 1814, the owner of the inheritance executed a marriage settlement; and in 1816, conveyed his life interest in the estate to a purchaser, as a security for a debt; but no assignment of the term, or delivery of the deeds relating to it, took place on either occasion. In 1819, an actual assignment of the term was made by an administrator of the trustee in 1779, to a new trustee, for the purchaser in 1816. It was holden, that under these circumstances, on an ejectment brought by a prior incumbrancer against the purchaser, the jury were warranted in presuming that the term had been surrendered previously to 1819. This decision*, (which was called in question by Lord *Eldon*, C., and by *Richards*, C. B., and *Graham*, B.,) may now be considered as overruled.

* See *Aspinall* v. *Kempson*, 3 Sug. V. & P. 65, 10th edition; *Doe* v *Putland, ib.* 59. Matthews on the Doctrine of Presumption, 226.

against C., can C. dispute (o) the title of A.; nor where tenant in possession has paid the rent to the lessor of plaintiff, can a third person come in and defend as landlord without the tenant, and dispute the lessor of plaintiff's title (p). " Neither the tenant, nor any one claiming by him, can controvert the landlord's title. He cannot put another person in possession, but must deliver up the premises to his own landlord (q)." There is not any distinction between the case of a tenant and that of a common licensee. The licensee, by asking permission, admits that there is a title in the landlord. Hence, where the lessor of the plaintiff being in possession of a house, &c., defendant asked leave to get vegetables in the garden, and having obtained the keys for this purpose, fraudulently took possession of the house and set up a claim of title : it was holden (r), that defendant having entered by leave of the party in possession, she could not defend an ejectment, but was bound to deliver up possession to the party by whom she was let in, for she could not contest the title.

' Where a copyholder (s) has been admitted to a tenement and done fealty to the lord of a manor, he is estopped, in an action by the lord for a forfeiture, from showing that the legal estate was not in the lord at the time of admittance. In a case, however, where the lessor of the plaintiff holding an estate under a lease for twenty-one years (t), underlet the same to the defendant for a year, and the defendant held over after the expiration of the twenty-one years, after which the lessor of the plaintiff gave the defendant a regular notice to quit, which not being complied with, an ejectment was brought; it was holden, that it was competent to the defendant to show, that the lessor's title had expired, and that he had no right to turn him out of possession. So where the tenant has not received possession from a person, to whom, however, under a misrepresentation or by mistake, he has paid rent, such payment of rent will not estop the tenant from setting up the title of the real owner (u). M., being seized in fee of land, mortgaged to O., but remained in possession, and afterwards demised part for a term to B., who also entered; after which, M. mortgaged to H. H., after this, received rent from B., and demised the other part to A. Afterwards B. and A., on notice from O., paid O. rent. H. then

(o) *Barwick* v. *Thompson*, 7 T. R. 488.

(p) *Doe d. Knight* v. *Smythe*, 4 M. & S. 347, recognized in *Doe d. Bullen* v. *Mills*, 2 Ad. & Ell. 17. See *infra*, *Balls* v. *Westwood*, 2 Campb. 11.

(q) Per *Dampier*, J., *S. C.*, 4 M. & S. 348, 9, cited by *Parke*, J., *Doe d. Manton* v. *Austin*, 9 Bingh. 45, 6. See also *Cooper* v. *Blandy*, 1 Bingh. N. C. 45. But see a distinction in *Hopcraft* v. *Keys*, 9 Bingh. 613.

(r) *Doe d. Johnson* v. *Baytup*, 3 Ad.

& Ell. 188.

(s) *Doe on the demise of Sir E. Nepean* v. *Budden*, 5 B. & A. 626.

(t) *England d. Syburn* v. *Slade*, 4 T. R. 682; *Doe* v. *Ramsbottom*, 3 M. & S. 516, S. P.; *Doe d. Lowden* v. *Watson*, 2 Stark. N. P. C. 230, S. P. See *Gravenor* v. *Woodhouse*, 1 Bingh. 38; *Cornish* v. *Searell*, 8 B. & C. 471; *Brook* v. *Biggs*, 2 Bingh. N. C. 572.

(u) *Fenner* v. *Duplock*, 2 Bingh. 10.

brought ejectment (after notice to quit) against B. and A. It was holden (*x*), that B. as well as A. might show in defence the prior mortgage to O., O.'s notice to them, and their payment of rent to O.; for, although B. could not dispute M.'s title at the time of the demise, yet he might show that H. had not any derivative title from M., and he was not precluded by having paid rent to H., under a mistake of the facts.

Premises being in possession of a tenant under an indenture of lease, a party claiming them by an alleged title adverse to that of the lessor, and prior to the lease, demanded them of the lessee, and ultimately obtained possession by paying him 20*l.* The landlord afterwards brought ejectment against the party so in possession, the term having been forfeited by non-payment of rent, and there being no sufficient distress on the premises. It was holden, that this case fell within the rule whereby the tenant is precluded from contesting his landlord's title. *Doe d. Bullen* v. *Mills*, 2 Ad. & Ell. 17.

II. *By whom an Ejectment may be brought.*

An ejectment may be brought by the following persons:

1. Bargainee, under a commission of bankrupt, 1 Wils. 276.
2. Conusee of a statute merchant or staple.
3. Copyholders (7), Moor, 569; 1 Leon. 4; Cro. Eliz. 535; 4 Rep.

(*x*) *Doe d. Higginbotham* v. *Barton*, 11 A. & E. 307; 3 P. & D. 194.

---

(7) If a copyholder, without license, makes a lease for one year, or, with license, makes a lease for many years, and the lessee be ejected, he shall not sue in the lord's court by plaint, but shall have an *ejectio firmæ* at the common law; because he has not a customary estate by copy, but a warrantable estate by the rules of the common law. Co. Cop. s. 51. A lessee for years of a copyholder may maintain ejectment, though there be no custom in the manor to lease, and no license has been obtained, such lease being void only as against the lord. *Doe d. Tressidder* v. *Tressidder*, 1 G. & D. 70. If the copyholders of a manor belonging to a bishoprick, during the vacancy of the see, commit a forfeiture by cutting timber, the succeeding bishop may bring ejectment. *Read* v. *Allen*, Oxford Circuit, 1730, per *Comyns*, Bull. N. P. 107. The lord may seize copyhold land *quousque*, in virtue of a right which accrued to the preceding lord, on default of the heir coming in to be admitted; and that, although he be the devisee, and not the heir of the preceding lord; but, to entitle the lord to make such seizure, there must be three proclamations made, at three consecutive courts. *Doe d. Bover* v. *Trueman*, 1 B. & Ad. 736. An heir to whom a copyhold descends, may surrender before admittance, because he is in by course of law, and the custom, which makes him heir to the estate, casts the possession upon him from his ancestor; consequently such heir may maintain

26, a; Cro. Jac. 31; Yelv. 144; 1 T. R. 600. A copyholder cannot make a lease for more than one year without a license, or by special custom, without incurring a forfeiture of his estate: but a lease for one year is good without either, and a copyholder may maintain an ejectment upon it. *Frosel* v. *Welsh*, Cro. Jac. 403; *Erish* v. *Rives*, Cro. Eliz. 717.

---

ejectment before admittance [*]. So the *grantee* of a copyhold in *reversion* has a good and perfect title by the grant, without admittance, and may maintain ejectment on the death of the tenant for life. *Roe* v. *Loveless*, 2 B. & A. 453. But a stranger, to whom a copyhold is *surrendered*, has nothing before admittance, because he is a purchaser. Until the admittance of surrenderee, the copyhold remains in the surrenderor, and if he die, his heir may bring ejectment. *Wilson* v. *Weddell*, Yelv. 144. But after admittance, surrenderee may maintain ejectment against surrenderor, and lay his demise on a day between the times of surrender and admittance. *Holdfast* v. *Clapham*, 1 T. R. 600. Admittance of tenant for life is admittance of him in remainder, without any other admittance. *Auncelme* v. *Auncelme*, Cro. Jac. 31; *Warsopp* v. *Abell*, 5 Mod. 307. But if a copyhold be surrendered to one for life, remainder to another in fee, if the lord is to have a fine from the remainder-man there is occasion for a new admittance. *Gipping* v. *Bunning*, Moor, 465. And a custom that the remainder-man coming into possession on the death of tenant for life shall be admitted and pay a fine, is a good custom. *Doe d. Whitbread* v. *Jenny*, 5 East, 522. An heir at law may devise his copyhold estate, without having been admitted, and without previous payment of the lord's fine. *Wright* v. *Banks*, 3 B. & Ad. 664. The devisee of a copyhold or customary estate, which had been surrendered to the use of the will, having died before admittance, it was holden, that her devisee, though afterwards admitted, could not recover in ejectment; for the admittance of the second devisee had no relation to the last legal surrender, and the legal title remained in the heir of the surrenderor. *Doe d. Vernon* v. *Vernon*, 9 East, 8, cited per *Cur.*, *Doe d. Winder* v. *Lawes*, 7 A. & E. 213. But see now 7 Will. IV. & 1 Vict. c. 26, s. 3. A copyhold tenant surrendered his estate to the use of another, and afterwards committed and was convicted of felony before admittance of the surrenderee: it was holden, that the estate was by the custom forfeited to the lord. *Rex* v. *Lady St. John Mildmay*, 5 B. & Ad. 254. Where a copyholder was convicted of a capital felony, but pardoned, upon condition of remaining two years in prison, and the lord did not do any act towards seizing the copyhold; it was holden, that at the expiration of the two years, the copyholder might maintain ejectment against one who had ousted him; inasmuch as the pardon, by virtue of stat. 6 Geo. IV. c. 25, s. 7, restored him to his competency, and the estate would not vest in the lord without any act done by him. *Doe d. Evans* v. *Evans*, 5 B. & C. 584. Copyholds are within the statute against fraudulent conveyances, 27 Eliz. c. 4. *Doe d. Tunstall* v. *Bottriell*, 5 B. & Ad. 131, overruling the dictum of *Blencowe*, J., in Bull. N. P. 108.

[*] Adm. per *Cur.* in *Roe d. Jeffereys* v. *Hicks*, 2 Wils. 15, and per *Kenyon*, C. J., in *Doe* v. *Hellier*, 3 T. R. 169, S. P.

4. Corporation aggregate, Carth. 390 ; 12 Mod. 113, or sole.

5. Devisee, 1 Inst. 240, b.

6. Grantee of rent-charge, with a power to retain until satisfaction, 1 Saund. 112.

7. Guardian in socage (8). ·

8. Infant, per *Mallet*, J., March, 143.

9. Legatee of a chattel real may maintain ejectment against executor (*y*) or a stranger (*z*) ; but the assent of the executor to the bequest must be proved.

10. Mortgagee, Doug. 21 ; Salk. 245 ; Str. 413 (9).

(*y*) *Doe* v. *Guy*, 3 East, 120.   (*z*) 1 Str. 70.

---

(8) Guardian in socage may make a lease for years, and his lessee may have an *ejectio firmæ*, per three justices, Cro. Jac. 99; Adm. Hutt. 16, 17.   Guardian in socage may make a lease of the infant's estate until his age of fourteen years, and upon such lease the lessee may maintain an ejectment.   2 Roll. Abr. 41, (Q) pl. 4.   Guardian in socage may bring trespass or ejectment in his own name, or make a lease of the land in his own name, until the infant arrive at the age of fourteen.   Per *Cur.*, Lord Raym. 131.   Guardian appointed by deed, or will in writing, attested by two witnesses under the stat. 12 Car. II. c. 24, ss. 8 and 9, has the same interest in all respects as a guardian in socage had before, with these exceptions : 1st, such guardian may hold his office for a longer time than the guardian in socage could ; *viz.* until the heir attain the age of twenty-one; 2nd, the next of kin not inheritable were the persons entitled to be guardians in socage; but, under the statute, the person appointed by the father shall be guardian.   See Vaughan, 179, and 1 P. Wms. 102.   See also several learned notes on the subject of guardianship in Harg. Co. Litt. 88, b.

(9) But by stat. 7 Geo. II. c. 20, s. 1, " Where any action of ejectment shall be brought by any mortgagees, their heirs, executors, &c., *and no suit shall be depending in equity for foreclosing or redeeming such mortgaged lands*, if the person having right to redeem, and who shall appear and become defendant, shall, *pending such action*, pay unto the mortgagees, or, in case of refusal, bring into court, principal, interest, and costs, expended, either in law or in equity, upon such mortgage; the monies so paid or brought into court, shall be in satisfaction of such mortgage, and the court shall discharge the mortgagor or defendant from the same, and compel the mortgagees, by rule of court, at the costs of the mortgagor, to reconvey the mortgaged lands, and deliver up all deeds and writings in their custody relating to the title."   N. There must be an affidavit that there is not any suit in equity depending.   After judgment for the plaintiff in ejectment, the mortgagor prayed to bring the money into court on the preceding statute; but per *Page* and *Chapple*, Js., the statute gives liberty to do it, *pending* the action : but, after judgment, the action is not depending; the application, therefore, was refused.   *Wilkinson d. Lock* v. *Traxton*, B. R. M.; 14 Geo. II. Serjeant Leeds' MSS.

11. Personal representative, stat. 4 Edw. III. c. 7 ; 4 Rep. 94, a. ; 1 Vent. 30.

12. Provisional assignee of Insolvent Debtors Court. *Doe d. Clark* v. *Spencer*, 3 Bingh. 203, even without the authority of that court or the creditors to sue. *Doe d. Spencer* v. *Clark*, 3 Bingh. 370. But insolvent himself, after such assignment, cannot maintain ejectment (a) ; although provisional assignee has not taken possession, nor permanent assignee been appointed, nor rent withheld from lessor. See stat. 1 & 2 Vict. c. 110, ss. 37, 50.

13. Tenant by elegit.

14. Tenant in common may maintain ejectment against his companion upon an actual ouster, Litt. sect. 322 ; *Doe d. Wawn* v. *Horn*, 3 M. & W. 333.

N. Committee of a lunatic's estate cannot bring an ejectment, Hob. 215 ; Hutt. 16.

The stat. 11 Geo. II. c. 19, s. 16, extended by stat. 57 Geo. III. c. 52, authorizes two justices under certain regulations to put landlords into possession, where tenants desert the premises, and leave the same uncultivated or unoccupied, so as no sufficient distress can be had. Where a tenant ceased to reside on the premises for several months, and left them without any furniture or other property sufficient to answer the year's rent ; it was holden, that the landlord might proceed under the stat. 11 Geo. II. c. 19, s. 16, although he knew where the tenant then was, and although the justices found a servant of the tenant on the premises, when they first went to view the same. *Exp. Pilton*, 1 B. & A. 369.

Difficulties having frequently arisen, and considerable expenses having been incurred by reason of the refusal of persons, who had been permitted to occupy, or who had intruded themselves into parish houses, to deliver up possession of such houses, by stat. 59 Geo. III. c. 12, s. 24, two justices are empowered, in such cases, to cause possession to be delivered to churchwardens and overseers. The mode of proceeding is prescribed by the statute. This statute was not intended to take away a right which the owner of property had at common law to enter and take possession, if it could be done peaceably, but to provide an expeditious mode, whereby parish officers might obtain possession where it was obstinately withheld ;

(a) *Doe* v. *Andrews*, 4 Bingh. 348, *Best*, C. J., diss.

This statute contains a proviso (sect. 3), that it shall not extend to any case, where the party praying a redemption has not a right to redeem, &c. Hence, where the mortgagor has agreed to convey the equity of redemption to the mortgagee, the court will not stay proceedings. *Goodtitle d. Taysum* v. *Pope*, 7 T. R. 185.

and that they might not do that which had before been sometimes done, *viz.* might not turn occupiers out *vi et armis*, which led to further expense and litigation. The provisions of the statute are equally applicable, whether the party has wrongfully intruded himself into the premises, or has been suffered by the parish officers to occupy them.

The 17th section (*b*) vests all real property belonging to the parish in the churchwardens and overseers in succession, as a corporation. In ejectment (*c*), by or against parish officers claiming to hold premises for the parish under the foregoing section, rated inhabitants are competent witnesses for the officers under stat. 54 Geo. III. c. 170, s. 9. In a case where it did not appear who had the legal property at the time of the act passing, but rent had been paid to the churchwardens and overseers as such; it was holden (*d*), that the property belonged to the parish, and that the present churchwardens and overseers might recover the same, having given a notice to quit, although defendant claimed to hold under a lease granted by former churchwardens and overseers, for an unexpired term ; inasmuch as such lease having been granted before the act, it conveyed no legal interest ; and the defendant therefore might be treated as a tenant from year to year, whose tenancy had been determined by the notice.

By stat. 5 & 6 Will. IV. c. 69, s. 5, the powers given by the 59 Geo. III. c. 12, are extended to houses and lands vested in guardians of an union or parish.

A pauper had removed from a parish house ; the overseers entered, resumed possession, and afterwards carried away the furniture which belonged to them : it was holden (*e*), that they were justified in so doing, without giving any notice to quit, and were not bound to pursue the mode pointed out by the foregoing statute ; for that did not apply. Under this act, property held by trustees for the benefit of a parish, vests in the churchwardens and overseers (*f*), where there are not any known feoffees in existence, nor any other person in whom the legal estate is vested (*g*) ; and the statute extends to tenements, the profits of which are applicable to the purpose for which a church-rate is levied (*h*) ; but not to a case where the trust is for a special and not for general purposes, and where the land for which the profits are to be applied cannot be called parish property (*i*).

By a late act, 1 & 2 Vict. c. 74, for facilitating the recovery of

(*b*) See now 5 & 6 Will. IV. c. 69, ss. 7 and 8, similar provisions as to guardians.

(*c*) *Doe d. Boultbee* v. *Adderley*, 8 A. & E. 502.

(*d*) *Doe d. Higgs* v. *Terry*, 4 Ad. & Ell. 274, recognizing *Doe* v. *Hiley ; Doe d. Hobbs* v. *Cockell*, 4 Ad. & Ell. 478, S. P.

(*e*) *Wildbor* v. *Rainforth*, 8 B. & C. 4.

(*f*) *Doe d. Jackson* v. *Hiley*, 10 B. & C. 885.

(*g*) Per *Denman*, C. J., *Allason* v. *Stark*, 9 A. & E. 255.

(*h*) *Doe d. Jackson* v. *Hiley*, 10 B. & C. 885.

(*i*) *Allason* v. *Stark*, 9 A. & E. 255.

possession of tenements after due determination of the tenancy, in cases where there is no rent, or where the rent does not exceed 20*l.*, and when the tenancy is either at will or for a term not exceeding seven years, summary proceedings may be had.

III. *For what Things an Ejectment will lie.*

In general an ejectment will lie to recover the possession of any thing whereon an entry can be made, and whereof the sheriff can deliver possession. Hence an ejectment will lie for the recovery of ——— acres of alder carr in Norfolk, because alder carr is a term well known in that county, and signifies the same as alnetum, *Barnes* v. *Peterson*, Str. 1063.

Beastgate in Suffolk, *Bennington* v. *Goodtitle*, Str. 1084.

Bedchamber, 3 Leon. 210.

——— acres of bogge in Ireland, Cro. Car. 512.

Cattlegate in Yorkshire (10), *Metcalf* v. *Roe*, B. R. M. 9 Geo. II. Ca. Temp. Hardw. 167.

Church, by the name of a messuage, Salk. 256.

Coalmine, *Comyn* v. *Kyncto*, Cro. Jac. 150.

——— de mineris carbonum in county palatine of Durham, Carth. 277.

Common of pasture adjudged good after verdict; for it shall be intended such common of pasture as an ejectment will lie for, *viz.* common appendant or appurtenant, *Newman* v. *Holdmyfast*, Str. 54.

Cottage, *Hill* v. *Giles*, Cro. Eliz. 818.

——— acres of furze and heath, and ——— acres of moor and marsh, *Connor* v. *West*, 5 Burr. 2673.

House, *Royston* v. *Eccleston*, Cro. Jac. 54.

——— part of a house, known by the name of the Three Kings in A., *Sullivan* v. *Seagrave*, Str. 695.

Land, and coalpit in the same land. Objection, that it is *bis*

---

(10) Ejectment for ten acres of pasture cattlegates with their appurtenances, in a close called, &c. in Yorkshire. Motion after verdict in arrest of judgment, on the ground of uncertainty of description. Per *Cur.* Either cattlegate must be considered as pasture, and then it is synonymous with the word pasture preceding it; or else it must be taken for common of pasture for cattle; and then being after verdict it must be taken for common appurtenant, which is recoverable in ejectment. *Metcalf* v. *Roe*, M. 9 Geo. II. B. R.

petitum. Answer, *ejectio firmæ* is a personal action, and plaintiff demands nothing certainly, *Harebottle* v. *Placock*, Cro. Jac. 21.

N. Under the description of land, the owner of the soil may recover land which is subject to a public easement, such as the king's highway: and a wall being built on the land, shall not vitiate the description, *Goodtitle d. Chester* v: *Alker*, 1 Burr. 133.

Messuage or tenement, *called the Black Swan*, 1 Sidf. 295.

—— acres of mountain in Ireland, *Lord Kildare* v. *Fisher*, Str. 71; *Lord Kingston* v. *Babbington*, 1 Bro. P. C. 71, Tomlin's edition.

Orchard, *Wright* v. *Wheatley*, Cro. Eliz. 854.

Rectory of B., and a certain place there called the Vestry, 3 Lev. 96, 97; *Hutchinson* v. *Puller*, adjudged on error in the Exchequer Chamber, and recognized in 2 Lord Raym. 1471.

Stable, 1 Lev. 58.

Where an Ejectment will not lie.—But an ejectment cannot be maintained for a—

Canonry; for it is an ecclesiastical office only, *Doe d. Butcher* v. *Musgrave, Clerk, Canon of Windsor*, 1 M. & Gr. 625.

Close, 11 Rep. 55, Godb. 53.

Manor, without describing the quantity and nature of land therein, Latch, 61; Lit. Rep. 301; Hetl. 146.

Messuage *and tenement, Doe* v. *Plowman*, 1 East's R. 441, (11), messuage, garden, *and tenement, Goodtitle* v. *Walton*, Str. 834. But no ground for reversal on error, if demanded in same count; because when same count contains two demands, for one of which action lies and not for the other, all the damages shall be referred (*k*) to the good cause of action.

Messuage *or tenement, Goodright on d. Welch* v. *Flood*, 3 Wils. 23.

Messuage, situate in Coventry (*l*), in the parishes of *A. and B.*, *or one of them.* Holden bad for uncertainty, after verdict, and that the words, "or one of them," could not be rejected.

De peciâ terræ, Moor, 702, pl. 976.

(*k*) *Doe d. Laurie* v. *Dyeball*, 8 B. & C. 70.

(*l*) *Goodright d. Griffin* v. *Fawson*, 7 Mod. 457, 8vo edit.; 1 Barn. 150, *S. C.*

---

(11) But *after verdict* the court will give leave (even pending a rule to arrest the judgment on this ground) to enter the verdict according to the judge's notes for the messuage only. *Goodtitle d. Wright* v. *Otway*, 8 East, 357.

De castro, villâ et terris, Yelv. 118.

Ejectment will not lie for things that lie merely in grant, which are not in their nature capable of being delivered in execution, as an advowson, common in gross, Cro. Jac. 146.

An ejectment will not lie for libera piscaria, Cro. Jac. 146; Cro. Car. 492; 8 Mod. 277; 1 Brownl. 142, contra per *Ashhurst*, J., 1 T. R. 361.

Nor pro quodam rivulo sive aquæ cursu, called D., Yelv. 143; nor for Pannage, 1 Lev. 212.

Nor for a tin-bound, *Doe d. E. of Falmouth* v. *Alderson*, 1 M. & W. 210.

The owner of the fee by indenture granted to A., his partners, fellow-adventurers, &c., free liberty to dig for tin and all other metals throughout certain lands therein described, and to raise, make merchantable, and dispose of the same to their own use; and to make adits, &c. necessary for the exercise of that liberty, together with the use of all waters and watercourses, excepting to the grantor, liberty for driving any new adit within the lands thereby granted, and to convey any watercourse over the premises granted, habendum for twenty-one years; covenant by the grantee to pay one-eighth share of all ore to the grantor, and all rates, taxes, &c., and to work effectually the mines during the term; and then, in failure of the performance of any of the covenants, a right of re-entry was reserved to the grantor: it was holden (*m*), that this deed did not amount to a lease, but contained a mere license to dig and search for minerals; and the grantee could not maintain an ejectment for mines lying within the limits of the set, but not connected with the workings of the grantee.

IV. *In what Cases previous Steps must be taken before Ejectment brought.*

In some cases, before an ejectment can be brought, some previous steps must be taken, in order to entitle the plaintiff to the action. Under what circumstances these proceedings will be necessary, will appear from the following remarks:—

An actual entry is necessary, to avoid a fine levied with proclamations, according to the stat. 4 Hen. VII. c. 24 (12); and an

(*m*) *Doe d. Hanley* v. *Wood*, 2 B. & A. 724.

---

(12) See 3 & 4 Will. IV. c. 74, abolition of fines after 31st Dec. 1833.

ejectment cannot be brought until such entry has been made (n). And by stat. 4 Ann. c. 16, the action must be commenced within one year next after the making such entry, and prosecuted with effect; the plaintiff laying his demise on a day subsequent to the day of the entry (o). But an actual entry is not necessary to avoid a fine at common law, without proclamations (p); nor a fine with proclamations, if all the proclamations were not made at the time when the ejectment was brought (q); nor a fine which has no operation, as a fine levied by son of tenant at sufferance (r), or a fine levied by a tenant for years (s); nor to maintain an ejectment on a clause of re-entry for non-payment of rent (t). So if one of two tenants in common of a reversion levy a fine of the whole, such fine does not require an actual entry by the other tenant in common to avoid it (u). Where tenant for life levies a fine with proclamations, although it is not any bar to those in remainder, yet a remainder-man must make an actual entry, in order to avoid it, before he can maintain an ejectment (x); but he need not enter until five years after the death of a tenant for life (y). An entry upon an estate generally, is an entry for the whole (z); if it be for less, it should be so defined at the time. But it is a sufficient entry to avoid a fine, if the party enters expressly to claim the premises as his own (a); it is not necessary for him to say that he enters to avoid all fines, or to specify what particular act, adverse to his own interest, he means to defeat. In a case where a party had a right of entry upon condition broken (b); and a stranger entered, and afterwards the plaintiff assented to such entry, and brought an ejectment, laying the demise after the assent, it was holden sufficient. Where an ejectment is brought by a corporation aggregate, they must execute a letter of attorney to some person, empowering him to enter on the land; but a verbal notice to quit, given by a steward of a corporation, is sufficient (c). Where lands are in the possession of a receiver (d), under an appointment of the Court of Chancery, an ejectment cannot be brought for the recovery of such lands, without leave of the court.

(n) Berrington v. Parkhurst, 2 Str. 1086; Compere v. Hicks, 7 T. R. 727.
(o) 2 Str. 1086; 7 T. R. 727.
(p) Jenkins on d. Harris and Wife v. Prichard, 2 Wils. 45.
(q) Doe d. Ducket and Ladbrooke v. Watts, 9 East, 17, in which Tayner d. Peckham v. Merlott, Willes, 177, was overruled.
(r) Doe v. Perkins, 3 M. & S. 271.
(s) Per Lord Kenyon, C. J., in Peaceable v. Read, 1 East, 575.
(t) Goodright v. Cator, Dougl. 477.

(u) Roe v. Elliot, 1 B. & A. 85. See also Doe v. Harris, 5 M. & S. 326.
(x) Compere v. Hicks, 7 T. R. 433, 727.
(y) Pomfret v. Windsor, 2 Ves. 481.
(z) Per Ld. Kenyon, C. J., 3 T. R. 170.
(a) Doe d. Jones v. Williams, 5 B. & Ad. 783.
(b) Fitchet v. Adams, 2 Str. 1128.
(c) Roe d. Dean and Ch. of Rochester v. Pierce, 2 Campb. 96.
(d) Angel v. Smith, Eldon, C., 10 Ves. jun. 335.

V. *In what Cases a Notice to quit must be given before Ejectment brought, p. 698; Requisites of Notice, p. 701; Waiver of Notice, p. 705; Where Notice is not required, p. 710; Stat. 1 Geo. IV. c. 87, for Recovery of Lands, &c. unlawfully held over, p. 712.*

THE old tenancy at will being attended with many inconveniences, the inclination of the courts has of late been to make every tenancy a holding from year to year, *if they can find any foundation for it* (*e*), as if the lessor accepts yearly rent, or rent measured by any aliquot part of a year : and it has been considered as more advantageous to the parties, that such demises should be construed to be tenancies from year to year, so long as it shall please both parties; for in that case one party cannot determine the tenancy, without giving a reasonable notice to quit to the other ; with respect to which it may be laid down as a general rule, that half a year's (13) notice (*f*), expiring with the year of the tenancy, is a reasonable notice in all cases, except where a different period is established, either by express agreement, or the custom (*g*) of particular places (14). If the tenant die, his personal representative, having the same interest in the land which the tenant had, will be entitled to the same notice ; that is, half a year's notice ending with the year (*h*). So if an infant becomes entitled to the

(*e*) See *Richardson* v. *Langridge*, 4 Taunt. 128, where the agreement was holden to be a tenancy at will; the premises being let so long as both parties liked, and a compensation reserved accruing *de die in diem*, and not referrible to a year or any aliquot part of a year. In *Freeman* v. *Jury*, M. & Malk. 19, and *post*, tit. "Use and Occupation," where rent had been paid for a single quarter only, *Abbott*, C. J., held that not to be evidence of a new continuing tenancy.

(*f*) 13 Hen. VIII. 15, b.

(*g*) *Roe d. Brown* v. *Wilkinson*, Harg. & But. Co. Litt. 270, b. n. 1 ; *Roe d. Henderson* v. *Charnock*, Peake's N. P. C. 4, 5.

(*h*) *Doe d. Shore* v. *Porter*, 3 T. R. 13. See also 3 Wils. 25, and *Lawrence*, J., in *Rex* v. *Stone*, 6 T. R. 298.

(13) By legal computation half a year contains 182 days ; for the odd hours are rejected. 1 Inst. 135, b. But a notice served on the 28th of September to quit on the 25th of March, although the period contain only 179 days, has been holden to be a good notice. *Doe d. Harrop* v. *Green*, 4 Esp. N. P. C. 199. And Lord *Ellenborough*, in the same case, said, that a notice on the 29th of September to quit at Lady-day following had been holden good. See *R.* v. *Swyer*, 10 B. & C. 486, where it was holden, that the words, "Three Years" in the prohibitory clause of a charter, imported years of office, and not calendar years.

(14) By the custom of London, a tenant at will, under 40s. rent, shall not be turned out without a quarter's warning. *Dethik* v. *Saunders*, 2 Sidf. 20. See also *Tyley* v. *Seed*, Skin. 649.

reversion of lands leased to a tenant from year to year, he cannot maintain an ejectment, unless he has given the tenant a proper notice to quit (i). There is not any distinction between houses and land, in this respect. Half a year's notice to quit, ending with the year of the tenancy, must be given in both cases (k). Neither will the circumstance of the rent being reserved quarterly, vary the case, if the tenancy be from year to year (l) (15). So if a house be let *from year to year*, to quit at a quarter's notice, the notice must be given to quit at the end of a quarter expiring with a year of the tenancy (m). But if the demise be for one year only, and then to continue tenant afterwards, and to quit at a quarter's notice, a quarter's notice ending at any time will be sufficient (n). So where premises are taken under an agreement by which the "tenant is always to be subject to quit at three months' notice," this constitutes a quarterly tenancy, which may be determined by a three months' notice to quit, expiring at the same time of the year it commenced, or any corresponding quarter-day. But although the tenant under such an agreement enters in the middle of one of the usual quarters, if there appears to be no agreement to the contrary, he will be presumed to hold from the day he enters, and the tenancy can only be determined by a notice expiring on that day of the year, or some other quarter-day calculated from thence (o). An insufficient notice to quit, accepted by the landlord, will not amount to a surrender by operation of law (p).

A demise, "not for one year only, but from year to year," enures as a demise for two years at least; and consequently, the tenant cannot be ejected after a notice to quit at the expiration of the first year (q). And where land was let for one year, and so on from year to year, until the tenancy should be determined as after mentioned, with a proviso that three months should be sufficient notice to be given from either party, and another proviso that it should be lawful for either party to determine the tenancy by giving three months' notice; it was holden (r), that the tenancy was not determinable by three months' notice expiring before the end of the second year. But where furnished apartments were taken (s) "*for twelve months certain, and six months' notice afterwards,*" it was contended, that the defendant, under the above taking, was not at

(i) *Maddon* v. *White*, 2 T. R. 159.

(k) *Right* v. *Darby*, 1 T. R. 162.

(l) *Shirley* v. *Newman*, 1 Esp. N. P. C. 267, *Kenyon*, C. J.

(m) *Doe d. Pitcher* v. *Donovan*, 2 Campb. 78; 1 Taunt. 555, *S. C.*

(n) Per *Chambre*, J., *S. C.*

(o) *Kemp* v. *Derrett*, 3 Campb. 510.

(p) Per *Parke*, B., *Doe d. Murrell* v. *Milward*, 3 M. & W. 332, and *post*, p. 703.

(q) *Denn* v. *Cartwright*, 4 East, 31.

(r) *Doe d. Chadborn* v. *Green*, 9 A. & E. 658.

(s) *Thompson* v. *Maberly*, 2 Campb. 573.

(15) But where a house is taken by the month, a month's notice will be sufficient. *Doe d. Parry* v. *Hazell*, 1 Esp. N. P. C. 94.

liberty to quit till six months' notice had been given after the expiration of the first year; but Lord *Ellenborough* was clearly of
opinion, that the defendant was only bound to remain the twelve
months certain, and that he was at liberty to quit at the end of that
period, by giving six months' previous notice. His lordship laid
considerable stress upon the word *certain*, applied to the first twelve
months, which showed that every thing afterwards was *uncertain*
and depended on the notice. If a lessee, after the expiration of the
lease, holds over and pays rent, the law presumes an agreement
between the parties, that the tenant shall continue the possession
according to the terms of the original demise, as far as those terms
are consistent with a tenancy from year to year; in which case, if
the landlord means to determine the tenancy, he must give the
tenant half a year's notice to quit, corresponding with the time of
the original taking. In this case, the tenancy from year to year
commences at the same time when the lease began (*t*); and if the
tenant assign the premises, the assignee will be tenant from year to
year from the same time, and notice to quit must be given accordingly: *e. g.* if the original term began from Michaelmas, the notice
must be to quit at Michaelmas. The receipt of rent is evidence to
be left to a jury that a tenancy was subsisting during the period
for which that rent was paid; and if no other tenancy appear, the
presumption is, that that tenancy was from year to year. A., being
tenant for life (*u*), with remainder to the lessor of the plaintiff in fee,
on 22nd June, 1785, demised to defendant, for twenty-one years, to
commence from old Lady Day then past. On 30th of September,
1785, A. died; defendant continued in possession, and paid rent to
the lessor of the plaintiff for two years, on old Lady Day and old
Michaelmas Day; before old Michaelmas Day, 1787, lessor of plaintiff gave defendant notice to quit on old Lady Day then next.
Adjudged, per *Cur.*, that the notice was good, on the ground, that
payment of rent on the 5th of April was evidence of an agreement
for a tenancy from year to year to hold from that day; although it
was objected, that the interest of the tenant for life having expired
on the 30th of September, the notice ought to have been to quit at
the end of the year from that time. In January, 1790, A. (*x*) let
a farm to defendant for *seven* years *by parol*. Defendant was to
enter at old Lady Day on the land, and on the house on the 25th
of May, and he was to quit at Candlemas. On the 22nd of September, 1792, a notice to quit at Lady Day next was served on
defendant. The court held, that this notice was improper, Lord
Kenyon, C. J., observing, that though the agreement be void by the
statute of frauds, as to the duration of the lease, yet it must regulate the terms, on which the tenancy subsisted, in other respects,

(*t*) *Doe d. Castleton* v. *Samuel*, 5 Esp. 97.
N. P. C. 173.
(*u*) *Doe d. Jordan* v. *Ward*, 1 H. Bl.
(*x*) *Doe d. Rigge* v. *Bell*, 5 T. R. 471.

i. e. as to the rent, the time of year when the tenant was to quit, &c. The agreement was, that defendant should quit at Candlemas. If the lessor, therefore, chose to determine the tenancy before the expiration of the seven years, he could put an end to it at Candlemas only.

Where the in-coming tenant enters upon different parts of the demised premises (*y*), at different times, half a year's notice to quit, with reference to the substantial time of entry, that is, with reference to the original time of entry on the substantial part of the premises demised, is sufficient, the whole being demised at one entire rent. It is not necessary that the notice to quit should be given with reference to the time of entry on the other parts, which are only auxiliary to the principal subject of the demise. Neither is it necessary that separate notices to quit the other parts should be given, where all the parts are demised as one entire thing. One notice, given in conformity with the rule laid down, is sufficient. The substantial time of entry is not necessarily to be collected from the rent days ; per *Le Blanc*, J., 7 East, 557, though it happened in the case of *Doe* v. *Spence*, that the tenant entered on the substantial part of the premises on the day from which the rent was reckoned. It is a question of fact for the jury to decide, which is the principal and which the accessorial subject of demise (*z*). This being found, the judge may then determine, whether the notice to quit has been given in due time.

Requisites of Notice.—With respect to the notice to quit, it may be observed, that although a parol notice is sufficient (*a*), yet it is more advisable to give a written notice ; but not attested by a witness ; for, if so attested, that witness (*b*) must be called, or his absence must be accounted for. The terms in which the notice is expressed should be clear and definite, in order to avoid any objection on this ground at the trial of the ejectment ; for it has been holden, that where an irregular (*c*) notice is given, it is not incumbent on the party served with it, to make an objection to it at the time of service ; it is sufficient if he object to it at the trial. The courts, however, seem to listen to these objections with reluctance, and will, if possible, so construe the notice as to give effect to it (*d*), for it is not required that a notice should be worded with the accuracy of a plea (*e*). Hence, " I desire you to quit on the

(*y*) *Doe* v. *Spence*, 6 East, 120 ; *Doe* v. *Watkins*, 7 East, 551. See also *Doe* d. *Dagget* v. *Snowdon*, 2 Bl. Rep. 1224.

(*z*) *Doe on d. of Heapy* v. *Howard*, 11 East, 498, recognized by *Parke*, B., in *Doe* d. *Kindersley* v. *Hughes*, 7 M. & W. 139.

(*a*) Per Lord *Ellenborough*, C. J., in *Doe* d. *Ld. Macartney* v. *Crick*, 5 Esp. N. P. C. 197 ; *Roe* v. *Pierce*, 2 Campb.

96.

(*b*) *Doe* d. *Sykes* v. *Durnford*, 2 M. & S. 62.

(*c*) *Oakapple* d. *Green* v. *Copous*, 4 T. R. 361 ; but see *Doe* d. *Leicester*, 2 Taunt. 109.

(*d*) See *Doe* v. *Archer*, 14 East, 245.

(*e*) Per *Patteson*, J., in *Doe* d. *Williams* v. *Smith*, 5 A. & E. 353.

25th of March, *or I shall insist on double rent*," has been holden a good notice (*f*). So upon a taking from old Michaelmas to old Michaelmas, a notice to quit at Michaelmas will be sufficient (*g*); at least if it be proved, that the tenancy commenced at old Michaelmas (*h*). So a notice delivered at Michaelmas, 1796, "to quit at Lady Day *which will be* in the year 1795," was adjudged to be good; for the intention is clear, and the words, " in the year 1795," may be rejected (*i*). So a notice to quit at the expiration of the current year of the tenancy, which shall expire next after the end of one half year from the date of the notice, is sufficient, although no particular day is mentioned (*k*). It is, however, essentially necessary, that the notice should be to quit at the expiration of the current year of the tenancy; that is, if the defendant hold from Michaelmas, the notice must be given half a year before Michaelmas, to quit at Michaelmas; if from Lady Day at Lady Day, &c.; for, if a notice to quit at Midsummer be given to a tenant holding from Michaelmas, or *vice versâ*, it will be insufficient (*l*); and a notice to quit at a particular day is not *primâ facie* evidence of a holding from that day (*m*), though a contrary doctrine was formerly holden (*n*), unless it is served personally on the tenant, who makes no objection at the time (*o*). In a case where the notice (which was delivered on the 29th of September) was to quit on the 25th of March, or the 8th day of April, next ensuing, defendant having objected to it on the ground that it did not express with sufficient accuracy the end of the tenancy, and the time when the defendant was to quit, and that at all events it was incumbent on the lessor of the plaintiff to show that the defendant's tenancy commenced either on the 25th of March or 8th of April, Lord *Kenyon*, C. J., ruled the notice to be sufficient, and that the onus of proving the commencement of his tenancy lay on the defendant (*p*). N. In this case the demise was laid on a day subsequent to the 8th of April. A notice (*q*) to a weekly tenant to quit at the end of his tenancy, next after a week from the date of the notice, was holden sufficient; where the ejectment was brought after a sufficient time had elapsed for covering

(*f*) *Doe d. Matthews* v. *Jackson*, Doug. 175.

(*g*) *Denn d. Alstone* v. *Waine*, C. B. E. 32 Geo. III., cited by *Heath*, J., Peake's A. C. 195.

(*h*) *Doe d. Hinde* v. *Vince*, 2 Campb. 256, per Sir *A. Mc. Donald*, C. B., and S. P., per Lord *Ellenborough*, C. J., in *Doe* v. *Brookes*, 2 Campb. 257, n.

(*i*) *Doe d. D. of Bedford* v. *Knightley*, 7 T. R. 63.

(*k*) *Doe d. Phillips* v. *Butler*, 2 Esp. N. P. C. 589; *Doe d. Williams* v. *Smith*, 5 A. & E. 350; *Hirst* v. *Horn*, 6 M. & W. 393.

(*l*) *Oakapple d. Green* v. *Copous*, 4 T. R. 361; see *Doe d. Murrell* v. *Milward*, 3 M. & W. 328.

(*m*) 2 Campb. 258, n.; *Doe d. Ash* v. *Calvert*, 2 Campb. 388.

(*n*) *Doe d. Puddicombe* v. *Harris*, per *Eyre*, Baron, Dorset Sum. Ass. 1784, 1 T. R. 161.

(*o*) *Doe d. Clarges* v. *Foster*, 13 East, 405; *Thomas* v. *Thomas*, 2 Campb. 647.

(*p*) *Doe d. Matthewson* v. *Wrightman*, 4 Esp. N. P. C. 5. But see *Doe* v. *Forster*, *sup*.

(*q*) *Doe d. Campbell* v. *Scott*, 6 Bingh. 362.

a tenancy commencing with any day of the week. It will be proper to remark, that where the tenant, being applied to by his landlord respecting the commencement of his holding, informs him that it began on a certain day, and the landlord gives the tenant notice to quit agreeably to the information received (r), the tenant will be precluded from contending that his tenancy commenced on a different day, even though he can prove that the information which he gave his landlord proceeded on a mistake, and not from an intention to deceive. But where a tenant from year to year, believing that his tenancy determined at Midsummer, gave a written notice to quit at that time, which the landlord accepted, without making any objection to it, but gave no assent in writing. The tenant having afterwards discovered that his tenancy expired at Christmas, gave his landlord another notice accordingly, and on possession being demanded at Midsummer refused to quit. An ejectment having been brought; it was holden (s), that the tenancy was not determined by the first notice; for it was not good as a notice to quit; and that it could not operate as a surrender, by note in writing, within the statute of frauds, being to take effect in futuro. A receipt for rent up to a particular day is *primâ facie* evidence of the commencement of the tenancy at that day (t). Upon a parol demise, rent to commence from the following Lady Day (u), evidence of the custom of the country is admissible to show that by "Lady Day," the parties meant "old Lady Day." It is not essentially necessary that the notice should be directed to the defendant (x), if the terms of it show that the defendant is tenant to the plaintiff, and if it is proved to have been served on the defendant at the proper time. Neither is it necessary for a landlord to give notice to any one but his own tenant (y), although such tenant may have underlet part of the demised premises. A., tenant from year to year (z) to B., from Michaelmas, 1801, underlet part of the premises to C. A., without receiving any regular notice to quit from B., agreed to give him up possession at Michaelmas, 1810, and B. then took possession of all that A. had continued to occupy; but C. having before refused to deliver his part, was served, in the February preceding, with a notice to quit at Michaelmas, 1810, from B., to whom he had never paid rent, or otherwise acknowledged as his immediate landlord, but had paid his rent to A. up to Michaelmas, 1808, and had tendered him the rent which

(r) *Doe d. Eyre* v. *Lambly*, 2 Esp. N. P. C. 635.

(s) *Doe d. Murrell* v. *Milward*, 3 M. & W. 328, recognizing *Johnstone* v. *Huddlestone*, 4 B. & C. 922, *post*, p. 709, n., and *Weddall* v. *Capes*, 1 M. & W. 50.

(t) Per Lord *Ellenborough*, C. J., in *Doe d. Castleton* v. *Samuel*, 5 Esp. N. P. C. 174.

(u) *Doe d. Hall* v. *Benson*, 4 B. & A. 588.

(x) *Doe d. Matthewson* v. *Wrightman*, 4 Esp. N. P. C. 5.

(y) *Roe* v. *Wiggs*, 2 Bos. & Pul. N. R. 330. See also 3 Taunt. 95.

(z) *Pleasant d. Hayton* v. *Benson*, 14 East, 234. See *Roe d. Blair* v. *Street*, 2 Ad. & Ell. 329.

had accrued since that time, which A. had refused to receive.
B. brought an ejectment against C.; it was holden, that the notice
was insufficient, B. not having given any regular notice to A., his
immediate tenant; and A. not having given any such notice to C.;
for without one or other of such notices, C.'s interest in the part
underlet continued. Lord *Ellenborough* observed, "that a tenancy
from year to year was determinable either by a regular notice to
quit, or, he might say, for the purpose of this case, by a surrender
of a part of the premises in the name of the whole; but A. had
not done even that; for he merely ceased to reside on the part which
he had retained in his own possession, without making a surrender
in the name of the whole. But while he was tenant from year to
year of the whole, he let off a part to the defendant; and nothing
has been done to put an end to the tenancy as to that part."
Evidence that the notice was delivered and explained *to the servant*
of the tenant at his dwelling-house, though such dwelling-house be
not situated on the demised premises, is presumptive evidence
that the notice came to the hands of the tenant (a), *the servant not
being called*. But evidence of the notice having been left at the
tenant's house (b), without further proof of its having been delivered
to a servant, who is not called, or that it came to the tenant's
hands, is not sufficient. Evidence of the notice being served on the
premises (c), on one of two joint-tenants, who resided on the premises, is presumptive evidence that the notice reached the other
joint-tenant, who resided elsewhere. A lease contained a proviso
making it determinable by a notice in writing given by the lessor or
his executors *under his or their respective hands*. Holden (d),
that a notice signed by two only of three executors of the lessor to
whom he had bequeathed the freehold as joint-tenants, expressing
the notice to be given on behalf of themselves, and the third executor, was not good. Neither could such notice be sustained
under the general rule of law that one joint-tenant may bind his
companion by an act done for *his benefit*; for non constat that the
determination of the lease was for the benefit of the co-joint tenant,
which it was incumbent on the party who wished to avail himself of
it to prove. And the notice to quit being such as the tenant was
to act upon at the time, no subsequent recognition of the third
executor would make it good by relation; nor was his joining in
the ejectment evidence of his original assent to bind the tenant by
the notice. In the foregoing case a mode was specifically pointed
out to be pursued, in order to put an end to a subsisting term, and

(a) *Jones d. Griffiths* v. *Marsh*, 4 T. R.
464.

(b) *Doe d. Buross* v. *Lucas*, 5 Esp. N.
P. C. 153.

(c) *Doe* v. *Watkins and another*, 7 East,
551; *Doe d. Lord Macartney* v. *Crick*

and another, 5 Esp. N. P. C. 196, S. P.,
Ellenborough, C. J.

(d) *Right* v. *Cuthell*, 5 East, 491. See
Doe d. Mann v *Walters*, 10 B. & C.
626.

that mode required the concurrence of all the joint-tenants; hence a notice by some of the joint-tenants only would have no operation. But where a notice to quit was signed by one of the several joint-tenants, on behalf of all, it was holden (e) sufficient to determine a tenancy from year to year as to all, inasmuch as a notice to quit by one of several joint-tenants puts an end to the tenancy on behalf of all. So a notice to quit given by a person authorized by one of several lessors, joint-tenants, determines the tenancy as to all (f). Where there is a mere tenancy at will, any thing which amounts to a demand of possession (g), although not expressed in precise and formal language, is sufficient to indicate the determination of the landlord's will.

A receiver appointed by the Court of Chancery, with a general authority to let the lands to tenants from year to year, has also authority (h) to determine such tenancies by a notice to quit; and an agent to receive rents and let has been holden (i) to have a similar authority; but a mere receiver of rents, as such, has no authority to determine a tenancy (k). A verbal notice to quit given by the steward of a corporation is sufficient (l), without evidence that he had an authority under seal; but a notice to quit given by an agent of an agent is not sufficient (m) without a recognition by the principal.

Waiver of Notice.—Where a notice to quit has been given, the lessor must be careful not to do any act which may be construed as an affirmance of the tenancy and a waiver of the notice. A distress for rent, which accrued after the expiration of the time, at which, by the notice, the tenant is to quit, is an acknowledgment of the tenancy (n); so is the acceptance of rent so due (o); but it shall be left to the jury to say whether the money received was received as rent; for whether it shall be a waiver of the notice depends on the intention of the parties, which is a matter of fact to be left to the jury (p) (16). Ejectment for recovering possession of a farm (q),

(e) *Doe d. Aslin and another* v. *Summersett,* 1 B. & Ad. 135.

(f) *Doe d. Kindersley* v. *Hughes,* 7 M. & W. 139, recognizing *Doe d. Aslin* v. *Summersett.*

(g) *Doe d. Price* v. *Price,* 9 Bingh. 356.

(h) *Doe d. Marsack* v. *Read,* 12 East, 57.

(i) *Doe d. Manvers* v. *Mizem,* 2 M. & Rob. 56, *Patteson,* J.

(k) *Doe d. Mann* v. *Walters,* 10 B. & C. 626.

(l) *Roe* v. *Pierce,* 2 Campb. 96, recognized in *Smith* v. *Birmingham Gas Company,* 1 A. & E. 531.

(m) *Doe d. Rhodes* v. *Robinson,* 3 Bingh. N. C. 677.

(n) *Ward* v. *Willingale,* 1 H. Bl. 311.

(o) *Goodright d. Charter* v. *Cordwent,* 6 T. R. 219.

(p) *Doe* v. *Batten,* Cowp. 243.

(q) *Doe d. Williams* v. *Humphreys,* 2 East's R. 237.

(16) In the case of a tenancy from year to year, if, at the expiration of the year, the landlord consents to accept another person as his tenant, the

tried before *Lawrence*, J., at Salop Sum. Ass. 1801. The farm consisted of lands of different descriptions, to be quitted at different times; the arable on the 29th of September, 1800; the pasture and meadow on the 30th of November; the dwelling-house, &c. on the 1st of May, 1801. The lessor, on the 21st of March, 1800, served the defendant with a notice to quit the farm at the several times above stated: and the defendant not having quitted the arable on the 29th of September, or the meadow and pasture on the 30th of November, the lessor brought his ejectment: pending which he delivered to the defendant another notice (17), dated the 20th of March, 1801, to quit the messuage and dwelling-house, &c., together with the lands &c., to wit, the arable on the 20th of September, 1801; the meadow and pasture on the 30th of November, 1801; the dwelling-house, &c. on the 1st of May, 1802. It was objected, at the trial, that the second notice was a waiver of the first, being a recognition of the tenancy still subsisting; but the learned judge overruled the objection, and a verdict was found for plaintiff. The court (after argument on motion to enter a nonsuit) concurred in opinion with *Lawrence*, J., observing, that it had been admitted, in the course of argument, that if the plaintiff had not intended that the second notice should operate as a waiver of the first, he might have so explained his intention, by adding that the second notice was to enable him to recover the premises at a subsequent assizes, if, by any accident, he should fail at those then ensuing. And, under the circumstances, the defendant must have understood, that this notice was given for that purpose; and it was not possible for the defendant to suppose, that the plaintiff intended to waive the first notice, when he knew the plaintiff was, on the foundation of that notice, proceeding by ejectment to turn him out of the farm (18). Where rent

---

first tenant is thereby discharged, although he has not given any notice to quit, or made any surrender in writing of his interest. *Sparrow* v. *Hawkes*, 2 Esp. N. P. C. 505.

(17) The second notice was copied verbatim from the first, with the alteration only of the dates; and the reason suggested at the bar, why it was given, was, because the person who was to prove the service of the first notice was dangerously ill, and it was apprehended, that the lessor would not be able to prove the notice.

(18) In *Messenger* v. *Armstrong*, 1 T. R. 53, which was an action for double the yearly value, it appeared that the defendant was tenant to the plaintiff, under a demise for three years, from Whitsuntide, 1781. Two months previously to Whitsuntide, 1784, plaintiff gave the defendant notice to quit at that time. After the expiration of this notice, *viz.* on the 3rd of June, 1784, the plaintiff gave the defendant another notice to quit at the Martinmas following, or to pay double rent. It was contended, that the first notice was waived by the second; but the objection was overruled; Lord *Mansfield*, C. J., observing, that where a term is to

is usually paid at a banker's, if the banker, without any special authority, receives rent accruing after expiration of notice to quit, it will not operate as a waiver (r).

Here it may be proper to take notice of a doctrine analogous to the subject of the preceding remarks, *viz.* that acceptance (s) of, or a distress (t) for, rent due after condition broken, with notice of the breach, is a waiver of the forfeiture. Ejectment, by a landlord, against his tenant (u), on a proviso for re-entry for non-payment of rent arrear; it appeared, that the lessor had brought covenant for half a year's rent, due on a day subsequent to the day of the demise laid in the declaration in ejectment, and a rule had been obtained to pay the rent arrear into court in that action: it was holden, that the plaintiff had waived the right of entry for the forfeiture; because, by bringing the action of covenant on the lease, he admitted the defendant to be tenant in possession by virtue of the lease; and the tenant having brought the money into court was equivalent to acceptance. The law will always incline against forfeitures, as courts of equity relieve against them: and the general rule is, that

(r) *Doe* v. *Calvert,* 2 Campb. 387.
(s) *Goodright d. Walter* v. *Davids,* Cowp. 803; *Arnsby* v. *Woodward,* 6 B. & C. 519. See *Doe d. Griffith* v. *Pritchard,* 5 B. & Ad. 765; 2 Nev. & M.

489.
(t) Adm. *Green's* case, Cro. Eliz. 3.
(u) *Roe d. Crompton* v. *Minshal,* Bull. N. P. 96, and MSS.

---

end on a precise day, there is not any occasion for a notice to quit; that here it ended at Whitsuntide; that the meaning of the first notice was, that if the tenant did not quit, the landlord would insist on double rent; and the second notice only expressed what was meant by the first. So where after the expiration of a notice to quit, the landlord gave the defendant a fresh notice, that unless he quitted in fourteen days, he would be required to pay double value. Lord *Ellenborough,* C. J., held, that the second notice was not a waiver of the first. *Doe d. Digby* v. *Steel,* 3 Campb. 117. A tenant held under a demise from the 26th day of March for one year then next ensuing, and so from year to year, for so long as the landlord and tenant should respectively please. The tenant, after having held more than one year, gave a parol notice to the landlord less than six months before the 25th day of March, that he would quit on that day, and the landlord accepted and assented to the notice; it was holden, on demurrer in replevin, that the tenancy was not thereby determined, there not having been either a sufficient notice to quit, or a surrender in writing, or by operation of law within the statute of frauds. It was holden, also, that the tenant having holden over after the expiration of the time mentioned in the notice to quit, the landlord was not entitled to distrain for double rent, under stat. 11 Geo. II. c. 19, s. 18, inasmuch as that statute applies only to those cases where the tenant has the power of determining his tenancy by a notice, and where he actually gives a valid notice, sufficient to determine it. *Johnstone* v. *Hudlestone,* 4 B. & C. 922; see *Doe d. Murrell* v. *Milward,* 3 M. & W. 328; *ante,* p. 703.

a clause of re-entry be construed strictly (*x*). Proviso in a lease (*y*), giving power of re-entry if the lessee "shall do, or cause to be done, any act, matter, or thing, contrary to, and in breach of, any of the covenants," does not apply to a breach of the covenant to repair, the omission to repair not being an act done within the meaning of the proviso. In ejectment for not insuring according to covenant; it was holden (*z*), that it was incumbent on the plaintiff to prove that no insurance had been effected, and that the circumstance that the defendant refused to show the policy, when the plaintiff required him, and the non-production of it on the trial after notice, were not *primâ facie* evidence against him; for the lessor of the plaintiff has chosen to make the forfeiture depend on a condition peculiarly within the knowledge of the defendant, and has therefore brought the difficulty on himself. *Littledale*, J., said, in *covenant* for not insuring, perhaps it might be for the defendant to prove affirmatively that he had insured, but not in an action like the present for a forfeiture. It has been holden (*a*), that a landlord does not waive a forfeiture by merely lying by and witnessing the act, but that there must be some act affirming the tenancy. Acceptance of rent, *without notice* of forfeiture, will not amount to a waiver (*b*). So a lessor who has a right of re-entry reserved on a breach of covenant not to underlet, does not, by waiving his re-entry, on one underletting, lose his right to re-entry on a subsequent underletting (*c*). A landlord of premises, about to sell them, gave his tenant notice to quit, on the 11th of October, 1806, but promised him not to turn him out (*d*), unless they were sold; and not being sold till February, 1807, the tenant refused, on demand, to deliver up possession; and on ejectment brought, laying the demise on the 12th of October, 1806, it was holden, that the promise, which was performed, was no waiver of the notice, nor operated as a license to be on the premises otherwise than subject to the landlord's right of acting on such notice, if necessary; and, therefore, that the tenant, not having delivered up possession on demand, after a sale, was a trespasser from the expiration of the notice to quit. Acceptance of rent, as rent by a remainder-man, will not amount to a confirmation of a lease void as against him (*e*); but it is an admission of a tenancy from year to year, and the lessee will thereby be entitled to half a year's notice to quit (*f*). In order to raise an implied tenancy (*g*)

(*x*) Per *Tenterden*, C. J., in *Doe d. Palk v. Marchetti*, 1 B. & Ad. 720.

(*y*) *Doe d. Abdy v. Stevens*, 3 B. & Ad. 299.

(*z*) *Doe d. Bridger v. Whitehead*, 3 Nev. & P. 557; 8 A. & E. 571.

(*a*) *Doe d. Sheppard v. Allen*, 3 Taunt. 78.

(*b*) *Gregson v. Harrison*, 2 T. R. 425.

(*c*) *Doe d. Boscawen v. Bliss*, 4 Taunt. 735.

(*d*) *Whiteacre d. Boult v. Symonds*, 10 East, 13. See also *Doe d. Leeson v. Sayer*, 3 Campb. 8.

(*e*) Doug. 51; Cowp. 201, 483.

(*f*) *Doe d. Martin v. Watts*, 7 T. R. 83; recognized in *Doe d. Tucker v. Morse*, 1 B. & Ad. 365.

(*g*) *Right v. Bawden*, 3 East, 260. See also 10 East, 188, 9; *Doe v. Quigley*, 2 Campb. 505.

from the receipt of rent, it must appear that the rent was paid and received, as between landlord and tenant, so as to raise a presumption of an agreement for a tenancy from year to year, and not as in the case of a conventionary rent, where the payment is made with reference to a supposed tenancy of another kind. Where, however, tenant in tail (h) had received an ancient rent of 1*l.* 18*s.* 6*d.* from the lessee in possession, under a void lease, granted by tenant for life under a power, the rack rent value of which was 30*l.* a-year; it was holden, that such tenant in tail could not maintain an ejectment, laying his demise on a day before the delivery of the declaration, without giving the lessee some notice to quit, so as to make him a trespasser at the time of the action brought, after such recognition of a lawful possession, if not as tenant from year to year, at least as tenant at will. An indenture of lease contained a general covenant to repair, and a further covenant that the tenant should, within three months after notice, repair all defects, of which notice had been given. The lease contained the usual clause of re-entry. It was holden (i), that the landlord, who had served a notice to repair *forthwith*, might maintain ejectment, before the expiration of the three months, for a breach of the general covenant to repair; for the notice was not any waiver of the forfeiture. But where the notice required the tenant to repair within three months, this was holden (k) to operate as a waiver of the forfeiture. From this last decision it appears that, in cases where a notice to repair has been given, it will be prudent neither to serve the ejectment nor to lay the demise until the time allowed by the notice has expired. In a case (l) where there was a general covenant to repair, but no specific power of re-entry for breach of that covenant, but a proviso for re-entry in case of non-repair within three months after notice, or in case of breach of the other covenants: notice (dated 6th of January) was given to repair within three months; and ejectment was brought before the expiration of the three months. At the Spring Assizes, by consent of parties, an order of court was made that a juror should be withdrawn, and the repairs be performed on or before the 24th of June. The repairs not being performed on that day, another ejectment was brought, and the plaintiff had a verdict, and the court refused a rule for a new trial, for the right of entry was at all events only suspended, *Parke*, J., observing, that "the lessor of the plaintiff had put an end to the first action by consenting to the order of court. It was the same as if the parties, after the 6th of January, and before the expiration of the three months, had agreed, that the time for repairing should be extended

---

(h) *Denn d. Brune* v. *Rawlins*, 10 East, 261.

(i) *Roe d. Goatly* v. *Paine*, 2 Campb. 520.

(k) *Doe* v. *Meux*, 4 B. & C. 606, cited

by *Patteson*, J., in *Doe d. de Rutzen* v. *Lewis*, 5 A. & E. 289.

(l) *Doe d. Rankin* v. *Brindley*, 4 B. & Ad. 84, cited by *Patteson*, J., in *Doe d. de Rutzen* v. *Lewis*, 5 A. & E. 289.

to the 24th of June: it was merely a consent to postpone the time of completing the repair for the benefit of the defendant; and on his failing to comply with the terms, the lessor of the plaintiff might justly insist on his right of entry, and bring a new ejectment after the expiration of the enlarged time."

Where Notice to quit is not required.—The doctrine relative to notices to quit, is only applicable to those tenancies where the time of quitting is not agreed upon between the parties; for, where a lease is determinable upon a certain event, or at a fixed time, it is not necessary to give such notice, both parties being apprized of the determination of the term (19). Neither is such notice necessary in a case where the possession is adverse (*k*), or where the relation of landlord and tenant does not subsist; *e. g.*, if the tenant has attorned to some other person, or done some other act disclaiming to hold as tenant to the landlord (*l*); and, in the case of a tenancy from year to year, it does not appear to be necessary that any act should be done as distinguished from a verbal disclaimer; a disavowal by the tenant of the holding under the particular landlord by words only is sufficient. But in order to make a verbal or written disclaimer sufficient, it must amount to a direct repudiation of the relation of landlord and tenant, or to a distinct claim to hold possession of the estate upon a ground wholly inconsistent with the existence of that relation (*m*). But if the acts done by the tenant do not amount to a disavowal of the landlord's title, *e. g.*, a refusal to pay rent to a devisee under a contested will, accompanied with a declaration (*n*), that he (the tenant) was ready to pay the rent to any person entitled to receive it, then the tenant is entitled to notice. It is sometimes said that a tenancy from year to year is forfeited by disclaimer; but it would be more correct to say that a disclaimer furnishes evidence in answer to the disclaiming party's assertion, that he has had no notice to quit; as it would be idle to prove such a notice where the tenant has asserted that there is no

(*k*) *Doe* v. *Williams*, Cowp. 622.
(*l*) *Throgmorton* v. *Whelpdale*, H. 9 Geo. III., Bull. N. P. 96.
(*m*) Per *Parke*, B., delivering judgment of court in *Doe d. Gray* v. *Stanion*,

1 M. & W. 702.
(*n*) *Doe d. Williams* v. *Pasquali*, Peake's N. P. C. 3rd edit. 259; see also *Doe d. Dillon* v. *Parker*, Gow's N. P. C. 180.

(19) "If there be a lease for a year, and, by consent of both parties, the tenant continue in possession afterwards, the law implies a tacit renovation of the contract. They are supposed to have renewed the old agreement, which was to hold for a year. But then it is necessary, for the sake of convenience, that, if either party should be inclined to change his mind, he should give the other half a year's notice before the expiration of the next or any following year." Per Lord *Mansfield*, C. J., in *Right* v. *Darby*, 1 T. R. 162.

longer any tenancy (o). A tenant for a definite term of years does not forfeit his term by *orally* refusing, upon demand made by his landlord, to pay the rent, and claiming the fee as his own (p).

A mortgagor in possession stands in a peculiar character; and is liable to be treated as tenant or trespasser, at the option of the mortgagee; and consequently is not entitled to a notice to quit, or even a demand of possession (q); and if a mortgagor lets another person into possession, as tenant from year to year, such tenant is not entitled to a notice to quit, either from the mortgagee (r), or his assignee (s); and this rule holds, although the tenant has been let into possession before the assignment of the mortgage. A. *agreed* to demise a house to B., during the joint lives of A. and B.; B. entered, in pursuance of the agreement, and before any lease was executed, died (t); after which, B.'s executor took possession of the house: it was holden, that A. might maintain ejectment against the executor, *without a notice to quit;* because the death of B. determined his interest, and consequently there was not any interest vested in the executor. So where the tenant had occupied under an agreement for a lease for seven years, which period had expired (u).

Where a person obtains possession of a house without the privity of a landlord, and afterwards a negociation takes place for a lease, upon the terms of which the parties eventually differ, a notice to quit is not necessary (x). So where a person enters under an agreement for a lease, without a stipulation that in case a lease is not executed he shall hold for one year certain; if a lease be tendered to the occupier and he refuses to execute it, the lessor may eject him without any notice to quit (y). But where the lessor of the plaintiff had put the defendant into possession under an agreement for the purchase of the land, it was holden (z), that he could not, without a demand of the possession again, and a refusal by the defendant, or some wrongful act by him to determine his lawful possession, treat the defendant as a wrong-doer and a trespasser, as he assumed to do by his declaration in ejectment. A minister of a dissenting congregation, after his election, was put into possession of a chapel and dwelling-house, by persons in whom the legal fee was vested in trust, to permit and suffer the chapel to be used for the purpose of religious worship; afterwards, at a meeting of the

(o) Per *Patteson,* J., in *Doe d. Graves* v. *Wells,* 10 A. & E. 427.

(p) S. C.

(q) *Doe d. Robey* v. *Maisey,* 8 B. & C. 767.

(r) *Keech* v. *Hall,* Doug. 22.

(s) *Thunder d. Weaver* v. *Belcher,* 3 East, 449.

(t) *Doe d. Bromfield* v. *Smith,* 6 East, 530.

(u) *Doe d. Tilt* v. *Stratton,* 4 Bingh. 446; *Doe* v. *Day,* B. R. Middlesex Sittings, 1 Will. IV., coram *Park,* J., S. P.

(x) *Doe d. Knight* v. *Quigley,* 2 Campb. 505.

(y) Per *Curiam, Hegan* v. *Johnson,* 2 Taunt. 148; see also *Doe d. Leeson* v. *Sayer,* 3 Campb. 8.

(z) *Right d. Lewis* v. *Beard,* 13 East, 210.

congregation, it was determined, by a large majority, that the minister should be changed; but another was not elected. Possession of the premises was demanded on behalf of the trustees; this was holden (a) sufficient, without any notice to quit; as the minister was a mere tenant at will to the trustees. The same point was ruled (b) in a subsequent case, where the defendant had an annual salary of 20l., and the ejectment had been served immediately after the demand of possession; although it was urged that the defendant was entitled to a reasonable notice. It is not necessary that this demand should be made on the premises; and even where made on a Sunday, it was holden (c) good. The defendant's confession of a lease from the lessor to the plaintiff, under the common rule, is not sufficient to determine the possession; for the rule is only entered into after the delivery of the declaration in ejectment, and can never prove that the defendant was a trespasser before that time.

By stat. 1 Geo. IV. c. 87, s. 1, after reciting that it was expedient to provide in certain cases a more expeditious mode for recovering the possession of lands and tenements unlawfully held over by tenants, it is enacted, that, " where the term or interest of any tenant holding under a *lease* or *agreement in writing* any lands or hereditaments for any *term or number of years* certain, or from year to year, shall have expired, or been determined either by the landlord or tenant by regular notice to quit, and such tenant, or any one holding or claiming by or under him, shall refuse to deliver up possession, after lawful *demand in writing made and signed* by the landlord or his agent, and served personally upon or left at the dwelling-house or usual place of abode of such tenant or person, and the landlord shall thereupon proceed by ejectment for the recovery of possession, he may, at the foot of the declaration, address a notice to such tenant or person, requiring him to appear in the court in which the action shall be commenced on the first day of the term next following, there to be made defendant, and to find bail if ordered by the court; and upon appearance, or in case of nonappearance, or making the usual affidavits of service, the landlord producing the lease or agreement, or some counterpart or duplicate thereof, and proving the execution by affidavit, and upon affidavit that the premises have been enjoyed under such lease or agreement, and that the interest of the tenant has expired or been determined by regular notice to quit, and that possession has been lawfully demanded in manner aforesaid, may move the court for a rule for such tenant or person to show cause, within a time to be fixed by the court, on a consideration of the premises, why such tenant or person, upon being admitted defendant, besides entering into the

(a) *Doe d. Jones* v. *Jones*, 10 B. & C. 718.

(b) *Doe d. Nicholl* v. *M'Kaeg*, 10 B.

& C. 721.

(c) *Doe d. Turner* v. *Benallack*, B. R. E. 10 Geo. IV.

common rule, should not undertake, in case a verdict should pass for the plaintiff, to give him a judgment, to be entered up against the real defendant of the term next preceding the trial; and also why he should not enter into a recognizance by himself and two sufficient sureties, in a reasonable sum, conditioned to pay the costs and damages recovered by the plaintiff in the action; and the court, on cause shown, or affidavit of service, may make the rule absolute in the whole or in part, and order such tenant or person, within a time fixed, to give such undertaking, and find such bail, with such conditions, and in such manner, as shall be specified in the rule, or such part of the same so made absolute; and if the party shall neglect or refuse so to do, and shall lay no ground to induce the court to enlarge the time for obeying the same, then upon affidavit of service of the order, the rule may be made absolute to enter judgment for the plaintiff."

The effect of this statute is to save the landlord the necessity of going to trial when the tenant holds over vexatiously, and when the trouble and expense of an ejectment may be very disproportionate to the value of the premises. Hence a tenancy by virtue of an agreement for three months certain, is a tenancy "for a term" within the meaning of the statute (d); but a tenancy for years, determinable *on lives* (e), is not: and where the tenant holds from year to year without a lease or agreement in writing, that is not a case within the meaning of the statute (f).

This statute does not apply in cases where the title is disputed (g); nor to the case of a tenant who holds over after notice to quit given by himself, where his tenancy has not expired by efflux of time (h); nor to the case of a tenant who has surrendered his term, but refuses to quit the premises (i).

Under this statute there must be a separate and distinct demand signed by the landlord, besides the demand of possession by John Doe at the foot of the declaration (k).

(d) *Doe d. Phillips* v. *Roe*, 5 B. & A. 766.

(e) *Doe d. Pemberton* v. *Roe*, 7 B. & C. 2.

(f) *Doe d. Bradford* v. *Roe*, 5 B. & A. 770.

(g) *Doe d. Sanders* v. *Roe*, 1 Dowl. P. C. 4.

(h) *Doe d. Cardigan* v. *Roe*, 1 Dow. & Ry. 540.

(i) *Doe d. Tindal* v. *Roe*, 2 B. & Ad. 922.

(k) *Anon.* E. T. 2 Geo. IV. B. R., 1 Dow. & Ry. 435, n.

VI. *Of the Mode of Proceeding in Ejectment, and herein of the Declaration.*

THE mode of proceeding in the action of ejectment now in use, is not, as in other actions, by suing out a writ; but A., the party claiming title, before the first day of the term, serves a copy of a declaration, with a notice subscribed, upon B. the tenant in possession of the lands or tenements; or, if there be several tenants, on each (*l*) of them. Declarations in ejectment may be served before the first day of any term, and thereupon the plaintiff shall be entitled to judgment against the casual ejector in like manner as upon declarations served before the essoign, or first general return day. R. G. T. T. 1 Will. IV. 11th Rule.—The Rule of Court, that every declaration shall be entitled of the day of the month and year on which it is filed and delivered, does not apply to declarations in ejectment (*m*). Where the declaration was entitled, "In the Common Pleas, June 12, 1834," it was holden (*n*) sufficient, although it was urged, that it should have been entitled of some term, or if of a particular day, *as* of some term. The declaration states that A. on a certain day, (that is, some day after A.'s title to the land, &c. accrued,) demised to John Doe, two messuages, one hundred acres of land, &c. situate, &c. for the term of —— years, by virtue of which demise the said John Doe entered and was possessed, until Richard Roe afterwards ejected him. Such is the outline of the declaration, which is for the most part a fiction; for, except in a few instances, there is neither lease, entry, nor ouster; and the parties, *viz.* the plaintiff, and the defendant, the ejector, usually termed the casual ejector, are fictitious persons. In some respects, however, care and accuracy are necessary in framing this declaration; as, 1st, The venue must be laid in the county in which the lands lie; for this is a local action. But where the venue stated in the body of the declaration was correct, it was holden (*o*) to be sufficient, although the county in the margin was wrong; and it is sufficient also to state the lands only "in the county" (*p*). 2nd, If there be several lessors, the demise stated in the declaration must be such as their title will warrant; as if the lessors of the plaintiff be joint-tenants (*q*), or parceners (20),

(*l*) Bull. N. P. 98.
(*m*) *Doe d. Evans* v. *Roe*, 2 Ad. & E. 11; *Doe d. Gillett* v. *Roe*, 1 Cr. M. & R. 19.
(*n*) *Doe d. Ashman* v. *Roe*, 1 Bingh.

N. C. 253.
(*o*) *Doe d. Goodwin* v. *Roe*, 3 Dowl. (P. C.) 323.
(*p*) *Doe* v. *Gunning*, 2 Nev. & P. 260.
(*q*) Bull. N. P. 107.

(20) In an action of *ejectio firmæ*, a lease was made by two parceners, and it was declared *quod dimiserunt*: an exception was taken, on the

the declaration must allege a *joint* demise; if tenants in common, a several demise by each of their several parts (r) (21). In the latter case the declaration must contain as many counts as there are tenants in common lessors of the plaintiff. But tenants in common may join in a lease to a third person, and then the declaration may state a demise by such lessee. 3rd, The day, on which the demise is stated to have been made, must be some day after the title of the lessor of the plaintiff accrued; otherwise the plaintiff will be non-suited: for not being entitled to the possession he cannot make a

(r) *Mantle* v. *Wollington*, Cro. Jac.   *Heatherley* v. *Weston*, 2 Wils. 232, S. P.
166; *Moore* v. *Pursden*, Show. 342;

---

ground, that the lease was the several lease of each of them for her moiety, and holden good. Moor, 682, pl. 939. This case was denied by *Holt*, C. J., in Ld. Raym. 726, who ruled, that parceners *might* join in eject-ment. *Holt's* opinion is confirmed by a passage in 1 Inst. 180, b., where it is said, that joint-tenants must jointly implead, and jointly be impleaded by others, which property is common between them *and parceners;* and *Holt's* opinion is adopted in Buller's N. P. 107. It is corroborated by the following position in Roll. Abr. 878, pl. 5. If two parceners join in a lease for years by indenture, this is but one lease; for they have not several frank tenements, but shall join in an assize. And in *Stedman* v. *Bates*, Ld. Raym. 64, it was holden that parceners must join in an avowry for rent arrear. It seems, that where a power of re-entry for breach of covenant is reserved in a lease, and the reversion descends to parceners at common law, one alone cannot maintain ejectment for breach of the covenant. *Doe d. de Rutzen* v. *Lewis*, 5 A. & E. 277.

(21) " Declaration in ejectment was of a joint demise of A. and B., and on the evidence it appeared that they were tenants in common; the plaintiff failed." M. 3 Jac. *Blackasper's* case, Noy, n. 43; Hal. MSS. cited and recognized in *Doe d. Poole* v. *Errington*, 1 Ad. & Ell. 750, 3 Nev. & Man. 646, where S. P. was adjudged. See Noy, 13, cited in Hargrave's n. (7) 1 Inst. 45, a. But payment of rent to the agent of A., B., and C. is an admission that the party holds under A., B., and C. jointly, and will support a joint demise, unless it be expressly proved that they were entitled in a different manner. *Doe d. Clarke and others* v. *Grant*, 12 East, 221. See also *Doe* v. *Read*, 12 East, 57. In *Roe d. Ruper* v. *Lonsdale*, 12 East, 39, it was holden that a copyhold descend-ing by custom to all the children equally of the tenant last seised, one of the joint-tenants might maintain ejectment on his single demise for his own share. In *Doe d. Lulham* v. *Fenn*, 3 Campb. 190, Lord *Ellen-borough*, C. J., held, that in ejectment on the several demises of three persons, each demise being of the whole, the lessors of the plaintiff were entitled to a verdict, upon evidence, that they had jointly granted a lease to the defendant under which he had paid rent, but which had expired.— N. It was objected, that it must be taken that the lessors of the plaintiff were joint-tenants, and as there was not any joint demise, the plaintiff could not recover, but Lord *Ellenborough* overruled the objection. See *Worrall* v. *Beck*, M. 8 Geo. II. cited 1 Wils. 1.

lease. The surrenderee of a copyhold estate *after admittance*, may
maintain an ejectment against the surrenderor, on a demise laid on
a day between the time of surrender and admittance; because, as
against all persons, but the lord, the title of the surrenderee, after
admittance, is perfect as from the time of the surrender, and shall
relate back to it (*s*). So in ejectment by an administrator, the
demise may be laid on a day after the intestate's death, but before
administration granted (*t*). 4th, The demise may be for any number
of years; this part of the declaration being a fiction, it will not be
any objection that the lessor of the plaintiff had not power to grant
a term of equal duration with that alleged. Hence, tenant from year
to year may declare on a demise for seven years (*u*). Care should
be taken that the term stated be long enough to admit of the plaintiff's recovering possession before it expires (22). 5th, If the ejectment be brought by a corporation aggregate (*x*) (23), an infant, or
for tithes (*y*), regularly the declaration ought to state that the
demise was by deed; and in the case of the infant, it ought to
appear that some rent was reserved; but it is not necessary that
the deed should be proved (*z*). In ejectment for tithes, the declaration used to set forth the nature of the tithe (*a*). 6th, With
respect to the description of the thing demised, it may be observed,
that it ought to be made with such certainty, that the sheriff may
know, from an inspection of the record, what he is to deliver pos-

(*s*) *Holdfast* v. *Clapham*, 1 T. R. 600.
(*t*) *Lessee of Patten* v. *Patten*, Alcock
& Napier, 493, Ireland, B. R.
(*u*) *Doe* v. *Porter*, 3 T. R. 13.
(*x*) Carth. 390. This omission will be
aided by verdict. Bull. N. P. 98.

(*y*) *Swadling* v. *Piers*, Cro. Jac. 613.
Omission cured by verdict, *Partridge* v.
Ball, Ld. Raym. 136.
(*z*) *Furley* v *Wood*, 1 Esp. N. P. C.
198, *Kenyon*, C. J.
(*a*) Bull. N. P. 99.

(22) But the courts have been very liberal in permitting plaintiffs to
amend in this instance. In the case of *Power d. Boyce and another* v.
Rowe, (in Ireland, Pasch. 1802,) the term expired, whilst the case was
depending in the Exchequer Chamber; the judgment having been affirmed, a motion was made to enlarge the term, and the court, (Lord
Redesdale, C., assisted by the chief justices,) on the authority of *Dickens*
v. *Greenvill*, Carth. 3, and *Vicars* v. *Haydon*, Cowp. 841, made an order
to amend the record by enlarging the term. A writ of error was then
sued, returnable in Parliament, and upon the record so amended being
transmitted, the plaintiff in error complained, by petition to the House of
Lords, of the amendment made by the Court of Exchequer Chamber as
an alteration of the record, and prayed a writ of *certiorari* to be directed
to the Court of Exchequer Chamber to transmit the record in its original
form. Upon debate, their lordships refused the writ, holding the amendment to have been properly made, and finally affirmed the judgment on
the merits. See *Lessee of Lawlor* v. *Murray*, 1 Sch. & Lef. 81, n. (a).

(23) A corporation aggregate cannot make a lease for years without
deed, in respect of the quality of the incorporation. 1 Inst. 85, a.

session of. But the strictness of this rule has been relaxed in many instances, on the ground that the sheriff is to take his information from the party recovering (24). 7th, The ejectment or ouster must be stated to have been made after the commencement of the supposed lease : but it is not necessary, although usual, to mention any particular day (b). It is sufficient, if it appear on the face of the declaration, that the ouster was after the term commenced, and before action brought. It was formerly usual for the declaration in ejectment by original, to repeat the whole of the original writ ; but now, by a general rule of all the courts (c), the rules heretofore made in the Courts of King's Bench and Common Pleas respectively, for avoiding long and unnecessary repetitions of the original writ in certain actions therein mentioned, shall be extended and applied, in the Courts of King's Bench, Common Pleas, and Exchequer of Pleas, to all personal and mixed actions ; and in none of such actions shall the original writ be repeated in the declaration, but only the nature of the action stated in manner following : viz. "A. B. was attached to answer C. D. in a plea of trespass, or in a plea of trespass and ejectment (d), or as the case may be ; and any further statement shall not be allowed in costs."

Of the Notice subscribed to the Declaration.—To the declaration is subscribed a notice to the tenant in possession, from the casual ejector, and subscribed with his name, signifying, that unless the tenant appear, &c. in the term next ensuing that in which the declaration is served, and by rule of court cause himself to be made defendant, in the room of the casual ejector, he shall suffer judgment to be entered against him, and the tenant will be turned out of possession. It is not necessary that there should be any date to the notice (e). At the time when the copy of the declaration and notice is delivered to the tenant in possession, he must be informed of the nature of the proceeding, and the notice should be read to him, or the substance of it fully explained. The delivery of the declaration and notice accompanied with the explanation above-mentioned, is called *service* of a declaration in ejectment.

(b) *Merrell* v. *Smith*, Cro. Jac. 311.   see above rule.
(c) R. G. H. T. 2 Will. IV. Reg. IV.   (e) Per *Patteson*, J., *Doe d. Evans* v.
(d) For form of declaration by original,   *Roe*, 2 A. & E. 12.

---

(24) *Ejectio firmæ* of 30 acres of land in D. and S. The defendant was found guilty of 10 acres, and as to the residue, not guilty ; and it was moved, in arrest of judgment, that it is uncertain in which of the vills this land lay, and therefore no judgment can be given, nor any execution. But the objection was overruled ; and it was adjudged for the plaintiff ; *for the sheriff shall take his information from the party* for what 10 acres the verdict was. *Portman* v. *Morgan*, Cro. Eliz. 465. See also, to the same effect, *Cottingham* v. *King*, 1 Burr. 623, and *Connor* v. *West*, 5 Burr. 2673.

Formerly, landlords, to whom a right of entry had accrued during or immediately after Hilary and Trinity Terms respectively, were unable to prosecute ejectments, so as to try the same *at the assizes* immediately ensuing; but now, by stat. 11 Geo. IV. and 1 Will. IV. c. 70, s. 36, [23rd July, 1830,] "in all actions of ejectment by any landlord against his tenant, or against any person claiming through or under such tenant, for the recovery of any lands or heredi- taments where the tenancy shall expire, or the right of entry shall accrue in (25) or after *Hilary* or *Trinity* Terms respectively, it shall be lawful for the lessor of the plaintiff, *at any time* within ten days after such tenancy shall expire, or right of entry accrue, to serve a declaration in ejectment, entitled of the day next after the day of the demise in such declaration, whether the same shall be in term or in vacation, with a notice thereunto subscribed, requiring the tenant in possession to appear and plead within ten days; and proceedings shall be had, and rules to plead entered and given, as nearly as may be, as if such declaration had been duly served before the preceding term. Provided, that no judgment shall be signed against the casual ejector, until default of appearance and plea within such ten days, and that at least six clear days' notice of trial shall be given to the defendant, before the commission day of the assizes at which such ejectment is intended to be tried (26). Provided also, that defendant may, at any time before trial, apply to a judge, by summons in the usual manner, for time to plead, or for staying or setting aside the proceedings, or for postponing the trial until the next assizes, and the judge may make such order as to him shall seem expedient." By sect. 37, the declaration may be entitled specially of the day next after the day of demise, whether in term or in vacation. The foregoing statute is confined to issu- able terms. *Doe* v. *Roe*, 2 C. & J. 45.

VII. *Of the Service of Declaration.*

THE tenant or tenants in possession may be served personally at any place. But in cases where tenant in possession cannot be

---

(25) That is, in full term. Trinity Term begins on the 22nd of May, (s. 6). Where the right accrued on the 20th of May, after the essoign day, but before the first day of term, it was holden, that the statute did not apply. *Doe* v. *Roe*, 1 Dowl. P. C. 79.

(26) It is not necessary to prove, at the trial, under this section, the notice of trial. *Doe d. Antrobus* v. *Jephson*, B. R. E. T. 1832. Jervis's New Rules and Statutes, 3rd edit. p. 143, n.

served, service on the wife of tenant in possession must be either on the land in question, or at the dwelling-house of the husband. In this case, from the fact of the wife being served on the premises (*f*), or at the dwelling-house of the husband though not on the premises, the court presumes that the parties are living together as man and wife, and that the husband has notice of the proceedings: and on this presumption, such service is deemed good. Where premises demised on lease to one person, have been underlet to others, it is necessary to serve separately all the under-tenants (*g*). Service on one of several joint-tenants has been holden (*h*) sufficient. So service on the messenger in possession of the premises, and on the official assignee, tenant being bankrupt (*i*). Where the tenant in possession had rendered the premises inaccessible, and had evaded personal service, the court held it sufficient to leave the declaration and notice at the counting-house (*k*) of the tenant in possession. Where a tenant in possession had absconded, leaving the key of his house in the hands of a broker, with instructions to let the house, it was holden (*l*), that service of the declaration on the broker, and fixing a copy on the door of the house, was sufficient.

Service on the servant, child, or niece, of the tenant in possession, *on the premises*, is good service, provided the service be afterwards acknowledged by the *tenant* himself, and it appears that he has received it before the term (*m*), but not otherwise (*n*) ; and a mere acknowledgment of the wife is not sufficient (*o*). If the tenant or his wife refuse to receive the declaration, &c., a copy of it should be left for them, or affixed to the premises ; so if there be not any person in possession of the thing demised, a copy of the declaration and notice should be affixed to some conspicuous part. Where there is any thing unusual in the manner of serving the declaration, it should be mentioned to the court on moving for judgment against the casual ejector ; and if the court are satisfied that the tenant has had notice of the declaration, they will make the rule for judgment absolute in the first instance ; if doubtful, they will grant a rule requiring the tenant to show cause why the service should not, under the special circumstances, be deemed sufficient, and they will prescribe the mode of serving the rule (*p*). Service (*q*) before the first day of the term is now sufficient. Semble, that although

(*f*) *Doe d. Morland* v. *Bayliss*, 6 T. R. 765.

(*g*) *Doe d. Lord Darlington* v. *Cock*, 4 B. & C. 259.

(*h*) *Doe d. Clothier* v. *Roe*, 6 Dowl. (P. C.) 291.

(*i*) *Doe d. Baring* v. *Roe*, 6 Dowl. (P. C.) 456.

(*k*) *Doe d. Barrow* v. *Roe*, 1 Man. & Gr. 238.

(*l*) *Doe d. Scott* v. *Roe*, 6 Bingh. N. C. 207.

(*m*) *Roe, Lessee of Hambrook*, v. *Doe*, 14 East, 441.

(*n*) *Doe d. Lord Dinorben* v. *Roe*, 2 M. & W. 374.

(*o*) 1 Bos. & Pul. 384.

(*p*) See *Sprightly* v. *Dunch*, 2 Burr. 1116 ; *Fenn* v. *Denn*, 2 Burr. 1181 ; *Lessee of Methold* v. *Noright*, 1 Bl. R. 290 ; *Gulliver* v. *Wagstaff*, 1 Bl. R. 317 ; *Doe d. Hindle* v. *Roe*, 3 M. & W. 279.

(*q*) R. G. T. T. 1 Will. IV. See *ante*, p. 714.

an administrator may lay the demise on a day after the death of intestate, and before grant of administration, yet the declaration ought not to be served until after administration has been granted (r).

VIII. *Of the subsequent Proceedings, Judgment against Casual Ejector, p. 720; Appearance of Defendant, p. 721; Consent Rule, p. 721; Stat. 11 Geo. II. c. 19, s. 13, enabling Landlord to defend, p. 722.*

I<small>F</small> the tenant in possession does not appear according to the notice subscribed, and enter into a rule called the consent rule, the plaintiff may, at the beginning of the term in which the tenant in possession ought to have appeared, move the court for judgment against the casual ejector. Before this motion can be made, a rule to plead must be given (s), and the motion itself must be founded on an affidavit of service of declaration, either on the tenant in possession, or in such manner as shall satisfy the court, that the tenant in possession has had notice of the proceeding; and the affidavit must state that the declaration has been *explained* (t) as well as read over at the time of service. The time for appearance depends on the situation of the premises.

1. *Where the Premises lie in London or Middlesex.*

The tenant in possession must appear within four days, inclusive, next after the motion for judgment, if such motion be made at the beginning of the term. But where it is in a more advanced stage of the term, the court will exercise their discretion, and order the tenant to appear immediately, or within one or two days, so that the plaintiff may give notice of trial within the term. If the motion for judgment is made within the last four days of the term, the tenant has until two days before the essoign day of the subsequent term to appear in.

By R. G. C. P. (u), motion for judgment against casual ejector in ejectment in London and Middlesex, may be made on any day during term.

2. *Where the Premises lie elsewhere than in London or Middlesex.*

[See *ante*, p. 718, stat. 11 Geo. IV. and 1 Will. IV. c. 70, s. 36.]

(r) See argument in *Keene* v. *Dee*, B. R. Ireland, Alcock & Napier, 496, n.

(s) R. T. 18 Car. II. B. R.

(t) *Doe d. Wade* v. *Roe*, 6 Dowl. P. C. 51.

(u) 4 Bingh. N. C. 366.

The motion for judgment in this case may be made at any time within the term, in which the tenant is called on to appear; because the tenant has four days after the end of such term to appear in. This motion may also be made in the term after that (*x*) in which the tenant is required to appear.

By R. G. H. 4 Vict., a party entitled to appear to a declaration in ejectment, may appear and plead thereto at any time after service of such declaration, and before the end of the fourth day after the term on which the tenant is required by the notice to appear, and may proceed to compel the plaintiff to reply thereto, or may sign judgment of non pros, notwithstanding such plaintiff may not have obtained a rule for judgment on such service of declaration; and a plaintiff who may have omitted to obtain a rule for judgment within the time prescribed by the present rules and practice, shall be entitled, on production of such plea, to an order of a judge for leave to draw up a rule for judgment, as of the time of which such rule for judgment should have been obtained.

If the tenant appears, then he enters into the consent rule, the substance of which is as follows:—1st, He consents to be made defendant instead of the casual ejector. 2nd, To appear at the suit of the plaintiff; and if the proceedings are by bill, to file common bail. 3rd, To receive a declaration and plead, Not Guilty. 4th, At the trial of the issue, to confess lease, entry, and ouster, and insist upon title only. To this rule are added the following conditions:—1st, If at the trial the defendant shall not confess lease, entry, and ouster, whereby plaintiff shall not be able to prosecute his suit, defendant shall pay to plaintiff the costs of the non pros, and judgment shall be entered against the casual ejector by default. 2nd, If a verdict shall be given for defendant, or plaintiff shall not prosecute his suit for any other cause than the non-confession of lease, entry, and ouster, the lessor of the plaintiff shall pay costs to the defendant. Defendants having, in many instances, put the plaintiff, after the title had been established, to give evidence that the defendant was in possession at the time of ejectment brought, and many plaintiffs having been nonsuited for want of such proof, and such practice being considered as contrary to the true meaning of the consent rule, it was ordered (*y*), that the defendant should specify, in the consent rule, for what premises he intends to defend, and should consent to confess, that he or (if he defends as landlord) his tenant was in possession thereof at the time of the service of declaration; and if upon the trial he should not confess such possession, as well as lease, entry, and ouster, whereby the plaintiff

(*x*) *Doe d. Barth* v. *Roe*, 4 Bingh. N. C. 675.
(*y*) Reg. Gen. B. R. M. T. 1820; 4 B.
& A. 196; C. B. H. T. 1821; 2 B. & B. 470; Exch. 2 Geo. IV.

should not be able further to prosecute his suit, then no costs should be allowed for not further prosecuting the same, and the defendant should pay costs to the plaintiff. N. It is not incumbent on the plaintiff, in ordinary cases, to produce the consent rule (z); the only instance in which it can now be necessary to produce the rule is, where the plaintiff, directing his case to certain premises, the other party contends that he does not defend for those; there it may be requisite to produce the rule, to show for what he does defend.

Formerly, by the practice of Q. B., the plea and consent rule were filed at the chambers of one of the judges of that court; but now (a), the plea, with the consent rule annexed thereto, is to be delivered in like manner as pleas in other actions.

Where the tenant in possession is merely an under-tenant to some other person, as soon as the declaration in ejectment is delivered to him, he is obliged, by stat. 11 Geo. II. c. 19, s. 12, to give notice of such delivery to his landlord, under pain of forfeiting three years' improved (b) or rack rent of the premises holden. N. This penalty does not attach on the tenant of mortgagor, who omits to give him notice of ejectment brought by mortgagee, 1 T. R. 647; because the statute only extends to cases where ejectments are brought inconsistent with landlord's title. This wise provision of the statute was intended to prevent fraudulent recoveries of the possession, by collusion with the tenant of the land. And by the same statute, s. 13, the court where the ejectment is brought, is empowered to suffer the landlord (c) to make himself defendant with tenant, if he shall appear; and by the same clause, although if the tenant shall refuse or neglect to appear, judgment shall be signed against the casual ejector; yet the landlord shall be permitted to appear by himself, on his consenting to enter into the usual rule; and judgment against the casual ejector shall be stayed *until further order* (d). Who shall be considered a landlord, within the meaning of this act, is sometimes a difficult question to determine: the following persons have been so considered: 1. Devisee in trust, 4 T. R. 122. 2. In *Doe d. Tilyard* v. *Cooper*, a mortgagee under the defendant was permitted to defend with him (e). The following persons have not been deemed landlords within the meaning of this act: 1. A devisee, where the ejectment was brought by the heir; *Roe d. Leake* v. *Doe*, M. 29 Geo. II. C. B. Bull. N. P. 95. 2. A mortgagee, who had never received rent, *ib.* The question to be considered in all cases is, whether the party applying

(z) *Doe d. Greaves* v. *Raby*, 2 B. & A. 948.

(a) R. G. H. 1 Vict. 7 A. & E. 972.

(b) See *Crocker* v. *Fothergill*, 2 B. & A. 652.

(c) Landlord might have defended with tenant before this statute, Salk. 257; 7 Mod. 70; 3 Burr. 1301; but the 2nd provision in this section is new.

(d) See *Jones* v. *Edwards*, Str. 1241.

(e) 8 T. R. 645.

to defend as landlord, be himself interested in the event of the suit; or whether he be merely set in motion for the purposes of some other person: if the latter be the case, the court will not permit a mortgagee to defend as landlord (*d*). 3. *Cestui que trust*, not having been in possession. 3 T. R. 783. In all cases of vacant possession (*e*), unless such as are within stat. 4 Geo. II. c. 28, (which see in next section,) no person claiming title will be let in to defend; but he who can first seal a lease on the premises, must obtain possession, and any other person claiming title may eject him if he can; and by the course of the court, no defence can be made in these cases but by the defendant in the ejectment, who is a real ejector. In *Martin* v. *Davis*, Str. 914, the court refused to let the parson of Hampstead chapel defend for right to enter and perform divine service only; notwithstanding the case of *Hollingsworth* v. *Brewster*, Salk. 256, observing, that that case had often been denied since. If a party should be admitted to defend as landlord, whose title is inconsistent with the possession of the tenant, the lessor of the plaintiff may apply to the court, or to a judge at chambers, and have the rule discharged with costs (*f*).

IX. *Of the Proceedings in Ejectment, directed by Stat.* 4 *Geo. II. c.* 28, *s.* 2, *in order to obviate the Difficulties attending Re-entries at Common Law, for Non-payment of Rent Arrear, p.* 723; *Of the Proceedings where the Possession is vacant, p.* 725.

By stat. 4 Geo. II. c. 28, s. 2, it is enacted, "That in *all* cases between landlord and tenant, when half a year's rent shall be in arrear, and the landlord has a right of entry for non-payment thereof, he may, *without a formal demand or re-entry*, serve a declaration in ejectment; *or*, in case the same cannot be legally served, or no tenant be in actual possession, affix the same upon the door of any demised messuage; *or*, in case such ejectment shall not be for the recovery of any messuage, then upon some notorious place of the lands, &c., comprised in the declaration in ejectment, and such affixing shall be deemed legal service; and in case of judgment against the casual ejector, or nonsuit for not confessing lease, entry, and ouster, it shall appear by affidavit, or be proved on the trial, in case the defendant appears, that half a year's rent was due before the declaration served, and that *no sufficient distress was*

(*d*) *Doe d. Pearson* v. *Roe*, 6 Bingh. 613.

(*e*) Arg. per *Eyre*, Serjt., and said by the reporter to be the constant practice.

Esp. Beauchamp, Barnes, 4to edit. 177.

(*f*) *Doe d. Harwood* v. *Lippincott*, Ad. Eject. 230.

to be found on the premises (*g*), countervailing the arrears then due, and that the lessor had power to re-enter; *then, and in every such case*, the lessor in ejectment shall recover judgment and execution, in the same manner as if the rent in arrear had been legally demanded, and re-entry made; provided (*h*), that if the tenant, at any time *before the trial* in such ejectment, shall pay or tender to the landlord or his attorney, or pay into court, the rent arrear and costs, all further proceedings on the ejectment shall be discontinued" (27). It has been supposed that the preceding statute only applied to cases of ejectment brought after half a year's rent due, *where no sufficient distress was to be found upon the premises.* But in a late case, (*Roe* v. *Davis*, 7 East, 363,) it was holden, that the statute was more general in its operation. And, according to Lord *Tenterden*, these words, "no sufficient distress was to be found on the premises," must mean no sufficient distress, which can be got at; hence, where the outer door was locked, so that the landlord could not get at the premises, Lord *T.* held, that there was not any sufficient distress; for there was not any available distress. *Doe* v. *Dyson*, M. & Malk. 77. The application to the court (*i*), on the part of the tenant, to stay proceedings, must, by the very terms of the act, be made *before* trial. In ejectment by a land-

(*g*) See *Doe d. Smelt* v. *Fuchau*, 15 East, 286.

(*h*) Sect. 4.
(*i*) *Roe* v. *Davis*, 7 East, 363.

---

(27) Before this statute, courts of law and equity exercised a discretionary power of staying the lessor from proceeding at law, in cases of forfeiture for non-payment of rent, by compelling him to take the money due to him. See the opinion of *Lee*, C. J., in *Archer* v. *Snapp*, Andr. 341; 2 Salk. 597; 8 Mod. 345; 10 Mod. 383; 2 Vern. 103; 1 Wils. 75; 2 Str. 900. By this statute, the service of the declaration in ejectment is substituted for the demand of rent, which, at common law, must have been made upon the exact day when the forfeiture accrued, in case of non-payment, for the precise rent, at the proper place of payment, at a convenient hour before sunset. See these particulars fully commented upon in the note to *Duppa* v. *Mayo*, 1 Saund. 287, a. Ejectment on a demise laid on the 10th May, 1824. Defendant was tenant under a lease, by which the rent was made payable at Lady-day and Michaelmas, and in which there was a proviso for re-entry on non-payment of rent for thirty days. Half a year's rent was due at Lady-day, 1824, and there was no sufficient distress on the premises; the declaration was served on the 14th May, 1824. It was holden, that, although the service of declaration was on a day subsequent to the day of demise, the plaintiff was entitled to recover, inasmuch as the title must be taken to have accrued on the 30th day after the rent became due, *viz.* the 24th of April. The statute does not require that the day of demise must be the very day when declaration is served. *Doe d. Lawrence* v. *Shawcross*, 3 B. & C. 752.

lord (*k*), the tenant moved to stay proceeding, upon payment of rent arrear and costs. On a rule to show cause, it was insisted, for the plaintiff, that the case was not within the preceding statute; because it was not an ejectment founded singly on the act, but it was brought likewise on a clause of re-entry in the lease for not repairing, and the lease was produced in court. However, the rule was made absolute, with liberty for the plaintiff to proceed upon any other title. Where an ejectment is brought on the preceding statute for the forfeiture of a lease (*l*), acceptance of rent afterwards, by the landlord, has been holden a waiver of the forfeiture; for it is a penalty, and by accepting the rent, the party waives the penalty (*m*). Landlord having a right of re-entry for non-payment of rent, brought an ejectment, and proved a demand of half a year's rent, *after* the day on which it was due, and a refusal on the part of the defendant to pay it before the re-entry. It appeared that there was a sufficient distress on the premises during the whole time. It was holden (*n*), that the lessor of the plaintiff could not recover either at common law, or under the preceding statute: not by the former, because the rent was not demanded on the day when it became due; Co. Litt. 201; 7 Rep. 28; nor by the latter, because there was a sufficient distress on the premises. Upon a lease reserving rent payable quarterly, with a proviso, that if the rent be in arrear twenty-one days next after day of payment, *being lawfully demanded*, the lessor may re-enter: it was holden (*o*), by three judges (dissentiente Lord *Ellenborough*, C. J.), that five quarters being in arrear, and no sufficient distress on the premises, the lessor might re-enter without a demand. Lands were devised in fee, charged with an annuity; and power was given to the annuitant to distrain, if the annuity were in arrear for twenty days after the day of payment, *being lawfully demanded;* power was also given, if the annuity should be in arrear for forty days, to enter and take the profits, until the annuitant should be thereby paid all arrears with costs; it was holden (*p*), that upon the annuity being forty days in arrear, the annuitant was entitled to recover in ejectment, although no demand was made; for this was not a case of forfeiture for non-payment of an annuity, but only a right to enter and receive the profits until the arrears were satisfied.

Of the Proceedings where the Possession is vacant.—In cases between landlord and tenant, where one half-year's rent is in arrear, and the landlord has a right of entry, the mode of proceed-

---

(*k*) *Pure d. Withers* v. *Sturdy,* H. 1752; Bull. N. P. 97.

(*l*) Per *Aston,* J., in *Doe* v. *Batten,* Cowp. 247.

(*m*) See further as to waiver of forfeiture, *ante,* p. 707.

(*n*) *Doe d. Forster* v. *Wandlass,* 7 T. R. 117.

(*o*) *Doe d. Scholefield* v. *Alexander,* 2 M. & S. 525.

(*p*) *Doe d. Biass* v. *Horsley,* 1 A. & E. 766; 3 Nev. & Man. 567, cited by *Patteson,* J., in *Doe d. Chawner* v. *Boulter,* 6 A. & E. 687.

ing, where the premises are untenanted, is marked out by the preceding statute. In other cases of a vacant possession the mode of proceeding is thus: A. (the person claiming title) by letter of attorney empowers B. to execute a lease, in the name of A., of the premises in question, to C. This lease is executed on the premises, B. and C. only being thereon; then B. leaves C. in possession, who is turned out by D., to whom, while on the premises, E. delivers a declaration in ejectment. A rule to plead having been given, and not complied with, a motion is made for judgment, which is granted of course. This motion must be supported by an affidavit of the above-mentioned proceedings, *viz.* the execution of the power of attorney, the lease, entry, ouster, and delivery of declaration; a copy whereof is annexed to the affidavit. A. made a lease of an alehouse in London (*q*), for years. The lessee, before the expiration of the term, left it, and took another house in Wapping; but there was some liquor and old vessels left in the first-mentioned house, and the doors were locked. Upon this the landlord sealed a lease on the premises, and brought an ejectment, as on a vacant possession, and accordingly, had judgment and execution; to set aside which, a motion was made. In addition to the foregoing facts it appeared, that only one quarter's rent was in arrear, and that the landlord had seen his tenant a short time only before he brought the ejectment. Lord *Hardwicke*, C. J.—"If only one quarter's rent was in arrear, the landlord could not proceed against the tenant on the statute 4 Geo. II. c. 28. But then, taking this as it stood at common law, the question will be, whether this was such a vacant possession as to enable the landlord to bring an ejectment in this manner. For though a tenant does not live on the premises, yet it cannot, from that circumstance alone, be called a vacant possession; as if a person uses one house and lives in another, that will be a good possession of both. Here the tenant had actual possession of the premises, by keeping his liquor there, and, as appears, was such a person as the landlord might have served personally with an ejectment; for a declaration in ejectment may be served on the tenant himself any where, though the wife can be served with it only on the premises (28). I remember a case where a person in the Fleet was served with an ejectment. If the tenant, in this case, sometimes absconded, and only appeared on Sundays, then the landlord should have applied to the court for a special rule, as to the service of the declaration in ejectment." *Probyn*, J., mentioned a case where hay was left in a barn by a

(*q*) *Savage* v. *Dent*, M. 10 Geo. II.   *S. C.* shortly stated.
B. R. MSS.; 2 Str. 1064; Bull N. P. 97,

---

(28) Or at the dwelling-house of the husband, if it appears that wife is living with husband. *Vid.* 4 T. R. 465.

tenant, and that was holden sufficient to keep the possession. The court ordered the judgment and execution to be set aside with costs. Where the premises to be recovered consisted of unfinished houses, it was holden (r), that the course was to proceed as on a vacant possession; and not by affixing the declaration on the doors of the houses. The stat. 11 Geo. II. c. 19, s. 16, authorizes two or more Js. P., in cases where tenants holding premises at rack rent or three quarters of yearly value, who are in arrear *one year*, desert them and leave them unoccupied so as no sufficient distress can be had, to go and view and affix on the most notorious part of the premises a notice in writing what day (at the distance of fourteen days at least) they will return to take a second view; and if upon such second view the tenant or some person in his behalf does not appear and pay the rent, or there shall not be sufficient distress upon the premises, then the justices may put the landlord into possession. The statute 57 Geo. III. c. 52, extends the foregoing provision as against tenants who are in arrear for one half-year. By the 17th section of the 11 Geo. II. an appeal is given to the judges at the next assize; the tenant, therefore, may have summary redress, if any wrong has been done; and the appeal is not attended with any great risk, for, if it is dismissed, the amount of costs to be awarded against the tenant cannot exceed 5*l*. It is not necessary that any complaint should be made *on oath* (s) in order to justify the interference of the magistrates. The *request* of the lessor or landlord, or his or her bailiff or receiver, is sufficient. Although the tenant has a summary remedy by appeal to the justices of assize, yet the record of the proceedings in pursuance of the statute unappealed from, is conclusive as to the magistrates, and will afford a complete defence to them in an action of trespass. In a case (t) where the magistrates had adjudicated erroneously on the fact of desertion, and the judges of assize on appeal had made an order for the restitution of the farm to the tenant with costs; and he tenant afterwards brought trespass for the eviction, against tthe magistrates, the constables, and the landlord; it was holden, that the record of the proceedings before the magistrates was an answer to the action on the behalf of all the defendants.

(r) *Doe d. Showell* v. *Roe,* 2 Cr. M. & R. 42.

(s) *Basten* v. *Carew,* 3 B. & C. 649.

(t) *Ashcroft* v. *Bourne and others,* 3 B. & Ad. 684.

X. *Of the Pleadings and Defence, p.* 728; *Entry barred by Fine
and Non-claim, p.* 726; *Entry barred by Statute of Limitations,* 21 *Jac. I. c.* 16, 3 *& 4 Will. IV. c.* 27, *p.* 732.

SPECIAL pleas, either in bar or abatement, are seldom pleaded to
this action; because, according to the modern practice, if the defendant appears, he generally enters into the consent rule, by the
terms of which he is bound to plead the general issue, Not Guilty (*u*).
Although the rule of H. T. 4 Will. IV. requiring pleadings subsequent to the declaration to be delivered between the parties, did
not apply to actions of ejectment (*x*), yet now, by R. G. H. 1 Vict.
(*ante,* p. 720,) the plea, with the consent rule annexed, is to be
delivered in like manner as pleas in other actions: with regard to
the declaration, it has been holden (*y*), that it must commence and
conclude in the usual form, for it is not within the rules of M. T.
3 Will. IV.

Of the Defence.—As an action of ejectment is founded on a
right of entry in the party claiming title, if the defendant can show
that such right has been tolled or taken away, it will be a sufficient
defence to the action.   Under the old law, as it stood before the
31st December, 1833, (for which, see former editions of this work,)
a right of entry might have been taken away by descent cast, discontinuance, or warranty; but that operation and effect has been
removed by a late statute (*z*).   Another mode of defeating the right
of entry, and thereby barring the ejectment, was by fine and non-
claim,—but since the same day, that is, 31st December, 1833, fines
and recoveries have been abolished (*a*), and more simple modes of
assurance substituted in their room.   As cases, however, may still
arise, upon this species of bar, it may be convenient to retain that
portion of the work.

Entry barred by Fine and Non-claim.—A fine at the common
law, or fine without proclamations, levied by a tenant of the freehold, not being under any disability (*b*), was a perpetual bar to all
persons who had right and no impediment at the time of fine levied,
and who did not claim within a year and a day after the fine levied,
and execution thereupon.   But this puissance of a fine was taken
away by stat. 34 Edw. III. c. 16, by which it was enacted, "that
the plea of non-claim should not be any bar in future."   Great inconveniences having resulted from the provisions of this statute, the
legislature again interposed, and by statute 1 Ric. III. c. 7, and 4
Hen. VII. c. 24, the ancient law was revived, though with some

(*u*) Runn. Eject. 233.
(*x*) *Doe d. Williams* v. *Williams,* 4
Nev. & Man. 259.
(*y*) *Doe d. Gillett* v. *Roe,* 1 Cr. M. &
R. 19; 4 Tyrw. 649.

(*z*) Stat. 3 & 4 Will. IV. c. 27, s. 39,
and 3 & 4 Will. IV. c. 74, s. 14.
(*a*) 3 & 4 Will. IV. c. 74.
(*b*) Shep. Touch. 19; Hargrave's Co.
Litt. 121, a. n. (1).

modification: proclamations being required to make fines more notorious, and the time for claiming being enlarged from one year to five years. The statute 4 Hen. VII. c. 24, (which is nearly a transcript of statute 1 Ric. III.) having directed, in the first place, that every fine, after the engrossing thereof, shall be read and proclaimed openly in court the same term, and the three next following terms, at four several days in each term, proceeds to enact, " that the proclamations being thus made, the fine shall conclude as well privies (29) as strangers: *except* women covert, persons within twenty-one years of age, in prison, or out of the realm, or not of whole mind at the time of the fine being levied, not parties to such fine, so as the said women covert, persons within age, &c., or their heirs (30), pursue their right by action or entry, within five years after the removal of their respective disabilities." Then follow the

---

(29) Although the issue in tail were privies to the ancestor, yet inasmuch as the statute *de donis* (13 Edw. I. c. 1,) had *expressly* ordained that tenants in tail should not have power to alien the lands entailed, doubts were raised, whether fines, levied with proclamations by the ancestor, would by force of this statute 4 Hen. VII. c. 24, bar the issue in tail. To remove these doubts, it was enacted by statute 32 Hen. VIII. c. 36, s. 1, " that all fines levied with proclamations according to statute 4 Hen. VII. c. 24, by any person of twenty-one years of age, of lands, &c. before the fine levied entailed to the person levying the fine, or to any ancestor of the same person, in possession, reversion, remainder, or use, immediately after proclamations made, should be adjudged a bar against him and his heirs claiming only by force of such entail, and against all others claiming only to his use, or to the use of any heir of his body." This statute, however, contained several exceptions, particularly one of fines of lands, of which the reversion is in the crown. In consequence of this exception, the question again arose in the *Earl of Derby's* case, whether a fine depending wholly on the 4 Hen. VII. was a bar to the issue in tail; eight judges against three held that it was. T. Raym. 260, 286, 319, 338; Pollexf. 491; Skin. 95; 2 Show. 104; T. Jo. 237. See further on this subject Mr. Hargrave's excellent note, Co. Litt. 121, a. n. (1). N. A fine levied by tenant in tail bars the estate tail, but not the remainders or reversion expectant thereon. Where a fine is levied by tenant in tail, who dies before all the proclamations are past, yet will the issue in tail be barred, provided the proclamations are afterwards duly made. *Parslow's* case, cited 3 Rep. 90, b.

(30) By this provision, the rights of those persons who are under disabilities, and of their heirs, are saved as long as the disabilities continue, and five years after, but no longer. A., seised in fee of lands, died, leaving B. his heir, a feme covert. Upon the death of A., a stranger made a tortious entry on the lands, continued in possession, and levied a fine *sur cognizance de droit come ceo, &c.* with proclamations. B. afterwards died under coverture, no entry having been made on her behalf to avoid the fine, leaving C. her heir not affected with any of the disabilities mentioned in the statute. It was holden, that C., who had not pursued his right

saving clauses, which are, 1st, Saving to every person and their heirs (*other than parties*) such right as they have at the time of such fine engrossed, so that they pursue their claim by action or entry within five years after the proclamations (31). 2nd, Saving to all other persons such right, claim, and interest, as first (32) shall accrue after the proclamations, by force of any gift in tail, or by any other matter had and made *before* the fine levied, so as they pursue their right within five years after the same shall grow due; and further, if the said persons are under any of the before mentioned disabilities at the time when their right first accrues, they or their heirs may pursue their right within five years next after the removal of the disability. 3rd, Saving to every person, not party nor privy to the fine, their exception to avoid the fine, by that, that those which were parties to the fine, nor any person to their use, had nothing in the lands at the time of the fine levied. Such are the provisions of the statute on which the force and effect of fines heretofore levied, principally depended, and by virtue of which, a fine levied by tenant of the freehold, with five years' nonclaim, operates as a bar to an ejectment, except in those cases which are specially provided for by the statute. The statute, as to the engrossment of the fine before the proclamation, is only directory (c). Where the fine being levied at the great sessions, the indorsement of the proclamations was headed, "according to the

(c) *Doe d. Fleming* v. *Ford*, 1 A. & E. 765.

within five years after the death of B., was barred by the fine. *Dillon* v. *Leman*, 2 H. Bl. 584.

(31) By force of this clause, persons having a present right to lands whereof a fine is levied, and not being parties to such fine, may pursue their claim within five years, to be computed from the day on which the last proclamation was made.

(32) One who had a future interest, but no present right of entry at the time of the fine levied, died, and the five years passed, and afterwards administration was granted; it was holden, that the administrator should have five years to sue from the granting of the letters of administration, *for none had title of entry before*. *Sanders* v. *Stanford*, cited in *Saffyn* v. *Adams*, Cro. Jac. 61. But where a lease for years of land was made to commence from the end of a term for years then in being; the first term expired, the second lessee did not enter, but the reversioner entered and made a feoffment, and levied a fine with proclamations; five years passed; it was holden, that the fine and the nonclaim of the second lessee had barred him of his term : for although lessee for years has not such an estate as will enable him to levy a fine, yet shall his interest be barred by the statute; for the words of the statute are general; ("*the said fine with proclamations shall be a final end, and conclude as well privies as strangers to the same ;*") and the words of the saving are, (*such right, claim, and interest,*) and tenant for term of years has an interest. *Saffyn* v. *Adams*, 5 Rep. 123, b.; Cro. Jac. 60, *S. C.*

form of the statute;" it was holden (d), that the omission afterwards to state the place where the sessions were holden, was immaterial. A., tenant for life, with remainder to his own executors
for forty years, with remainder to B. in fee, levied a fine *sur conusance de droit*, with proclamations, in Hil. T. 1733-4. B., not
having made an entry to avoid the fine, in 1735, devised to C. for
life, with remainder to D. in tail, and died in that year; in 1738,
A. died; C. died in 1803, not having made an entry; in 1805, D.
entered for the purpose of avoiding the fine, and brought ejectment. It was holden, that D. was not entitled to recover; for
the right of entry was confined to five years after the expiration of the term of forty years, that is, to five years after 1778;
and B. could not by his will give a right to avoid this fine at a more
distant period than the end of the five years; that the devisee was
exactly in the same state as the heir; and that, as the title of D.
did not "first accrue to him after the fine by matter *before* the
fine," but by the will of B., which was after the fine, D. could not
claim the benefit of the second saving (e). This statute extends to
copyholds (f). With respect to the clauses relating to disabilities,
it may be observed, that if he who has a present right, and is not
under any disability, brings on himself a disability; as if, being
within the realm at the time of the fine levied, he should afterwards go beyond sea, or the like; in these cases he will not be
allowed any longer time to pursue his right than during the first
five years after proclamation had (g). So when the disability is
once removed, the five years begin to run, and will continue to run,
notwithstanding any subsequent disability, either voluntary or involuntary (h). It will be proper to remark also, that the exceptions in favour of infants, femes covert, &c. extend to those only
to whom a right first accrues, and in whom it first attaches; for
if a person to whom a right first accrues, dies before the expiration
of the five years, and such right descends to his son, or heir at law,
who is then under age, or labours under any of the other disabilities mentioned in the act, such son or heir must pursue his right
within the five years, which began to run in the time of his ancestor, otherwise he will be barred (i). A fine levied by tenant for
life divests and displaces all estates in reversion or remainder (k),
and leaves nothing in the reversioner or remainder-man but a
mere right of entry (33); and where the fine is levied by tenant

(d) *Doe d. Jones* v. *Harrison*, 3 B. &
Ad. 764.

(e) *Goodright* v. *Forester*, Exch. Chr.
1 Taunt. 578.

(f) 9 Rep. 105, a.

(g) Shep. Touch. 29.

(h) *Doe d. Duroure* v. *Jones*, 4 T. R.
300.

(i) *Stowell* v. *Zouch*, Plowd. 355.

(k) *Goodright* v. *Forrester*, 8 East,
552.

(33) This right of entry was not devisable, *S. C.* But see 1 Vict.
c. 26, s. 3.

for life of parcel of a manor, the reversion of which parcel is in the tenant in fee in possession of the other parts of the manor, the effect of the fine is to sever such parcel from the manor. Where tenant in tail, under a settlement, (which also created a term of years,) levied a fine; it was holden (*l*), that being seised of the immediate estate of freehold, the fine worked a discontinuance and displaced the remainders, whereby he acquired a tortious fee; and no step having been taken to set aside the tortious estate, it became descendible and capable of being devised, and the devisee therefore entitled to recover; for a person seised of a base fee can devise it like a fee simple.

Proof of Fine.—The chirograph of a fine is evidence of such fine; because the chirographer is appointed to give out copies of the agreement between the parties, which are lodged of record (*m*). But where a fine is to be proved with proclamations, an examined copy of the proclamations must be produced in evidence (*n*); for although the chirographer is authorized by the common law to make out copies to the parties of *the fine*, yet he is not appointed by the statutes to copy the proclamations, and therefore his indorsement on the back of the fine, that the proclamations have been duly made, will not be sufficient evidence (*o*).

Entry barred by Stat. of Limitations, 21 *Jac. I. c.* 16, 3 & 4 *Will. IV. c.* 27.—By the statute of James, no person could make an entry into any lands, tenements, or hereditaments, but within twenty years next after his right or title *first* descended or accrued. The plaintiff, therefore, in ejectment, must have proved either actual possession or a right of entry within twenty years, or have accounted for the want of it; for, by force of that statute, an uninterrupted adverse possession for that period operated as a complete bar, except in those cases which fell within the second section, which comprehend five disabilities, *viz.* infancy, coverture, non compos mentis, imprisonment, and absence beyond seas (34).

(*l*) *Doe d. Cooper* v. *Finch,* 4 B. & Ad. 283.
(*m*) Bull. N. P. 229.
(*n*) *Chettle* v. *Pound,* Bull. N. P. 229;

Allen's case, Clayt. 51, S. P.
(*o*) See *Doe d. Hatch* v. *Bluck,* 6 Taunt. 486, 7.

---

(34) Ireland was a place beyond the seas within this clause, *Anon.* 1 Show. 91. But this has been altered by the new statute. See *post,* Sect. 19, p. 738. The statute of Jac. runs against the lord of a manor as well as against any other person; *Greeby* v. *Preston,* Norfolk Summ. Ass. 1728, Lord *Raymond,* C. J.; Serjt. Leeds MSS. Hence, if a house, &c. be built on the waste, the lord should take care to have some entry made of it on his books, and reserve some rent or service; otherwise he will lose his right. See *Doe d. Watt* v. *Morris,* 2 Bingh. N. C. 189, on the construction of the 21 Jac. I. c. 14, limiting the right of the crown to twenty

Under this clause, if the party to whom the right of entry first accrued was under disabilities at that time, he was allowed to bring his action, although the twenty years might have expired, so as he brought it within ten years after the removal of the disability. And in the case of his death, the heir had ten years from that time to bring his action (p). An opinion at one time prevailed, that, under the foregoing statute, successive tenants in tail had distinct and successive rights, but that has been decided otherwise; and it is now settled, that the twenty years under the foregoing statute begin to run when the title descends to the first heir in tail, not being under a disability (q). After the removal of the disability, when the time once begins to run, nothing can stop it (r).

Notwithstanding the foregoing statute, the right of bringing an ejectment frequently existed long after the power of trying a real action had determined; for either when disabilities lasted for sixty years after the death of the ancestor, or when estates in remainder did not come into possession until after that time, real actions were barred by the 32nd of Hen. VIII. c. 2, but the right of entry was saved by the provisions of the 21 Jac. I. c. 16 (s). But now by stat. 3 & 4 Will. IV. c. 27, s. 2, no person shall make an entry or distress, or bring an action to recover any land or rent, but within twenty years next after the time at which the right to make such entry or distress, or to bring such action, shall have first accrued to some person through whom he claims; or if such right shall not have accrued to any person through whom he claims, then within twenty years next after the time at which the right to make such entry or distress, or to bring such action, shall have first accrued to the person making or bringing the same. In the construction (t) of this act, the right to make an entry or distress, or bring an action to recover any land or rent, shall be deemed to have first accrued at such time as hereinafter is mentioned; (that is to say,) 1. When the person claiming such land or rent, or some person through whom he claims, shall, in respect of the estate or interest claimed, *have been in possession or in receipt of the profits of such land,* or *in receipt of such rent, and shall, while entitled thereto, have been dispossessed,* or *have discontinued such possession or receipt,* then such right shall be deemed to have *first* accrued at the time of such dispossession or discontinuance of possession, or

(p) *Doe* v. *Jesson*, 6 East, 80.
(q) *Tolson* v. *Kaye*, 3 Brod. & Bingh. 217; *Cotterell* v. *Dutton*, 4 Taunt. 826.
(r) *Doe* v. *Jones*, 4 T. R. 300.

(s) See Tyrrell's Suggestions on the Laws of Real Property, (not published,) p. 99.
(t) Sect. 3.

years. Possession of lands is not possession of mines under them, where there has ever been a distinct grant of mines. *Hodgkinson* v. *Fletcher*, 3 Doug. 31.

at the last time at which any such profits or rent were so received; 2. And when the person claiming such land or rent shall claim the estate or interest of *some deceased person who shall have continued in such possession or receipt, in respect of the same estate or interest, until the time of his death, and shall have been the last person entitled to such estate or interest, who shall have been in such possession or receipt,* then such right shall be deemed to have *first* accrued at the time of such death; 3. And when the person claiming such land or rent shall claim *in respect of an estate or interest in possession, granted, appointed, or otherwise assured by any instrument (other than a will,) to him, or some person through whom he claims, by a person being in respect of the same estate or interest in the possession or receipt of the profits of the land, or in the receipt of the rent, and no person entitled under such instrument shall have been in such possession or receipt,* then such right shall be deemed to have *first* accrued at the time at which the person claiming, or the person through whom he claims, became entitled to such possession or receipt by virtue of such instrument; 4. And when the estate or interest claimed shall have been *an estate or interest in reversion or remainder, or other future estate or interest, and no person shall have obtained the possession or receipt of the profits of such land, or the receipt of such rent in respect of such estate or interest,* then such right shall be deemed to have *first* accrued at the time at which such estate or interest became an estate or interest in possession; 5. And when the person claiming such land or rent, or the person through whom he claims, shall have become entitled by *reason of any forfeiture or breach of condition,* then such right shall be deemed to have *first* accrued when such forfeiture was incurred or such condition was broken.

In *James* v. *Salter*, 3 Bingh. N. C. 553, *Tindal*, C. J., expressed an opinion, that the object and intent of the 3rd section of this statute is to explain and give a construction to the enactment contained in the 2nd section, as to "the time at which the right to make a distress for any rent shall be deemed to have first accrued," in those cases only, in which doubt or difficulty might occur; leaving every case which plainly falls within the general words of the 2nd section, but is not included among the instances given by the 3rd, to be governed by the operation of the 2nd. Therefore, a distress or action for an annuity accruing by will, and charged on land, must be resorted to within twenty years from the death of the testator (*u*).

In 1788, estates were settled by marriage settlement, to the use of the wife for life, with remainders to her issue in tail, with remainder to the settlor (whose heiress at law she was) in fee. In 1818, by deeds to which the husband and wife, and their only son,

---

(*u*) The court of C. B. had previously decided this otherwise; *James* v. *Salter*, 2   Bingh. N. C. 505.

R. G., were parties, and by a recovery suffered in pursuance thereof, the estates were limited to the use of the husband for life, remainder to the wife for life, remainder to R. G. the son for life, remainder to his issue in tail, remainder to J. F. his sister for life, with other remainders over. The husband died in 1819, the wife in 1822, and R. G. in 1828; it was holden (*x*), that inasmuch as the estate of J. F. was carved out of the estate tail of R. G., she had the same time for bringing an ejectment as he would have had if he had continued alive, *viz.* twenty years, from the year 1822, when his remainder came into possession.

Where the lessor permits his lessee, during the continuance of the lease, to pay no rent for twenty years, (but there has been no adverse claim, and no payment of rent to any other person,) the lessor is not therefore barred by the 2nd section from recovering the premises in ejectment. The case falls within the latter branch of the 3rd section, which, in the case of an estate in reversion, provides that the right shall be deemed to have first accrued when it became an estate or interest in possession. The lessor therefore may recover in ejectment at any time within twenty years after the determination of the lease (*y*).

When (*z*) any right to make an entry, &c. by reason of any forfeiture or breach of condition, shall have first accrued in respect of any *estate or interest in reversion or remainder*, and the land or rent shall not have been recovered by virtue of such right, the right to make an entry, &c. shall be deemed to have first accrued in respect of such estate or interest, at the time when the same shall have become an estate or interest in possession, as if no such forfeiture or breach of condition had happened.

Provided (*a*), that a right to make an entry, &c. shall be deemed to have *first* accrued in respect of an *estate or interest in reversion*, at the time at which the same shall have become an estate or interest in possession, by the determination of any estate or estates in respect of which such land shall have been held, or the profits thereof or such rent shall have been received, notwithstanding the person claiming such land, or some person through whom he claims, shall, at any time previously to the creation of the estate which shall have determined, have been in possession or receipt of the profits of such land, or in receipt of such rent.

For (*b*) the purposes of this act, an administrator claiming the estate or interest of the deceased person, of whose chattels he shall be appointed administrator, shall be deemed to claim as if there had been no interval of time between the death of such deceased person and the grant of the letters of administration.

(*x*) *Doe d. Curzon* v. *Edmonds*, 6 M. & W. 295.

(*y*) *Doe d. Davy* v. *Oxenham*, 7 M. & W. 131.

(*z*) Sect. 4.
(*a*) Sect. 5.
(*b*) Sect. 6.

When any person (*b*) shall be in possession or in receipt of the profits of any land, or in receipt of any rent, *as tenant at will*, the right of the person entitled, subject thereto, or of the person through whom he claims, to make an entry, &c., shall be deemed to have *first* accrued, either at the determination of such tenancy, or at the expiration of one year next after the commencement of such tenancy (*c*), at which time such tenancy shall be deemed to have determined (35) : Provided, that no mortgagor or *cestui que trust* shall be deemed to be a tenant at will, within the meaning of this clause, to his mortgagee or trustee. And when any person (*d*) shall be in possession, &c. as *tenant from year to year, or other period,* without any lease in writing, the right of the person entitled, subject thereto, or of the person through whom he claims to make an entry, &c., shall be deemed to have *first* accrued at the determination of the first of such years or other periods, or at the last time when any rent payable in respect of such tenancy shall have been received (which shall *last* happen). And when any person (*e*) shall be in possession, &c. by virtue of a lease in writing, by which a rent, amounting to the yearly sum of twenty shillings or upwards shall be reserved, and the rent reserved by such lease shall have been received by some person wrongfully claiming to be entitled to such land or rent in reversion immediately expectant on the determination of such lease, and no payment in respect of the rent reserved by such lease shall afterwards have been made to the person rightfully entitled thereto, the right of the person entitled to such land or rent, subject to such lease, or of the person through whom he claims to make an entry, &c. after the determination of such lease, shall be deemed to have *first* accrued at the time at which the rent reserved by such lease was first so received by the person wrongfully claiming, and no such right shall be deemed to have first accrued upon the determination of such lease to the person rightfully entitled.

No person (*f*) shall be deemed to have been in possession of any land within the meaning of this act, merely by reason of having made an entry thereon. No continual or other claim (*g*) upon or

(*b*) Sect. 7.
(*c*) See *Doe d. Bennett v. Turner,* 7 M. & W. 226.
(*d*) Sect. 8.

(*e*) Sect. 9.
(*f*) Sect. 10.
(*g*) Sect. 11.

(35) Under this act, no title accrues to a party who was tenant at will, and held without interruption or payment of rent for twenty years after the expiration of the first year, but who had *quitted possession* before the act passed ; nor can he recover in ejectment even against a stranger. *Doe d. Thompson* v. *Thompson,* 6 A. & E. 721.

near any land, shall preserve any right of making an entry or distress, or of bringing an action.

When any one or more of several persons entitled to any land or rent as coparceners, joint tenants, or tenants in common, shall have been in possession (*h*) or receipt of the entirety, or more than his undivided share, for his own benefit, or for the benefit of any person other than the person entitled to the other share of the same land or rent, such possession or receipt shall not be deemed to have been the possession or receipt of or by such last-mentioned person. This section has relation back, and makes the possession of one coparcener joint tenant or tenant in common who has been in possession of the entirety, separate, from the time of his coming into possession; therefore, where one tenant in common has been out of possession for twenty years prior to the act, he is barred by sections 2 and 12 from bringing an ejectment (*i*).

The possession of a younger brother or other relation of the person entitled is no longer to be deemed the possession of that person (*k*).

When (*l*) any acknowledgment of the title of the person entitled to any land or rent shall have been given to him or his agent in writing signed by the person in possession or in receipt of the profits of such land, or in receipt of such rent, then such possession or receipt of or by the person by whom such acknowledgment shall have been given, shall be deemed, according to the meaning of this act, to have been the possession or receipt of or by the person to whom or to whose agent such acknowledgment shall have been given at the time of giving the same, and the right of such last-mentioned person, or any person claiming through him, to make an entry or distress, or bring an action to recover such land or rent, shall be deemed to have first accrued at and not before the time at which such acknowledgment, or the last of such acknowledgments, if more than one, was given. Whether a writing amounts to an acknowledgment of title under this section is a question for the judge and not for the jury to decide (*m*). If at the time (*n*) at which the right of any person to make an entry or distress, or bring an action to recover any land or rent, shall have first accrued as aforesaid, such person shall have been under any of the disabilities hereinafter mentioned, (that is to say,) infancy, coverture, idiotcy, lunacy, unsoundness of mind, or absence beyond seas, then such person, or the person claiming through him, may, notwithstanding the period of twenty years before limited shall have expired, make an entry or distress, or bring an action to recover such land or rent, at any time

(*h*) Sect. 12.
(*i*) *Culley* v. *Doe d. Taylerson*, 3 P. & D. 539.
(*k*) Sect. 13.
(*l*) Sect. 14.
(*m*) *Doe d. Curzon* v. *Edmonds*, 6 M. & W. 295.
(*n*) Sect. 16.

within ten years next after the time at which the person to whom such right shall first have accrued, shall have ceased to be under any such disability, or shall have died, which shall have first happened. Provided (o), that no entry, distress, or action, shall be made or brought by any person who, at the time at which his right to make an entry, &c. shall have first accrued, shall be under any of the disabilities before mentioned, or by any person claiming through him, but within forty years next after the time at which such right shall have first accrued, although the person under disability at such time may have remained under one or more of such disabilities during the whole of such forty years, or although the term of ten years from the time at which he shall have ceased to be under such disability, or have died, shall not have expired.

A feme sole, seised in fee, married, and she and her husband ceased to be in possession or enjoyment of the land, and went to reside at a distance from it. They both died at times which were not shown to be within forty years from the ceasing to occupy. The heir at law brought ejectment against the person in possession within twenty years of the husband's death, and within five years of the passing of the foregoing act. Evidence was offered that the wife had not levied any fine. It was holden (p), that the ejectment was barred under the foregoing 17th section, although it did not appear how or when the defendant came into possession.

When (q) any person shall be under any of the disabilities before mentioned, at the time at which his right to make an entry, &c. shall have *first* accrued, and shall depart this life without having ceased to be under any such disability, no time to make an entry, &c. beyond the said period of twenty years next after the right of such person to make entry, &c. shall have first accrued, or the said period of ten years next after the time at which such person shall have died, shall be allowed by reason of any disability of any other person. No part (r) of Great Britain and Ireland (36), nor the Islands of Man, Guernsey, Jersey, Alderney, or Sark, nor any island adjacent to any of them, (being part of the dominions of his Ma- es ,) shall be deemed to be beyond seas, within the meaning of this act.

(b) Sect. 17.

(p) *Doe d. Corbyn* v. *Bramston*, 3 A. & E. 63. See the remarks of Sir *E. Sugden* on this case, in 2 Sugd. V. & P. 348,

353, 10th edition.

(q) Sect. 18.

(r) Sect. 19.

(36) Ireland is still a place beyond the seas, within the meaning of the 19th section of the stat. 4 Ann. c. 16, (which see *ante*, p. 145,) notwithstanding the Act of Union and this 19th clause of the 3 & 4 Will. IV. c. 27. *Lane* v. *Bennett*, 1 M. & W. 70. See also *Battersby* v. *Kirk*, 2 Bingh. N. C. 603.

When the right (*s*) of any person to make an entry, &c. for an estate or interest in possession, shall have been barred by the determination of the period before limited, which shall be applicable in such case, and such person shall, at any time during the said period, have been entitled to any other estate, interest, right, or possibility in reversion, remainder, or otherwise, in or to the same land or rent, no entry, distress, or action, shall be made or brought, by such person, or any person claiming through him, to recover such land or rent, in respect of such other estate, interest, right, or possibility, unless, in the mean time, such land or rent shall have been recovered by some person entitled to an estate, interest, or right, which shall have been limited, or taken effect, after or in defeasance of such estate or interest in possession. When the right of a tenant in tail (*t*) of any land or rent to make an entry, &c. shall have been barred by reason of the same not having been made or brought within the period before limited, which shall be applicable in such case, no such entry, distress, or action, shall be made or brought by any person claiming any estate, interest, or right, which such tenant in tail might lawfully have barred. When a tenant in tail of any land or rent, entitled to recover the same, shall have died (*u*) before the expiration of the period before limited, which shall be applicable in such case, for making an entry, &c., no person claiming any estate, interest, or right, which such tenant in tail might lawfully have barred, shall make an entry or distress, or bring an action to recover such land or rent, but within the period during which, if such tenant in tail had so long continued to live, he might have made such entry or distress, or brought such action. When a tenant (*x*) in tail of any land or rent shall have made an assurance thereof, which shall not operate to bar an estate to take effect after or in defeasance of his estate tail, and any person shall, by virtue of such assurance, at the time of the execution thereof, or at any time afterwards, be in possession or receipt of the profits of such land, or in receipt of such rent, and the same person, or any other person (other than some person entitled to such possession or receipt in respect of an estate, which shall have taken effect after or in defeasance of the estate tail), shall continue or be in such possession or receipt for the period of twenty years next after the commencement of the time at which such assurance, if it had then been executed by such tenant in tail, or the person who would have been entitled to his estate tail, if such assurance had not been executed, would, without the consent of any other person, have operated to bar such estate or estates as aforesaid, then, at the expiration of such period of twenty years, such assurance shall be, and be deemed to have been, effectual as against any person claiming any estate, interest, or right, to take effect after or in defeasance of such estate tail.

When a mortgagee (y) shall have obtained the possession or receipt of the profits of any land, or the receipt of any rent comprised in his mortgage, the mortgagor, or any person claiming through him, shall not ring a suit to redeem the mortgage, but within twenty years next after the time at which the mortgagee obtained such possession or receipt, unless in the mean time an acknowledgment of the title of the mortgagor, or of his right of redemption, shall have been given to the mortgagor, or some person claiming his estate, or to the agent of such mortgagor, or person, in writing, signed by the mortgagee, or the person claiming through him; and in such case no such suit shall be brought, but within twenty years next after the time at which such acknowledgment, or the last of such acknowledgments, if more than one, was given; and when there shall be more than one mortgagor, or more than one person claiming through the mortgagor or mortgagors, such acknowledgment, if given to any of such mortgagors or persons, or his or their agent, shall be as effectual, as if the same had been given to all such mortgagors or persons; but where there shall be more than one mortgagee, or more than one person claiming the estate or interest of the mortgagee or mortgagees, such acknowledgment, signed by one or more of such mortgagees or persons, shall be effectual only as against the party or parties signing as aforesaid, and the person or persons claiming any part of the mortgage money, or land, or rent, by, from, or under him or them, and any person or persons entitled to any estate or estates, interest or interests, to take effect after or in defeasance of his or their estate or estates, interest or interests, and shall not operate to give to the mortgagor or mortgagors a right to redeem the mortgage, as against the person or persons entitled to any other undivided or divided part of the money, or land, or rent; and where such of the mortgagees or persons aforesaid, as shall have given such acknowledgment, shall be entitled to a divided part of the land or rent comprised in the mortgage, or some estate or interest therein, and not to any ascertained part of the mortgaged [*Sic*] money, the mortgagor or mortgagors shall be entitled to redeem the same divided part of the land or rent, on payment, with interest, of the part of the mortgage money, which shall bear the same proportion to the whole of the mortgage money, as the value of such divided part of the land or rent shall bear to the value of the whole of the land or rent comprised in the mortgage. By stat. 1 Vict. c. 28, (3rd July, 1837,) reciting that doubts had been entertained as to the effect of the foregoing act, so far as the same related to mortgages (z), and that it was expedient that such doubts should be

(y) Sect. 28.　　　　(z) See *Doe d. Jones* v. *Williams*, 5 A. & E. 291.

removed, it is *declared* and enacted, that any person entitled to or claiming under any mortgage of land, within the definition contained in the first section of the act, may make an entry or bring an action at law or suit in equity, to recover such land at any time within twenty years next after the last payment of any part of the principal money or interest secured by such mortgage, although more than twenty years may have elapsed since the time at which the right to make such entry or bring such action or suit shall have first accrued.

Any archbishop (a), &c. may make an entry, &c. within such period as hereinafter is mentioned, next after the time at which the right of such corporation sole, or of his predecessor, to make such entry, &c. shall first have accrued, (that is to say,) the period during which two persons in succession shall have held the office or benefice, in respect whereof such land or rent shall be claimed, and six years after a third person shall have been appointed thereto, if the times of such two incumbencies, and such term of six years, taken together, shall amount to sixty years; and if such times, taken together, shall not amount to sixty years, then during such further number of years, in addition to such six years, as will, with the time of the holding of such two persons, and such six years, make up sixty years; and after the 31st December, 1833, no such entry, &c. shall be made or brought at any time beyond the determination of such period.

At the determination (b) of the period limited to any person for making an entry, or distress, or bringing any writ of quare impedit, or other action or suit, the right and title of such person to the land, &c. for the recovery whereof such entry, &c. might have been made or brought within such period, shall be extinguished.

By sect. 35, the receipt of the rent payable by any tenant from year to year, or other lessee, shall, as against such lessee, or any person claiming under him, (but subject to the lease,) be deemed to be the receipt of the profits of the land for the purposes of this act.

By stat. 3 & 4 Will. IV. c. 106, s. 2, descent shall be traced from the purchaser; and the person last entitled to the land shall, for the purposes of this act, be considered to have been the purchaser, unless it shall be proved that he inherited the same, in which case the person from whom he inherited the same shall be considered to have been the purchaser, unless it shall be proved that he inherited the same; and in like manner, the last person from whom the land shall be proved to have been inherited, shall in every case be considered to have been the purchaser, unless it shall be proved that he inherited the same.

(a) 3 & 4 W. IV. c. 27, s. 29.   (b) Sect. 34.

Where land (d) descends to the son of an illegitimate father, who is proved to have been the purchaser thereof, and the son dies seised and intestate and without issue, such land does not devolve on the heir *ex parte maternâ*, but escheats to the crown.

By section 3 of this act, when land shall have been devised by any testator who shall die after the 31st December, 1833, to the heir, or to the person who shall be the heir of such testator, such heir shall take as a devisee, and not by descent; and when land shall have been limited by any assurance executed after the 31st December, 1833, to the person or to the heirs of the person who shall thereby have conveyed the same land, such person shall be considered to have acquired the same as a purchaser, by virtue of such assurance, and not to be entitled thereto as his former estate, or part thereof.

By sect. 4, when any person shall have acquired any land by purchase, under a limitation to the heirs, or to the heirs of the body of any of his ancestors, contained in an assurance executed after the 31st December, 1833, or under a limitation to the heirs, or to the heirs of the body of any of his ancestors, or under any limitation having the like effect, contained in a will of any testator who shall die after the 31st December, 1833, such land shall descend and the descent thereof shall be traced as if the ancestor named in such limitation had been the purchaser of such land.

By sect. 5, no brother or sister shall inherit immediately from brother or sister, but every descent from a brother or sister shall be traced through the parent.

By sect. 6, every lineal ancestor is made capable of being heir to any of his issue; and where there shall be no issue of the purchaser, his nearest lineal ancestor shall be his heir in preference to any person who would have been entitled to inherit, either by tracing his descent through such lineal ancestor, or in consequence of there being no descendant of such lineal ancestor, so that the father shall be preferred to a brother or sister, and a more remote lineal ancestor to any of his issue other than a nearer lineal ancestor or his issue.

By sect. 7 and 8, it is declared that the male line is to be preferred, and the mother of the more remote male paternal ancestor to be preferred to the mother of the less remote.

By sect. 9, persons of the half blood are made capable of inheriting; those of the half blood on the part of the male ancestor to inherit next after the relation in the same degree of the whole blood and his issue; and those of the half blood on the part of a female ancestor next after such female ancestor.

(d) *Doe d. Blackburn* v. *Blackburn*, 1 M. & Rob. 547.

By sect. 10, where a person through whom a descent is to be traced shall have been attainted, and died before such descent shall have taken place, the attainder shall not prevent the heir from inheriting, unless the land shall have escheated in consequence of such attainder, before the 1st January, 1834.

The act does not extend (e) to any descent which takes place on the death of any person who died before the 1st January, 1834; and where (f) the heir or heirs of any person take an estate by purchase, under an assurance executed before the 1st January, 1834, or a will of any testator dying before the same day, such heir or heirs will be determined by the old law, whether the person named as the ancestor shall be living or not on the 1st January, 1834.

XI. *Evidence.*

Evidence on the Part of the Lessor of the Plaintiff.—The evidence required to support an ejectment will vary according to the title of the lessor of the plaintiff.

Possession is *primâ facie* evidence of seisin in fee simple: the declaration of a deceased possessor that he was tenant to another, makes most strongly against his own interest, and consequently is admissible (g). So the admission of a deceased person in receipt of the rent, that he held under another, whether as tenant by sufferance, or as receiver of the rents, is evidence (h) that he himself was not the owner of the legal estate.

Devisee of a Term.—Where the lessor of the plaintiff is devisee of a term, he must produce in evidence the probate of the will, and prove the assent of the executor to the devise (i); for where a person devises, either specially or generally, goods or chattels, real or personal, and dies, the devisee cannot take them without the assent of the executor. Lessee for years devised the term to his executor for life (k), paying £50 to J. S., remainder to the lessor of the plaintiff. The executor dying, his executrix entered upon the residue of the lease, and possessed herself of the term. An ejectment having been brought; it was holden, that the executor took as executor, and not as legatee; and then the remainder over was not executed, and that it was incumbent on the remainder-

---

(e) Sect. 11.
(f) Sect. 12.
(g) *Peaceable* v. *Watson*, 4 Taunt. 16, recognized in *Carne* v. *Nicoll*, Trial at Bar on writ of right, 1 Bingh. N. C. 430;

Gow's N. P. C. 227, S. P.
(h) *Doe d. Daniel* v. *Coulthred*, 7 A. & E. 239.
(i) 1 Inst. 111, a.
(k) *Young* v. *Holmes*, Str. 70.

man to prove a special assent thereto, as to a legacy; whereupon plaintiff proved payment of the £50; and that was holden to be a sufficient assent, and the plaintiff recovered. To prove the title of a lessor of the plaintiff in ejectment, claiming as executor, the will was produced from the registrar's office, with a memorandum at the foot of it, signed by the surrogate, that the executor had proved the will, and that the probate had been sealed. The probate was not produced, or accounted for; but it was proved that such a memorandum was never made till probate had been granted, and that, by the practice of the particular court, no other record of such grantsywas kept. The evidence was holden sufficient (*l*).

Administrator.—Where the lessor of the plaintiff claims title as administrator, in strictness he ought to produce the letters of administration under the seal of the Ecclesiastical Court. But the original book of acts (*m*), wherein the orders of the court for granting letters of administration are entered, or an examined copy (*n*) of the entry in that book, or an exemplification (*o*) of the letters of administration, will also be evidence. If the lessor of the plaintiff make title as assignee of a term from an administrator (*p*), *cum testamento annexo*, an exemplification, though not in *hæc verba*, yet agreeably to the form of the Ecclesiastical Court, will be good evidence (37).

Boundary.—Reputation is admissible evidence in questions of boundary. Hence where the question was, whether land was in the parish of A., or the parish of B., the land in B. being tithe-free; it was holden (*q*), that ancient leases granted by the ancestor of the plaintiff's landlord, in which the land was described as being in parish B., were admissible as evidence of reputation, that the land was in that parish.

Copyhold.—If the plaintiff make title in the lessor as lord of a manor (*r*), who has a right by forfeiture of copyhold, he ought to prove that his lessor is lord, and the defendant a copyholder; and that he committed a forfeiture: but the presentment of the for-

(*l*) *Doe d. Bassett* v. *Mew*, 7 A. & E. 240, recognizing *Cox* v. *Allingham*, Jacob, 514.

(*m*) *Garrett* v. *Lister*, 1 Lev. 25; *Peawelie's* case, 1 Lev. 101; *Elden* v. *Keddell*, 8 East, 187.

(*n*) *Ray* v. *Clerk*, London Sittings, after H. T. 1775; Lord *Mansfield*, C. J.,

13 East, 238.

(*o*) Per Lord *Hardwicke*, C. J., in *Kempton* v. *Cross*, Ca. T. H. 108.

(*p*) *Kempton* v. *Cross*, Ca. T. H. 108.

(*q*) *Plaxton* v. *Dare*, 10 B. & C. 17.

(*r*) *Peters d. Bp. of Winton* v. *Mills*, per Tracy, Surrey, 1707; Bull. N. P. 107.

(37) For the evidence necessary to establish a title by the heir, see Peake's Evid. Part II. Chap. 14, where this subject is treated with great perspicuity. For evidence on ejectment brought by the devisee of land, see *post*, tit. "Statute of Frauds," Sect. III,

feiture need not be proved, nor the entry or seizure of the lord for the forfeiture.

Tenant by Elegit.—As under an elegit the sheriff cannot deliver the land extended (s), the tenant by elegit must bring an ejectment (38); to support which he must either produce in evidence an examined copy of the judgment; of the writ of elegit taken out upon it, and the inquisition and return thereupon; or an examined copy of the judgment roll, containing the award of elegit and return of the inquisition (t). In an action by the lessee against the assignee of a lease, the plaintiff having proved the delivery of the original lease to the defendant, and the execution of the counterpart, the defendant put in the original lease, which was produced by a party to whom defendant had assigned it, by a deed reciting the lease; it was holden (u), that it was necessary for the plaintiff to call the subscribing witness to prove the execution of the lease. It is not competent to a party, who *has* taken under a deed all the interest which that deed was calculated to give, to dispute its execution.

The sheriff's return to an elegit stated, that he had caused to be delivered to J. S., one equal moiety of a house; it was holden (x), that this return was void, for not setting out the moiety by metes and bounds, and that the objection might be taken at nisi prius to an ejectment brought by J. S. claiming as a tenant by elegit. But on elegit sheriff may deliver entire (y) farms as moiety of the defendant's lands. A verdict was found for the lessor of the plaintiff, who claimed under a judgment recovered against the defendant, and writ of elegit and inquisition thereon taken and returned. Upon motion to enter nonsuit, the objection was, that by a deed executed 23d June, 1809, long before the judgment was recovered, the legal

---

(s) Per Lord *Kenyon*, C. J., in *Taylor v. Cole*, 3 T. R. 295.
(t) *Ramsbottom v. Buckhurst*, 2 M. & S. 565.
(u) *Burnett v. Lynch*, 5 B. & C. 589.

(x) *Fenny d. Masters v. Durrant*, 1 B. & A. 40.
(y) *Doe d. Taylor v. Lord Abingdon*, B. R. M. 21 Geo. III., 2 Doug. 473.

---

(38) "I am aware that it has in several places been said, that the tenant by elegit cannot obtain possession without an ejectment, but I have always been of a different opinion. I have no doubt that the sheriff may deliver actual possession of a moiety, except where the land is under a previous demise; in which case the sheriff sets out the moiety by metes and bounds; for the sheriff cannot disturb the previous title of the tenant in possession. Where the sheriff has set out the moiety, the tenant is bound to pay rent for his moiety to the tenant by elegit. In a case of this kind, attornment was not necessary, even before the statute of attornments, because tenant by elegit was in by judgment of law, to whom attornment was not necessary." Per *Gibbs*, C. J., 6 Taunt. 206, 7.

estate was vested in trustees for the purpose of securing an annuity to the defendant's mother, with permission to the defendant to take the rent, until the annuity should be in arrear. The trustees were empowered to enter in case the annuity was in arrear, which they did in 1817. But at the time of the execution of the elegit, and of commencing the action, there was nothing in arrear. It was contended that the case fell within 29 Car. II. c. 3, s. 10, (by which the sheriff can take under an elegit such lands only as the party against whom it issues is legally or beneficially entitled to,) as the premises were held in trust for the defendant. It was adjudged (z), that the plaintiff could not recover, because the estate was vested in trustees, though partly for the defendant's benefit.

Judgment.—Where the lessor of the plaintiff claims under an assignment from the sheriff (a), if he be a party in the original action in which the execution issues, he must not only produce the writ of fieri facias, but also the judgment. A judgment recovered by the defendant in a former ejectment is admissible in evidence against the lessor of the plaintiff, on the trial of a second eject- ment, where the lessor of the plaintiff and the defendant are the same parties (b).

Landlord.—In ejectment by a landlord against his tenant, it will not be necessary for the landlord to give any evidence of his title anterior to the lease; for the tenant will not be permitted to im- peach the title of the person under whom he came into possession. In ejectment upon a clause of re-entry (c) in a lease, for non-pay- ment of rent, against the assignee of the term, the lessor proved, by the subscribing witness, the execution of the counterpart of the lease; this was ruled to be sufficient proof of the holding upon the condition of re-entry in case of non-payment of rent, without pro- ducing the lease itself, or proving that notice had been given to the defendant to produce it (39). In ejectment for a leasehold estate, the lessor of the plaintiff produced the original lease, which was for a term of 1000 years, granted in the time of Queen Elizabeth; and one mesne assignment in the time of King James; and then proved possession in himself and those under whom he claimed, for seventy years prior to the ejectment; it was holden (d), that the jury might be directed to presume all the mesne assignments.

(z) *Doe d. Hull* v. *Greenhill*, 4 B. & A. 684, recognized in *Harris* v. *Booker*, 4 Bingh. 96.
(a) *Doe d. Bland* v. *Smith*, Holt's N. P. C. 589.

(b) *Doe d. Strode* v. *Seaton*, 2 C. M. & R. 728.
(c) *Roe* v. *Davis*, 7 East, 363.
(d) *Earl d. Goodwin* v. *Baxter*, 2 Bl. R. 1228.

---

(39) It is sufficient to prove assignment of lease by subscribing witness, without calling the subscribing witness to the original lease. *Nash* v. *Turner*, 1 Esp. N. P. C. 217, per *Kenyon*, C. J. In this case, the assign- ment was by indorsement.

In ejectment by landlord against tenant (e), the landlord proved payment of rent and half a year's notice to quit. But on the cross-examination of the plaintiff's witness, he was asked, whether there was not an agreement in writing relative to the holding of these lands? to which he answered, that an agreement in writing relative to these lands was produced at the last trial of this ejectment (this being the second trial); but he did not know the contents of it; and then another witness was called, who proved that he had seen the same paper in the hands of Sir M. Wood's attorney, on the same morning (i. e. of this trial). Whereupon it was objected, on the par of the defendant, that no parol evidence of the tenancy could be given, when it appeared that there was an agreement in writing concerning it; and it did not appear that the landlord had any right to determine the tenancy in the manner he had done. Lord *Ellenborough*, C. J. If there were any writing relative to this holding, in the possession of the landlord, the defendant ought to have given him a regular notice to produce it; otherwise, in this collateral way, he would get the whole benefit of it, without giving such a notice: when if notice had been given, and the paper were produced, it might not support the objection. How can we say that the plaintiff ought to have been nonsuited, for want of giving the best evidence of the tenancy, unless it appeared that there was other and better evidence of it in an agreement in writing between the landlord and his tenant, which the landlord kept back? Enough, at least, ought to appear to show that the paper not produced was better evidence of the terms of the tenancy than the evidence which was received; but it did not appear that it was an agreement between these parties, or that it was an existing agreement at this time: it might have been an agreement between the defendant and his former landlord; or it might have related to a former period of the tenancy (41). The witness did not profess to know any thing of the contents of the paper, only that it was an agreement relative to the lands in question. In ejectment against a bailiff, the tenant in possession is not competent to prove that the witness, and not the defendant, is the possessor of the land (f). Defendant enclosed a small piece of waste land by the side of a public highway, and occupied it for thirty years without paying any rent; at the expiration of that time the owner of the adjoining land demanded 6d.

(e) *Doe d. Sir M. Wood* v. *Morris*, 12 East, 237, recognized in *Stevens* v. *Pinney*, 8 Taunt. 327; 2 Moore, 349, *S. C.*; and in *Fielder* v. *Ray*, 6 Bingh. 337.

(f) *Doe d. Jones and others* v. *Wilde*, 5 Taunt. 183, cited in *Doe d. Willis* v. *Birchmore*, 9 A. & E. 663.

(41) Or it might have been unstamped, in which case it could not have been received in evidence. *Stevens* v. *Pinney*, and *Fielder* v. *Ray*, *ubi sup.*

rent, which defendant paid on three several occasions; it was holden (g), that this, in the absence of other evidence, was conclusive to show that the occupation of defendant began by permission, and entitled plaintiff to a verdict. So where a cottage standing in the corner of a meadow, (belonging to the lord of a manor,) but separated from the meadow and from the high road by a ditch, had been occupied for a period of more than twenty years without any payment of rent; then the lord demanded possession, which was reluctantly given; and the occupier was told, that if he were allowed to resume possession, it would only be during pleasure. He was allowed to resume, and kept possession for fifteen years more, but did not pay any rent; it was holden (h), that it was a question for the jury, whether the possession commenced and continued by adverse title or by the permission of the lord: and the jury having found that the occupation was by permission of the lord, the court refused to disturb the verdict. Where the question was, whether a slip of land between some old inclosures and the highway vested in the lord of the manor or the owner of the adjoining freehold; it was holden (i), that evidence might be received of acts of ownership by the lord of the manor, on the greens and wastes in other parts of the manor, at a distance, although the lord was not the owner of the adjoining freehold, provided such evidence were confined to the road, which passed by the spot claimed by plaintiff. Payment of the same and a small sum of money, annually, for a long series of years, for a piece of land, to the lord of a manor, has been holden (k) not to be evidence of a title to the land, but to the rent only. It had been paid nearly forty years, and the judge said, the presumption was, it was a quit rent.

In a case where the plaintiff proved that the premises had been leased to him and a year's possession; this was held sufficient, although it was not shown what the title of the demising parties was; the defendant being a mere wrong doer (l). The lessor of the plaintiff proved, that his father and himself held the premises, and during that time received and increased the rent. It did not appear that the father had any other son; but the defendant proved, that he had been in possession for ten years before ejectment brought. A verdict having been found for the plaintiff, the court refused to disturb it (m); *Tindal*, C. J., observing, that the earlier presumption must prevail, until better title is shown.

Legitimacy.—In this action, the legitimacy of the parties fre-

(g) *Doe d. Jackson* v. *Wilkinson*, 3 B. & C. 413.

(h) *Doe d. Thompson* v. *Clark*, 8 B. & C. 717.

(i) *Doe d. Barrett* v. *Kemp*, 2 Bingh. N. C. 102, recognized by *Parke*, B., in *Jones* v. *Williams*, 2 M. & W. 326, in the case of a river.

(k) Per *Holroyd*, J., confirmed by court; *Doe d. Whittick* v. *Johnson*, Gow, N. P. C. 173.

(l) *Doe d. Hughes* v. *Dyeball*, M. & Malk. 346.

(m) *Doe d. Harding* v. *Cooke*, 7 Bingh. 346.

quently comes in question. An opinion appears to have prevailed at one time, that unless the husband was *extra quatuor maria*, that is, out of the kingdom during all the time of the wife's going with child, access must be presumed, and the child must be deemed legitimate (n). But, on examination of this doctrine, it was found unsatisfactory; and it is now holden (o), that non-access may be proved to bastardize the issue, although it should appear that the husband was within the kingdom during the period of gestation. So where the husband, in the course of nature, cannot have been the father of his wife's child, the child is by law a bastard, whether the husband be within reach of access or not; as in the case of a natural impossibility, the husband being within the age of puberty (p); or disabled by bodily infirmity (q). So where it was proved that the husband had not access, until a fortnight before the birth of the child, the child was adjudged (r) to be illegitimate. Access is such access as affords an opportunity of sexual intercourse; and where there is evidence of such access between a husband and wife, within a period capable of raising the legal presumption as to the legitimacy of an after-born child, the court will not direct an issue upon evidence showing the continued adulterous intercourse with another man, and the improbability of the husband being the father, but will declare the legitimacy of the child (s).

The wife is a witness of necessity, as to the fact of adulterous intercourse, because that lies within her own knowledge (t), and she is the only person who may be supposed privy to it, except the adulterer. This case, therefore, affords an exception to the general rule, which prohibits the wife from being examined against her husband in any matter affecting his interest or character. But *non-access* must be proved by other testimony (u) than that of the wife; and this rule holds, although the husband be dead (x). It is clear and indisputable law, that, for the purpose of proving non-access, neither husband nor wife can be a witness; and this rule excludes all questions which have a tendency to prove access or non-access (y). The presumption of legitimacy arising from the birth of a child during wedlock, the husband and wife not being proved to be impotent, and having opportunity of access to each other during the period in which a child could be begotten and born in the course of nature, may be rebutted by circumstances inducing a contrary presumption (z).

(n) *Queen* v. *Murrey*, Salk. 122.
(o) *Pendrell* v. *Pendrell*, Str. 925; *R.* v. *Bedall*, Str. 1076; Rep. Temp. Hardw. 379, and Andr. 9.
(p) 1 Hen. VI. 3, b.
(q) 1 Rol. Abr. 359, cited by Lord *Ellenborough*, 8 East, 205.
(r) *R.* v. *Luffe*, 8 East, 193.
(s) *Bury* v. *Philpot*, Sir *John Leach*, M. R., 2 Mylne & K. 349.

(t) *R.* v. *Reading*, Rep. Temp. Hardw. 79; *R.* v. *Rook*, 1 Wils. 340, and Andr. 10.
(u) *Ib.*
(x) *R.* v. *Kea*, 11 East, 132.
(y) *R.* v. *Sourton*, 5 A. & E. 180; 6 Nev. & M. 575, recognizing *Goodright* d. *Stephens* v. *Moss*, 2 Cowp. 591, as to the general rule.
(z) *Banbury Claim of Peerage*, D. P., 2 May, 1811; opinion of the judges.

The fact of the birth of a child from a woman united to a man by lawful wedlock, is generally, by the law of England, *primâ facie* evidence, that such child is legitimate (*a*). Such *primâ facie* evidence of legitimacy may always be lawfully rebutted by satisfactory evidence that such access did not take place between the husband and wife, as by the laws of nature is necessary, in order for the man to be in fact the father of the child (*b*). The physical fact of impotency, or of non-access, or of non-generating access, as the case may be, may always be lawfully proved by means of such legal evidence as is strictly admissible in every other case in which it is necessary, by the law of England, that a physical fact be proved (*c*). After proof given of such access of the husband and wife, by which, according to the laws of nature, he might be the father of a child, (by which is to be understood proof of sexual intercourse between them,) no evidence can be received, except it tend to falsify the proof that such intercourse had taken place (*d*). Such proof must be regulated by the same principles as are applicable to the establishment of any other fact (*e*). In every case where a child is born in lawful wedlock, the husband not being separated from his wife by a sentence of divorce, sexual intercourse is presumed to have taken place between the husband and wife, until that presumption is encountered by such evidence as proves, to the satisfaction of those who are to decide the question, that such sexual intercourse did not take place at any time when, by such intercourse, the husband could, according to the laws of nature, be the father of such child (*f*). The presumption of the legitimacy of a child born in lawful wedlock, the husband not being separated from his wife by a sentence of divorce, can be legally resisted only by evidence of such facts or circumstances as are sufficient to prove, to the satisfaction of those who are to decide the question, that no sexual intercourse did take place between the husband and wife, at any time when, by such intercourse, the husband could, by the laws of nature, be the father of such child (*g*). Where the legitimacy of a child in such a case is disputed, on the ground that the husband was not the father of such child, the question to be left for the jury is, whether the husband was the father of such child; and the evidence to prove that he was not the father, must be of such facts and circumstances, as are sufficient to prove, to the satisfaction of a jury, that no sexual intercourse took place between the husband and wife at any time when, by such intercourse, the husband could, by the laws of nature, be the father of such child (*h*) (42). The mere circumstance

(*a*) *Banbury Claim of Peerage*, D. P., opinion of the judges, 13 May, 1811. N. This claim was disallowed, D. P., 9 March, 1813, 21 peers to 13.
(*b*) *Ib.*
(*c*) *Ib.*

(*d*) *Ib.*
(*e*) *Ib.*
(*f*) *Ib.*, *S. C.*, 4 July, 1811.
(*g*) Opinion of the judges, *S. C.*, 4 July, 1811.
(*h*) *Ib.*

(42) "The non-existence of sexual intercourse is generally expressed

of the wife living in notorious adultery is not sufficient to warrant a finding of illegitimacy (*i*). A child begotten after a divorce *a mensâ et thoro*, shall be taken to be a *bastard* (*k*); otherwise after voluntary separation, unless found that the husband had no access. Upon the question of marriage, it is part of the law of England that the law of the country where the marriage is solemnized shall be adopted; and the same observation applies to the distribution of personal property according to the law of the domicile. But the same principle does not apply to the inheritance of real property; to that the *lex loci* is alone applicable. Legitimacy alone is not sufficient to make a person inherit socage lands; it must be legitimacy *sub modo*; the heir must be a child born after marriage. Hence a child born in Scotland of unmarried parents (*l*), domiciled in that country, and who afterwards intermarry there, is not by such marriage rendered capable of inheriting lands in England.

Mortgagee.—In ejectment by a mortgagee, if the mortgagor be in possession (*m*), proof of the execution of the mortgage deeds by the subscribing witness, will be sufficient to support the mortgagee's title; but if a third person is in possession, the mortgagee should also prove, that such third person has paid rent to, or otherwise acknowledged the title of, the mortgagor. It is not necessary to prove either notice to quit or demand of possession (*n*). Where the mortgagee recognizes a party as being in lawful possession of the premises at a given time, it is not competent to him to say afterwards that at that time he was a trespasser (*o*); but mere payment of interest in respect of the original debt, for a period covering the day of the demise (*p*), is not a recognition of the right of mortgagor, or his tenant, to hold possession.

Rector.—In ejectment by a rector for a rectory (*q*), it seems

(*i*) Per Lord *Denman*, C. J., *R.* v. *Mansfield*, June 19, 1841, 1 G. & D. 7.

(*k*) *Parishes of St. George and St. Margaret's, Westminster*, 1 Salk. 123.

(*l*) *Doe d. Birtwhistle* v. *Vardill*, 5 B. & C. 438. See the report of writ of error in this case in D. P. 2 Cl. & Fi. 571; 9 Bligh, N. R. 32; judgment affirmed in D. P., 6 Bingh. N. C. 385.

(*m*) Peake's Evid. 324.

(*n*) *Doe d. Fisher* v. *Giles*, 5 Bingh.

421; and *Doe d. Roby* v. *Maisey*, 8 B. & C. 767; *Doe d. Austen* v. *Cowdry*, B. R. M. T. 1 Vict. S. P.

(*o*) *Doe d. Whitaker* v. *Hales*, 7 Bingh. 322.

(*p*) *Doe d. Rogers* v. *Cadwallader*, 2 B. & Ad. 473.

(*q*) See *Monk* v. *Butler*, 1 Roll. Rep. 83; recognized in *Powel* v. *Milbank*, 2 Bl. R. 853. See also *Williams* v. *East India Company*, 3 East, 199.

by the words, ' non-access of the husband to the wife.' And we understand those expressions as applied to the present question as meaning the same thing; because, in one sense of the word ' access,' the husband may be said to have access to his wife, as being *in the same place*, or *in the same house*, and yet under circumstances such as instead of proving, tend to disprove, that any sexual intercourse had taken place between them." Remark of the judges.

that it is not necessary for the plaintiff to prove that he subscribed and publicly read the thirty-nine articles; for where any act is required to be done, so that the party neglecting it would be guilty of a criminal neglect of duty in not having done it, the law presumes the affirmative, and throws the burthen of proving the contrary on the other side. Hence where a prebendary brought ejectment for a house, belonging to his prebend, and was required to show that he had performed the requisites necessary by law to make him prebendary; *Wilmot*, J., held (r), that it ought to be presumed that he had performed them, until something appeared to the contrary. In addition to the proof of his title, formerly, the lessor of the plaintiff was obliged to prove (s) the defendant in possession of the lands, &c. to which he makes title. But this is now rendered unnecessary by the consent rule, which see *ante*, p. 721. N. A tenant in possession cannot be a witness to support his own possession (t). If a material witness for the defendant be made a co-defendant, he should suffer judgment by default (43). Where there are several demises of two persons, although the evidence shows the title to be exclusively in one of them, the other cannot be *compelled* by the defendant to be examined as a witness for him; because the lessor of the plaintiff in ejectment is substantially the plaintiff on the record (u).

The parish register, or an examined copy thereof, will be evidence to prove baptisms, marriages, or burials. A register of baptism is not, per se, evidence (x) of the place of the birth of the party baptized. Reputation is sufficient evidence (y) of a marriage, even where the party adducing it seeks to recover as heir at law to his brother, the person last seised, and the father is still living. Under the stat. 6 & 7 Will. IV. c. 86, for providing means for a complete register, by s. 38, certified copies of entries, sealed or stamped with the seal of office, are to be received as evidence of the birth, death, or marriage, to which the same relates, without

---

(r) *Sherard's* case, cited by *De Grey*, C. J., delivering the opinion of the court in *Powel* v. *Milbank*, 2 Bl. R. 853.

(s) *Smith* v. *Mann*, 1 Wils. 220; *Fenn d. Blanchard* v. *Wood*, 1 Bos. & Pul. 573; *Goodright* v. *Rich*, 7 T. R. 327, in which *Doe d. Jesse* v. *Bacchus*, Bull. N. P. 110, was overruled.

(t) *Doe d. Foster* v. *Williams*, Cowp.

621; see *post*.

(u) *Fenn on the several demises of Pewtriss and Thompson* v. *Granger*, 3 Campb. 177.

(x) *R.* v. *North Petherton*, 5 B. & C. 508.

(y) *Doe d. Fleming* v. *Fleming*, 4 Bingh. 266.

---

(43) One of two defendants, who has suffered judgment by default, may be called to prove the other defendant in possession. *Doe d. Harrop* v. *Green*, 4 Esp. N. P. C. 198; *sed quæ.*, and see *Chapman* v. *Graves*, 2 Campb. 333, n.; but see *Worrall* v. *Jones*, 7 Bingh. 395, where it was adjudged, that a party to the record is a competent witness, provided he be disinterested. See also stat. 3 & 4 Will. IV. c. 42, s. 26.

any further or other proof of such entry. As to marriages, see *ante*, p. 18. If persons for whose lives estates have been granted, remain beyond the seas, or absent themselves in this realm for seven years together, and no sufficient proof be made of the lives of such persons, in any actions commenced by the lessors or reversioners for the recovery of the estates, they shall be accounted as naturally dead. Stat. 19 Car. II. c. 6. Where a party has been absent seven years without having been heard of, he is presumed to be dead; but there is not any legal presumption as to the time of his death. The presumption of law relates only to the fact of death; the time of death, whenever it is material, must be a subject of distinct proof by the party relying on it (*z*).

The original visitation-books of heralds (*a*) compiled when progresses were solemnly and regularly made into every part of the kingdom, to inquire into the state of families, and to register such marriages and descents as were verified to them on oath, are allowed to be good evidence of pedigrees (*b*). Although it is a general rule that hearsay evidence is not admissible, yet in some cases, where a strict adherence to that rule would utterly prevent the party from establishing his case, the law sanctions a departure from it (44). Hence the declarations of the members of a family are received in

(*z*) *Doe d. Knight* v. *Nepean*, 5 B. & Ad. 86, adopted on error in Exchequer Chamber, 2 M. & W. 914.

(*a*) *Matthew* v. *Port*, Comb. 63; 3 Bl. Comm. c. 7, 11.

(*b*) See further as to evidence of pedigrees, the remarks of *Tindal*, C. J., in *Davies* v. *Lowndes*, 5 Bingh. N. C. 167.

---

(44) " Hearsay is good evidence to prove, who is my grandfather, when he married, what children he had, &c., of which it is not reasonable to presume that I have better evidence; so to prove that my father, mother, cousin, or other relation beyond the sea is dead, and the common reputation and belief of it in the family, gives credit to such evidence." Gilb. L. Ev. 212, edit. 1761. See also *Doe d. Banning* v. *Griffin*, 15 East, 293, where it was proved by one of the family, that, many years before, a younger brother of the person last seised had gone abroad, and according to the repute of the family had died, and that witness had never heard in the family of his having been married. This was holden to be sufficient *primâ facie* evidence, that the party was dead without lawful issue. Ejectment on a demise laid in the year 1818. To establish the case for the lessors of the plaintiff, it became necessary to prove the death of A. who had been tenant for life; it appeared that he was born in February, 1759, and had been a wanderer during the greater part of his life, having been absent from his relations from 1787 to 1804. In 1804 he returned, and having remained a short time, went away again; since that time he had not been seen in the neighbourhood. These facts were deposed to by a person who resided near the spot; but no one of the family was called as a witness. It was holden, that this was *primâ facie* evidence, from which the jury might presume A.'s death. *Doe d. Lloyd* v. *Deakin*, 4 B. & A. 433.

evidence as to pedigrees (*b*) ; but evidence of what a mere stranger has said has ever been rejected in such cases (45) : so the declarations of an illegitimate child (*c*) have been rejected. So the dying declarations (*d*) of a person, who had, as she herself stated, been servant to M. W., through whom the pedigree was traced, as to the relationship of the lessor of the plaintiff to the person last seised, have been rejected. An entry, in an almanack, by the father, of the nativity (*e*) [the *time* of the birth] of his son, has been admitted to be good evidence, to show that the son was under age at the time of making his will; on the ground, as it should seem, of the peculiar means of knowledge of the fact by the father, and the absence of all interest in him at the time of the memorandum made. A written memorandum by a deceased man-midwife, stating that he had delivered a woman of a child on a certain day, and referring to his ledger, in which a charge for his attendance on that occasion was marked as *paid*, was holden (*f*) to be good evidence, upon an issue as to the child's age; on the ground, that if a person have peculiar means of knowing a fact, and make a declaration of that fact, which is against his interest, it is evidence after his death. It will be observed, that in this case, the memorandum of the payment of the midwife's charge was holden to be evidence of the *date* of the birth; and in *Doe* v. *Robson* (*g*), the entry of charges paid for a lease, as drawn on a certain day, was holden to be evidence that the lease was so drawn, which the proof by an eye-witness of the same payment on account of such charges, would not have been; and there are other cases to the same effect. The result of these authorities is, that the entry of a payment against the interest of the party making it, may have the effect of proving the truth of other statements contained in the

---

(*b*) Per Lord *Kenyon*, C. J., in *R.* v. *Eriswell*, 3 T. R. 723.

(*c*) *Doe* v. *Barton*, 2 M. & Rob. 28, *Patteson*, J.

(*d*) *Doe d. Sutton* v. *Ridgway*, 4 B. & A. 53.

(*e*) *Herbert* v. *Tuckal*, Sir T. Raym.

84, cited, with remarks, by *Ellenborough*, C. J., in *Roe* v. *Rawlings*, 7 East, 290.

(*f*) *Higham* v. *Ridgway*, 10 East, 116; see the remarks of *Bayley*, B., on the report of his opinion in East, in *Gleadow* v. *Atkins*, 1 Cr. & M. 423, 4.

(*g*) 15 East, 32.

---

(45) In ejectment brought by the Duke of Athol, Mr. Sharpe, attorney, was *at first* permitted to give in evidence what he had heard an old servant of the family (since dead) say concerning this pedigree; but it being strongly objected to, and Hollings relying on the objection, they afterwards gave other evidence. MS. Mr. Wegg. See a different statement of this case in Gilb. Law of Evid. 112, and Bull. N. P. 290, under the name of *Duke of Athol* v. *Lord Ashburnham*. But *quæ*. if the foregoing be not more correct. Declarations of servants and intimate acquaintance are not admissible; the rule is confined to members of the family. *Johnson* v. *Lawson*, 2 Bingh. 86; 9 Moore, 183, *S. C.*

same entry, and connected with it (*h*). But hearsay evidence of the declaration of a deceased father, as to the *place* (*i*) of birth of his bastard child, is not admissible to prove the birth settlement of such child. The husband has been considered as a member of the wife's family within the exception (*k*); and, consequently, his declarations as to the illegitimacy of his wife are admissible in evidence. So a widow has been allowed to prove the declarations of her deceased husband in support of her son's title, although the husband, if living, would have had the right which the declarations went to establish (*l*). So declarations of a person entitled to a remainder upon failure of issue of the then possessor are admissible (*m*), although the title of the plaintiff was that which the person making the declarations would have had, if living. But in all cases, if it appears that the declarations have been made post litem motam, that is, not merely after the commencement of the suit, but after the dispute has arisen (*n*), they are not to be received. In the case of the *Banbury Claim of Peerage*, D. P., 23d February, 1809, the counsel for the petitioner stated that he would offer in evidence certain depositions taken upon a bill (seeking relief), filed in the Court of Chancery on the 9th of February, 1640, by Edward, the eldest son of the first Earl of Banbury, an infant, by his next friend. This evidence having been objected to, and the point argued, the following questions were proposed to the judges:— Upon the trial of ejectment brought by E. F. against G. H. to recover the possession of an estate, E. F., to prove that C. D., from whom E. F. was descended, was the legitimate son of A. B., offered in evidence a bill in Chancery, purporting to have been filed by C. D. 150 years before that time by his next friend, such next friend therein styling himself the uncle of the infant, for the purpose of perpetuating testimony of the fact that C. D. was the legitimate son of A. B., and which bill stated him to be such legitimate son (but no persons claiming to be heirs at law of A. B., if C. D. was illegitimate, were parties to the suit, the only defendant being a person alleged to have held lands under a lease from A. B., reserving rent to A. B. and his heirs) : and also offered in evidence depositions taken in the said cause; some of them purporting to be made by persons styling themselves relations of A. B.; others styling themselves servants in his family; others styling themselves to be medical persons attendant upon the family; and in their respective depositions stating facts, and declaring that C. D. was

---

(*h*) Per *Parke*, B., delivering judgment of court in *Davies* v. *Humphreys*, 6 M. & W. 166.

(*i*) *R.* v. *Erith*, 8 East, 539.

(*k*) *Vowles* v. *Young*, 13 Ves. 143, Lord *Erskine*, C.; *Doe d. Northey* v. *Harvey*, Devon Summ. Ass. 1825, S. P., per *Littledale*, J., Ry. & M. 297.

(*l*) Peerage case cited by *Abbott*, C. J., in *Doe d. Filmer* v. *Tarver*, Ry. & M. 141.

(*m*) *S. C.*

(*n*) *Berkley Peerage* case, 4 Campb. 401; *Walker* v. *Beauchamp*, 6 C. & P. 560.

the legitimate son of A. B., and that he was in the family, of which they were respectively relations, servants, and medical attendants, reputed so to be:—

1st Question. Are the bill in equity, and the depositions respectively, or any and which of them, to be received in the courts below, upon the trial of such ejectment, (G. H. not claiming or deriving, in any manner, under either the plaintiff or defendant in the said chancery suit,) either as evidence of facts therein [alleged, denied, or] deposed to, or *as declarations respecting pedigree?* and are they, or any and which of them, evidence to be received in the said cause, that the parties filing the bill, and making the depositions, respectively sustained the characters of uncle, relations, servants, and medical persons, which they describe themselves therein sustaining?

Answer (46). Neither the bill in equity, nor the depositions, are to be received in evidence in the courts below, on the trial of the ejectment, either as evidence of the facts therein [alleged, denied, or] deposed to, or as *declarations respecting pedigree;* neither are any of them evidence that the parties filing the bill, or making the depositions, respectively sustained the characters of uncle, relations, servants, and medical persons, which they describe themselves therein sustaining. The judges further added, that it would not make any difference in their opinion, if the bill, stated to have been filed by C. D., by his next friend, had been a bill seeking relief.

2nd Question. Whether any bill in chancery can ever be received as evidence in a court of law, to prove any facts either alleged or denied in such bill?

Answer. Generally speaking, a bill in chancery cannot be received as evidence in a court of law, to prove any fact either alleged or denied in such bill (47). But whether any possible case might be put which would form an exception to such general rule, the judges could not undertake to say.

3rd Question. Whether depositions, taken in the Court of Chan-

---

(46) The C. J. of C. B. delivered the opinion of the judges on the 30th of May, 1809.

(47) In *Pennell* v. *Meyer*, 2 M. & Rob. 98, the plaintiff tendered in evidence the answer of the defendant to a bill in equity: the defendant insisted that the bill should be produced and read: *Tindal*, C. J., said, he thought he must order the whole bill to be read if the defendant required it, though it was certainly unusual to require this to be done; and he should tell the jury, that the statements in the bill were not to be considered as admissions of the facts so stated, it being notorious that allegations, not corresponding with the facts, were frequently introduced into bills for the purpose merely of eliciting the truth from the other party.

cery, in consequence of a bill to perpetuate the testimony of witnesses, or otherwise, would be received in evidence to prove the facts sworn to, in the same way and to the same extent as if the same were sworn to at the trial of an ejectment by witnesses then produced?

Answer. Such depositions would not be received in evidence, in a court of law, in any cause in which the parties were not the same as in the cause in the Court of Chancery, or did not claim under some or one of such parties.

In an ejectment brought to try the validity of a recovery suffered by the father of the lessor of plaintiff, tenant in tail; it was holden (o), that a party being a remainder-man in the entailed property after the tenant in tail, was not a competent witness for the plaintiff. But heir (p) apparent is competent witness in support of claim of ancestor; for the heirship is a mere contingency.

If the question be, whether a certain manor be ancient demesne or not, the trial shall be by Domesday Book, which will be inspected by the court (q). In ejectment for the manor of Artam (r), the defendant pleaded ancient demesne, and when Domesday Book was brought into court, would have proved that it was anciently called Nettam, and that Nettam appears by the book to be ancient demesne; but he was not permitted to give such evidence; for if the name be varied, it ought to have been averred on the record. An ancient writing, found among the court rolls of a manor, stated to be *ex assensu omnium tenentium*, and proved to have been delivered down from steward to steward, is admissible evidence, although not signed by any person, to prove the course of descent within the manor (s).—And the same rule holds, with respect to an entry in the court rolls of a presentment made by the homage of the customary mode of descent within the manor, although no instances be proved of any person having taken according to the mode of descent pointed out in the presentment (t). Custom is of the very essence of a copyhold; and if the custom be silent, the common law must regulate the course of descent.—Customs are to be taken strictly, and cannot be extended by implication.—Hence, where the custom is, that the elder sister shall inherit, yet, by that custom, the eldest aunt of the eldest niece shall not inherit the land (u). So if the custom be that the *youngest son* shall inherit, and a man has issue two sons and dies, and the land descends to the younger son, who dies without issue, the *eldest son* of the *eldest brother* shall have the land; because the custom does not hold in the transversal line,

---

(o) *Doe d. Lord Teynham* v. *Tyler*, 6 Bingh. 390.

(p) Per *Treby*, C. J., Salk. 283.

(q) Hob. 188.

(r) *Gregory* v. *Withers*, H. 28 Car. II., Gilb. Ev. 44; 3 Keb. 588, S. C.

(s) *Denn d. Goodwin* v. *Spray*, 1 T. R. 466.

(t) *Roe d. Beebee* v. *Parker*, 5 T. R. 26.

(u) *Ratcliff* v. *Chapman*, 4 Leon. 242.

but only in the lineal descent (*x*). Evidence of reputation of the custom of the manor (*y*), that in default of sons, the *eldest daughter*, and in default also of daughters, the *eldest sister*, and in case of the death of all, the *descendants* of the eldest daughter or sister respectively of the person last seised should take, is proper to be left to the jury of the existence of such a custom, as applied to a *great nephew*, (the grandson of an eldest sister,) of the person last seised; although the instances in which it was proved to have been put in use extended no further than those of eldest daughter and eldest sister, and the son of an eldest sister. The existence of such extended custom in adjacent manors seems to be no evidence of the custom in the particular manor. The premises were laid in the declaration to be in the parish of Farnham, and at the trial were proved to be in the parish of Farnham Royal; but it was not shown by the defendant that there were two Farnhams. The variance was holden to be immaterial (*z*). And where lands were described in the declaration to be in the parish of Westbury, in the county of Gloucester, and it was proved at the trial that there were two parishes of Westbury in that county; *viz.* Westbury upon Trim and Westbury upon Severn; still it was holden (*a*) not to be a variance; although, if there had been any plea in abatement in ejectment, it might have been a good objection on such plea.

To an indenture of feoffment by the Bank of England, the seal of the bank was affixed by a paper, wafered to the indenture, on which was written, " Sealed by order of the Court of Directors of the Governor and Co. of the Bank; J. K. Secretary; " it was holden (*b*), that J. K. was not an attesting witness, and that the execution of the feoffment might be proved by the seal without calling J. K.

Evidence on the part of the Defendant.—If the defendant prove a title out of the lessor of the plaintiff, it is sufficient, though he have not any title himself: but he ought to prove a subsisting title out of the lessor; for producing an ancient lease for 1000 years will not be sufficient, unless he likewise prove possession, under such lease, within twenty years (*c*). So if the defendant produce a mortgage deed, where the interest has not been paid, and the mortgagee never entered, it will not be sufficient to defeat the lessor, who claims under the mortgagor (*d*); because it will be presumed that the money was paid at the day, and consequently, that it is not a subsisting title; but if the defendant prove interest paid upon such mortgage, after the time of redemption, and within

(*x*) 1 Rol. Abr. 624, pl. 2.
(*y*) Doe d. Foster and another v. Sisson, 12 East, 62.
(*z*) Doe d. Tollet v. Salter, 13 East, 9.
(*a*) Doe d. James and Wife v. Harris, B. R. M. T. 57 Geo. III., MS.; and 5 M.
& S. 326, S. C.
(*b*) Doe d. Bank of England v. Chambers, 4 Ad. & Ell. 410.
(*c*) Bull. N. P. 110.
(*d*) Wilson v. Witherby, per Holt, C. J., Bull. N. P. 110.

twenty years, it will be sufficient to nonsuit the plaintiff. No less time than twenty years will raise a presumption that a mortgaged term has been assigned or surrendered; although the defendant neither proves that interest continues to be paid, nor in any way accounts for his possession of the mortgage deed (e).

The defendant produced a mortgage for years (f), by deed, from the plaintiff's ancestor, upon which was an indorsement in *hæc verba*, "Received of M. O. £500 on the within recited mortgage, and all interest due to this day; and I do hereby release to the said M. O., and discharge the mortgaged premises from the said term of 500 years." On a case reserved, the court held, 1st, that these words amounted to a surrender of the term; 2nd, that such surrender might be by note in writing, without deed, by the statute of frauds (29 Car. II. c. 3, s. 3); 3rd, that a note in writing was not required to be stamped (48).

The mother of a defendant who claimed to retain possession as heir at law to his father, is a competent witness (g) for defendant, although the effect of her testimony be to prove a seisin in law in her husband, which would give her a claim to dower.

In ejectment (h) by one who claims as heir of B., the son of an elder brother of B. is a competent witness for the defendant.

XII. *Verdict, p.* 759; *Judgment, p.* 760; *Execution, p.* 761; *Costs, p.* 762.

Verdict.—In an *ejectio firmæ* of a messuage (i), if it be found that a small part of the house is built, by encroachment, upon the land of the plaintiff, and not the residue, yet plaintiff shall recover for that parcel by the name of a messuage. Upon trial at bar in

(e) *Doe* v. *Calvert,* 5 Taunt. 170.
(f) *Farmer d. Earl* v. *Rogers and another,* T. 1755, C. B., Bull. N. P. 110; 2 Wils. 26, S. C.
(g) *Doe d. Nightingale* v. *Maisey,* 1 B.

& Ad. 439, cited by *Park,* J., in *Doe d. Bath* v. *Clarke,* 3 Bingh. N. C. 432.
(h) *Doe d. Bath* v. *Clarke,* 3 Bingh. N. C. 429.
(i) 2 Roll. Abr. 704.

---

(48) So in *Hodges* v. *Drakeford,* 1 Bos. & Pul. N. R. 270, it was holden, that an assignment in writing, not under seal, indorsed on a lease, did not require a stamp duty before the statute 44 Geo. III. c. 98. But now, by that statute, a deed or *other instrument* of assignment is made subject to a stamp duty. The like provision has been made by the last Stamp Act, 55 Geo. III. c. 184. See Schedule, Part. I. tit. Mortgage.

an *ejectio firmæ* (*k*), by a jury from Kent, the declaration was of a fourth part of a fifth part; and the title of the plaintiff was only to one-third of one-fourth of one-fifth, being only one-third of what was declared for. And it was said, that plaintiff could not have a verdict, because the verdict ought to agree with the declaration. But *per Cur.* The verdict may be taken according to the title. In ejectment, declaration was for a moiety of land of gavelkind tenure, in Kent (*l*); and the question was, whether the lessor of the plaintiff could recover a third part of the land described, having claimed a moiety in the declaration? Lord *Mansfield*, C. J., " The lessor of the plaintiff shall recover according to his title, and it is not any objection to his recovering what he has really a title to, that he has demanded more." If an ejectment is brought for forty acres, plaintiff may recover twenty acres (*m*). *Denison*, J., "In ejectment, plaintiff generally declares for more than he hopes to recover. If he claims a messuage in the declaration, he may recover a moiety." The plaintiff may recover, by way of damages, costs incurred by him in a court of error, in reversing a judgment in ejectment obtained by defendant (*n*).

By stat. 11 Geo. IV. and 1 Will. IV. c. 70, s. 38, "in all cases of trials of ejectments at nisi prius, where a verdict shall be given for the plaintiff, or the plaintiff shall be nonsuited for want of the defendant's appearance to confess lease, entry, or ouster; it shall be lawful for the judge before whom the cause shall be tried to certify his opinion on the back of the record, that a writ of possession ought to issue. *immediately;* and upon such certificate, a writ of possession may be issued *forthwith;* and the costs may be taxed, and judgment signed and executed afterwards at the usual time, as if no such writ had issued: Provided, that such writ, instead of reciting a recovery by judgment in the form now in use, shall recite shortly, that the cause came on for trial at nisi prius, at such time and place and before such a judge, (naming the time, place, and judge,) and that thereupon the said judge certified his opinion that a writ of possession ought to issue *immediately.*" The stat. 1 & 2 Will. IV. c. 7, which, by sect. 4, allows of judgments, which have been signed by virtue of that act, being vacated, executions stayed, and new trials granted, if justice requires it, contains an express provision in sect. 5, that it shall not be deemed to *frustrate or make void* the foregoing provision in the stat. 11 Geo. IV. and 1 Will. IV. c. 70, s. 38, relating to the issuing of the *habere facias possessionem.*

Judgment.—The form of the judgment, after verdict for the

(*k*) *Ablett d. Glenham* v. *Skinner*, 1 Sidf. 229.

(*l*) *Denn d. Burgess* v. *Purvis*, 1 Burr. 326, and MSS.; see Comb. 101.

(*m*) See *Guy* v. *Rand*, Cro. Eliz. 13,

and *Meredith* v. *Rand*, 43 Eliz., Dyer, 115, b., pl. 67, in marg. S. P.

(*n*) *Nowell* v. *Roake*, 7 B. & C. 404, cited in *Symonds* v. *Page*, 1 Cr. & J. 29.

plaintiff in ejectment on a single demise, is, "that the plaintiff do recover his term aforesaid, yet to come and unexpired, of and in the said tenements, with the appurtenances above mentioned, whereof it has been found by the jurors aforesaid, that the defendant is guilty of the trespass and ejectment aforesaid, and his damages aforesaid, by the jurors aforesaid, in form aforesaid assessed; and also ——*l.* to plaintiff at his request, for his costs and charges aforesaid, by the court here for an increase adjudged, which said damages in the whole amount to ——*l.* And let the said defendant be taken, &c." Where the ejectment is brought on several demises, a slight alteration of the language in the preceding form will be necessary, in order to adapt it to the particular case. The court will make every possible intendment to support the judgment. A bare possibility of title, consistent with the judgment, will be sufficient. Hence, where in the declaration two demises were alleged for the *same* term (*o*), both as to commencement and duration, by two different persons, of the *same* premises; and the judgment was, "that the plaintiff should recover his *terms;* it was objected on error, that it was impossible the plaintiff could have a right to recover the two terms, according to the words of the declaration; because if A. demise to a man an estate for forty years, and then B., at the same moment, demise the same estate to a man for forty years, it is impossible both can have a right. But the court overruled the objection, observing, that it might be *in rerum naturâ,* that the estate might have belonged to two joint tenants, who might have refused to concur in one lease, but each might have made a lease of the whole, which would operate as a lease of the moiety. So where the declaration in ejectment contained two demises (*p*), each of an undivided third of the same estate, for the same term, but by different lessors; and the judgment was, "that the plaintiff should recover his said *terms.*" It was objected, on error, that the judgment being for the recovery of two undivided thirds, (under a title, explained by the facts disclosed by the bill of exceptions, even in the parts stating the proof for the defendant in error, to be only for one undivided third, and confessed to be in fact to no greater extent,) was erroneous. But the court overruled the objection, observing, that this did not come before the court by special verdict, but by bill of exceptions; consequently what other evidence was given, besides that stated in the bill, did not appear; that it did appear that a great deal of other evidence was given, and for any thing that appeared, there might be a title to another undivided third of the estate.

Execution.—It is usual for the plaintiff to indemnify the sheriff, and then the sheriff gives the plaintiff execution of what he de-

(*o*) *Morres* v. *Barry,* Str. 1180; 1 Wils. 1, *S. C.*

(*p*) *Roe* v. *Power,* D. P. 2 Bos. & Pul. N. R. 1.

mands. If the plaintiff take out execution for more than the recovery warrants (*q*), the court will interpose in a summary way, and restore the tenant to the possession of such part as was not recovered. If the execution be for twenty acres (*r*), the sheriff must give possession of twenty acres, according to the estimation of the county where the lands lie. When a person has obtained leave to defend as landlord, and does not attend at the trial, application must be made to the court for leave to take out execution; but after trial and verdict against landlord, no such application is necessary (*s*). It is at the election of the plaintiff whether the sheriff shall return the writ of *hab. fac. pos.* or not (*t*). The court will not oblige the sheriff to return it, except at the instance of the plaintiff. But after possession has been given under the writ (*u*), the plaintiff cannot sue out another writ, although he is disturbed by the same defendant, and though the sheriff have not returned the former writ; for an alias cannot issue after a writ is executed; if it could, the plaintiff, by omitting to call on the sheriff to make his return to the writ, might retain the right of suing out a new *habere facias possessionem*, as a remedy for any trespass which the same tenant might commit within twenty years next after the date of the judgment. Formerly, in B. R., but not in C. B., it was necessary to lodge a *præcipe* with the officer of the court, before a writ of *habere facias possessionem* could be sued out; now, by R. G. H. T. 2 Will. IV., the lodging the *præcipe* is dispensed with. See Rule 76.

Where an ejectment was brought on two counts on several demises, and a verdict, by direction of the judge, was found for the plaintiff on the first, and for the defendant on the other, with liberty to the plaintiff to move to enter a verdict for him on the second; and the plaintiff's counsel had obtained leave to issue early execution on the first count, and possession was shortly after taken accordingly; it was holden, that as leave was reserved, the early execution on the first count did not form any objection to moving for the rule to enter a verdict on the second. *Doe on the several demises of the Governor and Company of the Bank of England, and Gregory* v. *Chambers*, 4 A. & E. 410.

Costs.—The court will compel the real defendant to pay the costs (*x*), although he is not a party to the record. Where three ejectments were brought against a landlord and his two tenants, and the landlord obtained a rule for the consolidation of the three actions, and that the ejectment against one of the tenants (a

(*q*) 1 Burr. 629; 2 Burr. 2673; *Doe d. Saul* v. *Dawson*, C. B., 3 Wils. 49.
(*r*) 1 Rol. Rep. 420; 1 Rol. Abr. 886, (H.) pl. 4.
(*s*) *Doe d. Lucy* v. *Bennett*, 4 B. & C. 897.
(*t*) Palm. 289.
(*u*) *Doe d. Pate* v. *Roe*, 1 Taunt. 55.
(*x*) *Doe d. Masters* v. *Gray*, 10 B. & C. 615.

pauper,) should abide the event of the ejectment against the other, and that action was tried, and the lessor of the plaintiff obtained judgment, and took possession of all the three tenements, the court (y) compelled the landlord to pay the costs of that ejectment.

XIII. *Writ of Error.*

By stat. 16 & 17 Car. II. c. 8, s. 3, it is enacted, that "No execution shall be stayed by writ of error upon any judgment *after verdict in ejectio firmæ*, unless the plaintiff in error shall become bound in such reasonable sum as the court of error shall think fit, to pay the plaintiff in ejectment all such costs, damages, and sums of money, as shall be awarded upon, or after such judgment affirmed, discontinuance or nonsuit had." The practice as to the amount of the recognizance varied in the different courts (z); but now, by R. G. H. T. 2 Will. IV. No. 27, the recognizance of bail in error shall be taken in double the yearly value and double the costs. Although the words of the statute seem to require a recognizance *by the plaintiff in error himself* (a), yet it has been holden, that the intention of the legislature will be satisfied by plaintiffs in error procuring responsible persons to enter into the obligation required. The plaintiff in error is not bound to give the defendant in error notice of his entering into the recognizance (b). By another clause (c) of the same statute, "in case of affirmance, discontinuance, or nonsuit, the courts are to issue a writ to inquire as well of the mesne profits, as of the damages, by any waste committed, after the first judgment; and are thereupon to give judgment; and award execution for the same, and also for costs of suit." Under 1 Geo. IV. c. 87, s. 3, defendant must give two additional *sureties on bringing* writ of error (d).

XIV. *In what Cases a Court of Equity will restrain the Party from bringing further Ejectments, by granting a perpetual Injunction.*

Where several verdicts had been obtained in ejectment upon the same title, to the satisfaction of the court, a perpetual injunction .

(y) *Thrustout* v. *Shenton*, 10 B. & C. 110.
(z) 8 East, 298; 7 Taunt. 427.
(a) *Keene* v. *Deardon*, 8 East, 298.
(b) *Doe d. Webb* v. *Goundry*, 7 Taunt.

427.
(c) Sect. 4.
(d) *Roe d. Durant* v. *Moore*, 7 Bingh. 124.

was granted, in the case of *Earl of Bath, Infant, and others,* v. *Sherwin and others,* D. P., 17th January, 1709 (*e*), reversing the decree of Lord Chancellor *Cowper.* N. Lord *Cowper* and Lord *Sommers* were present in the House of Lords when this decree was reversed. After this reversal of Lord *Cowper's* decree, it was usual to grant perpetual injunctions under the like circumstances, as was said by Baron *Price,* in the case of *Barefoot* v. *Fry,* in the Court of Exchequer. The case of *Barefoot* v. *Fry* (*f*) was determined by *Eyre,* C. B., and *Price, Page,* and *Gilbert,* Barons, on the 20th of February, 1723, in Serjeant's-Inn Hall, on a bill filed for a perpetual injunction to restrain defendant, Fry, from any further proceeding in ejectment, and to quiet plaintiff in his possession. The defendant, having brought five ejectments, had been nonsuited upon full evidence in three, and verdicts found for the lessor of the plaintiff in the other two. A perpetual injunction was granted, although it was said by Mr. Ward (defendant's counsel), that courts of equity did not decree perpetual injunctions upon ejectments, and only upon an issue directed. *Eyre,* C. B., observed, that real actions could not be brought twice for the same thing, but now ejectments having been introduced in the place of real actions, a party might bring as many ejectments as he should think fit; and this was a reason why courts of equity should settle and quiet the rights of parties. In *Calvert and another* v. *Saunders,* in 1739, West's Cases Temp. Hardwicke, p. 693, a perpetual injunction was decreed against plaintiffs, to recover, in ejectment, possession of premises, the right to which had been established against them upon a trial at bar, and upon a decree for giving effect to the verdict. In *Harwood* v. *Rolph,* after three verdicts in ejectment, another ejectment was brought, in 1772, upon which a special verdict was found and argued in C. B., in Easter and Trinity Terms, 1773; and in Hil. T. 1774, judgment was given for the lessor of the plaintiff (3 Wils. 497; 2 Bl. 937, *S. C.*); and upon error brought in the Court of King's Bench, the cause was argued there in Trinity and Michaelmas Terms, 1774, and the judgment of the Court of C. B. was reversed (see Cowp. 87); whereupon the lessors of the plaintiff brought a writ of error in parliament, and on the 9th May, 1775, the judgment of the Court of B. R. was affirmed. Upon a bill filed in the Court of Chancery, a motion was made for a perpetual injunction, to restrain defendants from any further proceeding in ejectment, which was finally heard before Lord *Bathurst,* Ch., assisted by Sir *Thomas Sewell,* M. R., on the 13th June, 1776, when an order was made for a perpetual injunction.

(*e*) This case was recognized in *Leighton* v. *Leighton,* Str. 404, affirmed D. P. 3rd March, 1720; 2 Bro. P. C. 217; Journals H. of Lords, vol. 21, fo. 455.

(*f*) Bunb. 158, pl. 228.

XV. *Of the Action of Trespass for Mesne Profits.*

ALTHOUGH the judgment in ejectment is for the recovery of damages, as well as of the term, yet, from the nature of the declaration in that action, such damages are necessarily confined to a compensation for the injury sustained by the ejectment, which being fictitious, the damages must of course be nominal. For the real injury sustained by the plaintiff, *viz.* the perception of the mesne profits by the tenant in possession, the law has provided another remedy, namely, by an action of trespass, *vi et armis*, which may be brought by the lessor of the plaintiff in ejectment, either in his own name, or in the name of the fictitious lessee (49), against the person in actual possession and trespassing; and in which the plaintiff may declare, not only for the loss of the mesne profits, but also for the costs of the ejectment, where the case requires it, as after judgment in ejectment by default against the casual ejector. This action is local in its nature, and must be brought in the county where the lands lie. It was formerly doubted, whether an action for mesne profits could be brought, in the name of the fictitious lessee or nominal plaintiff in ejectment, *after a judgment by default* against the casual ejector: but in the case of *Aslin* v. *Parkin*, 2 Burr. 665; Barnes, 472, 4to edit. *S. C.*, it was determined that it might be so brought, as well as after a judgment upon a verdict, against the tenant in possession. The action for mesne profits may be brought by one tenant in common, who has recovered in an action of ejectment by default, against his companion (*g*). By stat. 1 Geo. IV. c. 87, s. 2, it is enacted, that "wherever hereafter it shall appear on the trial of any ejectment, at the suit of a landlord against a tenant, that such tenant or his attorney hath been served with due notice of trial, the plaintiff shall not be nonsuited for the default of the defendant's appearance or of confession of lease, entry, and ouster; but the production of the consent rule and undertaking of the defendant shall, in such cases, be sufficient evidence of lease, entry, and ouster; and the judge before whom such cause shall come on to be tried shall, whether the defendant shall appear upon such trial or not, permit the plaintiff, on the trial, after proof of his right to recover possession of the whole or of any part of the premises mentioned

(*g*) *Goodtitle* v. *Tombs*, 3 Wils. 118.

---

(49) Where the action is brought in the name of the fictitious lessee, the court will, upon application, stay the proceedings, until security is given for answering the costs. Bull. N. P. 89.

in the declaration, to go into evidence of the mesne profits thereof, which shall or might have accrued from the day of the expiration or determination of the tenant's interest in the same, down to the time of the verdict given in the cause, or to some preceding day to be specially mentioned therein: and the jury, on the trial, finding for the plaintiff, shall, in such case, give their verdict upon the whole matter, both as to the recovery of the whole or any part of the premises, and also as to the amount of the damages to be paid for such mesne profits: provided that nothing hereinbefore contained shall be construed to bar any such landlord from bringing an action of trespass for the mesne profits, which shall accrue from the verdict, or the day so specified therein, down to the day of delivery of possession of the premises recovered in the ejectment."

Evidence.—The evidence necessary to support this action, (after judgment, upon a verdict of ejectment against the tenant in possession, who has appeared and confessed lease, entry, and ouster,) is as follows: an examined copy of the judgment in ejectment, and of the rule of court to confess lease, entry, and ouster (50), proof of the length of time during which the defendant has occupied, and of the value of the mesne profits, and of the costs of executing the writ of possession.

Where the judgment in ejectment has been by default against the casual ejector, and so no rule for the confession of lease, entry, and ouster, the plaintiff, in the action for mesne profits, ought to be prepared with an examined copy, not only of the judgment, but of the writ of possession also; and the return of execution thereon, and proof of the costs in the ejectment, and in executing the writ of possession: proof of the value of the mesne profits will be required in this case as in the former. The judgment in ejectment

---

(50) " Where the judgment is had against the *tenant in possession,* and the action of trespass brought against him, it seems sufficient to produce the judgment without proving the writ of possession executed, because, by entering into the rule to confess, the defendant is estopped both as to the lessor and the lessee, so that either may maintain trespass without proving an actual entry; but where the judgment is had against the *casual ejector,* and so no rule entered into, the lessor shall not maintain trespass without an actual entry, and therefore ought to prove the writ of possession executed." *Thorp* v. *Fry*, coram *Blencowe*, J., 11 Will. III. MSS. Bull. N. P. 87; *Northeron* v. *Bowler*, at Exon Ass.; *Button* v. *Box*, coram *Abney*, J., Oxford Summ. Ass. 1742, S. P. Notwithstanding the distinction taken in the preceding case, it may be prudent, in general, to be prepared with an examined copy of the writ of possession and return of execution. But N. If the plaintiff has been let into possession by the defendant, that will supersede the necessity of proving that the writ of possession has been executed. Per *Ellenborough*, C. J., in *Calvert* v. *Horsfall*, 4 Esp. N. P. C. 167.

will be conclusive evidence against the tenant in possession of the plaintiff's title, from the day of demise laid in the declaration in ejectment; consequently, in the action for mesne profits, it is not necessary for the plaintiff to be prepared with proof of title, except where he seeks to recover property antecedent to the day of the demise, or brings his action against a precedent occupier (h) (51). But in order to render the judgment by default conclusive evidence of the title, it must be pleaded as an estoppel (i); for a judgment is in no case conclusive unless pleaded by way of estoppel (k). If the plaintiff declares against the defendant for having taken the mesne profits for a longer period of time than six years, before action brought, the defendant may plead the statute of limitations; viz. not guilty within six years before the commencement of the suit, and thereby protect himself from all but six years. This action being for the recovery of damages (l), which are uncertain, the bankruptcy of the defendant cannot be pleaded in bar; and on the same principle, a plea of discharge under an insolvent debtors act is no bar (m). A judgment, recovered in ejectment against the wife (n), cannot be given in evidence in an action against the husband and wife, for the mesne profits; because the husband was no party to that suit. So a recovery in ejectment against a former tenant in possession is not (o) producible in evidence, against a person who is afterwards found in possession, without proving that he came in under the defendant in ejectment, so as to make him a privy to the judgment in ejectment; the rule of law being, that judgments bind only parties and privies, and as to strangers are considered as res inter alios actæ and consequently not producible against them. If there be two counts, and the defendant pleads to the first, Not Guilty, and on the last suffers judgment by default, the defendant will be entitled to a verdict on the first count, if plaintiff cannot prove that defendant had committed another and a different act of trespass from that confessed by the defendant. Trespass for mesne profits. The declaration contained two counts; the first of which stated the entry and expulsion on the 25th of March, 1794; and the last stated the entry and expulsion on the 3rd of June, 1797. To the first count the defendant pleaded, Not Guilty, and on the last he suffered judgment to go by default. The venire was awarded as well to try the issue joined on the first count as to assess damages on the last. At the trial the plaintiff proved one act of trespass

---

(h) *Decosta* v. *Atkins*, Bull. N. P. 87.
(i) *Doe* v. *Huddart*, 2 Cr. M. & R. 316.
(k) Per *Parke*, B., *Doe* v. *Seaton*, 2 Cr. M. & R. 732, and *ante*, p. 746.

(l) *Goodtitle* v. *North*, Doug. 583.
(m) *Lloyd* v. *Peell*, 3 B. & A. 407.
(n) *Denn* v. *White and Wife*, 7 T. R. 112.
(o) *Doe* v. *Harvey*, 8 Bingh. 242.

---

(51) In these cases the action should be brought in the name of the lessor of the plaintiff.

only, which was covered by the last count: it was holden (*p*), that a verdict should be entered up for the defendant on the first, and damages assessed on the last. The plaintiff brought ejectment in C. B., judgment was given for defendant; that judgment was afterwards reversed on error in B. R. The plaintiff afterwards brought trespass for mesne profits in B. R., and claimed to recover, by way of damages, the costs in error. It was holden (*q*), that he was entitled to recover those costs as part of the damage sustained, and that the jury might consider the costs between attorney and client as the measure of the damage.

On the subject of costs see stat. 3 & 4 Vict. c. 24, *ante*, p. 37 (52).

(*p*) *Compere* v. *Hicks*, 7 T. R. 727.   (*q*) *Nowell* v. *Roake*, 7 B. & C. 404.

---

(52) As to cases wherein verdicts have been returned before the passing of this act, see stat. 4 & 5 Vict. c. 28.

CHAPTER XIX.

EXECUTORS AND ADMINISTRATORS.

I. *Of Bona Notabilia, p.* 769.

II. *Of the Nature of the Interest of an Executor or Administrator in the Estate of the Deceased, p.* 774; *in what Cases
it is transmissible, p.* 777; *and where an Administration
de bonis non is necessary, p.* 778.

III. *Of limited or temporary Administrations, p.* 779.

IV. *Of an Executor de son Tort, p.* 781.

V. *Of the Disposition of the Estate of the Deceased, and of
the Order in which such Disposition ought to be made,
p.* 784.

VI. *Of Admission of Assets, p.* 788.

VII. *Of Actions by Executors and Administrators, p.* 791.

VIII. *Of Actions against Executors and Administrators, p.* 796.

IX. *Of the Pleadings, p.* 801; *and herein of the Right of
Retainer, p.* 805; *Evidence, p.* 806; *Judgment, p.* 808;
Costs, p. 808.

I. *Of Bona Notabilia.*

BY the 92nd canon (1), "If a testator or intestate dies in one
diocese, and has, at the time of his death, goods or good debts to

---

(1) This and the following will be found among the canons made by the
clergy in a convocation holden in the first year of the reign of King
James the First, A. D. 1603. They received the royal assent, *but were
not confirmed by parliament.* And on this ground it was holden, in *Middleton* v. *Croft*, Str. 1056, that the canons of 1603 did not *proprio
vigore* bind the laity. " I say *proprio vigore*, by their own force and
authority; for there are many provisions contained in these canons, which
are declaratory of the ancient usage and law of the Church of England

the value of £5, in any other diocese or peculiar jurisdiction, within the same province, the probate of the will, or granting letters of administration, belongs to the Prerogative Court of the arch-bishop of that province; and every probate or administration not so granted, is declared void; with this proviso, that if any man die *in itinere*, the goods he has about him at the time shall not cause his will or administration to be liable to the Prerogative Court."

The principle appears to be, that the goods of a party who dies *in itinere*, are supposed to be, for the purposes of the jurisdiction of the ordinary, in the place where he is domiciled, notwithstanding his personal absence. A person whose domicile and property were in the diocese of Gloucester, was proceeding on temporary business to Bristol, and met with an accident, in consequence of which he was taken to the Bristol Infirmary, which is in the diocese of Bristol, and within a few days after died. Probate of his will having been granted by the Bishop of Gloucester, it was holden regular; for the testator had died *in itinere*. *Doe d. Allen* v. *Ovens*, 2 B. & Ad. 423.

By the 93rd canon, "goods in different dioceses, unless of the value of £5, shall not be accounted *bona notabilia*" (2); with this proviso, "that this shall not prejudice those dioceses, where, by custom or composition, *bona notabilia* are rated at a greater sum." Where there are *bona notabilia* (a) in one diocese of Canterbury and one of York, the bishop of each diocese must grant an admi-nistration. Where in two dioceses of Canterbury (b), and two of York, there must be two prerogative administrations. It appears from the 92nd canon, before stated, that if an ordinary of a diocese commits administration, when the party has *bona notabilia* in different dioceses within the same province (c), such administration is merely void; and it was so decided according to Moor, 145, in 19 Eliz. (3).

(a) *Burston* v. *Ridley*, Salk. 39.　　(c) See *Stokes* v. *Bate*, 5 B. & C. 491,
(b) Per *Cur. ib.*　　　　　　　　　and *post*, 773.

---

received and allowed here, which in that respect and by virtue of such ancient allowance will bind the laity, but that is an obligation antecedent to, and not arising from, this body of canons;" per Lord *Hardwicke*, delivering judgment. See judgment, very fully reported, and probably from a MS. of the Chief Justice, Lord Hardwicke, 2 Atk. 653.

(2) " It seems that this canon has changed the law, if that were other-wise before, inasmuch as the granting administration belongs to the eccle-siastical law, and our law only takes notice of their law in this; and therefore they may alter it at their pleasure." 1 Rolle's Abr. 909, Exe-cutors, (1) pl. 5. But see the preceding note.

(3) The name of the case is not mentioned in Moor; but there is a case in 2 Leon. 155, by the name of *Dunne's* case, of this year, and on this

But where A. (*d*) had goods only in one inferior diocese, and the metropolitan of the same province, pretending that he had *bona notabilia* in several dioceses, granted administration; it was adjudged, that the administration was only voidable by sentence, and the reason assigned for this in 5 Rep. 29, b. (where this case is cited) is, that the metropolitan has jurisdiction over all the dioceses within his province. Goods of the value of £5 in one diocese (*e*), and a lease for years of the same value in another diocese of the same province, though a chattel real, make *bona notabilia*, and require a prerogative administration. Judgments are *bona notabilia* at the place where they are recorded (*f*). Debts by specialty are *bona notabilia*, not at the place where the securities were made (*g*), nor where the testator or intestate died (*h*), but at the place where the securities are at the death of the testator or intestate. Hence if a man becomes bound in an obligation in London (*i*), and dies

(*d*) *Veere* v. *Jeofferies*, Moor, 145; *Nedham's* case, 5 Rep. 135, a., S. P., agreed; *Lysons* v. *Barrow*, 2 Bingh. N.C. 486.

(*e*) 1 Rol. Abr. 909, (H) pl. 1.

(*f*) *Adams* v. *Savage*, Lord Raym. 855, agreed in *Gold* v. *Strode*, Carth. 149; *Boon* v. *Hayman*, E. 6 Geo. II. B. R., MSS.; S. P. *Anon.* 8 Mod. 244.

(*g*) *Lunn* v. *Dodson, post.*

(*h*) *Byron* v. *Byron*, Cro. Eliz. (472).

(*i*) *Lunn* v. *Dodson*, adjudged in an action brought by administrator in London, supposing the obligation to be there made, and showed the administration to be granted by Bishop of Exeter; and on demurrer to declaration, judgment for plaintiff. Affirmed on error, M. 15 Car., 1 Rol. Abr. 908, (G) pl. 4.

point; from which it appears that the court were divided in opinion. But Sir *Edward Coke*, in 5 Rep. 30, a., lays down the position agreeably with the decision mentioned in Moor; and *Holt*, C. J., in *Blackborough* v. *Davis*, Salk. 38; 1 P. Wms. 43, *S. C.*, speaking of an administration granted to a wrong person, says, "It is not void, *as where administration is granted in a wrong diocese*, but only voidable." So *Weston*, Baron, in Bull. N. P. 141, "Where administration is granted in a wrong diocese, it is void: where to a wrong person, voidable." So per Lord *Macclesfield*, Ch., in *Comber's* case, 1 P. Wms. 767, 768, (where a question arose upon the validity of a *probate* granted by the archdeacon of Surrey, the testator having died possessed of *bona notabilia* in two dioceses within the province of Canterbury,) "if this had been an *administration* granted by the archdeacon or ordinary, where there were *bona notabilia* in divers dioceses, the administration had been merely void: for the administrator receives his right entirely from the administration; but the right of the executor is derived from the will, and not the probate, as appears from an executor's having power to release or assign any part of the personal estate before probate; and a defendant at law cannot plead to any action brought by an executor, that the plaintiff has not proved the will, though it is true he may demur, if the plaintiff does not in his declaration show the probate." Probate in the Court of the Archdeacon of Sudbury, to whom the bishop granted full power to prove the wills of all persons deceased within the archdeaconry, was held good, the testator having died within the archdeaconry; although he was possessed of a term of years in lands lying within another archdeaconry in the same diocese. *Rex* v. *Yonge*, 5 M. & S. 119.

intestate in Devon, and there had the obligation at the time of his death, administration ought to be granted by the Bishop of Exon, where the obligation was at his death, and not by the Bishop of London, where the obligation was made: for the debt shall be accounted goods as to the granting the administration, where the deed was at his death, and not where it was made. So in covenant on a policy of insurance under seal, whereby three of the directors of the insurance company did order, direct, and appoint, that, if T. S., the insured, should die, &c., the capital, stock, and funds of the company should stand charged and be liable to pay to the executors, administrators, and assigns of the said T. S., within three calendar months after his decease should be certified, the sum of £500. The insured died in the diocese of Exeter, and the policy was in that diocese at the time of his death; it was holden (*k*), that a probate from the Diocesan Court of Exeter was sufficient to enable the executors to recover on the policy, though the defendants resided, and all the stock and funds of the company were situate, in the diocese of London. But simple contract debts, as debts due on bills of exchange (*l*), &c., follow the person of the debtor, and the will must be proved, or administration granted, in that place where the debtor resided at the time of the death of the testator or intestate. From the case of *Scarth* v. *Bishop of London* (*m*), it appears that stock in the public funds is *bona notabilia* within the diocese of London. In *indebitatus assumpsit* by an administrator (*n*), for goods sold and delivered by the intestate, on an administration committed by the archdeacon of Berkshire, the defendant pleaded in bar, that he, the defendant, at the time of the death of the intestate, was an inhabitant and resiant in the city of Oxford, which was within the diocese of Oxford, and that the archdeaconry and whole county of Berks were within the diocese of Salisbury. On special demurrer, because it did not appear that the defendant was not an inhabitant within the diocese of Salisbury, the court overruled the demurrer, and adjudged the plea to be good (4). In debt by an administrator (*o*), it appeared that the

_____

(*k*) *Gurney* v. *Rawlins*, 2 M. & W. 87.
See *Huthwaite* v. *Phaire*, 1 M. & Gr. 159.
   (*l*) *Yeomans* v. *Bradshaw*, Carth. 373, 4.

(*m*) 1 Hagg. Ecc. R. 625.
(*n*) *Hilliard* v. *Cox*, Salk. 37.
(*o*) *Griffith* v. *Griffith*, Say. R. 83.

_____

(4) There is evidently a mistake in Salkeld's report of this case*; the pleadings are stated in the text as they appeared on the record, a copy of which will be found at the end of Salkeld's Reports, p. 747. See also this case *ex relatione* M'ri Jacob, Ld. Raym. 562, where it is said, that Northey took exception to the plea, because the defendant did not traverse his residence in Berks within the peculiar. *Holt*, C. J. "If the debtor has two houses, in several dioceses, and at the time of the death of the

* See *Griffith* v. *Griffith*, Say. R. 83, where this mistake is noticed by *Lee*, C. J.

letters of administration were granted by the Bishop of Bristol. Plea, that the plaintiff's intestate died on the high sea, out of the jurisdiction of the Bishop of Bristol, and that therefore the letters of administration were void. On demurrer, it was holden, that the letters of administration were good ; for the right of granting them is not founded upon the dying of an intestate within a diocese, but upon his leaving goods therein. It has been holden (p), that where a party dies out of any province, having *bona notabilia* in one of its dioceses exclusively, the Prerogative and Diocesan Courts have concurrent jurisdiction. If one take administration to a person who was *felo de se*, and receive effects under it, he shall be liable to creditors (q), though, by law, the effects belong to the king. Administration was granted in Bengal to B. as attorney to A., a creditor in Bengal, and he receives money under that. Afterwards C. obtains administration in England,—A. sues B. for money had and received to his use; and it was holden (r), that he was entitled to recover.

In assumpsit by an administratrix upon a promissory note, given to her intestate, it was averred in the declaration, that administration of all and singular the goods and chattels of the intestate was duly granted by the Bishop of Chester. Plea, that the plaintiff never had been nor was administratrix, &c.; and issue being joined thereon, letters of administration granted by the Bishop of C. were there produced by plaintiff; but it was also proved that the intestate at the time of his death had *bona notabilia* in another diocese in a different province, and no evidence was given as to the residence of the defendant at the death of the intestate; it was holden (s), 1st, that the letters of administration were not void, inasmuch as the other diocese in which the intestate had *bona notabilia* was in a different province; and, secondly, that the only question raised upon the issue was, whether the letters of administration were duly granted by the Bishop of C., and that it was no part of the issue, whether the defendant, at the death of the intestate, resided within the diocese of C. The fact of his residence elsewhere, if relied upon, ought to have been pleaded specially. By stat. 55 Geo. III. c. 184, s. 37, " Persons administering personal estates, without obtaining probate or letters of administration within six calendar months after the death, or within two calendar months after termination of suit, if there be any, which shall not be

---

(p) *Scarth* v. *Bishop of London*, 1 Hagg. Ecc. R. 625.
(q) *Megit* v. *Johnson*, 2 Doug. 542.

(r) *Farringdon* v. *Clerk*, 3 Doug. 124.
(s) *Stokes* v. *Bate*, 5 B. & C. 491.

---

debtee and commission of administration, is inhabitant and resident at one of the houses, that will exclude the jurisdiction of the ordinary of the diocese, in which the other house stood." Judgment for defendant.

ended within four calendar months after the death, shall forfeit the sum of £100, and 10 per cent. on the duty."

II. *Of the Nature of the Interest of an Executor or Adminis-trator in the Estate of the Deceased, p. 774; in what Cases it is transmissible, p. 777; and where an Administration de bonis non is necessary, p. 778.*

EXECUTORS or administrators so entirely represent the personal estate of the testator or intestate (t), that they are liable to the payment of all debts, covenants, &c. of the deceased, as far as the assets which have come to their hands will extend to pay (5).

The executors (u) more actually represent the person of the testator, then the heir does the person of the ancestor; for if a man bind himself, his executors are bound, though they are not named; but the heir is not bound, unless he be expressly named. Executors may release (x), or take a release (y), before probate (6), if they prove afterwards. So executors may *commence* an action before probate (z), and it is sufficient if at the time of declaring they produce in court the letters testamentary (7). Each executor

(t) 1 Inst. 209, a, b.
(u) Ib. 292, b.
(x) Ib. 209, a.

(y) 1 Rol. Abr. 917, (A) pl. 1; Plowd. 281, a., S. P.
(z) 1 Rol. Abr. 297, (A) pl. 2.

(5) "It is a maxim and principle, that an executor, where no default is in him, shall not be bound to pay more for his testator than his goods amount unto." Went. Off. Exor. c. 12.

(6) Before probate, and before any seizure, the law adjudges the pro-perty of the goods of the testator in the executors. Hence if any person takes the goods of the testator before the executors have seized them, the executors shall have action of trespass* or replevin: by *Walsh*, J., and *Dyer*, C. J., Plowd. 281, a. So if a man die possessed of goods, and a stranger takes and converts them to his own use, and afterwards adminis-tration is granted to J. S.; J. S. may maintain trover for the conversion before administration granted to him. 2 Rol. Abr. 399, (A) pl. 1.

(7) So where an executor, before probate, files a bill in a court of equity, and afterwards proves the will, such subsequent probate makes the will good. Per *Talbot*, Ch., 3 P. Wms. 351. So where plaintiffs, after bill filed, took out letters of administration, and charged the same by way of

* 2 Inst. 398.

has the entire control of the personal estate of the testator, and may release or pay a debt, or transfer any part of the testator's property, without the concurrence of the other executor (a). And it seems, that the same rule holds with respect to administrators (b) (8).

If two have a lease for years as executors, and one sells the whole, this shall bind the other; and the whole shall pass; for each had the entire power of disposing of the whole, both being possessed in the right of the testator (c). So if one dispose of all the goods of the testator without the other (d). As an executor is not entitled in his own right, but in *auter droit* (e), to the property of the deceased, the goods of a testator, in the hands of his executor, cannot be seized in execution for the proper debt of the executor (f) (9). But if an executrix use the goods of her testator

(a) Per Sir *J. Strange*, M. R., 2 Ves. 267.
(b) *Willand* v. *Fenn*, see note (8).
(c) *Pannell* v. *Fenn*, 1 Rol. Abr. 924, (O) pl. 1 ; Gouldsb. 185, *S. C.*

(d) Dyer, 23, b., in marg.
(e) 2 Inst. 236.
(f) *Farr* v. *Newman*, 4 T. R. 621 ; *Buller*, J., dissentiente.

amendment to the bill, having obtained an order for such amendment, it was holden good; for the letters of administration, when granted, relate to the time of the death of the intestate. *Humphreys* v. *Humphreys*, 3 P. Wms. 351.

(8) In *Willand* v. *Fenn*, E. 11 Geo. II. B. R., MSS., a question arose, whether the release of one administrator would bind his companion? The case was argued in E. 11 Geo. II., when the court, entertaining doubts, directed a second argument. The second argument was heard Trin. 11 & 12 Geo. II., when *Lee*, C. J., expressed a strong opinion in favour of the affirmative, observing, that it was extremely difficult to form a distinction between executors and administrators upon any reasonable foundation; and that although it had not ever been determined at law, that the administration survived, yet having been so determined in equity, in *Adams* v. *Buckland*, 2 Vern. 514, cited 2 P. Wms. 121, n.; and by Lord *Talbot* in the case of *Hudson* v. *Hudson*, Ca. Temp. Talbot, 127; he thought those authorities were so strong, that they ought not to be departed from. The other judges were inclined to the same opinion, but as the case was new, and of general consequence, they ordered it to be argued again. According to Sir *J. Strange*, M. R., in *Jacomb* v. *Harwood*, 2 Ves. 267, the case was decided in the affirmative after the third argument; but from a MS. note in my possession, it appears to have been compromised before the third argument took place. In Mr. J. Gundry's MS. note, 13 Gundr. 33, a, it is said to have been adjudged for defendant; that is, that the release of one administrator did bind his companion. *Hudson* v. *Hudson*, before Lord *Hardwicke*, will be found in 1 Atk. 460, and in West's Reports from Lord Hardwicke's MSS. p. 155. See the observations of Sir *J. Nichol*, in *Warwick* v. *Greville*, 1 Phillim. 126; *Stanley* v. *Bernes*, 1 Hagg. Ecc. R. 222.

(9) " If an executor become bankrupt, the commissioners cannot seize

as her own, and afterwards marry, and then the goods are treated as the goods of the husband, they may be taken in execution for the husband's debt (g). Executors and administrators have a joint interest in the estate of the deceased. Hence, if there are two or more executors (h) or administrators (i), and one or more of them die, the administration of the estate of the deceased belongs to the survivor or survivors; and it seems, that an action may be brought by a surviving administrator without procuring a new grant of letters of administration (k).

Formerly, where testators, by their wills, appointed executors without making express disposition of the residue of their personal estate, the executors became by law entitled to the whole residue, and courts of equity to a certain extent followed the law; but now, by stat. 11 Geo. IV. and 1 Will. IV. c. 40, executors shall be deemed by courts of equity to be trustees for persons entitled under the statute of distributions, in respect of residue not expressly disposed of, unless it shall appear by will or codicil, that the executor was to take the same beneficially. But by sect. 2, it is provided, that the executor's right shall not be affected where there is not any person entitled to the residue.

A probate, as long as it remains unrepealed (l), cannot be impeached in the temporal courts. Hence, payment of money to an executor, who has obtained probate of a forged will, is a discharge to the debtor of the intestate; although the probate be afterwards declared null, and administration be granted to the intestate's next of kin; for the law will not compel a person to pay a sum of money a second time, which he has once paid under the sanction of a court having competent jurisdiction (10). The spiritual court has not only jurisdiction over wills, but exclusive jurisdiction (m); and they are not exceeding that jurisdiction, when they order the will to be

---

(g) *Quick* v. *Staines*, 1 Bos. & Pul. 293.

(h) 3 Atk. 510.

(i) *Hudson* v. *Hudson*, Ca. T. Talb. 127; *Adams* v. *Buckland*, 2 Vern. 514.

(k) Per Sir *J. Strange*, M. R., 2 Ves.

268, cites Rastall, 560, which was replevin by a surviving administrator, but no judgment.

(l) *Allen* v. *Dundas*, 3 T. R. 125.

(m) *Exp. Law*, 2 Ad. & Ell. 47.

---

the *specific* effects of his testator." Per Lord *Mansfield*, C. J., 3 Burr. 1369.

(10) In like manner, it is no defence to an action for a debt due, that the plaintiff is a trader, and has committed an act of bankruptcy, of which the defendant had notice, *no commission having issued nor proceedings had for that purpose;* for though voluntary payments under such circumstances are not protected, yet payments enforced by coercion of law are valid against the assignees, in case any commission should afterwards be taken out. *Foster* v. *Allanson*, 2 T. R. 479.

brought in. In an action of *indebitatus assumpsit* (n), brought by the plaintiff, as executor of J. S., deceased, for money due to the testator, but received by the defendant, after the testator's death, it appeared in evidence, that before the will was found, administration had been granted, and that the administrator had made a warrant of attorney to the defendant to receive the money, which he had done accordingly, and had paid it over to the administrator without notice of the will. *Holt*, C. J., was of opinion, that although all acts done by an administrator, where there is a will, are void, and consequently in this case an action might have been maintained against the administrator, yet the defendant, having paid over the money without notice of the will, was not liable (11). The property of a deceased person (o) vests in his executor from the time of his death; in an administrator from the time of the grant of the letters of administration. Where A. had obtained probate of a will, by which he was appointed executor, and after notice of a subsequent will, sold the goods of the testator: it was holden, that the rightful executor, in an action of trover, was entitled to recover the full value of the goods sold, and that A. was not entitled, in mitigation of damages, to show that he had administered the assets to that amount. For *some* purposes, letters of administration relate back to the death of the intestate; thus, an administrator may bring trover (p) for goods of the intestate taken by one before the grant of the letters; so, in ejectment (q), the demise may be laid on a day after the intestate's death, but before administration granted. So also, if one (r) sanctions an expensive funeral, ordered by a relation of the deceased, and afterwards takes out administration, he is liable in the capacity of administrator for the expenses. But where a landlord is entitled to a term of years, and dies without appointing an executor, a distress for rent made after his death and before administration granted cannot be justified (s).

In what Cases the Executor's Interest is transmissible.—The

(n) *Pond* v. *Underwood*, per *Holt*, C. J., London Sittings, M. 1705, Ld. Raym. 1210.

(o) *Woolley, Executrix of Woolley deceased, against Clark and another*, 5 B. & A. 744.

(p) *Long* v. *Hebb*, Style, 341; 2 Rol.

Abr. 399, tit. Relation (A).

(q) *Ante*, p. 716.

(r) *Lucy* v. *Walrond*, 3 Bingh. N. C. 841.

(s) *Keene* v. *Dee*, B. R. Ireland, Alcock & Napier, 496, n.

---

(11) *Trevor*, C. J., had ruled differently in *Jacob* v. *Allen*, London Sittings, M. 2 Ann., Salk. 27: but see *Sadler* v. *Evans*, 4 Burr. 1986; where Lord *Mansfield*, C. J., expressed his disapprobation of the decision in *Jacob* v. *Allen*, and recognized *Pond* v. *Underwood*. When the action for money had and received shall be brought against the principal, and when against the agent, see *ante*, p. 84, n. (36).

interest vested in B., the sole executor named in the will of A., is
(if B. has proved (*t*) the will,) transmissible to C., the executor of
B.; that is, the executor of an executor having proved the will is
the executor or personal representative of the first testator (*u*).
By 25 Edw. III. stat. 5, c. 5, " Executors of executors shall have
actions of debts, accounts, and of goods carried away of the first
testators; and execution of the statutes merchants, and recognizances made in courts of record to first testator, *in the same
manner as the first testator should have had if* he were living: and
the executors of executors shall answer to others for as much as
they have recovered of the goods of the first testators, as the first
executors should do, if they were living." The executor of the
administrator of A. is not the personal representative of A. (*x*);
for the administrator of A. is merely the officer of the ordinary,
in whom the deceased has not reposed any trust, and, therefore, on
the death of such administrator, it results back to the ordinary to
appoint another. Neither is the administrator of the executor of
A., the personal representative of A. (*y*). In these cases, when
the course of representation from executor to executor is interrupted by an intestacy, it becomes necessary that the ordinary
should grant a new administration of the goods of the deceased,
not administered by the former executor or administrator, as the
case may be. Such administrator, usually termed an administrator *de bonis non*, is the legal personal representative of the deceased.

Where an Administration de bonis non is necessary.—I shall here
briefly enumerate the cases where an administration de bonis non
is necessary. 1. Where the executor of the deceased, having
proved the will, dies intestate. N. If an executor die before probate (*z*), although he should have administered part of the personal estate of the testator, an immediate administration must be
granted. 2. Where there are several executors, and the surviving
executor, having proved the will, dies intestate (*a*). 3. Where an
administrator dies before he has administered the whole personal
estate of the deceased. In an assumpsit by an administrator *de
bonis non* (*b*), the promise was alleged in the declaration to have
been made to J. H., the first administrator of the intestate, without stating any promise to the plaintiff. After verdict for the
plaintiff, an exception was taken in arrest of judgment, that it was
not sufficient to allege the promise made to the former administrator, between whom and the plaintiff there was not any privity;

(*t*) *Hayton* v. *Wolfe*, Cro. Jac. 614.
(*u*) Bro. Abr. tit. Administration, pl. 7.
If the original executor takes prerogative
probate, and the executor of the executor
takes diocesan probate, it is doubtful whether the chain of representation is maintained. *Fowler* v. *Richards*, 5 Russ. 39;

Jernegan v. *Baxter*, 5 Sim. 568.
(*x*) Bro. Abr. tit. Administration, pl. 7.
(*y*) *Ley* v. *Anderton*, Sty. 225.
(*z*) Per *Holt*, C. J., Salk. 305.
(*a*) Bro. Abr. Executors, pl. 149.
(*b*) *Hirst* v. *Smith*, 7 T. R. 182.

and that it ought to have appeared on the record, that the promise was made either to the intestate or the plaintiff. *Kenyon*, C. J., and *Ashhurst*, J., refused to grant a rule to show cause, observing, that there was a privity of estate in law between the former administrator, from whom the plaintiff deduced his title, and the plaintiff.

Stat. 17 *Car. II. c.* 8, *made perpetual by Stat.* 1 *Jac. II. c.* 17, *s.* 5.—" Where any judgment after a verdict shall be had, by or in the name of any executor or administrator, in such case an administrator *de bonis non* may sue forth a *scire facias* and take execution upon such judgment." And it has been holden to be within the equity of this statute, that an execution commenced by an administrator may be perfected by an administrator *de bonis non* (c).

III. *Of limited or temporary Administrations.*

1. *During the Minority of Executor.*—An infant, however young, may be an executor; but administration shall be granted to another during his minority (12). At the common law, such administration determined as soon as the infant executor attained the age of seventeen years, for then the infant was considered as capable of administering. But now, by stat. 38 Geo. III. c. 87, s. 6, reciting, that inconveniences had arisen from granting probates to infants under the age of twenty-one, it is enacted, " That where an infant is sole executor, administration with the will annexed shall be granted to the guardian, or such other person as the spiritual court shall think fit, until such infant shall attain the age of twenty-one years." A *general* administrator, *ratione minoris ætatis*, shall not only have actions to recover debts and duties, but may also grant leases (d). An administrator, *durante minori ætate*, of an *administrator* may act and sue until the administrator be of the age of twenty-one years (e); for administrators are by the statute, and one is not a legal person in the eye of the law capable to act for another as trustee until twenty-one. See further, 3 Atk. 604.

2. *During the Absence of Executor beyond Sea.*—When the executor, or next of kin, is out of the realm, administration may be granted during his absence. Such limited administration is grantable at common law before probate has been obtained, or letters of administration granted to the absent executor or next of

(c) *Clerk* v. *Withers*, Salk. 323.   (e) *Freke* v. *Thomas*, Salk. 39.
(d) 6 Rep. 67, b.

---

(12) See the form of this administration in *Prince's* case, 5 Rep. 29, b.

kin (13), but it is not so after probate or letters of administration
obtained. To remedy this, by stat. 38 Geo. III. c. 87, s. 1, " If at
the expiration of twelve calendar months after the death of the testator, the executor, to whom probate has been granted, is residing
out of the jurisdiction of the king's courts, the Ecclesiastical Court,
which has granted the probate, may, upon the application of any
creditor, next of kin, or legatee, grounded on affidavit (f), grant
a special administration (g) to such creditor, &c. for the purpose of
being made a party to a bill in equity, to be exhibited against him
and to carry the decree into effect, and no further, or otherwise.
And by sect. 4, the court of equity, in which the suit shall be depending, may appoint any person to collect the debts due to the
estate, and give discharges for the same. But by sect. 5, if the
executor, capable of acting as such, shall return to, and reside
within the jurisdiction of any of the king's courts, pending such
suit, such executor shall be made party to such suit; and the costs
incurred by granting such administration, and by proceeding in
such suit against such administrator, shall be paid by such person,
or out of such fund, as the court shall direct." In an action by a
person to whom such administration is granted, the absence of the
executor in parts beyond the seas ought to be averred in the
declaration (h). The plaintiff, having taken out letters of administration (i), according to the form prescribed by the preceding
statute, and having been appointed by order of the Court of Chancery, in a suit instituted against him, to collect the debts of the
deceased, brought an action to recover a debt due to the testator;
the defendant pleaded, that on a day prior to the commencement
of the action, the executor, to whom probate of the will had been
granted, died. On demurrer, the plea was holden bad by *Rooke* and
Chambre, Js. (*Alvanley*, C. J., *dissentiente*,) on the ground, that the
authority of the special administration continued, until the appointment of a new representative, notwithstanding the death of the executor. Mr. J. *Chambre* observed (k), that although this act was made
for very beneficial purposes, yet many of its provisions had been
framed with a very short-sighted view of legal consequences. However, where a common law administration (l) has been granted to one
as the attorney, and for the benefit of the absent executor named in
a will, he, and not the executor, is the legal representative of the

(f) See form in second section.
(g) See form in third section.
(h) *Slater* v. *May*, 2 Ld. Raym. 1071.
(i) *Taynton* v. *Hannay*, 3 Bos. & Pul.

26.
(k) 3 Bos. & Pul. 33.
(l) *Suwerkrop* v. *Day*, 8 A. & E. 624 ;
3 N. & P. 670.

(13) In *Clare* v. *Hedges*, (said, in 1 Lutw. 342, to have been adjudged
in E. T. 3 Will. & Ma. B. R.) it was holden, that such administration
was grantable by law : and the case was put of the next of kin being in
parts beyond the seas, in which case the debt due to the intestate might be
lost, if such an administration could not be granted.

testator, and he continues to be so during the life of the executor, or, at all events, until he himself takes out probate; but the grant, *ipso facto*, ceases on the death of the executor.

3. *Pendente Lite, or pending Litigation.*—When a suit is commenced in the Ecclesiastical Court touching the validity of a will (*m*) or right of administration, an administration may be granted pending the suit, and the person to whom it is granted may bring actions to recover debts due to the deceased, averring that the suit is still depending; and such administrator may be sued, inasmuch as he is for the time complete administrator (*n*).

4. *During Lunacy.*—Where a sole executor, or next of kin, happens to be a lunatic at the time of the testator's or intestate's. decease, the practice is to make a limited grant of administration to his committee (*o*), if he has been found a lunatic by inquisition, if not, to a residuary legatee (*p*) in the case of a will, or to the next of kin (*q*) of the person entitled to administration in the case of intestacy. In a case (*r*) where a widow administratrix became lunatic, the court declined to revoke the administration, but granted administration to the son of the deceased, the letters granted to the widow being first brought into and impounded in the registry, in order to be re-delivered out in case of her recovery. In a case (*s*) where one of two executors became lunatic, the court granted a fresh probate, (the former probate having been brought in,) with power reserved of making a like grant to the lunatic, when he should become of a sound mind and apply.

IV. *Of an Executor de son Tort.*

An executor *de son tort* is a person who, without any authority derived from the deceased or ordinary, does such acts as belong to the office of an executor or administrator. As to the acts which will render a person liable as executor *de son tort*, it will be observed: 1st, In the case of *intestacy*, if a stranger takes the goods of the intestate, and uses them, or sells (*t*) them, this will make such stranger an executor *de son tort* (*u*). 2ndly, In the case of a *will* (*x*), and a regular appointment of an executor, who proves the

(*m*) *Woollaston* v. *Walker*, Str. 917; 2 P. Wms. 567, *S. C.*, recognized by Lord *Hardwicke* in *Wills* v. *Rich*, 2 Atk. 285.

(*n*) Agreed in *Impe* v. *Pitt*, 2 Show. 69.
(*o*) *In the goods of Phillips*, 2 Add. 336, n. (*b*).
(*p*) *In the goods of Milnes*, 3 Add. 55.

(*q*) *Exp. Evelyn*, 2 M. & K. 3.
(*r*) *In the goods of Binckes*, 1 Curt. 286; and see 1 Cas. Temp. Lee, 625.
(*s*) *In the goods of Marshall*, 1 Curt. 297.
(*t*) *Read's case*, 5 Rep. 33, b.
(*u*) 2 T. R. 97.
(*x*) 5 Rep. 34, a.

will; if a stranger takes the goods, and, *claiming to be executor*, pays debts, &c. and intermeddles, *as executor*, he may for such express administration, as executor, be charged as an executor *de son tort*, although there is another executor of right (14). But if, *after* the executor has proved the will, and administered, a stranger takes any of the goods, and, *claiming them as his own*, uses and disposes of them accordingly, this will not make him in construction of law an executor *de son tort*; because there is a rightful executor, who may be charged with these goods so taken from his possession, as assets, and to whom the stranger will be answerable in trespass for taking the goods. 3dly, In the case of a *will*, if a stranger takes the goods *before* the rightful executor has proved the will or taken upon him the execution thereof, the stranger may be charged as an executor *de son tort*; for the rightful executor shall not be charged with any goods except those which came to his hands after he had taken upon him the charge of the will. If a creditor takes an absolute bill of sale of the goods of his debtor (*y*), but agrees to leave them in his possession for a limited time, and in the mean time the debtor dies, whereupon the creditor sells the goods, he thereby becomes an executor *de son tort*. The slightest acts have been deemed sufficient to constitute an executor *de son tort* (*z*) (15); as where a widow milked her late husband's cows, she was adjudged to be an executrix *de son tort*. So, living in the house and carrying on the trade of the deceased (*a*) (a victualler). Where, however (*b*), a party receives a debt due to the estate of a person deceased, for the purpose of providing the funeral, he will not thereby become chargeable as executor *de son tort*, unless he receive a greater sum than is reasonable for that purpose, regard being had to the estate and condition of the deceased, which is a question for the jury. But a single act of wrong in taking the goods of the intestate, though it may be sufficient to make the party an executor *de son tort*, with respect to creditors who may choose to sue him in that character, yet will not give him any right to retain them as against the lawful administrator. In trover for a quantity of iron (*c*), it appeared that the goods in question had been originally sold by the

(*y*) *Edwards* v. *Harben*, 2 T. R. 587.   (*b*) *Camden* v. *Fletcher*, 4 M. & W. 378.
(*z*) Dyer, 166, b., in marg.   (*c*) *Mountford* v. *Gibson*, 4 East, 441.
(*a*) *Hooper* v. *Summerset*, Wightw. 16.

(14) This, however, has been denied by Lord *Kenyon*, in *Hall* v. *Elliot*, Peake N. P. C. 87, and by Sir *T. Plumer*, in *Tomlin* v. *Beck*, T. & R. 438; those judges maintaining that there cannot be a rightful executor and an executor *de son tort* at the same time.

(15) The jury are to determine whether the acts are sufficiently proved; but the question, whether executor *de son tort*, or not, is a conclusion of law. 2 T. R. 99.

defendant to the intestate; that on his death, they not having been
paid for, on application to the intestate's widow for that purpose,
she delivered them back to the defendant in satisfaction of his
demand. No other acts were stated to have been done by the
widow, to show that she had before taken upon herself to act as executrix. It was holden, that the plaintiff, as rightful administrator,
was entitled to recover the value of his goods.

A. had pledged goods to B. for a debt; B. died, and the parish
officers took the goods, and gave them to J., the carpenter, who
made B.'s coffin, on condition of his paying B.'s rent and the
funeral expenses: it was holden (d), that by taking these goods,
the parish officers became executors *de son tort*; and that if they
sold the goods to J., they would be liable to A. in trover, because
such a sale was so inconsistent with the bailment, as to revest the
right of possession in A. A person who possesses himself of the
effects of the deceased (e), under the authority, and as agent for,
the rightful executor, cannot be charged as an executor *de son
tort*. The plaintiff having received a horse belonging to the intestate (f), from the defendant, in remuneration of services performed at the request of the defendant, about the funeral of the
intestate, afterwards administered to the estate, and brought
trover against the defendant for the value of the horse, so received
by himself before he became administrator. It was holden, by
Dolben and *Eyres*, Js., that the plaintiff, being a *particeps criminis* in the very act he complained of, should not be permitted to
recover upon it against the person with whom he had colluded.
But *Holt*, C. J., was of a different opinion, conceiving that in this
case, if a stranger, or third person, had taken out letters of administration, an action might have been maintained against the defendant by such an administrator for the recovery of the horse;
and here the plaintiff was a third person; *for being administrator,
he sued, and would recover*, in the right of the intestate. An act
done by a person as executor *de son tort*, will not bind (g) him after
he becomes rightful administrator. An executor *de son tort* must
be declared against as a rightful executor (h). See further on the
subject of executor *de son tort* under Sect. IX. post, p. 805, tit.
" *Pleadings;" and of the Right of Retainer.*

(d) *Samuel* v. *Morris*, 6 C. & P. 620, *Alderson*, J.

(e) *Hall* v. *Elliot*, Peake's N. P. C. 86.

(f) *Whitehall* v. *Squire*, Carth. 103;

Salk. 294; Skin. 274; 3 Mod. 276, S. C.

(g) *Doe d. Hornby* v. *Glenn*, 1 Ad. & Ell. 49; 3 Nev. & M. 837.

(h) Yelv. 137.

V. Of the Disposition of the Estate of the Deceased, and of the Order in which such Disposition ought to be made.

THE order of payment, which ought to be observed by executors and administrators in the disposition of the estate of the deceased, is as follows:—1. Funeral charges (16), expenses of probate, or taking out letters of administration (*i*). 2. Debts due to the king (17), by record (18), or specialty (19). 3. Debts due to the

(*i*) 1 Rol. Abr. 926, (S) pl. 1; Dr. and Stud. Dial. 2, c. 10.

---

(16) In strictness, no funeral expenses are allowed against a creditor, except for the coffin, ringing the bell, parson, clerk, and bearer's fee; but not for the pall or ornaments. Per *Holt*, C. J., in *Shelley's* case, Salk. 296. The usual method is to allow 5*l*. Bull. N. P. 143. This sum was allowed by Lord *Hardwicke*, C. J., in *Smith* v. *Davis*, Middlesex Sittings after M. T. 10 Geo. II., MSS. As against a creditor, the rule of law is, that no more shall be allowed for funeral expenses, than is necessary; in considering what is necessary, regard must be had to the degree and condition in life of the party; *Hancock* v. *Podmore*, 1 B. & Ad. 260, in which case 79*l*. was holden to be too large a sum as against a creditor for the funeral expenses of a captain in the army on half-pay. See further on this point, *Edwards* v. *Edwards*, 4 Tyr. 444; 2 Cr. & M. 612. An executor who gives no order for the funeral, is liable only to the extent of the expenses suitable to the rank and circumstances of the testator, unless he, as an individual, and not in his character of executor, ratifies the orders given, in which case he is liable for the whole expense. *Brice* v. *Wilson*, 3 Nev. & M. 512; 8 A. & E. 349, n. Whether the funeral is ordered by the executor or another person, the estate must pay the reasonable expenses, and can in no event be liable beyond them. *Green* v. *Salmon*, 8 A. & E. 348. See also *Lucy* v. *Walrond*, 3 Bingh. N. C. 841, *ante*, p. 777; *Rogers* v. *Price*, 3 Y. & J. 28. But if there are assets, the allowance shall be according to the estate and degree of the deceased. In *Stag* v. *Punter*, 3 Atk. 119, the testator having desired to be buried at a church thirty miles distant, and it not being clear that there would be a deficiency, Lord *Hardwicke*, Ch., allowed 60*l*. for funeral expenses. So in *Offley* v. *Offley*, Prec. Ch. 26, 600*l*. were allowed, in respect of the testator's quality, and his having been buried in his own country.

(17) The king, by his prerogative, shall be preferred by executors in satisfaction of his debt before any other. 2 Inst. 32.

(18) Fines and amerciaments, in the king's courts of record, are debts of record. Went. Off. Exor. ch. 12.

(19) By statute 33 Hen. VIII. c. 39, it is enacted, "that all obligations and specialties for any cause concerning the king shall be taken *domino regi*, and shall be of the same force and effect as a statute staple."

post-office, not exceeding 5l. (k) ; debts due from an overseer of
the poor, by virtue of his office (l) (20). 4. Debts by judgments
in the Court of King's Bench, Common Pleas, and Exchequer,
doggetted (21) according to directions of stat. 4 & 5 Will. & Ma.
c. 20; by judgments in other courts of record; by decrees in

(k) Stat. 9 Ann. c. 10, s. 30.   (l) Stat. 17 Geo. II. c. 38, s. 3.

---

(20) By statute 17 Geo. II. c. 38, s. 3, executors of overseer shall pay,
out of his assets, all monies due received by virtue of office, before any of
his own debts are satisfied. A similar provision is contained in statute 4
& 5 Will. IV. c. 40, s. 12, respecting executors of persons intrusted with
the monies or effects of friendly societies; and by statute 3 & 4 Will. IV.
c. 14, s. 28, respecting executors of officers of savings banks.

. (21) At common law, executors and administrators were bound at their
peril to take conusance of debts of the testator upon record.* Hence to
an action on a judgment recovered against testator or intestate, executors
or administrators could not plead, that they had exhausted the assets in
payment of debts of an inferior nature without notice of the judgment.
To obviate the mischiefs to which personal representatives were liable, from
the difficulty of finding such judgments, the statute 4 & 5 Will. & Ma.
c. 20, s. 2, directed, "that the proper officers of the Courts of Common
Pleas, King's Bench, and Exchequer, should make a doggett of all judgments entered in the respective courts." The mode in which the doggett
was to be made was detailed in the second section; and by sect. 3, "judgments not doggetted as the second section directed had not any preference
against executors and administrators in the administration of their testator's or intestate's estates." The construction which was put on this section was, that the judgments not doggetted are thereby placed on a level
with simple contract debts. *Hickey* v. *Hayter*, 6 T. R. 384. Hence, to
an action on a simple contract debt of testator or intestate, the personal
representative could not plead an outstanding judgment recovered against
testator or intestate, in C. B., B. R., or Exchequer, if it had not been
doggetted as the statute directs. *Steel* v. *Rorke*, 1 Bos. & Pul. 307, cited
in *Hall* v. *Tapper*, 3 B. & Ad. 655. But now, by an Act for the better
Protection of Purchasers against Judgments, &c. (2 & 3 Vict. c. 11), s. 1,
no judgment shall hereafter be docketted under the provisions of the foregoing statute (4 & 5 Will. & Ma. c. 20), but all such dockets shall be
finally closed after the 4th June, 1839, without prejudice to the operation
of any judgment already docketted and entered under that act, except so
far as any such judgment may be affected by the provisions contained in
the 2 & 3 Vict. c. 11; and by sect. 2, no judgment already docketted shall,
after the 1st Aug. 1841, affect any lands, tenements, or hereditaments, as
to purchasers, mortgagees, or creditors, unless and until such memorandum or minute thereof, as is prescribed in 1 & 2 Vict. c. 110, s. 19,
shall be left with the senior Master of the Court of Common Pleas at
Westminster, who shall forthwith enter the same in manner thereby

* *Littleton* v. *Hibbins*, Cro. Eliz. 793.

courts of equity (*m*) (22); according to their respective priorities.
5. Recognizances at common law; statutes merchant and staple (*n*);
and recognizances in the nature of statute staple, pursuant to stat.
23 Hen. VIII. c. 6 (23). 6. Arrears of rent due at the death of

---

(*m*) *Searle* v. *Lane*, 2 Vern. 88; *Bishop*
v. *Godfrey*, Prec. in Chanc. 179, Finch's
ed.; 1 & 2 Vict. c. 110, s. 18.

(*n*) 4 Rep. 59, b., 60, a.; 1 Rol. Abr.
925; 4 Rep. 28, b.

---

directed in regard to judgments, together with the date of the year and
day of the month when such memorandum or minute was left; for which
the officer is entitled to the sum of *5s*. And by sect. 4, all judgments
of any of the superior courts, decrees or orders in any court of equity,
rules of a court of common law, and orders in bankruptcy, or lunacy,
which have been registered under the 1 & 2 Vict. c. 110, or shall hereafter
be so registered, shall be void after five years from entry, unless a like
memorandum is left with the senior Master who shall re-enter, and so,
toties quoties, at the expiration of every five years. See also stat. 3 & 4
Vict. c. 82. If a judgment be satisfied, or only kept on foot to injure
other creditors, or if there be any defeasance of the judgment then in force,
then the judgment will not avail to keep off other creditors from their
debts. Went. Off. Exor. c. 12. Between one judgment and another,
precedency or priority of time is not material, but he who first sueth the
executor must be preferred; and before execution sued, it is at the election
of the executor to pay whom he will first. Went. Off. Exor. c. 12.

(22) It is now become the established doctrine, that a decree of the
Court of Chancery is equal to a judgment in a court of law*: and where
an executrix of A., who was greatly indebted to divers persons, in debts
of different natures, being sued in chancery by some of them, appeared
and answered immediately, admitting their demands, (some of the plaintiffs being her own daughters,) and others of the creditors sued the executrix at law, where the decree not being pleadable, they obtained judgments; yet the decree of the Court of Chancery, being for a just debt,
and having a real priority in point of time, (not by fiction and relation to
the first day of term,) was preferred in the order of payment to the judgments; and the executrix protected and indemnified in paying obedience
to such decree, and all proceedings against her at law stayed by injunction. *Morice* v. *The Bank of England*. Decreed first at the Rolls by
Sir *Joseph Jekyll*, Aug. 1735, which decree was affirmed by Lord *Talbot*,
Ch.†, Nov. 1736, and Lord *Talbot's* decree was afterwards affirmed in
parliament‡, May 24, 1737. See also *Shafto* v. *Powell*, 3 Lev. 355.

(23) This must be understood of recognizances and statutes *forfeited*,
where the recognizances are for keeping the peace, good behaviour, &c.
and the statutes are for performing covenants, &c. A recognizance not

---

* 3 P. Wms. 401, n. (P).
† Ca. Temp. Talb. 217.
‡ 4 Bro. P. C. 287, ed. fo.; 2 Bro. P. C. 465, Tomlin's ed.

the testator or intestate, either on a parol lease (24) or lease by deed (25) ; debts by specialty, as bonds (26) ; damages upon covenants broken (27), &c. 7. Debts by simple contract, as bills of

---

enrolled was considered in *Bothomly* v. *Fairfax*, 1 P. Wms. 334, as a bond, (the sealing and acknowledging of the recognizance supplying the want of delivery,) and to be paid as a specialty debt. A recognizance, in its proper sense, is nothing more than a debt of record to the crown, defeasible in a particular event. *Rex* v. *Dover, Mayor, &c.*, 1 Cr. M. & R. 726 ; 5 Tyrw. 279.

(24) Arrears of rent on a parol lease, which is determined, are in equal degree with a bond debt; because the contract remains in the realty, though the term be determined. *Newport* v. *Godfrey*, 3 Lev. 267, and 2 Ventr. 184. See an exposition of this case by *Holt*, C. J., in *Cage* v. *Acton*, Ld. Raym. 516.

(25) A debt due for rent reserved upon a demise by deed, or by parol*, is in equal degree with a bond debt. *Gage* v. *Acton*, Carth. 511 ; 1 Salk. 236, cited by *Denman*, C. J., and *Littledale*, J., in *Davis* v. *Gyde*, 2 Ad. & Ell. 626, and *ante*, p. 672.

(26) A bond with a penalty conditioned for the payment of a less sum of money on a day, not arrived at the death of testator, may be pleaded by his executor as a specialty debt†, as well as a forfeited bond ; but there is this distinction between them,—that in the case of a bond forfeited, the penalty is the legal debt, and assets may be covered to that amount ; but in the case of a bond not forfeited, as the executor by discharging it may save the penalty, the assets can be covered only to the amount of the sum mentioned in the condition ‡. Where there are several debts by specialty, all due and payable at the death of the testator, if suit is not commenced by any of the creditors, and notice thereof given to the executor, he may give the preference to whom he pleases : and if he be a creditor himself, he may pay himself first. Went. Off. Exor. c. 12. Any voluntary bond is good against an executor or administrator, unless some creditor be thereby deprived of his debt. Indeed, if the bond be merely voluntary, a real debt, though by simple contract only, shall have the preference ; but if there be not any debt, then a bond, however voluntary, must be paid by an executor. Voluntary bonds given to be paid after death, take place of legacies, but not of debts by simple contract. Per Ld. Ch. *Harcourt*, *Powell* v. *Wood*, MS. Cases in Chancery, p. 84, Lincoln's-Inn Library, Bookcase A. A voluntary bond is postponed in equity to debts by simple contract. Cases Temp. Hardwicke, by West, p. 240.

(27) Covenants running with the land are binding on the executors, although not expressly named. See Went. Off. of Exors. p. 178, edit. 1763.

---

* *Brown* v. *Holyoak*, Barn. 290.
† *Lemun* v. *Fooke*, 3 Lev. 57.
‡ *Bank of England* v. *Morice*, Str. 1028.

exchange (28), promissory notes, &c. 8. Legacies, &c. An executor should not be too precipitate in paying legacies; for in a case where it appeared that an executor, after discharging some debts, made over the residue of the assets to the residuary legatee *within six months* after the date of the probate, it was holden (o), that he could not plead such payment in discharge of his testator's liability on a covenant to repair a house, although the testator did not occupy the house, nor was any notice given to the executor of the state of the house.

VI. *Admission of Assets* (29).

WHILE an executor is passive, he is chargeable only in respect of the assets; but if he promises to pay a debt of the testator at a future day, he thereby makes it his own debt, and it shall be satisfied by his own goods (p). A judgment against an executor by default (q), is an admission of assets to satisfy the demand; and if a *fi. fa.* be sued out on such judgment, and the sheriff cannot find goods of the testator sufficient to answer the demand, the sheriff may return a *devastavit*. The preceding case has been considered as a leading case on this subject: hence, where A. having executed a bond for the payment of a sum of money at her death (r); and the defendant having brought an action on the

(o) *Davis* v. *Blackwell*, 9 Bingh. 5.
(p) Per *Yelverton*, J., in *Goring* v. *Goring*, Yelv. 11.
(q) *Rock* v. *Leighton*, from Holt's MSS.

3 T. R. 690; Salk. 310, *S. C.*, but not accurately reported.
(r) *Ramsden* v. *Jackson*, 1 Atk. 292; 1 West, Cas. Temp. Hardwicke, 237, *S. C.*

---

(28) See *Yeomans* v. *Bradshaw*, Carth. 373. A breach of trust is considered but as a simple contract debt, and can only fall upon the personal estate of a trustee. *Vernon* v. *Vawdry*, 2 Atk. 119.

(29) All sperate debts, mentioned in the inventory, shall be deemed assets in the executor's hands; but the executor may discharge himself by showing the demand and refusal of them. *Shelley's* case, per *Holt*, C. J., Salk. 296. In the inventory, which the defendant had exhibited in the Ecclesiastical Court, were inserted several debts due and outstanding, which defendant charged herself with when received or recovered; Lord *Hardwicke*, C. J., put the defendant on proof, that she could not recover those debts; for she ought in her inventory to have set forth which debts were sperate and which desperate. The defendant proved by a witness, who went to demand several of them, that he could not recover them; and accordingly they were allowed as desperate. *Smith* v. *Davis*, Middlesex Sittings after M. T. 10 Geo. II., MSS., recognized in *Young* v. *Cawdrey*, 8 Taunt. 734.

bond against the plaintiff as the executor of A., who pleaded *non est factum*, which was found against him, and judgment thereon: on a bill filed by the plaintiff to have the bond and judgment set aside, Lord *Hardwicke*, Ch., being of opinion, that the bond was good, it became a question, whether the plaintiff was not entitled to relief, on the ground that there was a deficiency of assets. Lord *Hardwicke* decided, that the plea of *non est factum*, and verdict thereon, amounted to an admission of assets; and that the case was the same with the preceding case of a judgment by default. So where in debt in the detinet against defendant (*s*), (as executor of A., administratrix of B.,) upon a judgment by default, obtained by plaintiff against A. as administratrix, suggesting that goods of the intestate had come to the hands of A. as administratrix, which she had wasted; defendant pleaded, 1. *Non detinet*, on which issue was joined; 2dly. That defendant had fully administered the goods of A. Replication, that the defendant had goods of A. sufficient to satisfy, &c., and issue. The jury on the last issue found assets of A. in the hands of defendant. On the other issue the plaintiff produced the judgment by default against A., on which he relied as evidence of assets admitted by A., and a devastavit by A. *Lee*, C. J., (delivering the opinion of the court,) said, that he could not do it better than in the words of *Holt*, C. J., in *Rock* v. *Leighton*. Having read that case from *Holt's* notes, he observed, that it appeared from that case, that if an executor will not take advantage by pleading, but suffers judgment to go by default, such judgment is an admission of assets, and is as strong against an executor, as if assets were found by verdict on a *plene administravit*; and, notwithstanding the objection, which had been raised on the ground of the statute 30 Car. II. c. 7 (30), and by 4 & 5 Will. & Ma. c. 24,

(*s*) *Skelton* v. *Hawling*, 1 Wils. 258, and MSS. See also 1 Saund. 219, d., where this case is correctly stated by Serjt. Williams, who examined the roll.

---

(30) By stat. 30 Car. II. c. 7, s. 2, (made perpetual and enlarged by 4 & 5 Will. & Ma. c. 24, s. 12,) "The executors and administrators of executors of their own wrong, or administrators who have wasted and converted the assets of the deceased to their own use, shall be chargeable in the same manner as their testator or intestate would have been if living." A doubt having arisen upon the preceding clause, whether it extended to the executors and administrators of any executor or administrator of right, who, from want of privity, were not before answerable for the debts due from the first testator or intestate, although such executor or administrator of right had been guilty of a devastavit or conversion, it was enacted by stat. 4 & 5 Will. & Ma. c. 24, s. 12, "that the executor and administrator of such executor or administrator of right, who should waste or convert to his own use the estate of his testator or intestate, should be chargeable in the same manner as his testator or intestate would have been."

s. 12, he was clear, that the action in the case then before the court was well brought. On the authority of the preceding cases of *Rock* v. *Leighton*, *Ramsden* v. *Jackson*, and *Skelton* v. *Hawling*, it was holden (*t*), that where an executor, (to an action of debt on bond,) had pleaded payment, which was found against him, and judgment accordingly, it operated as an admission of assets; and a writ of *fi. fa.* having been sued out on the judgment, to which the sheriff had returned a devastavit, and an action having been brought against the executor on the judgment suggesting a devastavit; it was holden, that the production of the record of the judgment, the writ of *fi. fa.*, and the sheriff's return, was sufficient evidence to support the action. If an executor pay interest on a bond due from his testator (*u*), it will not conclude him from alleging want of assets to pay the principal, but it relieves the creditor from the necessity of proving assets, and throws the onus on the other side. Where defendant binds himself as administrator (*x*), to abide by an award touching matters in dispute between his intestate and another, and the arbitrator awards, that defendant as administrator shall pay a certain sum, it operates as an admission of assets between those parties, and defendant cannot plead *plene administravit* to an action of debt on the bond; because the giving such bond is an undertaking to pay whatever the arbitrator may award. And in such case, if an attachment be moved for against the administrator (*y*), for the non-payment of the money awarded, he cannot defend himself against it, by suggesting a deficiency of assets; for a submission to arbitration by a personal representative is considered as a reference, not only of the cause of action, but also of the question, whether or not he has assets. And when the arbitrator awards that the personal representative do pay the amount of the plaintiff's demand, it is equivalent to determining as between those parties, that the personal representative had assets to pay the debt. But mere submission to arbitration is not of itself an admission of assets (*z*); for in a case where the arbitrator only ascertained the amount of the demand, without ordering the administrator to pay it, it was holden, that the administrator might plead *plene administravit*.

By stat. 3 & 4 Will. IV. c. 104, [29 Aug. 1833,] entitled, "An Act to render Freehold and Copyhold Estates Assets for the Payment of Simple Contract Debts," after reciting that it is expedient that the payment of all debts should be secured more effectually than is done by the laws now in force; it is enacted, "That from and after the passing of this act, when any person shall die, seised of or entitled to any estate or interest in lands, tenements, or heredi-

(*t*) *Erving* v. *Peters*, 3 T. R. 685.
(*u*) *Cleverly* v. *Brett*, B. R. 11 Geo. III., cited in *Pearson* v. *Henry*, 5 T. R. 8. See 2 Ves. 85.
(*x*) *Barry* v. *Rush*, 1 T. R. 691.
(*y*) *Worthington* v. *Barlow*, 7 T. R. 453.
(*z*) *Pearson* v. *Henry*, 5 T. R. 6.

taments, corporeal or incorporeal, or other real estate, whether freehold, customaryhold, or copyhold, which he shall not, by his last will, have charged with, or devised subject to the payment of, his debts, the same shall be assets to be administered in courts of equity for the payment of the just debts of such persons, as well debts due on simple contract as on specialty; and that the heirs at law, customary heirs, devisees of such debtor, shall be liable to all the same suits in equity at the suit of any of the creditors of such debtor, whether creditors by simple contract, or by specialty, as the heirs or devisees of any persons who died seised of freehold estates were before the passing of this act liable to in respect of such freehold estates, at the suit of creditors by specialty in which the heirs were bound: Provided, that in the administration of assets by courts of equity under this act, all creditors by specialty, in which the heirs are bound, shall be paid the full amount of the debts due to them before any of the creditors by simple contract or by specialty, in which the heirs are not bound, shall be paid any part of their demands."

VII. *Of Actions by Executors and Administrators.*

1. *What Actions may be brought by Executors and Administrators.*—By the common law, executors might have maintained actions to recover *debts* due to their testator, but they could not maintain actions for a wrong done to their testator in his life-time; *e.g.* a trespass in taking his goods, &c. But by stat. 4 Edw. III. c. 7, reciting, *that in times past executors had not had actions for a trespass done to their testators, as of the goods of the said testators carried away in their life*, it is enacted, "that the executors in such cases shall have an action against the trespassers, in like manner as they, whose executors they are, should have if they were living." This statute has been expounded largely, with respect to the persons and the actions. With respect to the persons (a), it has been holden, that an administrator is within the equity of this statute, and shall have trespass for goods carried away in the life-time of the intestate. With respect to the actions, it has been resolved (b), that where, upon a church becoming void, the bishop collated wrongfully and the patron died, the executor of the patron might by the equity of this statute maintain a *quare impedit* (31). So an executor may have an action of trover for the

---

(a) *Smith* v. *Colgay*, Cro. Eliz. 384.   *Mason* v. *Dixon*, Sir W. Jones, 174, 5.
(b) 4 Leon. 15, Case 53, cited in *Le*

---

(31) *Ejectio firmæ* will lie at the suit of an executor for the ouster of his testator. 7 Hen. IV. 6, b.; Bro. Abr. Exor. 45, *S. C.*

conversion of the testator's goods in his life-time (c) ; or an action of debt on stat. 2 & 3 Edw. VI. c. 13, for not setting out tithes due to the testator (d) ; or an action on the case against the sheriff for a false return made in the life of the testator to a *fi. fa.*, *viz.* that he had levied only so much, part whereof he had sold and part remained in his hands for want of purchasers (e) ; or an action of debt on a judgment against an executor, suggesting a devastavit in the life-time of plaintiff's testator (f). In like manner, it has been holden, that an administrator may maintain an action against the bailiff of a liberty for executing a *fi. fa.* and removing the goods off the premises, before the landlord (the intestate) was paid a year's rent, pursuant to stat. 8 Ann. c. 17 (g). Formerly there was not any remedy provided by law, for injuries to the real estate of any person deceased, committed in his life-time; but now, by stat. 3 & 4 Will. IV. c. 42, s. 2, "an action of trespass, or trespass on the case, as the case may be, may be maintained by the executors or administrators of any person deceased for any injury to the real estate of such person committed in his life-time, for which an action might have been maintained by such person, so as such injury shall have been committed within six calendar months before the death of such deceased person ; and provided such action shall be brought within one year after the death of such person ; and the damages, when recovered, shall be part of the personal estate of such person "(h). And by stat. 7 Will. IV. & 1 Vict. c. 26, s. 6, "If no disposition by will shall be made of any estate *pur autre vie* of a freehold nature, the same shall be chargeable in the hands of the heir ; if it shall come to him by reason of special occupancy, as assets by descent, as in the case of freehold land in fee simple ; and in case there shall be no special occupant of any estate *pur autre vie*, whether freehold or customary freehold, tenant right, customary, or copyhold, or of any other tenure, and whether a corporeal or incorporcal hereditament, it shall go to the executor or administrator of the party that had the estate thereof by virtue of the grant ; and if the same shall come to the executor or administrator, either by reason of a special occupancy or by virtue of this act, it shall be assets in his hands, and shall go and be applied and distributed, as the personal estate."

Every action (i) brought by an executor, that is founded upon a duty accrued in the testator's life-time, must be brought in the detinet only, that is, in his representative capacity. Where the cause of action (k) accrues after the testator's death, the executor may

---

(c) *Rutland* v. *Rutland*, Cro. Eliz. 377.

(d) *Moreron's* case, 1 Ventr. 30.

(e) *Williams* v. *Grey*, Lord Raym. 40.

(f) *Berwick* v. *Andrews*, Ld. Raym. 973.

(g) *Palgrave* v. *Windham*, Str. 212.

(h) See *Powell* v. *Rees*, 7 A. & E. 426, and *post*, p. 798.

(i) 1 Saund. 112, n. to *Dean and Chapter of Bristol* v. *Guyse*.

(k) *Gallant* v. *Bouteflower*, 3 Doug. 36, per *Buller*, J.

sue as such, or in his individual capacity, at his option. And generally, whenever (*l*) the subject matter of the action would, when recovered, be assets, the executor may sue in his representative capacity.

One of two executors, having alone proved the will, had received a debt due to the testator, which by his will was appropriated to the payment of specific legacies to his grandchildren, with interest thereon, and afterwards permitted the money to be lent out to a third person, by whom it was paid to A. A., on being applied to by the executor, acknowledged that he had received the money, and that it belonged to the testator's grandchildren, but refused to pay it over to the executor. It was holden (*m*), that both executors might join in an action brought to recover the money against A.

By stat. 11 Geo. II. c. 19 (32), s. 15, "Executor or administrator of tenant for life, on whose death any lease of lands, &c. determined, shall, in an action on the case, recover from the under tenant a proportion of the rent reserved, according to the time such tenant for life lived of the last year, or quarter of a year, or other time in which the said rent was growing due." By the common law (*n*), an executor or administrator could not have an action of account; because it was founded on a matter in the privity of the testator; but now, by stat. 13 Edw. I. c. 23, "An executor shall have an action of account upon an account with his testator." By 25 Edw. III. stat. 5, c. 5, "Executors of executors shall have actions of debts, accounts, and of goods carried away of the first testators, in the same manner as the first testator should have had." Administrators derive their authority to bring actions from the stat. 31 Edw. III. stat. 1, c. 11, which provides, that "where a man dies intestate, the ordinary shall depute the next and most loyal friends (33) to administer his goods, which deputies may bring actions to demand and recover, *as executors*, the debts due to the intestate." Plaintiff (*o*), as administrator, declared in assumpsit that defendant, for certain fees to be paid to him by intestate, undertook as an attorney to investigate the title of premises about to be conveyed to intestate. Breach, that he omitted to do so, and that intestate in consequence took an insufficient title, whereby his

---

(*l*) *Marshall* v. *Broadhurst*, 1 Cr. & J. 405.

(*m*) *Webster* v. *Spencer*, 3 B. & A. 360.

(*n*) 2 Inst. 404.

(*o*) *Knight* v. *Quarles*, 2 Brod. & B. 102.

---

(32) See 4 & 5 Will. IV. c. 22, amending this act, *ante*, p. 603, 4.

(33) A subsequent statute, 21 Hen. VIII. c. 5, s. 3, in case of intestacy or executors refusing to prove, directs the ordinary to grant administration to the widow or next of kin; and where two or more stand in equal degree, to accept which he pleases.

personal estate was injured. A demurrer to this declaration was overruled. And where (p) a vendor omits to make out a good title within the stipulated time, and the vendee dies, his executor may sue for damage incurred by the personal estate by loss of interest on the deposit money, and the expense of endeavouring to procure the title. An administrator cannot have an action for a breach of promise of marriage to the intestate, where no special damage to the personal estate is alleged (q). Although the decisions in the three last mentioned cases turned upon the damage to the personal estate, yet, it seems, the right of an executor or administrator to sue on a breach of contract made with the deceased is not confined to cases in which such damage can be stated. For instance, an executor (r) is entitled to sue the lessee of his testator for the breach of a covenant purely collateral, committed in the lifetime of the testator, without alleging special damage to the personal estate in his declaration. But an executor (s) cannot sue on a breach of a covenant which runs with the land, where a formal breach only has taken place in the testator's lifetime; in that case the real representative is entitled to recover for any substantial damage incurred after his death. ·

John Franklin, after devising his real estate, bequeathed all the monies which he might have at the time of his decease, in the Three per Cent. Consolidated Bank Annuities unto C.B., and then devised and bequeathed the residue of his real and personal estate, subject to the payment of debts and legacies, to Thomas Franklin, and appointed him sole executor. The executor finding a large sum in the Three per Cent. Consolidated Bank Annuities standing in the name of the testator, demanded permission of the Bank to transfer the whole of the said annuities to such persons as he should think fit, to enable him to pay debts and legacies; the Bank refused, on the ground that the stock was specifically bequeathed; whereupon the executor filed a bill in the Court of Chancery to compel the Bank to allow the executor to sell and transfer the stock. No evidence was given in the suit of any debts being due from the estate at the time of the demand: upon a case sent by the chancellor to B. R., the question was, whether the executor had any right of action against the Bank for not permitting the transfer? and that court was of opinion (t) the executor had such right.

2. *Executors and Administrators must join in bringing Actions.* —It is a general rule, that, if there are two or more executors, and one proves the will, they must all join in bringing actions; and

(p) *Orme* v. *Broughton*, 10 Bingh. 533.

(q) *Chamberlain* v. *Williamson*, 2 M. & S. 408.

(r) *Raymond* v. *Fitch*, 2 C. M. & R. 588.

(s) *Kingdon* v. *Nottle*, 1 M. & S. 355, and 4 M. & S. 53; *Jones* v. *King*, 4 M. & S. 188, *ante*, p. 478.

(t) *Franklin* v. *Bank of England*, 9 B. & C. 156.

if they do not, the defendant may plead in abatement, that there are other executors living not named (*u*). In this plea it is not necessary to aver, that the executors not named have administered (*x*); because they may administer at their pleasure. So where there are two or more administrators, it is necessary that they should join in bringing actions (*y*). And this rule, *viz.* that all the executors shall join, holds even where some of the executors refuse before the ordinary (*z*); because the refusing executors may come in at any time (*a*), and administer, notwithstanding their refusal, either during the lives of their co-executors, who have proved, or after their death (*b*). The like law is, where some of the executors are infants; they must all join, and they may all appear by attorney: for those of full age may appoint an attorney for those within age (*c*). So where there are two executors, one of full age, and the other within age; and the executor of full age is appointed administrator, *durante minori œtate* of the other executor. A. made B. and C., who was an infant under seventeen, executors; B. only proved the will, and brought debt as executor against defendant (omitting C.). Plea in abatement, that C. was made an executor with B., and is yet in full life, not named (*d*), &c. Replication, that C. was of the age of one year, that B. proved the will, and had administration committed *durante minori œtate*, and that C. is still under seven years of age. On demurrer, judgment for the defendant; for, although by the administration committed *durante minori œtate*, B. hath the full power, yet C., the infant, being executor, ought to be named. Action on the case for an injury alleged to be done to the reversionary interest of the plaintiffs in some houses by the negligent manner in which the defendant pulled down a house of his own adjoining them. The plaintiffs were entitled to the property, which was leasehold, as executors of one J. S. To prove their title, they produced the probate of the will of J. S., which was granted to one of them, liberty being reserved to make the like grant to the two other executors named in the will. This was holden (*e*) sufficient, per Lord *Tenterden*, C. J.

3. *Of joining several Causes in one Action by Executors.*—In order to join several causes in one action, the action must be brought as to all such causes in the same right (34). Hence, a

(*u*) Reg. 140, b.; Bro. Abr. Exors. pl. 69; Fitz. Abr. Exors. pl. 48.
(*x*) 41 Edw. III. 22, a.
(*y*) Reg. 140, b.
(*z*) *Hensloe's case*, 9 Rep. 36, b. See also 3 Atk. 239.
(*a*) Bro. Exors. 117; Fitz. Abr. Exors. 26.
(*b*) 21 Edw. IV. 23, b., 24, a., recog-

nized by *Holt*, C. J., in *Wankford* v. *Wankford*, Salk. 307, and by *Tenterden*, C. J., in *Walters* v. *Pfeil*, M. & Malk. 363.
(*c*) *Foxwist* v. *Tremaine*, 2 Saund. 212.
(*d*) *Smith* v. *Smith*, Yelv. 130; 1 Brownl. 101, S. C.
(*e*) *Walters and others* v. *Pfeil*, M. & Malk. 362.

(34) By new rule H. T. 4 Will. IV. several counts shall not be allowed,

plaintiff cannot join, in the same action, a demand, as executor or administrator, with another demand, which accrued in his own right. The reason is, because the funds, to which the money and costs, when recovered, are to be applied, or out of which the costs are to be paid, are different; and the damages and costs being entire, the plaintiff cannot distinguish how much he is to have in his representative character, and how much he is to hold as his own.

After much discussion, it is now finally settled (*f*), that in all actions by executors or administrators, if the money recovered on each of the counts will be assets, the counts may be joined in the same declaration. Thus, for instance, a count (*g*) for work by the plaintiff as administrator may be joined with counts for goods sold and work done by the intestate on promises to him. So also counts (*h*) on promises made to an intestate may be joined with counts on promissory notes, given to the administrator, *as administrator*, since the death of the intestate. The counts so joined to counts on promises to the testator should state (*i*) that the duty accrued to the plaintiff in his representative character, "*as executor*." In a late case (*k*), however, in a declaration by executors, a count stating that the defendant had accounted with the plaintiffs, "executors as aforesaid," was joined with counts stating promises to the testator: after verdict and judgment for plaintiffs, a writ of error was brought upon the ground of misjoinder, but the judgment was affirmed.

VIII. *Of Actions against Executors and Administrators.*

1. *What Actions may be maintained against Executors.*—Formerly an action, wherein the testator might have waged his law, could not be maintained against his executors or administrators (*l*). Hence, *debt* on a simple contract, as on a promissory note (*m*), would not lie against an executor or administrator.

But now wager of law is abolished (*n*); and debt (*o*) on simple

---

(*f*) 2 Saund. 117, d. (m), 5th edition.
(*g*) *Edwards* v. *Grace*, 2 M. & W. 190.
(*h*) *Partridge* v. *Court*, 5 Price, 412; 7 Price, 591, overruling *Betts* v. *Mitchell*, 10 Mod. 315.
(*i*) 2 Saund. 117, d. 5th edition.
(*k*) *Lancefield* v. *Allen*, 1 Bligh, N. S.

592.
(*l*) Bro. Exors. 80.
(*m*) *Barry* v. *Robinson*, 1 Bos. & Pul. N. R. 293.
(*n*) Stat. 3 & 4 Will. IV. c. 42, s. 13.
(*o*) *Id. s.* 14.

---

unless a distinct subject matter of complaint is intended to be established in respect of each.

contract is maintainable in any court of common law against any executor or administrator. By stat. 4 Ann. c. 16, s. 27 (p), an action of account is given against executors and administrators of guardians, bailiffs, and receivers, and also by one joint tenant and tenant in common, his executors and administrators, against the other as bailiff, for receiving more than his share, and against the executor and administrator of such joint tenant or tenant in common. Assumpsit might always have been brought (q). But assumpsit will not lie against an executor (r) for a legacy payable out of the general funds of the testator, although assets be averred in the declaration ; for the law will not, from the mere circumstance of an executor's being possessed of assets, imply a promise by him to pay such legacy. But an action may be maintained by the legatee (s) of a specific chattel, against an executor, after his assent to the bequest. See *Hart* v. *Minors*, 2 Cr. & M. 700, where under the peculiar circumstances the action on account stated was holden to be maintainable against an executor, on the ground that he had debited himself, and ceased to hold the money in his character of executor.

An action at law cannot be maintained (t) for a distributive share of an intestate's property against the administrator, nor against his executor, although such executor may have expressly promised to pay. The neglect or refusal of the administrator to distribute the surplus or residue of the effects of the intestate among the next of kin, according to the statute of distribution without the previous decree or sentence of the court, is not (u) a breach of the condition of the administration bond.

An acting executor having once received (x), and fully had under his control, assets of the testator applicable to the payment of a debt, is responsible for the application thereof to that purpose ; and such application having been disappointed by the misconduct of his co-executor, whom he employed to make the payment in question, he is liable at law for the consequences of such misconduct, as much as if the misapplication had been made by any other agent of a less accredited and inferior description (35). Where a sheriff levies

(p) See *ante*, p. 3.
(q) *Palmer* v. *Lawson*, 1 Lev. 201 ; *Norwood* v. *Read*, Plowd. 181 ; *Carter* v. *Fosset*, Palm. 329 ; *Pinchon's case*, 9 Rep. 866 ; Cro. Jac. 662 ; *Cottington* v. *Hulett*, Cro. Eliz. 59.
(r) *Deeks* v. *Strutt*, 5 T. R. 690.

(s) *Doe* v. *Guy*, 3 East, 120.
(t) *Jones* v. *Tanner*, 7 B. & C. 542.
(u) *The Archbishop of Canterbury* v. *Tappen*, 8 B. & C. 151.
(x) *Crosse* v. *Smith and another*, 7 East, 246.

(35) By the old law, there was a distinction between executors and trustees. It was laid down as a general rule, that where executors joined in a receipt, both having the whole power over the fund, both were chargeable ; where trustees joined, each not having the whole power, and the

money under a *fi. fa.* and dies, an action may be maintained against his executors for the money so received (y).

Formerly, no remedy was provided by law for certain wrongs done by a person deceased in his lifetime to another, in respect of his property, real or personal (z) (36); but now, by stat. 3 & 4 Will. IV. c. 42, s. 2, " An action of trespass, or trespass on the case, as the case may be, may be maintained against the executors or administrators of any person deceased, for any wrong committed by him in his lifetime to another, in respect of his property, real or personal, so as such injury shall have been committed within six calendar months before such person's death, and so as such action shall be brought within six calendar months after such executors or administrators shall have taken upon themselves the administration of the estate and effects of such person; and the damages to be recovered in such action shall be payable in like order of administration as the simple contract debts of such person." An intestate (a) was lessee of some coal mines of the plaintiff's, and had worked the coal under a portion of land excepted from the demise; part of such coal was raised more than six months before the intestate's death, and part within six months; the plaintiffs may bring trespass under this statute for so much as was raised within the six months, and also money had and received for so much as was raised before, the acts being distinct, and, therefore, the two actions not incompatible. The foregoing statute is confined in terms to injuries in respect of *property*, real or personal; the law, therefore, in respect of injuries to the person remains unaltered, as to which Serjeant Williams's note, above referred to, may be consulted with advantage.

By stat. 29 Car. II. c. 3, s. 4, " No action shall be brought to charge any executor or administrator upon any special promise, to answer damages out of his own estate, unless the agreement upon which such action shall be brought, or some memorandum or note thereof, shall be in writing, and signed by the party to be charged therewith, or some other person thereunto by him lawfully autho-

---

(y) *Perkinson* v. *Gilford*, Cro. Car. 539.

(z) *Hambly* v. *Trott*, Cowp. 371.
(a) *Powell* v. *Rees*, 7 A. & E. 426.

---

joining being necessary, only the person receiving the money was chargeable; but the rule as to executors has been in some degree relaxed. See the opinion of *Eldon*, Ch., in *Chambers* v. *Minchin*, 7 Ves. jun. 197, 8. In *Walker* v. *Symonds*, 3 Swans. 64, the same learned judge said, " It may be laid down now, as in *Brice* v. *Stokes*, 11 Ves. 319, that though one executor has joined in a receipt, yet whether he is liable shall depend on his acting."

(36) See Serjeant Williams's note (1) to the case of *Wheatley* v. *Lane*, 1 Saund. 216.

rized." At the common law, an executor or administrator could not have been charged on any special promise to answer damages out of his own estate, unless such promise had been made on a sufficient consideration. The statute has not made any alteration in this respect. The promise, though in writing, still requires a sufficient consideration to support it (b). And (c) the consideration as well as the promise must be expressed in the written memorandum or note.

The provisional assignee of the Insolvent Debtors Court, under stat. 1 Geo. IV. c. 119, s. 7, assigned the estate of an insolvent to an assignee, who assented to such assignment, and acted under it as tenant of premises, which the insolvent held as lessee for years: it was holden (d), that the executor of such last mentioned assignee was liable to the lessor for breaches of covenants in the lease, subsequent to his testator's death; it not appearing that the Insolvent Debtors Court had appointed fresh assignees.

2. *What Causes of Action may be joined* against *Executors.*—
Several demands, some of which accrue from the defendant in his own right, and others in right of another, ought not to be joined in the same action; because such demands require different pleas and different judgments. Hence, if a declaration against an executor or administrator contain counts which charge him in his representative character, and counts which charge him in his own right, such declaration will be bad, for misjoinder of cause of action, either on general demurrer (e), or in arrest of judgment, or on writ of error. The four first counts in the declaration were on promises made by the intestate (f): the fifth stated, that *after the death of the intestate*, the defendant as administratrix, was indebted to the plaintiff for money, by the defendant, as such administratrix, had and received to the use of the plaintiff. On special demurrer, assigning for cause that the two causes of action, the one from the intestate and the other from the administratrix, could not be joined, the court were clearly of opinion that they could not; because the last count stated a cause of action after the intestate's death, which would exclude one of the pleas that might be pleaded to the other counts, and would warrant a different judgment. So counts on promises by the testator cannot be joined with counts for money had and received by the defendant as executor (g), or for money lent to defendant as executor (h), or on an account stated of money *due from defendant as executor* (i),

(b) *Rann* v. *Hughes*, 7 T. R. 350, n.
(c) *Wain* v. *Warlters*, 5 East, 10, recognized in *Saunders* v. *Wakefield*, 4 B. & A. 595; *Clancy* v. *Piggott*, 2 A. & Ell. 481; *Hawes* v. *Armstrong*, 1 Bingh. N. C. 761.
(d) *Abercrombie* v. *Hickman*, 8 A. & E. 683.

(e) *Brigden* v. *Parks*, 2 Bos. & Pul. 424.
(f) *Jennings* v. *Newman*, 4 T. R. 347.
(g) *Brigden* v. *Parks*, 2 Bos. & Pul. 424, and *Rose* v. *Bowler*, 1 H. Bl. 108.
(h) 1 H. Bl. 108.
(i) *Ibid.*

because the former charge the defendant in right of the testator, whereas the latter charge him in his own right. But where an action was brought against an administratrix (*k*), and the three first counts of the declaration were on promises by the intestate, and the last was on an account stated between plaintiff and defendant, as administratrix, of money *owing from the intestate*, and in consideration of the intestate being found indebted, a promise by defendant, as administratrix, to pay, the court were of opinion that there was not any misjoinder of action, that the defendant was charged as administratrix in all the counts, and that this was the common mode of declaring, to save the statute of limitations. A promise made upon good consideration by a testator, that his executor shall pay, is a sufficient consideration for an action in assumpsit against the executor (*l*). And in such action, it is neither necessary (*m*) to aver assets (the want of assets being matter of defence); nor a promise by the executor. On a count averring an account stated by the defendant of monies due from him as executor, the judgment shall be *de bonis testatoris*. It may, therefore, be joined (*n*) with counts on promises of the testator. Counts for goods sold to, and work and labour done for, the defendant, as executor cannot be joined (*o*) with a count for money found to be due on an account stated with the defendant as executor; for the two first counts are necessarily for debts due from the defendant in his own right, and charge the defendant personally, whereas the last count charges the defendant in his own representative character: and consequently there is a misjoinder. To a count in covenant charging the defendants, as executors, for breaches of covenant by their testator as lessee (*p*), who had covenanted for himself, his executors, and assigns, may be joined another count, charging them, that after the testator's death, and their proving the will, and during the term, the demised premises came by assignment to one D. A., against whom breaches were alleged; and concluding, that so neither the testator, nor the defendants after his death, nor D. A. since the assignment to him, had kept the said covenant, but had broken the same.

3. *What Executors are to be made Defendants.*—It has been observed, that in actions brought *by* executors, it is necessary that, where there are two or more, they should all join, whether they administer or not, if one of them has proved the will. But this is not necessary when actions are brought *against* them (*q*); for the mere circumstance of a person being named executor does not compel the plaintiff to make him a defendant, unless he has administered. Hence, where executors, *defendants*, plead in abatement, that there

---

(*k*) *Secar* v. *Atkinson*, 1 H. Bl. 102.
(*l*) *Powell* v. *Graham*, 7 Taunt. 580.
(*m*) *S. C.*, per three Js. ; *Burrough*, J., dissentiente.

(*n*) *S. C.*
(*o*) *Corner* v. *Shew*, 3 M. & W. 350.
(*p*) *Wilson* v. *Wigg*, 10 East, 313.
(*q*) Bro. Exors. pl. 69.

are other executors not named, they must add (r), that the executors not named have administered; for the plaintiff is bound to take notice of such executors only as have administered. Although executors cannot sever in declaring, yet they may in pleading. Hence, although infant executors may sue by attorney with executors of full age (s), because those of full age may appoint an attorney for those within age, yet they must defend by guardian. If any of the executors die (t), actions must be brought, not against the surviving executors and executors of deceased executors, but against surviving executors only. If there are two or more administrators, they must all be made defendants (u). An executor *de son tort* must be declared against as a rightful executor (x). In an action (y) against a married woman executrix, the husband must be joined as a defendant.

IX. *Of the Pleadings, p.* 801, *and herein of the Right of Retainer, p.* 805; *Evidence, p.* 806; *Judgment, p.* 808; *Costs, p.* 808.

An executor may plead the same plea in bar (z), that his testator might have pleaded; as, in an action of assumpsit, he may plead, that his testator did not undertake or promise; or in covenant, or debt on bond, that it is not the deed of the testator. So an executor may plead in bar, that he has fully administered all the goods and chattels which were of the deceased at the time of his death. The plea is termed a plea of *plene administravit*. A testator (a) being indebted to R., deposited with him a policy of insurance on testator's life, as a security for the debt, or for a further advance then made by R., and died, leaving R. and M. his executors. R., still holding the policy, applied to the insurers for the amount due on it (£200); which they refused to pay, unless R. and M. gave a receipt for it as executors. They did so; R. making protest that he signed as executor, merely to satisfy the insurers. In an action by a judgment creditor, to which the executors pleaded *plene administraverunt*, except as to £4 (the surplus out of the £200 after payment to R.), it was holden, that the executors were not chargeable with the £200 as assets, but only with the surplus after payment to R. In like manner an executor may plead an outstanding debt, as a judgment, in which plea it is not necessary for the executor to aver that the judgment was had for a true and just

(r) *Swallow* v. *Emberson*, 1 Lev. 161.
(s) *Frescobaldi* v. *Kinaston*, Str. 783; Fitz. Ab. Exor. 22.
(t) 4 Leon. 193; Bro. Exors. 99; Fitz. Abr. Exor. 22.

(u) Reg. 140, a. b.
(x) *Alexander* v. *Lane*, Yelv. 137.
(y) Com. Dig. Administration (D).
(z) Com. Dig. Pleader (2 D. 8).
(a) *Glaholm* v. *Rowntree*, 6 A. & E. 710.

debt (*b*); for this shall be presumed. So where an executor pleaded (*c*) that his testator entered into a bond conditioned for the payment of a sum of money at a day past, beyond which he had not assets; it was holden sufficient, although it was not averred that the bond was entered into for a true and just debt; for it shall be intended that it was. And the same intendment shall be made, where an executor or administrator pleads a bond debt due to himself and retainer (*d*). The ancient way of pleading an outstanding bond was to set forth the bond only; but the modern way is to set forth the condition also. When the day of payment (*e*), mentioned in the condition of the bond, is past in the lifetime of the testator, the penalty is the legal debt; and although an executor, in pleading it as an outstanding debt, sets forth the condition of the bond, yet that will not deprive him of the advantage of covering the assets to the amount of the penalty. But when the day of payment is not arrived at the death of the testator, if the executor sets forth the condition, the assets can be covered only to the amount of the sum mentioned in the condition; for the force of the bond is suspended until the condition is broken. To an action of debt on bond for £300 (*f*) against defendant, as executor, he pleaded that the testator was bound in a statute for the same sum, and that he had assets to the amount of £80 only, to satisfy that statute, which remained yet in force and not paid. On demurrer, it was objected, that it was not averred in the plea, that the statute was made for *debt*, and that the debt was not satisfied: for if it were for the performance of covenants, it was not reasonable that it should be a bar to a debt on a bond already due, when, perhaps, the covenants would never be broken (37), in which case there would not be any cause of suit or extent thereon. But the court resolved, that the plea was good; for it was averred that the statute was in force, and the money not paid; it was good enough *primâ facie;* and it should be intended to be made for a just debt, until the contrary was shown. It was holden, that an executor (*g*) might plead an outstanding judgment recovered in an action of *debt* on a simple contract against the executor, although the executor might have reversed such judgment, while debt could not be maintained against an executor on a simple contract. See *ante*, p. 796. If an action be brought against several administrators (*h*), they may plead an

---

(*b*) 1 Lev. 200.
(*c*) *Lake* v. *Raw*, Carth. 8.
(*d*) *Picard* v. *Brown*, 6 T. R. 550.
(*e*) *Bank of England* v. *Morice*, Str. 1028; *Hardwicke*, C. J., delivering the

opinion of the court.
(*f*) *Philips* v. *Echard*, Cro. Jac. 8.
(*g*) *Palmer* v. *Lawson*, 1 Lev. 200.
(*h*) *Further* v. *Further*, Cro. Eliz. (471).

---

(37) It was agreed by *Fenner*, *Gawdy*, and *Yelverton*, Js., that a statute for performance of covenants was not a bar in debt on bond, if none of the covenants were broken.

outstanding judgment recovered against one of the defendants; for a recovery against one administrator shall bind him and his companions. After the commencement of an action, an executor cannot pay another creditor before such other creditor has recovered judgment, but the executor may confess judgment in another action for the damages laid in the declaration (*i*), without ascertaining those damages by writ of inquiry, provided they do not exceed the real debt. If they do, the plaintiff may reply that such judgment was not for a true and just debt. An executor may confess a judgment to a creditor in *equal degree* with the plaintiff, pending the action, and plead it in bar (*k*). But if a plea of judgment, recovered on a simple contract, be pleaded by an executor to a debt on bond, it must be averred, that such recovery was had before notice of the bond debt (*l*).

An executor may plead, *puis darrein continuance* (*m*), unreversed judgments on simple contract debts of the testator, recovered against the executor in suits commenced since he pleaded the general issue in bar in the principal case; and though he might have demurred to such actions, he is not bound so to do (*n*). Where judgment was given against A., in the Common Pleas, who afterwards entered into a statute and died; and his administrator brought error on the judgment, and, pending that suit, paid the statute, and afterwards the judgment was affirmed; upon a *sci. fa.* to have execution thereon, the administrator pleaded payment of the statute, beyond which he had not assets. It was adjudged a good plea, because at the time of the execution of the statute, the administrator could not plead the judgment in C. P., because it was doubtful whether it would be affirmed or not (*o*). To a plea of an outstanding judgment, the plaintiff may reply, that the judgment was obtained by fraud and covin. And in a case where an executor, defendant, pleaded two outstanding judgments, to each of which the plaintiff replied fraud, and traversed that the debts recovered were due for just debts (*p*): the replication was holden good on a special demurrer, the court observing, that the plaintiff might traverse the special matter, or rely on the fraud generally, at his election. A judgment confessed by an executrix to a creditor of the testator, as well for his own debt as in trust for the debt of many of the creditors, cannot be pleaded in bar to an action brought against her by another creditor of the testator (*q*).

Where the statute of limitations (*r*) is pleaded to an action

(*i*) *Waring* v. *Danvers*, 1 P. Wms. 295; 10 Mod. 496; 3 P. Wms. 401.

(*k*) *Waring* v. *Danvers*, 1 P. Wms. 295; *Morrice* v. *Bank of England*, Ca. Temp. Talb. 225, S. P.

(*l*) *Sawyer* v. *Mercer*, 1 T. R. 690.

(*m*) As to pleading a plea *puis darrein* continuance, see R. G. H. T. 4 Will. IV. No. 2, *ante*, p. 134.

(*n*) *Prince* v. *Nicholson*, 5 Taunt. 665.
(*o*) *Rede* v. *Berelocke*, Yelv. 29.
(*p*) *Trethewy* v. *Ackland*, 2 Saund. 49.
(*q*) *Tolputt* v. *Wells*, 1 M. & S. 395.
(*r*) *Hickman* v. *Walker*, Willes, 27.

brought by an executor on a promise made to his testator, the six years are computed from the time when the action first accrued to the testator, and not from the time of proving the will. But where money belonging to the estate of an intestate is received by A. (s) after the death of the intestate, and more than six years afterwards B. takes out an administration, *it seems* that the time of limitation must be computed from the day on which the letters of administration were granted; and, consequently, if B., within six years from that day brings an action for money had and received against A., the statute of limitations will not operate as a bar. In an action by administrator upon a bill of exchange, payable to the intestate, but accepted after his death, the statute of limitations begins to run from the time of granting the letters of administration, and not from the time the bills become due, there being no cause of action until there is a party capable of suing. *Murray* v. *East India Company*, 5 B. & A. 204. See also *Pratt* v. *Swaine*, 8 B. & C. 287, per *Bayley*, J. " Where letters of administration have been granted, the administrator is entitled to all the rights which the intestate had at the time of his death vested in him; but no right of action accrues to the administrator, until he has sued out the letters of administration." For the statute of limitations, and the decisions thereon, see *ante*, p. 135, 139.

As to the proper mode in which an executor of an executor should frame his plea, the following case deserves attention : Plaintiff, assignee of lessee for years, sued the defendant as executor of B., executor of A., the lessor, in covenant upon the original indenture of lease, for a breach of the covenant for quiet enjoyment of A. (t), and since his decease by defendant. Defendant pleaded, that he had fully administered all the goods of A., the first testator. On demurrer, it was holden, that the plea was bad, inasmuch as it only gave an answer to one part of a case which pointed at two kinds of misapplication of those funds which were liable to the plaintiff's demand. *Le Blanc*, J., observed, that the defendant might discharge himself in two ways : either by showing that the first executor fully administered all the goods and chattels of A. which came to his hands, and that the defendant, since the death of the first executor, has duly administered all that he has received of A.'s assets; or he might show that he had received no assets of the first executor. But, as the plea now stands, he leaves unanswered every thing respecting the assets of the first testator which came to the hands of his executor, and merely answers as to his own application. *Bayley*, J., added, that the plaintiff was entitled to recover his debt in either of two events; if the defendant had received assets of the original testator, and had not properly applied them; or if the defendant had received assets of the first executor,

(s) *Curry* v. *Stephenson*, Carth. 335; Mod. 372.
Skinn. 555, *S. C.* See the record, 4   (t) *Wells* v. *Fydell*, 10 East, 315.

and the first executor had received assets of his testator, and had not duly applied them. The defendant has only answered as to one of those events, but the plaintiff may be entitled to satisfaction out of both funds: and, therefore, he is entitled to have the issue so framed, that if any thing be forthcoming to him out of either fund, he may be able to avail himself of it. See further as to pleading the statute of limitations, and statute of set-off, by and against executors, *ante*, tit. "Assumpsit," and tit. "Debt."

Of the Right of Retainer.—A lawful executor or administrator (*u*), when sued by a creditor of the deceased, may claim a right of retaining the assets in satisfaction of debt due to himself, provided such debt is equal or superior in degree to that claimed by the creditor. Where an action is brought against a defendant as *executor* (which is the case, as well where the defendant is charged as rightful executor, as when he is charged as executor *de son tort*), and he claims to retain as executor or administrator, he ought to set forth the letters testamentary (*x*), or the letters of administration (*y*), in order that it may appear to the court, that he is such a person as is entitled to retain; for an executor *de son tort* is not so entitled (*z*). But where the plaintiff sues the defendant as *administrator*, and he claims to retain as administrator, it is not necessary that the letters of administration should be set forth, because the plaintiff, by his declaration, admits him to be lawful administrator (*a*). An executor *de son tort* cannot retain for his own debt, although of a superior nature; neither will the consent of the rightful administrator to the retainer, given after action brought by creditor, alter the case (*b*); nor can such executor avail himself of a delivery over of the effects of the deceased to the rightful administrator after action brought, and before plea pleaded, so as to defeat the action of a creditor. In debt upon bond against the defendant as executor (*c*), he pleaded a judgment which he had recovered against the deceased, and so justified by way of retainer. Replication, that the defendant was executor *de son tort*. Rejoinder, that after the last continuance the defendant had obtained letters of administration. On demurrer, it was objected, that the rejoinder was a departure from the plea. But the court held, that it was well enough; because the plea did not expressly admit, that defendant had proved the will, but only admitted the defendant's executorship according to the declaration. By the replication it appeared, that the defendant was not charged as a rightful but as a wrongful executor, which could not appear on the declaration, the

---

(*u*) 1 Keb. 285; 2 Vent. 180; Sty. 337; *Vaughan* v. *Browne, infra.*
(*x*) *Atkinson* v. *Rawson*, 1 Mod. 208.
(*y*) *Caverly* v. *Ellison*, T. Jones, 23.
(*z*) *Coulter's case*, 5 Rep. 30; Yelv. 138.

(*a*) *Picard* v. *Brown*, 6 T. R. 550.
(*b*) *Vernon* v. *Curtis*, 2 H. Bl. 18; 3 T. R. 587.
(*c*) *Vaughan* v. *Browne*, Str. 1106; Andr. 328; 7 Mod. 274, Leach's edit., and MSS.

method of declaring against both of them being the same. And the rejoinder set forth a matter, which made the acting as unlawful executor justifiable; for the subsequent administration related to the death of the intestate, and purged the precedent wrongful executorship, so as to give the defendant the benefit of retaining. Although an executor *de son tort* cannot avail himself of his own wrongful act in taking possession of the goods of the deceased, in order to retain a debt for his own benefit, yet he may plead (*d*) in answer to the claim of a simple contract creditor, that after action brought, he had disposed of the assets in that course of administration which the law allows, *viz.* by discharging a debt of higher degree, as a specialty debt; for if, at any time before plea pleaded, an executor comes to the knowledge of such a debt, he is bound to pay it before a simple contract debt, whether he be a rightful or wrongful executor.

Evidence.—In all questions respecting *personalty*, the probate or letters of administration, with the will annexed, are the only legal evidence of the will (*e*). Trespass for taking goods (*f*). On not guilty, the defendant admitted that the goods had been in the possession of the plaintiff, but insisted that he, the defendant, had a property in them as executor of I. S., and then produced the original will, by which he was appointed executor. But, per *Raymond*, C. J., "I cannot allow the original will to be evidence to prove a property in an executor; *the probate must be produced;* for, perhaps, the Ecclesiastical Court will not allow this to be the testator's will. Besides, until probate, a man dies intestate; and, if the executor dies before probate, his executor shall not be executor to the first testator." Where a probate of a will is lost, the Ecclesiastical Court never grants a second probate; but they will exemplify the first, and such exemplifications are admissible in evidence (*g*). Upon issue joined on a plea by executors of *plene administravit*, the amount of the stamps upon the probate is admissible in evidence (*h*); but semb. that this is not even *primâ facie* evidence of the amount of assets received. Probate is not admissible to prove declarations of the testator as reputation in questions of pedigree (*i*). After notice to defendant's executors to produce probate, and refusal, it has been holden (*k*), that an instrument, produced by the officer of the Ecclesiastical Court, purporting to be the will of the defendant's testator, and indorsed by the officer as

(*d*) *Oxenham* v. *Clapp*, 2 B. & Ad. 309.
(*e*) But see *Doe d. Bassett* v. *Mew*, 7 A. & E. 240, *ante*, p. 744.
(*f*) *Coe* v. *Westernham*, Norfolk Summ. Ass. 1725; Serjt. Leeds' MSS.; *Pinney* v. *Pinney*, 8 B. & C. 335, S. P.
(*g*) Per *Cur.* in *Shepherd* v. *Shorthose*, Str. 413.

(*h*) *Mann* v. *Lang*, 3 A. & E. 699, overruling *Curtis* v. *Hunt*, 1 C. & P. 180; and *Foster* v. *Blakelock*, 5 B. & C. 328.
(*i*) *Doe d. Wild* v. *Ormerod*, 1 Mo. & Rob. 466, *Alderson*, J., on the authority of Bull. N. P. 246.
(*k*) *Gorton* v. *Dyson*, 1 Broderip & Bingh. 219.

being the instrument whereof probate had been granted to the defendants, and that they had sworn to the value of the effects, is admissible in evidence in an action against defendants for money had and received by their testator. An examined copy of the act book in the registry of the Prerogative Court of Canterbury, stating that administration was granted to the defendant of her husband's goods and chattels at such a time, is proof (*l*) of her being such administratrix in an action against her as such, without giving her notice to produce the letters of administration. Where a bill of exchange was indorsed, generally, but delivered to A., as administratrix of B., for a debt due to the intestate, and A. died intestate after the bill became due, and before it was paid: it was holden (*m*), that the administrators *de bonis non* of B. might sue upon the bill; and that their title was sufficiently proved by the letters of administration *de bonis non*, without producing those granted to A., the administratrix. A retainer may be given in evidence on *plene administravit* (*n*); but debts of a higher nature subsisting cannot (*o*). In an action against executors for a debt of testator, a person entitled to an annuity under the will, was holden not to be disqualified by interest from giving evidence for the defendants (*p*). But where the action was by a bond creditor of the testator against the devisee of his real estate, out of which an annuity was payable, the defence being, that the testator's signature was a forgery; it was holden (*q*), that the annuitant was not a competent witness for defendant; for he was directly interested, the object of the evidence being to prevent the plaintiff from recovering against the very estate devised for payment of the annuity. By stat. 1 Vict. c. 26, s. 17, no person shall, on account of his being an executor of a will, be incompetent to be admitted a witness to prove its execution, or validity or invalidity. Upon *plene administravit et issint riens inter mains* (*r*), if it be proved that executor hath goods in his hands, which were the testator's, he may give in evidence, that he hath paid to that value of his own money, and need not plead it specially. In case against executor, upon *plene administravit* (*s*), the plaintiff must prove his debt, otherwise he shall recover but one penny damages, though there be assets; for the plea admits the debt, but not the amount.

In all actions by and against executors or administrators, the character in which the plaintiff or defendant is stated on the record to sue or be sued, shall not in any case be considered as in issue (*t*), unless specially denied.

(*l*) *Davis* v. *Williams*, 13 East, 232.
(*m*) *Catherwood* v. *Chabaud*, 1 B. & C. 150.
(*n*) *Plumer* v. *Marchant*, 3 Burr. 1380.
(*o*) Bull. N. P. 141.
(*p*) *Nowell* v. *Davies*, 5 B. & Ad. 368; but see the remarks of *Parke*, B., on this case, in 7 M. & W. 240.
(*q*) *Bloor* v. *Davies*, 7 M. & W. 235.
(*r*) 1 Inst. 283, a.
(*s*) Per *Holt*, C. J., *Shelley's* case, Salk. 296.
(*t*) R. G. H. T. 4 Will. IV. 21.

Judgment.—On a plea of *plene administravit* generally, by an executor (*u*), the plaintiff may immediately take judgment of assets *quando acciderint* (38). In debt or *scire facias* on this judgment, evidence of such assets only as have come to the executor's hands since the judgment will be received (*x*). Judgment against an executor, in covenant broken by himself, shall be *de bonis testatoris*; for it is the testator's covenant which binds the executor as representing him; and therefore he must be sued by that name (*y*). In like manner, upon an obligation made by testator for the performance of covenants, judgment in debt on the bond for a breach of covenant by executor, shall be *de bonis testatoris* (*z*). So in debt against an executor on a bond made by testator (*a*), if the defendant plead *non est factum*, and it is found against him, judgment shall be for the debt and damages *de bonis testatoris*; for the executor cannot know whether it be the deed of the testator or not. In debt on bond against an executor, if the defendant plead "fully administered," and any assets are found in his hands, although they be not to the value of the debt, yet the plaintiff shall have judgment for his whole debt *de bonis testatoris* (*b*) (39). In debt against two executors (*c*), if they plead severally by several attorneys, "fully administered," and the jury find that the one has assets and the other has not, the judgment shall be against him only who is found to have assets, and the other shall go quit.

Costs.—Where the cause of action is such, that the executor might have declared in his own right, he is liable for costs, if he is nonsuited (*d*). Where an executrix pleaded first, *non assumpsit*; 2ndly, *ne unques* executrix; and 3dly, *plene administravit*; and issues on the first pleas were found for the plaintiff, and on the last for the defendant; it was holden (*e*), that the last plea being a complete answer to the action, the defendant was entitled to the general costs of the trial. Plaintiff sued as administratrix, upon promises to the intestate, and upon an account stated with her as administratrix of monies due to her in that character, and a promise to pay her: it was holden (*f*), that it thereby appeared that

(*u*) *Noell* v. *Nelson*, 2 Saund. 226.
(*x*) *Taylor* v. *Hollman*, Bull. N. P. 169.
(*y*) *Collins* v. *Thoroughgood*, Hob. 188.
(*z*) *Castilion* v. *Executor of Smith*, Hob. 283.
(*a*) Bro. Abr. Exor. pl. 109.
(*b*) *Lee* v. *Ridford*, adjudged on error, in Exch. Ch. Roll. Rep. 58.
(*c*) *Bellew* v. *Jackleden*, on error in

Exch. Ch., 1 Roll. Abr. 929, (B.) pl. 5. See also *Parsons* v. *Hancock*, 1 M. & Malk. 330.
(*d*) *Grimstead* v. *Shirley*, 2 Taunt. 116; *Jones* v. *Jones*, 1 Bingh. 249.
(*e*) *Edwards* v. *Bethel*, 1 B. & A. 254. See also *Ragg* v. *Wells*, 8 Taunt. 129.
(*f*) *Dowbiggin* v. *Harrison*, 9 B. & C. 666; *Jobson* v. *Forster*, 1 B. & Ad. 6.

(38) See the form of this judgment in 2 Saund. 216, 17.

(39) But see *Harrison* v. *Beccles*, cor. Lord *Mansfield*, C. J., London Sittings, 1769, cited in *Erving* v. *Peters*, 3 T. R. 688.

the contract was one made between *the plaintiff* and another person within the words of stat. 28 Hen. VIII. c. 15, and, therefore, that, after a nonsuit, the defendant was entitled to costs. Declaration by executor stated, that the defendant being indebted to the testator at the time of his death, in consideration thereof, promised the plaintiff as executor to pay him the amount. The statute of limitations was pleaded ; it was holden (*g*), that the plaintiff being nonsuited was entitled to costs, although he did not declare upon an account stated. And now, by stat. 3 & 4 Will. IV. c. 42, s. 31, in every action brought by any executor or administrator in right of the testator or intestate, such executor or administrator shall, *unless the court in which such action is brought, or a judge of any of the said superior courts, shall otherwise order*, be liable to pay costs to the defendant, in case of being nonsuited or a verdict passing against the plaintiff. An executor suing on a count upon promises to himself as executor, stating a consideration, partly of money due to testator in his life-time, and partly of an account stated with himself as executor, is liable to costs (*h*) if nonsuited, and cannot be relieved by the court or a judge under this statute. In order to induce the court to exempt an executor who has failed, from costs (*i*), it is not sufficient that the action has been brought *bonâ fide*, under counsel's advice, and that it has been defeated on a difficult point of law, unless there be improper conduct on the part of the defendant. Unnecessary prolixity in the pleadings is not such conduct : nor omitting to give the plaintiff information, which might have prevented his proceeding with the action, if the plaintiff did not apply for the information.

(*g*) *Slater* v. *Lawson*, 1 B. & Ad. 893.
(*h*) *Chesterman* v. *Lamb*, 2 A. & E. 129.
(*i*) *Farley* v. *Briant*, 3 A. & E. 839, recognizing *Wilkinson* v. *Edwards*, 1 Bingh. N. C. 301 ; *Southgate* v. *Crowley*, ib. 518 ; *Engler* v. *Twisden*, 2 Bingh. N. C. 263. See also *Godson* v. *Freeman*, 2 Cr. M. & R. 585.

CHAPTER XX.

FACTOR.

Of the Nature of the Employment of a Factor, p. 810; *Power and Authority, p.* 811; *Lien, p.* 817; *Liability of Principal, p.* 820; *Stat.* 4 *Geo. IV. c.* 83, 6 *Geo. IV. c.* 94, *p.* 820; *Evidence, p.* 825.

OF the Nature of the Employment of a Factor.—A Factor is an agent, who is commissioned by a merchant or other person to sell goods for him, and to receive the produce. Foreign factors are agents residing here, commissioned by merchants resident abroad, or the contrary. Home factors are agents resident in England, commissioned by merchants also resident in England. A factor is usually paid for his trouble by a commission of so much *per cent.* on the goods sold. But sometimes he acts under a *del credere* commission (1); in which case, for an additional premium beyond the

---

(1) " *Del credere* is an Italian mercantile phrase, which has the same signification as the Scotch word *warrandice,* or the English word *guarantee.* A factor who has *general* orders to dispose of goods for his principal to the best advantage, is bound to exercise that degree of diligence which a prudent man exercises in his own affairs, and consequently the factor is authorized to dispose of the goods according to the best terms which can be obtained at the time; and if it shall appear that he has done so, and that he has sold the goods to persons in reputed good circumstances at the time, and to whom at that time he would have given credit in his own affairs, he will not be liable to his principal, although some of these should fail; and for such trouble the factor is generally paid by a commission of so much per cent. upon the goods sold. According to the above practice, the principal runs all the risk, and the factor is sure of his commission whether the event be favourable or not. Many merchants do not choose to run this risk, and to trust so implicitly to the prudence and discretion of their factor; and, therefore, the agreement called *del credere* was invented, by which the factor, for an additional premium beyond the usual commission, when he sells his goods on credit, becomes bound to warrant the solvency of the purchasers." Arg. *Mackenzie* v. *Scott,* 6 Bro. P. C. 287, Tomlin's ed. In *Grove* v. *Dubois,* 1 T. R. 112, the effect of a commission *del credere* was discussed in the Court of King's Bench, and that court decided that it was not merely a conditional undertaking and gua-

usual commission, he undertakes for the credit of the persons to whom he sells the goods consigned to him by his principal.

Power and Authority.—By the common law, a factor, as such, had not any authority to pledge, so as to transfer his lien to the pawnee, or to barter (a), but only to sell the goods of his principal (b). Hence, if a factor pledged the goods of his principal, the latter might recover the value of them in trover, against the pawnee, on tendering to the factor what was due to him, without making any tender to the pawnee (c) (2). The same rule held with respect to a bill of lading which had been indorsed to a factor by his principal: for the bill of lading, which is the symbol of the delivery of possession, cannot give a factor a greater authority than the actual possession of the goods themselves. Hence, as a factor could not pledge the goods of his principal (d), by a delivery of the goods, so neither could he do it by an indorsement and delivery of the bill of lading; for, although the indorsement of a bill of lading gave the indorsee an irrevocable right to receive the goods, where it was intended as an assignment of the property in the goods, yet it would not have that operation, where it was intended as a deposit only, by a person who was not authorized to make such deposit. Nor did the factor acquire an authority to pledge, where bills were drawn by the principal in advance of a consignment made to the factor for sale. Where plaintiffs, at Liverpool, having a consignment of goods coming from abroad, transmitted the bill of lading, which was to deliver to their order, to B., their brokers in London,

(a) *Guerreiro* v. *Peile*, 3 B. & A. 616.
(b) *Paterson* v. *Tash*, Str. 1178, per *Lee*, C. J., *Martini* v. *Coles*, 1 M. & S. 140; *Shipley* v. *Kymer*, 1 M. & S. 484; *Boyson* v. *Coles*, 6 M. & S. 14. But see

stat. 4 Geo. IV. c. 83, *post*, p. 820, and stat. 6 Geo. IV. c. 94, *post*, p. 821.
(c) *Daubigny* v. *Duval*, 5 T. R. 604.
(d) *Newsom* v. *Thornton*, 6 East, 17.

---

rantee from the person taking it, that he would pay if some other person did not, but that it was an absolute engagement from him, and made him liable in the first instance; and the same doctrine was acquiesced in, and acted upon, in *Bize* v. *Dickason*, 1 T. R. 285, cited in *Koster* v. *Eason*, 2 M. & S. 112, *ante*, p. 262. Hence, where a factor, under a commission *del credere*, sold goods, and took accepted bills from the purchasers, which he indorsed to a banker at the place of sale, and having received the banker's bill (payable to the factor's order) on a house in London, indorsed and transmitted it to his principal, who got it accepted; it was holden, that on the failure of the acceptor and drawer of this bill, the factor was answerable for the amount. *Mackenzie* v. *Scott*, 6 Bro. P. C. 280, Tomlin's ed. But see further as to the effect of a *del credere* commission, *Morris* v. *Cleasby*, 4 M. & Sel. 574. *Hornby* v. *Lacy*, 6 M. & Sel. 171.

(2) Where a factor *pledges* the goods of his principal as his own, the pawnee cannot claim to retain against the principal for the amount of the factor's general lien at the time of the pledge. *M'Combie* v. *Davies*, 7 East, 5.

instructing them to sell, and on the arrival of the consignment drew on B., as on former occasions, in anticipation of the proceeds, authorizing B. to deal with the consignment at their discretion, which bills B. accepted, and placed the consignment in the hands of defendant, their factor, for sale, not disclosing to him that it was not their property, and drew on him on account, which bill he accepted and paid; and sold the goods, and rendered his account, including the sale therein to B., who, before their acceptances became due, failed, and the same were dishonoured; it was holden (e), that the plaintiffs were entitled to recover the proceeds of such sale from the defendant. A quantity of oats having been consigned by a merchant abroad, to be sold by I. S., who was a merchant as well as factor, he placed them in the hands of A., a cornfactor, as a security for advances made by him; but the oats were not to be sold, without the consent of I. S.: they remained in A.'s possession, upon these terms, for nine months, when they were transferred to A. by a sale at the market price. No money actually passed, nor was any account of sale rendered; but the amount of the price was allowed in account between I. S. and A., leaving a balance in favour of the latter: it was holden (f), that this was in substance a pledge, and not a sale by the factor; and that no property passed to A., although the jury had found it to be a bonâ fide transaction. The circumstance (g) of the merchant drawing bills upon the factor to whom the goods are consigned, against the consignment, does not raise an authority in the factor to raise money to meet the bills by pledging the goods. A., a merchant at Rio Janeiro, consigned cottons to B. in this country for sale, and sent bills of lading, which showed that the cottons were sent on account, and at the risk of the consignor. B. employed C., a broker at Liverpool, to effect the sales, which C. did, some at a credit of ten days, and bills at three months; others for cash in one month. C. made large advances to B., and received the proceeds of the cottons when due. Before that time B. had become bankrupt. In an action by A. against C. for money had and received, it was holden (h), that C. was not entitled to retain for the advances made by him to B.: for that B. was a factor for sale only, and had not any authority to pledge the goods; and that A. was entitled to recover the net proceeds, deducting such sums only as B. could have retained. A., when he consigned the cottons to B., requested him to make remittances in anticipation of sales; it was holden, that such request did not give B. any special authority to pledge. Where the goods are permitted to remain at a wharf in the name of a broker, who is accustomed to deal in the article, and the broker *sells* them, the principal will be bound by such sale, although

(e) *Graham* v. *Dyster*, 6 M. & S. 1.   (C. P.) 639.
(f) *Kuckein* v. *Wilson*, 4 B. & A. 443.   (h) *Queiroz* v. *Truman*, 3 B. & C. 342.
(g) *Fielding* v. *Kymer*, 2 Brod. & B.

he did not expressly authorize the broker to sell (*i*). A factor may sell on credit (*k*), although not particularly authorized by the terms of his commission so to do.

" An agent employed generally, to do any act, is authorized to do it only in the usual way of business. Hence, as stock is sold usually for ready money only, a broker employed to sell stock cannot sell it upon credit, without a special authority, although acting *bonâ fide*, and with a view to the benefit of his principal" (*l*). A person who employs a broker on the Stock Exchange, impliedly gives him authority to act in accordance with the rules there established, although such principal may himself be ignorant of the rules (*m*).

Where plaintiffs consigned goods to their factors, who, not having funds to pay the freight and duties, agreed with the defendants that they should take charge of the consignment, pay the freight and duties, and sell the goods, and have one half the usual commission on such sale; and the defendants accordingly paid the freight and duties, and received the goods, after which the factors became bankrupt, having before informed defendants that the goods were the plaintiff's; but defendants, notwithstanding, sold the goods: held, that, on trover by the plaintiffs, the defendants had not a right to retain for the freight and duties after deducting the balance due from the factors to the plaintiffs at the time of the bankruptcy (*n*). Where C. consigned goods to M., their broker, upon a *del credere* commission for sale, and drew bills on him in advance, which M. accepted, but never paid, and afterwards, without the knowledge of C., placed the goods with H., another broker, upon a *del credere* commission, and upon an agreement to divide the commission with him, and obtained his acceptances for the amount, and H. sold the goods and afterwards became bankrupt, and his assignees received the proceeds of those sales, and the acceptances of H. were proved under his commission, and a dividend received upon them: held, that the assignees of H. were liable to the assignee of C., who had also become bankrupt, for the amount of the proceeds, in an action for money had and received (*o*). Factors may be bankrupts (*p*). By stat. 31 Geo. II. c. 40, s. 11, factors, employed to buy or sell cattle by commission, are prohibited from buying either directly or indirectly, on their own account, (except for the necessary use of their families,) live cattle, sheep, or swine, in London, or within the bills of mortality, or at any place whilst the cattle are on the road to London for sale; and, by the same clause, such factors are prohibited from selling, either by themselves or their agents, such cattle, &c.

(*i*) *Pickering* v. *Busk*, 15 East, 38. See also *Whitehead* v. *Tuckett*, 15 East, 400.

(*k*) Per *Willes*, C. J., Willes, 406. Per *Chambre*, J., 3 Bos. & Pul. 489.

(*l*) Lord *Ellenborough*, C. J., *Wiltshire* v. *Sims*, 1 Campb. 258.

(*m*) Per Lord *Denman*, C. J., and *Littledale*, J., *Sutton* v. *Tatham*, 10 A. & E. 27; 2 P. & D. 308.

(*n*) *Solly* v. *Rathbone*, 2 M. & S. 298. See *Bailey* v. *Culverwell*, 8 B. & C. 448.

(*o*) *Cockran* v. *Irlam*, 2 M. & S. 301.

(*p*) Stat. 6 Geo. IV. c. 16, s. 12.

in London, or within the bills of mortality. Penalty, double the
value of the cattle sold; to be recovered by application to J. P.;
one moiety to prosecutor, and the other to the poor of the parish
where the offence was committed. When goods are consigned to
joint factors (q), they are in the nature of co-obligors, and are
answerable for one another for the whole.

According to the general rule of law, a sale by a factor creates a
contract between the owner and buyer (r); and this rule holds
even in cases where the factor acts upon a *del credere* commission (s). Hence, if a factor sells goods, and the owner gives notice
to the buyer to pay the price to him and not to the factor, the
buyer will not be justified in afterwards paying the factor; and the
owner will be entitled to recover the price in an action against the
buyer, unless the factor has a lien on such price (t). If a factor
sells goods in his own name, the purchaser has a right to set off (u)
a debt due from him in an action by the principal for the price of
the goods. Where a contract, not under seal, is made with an agent
in his own name, for an indorsed principal, either the agent or the
principal may sue upon it; the defendant, in the case where the
principal sues, being entitled to be placed in the same situation at
the time of the disclosure of the real principal, as if the agent had
been the contracting party. This is a well established rule of law,
frequently acted upon in sales by factors, agents, or partners, but
it may equally be applied to other cases. *Sims* v. *Bond*, 2 Nev. &
Man. 616. If goods are bought by a broker (x), who does not
mention the name of his principal until he (the broker) has become
insolvent, the principal cannot set off the price of the goods against
a debt due to him from the broker, but is still liable to the vendor.
But where a factor, acting under a *del credere* commission (y), sells
goods as his own, and the buyer does not know of any principal, the
buyer may, in an action brought against him by the principal, set
off a debt due to him from the factor (3). There is, however, a

(q) *Godfrey* v. *Saunders*, 3 Wils. 114.
(r) Per *Lee*, C. J., in *Scrimshire* v.
Alderton, London Sittings, Str. 1182,
where the jury, however, found a verdict
against the opinion of the judge. See
also *Exp.Murray*, Co. B. L. 379, 5th ed.
(s) *Hornby* v. *Lacy*, 6 M. & S. 166.
(t) See *Drinkwater* v. *Goodwin*, Cowp.
251.

(u) Per Lord *Tenterden*, C. J., delivering judgment, *Taylor* v. *Kymer*, 3 B. &
Ad. 334.
(x) *Waring* v. *Favenck*, 1 Campb. 85.
(y) *George* v. *Clagett*, 7 T. R. 359.
See *Morris* v. *Cleasby*, 1 M. & S. 576;
Blackburn v. *Scholes*, 2 Campb. 343, and
Carr v. *Hincliff*, 4 B. & C. 551; *Wynen*
v. *Brown*, B. R. E. T. 7 Geo. IV.

---

(3) Where a factor to a person beyond sea buys or sells goods for the
principal in his own name; an action will lie against him or for him, in
his own name; for the credit will be presumed to be given to him in the
first case, and in the last the promise will be presumed to be made to him
—and the rather so, as it is so much for the benefit of trade. *Gonzales*
v. *Sladen*, T. 1 Ann. London Sittings, Salk. MSS.; Bull. N. P. 130.

distinction between a factor and a broker. A factor is a person to whom goods are consigned for sale by a merchant residing abroad or at a distance from the place of sale, and he usually sells in his own name, without disclosing that of his principal; the merchant, therefore, with full knowledge of these circumstances, trusts him with the actual possession of the goods, and gives him authority to sell in his own name. But the broker is in a different situation, he is not trusted with the possession of the goods, and he ought not to sell in his own name. The principal who trusts a broker has a right to expect that he will not sell in his own name. Hence, where an action was brought by a merchant to recover the price of his own goods, and the demand was resisted on the ground that the defendants, who were buyers of the goods, did not purchase them of the plaintiffs, but of Coles and Co., and that they had a counter demand against Coles and Co., which they were entitled to set off against the price of the goods; it was holden (z), that the defendants had not any right of set off; for the plaintiffs had not enabled Coles and Co. to appear as proprietors of the goods; and although Coles and Co. had not disclosed the name of their principal, and were merchants as well as brokers, yet in this case they had delivered to the plaintiffs a sold note, in the proper form, supposing them to have sold in their character of brokers, and they had delivered to the defendants a bought note, and they had not taken any counter note from the defendants; there was enough, therefore, to have raised a strong presumption in the minds of the defendants that the sale was in the character of brokers. Coles and Co. did not say they sold the goods as their own; the defendants did not ask any questions; and further, it appeared that the delivery order had been signed by the plaintiffs. A bill broker who receives a bill merely for the purpose of procuring it to be discounted for his customer, has no right to mix it with bills of his other customers, and to pledge (a) the whole mass as an advance for the security of money. *Parke*, B., delivering judgment and commenting on the foregoing case in *Foster* v. *Pearson*, 5 Tyrw. 265, observed, that in the absence of evidence as to the nature of such an employment, a bill broker must be taken to be an agent to procure the loan of money on each customer's bill separately; and that he had there-

(z) *Baring* v. *Corrie*, 2 B. & A. 137.
(a) Per Ld. *Lyndhurst*, delivering judgment, *Haynes* v. *Foster*, 4 Tyrw. 66; 2 Cr. & M. 239, *S. C.*

"Where the principal resides abroad, he is presumed to be ignorant of the circumstances of the party with whom his factor deals, and therefore the whole credit is considered as subsisting between the contracting parties." Per *Chambre*, J., in *Houghton* v. *Matthews*, 3 Bos. & Pul. 490. "There may be a particular course of dealing with respect to trade in favour of a foreign principal, that he shall not be liable in cases where a home principal would be liable." Per *Bayley*, J., 15 East, 69.

fore no right to mix bills together, and pledge the mass for one entire sum. In truth, a bill broker is not a person known to the law with certain prescribed duties, but his employment is one which depends entirely upon the course of dealing. It may differ in different parts of the country; it may have bounds more or less extensive in one place than in another. What is the nature of its powers and duties in any instance is a question of fact, and is to be determined by the usage and course of dealing in the particular place.

The law has been settled, by a variety of cases, that an unknown principal, when discovered, is liable on the contracts which his agent makes for him (4), but this rule must be taken with some qualification; for a party may preclude himself from recovering over against the principal, by knowingly making the agent his debtor (b).

Evidence is admissible, on behalf of one of the contracting parties, to show that the other was agent only, though contracting in his own name, and so to fix the real principal; but if the agent contracts in such a form as to make himself personally responsible, he cannot afterwards, whether his principal were or were not known at the time of the contract, relieve himself from that responsibility (c). Thus where L. and Co., brokers at Liverpool, sold hemp by auction at their rooms, and gave an invoice, describing the goods as "bought of L. and Co.," and received part of the price, but failed to deliver the goods. An action being brought against them by the purchaser for the non-delivery, and for money had and received; it was holden (d), that L. and Co. had made themselves responsible as sellers, by the invoice; and could not defend themselves by evidence tending to show that they sold as agents, and had intimated that fact before and at the time of the sale, and that, the principals being indebted to L. and Co., the invoice had been made out in their names, according to a custom of brokers in Liverpool, to secure the passing of the purchase-money through their hands.

In *Trueman* v. *Loder* (e), it was holden, that it was not competent to defendant to give evidence, that by the custom of the tallow trade, under certain contracts, a party may reject the undis-

(b) Per Ld. *Ellenborough*, in *Paterson* v. *Gandasequi*, 15 East, 68.
(c) Per Ld. *Denman*, C. J., delivering judgment of court in *Jones* v. *Littledale*,

6 A. & E. 490.
(d) S. C.
(e) 3 P. & D. 267; 11 A. & E. 589.

(4) This rule has been applied to a case, where the agent, at the time when he bought the goods of plaintiff at Liverpool, said that he bought them for a house at Dumfries, for which house he had bought goods of the plaintiff the season before, but did not name the principal, nor did the seller ask it; and the court said he was not bound to ask it. *Thomson* v. *Davenport*, in error, from Borough Court of Liverpool, 9 B. & C. 78.

closed principal, and look to the broker for the completion of the contract. But in *Johnston* v. *Usborn* (*f*), evidence of a custom in the corn trade for the corn-factors to sell in their own name was holden to be admissible.

Goods sold by a broker for a principal not named, upon the terms, as specified in the usual bought and sold notes, (delivered over to the respective parties by the broker,) of "*payment in one month, money,*" may be paid for by the buyer to the broker within the month, and that payment may be made by a bill of exchange accepted by the buyer and discounted by him within the month, although such bill had a longer time to run before it became due (*g*). A person who has made a contract as agent for a third person cannot sue (*h*) as principal without giving notice to the defendant, before action brought, that he is the party really interested. But where money is paid by an agent upon an agreement made with him in his own name, the principal (*i*) may recover it back upon the rescinding of the agreement. The plaintiffs, who were brokers, bought goods of the defendant on account of H. and by his authority. The purchase was made in their own names, but the vendor was told that there was an unnamed principal. The plaintiffs afterwards, under a general authority from H., contracted to sell the same goods, which the defendant had not yet delivered. H., on hearing of the latter contract, told the plaintiffs that he would have nothing to do with the goods, either as buyer or seller; and to this the plaintiffs assented. The defendant then refused to deliver the goods, and the plaintiffs sued him for damages sustained by them in consequence: it was holden (*k*), that the renunciation of the contract by H., and the plaintiff's assent thereto, formed no objection to the plaintiff's right to recover, of which the defendant could take advantage.

Lien.—By the general usage of trade, where there is a course of dealings and general account between the merchant and factor, and a balance is due to the factor, he has a lien on all goods in his hands for such balance of the general account, without regard to the time when, or on what account, he received the goods (*l*).

With respect to this general lien, it is to be observed:

First, That it will not attach until the goods come into the possession of the factor (*m*).

Secondly, The lien exists during such time only as the factor has possession of the goods; for if he should part with the possession

---

(*f*) 3 P. & D. 236; 11 A. & E. 549.
(*g*) *Favenc* v. *Bennett*, 11 East, 36.
(*h*) *Bickerton* v. *Burrell*, 5 M. & S. 383.
(*i*) *D. of Norfolk* v. *Worthy*, 1 Campb. 337.
(*k*) *Short and others* v. *Spackman*, 2

B. & Ad. 962.
(*l*) *Kruger* v. *Wilcox*, Ambl. 252; 1 Kenyon, 32, *S. C.*; *Gardiner* v. *Coleman*, cited 1 Burr. 494; and per *Buller*, J., 6 East, 28, n. S. P.
(*m*) *Kinloch* v. *Craig*, 3 T. R. 119, 783.

after the lien has attached, the lien is gone (*n*). But where a factor is in advance for goods by actual payment, or where he sells under a *del credere* commission, whereby he becomes responsible for the price, he has a lien on the price, although he should have parted with the possession of the goods (*o*). And this rule holds, although money should have been advanced by the factor, at the time when he knew that the principal was in insolvent circumstances (*p*). The owner of goods, being indebted to a factor in an amount exceeding their value, consigned them to him for sale : the factor, being also similarly indebted to J. S., sold the goods to him. The factor afterwards became bankrupt ; and on a settlement of accounts between J. S. and the assignees, J. S. allowed credit to them for the price of the goods, and he then proved the residue of the claim against the estate : it was holden (*q*), that as the factor had a lien on the whole price of the goods, such settlement of accounts between the vendee and the assignees afforded a good answer to an action against the vendee for the price of the goods, brought either by or on the account of the original owner. But where a factor has not any special claim on the goods, and he has disposed of them, whereby he has lost the advantage arising from possession, the debt is to be considered as the debt of the principal, and the factor has no lien on the price. The plaintiff, who was resident in Ireland, employed two persons, as his factors in London, to sell goods for him, which he had sent to them (*r*). The factors sold these goods to J. S. for a certain sum ; the plaintiff not knowing to whom they were sold, and J. S. not knowing that they belonged to the plaintiff, the goods having been delivered to him as the goods of the factors. The factors, before payment, became bankrupts, and their debts were assigned by the commissioners to the defendants, who afterwards received from J. S. the money for the goods. The plaintiff having brought an action against the defendants for money had and received, the case was reserved by *Holt*, C. J., for the opinion of the Court of King's Bench, who gave judgment, after argument, for the plaintiff. This case was afterwards cited before *Parker*, C. J., at the London Sittings, and allowed to be law ; because, although it was agreed, that payment by J. S. to the factors, with whom the contract was made, would have discharged J. S. as against the principal, *yet the debt was not in law due to the factors ; but to the person whose goods they were ;* and therefore it was not assigned to the defendants, by a general assignment of their debts, but remained due to the plaintiff as before ; and having been paid to

(*n*) See *Sweet* v. *Pym*, 1 East, 4, and *Buller*, J., in *Lickbarrow* v. *Mason*, 6 East, 27, n.

(*o*) See *Drinkwater* v. *Goodwin*, Cowp. 251 ; *Hudson* v. *Granger*, 5 B. & A. 27.

(*p*) *Foxcroft* v. *Devonshire*, 2 Burr. 931.

(*q*) *Hudson* v. *Granger*, 5 B. & A. 27.

(*r*) *Garratt* v. *Cullum*, T. 9 Ann. B. R., stated by *Willes*, C. J., delivering the opinion of the court in *Scott* v. *Surman*, Willes, 405 ; reported also in Bull. N. P. 42, ed. 6th, by the name of *Garratt* v. *Cullum*.

the defendants, who had not any right to have it, it must be considered in law as paid for the use of him to whom it was due; and, consequently, an action might be maintained by him as for money had and received to his use. The plaintiffs, who were partners, resident beyond sea, consigned a quantity of tar to R. S., the bankrupt, brother of one of the plaintiffs, as their factor (s). There had been mutual dealings between the two brothers, the accounts of which were then unsettled. The ship and goods arrived in the Thames, from Carolina. The factor, having received the bill of lading, sold the tar to J. S., upon an agreement that it should be paid for in promissory notes, payable four months after the delivery of the goods. A few days after the sale, the vendee gave the factor, in part payment, two promissory notes. Soon afterwards the factor committed an act of bankruptcy, and the defendants were chosen assignees under the commission. The bankrupt delivered up the two notes to the assignees, and they received the money due upon them. They likewise confirmed the sale, and settled the account with the vendee, and received the balance. An account for money had and received having been brought by the plaintiffs against the assignees, for the recovery of the money received on the notes, and the money received on the settlement of the account, it was holden, that the plaintiffs were entitled to recover both sums; *Willes*, C. J., (who delivered the opinion of the court,) observing, as to the first, that the notes, having been in the hands of the bankrupt at the time of his bankruptcy, were capable of being distinguished from the rest of the bankrupt's estate, and therefore could not be applied to the bankrupt's debts; consequently the plaintiffs were entitled to recover the value of those notes which had been received by the defendants in like manner as, if the goods had remained in specie, unsold in the bankrupt's hands at the time of the bankruptcy, the plaintiffs might have recovered them in an action of trover. As to the second sum, the general rule was, that if a person received money, which ought to be paid to another, an action would lie as for money had and received; that the assignees having received the money, which belonged to the plaintiffs, they ought to have paid it to the plaintiffs; and not having done so, this action would lie against them for so much money had and received to the use of the plaintiffs.

Thirdly, A factor has not a lien in respect of debts which have accrued previously to the time at which his character of factor commenced. A., a factor, sold the goods of B., in his own name (t), to C.: C., without paying for these goods, sent another parcel of goods to A., to sell for him, not having employed A. as a factor

(s) *Scott and another* v. *Surman and others, Assignees of R. S., a Bankrupt,* Willes, 400, cited by Lord *Ellenborough,* delivering judgment in *Taylor* v. *Plumer,*

3 M. & S. 575.
(t) *Houghton* v. *Matthews,* per *Heath, Rooke,* and *Chambre, Js., Alvanley,* C. J., dissentiente, 3 Bos. & Pul. 485.

before. C. became bankrupt, and his assignees claimed the goods sent by C. to A., which still remained unsold, tendering the charges upon those goods. A. refused to deliver them, claiming a lien upon them for the price of the former goods sold by him to C., the balance between A. and B. being in favour of A. An action of trover having been brought by the assignees against A., for the value of the goods sent by C., it was holden, that they were entitled to recover.

Liability of Principal.—The maxim, that the principal is *civilly* responsible for the acts of his agent, universally prevails both in courts of law and equity (*u*). Upon this principle it was holden, by *Holt*, C. J., that a merchant was answerable for the deceit of his factor who had sold some silk to the plaintiff, as silk of a superior quality, knowing it to be silk of an inferior quality (*x*) (5). Notice to the principal is notice to all his agents, if there be reasonable time to communicate that notice to the agents before the event which raises the question happens (*y*).

The law, established by the decisions, relating to goods shipped in the names of persons who were not the actual proprietors thereof, and to the deposit or pledge of goods, having been found to afford great facility to fraud, and to produce frequent litigation, and proving in its effects highly injurious to the interests of commerce, the legislature interposed; and by stat. 4 Geo. IV. c. 83, [18th July, 1823,] it was enacted, "That any person intrusted for the purpose of sale with any goods, and by whom such goods shall be shipped in his own name, or in whose name any goods shall be shipped by any other person, shall be deemed to be the true owner, so as to entitle the consignee to a lien thereon, in respect of any money or negotiable security, advanced or given by such consignee, to or for the use of the person in whose name such goods shall be shipped, or in respect of any money or negotiable security received by him to the use of such consignee, in like manner as if such person was the true owner, PROVIDED such consignee shall not have notice by the bill of lading, at or before the advance or receipt of the money or negotiable security, that the person shipping, or in whose name the goods are shipped, is not the actual and *bonâ fide* owner: PROVIDED ALSO, that the person in whose name such goods

(*u*) 4 T. R. 66, per *Kenyon*, C. J.
(*x*) *Hern* v. *Nichols*, Salk. 289. Per *Holt*, C. J., at Nisi Prius.
(*y*) *Mayhew* v. *Eames*, 3 B. & C. 601,

recognized in *Willis* v. *Bank of England*, 5 Nev. & Man. 490; 4 Ad. & Ell. 21, S. C.

---

(5) But see 9 Hen. VI. 53, b., cited in Bro. Abr. Actions sur le Case, pl. 8, where it was said by the court, if my servant sell false stuff, an action on the case does not lie against me, unless he sold it through my covin or by my command.

are shipped shall be taken for the purposes of this act to have been intrusted therewith, unless the contrary shall appear or be shown in evidence by the person disputing such fact." By sect. 2, " Any person, body politic or corporate, may accept any goods or bill of lading, in deposit or pledge from any consignee, and enforce the right possessed by such consignee, but shall acquire no further right than was possessed by the consignee at the time of the pledge." The 3rd section provides, that this act shall not be construed so as to prevent the owner from demanding and recovering the goods from the factor before they have been pledged, or from his assignees in the event of his bankruptcy; nor from demanding or recovering from any person, or his assignees in case of his bankruptcy, or from any body corporate, the goods deposited or pledged, upon repayment of the money, or on restoration of the negotiable security, or on payment of a sum of money equal to the amount of such security; nor from recovering from such person, or body corporate, any balance remaining in his hands as the product of the sale of such goods, after deducting thereout the amount of the money or negotiable security; provided that in case of the bankruptcy of such factor, the owner of the goods so pledged and redeemed shall be held to have discharged, *pro tanto*, his debt to the bankrupt's estate.

Shortly afterwards it was found expedient to alter and amend the foregoing statute, and to make further provisions; and therefore, by stat. 6 Geo. IV. c. 94, [5th July, 1825,] it was enacted, that any person intrusted for the purpose of *consignment* or sale with any goods, and who shall have shipped such goods in his own name, and any person in whose name any goods shall be shipped by any other person, shall be deemed to be the true owner, so far as to entitle the consignee to a lien thereon, in respect of any money or negotiable security advanced or given by such consignee to or for the use of the person in whose name such goods shall be shipped, or in respect of any money or negotiable security received by him to the use of such consignee, in the like manner and *to all intents and purposes*, as if such person was the true owner; *provided such consignee shall not have notice* by the bill of lading or otherwise, at or before the advance or receipt of the money or negotiable security, that the person shipping, or in whose name the goods are shipped, is not the actual and *bonâ fide* owner; provided also, that the person in whose name any such goods are to be shipped, shall be taken, for the purpose of this act, to have been intrusted therewith for the purpose of consignment or of sale, unless the contrary be made to appear, by bill of discovery or otherwise, or be made to appear or be shown in evidence by any person disputing such fact; and by sect. 2, that any person *intrusted with* (z),

(z) See *Phillips and others* v. *Huth and others*, 6 M. & W. 572, and *post*, p. 824.

and in possession of, any bill of lading, India warrant, dock warrant, warehouse keeper's certificate, wharfinger's certificate, warrant or order for delivery of goods, shall be deemed to be the true owner of the goods described in the said several documents, so far as to give validity to any agreement (6), thereafter entered into by such person with any person, for the sale or disposition of the goods, or any part thereof, or for the deposit or pledge thereof, or any part thereof, as a security for any money or negotiable instrument advanced or given by such persons, &c. upon the faith of such several documents; provided such persons, &c. *shall not have notice* by such documents, or otherwise, that the person intrusted is not the actual and *bonâ fide* owner of the goods so sold or pledged : provided (a) that in case any person, &c. shall accept any such goods in deposit or pledge from any such person so in possession and intrusted, *without notice*, as security for any debt or demand due from such person so intrusted and in possession to such person, &c. before such deposit or pledge, then such person, &c. so taking such goods in deposit or pledge, shall acquire no further right in the goods or any such document than was possessed by the person so possessed and intrusted at the time of such deposit or pledge as a security ; but such person, &c. so taking such goods in deposit or pledge, shall and may acquire and enforce such right as was possessed by such person so possessed and intrusted : and, by sect. 4, any person, &c. may contract with any *agent intrusted with any goods* (7), or to whom the same may be consigned, *for the purchase* of any such goods, and receive the same of, and pay the same to, such agent; and such contract and payment shall be binding against the owner of such goods, *notwithstanding such person, &c. shall have notice,* that the person making such contract, or on whose behalf such contract is made, is an agent, provided such contract and payment be made in the usual and ordinary course of business, and that such person, &c. shall not, when such contract is entered into or payment made, have *notice* that such agent is not authorized to sell the goods or to receive the purchase-money. And *by the 5th*

(a) Sect. 3.

---

(6) Persons who would avail themselves of the provisions of this act, must prove the agreement. *Evans* v. *Truman,* 2 B. & Ad. 886. In this case the defendant had received, by way of pledge, India warrants from the plaintiff's broker, who had been intrusted with them, without any authority to pledge or sell, under a written agreement. It was holden, that defendant was bound to produce the agreement.

(7) It is difficult to say precisely what is meant by " an agent intrusted with goods :" but a wharfinger is not such a person. *Monk* v. *Whittenbury,* 2 B. & Ad. 486.

section (8), any person, &c. may take any such goods or any such *document* in deposit or pledge from any such factor or agent, *notwithstanding such person, &c. shall have notice*, that the person making such deposit or pledge is a factor or *agent*; but then such person, &c. shall acquire no further right to the goods, or document for the delivery thereof, than was possessed or might have been enforced by the factor or agent at the time of such deposit or pledge as security; but such person, &c. shall and may possess and enforce such right as was possessed and might have been enforced by such factor or agent at the time of such deposit or pledge. The right of a factor to pledge under this section depends upon the question whether, upon the face of the *whole* account between them, the principal is indebted to the factor (a).

It is, however, provided (b), that "nothing herein contained shall be construed to prevent the true owner of the goods from recovering the same from his factor or agent *before* a sale, deposit, or pledge, or from the assignees of such factor or agent in the event of his bankruptcy; nor to prevent the owner from recovering from any person, &c. the price agreed to be paid for the purchase of such goods, subject to any right of set-off on the part of such person, &c. against such factor or agent; nor to prevent the owner from recovering from such person, &c. the goods deposited or pledged, upon repayment of the money, or on restoration of the negotiable instrument advanced on the security thereof by such person, &c. to the factor or agent, and upon payment of such further sum of money or on restoration of such other negotiable instrument (if any) as may have been advanced by the factor or agent to the owner, or on payment of money, equal to the amount of such instrument; nor to prevent the owner from recovering from such persons, &c. any balance remaining in his hands as the produce of the sale of the goods, after deducting the money or negotiable instrument advanced on the security thereof; and in case of the bankruptcy of the factor or agent, the owner of the goods so pledged and redeemed shall be held to have discharged *pro tanto* his debt to the estate of such bankrupt." See *Taylor* v. *Kymer*, 3 B. & Ad. 320, where the

(a) *Robertson* v. *Kensington*, 5 M. & Ry. 381. (b) Sect. 6.

---

(8) A broker having accepted bills for his principal on the security of goods then in his hands, pledged the goods with a person who had notice of the agency, but did not inform the principal of this transaction; it was holden *, that under this section the broker could transfer such right only as he had, which was a right to be indemnified against the bills which he had accepted, and that the principal, having satisfied those bills, was entitled to have back his goods from the pawnee without paying the amount for which they were pledged.

* *Fletcher* v. *Heath*, 7 B. & C. 517. The provision in this section refers to a deposit or pledge only, made distinctly as such. *Thompson* v. *Farmer*, M. & Malk. 48.

transfer of India warrants under the circumstances was holden not to be a *sale* or *disposition* within the meaning of the foregoing statute. The remaining sections of this statute relate to the prosecution of agents fraudulently pledging the goods of their principal.

Before the passing of this act, or rather the previous act, the 4 Geo. IV. c. 83, it was settled, that a factor or agent for sale had not any power to pledge, whether he was in possession either of the goods themselves, or of the symbol of the goods, and even though the symbol might bear on the face of it some evidence of the property being in himself; as in the case of a bill of lading, in which he was the consignee or indorsee. This rule was thought to be attended with hardship on persons dealing with factors on the faith of their being principals, and the legislature, by the 4 Geo. IV. first relaxed this rule, and by the 6 Geo. IV. extended that relaxation.

This statute gives validity only to pledges by a factor of documents with which the real owner has previously intrusted him, and does not extend to the pledge of documents created by the factor himself (c).

The 2nd section of the 6th Geo. IV. came under the consideration of a court in *Phillips* v. *Huth* (d), when *Parke*, B., delivered a very elaborate judgment of the court, for the express purpose of distinctly defining the meaning of the statute: adverting to the 2nd section, he said, "It is very clear, that this section relaxes the rule of the common law only with respect to those who deal with persons who are not merely in possession of, but are also intrusted with, the symbol of property. However great the hardship may be on innocent persons, and whatever they may have supposed from finding another in possession of a document bearing the indicia of property in himself, still the statute does not apply, and they can acquire no title by virtue of it, unless the document has been intrusted to that person. If the legislature had intended to make the simple possession of such instruments sufficient to enable the party having them to make a good title, they no doubt would have so provided; if they had, the innocent party dealing with him would have been protected, but the innocent owner would, in that case, have suffered, if the document had been taken from him by felony or fraud. But by providing that a person should be *intrusted* as well as in possession, the inconvenience is obviated. The statute applies only to written documents relating to goods, and not to goods themselves; and for this reason—these documents may be made to designate the owner's name, which the goods themselves, generally speaking, cannot; and it is clear that the legislature intended that those persons only should suffer by the frauds of their agents, who have intrusted them with the evidence of title, and

. (c) Per *Alderson*, B., in *Close* v. *Holmes*, 2 M. & Rob. 25.   (d) 6 M. & W. 572.

omitted to take those precautions which might have prevented them deceiving others. It is therefore necessary, in order to give effect to this clause, that the owner should have "*intrusted*" the factor with the document ; not that it is necessary that the owner should have had personal possession of the document, so as to be able to mark it with his name, and himself delivered it to the factor; for if his own agent, general or special, puts it into the hands of the factor with the factor's name on it, or if the factor be instructed by the owner to obtain the document in that state, and does so, no doubt he is "*intrusted*" by the owner with it within the meaning of the act. But in order to constitute an *intrusting* of such a document, it is necessary that the owner should have intended the factor to *possess* it in that form, at the time when he had the possession. *Intrusting* with the document is essentially different from enabling a person to become possessed of it—from giving him the means of obtaining it.

Evidence.—It is a general rule of evidence, that where a witness has a direct interest in the event of a cause, his testimony cannot be received (9). But, from necessity, an exception has been introduced in the case of factors and brokers, because, from the nature of the transactions in which they are engaged, the contracts they make for other persons cannot be proved without them. Hence

---

(9) By statute 3 & 4 Will. IV. c. 42, s. 26, in order to render the rejection of witnesses, on the ground of interest, less frequent, it is enacted, " that if any witness shall be objected to as incompetent, on the ground that the verdict or judgment would be admissible in evidence for or against him, such witness shall nevertheless be examined; but, in that case, a verdict or judgment in that action in favour of the party on whose behalf he shall have been examined, shall not be admissible in evidence for him, or any one claiming under him, nor shall a verdict or judgment against the party, on whose behalf he shall have been examined, be admissible in evidence against him or any one claiming under him." And by sect. 27, " the name of every witness objected to as incompetent, on the ground that such verdict or judgment would be admissible in evidence for or against him, shall, at the trial, be indorsed on the record or document on which the trial shall be had, together with the name of the party on whose behalf he was examined, by some officer of the court, at the request of either party, and shall be afterwards entered on the record of the judgment; and such indorsement or entry shall be sufficient evidence that such witness was examined, in any subsequent proceeding in which the verdict or judgment shall be offered in evidence." The object of this statute is to supersede the necessity and to save the expense of a release. The effect is to make the witness competent where the only interest is, that the verdict or judgment may be used for or against the witness. If the interest extend beyond that, then a release is necessary. See *Bowman* v. *Willis*, 3 Bingh. N. C. 669; *Yeomans* v. *Legh*, 2 Mee. & Wels. 419, and the other cases on this statute cited *ante*, p. 375, 650.

it has been holden (e), that a factor is a good witness to prove the contract of sale, in an action by the principal, for the price of the goods sold. And, in a later case (f), it was determined, that there was not any difference, in point of interest, between a person who sells upon commission, and one who is to have a share of the profit; and, consequently, that a person who was employed to sell goods, and was to receive for his trouble whatever money he could procure for them beyond a stated sum, was a competent witness to prove the contract between the seller and buyer. So a broker, who has effected a policy and has a lien on it for his premiums, is a competent (g) witness, (notwithstanding his lien,) to prove all matters connected with the policy.

(e) *Dixon* v. *Cooper*, 3 Wils. 40.   (g) *Hunter* v. *Leathley*, 10 B. & C.
(f) *Benjamin* v. *Porteus*, 2 H. Bl.   858.
590, per *Heath* and *Rooke*, Js.

CHAPTER XXI.

FISHERY.

I. *Of the Right of Fishery in the Sea, and in the Creeks and Arms thereof, and in fresh Rivers, p. 827.*

II. *Of the different Kinds of Fishery, p. 829 ; Several Fishery, p. 829 ; Free Fishery, p. 830 ; Common of Fishery, p. 832.*

I. *Of the Right of Fishery in the Sea, and in the Creeks and Arms thereof, and in fresh Rivers.*

" THE right of fishing in the sea (a), and the creeks and arms thereof, is originally lodged in the crown, in like manner as the right of fishing in a private or inland river is originally lodged in the owner thereof. But although the king is the owner, and, as a consequence of his property, hath the primary right of fishing in the sea, or creeks or arms thereof, yet all the king's subjects in England have regularly a liberty of fishing in the sea, and the creeks and arms thereof, as a public common of piscary, and may not, without injury to their right, be restrained of it, unless in such places, creeks, or navigable rivers, where the king, or some particular subject, hath gained a propriety exclusive of that common liberty, either by the king's charter or grant, or by custom and usage, or prescription." It appears from this passage, that Lord *Hale* thought an exclusive right of fishery in an arm of the sea might belong to a subject (b). And of this opinion were the Court of B. R. in *Carter and another* v. *Murcot and another*, 4 Burr. 2162, where it was decided, that a plea which prescribed for a several fishery in an arm of the sea, was good; but it was there said, that, as the presumption in such case was in favour of the king and public, it was incumbent on the plaintiff to prove his exclusive right, agreeably to the rule laid down by Lord *Hale*, in 1 Mod. 105, that if any one will appropriate a privilege to himself, the

---

(a) Ld. *Hale*, De Jure Maris, p. 1, c. 4 ; Hargrave's Tracts, vol. 1, p. 11. See also the case of *The Royal Fishery of the Banne*, Dav. R. 55.

(b) See also 8 Edw. IV. 19, a. ; 4 T. R. 439, S. P., admitted by *Kenyon*, C. J., and *Ashhurst*, J.

proof lies on his side. In *Ward* v. *Cresswell*, Willes' Rep. 265, and 16 Vin. Abr. 354, tit. "Piscary" (B.) *S. C.*, the court held, that all the subjects of England, of common right, might fish in the sea, it being for the good of the commonwealth, and for the sustenance of the people of the realm, and that therefore a prescription for it, as appurtenant to a particular township, was void, and as absurd as a prescription would be for travelling the king's highway, or for the use of the air as appurtenant to a particular estate. To trespass for fishing in the plaintiff's fishery (c), defendant pleaded, that the place is an arm of the sea, in which every subject has a right to fish; the plaintiff in his replication claimed an exclusive right by prescription, traversing the general right. It was holden, that this was a bad and immaterial traverse, and might be passed over by the defendant, and that it was competent to him to traverse the prescriptive right of the plaintiff stated in the replication. The preservation of the spawn, fry, or brood of fish, has been, for centuries, a favourite object of legislation, and the statutes passed for the purpose are extremely numerous; thus dredging for oyster spat in a common navigable river is illegal under the stat. 13 Ric. II. stat. 1, c. 19, which has never been repealed, but frequently recognized (d). In *Bagott* v. *Orr*, 2 Bos. & Pul. 472, the court seem to have been of opinion, that *primâ facie* every subject has a right to take fish found on the sea shore between high and low water mark, but that such general right might be restrained by an exclusive right in an individual.

Fresh rivers, of what kind soever, of common right belong to the owners of the soil adjacent (e); so that the owners of the one side have, of common right, the propriety of the soil, and consequently the right of fishing, *usque filum aquæ*, and the owners of the other side the right of soil or ownership, and fishing unto the *filum aquæ* on their side. And if a man be owner of land on both sides, in common presumption he is owner of the whole river, and hath the right of fishing according to the extent of his land in length. But special usage may alter that common presumption; for one may have the river, and others the soil adjacent; or one may have the river and soil thereof, and another the free or several fishery in that river. "Where a private river is the boundary of two persons' lands, the soil *ad filum aquæ* belongs to the owners of the lands on each side *ad filum aquæ*, unless there have been immemorially acts of ownership exercised by one or the other" (f).

(c) *Richardson* v. *The Mayor, &c. of Orford*, 2 H. Bl. 182.

(d) *Mayor, &c. of Maldon* v. *Woolvet*, 4 P. & D. 26.

(e) Ld. Hale, De Jure Maris, p. 1, c. 1; Hargrave's Tracts, vol. 1, p. 5; Davis's R. 57, a. b. See as to the evidence of ownership of rivers, *Jones* v. *Williams*, 2 M. & W. 326.

(f) Per *Wilmot*, J., *Sparks* v. *Lloyd*, Worcester Spring Ass. 1757, MSS.

II. Of the different Kinds of Fishery, p. 829; Several Fishery, p. 829; Free Fishery, p. 830; Common of Fishery, p. 832.

A *several* fishery is where a person has an exclusive right of fishery, either in his own soil or in the soil of another (g). " In order to constitute a *several* fishery, it is requisite that the party claiming it should so far have the right of fishing independently of all others, as that no person should have a co-extensive right with him in the object claimed. But a partial independent right in another, or a limited liberty, does not derogate from the right of the general owner" (h). He who has a several fishery is not necessarily the owner of the soil (i); but as the exclusive right of fishing is an incident to the ownership of the soil, it will be presumed (k), until the contrary be shown, that such right resides in the owner of the soil. Hence, to an action of trespass for an injury to a right of several fishery, it is a good plea that the soil and freehold belong to the defendant (l) (1). To this, however, the plaintiff may reply title to the several fishery, either by prescription or grant, thereby rebutting the presumption of the right of several fishery being still vested in the owner of the soil. Where a subject was owner of a several fishery in a navigable river, where the tide flows and reflows, which fishery had been granted to him before Magna Charta, by the description of *separalis piscaria;* it was holden (m), that it was an incorporeal and not a territorial hereditament, and that a term for years in it could not be created without deed.

If a person be seised of a river (n), and by deed grant a several fishery in the same, and makes livery of seisin *secundum formam cartæ,* the soil does not pass; and if the river become dry, the grantor may take the benefit of the soil, for a particular right only passed to the grantee. A prescriptive right to a several fishery in

(g) Fitz. Abr. Barre, pl. 27, cites M. 20 Hen. VI. 4.

(h) Per Ld. *Mansfield,* C. J., delivering the resolution of the court, *Seymour and others* v. *Ld. Courtenay and others,* 5 Burr. 2814.

(i) Hargrave's Note, Co. Litt. 122, a. n. (7).

(k) See 5 B. & C. 886.

(l) 17 Edw. IV. 6, b.; 18 Edw. IV. b. Per *Paston,* J., 18 Hen. VI. 30, a.; Fitz. Abr. Barre, pl. 20, *S. C.*

(m) *D. of Somerset* v. *Fogwell,* 5 B. & C. 875.

(n) 1 Inst. 4, b. But see Hargrave's note.

---

(1) See also 10 Hen. VII. 24, b., 28, b., a case very clearly reported; but it is said there, that the plea is not good, unless it conclude with praying, *whether plaintiff shall have his action without showing title.* Per *Brian,* J., but in 20 Hen. VI. 4, a., *Newton,* C. J. C. B., was of opinion, that the plea might be concluded either way.

a navigable river may pass as appurtenant to a manor (o). A right of fishery is divisible, and may be abandoned as to part, while another part is preserved. Hence, an exclusive right to dredge for oysters may subsist as appurtenant to a manor, although it be lawful for all the king's subjects to catch floating fish therein. Trespass for breaking and entering his close, and fishing in *separali piscariâ suâ*, and for taking pisces *suos* (p). After verdict, exception was taken to the declaration in arrest of judgment, because it is said pisces *suos*. But the court were of opinion, that being in *separali piscariâ*, it might well be said pisces *suos*, because they could not be taken by any other person. In *Fontleroy* v. *Aylmer*, Lord Raym. 239, where the declaration stated that defendant, in *separali suâ piscaria piscatus fuit, et pisces cepit,* after verdict for plaintiff, an exception in arrest of judgment, directly the reverse of that in the foregoing case, was taken, *viz.* that the declaration had omitted the word *suos;* but the court thought the objection entitled to very little weight; because the plaintiff having alleged that it was his fishery, the fish there should be intended *primâ facie* to be his fish. A., being seised of a mill, and having a sole fishery in the waters of the mill, granted the mill, with all waters, streams, &c. necessary in working the same, "except, and always reserving, the right and privilege of fishing in the waters of the said mill." It was holden (q), that this was an exception of the sole fishery, and not a reservation of a new easement.

Free Fishery.

IT is to be lamented, that the books do not afford materials for an accurate description of a free fishery. That this subject is involved in doubt and uncertainty, will appear from the following passages, extracted from the writings of Mr. Justice Blackstone and Mr. Hargrave:—

Mr. J. Blackstone, having defined common of fishery to be a liberty of fishing in another man's water (r), states a free fishery to be an exclusive right of fishing in a public river, and adds, "that it is a royal franchise, and is considered as such in all countries where the feodal polity has prevailed; though the making such grants, and thereby appropriating what seems to be unnatural to restrain, the use of running water, was prohibited for the future by King John's great charter; and the rivers that were fenced in his

(o) *Rogers* v. *Allen*, 1 Campb. 309.
(p) *Child* v. *Greenhill*, Cro. Car. 553; Sir Wm. Jones, 440, *S. C.*

(q) Ld. *Paget* v. *Milles*, 3 Doug. 43.
(r) 2 Bl. Com. 39, 40; Edn. 12.

time were directed to be laid open. This opening was extended by the second and third charters of Henry III. to those also which were fenced under Richard I., so that a franchise of free fishery ought to be as old as the reign of Henry II. This differs from a *several* fishery, because he that has a *several* fishery must also be (or at least derive his right from) the owner of the soil, which in a free fishery is not requisite. It differs from a common of piscary, in that the free fishery is an *exclusive* right; the common of piscary is not so; and therefore, in a free fishery, a person has a property in the fish before they are caught; in a common of piscary, not until afterwards. Some, indeed, have considered a free fishery, not as a royal franchise, but merely as a private grant of a liberty to fish in the *several* fishery of the grantor. But the considering such right as originally a flower of the prerogative, till restrained by Magna Charta, and derived by royal grant, previously to the reign of Richard I., to such as now claim it by prescription, and to distinguish it, as we have done, from a *several* and a *common* of fishery, may remove some difficulties, in respect to this matter, with which our books are embarrassed." On this passage Mr. Hargrave made the following remark (s): "Both parts of this description of a free fishery seem disputable. With regard to the first part, although for the sake of distinction it might be more convenient to appropriate free fishery to the franchise of fishing in public rivers by derivation from the crown; and although in other countries it may be so considered, yet, from the language of our books, it seems as if, in our law, practice had extended this kind of fishery to all streams, whether private or public: neither the register nor other book professing any discrimination. Reg. 95, b. *F. N. B.* 88, *G.*; Fitz. Abr. Ass. 422; 17 Edw. IV. 6, b. 7. a.; 7 Hen. VII. 13, b. With respect to the 2nd part, it is true, that in *Smith* v. *Kemp*, 2 Salk. 637; Carth. 285, *S. C.*, the court held free fishery to import an exclusive right equally with several fishery, chiefly relying on the writ in the Register, 95, b. and the 46 Edw. III. 11, a. But then this was only the opinion of two judges (t) against one (u), who strenuously insisted, that the word *libera, ex vi termini*, implied common, and that many judgments and precedents were founded on Lord Coke's so construing it. That the dissenting judge was not wholly unwarranted in the latter part of his assertion, appears from two determinations a little before the case in question, viz. *Upton* v. *Dawkin*, 3 Mod. 97, where judgment was arrested in trespass for breaking and entering a free fishery; because the declaration alleged the fish taken to be the fish *of the plaintiff;* and *Peake* v. *Tucker*, cited in margin, Carth. 286, where judgment was arrested on the same ground." After the preceding remarks were published, Mr. J. *Blackstone*, with that candour and liberality

(s) Hargrave's Co. Litt. 122, a. n. 7.   (u) *Eyre*, J.
(t) *Holt*, C. J., *Dolben*, J.

which are the inseparable companions of true learning, added the following observation, in a subsequent edition of his Commentaries: " It must be acknowledged, that the right and distinctions of the three species of fishery are very much confounded in our law books; and there are not wanting respectable authorities (see them well digested in Hargrave's notes on Co. Litt. 122 (23),) which maintain that a *several* fishery may exist distinct from the property of the soil, and that a *free* fishery implies no exclusive right, but is synonymous with common of piscary." Whatever be the nature of free fishery, whether it be, as Mr. J. Blackstone supposes, an exclusive right, or as Mr. Hargrave seems to think, only the same with common of fishery; since the case of *Smith* v. *Kemp*, before mentioned, it is too late now to contend, that an action of respass *vi et armis* will not lie for an injury to it (2). But it may admit of a question, whether the declaration ought to state the fish taken to be the fish *of the plaintiff.* It seems, that such allegation ought to be made.

Common of Fishery.

A COMMON of fishery is a right of fishing in common with other persons in a stream or river, the soil whereof belongs to a third person. This does not differ in any respect from any other right of common (x), and trespass will not lie for an injury to it. A person having a common of fishery in another's land, cannot cut (y) the grass growing on the bank. Under ancient deeds recognizing a right in the owner of an estate to have a weir across a river for taking fish (z), if it appear that such weir was heretofore made of brushwood, through which the fish might escape into the upper part of the river, he cannot convert it into a stone weir, whereby the possibility of escape is debarred, except in times of extraordinary flood. Weirs erected in public rivers before the time of Edw. I., although an obstruction to navigation, are legalized by subsequent acts of the legislature (a). The right of the public to navigate a public river is paramount to any right of property in the crown, which never had the power to grant a weir so as to obstruct the public navigation; and if a weir, which was legally granted in such a river caused obstruction at any subsequent time, it became a nuisance (b).

(x) Salk. 637.
(y) 13 Hen. VIII. p. 15, b.
(z) *Weld* v. *Hornby*, 7 East, 195.

(a) *Williams* v. *Wilcox*, 3 Nev. & P. 606.
(b) S. C.

---

(2) It should be remarked, however, that the declaration in *Smith* v. *Kemp* was for breaking and entering the *close* of the plaintiff, and fishing in the free fishery of the plaintiff *in the said close.* See Carthew's Rep. p. 285.

CHAPTER XXII.

FRAUDS, STATUTE OF.

Stat. 29 Car. II. c. 3, entitled, An Act for Prevention of Frauds and Perjuries.

I. *Introduction.—The first, second, and third Sections, relating to parol Demises, Assignments and Surrenders, p. 833.*

II. *The fourth and seventeenth Sections, relating to Agreements, p. 838; On the Effect of Parol Evidence of a Variation or Waiver of a written Agreement, p. 867.*

III. *The fifth and sixth Sections, relating to the Execution and Revocation of Wills, p. 870; and the Stat. 1 Vict. c. 26, for the Amendment of the Laws with respect to Wills, p. 889.*

I. *Introduction.—The first, second, and third Sections, relating to parol Demises, Assignments, and Surrenders.*

INTRODUCTION.—This statute, the wise provisions of which have been so often and so justly commended (1), originated with Lord *Nottingham,* who probably was assisted by Sir *Matthew Hale,* Sir *F. North,* and Sir *Leoline Jenkins,* an eminent civilian (a). Sir *M. Hale,* however, died a few months before the act passed into a

(a) See *Ash* v. *Abdy,* 3 Swanst. 664; *Guildford's Life,* p. 109.
Gilb. Eq. R. 171, and Lord Keeper

---

(1) Lord *Nottingham* used to say of this statute, that every line of it was worth a subsidy. Lord Keeper Guildford's Life by R. North, p. 109. See also *Chaplin* v. *Rogers,* 1 East, 194, where Lord *Kenyon,* C. J., said, "It is of great consequence to preserve unimpaired the several provisions of the statute of frauds, *which is one of the wisest laws in our statute book.*"

law (2) ; and this circumstance may possibly account for the inaccuracies which have been discovered in the composition (*b*). To detail all the clauses of this statute, and to notice the construction which they have received in a variety of decisions, would far exceed the limits prescribed to this Abridgment. The object of the present chapter will be merely to select such of the provisions of the statute of frauds as will fall within the scope of this work, and to subjoin, in a regular series, the cases which have arisen, and the decisions thereon.

1st Section.—By this statute, *for prevention of many fraudulent practices, which are commonly endeavoured to be upheld by perjury and subornation of perjury*, it is enacted, that " All leases, estates, interests of freehold, or terms of years, or any uncertain interest of, in, to, or out of any messuages, manors, lands, tenements, or hereditaments, made or created by livery and seisin only, or by parol, and not put in writing, and signed by the parties so making or creating the same, or their agents thereunto lawfully authorized *by writing*, shall have the force and effect of leases or estates at will only."

2nd Section.—" Except all leases, not exceeding the term of three years from the making thereof, whereupon the rent reserved to the landlord, during such term, shall amount unto two third parts, at the least, of the full improved value of the thing demised."

Collecting the meaning of the first section (*c*), by aid derived from the language and terms of the second, and the exception therein contained, I think, that the *leases*, &c. meant to be vacated by the first section, must be understood as *leases* of the *like* kind with those in the second section, but which conveyed *a larger interest* to the party *than for a term of three years*, and such also as were made *under a rent reserved thereupon*. Hence, where the plaintiff (*d*) agreed *by parol*, with the defendant, for the purchase of a standing crop of mowing grass, then growing in a close of the defendant's, for a certain sum ; it was holden, that the agreement was not a lease, estate, interest of freehold, or term of years, " or

(*b*) See Doug. 244, n.
(*c*) Per *Ellenborough*, C. J., in *Crosby*
v. *Wadsworth*, 6 East, 602.
(*d*) S. C.

---

(2) Sir M. Hale died on the 25th of December, 1676. The parliament met on the 15th February following, and this statute received the royal assent on the 16th April, 1677. From the circumstance of this statute not having passed until after the death of Sir M. Hale, Lord Mansfield inferred, that it could not have been drawn by him ; more especially as the bill was introduced in the usual manner, and not upon any reference to the judges. See *Wyndham* v. *Chetwynd*, 1 Burr. 418.

an uncertain interest of, in, to, or out of lands created by parol," within the meaning of the first section, so as to be void on the ground of not *having been in writing*. A lease by parol for a year and a half, to commence after the expiration of a lease which wants a year of expiring, is good; for it does not exceed three years from the making. *Ryley* v. *Hicks*, M. 2 Geo. II. per *Raym.*, Bull. N. P. 173; 1 Str. 651, *S. C.*, but probably from a different note. But a parol lease for three years, to commence from a future day, is void. *Baker d. Nelson* v. *Reynolds*, B. R. E. 1785, from Mr. Balguy's note, Serjt. Hill's MSS. vol. 21, p. 167. In *Inman* v. *Stamp*, B. R. Trin. 55 Geo. III. *Dampier*, J., said, the practice had been with the foregoing case of *Ryley* v. *Hicks*, although he rather inclined to think that the second section of this statute, taken with sect. 4, was confined to leases executed by possession, on which two thirds of the improved rent were reserved. This opinion of *Dampier*, J., was discussed in *Edge* v. *Strafford*, 1 Tyrw. 295; 1 Cr. & Jerv. 391, *S. C.*, (recognizing *Inman* v. *Stamp*, 1 Stark. N. P. C. 12,) in which it was holden, that a verbal agreement to take ready furnished lodgings "for two or three years," inasmuch as it did not exceed three years, was valid as a lease; and whatever remedy could be had upon it, in the character of a lease, might be resorted to; but being a contract for an interest in land, and consequently falling within the 4th section, which requires a note in writing, no action would be supported for not entering on or occupying the demised premises. A parol demise (e), valid under the 2nd section, may contain the same special stipulations as a regular lease, and such stipulations may be proved by parol. In an action for the breach of an agreement, whereby the defendant agreed to take of the plaintiff certain premises for fifteen years (f), it appeared, by the evidence of an attorney, that he had prepared a draft of a lease, which he had sent to an attorney on the part of the defendant for perusal, who made some alterations in it, and returned it; that soon after, the defendant, being unable to perform the agreement, applied to the plaintiff to cancel it; to which the plaintiff did not object, upon being indemnified against the expense which he had incurred; but before he would try to let it again, he required the defendant to relinquish the agreement by writing, whereupon the defendant wrote on the draft of the lease as follows: "I hereby request Mr. Shippey to endeavour to let the premises to some other person, *as it will be inconvenient to me to perform my agreement for them*, and for so doing, this shall be a sufficient authority. I. Derrison." The defendant having refused to make any compensation, this action was brought. It was admitted, that at the time when the agreement for the lease was entered into, it was not reduced into writing, nor was any

---

(e) Lord *Bolton* v. *Tomlin*, 5 A. & E. 856.

(f) *Shippey* v. *Derrison*, 5 Esp. N. P. C. 190.

memorandum or note made of it. It was objected, that the agreement was void by the statute of frauds; and *Hawkins* v. *Holmes*, 1 P. Wms. 770, was cited. But per Lord *Ellenborough*, C. J., "It is not necessary that the note in writing should be contemporaneous with the agreement. It is sufficient if it has been made at any time, and adopted by the party afterwards; and then any thing under the hand of the party, expressing that he had entered into the agreement, will satisfy the statute, which was only intended to protect persons from having parol agreements imposed on them. In this case, the indorsement says, that he was unable to perform the agreement for the premises, and it is written on the draft of the lease of those premises, which had been perused and altered by his own attorney. It is sufficient with respect to the case from Peere Williams, to observe, that was an agreement purely executory, and nothing more than the bare draft of the lease, which was not signed by the party." Where the lessee of a house, and his partner in trade, agreed to pay the lessor annually, during the residue of the lessee's term, ten per cent. on the cost of new buildings if the lessor would erect them; it was holden (g), 1. That this agreement was not required by the statute of frauds to be in writing; 2. That although the partner quitted the premises, he was liable on this collateral agreement during the residue of the term. So where a landlord who had demised premises by a lease for a term of years at 50*l.* a year, after some years were expired, agreed with the tenant to lay out 50*l.* in making improvements upon them, the tenant undertaking to pay the landlord an increased *rent* of 5*l.* a year during the remainder of the term, to commence from the quarter preceding the completion of the work: the agreement was reduced into writing, but the defendant refused to sign it. The improvements were finished in November, 1827, and the defendant, after the Christmas following, paid the increased rent for that quarter; but refused to pay it afterwards. An action of assumpsit having been brought for the arrears for two years and upwards; it was holden (h), that the landlord was entitled to recover; for this case did not fall within the statute, for though called a rent, it was not so in the strict technical meaning of the term; it was a matter of mere personal contract, and that this case was governed by the foregoing of *Hoby* v. *Roebuck.*

Any unknown Interest in Land.]—The defendant had agreed (i), by parol, that the plaintiff should have the liberty of stacking coals

---

(g) *Hoby* v. *Roebuck and another*, 7 Taunt. 157.

(h) *Donellan* v. *Read*, 3 B. & Ad. 899.

(i) *Wood* v. *Lake*, Say. Rep. 3 (3).

A short note of this case, when it was first argued and adjourned, will be found in Serjt. Hill's MSS. vol. 26, p. 287.

---

(3) This authority appears questionable, upon the ground that an easement cannot be granted even for a term of years without deed. *Bird* v.

upon part of a close belonging to the defendant, for the term of seven years; and that, during this term, the plaintiff should have the sole use of that part of the close (4). After the plaintiff had, pursuant to this agreement, enjoyed the liberty of stacking coals for three years, the defendant locked up the gate of the close. The question was, whether this agreement was good for seven years! *Lee,* C. J., and *Denison,* J., were of opinion that it was; observing, that in the case of *Webb* v. *Paternoster,* Palm. 71, it was laid down that the grant of a license to stack hay upon land did not amount to a lease of the land; and although it was said in that case, that such a license, provided the grant were for a time certain, was irrevocable, yet it did not follow, that an interest in the land did thereby pass. As the agreement, in the present case, was only for an easement, and not for an interest in the land, it did not amount to a lease; and, consequently, it was, notwithstanding the statute, good for seven years. *Foster,* J., concurred in opinion, that the agreement did not amount to a lease; but he inclined to be of opinion, that the words in the statute, " any uncertain interest in land," extended to this agreement, and, consequently, that it was not good for more than three years. *Lee,* C. J., and *Denison,* J., were of opinion, that these words related only to interests which are uncertain *as to the time of their duration.* After consideration, it was holden, that the agreement, though by parol, was good for seven years.

Shall have the Force and Effect of Leases at will ONLY.] Notwithstanding these words, a lease by parol, for a longer term than three years, will enure as a tenancy from year to year. In an action against a tenant (*k*), for double rent, for holding over after the expiration of his term, and a regular notice to quit, the first count in the declaration stated a holding under a certain term, determinable on the 12th of May then last past; and other counts stated a holding from year to year, determinable on the same day. It appeared in evidence, that the defendant had held the premises for two or three years, under a parol demise for twenty-one years from the day mentioned, to which the notice to quit referred. It was contended, at the trial, that the holding should have been stated according to the legal operation of it, as a tenancy at will;

(*k*) *Clayton* v. *Blakey,* 8 T. R. 3.

Higginson, 4 Nev. & M. 505. Although the parol grant of an easement cannot be enforced, yet it may operate as a license, and may be set up as a defence to an action of trespass. *Wood* v. *Manley,* 11 A. & E. 34; 3 P. & D. 5. See Sugden's Law of Vendors and Purchasers, vol. 1, p. 138, 10th ed., on the case of *Wood* v. *Lake.*

(4) From a MS. note of this case it appears, that the consideration to be paid by the plaintiff for the liberty of stacking the coals, was 20*s.* for every stack.

and as there was not any count adapted to that statement, the plaintiff ought to be nonsuited. *Rooke*, J., however, considering that it amounted to a tenancy from year to year, overruled the objection, and plaintiff obtained a verdict. On motion to set aside the verdict, on the ground of a misdirection, Lord *Kenyon*, C. J., said, that the direction was right, for such holding now operates as a tenancy from year to year. The meaning of the statute was, that such an agreement should not operate as a term; but what was then considered as a tenancy at will has since been properly construed to enure as a tenancy from year to year. If a landlord lease for seven years by parol (*l*), and agree that the tenant shall enter at Lady-day and quit at Candlemas, though the lease be void by the statute of frauds, as to the duration of the term, the tenant holds under the terms of the lease, in other respects; and therefore the landlord can only put an end to the tenancy at Candlemas.

3rd Section.—"And moreover, that no leases, estates, or interests, either of freehold, or terms of years, or any uncertain interest, not being copyhold or customary interest, of, in, to, or out of any messuages, manors, lands, tenements, or hereditaments, shall be assigned, granted, or surrendered, unless it be by deed, or note in writing signed by the party so assigning, granting, or surrendering the same, or their agents thereunto lawfully authorized *by writing*, or by act and operation (*m*) of law." The mere cancelling, in fact, of a lease (*n*), cannot be considered as either a deed or note in writing within the meaning of this clause, and, consequently, will not be a surrender. A parol assignment of a lease from year to year is void under this clause (*o*). So a parol surrender of a lease (*p*). An insufficient notice to quit, accepted by the landlord, does not amount to a surrender by operation of law; and there cannot be a surrender to operate in futuro (*q*).

II. *Fourth and seventeenth Sections relating to Agreements, p. 838; On the Effect of Parol Evidence of a Variation or Waiver of a Written Agreement, p. 867.*

4th Section.—"No action shall be brought, whereby to charge any executor or administrator, upon any special promise, to answer

(*l*) *Doe d. Rigge* v. *Bell*, 5 T. R. 471.
(*m*) *Thomas* v. *Cook*, 2 B. & A. 119.
(*n*) *Roe d. Berkeley* v. *Abp. of York*, 6 East, 86; *Doe d. Courtail* v. *Thomas*, 9 B. & C. 288.
(*o*) *Bottina* v. *Martin*, 1 Campb. 318.

(*p*) *Matthews* v. *Sawell*, 8 Taunt. 270; 2 Moore, 262, S. C.
(*q*) *Johnstone* v. *Hudlestone*, 4 B. & C. 922, cited by *Parke*, in *Doe d. Murrell* v. *Milward*, 3 M. & W. 332.

damages out of his own estate; or to charge the defendant, upon any special promise, to answer for the debt, default, or miscarriage of another person; or to charge any person, upon any agreement made upon consideration of marriage; or upon any contract or sale of lands, tenements, or hereditaments, or any interest in or concerning them; or upon any agreement that is not to be performed within the space of one year from the making thereof, unless the *agreement* upon which such action shall be brought, or some memorandum or note thereof, shall be in writing, and signed by the party *to be charged* therewith, or some other person thereunto by him lawfully authorized." This section was intended for the relief of personal representatives and others, and it was not thereby intended that they should be charged further or otherwise than by common law they were chargeable. Before the statute, a promise made, with reference to any of the subjects mentioned in this section, would not have made the party promising liable, unless such promise had been founded on a sufficient consideration (r). The same rule holds since the statute, with this addition, that such promise, and the consideration (s) on which it is founded, must be in writing, and be signed by the party to be charged, or his agent. It is not, however (t), necessary that such consideration should appear in express terms; it would undoubtedly be sufficient in any case, if the memorandum is so framed that any person of ordinary capacity must infer from the perusal of it, that the consideration stated in the declaration, and no other, was the consideration upon which the undertaking was given. If an action is brought for the non-performance of the promise, it is not necessary that it should be stated in the declaration (u), that the agreement was in writing; it will be sufficient for the plaintiff to produce a written agreement in evidence at the trial (5); but if such agreement be pleaded in bar of another action, it must be shown, on the face of the plea, that it was in writing; for, otherwise, it would not appear, that it was an agreement whereon an action might be maintained (x).

(r) *Barrell* v. *Trussell*, 4 Taunt. 117.

(s) *Wain* v. *Warlters*, 5 East, 10; recognised in *Saunders* v. *Wakefeld*, 4 B. & A. 595, and *Jenkins* v. *Reynolds*, 3 B. & B. 14; although Ld. *Eldon*, in *Exp. Minet*, 14 Ves. 189, and in *Exp. Gardom*, 15 Ves. 286, had questioned the authority of *Wain* v. *Warlters*, according to the remark of *Dallas*, C. J., in *Boehm* v. *Campbell*, 8 Taunt. 682. But see the observations of *Best*, C. J., on the two cases in Chancery in *Morley* v. *Boothby*, 3 Bingh. 113. See also *Clancy* v. *Piggott*, 2 Ad. & Ell. 481.

(t) *Hawes* v. *Armstrong*, 1 Bingh. N. C. 761, and see *Raikes* v. *Todd*, 8 A. & E. 846; 1 P. & D. 138; *Kennaway* v. *Treleavan*, 5 M. & W. 498.

(u) *Anon.*, Salk. 519; 3 Burr. 1890; per *Yates*, J., S. P.

(x) *Case* v. *Barber*, T. Raym. 450.

---

(5) A plea of tender to the action will supersede the necessity of this proof; for by payment of money into court upon that plea, the defendant admits the cause of action. *Middleton* v. *Brewer*, Peake's N. P. C. 15.

The objection (*y*), that there is no contract in writing, need not be pleaded specially, but may be set up under *non assumpsit*. The word "action," duly interpreted, embraces every suit in equity (*z*). Having premised that the preceding remarks apply to each of the clauses in this section, and that they are introduced in this place for the sake of avoiding repetition, I shall proceed to consider the several clauses separately.

No Action shall be brought to charge any Executor or Administrator, upon any special Promise, to answer Damages out of his own Estate.]—The leading case on this clause is that of *Rann* v. *Hughes*. It was stated in the declaration (*a*), "that disputes had arisen between the testatrix and the intestate, which had been referred to arbitration ; that the arbitrator awarded, that the intestate should pay to the testatrix a sum of money on a day appointed ; that afterwards the intestate died, possessed of effects sufficient to pay the sum awarded ; that at the time of the death of the testatrix, the sum awarded remained unpaid, by reason of which the defendant, as administratrix, became liable to pay the plaintiffs, as executors, the said sum, and, being so liable, the defendant, (not saying as administratrix,) in consideration thereof, promised to pay the same." Pleas.—1. *Non assumpsit.* 2. *Plene administravit.* 3. An outstanding debt, on bond, and *plene administravit præter.* The replication took issue on all the pleas. Verdict for the plaintiffs on the first issue, and damages assessed : on the other issues, for the defendant. The plaintiffs entered judgment for the damages assessed and costs, against the defendant *generally*. On a writ of error in the Exchequer Chamber, it was assigned for error, that the defendant was impleaded as administratrix of the intestate, yet judgment was given against her *generally*, and without any regard to her having goods of the intestate in her hands to be administered. The Court of Exchequer Chamber reversed the judgment. Upon a writ of error from this judgment, in the House of Lords, the following question was put to the judges : Whether sufficient matter appeared upon the declaration to warrant, after verdict, the judgment entered up against the defendant in error in her personal capacity (*b*) ? *Skynner*, C. B., delivered the unanimous opinion of the judges, 1. That there was not a sufficient consideration to support this demand, as a personal demand against the defendant : inasmuch as the defendant did not derive any advantage from the promise, for it was a promise generally to pay upon request, what she was liable to pay upon request in another right, and the promise was not founded on any consideration of forbearance, or the

---

(*y*) *Eastwood* v. *Kenyon*, 3 P. & D. 276 ; 11 A. & E. 438 ; *Buttemere* v. *Hayes*, 5 M. & W. 456, *ante*, p. 118.

(*z*) Per Lord *Eldon*, C., *Cooth* v. *Jackson*, 6 Ves. 31.

(*a*) *Rann and another, Executors of Mary Hughes*, v. *Isabella Hughes, Administratrix of John Hughes*.

(*b*) D. P. 14 May, 1778 ; 4 Bro. P. C. p. 27, Tomlin's ed. ; 7 T. R. 350, n.

like, which might have supported it. 2. That the promise not being founded on any consideration, the circumstance of its being in writing (which might be presumed after verdict,) would not assist the case; for by the law of England, an agreement merely written, and not being a specialty, required a consideration. 3. That the statute of frauds had not taken away the necessity of a consideration; for that statute was made for the relief of personal representatives, and did not intend to charge them further, than by common law they were chargeable.

Or to charge the Defendant upon any special Promise to answer for the Debt, Default, or Miscarriage of another Person.]—In order to bring a case within this clause of the statute, it is essentially necessary that the person, on whose behalf the promise is made, should be liable, as well as the promiser, or, as it is sometimes expressed, (though the propriety of the expression has been questioned,) (6) that the promise should be collateral, and not original. This distinction will be illustrated by the following cases, which are arranged under two divisions: first, cases within the statute; secondly, cases not within the statute.

1. *Cases within the 2nd Clause of the 4th Section.*—In an action upon the case, the plaintiff declared, that the defendant, in consideration that the plaintiff would let his gelding out to hire to J. S. (c), promised the plaintiff that J. S. should re-deliver the gelding, but that J. S. never did re-deliver him. It was objected, that the plaintiff had not any remedy against the party upon the contract, for not re-delivering the gelding, except by an action of trover upon the subsequent tort, in case of demand and refusal; and, therefore, as such remedy accrued from a wrong, subsequent to the contract, the present case was not within the meaning of the statute; but the court overruled the objection, observing, that the party was also liable in detinue upon the original delivery or bailment, the bailment having been such as in its nature required a re-delivery; and if the bailee will not re-deliver the thing bailed, the only adequate remedy is an action of detinue against the bailee; consequently, this promise of the defendant's, that J. S. should re-deliver the horse bailed, for which there was a remedy against J. S. upon the bailment, was a collateral promise, and, therefore, a promise to answer for the act and default of another, within the statute. A. had wrongfully, and without the license of B., ridden his horse, and thereby caused his death; it was holden (d), that

(c) *Buckmyr* v. *Darnall*, Ld. Raym. 1085; Salk. 27, B. R.; 6 Mod. 248, S. C.

(d) *Kirkham* v. *Marter*, 2 B. & A. 613.

(6) "Many of the doubts upon this statute have arisen from making use of the word collateral, which is not a word used in the statute." Bull. N. P. 281.

a promise by a third person to pay the damage thereby sustained, in consideration that B. would not bring any action against A., is a collateral promise within the statute of frauds, and must be in writing. The defendant, in consideration that the plaintiff would not sue J. S. (e), promised to pay the plaintiff the money due from J. S.: this was holden to be within the statute, for there was not any consideration stated for which the plaintiff had promised not to sue; and if there had, J. S. could not have availed himself of this agreement between the defendant and plaintiff, but the debt would still have subsisted, and, consequently, the promise was collateral. J. S. was indebted to the plaintiff in a sum of money (f), for the recovery of which the plaintiff had commenced an action; whereupon the defendant, in consideration that the plaintiff would stay his action against J. S., promised to pay the plaintiff the money owing to him by J. S. This was holden to be clearly within the statute; on the ground that there was a debt of another still subsisting, and a promise to pay it. So also, if plaintiff (g) become bail for a stranger, in consideration of defendant's request, and of defendant promising to indemnify plaintiff against the consequences, an action cannot be maintained unless the promise be in writing.

An opinion formerly prevailed, that, in order to bring a case within the statute, it was necessary that there should be an existing debt owing from the person on whose behalf the undertaking was made, *at the time* of such undertaking. Hence, a promise on the behalf of another, for the payment of the price of goods, *before* the delivery of such goods, was holden not within the statute: because at the time of the promise there was not any debt (h) (7). But this distinction was overruled in the following cases:—In an action for goods sold and delivered (i), it appeared in evidence, that the goods in question had been delivered to J. S. in consequence of a *parol* promise by the defendant to the plaintiff in these words, "*I will pay you, if J. S. will not.*" J. S. was entered as the debtor in the plaintiff's books. The court were of opinion, that

(e) *Rothery* v. *Curry*, Bull. N. P. 281.
(f) *Fish* v. *Hutchinson*, 2 Wils. 94.
(g) *Green* v. *Cresswell*, 10 A. & E. 453; 2 P. & D. 430; questioning the decision in *Thomas* v. *Cook*, 8 B. & C.

728.
(h) *Mawbrey* v. *Cunningham*, Sittings after H. T. 1773, cited in *Jones* v. *Cooper*, Cowp. 228.
(i) *Jones* v. *Cooper*, Cowp. 227.

---

(7) In *Legge* v. *Gibson*, B. R. M. 29 Geo. III., MS., *Buller*, J., said, "that he had always been of opinion that Lord *Mansfield's* doctrine in *Cunningham* v. *Mowbray* was right, and warranted by the statute; because in these cases, when a third person is called in, the real meaning is, that the party will not trust the person first applying, and gives credit to the last; that Lord *Mansfield's* distinction between a promise made at the time and afterwards was sound. This case had been overruled, but he had seen no reason to alter his opinion."

this promise by the defendant was a collateral undertaking within the statute. The defendant had asked M. (*k*) (one of the plaintiffs,) whether he was willing to serve J. S. with goods? M. answered, that he did not know J. S.; to which the defendant replied, "*If you do not know him, you know me, and I will see you paid.*" M. then said, he would serve him; to which the defendant answered, "He is a good chap; *but I will see you paid.*" A letter was afterwards received by the plaintiffs from J. S. containing an order for certain goods, which were afterwards sent to him. The plaintiffs made J. S. the debtor for these goods in their books; J. S. having refused to pay for the goods, an action for goods sold and delivered was brought against the defendant. The court held, that the case was within the statute, there not having been any promise in writing, and gave judgment for the defendant; *Buller, J.*, observing, that the general rule now was, that *if the person for whose use the goods are furnished be liable, any other promise by a third person to pay that debt must be in writing.*

The plaintiff, a woollen-draper, in London (*l*), employed a rider to receive orders from his customers in the country. The defendant, meeting with the rider at Deal, desired him to write to the plaintiff, to request him to supply the defendant's son (who traded in the West Indies,) with whatever goods he might want, *on his, the defendant's credit*; and at the same time said, "Use my son well; charge him as low as possible, and *I will be bound for the payment of the money, as far as* £800 *or* £1000." The rider accordingly wrote to the plaintiff the following letter: "Mr. Hayman of this town says, his son will call on you, and leave orders; and he has promised me to see you paid, if it amounts to £1000. N. B. If deal for twelve months' credit, and pay in six or eight months, expects discount in proportion." Soon after the son received goods from the plaintiff to the amount of £800, which were delivered to him in consequence of the before mentioned engagement of the father. *The son was debited in the plaintiff's books*, and having been applied to for payment, wrote the following answer to the plaintiff: "In answer to your letter, I can only say, that I understand your credit for the goods was twelve months, which was also mentioned by your rider to my father: I shall, at this rate, make you remittances for the different parcels as they become due." The son afterwards became a bankrupt, and this action was brought against the father, to recover the value of the goods. *Heath, J.*, (who tried the cause,) directed the jury to consider whether the plaintiff gave credit to the defendant *alone*, or to him *together with his son*; that in the former case they should find a verdict for the plaintiff; in the latter for the defendant; being of opinion, that if any credit was given to the son, the promise of the defendant, not being in writing, was void by the statute. A verdict was found for the defendant, and a rule obtained to set it aside; which the court afterwards discharged; being clearly of opinion, that this promise, not being in writing, was void by the statute, as it appeared from the letter of Hayman, the son, that credit was given to him as well as to the defendant. Where a parol agreement is entered into for the payment of the debt (*n*), or part of the debt, of another person, and also for the performance of some other act, the promise to perform which would not of itself be required to be in writing, an action cannot be maintained on such agreement; because the agreement being entire, it is incapable of separation, so as to enable the plaintiff to recover on one part alone. J. S. being indebted to several persons (*o*), and among others to the plaintiff, (who had incurred considerable expenses in law proceedings against J. S. for the recovery of his debt), and a proposal having been made, at a meeting of the creditors, that they should receive a composition of 10*s*. in the pound; all the creditors consented to take it except the plaintiff, who refused to consent, unless the law expenses before mentioned were also paid; whereupon the defendant promised to pay those expenses, and to accept bills drawn by the plaintiff on him to the amount of the composition. The plaintiff accordingly drew bills on the defendant to that amount, which he accepted and paid; but the defendant having refused to pay the law expenses, the plaintiff paid them to his own attorney, and then brought an action against the defendant, declaring on the special agreement, and also for money paid: it was holden, 1st, That the agreement *being by parol*, the plaintiff could not recover on the special count; for, though the agreement was to do something beyond payment of part of the debt of another, yet, being entire, the plaintiff could not separate it, and recover on one part only. 2dly, That the plaintiff could not recover on the count for money paid; because, in order to support that count, there should have been evidence of the plaintiff having paid a sum of money which defendant was bound to pay; whereas here the plaintiff, not the defendant, was bound to pay the law expenses. Where a defendant, having entered into a guarantee in writing, and become liable upon it, at a period of more than six years before the commencement of suit, verbally promised within six years that the matter should be arranged, and afterwards, upon an action being brought, pleaded *actio non accrevit*, &c.; it was holden (*p*), that the statute of frauds having been once satisfied by the original promise being in writing, it was not necessary, in order to take the case out

(*n*) *Lexington* v. *Clarke*, 2 Ventr. 223.
(*o*) *Chater* v. *Beckett*, 7 T. R. 201, recognized in *Thomas* v. *Williams*, 10 B.
& C. 664, and *post*, p. 847.
(*p*) *Gibbons* v. *M'Casland*, 1 B. & A. 690.

of the statute of limitations, that the latter promise should also be in writing. But see stat. 9 Geo. IV. c. 14, s. 1, *ante*, p. 139.

A., an agent for some manufacturers, sells to B., who likewise acted as an agent, a quantity of shoes, and receives bills of exchange in payment. B., being pressed to indorse them, refuses; but writes a letter to A., in which he incloses the bills; and adds, " that should they not be honoured when due, he (B.) would see them paid;"—it was holden (*q*), that this was a sufficient agreement within the statute to bind B. to pay for the goods, in default of his principal.

2. *Cases not within the 2nd Clause of the 4th Section.*—An action having been brought against the defendant, an attorney, and two others, for appearing for the plaintiff without a warrant, the record was carried down to be tried at the assizes (*r*), when the defendant promised, in consideration that the plaintiff would not further prosecute the action, defendant would pay £10 and costs of suit. In an action on this promise, the question was, whether this was a promise within the statute; and it was holden, that it was not ; as not being a promise to pay the debt of another, but to pay the party's own debt. A., the plaintiff's testator (*s*), brought an action of assault and battery against J. S.; the cause being at issue, the record entered, and just coming on to be tried, the defendant, in consideration that A. would withdraw the record, promised to pay him a sum of money, and the costs to that time; whereupon A. withdrew his record; A. died : the plaintiff, his executor, brought this action upon the special promise of defendant. The defendant pleaded the statute of frauds, *viz.* that there was not any agreement in writing, touching the promise. On demurrer, the court gave judgment for the plaintiff; being of opinion, that this promise was not within the statute; that it was an original promise sufficient to found an assumpsit against the defendant; that it was a lien upon the defendant, and upon him only; that J. S. was not a debtor; the cause was not tried; it did not appear that J. S. had been guilty of any default or miscarriage; there might have been a verdict for him, if the cause had been tried ; J. S. never was liable to the particular debt, damages, or costs; that the true difference was between an original promise, and a collateral promise; the former promise was not within the statute, the latter was. In an action of *indebitatus assumpsit*, for money laid out to the use of defendant (*t*), by the plaintiff, at the request of the defendant, the evidence was that one D. coming to the plaintiff, by the defendant's order, for money to pay some workmen who had been employed in the garden of J. S., the infant grandson of

(*q*) *Morris* v. *Stacey*, Holt's N. P. C. 153.

(*r*) *Stephens* v. *Squire*, 5 Mod. 205.

(*s*) *Read* v. *Nash*, 1 Wils. 305, recog-
nized in *Bird* v. *Gammon*, 3 Bingh. N. C. 889 ; 5 Scott, 213, *ante*, p. 140.

(*t*) *Harris* v. *Huntbach*, 1 Burr. 373, and MSS.

defendant, the plaintiff refused to pay the money unless the defendant would sign a receipt. Whereupon the defendant wrote the following note, *viz.* " This is to certify, that it is my request that you pay to Mr. D., on the account of J. S., for the workmen's use, the sum of £   ;" signed by the defendant. It was objected, that this was evidence only of a collateral security, and not of a debt from the defendant. But *per Cur.*, the money was manifestly advanced on the defendant's credit; and its being on account of the defendant's grandson, an infant, is a matter merely between the defendant and the infant. The defendant is the debtor to the plaintiff; the objection arises from an ambiguous use of the term *collateral* promise; by which the defendant must mean a special undertaking upon a special contingency; as, if such a one does not pay, I will. It is also applied to a joint undertaking, which is joint and several, and it is called collateral as between the two debtors, but it is original in each of them as to the creditor; so in this case, there is an original undertaking by the defendant, though, perhaps, she may undertake this as a security for her grandson, as between him and her. The defendant is the only original debtor; for the infant never could be liable. A., being indebted to the plaintiff for the rent of a dwelling-house (*u*), in arrear for three quarters of a year, and becoming insolvent, made a bill of sale of all his goods in the house, to the defendant Leaper, in trust, to be sold by him as broker, for the benefit of A.'s creditors; defendant accordingly advertised a sale: on the morning of the sale, and while the defendant was in possession of the goods upon the premises, the plaintiff (the landlord) came there to distrain for his rent; whereupon the defendant, in consideration that the plaintiff would not distrain, promised to pay the plaintiff the rent in arrear. Upon this promise of the defendant an action was brought, and the question was, whether the promise was within the statute. It was holden, that it was not (8). In the foregoing case, although

(*u*) *Williams* v. *Leaper*, 2 Wils. 308; 3 Burr. 1886; *S. C.*, recognized by *Ellenborough*, C. J., and *Grose*, J., in *Castling* v. *Aubert*, 2 East, 325; *Edwards* v. *Kelly*, 6 M. & S. 204; and in *Bampton* v. *Paulin*, 4 Bingh. 264.

(8) It is extremely difficult to collect from the reports the precise ground on which this case was decided. Lord *Mansfield*, C. J., and *Wilmot*, J., seem to have founded their opinion on a supposition that the plaintiff had actually distrained and was in possession of the goods at the time when the promise was made; but the fact was, that the plaintiff was not in possession, (see 2 Wils. 308,) he had merely given notice to distrain. See the remark of *Lawrence*, J. (2 East, 330). *Yates*, J., argued upon the ground of the defendant being in possession, and seems to have thought that the defendant derived an advantage from the plaintiff's permitting him to proceed in the sale of the goods; and that this was an original consideration to the defendant. *Aston*, J., considered the goods

there was no actual distress, yet there was a power of immediate distress, and an intention to enforce it ; it should seem, therefore, that the judges must have considered that power as equivalent to an actual distress ; and the promise extended only to the amount of the arrears and rent then due, and for which the right of distress might have been immediately exercised. But where the promise was to pay the arrears of rent then due, and also the accruing rent up to a future day, and this promise was by word only, it was holden, that the promise to pay the accruing rent exceeded the consideration, and could not be sustained on the ground on which former cases had been sustained, and was nothing more than a promise to pay money that would become due from a third person (*x*); and consequently, being within the mischief intended to be remedied by the statute, was void ; and being void in part, could not be held good as to the other part (*y*). The words of this section have always been construed to mean, that the person for whose debt the collateral promise is made, must still remain him-

(*x*) *Thomas* v. *Williams*, 10 B. & C. 664.   *Chater* v. *Becket*, 7 T. R. 201.   See also
(*y*) *Lexington* v. *Clarke*, 2 Ventr. 223;   *Mechelen* v. *Wallace*, 7 A. & E. 49.

---

as the only debtor; and consequently that the promise was not a promise to pay the debt of the tenant. Such is the report of this decision ; but whatever may have been the grounds on which it proceeded, the case has since been recognized. In assumpsit for the repair of a carriage, it appeared that the carriage had been bought by J. S., but had been sent to be repaired by the defendant. When the repairs were done, the defendant directed the plaintiff to pack up the carriage, and send it on board ship Upon the plaintiff's inquiring who was to pay for the repairs, the defendant said, as he had sent the carriage, he would pay for the repairs. Accordingly, the carriage was packed up and sent on board ship, and a bill made out and delivered to the defendant. It was contended, on the part of the defendant, that the undertaking ought to have been in writing ; but per Lord *Eldon*, C. J., in general cases to make a person liable for goods delivered to another, there must be either an original undertaking by him, so that the credit was given solely to him ; or there must be a note in writing. There may, however, be cases where this rule does not apply : *If a person obtains possession of goods, on which the landlord has a right to distrain for rent, and he promises to pay the rent, though it is clearly the debt of another, yet a note in writing is not necessary.* That applies precisely to the present case. The plaintiff had, to a certain extent, a lien on the carriage, and he parted with it on the defendant's promise to pay. This takes the case out of the statute. *Houlditch* v. *Milne*, 3 Esp. N. P. C. 86. So where plaintiff having distrained for rent arrear, goods, which the tenant was at that time about to sell, agreed with defendants to deliver up the goods, and to permit them to be sold by one of defendants for the tenant, upon defendant's joint undertaking to pay to plaintiff all such rent as should appear to be due to him from the tenant. *Edwards* v. *Kelly*, 6 M. & S. 204.

self liable to the debt. Hence, where a defendant, taken on a *ca. sa.*, is discharged out of custody by consent of the plaintiff, the debt itself is extinguished; and therefore a promise by a third person to pay that debt on condition of that discharge is an original promise, and not within the statute (*z*).

The case of *Keate* v. *Temple*, 1 Bos. & Pul. 158, where a question arose on the clause of the statute now under consideration, is omitted on account of its special circumstances.

The plaintiff, who was the broker of J. S. (*a*), having policies of assurance of great value in his hands, belonging to J. S., accepted several bills for the accommodation of J. S. A loss having happened on the policies, which the underwriters had agreed to pay, but which J. S. could not receive without having the policies to produce, the plaintiff was applied to, to give them up for that purpose to the defendant, into whose hands J. S. had at that time transferred the management of his insurance concerns. Some of the plaintiff's acceptances being then outstanding, (and particularly an acceptance on a bill in the hands of J. N.) upon which writs had been sued out (though not then executed) against J. S. as drawer, and the plaintiff as executor, the plaintiff refused to deliver up the policies, they being the only securities he had against his acceptances, without an indemnity; whereupon it was *verbally* agreed between plaintiff, defendant, and J. S., that the defendant, upon the policies being made over to him, should pay the amount of the bill in the hands of J. N., with the costs incurred, and should lodge money in a banker's hands for the satisfaction of the remainder of the acceptances as they became due. In pursuance of this agreement, the defendant paid into the bankers' hands the sum agreed on, and the plaintiff delivered up the policies to the defendant. The defendant received from the underwriters the amount of their subscriptions, far exceeding the sum in dispute; but refused to pay the debt and costs on the bill in J. N.'s hands; in consequence of which refusal the plaintiff was arrested at the suit of J. N. Upon this the plaintiff brought an action against the defendant, declaring upon the special agreement, and also for money had and received. The question was, whether the promise of the defendant to pay the sum due from J. S. for the debt and costs, on having the policies of assurance delivered to him, was within the statute? The court were of opinion, that it was not; *Lawrence*, J., observing, that "this was to be considered as a purchase by the defendant of the plaintiff's interest in the policies. It was not a bare promise to the creditor to pay the debt of another due to him, but a promise by the defendant to pay what the plaintiff

(*z*) *Goodman* v. *Chase*, 1 B. & A. 297.
(*a*) *Castling* v. *Aubert*, 2 East, 325, cited by *Parke*, B., in *Andrews* v. *Smith*, 2 Cr. M. & R. 631, as an exception to

the general rule that the undertaking is collateral, wherever there is an original debt.

would be liable to pay, if the plaintiff would furnish him with the means of doing it." And per *Le Blanc*, J. "This is a case where one man, having a fund in his hands, which was adequate to the discharge of certain incumbrances, another party undertook, that if the fund were delivered up to him, he would take it with the incumbrances; this, therefore, has not any relation to the statute of frauds." To an action of assumpsit for not replacing some bank annuities (b), the produce of which had been paid by the plaintiff to the defendant, on his undertaking to replace the same within a certain time; the defence was, that the defendant being indebted to the plaintiff, as stated in the declaration, and also to several other persons, an investigation was had of his affairs, and it was found that his estate was inadequate to the payment of his debts; whereupon it was agreed between the plaintiff, and the other creditors, and one J. S., that J. S. should, out of his own money, pay the plaintiff and the other creditors 10s. in the pound on the amount of their debts, to be received by them in full satisfaction, and that they should assign their debts to J. S.; that J. S., in pursuance of this agreement, tendered out of his own money, a sum amounting to 10s. in the pound on the debt of the plaintiff, which he refused to accept. It was objected, that the undertaking of J. S. not being in writing, this defence could not be sustained. But the court overruled the objection, *Chambre*, J., observing, that this was a contract to purchase the debts of the several creditors, and not a contract to pay the debt of the defendant. It was of the substance of the agreement, that the debts should remain in full force to be assigned to J. S., and J. S. had a right to make use of the names of the original creditors to recover the same to the full amount, if defendant had effects to satisfy the debts. He concluded with this remark: "We all agree upon the point, that it is a contract for the purchase of the debts of the defendant, which is not prohibited by the statute of frauds."

A promise (c) to a *debtor* to pay his debt to a third person, is not a promise to answer for the debt of another within this section, which applies only to promises made to the person, to whom another is answerable.

To bring a case within this clause there must be a good consideration for the promise in writing (d). A count averring that J. A. made a bill of sale of goods to the plaintiff, in consideration of a debt of £122 19s. due from J. A. to the plaintiff, and the plaintiff being about to sell his goods in satisfaction of his debt, the defendant undertook to pay him £122 19s. if he would forbear to sell, does not show that this is a promise to pay the debt of another with sufficient distinctness to bring the case within the statute (e).

(b) *Anstey* v. *Marden*, 1 Bos. & Pul. N. R. 124.
(c) *Eastwood* v. *Kenyon*, 3 P. & D. 276; 11 A. & E. 438.
(d) *Barrell* v. *Trussell*, 4 Taunt. 117.
(e) *Ib.*

A written proposal to pay a moiety of the debt of another, if the creditor will at a specified time of meeting accept this proposal and discharge the debtor, is not binding unless the creditor accede to the terms in writing (*f*).

Or to charge any Person upon any Agreement made in Consideration of Marriage.]—It is now settled, notwithstanding former decisions to the contrary (*g*), that this clause does not extend to mutual promises to marry: consequently, such promises are binding, although they are not reduced into writing and signed by the party. The plaintiff declared (*h*), that in consideration of her having promised to marry the defendant, he promised to marry her at his father's death; and averred, that the father was dead, but the defendant had refused to marry plaintiff, and had since married A. B. On non-assumpsit pleaded, and verdict for plaintiff, it was moved, in arrest of judgment, that this parol promise was not good in law. But (after argument) it was holden, that the case was not within the statute; for that this clause in the statute related only to contracts in consideration of marriage; and the defendant, having married another person, had disabled himself from performing the promise; the plaintiff, therefore, could not apply to the spiritual court to have a performance decreed, and consequently was entitled to a compensation in damages.

Or upon any Contract or Sale of Lands, &c., or any Interest in or concerning them.]—It must be observed, that the statute does not expressly and immediately vacate such contract, if made by parol; it only precludes the bringing an action to enforce it, by charging the contracting party, or his representatives, on the ground of such contract, and of some supposed breach thereof. Hence, if the contract be executed, the parties cannot treat it as a nullity (*i*). An agreement conferring an exclusive right to the vesture of land (*k*), during a limited time and for given purposes, is a contract or sale of an interest in, or at least an interest concerning, lands; therefore, an agreement to sell a growing crop of mowing hay, to be mowed and made into hay by the purchaser, requires a written agreement. So also a sale of growing poles (*l*), or of growing underwood (*m*), is within the 4th section. *Indebitatus assumpsit* for a crop of potatoes bargained and sold (*n*), and dug up and carried away by virtue of such bargain and sale. On the 21st day of November, 1807, the defendant purchased of the plaintiff,

(*f*) *Gaunt* v. *Hill*, 1 Stark. N. P. C. 10.

(*g*) *Philpott* v. *Wallet*, 3 Lev. 65; Freem. 241, *S. C.*

(*h*) *Cork* v. *Baker*, 1 Str. 34; *Harrison* v. *Cage*, Ld. Raym. 386; S. P. per *Ward*, C. B., Carth. 467, 8.

(*i*) Per *Ellenborough*, C. J., delivering the opinion of the court in *Crosby* v. *Wadsworth*, 6 East, 602.

(*k*) *Crosby* v. *Wadsworth*, 6 East, 602; *Carrington* v. *Roots*, 2 M. & W. 248.

(*l*) *Teal* v. *Auty*, 2 Brod. & Bingh. 99; 4 Moore, 542. See, however, *Smith* v. *Surman*, 9 B. & C. 561; 4 M. & Ry. 455.

(*m*) *Scorell* v. *Boxall*, 1 Y. & J. 396.

(*n*) *Parker* v. *Staniland*, 11 East, 362. But see *Mayfield* v. *Wadsley*, 3 B. & C. 364; 5 D. & Ry. 224.

by parol, at so much per sack, a crop of potatoes then in the ground. The defendant was to dig them up and remove them without delay, as the plaintiff wanted the ground for other purposes. The defendant accordingly dug up and carried away more than half the crop, but was prevented by the frost from taking the remainder. The plaintiff brought his action to recover the value of the whole crop. The defendant paid into court a sum of money equivalent to the value of that portion of the crop which he had taken. It was objected, that this was a contract or sale of an interest in land. But per Lord *Ellenborough*, C. J. The liberty which the defendant had of entering the close for the purpose of taking the crop, amounted to an easement, and nothing more. No interest in the land itself passed, or was intended to pass, by the contract. The defendant could not have maintained ejectment to recover possession of the crop. In this respect this case differed materially from that of *Crosby* v. *Wadsworth*, which he was not disposed to extend; in that case the subject matter of the contract was the *prima vestura*, for which ejectment lies, as does also trespass *quare clausum fregit*. But trespass *quare clausum fregit* could not be brought by this defendant for a trespass to the close in which the crop of potatoes grew. It did not follow, that, because the crop of potatoes was not at the time of the contract a chattel, it was, therefore, an interest in land. *Bayley*, J., said, it was a thing whose growth was at an end, and in this respect distinguishable from the case of *Bristow* v. *Waddington* (o), which was a contract for the next year's crop of hops ; and that he considered the land merely as a warehouse, and that the contract was substantially the same thing, as if the potatoes had been deposited in a warehouse at the time of the sale. And if the potatoes had been sold while growing, and at so much per acre (p), to be dug and carried away by the purchaser, without any time limited ; or if they had been in a growing state, and sold by the cover (q), to be turned up by the seller ; or if they had been sold in a similar state at so much per sack (r), to be dug by the purchaser at the usual time, and to be then paid for ; the decision would have been the same, that such sales do not fall within the 4th section. Plaintiff (s) and defendant orally agreed, (in August,) that defendant should give £45 for the crop of corn on plaintiff's land, and the profit of the stubble afterwards ; that plaintiff was to have liberty for his cattle to run with defendant's ; and that defendant was also to have some potatoes growing on the land, and whatever lay grass was in the fields ; defendant was to harvest the corn and dig up the potatoes ; and plaintiff was to pay the tithe. It was holden, that it did not appear to

---

(o) 2 Bos. & Pul. 452, in which case the question indirectly arose, but did not require decision.

(p) *Warwick* v. *Bruce*, 2 M. & S. 205.

(q) *Evans* v. *Roberts*, 5 B. & C. 829 ;

8 D. & Ry. 611.

(r) *Sainsbury* v. *Matthews*, 4 M. & W. 343.

(s) *Jones* v. *Flint*, 10 A. & E. 753 ; 2 P. & D. 594.

be the intention of the parties to contract for any interest in land, and, therefore, not within the statute of frauds, but a sale of goods and chattels, as to all but the lay grass, and, as to that, a contract for the agistment of the defendant's cattle. A parol agreement for the sale of crops may be good between an outgoing and incoming tenant, for there would be no sale of any interest in the land, for that would come from the landlord (s). But where a landlord agreed to let a farm by parol, and the tenant was to take the growing crops and pay for them, and also for the work, labour, and materials in preparing the land for tillage, it was holden, that the case was within the 4th section. At the time when the contract was made, the crops were growing upon the land, the tenant was to have had the land as well as the crops, and the work, labour, and materials were so incorporated with the land as to be inseparable from it (t). An action of *indebitatus assumpsit* (u), with a count on a *quantum meruit*, for moieties of crops of wheat sold by the plaintiff to the defendant, and accordingly reaped for his, the defendant's, own use; and also a count for money had and received. The case was, that the plaintiff, by a parol agreement, had let land to the defendant, for which he was to take two successive crops, and to render the plaintiff a moiety of the crops in lieu of rent. While the crops of the second year were on the ground, an appraisement of them was taken by both parties, and the value ascertained. The defendant having afterwards refused to pay a moiety of the value, this action was brought. It was objected, on a case reserved, that the agreement was within the statute, because it related to land; but the court overruled the objection; *Eyre*, C. J., observing, that the circumstance of the appraisement seemed to put an end to this point. It was true, that, as the case originally stood, the plaintiff had a claim to a moiety of the produce of the land, under a special agreement; but that special agreement was executed by the appraisement. This circumstance of the appraisement afforded clear proof that the plaintiff sold what the defendant had agreed was his; and the price having been ascertained, brought this to the case of an action for goods sold and delivered (9). Where tenant, on expiration of term being about to remove fixtures, to

(s) *Mayfield* v. *Wadsley*, 3 B. & C. 357; 5 D. & Ry. 224.
(t) *E. of Falmouth* v. *Thomas*, 1 Cr. & M. 89; 3 Tyrw. 26.
(u) *Poulter* v. *Killingbeck*, 1 Bos. & Pul. 397.

---

(9) "The contract, if it had originally concerned an interest in land, after the agreed substitution of pecuniary value for specific produce, no longer did so: it was originally an agreement to render what should have become a chattel, *i. e.* part of a severed crop in that shape, in lieu of rent, and by a subsequent agreement it was changed to money instead of remaining a specific render of produce." Per *Ellenborough*, C. J., 6 East, 612.

which he was entitled, agreed to sell them to his landlord at a valuation, which was afterwards, and after the time expired, made and signed by the two brokers; it was holden (x), that this was not a sale of any interest in land. But although the contract is not itself wholly void (y) under the statute, merely on account of its being by parol, so that, if the same is executed, the parties cannot treat it as a nullity; yet, while it remains executory, it may be discharged by parol, before any thing is done under it which can amount to a part execution of it. An agreement to occupy lodgings at a yearly rent, payable in quarterly portions, (the occupation to commence on a future day,) is an agreement relating to an interest in land, within the meaning of this clause (z). A., being possessed of a messuage and premises for the residue of a certain term of years, agreed with B. to relinquish possession to him, and to suffer him to become tenant thereof for the residue of the term, in consideration of B.'s paying a sum of money towards completing some repairs. It was holden (a), that this was an agreement relating to the sale of an interest in land. This clause comprehends sales of land by auction as well as other sales (b); hence, where land had been sold by auction, and the contract having been abandoned, an action was brought to recover the deposit, in which action the plaintiff declared specially on the contract; it was holden, that it was incumbent on the plaintiff to prove a contract in writing (c), in the manner specified in the statute; and that the entry by the auctioneer of the buyer's name could not be considered as a sufficient memorandum and signature of the agreement so as to satisfy the requisitions of the statute: although a different doctrine had been laid down with regard to the 17th section, relating to the sale of goods, upon the construction of which it has been holden (d), that the auctioneer must be considered as the agent of both parties, and a memorandum made by him sufficient to bind the bargain. But in a latter case of *Emmerson* v. *Heelis* (e), it was solemnly decided that a signing by the auctioneer is a signing by an agent for the purchaser, although the contract be a contract for the sale of an interest in land. N. The purchaser was not present at the sale, but bid by an agent. The entry of the name of the best bidder by the auctioneer in his book, is just the same as if the bidder had written his own name. But putting down the name in

(x) *Hallen* v. *Runder*, 1 Cr. M. & R. 266.

(y) *Crosby* v. *Wadsworth*, 6 East, 602.

(z) *Inman* v. *Stamp*, 1 Stark. N. P. C. 12, Ld. *Ellenborough*, C. J., recognized in *Edge* v. *Strafford*, *ante*, p. 835.

(a) *Buttemere* v. *Hayes*, 5 M. & W. 456.

(b) *Walker* v. *Constable*, 2 Esp. N. P. C. 659; 1 Bos. & Pul. 306, per *Erskine*, C., in *Buckmaster* v. *Harrop*, 7 Ves. 341.

(c) *Stansfield* v. *Johnson*, coram *Eyre*, C. J., 1 Esp. N. P. C. 101. But see the remarks of *Eldon*, C., in *Coles* v. *Trecothick*, 9 Ves. jun. 249, adopted by *Erskine*, C., in *Buckmaster* v. *Harrop*.

(d) *Simon* v. *Metivier*, 1 Bl. R. 599; 3 Burr. 1921, recognized as to this point in *Hinde* v. *Whitehouse*, 7 East, 558.

(e) 2 Taunt. 38, recognized in *White* v. *Proctor*, 4 Taunt 209.

catalogue, neither attached to, nor referring to, conditions of sale, will not suffice (*f*). See cases decided upon the 17th section, *post*, p. 863, and *ante*, tit. "Auction," p. 172.

Or upon any Agreement that is not to be performed within the Space of One Year from the making thereof.]—This clause extends to those cases only, where, by the express agreement of the party, the act is not to be performed within a year. Hence it has been holden (*g*), that a promise to pay money on the return of a ship, which happened not to return within two years after the promise made, was not within the statute; for, by possibility, the ship might have returned within a year. So where an action was brought upon an agreement (*h*), in which the defendant promised, for one guinea, to give the plaintiff so many on the day of his marriage. The marriage did not take effect until nine years after the agreement; and the question was, whether the agreement ought to have been in writing. *Holt*, C. J., (before whom the cause was tried,) advised with all the judges, and it was said by the majority of them, (for there was a diversity of opinion, and *Holt* differed from the majority) (10), "Where the agreement is to be performed upon a contingency, *and it does not appear on the face of the agreement* that it is to be performed after the year, there a note in writing is not necessary; for the contingency might happen within the year; but where it *appears*, from the whole tenor of the agreement, that it is to be performed *after* the year, there a note in writing is necessary." So where the plaintiff declared (*i*), that the defendant's testator, in consideration that the plaintiff would become his housekeeper, and take upon herself the care and management of his family, as long as it should please both parties, undertook to pay her wages at the rate of £   for one year; *and also by his will to bequeath to her an annuity of £   for life, payable yearly from the day of his death;* and then averred, that she became his house-

---

(*f*) *Kenworthy* v. *Schofield*, 2 B. & C. 945.

(*g*) By the judges, ex. rel. *Treby*, C. J., *Anon.*, Salk. 280, recognized by *Wilmot*, J., in 3 Burr. 1281.

(*h*) *Peter* v. *Compton*, Skin. 353, cited by *Denison*, J., in *Fenton* v. *Emblers*, 3 Burr. 1281.

(*i*) *Fenton* v. *Emblers*, *Exor.*, 3 Burr. 1278; 1 Bl. R. 353, *S. C.*

---

(10) If the marriage had taken effect within the year, all the judges agreed no writing was necessary; but as, in the case before them, the marriage did not happen within the year, but nine years after the promise, *Holt*, C. J., and the minority of the judges, were of opinion that it ought to have been in writing, because the design of the statute was, not to trust to the memory of witnesses for a longer time than one year. See *Smith* v. *Westall*, Lord Raym. 316, 7. *Holt*, C. J., had expressed the same opinion with respect to the necessity of the contingency happening within the year in order to take a case out of the statute, in *Francam* v. *Foster*, Skin. 326.

keeper, and so continued for three years and upwards, but that the defendant's testator had not bequeathed her the annuity; the agreement having been by parol, it was contended, that the case was within the statute, for it could not be performed on the part of the testator within a year; for a whole year from his death was to elapse, before the annuity, or any part of it, would become payable. To this it was answered, that the action was brought for the testator not having done what he ought to have done in his lifetime, *viz.* bequeathing the annuity by will, which might have been done within the year. The court held the case not within the statute; and *Denison*, J., said, "The statute of frauds plainly means an agreement not to be performed within the space of a year, and expressly and specifically so agreed. A contingency is not within it, nor any case that depends upon a contingency. It does not extend to cases, where the thing *may* be performed within the year." Nor to a case, where the work agreed to be done was done entirely within the year (*k*), and it was the intention of the parties, founded on a reasonable expectation that it should be so; although no time was fixed by the agreement for the performance. So where A., being indebted to the plaintiff, promised plaintiff that in consideration of his forbearing to sue, A.'s executor should pay him £10,000; it was holden (*l*), that the statute did not require this promise to be in writing.

An objection upon this clause was taken in the case of *Poulter* v. *Killingbeck*, 1 Bos. & Pul. 397, (*ante*, p. 852,) but the court were of opinion, that the subsequent agreement relieved the case from the objection. By the word *performed*, in this clause, the legislature meant a complete and not a partial performance. Hence, if it appear to have been the understanding of the parties to a contract at the time, that it was not to be completed within a year (*m*), although it might, and was in fact in part performed within that time, such contract is within this clause, and if the requisites of the statute are not complied with, it cannot be enforced. A contract for a year's service, to commence at a subsequent day, being a contract not to be performed within the year, is within this clause, and must be in writing (*n*). A contract (*o*), whereby a coachmaker agreed to let a carriage for a term of five years, in consideration of receiving an annual payment for the use of it, but which, by the custom of the trade, is determinable at any time within that period upon the payment of a year's hire, is an agreement not to be performed within a year, within the meaning of this clause, and, therefore, must be in writing.

(*k*) *Donellan* v. *Read*, 3 B. & Ad. 906, distinguishing *Boydell* v. *Drummond.*

(*l*) *Wells* v. *Horton*, 4 Bingh. 40.

(*m*) *Boydell* v. *Drummond*, 11 East, 142.

(*n*) *Bracegirdle* v. *Heald*, 1 B. & A. 722; *Snelling* v. *Lord Huntingfield*, 1 Cr. M. & R. 20, S. P.

(*o*) *Birch* v. *E. of Liverpool*, 9 B. & C. 392.

*Unless the Agreement or some Memorandum or Note thereof shall
be in Writing.*]—The word *agreement* is not to be understood in the
loose incorrect sense, in which it is sometimes used as synonymous
to *promise or undertaking*, but in its proper and correct sense, as
signifying a mutual contract on consideration between two or more
parties. Hence, the whole agreement, that is, not the promise
only, but the consideration on which it is founded, must be in
writing (*p*). The word "*agreement*," however, is satisfied (*q*), if
the writing states the subject matter of the contract, the consideration, and is signed by the party to be charged; and it is sufficient
if the consideration appear by necessary inference and implication.
But where (*r*) B. contracted, by a writing signed by him alone, to
work for plaintiff in his trade, and for no other person during twelve
months, and so on from twelve months to twelve months, until B.
should give notice of quitting; it was holden, that such agreement
was invalid for want of mutuality; for admitting that a promise must
be implied on the master's part, to pay B. for his labour, yet that
would be the same in any service to which B. might engage himself.
An action was brought to recover the value of goods, which had
been furnished by the plaintiff to one Nichols (*s*), under a written
agreement signed by the defendant in the following words: " I guarantee the payment of any goods which Mr. John Stadt delivers
to I. Nichols." It was objected, that this guarantee was void,
because it did not express any consideration for the defendant's promise to answer for the debt of another person; that, in order to
ascertain whether there was any consideration expressed for this
purpose, the proper way was, to consider, whether any action could
have been brought on the supposed agreement, by the defendant
against the plaintiff. But here there was no undertaking on the
part of the latter to deliver goods to Nichols, and no action would
have lain against him, had he refused to deliver any; Lord *Ellenborough* said, that though by the agreement the plaintiff was not
obliged to deliver goods, there appeared a sufficient consideration
for the defendant's promise to be answerable, if any should be delivered; the stipulated delivery of the goods to Nichols was a consideration appearing on the face of the writing, and when the delivery took place, the consideration attached: he should therefore
admit evidence of the delivery of the goods. V. for plaintiff. Upon
an application to the court to set aside this verdict, the court said,
that this case differed from *Wain* v. *Warlters*, as the agreement
here contained the thing to be done by the plaintiff, which was the
foundation of the defendant's promise; and that the delivery of the
goods was a sufficient consideration, although no cross action upon

---

(*p*) *Wain* v. *Warlters*, 5 East, 10, re-
cognized in *Saunders* v. *Wakefield*, 4 B.
& A. 595, and *Jenkins* v. *Reynolds*, 3 B.
& B. 14, and *Hawes* v. *Armstrong*, 1
Bingh. N. C. 761.

(*q*) *Laythoarp* v. *Bryant*, 2 Bingh. N.
C. 744.
(*r*) *Sykes* v. *Dixon*, 9 A. & E. 693.
(*s*) *Stadt* v. *Lill*, 1 Campb. 242; 9
East, 348, *S. C.*

the agreement could have been brought against the plaintiff, either at the suit of the defendant or of Nichols. Rule nisi refused. If the writing contain a promise to pay the *debt* of another, it is sufficient without mentioning the amount (*t*).

17th Section.—" No contract for the sale of any goods, wares, and merchandizes, for the *price* of ten pounds or upwards, shall be good, except the buyer shall accept part of the goods so sold, and actually receive the same; or give something in earnest to bind the bargain, or in part of pa men ; or that some note or memorandum in writing, of the said bargaih, be made and signed by the parties to be charged by such contract, or their agents thereunto lawfully authorized."

No Contract for the Sale of any Goods.]—This branch of the statute extends to executory contracts, that is, contracts to be completed at a future time, as well as other contracts; but in many cases a distinction used to be taken between those contracts, where the thing contracted for was existing *in solido*, and capable of being delivered at the time of the contract, or would be at the time of delivering a personal chattel (*u*), and those, where it was requisite that something should be done, in order to put the thing into the state in which it was to be delivered according to the contract; the former having been holden to be within (*x*) the statute, the latter not (*y*). But now, by 9 Geo. IV. c. 14, s. 7, it is provided, that the enactment of this 17th section shall extend to all contracts for sale of goods of the value of £10 sterling and upwards, notwithstanding the goods may be intended to be delivered at some future time, or may not at the time of such contract be actually made, procured, or provided, or fit or ready for delivery, or some act may be requisite for the making or completing thereof, or rendering the same fit for delivery. This last act has the word *value*, and not *price;* hence where an executory contract is entered into for the fabrication of goods, without any agreement as to price, the memorandum of the contract required by the statute of frauds, is sufficient without specification of price (*z*).

The statute of frauds does not exclude parol evidence that a written contract for sale of goods, purporting to be made between A. the seller, and B. the buyer, was on B.'s part made by him only as agent for C. (*a*).

Goods, Wares, and Merchandizes.]—Shares in a joint stock banking company are not (*b*) within these words; but the sale of a

(*t*) *Bateman* v. *Phillips*, 15 East, 272.
(*u*) *Watts* v. *Friend*, 10 B. & C. 446.
(*x*) *Rondeau* v. *Wyatt*, 2 H. Bl. 63; *Garbutt and another* v. *Watson*, 5 B. & A. 613; *Smith* v. *Surman*, 9 B. & C. 568.
(*y*) *Clayton* v. *Andrews*, 4 Burr. 2101;

Groves v. *Buck*, 3 M. & S. 178.
(*z*) *Hoadly* v. *M'Laine*, 10 Bingh. 482; 4 M. & Sc. 340.
(*a*) *Wilson* v. *Hart*, 7 Taunt. 295.
(*b*) *Humble* v. *Mitchell*, 3 P. & D. 141.

share in a mining company has been holden (c) by the Court of King's Bench, in Ireland, to be within the statute.

Except the Buyer shall accept Part of the Goods so sold, and actually receive the same.]—In order to take a contract for the sale of goods, of the price of £10 or upwards, out of the statute, there must be either a receipt and acceptance, by the vendee, of the whole or a part of the thing sold, or something given in earnest, or a part payment of the consideration; otherwise the agreement must be reduced to writing in the manner specified by this section. Where goods are sold under a parol order subject to approval (d), the vendee must refuse to accept them within a reasonable time; otherwise he will be considered as having accepted them. Where goods are ponderous, and incapable of being handed over from one to another, there need not be an actual delivery (12), but it may be done by that which is tantamount, such as the delivery of a key of the warehouse, in which the goods are lodged, or by delivery of other indicia of property. So if the purchaser deals with the commodity, as if it were in his actual possession, this will supersede the necessity of proving actual delivery. Hence (e), after a bargain and sale of a stack of hay between the parties on the spot where the stack stood, evidence that the vendee actually sold part of it to another person, by whom, though against the vendee's approbation, it was taken away, is sufficient to warrant the jury in finding a de-

(c) *Boyce* v. *Green*, Batty, 608.

(d) *Coleman* v. *Gibson*, 1 M. & Rob.

168, Lord *Tenterden*, C. J.

(e) *Chaplin* v. *Rogers*, 1 East, 192.

---

(12) In an action for not delivering a quantity of rice, it appeared that the defendant had informed the plaintiff that defendant had a quantity of rice to sell; there was no evidence to prove any contract made, but the plaintiff produced an order on Bennett and Co. to deliver to him twenty barrels of rice, which was signed by defendant; and a witness proved that defendant had told him that he had sold twenty barrels of rice to the plaintiff, at 17s. per hundred. The plaintiff then proved the delivery of the order for the rice to the warehouseman of Bennett and Co. The rice not having been taken away immediately, the defendant afterwards countermanded the delivery, in consequence of which Bennett and Co. refused to deliver the rice to the plaintiff, who sent for it some days after the order had been countermanded. *Eyre*, C. J., was of opinion, that the order for delivery, directed to the persons in whose possession the rice was, amounted to a delivery, so as to take the case out of the statute. *Searle* v. *Keeves*, 2 Esp. N. P. C. 598. But where a hogshead of wine in the warehouse of the London Dock Company was sold for a sum exceeding 10l., and a delivery-order given to the vendee, and there was not any contract in writing: it was holden, that the acceptance of the delivery-order by the vendee was not equivalent to an actual acceptance of the wine, so as to take the case out of the statute. *Bentall* v. *Burn*, Ry. & M. 107; 3 B. & C. 423.

livery to, and an acceptance by, the vendee, so as to take the case out of the statute. So where a person having purchased a horse of a horse-dealer, desired him to keep the horse at livery for him, and the horse-dealer accepted the order, and put the horse out of his sale-stable into another stable: this was holden (*f*) to be a sufficient delivery, so as to take the case out of the statute. But where a horse was sold by verbal contract, but no time was fixed for the payment of the price; the horse was to remain with the vendors for twenty days without any charge to the vendee; at the expiration of that time the horse was sent to grass, by the direction of the vendee, and by his desire entered as the horse of one of the vendors: it was holden (*g*), that there was no acceptance of the horse by the vendee. So where a vendee verbally agreed, at a public market, with the agent of the vendor to purchase twelve bushels of tares, (then in vendor's possession, constituting part of a larger quantity in bulk,) to remain in vendor's possession until called for, and the agent, on his return home, measured the twelve bushels and set them apart for the vendee; it was holden (*h*), that this did not amount to an acceptance by the latter, so as to take the case out of the statute, for there cannot be any actual acceptance, so long as the buyer continues to have a right to object, either to the quantum or quality of the goods. So where A. agreed to purchase a horse from B. for ready money, and to take him within a time agreed upon; about the expiration of that time, A. rode the horse, and gave directions as to its treatment, &c., but requested that it might remain in B.'s possession for a further time, at the expiration of which he promised to fetch it away and pay the price, to which B. assented, the horse died before A. paid the price or took it away: it was holden (*i*), that there was not any acceptance within the statute. So where A., a merchant in London (*k*), had been in the habit of selling goods to B., resident in the country, and of delivering them to a wharfinger in London, to be forwarded to B. by the first ship; and in pursuance of a parol order from B., goods were delivered to, and accepted by, the wharfinger, to be forwarded in the usual manner: it was holden, that this was not an acceptance by the buyer sufficient to take the case out of the statute. So where defendant employed plaintiff to construct a waggon, and, whilst the vehicle was in the plaintiff's yard unfinished, procured a third person to fix on the iron-work and a tilt; it was holden (*l*), that this did not constitute an acceptance. If a purchaser of goods draws the edge

(*f*) *Elmore* v. *Stone*, 1 Taunt. 458.
(*g*) *Carter and another* v. *Toussaint*, 5 B. & A. 855.
(*h*) *Howe* v. *Palmer*, 3 B. & A. 321.
(*i*) *Tempest* v. *Fitzgerald*, 3 B. & A. 680.

(*k*) *Hanson and another* v. *Armitage*, 5 B. & A. 557, recognizing *Howe* v. *Palmer*.
(*l*) *Maberley* v. *Sheppard*, 10 Bingh. 99.

of a shilling over the hand of the vendor, and returns the money into his own pocket, which in the north of England is called the striking off a bargain, this is not a part payment (m) within the statute. A. having sent to B. (n) a bale of sponge (in consequence of a verbal order from B.), for which he charged 11s. per pound; B. returned it, and at the same time wrote a letter to A., stating, that the sponge had been examined, and having been found not to be worth more than 6s. per pound, he had sent it back. It was holden, that there was not such a receipt and acceptance of the goods as would take the case out of the statute. So where a corn-factor, at Nottingham, and who also had a warehouse at Derby, on the 18th November agreed to sell to the defendant a quantity of barley, the property of the plaintiff, and then in the hands of J. S. for the purpose of being kiln-dried, at 38s. per quarter, to go by the corn-factor's first boat, and to be delivered at Derby at the corn-factor's warehouse. The 38s. per quarter was a higher price on account of the delivery being at the corn-factor's expense. Afterwards the defendant went to J. S., told him he had bought the barley, and desired him to see it delivered and measured, and put up properly. Two or three days afterwards the barley was sent by the first boat, and on the 26th November the corn-factor's clerk saw the defendant at Derby, and delivered him the invoice, which the defendant took and requested a week longer for payment, which was allowed him, but on the same day gave notice that he would not accept the barley. The barley arrived at the warehouse at Derby on the 1st of December. In assumpsit for goods sold and delivered, it was holden (o), that there being no note in writing, the contract was void. A. went to the shop of B. and Co., linen-drapers, and contracted for the purchase of various articles, each of which was under the value of £10, but the whole amounted to £70. A separate price for each article was agreed upon; some A. marked with a pencil, others were measured in his presence, and others he assisted to cut from larger bulks. He then desired that an account of the whole might be sent to his house, and went away. A bill of parcels was accordingly sent, together with the goods, when A. refused to accept them. It was holden (p), that this was all one contract, and therefore within the statute. Secondly, that there was no delivery and acceptance of any of the goods so as to take the case out of the operation of this section. Where a joint order (q) is given for several classes of goods, the acceptance of one class is a part acceptance of the whole. But if goods are ordered verbally, the delivery of them to

(m) *Blenkinsop* v. *Clayton*, 7 Taunt. 597.

(n) *Kent* v. *Huskinson*, 3 Bos. & Pul. 233, cited in *Astey* v. *Emery*, 4 M. & S.

262.

(o) *Astey* v. *Emery*, 4 M. & S. 262.
(p) *Baldey* v. *Parker*, 2 B. & C. 37.
(q) *Elliott* v. *Thomas*, 3 M. & W. 170.

a carrier is sufficient to bind the contract, where the purchaser has been in the habit of receiving goods from the vendor by the same mode of conveyance (r). Where a sample is delivered to and accepted by the purchaser (s), and such sample is to be accounted for as part of the commodity sold, this will be considered as a sufficient acceptance and receiving of part of the goods, so as to take the case out of the statute. But the delivery of a sample, which is no part of the things sold, will not (t). Where goods were made to order, and remained in the possession of the vendor at the request of the vendee, with the exception of a small part, which the vendee took away; it was holden (u), that there was not any acceptance of the residue of the goods. To satisfy the statute, there must be a delivery of the goods by the vendor, with an intention of vesting the right of possession in the vendee; and there must be an actual acceptance by the vendee, with an intention of taking to the possession as owner (x). The later cases of *Howe* v. *Palmer*, 3 B. & A. 321; *Hanson* v. *Armitage*, 5 B. & A. 557; *Carter* v. *Toussaint*, 5 B. & A. 855; *Tempest* v. *Fitzgerald*, 3 B. & A. 680; have established, that unless there has been such a dealing on the part of the purchaser as to deprive him of any right to object to the quantity or quality of the goods, or to deprive the seller of his right of lien, there cannot be any part acceptance. See the remark of *Parke*, J., 9 B. & C. 577. Plaintiff entered into a parol agreement to sell to defendant a mare for £20, subject to the condition that, if it should prove to be in foal, defendant should, on receiving £12 from plaintiff, return it on request. Plaintiff delivered the mare and received £20. On its proving to be in foal, he tendered to defendant £12, and requested him to return the mare, which defendant refused to do. It was holden (y), that the contract to return it on payment of £12, was not a distinct contract of sale, but one of the conditions of the original sale to the defendant, and that the delivery of the mare to the defendant took the whole agreement out of the statute.

Or that some Note or Memorandum in Writing of the Bargain be made, and signed by the Parties to be charged by such Contract or their Agents.]—An action on the case was brought against the defendants (z), for not accepting and paying for goods which they had contracted to purchase by the following memorandum in writing: " We agree to give Mr. Egerton 19*d.* per pound for thirty bales of Smyrna cotton, customary allowance, cash three per cent., as soon as our certificate is complete. (Signed) Matthews and Turnbull; and dated 2nd of September, 1803." The defendants had before

(r) *Hart* v. *Sattley*, 3 Campb. 528.
(s) *Hinde* v. *Whitehouse and another*, East, 558; *Kilnitz* v. *Surrey*, 5 Esp. N. P. C. 267.
(t) *Talver* v. *West*, Holt's N. P. C. 178.
(u) *Thompson* v. *Maceroni*, 3 B. & C. 1.

(x) Per *Cur.* in *Phillips* v. *Bistolli*, 2 B. & C. 511.
(y) *Williams* v. *Burgess*, 10 A. & E. 499.
(z) *Egerton* v. *Matthews and another*, 6 East, 307.

become bankrupts, and their certificate was then waiting for the
Lord Chancellor's allowance, and after it was allowed they signed
the memorandum again. It was objected, on the authority of *Wain*
v. *Warlters*, that the contract being altogether executory, and no
consideration for the promise appearing on the face of the writing,
nor any mutuality in the engagement, it was void; but the court
overruled the objection on this ground—that the object and wording of the 17th section was different from that of the 4th section,
in which the word *agreement* was introduced, and upon which
the decision in *Wain* v. *Warlters* proceeded. And Lord *Ellenborough*, C. J., observed, that in this case of *Egerton* v. *Matthews*,
the words of the statute were satisfied, if there were some note or
memorandum in writing, of the *bargain*, signed by the parties to
be charged by such contract. And this was a memorandum of the
bargain, or at least of so much of it as was sufficient to bind the
parties to be charged therewith, and whose signatures to it was all
that the statute required (13). Assumpsit (a) for goods sold and
delivered. Plea, N. A. The plaintiffs, on the 25th January, 1826,
had sent from Worcester to the defendant at Derby, an invoice of
five pockets of hops, and delivered the hops the same day to a carrier to be conveyed from Worcester to Derby, and informed the
defendant, at the same time, that they were so forwarded. The
invoice described the plaintiffs as the sellers, and the defendant as
the purchaser of the hops. The defendant afterwards wrote to the
plaintiffs as follows: "The hops which I bought on the 25th of last
month are not yet arrived, nor have I ever heard of them. I received
the invoice: the last were much longer on the road than they ought
to have been; however, if they do not arrive in a few days, I must
get some elsewhere, and consequently cannot accept them." It was
holden, that this was not a sufficient note in writing.

Signed by the Parties.]—The place of the signature is immaterial. If a person draw up an agreement in his own handwriting,
beginning, "I, A. B., agree, &c." and leave a place for a signature

---

(a) *Richards and another* v. *Porter*, 6 B. & C. 437.

---

(13) It will be observed, that in this case the name of the purchaser,
as well as the seller, appeared in the memorandum, although the purchaser only regularly signed it: but in *Champion* v. *Plummer*, 1 Bos. &
Pul. N. R. 252, where the seller only signed, and the name of the purchaser did not appear on the bill of parcels; it was holden, that the bill
of parcels was an insufficient memorandum of the bargain, because there
cannot be a contract without two parties. See *Cooper* v. *Smith*, 15
East, 103, recognized in *Richards and another* v. *Porter*, 6 B. & C.
439. The price must also be stated in the memorandum. *Elmore* v.
Kingscote, 5 B. & C. 583, recognized in *Acebal* v. *Levy*, 10 Bingh. 383.
But see *ante*, p. 857.

at the bottom, but does not sign it, the agreement will be considered as sufficiently signed (*b*).   In such cases (*c*), however, the question is always open to the jury, whether the party, not having signed it regularly at the foot, meant to be bound by it as it stood, or whether it was left so unsigned because he refused to complete it.   So it seems, if a person be in the habit of printing instead of writing his name, he may be said to sign by his printed name, as well as his written name (*d*).   In an action on the case for the non-delivery of a quantity of gin, bought of the defendants (*e*), it appeared, that at the time the order for the gin was given by the plaintiff to the defendants, a bill of parcels was delivered to the former, the printed part of which was, " London.   Bought of Jackson and Hankin, distillers ;" and then followed in writing "1000 gallons of gin, 1 in 5, gin 7*s*. 350*l.*"   The name of the purchaser was inserted in the bill of parcels (*f*).   About a month after, the defendants also wrote the following letter to the plaintiff : " Sir, we wish to know what time we shall send you part of your order, and shall be obliged for a little time in delivery of the remainder ; must request you to return our pipes. Your's, &c. Jackson and Hankin." It was holden, that by connecting the bill of parcels with the subsequent letter of the defendants, the requisites of the statute were sufficiently complied with.   So where the name of the seller was printed on the bill of parcels, but he had written thereon the name of the purchaser, that was holden to be a recognition of the contract and adoption of the printed name, so as to satisfy the words of the statute (*g*).

Or their Agents thereunto lawfully authorized.]—A sale of goods by auction, has been holden to be within the 17th section of the statute, as a sale of lands by auction is within the 4th section ; see *Kenworthy* v. *Schofield,* 2 B. & C. 945 ; *Walker* v. *Constable,* 1 Bos. & Pul. 306. *ante,* p. 172, tit. " Auction ;" and it has been uniformly holden, ever since the case of *Simon* v. *Metivier* (*h*), that the auctioneer or broker is the agent of both parties, and a memorandum made by him of the bargain, is a sufficient compliance with the terms of the statute, to make the contract of sale binding on each (14).   But the memorandum by the auctioneer must be a

---

(*b*) *Knight* v. *Crockford,* 1 Esp. N. P. C. 190, per *Eyre,* C. J.

(*c*) Per Lord *Abinger,* in *Johnson* v. *Dodgson,* 2 M. & W. 653.

(*d*) Per *Eldon,* C. J., in 2 Bos. & Pul. 239.

(*e*) *Saunderson* v. *Jackson and another,* 2 Bos. & Pul. 238, recognized in *Dobell* v. *Hutchinson,* 3 A. & E. 372, and *post,*

866.

(*f*) See *Champion* v. *Plummer,* 1 Bos. & Pul. N. R. 254.

(*g*) *Schneider* v. *Norris,* 2 M. & S. 286.

(*h*) Per *Ellenborough,* C. J., delivering the opinion of the court in *Hinde* v. *Whitehouse,* 7 East, 569.

---

(14) In like manner, the memorandum in a broker's book, and the bought and sold notes transcribed therefrom, and delivered to the buyers

sufficient memorandum; for where, at a sale by auction of sugars, the auctioneer (having before him the printed catalogue of sale, containing the lots, marks, and number of hogsheads, and the gross

---

and sellers respectively, are sufficient to bind the bargain, the broker being considered as the agent of both parties. *Rucker* v. *Cammeyer*, 1 Esp. N. P. C. 105, ruled by *Kenyon*, C. J., on the authority of *Simon* v. *Metivier;* and per *Ellenborough*, C. J., in *Hinde* v. *Whitehouse*, 7 East, 569, S. P. The broker is the agent of both parties, and, as such, may bind them by signing the same contract on behalf of buyer and seller. But if he does not sign the *same* contract for both parties, neither will be bound. Hence, where the broker, having made a contract, entered it in his book, but did not sign it, and afterwards signed and delivered to the contracting parties bought and sold notes materially differing from each other; it was holden, that there was not any valid contract in writing to bind the parties. *Grant* v. *Fletcher*, 5 B. & C. 436. A material alteration in a sale-note by the broker, after the bargain made, at the instance of the seller, without the consent of the purchaser, annuls the instrument, so as to preclude the seller from recovering upon the contract, evidenced by the instrument so altered by him. *Powell* v. *Divett*, 15 East, 29. "If the broker deliver a different note of the contract to each party contracting, there is no valid contract. Each is bound by the note which the broker delivers; and if different notes are given to the parties, neither can understand the other." Per *Gibbs*, C. J., *Cumming* v. *Roebuck*, Holt's N. P. C. 172, recognized by *Taunton*, J., *Smith* v. *Reynolds*, Somerset Lent Ass. 1831, MS. The traveller of the defendant had sold a quantity of tallow to the plaintiff, to be delivered at a certain time. The plaintiff had signed the bought note, and the traveller had signed the sold note for the defendant and left it with the plaintiff. The tallow not having been delivered at the time specified, plaintiff brought an action and produced in evidence the sold note. The defendant produced in evidence the bought note; between which and the sold note there was a material variance. The plaintiff was nonsuited. This doctrine renders it essentially necessary that a plaintiff should procure an inspection of the other note, before he can commence his action with safety, unless he has retained a copy. Where a broker made an entry of a contract in his book, which he did not sign, but sent to the vendor and purchaser bought and sold notes copied from the book, and signed by him; it was holden, that these were a sufficient memorandum of the bargain, and the parties were bound by the contract so made. *Goom* v. *Aflalo*, 6 B. & C. 117. The bought and sold notes delivered to the parties, and not the entry in the broker's book, are the proper evidence of the contract. *Abbott*, C. J., *Thornton* v. *Meux*, M. & Malk. 43. See *Trueman* v. *Loder*, 11 A. & E. 589; 3 P. & D. 267. The entry in the broker's book is, properly speaking, the original, and ought to be signed by him. The bought and sold notes delivered to the parties ought to be copies of it: a valid contract may probably be made by perfect notes signed by the broker, and delivered to the parties, although the book be not signed, but if the notes are imperfect, an unsigned entry in the book will not supply the defect. *Abbott*, C. J., *Grant* v. *Fletcher*, 5 B. & C. 437.

weights of the sugars; and also another written paper, containing the conditions of sale, which latter he read to the bidders, as the conditions on which the sugars were to be sold; but the two papers were neither externally annexed nor contained any internal reference to each other,) wrote down on the catalogue the name of the highest bidder, and the sum bid for the particular lots; it was holden (i), that the minute made on the catalogue of sale (which catalogue was not by any reference incorporated with the conditions of sale,) was not a sufficient memorandum of a bargain under those conditions of sale. Where, however, goods were sold by auction to an agent (k), and the auctioneer wrote the initials of the agent's name, together with the prices, opposite the lots purchased by him, in the printed catalogue, and the principal, afterwards, in a letter to the agent, recognized the purchase; it was holden, that the entry in the catalogue, and the letter, coupled together, were a sufficient memorandum of the contract. But the agent contemplated by the 17th section, who is to bind a defendant by his signature, must be a third person, and not the other contracting party; and therefore, where an auctioneer wrote down the defendant's name by his authority, opposite to the lot purchased; it was holden (l), that in an action brought in the name of the auctioneer, the entry in such book by the plaintiff, the auctioneer, was not sufficient to take the case out of the statute. But if the entry be made by the auctioneer's clerk, it will suffice (m); for the clerk is not identified with the plaintiff who sues; and in the business which he performs, of entering the name, he is impliedly authorized by the purchaser. A buyer of goods requested D., the agent of the seller, to write a note of the contract in the buyer's book: D. did so, and signed the note with his own name. It was holden (n), that such note was not sufficient to bind the buyer, inasmuch as D. was not his agent. The defendant purchased leasehold premises at an auction, and signed a memorandum of the purchase on the back of the particular of sale, containing the name of the owner and the conditions: it was holden (o), that the defendant was bound, although there was not any signature by the vendor. In *Boydell v. Drummond*, 11 East, 142, it was holden, that the signature of the defendant, in a book intituled "Shakspeare Subscribers, their Signatures," not referring to a printed prospectus which contained the terms of the contract, and which was delivered at the time to the subscribers to the Boydell Shakspeare, could not be connected with the prospectus, so as to take the case out of the statute, inasmuch as such connection could not be established without the intervention of parol evidence,

(i) *Hinde* v. *Whitehouse*, 7 East, 558; *Kenworthy* v. *Schofield*, 2 B. & C. 945, S. P.

(k) *Phillimore* v. *Barry*, 1 Campb. 513.

(l) *Farebrother* v. *Simmons*, 5 B. & A. 333.

(m) *Bird* v. *Boulter*, 4 B. & Ad. 443; 1 Nev. & M. 313.

(n) *Graham* v. *Musson*, 5 Bingh. N. C. 603.

(o) *Laythoarp* v. *Bryant*, 2 Bingh. N. C. 735.

and that would open a door for perjury, which it was the object of the statute to prevent. But where the purchaser of lands by auction signed a memorandum of the contract indorsed on the particulars and conditions of sale, and referring to them, and afterwards he wrote to the vendor, complaining of defect in the title, referring to the contract expressly, and renouncing it; the vendor wrote and signed several letters, mentioning the property sold, the names of the parties, and some of the conditions of sale, insisting on one of them as curing the defect, and demanding the execution of the contract; it was holden (*p*), that these letters might be connected with the particulars and conditions of sale, so as to constitute a memorandum in writing, binding the vendor, although neither the original conditions and particulars, nor the memorandum signed by the purchaser, mentioned, or were signed by, the vendor. If, on the sale by auction of goods, the same person is declared the highest bidder for several lots, a distinct contract arises for each lot; and although all the lots together purchased by the same person exceed £10 in value, yet if the lots are separately of less value than £10 a memorandum in writing is not necessary (*q*). It is to be observed, that neither the 4th nor 17th sections of this statute require that the agent should be authorized *by writing*. A parol authority, therefore, is sufficient (*r*) (15). But the character of agent cannot be supported by one of the contracting parties (*s*). Where A. and B. being jointly interested in a quantity of oil, A. entered into a contract for the sale of it without the authority or knowledge of B., who, upon receiving information of the circumstance, refused to be bound, but afterwards assented by parol, and samples were delivered to the vendees; it was holden (*t*), in an action against the vendees, that B.'s subsequent ratification of the contract rendered it binding. So in *Kinnitz* v. *Surry*, Paley, Pr. and Ag. 143, n. 2nd ed., where the broker, who signed the broker's note upon a sale of corn was the seller's agent, Lord *Ellenborough* held, that if the buyer acted upon the note, that was such an adoption of his agency, as made the note sufficient within the statute. So where A., without authority, made a contract in writing for the purchase of goods by B., and B. subsequently ratified the contract; it was holden (*u*), that such ratification rendered A. an agent lawfully authorized within the statute.

(*p*) *Dobell* v. *Hutchinson*, 3 A. & E. 355.

(*q*) *Emmerson* v. *Heelis*, 2 Taunt. 38.
(*r*) Per *Kenyon*, C. J., in *Rucker* v. *Cammeyer*, 1 Esp. N. P. C. 106. See also *Emmerson* v. *Heelis*, 2 Taunt. 46.

(*s*) *Wright* v. *Dannah*, 2 Campb. 203.
(*t*) *Soames* v. *Spencer*, 1 Dow. & Ry. 32.

(*u*) *Maclean* v. *Dunn*, 4 Bingh. 722. See *Gosbell* v. *Archer*, 2 Ad. & Ell. 500; 4 Nev. & Mann. 485.

(15) The third section, relating to assignments and surrenders of leases, &c., requires that the agent should be authorized in *writing*.

On the Effect of Parol Evidence of a Variation or Waiver of a Written Contract.

The question as to the admissibility of parol evidence to vary or annul a written contract, has recently been before the courts on several occasions. The judgments then delivered, render it unnecessary to insert the earlier decisions. By an agreement in writing, the plaintiff contracted to sell the defendant several lots of land, and to make a good title to them ; and a deposit was paid. It was afterwards discovered, that a good title could not be made to one of the lots ; and it was then verbally agreed between the parties, that the vendee should waive the title as to that lot. The vendor delivered possession of the whole of the lots to the vendee, which he accepted. In an action brought by the vendor to recover the remainder of the purchase-money, the declaration stated, that the defendant agreed to deduce a good title to all the lots except one, and that the vendee discharged and exonerated him from making out a good title to that lot, and waived his right to require the same. Lord *Denman,* C. J., in delivering the opinion of the court (*x*), after reading the 4th section of the statute of frauds, said: " It is to be observed, that the statute does not say, in distinct terms, that all contracts or agreements concerning the sale of lands shall be in writing; all that it enacts is, that no action shall be brought unless they are in writing. And as there is no clause in the act, which requires the dissolution of such contracts to be in writing, it should rather seem that a written contract concerning the use of the lands may still be waived and abandoned, by a new agreement not in writing, and so as to prevent either party from recovering on the contract which was in writing. It is not, however, necessary to give an opinion upon that point; as this is not a waiver and abandonment of the whole written agreement, but only a part of it; and the question is, what is the effect of that? It may be said by the plaintiff, that this does not in any degree vary what is to be done by either party ; that the same land is to be conveyed, there is to be the same extent of interest in the land, and it is to be conveyed at the same time, and the same price is to be paid ; and that it is only an abandonment of a collateral point. But we think the object of the statute of frauds was to exclude all oral evidence as to contracts for the sale of lands, and that any contract which is sought to be enforced, must be proved by writing only. But, in the present case, the written contract is not that which is sought to be enforced, it is a new contract which the parties have entered into, and that new contract is to be proved, partly by the former written agreement, and partly by the new

(*x*) *Goss* v. *Lord Nugent,* 5 B. & Ad. 58.

verbal agreement; the present contract, therefore, is not a contract entirely in writing; and as to the title being collateral to the land, the title appears to us to be a most essential part of the contract, for, if there be not a good title, the land may, in some instances, better not be conveyed at all; but our opinion is not formed upon the stipulation about the title being an essential part of the agreement, but upon the general effect and meaning of the statute of frauds, and that the contract now brought forward by the plaintiff is not wholly a contract in writing." A rule nisi, which had been obtained for entering a nonsuit, was accordingly made absolute.

In a subsequent case (*y*), the written agreement was, that the plaintiff should grant a lease to the defendants, and the defendants should take certain quantities of straw and other things at a valuation, to be made by persons named respectively by plaintiff and defendants, or their umpire, in the usual way; and the defendants entered under the agreement, and took possession of the straw, &c. A parol agreement was afterwards entered into, that the valuation should be made by one D. The defence set up to an action to recover the amount of D.'s valuation was, that no valuation had been made pursuant to the original agreement. It was holden, on demurrer, that, although the part of the written agreement which was varied by parol might have been good of itself without writing, by reason of the acceptance of the straw, &c., yet it was not competent to the parties, by agreement not in writing, to separate into two parts the subject matters of the original agreement, and to substitute a new agreement, not in writing, as to the straw, &c.; and judgment was given for the defendants. In deciding this case, the court adverted to *Goss* v. *Lord Nugent*, as a case in which it was doubted whether it was competent to the parties to waive and abandon an agreement in writing by parol, but expressed no direct opinion on the subject.

In another case, the plaintiff brought his action to recover the deposit paid by him on entering into a written contract, by which the defendant agreed to sell the lease of a house and deliver possession by a day named. It appeared, at the trial, that on that day neither of the parties were in a situation to carry the contract into effect, but within a reasonable time afterwards the obstacles might have been removed; but before that time arrived, the plaintiff insisted that the contract was at an end, and demanded the return of the deposit. The count, upon which the court held the plaintiff might recover, was one for money had and received. Lord *Tindal*, C. J., in delivering the opinion of the court, stated (*z*), that the question was, "Can the day for the completion of the purchase of an interest in land, inserted in a written contract, be waived by a parol agreement, and another day be substituted in its place, so as to

(*y*) *Harvey* v. *Grabham*, 5 A. & E. 61.
(*z*) *Stowell* v. *Robinson*, 3 Bingh. N. C. 928; 5 Scott, 196.

bind the parties? We are of opinion that it cannot. This is an agreement for the sale of land, upon which, by the statute of frauds, section 4, no action can be brought, ' unless it is in writing, and signed by the party to be charged therewith, or his agent thereunto lawfully authorized.' Now we cannot get over the difficulty which has been pressed upon us, that to allow the substitution of a new stipulation as to the time of completing the contract, by reason of a subsequent parol agreement between the parties to that effect, in lieu of a stipulation as to time contained in the written agreement signed by the parties, is virtually and substantially to allow an action to be brought on an agreement relating to the sale of land, partly in writing signed by the parties, and partly not in writing, but by parol only, and amounts to a contravention of the statute of frauds."

In the following case, *in assumpsit* (a), the declaration stated, that plaintiff agreed to buy, and defendant to sell, a cargo, to be delivered " on the 20th to the 22nd instant," to be paid for by an acceptance three months from delivery; and that afterwards, before the 22nd, plaintiff, at request of defendant, gave time for the delivery to the 24th: breach, that defendant, though requested (to wit, on 24th,) to deliver, had not, on 24th or any other time, delivered: special damage by rise of price between the agreement and breach. Plea, that the giving of time was part of a contract for the sale of goods at the price of above £10; and that there was no part acceptance, or earnest, or note or memorandum in writing. Replication, that the giving of time was not part of the contract, &c. It appeared that there was a written contract, as stated in the declaration, for the delivery, " on the 20th to the 22nd," but the 22nd falling on Sunday, plaintiff, at defendant's request, verbally agreed to enlarge the time to the 23rd or 24th. The price fluctuated between the time of the agreement, and the 24th, being higher on the last day. It was understood that the enlargement of time would postpone the delivery of the three months' acceptance. It was holden, that, on these facts, defendant was entitled to the verdict, the enlargement of time having materially varied the contract, substituting for it a new contract on a similar consideration, and not being merely a dispensation from performance on a particular day. The judgment of the court, delivered by Lord *Denman*, contains the following passage, which appears, however, to apply more accurately to the 4th than to the 17th section:—" It was urged by the plaintiff's counsel, that the defendant's argument reduced him to an inconsistency; that he alleged, on the one hand, an alteration of the contract by parol, and yet, on the other, asserted that such alteration by parol could not be made. But this is, in truth, to confound the contract with the remedy upon it.

(a) *Stead* v. *Dawber*, 10 A. & E. 57; M. & S. 21.
2 P. & D. 447, overruling *Cuff* v. *Penn*, 1

Independently of the statute, there is nothing to prevent the total waiver, or the partial alteration, of a written contract not under seal, by parol agreement; and, in contemplation of law, such a contract so altered subsists between these parties; but the statute intervenes, and, in the case of such a contract, takes away the remedy by action."

Plaintiff entered into a written agreement with the defendant, for the purchase of a cargo to be shipped on board a vessel on her next arrival at a certain port. On the arrival of the vessel, the defendant verbally requested a postponement of the shipment, until she should have completed another voyage. Plaintiff assented to this proposal, and the voyage was made. The defendant, on the second arrival of the vessel, declined taking the goods, which were resold by the plaintiff, who brought his action to recover the loss sustained by the defendant's non-performance of the contract. It was holden (b), that the plaintiff could not recover. *Parke,* B., said, "Here there was an original contract in writing to send these goods by the first vessel; an alteration as to the time of their delivery was subsequently made by parol; and the point to be decided is, whether such an alteration, by parol, of the written contract, can be binding. It appears to me that it cannot; and that the same rule must prevail as to the construction of the 17th section, which has already prevailed (c) in the construction of the 4th section." " It appears to me that no distinction can be made; and that it is unnecessary to inquire, what are the essential parts of a contract, and what not; and that every part of the contract, in regard to which the parties are stipulating, must be taken to be material."

III. *The Fifth and Sixth Sections, relating to the Execution and Revocation of Wills, p.* 870; *and the Stat.* 1 *Vict. c.* 26, *for the Amendment of the Laws with respect to Wills, p.* 889.

5th *Section.*—" All devises and bequests of any lands or tenements, devisable either by force of the statute of wills, or by this statute, or by the custom of Kent, or of any borough, or any other particular custom, shall be in writing, and signed by the party so devising the same, or by some other person in his presence, and by his express directions, and shall be attested and subscribed in the presence of the devisor, by three or four credible witnesses, or else they shall be utterly void and of none effect."

(b) *Marshall* v. *Lynn,* 6 M. & W.   (c) *Goss* v. *Lord Nugent,* 5 B. & Ad.
109.   58.

" All facts relating to the subject matter and object of the devise, such as that it was or was not in the possession of the testator, the mode of acquiring it, the local situation, and the distribution of the property, are admissible to aid in ascertaining what is meant by the words used in the will " (*d*).

All Devises of any Lands or Tenements.]—Although these words are very general, and extend to customary freeholds (*e*), not passing by surrender, yet it has been holden, that copyhold land (*f*) and customary (*g*) estates, passing by surrender, are not comprehended within them. In these cases, the estate is considered as passing by the surrender of which the will only directs the uses. Consequently, it is not necessary that such will should be executed with the solemnities required by this statute. Hence, a mere draught of a will, the signing and publication of which were prevented by the sudden death of the testator, has been holden sufficient to pass copyhold land surrendered to the use of the will. N. By stat. 55 Geo. III. c. 192, dispositions by will, by any person dying after 12th July, 1815, of copyhold estates, are made effectual without any previous surrender to the use thereof. But this statute only supplies the want of a formal surrender, and does not extend to a case where the surrender is a matter of substance, as where it is required to be accompanied by the separate examination of wife (*h*). Since this statute, a copyhold will pass (*i*) under a general devise of real estate, although there be no surrender to the use of the will. But the will must contain a disposition of the copyhold, either express or implied (*k*). The statute applies to wills made before the statute, as well as those which were made after (*l*). An heir at law, who has not been admitted to a copyhold estate, which has descended to him, nor paid the lord's fine due on admission, may, notwithstanding, devise (*m*) the same.

Shall be in Writing.]—This provision is merely a repetition of what had been required by the stat. 32 Hen. VIII. c. 1, which first gave power of disposing of land by will. But writing was the only solemnity which that statute required. Hence, before the statute of frauds, short notes, taken by a lawyer from the testator's mouth, for the purpose of being reduced into form (*n*), were holden to be a good will, though the testator died before they were so reduced into

(*d*) Per *Parke, J., Doe d. Templeman* v. *Martin,* 4 B. & Ad. 785.

(*e*) *Hussey* v. *Grills,* Ambl. 299.

(*f*) *Roe d. Gilman* v. *Heyhoe,* 2 Bl. R. 1114. See also *The Attorney General* v. *Barnes,* 2 Vern. 598 ; *Attorney General* v. *Andrews,* 1 Ves. 225 ; *Tuffnell* v. *Page,* 2 Atk. 37.

(*g*) *Doe d. Cook* v. *Danvers,* 7 East, 299 ; *Carey* v. *Askew,* coram Sir *L. Kenyon,* M. R., May 9, 1786, 2 Bro. C. C. 58, and in a note to *Wagstaff* v. *Wagstaff,*

2 P. Wms. 259, Cox's ed., recognized by *Ellenborough,* C. J., in 7 East, 324.

(*h*) *Doe d. Nethercote* v. *Bartle,* 5 B. & A. 492.

(*i*) *Doe d. Clarke* v. *Ludlam,* 7 Bingh. 275.

(*k*) *Doe* v. *Bird,* 5 B. & Ad. 695.

(*l*) See the words.

(*m*) *Right* v. *Banks,* 3 B. & Ad. 664.

(*n*) 1 Anderson, 34, cited by Lord *Ellenborough,* C. J., 7 East, 324.

form. In like manner, a scrap of writing, though it was not signed, sealed, or written by the testator, might have been established as a will by the testimony of a single witness. This did in fact happen in a very remarkable case, that of Sir *Francis Worseley's* will (o).

And signed by the Party devising.]—What shall be considered as a sufficient signature within this clause, will appear from the following cases.—The devisor wrote his will with his own hand, thus: "I, John Stanley, make this my last will and testament;" and thereby devised the land in question, and put his seal thereto, but did not subscribe his name. The will was subscribed by three witnesses in his presence. This was holden (p) to be a good will to pass the land; for the will having been written by the devisor, and his name being in the will, it was a sufficient signing within the statute, which has not appropriated any particular place in the will, where it shall be signed, either at the top or bottom, or in the margin. It seems, that if the devisor cannot write, a mark made by him will be a sufficient signing (q) within the statute (16). It is immaterial whether the devisor can write at the time or not, and no collateral inquiry of that sort ought to take place (r). Whether the devisor, by merely affixing his seal to the will, can be considered as having sufficiently signed within the meaning of the statute, seems to be a *vexata quæstio.* Affirmed per *North, Wyndham,* and *Charlton,* in *Lemayne* v. *Stanley,* 3 Lev. 1, Dub. per *Levinz,* S. C. Affirmed per *Holt,* C. J., in *Lee* v. *Libb,* 1 Show. 69. Affirmed per Lord *Raymond,* C. J., at *nisi prius,* in *Warneford* v. *Warneford,* 2 Str. 764. Negatived per three Barons (including *Parker,* C. B.) in *Smith* v. *Evans,* 1 Wils. 313; also per

(o) Reported in 1 Sidf. 315, pl. 33; 2 Keb. 128, pl. 82, by the name of *Stevens, Lessee of Gerrard* v. *Lord Manchester,* 18 Car. II.

(p) *Lemayne* v. *Stanley,* 3 Lev. 1; adjudged after several arguments by the whole court, *S. C.; North,* C. J., *Wynd-*

ham, Charlton, and *Levins, Js.,* on special verdict in ejectment, Easter T. 1681, C. B.

(q) See in *Lemayne* v. *Stanley,* Freem. 538, a dictum to this effect.

(r) *Baker* v. *Dening,* 8 A. & E. 94; 3 N. & P. 228.

---

(16) See *Harrison* v. *Harrison,* 8 Ves. jun. 185, where it was holden by Lord *Eldon,* C., on the authority of *Gurney* v. *Corbet**, C. B., that a will was duly executed to pass freehold land, although one witness only had subscribed his name, and the other two had attested by setting their marks. See also *Addy* v. *Grix,* coram Sir *W. Grant,* M. R., 8 Ves. jun. 504, S. P.

* Not printed, but said by Lord *Eldon* to be in a note-book which was the property of Mr. J. Burnet. This book is now in Lincoln's Inn Library, forming a part of Serjeant Hill's MSS. purchased by the Society. This case is in 9 Burnet, p. 138. Another note of the same case is in vol. 30, p. 51, of Serjeant Hill's MSS.

Willes, C. J., Sir *John Strange*, M. R., and per *Parker*, C. B. (17), sitting with Lord *Hardwicke*, C., in *Ellis* v. *Smith*, as assistants, 1 Ves. jun. 11 ; 1 Dickens, 225. It is not required by the statute, that the witness should see the devisor sign, or that he should sign in their presence (*s*). It is sufficient, that the devisor should declare to the witnesses, that the instrument offered to them to be subscribed is his will, and that the signature is his handwriting.

Attested and subscribed] (18).—It is not necessary that the will should be attested and subscribed by all the witnesses at the same time. Hence, where the devisor published his will in the presence of two witnesses (*t*), who subscribed it in his presence, and some time after he sent for a third witness, and published it in his presence ; the will was holden to be duly attested. If the will be subscribed by three witnesses in the presence and at the request of the testator, it is sufficiently attested (*u*), although none of the witnesses saw the testator's signature, and only one of them knew what the paper was. A will more than thirty years old proves itself, without calling any witnesses, even where they are all alive (*x*).

(*s*) *Grayson* v. *Atkinson*, 2 Ves. 454 ; *Ellis* v. *Smith*, 1 Ves. jun. 11 ; Dickens, 225, *S. C.*

(*t*) *Jones* v. *Lake*, 16 Geo. II. B. R., on special verdict in ejectment ; 2 Atk.

176, n. S. P. admitted per *Hardwicke*, Ch., 2 Ves. 458.

(*u*) *Wright* v. *Wright*, 7 Bingh. 457.

(*x*) Per *Cur.*, *Doe d. Spilsbury* v. *Burdett*, 4 A. & E. 19, *ante*, p. 540.

---

(17) *Parker*, C. B., observed, however, (according to the report in 1 Ves. jun. 12,) that, as in some cases it was thrown out obiter, that sealing was signing, and *in one case decreed*, that it was equal to signing, he should submit his opinion. But in Dickens's Rep. of *Ellis* v. *Smith*, vol. 1, p. 228, and in a MS. note, this remark does not appear; and *Parker's* dissent from the opinion of the three judges in *Lemayne* v. *Stanley*, and Lord *Raymond* in *Warneford* v. *Warneford*, stands unqualified.

(18) It is not necessary that the witnesses should be informed of the nature of the instrument they are about to attest, or that it is a will. Hence, in *Trymmer* v. *Jackson*, determined in the Court of King's Bench, upon a trial at bar[*] of an issue directed by the Court of Chancery, cited in 1 Ves. 487, recognized by Lord *Hardwicke*, Ch., in *Rigden* v. *Vallier*, 2 Ves. 258, and by *Denison*, J., in *Wallis* v. *Wallis*, Lincoln Summ. Ass. 1762 ; 4 Burn's E. L. p. 127, 6th ed., the witnesses to the will were induced, from words made use of by Anna Lordell, the testatrix, at the time of the execution, to believe that the instrument they attested was a deed, and not a will. The testatrix delivered it " as her act and deed," and the words " sealed and delivered" were written above the place where the three witnesses were to subscribe their names. The court were of opinion that this was a sufficient execution of the will.

[*] On the 7th of May, 1749. See Reg. Lib. B. 1749, p. 191.

A will was dated more than thirty years before the trial, but one of the subscribing witness was proved to be still living; it was holden (y), that it was not necessary to call such witness to prove the execution, although the devisor had died within thirty years.

The devisor wrote upon a sheet of paper a devise of land, and subscribed the paper, but did not seal it, nor was it attested (z); on a subsequent day he wrote a memorandum on another side of the same sheet of paper, containing a bequest of personal estate, and subscribed this memorandum in the presence of three witnesses. He then took the sheet of paper in his hand, and declared it to be his last will, in the presence of the three witnesses, and then delivered it to them, and desired them to attest and subscribe it, in his presence, and in the presence of each other, which they accordingly did. It was holden, that this was to be considered as one entire instrument, though made at different times; and that it was duly executed and attested to pass the real estate; that the memorandum relating to personalty only, the having three witnesses must have been merely for the purpose of authenticating the former devise; and the court observed, that a person was not obliged to make his whole will at the same time. In the case of *Stonehouse* v. *Evelyn*, at the Rolls, 3 P. Wms. 254, it was proved, that the three subscribing witnesses to the will had subscribed their names in the presence of the testatrix; but one of them said he did not see testatrix sign the will, but that she owned at the time when the witnesses subscribed, that the name signed to the will was her own hand-writing. This was holden to be sufficient by Sir *Joseph Jekyll*, M. R. Where a will consisted of two sheets of paper (a), and the first sheet was regularly connected with the second, and in the first sheet the testator devised land to trustees thereinafter named upon trusts therein specified, and in the last sheet, which was duly executed and attested, appointed certain persons to be trustees; although the testator did not execute the first sheet, and the witnesses never saw it, it was the opinion of all the judges in England, that if the first sheet were in the room at the time of the execution of the second, that was sufficient.

In the Presence of the Devisor.]—It is required by the statute, that the attestation and subscription of the witnesses should be in the presence of the devisor, in order to prevent another will being obtruded in the place of the true will; but it is sufficient, if it be proved, that the testator *might see* the witnesses subscribing their attestation; it is not necessary that it should be proved, that the testator did actually see the witness subscribe. Hence, where the

(y) *Doe d. Oldham and Wife* v. *Wolley,* 8 B. & C. 24.
(z) *Carleton d. Griffin* v. *Griffin,* 1 Burr. 549, on a case reserved.

(a) *Bond* v. *Seawell,* on case reserved, 3 Burr. 1773; 1 Bl. R. 407; Bull. N. P. 264, *S. C.*

devisor, being in bed (b), made his will, which he signed in the presence of three witnesses, but he being very ill, the witnesses withdrew into a gallery, and there subscribed their names as witnesses to the will. Between the gallery and the bedchamber, where the devisor lay, there was a lobby with glass doors, and the glass broken in some places; it was proved, that the devisor *might* see from his bed where he lay (through the lobby and the broken glass windows) the table in the gallery, where the witnesses subscribed their names; it was adjudged, that the will was duly executed in the presence of the devisor, within the intent of the statute. Honora Jenkins (c), having directed her will to be prepared, went to the office of her attorney at York, in order to execute it. H. J. being asthmatical, and the office very hot, she retired to her carriage in order to execute the will, the witnesses attending her, who, after having seen her execute, returned into the office, to attest the will, and the carriage was put back to the window of the office; it was proved by a person who was in the carriage with H. J., that the testatrix *might* see what passed through the window of the office. Immediately after the attestation, one of the witnesses took the will to the testatrix, which she folded up and put into her pocket. Lord *Thurlow*, Ch., thought the will well executed; and the case of *Sheers* v. *Glasscock* was relied upon as an authority. But the testator must be in a situation that he *may* see the witness attest: therefore, where the attesting witnesses retired from the room where the testator had signed, and subscribed their names in an adjoining room, and the jury found that from one part of the testator's room a person by inclining himself forwards, with his head out at the door, might have seen the witnesses, but that the testator was not in such a situation in the room that he might by so inclining have seen them; held, that the will was not duly attested (d). It was proposed in the new law, to omit the words "in the presence of the testator;" but they are retained, so that the foregoing cases will be applicable. See 1 Vict. c. 26, s. 9. Although it is required by the statute of frauds (e), that the attestation of the witnesses should be in the presence of the devisor, yet it is not necessary that it should be inserted in the form of the attestation, that the witnesses subscribed their names in the presence of the devisor; whether they did so subscribe is matter of evidence to be left to the jury (f). Hence, where the attestation was "signed, sealed, published, and declared, in the presence of us," the witnesses being dead, and their

---

(b) *Sheers* v. *Glasscock*, C. B. Carth. 81; Salk. 688; 1 Eq. C. Abr. 403; *Todd* v. *Earl of Winchelsea*, coram *Abbott*, C. J., S. P., 1 M. & Malk. 12.

(c) *Casson* v. *Dade*, 1 Bro. C. C. 99.

(d) *Doe* v. *Manifold*, 1 M. & S. 294.

(e) *Brice* v. *Smith*, Willes, 1.

(f) *Hands* v. *James*, Comyn's R. 531; cited by the name of *Head* v. *James*, by *Willes*, C. J., in *Brice* v. *Smith*, Willes, 2.

hand-writing proved (*g*) ; the court held, that it was the province of the jury to determine upon circumstances, without any positive proof, whether the witnesses had subscribed in the presence of the devisor.   So where there had been possession under a will for more than thirty years, although the will did not (in the attestation) state that the witnesses signed in the presence of the testator, yet *Lee*, C. J., held (*h*), that it might be presumed that the requisites of the statute had been complied with.   Under the stat. 1 Vict. c. 26, s. 9, a form of attestation is not necessary.

By three or four credible Witnesses.]—The witnesses must be persons who have the use of their reason, and such religious belief as to feel the obligation of an oath ; who have not been convicted of any infamous crime, and are not influenced by interest (19).

1. The witnesses must be persons who have the use of their reason.   Persons excluded from giving testimony (*i*), for want of skill and discernment, are idiots, persons of insane mind, and children. In regard to children, there seems not to be any precise time or age fixed, before which they are excluded from giving evidence; this will depend in a great measure on the sense and understanding of the child, as it shall appear to the court upon examination of the infant.

2. The witnesses must be persons who have such religious belief as to be sensible of the obligation of an oath.   " An infidel is not to be admitted as a witness (*k*) ; the consequence of which would be, that a Jew, who acknowledges the Old Testament only, could not be a witness.   But I take it, that although the form of the oath, as administered according to the laws of England, is, ' *tactis sacrosanctis Dei Evangeliis,*' by which it is presumed that the witness is a Christian ; yet in cases of necessity, as in foreign contracts between merchant and merchant, frequently transacted by Jewish brokers, the testimony of a Jew, ' *tacto libro legis Mosaicæ,*' is not to be rejected, and is used (as I have been informed) among all nations."   The depositions of witnesses (*l*), professing the Gentoo religion, who were sworn according to the ceremonies of their religion, taken under a commission out of chancery, were holden to be

(*g*) *Croft* v. *Pawlet*, Str. 1109. See *Doe d. Spilsbury* v. *Burdett*, 4 A. & E. 1, as to execution of a will under a power.

(*h*) *Higbed d. Marshall* v. *Breeding*, Bedford Summ. Ass. 1738; Serjt. Hill's MSS. vol. 33, p. 99; *Doe d. Restorick* v. *Purse*, Devon. Summ. Ass. 1832. Attestation of will 30 years old, stated that testator signed in the presence of wit-

nesses, but omitted to state that witnesses had signed in presence of testator ; it was proved, that there had been uninterrupted possession under the will; held sufficient by *Taunton*, J., on the authority of some of the foregoing cases.

(*i*) Gilb. Evid. 109.

(*k*) 1 Inst. 6, b.

(*l*) *Omichund* v. *Barker*, Willes, 538.

(19) This is a general rule of evidence.

admissible in evidence, in the great case of *Omichund* v. *Barker*; *Willes*, C. J., remarking, " that if an oath were merely a Christian institution, as baptism, the sacrament, and the like, he should have been compelled to admit, that none but a Christian could take an oath. But oaths were instituted long before Christianity, were made use of to the same purposes as now, were always held in the highest veneration, and were almost as old as the creation. ' *Juramentum* (according to Sir *Edward Coke*,) *nihil aliud est quam Deum in testem vocare;*' and, therefore, ' *nothing but the belief of a God, and that he will reward and punish us according to our deserts, is necessary to qualify a man to take an oath.*' Therefore, the proper questions to be put to a witness, in order to ground an objection to his competency (*m*), is not whether he believes in Jesus Christ, or the Holy Gospels, but whether he believes in God, the obligation of an oath, and a future state of rewards and punishments."

3. Persons who have been convicted of any infamous crimes cannot be witnesses. There are several crimes, the commission of which evince such a moral depravity, as utterly to exclude the offender from becoming a witness. Hence, where a person has been convicted of treason or felony, his testimony cannot be received in a court of justice. At the common law, a person convicted of petty larceny was holden not to be a competent witness, and consequently was incapable of attesting a devise of land (*n*). The stat. 31 Geo. III. c. 35, reciting, that persons convicted of grand larceny are by their punishment restored to their credit, removed the incompetency by reason of a conviction for petty larceny. This statute was repealed in 1827, when the distinction between grand and petty larceny was abolished. Every species of the *crimen falsi*, as it is termed, such as perjury, forgery, and the like, renders persons convicted thereof incompetent to be witnesses. Standing in the pillory being the usual punishment inflicted on those who are convicted of the *crimen falsi*, it was formerly holden, that no person, who had suffered this punishment, or even had been sentenced to it, could be a witness: but the rule now laid down is, that it is the *crime*, and not the *punishment*, which makes a man infamous; and, consequently, although a person be sentenced to stand in the pillory, yet if it be not for an infamous offence, such person is still a competent witness (*o*). If one found guilty on an indictment for perjury at common law be pardoned by the king, he will be a good witness (*p*); because the king has power to take off every part of the punishment: but if a person be indicted of perjury on the stat. 5 Eliz. c. 9, and convicted, the king cannot restore such person to

(*m*) *R.* v. *Taylor*, Peake's N. P. C. 11, per *Buller*, J.
(*n*) *Pendock* v. *Mackinder*, Willes, 665; 2 Wils. 18, *S. C.*

(*o*) *Chater* v. *Hawkins*, 3 Lev. 426.
(*p*) Gilb. Evid. 108; *Dover* v. *Mestaer*, B. R. M. T. 1803; London Sittings, *Ellenborough*, C. J., *ante*, p. 634.

his competency as a witness; for the king is divested of that prerogative by the express words of the statute. In this case the disability forms a part of the judgment on the statute, *viz.* " that the oath of such person or persons, so offending, thenceforth shall not be received in any court of record within England or Wales, or the marches, until the judgment shall be reversed by attaint or otherwise" (*q*). But on an indictment at common law, the disability is only a consequence of the infamous judgment (*r*). N. The party who would object to the testimony of a witness, on the ground of his having been convicted of an infamous offence, must be prepared with a copy of the judgment, regularly entered upon the verdict of conviction ; for, until such judgment is entered, the witness is not deprived of his legal privileges (*s*). A mere conviction, unless followed by a judgment, is not sufficient to destroy the competency of a witness (*t*). The admission of a witness, that he has been convicted of the offence, will not supersede the necessity of producing the record of conviction, or copy thereof (*u*).

4. The witness must not be biassed or influenced by interest. Previously to the stat. 25 Geo. II. c. 6, it was holden (*x*), that if one of the subscribing witnesses to a will of land was a legatee named in the will, and the land was charged with the payment of the legacy, such witness, not having received the legacy, or otherwise discharged himself of his interest at the time of examination, was not a credible witness within the intent of the statute of frauds. Whether a witness who was a creditor or a legatee, was competent to be examined in support of a will, containing a charge on the land for payment of debts and legacies, if after the death of the devisor, and before examination, he had received or released, or upon tender made had refused to receive, the debt or legacy, seems to have been a *vexata quæstio* (*y*) ; but by stat. 25 Geo. II. c. 6, it was enacted, " That if any person shall attest the execution of any will or codicil, to whom any beneficial devise, legacy, estate, interest, gift, or appointment, of or affecting any real or personal estate, other than charges on lands, &c., for payment of any debt or debts, shall be thereby given or made; such devise, &c. shall, so far only as concerns such person attesting the execution of such will or codicil, or any person claiming under him, be void ; and such person shall be admitted as a witness to the execution of such will or codicil, within the intent of the said act, notwithstanding such devise, &c." And by sect. 2, " In case, by any will or codicil, any lands, &c. shall be charged with debts, and any creditor, whose

(*q*) Co. Ent. 368, b., 2nd edit.
(*r*) Per *Holt*, C. J., in *R.* v. *Crosby*, Salk. 689.
(*s*) Peake's Evid. 128, 2nd ed.
(*t*) *Lee* v. *Gansel*, Cowp. 3.
(*u*) *R.* v. *Castell Careinion*, 8 East, 77.
(*x*) *Holdfast d. Anstey* v. *Dowsing*, Str. 1253.
(*y*) See *Wyndham* v. *Chetwynd*, 1 Burr. 414 ; 1 Bl. R. 65. Special verdict. Ld. Kenyon, 121, *S. C.*, and *Hindson* v. *Kersey*, C. B., on case reserved from Westmorland Assizes, 4 Burn. E. L. 97.

debt is so charged, shall attest the execution of such will or codicil, every such creditor, notwithstanding such charge, shall be admitted as a witness to the execution of such will or codicil, within the intent of the said act : Provided (*z*), that the credit of every such witness, and all circumstances relating thereto, shall be subject to the consideration and determination of the court and the jury, before whom any such witness shall be examined, or his testimony or attestation made use of; or of the court of equity in which the testimony or attestation of any such witness shall be made use of; in like manner as the credit of witnesses in all other cases ought to be .considered of and determined." An estate in fee upon the determination of a life estate was devised to the wife of A. B.; A. B. was one of the attesting witnesses to the will. The testator died in 1779, and the wife of A. B. died in 1813, before the previous life estate was determined; it was holden (*a*), that A. B. was not a good attesting witness to this will. But where, in ejectment against a devisee, the question turned upon the sanity of the testator at the time of making the will; it was holden (*b*), that an executor, who took a pecuniary interest under the will, but who was not an attesting witness, was a competent witness to support it ; for the verdict in this case would have the effect of establishing the will as to the real property only. It does not appear that the legislature (*c*), when they passed the statute of frauds, had in their contemplation executions of wills by blind men. It seems, however, that, in the case of a blind man, stronger evidence will be required than the mere attestation of signature ; but it is not necessary that the will should be read over to him in the presence of the attesting witnesses.

Heir apparent to an estate is competent to give evidence in support of the claim of the ancestor, although one who has a vested interest as a remainder-man is incompetent ; for he hath a present estate in the land; but the heirship is a contingency (*d*). So a remainder-man after a tenant in tail is not a competent witness (*e*), for the tenant in tail, in ejectment for the entailed estate.

Of the Proof by the subscribing Witnesses.]—To prove the due execution of a devise of lands, the original will must be produced, and one of the subscribing witnesses, if living, must be examined, to prove that the solemnities prescribed by the statute have been complied with, agreeably to the rule of law, that where a witness has subscribed an instrument, he must be produced, because it is the best evidence (20) ; and, even where the will is in the hands of

(*z*) Sect. 6.
(*a*) *Hatfield* v. *Thorp*, 5 B. & A. 589.
(*b*) *Doe d. Wood* v. *Teage*, 5 B. & C. 335.
(*c*) *Longchamp d. Goodfellow* v. *Fish*,

2 Bos. & Pul. N. R. 415.
(*d*) Per *Treby*, C. J., in *Smith* v. *Blackham*, Salk. 283.
(*e*) *Doe d. Ld. Teynham* v. *Tyler*, 6 Bingh. 390.

(20) " Although the common course is to call one witness only to

the adverse party, who has notice to produce it, and in consequence of such notice does produce it at the trial, the party calling for it is bound to call one of the subscribing witnesses to prove it (*f*). If all the subscribing witnesses are dead, or insane (*g*), their hand-writing and that of the devisor must be proved. A devisee or exe-cutor in trust (*h*), who has acted, may be examined as a witness in support of the will. In like manner an executor, who does not take any beneficial interest under the will, is a competent witness to prove the sanity of the testator. So the wife of an acting executor, who does not take any beneficial interest under the will, is a com-petent witness to prove the execution of it (*i*). So an executor of a testator possessed of real and personal estate, clothed with a trust to pay debts, and to lay out money for the benefit of the testator's children, and with a power to sell freehold lands in fee, but taking no beneficial interest under the will, is a good attesting witness (*k*) to the will. If a person who is interested, execute a surrender or release of his interest (*l*), he may be examined as a witness,

---

(*f*) Per Lord *Kenyon*, C. J., in a case cited by *Lawrence*, J., in *Gordon* v. *Se-cretan*, 8 East, 548.

(*g*) *Bernett* v. *Taylor*, 9 Ves. 381.

(*h*) *Lowe* v. *Jolliffe*, 1 Bl. R. 365.
(*i*) *Bettison* v. *Bromley*, 12 East, 250.
(*k*) *Phipps* v. *Pitcher*, 6 Taunt. 220.
(*l*) *Goodtitle* v. *Welford*, Doug. 139.

---

prove the will*, yet that is only where there is no objection made to the execution of the will by the heir; for he is entitled to have all the wit-nesses examined, but then he must produce them; for the devisee need not produce more than one, if such witness shall prove all the requisites; and though they should all swear that the will was not duly executed, yet the devisee would be permitted to adduce evidence of circumstances to prove the due execution: as was the case of *Austin* and *Willes*, cited by Lord *Hardwicke*, C., in *Blacket* and *Widdrington*, M. T. 4 Geo. II.; in which case, notwithstanding the three witnesses swore that the will was not duly executed, the devisee obtained a verdict.† In *Pike* and *Bradbury* ‡, before Lord *Raymond*, upon an issue of *devisavit vel non*, the witnesses denying their hands, the devisee would have avoided calling them; but the C. J. obliged him to call them; whereupon the first and second denying their hands, it was contended that he should go no fur-ther; for it was argued, that though if you call one witness, who proves against you, you may call another, yet if the second also prove against you, you can go no further; but the C. J. permitted the devisee to call other witnesses to prove the will, and he obtained a verdict." Gilb. Evid. 69; Bull. N. P. 264. If three witnesses to a will are dead, the hand-writing of all must be proved, unless the will be thirty years old. Per Cur. in *Hans d. Gurney* v. *Corbett*, C. B. H. T. 17 Geo. II., Serjeant Hill's MSS. vol. 30, p. 51.

---

* Per *Lee*, C. J., in *Anstey* v. *Dowsing*. See also the opinion of *Kenyon*, C. J., in *Doe* v. *Smith*, 1 Esp. N. P. C. 391.

† See also *Lowe* v. *Jolliffe*, 1 Bl. R. 365, S. P.

‡ Q. *Pike* v. *Badmering*, cited in Str. 1096, and there said to have been determined by *Pratt*, C. J.

although the surrenderee, &c. refuse to accept the surrender or release.

6th Section.—" No devise, in writing, of lands, tenements, or hereditaments, nor any clause thereof, shall be revocable, otherwise than by some other will or codicil, in writing, or other writing declaring the same; or by burning, cancelling, tearing, or obliterating the same, by the testator himself, or in his presence, and by his directions and consent; but all devises and bequests of lands and tenements shall remain and continue in force, until the same be burnt, cancelled, torn, or obliterated by the testator, or by his directions, in manner aforesaid; or unless the same be altered by some other will or codicil, in writing, or other writing of the devisor, signed in the presence of three or four witnesses, declaring the same."

No Devise in Writing, of Lands, &c., shall be revocable, otherwise than by some other Will or Codicil, in Writing; or other Writing of the Devisor, signed in the Presence of three or four Witnesses declaring the same.—Having premised that before this statute, devises of lands, made under the particular customs of boroughs, or by virtue of the statute of wills, (32 Hen. VIII. c. 1,) might have been revoked by any *express* words without writing (*m*), the statute of wills having given power to any person seised in fee of lands, to devise such lands by will *in writing*, but being silent as to revocations, I shall proceed to consider the several methods prescribed by the statute of frauds for the revocation of wills of lands, and then subjoin some remarks on implied revocations. This section prescribes three methods, by which a devise of lands may be revoked: either by another will or codicil in writing, or by other writing, declaring the intention of the devisor to revoke the former devise; or by burning, cancelling, &c. With respect to the first method, (the only subject now under consideration,) it is to be observed, that the words " signed in the presence of three or four witnesses," having been holden to refer to the next preceding words, " *other writing*," only, and not to the words, " *will or codicil in writing,*" it is not necessary that a *will*, whereby a former will is revoked, should be signed by the devisor in the presence of three witnesses (*n*); but that a second will may operate as a revocation of a former, it is necessary, 1. That the second will should expressly revoke or be clearly inconsistent with the first devise, *quoad* the particular subject matter of such devise (*o*). If it be merely found, that another or even a different disposition has been made by the testator from that which he had first willed, yet if it do not appear

(*m*) Dyer, 310, b. pl. 81. Adm. in *Symson* v. *Kirton*, Cro. Jac. 115, and *Cranwell* v. *Sanders*, Cro. Jac. 497; Gilb. Dev. 93, ed. 1739.

(*n*) See *Heil* v. *Clerk*, 3 Mod. 218, re-

cognized by Ld. *Hardwicke*, C., in *Ellis* v. *Smith*, 4 Burn. E. L. 199.

(*o*) See Cox's note to *Onions* v. *Tyrer*, 1 P. Wms. 345.

to the court, what that difference is, it will not be a revocation (*p*).
2. It is necessary that the second will should be subsisting and
effective at the time of the death of the testator; consequently, if
the second will be not executed with the formalities prescribed by
the fifth section of the statute (*q*), or if the second will be effectually cancelled in the lifetime of the testator (*r*), the first will
shall operate, as if no other had existed (21). 3. As, before the
statute of frauds, parol declarations of an intention to revoke in
future, were holden not to amount to a present revocation (*s*); so,
since the statute, such declaration, although executed with the
formalities required by the statute, will not operate as a revocation (*t*). 4. It is an established principle, that an instrument,
which is intended to operate as a devise, if it cannot take effect as
such, shall never operate as a revocation (*u*).

*Or other Writing of the Devisor declaring the same, signed in
the Presence of three or four Witnesses.*]—An instrument of revocation, intended merely to operate as such, and not as a devise,
would, according to the opinion of Lord *Cowper*, C., in *Onions* v.
Tyrer, 1 P. Wms. 345, Cox's edit., be effective, if signed by the
devisor in the presence of three witnesses, as this clause directs,
and without the other formalities required in the case of wills by
the 5th section, *viz.* the attestation and subscription of the witnesses in the presence of the devisor.

*3d. Method of express Revocation. By burning, &c. Or by
burning, cancelling, tearing, or obliterating the same, by the
Testator himself, or in his Presence, and by his Directions and
Consent.*—The acts here mentioned are in themselves equivocal
acts: and, consequently, in order to make them operate as revocations, it must be shown that they were done *animo revocandi*,
that is, with an intention to revoke; for unless that appears, the
prior devise will not be revoked (*x*). Hence, if the devisor were to
throw his ink upon his will, instead of the sand; though it might
be a complete defacing of the instrument, it would not be a revo-

---

(*p*) *Hitchins* v. *Basset*, Salk. 592; 1
Show. 537; 3 Mod. 203; Show. P. C.
146; *Harwood* v. *Goodright*, Cowp. 87;
S. C. in C. B., 3 Wils. 497; 2 Bl. R.
937, and in Dom. Pro. 7 Bro. P. C. p.
344, but in Tomlins's edit. p. 489;
Thomas v. *Evans*, 2 East, 488.
(*q*) *Eccleston* v. *Speke*, 1689, Carth.
81; *Onions* v. *Tyrer*, 1716, 1 P. Wms.

344.
(*r*) *Goodright* v. *Glazier*, 4 Burr. 2512.
(*s*) *Cranvell* v. *Sanders*, Cro. Jac. 497.
(*t*) *Thomas* v. *Evans*, 2 East, 488.
(*u*) *Exp. Earl of Ilchester*, 7 Ves. jun.
348.
(*x*) Per Ld. *Mansfield*, C. J., in *Burtenshaw* v. *Gilbert*, Cowp. 52.

---

(21) Where an effective devise appears to have been once made in dis-
herison of the heir at law, it will lie upon the heir to prove, that such
devise has been effectively defeated. Cowp. 87.

cation; or suppose a person having two wills of different dates by him, should direct the first will to be cancelled, and, through mistake, the person to whom the devisor gave his directions, should cancel the last will; such an act would not be a revocation of the last will: or, suppose a person having a will consisting of two parts, throws one unintentionally into the fire, where it is burnt, it would not be a revocation of the devises contained in such parts. The intention, therefore, must govern in such cases. A., by will, duly executed and attested (*y*), devised land to trustees to several uses; and at the same time executed a duplicate thereof, with all the solemnities prescribed by the fifth section of this statute. Some time after, having been desirous to change one of his trustees, he ordered his will to be written over again, without any variation from the first, except only in the name of that trustee, and a clause revoking all former wills. When it was so written over he executed it in the presence of three witnesses, and the three witnesses subscribed their names, but not in his presence, (as the 5th section directs). Some evidence was adduced, that the testator afterwards cancelled the duplicate of the first will, by tearing off the seal. The question was, whether the cancelling the duplicate of the first will should be a revocation thereof within this clause. It was admitted, that if a devisor, having duplicates of his will, cancels one of them *animo revocandi*, this is a good revocation of the whole will, and of both the duplicates (22). But it was decreed in the present case (*z*), *that it was plain the testator did not mean to revoke his former will by cancelling, but by substituting another perfect will in lieu thereof*, and not otherwise; and, therefore, the cancelling thereof (if any) was but a circumstance showing that he thought he had made a good disposition by the second will, and in confidence thereof it was done with no other intent, but that the second will should thereby more surely take place." The cancelling of a will under this section may be proved (*a*) in any manner consistent with the general law of evidence, the statute not introducing any new rule of proof. In order to effectuate a revocation, it is not necessary that the will should be actually destroyed: hence a slight *tearing of a will* and throwing it on the fire, with a deliberate intent to consume it, by the testator, though it fell off, and was preserved by a bystander without

(*y*) *Onions* v. *Tyrer*, 2 Vern. 741; Prec. in Chan. 459; Gilb. Rep. 130; 1 Eq. Ca. Abr. 407, pl. 1; but best reported in P. Wms. vol. 1, p. 344, Cox's ed.

(*z*) Reg. Lib. B. 1716, fol. 242; Cox's P. Wms. vol. 1, p. 345.
(*a*) *Doe d. Reed* v. *Harris*, 6 A. & E. 209; 1 Nev. & P. 405.

---

(22) "Where there are duplicates of a will, one in the possession of the devisor, the other not; and the devisor cancels that which is in *his* custody, it is an effectual cancelling of both." Per *Aston*, J., in *Burtenshaw* v. *Gilbert*, Cowp. 54.

his consent or knowledge, has been holden (b) to be a sufficient revocation. But where a testator, intending to destroy his will, threw it upon the fire, and another person snatched it off; a corner of the envelope only, and no part of the will itself being burnt; it was holden, that the will was not revoked as to the freehold (c), but, as to the copyhold (d), to which the statute of frauds does not extend, it was revoked by the attempt to burn. A. having made a will of land (e) and a duplicate thereof, (both duly executed and attested,) but declaring that it was not a will to his liking, and that he should alter it, delivered a duplicate to B. (a devisee named therein). Afterwards A. executed another will, disposing of his estate in a different manner from what he had done under the former will, and thereby revoked all former wills, and at the same time cancelled the first will, which remained in his own custody, observing to the person who made the second will, that there was a duplicate of his first will in the hands of B. A short time before A.'s death, one of the principal devisees in the last will died; whereupon A. sent for an attorney to prepare another will, but, before the attorney arrived, A. became senseless, and shortly afterwards died. After his death, the first and second wills were found together in a paper, both cancelled; but the duplicate of the first will (which duplicate had been delivered to B.) was found among some deeds and papers of the testator *uncancelled*. It did not appear how the duplicate came to be found among the testator's papers. It was holden, that at the time of making the second will, the first was clearly revoked, and that it was not set up again by cancelling the second will. The testator, after devising all his land (f) to trustees upon trust to sell, "except the house at Bath," gave to his wife his house in Bath for her life, and after her death to his eldest son; and after the execution of the will sold his house at Bath, and struck out of his will the exception and the devise respecting it. It was holden, that the devise to the trustees was not revoked by the erasure, as to the house at Bath (23). So where a testator, by will duly executed and attested (g), devised

---

(b) *Bibb d. Mole* v. *Thomas*, 2 Bl. R. 1043. But see the 20th section of the new act, 1 Vict. c. 26, *post*, p. 892.
(c) *Doe d. Reed* v. *Harris*, 6 A. & E. 209; 1 Nev. & P. 405.

(d) *Doe d. Reed* v. *Harris*, 8 A. & E. 1.
(e) *Burtenshaw* v. *Gilbert*, Cowp. 49.
(f) *Sutton* v. *Sutton*, Cowp. 812.
(g) *Larkins* v. *Larkins*, 3 Bos. & Pul. 16.

---

(23) If A. by his will devises all the residue of his personal estate to B. and C., and makes them executors; and after, by a codicil, cancels and revokes every thing relating to B., and also revokes the appointment of B. as executor, C. shall have the whole. A revocation, without a new gift, shall have the same effect as if it had been expressly given; and whether it be by codicil or obliteration, it is the same. *Humphries* v. *Taylor*, in Canc. Hil. 25 Geo. II., 7 Bac. Abr. by Gwillim, p. 363.

lands to A. and B., as joint tenants in fee, and afterwards struck out the name of B. by drawing a pen through it. It was holden that the erasure was to be considered as a revocation of the devise *pro tanto* only (24). A., by will duly executed and attested (*h*), devised land to B. and C. in trust, and afterwards struck out the name of C. and inserted the names of D. and E., leaving the general purposes of the trust unaltered, though varying in certain particulars, and did not republish his will. It was holden, that the intent of the testator appeared to be to revoke by the substitution of another good devise to the new trustees, and not by the obliteration; but such devise, not having been executed with the proper solemnities, would not operate as a revocation; and, admitting that the obliteration of the name of C. would have revoked the devise to C., yet the heir could not recover, inasmuch as the devise to B. remained unrevoked, and competent to sustain all the trusts in the will in exclusion of the heir.

Implied Revocations.]—Although the section of the statute of frauds now under review has enumerated several methods by which a devise of lands may be revoked, and although it should seem to have been the intention of the legislature to have excluded every other method of revocation, yet has it been holden, that implied revocations are not within the statute. Implied revocations, strictly so termed, are, 1st, when certain acts are done by the testator, inconsistent with or contradictory to the dispositions made by the will, so necessarily inferring an intention to revoke, that the law will presume such an intention. As where the devisor (*i*), by a subsequent deed, gives the devisee in fee a lesser interest, *e. g.* an estate for years, to commence after the death of the devisor: in such case the intended devisee cannot have both interests; that which is conveyed by the deed must take effect, and, therefore, the law makes a necessary implication, that the first disposition, which is by the will, is revoked. In like manner, where the devisor having devised a reversion to A., afterwards grants the same to B., this will be a revocation, even though the lessee has not attorned. So where the testator, having devised land to A., bargains and sells the same land to B., although the deed be not inrolled within six months, according to the statute, and, consequently, nothing can pass to the bargainee, yet this will amount to a revocation, because here is a solemn act done, whereby the testator has clearly evinced

(*h*) *Short d. Gastrell* v. *Smith*, 4 East, 419.

(*i*) *Coke* v. *Bullock*, Cro. Jac. 49, cited

in *Harkness* v. *Bayley*, Pr. Ch. 514, and 2 Atk. 72.

---

(24) A mere change of trustees will not revoke a prior devise of the equitable estate. *Willet* v. *Sandford*, 1 Ves. 178, 186; *Doe* v. *Pott*, Doug. 710; *Watts* v. *Fullarton*, (cited) Doug. 718.

his intention, that the devisee should not have the land devised (25).
2. It has been holden, that revocations are necessarily to be implied
or presumed, from a total change in the circumstances of the testator's family after the execution of the will. This head of revocation was originally borrowed from the civil law (26), and applied
in the first instance to bequests of personal estate (k), and afterwards extended to devises of land, such revocation not having been
considered as excluded by the provisions of the 6th section of the
statute of frauds. What changes or alteration in the circumstances
of the testator will be sufficient to work a revocation of a devise
of land, may often be difficult to decide. It has, however, been
solemnly determined, that a subsequent marriage, *and* the birth of
a child, *without provision (l) made for the objects of these relations,* is such a material change in the circumstances of the testator's family, as will work a revocation of the devise of land (27).

(k) *Lugg* v. *Lugg*, Salk. 592; *Over-*   (l) See *Exp. E. of Ilchester*, 7 Ves.
bury v. *Overbury*, 2 Show. 242.   jun. 242.

---

(25) I am not aware, that the two last-mentioned instances have ever
been solemnly decided. They are mentioned in 1 Roll. Abr. 615, (P)
pl. 5, 6, as the opinions of *Popham* and *Gawdy*, Js.; but, from subsequent cases, where they have been cited, it appears that they have been
considered as law. Gilbert has inserted them in his Treatise on Devises,
p. 95, 96, ed. 1739.

(26) N. By the common law, before the statute of frauds, a subsequent marriage was holden to revoke a will of land made by a feme sole;
although such marriage was had with the person in whose favour the will
was made. *Forse* v. *Hemblinge*, 4 Rep. 60, b.

(27) An opinion has been expressed in *Brown* v. *Thompson*, at the
Rolls, 8 Dec. 1731, by Sir *John Trevor*, M. R., and afterwards in the
same case by Lord Keeper *Wright*, (1 P. Wms. 304, n.; 1 Eq. Ca. Abr.
413,) that revocations of a devise of land might be implied from subsequent marriage and birth of a child, notwithstanding the provision of the
6th section of the statute of frauds; but this point was not considered as
settled until the case of *Christopher* v. *Christopher*, 2 Dickens, 445,
when it was solemnly determined by *Adams*, B., *Smythe*, B., and *Parker*,
C. B., against the opinion of *Perrot*, B., who thought the case within
the statute, and that the dispute concerning the reality of a subsequent
marriage, and the legitimacy of children, was as open to perjury as any
other, and that the statute intended an actual and not a presumptive revocation. The case of *Christopher* v. *Christopher* has been recognized in
several subsequent cases, viz. in *Spraage* v. *Stone*, Ambl. 721; *Brady*
v. *Cubitt*, Doug. 31; *Doe* v. *Lancashire*, 5 T. R. 49; in *Kenebel* v.
Scrafton, 2 East, 530; *Exp. E. Ilchester*, 7 Ves. 348; *Sheath* v. *York*,
1 Ves. & Beames, 397. N. Marriage alone, or the subsequent birth of
children unprovided for alone, is not sufficient to operate as a revocation

In a subsequent case the rule was thus laid down (*m*) : that, in the case of the will of an unmarried man having no children by a former marriage, whereby he devises away the whole of his property which he has at the time of making his will, and leaves no provision for any child of the marriage, the law annexes the tacit condition that subsequent marriage and the birth of a child operates as a revocation. And in a case where, after making his will, the testator married, and his wife became pregnant with his knowledge, the post umous child was considered for this purpose in the same condition as a child born during the testator's lifetime (*n*). This rule of revocation, like the preceding, was formerly considered as grounded upon a presumed alteration of intention in the testator ; but Lord *Kenyon*, C. J. (*o*), thought it was founded "on a tacit condition annexed to the will when made, that it should not take effect if there should be a total change in the situation of the testator's family" (28). But this rule has been holden to apply only in cases where the wife and children, the new objects of duty, are wholly unprovided for, and where there is an entire disposition of the whole estate to their exclusion and prejudice. Hence (*p*), where A. devised certain lands to B. in trust, and directed him to pay, out of the rents and profits, an annuity to M. S., with whom he cohabited, and in case he should leave any child or children by M. S., to raise a sum of money to be paid among his children, and then devised the remainder of his estate to several of his relatives ; and afterwards A. married M. S., by whom he had several children : it was holden, that the will was not revoked ; either, 1st, on the ground of a tacit condition annexed to the will, *viz.* that it should be void in the event of a marriage and children, *without provision* ; inasmuch as that condition, *viz.* of marriage, and of the birth of children *unprovided for*, had not taken effect ; or 2ndly, on the ground of an intention to revoke, to be presumed, in favour of a wife and children unprovided for ; because the fact, upon which such presumption could be formed, did not exist in the present case. And it must further be remarked, that both the circum-

(*m*) By *Tindal*, C. J., delivering judgment in Exch. Chamb. in *Marston* v. *Roe d. Fox*, 8 A. & E. 60 ; 2 Nev. & P. 504.

(*n*) *Doe* v. *Lancashire*, 5 T. R. 49.

(*o*) *Ib.*, recognized by *Tindal*, C. J.,

delivering judgment in *Marston* v. *Roe d. Fox*, on error in Exch. Chamb., 8 A. & E. 57, 8 ; 2 Nev. & P. 504.

(*p*) *Kenebel* v. *Scrafton*, 2 East, 530.

of a will of personal estate*. Per Dr. *Hay*, in *Shepherd* v. *Shepherd*, Hil. 1770, in the Prerogative Court. Nor of real estate. *Doe* v. *Barford*, 4 M. & S. 10.

(28) Lord *Ellenborough*, C. J., delivering the judgment of the court in *Kenebel* v. *Scrafton*, seems to have approved of Lord *Kenyon's* opinion.

* *Jackson* v. *Hurlock*, Lord *Northington*, Ch., S. P., Amb. 494 ; 2 Eden, 63, *S. C.*

stances of a subsequent marriage and the having of child or children must concur to work an implied revocation: the birth of a posthumous child alone, although the testator die childless, is not sufficient (*q*).

Having endeavoured to illustrate the nature of implied revocations, strictly so called, it will be proper, in the next place, to take notice of those acts, by which a devise of land may more properly be said to be annulled than revoked; though the latter term is most frequently applied to this subject. The acts here alluded to are such, whereby a material alteration is made by the testator, in his seisin of the estate devised, after the execution of the will. The authorities on this subject are of very ancient date, beginning in the latter end of Queen Elizabeth's reign, and continued down in a regular series to the present time, with a few exceptions. The rule to be collected from these authorities appears to be this,—that *where a person seised of an estate, devises it, and afterwards conveys his whole interest, either by feoffment, lease and release* (*r*), *bargain and sale, fine* (*s*), *or recovery* (*t*), *though but for an instant, and though he takes back the estate to the same use as before, or though the old use results to him again so as to descend in the same line as before, still the conveyance operates to annul his will.* This rule is founded on a technical principle of law, introduced, as it should seem, originally in favour of the heir; *viz.* that in order to render a devise valid and effectual, it is necessary that the seisin of the devisor should remain unaltered from the execution of the will until the death of the devisor. The foundation of the rule being wholly independent of the intention of the testator to revoke, the rule will operate where the provisions of the subsequent conveyance are consistent with the provisions of the will; and even where such conveyance is made for the express purpose of confirming the will. Hence, also, parol evidence to show that the testator did not intend, by the subsequent conveyance, to revoke his will, is inadmissible (*u*). In conformity with the preceding rule (*x*), it has been holden, that where *the whole estate* is conveyed by lease and release to uses, although there be a resulting use in the ultimate reversion to the grantor by the same instrument, yet the conveyance will operate as a revocation of a prior will. It will be observed that, in the preceding instances, the *whole* estate was conveyed; and therefore the party did not die seised of that estate which he had at the time of making his will; and consequently the devise, which will only operate upon that seisin, which the testator had at the time of making his will, was annulled or revoked: but where the devisor does not

(*q*) *Doe d. White* v. *Barford*, 4 M. & S. 10.

(*r*) *E. of Lincoln's* case, 2 Freem. 202; Show. P. C. 154, *S. C.*

(*s*) *Doe d. Dilnot* v. *Dilnot*, 2 N. R. 401; *Parker* v. *Biscoe*, 8 Taunt. 699; 3 Moore, 24, *S. C.*

(*t*) *Doe d. Lushington* v. *Bp. of Llandaff*, 2 N. R. 491.

(*u*) *Goodtitle* v. *Otway*, 2 H. Bl. 516.

(*x*) *Goodtitle* v. *Otway*, 1 Bos. & Pul. 576; 7 T. R. 399.

part with his whole estate, *e. g.* where he grants an estate for years only, to the devisee, to commence in the life of the devisor, in such case, the conveyance will not operate as a revocation of the fee (*y*). In like manner, if a man devises land in fee to A., and afterwards makes a mortgage thereof in fee, either to the devisee (*z*) or a stranger (*a*), this mortgage in fee, though a revocation of the will in law, will not operate as such in equity, and the right of redemption will pass by the will. And the same rule holds in equity with respect to a conveyance in fee for payment of debts (*b*).

The foregoing sections of the statute of frauds, and the construction thereof, are applicable to all wills made before the 1st of January, 1838, at which time the Act for the Amendment of the Laws with respect to Wills, 1 Vict. c. 26, came into operation. The general object (*c*) of this act is to collect the provisions of the several statutes relating to wills into one act, and to make in those provisions such modifications as may afford additional securities for the prevention of spurious wills, and additional facilities for making genuine wills. The particular provisions relate to the property which may be disposed of by will; the persons by whom wills may be made; the forms which are to be observed in making them; and the modes of revoking, altering, and reviving them; to which are added, other provisions for correcting certain rules of construction, by which the intentions of testators were often defeated.

The 1st section defines the meaning of the following words in this act: "Will" shall extend to a testament, and to a codicil, and to an appointment by will or by writing in the nature of a will in exercise of a power, and also to a disposition by will and testament or devise of the custody and tuition of any child, by virtue of stat. 12 Car. II. c. 24, or of stat. 14 & 15 Car. II. (I.), and to any other testamentary disposition; "real estate," shall extend to manors, advowsons, messuages, lands, tithes, rents, and hereditaments, whether freehold, customary freehold, tenant right, customary or copyhold, or of any other tenure, and whether corporeal, incorporeal, or personal, and to any undivided share thereof, and to any estate, right, or interest (other than a chattel interest) therein; "personal estate" shall extend to leasehold estates and other chattels real, and also to monies, shares of government and other funds, securities for money (not being real estates), debts, choses in action, rights, credits, goods, and all other property, which by law devolves upon the executor or administrator, and to any share or interest

---

(*y*) 2 Atk. 72; *Vawser* v. *Jeffery*, 3 B. & A. 462.

(*z*) *Baxter* v. *Dyer*, 5 Ves. jun. 656.

(*a*) Admitted to be a settled point in *York* v. *Stone*, Salk. 158. Adjudged by Sir *John Churchill*, M. R., and Lord

Jefferies, Ch., in *Hall* v. *Dunch*, 1 Vern. 329, 342.

(*b*) Adm. in *Cave* v. *Holford*, 3 Ves. jun. 654.

(*c*) See Ld. *Langdale's* speech, February 23, 1837.

therein; and every word importing the singular number only shall extend to several persons or things, as well as one person or thing; and every word importing the masculine gender only, shall extend to a female as well as a male. By sect. 2, 32 Hen. VIII. c. 1; 34 & 35 Hen. VIII. c. 5; 10 Car. I. sess. 2, c. 2, (I.); sections 5, 6, 12, 19, 20, 21 and 22 of the statute of frauds; 29 Car. II. c. 3; 7 Will. III. c. 12, (I.); 4 & 5 Ann. c. 16, s. 14; 6 Ann. c. 10, (I.); section 9 of 14 Geo. II. c. 20; 25 Geo. II. c. 6, except as to colonies. 25 Geo. II. c. 11, (I.); and 55 Geo. III. c. 192, are repealed, except so far as the same respectively relate to any will or estates *pur autre vie*, to which this act does not extend. Formerly, such real estates only as a person was seised of at the time of making his will, would pass by the will; real estate purchased intermediately between the making the will and the death, would not so pass: but now, by sect. 3, every person may devise, bequeath, or dispose of, by his will executed in manner hereinafter required, all real estate and all personal estate which he shall be entitled to, either at law or in equity, at the time of his death, and which if not so devised would devolve upon the heir at law, or customary heir of him, or, if he become entitled by descent, of his ancestor, or upon his executor, or administrator; and the power hereby given shall extend to all real estate of the nature of customary freehold or tenant right, or customary or copyhold, notwithstanding that the testator may not have surrendered the same to the use of his will, or notwithstanding that, being entitled as heir, devisee, or otherwise to be admitted thereto, he shall not have been admitted thereto, or notwithstanding that the same, in consequence of the want of a custom to devise or surrender to the use of a will or otherwise, could not at law have been disposed of by will if this act had not been made, or notwithstanding that the same, in consequence of there being a custom that a will or a surrender to the use of a will should continue in force for a limited time only, or any other special custom, could not have been disposed of by will according to the power contained in this act, if this act had not been made; and also to estates *pur autre vie*, whether there shall or shall not be any special occupant thereof, and whether the same be freehold, customary freehold, tenant right, customary or copyhold, or of any other tenure, and whether the same shall be a corporeal or incorporeal hereditament: and also to all contingent, executory, or other future interests in any real or personal estate, whether the testator may or may not be ascertained as the person or one of the persons in whom the same respectively may become vested, and whether he may be entitled thereto under the instrument by which the same respectively were created, or under any disposition thereof by deed or will; and also to all rights of entry for conditions broken, and other rights of entry; and also to such of the same estates, interests, and rights respectively, and other real and personal estate, as the testator may be entitled to at the time of his death, notwithstanding that he may become entitled to the same subsequently to the execution of his will.

The 4th section requires, where estates have not been surrendered to the use of will, the payment of fees, fines, and stamp duties, by the devisees of customary freehold, copyhold and customary estates.

The 5th section enacts, that the wills or extracts of wills of customary freeholds, &c. shall be entered on the court rolls, and that the lord shall be entitled to the same fine, &c. when such estates could not have been disposed of by will if this act had not been made, as he would have been from the customary heir in case of descent.

For the 6th section, which relates to estates *pur autre vie*, see *ante*, p. 792.

By sect. 7, no will made by any person under the age of twenty-one years shall be valid; and sect. 8 provides, that no will made by any married woman shall be valid, except such a will as might have been made by a married woman before the passing of this act. By sect. 9, no will shall be valid unless it shall be in writing and executed in manner hereinafter mentioned, (that is to say,) it shall be signed at the foot or end thereof by the testator, or by some other person in his presence and by his direction; and such signature shall be made or acknowledged by the testator in the presence of two or more witnesses present at the same time, and such witnesses shall attest and shall subscribe the will in the presence of the testator, but no form of attestation shall be necessary. By sect. 10, no appointment made by will, in exercise of any power, shall be valid, unless the same be executed in manner before required; and every will executed in manner before required shall, so far as respects the execution and attestation thereof, be a valid execution of a power of appointment by will, notwithstanding it shall have been expressly required that a will made in exercise of such power should be executed with some additional or other form of execution or solemnity.

Sect. 11 excepts wills of personal estate made by soldiers in actual service, or mariners or seamen at sea.

Sect. 12 leaves untouched the provisions of 11 Geo. IV. and 1 Will. IV. c. 20, with respect to wills of petty officers and seamen and marines. By sect. 13, every will executed in manner before required shall be valid without any publication thereof; and by sect. 14, if any person who shall attest the execution of a will shall, at the time of the execution thereof, or at any time afterwards, be incompetent to be admitted a witness to prove the execution thereof, such will shall not, on that account, be invalid. By sect. 15, if any person shall attest the execution of any will, to whom, or to whose wife or husband, any beneficial devise, legacy, estate, gift, or appointment, of or affecting any real or personal estate, (except charges and directions for the payment of any debt,) shall be thereby given or made, such devise, &c. shall, so far only as concerns such person attesting the execution of such will, or the wife or husband of such person, or any person claiming under them, be utterly void; and such person so attesting shall be admitted as a witness to prove the execution of such will, or to prove the validity or invalidity thereof, notwithstanding such devise, &c. By sect. 16, in case by any will any real or personal estate shall be charged with any debt, and any creditor, or the wife or husband of any creditor, whose debt is so charged, shall attest the execution of such will, such creditor, notwithstanding such charge, shall be admitted a witness to prove the execution of such will, &c.

By sect. 17, no person shall, on account of his being an executor of a will, be incompetent to be admitted a witness to prove the execution of such will, &c.

By sect. 18, every will made by a man or woman shall be revoked by his or her marriage, (except a will made in exercise of a power of appointment, when the real or personal estate thereby appointed would not, in default of such appointment, pass to his or her heir, customary heir, executor, or administrator, or the person entitled as his or her next of kin, under the statute of distributions). By sect. 19, no will shall be revoked by any presumption of an intention on the ground of an alteration in circumstances.

By sect. 20, no will or codicil, or any part thereof, shall be revoked otherwise than as aforesaid, or by another will or codicil executed in manner before required, or by some other writing declaring an intention to revoke the same, and executed in the manner in which a will is hereinbefore required to be executed, or by the burning, tearing, or otherwise destroying the same by the testator, or by some person in his presence and by his direction, with the intention of revoking the same. It has been decided in the ecclesiastical courts, that cutting out (d) the signature amounts to a revocation under this section.

By sect. 21, no obliteration, interlineation, or other alteration made in any will after the execution thereof, shall be valid or have any effect, except so far as the words or effect of the will before such alteration shall not be apparent, unless such alteration shall be executed in like manner as hereinbefore is required for the execution of the will; but the will, with such alteration as part thereof, shall be deemed to be duly executed if the signature of the testator and the subscription of the witnesses be made in the margin or on some other part of the will opposite or near to such alteration, or at the foot or end of or opposite to a memorandum

(d) *Hobbs* v. *Knight*, 1 Curt. Eccles. Rep. 768.

referring to such alteration, and written at the end or some other part of the will.

By sect. 22, no will or codicil, or any part thereof, which shall be in any manner revoked, shall be revived otherwise than by the re-execution thereof, or by a codicil executed in manner hereinbefore required, and showing an intention to revive the same; and when any will or codicil which shall be partly revoked, and afterwards wholly revoked, shall be revived, such revival shall not extend to so much thereof as shall have been revoked before the revocation of the whole thereof, unless an intention to the contrary shall be shown.

By sect. 23, no conveyance or other act made or done subsequently to the execution of a will of or relating to any real or personal estate therein comprised, except an act by which such will shall be revoked as aforesaid, shall prevent the operation of the will with respect to such estate or interest in such real or personal estate as the testator shall have power to dispose of by will at the time of his death.

By sect. 24, every will shall be construed, with reference to the real estate and personal estate comprised in it, to speak and take effect as if it had been executed immediately before the death of the testator, unless a contrary intention shall appear by the will. By sect. 25, unless a contrary intention shall appear by the will, such real estate or interest therein as shall be comprised or intended to be comprised in any devise in such will contained, which shall fail or be void by reason of the death of the devisee in the lifetime of the testator, or by reason of such devise being contrary to law or otherwise incapable of taking effect, shall be included in the residuary devise (if any) contained in such will.

By sect. 26, a general devise of the testator's lands shall include copyhold and leasehold as well as freehold lands. By sect. 27, a general devise shall include estates over which the testator has a general power of appointment. By sect. 28, where any real estate shall be devised to any person without any words of limitation, such devise shall be construed to pass the fee simple, or other the whole estate or interest which the testator had power to dispose of by will in such real estate, unless a contrary intention shall appear by the will. By sect. 29, the words "die without issue," or "die without leaving issue," shall be construed to mean, die without issue living at the death. By sect. 30, where any real estate (other than or not being a presentation to a church) shall be devised to any trustee or executor, such devise shall be construed to pass the fee simple or other the whole estate or interest which the testator had power to dispose of by will in such real estate, unless a definite term of years, absolute or determinable, or an estate of freehold, shall thereby be given to him expressly or by implication. By sect. 31, where any real estate shall be devised to a trustee, without any express limitation of the estate to be taken by such trustee, and the beneficial interest in such real estate, or in the surplus rents and profits thereof, shall not be given to any person for life, or such beneficial interest shall be given to any person for life, but the purposes of the trust may continue beyond the life of such person, such devise shall be construed to vest in such trustee the fee simple, or other the whole legal estate which the testator had power to dispose of by will in such real estate, and not an estate determinable when the purposes of the trust shall be satisfied.

By sect. 32, where any person to whom any real estate shall be devised for an estate tail, or an estate in quasi entail, shall die in the lifetime of the testator leaving issue who would be inheritable under such entail, and any such issue shall be living at the time of the death of the testator, such devise shall not lapse, but shall take effect as if the death of such person had happened immediately after the death of the testator, unless a contrary intention shall appear by the will. By sect. 33, where any person being a child or other issue of the testator, to whom any real or personal estate shall be devised or bequeathed for any estate or interest not determinable at or before the death of such person, shall die in the lifetime of the testator leaving issue, and any such issue of such person shall be living at the time of the death of the testator, such devise or bequest shall not lapse, but shall take effect as if the death of such person had happened immediately after the death of the testator, unless a contrary intention shall appear by the will. By sect. 34, this act shall not extend to any will made before 1st of January, 1838, and every will re-executed or republished, or revived by any codicil, shall, for the purposes of this act, be deemed to have been made at the time at which the same shall be so re-executed, re-published, or revived; and this act shall not extend to any estate *pur autre vie* of any person who shall die before the 1st of January, 1838. By sect. 35, this act shall not extend to Scotland.

CHAPTER XXIII.

GAME.

I. *Of the Right of taking and destroying the Game at Common Law, and of the Stat. 1 & 2 Will. IV. c. 32, p. 895.*

II. *Of the Appointment and Authority of Gamekeepers, p. 902.*

III. *Of the Destruction of the Game at improper Seasons of the Year, p. 904.*

IV. *Of the Duties made Payable in respect of Game Certificates, p. 904.*

I. *Of the Right of taking and destroying the Game at Common Law, and of the Stat. 1 & 2 Will. IV. c. 32.*

IT has been asserted by Sir W. Blackstone, in his Commentaries, that, by the common law, the sole property of all the game in England is vested in the king alone, and that the sole right of taking and destroying the game belongs exclusively to the king; and, consequently, that no person, of whatever estate or degree, has a right to kill game, even upon his own land, unless by license or grant from the king. This position, however, has been questioned by Mr. Christian, in a note to his edition of the Commentaries, vol. 2, p. 419, n. 10. See also Mr. Justice *Coleridge's* note, vol. 2, p. 419. If A. start a hare in the ground of B., and hunt and kill it there, the property continues all the while in B.; but if A. start a hare in the ground of B., and hunt it into the ground of C., and kill it there, the property is in A., the hunter, but A. is liable to an action of trespass for hunting in the ground, as well of B. as C. (a). Trespass for a dead hare, the property of plaintiff.— The plaintiff, a farmer, being out hunting with hounds of which he had in part the management, and actually had such management at the time, though the hounds belonged to other persons,

(a) Per *Holt*, C. J., in *Sutton* v. *Moody*, 1 Ld. Raym. 251; 2 Salk. 556; 5 Mod. 375, S. C.; *Deane* v. *Clayton*, 7 Taunt. 489.

the hounds put up a hare in a third person's ground, and followed her into a field of the defendant, where, being quite spent, she ran between the legs of a labourer who was accidentally there, where one of the dogs caught her, and she was taken up alive by the labourer, from whom the defendant immediately afterwards took the hare and killed her. Shortly after the plaintiff came up, and claimed to have the hare as his own, but the defendant refused to give it up, and questioned the right of the plaintiff to be where he then was. The labourer, upon his examination at the trial, swore that when he took the hare from the dogs, he did not mean to take it for his own use, but in aid of the hunters. Verdict for the plaintiff, 40s. damages. Rule for new trial, after argument, was discharged; Lord *Ellenborough*, C. J. (b), observing, that the plaintiff, through the agency of his dogs, had reduced the hare into his possession. The labourer took it for the benefit of the hunters, which is the same as if it had been taken by one of the dogs. Secus, if the labourer had taken it up for the defendant, before it was caught by the dogs, or if he had taken it as an indifferent person in the nature of a stakeholder. An exception in a conveyance made in the year 1655, of the free liberty of hawking and hunting, does not (c) include the liberty of shooting feathered game with a gun. Rooks are a species of birds feræ naturæ, destructive in their habits, not known as an article of food, and not protected by any statute; hence a person cannot have any property (d) in them, or show any right to have them resort to his trees.

The franchise of free warren is of great antiquity, and very singular in its nature. It gives a property in wild animals; and that property may be claimed in the land of another, to the exclusion of the owner of the land. Such a right ought not to be extended by argument and inference to any animals not clearly within it. There is not any book in the law which has mentioned grouse as a bird of warren. Manwood confines his description to two species, pheasants and partridges. Hence it has been holden (e), that the owner of a free chase and free warren cannot maintain an action for killing and taking away grouse shot within the limits of the free warren. In a case where it did not appear that, at the time of the grant, the locus in quo was applied to purposes of warren, or that any distinct right of free warren, independent of the general forest right, was then subsisting on it; and the grant did not contain any words showing an intention of the crown to create such right, and pass it de novo, it was holden (f), that free warren would

(b) *Churchward* v. *Studdy*, 14 East, 249.

(c) *Moore* v. *Lord Plymouth*, 7 Taunt. 614.

(d) *Hannam* v. *Mockett*, 2 B. & C. 934.

(e) *Duke of Devonshire* v. *Lodge*, 7 B. & C. 36.

(f) *Smith* v. *Carr*, B. R. Trin. 53 Geo. III., shortly reported in a note to *Attorney General* v. *Parsons*, 2 Tyrw. 243; 2 Cr. & Jer. 270; S. C. will be found among the paper books of Dampier, J. P. B. D. No. 27, Dampier MSS. Lincoln's Inn Library.

not pass by general words in a grant from the crown of lands within a forest of the crown. A grant, by the king, of free warren of land of which he is seised in fee, is a grant of free warren in gross (*g*).—James I. granted to R. T. and his heirs, the king's manor and town of Aulton, and the king's hundred of Aulton, with its rights, and all other things to the said manor and hundred belonging; and also, that they should have free warren and free chase in all their demesne lands in the hundred, manor, town, tenements, and hereditaments, aforesaid, and on all other lands and woods being in the same hundred, &c., although the same demesne and other lands were within the king's forest, &c.; it was holden (*h*), that this grant did not confer a right of free warren over the king's lands within the hundred, but that the term "demesne" applied to lands held by R. T. as lord of the manor of Aulton, and that "other lands" applied to tenemental lands held by R. T. in fee of the king, or of any other lord within the limits of the grant. The term "demesne lands" properly signifies lands of a manor, which the lord either has, or potentially may have, in propriis manibus.

The right of taking and destroying the game can only be exercised on a person's own estate; and not even a lord of a manor (1), or his gamekeeper, can go into any part of the manor, which is not the lord's own estate or waste, without being a trespasser, as any other person would be; unless a right of entry in pursuit of the game be specially reserved to him. A grant to a person, *his heirs and assigns*, of the liberty with servants or otherwise, to come upon certain land, and there to hawk, hunt, &c. at their will and pleasure, is a grant of a profit *à prendre*, and not a mere personal license of pleasure; and therefore enables the grantee to hawk, hunt, &c. on the land, and carry away the game, or authorize his servants to do so in his absence (*i*). But a grant of full liberty to a person, his executors and administrators, and his and their friends, in his or their company, or with his or their permission, and to and for his or their gamekeeper, to hunt, course, shoot, and fish, over lands, is not such an interest as can pass under the execution of a power to

(*g*) *Morris* v. *Dimes*, 1 Ad. & Ell. 654.   (*i*) *Wickham* v. *Hawker*, 7 M. & W.
(*h*) *Attorney General* v. *Parsons*, 2   63.
Cr. & Jer. 279; 2 Tyrw. 243, S. C.

---

(1) Mr. Christian has remarked, that the common opinion, that the lord of the manor has a peculiar right to the game, superior to that of any other duly qualified landowner within the manor, is erroneous. He conceives that this opinion owes its rise to the power which lords of manors have of appointing gamekeepers, a power originally given to them by stat. 22 & 23 Car. II. c. 25, the first statute in which lords of manors are distinguished from other landowners with respect to the game.

lease lands or any part or parts thereof (*k*). " It is the land itself which gives the right of shooting, and the lessor has no power to separate the land from one of its incidents" (*l*).

For the qualifications of estate and degree, which were necessary under the old statutes, to entitle a person to keep and use guns, &c. for the destruction of the game, and the construction thereof, the reader is referred to the eighth and former editions of this work. These qualifications, with the other acts relating to the game, were repealed by stat. 1 & 2 Will. IV. c. 32, the 6th section of which enacts, that every person, who shall have obtained an annual game certificate, shall be authorized to kill and take game, subject to an action or such other proceedings as are mentioned in the statute. By sect. 2, the word game shall, for all the purposes of this act, be deemed to include hares, pheasants, partridges, grouse, heath or moor game, black game, and bustards.

By sect. 7, in all cases, where any person shall occupy any land under any lease or agreement made previously to the passing of this act, excepting in the cases hereinafter next excepted, the lessor or landlord shall have the right of entering upon such land, or of authorizing any other person who shall have obtained any annual game certificate to enter upon such land, for the purpose of killing or taking the game thereon; and no person occupying any land under any lease or agreement, either for life or for years, made previously to the passing of this act, shall have the right to kill or take the game on such land, except where the right of killing the game upon such land has been expressly granted or allowed to such person by such lease or agreement, or except where, upon the original granting or renewal of such lease or agreement, a fine or fines shall have been taken, or except where, in the case of a term for years, such lease or agreement shall have been made for a term exceeding twenty-one years.

By sect. 8, nothing in this act contained shall authorize any person seised or possessed of, or holding, any land, to kill or take the game, or permit any other person to kill or take the game, upon such land, in any case where, by any act, deed, grant, lease, or any written or parol demise or contract, a right of entry upon such land for the purpose of killing or taking the game hath been or hereafter shall be reserved or retained by or given or allowed to any grantor, lessor, landlord, or other person; nor shall any thing in this act contained, defeat or diminish any reservation, exception, covenant, or agreement already contained in any private act of parliament, deed, or other writing relating to the game upon any land, nor in any manner prejudice the rights of any lord or owner of any forest, chase, or warren, or of any lord of any manor, lordship, or

(*k*) *Dayrell* v. *Hoare*, 4 P. & D. 114.   (*l*) Per *Patteson*, J., *ibid*.

royalty, or reputed manor, &c., or of any steward of the crown of any manor, &c. appertaining to his Majesty.

By sect. 9, this act is not to affect any of his Majesty's forest rights, &c.; nor, by sect. 10, any cattle-gates or rights of common; and lords of manors are to have the game on their wastes.

By sect. 11, where the lessor or landlord shall have reserved to himself the right of killing the game upon any land, it shall be lawful for him to authorize any other person who shall have obtained an annual game certificate, to enter upon such land for the purpose of pursuing and killing game thereon.

By sect. 12, where the right of killing the game upon any land is by this act given to any lessor or landlord, in exclusion of the right of the occupier of such land, or where such exclusive right hath been or shall be specially reserved by or granted to, or doth or shall belong to the lessor, landlord, or any person other than the occupier of such land, then and in every such case, if the occupier of such land shall pursue, kill, or take any game, upon such land, or shall give permission to any person so to do, without the authority of the lessor, landlord, or other person having the right of killing the game upon such land, such occupier shall, on conviction thereof before two J. P., pay a sum not exceeding two pounds, and for every head of game so killed or taken a sum not exceeding one pound, with costs.

By sect. 23, persons killing or taking any game, or using any dog, net, gun, or other engine or instrument for the purpose of searching for or killing or taking game, not being authorized so to do for want of a game certificate, shall, on conviction before two J. P., forfeit for every such offence a sum not exceeding five pounds, with costs: provided, that no person so convicted shall, by reason thereof, be exempted from any penalty or liability under any statute relating to game certificates, but that the penalty imposed by this act shall be deemed to be a cumulative penalty.

By sect. 30, reciting, that after the commencement of this act, game will become an article, which may be legally bought and sold, and it is therefore just to provide some more summary means than now by law exist for protecting the same from trespassers: it is enacted, that if any person shall commit any trespass, by entering or being in the day time upon any land in search or pursuit of game, or woodcocks, snipes, quails, landrails, or conies, such person shall, on conviction thereof before a J. P., forfeit a sum not exceeding two pounds, with costs; and if any persons to the number of five or more together shall commit any trespass, by entering or being in the day time upon any land in search or pursuit of game, or woodcocks, snipes, quails, landrails, or conies, each of such persons shall, on conviction thereof before a J. P., forfeit a sum not exceeding five pounds, with costs: provided, that any person charged with any such trespass shall be at liberty to prove, by way of defence, any matter which would have been a defence to an action at law for such trespass; save and except that the leave and license of the occupier of the land so trespassed upon shall not be a sufficient defence in any case, where the landlord, lessor, or other person shall have the right of killing the game upon such land by virtue of any reservation or otherwise, as before mentioned; but such landlord, lessor, or other person shall, for the purpose of prosecuting for each of the two offences herein last before mentioned, be deemed to be the legal occupier of such land, whenever the actual occupier thereof shall have given such leave or license; and that the lord or steward of the crown of any manor, lordship, or royalty, or reputed manor, lordship, or royalty, shall be deemed to be the legal occupier of the land of the wastes or commons within such manor, &c. or reputed manor, &c.

By sect. 31, where any person shall be found on any land, or upon his Majesty's forests, parks, chases, or warrens, in the day time, in search or pursuit of game, or woodcocks, snipes, quails, landrails, or conies, the person having the right of killing the game upon such land, by virtue of any reservation or otherwise, as before mentioned, or the occupier of the land (whether there shall or shall not be any such right by reservation or otherwise), or the game-keeper or servant of either of them, or any person authorized by either of them, or the warden, ranger, verderer, forester, master-keeper, underkeeper, or other officers of such forest, &c., may require the person so found forthwith to quit the land whereon he shall be so found, and also to tell his christian name, surname, and place of abode; and in case such person shall, after being so required, offend by refusing to tell his real name, or place of abode, or by giving such a general description of his place of abode as shall be illusory for the purpose of discovery, or by wilfully continuing or returning upon the land, the party so requiring as aforesaid, and any person acting by his order and in his aid, may apprehend such offender, and convey him as soon as conveniently may be before a J. P.; and such offender (whether so apprehended or not), upon being convicted of any such offence before a J. P., shall forfeit a sum not exceeding five pounds, with costs: provided, that no person so apprehended shall, on any pretence, be detained for a longer period than twelve hours from the time of his apprehension until he shall be brought before some J. P., and that if he cannot, on account of the absence or distance of the residence of any such J. P., or owing to any other reasonable cause, be brought before a J. P. within such twelve hours, then the person so apprehended shall be discharged, but may nevertheless be proceeded against for his offence by summons or warrant, according to the provisions hereinafter mentioned, as if no such apprehension had taken place.

By sect. 34, for the purposes of this act, the *day time* shall be deemed to commence at the beginning of the last hour before sunrise, and to conclude at the expiration of the first hour after sunset.

By sect. 35, the aforesaid provisions against trespassers and persons found on any land, shall not extend to any person hunting or coursing upon any lands with hounds or greyhounds, and being in fresh pursuit of any deer, hare, or fox, already started upon any other land, nor to any person *bonâ fide* claiming and exercising any right or reputed right of free warren or free chase, nor to any gamekeeper lawfully appointed within the limits of any free warren, or free chase, nor to any lord or any steward of the crown of any manor, lordship, or royalty, or reputed manor, &c., nor to any gamekeeper lawfully appointed by such lord or steward within the limits of such manor, &c: or reputed manor, &c.

By sect. 36, when any person shall be found by day or night upon any land, or in any of his Majesty's forests, parks, chases, or warrens, in search or pursuit of game, and shall then and there have in his possession any game which shall appear to have been recently killed, it shall be lawful for any person having the right of killing the game upon such land by virtue of any reservation or otherwise, as before mentioned, or for the occupier of such land, (whether there shall or shall not be any such right, reservation, or otherwise,) or for any gamekeeper or servant of either of them, or for any officer as aforesaid of such forest, &c., or for any person acting by the order and in aid of any of the said several persons, to demand from the person so found such game in his possession, and in case such person shall not immediately deliver up such game, to seize and take the same from him, for the use of the person entitled to the game upon such land, forest, park, chase, or warren. For the best manner of pleading a justification for an act done under the authority of this section, see *Wisdom* v. *Hodson*, 3 Tyrw. 811.

By sect. 46, nothing in this act shall prevent any person from proceeding, by way of civil action, to recover damages in respect of any trespass upon his land, whether committed in pursuit of game or otherwise, save and except that where any proceedings shall have been instituted under the provisions of this act, against any person for or in respect of any trespass, no action at law shall be maintainable for the same trespass by any person at whose instance or with whose concurrence or assent such proceedings shall have been instituted, but that such proceedings shall, in such case, be a bar to any such action, and may be given in evidence under the general issue. (See new Rule as to plea " by statute," *ante*, p. 29.)

By sect. 47, for the protection of persons acting in the execution of this act, it is enacted, that all actions and prosecutions to be commenced against any person for any thing done in pursuance of this act, shall be laid and tried in the county where the fact was committed, and shall be commenced within six calendar months after the fact committed, and not otherwise; and notice in writing of such action, and of the cause thereof, shall be given to the defendant one calendar month at least before the commencement of the action; and the defendant may plead the general issue, and give this act and the special matter in evidence; and no plaintiff shall recover in such action, if tender of sufficient amends shall have been made before such action brought, or if a sufficient sum of money shall have been paid into court after such action brought, by or on behalf of the defendant.

A person acting as a gamekeeper by virtue of a deputation, granted under stat. 48 Geo. III. c. 93, is not entitled (m) to a month's notice of action under this section, for " no one is a gamekeeper under the late act, unless he be registered with the clerk of the peace under it; the defendant is excluded, therefore, from the privileges conferred by the act, by the express language of sect. 16 (n), the deputation being not only given, but registered, under the old law.

The foregoing act does not extend to Scotland or Ireland. As to Scotland, see 2 & 3 Will. IV. c. 68. For offences relating to the game, which are the subject of indictment, or other penal enactment, see stat. 9 Geo. IV. c. 69, for the more effectual prevention of persons going armed by night for the destruction of game.

II. *Of the Appointment and Authority of Gamekeepers under the New Act.*

By stat. 1 & 2 Will. IV. c. 32, s. 13, any lord of a manor, lordship, or royalty, or reputed manor, &c., or any steward of the crown of any manor, lordship, or royalty appertaining to his Majesty, may, by writing under hand and seal, or in case of a body corporate, then under the seal of such body corporate, appoint one or more persons as gamekeepers, to preserve or kill the game within the limits of such manor, &c. or reputed manor, &c., for the use of such lord or steward thereof, and may authorize such gamekeeper, within the same limits, to seize and take for the use of such lord or steward, all such dogs, nets, and other engines and instruments for the killing or taking of game as shall be used within the said limits by any person not authorized to kill game for want of a game certificate. By sect. 14, any lord of a manor, &c.

(m) Per *Tindal*, C. J., in *Bush* v. *Green*, 4 Bingh. N. C. 41; 5 Scott, 289; recognized in *Lidster* v. *Borrow*, 9 A. &

E. 654, S. P.
(n) See p. 903, where this section is set out.

or reputed manor, &c., or any steward of the crown of any manor, &c. appertaining to his Majesty, may appoint and depute any person, whether acting as a gamekeeper to any other person or not, or whether retained and paid for as the male servant of any other person or not, to be a gamekeeper for any such manor, &c. or reputed manor, &c., or for such district of such manor, &c., as such lord or steward of the crown shall think fit, and may authorize such person, as gamekeeper, to kill game within the same for his own use, or for the use of any other person who may be specified in such deputation, and also may give to such person all such power and authorities as may, by virtue of this act, be given to any gamekeeper of a manor; and no person so appointed gamekeeper, and empowered to kill game for his own use, or for the use of any other person so specified as aforesaid, and not killing any game for the use of the lord or steward of the crown of the manor, &c. or reputed manor, &c., for which such deputation shall be given, shall be deemed to be or shall be entered or paid for as the gamekeeper or male servant of the lord or steward making such deputation. By sect. 6, it is provided, that no game certificate, on which a less duty than £3 13s. 6d. is chargeable, under the act relating to game certificates, shall authorize any gamekeeper to kill or take any game, or to use any dog, gun, net, or other engine or instrument for the purpose of killing or taking game, except within the limits included in his appointment as gamekeeper.

Sect. 15 contains regulations as to the appointment of gamekeepers by landowners of a certain value in Wales.

By sect. 16, no appointment or deputation of any person as a gamekeeper by virtue of this act shall be valid, unless, and until, it shall be registered with the clerk of the peace for the county, riding, division, liberty, franchise, city, or town, wherein the manor, lordship, or royalty, or reputed manor, &c., or the lands, shall be situate, for or in respect of which such person shall have been appointed gamekeeper; and in case the appointment of any person as gamekeeper shall expire or be revoked, by dismissal or otherwise, all powers and authorities given to him by virtue of this act shall immediately cease.

Sect. 17 authorizes persons who have obtained an annual game certificate, to sell game to any person licensed to deal in game. Provided, that no game certificate on which a less duty than £3 13s. 6d. is chargeable under the acts relating to game certificates shall authorize any gamekeeper to sell any game, except on the account and with the written authority of the master, whose gamekeeper he is; but that any such gamekeeper selling any game not on the account and with the written authority of such master, may be proceeded against under this act, in the same manner as if he had no game certificate.

III. *Of the Destruction of the Game at improper Seasons of the Year.*

By stat. 1 & 2 Will. IV. c. 32, s. 3, persons killing or taking any game, or using any dog, gun, net, or other engine or instrument for the purpose of killing or taking any game, on a Sunday or Christmas-day, on conviction before two J. P. shall forfeit a sum not exceeding £5, with costs; and persons killing or taking any partridge between the 1st of Feb. and the 1st of Sept., or any pheasant between the 1st of Feb. and the 1st of Oct., or any black game, (except in the county of Somerset or Devon, or in the New Forest,) between the 10th of Dec. and the 20th of Aug. in the succeeding year, or in the county of Somerset or Devon, or in the New Forest, between the 10th of Dec. and the 1st of Sept.; or any grouse, commonly called red game, between the 10th of Dec. and the 12th of Aug.; or any bustard, between the 1st of March and the 1st of Sept., shall, on conviction before two J. P., forfeit, for every head of game so killed or taken, a sum not exceeding £1, with costs; and persons, with intent to destroy or injure any game, putting poison or poisonous ingredients on the ground, whether opened or enclosed, where game usually resort, or in any highway, shall, on conviction before two J. P., forfeit a sum not exceeding £10, with costs. By sect. 4, the possession of birds of game is made illegal after ten days in licensed dealers, and forty days in other persons, from the expiration of the season limited by the foregoing section.

IV. *Of the Duties made payable in respect of Game Certificates.*

By the Game Act, 1 & 2 Will. IV. c. 32, s. 5, the existing laws respecting game certificates are to remain unaltered.

By stat. 48 Geo. III. c. 55, entitled (*inter alia*) An Act for repealing the Duties on Game Certificates, and granting new Duties to be placed under the Management of the Commissioners of Taxes, " Every person using any dog, gun, net, or other engine, for the purpose of taking or killing game, or any woodcock, snipe, quail, or landrail, or any conies in G. B., if such person be a servant to a person charged in respect of such servant by this act, and shall use any dog, &c. for any of the before-mentioned purposes, upon a manor or royalty in England, Wales, or Berwick-on-Tweed, or Scotland, by virtue of a deputation or appointment duly registered or entered as gamekeeper, is charged with the annual sum of

£1 1s. (1), and if not a servant for whom the duties on servants shall be charged, the annual sum of £3 3s. (2): and every other person using any dog, &c. for any of the purposes before mentioned, is chargeable with the annual sum of £3 3s. with two exceptions only; 1st, the taking woodcocks and snipes, with nets and springes; and 2nd, the taking or destroying conies in warrens, or in any enclosed ground, or by any person in land in his occupation, either by himself or by his direction." These duties are to be paid to the collector of assessed taxes for the place where party resides; and the collector is authorized to give a receipt, and to demand 1s. of the party for the same, over and above the duty, as a compensation for his trouble. The receipt being delivered to the clerk of the commissioners of the district, he will exchange it for a certificate, gratis. Gamekeepers, in whose behalf a receipt and certificate have been obtained by their masters, are not required to obtain a certificate for themselves; but it is provided that the certificate shall be void upon the revocation of the deputation, but the same may be renewed, for the remainder of the year, in behalf of the new gamekeeper. The same statute provides that unqualified persons shall not be protected by the certificate; and that the protection of gamekeepers' certificates shall not extend beyond the limits of the manor for which they are appointed. The following persons may demand the production of certificate, and permission to read or take a copy of it, viz. the assessor or collector of the parish where the party is using dog, &c.; commissioners of assessed taxes for the county, riding, division, or place; lord, lady, or gamekeeper of the manor; inspector of taxes for the district; any person duly assessed to these duties for killing game; and lastly, the owner, landlord, lessee, or occupier of the land. If certificate is not produced, then the party who has made the demand, may require the person using the dog, gun, &c., under a penalty of £20, to declare his christian and surname, and place of residence, and parish or place in which he has been assessed; lastly, persons who use dogs, guns, &c. without having obtained certificate, are to pay the duty of £3 3s. by way of surcharge, and a penalty of £20. It is not necessary, that the demand of the certificate should be made on the land (o) on which the party was sporting; but if not, the demand must be made immediately, and so as in some degree to form a part of the same transaction. Nor is it necessary, that the party making the demand should produce any certificate; and if the other party

(o) *Scarth* v. *Gardener*, 5 C. & P. 40, *Tenterden*, C. J.

---

(1) Four shillings were added by stat. 52 Geo. III. c. 93.

(2) Ten shillings and sixpence added to this and the following sum by stat. 52 Geo. III. c. 93.

refuse to produce (*p*) his certificate, he does so at the risk of whether the party demanding it is a gamekeeper, or other person having a right to demand it.

By stat. 52 Geo. III. c. 93, Sched. (L.) XIII. the penalties are recoverable before any two or more commissioners for the affairs of taxes, who shall give judgment for the penalty; or for such part thereof as the commissioners shall think proper to mitigate, not being less than one moiety. By stat. 54 Geo. III. c. 141, (27 July, 1814,) the duties and penalties contained in the schedule of the 52 Geo. III. c. 93, relating to persons aiding or assisting or intending to aid or assist in the taking or killing of any game, or any woodcock, snipe, quail, landrail, or coney, shall, after the passing of this act, severally cease and determine; provided that the act of aiding and assisting as aforesaid, and in the said act mentioned, shall be done in the company or presence and for the use of another person who shall duly have obtained a certificate in his own right, according to the directions of the said act, and who therein shall, by virtue of such certificate, then and there use his own dog, gun, net, or other engine, for the taking or killing of such game, &c., and who shall not act therein by virtue of any deputation or appointment.

By stat. 2 & 3 Vict. c. 35, s. 3, all game certificates are to expire on the 5th July instead of the 5th April; and by sect. 4, justices of the peace are authorized to hold special sessions, for the purpose of granting licenses to deal in game, at any time after July in every year, as well as in July, as enacted by stat. 1 & 2 Vict. c. 32, s. 18, and under similar regulations as to notice, &c., and the licenses are to continue till the 1st July next following.

(*p*) *Scarth* v. *Gardener*, 5 C. & P. 40, *Tenterden*, C. J.

CHAPTER XXIV.

IMPRISONMENT.

I. *Of the Nature of the Action for false Imprisonment, and in what Cases it may be maintained, p. 907.*

II. *Statutes relating to the Action for false Imprisonment,* 21 *Jac. I. c.* 12, *p.* 913; 24 *Geo. II. c.* 44, *p.* 914.

III. *Of the Pleadings, p.* 920.

I. Of the Nature of the Action for false Imprisonment, and in what Cases it may be maintained.

FALSE imprisonment is a restraint on the liberty of the person without lawful cause; either by confinement in prison, stocks, house, &c., or even by forcibly detaining the party in the streets, against his will (a). For this injury an action of trespass *vi et armis* lies, usually termed an action for false imprisonment. An unlawful detention is a new caption, and may be declared on as such (b). An arrest on mesne process, which is not returned, is wrongful (c), and false imprisonment will lie against the sheriff (d); so if an officer of an inferior court does not return the process directed to him, he is a trespasser *ab initio,* and false imprisonment lies against him; for he is as sheriff within the jurisdiction. The sheriff must, at his peril, execute the writ upon the person really named therein (e); and if he mistakes the person, he is liable to an action for false imprisonment. A. B. brought false imprisonment against C. (f), who justified that he had a warrant to arrest *J. S.,* and having asked A. B., the plaintiff, what his name was, he answered *J. S.,* whereupon C. arrested A. B. Plaintiff demurred, and

(a) Per *Thorpe,* C. J., 22 Ass. fo. 104, pl. 85.
(b) Cro. Jac. 379.
(c) 2 Rol. Ab. 563, pl. 9.
(d) *Id.* pl. 18.

(e) Per *Hankford,* J., 11 Hen. IV. 91, a. See also *Thurbane and another,* Hardr. 323, per *Hale,* C. B.
(f) Moor, 457; Hardr. 323, S. P.

judgment for plaintiff, because C., the defendant, ought, at his peril, to have taken notice of the person named in the writ. A commission of rebellion issued against I. G. appeared before the commissioners, and affirmed himself to be the person, whereupon they apprehended him by virtue of their commission. Per *Hale*, C. B. (*g*), "If a wrong man be taken, though he affirm himself to be the person against whom the commission is awarded, yet the commissioners having no warrant to take him by the commission, his affirming himself to be the person will be no excuse in false imprisonment, as has been held on the execution of a capias." A sheriff's officer (*h*) having received a warrant to arrest A., whose person he had never seen, went to her house, where he found her and the plaintiff together. Addressing himself to the plaintiff, he said, "I have a writ against you;" upon which A. desired the plaintiff to go with the officer. The officer immediately took plaintiff to a sponging house, where he kept her all night; but the next morning, having discovered his mistake, he released her. *Kenyon*, C. J., admitted the law to be as stated in the preceding case; but considering this as a trick on the officer, directed the jury to give the plaintiff nominal damages only, which they did accordingly. But if a person whose real name is W. is asked, before process issues against him, whether his name is not John, and he says it is, he cannot maintain trespass for imprisonment under process against him by the wrong name (*i*). If a magistrate's warrant is shown by the constable (*k*), who has the execution of it, to the person charged with an offence, and he thereupon *voluntarily, and without any, even the slightest, compulsion,* attends the constable to the magistrate, who after examination dismisses him, it seems that this will not constitute an arrest, so as to enable the party to maintain trespass for an assault and false imprisonment (1). So where a sheriff's officer, to whom a warrant upon a writ against A. was delivered, sent a message to A. and asked him to fix a time to call and give bail; and A. accordingly fixed a time, attended, and gave bail; it was holden (*l*), that this was not either an actual or constructive arrest. The sheriff's officer did not take a warrant with him, nor did he tell A. that he came to arrest him, but merely gave notice of the writ, and asked him to fix a time for giving bail.

An action for false imprisonment was brought by a native and

(*g*) Hardr. 323, upon motion for an attachment against G. which was granted.

(*h*) *Oxley* v. *Flower*, B. R. Middx. Sittings, Dec. 4, 1800, MSS. See *Morgans* v. *Bridges*, 1 B. & A. 647, and *Brunskill* v. *Robertson*, 9 A. & E. 840.

(*i*) Per Ld. *Ellenborough*, C. J., *Price*

v. *Harwood*, 3 Campb. 108.

(*k*) *Arrowsmith* v. *Le Mesurier*, 2 Bos. & Pul. N. R. 211. See also *Bisten* v. *Burridge*, 3 Campb. 139; *Peters* v. *Stanway*, 6 C. & P. 737; *Wood* v. *Lane*, 6 C. & P. 774.

(*l*) *Berry* v. *Adamson*, 6 B. & C. 528.

(1) Words merely will not make an arrest. *Genner* v. *Sparks*, Salk. 79.

inhabitant of Minorca (*m*), (then part of the dominions of the
crown of Great Britain,) against the governor of the island, for
imprisoning the plaintiff at Minorca, and causing him to be carried
thence to Carthagena, in Spain. The plaintiff laid the venue in
London, stating the injury to have been committed at Minorca, to
wit, at London, &c. The defendant justified, on the ground that
the plaintiff had endeavoured to create a mutiny among the inhabitants of Minorca, whereupon the defendant, as governor, was
obliged to seize the plaintiff, and imprison him, &c. The plaintiff
replied *de injuriâ suâ propriâ.* After verdict for plaintiff, with
£3000 damages, a bill of exception was tendered, and error having
been assigned thereon, it was contended, among other things,
1st, That the plaintiff, being a Minorquin, was incapacitated from
bringing an action in the king's courts in England; but it was
holden, that a subject born in Minorca was as much entitled to
appeal to the king's courts as a subject born in Great Britain; and
that the objection of its not being stated on the record, that the
plaintiff was born since the treaty of Utrecht, did not make any
difference. 2ndly, It was objected, that the injury having been
done at Minorca, out of the realm, could not be tried in the king's
courts in England; but it was holden, that an action for false imprisonment being a transitory action, it was competent to the
plaintiff to lay it in any county of England, although the matter
arose beyond the seas (2). If a person causes another to be impressed, he does it at his own peril, and is liable in damages, if
that person can show that he was not subject to the impress service.
The defendant went to the place of rendezvous (*n*) for the impress
service, near the Tower, and gave information that there was a
young man (meaning the plaintiff) at a house she described, who
was liable to be impressed, and who was a fit person to serve his
Majesty. In consequence of this, the plaintiff was seized by the
press-gang, and carried on board the tender, where he was detained,
until it was discovered that he had never been in a ship before,
except once, when he had been in like manner wrongfully impressed.
An action for trespass and false imprisonment having been brought,
it was objected, that the form of action should have been an action
on the case, and not an action of trespass; but Lord *Ellenborough,*
C. J., was of a different opinion, observing, that this was not like
a malicious prosecution, where a party gets a valid warrant or writ,
and gives it to an officer to be executed. There was clearly a
trespass here in seizing the plaintiff, and the defendant therefore

(*m*) *Mostyn* v. *Fabrigas,* in error, M.   (*n*) *Flewster* v. *Royle,* 1 Campb. 187,
T. 15 Geo. III. B. R. Cowp. 161 (2).   Ld. *Ellenborough,* C. J.

(2) The proceedings in all the stages of the cause will be found reported at great length in the eleventh volume of the State Trials, p. 162,
edited by Mr. Hargrave.

was a trespasser in procuring it to be done. An action will not lie
at common law for false imprisonment (o), where the imprisonment
was merely in consequence of taking a ship *as prize*, although the
ship has been acquitted. Trespass for false imprisonment will lie
against overseers of the poor for imprisoning a man under a justice's
warrant (p), until he should pay a sum of money for the maintenance of a child which should be born of a woman then pregnant
by plaintiff, but who had not as yet been delivered. Trespass will
lie (q) against an attorney and client for suing out an illegal *ca. sa.*
and causing a party to be arrested. So where A. employed B., an
attorney, to enforce payment of a debt; B. directed his agent to
sue out a justicies in the county court. Before the return of the
justicies the debtor paid debt and costs to B. B.'s agent, not
knowing of such payment, afterwards entered up judgment in the
county court, although the defendant had not appeared, and sued
out execution: it was holden (r), that A. and B. were liable as
trespassers; for A. was answerable for the act of B., his attorney,
and B. and his agent were to be considered as one person. And
where an arrest is made under process which is afterwards set aside
for irregularity, the attorney in the suit is liable in trespass, as
well as the plaintiff (s). If A., having been robbed (t), suspect B.
to be guilty of the robbery, and take B., and deliver him into the
charge of a constable present, B. (if innocent) may maintain
trespass and false imprisonment against A. If a prisoner *in execution* escape by the voluntary permission of the gaoler, and the
gaoler retake him, he is liable to an action for false imprisonment (u). But an officer who has arrested a prisoner on *mesne
process*, and voluntarily permitted him to escape, may retake him
before the return of the writ, without being liable to such action.
Trespass for false imprisonment will lie for a detention under a
lawful process, if it be executed at an unlawful time, as on a
Sunday (x); for by stat. 29 Car. II. c. 7, s. 6, it is provided, " That
no person upon the Lord's day shall serve or execute any writ,
process, warrant, order, judgment, or decree, (except in case of
treason, felony, or breach of the peace) (3); the service of such

(o) *Le Caux* v. *Eden*, Doug. 594.
(p) *Wenman* v. *Fisher*, M. 2 Geo. II.,
B. R. MSS., cited in *R.* v. *Banghurst*,
H. 5 Geo. II. B. R., Sess. Ca. vol. 1, p.
149.
(q) *Barker* v. *Braham*, 3 Wils. 368.
(r) *Bates* v. *Pilling and another*, 6 B.
& C. 38.
(s) *Codrington* v. *Lloyd*, 8 A. & E.
449.
(t) *Stonehouse* v. *Elliott*, 6 T. R. 315.
(u) *Atkinson* v. *Matteson*, 2 T. R. 172.
(x) *Wilson* v. *Tucker*, Salk. 78; 5
Mod. 95, *S. C.*

(3) In *Taylor* v. *Freeman and another*, Glouc. Lent Ass. 1757,
MSS., it appeared that the defendants, as constables, had arrested the
plaintiff upon a Sunday, by virtue of a warrant from a justice of the
peace, for getting a bastard child. An action for false imprisonment having
been brought, *Adams*, Baron, held, that plaintiff was entitled to recover.

writ, &c. shall be void, and the person serving or executing the same shall be as liable to the suit of the party grieved, and to answer damages to him for doing thereof, as if he had done the same without any writ, process, &c." This statute forbids serving *original* process only on a Sunday. Where, therefore, there has been an escape against the will of bailiff, he may retake on a Sunday. Secus, if voluntary. 2 Gundry, 14 MSS. Trespass for false imprisonment may be maintained against the sheriff for an arrest made by his bailiff after the return day of the writ (*y*).

When a court has jurisdiction of the cause (*z*), and proceeds *inverso ordine*, or erroneously, an action does not lie against the party who sues, or the officer or minister of the court who executes the precept or process of the court; but when the court has not jurisdiction of the cause, the whole proceeding being *coram non judice*, an action will lie against them, without any regard to the precept or process (4). Hence, where one of the bail had been arrested by process out of the Marshalsea (*a*) for the purpose of satisfying a judgment obtained against the principal in a cause, of which the Marshalsea Court had no jurisdiction, it was holden, that an action for false imprisonment would lie against the party who sued, the marshal who directed the execution of the process, and the officer who executed the same. In the case of a warrant, illegal on the face of it, for an excess of jurisdiction in the magistrate, trespass is maintainable against the committing magistrate, although the conviction has not been quashed (*b*); but where the justice has competent jurisdiction, his judgment is conclusive, until reversed or quashed, and the conviction cannot be controverted in evidence (*c*). A conviction stated that plaintiff, having been brought before a magistrate on an information charging him with having unlawfully returned without a certificate to a parish from whence he had been removed, and that upon that occasion he confessed himself guilty; it was holden (*d*), that this conviction was good upon the face of it, and that it was not necessary to state in it expressly any act of vagrancy, it being for the party convicted to show in his defence, that he did not return in a state of pauperism. A magistrate had committed the plaintiff for re-examination for a

---

(*y*) *Parrot* v. *Mumford*, 2 Esp. N. P. C. 585, *Prior*, C. J.

(*z*) Second resolution, *Marshalsea* case, 10 Rep. 76, a.

(*a*) *Marshalsea* case, 10 Rep. 68, b.

(*b*) *Groome* v. *Forrester*, 5 M. & S. 314.

(*c*) *Strickland* v. *Ward*, 7 T. R. 633, n.; *Fawcett* v. *Fowlis*, 7 B. & C. 394..

(*d*) *Mann* v. *Davers*, 3 B. & A. 103.

---

(4) This principle has been recognized in several cases. See *Nichols* v. *Walker*, Cro. Car. 395; *Hill* v. *Bateman*, Str. 711; *Shergold* v. *Holloway*, Str. 1002. Sessions Cases, vol. 2, p. 100, *S. C.*; *Perkin* v. *Proctor*, 2 Wils. 384, and since in *Brown* v. *Compton*, 8 T. R. 424.

period of fourteen days. The jury found that the commitment was *bonâ fide*, and without any improper motive, but that the time for which the commitment was made was unreasonable. In such case trespass (*e*) is the proper remedy, and not case; for the better opinion is, that such commitment is wholly void. A magistrate, who commits a party in a case where he has not any jurisdiction, is liable to an action of trespass; but if the charge be of an offence over which, if the offence charged be true in fact, the magistrate has jurisdiction, the magistrate's jurisdiction cannot be made to depend upon the truth or falsehood of the facts, or upon the evidence being sufficient or insufficient to establish the *corpus delicti* brought under investigation (*f*). If a justice of the peace make a warrant to a constable to bring A. B. before him, for a matter of which he has a general cognizance, though the J. P. had no foundation in fact for granting such a warrant, or though the warrant itself be defective in point of form, yet the constable may justify under it; but if the J. P. make a warrant to take up A. B. to answer in a plea of debt, a constable cannot justify under such a warrant, because the justice has not any jurisdiction of debts (*g*). Where a magistrate has a general jurisdiction over the subject matter, and a party comes before him and prefers a complaint, upon which the magistrate makes a mistake in thinking it a case within his authority, and grants a warrant which is not justifiable in point of law, the party complaining is not liable as a trespasser, but the only remedy against him is by an action upon the case, if he has acted maliciously. The magistrate acting without any jurisdiction at all is liable as a trespasser in many cases; but this liability does not extend to the constable, who acts under a warrant, and the statute 24 Geo. II. cap. 44, was passed with the object of protecting such officers (*h*).

Where a statutory protection is given to persons having acted in pursuance of the statute, a party is not entitled to the protection merely because he believed, *bonâ fide*, that he was so acting; there must be reasonable ground for the belief. If the party acted under a reasonable, though mistaken persuasion, from appearances, that the facts were such as made his proceeding justifiable by the statute, he is entitled to protection, though the real facts were such that the statute clearly affords no justification (*i*).

Trespass *vi et armis* will not lie against commissioners of bankrupt (*k*), for a commitment by them for not fully answering to their satisfaction lawful questions proposed by them to a party whom

(*e*) *Davis* v. *Capper*, 10 B. & C. 38.
(*f*) *Cave* v. *Mountain*, 1 Man. & Gr. 257.
(*g*) *Shergold* v. *Holloway*, Str. 1002.
(*h*) Per Lord *Abinger*, C. B., in *West* v. *Smallwood*, 3 M. & W. 420.

(*i*) *Cann* v. *Clipperton*, 10 A. & E. 582, and see *Cook* v. *Leonard*, 6 B. & C. 351; *Beechey* v. *Sides*, 9 B. & C. 806; *Reed* v. *Cowmeadow*, 6 A. & E. 661; *Wedge* v. *Berkeley*, 6 A. & E. 663.
(*k*) *Doswell* v. *Impey*, 1 B. & C. 163.

they have authority to examine, and upon a subject into which they have authority to inquire. But the commissioners have not authority to commit (*l*) a person brought before them to be examined for giving an unsatisfactory answer to an immaterial question. A witness summoned by commissioners of bankrupt under the 6 Geo. IV. c. 16, s. 33, was required by them to read certain entries in a ledger, and on his refusal to do so was committed by them for refusing to answer a question. It was holden (*m*), that the commitment was illegal, inasmuch as the request to read was neither in form nor in substance a question. By stat. 5 & 6 Will. IV. c. 29, s. 25, Court of Review and subdivision courts are declared to have been courts of record from the passing of 1 & 2 Will. IV. c. 56, but no single judge or commissioner is authorized to impose a fine or commit for a contempt, but every contempt of single judge or commissioner is cognizable by Court of Review. An action for false imprisonment will lie (*n*) against a superior officer, where the imprisonment at first was legal, but was afterwards aggravated with many circumstances of cruelty, and continued beyond ordinary bounds. So where a captain of a man-of-war imprisoned a person three days for a supposed breach of duty, without hearing him, and then released (*o*) him without bringing him to a court-martial.

II. *Statutes relating to the Action for False Imprisonment*, 21 *Jac. I. c.* 12, *p.* 913; 24 *Geo. II. c.* 44, *p.* 914.

Stat. 21 *Jac. I. c.* 12.—By this stat. sect. 5, "if any action, bill, plaint, or suit, for false imprisonment, shall be brought against any J. P., mayor, or bailiff of city, or town corporate, headborough, portreve, constable, tithing-man, churchwarden, or overseer of the poor, and their deputies, or any other, (who in their aid, or by their commandment, shall do any thing concerning their office,) concerning any thing by them done by virtue of their office, such action, bill, &c. shall be laid within the county where the trespass was committed." 2. "The above-mentioned persons may plead the general issue, and give the special matter in evidence." 3. "If upon the trial, the plaintiff shall not prove that the trespass was committed within the county wherein the action, &c. is laid, then the jury shall find the defendant, without respect to the plaintiff's evidence, *not guilty*." 4. "If the verdict shall pass with the defendant, or plaintiff become nonsuit, or suffer any discontinuance, defendant shall have double costs." N. The officer or person acting in aid, in

(*l*) *Exp. Baxter*, 7 B. & C. 673.
(*m*) *Isaac* v. *Impey*, 10 B. & C. 442.
(*n*) *Wall* v. *M'Namara*, 1 T. R. 536.
(*o*) *Swinton* v. *Molloy*, 1 T. R. 537, n.

order to entitle himself to double costs, must obtain a certificate
from the judge, that, at the time of the trespass, he was a mayor,
constable, &c. and in the execution of his office, or that he was
acting in aid of mayor, constable, &c. (p). But it is not necessary that this certificate should be granted at the trial (q). The
provisions of the preceding statute having been found very salu-
tary, they were, by stat. 42 Geo. III. c. 85, s. 6, extended to all
persons holding a public employment, or any office, station, or
capacity, civil or military, either in or out of this kingdom, and
who, by virtue of such employment, have power to commit persons to safe custody; provided, that where any action shall be
brought against such persons in this kingdom, for any thing done
out of this kingdom, the plaintiff may lay the act to have been done
in Westminster, or in any county where the defendant shall reside.
By stat. 24 Geo. II. c. 44, s. 1, " No writ shall be sued out against,
nor any copy of any process at the suit of a subject shall be served
on, any J. P. (5), for any thing by him done in the execution of
his office, until notice in writing of such intended writ or process
shall have been delivered to him, or left at the usual place of his
abode, by the attorney or agent for the party who intends to sue, at
least one calendar month (6) before the suing out or serving the
same, in which notice shall be clearly and explicitly contained the
cause of action; on the back of which notice shall be indorsed the
name of such attorney or agent, with the place of his abode (7), who

(p) *Anon.* 2 Ventr. 45.   (q) *Harper* v. *Carr*, 7 T. R. 449.

---

(5) A Secretary of State* is not a justice of a peace within this statute,
and, therefore, his warrant, if bad, will not justify the officer who executes
it, nor is it necessary to demand a copy of the warrant before the bringing
of an action. So a king's officer is not within the statute, which means
to protect those officers only, who are bound to execute warrants directed
to them, as constables, &c.

(6) In computing the month, the day of giving the notice, and the day
of suing out the writ, are both to be excluded. *Young* v. *Higgon*, 6 M.
& W. 49, *ante*, p. 207, n.

(7) A notice written by the attorney, and signed by him thus: " Given
under my hand at Durham," was holden insufficient, because it did not
expressly state that Durham was the place of attorney's residence.
Taylor v. *Fenwick*, 3 Doug. 178, cited by *Lawrence*, J., in *Lovelace*
v. *Curry*, 7 T. R. 635. But a notice, indorsed with the name of the
plaintiff's attorney, with the addition of the words " of Birmingham,"
has been holden sufficiently descriptive of the attorney's place of residence. *Osborn* v. *Gough*, 3 Bos. & Pul. 551. So it is sufficient in
indorsing the attorney's name to put the initial only of his christian name:
as where the indorsement was thus, " D. Shuter," with the place of

* *Entick* v. *Carrington*, 2 Wils. 290.

shall be entitled to the fee of 20s. for preparing and serving such notice."

Two things are required by this clause before an action can be brought against a magistrate, one that the plaintiff shall give notice of the writ or process which he intends to sue out; the other, that such notice shall also contain the cause of action. This form, prescribed by the statute, must be religiously adhered to, as will appear by the following case:—

Plaintiff gave defendant notice, which, after reciting the cause of complaint, stated, that plaintiff would cause an action to be commenced against defendant; such notice was holden insufficient because it did not mention any writ or process (r). It is not necessary, however, that the *form of action* should be stated in the notice (s); but the plaintiff having given notice of one form of action cannot declare in another: Plaintiff gave notice of an action *on the case* for false imprisonment, and afterwards brought an action of *trespass* and false imprisonment. *Yates*, J., held the notice insufficient, as tending to mislead the J. P., who might know that an action on the case was improper, and such whereon the plaintiff might be nonsuited, and neglect to tender amends (t). But where the notice given was of an action against a magistrate alone, it was holden sufficient (u) to warrant proceedings against the magistrate and constable jointly. Where the subject matter is within the jurisdiction of the magistrate, and he intends to act as a magistrate at the time, however mistaken he may be, he is still within the protection of the statute. Hence, where *one* magistrate committed the mother of a bastard to custody for not filiating, it was holden that such magistrate was entitled to the notice prescribed by this statute, before an action for false imprisonment was brought against him, although the statute 18 Eliz. c. 3, s. 2, only gave jurisdiction in such matter to *two* justices of the peace (x). So where a magistrate acts upon a subject matter of complaint over which he has authority, but which arises out of his jurisdiction, he is entitled to notice (y).

By sect. 2, " Such J. P. may, at any time within one calendar month after such notice given, tender amends to the party complaining, or to his attorney, and in case the same is not accepted, may plead such tender in bar to any action grounded on such writ or process, together with the plea of not guilty, and any other plea,

(r) *Lovelace* v. *Curry*, 7 T. R. 631.

(s) *Sabin* v. *De Burgh*, 2 Campb. 196.

(t) *Strickland* v. *Ward*, Winchester Sum. Ass. 1767, reported in a note to *Lovelace* v. *Curry*, 7 T. R. 631.

(u) *Jones* v. *Simpson and another*, 1 Cr. & J. 174, recognizing *Robson* v. *Spearman and another*, 3 B. & A. 493.

(x) *Weller* v. *Toke*, 9 East, 364.

(y) *Prestidge* v. *Woodman*, 1 B. & C. 12.

abode in words at length. *Mayhew* v. *Locke*, 2 Marsh. R. 377 ; 7 Taunt. 63, *S. C.*

with leave of the court; and if upon issue joined the jury find the amends so tendered to have been sufficient, they shall give a verdict for the defendant; and in such case, or in case the plaintiff become nonsuit, or discontinue his action, or judgment be given for such defendant upon demurrer, such J. P. shall be entitled to the like costs as if he had pleaded the general issue only; and if the jury find that no amends were tendered, or that the same were not sufficient, and also against the defendant on such other plea, they shall give a verdict for the plaintiff, and such damages as they think proper, which he shall recover, together with his costs." And by sect. 3, " No such plaintiff shall recover any verdict against such J. P. where the action is grounded on any act of the defendant, as J. P., unless it is proved upon the trial that such notice was given; but in default thereof, such J. P. shall recover a verdict and costs." And by sect. 4, " In case such J. P. neglect to tender any amends, or have tendered insufficient amends before the action brought, he may, by leave of the court where such action depends, at any time before issue joined, pay into court such sum as he shall see fit; whereupon such proceeding shall be had as in other actions where the defendant is allowed to pay money into court." And by sect. 5, " No evidence shall be given by the plaintiff, on the trial of any such action, of any cause of action, except such as is contained in the notice." And by sect. 6, " No action shall be brought against any constable, headborough, or other officer (8), or against any person acting by his order and in his aid, for any thing done in obedience to any warrant under the hand or seal of any J. P., until demand has been made or left at the usual place of his abode, by the party intending to bring such action, or by his attorney, in writing (9), signed by the party (10) demanding the same, of the perusal and copy of such warrant, and the same has been refused or neglected for six days after such demand: and in case, after such demand and compliance therewith, any action be brought against such constable, &c. for any such cause as aforesaid, without making

---

(8) Churchwardens*, and overseers of the poor†, acting under a magistrate's warrant of distress for a poor's rate, are within the meaning of the words " other officer " in this statute, and consequently entitled to the protection which it affords, when sued in those actions to which the statute extends, *e. g.* trespass, &c.; but *secus* when sued in replevin, that being a proceeding not within the statute. See *post*, p. 917, 8.

(9) A duplicate original of demand is sufficient evidence. *Jory* v. *Orchard*, 2 Bos. & Pul. 39.

(10) Demand, signed by attorney, is within the meaning of this section. *Ib.* per *Buller*, J.

* *Harper* v. *Carr*, 7 T. R. 271.
† *Nutting* v. *Jackson*, E. 3 Geo. III. B. R., Bull. N. P. 24.

the J. P. who signed or sealed the warrant, defendant, on producing and proving such warrant at the trial, the jury shall give their verdict for the defendant, notwithstanding any defect of jurisdiction in such J. P.; and if such action be brought jointly against such J. P. and such constable, &c. then, on proof of such warrant, the jury shall find for such constable, &c., notwithstanding such defect of jurisdiction; and if the verdict be given against the J. P., the plaintiff shall recover his costs against him, to be taxed in such manner as to include the costs which the plaintiff is liable to pay to the defendant for whom such verdict is found (11).

This section does not extend to actions of assumpsit. Hence, where an action for money had and received was brought against an officer, who had levied money on a conviction by a J. P., the conviction having been quashed, it was holden, that a demand of the copy of the warrant was not necessary (z). Whether the term "action" extended to replevin or not, seems formerly to have been a *vexata quæstio*. In *Pearson* v. *Roberts and another*, Willes, 668, it was holden to extend to actions of replevin to *recover damages* (a); but *Willes*, C. J., in delivering the opinion of the court, took a distinction between a replevin by plaint, in the sheriff's court, for the recovery of the goods, and replevin by way of action, to recover damages, admitting that the former could not be considered as an action within the meaning of the statute. In *Milward* v. *Caffin*, 2 Bl. R. 1330, it was holden, that replevin was a proceeding, to which the statute had never been held to extend. On the last cited case, Lord *Kenyon* made the following observation, in *Harper* v. *Carr*, 7 T. R. 270:—"I will not now enter into an examination of the case of *Milward* v. *Caffin*, because that was decided on the form of the action, *replevin*, to which it was ruled this statute did not extend: had it not been for that decision I should have thought that the act *did* extend to a replevin, and certainly convenience requires that it should; otherwise it is in the plaintiff's power to evade the provisions of the act, by adopting a particular mode of proceeding, which depends on his own choice. Perhaps, however, it may be shown, on examination, that this case was rightly decided, whatever doubts may have been concerning it." Such was the opinion of Lord *Kenyon*; but the question to which it relates is now completely at rest: for, in *Fletcher* v. *Wilkins*, 6 East, 283, it was

(z) *Feltham* v. *Terry*, Bull. N. P. 24, E. 13 Geo. III. B. R.

(a) Q. Whether there be any mode of proceeding, by action of replevin, to recover damages, as contradistinguished from proceedings to have the goods again? See 6 East, 286.

(11) A similar protection is extended to messengers acting in obedience to warrants of commissioners of bankrupt, by stat. 6 Geo. IV. c. 16, s. 31, which see *post*, tit. "Trespass, Process."

expressly determined, that replevin was not an action within the
meaning of this statute; Lord *Ellenborough*, C. J., (who delivered
the judgment of the court,) observing, that the reason assigned by
Lord *Kenyon*, *ab inconvenienti*, had undoubtedly great weight; but
on the other hand, it appeared to the court, that the inconvenience
of depriving the subject of his remedy by replevin was full as great;
for it might happen, that no damages which a jury was properly
authorized to give, could compensate for the loss of a particular
chattel, which the owner might be for ever deprived of, if he could
not sue a replevin.   A constable acting under a warrant commanding him to take the goods of A., takes the goods of B., believing
them to belong to A.: it was holden (*b*), that he was entitled to
the protection of the statute, and that an action against him must
be brought within six calendar months.

   The officer must prove that he acted in obedience to the warrant;
and where the J. P. cannot be liable, the officer is not entitled to
the protection of the statute (*c*).   The act was intended to make
the justice liable instead of the officer; where, therefore, the officer
makes such a mistake as will not make the justice liable, the officer
cannot be excused.   Hence, an officer executing a warrant of a
justice of Norfolk at large, in the county of the city of Norwich,
was held not to be justifiable (*d*).   So where, under a warrant to
take up loose and disorderly persons, the constable took up a woman
of character. *Dawson* v. *Clerk*, Middlesex Sittings, 1 Bl. R. 563.
So where the warrant was to take up the authors, printers, and publishers of a libel, and the officers took up persons who did not fall
under any of those descriptions (*e*).   But if the officer act in obedience to the warrant, it is immaterial whether the warrant be legal
or not.   If the warrant direct the officer to seize "stolen goods,"
and he seizes goods which fall within the description contained in
the warrant in other respects, although they turn out not to be
stolen, he is still under the protection of the statute (*f*).

   Sect. 7.—" Where plaintiff in any such action against any J. P.
obtains a verdict, he shall be entitled to double costs, if the judge
(before whom the cause is tried) in open court will certify, on the
back of the record, that the injury, for which such action was
brought, was wilfully and maliciously committed."   This enactment
relates only to the costs incurred in the ordinary course of law (*g*).

   Sect. 8.—" No action shall be brought against any J. P. for any
thing done in the execution of his office, or against any constable,

(*b*) *Parton* v. *Williams and another*,
3 B. & A. 330, recognized in *Smith* v.
Wiltshire, 2 Brod. & Bingh. 619, and
Smith v. *Shaw*, 10 B. & C. 284.

   (*c*) *Money* v. *Leach*, 3 Burr. 1766; 1
Bl. R. 555, *S. C.*; *Milton* v. *Green*, 5
East, 233; *Bell* v. *Oakley*, 2 M. & S.
259.

   (*d*) Coram Ld. *Mansfield*, C. J., Norfolk Ass. 1761, 1 Bl. R. 563.
   (*e*) *Money* v. *Leach*, 1 Bl. R. 555; 3
Burr. 1766, *S. C.*
   (*f*) *Price* v. *Messenger*, 2 Bos. & Pul.
158.
   (*g*) Per *Taunton*, J., *Thomas* v. *Saunders*, 1 A. & E. 553.

&c. *acting as aforesaid,* unless commenced within six calendar months after the act committed."

" Acting as aforesaid," that is, under the warrant of a magistrate. If, therefore, a constable acts without a warrant, this statute does not apply, and the action against such constable may be brought after the expiration of six calendar months, and at any time within the period allowed by the statute of limitations, 21 Jac. I. c. 16 (*h*). Where a constable acting under a warrant commanding him to take the goods of A., took the goods of B., it was holden (*i*), that the constable not having acted in obedience to the warrant, which directed him to take the goods of A., the magistrate could not be responsible; and therefore there was not any necessity for demanding a copy of the warrant. So where, under a warrant against the goods of A., the defendant, an overseer took goods, already in the hands of the bailiff of A.'s landlord as a distress for rent (*k*). A perusal and copy of the warrant need not be demanded, where the officer does not act within his jurisdiction in obedience to the warrant (*l*).

If a man be imprisoned by a warrant of J. P. on the 1st day of January, and kept in prison till the 1st day of February, he may bring his action within six months after the 1st of February, for the whole is one entire trespass (*m*). In *Hardy* v. *Ryle*, 9 B. & C. 609, the question was moved, whether the last day of the imprisonment was to be considered as inclusive or exclusive. The month's imprisonment terminated on 14th December, and the writ was sued out on the 14th June following; it was holden, that the 14th December ought to be excluded in computing the six months, and consequently the action was commenced in due time. Where an act is required by statute to be done so many days *at least* before a given event, the time must be reckoned, excluding both the day of the act, and that of the event (*n*), for the rule is now clearly established, that so many days " at the least," mean so many clear days (*o*).

For the further protection of magistrates, it is enacted, by stat. 43 Geo. III. c. 141, that in all actions brought against any J. P., on account of any *conviction* made by virtue of any act of parliament, or by reason of any thing done, or commanded to be done, by such J. P., for the levying of any penalty, apprehending any party, or for or about the carrying such conviction into effect, *in case such*

(*h*) *Postlethwaite* v. *Gibson*, Middx. Sittings after M. T. 41 Geo. III., *Kenyon*, C. J., MSS., and 3 Esp. 226, *S. C.*
(*i*) *Parton* v. *Williams*, 3 B. & A. 330.
(*k*) *Kay* v. *Grover*, 7 Bingh. 312. See *Smith* v. *Wiltshire*, 2 B. & B. 619.
(*l*) Per *Parke*, B., *Gladwell* v. *Blake*, 5 Tyrw. 194; 1 Cr. M. & R. 645.

(*m*) *Pickersgill* v. *Palmer*, Bull. N. P. 24.
(*n*) *R.* v. *Js. of Shropshire*, (*Tibberton* v. *Newport*,) 8 A. & E. 173, recognizing *Zouch* v. *Empsey*, 4 B. & A. 522; and see *Young* v. *Higgon*, 6 M. & W. 49, *ante*, p. 914, n.
(*o*) *Mitchell* v. *Foster*, 4 P. & D. 150.

conviction shall have been quashed, the plaintiff, in such action, (besides the value and amount of the penalty, which may have been levied upon the plaintiff, in case any levy thereof shall have been made,) shall not be entitled to recover any more or greater damages than the sum of two-pence, nor any costs of suit, unless it shall be expressly alleged in the declaration in the action wherein the recovery shall be had, *and which shall be in an action upon the case only,* that such acts were done maliciously, and without any reasonable and probable cause. *Sect.* 2.—And further, that such plaintiff shall not be entitled to recover against such justice any penalty which shall have been levied, nor any damages or costs, in case such justice shall prove at the trial, that such plaintiff was guilty of the offence whereof he hath been convicted, or on account of which he hath been apprehended, or had otherwise suffered, and that he had undergone no greater punishment than was assigned by law for such offence. This statute applies to those cases only where there has been a conviction (*p*).

As to the circumstances under which a person is entitled to a statutory protection, see *Cann* v. *Clipperton,* 10 A. & E. 582, and *ante,* p. 912, and the cases there cited.

III. *Of the Pleadings.*

Money cannot be paid into court in this action. See stat. 3 & 4 Will. IV. c. 42, s. 21. The general issue to an action for false imprisonment is, Not Guilty. By stat. 7 Jac. I. c. 5, (made perpetual by 21 Jac. I. c. 12,) in an action upon the case, trespass, battery, or false imprisonment, against a J. P., mayor, bailiff, constable, &c. for any thing done by virtue of their offices, or against any other persons acting in their aid, and by their command, concerning their offices, the defendant may plead the general issue, and give the special matter in evidence. The power enjoyed by J. P., &c. under the foregoing statute, of giving the special matter in evidence under the plea of the general issue, is not taken away by the new rules of pleading, H. T. 4 Will. IV., the statute 3 & 4 Will. IV. c. 42, s. 1, having, by a proviso (*q*), expressly reserved such powers when given by act of parliament (*r*). But by R. G. T. 1 Vict. (*s*), unless the defendant insert in the margin of such plea the words, "by statute," such plea is to be taken not to have been pleaded by virtue of any act of parliament. Where a statute enables defendants to plead the general issue and give the special

(*p*) *Massey* v. *Johnson,* 12 East, 67.   *Haine* v. *Davey,* 4 A. & E. 892.
(*q*) See *ante,* p. 148.   (*s*) 4 Bingh. N. C. 816; 8 A. & E.
(*r*) See stat. 43 Eliz. c. 2, s. 19, and   279.

matter in evidence, the plea of Not Guilty, so pleaded, is not affected by the new rules of Hil. 4 Will. IV. but has the same operation as it had before they were made, putting in issue not only the defences peculiar to the statute, but all that would have arisen at common law (*t*). In other cases, matter of justification must be pleaded specially. Every plea of justification must admit the trespass. To an action for false imprisonment brought by A. against B., C., and D. (*u*), they pleaded a plea of justification, under process, wherein B. said, that he, as attorney for the plaintiff in the original action, delivered the warrant made by the sheriff upon the process to C. and D. as his bailiffs, to be executed in due form of law, and that C. and D. thereupon arrested the plaintiff A., and detained him in prison. This was holden to be a sufficient admission by B. of the trespass, for the purpose of his justification; for he who commands or directs another to do a trespass is guilty of the trespass, if done by the other person pursuant to his direction. To trespass for false imprisonment, the defendant may plead that he did it by lawful authority. It is a general rule of pleading, that where a party justifies a trespass under an authority given, he must show that authority (*x*). There is a difference, however, in this respect, where the justification is under judicial process, between the party to the cause, or a mere stranger, and the officer who executes the process of the court. The party to the cause, or mere stranger, must set forth in their plea the judgment (*y*), as well as the writ; but the officer need only show the writ (*z*) (12) under which he acted, for he is bound to execute the process of the

---

(*t*) *Ross* v. *Clifton*, 11 A. & E. 631; 1 G. & D. 72. See also *Williams* v. *Jones*, 11 A. & E. 643.

(*u*) *Rowe* v. *Tutte*, Willes, 14.

(*x*) 1 Inst. 283, a.; *Matthews* v. *Cary*, 3 Mod. 137; Carth. 73, S. C.

(*y*) Per *Holt*, C. J., *Britton* v. *Cole*, Carth. 443.

(*z*) *Turner* v. *Felgate*, 1 Lev. 95; *Cotes* v. *Michill*, 3 Lev. 20.

---

(12) Where final process issues, a return is not necessary, (*Hoe's* case, 5 Rep. 90;) consequently, it is not necessary to allege that such process was returned. (*Rowland* v. *Veale*, Cowp. 18, recognized in *Cheasely* v. *Barnes*, 10 East, 73; but there said by Lord *Ellenborough*, C. J., that if any ulterior process in execution is to be resorted to, to complete the justification, there it may be necessary to show to the court the return of the prior writ, in order to warrant the issuing of the other.) But an officer who justifies under process, which he ought to return, (and all mesne process ought to be returned,) must show that such process was returned. · *Middleton* v. *Price*, Str. 1184. " There is a difference, however, between the principal officer, to whom the writ is directed, and a subordinate officer; the former shall not justify under the process, unless he has obeyed the order of the court in returning it; otherwise it is of one who has not the power to procure a return to be made." Per *Holt*, C. J., in *Freeman* v. *Blewett*, Ld. Raym. 633, 634.

court, having competent jurisdiction, without inquiring after the judgment. And it is to be observed, that where the party to the cause and the officer join in pleading, the plea must contain all the requisites which would be necessary in case they had pleaded separately (a); for it is a general rule, that where two or more join in a defence, although the justification may be sufficient for one or more, yet if it be not sufficient for the rest, it will be bad as to all the defendants. Such are the rules of pleading, where the justification is founded on process out of the superior courts: but in justifying under process issuing out of inferior courts, greater strictness is required (b); as, 1, The nature and extent of the jurisdiction of the court below ought to be set forth (13); for the judges of the superior courts are not bound to take cognizance of it. N. This rule holds even in justifications by officers. 2. It ought to be stated, that the cause of action below arose within the jurisdiction of the court below: on this point, indeed, there has been a diversity of opinion; for in *Gwynne* v. *Poole and others,* Lutw. 935, it was holden, that a justification by the party, judge, and officer, to whom the process was directed, was good, although it did not state that the cause of action below arose within the jurisdiction of the court below: but in *Moravia* v. *Sloper and others,* Willes, 30, (where *Willes,* C. J., controverts with great ability the reasoning of *Powell,* J., in *Gwynne* v. *Poole,*) the propriety of this decision was questioned, and it was ruled, that although it might not be necessary for the *officers* (14) of the court below to make this averment in their plea, because they were punishable if they did not obey the process of the court; yet when the party, or his attorney, or a mere stranger, pleaded a justification under process of an inferior court of record, it was necessary for them to state, that the cause of action arose within the jurisdiction of the court (15). Merely

<hr>

(a) *Phillips* v. *Biron,* Str. 509; *Smith* v. *Bouchier,* Str. 993; *Middleton* v. *Price,* Str. 1184.

(b) *Moravia* v. *Sloper,* Willes, 37, recognized by *Lawrence,* J., in *Evans* v. *Munkley,* 4 Taunt. 50.

<hr>

(13) It is not necessary, however, to make a profert of the letters patent by which the court is erected. *Titley* v. *Foxall,* Willes, 689.

(14) But see *Morse* v. *James,* Willes, 128; where it was holden, that though an officer need not set forth the proceedings at length, and though he may justify under an erroneous process, yet it must appear that the process issued in a cause wherein the court below had jurisdiction.

(15) But it is not necessary to set forth the cause of action. *Rowland* v. *Veale,* Cowp. 18, recognized in *Belk* v. *Broadbent,* 3 T. R. 183, where the same doctrine was applied to a justification under mesne process issuing out of a *superior* court, and in which the defendant merely stated, that the writ upon which the plaintiff had been arrested had been issued upon an affidavit to hold to bail, without stating any cause of action for which the plaintiff was liable to be arrested.

stating in the plea the declaration in the court below, which contained an averment that the cause of action arose within the jurisdiction, is not sufficient, for such averment is not traversable (c).
3. Before the time of Charles the Second, it was necessary to set forth the proceedings had in the inferior court at length (16); but now they may be set out shortly with a *taliter processum est* (d); but if the party justify under a *capias ad respondendum*, a precedent summons ought to be set forth (e), or at least the plea ought to be so framed, that the court may intend that a precedent summons had issued (f); for a *capias* without a summons is illegal. Where it is stated that the *capias* issued at the same court at which the plaint was levied, this intendment cannot be made (g); but where it appears on the plea, that the plaint was levied at one court, and the *capias* issued at a subsequent court, and this allegation is introduced by a *taliter processum est*, there such intendment may be made (h). In justifying a trespass under the process of a foreign court, it seems that the plea should be formed in analogy to similar justifications under the process of our inferior courts; but, at any rate, a plea which only states that the court abroad was governed by foreign laws, that the property seized was within its' jurisdiction, that certain legal proceedings were had, according to such foreign laws, against the property in question, in such court having competent jurisdiction in that behalf, *et taliter processum, &c.*, that

(c) *Adney* v. *Vernon*, 3 Lev. 243.
(d) *Patrick* v. *Johnson*, 3 Lev. 403; *Rowland* v. *Veale*, Cowp. 18; *Higginson* v. *Martin*, 2 Mod. 197.
(e) *Marpole* v. *Basnett*, Willes, 38, n. (a).
(f) See *Titley* v. *Foxall*, Willes, 688.

(g) *Marpole* v. *Basnett, ubi sup.; Murphy* v. *Fitzgerald*, Willes, 38, n. (a).
(h) *Titley* v. *Foxall*, Willes, 688; *Adams* v. *Freeman*, reported in Say. 81, and 2 Wilson, 5, and illustrated by Durnford, Willes, 39.

---

(16) There is an *obiter dictum* in *Morse* v. *James*, Willes, 128, that the plaintiff, or a mere stranger, must set forth the proceedings at length, and it is there said to have been established in *Moravia* v. *Sloper*. Upon an examination of that case, I cannot find that any such point was expressly decided in it. The court, indeed, in that case, were of opinion, that the party, having set forth a capias, ought to have shown a precedent summons, and that from the *taliter processum est*, as there pleaded, a summons could not be presumed. It is worthy of remark, that *Willes*, C. J., speaking of *Moravia* v. *Sloper*, in *Titley* v. *Foxall* *, says, "He held, in *Moravia* v. *Sloper, that taliter processum est would be sufficient,* if it did not appear (as it did in that case) that there could not have been a precedent summons." So in *Johnson* v. *Warner*, Willes, 528, it was holden, that this mode of pleading, *by taliter processum est*, was good, and the modern practice is in conformity with it. *Rowland* v. *Veale*, Cowp. 18, and 1 Wms. Saund. 92, n. (2).

* Willes, 690.

the defendant was ordered, by the said court having competent authority in that behalf, to seize the property, is bad, as being too general, and not giving the plaintiff notice, whether the defendant justified as an officer of the court, or party to the cause, or of what nature the charge was, or by whom instituted, or what the order of seizure was, whether absolute or *quousque*, &c. (*i*).

Regularly, process ought to describe the party against whom it is meant to be issued, and the arrest of one person cannot be justified under a writ sued out against another. To trespass for false imprisonment (*k*) by A. B., the defendant pleaded, that J. S. sued out a writ of *latitat against the plaintiff*, A. B., therein called by the name of C. B., directed to the sheriff of L., and then set forth the writ, authorizing the sheriff to arrest C. B., &c., who directed his warrant to the defendant, and thereby commanded him to take *the said A. B., therein called by the name of* C. B., &c., concluding with an averment, that the said A. B. and C. B., in the said writ and warrant mentioned, are *one and the same person*. On general demurrer, the plea was holden to be bad, Lord *Ellenborough*, C. J., observing, that this case was exactly the same in principle as *Cole* v. *Hindson*, 6 T. R. 234 (17). And *Lawrence*, J., said, " In *Cole* v. *Hindson*, Lord *Kenyon* observed, that there was not any averment that the plaintiff was as well known by the one name as the other; neither was there any such averment in this case." A *peace-officer* may justify an arrest in the day-time on a reasonable charge of felony without a warrant, although it should afterwards appear that a felony had not been committed (*l*). So a *constable*, having reasonable ground to suspect that a felony has been committed, is authorized (*m*) to detain the party suspected, until inquiry can be made by the proper authorities; although it appear afterwards that a felony has not been committed. So

---

(*i*) *Collett* v. *Ld. Keith*, 2 East, 260.
(*k*) *Shadgett* v. *Clipson*, 8 East, 328.
(*l*) *Samuel* v. *Payne*, Doug. 359. See also Cald. 291; 2 Esp. N. P. C. 540,

and 3 Campb. 420.
(*m*) *Beckwith* v. *Philby and others*, 6 B. & C. 635; *Nicholson* v. *Hardwick*, 5 C. & P. 495, S. P., *Gurney*, B.

---

(17) In that case, to trespass for taking the goods of A. B., the defendant (an officer) pleaded, that he took them under a *distringas* against C. B., meaning the said A. B., to compel an appearance, averring that A. B. and C. B. were the same person. N. A. B. had not appeared in the original action. On demurrer, the plea was holden to be bad; Lord *Kenyon*, C. J., observing, that this was distinguishable from *Crawford* v. *Satchwell*, Str. 1218, where it was determined, that the defendant might be taken in execution by virtue of a *ca. sa.* under a wrong name; *for there the party had appeared in the original action, and done an act to avow that he was sued by the right name.* See *Price* v. *Harwood*, 3 Campb. 108, and *ante*, p. 908.

watchmen and beadles have authority at common law to arrest, and detain in prison for examination, persons walking in the streets *at night*, whom there is reasonable ground to suspect of felony, although there is no proof of a felony having been committed (n). But when a *private person* apprehends another on suspicion of felony, he does it at his peril, and is liable to an action, unless he can establish in proof that the party has actually been guilty of a felony (o). Proof of mere suspicion will not bar the action, although it may be given in evidence in mitigation of damages (p). And the plea justifying an arrest by a private person, on suspicion of felony, must show the circumstances, from which the court may judge whether the suspicion were reasonable (q). Suspicion that a person has on a former occasion committed a misdemeanour is not any justification for giving him in charge to a constable without a justice's warrant (r); and there is not any distinction in this respect between one kind of misdemeanour and another, as breach of the peace and fraud. Where a warrant is directed to a constable in his official character, without naming him, as, "To the constable of the parish of W.," the warrant ought to be executed (s) within the limits of the district for which he is constable. If a warrant be directed to a constable by name, commanding him to execute it (t), though he is not compellable to go out of his own precinct, yet he may if he will, and shall be justified by the warrant for so doing; but if the warrant be directed to all constables, &c. generally, it shall be taken respectively, and no constable can execute the same out of his precinct. Where a constable, authorized by a warrant to seize certain articles suspected to have been stolen, took away others also, not specified, nor likely to furnish evidence as to the identity of others; it was holden (u), that he was not protected. It is lawful for a private person to do any thing to prevent the perpetration of a felony. Hence, the imprisonment of a husband by a private person, to prevent him committing murder on his wife, is justifiable (x). So if two persons are fighting, and there is reason to fear that one of them will be killed by the other, it is lawful to part them and imprison them, until their anger is cooled (y). A justice of the peace may commit a feme covert who is a material witness, upon a charge of felony brought before him, and who refuses to appear at the sessions to give evidence or to find sureties for her appearance (z). A justice of the peace cannot, for a

(n) *Lawrence* v. *Hedger*, 3 Taunt. 14.
(o) *Adams* v. *Moore*, C. B. Middlesex Sittings after H. T. 51 Geo. III., coram Heath, J., MS.
(p) *S. C.*
(q) *Mure* v. *Kaye*, 4 Taunt. 34; *Hall* v. *Booth*, 3 Nev. & Man. 316.
(r) *Fox* v. *Gaunt*, 3 B. & Ad. 798.
(s) *R.* v. *Weir*, B. R. Sittings after

H. 3 & 4 Geo. IV., per three justices, absente C. J., 1 B. & C. 288.
(t) Per *Holt*, C. J., in case of *The Village of Chorley*, Salk. 175.
(u) *Crozier* v. *Cundey*, 6 B. & C. 232.
(x) *Handcock* v. *Baker*, 2 Bos. & Pul. 260.
(y) 2 Roll. Abr. 559, (E.) pl. 3.
(z) *Bennet* v. *Watson*, 3 M. & S. 1.

contempt of himself in his office, commit (a) for punishment unless
by warrant in writing.   In general, where an affray takes place in
the presence of a constable (b), he may keep the parties in custody
until the affair is over, or he may carry them *immediately* before a
magistrate.   But to justify a constable in apprehending a party without a warrant for an affray, it is essential that the party should have
been engaged in the affray, and that the constable should have had
view (c) of the affray, while the party was so engaged in it, and that
the affray was still continuing at the time of the apprehension.   A
constable may justify under the general issue, although he acted
without a warrant, provided there were a reasonable charge of felony
made;   although he afterwards discharges the prisoner without
taking him before a magistrate;   and although it should eventually
appear that no felony was committed.   But a private individual
who makes the charge and puts the constable in motion, cannot
justify under the general issue;   he must plead the special circumstances, by way of justification, in order that it may be seen whether his suspicions were reasonable (d).   If a plea of justification
consist of two facts (e), each of which would, when separately
pleaded, amount to a good defence, it will sufficiently support the
justification if one of these facts be found by the jury.   Hence,
where, to an action for false imprisonment against a sheriff, he
pleaded that, at the time when the trespass was committed, the
defendant was sheriff of the county of S., and in that character
was presiding at the election of knights of the shire to serve for
the county in parliament;   and because the plaintiff assaulted the
defendant, and made a great noise and disturbance, and obstructed
the defendant in the execution of his duty, he ordered a constable
to take the plaintiff into custody and carry him before a J. P.;   and
the jury found that the plaintiff, who was a freeholder, did not
assault the defendant, but that all the other facts contained in the
plea were proved;   it was holden, that that part of the plea, which
the jury had found, constituted a good defence;   for although the
sheriff had not any authority to commit, yet it was his duty to preserve order and decency in the county court.

In an action for false imprisonment, if the defendant can take
advantage of the statute of limitations, he must plead that he was
not guilty within four years.   If an action be brought for detaining
plaintiff in prison (f) from ———— to ————, and defendant
plead (as he may) as to part, *not guilty within four years*, plaintiff
may reply, that it was one continued imprisonment, and so oust the

(a) *Mayhew* v. *Locke*, 2 Marsh. R.
377; 7 Taunt. 63, *S. C.*

(b) *Churchill* v. *Matthews, Nutt, and
Hill*, Somerset Summ. Ass. 1808, *Bayley*, J.

(c) *Cook* v. *Nethercote*, 6 C. & P. 741,
Alderson, B.

(d) *M'Cloughan* v. *Clayton*, Holt's N.
P. C. 478, *Bayley*, J.

(e) *Spilsbury* v. *Micklethwaite*, 1 Taunt.
146.

(f) *Coventry* v. *Apsley*, Salk. 420.

defendant of the benefit of the statute. Where a declaration for false imprisonment against A. and B. contained two counts (g), to both of which the defendants pleaded *not guilty*, and justified the first under *mesne process*, A. as the plaintiff in that action, and B. as the bailiff; and the plaintiff, by a new assignment, admitting the arrest to be lawful, replied that B., with the consent of A., voluntarily released him, and that they afterwards imprisoned him for the time mentioned in the first count; the plaintiff having failed in proving the new assignment, by not showing the consent of A.; it was holden, that he should not be permitted to prove the same trespass against B. under the other count.

Costs.—If the damages are less than 40s. the plaintiff is not entitled to recover costs, unless the judge immediately after trial certify that the trespass or grievance was wilful and malicious. See stat. 3 & 4 Vict. c. 24, s. 2, *ante*, p. 37, explained, as to actions in which verdicts had been returned before the passing of that act, by stat. 4 & 5 Vict. c. 28.

(g) *Atkinson* v. *Matteson*, 2 T. R. 172.

CHAPTER XXV.

INSURANCE.

I. *Of Insurance in general*, p. 929.

II. *Of Marine Insurance*, p. 930; *The Policy*, p. 930; *Different Kinds*, p. 931; *Requisites*, p. 932; *Rule of Construction*, p. 947.

III. *What Persons may be insured*, p. 948; *Who may be Insurers*, p. 948; *What may be Insured*, p. 950.

IV. *Of Losses*,
    1. *By Perils of the Sea*, p. 953.
    2. *By Capture*, p. 955.
    3. *By Arrests*, p. 957, *and herein of the Effect of an Embargo on the Contract of Insurance*, p. 959.
    4. *By Barratry*, p. 959.
    5. *By Fire*, p. 963.
    6. *By other Losses*, p. 963.

V. *Of Total Losses and of Abandonment*, p. 965.

VI. *Of Partial Losses*, p. 976.

VII. *Of Adjustment*, p. 979.

VIII. *Of the Remedy by Action for Breach of the Contract of Insurance, and herein of the Declaration*, p. 980; *Pleadings*, p. 983; *Consolidation Rule*, p. 984.

IX. *Of the several Grounds of Defence on which the Insurer may Insist;*
    1. *Alien Enemy*, p. 985.
    2. *Illegal Voyage or Illegal Commerce*, p. 985.
    3. *Misrepresentation, Concealment, and Suppression*, p. 989.

4. *Breach of Warranty*, p. 994.

Express
- 1. *Time of Sailing*, p. 994.
- 2. *Safety of a Ship at a particular Time*, p. 996.
- 3. *To depart with Convoy*, p. 997.
- 4. *Neutral Property*, p. 999.

Implied
- 1. *Not to deviate*, p. 1004.
- 2. *Seaworthiness*, p. 1010.

5. *Re-assurance*, p. 1013.

6. *Wager Policy*, p.1013.

X. *Evidence*, p. 1016; *Damages*, p. 1022.

XI. *Premium, Return of*, p. 1022.

XII. *Of Bottomry and Respondentia*, p. 1028.

XIII. *Insurance upon Lives*, p. 1030.

XIV. *Insurance against Fire*, p. 1033.

I. *Of Insurance in general.*

INSURANCE is an agreement whereby one party, in consideration of a sum of money, either given or contracted for, undertakes to pay to the other party a certain sum of money upon the happening of some event. *A policy of insurance* is the instrument in which the terms of this agreement are set forth. To this instrument the insurer having subscribed his name, and, in the case of marine insurances, the sum which he undertakes to pay in case the contingency happens, is termed the *insurer* or *underwriter*. The sum of money, received by the insurer as a consideration for his undertaking, is termed the *premium;* and the party protected by the insurance, the *insured* or *assured*. The subject matter of insurance is as various as the different species of property, and the different risks to which they may be exposed. In some cases, however, a contract of insurance may be void, as being against the policy of the common law; in other cases, as being contrary to the express provisions of a statute (1). These are the only limits to

---

(1) The interference of the legislature has frequently been deemed necessary to provide against the mischiefs arising from insurances calculated merely to excite and encourage a spirit of gaming, and thereby to subvert the morals and impair the industrious habits of the people. See the stat. 9 Ann. c. 6, s. 57, whereby a penalty is imposed on persons

the subject of insurance. The following sections will be confined
to an investigation of three species of insurance only :—1. Marine
insurance. 2. Insurance upon lives. 3. Insurance against losses
by fire.

II. *Of Marine Insurances, p.* 930; *The Policy, p.* 930; *Different
Kinds, p.* 931; *Requisites, p.* 932; *Rule of Construction, p.* 947.

Of Marine Insurance.—Marine insurances are made for the
protection of persons having an interest in ships, or goods on board,
from the loss or damage which may happen to them during a certain voyage, or a fixed period of time (*a*). Insurance on ships and
merchandize greatly conduces to the advancement of trade and
navigation, and the extension of commerce, by dividing a risk which
might be ruinous, and enabling parties to undertake larger adventures than it would otherwise be prudent for them to undertake.
The nature of this contract is a contract of indemnity (*b*), and this
principle ought always to be kept in view in considering questions
relative to insurance. But although indemnity is the principle of
insurance, yet the contract of insurance is, like other contracts,
subject to explanation and construction, regulated in some countries by positive law, in this country by usage (*c*); and it will be
found, that absolute and perfect indemnity cannot be attained in all
cases and under every possible event. One familiar instance may
be mentioned : if goods sustain damage on the voyage, but arrive at
the place of destination, the freight may become payable, although
by reason of the damage the value of the goods may fall short of
the amount of freight ; but the freight cannot be added to the
amount of the damage, and the assured has not a perfect indemnity
for his loss.

The Policy.—The policy of insurance, which has been defined
to be the instrument in which the terms of the agreement are set
forth, is generally printed, with a few terms superadded in writing,
calculated either to control and confine, or to enlarge and extend,
the printed language, and thereby to render it subservient to the

---

(*a*) Marsh. 2.
(*b*) *Godsall* v. *Boldero*, 9 East, 81, recognized by Lord *Ellenborough* in *Bainbridge* v. *Neilson*, 10 East, 344.

(*c*) Per Lord *Tenterden*, delivering
judgment, *Winter* v. *Haldimand*, 2 B. &
Ad. 656.

---

setting up offices for making assurances on marriages, births, christenings,
and service. See also stat. 27 Geo. III. c. 1, against fraudulent insurances upon lottery tickets.

intention of the parties in the particular contract. The form of
the policy is at this day nearly the same as that anciently used
among merchants (2); every policy still referring to those made in
Lombard Street, where the Italians (who introduced them into
England) used to meet at a house called the Pawn-house, or Lombard, for transacting business, before the building the Royal
Exchange. The instrument is inaccurate and ungrammatical; but
having acquired a sense from judicial decision and the usage (3) of
trade, it may be safer to adhere to the old form than to substitute
another, though more correct. It is a simple contract, by which
the heir is not bound, although the word "heirs" is erroneously
used in the present form of the policy. The parties are bound by
the contents of the instrument, and will not be permitted to give
parol evidence contradicting (d) or restraining (e) the express
terms thereof (4).

Different Kinds of Policies.— Policies are of four different kinds:
1. An interest policy. 2. A wager policy. 3. An open policy. 4.

(d) *Kaines* v. *Knightly*, Skinn. 54. See
also *Henkle* v. *The Royal Exch. Ass.
Comp.*, 1 Ves. 317; *Hoare* v. *Graham*, 3

Campb. 57; *Meyer* v. *Everth*, 4 Campb.
22.

(e) *Weston* v. *Emes*, 1 Taunt. 115.

(2) See the form of policy of insurance used in London on ship or goods
in the appendix to Mr. Justice *Park's* valuable treatise. See the Scotch
form, in Miller's Elements of the Law relating to Insurances, 8vo, 1787,
p. 30.

(3) How far the words of this written instrument ought to be controlled,
or any words supplied from the usage of merchants, is a question which
deserves great consideration, as it may affect a main principle in the law of
evidence.

(4) A mistake in a policy may be altered, *by consent*, after it is underwritten. *Bates* v. *Grabham*, Salk. 444. In a case where the clerk of
the underwriter had been guilty of a mistake, and had not pursued the
written instruction of the underwriter, a court of equity decreed relief.
Motteux v. *Gov. and Comp. of London Assurance*, 1 Atk. 545. A
policy was executed by defendant in the printed form *, without any
specific subject of insurance being inserted in writing, or value declared.
The subject matter was afterwards added in writing, and the addition
signed by other underwriters. It was holden, that the assured could not
recover against defendant, who had not signed, on the contract, as it
stood altered by the insertion. So if the assured, after subscription by
the underwriter, strikes out with a pen the time of warranty of sailing,
which stood in the body of the policy, and inserts in a memorandum in
the margin a different time for sailing, which the underwriter does not
sign, the policy is thereby destroyed. *Fairlie* v. *Christie*, 7 Taunt. 416.
See also *Campbell* v. *Christie*, 2 Stark. 64, to the same effect. But an
immaterial alteration will not vitiate the policy. *Sanderson* v. *Symonds*,
1 Brod. & Bingh. 426.

* *Langhorn* v. *Cologan*, 4 Taunt. 330.

A valued policy. 1. An *interest* policy is, where the assured has a real, substantial, assignable interest in the thing insured (*f*). 2. A *wager* policy is an insurance founded on an imaginary risk, where the assured has not any interest in the thing insured, and consequently cannot sustain any injury by the happening of the event insured against. 3. An open policy is, where the value of the thing insured is not inserted in the policy, and must therefore be proved at the trial, if a loss happens. 4. A *valued* policy is where the value of the thing insured has been settled by agreement between the parties, and that value inserted in the policy in the nature of liquidated damages, so as to supersede the necessity of proving it, in case of a total loss. The custom of making valued policies arose soon after the stat. 19 Geo. II. c. 37, and such policies were decided to be legal by *Lee*, C. J.; since which time the constant usage, in case of a total loss, has been to let the valuation stand, and the parties are estopped from altering it. That statute was made in order to prohibit mere wagering policies by persons insuring who had no interest in the thing insured, and therefore it avoids policies made, *interest or no interest*, or without further proof of interest than the policy itself. The effect, therefore, of a valued policy is not to conclude the underwriter from showing that the assured had no interest (*g*), and that in fact it was a mere wagering policy within the statute; but in order to avoid disputes as to the quantum of the interest of the assured, the parties agree that it shall be estimated at a certain value. If goods are fraudulently overvalued in a policy of insurance, with intent to cheat the underwriters, the contract is entirely vitiated, and the assured cannot recover even for the value actually on board (*h*). K., an East India captain, having borrowed money of R., in order to secure R. arranged with P. that K. should draw in favour of R. bills on C. (P.'s agent in Calcutta), payable thirty days after the arrival of the ship B., which bills R. was to indorse to P., and P. was to negotiate on Calcutta upon K.'s consigning to C. goods to double the amount of the bill; it was holden (*i*), first, that P. had no insurable interest in these bills; secondly, that even supposing he had, he could not recover upon a policy describing them as bills of exchange.

Requisites of the Policy.—In order to illustrate the nature of the policy, it will be proper to consider the essential parts of which it is composed, which are as follow:—1. The name of the party insured, or of his agent (p. 933). 2. The name of the ship (p. 935). 3. The subject matter of the insurance (p. 936). 4. The voyage insured (p. 936). 5. The perils against which the insurer undertakes to indemnify the assured (p. 939). 6. The memorandum (p. 939). 7. The date and subscription (p. 944). 8. The stamp (p. 944).

(*f*) Marshall, 199.
(*g*) Per *Lawrence*, J., in *Shawe* v.
Felton, 2 East, 116.

(*h*) *Haigh* v. *De la Cour*, 3 Campb.
319.
(*i*) *Palmer* v. *Pratt*, 3 Bingh. 185.

1. *The Name of the Party insured, or of his Agent.*

A custom prevailed formerly of effecting marine insurances in blank, that is, without specifying the name of the person for whose benefit such insurances were made. This practice having been found productive of great inconvenience, it was enacted, by stat. 25 Geo. III. c. 44, that where policies were made by persons residing in Great Britain, the names of the persons interested should be inserted therein, or the names of the persons who should effect the same, as agents for the persons interested, and in the case of persons not residing in Great Britain, the names of the agents. Soon after this statute was passed, a question arose upon it, whether, when an agent effected a policy for his principal residing abroad, it was necessary that the name of the agent should be inserted in the policy, *eo nomine*, as agent. The Court of King's Bench were clearly of opinion that it was necessary (*k*). It was holden also to be necessary that the names of *all* the persons interested should be inserted (*l*). The provisions of the preceding statute having been found to be injurious to the interests of the ship-owners and merchants, and inadequate to the purpose for which they were designed, the legislature again interposed, by repealing this statute, and enacting another (*m*), whereby it was declared, " that no person should effect any policy on any ship, goods, or other property, without first inserting the names, or usual style and firm of dealing (5), *of the persons interested* in such assurance ; or of *the consignors* or *consignees* of the property insured ; or of the persons residing in Great Britain who *receive* the order for, and effect the policy ; or of the persons who give the order to the agent immediately employed to effect the policy ; and that every policy made contrary to the meaning of this act should be void" (6). It is not necessary under this statute, (as it was under the former,) that, where an insurance is effected by an agent, the name of the agent should be inserted in the policy, *eo nomine*, as agent. Hence where a policy was effected by A. and Co. (*n*), (who were the brokers and

(*k*) *Pray* v. *Edie*, 1 T. R. 314.
(*l*) *Wilton* v. *Reaston*, London Sittings after M. T. 1787; Park, 20, 7th ed.

(*m*) 28 Geo. III. c. 56.
(*n*) *De Vignier* v. *Swanson*, B. R. M. 39 Geo. III., 1 Bos. & Pul. 346, n.

---

(5) The persons interested were denominated in the policy "The trustees of Messrs. K. F. and Co." Lord *Ellenborough* thought that this might be considered as their usual style and firm of dealing for the purposes of this act. *Hibbert* v. *Martin*, 1 Campb. 538.

(6) "This statute must receive the most liberal construction that the words will bear." Per *Buller*, J., 1 Bos. & Pul. 322.

general agents of the party interested,) and A. and Co. were not
described as agents in the policy; but it having been averred in the
declaration, that " A. and Co. were the persons residing in Great
Britain, who received the order for, and effected the insurance ;" it
was holden sufficient.   In a case where the policy was effected by
insurance brokers (o), who stated themselves in the policy to have
effected it " as agents ;" and it was averred in the declaration, that
they were the persons residing in Great Britain who received the
order for and effected the insurance ; but it did not appear that
they were in any other instance the agents of the party interested ;
it was objected, that a mere broker was not within the description
of persons mentioned in stat. 28 Geo. III., and that, by the expression " as agents," used in the policy, the underwriter had been
deceived, since he might have been led to suppose that the brokers
were the general agents of the plaintiff, which they did not appear
to have been.   But the court overruled the objection, conceiving
that the intention of the legislature had been satisfied by inserting
the names of the persons immediately employed to effect the policy.
A. having consigned a cargo to B. (p), transmitted the bills of
lading to C. his (i. e. A.'s) general agent, with directions to deliver
them to B., in order that B. might insure the cargo; shortly afterwards A. drew a bill of exchange on B. for the amount of the cargo
in favour of C., and remitted the same to C. to procure acceptance.
B. refused to accept the bill of exchange, and returned the bills of
lading to C., who thereupon caused an insurance to be effected on
the cargo in his own name, and having informed A. of what he
had done, A. approved of it.   A loss happened.   In an action on
the policy, it was averred in the declaration, that the interest was
in A., and that C. made the insurance as his agent, and for his use
and benefit, and that, at the time of making it, C. resided in Great
Britain.   It was holden, that C. fell within the description of
persons mentioned in the statute.   He might be considered, 1, as
the consignee, inasmuch as he was the general agent of A., and
had in his possession the bills of lading which had been returned
by B., the original consignee ; 2, as the person who had received
the order to insure ; for the subsequent approbation of A. was equivalent to a previous order, and consequently the policy was well
effected in the name of C.   A declaration stating that A. (the
plaintiff) caused to be effected a policy, containing that B. made
assurance, and averring the interest in C., with a promise by the
defendant to the plaintiff, in consideration of the premium paid by
the plaintiff, was holden good, after verdict (q).

(o) Bell v. Gilson, 1 Bos. & Pul. 345.   316.
(p) Wolff v. Horncastle, 1 Bos. & Pul.   (q) Mellish v. Bell, 15 East, 4.

2. *The Name of the Ship.*

The name of the ship should be truly described in the policy; for if the underwriter should be deceived, or prejudiced by a false name having been given to him, he will not be bound. To avoid any inconvenience which may arise from a mistake in the name of a ship, it is usual to add in the policy, to the name given, these words, " or by whatever other name or names the said ship should be called;" in which case, although it should appear that the real name of the ship was different from that inserted in the policy, yet, if the identity of the ship can be proved, and if it does not appear that the underwriter will sustain any prejudice, the variance will be immaterial. As where an insurance was made upon a ship called the Leopard (r), "or by whatsoever other name, &c.," whereof was master, for that voyage, A. B., and upon the evidence of A. B. it appeared, that the ship of which he was master was called the Leonard; and was never called by the name of the Leopard; it was holden by *Lee*, C. J., that by reason of the general words, "by whatsoever name, &c." it was only necessary to prove the identity, which was done here by A. B., who said that he was master of the Leonard. So where a broker had received instructions to insure goods on board an American ship, called " the President" (s), but by mistake had stated it in the policy all as one name of a ship, called " the American ship President," instead of stating it as part name and part description; it was holden, that the general words, or " by whatever other name called," had cured the mistake; the identity of the ship in which the goods were lost, with that in which they were insured for the voyage, being proved, and it not appearing that the underwriter could be prejudiced by the mistake. Where there is a policy on goods to be thereafter declared, by ship or ships, if the broker by mistake makes a written declaration upon goods by a wrong ship, to which the underwriters put their initials, he may afterwards, in compliance with the orders of the assured, declare upon goods by another ship, without the assent of the underwriters, and without a new stamp (t).

(r) *Hall* v. *Molineux*, coram *Lee*, C. J., cited and recognized by *Lawrence*, J., in *Le Mesurier* v. *Vaughan*, 6 East, 365.

(s) *Le Mesurier* v. *Vaughan*, 6 East,

382.

(t) *Robinson* v. *Touray*, 3 Campb. 158 (7); 1 M. & S. 217, *S. C.*

(7) " The declaration of interest does not require any assent on the part of the underwriters. They put their initials to it, not for the purpose of expressing their assent, but to authenticate the declaration, and to prevent fraud in changing the subject matter intended to be covered by the insurance. The contract between the parties is complete when the

3. *The Subject Matter of the Insurance.*

The subject matter of the insurance ought to be inserted in the policy, that is, whether it be ship, goods, freight, &c.; but it is not necessary that the particular kind of goods should be specified. But the assured should take care that the terms used are large and comprehensive enough to embrace accurately and precisely all the objects of the insurance (u). *Respondentia* cannot be insured under the denomination of *goods,* for by the custom of merchants, *respondentia* must be insured under a special denomination (x) (8). *Provisions* which are necessary for the use of the ship's crew, and on board at the time of insurance, are comprehended under the word "*furniture,*" and are protected by a policy on the ship and furniture (y).

4. *The Voyage Insured.*

The voyage insured must be truly and accurately described in the policy (z), namely, the time when, and place at which, the risk is to begin, the place of the ship's departure, the place of her destination, and the time when the risk shall end. A ship was insured "at and from Genoa," her loading consisting of perishable commodities (a). The loading was put on board at Leghorn, whence the vessel had sailed, bound for Dublin; but losing her convoy she had put into Genoa, where she lay nearly five months,

---

(u) See *Winter* v. *Haldimand,* 2 B. & Ad. 649.

(x) *Glover* v. *Black,* 3 Burr. 1394; 1 Bl. R. 405, recognized in *Simonds and Loder* v. *Hodgson,* 6 Bingh. 114.

(y) *Brough* v. *Whitmore,* 4 T. R. 206.

(z) *Marshall,* 227; *Smith* v. *Yelton,* D. P., 21 July, 1906.

(a) *Hodgson* v. *Richardson,* 1 Bl. Rep. 463.

---

underwriters have signed the policy. The declaration of interest is the mere exercise of a power conferred upon the assured. It is generally put upon the policy for convenience, but this is not necessary; nor is there any necessity for its being in writing." Per Lord *Ellenborough,* C. J., *S. C.*

(8) In *Gregory* v. *Christie,* Park, 14; Marshall, 94, 225; 3 Doug. 419, *S. C.,* an insurance had been made on behalf of the captain of an East Indiaman on "goods, specie, and effects," on board his ship; the plaintiff claimed to recover money which he had expended for the use of the ship, and for which he charged respondentia interest; it was proved by several East India captains, that this kind of interest was always insured under the denomination of "goods, specie, and effects." The court held, that under this express usage the plaintiff was entitled to recover.

and then sailed. The insurance was made a few days after the ship had sailed from Genoa, at which time the above-mentioned circumstances were known to the assured, but not communicated to the underwriter. A few days after the ship put to sea she was shattered by a storm, and the cargo considerably damaged. In an action on the policy, it was proved that it had been always considered as material to acquaint the underwriter, whether the insurance was to be at the commencement or in the middle of a voyage. It was holden, that the plaintiff was not entitled to recover. In an action upon a policy of insurance, *at, and from all, any, or every port and place on the coast of Brazil, and after the 17th day of September to the Cape of Good Hope, upon goods and ship,* beginning the adventure upon the goods from the loading thereof aboard the ship, *at all, any, or every port and place on the coast of Brazil, and from the 17th day of September,* 1800, *and* upon the ship in the same manner; it appeared that the goods, for the loss of which the plaintiff declared, had been put on board at the Cape. It was holden (b), that the plaintiff could not recover; for the obvious meaning of the policy was, that the adventure was to attach on goods and ship, after a loading of goods had taken place on the coast of Brazil; and as that circumstance or event never took place in the present instance, the policy of course never attached at all. A policy at and from G., on goods, beginning the adventure from the loading on board the ship, will not protect goods laden on board before the ship's arrival at G. (c). The foregoing cases have been considered as laying down a rule of strict construction not to be favoured: hence, if there be anything to indicate that a prior loading was contemplated, it will release the case from that strict construction; as where the policy was on goods at and from G., to any port in the Baltic, beginning the adventure from the loading thereof on board the ship, and the policy was declared to be in continuation of a former policy, which was a policy from V. to her port of discharge in the United Kingdom, or any ports in the Baltic, with liberty to take in and discharge goods, wheresoever, to return twelve per cent. if the voyage ended at G.; it was holden (d), that the assured were entitled to recover, although the goods were not loaded on board at G., but at V., and although the defendant was not an underwriter on the former policy. So where the policy was on goods at and from Pernambuco to Maranham, and thence to Liverpool, beginning the adventure on the goods from the loading thereof, on board the ship, *wheresoever;* it was holden (e), that it would cover

(b) *Robertson* v. *French*, 4 East, 130. See *Spitta* v. *Woodman*, 2 Taunt. 416; *Horneyer* v. *Lushington*, 15 East, 46.

(c) *Langhorn* v. *Hardy*, 4 Taunt. 628. See *Spitta* v. *Woodman*, 2 Taunt. 416, S. P.

(d) *Bell* v. *Hobson*, 16 East, 240; 3 Campb. 272, S. C. See also *Rickman* v. *Carstairs*, 5 B. & Ad. 651; 2 Nev. & M. 562.

(e) *Gladstone* v. *Clay*, 1 M. & S. 418.

goods previously loaded at Liverpool, and which arrived at P., but were not unloaded there, and afterwards sustained a partial loss by wreck in the voyage from P. to M. If a ship be insured for one voyage (*f*), and sails upon another, although she be taken before she arrives at the dividing point of the two voyages, the policy is discharged. So if a ship, insured from a certain time (*g*), sail *before* the time on a different voyage from that insured, the assured cannot recover, though she afterwards get into the course of the voyage described in the policy, and is lost after the day on which the policy was to have attached. It is to be observed (*h*), however, that if the termini of the intended voyage are the same with that described in the policy, a mere intention to touch at a particular port out of the usual track of the voyage insured, will be considered only as an INTENTION *to deviate*, and as such will not vacate the policy. The voyage is to be considered as the same, until the vessel arrives at the dividing point of the two voyages.

Goods were insured on board a vessel on a voyage from Liverpool to Palermo, Messina, and Naples. She cleared out for Naples only, and was captured before the dividing point. It was holden (*i*), that there was an inception of the voyage insured; that the voyage insured meant a voyage to all or any of the places, with this reserve only, that if the ship went to more than one place, she must visit them in the order described in the policy. Goods were insured on board a ship from London to Nantz, with liberty to call at Ostend, and she was cleared only for Ostend, but sailed directly for Nantz, that being the known course of the trade, in order to save certain duties both in England and France. It was holden (*k*), that there was not any fraud on the underwriter so as to vacate the policy. A ship insured from A. to B. sailed with directions to the captain to touch at C. (*l*); an intermediate point. To a certain point the voyage was the same; from that point there were three tracks to B., one by the way of C., the two others by different courses; there were advantages and disadvantages attending each, and it was usual for the captain to elect, according to circumstances; the ship took the track by C., with intent to put in there, but was taken before she actually came to the point, where she must have turned out of the track to B. by the way of C., for the purpose of putting into the harbour of C. It was holden, that the underwriter was discharged; because he was entitled to the advantage of the captain's judgment, in electing which of the three tracks it was best to pursue, when he came to the first dividing point. A liberty "to cruise six weeks," in a policy of insurance, has been holden to mean six weeks successively, from the commencement of the

(*f*) *Wooldridge* v. *Boydell*, 1 Doug. 16.

(*g*) *Way* v. *Modigliani*, 2 T. R. 30.

(*h*) *Kewley* v. *Ryan*, 2 H. Bl. 343, cited by *Bayley*, J., in *Hare* v. *Travis*, 7 B. & C. 18.

(*i*) *Marsden* v. *Reid*, 3 East, 572.

(*k*) *Planché and another* v. *Fletcher*, 1 Doug. 250.

(*l*) *Middlewood* v. *Blakes*, 7 T. R. 162.

cruise (*m*). A policy of insurance was effected on a ship for a certain voyage *with letters of marque, with leave to chase, capture, and man prizes.* It was holden (*n*), that acting as a convoy to a prize, which the ship insured had taken, and slackening sail in the course of the voyage insured, in order to make the sailing of the ship insured conform to that of the prize, was not within the meaning of the terms, *chasing, capturing, and manning prizes.* See further on this subject, *Parr* v. *Anderson,* 6 East, 202. Policy on a ship for four months, at and from a place to any port or ports; it was holden (*o*), that an open roadstead (being the usual place of loading and unloading,) was a port within the meaning of this policy.

So a place lying within a bay, with a roadstead and custom-house, and of which the British consul describes himself as vice-consul, has been holden (*p*) to be a port within the meaning of the policy. But upon a policy at and from a port of lading, it was holden (*q*), that a proceeding from the port of C. to B., within the same bay, but having different post-offices, although subject to the jurisdiction of the same custom-house, was a deviation.

5. *The Perils against which the Insurer undertakes to indemnify the Assured.*

These perils must be inserted in the policy. Molloy, in his Treatise De Jure Maritimo, says, that there is scarce any misfortune which is not provided against by the terms of the policy which was used in his time, and there is in the modern printed form of policy an enumeration of the same adventures and perils, that is, "of the seas, men of war, fire, enemies, pirates, rovers, thieves, jettisons, letters of mart and countermart, surprisals, taking at sea, arrests." In all our policies are inserted the words, "lost or not lost," by which the insurer not only takes upon himself the risk of future loss, but also the loss, if any, that may already have happened (*r*).

6. *Of the Memorandum.*

The underwriters of London, in order to protect themselves against small averages, which might be claimed in respect of perishable commodities, have inserted, at the foot of the policy, a memo-

(*m*) *Syers* v. *Bridge,* Doug. 527.
(*n*) *Lawrence* v. *Sydebotham,* 6 East, 45. See *Hibbert* v. *Halliday,* 2 Taunt. 423.
(*o*) *Cockey* v. *Atkinson,* 2 B. & A. 460.
(*p*) *Scotland Sea Insurance Company* v. *Gavin,* 4 Bli. 578; 2 Dow. & C. 129.
(*q*) *Brown* v. *Tayleur,* 5 Nev. & M. 472; 4 Ad. & Ell. 241.
(*r*) Marshall, 237; *Mead* v. *Davison,* 3 Ad. & Ell. 303; 4 Nev. & M. 701, and *post,* p. 947.

randum to the following effect: " N. B. Corn (9), fish, salt (10), fruit, flour, and seed, are warranted free from average, unless general, *or the ship be stranded;* sugar, tobacco, hemp, flax, hides, and skins, are warranted free from average under £5 per cent.: and all other goods, also the ship and freight, are warranted free of average under £3 per cent., unless general, *or the ship be stranded.*" The words in italics have been omitted for several years in the forms of policies adopted by the two insurance companies, viz. London Assurance and Royal Exchange Assurance. By virtue of this memorandum, the insurer is not bound to make good any average or partial loss upon the articles specified in the memorandum except a general average, or unless the ship be stranded.

The term *general average* requires explanation. Whatever damage or loss is incurred by any particular part of the ship or cargo *for the preservation of the rest,* such damage or loss shall be considered as *general average;* that is, the several parties interested in the ship, freight (s), or cargo, shall contribute their respective proportions to indemnify the owner of the particular part for the damage, which has been incurred *for the good of all.* From the preceding description, it appears, that in order to constitute a general average, the whole adventure must have been in jeopardy. A ship laden with coals and wheat (t), (which were the subject matter of insurance,) was forced, by stress of weather, into a harbour in Ireland, and there happening to be a great scarcity of corn there at that time, the people came on board in a tumultuous manner, took the government of her from the captain and crew, and weighed her anchor, by which she drove on a reef of rocks, where she was stranded, and they would not leave her till they had compelled the captain to sell all the corn except about ten tons, at a certain rate which was about three fourths of the invoice price. The ten tons were damaged in consequence of the stranding, and it became necessary that they should be thrown overboard. The ship afterwards arrived at her place of destination with the remainder of her cargo, which was about £25 worth of coals. It was contended, that the loss sustained was a general, and not a

(s) *Da Costa* v. *Newnham,* 2 T. R. 407; *Williams* v. *London Assurance,* 1 M. & S. 318.

(t) *Nesbitt and another* v. *Lushington,* 4 T. R. 783.

(9) The word *corn* comprehends peas, *Mason* v. *Skurray,* Marsh. 143; Park, 179, 7th edition; and malt; *Moody* v. *Surridge,* 2 Esp. N. P. C. 633, *Kenyon,* C. J.; but not rice. *Scott* v. *Bourdillon,* 2 Bos. & Pul. N. R. 213.

(10) The word *salt* does not comprehend saltpetre. *Journu* v. *Bourdieu,* Park, 179, per *Wilson,* J.

particular average; but the court were of a different opinion, Lord *Kenyon*, C. J., observing, that this was not a general average, because the whole adventure was never in jeopardy. There was not any pretence to say that the persons who took the corn intended any injury to the ship, or to any other part of the cargo, except the corn, which they wanted in order to prevent their suffering in a time of scarcity; therefore the plaintiffs could never have called on the rest of the owners to contribute their proportion as upon a general average.

It is not every object of value which has been held liable to a contribution for average, but such stores only as are termed merces. Merces has never been held to extend to provisions, but includes only the cargo put on board for the purposes of commerce. Hence it has been holden (u), that provisions do not contribute to general average, even where the cargo consisted of passengers only, in a convict ship.

Insurance at and from C. to L. on goods, in a ship by name, until the same should be there safely discharged and landed, *rice free of particular average*, and the ship with rice and other goods arrived within the limits of the port of L., but before she could be brought to her moorings or be at all unloaded, ran aground and was wrecked, and the whole cargo was greatly damaged, and was taken out of her in craft, and carried to the consignees at L. and sold, and produced upon the whole little more than sufficient to pay freight and salvage, but the rice did not produce sufficient to pay the freight: it was holden (x), that this was a case of particular average only, and therefore as to the rice the underwriter was exempted by the warranty.

Upon the other branch of the exception (y), *viz.* the words "unless the ship be stranded," it has been holden, that these are words of condition, and that if such condition happens, it destroys the exception and lets in the general words of the policy (z), and that the underwriter is liable for an average loss upon the articles specified in the memorandum, where there is a stranding, although no part of the loss happen in consequence of the stranding, provided such average loss arises from one of the perils insured against (11). And the underwriter is liable (a) for a loss, the proxi-

(u) *Brown* v. *Stapyleton*, 4 Bingh. 119.
(x) *Glennie* v. *The London Ass. Comp.*, 2 M. & S. 371.
(y) *Cantillon* v. *London Ass.*, cited by *Norton*, 3 Burr. 1553; 2 Mag. 385; *Burnett* v. *Kensington*, 7 T. R. 210. See note of former trial in Peake's Additional Cases, p. 71.

(z) *Burnett* v. *Kensington*, 7 T. R. 210, recognized by *Tindal*, C. J., delivering judgment of court in *Kingsford* v. *Marshall*, 8 Bingh. 463.
(a) *Busk* v. *R. E. A.*, 2 B. & A. 73; *Walker* v. *Maitland*, 5 B. & A. 171, cited by *Bayley*, J., in *Bishop* v. *Pentland*, 7 B. & C. 223.

(11) "When a ship is stranded, the underwriters agree to ascribe the

mate cause of which is one of the enumerated risks, although the remote cause may be traced to the negligence of the master and mariners.

To constitute a stranding, it is essential that the vessel should be stationary; the striking on a rock where the vessel remains for a minute and a half only, is not a stranding, though she thereby receives an injury which eventually proves fatal (b). A stranding (c) may be said to take place where a ship takes the ground not in the ordinary course of .the navigation, but by reason of some unforeseen accident; for the mere taking of the ground (d) in the ordinary course of the voyage, is not a stranding within the meaning of the policy. Upon the ebbing of the tide, a vessel took the ground in a tide harbour in the place where it was intended she should; but in so doing, struck against some hard substance, by which two holes were made in her bottom, and the cargo damaged; this was holden (e) not to be a stranding.

Where a ship being under conduct of a pilot, in her course up the river to Liverpool, was, against the advice of the master, fastened at the pier of the dock-basin, by a rope to the shore, and left there, and she took the ground, and when the tide left her, fell over on her side and bilged, in consequence of which when the tide rose she filled with water, and the goods were wetted and damaged: it was holden (f), that this was a stranding to entitle the assured to recover for an average loss upon the goods. So where, in assumpsit on a policy on goods warranted free from average, unless the ship were stranded, it appeared, that in the course of the voyage, the ship was, by tempestuous weather, forced to take shelter in a harbour, and in entering, it struck upon an anchor, and being brought to her moorings, was found leaky and in danger of sinking, and on that account was hauled with warps higher up the harbour, where she took the ground, and remained fast there for half an hour; it was holden (g), that this was a stranding within the meaning of the policy. Where, during the course of a voyage upon an inland navigation, it became necessary, in order to repair the navigation, to draw off the water: and the ship, in consequence, having been placed in the most secure situation that could be found, when the water was drawn off, went by

(b) *Macdougle* v. *The Royal Ex. Ass. Co.*, 1 Stark. N. P. C. 130.

(c) Per *Bayley*, J., in *Bishop* v. *Pentland*, 7 B. & C. 224. The case of *Bishop* v. *Pentland* was recognized in *Wells* v. *Hopwood*, 3 B. & Ad. 20, *Parke*, J., dissentiente.

(d) *Hearne* v. *Edmunds*, 1 Brod. & Bingh. 388.

(e) *Kingsford* v. *Marshall*, 8 Bingh. 458.

(f) *Carruthers* v. *Sydebotham*, 4 M. & S. 77.

(g) *Barrow* v. *Bell*, 4 B. & C

loss to the stranding, as being the most probable occasion of the damage, though that fact cannot always be ascertained." Per Lord *Kenyon*, C. J., 4 T. R. 787.

accident upon some piles, which were not previously known to be there: it was holden (*h*), that this was a stranding within the usual memorandum in the policy, the accident having happened not in the ordinary course of such voyage. So where a ship having goods on board, was compelled, in the course of her voyage, to put into a tide harbour, and was there moored alongside a quay, in the usual place for ships of her burthen. It became necessary, in addition to the usual moorings, to fasten her by tackle to posts on the shore, to prevent her falling over, upon the tide leaving her. The rope, not being of sufficient strength, broke when the tide left the vessel, and she fell over upon her side, and was thereby stove in and greatly injured: it was holden (*i*), that this was a stranding. So where the ship, having arrived in Hull harbour, was in the course of discharging her cargo at a quay alongside of which she was moored. At low water she grounded on the mud; but on one occasion, the rope by which her head was moored to the opposite side of the harbour stretched, and the wind blowing from a particular quarter, instead of grounding entirely on the mud, as it was intended she should have done, she partly grounded on a bank of rubbish and stones. This grounding was holden (*k*), by a majority of the judges, to be a stranding. It will be remarked, that all these cases were decided upon the principle, that the taking the ground was occasioned by some extraneous and accidental cause; and was not a taking of the ground in the usual course of navigation. According to Lord *Tenterden*, the rule which may fairly be collected from the greater number of the cases is this :—" *Where* (*l*) *a vessel takes the ground in the ordinary and usual course of navigation and management in a tide river or harbour, upon the ebbing of the tide or from a natural deficiency of water, so that she may float again upon the flow of tide or increase of water, such an event shall not be considered a stranding within the meaning of the memorandum. But where the ground is taken under any extraordinary circumstances of time or place, by reason of some unusual or accidental occurrence, such an event shall be considered as a stranding.*" Where goods were insured free from average, unless general or the ship be stranded, and a particular average loss was incurred by the stranding of a *lighter* conveying the goods from ship to shore; it was holden (*m*), that the insurer was not liable. The assured may recover an average loss upon a damage by stranding, occasioned by the neglect of a Liverpool pilot appointed under stat. 37 Geo. III. c. 78, while the ship was under his conduct (*n*).

Where there is neither general average nor stranding (*o*), it

(*h*) *Rayner* v. *Godmond*, 5 B. & A. 225.

(*i*) *Bishop* v. *Pentland*, 7 B. & C. 219.

(*k*) *Wells* v. *Hopwood*, 3 B. & Ad. 20.

(*l*) In *Wells* v. *Hopwood*, 3 B. & Ad. 34.

(*m*) *Hoffman* v. *Marshall*, 2 Bingh. N. C. 383; 2 Scott, 559.

(*n*) *Carruthers* v. *Sydebotham*, 4 M. & S. 77.

(*o*) *Mason* v. *Skurray*, London Sittings after H. T. 1780, coram Lord *Mansfield*, C. J., Park, 191, 2; *Cocking* v. *Fraser*. Park, 181; Marsh. 144.

seems that the underwriter is not liable at all, if the commodity specifically remain, although the damage sustained may amount to a total loss. The Royal Exchange Assurance Company is liable for a total loss upon a cargo of wheat, where the ship, from the perils insured against, becomes incapable of pursuing the voyage, and another vessel cannot be procured to forward the cargo (p).

7. The Date.

Regularly the policy should be dated (q), that is, to each subscription, for each subscription makes a distinct contract, the day on which, and the month and year in which, it is made ought to be added. The insertion of a date may tend to the discovery of fraud, and consequently ought not to be omitted. It is usual, although not essentially necessary, to specify the sum insured: and the mode of doing this is, by writing the sum in words, and not in figures, in order to prevent any alteration being made.

8. The Stamp.

The policy must be duly stamped (12), at the time when it is effected, for it cannot be legally stamped afterwards (r).

A policy of insurance was subscribed by the defendant on the 5th of February, 1800 (s), and duly stamped, purporting to be a policy " on goods and specie on board of ship or ships sailing between the 1st of October, 1799, and the 1st of June, 1800, being the property *which should first sail* to a certain amount, and upon the vessels carrying the goods." After the 1st of June, 1800, but before any notice of the determination of the risk (13) had been received, a memorandum was written on the policy, and subscribed by the defendant, whereby it was agreed to extend the time of sailing to the 1st of August, 1800. It was holden, that although

(p) Per Lord *Ellenborough*, C. J., *Wilson* v. *R.E. Ass. Comp.*, 2 Campb. 623. See also *Manning* v. *Newnham, ib.* 624, n.; 3 Doug. 130, *S. C.;* and *Anderson* v. *Wallis*, 2 M. & S. 240.

(q) Marsh. 241.
(r) *Roderick* v. *Hovil*, 3 Campb. 103.
(s) *Kensington* v. *Inglis*, in error, 8 East, 273.

---

(12) For the amount of the stamp duties, see stat. 3 & 4 Will. IV. c. 23.

(13) By these words, " determination of the risk," is to be understood either the loss or safe arrival of the thing insured, or the final end and conclusion of the voyage. Per Lord *Ellenborough*, C. J., delivering judgment of court in *Kensington* v. *Inglis*, 8 East, 291.

by this memorandum the time of sailing was extended, yet the object of the insurance continued the same; and consequently the memorandum, falling within the proviso contained in the 13th section of the stat. 35 Geo. III. c. 63, did not require a stamp.

The stat. 35 Geo. III. c. 63, s. 13, provides, " that the act shall not extend to prohibit the making any alteration which may lawfully be made in the terms or conditions of any policy of insurance, duly stamped, after the same shall have been underwritten, or to require any additional stamp duty by reason of such alteration, *so that such alteration be made before notice of the determination of the risk originally insured, &c., and so that the thing insured shall remain the property of the same persons; and so that such alteration shall not prolong the term insured beyond the period allowed by this act; and so that no additional or further sum shall be insured by means of such alteration.*" The words "the thing insured shall *remain* the property, &c." apply to one identical and continued subject matter *all along remaining* the property of the same proprietor, and will not comprehend a case where the thing last insured is not only in fact, but in name and kind, as a specific object of insurance, essentially different from the thing first insured, and which begins also to have an existence at a much later period than the other, and when the thing first insured scarcely, or in a small degree only, *remains* or continues to exist at all. Hence, where the original policy was " on ship *and outfit,*" at and from London to the South Seas, during the ship's stay and fishing there, and at and thence to Great Britain, &c.; and after the ship had sailed on the voyage insured, by consent of the underwriters, the policy was altered, and declared to be on the ship and *goods,* instead of the ship and *outfit.* It was holden, that as the outfit for such a voyage as was described in the policy differed materially from what was comprehended under the term *goods,* the policy in its altered state required an additional stamp within the meaning of the preceding section (*t*). It was holden afterwards, that the assured could not recover upon the policy in its original state, as an assurance on " ship and outfit," by reason of the alteration apparent on the face of the instrument, such alteration having been made by the parties interested (*u*). But where a broker instructed to effect a policy on goods, effected it on ship: and the mistake was afterwards rectified by the underwriter subscribing a memorandum in the margin: it was holden, that a new stamp was not necessary (*x*). So where a mistake was made by an agent in declaring the interest in the margin of the policy to be on a ship by a wrong name, it was holden, that it might be rectified by inserting the true name,

(*t*) *Hill* v. *Patten,* 8 East, 373, cited in *Bathe* v. *Taylor,* 15 East, 415.

(*u*) *French* v. *Patten,* 9 East, 351; 1

Campb. 72, cited in *Reed* v. *Deere,* 7 B. & C. 264.

(*x*) *Sawtell* v. *Loudon,* 5 Taunt. 359.

without a fresh stamp (*y*). A policy was effected at four guineas per cent. on hemp marked R. and valued, with certain returns of premium, upon arrival at certain ports, and warranted to sail before the 20th of August, which was a summer risk and premium. By a memorandum indorsed, the underwriter, for four guineas additional and the return of five shillings less for arrival, absolved the assured from the warranty of sailing before the 20th August, so making it a winter risk, and withdrew the mark of the hemp; it was holden (*z*), that these alterations might be made by stat. 35 Geo. III. c. 63, s. 13, without any new stamp. Policy on goods at and from Stockholm to Swinemunde; and the ship being driven into Wisby on the 20th May, and detained there till the 9th October, the assured, on 1st July, wrote to their agents in London, "that the captain had been ordered to proceed to Konigsberg, as they were not certain whether the enemy might be at Swinemunde or not, and that the passage to Konigsberg was nearly the same, . but rather the shortest and safest, and they desired the agents to arrange the matter with the underwriters;" which letter the agents receiving on the 12th July, applied to the underwriters for their consent to alter the policy, by adding the words "Konigsberg or Memel" after "Swinemunde," which consent was obtained; and the ship and goods were afterwards lost in their voyage to Konigsberg; it was holden (*a*), that this alteration did not require a new stamp. So where the policy was, "at and from Liverpool to Quebec," and afterwards, by a memorandum at the foot, it was changed to "from Liverpool to St. John's, New Brunswick;" it was holden (*b*), that a new stamp was not necessary. Policy of insurance on ship and goods at and from Cuba to Liverpool, with liberty, "in that voyage, to proceed and sail to, and touch and stay at, any ports or places whatsoever; and with leave to discharge and take in, at any ports or places she might touch at, without prejudice to that insurance;" the insured, after subscription of the policy, inserted in the body of it the words, "with leave to call off Jamaica," to which interpolation all the underwriters assented, without increase of premium, except the defendant, who, being out of the way, was not applied to. The captain sailed from Cuba with eight men, engaged to navigate to Liverpool, and two to Jamaica, being unable, at Cuba, to procure ten men (the proper complement of the crew) for Liverpool. She then touched at Jamaica, for the sole purpose of landing the two men, and procuring others in their stead; and, having accomplished this purpose, was lost on the voyage from Jamaica to Liverpool: it was holden (*c*), 1st, that this was a material alteration of the policy, and rendered it void; 2nd, that the

(*y*) *Robinson* v. *Touray*, 1 M. & S. 217.

(*z*) *Hubbard* v. *Jackson*, 4 Taunt. 169.
(*a*) *Ramstrom and another* v. *Bell*, 5 M. & S. 267.

(*b*) *Brockelbank* v. *Sugrue*, 1 B. & Ad. 81.

(*c*) *Forshaw* v. *Chabert*, 2 Brod. & Bingh. 158.

ship was not, as to the crew, seaworthy for the whole voyage, (as she ought to have been,) when she sailed from Cuba; 3rd, that the circumstance of her having become seaworthy after her leaving Cuba, and before the loss, did not entitle the plaintiff to recover.

A policy on a ship, lost or not lost, is good (d), the ship having been accepted for insurance and the premium paid before loss, although the policy was not actually executed and stamped till loss had happened, and both insurer and assured knew it.

Rule of Construction.—The same rule of construction which applies to all other instruments, applies equally to a policy of assurance (e), *viz.* that it is to be construed according to its sense and meaning, as collected in the first place from the terms used in it, which terms are to be understood in their plain, ordinary, and popular sense, unless they have generally, in respect to the subject matter, as by the known usage of trade or the like, acquired a peculiar sense distinct from the popular sense of the same words, or unless the context evidently points out that they must, in the particular instance, and in order to effect the immediate intention of the parties to that contract, be understood in some other special and peculiar sense. The only difference between policies of assurance and other instruments in this respect, is, that the greater part of the printed language of them, being invariable and uniform, has acquired, from use and practice, a known and definite meaning, and that the words superadded in writing, subject indeed always to be governed in point of construction by the language and terms with which they are accompanied, are entitled, nevertheless, if there should be any reasonable doubt upon the sense and meaning of the whole, to have a greater effect attributed to them than to the printed words; inasmuch as the written words are the immediate language and terms selected by the parties for the expression of their meaning, and the printed words are a general formula, adapted equally to their case, and that of all other contracting parties upon similar occasions and subjects.

(d) *Mead* v. *Davison*, 3 Ad. & Ell. 303; 4 Nev. & M. 701.

(e) Lord *Ellenborough*, C. J., delivering judgment of court in *Robertson* v. *French*, 4 East, 135, recognized by Lord *Tenterden*, C. J., delivering judgment of court in *Hunter* v. *Leathley*, 10 B. & C. 871.

III. *What Persons may be Insured, p.* 948; *Who may be Insurers,*
   p. 948; *What may be Insured, p.* 950.

What Persons may be Insured.

In this country all persons, whether British subjects or aliens,
may, in general, be insured. But an action cannot be maintained
on a policy at the suit or on the behalf of an alien enemy during
war, although the property insured be of British manufacture, and
exported from this country (*f*). A neutral, however, although
domiciled and carrying on trade in an enemy's country, in partnership with an alien enemy, may insure his interest in the joint property, and on coming into this country may sue for the recovery of
a loss arising from one of the perils insured against (*g*).

Where a ship belonging to an alien enemy is protected by the
king's license, an assurance may be effected on such ship by a
British subject, as trustee on the behalf of the ship-owner, and an
action on the policy may be maintained at the suit *of the trustee*
even in time of war, because the public policy of the country is not
contravened by sustaining and giving effect to such trust; and
although the king's license cannot, in point of law, have the effect
of removing the personal disability of the ship-owner, (being an
alien enemy,) in respect of suit, so as to enable him to sue in his own
name, yet it purges the trust in respect to him of all the injurious
qualities in regard to the public interest (*h*).

An English subject who lives and carries on trade under the protection and for the benefit of a hostile state, and who is so far a
merchant settled in the state that his goods would be liable to confiscation in a court of prize, is not to be considered as entitled to
sue as an English subject in an English court of justice. Residing
under the allegiance and protection of a hostile state, he may be
considered, to all civil purposes, as much an alien enemy as if he
were born there. But if he reside in a neutral country, he is entitled to all the privileges of a neutral country (*i*).

Who may be Insurers.

At the common law, any person in his individual and separate
capacity, or any number of persons forming a society or partner-

---

(*f*) *Brandon* v. *Nesbitt*, 6 T. R. 23;
Bristow v. *Towers*, 6 T. R. 35. See also
Flindt v. *Waters*, 15 East, 260, and *post.*
(*g*) *Rotch* v. *Edie*, 6 T. R. 413.
(*h*) *Kensington* v. *Inglis*, 8 East, 273,

recognized in *Flindt* v. *Waters*, 15 East,
266.
(*i*) See *M'Connell* v. *Hector*, 3 Bos.
& Pul. 113, and *Willison* v. *Patteson*, 7
Taunt. 449.

ship, might have been insurers; but it having been found by experience that particular underwriters, after having received large premiums for the insurance of ships, &c. at sea, became bankrupts, or otherwise failed in answering or complying with the terms of their policies of assurance, to the ruin of many merchants, and to the discouragement of adventurers at sea, and to the great diminution of the trade and public revenues of the kingdom, it was deemed advisable to establish two distinct corporations, with competent funds for assurance of ships, goods, or merchandizes at sea, or going to sea, on the supposition that merchants would think it much safer to depend on the assurances of either of these corporations, than on those of private or particular persons; at the same time leaving to the merchants their option to assure with private underwriters, if they should prefer it. To carry this design into effect, the stat. 6 Geo. I. c. 18, (A. D. 1719,) authorized the king to grant charters to two distinct companies for assurance of ships, goods, and merchandizes at sea, or going to sea, and for lending money on bottomry. In pursuance of the powers given by this statute, the Royal Exchange Assurance and the London Assurance Companies were established by charters, bearing date the 22nd day of June, 1720. By the 12th section of the before-mentioned statute, it was enacted, that "all corporations, societies, and partnerships (other than the two corporations) should be restrained from underwriting." By stat. 5 Geo. IV. c. 114, s. 1, this restraint was removed, and now any corporation or body politic, society, or partnership, or persons acting in any society or partnership, may grant, sign, and underwrite any policy of assurance, upon any ship or goods, at sea or going to sea, or lend money by way of bottomry. But by the 2nd section, it is provided, that this act shall not affect the rights and privileges of the corporations of the Royal Exchange and London Assurance, otherwise than by making it lawful for other corporations and bodies politic, and persons acting in societies or partnership, to grant and make such policies of assurance and contracts of bottomry. It may be remarked, that the object of the 12th section of the statute of George I. was merely to avoid *marine* insurances entered into by corporations and partnerships, other than the two privileged corporations: for it was expressly declared, at the close of that section, that any private persons might underwrite as fully and beneficially as before that statute (14), provided they did not underwrite upon the account or risk of a corporation, or persons acting in partnership.

---

(14) For the cases decided upon the statute 6 Geo. I. c. 18, s. 12, before its repeal, see the 9th edition of this work, p. 64, under title "Assumpsit."

What may be Insured.

The subjects of marine insurance are, ships, goods, merchandize, freight (*i*), bottomry, and respondentia interest; a special interest in goods, as the lien of a factor (*k*); money expended by the captain for the use of an East India ship (*l*): the captain's commission and privileges in an African trade ship (*m*) (15); the profits expected to arise from a cargo, as from a cargo of molasses (*n*), or from a cargo employed in the trade on the coast of Africa (*o*). But a mere expectation without any interest is not insurable; as where (*p*) a vessel not having strictly complied with the provisions of a French law by which a bounty is given to ships fishing in certain latitudes under certain conditions, and therefore not being entitled to the bounty as a matter of right, it was holden, that although it was the practice of the French government to allow the bounty to vessels under similar circumstances, without inquiry as to the strict performance of the conditions, such an expectation of the bounty was not an insurable interest. With respect to an insurance on freight, it is to be observed, 1st, that freight ought to be insured *eo nomine* as freight, and that it will not be covered by an insurance on goods (*q*); and 2ndly, unless an inchoate right to the freight has commenced, the assured will not be entitled to recover. The risk does not attach until the goods are either

(*i*) *Montgomery* v. *Eggington*, 3 T. R. 362.

(*k*) Park, 14.

(*l*) *Gregory* v. *Christie*, Park, 14; 3 Doug. 419.

(*m*) *King* v. *Glover*, 2 Bos. & Pul. N. R. 206.

(*n*) *Grant* v. *Parkinson*, Park, 402;

Marsh. Ins. 97, 2nd edit.; *S. C.* more fully reported, 3 Doug. 16 (16).

(*o*) *Barclay* v. *Cousins*, 2 East, 544. See also *Hodgson* v. *Glover*, 6 East, 316.

(*p*) *Devaux* v. *Steele*, 6 Bingh. N. C. 358.

(*q*) *Baillie* v. *Moudigliani*, Park, 90.

---

(15) The policy of the law considers the insurance of seamen's wages, or of any thing to be received at the end of the voyage in lieu of wages, as illegal[*]. The law of England, following the marine law, does not allow the mariners any wages, unless the ship earn freight. This law would be completely evaded, if the mariners could insure their wages; but there is not any such rule as to the captain. An insurance, however, on money lent to the captain, payable out of the freight, is illegal[†].

(16) An insurance may be effected on *profits* generally, without more description[‡], and engrafted upon a policy on ship and goods in the common printed form for a certain voyage; with a return of premium for short interest: the assured proving an interest in the cargo.

[*] See *Webster* v. *De Tastet*, 7 T. R. 157.

[†] *Wilson* v. *R. Ex. Ass. Com.*, 2 Campb. 626.

[‡] *Eyre* v. *Glover*, 16 East, 218; 3 Campb. 276.

actually shipped on board, or until there is an actual contract for
shipping them (r). In an action upon a policy of insurance upon
ship and freight (s), it appeared that the ship had been destroyed
by a tempest, before the goods, which were ready to be shipped,
were actually on board. *Lee*, C. J., was of opinion, that the plaintiff was not entitled to recover for freight, as the goods not having
been actually on board, the plaintiff's right to freight had not commenced. But where the right to freight has commenced, as if part
of the goods are on board, and the rest ready to be shipped, the
plaintiff will be entitled to recover on an insurance on freight (t).
So where (u) plaintiff, a ship-owner, effected a policy on freight at
and from the Coromandel coast to Bourbon: the ship put into port
on the Coromandel coast for repairs; the plaintiff purchased a
cargo, and had it ready to be sent on board in storehouses about
seven miles from the port. The ship was lost by an accident in
getting out of dock. It was holden, that the cargo being ready
when the ship was about to leave the dock, the risk attached. So,
where a ship was chartered for a voyage from London to Teneriffe,
where she was to take wine on board, and to carry it to the West
Indies, and it was covenanted that the owner was to receive for the
freight for the said voyage so much per pipe, and the vessel set sail,
but was captured before she arrived at Teneriffe (x); it was holden,
that, as in this case the inchoate right to freight commenced from
the inception of the voyage, that is, the instant the ship sailed from
London, the plaintiff was entitled to recover on a policy on freight.
N. In this case the policy was a valued policy on freight "at and
from London to Teneriffe, and at and from thence to the West
Indies." So where an insurance was made by ship-owners on
freight of a certain ship (y) "at and from Dominica," &c. to
London, and it appeared that the ship had been chartered for a
voyage *from London to Dominica, and back to London*, the charterers agreeing to pay a certain part of the freight which the ship
should make outwards, and also to procure for the ship at Dominica
a full cargo at the current freight for London; the ship having
arrived at Dominica, and delivered her outward-bound cargo, was
captured while she lay at Dominica, before any part of the home-
bound cargo, which was ready to be loaded, could be put on board.
An endeavour was made to distinguish this case from the preceding
case of *Thompson* v. *Taylor*, on the ground, that there the insurance
was on a valued policy upon freight on a chartered ship *at and from
London to Teneriffe*, and at and from thence to the West Indies;
and which, as it was said, turned on the entirety of the voyage
insured, the freight being covenanted to be paid for the said
voyage, according to a stipulated rate per pipe for 500 pipes of

(r) *Flint* v *Flemyng*, 1 B. & Ad. 45.
(s) *Tonge* v. *Watts*, Str. 1251.
(t) *Montgomery* v. *Eggington*, 3 T. R.
362.

(u) *Devaux* v. *J'Anson*, 5 Bingh. N. C.
519.
(x) *Thompson* v. *Taylor*, 6 T. R. 478.
(y) *Horncastle* v. *Suart*, 7 East, 400.

wine; whereas this was an open policy, and the freight was to be estimated according to the quantity of goods on board, of which there never were any, and, therefore, no inception of the freight, and, consequently, not of the insurance upon it: and this, it was argued, was the same as if the ship had sailed from Dominica without any goods on board; but the objection was overruled; Lord *Ellenborough*, C. J., observing, that it was clear that the underwriter was liable, upon the authority of *Thompson* v. *Taylor*, the voyage having commenced in which the freight was to be earned according to the terms of the charter-party, which made it one entire contract, and which voyage was insured by the policy; that in *Thompson* v. *Taylor*, the loss happened before the ship arrived at Teneriffe, where she was going to fetch her freight, and yet the underwriter was holden to be liable. Freight may be insured for part of an entire voyage (z); and if the ship be on the voyage insured when the loss happens, the assured will be entitled to recover, although the ultimate destination of the ship was not disclosed to the underwriter. On a policy on goods at and from Plymouth to Malta, with liberty to touch at Penzance, or any other port in the channel to the westward, for any purpose whatever, beginning the adventure from the loading the goods on board the ship as above, it was holden (a), that goods loaded at Penzance were protected by the policy. A policy on freight, at and from the ship's port of loading at J. to her port of discharge, with leave to call at intermediate ports, beginning the adventure on the goods from the loading, as aforesaid, *with leave to discharge, exchange, and take on board goods at any port she may call at*, without being deemed a deviation, covers the freight of goods loaded at an intermediate port; and therefore, where the ship having sailed with a cargo loaded at J. was, during the voyage, cast on shore at an intermediate port, and lost a part of her cargo, and took on board other goods at that port to complete her cargo, and arrived at her port of discharge, and earned freight; it was holden (b), that the assured, who had abandoned to the underwriter upon intelligence of the loss, and had adjusted with him as for a total loss, was liable to the underwriter for the freight of that part of the cargo loaded at the intermediate port, after deducting the expenses attendant upon procuring the said freight. In an action on a policy on freight it appeared, that the ship in the course of her voyage having been injured by a peril of the sea, was obliged to put into a port, and land the whole of her cargo. Part of her cargo had been so wetted by sea-water that it could not be reshipped without danger of ignition, unless it went through a process which would have detained the vessel six weeks, and have been attended with

---

(z) *Taylor* v. *Wilson*, 15 East, 324.
(a) *Violett* v. *Allnutt*, 3 Taunt. 419, recognized in *Leathly* v. *Hunter*, 7

Bingh. 529.
(b) *Barclay* v. *Stirling*, 5 M. & S. 6.

expense equal to the freight. Under these circumstances, the master sold these goods, and finding he could not obtain others, he sailed on his voyage, and arrived at his port of destination with the rest of his cargo. The master's proceedings were such as a prudent man uninsured would have adopted. It was holden (c), that the underwriters were not liable for the loss of the freight of these goods. A ship-owner is entitled (d) to recover upon a policy of insurance for freight for a loss accruing to him by reason of his having been deprived of the means of carrying his own goods in his own ship. A homeward policy on freight (e), at and from A., attaches when the ship is at A. in a condition to begin to take in her homeward cargo, which is a question of fact for the jury.

IV. *Of Losses,*

1. *By Perils of the Sea, p.* 953.

2. *By Capture, p.* 955.

3. *By Arrests, &c., p.* 957.

4. *By Barratry, p.* 959.

5. *By Fire, p.* 963.

6. *By other Losses, p.* 963.

1. *By Perils of the Sea.*—Losses by *perils of the sea* are understood to mean only such as proceed from mere sea damage (*f*); that is, such as arise from stress of weather, winds, and waves, from lightning and tempests, from striking against rocks, from sands, &c. A loss occasioned by another ship running down the ship insured, through gross negligence, is a loss by perils of the sea (*g*). If there has not been any intelligence received of a ship within a reasonable time after she has sailed (*h*), it will be presumed, that she foundered at sea, and the assured may maintain an action against the underwriter, stating the loss to have happened by the vessel sinking at sea (*i*). What shall be deemed a reasonable time, must depend on the distance and length of the voyage, &c. Evidence of the vessel having sailed on her intended voyage on such a day, and not having been heard of since, is the best

(c) *Mordy* v. *Jones,* 4 B. & C. 394 ; *Brocklebank* v. *Sugrue,* 1 M. & Rob. 102.

(d) *Flint* v. *Flemyng,* 1 B. & Ad. 45, recognised in *Devaux* v. *J'Anson,* 5 Bingh. N. C. 519.

(e) *Williamson* v. *Innes,* 1 M. & Rob. 88, *Lyndhurst,* C. B. See *Devaux* v. *J'Anson, ubi sup.*

(f) Marsh. 416.

(g) *Smith* v. *Scott,* 4 Taunt. 126.

(h) Park, 105.

(i) *Green* v. *Brown,* Str. 1199. See also *Newby* v. *Read,* Sittings after M. T. 1763, coram Lord *Mansfield,* C. J., Park, 106.

evidence of which the nature of such a case admits, and consequently will be sufficient to support the action. It is not necessary to call witnesses from the vessel's port of destination; it is sufficient to prove that she was not heard of in this country after she sailed (*k*). But it must be shown, that when the ship left the port of outfit, she was bound on the voyage insured (*l*). For this purpose the *convoy bond* (*m*) mentioning the port of destination in the common form, or a license (*n*), is *primâ facie* evidence. Insurance on goods by a certain ship from Leghorn to Lisbon. At the trial in 1826, the evidence was, that the vessel with the goods insured on board, sailed from Leghorn in April, 1821, for Lisbon; that she never arrived at that place; and that, a few days after her departure from Leghorn, the witness heard that she had foundered at sea, but that the crew were saved: holden (*o*), that this was sufficient *primâ facie* evidence of a loss by perils of the sea, and that it was not necessary for the plaintiff to call any of the crew, or to account for their non-attendance.

Upon a policy of insurance on goods, where the ship, being disabled by the perils of the sea from pursuing her voyage, was obliged to put into port to repair; and, in order to defray the expenses of such repairs, the master, having no other means of raising money, sold part of the goods, and applied the proceeds in payment of these expenses. It was holden (*p*), that the underwriter was not answerable for this loss. Under a count for a loss by perils of the sea (*q*), evidence that the ship was destroyed by a species of worms, which infest the rivers of Africa, was holden not to support the declaration. If a ship hove down on a beach within the tideway to repair, be thereby bilged and damaged, it is not a loss occasioned by the perils of the sea (*r*). A transport in the service of government, was insured for twelve months, during which she was ordered into a dry harbour, the bed of which was uneven, and on the tide having left her, she received damage by taking the ground; it was holden (*s*), that this was a loss by a peril of the sea. So in an insurance on goods in a ship warranted free from capture and seizure. The ship was stranded on a shoal within a few miles of the port of destination, and disabled from proceeding; but while she lay in the sand, she was seized by the commander of the place at which she was stranded; and the goods were confiscated by him: it was holden (*t*) a loss of the goods by the perils of the sea.

A policy was effected on living animals, warranted free from

(*k*) *Twemlow* v. *Oswin*, 2 Campb. 85.
(*l*) *Cohen* v. *Hinckley*, 2 Campb. 51;
Koster v. *Innes*, Ry. & M. 333.
(*m*) 2 Campb. 51.
(*n*) *Marshall* v. *Parker*, 2 Campb. 69.
(*o*) *Koster* v. *Reed*, 6 B. & C. 19.
(*p*) *Powell and another* v. *Gudgeon*, 5 M. & S. 431; *Sarquy* v. *Hobson*, 2 B. &

C. 7; judgment affirmed on error, in Ex. Chr. 4 Bingh. 131, S. P.
. (*q*) *Rohl* v. *Parr*, London Sittings after H. T. 1796, Park, 105.
(*r*) *Thompson* v. *Whitmore*, 3 Taunt. 227.
(*s*) *Fletcher* v. *Inglis*, 2 B. & A. 315.
(*t*) *Hahn* v. *Corbett*, 2 Bingh. 205.

mortality and jettison. In the course of the voyage some of the animals, in consequence of the agitation of the ship in a storm, were killed; and others, from the same cause, received such injury that they died before the termination of the voyage insured. It was holden (u), that this was a loss by a peril of the sea, for which the underwriters were liable. In a similar case, where it was found in the special verdict, that a certain usage, with respect to such policies, prevailed amongst the underwriters subscribing policies at Lloyd's Coffee-house in London, and merchants and others effecting policies there, and that the policy in question was effected at Lloyd's Coffee-house; but it was not found that the plaintiff was in the habit of effecting policies at that place: it was holden (x), that this usage was not sufficient to bind the plaintiff. An averment of loss by perils of the sea, is not supported by proof that the vessel was sunk in consequence of being fired upon by another vessel, under a mistake (y). It is the province of the jury to determine whether the cause of the loss be a peril of the sea or not (z). In cases of insurances upon goods, where, by the terms of the policy, the underwriter is to continue liable until the goods are safely landed, if one of the public lighters, entered at Waterman's Hally be employed for the purpose of landing the goods, and the goods sustain a damage on board such lighter, without any negligence on the part of the lighterman, the underwriter will be responsible for the loss (a); but if the owner of the goods chooses to employ his own private lighter to land them (b); or if after the goods are put on board a public lighter, the owner takes them into his own custody and possession, and discharges the lighterman (c), the underwriter in such cases will not be liable. See *Hoffman* v. *Marshall*, 2 Bingh. N. C. 383, and *ante*, p. 943.

2. *Loss by Capture.*

Capture is the taking the ship or goods by an enemy of the country to which the ship and goods belong, when in a state of public war.

To constitute a loss by capture within the meaning of the policy (d), it is not necessary that the ship should be condemned, or carried into any port or fleet of the enemy. In every case of

(u) *Lawrence* v. *Aberdein*, 5 B. & A. 107.

(x) *Gabay and another* v. *Lloyd*, 3 B. & C. 793.

(y) *Cullen* v. *Butler*, 1 Stark. N. P. C. 138, Ld. *Ellenborough*, C. J.

(z) Per *Kenyon*, C. J., in *Buller* v. *Fisher*, Abbott, 236.

(a) *Rucker* v. *London Assurance Comp.*,

London Sittings, June, 1784, per *Buller*, J.; *Hurry* v. *Royal Exch. Ass.*, 2 Bos. & Pul. 430.

(b) *Sparrow* v. *Carruthers*, Str. 1236.

(c) *Strong* v. *Natally*, 1 Bos. & Pul. N. R. 16.

(d) Per Lord *Mansfield*, C. J., in *Goss* v. *Withers*, 2 Burr. 694.

capture (e), the insurer is answerable to the extent of the sum insured for the loss actually sustained. This may be either *total*, as where the thing insured is not recovered again; or *partial*, as where the ship is recaptured or restored *before abandonment;* in which case the insurer is bound to pay the salvage, and any other necessary expense, which may have been incurred by the party for the recovery of his property. In assumpsit upon a policy of insurance (f), *interest or no interest*, against enemies, pirates, takings at sea, &c., it appeared, that the ship was taken by a Swedish pirate, and remained in his possession nine days, and then was retaken by an English man of war, and, after the suit commenced, brought into Harwich: it was holden, that the plaintiff was entitled to recover: for though the ship was retaken, yet the plaintiff had received a damage by the interruption of his voyage; and the question was not, whether the plaintiff had his ship, and did not lose his property, but what damage he had sustained. In a case where a privateer had been insured (g), *interest or no interest, free from average, and without benefit of salvage,* for a cruise of three months, and during that time she was captured, whereby she was prevented from finishing her cruise: it was holden, that the assured was entitled to recover for a *total* loss, although it did not appear, that the ship was ever carried *infra præsidia hostium*, and although the ship was retaken before the expiration of the three months. See further on this subject, *Whitehead* v. *Bance*, Park, 77, and *Dean* v. *Dicker*, Str. 1250.

A ship warranted neutral was captured as an enemy's ship, and the owners, after an interlocutory decree against them, agreed to a compromise (h); this being done *bonâ fide*, it was holden, that the insurer was liable for the sum paid by the insured under such compromise. Formerly, it was a common practice, when vessels were captured by the king's enemies, or by other persons committing acts of hostility, for persons to agree with the captors for ransom of the vessels, and for securing the stipulated ransom, not only to give hostages, but also to bind themselves, or the owners, for the payment thereof. The law of nations gave a sanction to this practice; but it having been found, by experience, liable to great abuse, and there being reason to apprehend, that upon the whole it operated more to the disadvantage than the benefit of his Majesty's subjects, the legislature interposed, and prohibited it. See stat. 22 Geo. III. c. 25, s. 1; 33 Geo. III. c. 66, s. 37, 38; 43 Geo. III. c. 160, s. 34, 35. Although by the terms of the policy, the underwriters undertake to indemnify the assured against *all* captures and detentions of princes, without any exception in respect to the acts of the government of their own nation, yet has

(e) Marsh. 422.
(f) *Depaba* v. *Ludlow*, Comyn's R. 360.
(g) *Pond* v. *King*, 1 Wils. 191.
(h) *Berens* v. *Rucker*, 1 Bl. R. 313.

the law engrafted an exception thereon of captures made by the authority of the government of the country to which the underwriters belong. Hence (i), it has been solemnly determined, that even after the cessation of hostilities between England and France, a Frenchman was not entitled to recover in the English courts upon a policy of insurance effected in England before the commencement of hostilities; for a policy, containing an insurance against British capture, *eo nomine*, would be illegal and void upon the face of it, as being directly and obviously repugnant to the interest of the state, having immediate tendency to render ineffectual, to the extent of the indemnity created thereby, all offensive operations by sea adopted on the part of his Majesty and his subjects, for the purpose of weakening the strength and diminishing the resources of the enemy. And if an insurance by a British subject, made in terms against British capture, would be void, an insurance indirectly producing the same effect, by the application afterwards of the general terms of the insurance to the particular event (*i. e.*) of British capture, which takes place afterwards, must upon principle be equally illegal; and no peril, the subject of insurance, can be recovered under the generality of the terms "capture," "detention of princes," or the like, which cannot, consistently with law, be specifically insured against in direct and express terms. Although, in cases of capture, the underwriter is responsible to the assured, yet, if *before a demand* the ship be recovered, he is liable for the amount only of the loss sustained at the time of the demand; or if the ship be restored after payment by the underwriter, he shall stand in the place of the assured.

3. *Loss by Arrests, &c.*

Among other perils, which the assurers, in the language of the policy, are contented to bear, and do take upon them in the voyage, are "arrests and detainments of all kings, princes (17), and people, of what nation, condition, or quality soever." The word people means the ruling and supreme power of the country, whatever it may be. This appears clearly from another part of the policy; for where the underwriters insure against the wrongful acts of indivi-

(i) *Furtado* v. *Rodgers*, 3 Bos. & Pul. 396; *Gamba* v. *Le Mesurier*, 4 East, 407. 191; *Kellner* v. *Le Mesurier*, 4 East,

(17) By the word "princes," according to the opinion of Lord *Mansfield*, in *Goss* v. *Withers*, 2 Burr. 696, must be understood, not enemies merely, but those in amity also. Hence it is said, that, by the general law, the assured may abandon in the case of an arrest or detainment by a prince, not an enemy.

duals, they describe them by the names of pirates, rogues, thieves. The words, therefore, " kings, princes, and *people*," must apply to nations in their collective capacity. Hence, where a party of rioters boarded a ship, and having taken the command, stranded her, and compelled the captain to sell the cargo, which consisted of wheat, at their own price, and much below its real value; it was holden (*k*), that the plaintiff, who had insured the cargo, could not recover on a count stating that the vessel was *arrested, distrained, and detained by people*, to the plaintiff unknown, by reason whereof the cargo was wholly lost to the plaintiff. Upon a common policy on goods, the underwriters are discharged, if the goods are landed at the port of destination by the officers of government there, and are lodged in the government warehouses, if this be the usual mode in which goods are landed at that port, although the goods insured are afterwards confiscated by the government, and are never in the possession of the consignees (*l*). Policy on goods at and from London to Archangel (*m*), " until the goods should be there discharged and safely landed." The declaration averred that the ship arrived at Archangel; but that before the goods were discharged or safely landed, they were seized and detained by the persons exercising the powers of government there. It appeared in evidence, that as soon as the vessel arrived at Archangel, her hatches were sealed down, and a custom-house officer remained constantly on board. Leave was refused to unload the cargo for several weeks; and at last it was unloaded into praams or lighters belonging to the government, under the inspection of an officer, and lodged in a government warehouse, where the consignees had no control over it, and were not even permitted to see it. The whole was afterwards condemned on the ground that the ship had come from London instead of Teneriffe, as was represented by the simulated papers which she carried. It appeared, however, to be the uniform course of transacting business at Archangel, that when a ship arrives, her hatches are sealed down, that a custom-house officer remains on board till she is unloaded, and that the goods must be carried in the first instance to the government warehouses, where they remain till the duties are paid. Under these circumstances Lord *Ellenborough* was of opinion, that there was not any evidence, that the goods were seized and detained by the Russian government before they were discharged and safely landed—that the goods were landed according to the usual course of trade at the port of Archangel; and consequently that the underwriters on such a policy as the present were not liable for any subsequent loss. In a declaration on a policy on goods it was averred, that the ship with the goods on board, when at C., was arrested by the persons exercising the powers of government there, and the goods were by

(*k*) *Nesbitt* v. *Lushington*, 4 T. R. 783.   (*m*) *Ibid*.
(*l*) *Brown* v. *Carstairs*, 3 Campb. 161.

the said persons seized and confiscated. It was proved, that on the ship's arrival at C., her hatches were sealed down, and her cargo was afterwards forcibly unloaded by the officers of government, and never delivered to the consignees. This was holden (n) to be sufficient proof of the averment, without the production of any sentence of condemnation.

Under this head it will be proper to consider the effect and operation of an embargo on the contract of insurance. An embargo is an arrest laid on ships or merchandize by public authority, or a prohibition of state, commonly issued to prevent foreign ships from putting to sea in time of war, and sometimes also to exclude them from entering our ports. Where a neutral insures (o) in this country a ship " at and from a port in a foreign country ;" and while the ship remains in that port, an embargo is laid on by the *foreign state*, the assured will, if the embargo continue, be entitled to abandon, and to recover for a total loss ; for such an embargo is within the meaning of the words, " arrests, restraints, and detainments by kings, princes, and people." What would be the effect of an embargo laid by the government of this country upon a ship insured here, has not been solemnly determined. It seems, however, that although one British subject might insure another British subject against the consequences of an embargo laid on by the British government (p), yet an insurance for the benefit of *a foreigner* against such an embargo would be illegal (q).

4. *Loss by Barratry* (18).

The original meaning of the term "barratry" is to be collected from the Italian language, and is, according to Dufresne's Glossary,

(n) *Carruthers* v. *Gray*, 3 Campb. 142.
(o) *Rotch* v. *Edie*, 6 T. R. 413.
(p) See Marsh. 437; *Green* v. *Young*, Ld. Raym. 840; Salk. 444; and Ld.

Alvanley's opinion in *Touteng* v. *Hubbard*, 3 Bos. & Pul. 302.
(q) Opinion of the judges in *Touteng* v. *Hubbard.*

---

(18) " It is extraordinary that this species of loss, occasioned by the misconduct of the master, selected and appointed as he is by the owners themselves, and liable to be dismissed by them only, should ever have been made the subject of insurance; and it is the more so, as it has an impolitic tendency to enable the master and owners, by a fraudulent and secret contrivance and understanding between them, to throw the ill success of an illegal adventure, of which the benefit, if successful, would have belonged solely to themselves, upon the underwriters. So, however, it is, that this description of loss has, from the earliest times, held its place as a subject of indemnity in British policies of insurance." Per Lord *Ellenborough*, C. J., delivering the judgment of the court in *Earle* v. *Rowcroft*, 8 East, 134.

(*verbum barratria*,) *fraus, dolus, qui fit in contractibus et venditio-nibus*" (r). He does not apply it in any marine sense, or with reference to the particular relation of masters and owners. In that sense, however, in which it is particularly used, as applied to sub-jects of British marine insurance, in the earliest reported case (s), which we find on the subject, it is considered as being precisely tantamount to fraud, in the particular relation which subsists between master mariners and owners, being such by which a loss may happen on the subject matter insured. And as no limitation is put upon the term "fraud," in that case, the court must be under-stood as holding, that fraud and barratry were in effect words of co-extensive import; that is, that barratry included *every species of fraud*, in the relation of the master to his owners, by which the subject matter insured might be endangered. In conformity with this opinion, *Willes*, J., in giving the judgment of the court in *Lockyer* v. *Offley*, 1 T. R. 252, defines *barratry* as including "every species of fraud or knavery of the master of the ship, by which the freighters or owners (the freighters in that case were owners *pro tempore*) are injured." Barratry may be committed either by a wilful deviation (t), in fraud of the owner, by smuggling (u), by running away with the ship, by sinking or deserting her, or by defeating or delaying the voyage (19) with a criminal intent. If by reason of these, or other similar acts, the subject matter insured is detained, lost, or forfeited, the assured will be entitled to recover against the underwriter for a loss by barratry; and such acts being in violation of that duty which the masters and mariners owe to the ship-owners, the circumstance of the master or mariners conceiving that they were acting for the benefit of the owners will not vary the case. Hence where the master (x), under letters of marque, which, for want of a certificate, were not valid, (and which had been put on board by the owners with a view to encourage seamen to enter, and without any intention of their being used for the pur-pose of cruising,) had cruised for and taken a prize, in consequence whereof the vessel was lost; it was holden to be an act of barratry, although the master had libelled the prize in a court of admiralty, for the benefit of the owners as well as himself. Neither is it necessary, in order to constitute barratry, that the master should derive, or even intend to derive, any benefit from the act done (20).

(r) Per Lord *Ellenborough*, C. J., de-livering the judgment of the court in *Earle* v. *Rowcroft*, 8 East, 134.

(s) *Knight* v. *Cambridge*, Str. 581.

(t) *Vallejo* v. *Wheeler*, Cowp. 143.
(u) 1 T. R. 252.
(x) *Moss* v. *Byrom*, 6 T. R. 379.

---

(19) "Even dropping anchor *with a fraudulent intent* is barratry." Per *Buller*, J., in *Ross* v. *Hunter*, 4 T. R. 38.

(20) But in some cases the circumstance of private benefit accruing to the master may be *evidence of fraud* in him.

Hence, where the master sailed out of port (y), without paying the port duties, whereby the ship was forfeited, it was holden to be barratry. So where the master (z), under general instructions from his owners to make the best purchases, with dispatch, went into an enemy's port and traded there, on account of which illegal traffic, the vessel insured was seized by a king's ship, and afterwards condemned; this illegal act, unauthorized by the ship-owners, was holden to be barratry, although it did not appear that the master would have been benefited by the act, or that he intended thereby anything more than to make the cheapest and speediest purchases for his employers (21). In order (a), however, to constitute barratry, it is essentially necessary that there should be fraud. Hence, a simple deviation, through the ignorance of the master, *without fraud* on his part, although it avoids the policy, will not amount to barratry (22). It is to be observed, that barratry, in the sense in which it is used in our policies, cannot be committed by any persons except masters or mariners, nor against any persons except the owners of the ship (b); but this term comprehends not only absolute owners, but owners *pro hâc vice* only, as general freighters. Hence, if A. be the owner of a ship (c), and let it out

---

(y) *Knight* v. *Cambridge*, as cited in 8 East, 135, 136.

(z) *Earle* v. *Rowcroft*, 8 East, 126.

(a) *Phyn* v. *Royal Exch. Ass. Comp.*, 7 T. R. 505.

(b) *Nutt* v. *Bourdieu*, 1 T. R. 323.

(c) *Vallejo* v. *Wheeler*, Cowp. 143.

But see *Hobbs* v. *Hannam*, 3 Campb. 94, where it was held, that if a chartered ship be lost, by means of the captain engaging in an illegal trade, in obedience to the orders of the charterer, this is not a loss by barratry for which ship-owner can recover against the underwriters.

---

(21) It was contended in this case, on the part of the defendant, that if the conduct of the master, although criminal in respect of the state, were, in his opinion, likely to advance the owner's interest, and intended by him to do so, it would not be barratry; but to this the court said they could not assent, for it was not for him to judge in cases not intrusted to his discretion; or to suppose that he was not breaking the trust reposed in him, but acting meritoriously, when he endeavoured to advance the interest of his owners by means which the law forbids, and which his owners also must be taken to have forbidden, not only from what ought to be, and therefore must be presumed to have been, their own sense of public duty, but also, from a consideration of the risk and loss likely to follow from the use of such means.

(22) "Barratry must be some breach of trust in the master, *ex maleficio*." Per *Lee*, C. J., in *Stamma* v. *Brown*, as cited by *Lawrence*, J., from a MS. note in 7 T. R. 508. "No case of deviation, unless it be accompanied with fraud or crime, is within the true definition of barratry." Per *Ellenborough*, C. J., in *Earle* v. *Rowcroft*, 8 East, 139. But where the deviation is such as amounts to barratry, the underwriter cannot insist on the deviation as a ground of objection against the right of the assured to recover.

to B. as freighter, who insures it for the voyage, and the barratrous act, whereby the vessel is lost, is committed with the knowledge of A.; yet if it be unknown to B., he may recover against the underwriter for a loss by barratry. So where the insurance is made by and in favour of the ship-owner, and the barratrous act is committed with the privity of the freighter, the underwriter is not discharged (d), unless he can show that the ship-owner also was privy to the barratry. It appears from the preceding remarks, that where the owner of the ship consents to the act done, such act is not barratry (e). So where the master of the ship is also owner (f), he cannot commit barratry, because he cannot commit fraud against himself. And the same rule holds in equity, where the owner, having mortgaged the ship, acts as master (g), for the mortgagor is considered in equity as the owner of the thing mortgaged. But proof of the master having committed barratry is *primâ facie* sufficient to entitle plaintiff to recover, without showing negatively that the master was not owner or general freighter. If the underwriter insists on this as a defence, it is incumbent on him to show that the master was also owner or general freighter. Barratry cannot be committed against the owner of the ship with his consent. It is not necessary that the loss, in consequence of the barratry, should happen in the very act of committing the barratry : it is sufficient if it happen at any time afterwards, and before the voyage insured is completed ; but it must happen during the voyage insured, and within the time limited by the policy ; for where the master, in the course of the voyage, committed barratry by smuggling, on his own account, by hovering, and running brandy on shore in casks under sixty gallons, and the ship afterwards arrived at the port of destination, and was there moored at anchor twenty-four hours in safety, after which she was seized by the revenue officers for the smuggling; it was holden (h), that the underwriter was discharged. The captain of a ship insured, barratrously carried her out of the course of her voyage, procured her to be condemned in a vice-admiralty court, sold her, and delivered her to the purchaser. In an action on the policy, to which the statute of (i) limitations was pleaded, Lord *Ellenborough* was of opinion, that the cause of action did not accrue, as the loss did not happen, until the master had divested himself of the possession of the ship, by delivering her to the purchaser ; and therefore, although the barratrous abandonment of the voyage, for the purpose of making away with the ship, and fraudulent condemnation, had taken place more than six years before the commencement of the action, yet as

(d) *Boutflower* v. *Wilmer*, London Sittings after T. T. 21 Geo. II., coram *Lee*, C. J., MSS.

(e) *Stamma* v. *Brown*, Str. 1173 ; *Nutt* v. *Bourdieu*, 1 T. R. 323.

(f) Admitted *S. C.*, and in *Ross* v. *Hunter*, 4 T. R. 33.

(g) *Lewin* v. *Suasso*, Postleth. Dict. vol. 1, p. 147, per Lord *Hardwicke*, Ch.

(h) *Lockyer* v. *Offley*, 1 T. R. 252.

(i) *Hibbert* v. *Martin*, 1 Campb. 539.

the sale and delivery were within six years, the plea did not operate as a bar. As it is not necessary to aver the fact whereby the loss is occasioned (*k*), in the very words of the policy, provided the fact alleged be within the meaning of these words; in a case where, by the policy, the insurance was against the barratry of the master, and the breach assigned in the declaration was, that the ship was lost by the fraud and neglect of the master, the declaration was holden to be good: for barratry imports fraud, and he who commits a fraud may properly be said to be guilty of neglect, *viz.* of his duty.

5. *Loss by Fire.*

Fire is expressly mentioned in the policy, as one of the perils against which the underwriters agree to indemnify the assured. In an action on a policy, where the loss was stated to be by fire, it appeared that the ship in question having been chased by an enemy of superior force, the captain, in order to prevent her from falling into the hands of the enemy, set her on fire. It was holden (*l*), that this loss was covered by the policy; Lord *Ellenborough*, C. J., observing, that if the ship is destroyed, it is immaterial whether it is occasioned by a common accident, or by lightning, or by an act done in duty to the state. Nor could it make any difference whether the ship was thus destroyed by third persons, subjects of the king, or by the captain and crew, acting with loyalty and good faith. Fire was still the *causa causans*, and the loss within the perils insured against. If a fire arises on board a ship from the damaged quality of the goods insured, the underwriters are not liable; but if the loss is not so occasioned, the policy will not be vitiated by the non-disclosure of the condition of the goods to the underwriter (*m*). Upon a policy on ship by which the underwriters insured against fire and barratry of the master and mariners, it was holden (*n*), that the underwriters were liable for a loss by fire, occasioned by the negligence of the master and mariners.

6. *By other Losses.*

These general words were not the immediate subject of judicial construction in our courts, until the case of *Cullen* v. *Butler*, 5 M. & S. 461. There the master and crew of a British ship, believing the ship insured to be an enemy's ship about to attack them, fired at her and sunk her with the goods on board. This loss was spe-

---

(*k*) *Knight* v. *Cambridge*, Lord Raym. 1349; Str. 581; 3 Mod. 230.
(*l*) *Gordon* v. *Rimmington*, 1 Campb. 123.
(*m*) *Boyd* v. *Dubois*, 3 Campb. 133.
(*n*) *Busk* v. *R. Exch. Ass.*, 2 B. & A. 73.

cially set forth in the second count of the declaration; and the court held, that the plaintiff was entitled to recover upon it, inasmuch as it fell within the general and comprehensive words in the policy subjoined to the particular causes of loss, *viz.* "All other perils, losses, and misfortunes, which had or should come to the damage of the goods and ship or any part thereof." In an action on a policy of insurance, from Spain to Cuba and the Spanish Main, the declaration stated the insurance to be on dollars. The interest was averred to be in a subject of the King of Spain. It stated that hostilities had commenced between Spain and South America. The loss was stated as follows: namely, that while the ship was on her voyage, an armed vessel proceeded from a ship acting under the authority of persons exercising the powers of government in South America, made up to the ship on board of which the dollars were, in order to attack her; and that the master, in order to prevent the dollars from falling into their hands, threw them overboard. It then stated, that the armed boat did attack the ship, and capture her. To this declaration there was a general demurrer; and the question was, whether this was a loss within the policy. It was holden (*o*), that it was; the court observing, that this was a general demurrer. Taking all the circumstances together, it must be considered that the master acted properly in throwing the dollars overboard. If the defendant had intended to dispute that, he should have gone to trial. They said they considered that this was a loss by jettison; which meant any throwing overboard *ex justâ causâ*. All the foreign writers agree that the master may set fire to a ship to prevent its falling into an enemy's hands. This case fell within the same principle. The dollars would have been useful to the enemy in the prosecution of the war. It was the master's duty to prevent the enemy from seizing them. The circumstance of the insurer not being a subject of Spain could make no difference. They said that this might also be considered as a loss by enemies, and would also fall within the general words "other losses." Where, in an action on a policy of insurance on a ship in the usual form, for twelve months, at sea and in port, the loss averred was as follows: that the ship having arrived at the harbour of St. J., and discharged her cargo, it became necessary to place her, and she was accordingly placed, in a graving-dock, there to be repaired, and near to a certain wharf in the graving-dock; and that whilst she was there, by the violence of the wind and weather, she was thrown over on her side, whereby she struck the ground with great violence and was bilged, &c. It was holden (*p*), that this was a loss within the general words of the policy, "all other perils, losses, and misfortunes, &c." for which the underwriters were liable. Held also, that the above facts, with the additional circumstance

(*o*) *Butler* v. *Wildman*, 3 B. & A. 398.   B. & A. 161. See *Devaux* v. *J'Anson*,
(*p*) *Phillips and another* v. *Barber*, 5   5 Bingh. N. C. 519.

of there being two or three feet water in the graving-dock when the accident happened, did not amount to a loss by perils of the sea. An underwriter is liable (*q*) for losses occurring in the transhipment of goods from the ship to the place of landing, where such transhipment is in the usual course of the voyage, although such risk be not specially mentioned in the policy.

V. *Of Total Losses and Abandonment.*

A TOTAL loss is of two kinds: one, where the whole property insured perishes; the other, where the property exists, but the voyage is lost (*r*), or the expense of pursuing it exceeds the benefit arising from it. In the latter case, the assured *may* elect (23) to abandon to the underwriter all right to such part of the property as may be saved, and having given due notice of his intention to do so, the assured will then be entitled to demand a compensation as for a total loss; but if the assured does not in fact abandon (24), or if he omits to give the underwriter notice (25) of his having abandoned, or if, being required by the underwriter to assign over his interest in the property insured, he refuses to do so (*s*) (26), he

---

(*q*) *Stewart* v. *Bell*, 5 B. & A. 238. Insurance from London to Jamaica.

(*r*) If the voyage be defeated, it is the same thing for this purpose as if the ship be lost. *Lawrence*, J., 6 T. R. 425. But see *Parsons* v. *Scott*, 2 Taunt. 363, and

Anderson v. *Wallis*, 3 Campb. 440; 2 M. & S. 240, and *post*, p. 973. See also *Hunt* v. *Roy. Exch. Ass.*, 5 M. & S. 47.

(*s*) *Havelock* v. *Rockwood*, 8 T. R. 268, more fully reported by N. Atcheson, 8vo. 1800.

---

(23) The assured is not in any case *bound* to abandon. See 15 East, 15.

(24) An assurance was effected on some hogsheads of sugar on a voyage from Ostend to Havre. The vessel sailed from Ostend, but was forced on shore, and the cargo damaged. The assured wrote to the underwriters, to inform them of the circumstances, and of the injury which the sugars had sustained. The underwriters, in answer, desired " that the assured would do the best with the damaged property." It was holden, that the letter, coupled with the answer, did not amount to abandonment. *Thelluson* v. *Fletcher*, 1 Esp. N. P. C. 73, per *Kenyon*, C. J.

(25) Notice of abandonment is necessary, although the ship and cargo have been sold and converted into money, when the notice of the loss was received. *Hodgson* v. *Blackiston*, Park, 281, n.

(26) In *Havelock* v. *Rockwood*, the insurers offer to settle with the assured, he first making an assignment of one fourth part of the value of

will not be entitled to claim as for a total loss; unless, in the conclusion, there be an actual total loss (t). If the subject matter of insurance ultimately exists in specie, so as to be capable of being restored to the hands of the assured, there cannot be a total loss, unless there has been an abandonment (u). And in order to justify an abandonment, there must have been that, in the course of the voyage, which at the time constituted a total loss (x). The question whether the loss be partial or total is precisely the same, whether the policy be valued or open (y). Capture, or the necessary desertion of the ship, constitutes a total loss (z); and the mere existence of a ship after a total loss and abandonment will not reduce it to a case of partial loss (a). The ship must be in esse in this kingdom under such circumstances, that the assured may, if they please, take possession. Insurance on goods. The vessel was wrecked, part of the goods were lost, and part got on shore, but (whilst on shore) were destroyed and plundered by the inhabitants of the coast of the Isle of France, so that no portion of them came again into the possession of the assured. It was holden (b), that this was a total loss by perils of the sea, and no abandonment was necessary. An insurance was effected on freight, and on the cargo from Quebec to London. This ship sailed from Quebec, and on her voyage sprung a leak, and in that state was run aground on a reef of rocks, and was in imminent danger of being carried away and destroyed; whereupon the captain, by the advice of a surveyor and of an agent for the owners, who was also a part owner himself, sold the ship and cargo. The ship was afterwards saved by the purchasers, and repaired, and brought a cargo to London. In an action by the assured against the underwriters on freight for a total loss, the jury found that, in effecting the sale, the master had acted fairly for the benefit of all concerned; and the court, upon special verdict, held (c), that the captain was justified in making such sale, and that an abandonment of freight was not necessary,

---

(t) *Mellish* v. *Andrews*, 15 East, 13.
(u) Per *Bayley*, J., in *Holdsworth* v. *Wise*, 7 B. & C. 798.
(x) *Ib.* 799.
(y) *Allen* v. *Sugrue*, 8 B. & C. 561.
(z) Per *Bayley*, J., *Holdsworth* v. *Wise*, 7 B. & C. 799.

(a) *M'Iver* v. *Henderson*, 4 M. & S. 576; *Cologan* v. *The London Assurance*, 5 M. & S. 447.
(b) *Bondrett* v. *Hentigg*, 1 Holt's N. P. C. 149, C. B., *Gibbs*, C. J.
(c) *Idle* v. *R. E. A. C.*, 8 Taunt. 755.

---

the ship for their benefit. The sum insured not amounting to one fourth, the plaintiff declined making the assignment. The court were of opinion, that, under these circumstances, the assured could not be considered as having abandoned; *Kenyon*, C. J., observing, that the refusal to assign seemed to him to be equivalent to a refusal to abandon; and *Grose*, J., intimating, that there should have been an offer on the part of the assured to assign such part as he was entitled to. See Atcheson's Report, p. 18.

inasmuch as there was nothing to abandon; for the sale being right, the ship and cargo were gone into different hands; and she could not earn freight for the underwriters. On this last point, see *Green* v. *R. E. A. C.*, 6 Taunt. 68, and *Mount* v. *Harrison*, 4 Bingh. 388. In a case (*d*) where hides insured from Valparaiso to Bordeaux, free of particular average, unless the ship were stranded, arriving at Rio Janeiro on their way to Bordeaux, in a state of incipient putridity occasioned by a leak, were sold for one quarter of the value at Rio, because, by the process of putrefaction, they would have been destroyed before they could have reached Bordeaux. The assured received news of the damage to the hides, and their sale at the same time. It was holden, that the assured might recover as for a total loss without abandonment. It was there observed by Lord *Abinger*, delivering the judgment of the court, that, if goods once damaged by the perils of the sea, and necessarily landed before the termination of the voyage, are, by reason of that damage, in such a state, that though the species be not utterly destroyed, they cannot with safety be reshipped into the same or any other vessel; if it be certain that before the termination of the original voyage the species itself would disappear, and the goods assume a new form, losing all their original character; if, though imperishable, they are in the hands of strangers not under the control of the assured; if, by any circumstance over which he has no control, they can never, or within no assignable period, be brought to their original destination; in any of these cases, the circumstance of their existing in specie at that *forced termination* of the risk is of no importance. The loss is, in its nature, total to him who has no means of receiving his goods, whether his inability arises from their annihilation or from any other insuperable obstacle. When the assured has received intelligence of such a loss as entitles him to abandon (*e*), it is incumbent on him to make his election to abandon, and to give notice thereof to the underwriter *within a reasonable time* (*f*) (27) after receipt of the intelligence; otherwise the

(*d*) *Roux* v. *Salvador*, in error, in Exch. Chr., 3 Bingh. N. C. 266.
(*e*) *Mitchell* v. *Edie*, 1 T. R. 608; *All-wood* v. *Henckell*, Park, 280.
(*f*) *Barker* v. *Blakes*, 9 East, 283; *Hudson* v. *Harrison*, 3 B. & B. 97.

(27) "An abandonment must be made within a reasonable time; and I rather conceive that it is the province of the judge to direct the jury as to what is a reasonable time, under the circumstances." Per Lord *Ellenborough*, C. J., in *Anderson* v. *Royal Exch. Ass.*, 7 East, 43, cited by Ld. *E.* in *Davy* v. *Milford*, 15 East, 563. "The assured must make his election speedily, whether he will abandon or not. He cannot lie by, and treat the loss as an average loss, and take measures for the recovery of it, without communicating that fact to the underwriters, and letting them know that the property is abandoned to them." Per Lord *Kenyon*, C. J., in *Allwood* v. *Henckell*, Park, 280, 1. The assured are bound to

assured will be considered as having waived his right to abandon, and in case any part of the property insured be saved, he can recover as for a partial loss only.   But the assured is entitled to a reasonable time for acquiring a full knowledge of the state of a damaged cargo, before he is bound to elect, whether he shall abandon; therefore, where a ship bound from Liverpool to Calais, put back to Liverpool on the 20th of December, when the cargo, consisting of sugar, was immediately relanded and surveyed;—the owners in London received a letter from their agents at Liverpool, dated 29th of December, stating, that the cargo was much damaged, but that it was still in contemplation to send it on; and another dated 7th of January, stating that, on further examination, the whole cargo was found to be damaged: it was holden (g), that the owners, on the receipt of the last letter, were still in time to abandon.

Insurance for £8000 on ship Vittoria, and £4000 on freight "at and from London to the East Indies, and back."   The ship sailed sea-worthy from Calcutta, on her voyage home, when, in addition to some damage which she sustained in the River Hooghly, she encountered two storms at sea, by which she was so shattered as to render it necessary for the captain to put back; and he returned to Calcutta on the 30th of August, 1820.   On his arrival at Calcutta, he gave notice of abandonment to the agents for Lloyd's resident there, and requested that their surveyor might be present at the surveys of the ship.   The agents said, they had no authority to accept the abandonment; but their surveyor attended the surveys, when it was found, that the ship was so seriously damaged, that the expense of repairing her would be nearly £5000.   The agents refused to undertake the repairs; and the captain, having in vain attempted to borrow money for that purpose by hypothecation of *ship*, sold the ship for £1200, conceiving that to be the best course for all parties.   On the 25th of April, 1821, the captain arrived in London, where the owner resided; and on the 3rd of May, the ship's papers were delivered.   On the 5th of May, the ship's brokers abandoned to the underwriters.   In an action on the policy on ship, the jury having found a verdict for the plaintiff, as for a total loss, and that the captain had sold the ship from a justifiable cause, the court (*Richardson*, J., *dissentiente*,) refused to grant a new trial, which was moved for, on the ground that the ship ought not to have been sold, and that notice of abandonment had not been given in due time (h).

(g) *Gernon* v. *R. E. Ass.*, 6 Taunt. 383 ; 2 Marsh. R. 88, *S. C.*
(h) *Read* v. *Bonham*, 3 Brod. & Bingh.

147, cited in *Roux* v. *Salvador*, 1 Bingh. N. C. 542 ; 1 Sc. 491, *S. C.*

give notice of abandonment at the earliest opportunity; notice given five days after they received intelligence of the loss was held too late.   *Hunt* v. *The R. E. Assurance*, 5 M. & S. 47.

If one of several, jointly interested in a cargo, effects an insurance for the benefit of all, he may give notice of abandonment for all (i). Abandonment is necessary to make a constructive total loss; but if there be an actual loss, the circumstance of the assured having previously given an ineffectual notice of abandonment, will not prejudice his claim (k). Where a ship was chartered from Liverpool to Jamaica, there to take on board a full cargo for Liverpool, at the current rate of freight, to be paid at one month from the discharge of her cargo at Liverpool; and the ship-owners effected a valued policy on the freight at and from Jamaica, to her port of discharge in the United Kingdom; and the ship arrived at Jamaica, and, after taking on board one half of her cargo, was lost by storm, the remainder of her cargo being on shore and ready to be shipped: it was holden (l), that the assured were entitled to recover, as for a total loss.

It may be collected, from the two following cases, under what circumstances the assured may elect to abandon and claim as for a total loss. A ship was freighted with fish, and was insured on a voyage from Newfoundland to the port of discharge in Portugal or Spain, without the Streights, or England. During the voyage a violent storm arose, in consequence of which it became necessary that part of the cargo should be thrown overboard, and the ship was so much disabled as to render it necessary for her to go into port to refit; but before she could reach any port, she was captured by the French, who took out nearly the whole of the crew and sent them into France. The ship having remained eight days in possession of the enemy, but not having been carried into port, nor within the enemies' fleet, was recaptured and brought into Milford Haven. The assured immediately gave notice of their intention to abandon. The remainder of the cargo was spoiled whilst the ship lay at Milford Haven, and before she could be refitted. It was holden (m), that the loss being in its nature a total loss, at the time when it happened, the assured had a right of election to abandon; that the subsequent title to restitution arising from the recapture of the ship, *which was not in a situation to pursue her voyage*, could not take away a right vested in the assured at the time of the capture; and consequently that the assured, having given immediate notice of abandonment, were entitled to recover against the insurers for a total loss. A ship and goods were insured for a voyage from Montserrat to London (n). The ship was taken by an enemy, who took out all the crew, part of the cargo, (which consisted of sugars,) and the rigging. She was afterwards recaptured, and carried into New York, where the captain arrived on the 23rd of June, and taking possession of her, found that part of

(i) *Hunt* v. *R. E. Ass.*, 5 M. & S. 47.   313.
(k) *Mellish* v. *Andrews*, 15 East, 13.   (m) *Goss* v. *Withers*, 2 Burr. 683.
(l) *Davidson* v. *Willasey*, 1 M. & S.   (n) *Milles* v. *Fletcher*, 1 Doug. 230.

what had been left of the cargo had been washed overboard; that
fifty-seven hogsheads of what remained were damaged; and that the
ship was in such a state, that she could not be repaired without
unloading her entirely. The owners had not any storehouses at
New York, where the sugars could have been deposited while the
ship was repairing, nor any agent there to advise the captain. No
sailors were to be had. There was an embargo on all vessels at
New York until the 27th of December; and by the destination of
the ship, she was to have arrived at London in July. Thus circumstanced, the captain sold the cargo, and contracted for the
sale of the ship, conceiving that he was thereby acting most beneficially for his employers. The captain did not know of the
insurance. The assured, upon receiving intelligence of what the
captain had done, offered to abandon to the underwriters, and made
a demand as for a total loss. An action having been brought to enforce this demand, it was holden, that the assured were entitled
to recover as for a total loss: Lord *Mansfield*, C. J., observing,
that it had been laid down, "that if the voyage was lost, or not
worth pursuing, if the salvage was high, if further expense was
necessary, if the insurers would not at all events undertake to pay
that expense, &c., the insured might abandon, notwithstanding a
recapture." The preceding cases were cases of peculiar circumstances, so that it ought not to be inferred from them, that in the
case of a mere capture, followed by a recapture, the insured may,
after the recapture (28), abandon, and demand as for a total
loss. The impropriety of making such an inference will appear
from the following case. A ship, valued at a certain sum, was
insured on a voyage from Virginia or Maryland to London; during
the voyage, the ship was captured by the French, who took
out nearly the whole of the crew, and put in a prize-master to
carry her to France. Having remained seventeen days in possession of the enemy, she was recaptured by an English man-
of-war, and carried into Plymouth, whence she was brought into
the port of London, by the order of the owners of the cargo and
the recaptors. The assured, having received intelligence of what
had happened, gave notice to the underwriters of his intention
to abandon. It appeared, that no damage had been sustained
from the capture, except what arose from the temporary interruption of the voyage, and a charge for salvage, which the underwriter
had offered to pay. The cargo had been delivered to the freighters,
who had paid freight for the same. An action having been brought,

---

(28) The assured, upon intelligence of a capture, may abandon, and
claim as for a total loss. Admitted per Lord *Kenyon*, C. J., in *M'Masters*
v. *Schoolbred*, 1 Esp. N. P. C. 237; but if they neglect this opportunity,
and afterwards the ship is recovered, the assured can only claim for the
loss actually sustained. *S. C.*

in which the assured claimed as for a total loss, it was holden (o), that in cases of insurance, the plaintiff's demand is for an indemnity, consequently his action must be founded upon the nature of the injury sustained at the time of action brought; that, as it was repugnant, upon a contract of indemnity, to recover as for a total loss, when the final event had decided that the real injury was an average loss only, the plaintiff in the present case was entitled to recover for an average loss only. At the conclusion of the judgment, Lord *Mansfield* said, that the court desired to be understood that the only point determined was, "that on a valued policy, the plaintiff could not recover more than the actual loss, which had happened at the time when he chose to abandon." A later decision on this subject, and which was admitted to be new in specie, must not pass unnoticed. The defendant had subscribed two policies (p), one on ship, and the other on freight of the same ship, on a voyage from Liverpool to Jamaica. The ship was captured on the 21st of September, and recaptured on the 25th; after which, the plaintiff having received intelligence on the 30th of the capture, but not of the recapture, gave notice of abandonment on the 31st, which he persevered in after the 6th of October, when news of the recapture arrived, and that the ship was safe in a port in Ireland, but which notice the underwriters did not accept. And it appeared, that instead of a total loss, there had been only a small partial loss of £13 and a fraction, for salvage and charges on the policy on freight, and £15 and a fraction on the ship and policy, and that no damage whatever was sustained by the ship whilst in the possession of the enemy. The question was, whether, that, which in the result turned out to be only a partial loss to a trifling extent, should, because of the notice of abandonment given when a total loss appeared to exist, be recovered as a total loss. The court were of opinion, that they must look to the real nature of the contract in a policy of insurance, which was nothing more than a contract of indemnity; and consequently, as that which was supposed to be a total loss at the time of the notice of abandonment first given had ceased, and as only a small loss had been incurred in the salvage, that was the real amount of the indemnification which the plaintiff was entitled to receive under this contract of indemnity. Lord *Ellenborough* observed, "that it has been said in argument, that the offer to abandon having been rightly made at the time, a right of action vested in the assured, which could not be defeated by the subsequent events: but that proposition is not only not true in the whole, but it is not true in its parts. The effect of an offer to abandon is truly this, that if the offer appear to have been properly made upon certain supposed facts which turn out to be true, the assured has put himself in a condition to insist upon his abandon-

(o) *Hamilton* v. *Mendes*, 2 Burr. 1198; 1 Bl. R. 276.

(p) *Bainbridge* v. *Neilson*, 10 East, 329.

ment ; but it is not enough that it was properly made upon facts, which were supposed to exist at the time, if it turn out that no such facts existed, or that other circumstances had occurred which did not justify such abandonment. It may be said to be properly made upon notice received, and *bonâ fide* credited, by an assured, of his ship having been wrecked, whether such intelligence were true or not, and though the letter conveying it turned out to be a forgery : and yet, clearly no right of action would vest in him, founded upon an abandonment made upon false intelligence, and without any thing, in fact, to warrant the giving of such notice. What is an abandonment more than this,—that the assured, having had notice of circumstances, which, if true, entitle him to treat the adventure as a total loss, he, in contemplation of those circumstances, casts a desperate risk on the underwriter, who is to save himself as he can? But does not all this presume the existence of those facts on which the right accrues to him to call upon the underwriter for an indemnity? And if they be all imaginary, or founded in misconception, or if at the time it had ceased to be a total loss, and there be no damage to the assured, or at least if the only damnification arise out of the very act (the recapture) which saves the thing insured from sustaining a total loss, the whole foundation of the abandonment fails. So where upon an insurance on ship from Rio de Janeiro to Liverpool, the ship was captured, and afterwards recaptured ; but in the interval, the assured, having received intelligence of the capture, gave notice of abandonment, and after the recapture the ship arrived at Liverpool, having sustained a partial damage ; it was holden (*q*), that the abandonment was not binding, and that the assured could recover for a partial loss only.

The loss of the voyage, occasioned by the detention of the ship, will not enable the owner to recover upon a policy on the ship as for a total loss, the ship having been released before abandonment (*r*). Where the ship was wrecked, but all the goods were brought on shore, though in a very damaged state, so that they became unprofitable to the assured : it was holden (*s*), that the underwriters on the goods, who were freed by the policy from particular average, could not be made liable as for a total loss, by a notice of abandonment. Policy of assurance on goods (copper and iron) at and from London to Quebec, warranted free of particular average, and the ship, owing to sea damage in the course of her voyage, was obliged to run into port and undergo repair, and some part of the goods were damaged, and the repairs detained her so long as to prevent her reaching Quebec that season, and no other ship could be procured at that or a neighbouring port, to forward the cargo in time,

(*q*) *Brotherston* v. *Barber*, 5 M. & S. 418.

(*r*) *Parsons* v. *Scott*, 2 Taunt. 363.

(*s*) *Thompson* v. *Roy. Ex. Ass. Comp.*, 16 East, 214.

so that the voyage was abandoned, and the ship afterwards sailed on another voyage; it was holden (t), that this was not a total loss of the goods, and that the assured could not abandon. A loss of voyage for the season by perils of the sea, is not a ground (u) of abandonment upon a policy on goods, with a clause of warranty, free from average, &c. where the cargo is in safety, and not of such a perishable nature as to make the loss of voyage a loss of the commodity, although the ship be rendered incapable of proceeding in the voyage. Insurance on ship. The ship, during her voyage, while loading her homeward cargo, was seized by the crew and carried away to a distant country and her cargo plundered, and the ship deserted, but was afterwards retaken by another ship, and was brought with a small remaining part of her cargo to an English port (not the port of her destination), and part of her rigging was gone, and she could not be made fit for a voyage again without considerable expense in providing a crew and stores : it was holden (x), that this was not a total loss so as to entitle the assured to abandon after notice of the recapture.

Where a ship with cargo was barratrously taken out of her course by the crew, and the ship and part of her cargo sold, and the remainder sent home by another vessel; it was holden (y), that this was a total loss of the cargo from the time of the committing of the act of barratry. Upon a hostile embargo in a foreign port, the ship-owner, who had separately insured ship and freight, abandoned them to the respective underwriters at the same time; the abandonment was accepted by the underwriters; afterwards the embargo was taken off, and the ship completed her voyage and earned freight. The freight having been paid by the freighters to the underwriters on the ship, the ship-owner, the assured, brought an action against one of the underwriters on freight, claiming as for a total loss; it was holden (z), that the assured could not recover, the freight not having been in fact earned; or supposing it to have been in any other sense lost to the assured, by the abandonment of the ship to the underwriters thereon, it was so lost, not by any peril insured against, but by the voluntary act of the assured in making such abandonment, with which, and the consequences thereof, the underwriters on freight had not any concern. Policy on fruit from Cadiz to London, with the usual memorandum. In the course of the voyage the fruit was so much damaged by the sea water that it became rotten and stunk, and on the ship's arrival at an intermediate port, into which she was driven, the government of the place prohibited the landing of the cargo. The ship also, being too much damaged to proceed

(t) Anderson v. Wallis, 2 M. & S. 240, recognized in Everth v. Smith, 2 M. & S. 278, and in Hunt v. Royal Exchange Assurance, 5 M. & S. 47.

(u) Hunt v. The Royal Exchange Assurance, 5 M. & S. 47.

(x) Falkner v. Ritchie, 2 M. & S. 290.
(y) Dixon v. Reid, 5 B. & A. 597.
(z) M'Carthy v. Abel, 5 East, 388. See post, p. 974, n. (29) Case v. Davidson.

on her voyage, was sold, and the cargo necessarily thrown overboard. It was holden (a), on a case reserved, that the assured were entitled to recover for a total loss; and *Chambre*, J., said, " the ship is expressed to have been so much damaged that she could not proceed, but was sold; now this must certainly have made a complete end of the voyage. We do not construe special cases so strictly as we do special verdicts ; on the whole, therefore, it seems to me that the loss was total, and though the cargo might be said to exist in specie, yet in value it did not exist at all. If that be so, the inference of law is plain. What is it against which the underwriters protect themselves by the memorandum? Against partial damage. For what reason? Because, as the commodities enumerated are perishable in their nature, it might be impossible to ascertain with exactness, what part of the loss arose from the nature of the commodity, and what from sea damage. If ever there was a case of total loss, it certainly is the present." After satisfaction made as to the goods themselves (b), if restored in specie, or compensation made for them, the assured stands as a trustee for the insurer, in proportion for what he has paid. A ship owner having chartered his ship to J. S., insured the ship and freight with different sets of underwriters. Having notice of an embargo laid on the ship in a foreign port, he abandoned the ship and freight to the respective underwriters, and received the whole amount of their subscriptions as for a total loss; first undertaking, by a memorandum on the ship policy, to assign to the underwriters thereon his interest in the ship, and to account to them for it: and afterwards undertaking, by a similar memorandum on the freight policy, to assign to the underwriters on freight all right of recovery, compensation, &c. The ship having been afterwards liberated, returned home, and earned freight, which was received by the assured; it was holden (c), that however the question of priority as to the title to the freight might have been, as between the different sets of underwriters litigating out of the same fund, and however the weight of argument might preponderate in favour of the underwriters on the ship (29), yet that the assured, who had received the

(a) *Dyson* v. *Rowcroft*, 3 Bos. & Pul. 478.
(b) *Randal* v. *Cockran*, 1 Ves. 98.

(c) *Thompson* v. *Rowcroft*, 4 East, 34. See also *Leatham* v. *Terry*, 3 B. & P. 479.

(29) See *Sharp* v. *Gladstone*, 7 East, 30, where Lord *Ellenborough*, C. J., observed, that as to the general question, whether an abandonment could be made to the underwriters on freight after an abandonment to the underwriters on ship, he desired to be understood as giving no opinion. But in *Case* v. *Davidson*, 5 M. & S. 79, by three justices, *Bayley*, J., dissent., it was determined on a special case that an abandonment to the underwriter on ship, transfers the freight subsequently earned as incident to the ship. Therefore, where ship and freight were

freight, was at all events liable on his express undertaking to pay it over to the underwriters on freight. But in a subsequent case (d), which arose on the same embargo, it was holden, that although the underwriter on freight was entitled to recover the freight received by the assured, yet the assured might deduct out of it the following expenses :—1. The expenses of the ship and crew in the foreign port, including port charges (besides the expenses of shipping the cargo, which exclusively belonged to the underwriters on freight). 2. Insurance thereon. 3. Wages and provisions of crew, from their liberation in the foreign port till their discharge here. 4. Wages, (provisions were supplied by the foreign government,) to the crew during their detention. But it was further holden, that the assured was not entitled to deduct out of such freight; 1. Charges paid at the port of discharge on ship and cargo. 2. Insurance on ship. 3. Diminution in value of ship and tackle by wear and tear on the voyage home. In case of a total loss, where the policy is a valued policy, the value inserted in the policy must be paid by the underwriter. Goods protected by a valued policy, being captured, are condemned as lawful prize, the captors paying freight. The assured may recover as for a total loss (e). Where the subject matter of the insurance is at first of the value mentioned in the policy, and there is not any imputation of fraud, the underwriter will be bound, in case of a loss, by the valuation in the policy, although the loss happens at the latter end of the voyage, at which time the property insured is considerably diminished in value; as where an insurance was made on ship (f) stores, and provisions, valued, on a certain voyage, and the ship foundered on her arrival at the port of discharge; it was holden, that the loss being total, and no fraud, the underwriter was liable to pay the value inserted in the polic , although it appeared that the provisions to the amount of half that value had been expended (30).

(d) *Sharp* v. *Gladstone*, 7 East, 24.   (f) *Shawe* v. *Felton*, 2 East, 109.
(e) *Marshall* v. *Parker*, 2 Campb. 69.

---

insured by separate sets of underwriters, and the ship, being a general ship, was captured, and ship and freight were abandoned to the respective underwriters, who paid each a total loss; and the ship being recaptured, performed her voyage and earned freight, which was received by the defendant for the use of those who were legally entitled thereto; it was holden, that the underwriter on ship was entitled to recover. This judgment was affirmed, on error, in Exchequer Chamber, 2 B. & B. 379. See further as to abandonment of freight, *Green* v. *R. E. A.*, 6 Taunt. 68.

(30) " Valuation at the sum insured is an estoppel in case of a total loss." Per *Lee*, C. J., in *Erasmus* v. *Bank*, M. 21 Geo. II., and *Smith* v. *Flexney*, Dec. 13, 1747.

The wages and provisions (*g*) of the crew of a ship during its detention for the purpose of repairing damages sustained by perils of the sea, are not chargeable to the underwriters of a policy on the ship. Where two ships, A. and B., come into collision, and both sustain damage, but ship A. having sustained less damage than ship B., the owners of A. are legally compelled to pay a sum of money to the owners of ship B., so as to equalize the loss sustained by each; it was holden (*h*), that the sum so paid was not a loss recoverable under a policy on the ship A., although the accident occurred under circumstances, that the loss, by the direct damage, sustained by the ship A. was recoverable.

An action upon a valued policy; the defendant paid into court £30 per cent. It was holden (*i*), that this was merely an admission that a loss of £30 per cent. had been sustained, and no more. Where there is not any valuation in the policy, the prime cost or invoice price, together with all charges until the goods are put on board, and the premium of insurance, will be the foundation upon which the loss will be computed. If part of a cargo, capable of distinct valuation, be lost, the value of such part must be paid (*k*). When there is an insurance on goods, as may be thereafter declared and valued, the assured may, by duly declaring and valuing before the loss, make it a valued policy: but if the assured do not so declare and value, it is then an open policy, and the interest must be proved at the trial.

VI. *Of partial Losses.*

A PARTIAL loss upon a ship or goods (*l*) is such a proportion of the prime cost as is equal to the diminution in value occasioned by the damage. In the case of a partial loss (*m*), although the policy be a valued policy, yet the computation must be by the real interest of the assured on board, and not by the value in the policy; that is, the policy, notwithstanding the valuation, must be considered as an open policy. In the case of a partial loss upon goods, by sea damage, the rule is, that the underwriter is not to be subjected to the fluctuations of the market (*n*), and that he is not liable for any loss which may be the consequence of the duties or charges to be paid after the arrival of the commodity at the place of its destina-

(*g*) *Devaux* v. *Salvador*, 6 Nev. & M. 713.
(*h*) S. C.
(*i*) *Rucker* v. *Palgrave*, 1 Taunt. 419.
(*k*) Per Lord *Ellenborough*, C. J., *Har-*man v. *Kingston*, 3 Campb. 152.
(*l*) Marsh. 535.
(*m*) *Le Cras* v. *Hughes*, Marsh. 541.
(*n*) *Lewis* v. *Rucker*, 2 Burr. 1167.

tion. Hence, in computing the average in a case of this kind, the difference between the respective *gross* proceeds (31) of the damaged goods, and of the goods if they had arrived sound *at the port of delivery*, must first be ascertained. Then, whatever aliquot part of the gross proceeds of the sound commodity at the port of delivery such difference constitutes, the same aliquot part of the original value will be the sum for which the underwriter will be liable: *e. g.* suppose a hogshead of sugar is insured on a voyage from London to Hamburgh, the original value is £30; being deteriorated by sea damage, the gross proceeds at Hamburgh amount to £40; whereas, if the sugar had not been damaged, the gross proceeds would have amounted to £50. The difference is £10, or one fifth part of £50. The sum, then, which the underwriter must pay will be one fifth of £30, the original value, or £6. In cases where the sums are more complicated than in the preceding instance, the calculation may be made as follows: as the gross proceeds of the sound : the gross proceeds of the damaged : : the original value : a fourth quantity, which being found by the rule of three, must be subtracted from the prime cost, and the difference will be the average loss or sum for which the underwriter is chargeable. The proportion of loss is calculated through the same medium, (that is, by comparing the selling price of the sound commodity with the damaged part of the same commodity at the port of delivery,) whether the policy be valued (*o*) or open (*p*). But the proportion of loss, when ascertained, is applied to different standards of value. For the original value in the case of a valued policy is the valuation in the policy; but in the case of an open policy, the original value is the invoice price at the port of delivery, including premiums of insurance and commission. A ship received considerable damage from tempestuous weather, and the crew, completely exhausted, deserted the ship on the high seas, for the mere preservation of their lives; and the ship was then taken possession of by a fresh crew, who succeeded in conducting her safely into port: it was

(*o*) *Lewis* v. *Rucker*, 2 Burr. 1167.   (*p*) *Usher* v. *Noble*, 12 East, 639.

(31) It was solemnly determined in *Johnson* v. *Sheddon*, 2 East, 581, recognized in *Hurry* v. *R. Ex. Ass.*, 2 Bos. & Pul. 308, that the gross proceeds, and not the net proceeds, must be taken as the basis of the calculation. A cargo insured by a valued policy was confiscated abroad and sold *; but the enemy permitted the foreign consignee to retain from the proceeds the amount of his acceptances which he had previously paid; the assured not having abandoned, the loss became partial only, and the assured was holden to be entitled to recover from the underwriter a sum bearing the same proportion to his subscription as the loss ultimately sustained bore to the whole value in the policy.

* *Goldsmid* v. *Gillies*, 4 Taunt. 803.

holden (*q*), that such desertion of the crew did not of itself amount
to a total loss; and secondly, that the ship having been sold under
the decree of the Admiralty Court to pay the salvage, and it not
appearing that the assured had taken any means to prevent such
sale, that they were not entitled to abandon, and that there was
only a partial loss.   In an action on a policy on ship and goods,
warranted free from American condemnation, it appeared, that the
ship and goods were damaged by the perils of the seas, and were
afterwards seized by the American government, and condemned.
It was holden (*r*), that the total loss by subsequent seizure and
condemnation took away from the assured the right to recover in
respect to the previous partial loss by sea damage: inasmuch as the
immediately operating cause of total loss was one from which, and
its consequences, the underwriter was by express provision in the
policy exempted; and as the other antecedent causes of injury
never produced any pecuniary loss to the plaintiff; and as there
never existed a period of time prior to the total loss, in which the
assured could have practically called on the underwriter for an indemnity against the temporary and partial injury.   The liability of
the underwriter is not restricted to the single amount of his subscription (*s*), but he may be subject either to several average losses,
or to an average loss and total loss, or to money expended and
labour bestowed about the defence, safeguard, and recovery of the
ship, to a much greater amount than the subscription; and it shall
be recoverable as an average loss.   Upon a policy on hogsheads of
sugar, warranted against particular average, some part of the sugar
in every hogshead being preserved, though less than three per cent.
on the cargo; it was holden (*t*), that this could not be a total loss.
Where an insurance was effected on wheat shipped in bulk, and
valued at £1600, free from average, except general, or the ship
were stranded, and the ship having sprung a leak, part of the wheat,
value £75, was pumped out with the water and lost; it was
holden (*u*), that the insured could not recover as for a total loss of
a part; the court observing, that "Where the insurance is on each
package separately, it is to be treated as a total loss upon each
package lost; but where it is an insurance upon the bulk, unless
the loss exceed a certain value upon the particular article, there is
no *average* loss; and there cannot in such a case be any *total* loss
of a portion only of the cargo."   On the memorandum "free from
average under £3 per cent.," the underwriter is liable (*x*) for the
amount of the aggregate of several partial losses, each less than
£3 per cent., but amounting together to more.

(*q*) *Thornely* v. *Hebson*, 2 B. & A. 513.
(*r*) *Livie* v. *Janson*, 12 East, 648.
(*s*) *Le Cheminant* v. *Pearson*, 4 Taunt.
367.
(*t*) *Hedburg* v. *Pearson*, 7 Taunt. 154.

(*u*) *Hills* v. *London Ass. Corp.*, 5 M.
& W. 569.   See *Davy* v. *Milford*, 15
East, 559.
(*x*) *Blackett* v. *R. E. A. Comp.*, 2 Cr.
& J. 244; 2 Tyrw. 266.

VII. *Of Adjustment.*

THE adjustment of a loss is the settling and ascertaining the amount of the indemnity which the assured (y), after all allowances and deductions are made, is entitled to receive under the policy, and fixing the proportion which each underwriter is liable to pay. An adjustment being indorsed on the policy, and signed by the underwriter, with a promise to pay in a given time, is to be considered as a note of hand (z), but it does not require a stamp (a). The (b) adjustment is only *primâ facie*, and not conclusive evidence against the underwriter. Hence where the witness (c), who proved the adjustment, swore that soon after the underwriters had signed it, doubts arose in their minds as to the honesty of the transaction, Lord *Kenyon*, C. J., was of opinion, that in such case the plaintiff should produce other evidence; and that shutting the door against inquiry, after an adjustment, would be putting a stop to candour and fair dealing amongst the underwriters. The court afterwards, on a motion for a new trial, concurred in opinion with the chief justice. The production of the policy by assured, with adjustment on it and name of defendant struck off, does not prove (d) payment of the sum adjusted; for it frequently happens, that the name is struck off, on the faith of an adjustment, where nothing is paid, but an arrangement made to pay at a future time. In *Herbert* v. *Champion*, 1 Campb. 134, Lord *Ellenborough* expressed a clear opinion, that an adjustment is merely an admission on the supposition of the truth of certain facts stated, that the assured are entitled to recover; and although it is incumbent on an underwriter, who has once admitted his liability by an adjustment, to make out a strong case, yet, until actual payment of the money, he may avail himself of any defence, which either the facts or the law of the case will furnish. In *Shepherd* v. *Chewter*, 1 Campb. 274, it was holden, that an adjustment was not binding, although the underwriter, at the time of signing it, had an opportunity of becoming acquainted with the history of the voyage, and the circumstances attending the loss, his attention not having been drawn to the fact which discharged his liability to the assured; Lord *Ellenborough*, C. J., observing, that the adjustment was *primâ facie* evidence against the defendant, but it certainly did not bind him, *unless there was a full disclosure of the circumstances of the case: unless they were all blazoned to him as they really existed.* But see Lord

---

(y) Marsh. 529.

(z) *Hog* v. *Gouldney*, Beawes, 310, *Lee*, C. J.

(a) Per *Kenyon*, C. J., in *Wiebe* v. *Simpson*, London Sittings after M. T. 41 Geo. III., MSS.

(b) Per *Kenyon*, C. J., in *Rodgers* v. *Maylor*, Park, 191.

(c) *De Garron* v. *Galbraith*, Park, 194; Peake's Additional Cases, 37, *S. C.*

(d) *Adams* v. *Sanders*, M. & Malk. 373, Ld. *Tenterden*, C. J.

Campbell's note on this case, in which he has shown, that, upon
principles of law, a mere adjustment is not in any case or under any
circumstances conclusive, and that the utmost effect which can be
given to it, is to transfer the burthen of proof from the assured to
the underwriters. A ship was insured, warranted free of capture,
in port. A letter announcing her capture stated it to be in port,
on which the underwriter and assured adjusted; the former returned, and the latter received back the premium. It afterwards
appeared the capture was not in port. It was holden (e), that the
assured was not precluded by the adjustment and repayment from
recovering on the policy; whether the underwriter's name had been
struck off the adjustment only (f), or of the policy also (g). An
underwriter has never been considered discharged as against the
assured, until his name has been struck off the policy, *Russell* v.
Bangley, 4 B. & A. 395, with the consent of the assured; *Bartlett*
v. *Pentland*, 10 B. & C. 760. An usage at Lloyd's does not bind
a person not cognizant of it. *Gabay* v. *Lloyd*, 3 B. & C. 793,
recognized by *Bayley*, J., in *Bartlett* v. *Pentland*, 10 B. & C.
767. In *Scott* v. *Irving*, 1 B. & Ad. 605, where the name had
been struck off the policy, but without the consent of the assured,
the court held the underwriter liable, and disallowed a set-off
between broker and underwriter as against the assured. A trustee
suing as a plaintiff in a court of law must be treated in all respects
as a party to the cause, and any defence against him is a defence in
that action against the cestui que trust, who uses his name. And
therefore, where a broker in whose name a policy of insurance under
seal was effected, brought covenant, and the defendants pleaded
payment to the plaintiff according to the tenor and effect of the
policy; and the proof was, that after the loss happened, the assurers
paid the amount to the broker by allowing him credit for premiums
due from him to them; it was holden (h), that although that was
no payment as between the assured and assurers, it was a good payment as between the plaintiff on the record and the defendants,
and, therefore, an answer to the action.

VIII. *Of the Remedy by Action for Breach of the Contract of
     Insurance, and herein of the Declaration, p.* 980; *Plead-
     ings, p.* 983; *Consolidation Rule, p.* 984.

THE usual remedy or form of action against the insurers or
underwriters, to recover a loss upon a policy of insurance, is an

(e) *Reyner* v. *Hall*, 4 Taunt. 725.   (h) *Gibson* v. *Winter*, 5 B. & Ad. 96;
(f) Ib.   2 Nev. & M. 737.
(g) Ib.

action on the case, founded upon the express special undertaking of the insurers who have signed the policy, or (as it is technically called) a special assumpsit. Two counts upon the same policy are not allowed. But a count upon a policy, and a count for money had and received to recover back the premium upon a contract implied by law, are allowed. R. G. H. T. 4 Will. IV. No. 5. The two insurance companies, namely, the Royal Exchange and the London Assurance, having been, in consequence of stat. 6 Geo. I. c. 18, incorporated by several charters granted, and having a common seal affixed to all their contracts, the proceedings against these companies must be by action of covenant or debt.

The policy must be stated in the declaration, and it must be alleged, that it was signed or subscribed with the name of the insurer against whom the action is brought; that in consideration that the assured had paid to the defendant the premium, the defendant had undertaken to indemnify the assured against the losses specified in the policy; that the goods, wares, and merchandizes, were laden on board the ship to the amount of £— (i. e. the value insured) (32); and further it must be alleged, that the plaintiffs were interested (33) therein, unless the insurance be on a foreign

---

(32) In an action on a policy of insurance of indigo and bale goods, after setting out the policy, it was averred in the declaration, that *divers goods* were loaded on board, and that the policy was made on the *said* goods; on special demurrer, because it was not averred, that the goods stated to have been loaded on board were indigo or bale goods, the court observed, that the allegation, in the declaration, that the policy was made on the goods put on board, completely answered the objection taken, since that could not be true, unless indigo or bale goods were loaded on board, which it would be necessary for the plaintiff to prove at the trial. *De Symons* v. *Johnston*, 2 Bos. & Pul. N. R. 77.

(33) It is immaterial to aver interest at any day previous to the commencement of the risk. In a declaration on a policy on freight, if it be averred that the plaintiff was interested at the time of the ship's sailing, or that the policy was made on a certain day, and that afterwards, on a subsequent day, the plaintiff acquired an interest, it will suffice. Per *Cur.*, *Rhind* v. *Wilkinson*, 2 Taunt. 242, 3. A change in the interest after the policy is effected, much less after the loss has happened, cannot be set up as an answer by the underwriters against a claim for such loss. *Sparkes* v. *Marshall*, 2 Bingh. N. C. 776.

A person who has several interests in a cargo, *viz.* as partner in $\frac{1}{17}$ths, as consignee of the whole, and as having a lien on the whole for advances, may protect them all by one insurance, without expressing in the policy the number or nature of his interests. *Carruthers* v. *Sheddon*, 6 Taunt. 14. Although the subject matter of the insurance must be properly described, the nature of the interest may in general be left at large. Hence, an insurance " on goods" is sufficient to cover the interest of car-

ship, in which case an averment of interest is not necessary (34).
The declaration then proceeds to state, that the property insured
was lost, and by what means it was lost, so as to bring the case
within some or one of the perils specified in the policy, and thereby
intended to be insured against; as by the barratry of the master or
mariners, &c.

---

riers in the property under their charge. *Crowley* v. *Cohen*, 3 B. & Ad.
478. Joint owners of property insured for their joint use and on their
own account, cannot recover upon a count on the policy averring the
interest to be in one of them only*.

(34) Whether, in such case, it may be necessary that any allegation
as to the property in the ship should be made on the part of the plaintiff,
or whether it be not incumbent on the defendant to show that the property
is not insurable within the statute 19 Geo. II. c. 37, s. 1, is a question
which has not been solemnly decided. In several cases, where actions
have been brought on foreign ships, averments as to the property have
been inserted in the declaration. In *Crauford* v. *Hunter*, 8 T. R. 15, it
was averred, that the ships insured were not belonging to his Majesty, or
any of his subjects, *before or at the time of the making the policy, or at
the time of the loss*. In *Nantes* v. *Thompson*, 2 East, 385, the averment was, " that the ship was not, at the time of effecting the policy, nor
of the happening of the loss, *nor at any other time*, the property of the
king, or any of his subjects." In neither of these cases was any objection
made to the form of the averment; but in *Kellner* v. *Le Mesurier*, 4 East,
396, (where an insurance was made in England on the ship Princess
Louisa, lost or not lost, " at and from Lisbon to Cadiz, &c.") the averment being that the ship was not, at the time of making the policy, nor
of the happening of the loss, the property of the king, or any of his
subjects, there was a special demurrer, assigning for cause that the declaration did not contain an averment of interest, and that it did not appear
that the ship, at the time of her departing from Lisbon, or at the beginning
of the adventure insured, was not the property of the king, or any of his
subjects. It was contended, on the part of the plaintiff, that supposing
the allegation in question to be insufficient, yet it might be rejected as
surplusage, for it was not necessary to make any allegation at all on the
subject, and that the onus lay on the defendant to show, that the property was not insurable in virtue of the provisions introduced by the
statute 19 Geo. II. c. 37, s. 1. The court being of opinion in favour of
the defendant, on another ground of objection, declined the consideration
of the question as to the averment.

Action lies in name of person who makes insurance, though made for
the benefit and on property of another, so averred in declaration. *Famin
and another* v. *Cawthorn*, B. R. H. 22 Geo. III. B. P. B. 194; Dampier
MSS. L. I. L. See *Fitzgerald* v. *Poole*, Law of Bills, 251, like declaration.

* *Bell* v. *Ansley*, 16 East, 141.

It is necessary to show who are the real contracting parties, and to describe truly the interest on which the policy is effected. Therefore, if A. and B., jointly interested in a ship, effect an insurance, and there be two counts, the one averring interest in A. and the other averring interest in B., the plaintiff can recover on neither count (*i*). If the plaintiff should allege in the declaration (*k*), that there was a total loss, and lay his damages accordingly, evidence of a partial loss will maintain the declaration, and plaintiff may recover the amount of his real loss. If there has been a double insurance (35), then it will be proper to consider against which of the underwriters (as the best man or in the best circumstances,) the action shall be brought.

Of the Pleadings.

The action of assumpsit being that form of action which is most usually brought upon policies of assurance, the defendant may of course plead any plea which the law permits to be pleaded to that action; as to which see *ante*, p. 115, and new rules there. As to the actions of debt and covenant, (which are the only forms of action which can be adopted in cases where the two insurance companies are defendants,) it has been provided by stat. 11 Geo. I. c. 30, s. 43, "that in all actions of debt against either of the said corporations, or upon any policies of insurance under their common seal, it shall be lawful for them to plead generally, that they owed nothing to the plaintiff in such action; and in actions of covenant upon such policies, to plead generally, that they have not broken the covenants in such policy contained, or any of them. And if issue be joined thereupon, it shall be lawful for the jury, if they see cause, to find a verdict for the plaintiff, and to give such part only

(*i*) *Cohen* v. *Hannam*, 5 Taunt. 101.   (*k*) 2 Burr. 904; 1 Bl. R. 198.

---

(35) Double insurance is, where there are two insurances made by the same person on the same risk, whereby the *assured* proposes to receive the said sum twice for the same loss, or, in other words, a double satisfaction. The policy of the law, however, will permit the recovery of a single satisfaction only. But although the assured is not entitled to two satisfactions, yet in an action upon the first policy, he may recover the whole sum insured *. Whether in such case the first insurers may recover a rateable satisfaction from the other insurers, seems to be a *vexata quæstio* †. See further on the subject of double insurance, *Godin* v. *London Assurance*, 1 Burr. 489; 1 Bl. R. 103.

* *Newby* v. *Read*, 1 Bl. R. 416.
† Aff. *Newby* v. *Read, ubi sup.*; *Rogers* v. *Davis*, Beawes, 242; *Davis* v. *Gildart*, all decided at N. P., by Lord *Mansfield*. Neg. *African Comp.* v. *Bull*, 1 Show. 132.

of the sum demanded, if in debt, or so much damages, if in covenant, as it shall appear to them, upon the evidence, such plaintiff
ought in justice to have."

Consolidation Rule.

In actions upon a policy of assurance against several underwriters (*l*), the court, by consent of the plaintiff, will make a rule, on
the application of the defendants, which is called the consolidation
rule, for staying the proceedings in all the actions except one, upon
the *defendants'* undertaking to be bound by the verdict in that
action, and to pay the amount of their several subscriptions and
costs, in case a verdict shall be given therein for the plaintiff.
This rule, though attempted before without success, was introduced
by Lord *Mansfield* into general use, to avoid the expense and delay
arising from the trial of a multiplicity of actions upon the same
question: and if the plaintiff will not give his consent, the court
have the power of granting imparlances in all the actions but one,
till the plaintiff has an opportunity of proceeding to trial in that
action.   On the other hand, if the plaintiff consent to the rule, the
court will make the defendant submit to reasonable terms, such as
admitting the policy, producing and giving copies of books and
papers, and undertaking not to file a bill in equity, or bring a writ
of error.   It was formerly supposed that the plaintiff as well as the
defendant was bound by the consolidation rule; but in *Doyle* v.
Stewart, 4 Nev. & M. 873, the contrary was holden, Lord *Denman*,
C. J., observing, " that the principle of the consolidation rule had
always been, that as the defendants asked for a *favour*, they might
reasonably be required to pay the price of it.   It may be that in
this case the consolidation rule would benefit the plaintiff, but we
cannot compel a party to accept a benefit for which he does not
ask."

By R. G. H. T. 2 Will. IV. Reg. 1, s. 104, where money is paid
into court in several actions, which are consolidated, and the plaintiff, without taxing costs, proceeds to trial on one, and fails, he shall
be entitled to costs on the others, up to the time of paying money
into court.

Two actions having been brought by the same plaintiff against
different defendants, on the same policy, the court consolidated
them after a declaration had been delivered in one, and an appearance entered in the other, at the instance of the defendant in the
latter action, though the plaintiff objected (*m*).

(*l*) Tidd's Prac. 635, 7th ed.
(*m*) *Hollingsworth* v. *Brodrick*, *Hollingsworth* v. *Collinson*, 4 A. & E. 646.

IX. *Of the several Grounds of Defence on which the Insurer may insist.*

1. *Alien Enemy*, p. 985.
2. *Illegal Voyage or Illegal Commerce*, p. 985.
3. *Misrepresentation, Concealment, Suppression*, p. 989.
4. *Breach of Warranty*, p. 994.

Express
$\begin{cases} 1. \ Time\ of\ Sailing,\ p.\ 994. \\ 2. \ Safety\ of\ a\ Ship\ at\ a\ particular\ Time,\ p.\ 996. \\ 3. \ To\ depart\ with\ Convoy,\ p.\ 997. \\ 4. \ Neutral\ Property,\ p.\ 999. \end{cases}$

Implied
$\begin{cases} 1. \ Not\ to\ deviate,\ p.\ 1004. \\ 2. \ Seaworthiness,\ p.\ 1010. \end{cases}$

5. *Re-assurance*, p. 1013.
6. *Wager Policy*, p. 1013.

1. *Alien Enemy.*

IF the parties interested in the insurance become alien enemies before the loss happens, this may be *pleaded* to an action brought in the name of the British agent who effected the insurance (n). But where parties interested became alien enemies after the loss happened, though before action commenced, it was holden, that the British agent, who effected the insurance, might recover against the underwriter, who had only pleaded the general issue (o). A plea stating, that plaintiff was born out of the ligeance of the king, and that the persons exercising the powers of government in the country where he was born are enemies of the king, is not good. It ought to state (p) that the plaintiff *himself* is an enemy.

2. *Illegal Voyage, or Illegal Commerce.*

Another ground of defence is, that the voyage insured was prohibited by law, or that the goods insured were intended for carrying on an illegal commerce. In neither of these cases can an action be supported against the underwriter for non-performance of the contract of insurance. The circumstance of the underwriter having been apprized of the illegality of the voyage or trade is wholly immaterial, but, in order to render the insurance illegal, it

---

(n) *Brandon* v. *Nesbitt*, 6 T. R. 23.
(o) *Flindt* v. *Waters*, 15 East, 260. See also *Harman* v. *Kingston*, 3 Campb. 153, S. P. An alien to whom a bill of exchange drawn on a British subject in England, by a British subject detained prisoner in France during war, payable to

another British subject detained there, is there indorsed by the latter, may sue on it in this country after the return of peace. *Antoine* v. *Morehead*, 6 Taunt. 237.
(p) *Casseres* v. *Bell*, Feb. 8, 1799, B. R., L. P. B. 264 ; *Dampier*, MSS. L. I. L.

is necessary that the illegality should exist during the course of the voyage insured. Hence, a policy on goods purchased with the proceeds of an illegal cargo is binding (p); and, in like manner, the assured may recover on a policy, although the ship, in a prior voyage, had been guilty of some transgression for which she was liable to be seized (q). Trading with an enemy (r), without the king's license, being illegal, the law will not enforce a contract of insurance made for the protection of such trade. But it is legal to trade with the subjects of an enemy's country by the king's license (s). If it be provided in such license, that the party acting under it shall give bond for the due exportation to the places proposed of the goods intended to be exported to such country, and they are exported without such bond having been given, such exportation is illegal, and the owners cannot recover on a policy to protect the goods. If a license to export and deliver goods to an enemy's country be granted for a limited time, it is not sufficient, that the goods were shipped before the expiration of the time, the ship not sailing until after that time. But if the adventure licensed be *bonâ fide* prosecuted within a part of the time limited, it will not become illegal, because, by some accident, the voyage was protracted beyond that period (t). Whenever the crown, for purposes of state policy and public advantage, licenses a description of trading with an enemy's country, which would otherwise be unquestionably illegal, such commerce must be regarded by all the subjects of the realm, and by the courts of law, as legal, with all the consequences of its being legal; one of which consequences is a right to contract with other subjects of the country for the protection of such property in the course of its conveyance to its licensed place of destination, through an enemy's country, and for the purpose of being there delivered to an alien enemy as consignee or purchaser (u).

A., a Spaniard by birth (x), who had been domiciled as a merchant in England for several years, having purchased and shipped goods in a neutral vessel, on account of a correspondent, a native of, and resident in, Spain, obtained a license from the British government for the vessel to proceed with her cargo on a voyage from an English port to a port in Spain. A. effected a policy on the goods, which was in the usual form, and stated to be made by A. "as well in his own name as in the name of any person to whom the same might appertain." The vessel, in the prosecution of the voyage, was captured by a French privateer, and carried into a port in Spain, where the vessel and cargo were condemned. At the time of the capture and condemnation, France and Spain were co-bel-

(p) *Bird* v. *Appleton*, 8 T. R. 562.
(q) S. C.
(r) *Potts* v. *Bell*, 8 T. R. 548.
(s) *Vandyck* v. *Whitmore*, 1 East, 475.

(t) *Schroeder* v. *Vaux*, 15 East, 52.
(u) *Usparicha* v. *Noble*, 13 East, 332.
(x) *Ibid.*

ligerent allies at war with England. A. having brought an action on the policy, averring interest in the purchaser; it was holden, that A. was entitled to recover, and that the action was well brought in his name for the benefit of the purchaser; that the legal result of the license was, that not only the plaintiff, the person licensed, might sue in respect of such licensed commerce in an English court of law, but that the commerce itself was to be regarded as legalized for all purposes of its due and effectual prosecution. That for the purpose of the licensed act of trading, (but to that extent only,) the person licensed was to be considered as virtually an adopted subject of this country, and his trading, as far as the disabilities arising out of a state of war were concerned, was British trading; that the plaintiff and the Spanish purchaser of the cargo were actually privy to the objects of the British government, and acting in furtherance thereof, and in direct opposition to the laws and policy of their own country; and that it could not be contended to be illegal to insure a trade carried on in contravention of the laws of a state at war with us, and in furtherance of the policy of our country and its trade, and which this trade in question, sanctioned as it was by his Majesty's license, must be deemed to have been. Although the authority of the preceding decision appears to have been doubted in *Mennett* v. *Bonham*, 15 East, 495, and *Flindt* v. *Crokatt*, 15 East, 522, yet on a review of these two cases in a court of error, the judgment of B. R. has been reversed. See 5 Taunt. 674; *Anthony* v. *Moline*, 5 Taunt. 711; and *Bazett* v. *Meyer*, 5 Taunt. 824. A license granted under an order in council to H. S., (a British resident merchant,) permitting a vessel bearing any flag, except the French, to proceed in ballast from any port north of the Scheldt to Archangel, there to load a cargo of such goods as are permitted by law to be imported, and proceed with the same to a port in the United Kingdom, was considered as not confined personally to H. S., or any particular class of persons (y): and, therefore, where Russian subjects at Archangel, who were alien enemies, had shipped goods under such license for the purpose of being brought into this country; it was held, that they were protected by it; and an insurance made for their benefit was legal. A license to I. H., of London, merchant, on behalf of himself and other British or neutral merchants, to import a cargo from certain limits, within which an enemy's port is situate, in any vessel, bearing any flag except the French, will protect a ship trading from that port, in which ship I. H. and an alien enemy are jointly interested (z); and therefore such interest was held insurable. By virtue of a treaty of commerce entered into between

---

(y) *Robinson* v. *Touray*, 1 M. & S. 217; S. P. *Same* v. *Cheesewright, ib.* 220, recognized in *Hullman* v. *Whitmore*, 3 M. & S. 340. The same subject was discussed again in *Rucker* v. *Ansley*, B. R. Sittings at Serjeant's Inn before E. T. 56 Geo. III., 5 M. & S. 35.

(z) *Hagedorn* v. *Reid*, 1 M. & S. 567.

Great Britain and the United States of America (36), the citizens of the United States may carry on trade between the British territories in the East Indies and the United States, in articles not entirely prohibited. It is not necessary that this trade should be a direct and immediate trade from the United States to the British territories (a); it may be carried on circuitously through any country in Europe, including Great Britain. A natural-born subject of Great Britain, admitted a citizen of the United States of America, either before or after the declaration of American independence, has been considered as a citizen of the United States, within the meaning of the above-mentioned treaty, and as such entitled to the commercial privileges thereby granted. Hence a policy of insurance, effected by or in favour of such adopted citizen of the United States, for the protection of such circuitous trade, is valid. A natural-born subject of this country, domiciled in a foreign country, in amity with this, may lawfully exercise the privileges of a subject of the country where he is domiciled, to trade with another country in hostility with this (b): therefore, where plaintiff, a British-born subject domiciled in America, effected a policy of assurance on ship, freight, and goods, at and from Virginia to any ports in the Baltic, and the ship was captured in her way to Elsineur, in Denmark; Denmark being in amity with America, but at war with this country; it was holden, that the plaintiff was entitled to recover. Although insurances upon goods, the exportation or importation of which is prohibited by the law of England, or by the law of nations, be illegal, yet where the prohibition is founded merely on the law of a foreign state, the insurance will be valid; because one nation never takes notice of the revenue laws of another (c). The mere circumstance of an alien (d) residing in an enemy's country will not invalidate an insurance effected by him on goods to be delivered at a neutral or friendly port. Though a state may be in the military possession of one of two belligerents, that will not constitute her subjects enemies to the other belligerent, if the sovereign power of the latter choose to permit a continuance of commerce with them (e): therefore, where an insurance was effected on property, shipped in this country, on account of per-

---

(a) *Wilson* v. *Marryat*, 8 T. R. 31, affirmed on error in the Excheq. Ch., 1 Bos. & Pul. 430.

(b) *Bell* v. *Reid*, 1 M. & S. 726.

(c) *Planche* v. *Fletcher*, Doug. 250.

(d) *Bromley* v. *Hesseltine*, 1 Campb. 75.

(e) *Hagedorn* v. *Bell*, 1 M. & S. 450.

---

(36) This treaty was entered into on the 19th of November, 1794, ratified by the United States on the 14th of August, 1795, and by his Majesty on the 28th of October in that year, and retrospectively confirmed by parliament. See stat. 37 Geo. III, c. 97. The articles of this treaty, relating to the subject now under consideration, will be found in a note to the report of *Wilson* v. *Marryat*, 8 T. R. 35.

sons who were domiciled at Hamburgh, at a time when that country was in the possession of French troops, the senate continuing to exercise the powers of civil government in the same manner as before; it was holden, that the assured were entitled to recover for a loss which happened in the course of a voyage permitted by his Majesty's orders in council. Where a particular trade is prohibited by express statute, insurances made for the protection of such trade are illegal (f). The owners of a vessel, who by performing the legal stipulations of a charterparty, provoke confiscation by the illegal and piratical act of a foreign state, do not thereby avoid their assurance (g). Trading in contravention of a proclamation, whereby an embargo is laid on, in time of war, is illegal: and consequently an insurance upon such trade, even when carried on by a neutral (h), is void. If a vessel brings hither from a hostile country, under a license, a cargo of enumerated goods, and also certain other goods not licensed, the insurance on the licensed goods is not thereby vitiated (i). If there be an infirmity in any part of an integral voyage, it will make the whole illegal, so that the insured cannot recover upon a policy on any part of it (k). So if a party insure goods altogether in one policy, and some of them are of a nature to make the voyage illegal, the whole contract is illegal and void. A policy was effected on goods to be thereafter specified to a certain amount (l); by the specification it appeared that the goods consisted principally of hardware, but partly of naval stores, the exportation of which was prohibited, under pain of forfeiting the stores, treble their value, and the ship. It was holden, that the exportation of the stores being illegal, all contracts for protecting the stores so exported were impliedly avoided; that the policy was one entire contract on goods to be thereafter specified, to which the underwriters subscribed; and the subsequent specification by the assured could not alter the nature of the contract with respect to the underwriters, so as to sever that which was originally one entire contract.

3. *Misrepresentation, Concealment, and Suppression.*

The allegation of a falsehood (m) or misrepresentation, (though by mistake) (n), or the concealment and suppression (o) of the truth,

(f) *Johnston* v. *Sutton*, Doug. 254.
(g) *Sewell* v. *Roy. Ex. Ass. Comp.*, 4 Taunt. 856.
(h) *Delmada* v. *Motteux*, Park, 234.
(i) *Pieschell* v. *Allnutt*, 4 Taunt. 792. See 1 M. & S. 450.
(k) Admitted by Lord *Kenyon*, C. J., in *Wilson* v. *Marryat*, 8 T. R. 46, and expressly laid down by the same learned judge in his charge to the jury, in *Bird* v. *Pigou*, London Sittings after H. T. 40

Geo. III. B. R., MSS.
(l) *Parkin* v. *Dick*, 2 Campb. 221; 11 East, 502, *S. C.*
(m) Skin. 327; *Roberts* v. *Fonnereau*, Park, 285.
(n) *Macdowall* v. *Fraser*, Doug. 260.
(o) *De Costa* v. *Scandret*, 2 P. Wms. 170; *Hodgson* v. *Richardson*, 1 Bl. R. 463; *Ratcliff* v. *Shoolbred*, Park, 180; *Willes* v. *Glover*, 1 Bos. & Pul. N. R. 14.

as to a fact or circumstance material to the risk, either by the assured or his agent (*p*), is considered as a fraud on the underwriter, and consequently will vacate the policy or annul the contract from the beginning. Hence, the underwriter may avail himself of this ground of defence, even where the loss arises from a cause wholly unconnected with the fact or circumstance misrepresented (*q*). The question of materiality is not a matter of law, but a question of fact (*r*) to be decided by a jury; and the proper evidence to guide their judgment is the evidence of persons conversant with the subject matter of the inquiry (*s*). But a misrepresentation as to the cargo with which a ship is to sail on a future day will not suffice as a defence, unless the misrepresentation (*t*) be fraudulently made.

Goods were insured as the goods of a Hamburgher, who was an ally, and the goods were, in fact, the goods of a Frenchman, who was an enemy; this was holden, by *Holt*, C. J., to be a fraud (*u*). So where a letter had been received (*x*), stating that a ship sailed on the 24th November, after which an insurance was made, and the agent of the assured told the insurer, that the ship sailed the latter end of December; this was holden by *Lee*, C. J., to be a fraud. So where a ship was insured in London, on the 30th of January (*y*), on a voyage from New York to Philadelphia, and the broker represented the ship to be safe in the Delaware, on the 11th of December, whereas in fact it was lost in that river on the 9th of December; it was holden, that as the representation was false in point of fact, and as it related to a material circumstance, namely, the safety of a ship at a certain time, the contract was annulled; and although it appeared that the assured, at the time, believed the representation to be true, yet the court were of opinion that this did not vary the case; for it was incumbent on the assured to make a fair and true representation, and if he represented material facts to the underwriter, without knowing the truth, he took the risk on himself (37).

(*p*) *Fitzherbert* v. *Mather*, 1 T. R. 12.
(*q*) Per *Lee*, C. J., in *Seaman* v. *Fonereau*, Str. 1183.
(*r*) *Lindenau* v. *Desborough*, 8 B. & C. 586.
(*s*) *Berthon* v. *Loughman*, 2 Stark. N. P. C. 258; *Rickards* v. *Murdock*, 10 B. & C. 540.

(*t*) *Flinn* v. *Tobin*, M. & Malk. 367.
(*u*) Skin. 327.
(*x*) *Roberts* v. *Fonnereau*, London Sittings after Trin. 1742, Park, 285.
(*y*) *Macdowall* v. *Fraser*, Doug. 260. See also *Stewart* v. *Dunlop*, 4 Bro. P. C. 483, Tomlin's ed.

---

(37) It was said by Lord *Mansfield*, in *Barber* v. *Fletcher*, Doug. 306, that it had been determined in a variety of cases *, that a representation to the first underwriter extended to the others. " By an extension of an equitable relief, in cases of fraud, if a man is a knave with respect to

* Q. If there be any in the printed books?

The same rule holds (z), where the misrepresentation is made by the proper agent of the assured, although the assured be not guilty of any improper conduct; for the act of the agent binds the principal, and it will be presumed, that the principal knows whatever the agent knows. In a case where the word *expected* was used, as that the vessel insured was *expected* to set sail at such a time, this was holden not to amount to a representation (a). A representation by the owner of goods insured as to the time of the ship's sailing is matter of expectation, and if made *bonâ fide* does not conclude him (b). In effecting a policy of insurance from Russia to this country while the ship was on the outward voyage, the broker represented to the underwriters *that a cargo was ready for her, and she was sure to be an early ship.* It was holden (c), that this amounted only to a representation of what was *expected* on the part of the assured, and that the underwriters were liable, although, from the delay in beginning to load the cargo, the voyage home was turned from a summer to a winter risk. A representation, as it does not form any part of the written policy, requires only to be *substantially* performed. It is distinguishable in this respect from a warranty, which, being part of the policy, must be *strictly* performed. Insuring a ship by *an English name* does not amount to a warranty, or a representation, that she is *an English ship* (d). A merchant having received intelligence (e) that a ship described like his was taken, insured her, without giving any information to the insurers of what he had heard; it was holden, that the conceal-

(z) *Fitzherbert* v. *Mather*, 1 T. R. 12.
(a) *Barber* v. *Fletcher*, Doug. 305.
(b) *Bowden* v. *Vaughan*, 10 East, 415.
(c) *Hubbard* v. *Glover*, 3 Campb. 313.
(d) *Clapham* v. *Cologan*, 3 Campb. 382.
(e) *De Costa* v. *Scandret*, 2 P. Wms. 170.

the first underwriter, and makes a false representation to him in a point that is material; as where, having notice of a ship being lost, he says she was safe, that shall affect the policy with regard to all the subsequent underwriters, who are presumed to follow the first." Per Lord *Mansfield*, C. J., in *Pawson* v. *Watson*, Cowp. 789. Agreeably to this doctrine, the Court of King's Bench, in the case of *Marsden* v. *Reid*, 3 East, 573, intimated an opinion, that where it appears that a material fact has been represented to the first underwriter, to induce him to subscribe the policy, it shall be taken to be made to all the rest, without the necessity of repeating it to each *. A representation made by an insurance broker, when the names of the underwriters are put upon a slip, is binding on the assured, unless there is evidence of its being altered or withdrawn between that time and the execution of the policy. *Edwards* v. *Footner*, 1 Campb. 530. The authority of the broker is revocable even after the underwriters have signed the slip, and until they have actually subscribed the policy. *Warwick* v. *Slade*, 3 Campb. 127.

* But a representation made to any underwriter, except the first, is not to be considered as made to subsequent underwriters. *Bell* v. *Carstairs*, 2 Campb. 543.

ment was a fraud on the underwriters. So where, in an action on a policy of assurance of a ship on a voyage from Lisbon to London (f), it appeared that the plaintiff had, on the 24th of November, received information of the ship having sailed on the 8th; it appeared also, that another vessel, which had sailed at the same time with the ship insured, had arrived in safety; after which, *viz.* on the 2nd of December, the plaintiff had effected the insurance in question, without making any disclosure to the underwriter: it was holden, that there was a concealment of circumstances sufficient to avoid the policy. But where a broker, in pursuance of instructions previously received from Sunderland, effected a policy at Lloyd's at a time when a letter lay on his table at the Coal-exchange unopened, announcing the ship's loss: it was holden (g), that the conduct of the broker did not avoid the policy; for he had a right to presume that he had possession of all the information on which he was to effect the policy (38). Where the plaintiffs effected a policy of assurance on wines from Oporto to London, on the 12th of November, at which time they were in possession of two letters from their correspondents at Oporto; the first of which, dated 11th of October, stated thus; " *We are loading the wines on the* Stag, *Captain* Wheatley, *who pretends to sail after to-morrow ;*" the other dated the 13th of October, enclosed the bills of lading, which were filled up "with convoy;" which letter the plaintiffs did not communicate to the underwriters: it was holden (h), that it was a material concealment. "The reason of the rule which obliges the party to disclose (i), is to prevent fraud, and encourage good faith: it is adapted to such facts as vary the nature of the contract, which one privately knows, and the other is ignorant of, and has no reason to suspect." The question, therefore, in cases of this kind, is,

(f) *M'Andrew* v. *Bell,* 1 Esp. N. P. C. 373.

(g) *Wake* v. *Atty,* 4 Taunt. 493.
(h) *Bridges and others* v. *Hunter,* 1 M. & S. 15.

(i) Per Ld. *Mansfield,* C. J., in *Carter* v. *Boehm,* 3 Burr. 1905, cited by Lord *Ellenborough,* C. J., delivering judgment in *Haywood* v. *Rodgers,* 4 East, 596.

(38) The nature of this work will not permit the insertion of all the cases relating to concealment; neither is it necessary, since the reader will perceive that they are cases depending wholly on their own special circumstances. If he is desirous of pursuing the subject, he may peruse the following cases: *Seaman* v. *Fonereau,* Str. 1183; *Carter* v. *Boehm,* 3 Burr. 1905; 1 Bl. R. 594; *Shirley* v. *Wilkinson,* 3 Dougl. 41; *Court* v. *Martineau,* 3 Doug. 161; *Webster* v. *Foster,* 1 Esp. N. P. C. 407; *Willes* v. *Glover,* 1 Bos. & Pul. N. R. 14; *Littledale* v. *Dixon,* 1 Bos. & Pul. N. R. 151; *Freeland* v. *Glover,* 7 East, 457; *Lynch* v. *Hamilton,* 3 Taunt. 37; *Bell* v. *Bell,* 2 Campb. 479; *Kirby* v. *Smith,* 1 B. & A. 672; *Weir* v. *Aberdeen,* 2 B. & A. 320; *Bufe* v. *Turner,* 6 Taunt. 338; 2 Marsh. Rep. 46, *S. C.; Rickards* v. *Murdock,* 10 B. & C. 527 *Elton* v. *Larkins,* 8 Bingh. 198; 1 M. & Sc. 323.

" Whether there were, under all the circumstances, at the time the policy was underwritten, a fair statement, or a concealment, fraudulent, if designed, or, though not designed, varying materially the object of the policy, and changing the risk understood to be run?" Information respecting the subject matter of warranty, either express or implied, need not be communicated to the underwriter, unless there be a specific request on his part for such information. Hence, in the case of *Shoolbred* v. *Nutt*, Park, 346, where the owner had received letters from his captain the day before he effected the insurance, stating, that the ship had arrived at Madeira, but was very leaky, and that the pipes of wine had been half covered with water, which letters were not communicated to the underwriters; Lord *Mansfield* told the jury, "That there should be a representation of every thing relating to the risk which the underwriter has to run, except it be covered by a warranty. It is a condition, or implied warranty, in every policy, that the ship is seaworthy, and therefore there need be no representation of that. If she sail without being so, there is no valid policy. Here the leak was stopped before she sailed from Madeira, and she sailed in good condition from thence, and there is no occasion to state the condition of a ship or cargo at the end of the former voyage." Verdict for plaintiff. So where in an action on a policy of insurance upon a ship from Trinidad to London (k), it appeared that the assured had received a letter from his captain, informing him that he had been obliged to have a survey on the ship at Trinidad, *on account of her bad character*, but the survey, which accompanied the letter, gave the ship a good character: it was holden, that the concealment of the letter and survey from the underwriter, did not vacate the policy, inasmuch as the assured impliedly warranted the ship to be seaworthy, and it did not appear that he had concealed any circumstance relative to the seaworthiness of the ship, or that at the time of effecting the policy he knew of any fact which rendered her, with reference to the risk, otherwise than seaworthy. It will be presumed that the underwriter is acquainted with the usage and circumstances of the branch of trade to which the policy relates (l), and consequently the assured is not bound to make a disclosure thereof; e. g. upon an insurance on an East India voyage, the underwriters are bound to know the course of the East India Company's charterparties and trade, and that the ship's destination is liable to be changed after the policy is effected (m). If the usage of the trade is general, it is immaterial for this purpose that it is not uniform (n).

(k) *Haywood* v. *Rodgers*, 4 East, 590.
(l) *Vallance* v. *Dewar*, 1 Campb. 503; *Ougier* v. *Jennings*, ib. 505, n.; *Kingston* v. *Knibbs*, ib. 508, n.; *Moxon* v. *Atkins*, 3 Campb. 200.
(m) *Grant* v. *Paxton*, 1 Taunt. 463.
(n) See cases in note (l), *ante.*

4. *Breach of Warranty:*

$$
Express \begin{cases} 1. \ \textit{Time of Sailing, p. 994.} \\ 2. \ \textit{Safety of a Ship at a particular Time, p. 996.} \\ 3. \ \textit{To depart with Convoy, p. 997.} \\ 4. \ \textit{Neutral Property, p. 999.} \end{cases}
$$

$$
Implied \begin{cases} 1. \ \textit{Not to deviate, p. 1004.} \\ 2. \ \textit{Seaworthiness, p. 1010.} \end{cases}
$$

ANOTHER ground of defence which may be taken by the under-writer to defeat the action, is the non-compliance with a warranty, either express or implied. Every warranty incorporated in the body of the policy, or appearing on the face of the instrument, *e. g.* in the margin (*o*), or at the bottom of the policy (*p*), or inserted in any print or writing, which is by reference incorporated with the policy (*q*), must be *strictly* and *literally* complied with (39): and in this respect it is distinguishable from a mere *representation*, which, if it be *substantially* fulfilled, it is sufficient. The most usual kinds of warranties inserted in policies, are, 1. As to the time of sailing; 2. The safety of the ship at a particular time; 3. Departing with convoy; 4. That the thing insured is neutral property.

Express Warranty.—1. *Time of Sailing.*—This means, that the ship shall be on her voyage on the given day; for which purpose she must be completely unmoored; it will not suffice that she then had cargo and passengers on board, and was only prevented from sailing by stress of weather (*r*). But if a ship quits her moorings, and removes only to a short distance, being quite ready to proceed upon her voyage, and is by some subsequent occurrence detained, that is, nevertheless, a sailing; it is otherwise, however, if, at the time when she quits her moorings and hoists her sails, she is not in

(*o*) *Bean* v. *Stupart*, Doug. 11; *De Hahn* v. *Hartley*, 1 T. R. 343.
(*p*) 3 T. R. 360.
(*q*) *Worsley* v. *Wood*, 6 T. R. 710;

Routledge v. *Burrell*, 1 H. Bl. 254.
(*r*) *Nelson* v. *Salvador*, M. & Malk. 309.

---

(39) " A warranty in a policy of insurance is a condition or a contin-gency, and unless that be performed, there is not any contract. It is perfectly immaterial for what purpose a warranty is introduced; but being inserted, the contract does not exist, unless it be *literally* complied with." Per Lord *Mansfield*, C. J., 1 T. R. 345, 6. The very meaning of a warranty is to preclude all questions, whether it has been *substan-tially* complied with; it must be *literally* so." Per *Ashhurst*, J., 1 T. R. 346.

a condition for completing her voyage (s); and no distinction can be drawn between taking in more ballast and receiving part of the cargo (t). The word "sailing" is not confined (u) to the mere act of hoisting the sails; the fair question in these cases is, whether, at the time of the loss, the voyage can be said to have commenced! A ship, which was insured *at* and *from* Jamaica to London, *warranted to have sailed on or before a particular day*, with a return of premium in case of convoy (x), *sailed* before the day from the port of her lading, with all her cargo and clearances on board, to the usual place of rendezvous at another part of the island, in order to join the convoy, which then lay ready, where she arrived in safety, but was detained there by an embargo *beyond* the day. It was holden, that although the place of rendezvous was out of the direct course of the voyage, yet as the ship, when she sailed from the port of lading, had not any view or object but to make the best of her way to England, and as she did not go to the place of rendezvous for any purpose independent of the immediate prosecution of her voyage, the voyage began from the port of lading, and consequently the warranty had been complied with. A French ship was insured " at and from Guadaloupe to Havre," *warranted to sail on or before a particular day*. The ship took in her complete lading, and all her clearances, at Point-a-Pitre, and sailed thence before the day for Basseterre; a condition having been inserted in one of the clearances, that the ship should pass that way to take the orders of government; and the captain also expecting, in consequence of a notice which had been given by his governor, that there would be a convoy at that place. It appeared that the captain had paid an extra fee in order to procure his clearances, that he might take the benefit of the convoy. The ship arrived at Basseterre two months before the day on which she was warranted to sail, and was detained there by the governor until after the day. It was proved that Basseterre was in the direct course of the voyage. Under these circumstances, it was holden (y), that there had been a *bonâ fide* and complete inception of the voyage, on the day the ship sailed from Point-a-Pitre, and consequently that the warranty had been complied with. Under a warranty to *depart* on or before a particular day, it is necessary not only that the ship should set sail on the voyage, but also, that she should be out of the port on or before the day (z). To "sail," is to sail on the voyage. To " depart," is to depart from some particular place (a).

(s) Per Ld. *Tenterden*, C. J., *Pittegrew* v. *Pringle*, 3 B. & Ad. 520, 1; *Graham* v. *Barras*, 5 B. & Ad. 1011; 3 Nev. & Mann. 125, S. P.

(t) Per *Park*, J., in *Pittegrew* v. *Pringle*, 3 B. & Ad. 522.

(u) Per *Denman*, C. J., delivering judgment on error in Exch. Chr., *Cockrane* v. *Fisher*, 1 Cr. M. & R. 818, 5 Tyrw.

501, 2.

(x) *Bond* v. *Nutt*, Cowp. 601.

(y) *Thellusson* v. *Fergusson*, 1 Doug. 361.

(z) *Moir* v. *The Royal Exchange Assurance*, 3 M. & S. 461.

(a) *Moir* v. *The Royal Exchange Assurance*, 6 Taunt. 245.

Goods were insured at and from Demerara to London in ship or ships warranted to sail from Demerara on or before the 1st of August, 1823. Small ships take in and discharge the whole of their cargoes in the river of Demerara; but there is a shoal off the coast, about ten miles out at sea, and large ships usually discharge and take in part of their cargoes on the outside of the shoal. Goods covered by the policy were laden on board a small vessel that completed her cargo in the river; and on the 1st of August, the captain, having obtained his clearance, set sail, proceeded down the river, and about two miles out to sea, and then anchored, the tide being low. On the 3rd of August he crossed the shoal, and on the 8th the vessel was lost by perils of the sea: it was holden (b), that the vessel sailed from Demerara on the 1st of August, within the meaning of the policy. Where a license is granted for a voyage to a hostile country, to continue in force till a given day, if the voyage is *bonâ fide* begun before that day, it continues to be protected by the license, though delayed beyond the day by stress of weather or other accident over which the assured have no control (c). So where there is a policy "*at and from*," if the ship has her cargo on board and is ready to sail before the day when the license expires, although she is detained in port till after the day by contrary winds, the policy remains valid (d).

2. *Safety of Ship at a particular Time.*—Goods were insured from the lading of them on board a certain ship, "lost or not lost," and at the bottom of the policy was added "*warranted well on a particular day.*" It appeared that the defendant underwrote the policy in the afternoon of that day, and that the ship was lost about eight o'clock in the morning of the same day. It was holden (e), that the warranty did not mean that the ship was well at the time when the defendant subscribed the policy, but at *any time* on that day, and consequently that it had been complied with. Action on policy of insurance against fire on ship Hero (f), for one month, on the terms that the ship should be safe moored in the harbour of Portsmouth during the period for which the insurance was made; the ship was accidentally burned within that time. It appeared in evidence, that the ship was first moored off the beach, in order to clear her bottom; she was then removed to Hardway, and lastly was moored at March's wharf, in order the more conveniently to take in her cargo, but had never been taken out of the harbour. It was insisted, for the defendant, that the removing the ship from her moorings at one place to the other, was a discontinuance of the risk: so also the laying her down on the beach to clear her bottom. But, per Lord *Ellenborough,* C. J., "Where a

(b) *Lang and others* v. *Anderdon,* 3 B. & C. 495.

(c) *Groning* v. *Crockett,* 3 Campb. 83.

(d) *Schroeder* v. *Vaux,* 3 Campb.

84, n.

(e) *Blackhurst* v. *Cockell,* 3 T. R. 360.

(f) *Clarke* v. *Westmore,* London Sittings B. R., 25 May, 1807.

vessel is only removed from one part of the harbour to the other, for the more convenient purpose of repairs, or of taking in her cargo, but does not go beyond the bounds of the harbour, and is safely moored at the different parts of the harbour, when she is so removed according to the policy, it is not such an act as will avoid the policy." Verdict for plaintiff. " When a broker (g) proposes a policy to an underwriter, on a ship at and from a certain place, it imports either that the ship is there at the time, or shortly will be there." A delay in the arrival of the vessel at the place where the risk is to attach, alters the risk.

8. *To depart with Convoy.*—The next species of warranty which falls under consideration, is a warranty that the ship insured shall sail or depart with *convoy*, by which term is to be understood " a naval force under the command of a person appointed by the government of the country, to which the vessel insured belongs." The form of expression, as to this warranty, is different in different policies; in some, that the ship shall depart with convoy; in others, that she shall depart with convoy *for the voyage.* In substance, however, these expressions are the same; for it has been solemnly decided, that, although the words of the policy are merely "to depart with convoy," yet those words must be understood to mean that the ship shall depart with convoy *for the voyage,* as much as if the words " for the voyage" had been added (h). If a ship does not sail with the convoy appointed by government, it is not a sailing with convoy within the terms of the warranty (i); hence the protection of a ship of war accidentally bound on the same voyage, although discharging the office of convoy, is not a convoy within the meaning of the warranty; but a convoy appointed by the admiral commanding in chief upon a foreign station, will be considered as a convoy appointed by government (k). It may be laid down also, as a general rule, that a warranty to depart with convoy is not complied with, unless sailing instructions are obtained before the ship leaves the place of rendezvous, if by due diligence of the master they can be obtained (40). When the policy is silent as to the

(g) Per *Ellenborough*, C. J., *Hull* v. *Cooper*, 14 East, 479, cited by *Tindal*, C. J., *Mount* v. *Larkins*, 8 Bingh. 123, recognized in *Freeman* v. *Taylor*, 8 Bingh. 139.

(h) Per *Holt*, C. J., and the greater part of the court, in *Jeffery* v. *Legendra*, 3 Lev. 321, after several arguments on special verdict, per *tot. Cur.*, Carth. 217; *Lilly* v. *Ewer*, Doug. 72, S. P.

(i) *Hibbert* v. *Pigou*, Park, 498; Marsh. 272; S. C. 3 Doug. 224.

(k) S. C. See also *Audley* v. *Duff*, 2 Bos. & Pul. 111.

(40) " The value of a convoy appointed by government, in a great measure arises from its taking the ships under control, as well as under protection. But that control does not commence until sailing instructions have been obtained, nor can it be enforced otherwise than by their means. Indeed, the reason of that rule, which requires that the convoy should be

place from which the vessel is to depart with convoy, the usage of merchants puts a construction on it, and the warranty must be understood to mean, that the ship shall sail with convoy from the place of general rendezvous, or that place where convoys are to be had: as, if a vessel be insured from London to the East Indies, warranted to depart with convoy, and the ship sail with *convoy from the Downs*, it is a fulfilment of the warranty (*l*) (41). It is not necessary that the vessel should in all cases sail with convoy bound precisely to the place of her destination (*m*). Whether the convoy be sufficient must depend on the usage of trade and the orders of government; and it is the province of the jury to determine whether, under the circumstances, the warranty has been satisfied (42). It sometimes happens (*n*), that the force first appointed is to accompany the ships only for a part of their voyage, and to be succeeded by another; at other times a small force is detached from the main body, to bring them up to a particular point: if a vessel sail under the protection of a force thus appointed (*o*) or detached (*p*), the warranty is complied with. Although the terms of this warranty do not express it, yet it is essentially necessary, that the ship should not only depart, but also *continue* with the convoy until the end of the voyage, unless she be prevented by absolute necessity. Case on a policy of insurance on

(*l*) *Lethulier's* case, Salk. 443, but *Holt*, C. J., *contra; Gordon* v. *Morley*, Str. 1265, per *Lee*, C. J.
(*m*) *D'Eguino* v. *Bewicke*, 2 H. Bl. 551.
(*n*) Abbott, 229.

(*o*) *Smith* v. *Readshaw*, Park, ch. 18, p. 510; *De Garay* v. *Clagget*, *ib.* 511.
(*p*) *Manning* v. *Gist*, Marsh. 367, 2nd edit. *S. C.;* more fully reported, 3 Doug. 74; *Audley* v. *Duff*, 2 Bos. & Pul. 111.

appointed by government, shows the necessity of having sailing instructions; since without them the ship does not stand in that relation, or under those circumstances in which she can take the full benefit of the government convoy." Per *Eldon*, C. J., in *Anderson* v. *Pitcher*, 2 Bos. & Pul. 169.

(41) No convoy ever sails from the port of London. Abbott's Law relative to Merchant Ships and Seamen, 5th ed. p. 227. Occasional convoys are appointed by the admiral on the station to sail from the Downs to Portsmouth, &c.; but such convoys are never appointed by the admiralty. Ships sailing from foreign ports are not within the Convoy Act, unless there are persons at these ports, authorized to grant convoy licenses. And it is not sufficient to show that convoys have been actually appointed from those ports, but proof must be given that there are persons stationed there, legally authorized by the admiralty to appoint them*.

(42) " It has always been understood, that provisions for a departure with convoy have relation to the custom of trade, and the orders of government, and ought, therefore, to receive a liberal construction." Per *Heath*, J., in *Audley* v. *Duff*, 2 Bos. & Pul. 115.

* *D'Aguilar* v. *Tobin*, 1 Holt's N. P. C. 185.

the ship Speedwell (*q*), from London to Lisbon, *warranted to depart from England with convoy*. The ship sailed from London in December, and arrived at Spithead, (the place where the Lisbon convoy was to be met with,) whence she sailed on the 25th of December, with the convoy. On the 26th December a storm arose, which separated her from her convoy, and rendered her so leaky, that she was obliged to sail for Plymouth, where she arrived on the 28th of December. Having been refitted and made a tight ship, as was supposed, she sailed again on the 13th of February following, but *without convoy*. A few days after, she encountered another violent storm, and on the 19th of February she was totally lost near Ireland. *Lee*, C. J., held, that the sense of the warranty was not to be taken literally; that the meaning was not only to *depart* with convoy, but to *keep with* convoy during the whole voyage, and that this had always been so holden: that absolute necessity alone, such as rendered it impossible to keep with convoy, could excuse; as being driven by a tempest to some foreign port or place where convoy could not be had; but that was not the present case, the ship having been driven into an English port. He, therefore, was of opinion, that this was not a loss within the policy; and, accordingly, a verdict was found for the defendant. But if a ship sails with convoy (*r*), and is separated by stress of weather, and does all in her power to rejoin the convoy, this will be considered as a sufficient compliance with the warranty, so as to render the insurers liable. The security of trade, in time of war, has been considered as depending so essentially on ships sailing with convoy, that by a statute (*s*) (43), (which continued in force during hostilities with France,) several enactments were made to enforce it.

Neutral Property.—If the insurance be effected in time of war, and the party insuring be the subject of a neutral state, it is usual for him, in order to induce the underwriter to accept a smaller premium, to warrant that the subject matter of the insurance is neutral property, which is usually done by inserting in the policy the words "warranted neutral," or "warranted neutral property;" by which (*t*) is to be understood, that the thing insured is neutral property at the time when the risk commences, not that it shall continue so during the whole voyage, for the risk of *future* war is

(*q*) *Morrice* v. *Dillon*, London Sittings after M. T. 22 Geo. II., coram *Lee*, C. J., MSS.

(*r*) *Jeffery* v. *Legendra*, 3 Lev. 320; Carth. 216; Salk. 443; 1 Show. 320; 4 Mod. 58; reported for the judgment only

in Holt, 465.

(*s*) Stat. 43 Geo. III. c. 57. See *Cohen* v. *Hinckley*, 1 Taunt. R. 249.

(*t*) *Eden* v. *Parkison*, Doug. 732, a.; *Tyson* v. *Gurney*, 3 T. R. 477, per *Buller*, J., in *Saloucci* v. *Johnson*, Park, 558.

(43) A similar statute was made during the preceding war. See stat. 38 Geo. III. c. 76.

undertaken by the insurer in every policy. But though it is not
necessary, that a ship, warranted neutral, should continue neutral
during the whole voyage; because, if she be neutral at the time of
sailing, the breaking out of war on the next day will not discharge the
underwriter; yet the ship must not forfeit its neutrality by the misconduct of the parties on board: hence where, on an insurance of a
ship warranted neutral (*u*), it appeared that the master and crew
had broken their neutrality, in the course of the voyage insured, by
forcibly rescuing the ship, which had been seized and carried into
port by a belligerent power, for the purpose of search; it was
holden, that the assured could not recover. That a warranty of
neutrality may be satisfied, it is necessary, 1. That the vessel
insured should belong to the subject of a neutral state; 2. That
the vessel should be navigated, not only according to the law of
nations, but also in conformity to the particular treaties subsisting
between the country to which she belongs and the belligerent
states (44). If, therefore, a state in amity with a belligerent power
has, by treaty, agreed that the ships of their subjects shall only
have that character when furnished with certain documents; whoever warrants the ship to be the property of such subject, should
provide himself, at the time when the ship sails, with those documents, which have, by the country to which she belongs, been
agreed to be the necessary proof of that character (45). In an
action on a policy upon a ship warranted Dutch property (*x*), it
appeared that the ship in question was originally a French privateer bearing a French name; that having been captured by the
English, she was carried into Liverpool, and there named the Three

---

(*u*) *Garrels* v. *Kensington*, 8 T. R. 230.   *rence*, J., in *Pollard* v. *Bell*, 8 T. R. 441;
(*x*) *Barzillai* v. *Lewis*, Park, 526, and   *S. C.* 3 Doug. 126.
MS. note of *Buller*, J., cited by *Law-*

---

(44) " Courts of admiralty are to proceed on the known *jus gentium*,
or on the treaties between particular states; such treaties do not alter the
jus gentium with respect to the rest of the world, but as between those particular states they are considered as engrafted on the *jus gentium*." Per
Lord *Kenyon*, C. J., in *Bird* v. *Appleton*, 8 T. R. 567.

(45) N. There is not an implied warranty on the part of the owner of
goods insured, that the ship shall be in all respects properly documented.
Where, through the negligence of the captain, the goods had not been
regularly entered in the ship's manifest, for exportation, as required by
statutes 13 & 14 Car. II. and other statutes; the loss not having been
occasioned by this omission, it was holden, that the underwriters were
liable. *Carruthers* v. *Gray*, 3 Campb. 142; 15 East, 35, *S. C.* In the
case of an insurance upon goods, in a certain ship, which ship is not
represented as a neutral at the time when the insurance is effected,
although she be in fact a neutral, it is not necessary that she should be
documented as such. *Dawson* v. *Atty*, 7 East, 367. See *Bell* v. *Carstairs*, 14 East, 393.

Graces.   A merchant there purchased her for a house at Amsterdam.   Having been insured by a Dutch name, and warranted as in the policy, she went to sea, was captured by the French, and finally condemned by the parliament of Paris, under her English name, as lawful prize.   The court were of opinion, that the sentence of the parliament of Paris was conclusive against the warranty.   So where it appeared, that a ship, warranted American, had not on board a passport, which was required by the treaty between France and America; it was holden (y), that the assured could not recover, inasmuch as the warranty had not been complied with; for that required that the ship should be entitled to all the privileges of the American flag, and in order to be entitled to these privileges, she should have had a passport.   But it is not necessary (z), in order to satisfy a warranty of neutrality, that the vessel should be navigated in conformity to an *ex parte* ordinance made by one of the belligerent states, and to which the neutral state is not a party. A neutral ship may carry enemy's property from its own to the enemy's country, without being guilty of a breach of neutrality (a); provided that neither the voyage nor commerce be of a hostile description, nor otherwise expressly or impliedly forbidden by the law of this country; although such ship, in consequence of carrying enemy's property, be liable to detention or to be carried into British ports for the purpose of search.   The evidence usually adduced to falsify this warranty (b), or to prove a breach or forfeiture of neutrality, which amounts to a breach or forfeiture of the warranty, is the judgment or sentence of a court of admiralty, or other court having jurisdiction in questions of prize, by which the ship or goods insured, and warranted neutral property, have been condemned as prize.   Since the judgment of the House of Lords in *Lothian* v. *Henderson* (c), it may be assumed as the settled doctrine of a court of English law, that all sentences of foreign courts of competent jurisdiction to decide questions of prize, are to be received here as conclusive evidence in actions upon policies of insurance, upon every subject immediately and properly within the jurisdiction of such foreign courts, and upon which they have professed to decide judicially.   Consequently, where such sentences are given in evidence, and it appears that they proceed on a ground which falsifies the warranty of neutrality, the assured will thereby be prevented from recovering.   In one case (d), indeed, where a ship was condemned as lawful prize in a foreign court of admiralty, and it was not stated in the sentence upon what ground the condemnation proceeded; it

(y) *Rich* v. *Parker*, 7 T. R. 705. See further on this subject, *Baring* v. *Christie*, 5 East, 398.

(z) *Mayne* v. *Walter*, Park, 531 ; *S. C.* 3 Doug. 79; *Pollard* v. *Bell*, 8 T. R. 434 ; *Bird* v. *Appleton*, 8 T. R. 562; *Price* v. *Bell*, 1 East, 663.

(a) *Barker* v. *Blakes*, 9 East, 283.

(b) Marsh. 288.

(c) 3 Bos. & Pul. 499, per *Ellenborough*, C. J., delivering the opinion of the court in *Bolton* v. *Gladstone*, 5 East, 155, and per Sir *J. Mansfield*, C. J., in *Siffken* v. *Lee*, 2 N. R. 489.

(d) *Saloucci* v. *Woodmass*, Park, 362 ; 3 Doug. 345, *S. C.*

was holden, that a sentence of condemnation, as lawful prize, afforded a presumption that the goods were enemy's property, unless the contrary appeared on the sentence. In *Baring* v. *Clagett*, 3 Bos. & Pul. 201, the court being of opinion that the sentence of condemnation proceeded either on the ground of the ship not being neutral property, or on the ground that she was not properly documented, so as to entitle herself to the privileges of a neutral, adjudged the sentence to be conclusive evidence against a warranty of neutrality. Whether the foreign sentence profess distinctly and directly to condemn the ship, on the ground of its being enemies' property, or whether it can be collected only from other parts of the proceedings, that such was the ground of decision (*e*), our courts are equally bound by the sentence; and this rule holds, although it appears on the face of the sentence, that the prize court arrived at the conclusion through the medium of rules of evidence, and rules of presumption, established only by the particular ordinances of their own country, and not admissible on general principles (*f*). In short, wherever the foreign courts adjudge the vessel to be good prize, upon a ground within their jurisdiction, and such ground falsifies the warranty, our courts will, by the comity of nations, which has always prevailed among civilized states, give credit to and consider themselves bound by their adjudication, without examining the reasons by which the foreign courts have arrived at their conclusion (46). Hence, as foreign courts of admiralty may decide on the construction of treaties (*g*), if they expressly adjudge a ship to be lawful prize for a breach of treaty, such sentence is conclusive in our courts against a warranty of neutrality, although, in this sentence, the foreign court may have referred to *ex parte* ordinances, and drawn inferences from such ordinances, in order to show an infraction of treaty. The sentence is equally to be regarded, as evidence of the facts inducing the condemnation, and upon which the condemnation proceeds, as of the judicial act of condemnation. In the case of an insurance upon ship, goods, and freight, all belonging to nearly the same American proprietors, which, as it appeared by the sentence, had been condemned on

(*e*) *Bolton* v. *Gladstone*, 5 East, 155.
(*f*) *Bolton* v. *Gladstone*, 2 Taunt. 85.
(*g*) *Baring* v. *Royal Exchange Assurance Company*, 5 East, 99.

---

(46) "A warranty of neutrality must, I conceive, now be understood, as containing in itself (among other things) a stipulation that the contract of assurance shall be void, if the subject-matter warranted neutral be condemned as enemies' property; and, if a warranty of neutrality contains this stipulation, the sentence of a court of competent jurisdiction, condemning a ship on account of its want of neutrality, is the proper evidence, according to every principle and rule of our law, to determine that fact." Per *Lawrence*, J., in *Lothian* v. *Henderson*, 3 Bos. & Pul. 524.

account of the common default of all the proprietors, *in their joint character of ship-owners*, in not having a regular passport on board, as required by the treaty of their own state with France: it was holden (*h*), that the assured could not claim from the underwriter an indemnity for a loss thus occasioned by themselves, although the ship was not warranted or represented to be an American; for the ship owner is bound to have such documents as are required by treaties with particular nations on board, to evince his neutrality in respect to such nations. By the sentence of a French court of admiralty, it appeared that the ship insured, "*warranted American*," had been condemned as enemy's property, for want of having on board a *role d'equipage*, or list of the crew, such as was required by a marine ordinance of France, and adjudged by the court there to be requisite within the meaning of the treaty of commerce between France and America; it was holden (*i*) to be conclusive evidence against the warranty of neutrality, though, in fact, the ship was American. So where the sentence states, that the ship was condemned on the ground of having violated her neutrality (*k*), and acted contrary to the law of nations and the faith of treaties, such sentence is conclusive evidence against the warranty of neutrality. But where the grounds of confiscation are stated obscurely, and the court cannot collect what the precise ground was (*l*) ; or where the sentence adjudges the ship to be lawful prize, not because it is enemies' property, but for reasons which lead to a contrary conclusion (*m*) ; or if it appear that the condemnation proceeded *solely* on the ground of the ship having violated an *ex parte* ordinance, to which the neutral country had not assented (*n*) ; in such cases the sentence is not conclusive evidence against the warranty of neutrality.

It is to be observed also, that the sentence of a foreign court, where it is conclusive, is conclusive only as to the grounds of the sentence, and not as to the premises which led to the conclusion (*o*). The preceding remarks, as to foreign sentences of condemnation, being conclusive evidence against the warranty of neutrality, must be confined to legal sentences, that is, sentences of a prize-court, acting and exercising functions either in the belligerent country, or in the country of a co-belligerent or ally in the war (*p*) ; for sentences of condemnation, pronounced by the authority of the capturing power, *within the dominions of a neutral country*, to which the prize may have been taken, are illegal (*q*), and consequently

(*h*) *Bell* v. *Carstairs*, 14 East, 374.
(*i*) *Geyer* v. *Aguilar*, 7 T. R. 681.
(*k*) *Garrels* v. *Kensington*, 8 T. R. 230.
(*l*) *Bernardi* v. *Motteux*, Doug. 575; *Fisher* v. *Ogle*, 1 Campb. 418.
(*m*) *Calvert* v. *Bovill*, 7 T. R. 523, recognized by *Tindal*, C. J., delivering judgment, *Dalgleish* v. *Hodgson*, 7 Bingh. 504.
(*n*) *Bird* v. *Appleton*, 8 T. R. 562.
(*o*) *Christie* v. *Secretan*, 8 T. R. 192.
(*p*) *Oddy* v. *Bovill*, 2 East, 473.
(*q*) *Havelock* v. *Rockwood*, 8 T. R. 268; *The Flad Oyen*, 1 Rob. A. R. 135.

inadmissible. And that is to be considered as a neutral country for this purpose (r), in which the forms of an independent neutral government are preserved, although a belligerent may have such a body of troops stationed there as in reality to possess the sovereign authority.

Free of Capture in Port.—If a vessel is taken at her moorings, being neither within the *caput portus*, nor within that part of a haven where ships unload, the underwriter is not discharged by a warranty against "capture in the ship's port of destination" (s). Whether a vessel warranted free of capture in port, be in a port or not at the time of her capture (t), is purely a question of fact for the jury. See further *Oom* v. *Taylor*, 3 Campb. 204, and *Maydhew* v. *Scott*, *ib.* 205. The assured upon a policy on ship, not having leave to carry simulated papers, cannot recover for a loss by capture; if it appear by the sentence of the foreign prize-court that one of the causes stated for the condemnation was the carrying of simulated papers (u).

Implied Warranty.—1. *Not to deviate.*—Another condition implied in the contract of insurance is, that the ship shall not deviate. Hence arises another ground of defence, on which the underwriter may insist, *viz.* that there has been a *deviation*, by which term is to be understood a wilful and unnecessary departure from the due course of the voyage insured, either with or without the consent of the assured, for any, even the shortest space of time. The effect of a deviation is not to avoid the contract *ab initio*, but only to determine it from the time of the deviation, and to discharge the insurer from all subsequent responsibility. Hence, damage sustained before the actual deviation must be made good by the underwriters (x). From the moment of deviation, however, the contract is at an end, and it is immaterial from what cause the subsequent loss arises. If two ports of discharge are named in the policy, and the ship intends going to both, she must take them in the order named in the policy. Hence, where a ship insured for A. and B., meaning to go to both, went first to B. in her way to A.; it was holden to be a deviation from the voyage insured, not being in the order named in the policy (y). Upon a policy from London to Trinidad or the Spanish Main, with leave to call at all or any of the West India Islands or settlements, and with liberty to touch and stay at any ports or places whatsoever and wheresoever, the assured must take all the ports at which he touches, in the same succession in which they occur in the course of his voyage insured (z). A policy

(r) *Donaldson* v. *Thompson*, 1 Campb. 429.

(s) *Keyser* v. *Scott*, 4 Taunt. 660.

(t) *Reyner* v. *Pearson*, 4 Taunt. 662.

(u) *Orwell* v. *Vigne*, 15 East, 70. But *secus*, if leave be given to carry simulated papers. *Bell* v. *Bromfield*, 15 East, 364.

(x) *Green* v. *Young*, 2 Raym. 840; Salk. 444.

(y) *Beatson* v. *Haworth*, 6 T. R. 531.

(z) *Gairdner* v. *Senhouse*, 3 Taunt. 16.

at and from Martinique *and all* and every West India Islands, warrants a course from Martinique to islands not in the homeward voyage (*a*). A ship having liberty to put into one port, put into another equally in her way; this was holden (*b*) to be a deviation, and to avoid the contract, though neither the risk nor the premium would have been greater, if the putting into such other port had been allowed by the policy. A ship was insured from Lisbon to England, with liberty to call at any one port in Portugal; it was holden (*c*), that under such a policy the party had only a liberty to call at some port in Portugal, in the course of the voyage to England. Where a ship insured to Martinique and all or any of the Windward and Leeward Islands, landed the greatest part of her cargo at Martinique, and sailed with the residue to Antigua, where she was wrecked while stopping partly to dispose of the residue of the outward cargo, and *partly to obtain a homeward cargo;* it was holden (*d*), that the underwriters were not liable; for, per Lord *Ellenborough*, C. J., when the disposal of the outward cargo ceased to be the sole reason for the stay at Antigua, the underwriters were discharged. A policy of insurance on goods at and from London to the ship's discharging port or ports in the Baltic (*e*), *with liberty to touch at any port or ports for orders*, or any other purpose, does not warrant the assured, after having touched at C. for orders, and gone on to S., a more distant port, in retouching at C. for orders: but if the policy be to any and all ports and places in the *Baltic, forwards and backwards*, and *backwards and forwards*, it is otherwise. Under a liberty to touch and stay at all ports for all purposes whatsoever, the stay must be for some purpose connected with the furtherance of the adventure (*f*). Whether the purpose is within the scope of the policy, is a question for the court solely, and not for the jury (*g*). If the policy does not limit the time of stay, whether a ship has stayed an unreasonable time, is purely a question for the jury (*h*). A policy of insurance " at and from London to Berbice," was effected upon the receipt of a letter from the captain, (which was shown to the underwriter,) stating that he had passed Barbadoes, and the words " at sea" were inserted in the policy after the printed clause describing the beginning of the adventure on the goods. It was holden (*i*), notwithstanding, that the policy was vacated by a deviation at Madeira, in a former part of the voyage. A ship was insured from London to the southern whale fishery and back again (*k*), " with leave

(*a*) *Bragg* v. *Anderson*, 4 Taunt. 229.

(*b*) *Elliot* v. *Wilson*, 7 Bro. P. C. 439; 4 Bro. P. C. 470, Tomlins' ed.

(*c*) *Hogg* v. *Horner*, Marsh. 197. But see *Leathly* v. *Hunter*, 7 Bingh. 528.

(*d*) *Inglis* v. *Vaux*, 3 Campb. 437; Ld. *Ellenborough*, C. J., *Moore* v. *Taylor*, 1 Ad. & Ell. 25; 3 Nev. & M. 406, S. P.

(*e*) *Mellish* v. *Andrews*, 16 East, 312.

(*f*) *Langhorn* v. *Allnutt*, 4 Taunt. 511.

(*g*) *Ib.*

(*h*) *Ib.*

(*i*) *Redman* v. *London*, 3 Campb. 503, C. B., per Sir *J. Mansfield*, and afterwards confirmed by the court.

(*k*) *Jarratt* v. *Ward*, 1 Campb. 263.

to carry letters of marque, and to cruise for, chase, capture, man, and *see into port*, any ships of the king's enemies." It was holden, that although the ship insured might be authorized under the terms of this policy, in accompanying prizes to any convenient port consistently with the main adventure, seeing them safely moored there, and perhaps stopping a reasonable time to give directions for their proceeding on their final destination, yet *remaining in port until a prize was repaired*, could not be considered as warranted by those terms. A deviation never puts an end to the insurance, unless it be the voluntary act of those who have the management of the ship. Hence, where a policy was effected on a ship carrying letters of marque, from Bristol to Newfoundland, and the orders of the owners were to put a few hands on board any prize that might be taken, and send her to Bristol, but that the ship should proceed to Newfoundland; notwithstanding *the crew obliged the captain* to go back to Bristol with a prize, taken during the voyage, and in so doing the ship was captured; it was holden (*l*), that this deviation was justifiable, and that the underwriter was not discharged from his obligation to indemnify the assured. The owner of a ship (which was about to sail on a voyage from Lisbon to Madeira, from Madeira to Saffi, on the coast of Africa, in ballast, and thence to Lisbon, with a cargo,) was desirous of having the insurance effected on part of the freight from Saffi to Lisbon. The underwriters objected, on account of the distant period at which the risk was to commence; however, on a representation some time afterwards, by the owner, that he had received intelligence of the ship's arrival at Madeira, and that she was about to proceed immediately on her voyage, the insurance was effected. When the ship arrived at Madeira, all the crew, except two, being alarmed by reports of some Moorish cruisers being off Saffi, and of their having captured and ill-treated a Dane and an American, quitted the ship, and refused to return to it, unless the captain would promise to sail immediately for Lisbon. Under these circumstances, the captain carried the ship back to Lisbon: but on his arrival there, the charterers insisted on his proceeding directly from thence to Saffi, which he accordingly did, and was captured in his return from Saffi to Lisbon. It was in evidence, that the difference of season, arising from this delay, did not vary the risk. It was holden (*m*), that the deviation was justified by the special circumstances. And this rule holds as well in the case of a limited as a general policy. Hence, where a policy was effected on goods on board a ship for a certain voyage, " against sea risk and fire only," and the ship was forcibly carried out of the course of her voyage, and detained by a king's ship, but afterwards was released, and permitted to proceed on the voyage insured, during which the goods insured sustained sea-damage; it was holden (*n*),

---

(*l*) *Elton* v. *Brogden*, 2 Str. 1264.　　Pul. 313.
　(*m*) *Driscol* v. *Passmore*, 1 Bos. & Pul. 　　(*n*) *Scott* v. *Thompson*, 1 Bos. & Pul.
200. See also *Driscol* v. *Bovil*, 1 Bos. &　　N. R. 181.

that the deviation having been occasioned by force, and without any consent on the part of those who had the management of the ship, the underwriter was liable, although the voyage was made longer than it otherwise would have been, by the detention of the king's ship.

An unreasonable delay *in performing the voyage insured,* is equivalent to a deviation (*o*); as where a ship insured "at and from the coast of Africa to the West Indies, with liberty to exchange goods and slaves," stayed several months beyond the usual stay of ships in that trade. It is immaterial whether the risk has or has not been thereby increased. So a *delay* (*p*) *in the commencement of the risk*, by the interposition of an intermediate voyage not communicated to the underwriters, will discharge the policy; unless such intermediate voyage was one, which was made usually and according to the trade in which the ship was then engaged, which would be equivalent to notice to the underwriters. So where the delay before the ship arrived at the port where the policy was first to attach was unreasonable and unjustifiable; it was holden (*q*), that the underwriter was discharged. So where the insurance was effected on January 28th, on a vessel afloat "at and from Bristol to London;" and the vessel (a yacht) did not sail until the 17th of May; it was holden, that the delay unaccounted for was unreasonable, and that the underwriter was discharged (*r*), although the vessel was one which did not usually sail in the winter. In a subsequent trial on the same policy, the jury found (*s*) that the delay was sufficiently accounted for, and plaintiff obtained a verdict.

Grounds of Necessity.—Going into port for the purpose of refitting or repairing (*t*), or stress of weather (*u*), or avoiding an enemy, or seeking for convoy (*x*), are grounds of necessity, and will justify a deviation.

A vessel may deviate somewhat from the straight line of her track to seek for convoy; and the captain, unless expressly prohibited by the terms of the policy, may always do what is necessary for the safety of the ship. A vessel insured may do whatever it would be expedient for the common security to do if uninsured (*y*). But where a ship was insured *from London to Berbice*, with an extensive liberty of touching and trading at all places; it was holden (*z*), that by putting into Madeira, and voluntarily stay-

(*o*) *Hartley* v. *Buggin*, M. 22 Geo. III., Park, 468 ; *S. C.*, 3 Doug. 39, recognized in *Mount* v. *Larkins*, 8 Bingh. 121.

(*p*) Admitted, *Vallance* v. *Dewar*, 1 Campb. 505 ; *Ougier* v. *Jennings*, *ib.* n.

(*q*) *Mount* v. *Larkins*, 8 Bingh. 108, recognized in *Freeman* v. *Taylor*, 8 Bingh. 139, and *ante*, p. 997.

(*r*) *Palmer* v. *Marshall*, 8 Bingh. 317.

(*s*) *Palmer* v. *Fenning*, 9 Bingh. 460.

(*t*) Admitted by Lord *Hardwicke*, Ch., in *Motteux* v. *London Ass.*, 1 Atkyns, 545.

(*u*) *Delany* v. *Stoddart*, 1 T. R. 22.

(*x*) *Bond* v. *Gonsales*, Salk. 445.

(*y*) *D'Aguilar* v. *Tobin*, 1 Holt's N. P. C. 185, C. B., *Gibbs*, C. J.

(*z*) *Williams* v. *Shee*, 3 Campb. 469, B. R., Lord *Ellenborough*, C. J.

ing there for the purposes of trade, after the convoy, with which she sailed, had proceeded on the voyage, she was guilty of a deviation which discharged the underwriters. Whenever such circumstances exist as render a deviation necessary (a), the voyage (which may then be termed a voyage of necessity,) must be pursued according to its due course in like manner as the original voyage. An intention to deviate from the due course, not carried into execution (b), will not be considered as a deviation. Where goods were insured from Heligoland to Memel, with liberty to touch at any ports, and to seek, join, and exchange convoy, warranted free from capture in the port of Memel, and the ship sailed from Heligoland with orders to go to Gottenburgh to know whether to proceed to Anholt or Memel, and was captured in her way to Gottenburgh, which is in the track either to Anholt or Memel: it was holden (c), that this was to be considered as a voyage to Memel, although it was subject to be changed according to circumstances upon the ship's arrival at Gottenburgh; and therefore the risk commenced on her leaving Heligoland; and the ship never having reached Gottenburgh, the purpose of going thither for orders was merely an intention to deviate, which did not vacate the policy; neither was it a restraint on the captain's judgment as to the place of seeking convoy, it not appearing that he could have met with convoy before the capture; and consequently the underwriter was liable. Policy of assurance on goods at and from London to the ship's discharging port or ports in the Baltic, with liberty to touch at any port or ports for orders or any other purpose, and to touch and stay at any ports or places whatsoever and wheresoever: it was holden (d), that the ship having touched at C. for orders and gone on to S., a more distant port, for further orders, and having received orders at S., because it was unsafe to land there, to return to C. and wait for orders, might so return to C. without being guilty of a deviation; it being found that she went to S. for orders in the prosecution of her voyage; and returned to C. to obtain orders as to the further progress of the voyage, and no fraud being found.

So where the policy was "at and from Singapore, Penang, Malacca, and Batavia, all or any, to the ship's port of discharge in Europe, with leave to touch, stay and trade at all or any ports or places whatsoever and wheresoever in the East Indies, Persia, or elsewhere, &c., upon goods in certain ships, beginning the adventure from the loading thereof aboard the said ships:" the ship took in part of her cargo at Batavia, and then went to Sourabaya, another port in the East Indies, (not in the course of a voyage from Batavia to Europe, and not mentioned by name in the policy,) and took in other goods; then returned to Batavia, whence she

(a) Lavabre v. Wilson, Doug. 284.
(b) Foster v. Wilmer, Str. 1249;
Thellusson v. Fergusson, Doug. 361;

Kewley v. Ryan, 2 H. Bl. 343.
(c) Heselton v. Allnutt, 1 M. & S. 46.
(d) Mellish v. Andrews, 2 M. & S. 27.

afterwards sailed to Europe, and was lost by perils of the seas; it was holden (e), that Sourabaya, being a place in the East Indies, might be considered as a loading port or *terminus a quo*, within the meaning of the policy; and consequently that the going there was not a deviation, and the goods there taken on board were protected.

In a policy on ship and freight, it is not an implied condition that the ship shall not trade in the course of her voyage, if that may be done without deviation or delay, or otherwise increasing the risk of the underwriters. Hence, where a ship was compelled in the course of her voyage to enter a port, for the purpose of obtaining a necessary stock of provisions, which she could not obtain before in the usual course, by reason of a scarcity at her loading ports, and during her justifiable stay in the port so entered for that purpose, she took on board bullion for freight, the jury having found that no delay in the voyage was occasioned thereby; it was holden (f), not to avoid the policy. So were a ship had liberty to touch at a port; it was holden (g), not to be any deviation to take in a quantity of salt during her stay there, the ship not having thereby exceeded the period allowed for her remaining there. N. In this case a communication had been made to the underwriter that the ship was to touch for the purpose of trade. It seems, however, that the words " liberty to touch" will not authorize a general trading (h). See further on this subject, *Phelps* v. *Auldjo*, 2 Campb. 350. Assumpsit on a policy on freight of a ship at and from Grenada to London. It was proved that there is only one custom-house for the whole island of Grenada, that the vessel arrived in safety at Grenada, and discharged parts of her outward cargo at three different bays, and she was proceeding to a fourth to discharge the residue of her outward cargo, and take in part of her homeward cargo, when she was lost by perils of the sea: it was holden (i), that the vessel, at the time of the loss, was proceeding to this fourth bay for a purpose connected with the voyage insured, and, consequently, that it was not a deviation.

There has been much doubt whether a deviation, for the purpose of succouring a vessel in distress, will avoid the policy. In *Lawrence* v. *Sydebotham* (k), Lord *Ellenborough* expressly avoided giving any judgment on the point, which has not yet arisen directly in a court of law; but the inclination of his opinion (which will probably be followed by the courts) was, that when such a case did arise, it would be found to be for the general benefit of all insurers, to allow

---

(e) *Hunter* v. *Leathley*, 10 B. & C. 858. Affirmed on error, 7 Bingh. 517.

(f) *Raine* v. *Bell*, 9 East, 195, recognised in *Laroche* v. *Oswin*, 12 East, 131.

(g) *Urquhart* v. *Barnard*, 1 Taunt. 450.

(h) Per Sir J. *Mansfield*, S. C., 1 Taunt. 456.

(i) *Warre* v. *Miller*, (in error,) 4 B. & C. 538.

(k) 6 East, 52.

such succour to be given without imputing deviation to the succour-ing ship.

2. *Seaworthiness.*—In every marine insurance, whether on ship or goods, there is an implied warranty, that the ship is seaworthy *at the commencement of the risk* (*l*), or, in the language of the charterparty, tight, staunch, and strong.   Any defect, which may endanger the ship, though unknown to the assured, will discharge the underwriter; for it is the duty of the assured to provide a good ship in such state and condition as to be able to perform the des-tined voyage, *i. e.* seaworthy.   As to any decay to which the loss of the ship may be attributed, the question will be, whether the same commenced previously to or after the insurance made.   If a ship, in a short time after having sailed, become leaky, and founders, or is obliged to return to port, there not having been any storm, ex-ternal accident, or cause adequate to the producing such effect, it may be presumed that she was not, at the time of sailing, sea-worthy: but the conclusion, in all cases of this kind, is to be drawn by the jury, to whom the several circumstances are to be submitted. If the ship be insured at and from a port, although in want of repairs, she is protected by the policy, whilst in the port.   The con-dition that she shall be seaworthy for the voyage, does not attach until her sailing (*m*).   Where a ship is insured at and from a foreign port, it is necessary that she should have once been *at* the place in good safety; for if she arrives at the outward port so shat-tered as to be a mere wreck, a policy on the homeward voyage never attaches (*n*).

In *Franco* v. *Natusch*, 1 Tyrw. & Gr. 401, where, in an action on a policy, the loss was alleged to be by perils of the sea, and the defendant pleaded, that the ship at the commencement of the risk was unseaworthy; *Parke,* B., observed, that it had been laid down in *Parker* v. *Potts*, 3 Dow. 23, that it must be taken *primâ facie* that a ship is seaworthy at the commencement of the risk ; but that if, soon after her sailing, it appears that she is not sound or fit for sea, without adequate cause of stress of weather, &c. to account for it, the rational inference is, that notwithstanding appearances, she was not seaworthy when the voyage commenced.

By the new rules, which see *ante,* p. 116, 7, unseaworthiness, misrepresentation, concealment, deviation, and various other de-fences must be pleaded.   And semble, that the burthen of proving unseaworthiness lies on the defendant.   See the opinion of Baron *Parke*, in the foregoing case of *Franco* v. *Natusch.*

It is also an implied condition, that the ship insured shall be furnished with every article necessary for the purpose of safe navi-

---

(*l*) *Hollingworth* v. *Brodrick*, 7 A. & E. 47, *Patteson*, J. "I do not know of any distinction on account of the risk
being for time."
  (*m*) *Annen* v. *Woodman*, 3 Taunt. 299.
  (*n*) *Parmeter* v. *Cousins*, 2 Campb. 235.

gation during her voyage, *i. e.* properly equipped with sails (*o*), a sufficient number of hands on board (47), an able captain, skilful pilots, and a crew of competent skill (*p*). In an action on a policy of insurance on ship and goods from Stettin to London, in which the plaintiff declared upon a loss, by reason of the vessel sinking before she had been moored twenty-four hours, in consequence of an anchor having been driven into her; it appeared, that the captain had taken a pilot on board at Orfordness, on entering the river Thames, who had quitted her at Half-way Reach; after which, and before she had come to her moorings higher up the river, the accident happened which occasioned the loss, and in consequence of which the vessel filled with water, before she had been moored twenty-four hours; but the precise time at which the damage was sustained within those limits, or by what particular default, was not ascertained. The captain had also left the ship before the time of the actual loss. It was holden (*q*), that the underwriter was discharged; Lord *Kenyon*, C. J., observing, that in this case the captain did not perform his duty; for he had no pilot on board at the time when the accident happened; and it is one of the things implied in contracts of this kind, that there shall be some person on board the ship apparently qualified to navigate her. If the underwriters had been previously informed, that there would be no pilot on board during the ship's sailing up the river Thames, probably they would not have undertaken the risk. On the ground, therefore, that there was no pilot on board the vessel when the accident happened, he was of opinion that the underwriter was discharged (48).

(*o*) *Wedderburn* v. *Bell*, 1 Campb. 1.
(*p*) Per Lord *Tenterden*, C. J, in *Shore* v. *Bentall*, 7 B. & C. 798, n.
(*q*) *Law* v. *Hollingsworth*, 7 T. R.
160; the authority of this case has been doubted. See *Dixon* v. *Sadler*, 5 M. & W. 405.

---

(47) In *Hunter* v. *Potts*, London Sittings after Trin. T. 45 Geo. III., Lord *Ellenborough*, C. J., said, that the vessel must not only be seaworthy, but the crew must be adequate to discharge the ordinary duties, and to meet the usual dangers to which she is exposed. " Underwriters are responsible for the misconduct or negligence of the captain and crew; but the owner, as a condition precedent, is bound to provide a crew of competent skill." Per Lord *Tenterden*, C. J., *Shore* v. *Bentall*, 7 B. & C. 798, n. If the captain of a vessel, about to enter a foreign harbour, uses due diligence to obtain a pilot and fails, and then in the exercise of a fair discretion attempts to enter, and the vessel is lost, the underwriter is responsible for the loss. *Phillips* v. *Headlam*, 2 B. & Ad. 380.

(48) Another question was agitated, *viz.* Whether the defendant would have been answerable, if there had been a pilot on board, whom the captain believed to be of sufficient skill, but who was not duly qualified under stat. 5 Geo. II. c. 20. The court declined giving an opinion, as in the case before them *no* pilot was on board. Pilotage from Dover, Deal,

When the assured have once provided a sufficient crew, the negligent absence of all the crew, at the time of the loss, is not (r) any breach of the implied warranty that the ship shall be properly manned. The principle (s) established by the more recent decisions is, that if the vessel, crew, and equipments be originally sufficient, the assured has done all that he has contracted to do, and is not responsible for the subsequent deficiency occasioned by any neglect or misconduct of the master or crew; and there is no distinction between a time policy and another. So a plea to an action on a policy that the ship became unseaworthy after the voyage commenced, and might have been made seaworthy with reasonable care, was holden insufficient on demurrer, assigning for cause, that it was not averred in the plea, that the loss was in anywise caused by reason of the plaintiff not repairing, amending, or rendering the said ship seaworthy (t).

Where a vessel, engaged in the southern whale and seal fishery, and with liberty to chase and capture prizes, was insured in August, 1807, with a retrospect to the 1st of August, 1806, although at the time of her insurance she was not competent to pursue all the purposes of her voyage, her crew being reduced by death and casualties; yet if she had a competent force to pursue *any* part of her adventure, and could be safely navigated home, she is to be deemed seaworthy (u).

(r) *Busk* v. *R. Exch. Ass.*, 2 B. & A. 73.

(s) Per *Parke*, B., delivering judgment of the court in *Dixon* v. *Sadler*, 5 M. & W. 405.

(t) *Hollingworth* v. *Brodrick*, 7 A. & E. 40.

(u) *Hucks* v. *Thornton*, Holt's N. P. C. 30, C. B., *Gibbs*, C. J.

---

and the Isle of Thanet, *up* the rivers Thames and Medway, is regulated by statutes 3 Geo. I. c. 13, 7 Geo. I. c. 21, and 43 Geo. III. c. 152. Pilotage *down* the Thames, and through the North Channel, to or by Orfordness, and round the Long Sand-Head into the Downs, and down the South Channel into the Downs, and from or by Orfordness up the North Channel and the Thames and Medway, by stat. 5 Geo. II. c. 20; and pilotage into or out of the port of Liverpool, by stat. 37 Geo. III. c. 78. See also modern regulations as to pilots in later statutes, 47 Geo. III. sess. 2, c. 70. Local, 48 Geo. III. c. 104, continued and amended by 52 Geo. III. c. 87; 6 Geo. IV. c. 125. This statute will be found in the Appendix to the 5th edition of the Law relative to Merchant Ships, published by Mr. J. H. Abbott, p. 530 to 572. The 6th section, which enacts that it shall be lawful for the Trinity House of Hull and Newcastle to appoint sub-commissioners of pilotage to examine and license pilots, is permissive and not imperative. *Beilby, q. t.* v. *Raper*, 3 B. & Ad. 284. The 6 Geo. IV. c. 125, has been amended by 9 Geo. IV. c. 86, and extended and altered by stat. 3 & 4 Vict. c. 68. See on the construction of the 6 Geo. IV. c. 125, *Lucey* v. *Ingram*, 6 M. & W. 302; *Beilby* v. *Scott*, 7 M. & W. 93.

5. *Re-assurance.*

Re-assurance is a contract made by the first insurer or under-writer, with a view of securing himself from a risk, by throwing it on other underwriters, who are termed re-assurers. This is allowed in almost all the trading countries in Europe, and was permitted by the law of England, until the stat. 19 Geo. II. c. 37, by the fourth section of which re-assurance is prohibited, except in three cases: 1. The insolvency; 2. The bankruptcy; 3. The death of the insurer; and even in these cases, it must be expressed in the policy to be a re-assurance, and the re-assurance must not exceed the amount of the sum before assured.

Although the first section of the above-mentioned statute does not extend to foreign ships (*x*), yet the fourth section does. Consequently a re-assurance, even by a foreigner, on a foreign ship, is illegal.

6. *Wager Policy—Stat.* 19 *Geo. II. c.* 37.—*Interest of Assured.*

An insurance being a contract of indemnity, its object is not to make a positive gain, but to avert a possible loss. Hence, as a person cannot be said to be indemnified against a loss which can never happen to him, a policy without interest is not an insurance, but a mere wager only. Such policy, therefore, is properly deno-minated a wager policy. Although contradictory decisions are to be found in the books, as to the legality of wager policies, before the statute 19 Geo. II., yet they have been recognized as legal con-tracts by modern judges; and it seems now to be admitted (*y*), that by the law of merchants, and particularly by the law of England, as it stood at the time of passing the act 19 Geo. II., a wager policy, in which the parties, by express terms, such as the words—" interest or no interest," or " without proof of interest," disclaimed the intention of making a contract of indemnity, was then (contrary to older determinations,) deemed a valid contract of insurance; but that a policy containing no such clause, disclaiming or dispensing with the proof of interest, was to be considered as a contract of indemnity only, upon which the assured could never recover without proof of an interest (49). But it having been

(*x*) *Andrée* v. *Fletcher*, 2 T. R. 161.   *Lucena* v. *Craufurd*, 3 Bos. & Pul. 101.
(*y*) See the opinion of *Chambre*, J., in

---

(49) This opinion of *Chambre*, J., is confirmed by an observation of Lord *Hardwicke*, in a case which was decided before the passing of the

found by experience, that the making assurances, "interest or no interest, or without further proof of interest than the policy," had been productive of many pernicious practices, and by introducing a mischievous kind of gaming or wagering, under the pretence of assuring the risk on shipping and fair trade, the institution and laudable design of making assurances had been perverted; and that which was intended for the encouragement of trade and navigation, had, in many instances, become destructive to the same: it was enacted, by stat. 19 Geo. II. c. 37, s. 1, "That no assurances should be made by any persons, bodies corporate or politic, on any ships *belonging to his Majesty, or any of his subjects* (50), on any goods laden, or to be laden, on board such ships, interest or no interest, or without further proof of interest than the policy, or by way of gaming or wagering, or without benefit of salvage to the assurer, and that such assurances should be void." But by sect. 2, it is provided, "That insurances on private ships of war, fitted out by any of his Majesty's subjects, solely to cruise against his enemies, may be made by or for the owners thereof, interest or no interest, free of average, and without benefit of salvage to the insurer." And by sect. 3, it is also provided, "That any effects, from any port or places in Europe or America, in possession of the crowns of Spain and Portugal, may be insured in the same manner as if this act had not been made." Having detailed the provisions of the stat. 19 Geo. II. c. 37, it will be necessary briefly to consider what that interest is, the protection of which is the proper object of a policy of assurance. And this is to be collected from considering what is the nature of such contract (z). Now insurance is a contract by which the one party, in consideration of a price paid to him adequate to the risk, becomes security to the other, that he shall not suffer loss or damage by the happening of the perils specified to certain things, which may be exposed to them. This being

(z) Per *Lawrence*, J., in *Lucena* v. *Craufurd*, D. P., 2 Bos. & Pul. N. R. 300, where this subject is very elaborately discussed.

---

stat. 19 Geo. II. c. 37. Speaking of the difference between insurances from fire and marine insurances, he says, "in the insurance of ships, ' interest or no interest' is almost constantly inserted, and, *if not inserted*, you cannot recover, unless you prove a property." Per Lord *Hardwicke*, C., in the *Sadlers' Company* v. *Badcock*, 2 Atk. 556.

(50) In consequence of these words, it has been holden, that this section does not apply to the case of foreign ships, and that insurances, "interest or no interest," may be made upon them. *Thellusson* v. *Fletcher*, Doug. 315. And although the words "interest or no interest" are omitted in the policy on a foreign ship, yet in declaring on such policy, it is not necessary to aver that the assured had an interest. *Craufurd* v. *Hunter*, 8 T. R. 13; *Nantes* v. *Thompson*, 2 East, 385.

the general nature of the contract, it follows, that it is applicable to protect persons against uncertain events, which may in anywise be of disadvantage to them; not only those persons, to whom positive loss may arise by such events occasioning the deprivation of that which they may possess, but those also, who, in consequence of such events, may have intercepted from them the advantage or profit which, but for such events, they would acquire according to the ordinary and probable course of things. That a person must somehow or other be interested in the preservation of the subject matter exposed to perils, follows, from the nature of this contract, when not used as a mode of wager, but as applicable to the purposes for which it was originally introduced; but to confine it to the protection of the interest which arises out of property, is adding a restriction to the contract which does not arise out of its nature. Interest, therefore, with reference to the subject under consideration, does not necessarily imply a right to the whole, or a part of a thing, nor necessarily and exclusively that which may be the subject of privation, but the having some relation to, or concern in, the subject of the insurance, which relation or concern, by the happening of the perils insured against, may be so affected as to produce a damage to the person insuring; and where a person is so circumstanced, with respect to matters exposed to certain risks, as to have a moral certainty of advantage but for those risks, he may be said to be interested in the safety of the thing. Having endeavoured to explain the nature of an insurable interest, it will be proper to add, that it is not necessary such interest should be indefeasible; for the consignee of goods under a bill of lading has an insurable interest in such goods, although they may be stopped in transitu on their passage home (a). So also has an executor before probate. In like manner it has been holden, that where a ship was taken as prize by the conjoint forces of the army and navy, the captors, before condemnation, had an insurable interest under stat. 45 Geo. III. c. 72, s, 3, whereby the crown gave up its right in the prize to the captors, although such interest was defeasible, as well by the release of the crown, as the adjudication of the Court of Admiralty (b). The owner of a ship, who has chartered her for a particular voyage, has an insurable interest in the ship during that voyage, although the charterparty contain a stipulation, that, in case the ship be lost, the charterer shall pay the owner the estimated value of the ship (c). Assumpsit on a policy of insurance. The plaintiffs were entitled, under a verbal agreement, to a cargo on board a ship when it should arrive at port. The ship was lost at sea: it was holden (d), that the plaintiffs had no insurable

(a) Per Lord *Ellenborough*, C. J., 11 East, 628.

(b) *Stirling* v. *Vaughan*, 11 East, 619; 2 Campb. 225; S. C., cited in *Robertson and others* v. *Hamilton*, B. R. M. 52

Geo. III.

(c) *Hobbs* v. *Hannam*, 3 Campb. 93.
(d) *Stockdale* v. *Dunlop*, 6 M. & W. 224.

interest in the goods, as the contract which they had entered into, being verbal only, was incapable of being enforced.

X. *Evidence, p.* 1016 ; *Damages, p.* 1022.

In order to support his action, the plaintiff must be prepared with the following proof: 1. The policy must be produced in evidence, and the subscription of the defendant must be proved. 2. Evidence must be given of the interest of the insured in the subject matter of the insurance (51) at the time of the loss (*e*). In insurances upon ships, the mere fact of the possession of the assured, as owners, is sufficient *primâ facie* evidence of ownership (*f*), without the aid of any documentary proof or title deeds on the subject, such as the bill of sale or ship's register, unless such further evidence is rendered necessary in support of the *primâ facie* evidence of ownership, in consequence of the adduction of some contrary proof on the other side. As in an action on a policy of insurance on freight, where the interest in a ship and its earnings were alleged to be in four persons, who were partners in trade, and it was proved by the plaintiffs, that the ship had been paid for by all the four partners; but the defendant having produced the register, wherein the ship was registered in the names of two of the partners only; it was holden (*g*), that as the title to freight arose only from ownership, and the register was conclusive evidence that only two were owners, and as there was not any count in the declaration, stating the interest to be in two only, the plaintiffs could not recover. Where the plaintiffs declared on a policy of assurance (*h*), and averred that they were the persons residing in *Great Britain*

(*e*) *Clay* v. *Harrison*, 10 B. & C. 106.
(*f*) *Robertson* v. *French*, 4 East, 136. See also *Thomas* v. *Foyle*, 5 Esp. N. P. C. 88.
(*g*) *Camden* v. *Anderson*, 5 T. R. 709,

recognized by *Le Blanc*, J., in *Marsh* v. *Robinson*, B. R., London Sittings after H. T. 42 Geo. III., 4 Esp. N. P. C. 98.
(*h*) *Bell* v. *Janson*, 1 M. & S. 201.

---

(51) In *Amery* v. *Rogers*, 1 Esp. N. P. C. 207, where an action was brought on a policy of insurance on a ship, Lord *Kenyon*, C. J., was of opinion, that the proof of the assured having exercised acts of ownership, in directing the loading, &c. of the ship, and paying the people employed, was sufficient proof of interest. And in *M'Andrew* v. *Bell*, 1 Esp. N. P. C. 373, where the insurance was on a ship and her cargo, the plaintiff, in order to prove interest, produced the bill of lading, and the captain proved that it was his bill of lading, and that he had the goods specified in it on board; Lord *Kenyon*, C. J., held that the interest was sufficiently proved.

who received the order for and effected the insurance; this was considered as a material averment, and not sustained by evidence of a letter received by them after the policy was effected, directing to make assurance; although the policy was originally on goods on board the ship called *The Ann*, or *ships*, or by whatsoever other name the ship should be named; and the plaintiffs, upon the receipt of the letter, procured a memorandum to be made on the policy, signed by the defendant, declaring the interest to be on board the Herald, the ship mentioned in the letter. In insurances upon goods, the mere production of a bill of parcels from the seller abroad, with the receipt to it, and proof of his hand-writing, has been holden (i) to be sufficient proof of the interest of the assured. In a declaration on a policy of insurance effected by the plaintiff (k), as agent of A. and B., it was averred, "that A. and B., at the time of effecting the policy, and thence until the time of the loss, were interested in the goods insured, *to a large amount, to wit, to the amount of all the money ever insured thereon.*" At the trial it appeared that, at the time when the policy was effected, another person was jointly interested in the goods, together with A. and B. The court were of opinion, that although A. and B. had not an exclusive interest, yet they had such an interest as would answer the terms of the averment; *Chambre*, J., observing, that the averment in substance was nothing more than that the parties for whose benefit the assurance was made, had an interest in the subject of that insurance. They were not bound by the terms of the averment to show any thing more than that they had an interest; and if they had shown an interest to the extent of one hundredth part of the cargo, it would be sufficient. The spirit of the stat. 19 Geo. II. only required that the policy should not be a gaming policy.

3. It must be proved, that the loss happened in the same manner as is stated in the declaration, that the underwriter may be apprized of the case, which he has to encounter by evidence. Goods were insured at and from Mogadore to London. The declaration averred, "that after the loading the goods, the ship departed on her intended voyage, and while in the course of her said voyage was lost by perils of the sea." It was holden (l), that this was a material allegation, and therefore, the ship having been lost while at her moorings, and before the cargo was completed, the insured could not recover. Where a loss is averred to be by *perils of the sea* (m), and some of the goods insured are spoiled, and others saved, the expenses of the salvage may be given in evidence (without stating them specially) on this averment, as being a damage within the cause of action as laid. If a total loss of the ship is stated in the declara-

<hr/>

(i) *Russel* v. *Boheme*, Str. 1127, per *Lee*, C. J.

(k) *Page* v. *Fry*, 2 Bos. & Pul. 240. But see *Bell* v. *Ansley*, 16 East, 141, recognized in *Cohen* v. *Hannam*, 5 Taunt.

108.

(l) *Abitbol* v. *Bristow*, 2 Marsh. Rep. 157; 6 Taunt. 464, S. C.

(m) *Cary* v. *King*, Ca. Temp. Hardw. B. R. 304.

tion (n), and damages laid accordingly, evidence of a partial loss may be received, and the plaintiff may recover to the amount of such loss as he is able to prove. Under an averment, that after loading the cargo, the ship sailed on the voyage, and was lost, the plaintiff cannot recover (o) on proof that the ship, before she had half of her cargo on board, was driven from her moorings and lost. In an action upon an insurance upon profits, the assured must prove a loss: for where, upon an insurance of profits of a cargo of slaves, valued at £400, the plaintiff declared for a total loss by perils of the seas, and it appeared that the vessel was wrecked, whereby many of the slaves were lost, but the remainder got into the market, and were there sold; it was holden (p), that, although the produce of the slaves sold did not give a profit upon the whole adventure, the plaintiff was not entitled to recover, because it did not appear, that if there had been no shipwreck, and all the slaves had got to market, any profit would have been produced. It is a general rule, that nothing which depends on the proceedings of a court can be proved by parol testimony (q); hence, in cases of capture, and recapture, neither the salvage, nor the expenses incurred for ascertaining the amount of the salvage, can be otherwise proved than by producing the proceedings of the Admiralty Court. The copy of a sentence of condemnation of a ship or cargo in a foreign Admiralty Court, is not made admissible evidence for the under-writers, by being handed over to them, by the assured, along with other papers, to satisfy them of the loss (r). A slip of paper, wherein the names of the underwriters were mentioned, in the order in which they had originally been applied to (s), and had agreed to underwrite, (and which was different from that in which their names appeared on the policy,) having been tendered in evi-dence to show the true order of the names, for the purpose of letting in evidence of a false representation made to the first under-writer in fact; the court were of opinion, that such paper could not be received in evidence, for want of a stamp, the effect of the evidence being to show, through the medium of writing, that the contract entered into between the parties was different from that which it appeared to be on the face of the policy. In a case where it appeared that a license to trade with an enemy (t), granted abroad, had been returned, after being used, to the secretary of the governor by whom it was issued, and the secretary was examined, who said that he had, as he believed, thrown it aside among the waste papers of his office, and did not know what was become of it; that he had afterwards searched for, but did not recollect the finding it, and thought that he had not found it: it was holden, that this was reasonable and proper evidence of the loss of such

(n) 2 Burr. 904.
(o) *Abitbol* v. *Bristow*, 6 Taunt. 464.
(p) *Hodgson* v. *Glover*, 6 East, 316.
(q) *Thellusson* v. *Shedden*, 2 Bos. &

Pul. N. R. 228.
(r) *Flindt* v. *Atkins*, 3 Campb. 215.
(s) *Marsden* v. *Reid*, 3 East, 572.
(t) *Kensington* v. *Inglis*, 8 East, 273.

license, so as to let in parol evidence of its contents; the paper not being considered as of any further use at the time, and the attention of the witness not having been then called particularly to the circumstances: and further, that the witness might speak to the contents of the license from memory, though he had made an entry of it in his memorandum book for the private information of himself and the governor, which book was not produced, he having given it to the governor, who was gone abroad without returning it to him; for such book, if in court, would not have been evidence *per se*, but could only have been used by the witness to refresh his memory. When a ship insured is captured in a voyage to an enemy's country (*u*), and the British license legalizing the voyage is lost; to show that she had such a license, it is necessary to prove the loss of the paper purporting to be a license put on board the ship, and to produce examined copies of the order in council for granting the license, and of the copy of the license preserved in the secretary of state's office. To support an averment in a declaration on a policy of insurance on goods, "that the ship, with the goods on board, when at A. was arrested by the persons exercising the powers of government there, and the goods were then and there by the said persons seized, detained, and confiscated;" it is enough to show, that the goods were forcibly taken on board the ship by the officers of government, and never delivered to the consignees; without putting in any sentence of condemnation (*x*). To prove a warranty, that a ship insured was of a particular nation, it is *primâ facie* evidence, that she carried the flag of that nation at times when she was free from all danger of capture, and that the captain addressed himself to the consul of that nation in a foreign port (*y*). The production of a letter dated abroad, and addressed to J. S. in England, with the English ship-letter post-mark upon it, which directed a policy to be effected, is sufficient to prove that J. S. was "the person residing in Great Britain who received the order for, and effected, such policy" (*z*). In an action on a policy on a voyage "to any port in the Baltic," evidence was admitted to prove that the Gulf of Finland is considered, in mercantile contracts, as within the Baltic, although the two seas are treated as separate and distinct by geographers (*a*). Upon a question concerning the seaworthiness of a ship (*b*), after the evidence of persons who have examined her condition, experienced shipwrights, who never saw her, may be called on to say whether, upon the facts sworn to, she was, in their opinion, seaworthy or not, in conformity to the rule of evidence, that where a matter of skill or science is to be decided, the jury may be assisted by the opinion of persons pecu-

(*u*) *Eyre* v. *Palgrave*, 2 Campb. 605.

(*x*) *Carruthers* v. *Gray*, 3 Campb. 142, Lord *Ellenborough*, C. J.

(*y*) *Arcangelo* v. *Thompson*, 2 Campb. 620.

(*z*) S. C.

(*a*) *Uhde* v. *Walters*, 3 Campb. 16. See *Moxon* v. *Atkins*, 3 Campb. 200.

(*b*) *Beckwith* v. *Sydebotham*, 1 Campb. 116.

liarly acquainted with it from their professions or pursuits. In an
action on a policy on goods on board a ship (c), the master and
owner was held not a competent witness to prove the ship seaworthy, until he had been released by the owner of the goods. So
in an action against an underwriter (d), for a loss by barratry of
master, it was holden, that the master could not be examined by
the defendant, to prove that the barratry was committed by the
consent, and with the privity, of the owners, without a release by
the defendant. In an action on a policy on goods (e), the declaration contained an averment that the plaintiffs were interested in
the subject matter of insurance; the defendant, meaning to dispute this at the trial, gave them notice to produce certain articles
of agreement executed by the plaintiffs and the captain (who was
not a plaintiff). The instrument was produced in pursuance of the
notice, when there appeared to be two subscribing witnesses to it;
the plaintiffs insisted that the defendant could not give it in evidence without calling one of those witnesses to prove it. Lord
Ellenborough being of that opinion, the plaintiffs recovered. A
motion was made for a new trial, on the ground that the instrument coming out of the hands of the plaintiffs, *parties* thereto,
upon notice to produce it, it was not necessary to be proved by one
of the subscribing witnesses, according to the rule laid down in *Rex*
v. *Middlezoy*, 2 T. R. 41. But Lord *Ellenborough* said, that that
case, which was much questioned at the time, had been since overruled, and that the production of the instrument, in pursuance of
the notice, did not supersede the necessity of proving it by one of
the subscribing witnesses, if any, as in ordinary cases. And *Lawrence*, J., said, that this had been so ruled by Lord *Kenyon*, in a
subsequent case respecting a will, which the adverse party, in
whose hands it was, had notice to produce, and did produce at the
trial, when it appeared that there were subscribing witnesses to it;
and Lord *Kenyon* held, that the party who gave the notice was
bound to call one of the subscribing witnesses to prove the will.
In the present case, however, the court made the rule absolute
for a new trial, on payment of costs, the defendant having made an
affidavit of his being surprised, and not prepared at the trial for
want of knowing who the subscribing witnesses were (52).

(c) *Rotheroe* v. *Elton*, Peake's N. P. C.
84, *Kenyon*, C. J.; *Fox* v. *Lushington*,
ib. n., S. P., per Lord *Kenyon*, C. J.

(d) *Bird* v. *Thompson*, 1 Esp. N. P. C.
339.

(e) *Gordon and others* v. *Secretan*, 8
East, 548; *Bateson* v. *Lewin*, Middlesex
Sittings after H. T. 52 Geo. III., Lord
Ellenborough, C. J., S. P.

---

(52) The doctrine established in *Gordon* v. *Secretan*, was recognized
by *Heath*, J., in *Wetherston* v. *Edgington*, 2 Campb. 94, and there
applied to an agreement not under seal. But although the mere possession of an instrument does not dispense with the necessity, which lies on

The plea of alien enemy, which goes merely in disability of the person, must be supported by the strictest proof. Hence, it is not sufficient merely to show that some time *before* action was brought, the party was domiciled in a territory which has become hostile, without showing that he was a native of that territory, or living there, at the time of action brought (*f*). The opinion of the underwriters as to the materiality of communicating information as to a particular fact, previously to the effecting a policy, is not admissible (*g*) in evidence. The materiality of such a communication is a question for the jury (*h*).

(*f*) *Harman* v. *Kingston*, 3 Campb. 153.

(*g*) *Campbell* v. *Rickards*, 2 Nev. & M.

(*h*) *S. C.*

542; 5 B. & Ad. 840, *S. C.*

---

the party calling for it, of producing the attesting witness, yet where a person is called on to produce a deed to which he is a party, and under which he claims to hold an estate, and he produces it, it shall be taken to be a good deed, so far as relates to the execution, as against himself. *Pearce* v. *Hooper*, 3 Taunt. 60 ; *Roe* v. *Wilkins*, 4 Ad. & Ell. 86, S. P.; 5 Nev. & Mann. 434, *S. C.*, by name of *Doe* v. *W.* See also *Orr* v. *Morrice*, 3 Brod. & Bingh. 139, where it was holden, in an action for use and occupation of premises, against the assignees of a bankrupt, that the deed of assignment of the bankrupt's effects, produced by the defendants, at the trial, under a notice from the plaintiff, was admissible in evidence, without proof of the execution by the subscribing witness, as it appeared that one of the assignees had continued to occupy the premises for some time after the bankruptcy. See also *Burnett* v. *Lynch*, 5 B. & C. 604. " It is not competent to a party, who has taken under a deed all the interest which that deed was calculated to give, to dispute its due execution, although at the time when the deed is produced, he has not any existing interest under it." Per *Bayley*, J.—N. This was an action by a lessee against the assignee of a lease, and the plaintiff having proved the execution of the counterpart, the defendant put in the original lease, which was produced by a person to whom he had assigned it; it was holden, that it was not necessary for the plaintiff to call the subscribing witness. See also *Doe d. Tyndale and others* v. *Heming and others*, 6 B. & C. 28, where the attorney for the lessors of the plaintiff obtained from one of the defendants, (the tenant in possession,) a lease of the premises granted to him for a term' not then expired, in order to prevent the defendants from setting it up, to defeat the action: it was holden, that, as the lessors of the plaintiff were to derive a benefit from the possession of the lease, and as the conduct of the attorney amounted to a recognition of it as a valid instrument, when produced in pursuance of notice from the defendants, it might be read without calling the subscribing witness. But if the instrument be in the possession of the party producing it at the trial, the execution must be proved by the subscribing witness: although the adverse party may claim under the deed. *Vacher and another, Assignees, &c.* v. *Cocks*, 1 B. & Ad. 147, 8.

Damages.—By stat. 3 & 4 Will. IV. c. 42, [14th August, 1833,] s. 29, the jury, on the trial of any issue, or on any inquisition of damages, may, if they shall think fit, give damages in the nature of interest over and above the money recoverable in all actions on policies of assurance made after the passing of this act.

XI. *Premium—Return of.*

THE general rule (*i*) is, that the broker is the debtor of the underwriter for the premiums, and the underwriter the debtor of the assured for the loss.

In cases where the contract of insurance is void, as on the ground of non-compliance with a warranty, *e. g.*, to sail with convoy, seaworthiness or the like, and fraud cannot be imputed to the assured, the assured will be entitled to a return of premium; because, where the contract does not attach, there is not any risk (53). Where there is an insurance on ship and freight, and the ship has arrived in safety, and earned freight, the assured cannot afterwards claim a return of premium, on the ground that he had no insurable interest, on account of a defect in his title to the ship (*k*). In cases where the risk is entire, and has once commenced, as in the case of a deviation, there shall not be any return or apportionment of premium (*l*) (54). A ship was insured

---

(*i*) Per Lord *Tenterden*, C. J., *Scott* v. *Irving*, 1 B. & Ad. 612.

(*k*) *M'Culloch* v. *Royal Exchange Assurance Company*, 3 Campb. 406.

(*l*) *Tyrie* v. *Fletcher*, Cowp. 668; *Meyer* v. *Gregson*, B. R. East. 24 Geo. III., Marsh. 568.

---

(53) " If the risk be not run, though it be by neglect, or even by *fault* of the insured, yet the insurer shall not retain the premium." Per Lord *Mansfield*, C. J., in *Stevenson* v. *Snow*, 3 Burr. 1240. " Where the risk has not been run, whether its not having been run was owing to the fault, pleasure, or will of the insured, or to any other cause, the premium shall be returned; *because a policy of insurance is a contract of indemnity.* The underwriter receives a premium for running the risk of indemnifying the assured, and to whatever cause it be owing, if he does not run the risk, the consideration for which the premium or money was put into his hands, fails, and therefore he ought to return it." Per Lord *Mansfield*, C. J., in *Tyrie* v. *Fletcher*, Cowp. 668.

(54) Upon an insurance at and from a place, if an usage can be proved warranting a division of the risk, the insured will be entitled to an apportionment of the premium, in case one of the risks be not run. *Long* v. *Allan*, B. R. E. 25 Geo. III., Marsh. 570.

" at and from London to any port or place, for twelve months, at £9 per cent., warranted free from capture by the Americans" (m). The ship sailed from the port of London and was taken by an American privateer about two months afterwards. It was contended, that a proportionate part of the premium ought to be returned; that £9 was much more than adequate to the risk actually run, viz. only two months. But the court were of opinion that there ought not to be a return of premium; Lord *Mansfield*, C. J., observing, " that there were two general rules established, applicable to the question: The first is, that where the risk has not been run, whether its not having been run was owing to the fault, pleasure, or will of the insured, or to any other cause, the premium shall be returned; *because a policy of insurance is a contract of indemnity.* The underwriter receives a premium for running the risk of indemnifying the insured; and to whatever cause it be owing, if he does not run the risk, the consideration for which the premium or money was put into his hands, fails, and therefore he ought to return it. 2d. Another rule is, that if that risk of the contract of indemnity has *once* commenced, there shall be no apportionment or return of premium afterwards. For though the premium is estimated, and the risk depends upon the nature and length of the voyage, yet, if it has commenced, though it be only for twenty-four hours or less, the risk is run, the contract is for the whole entire risk, and no part of the consideration shall be returned." The same rules were laid down by Lord *Mansfield*, C. J., in *Loraine* v. *Thomlinson*, Doug. 587. A ship, employed in the coasting trade, was insured against capture for twelve months (n); at 15s. per cent. per month, £18. The ship was lost in a storm, within the first two months. An action having been brought for the amount of the premium (£18), the defendant pleaded non-assumpsit as to all except £3, and as to that a tender. The jury found a verdict for the defendant upon the tender, and for the plaintiff upon the other issue, for the sum of £15, subject to the opinion of the court, whether he was entitled to recover that sum of £15, or the sum of £3 only. It was contended, on the part of the defendant, that this was not one entire contract for a year, but an insurance from month to month for twelve months; if the policy had been for a year, or twelve months, and the *premium* a gross sum, *the court* could not have apportioned it, because the risk in one month might be greater than in another, but here the *parties* have apportioned the *premium*; that the insurance was the same as if there had been twelve policies for each month. But per Lord *Mansfield*, C. J., it is an insurance for twelve months, for one gross sum of £18. They have calculated this sum to be at the rate of 15s. per month. But what was to be paid down? Not 15s. for the first month, and so from month to month; but £18 at once. A

(m) *Tyrie* v. *Fletcher*, Cowp. 668. (n) *Loraine* v. *Thomlinson*, Doug. 585.

ship with her cargo was insured " at and from Honfleur to the coast of Angola(*o*), during her stay and trade there, at and thence to her port or ports of discharge in St. Domingo, and at and from St. Domingo back to Honfleur, at a premium of £11 per cent." The ship sailed to A., but in this part of the voyage she was guilty of a deviation. It was contended, on the part of the plaintiff, that there ought to be an apportionment and return of premium; but the court were clearly of opinion that there ought not to be any return. Lord *Mansfield*, C. J., said, the question depends upon this: Whether the policy contains one entire risk on one voyage, or whether it is to be split into six different risks? for, by splitting the words, and taking "at," and "from," separately, it will make six; *viz.* 1. At Honfleur; 2. From Honfleur to Angola; 3. At Angola, &c. The argument must be, that, if the ship had been taken between Honfleur and Angola, there must have been a return. By an implied warranty, every ship must be seaworthy, when she first sails on the voyage insured, but she need not continue so throughout the voyage: so that, if this is one entire voyage, if the ship was seaworthy when she left Honfleur, the underwriters would have been liable though she had not been so at Angola, &c.; but, according to the construction contended for on the part of the plaintiff, she must have been seaworthy, not only at the departure from Honfleur, but also when she sailed from Angola, and when she sailed from St. Domingo. But if the insurance be in effect on two or more voyages, and one or more have not commenced, there shall be an apportionment and return of premium in respect of those voyages which have not commenced, as will appear from the following case:—

An insurance was effected upon a ship at five guineas per cent. (*p*), lost or not lost, at and from London to Halifax, warranted to depart with convoy from Portsmouth for the voyage (55). Before the ship arrived at Portsmouth, the convoy was gone. Notice of this was immediately given by the assured to the underwriter, and at the same time he was also desired either to make the long insurance, or to return part of the premium. The jury found that the usual settled premium, from London to Portsmouth, was one and one half per cent., and that it was usual, in cases like the present, for the underwriter to return part of the premium, but the quantum was uncertain. It was stated, that the plaintiff made to the defendant an offer of allowing him to retain one and one half per cent. for the risk from London to Portsmouth. It was holden, that the plaintiff

<hr>

(*o*) *Bermon* v. *Woodbridge*, Doug. 781.   (*p*) *Stevenson* v. *Snow*, 3 Burr. 1237.

<hr>

(55) In Mr. J. Blackstone's report of this case, 1 Bl. R. 315, the words of the policy are, " warranted to depart with convoy for the voyage," omitting the words " from Portsmouth."

was entitled to recover such part of the premium as had been given for insuring the ship on the voyage from Portsmouth to Halifax: *Denison*, J., observing, that it was most equitable that the defendant should retain the premium for such part of the voyage only as he had run the risk of; that the insured had a right to have the other part restored to him. And this was agreeable to the general principle of actions for money had and received to the plaintiff's use; where the defendant had no right to retain it, he must refund it. *Foster*, J., added, that there was not any consideration for the remainder of the premium, *i. e.* for the voyage from Portsmouth to Halifax, wherein no risk was run by the insurer, who only insured the voyage with convoy; therefore he had no right to retain the premium for this. *Wilmot*, J., said, that upon this policy there were two distinct points of time, in effect two voyages, which were clearly in the contemplation of the parties, and only one of the two voyages was made, the other not at all entered upon. It was a conditional contract, and the second voyage was not begun, therefore the premium must be returned; for upon the second part of the voyage the risk never took place. Lord *Mansfield*, C. J., commenting on the preceding case in *Tyrie* v. *Fletcher*, Cowp. 669, observed, " that the first object of insurance was from London to Halifax; but if the ship did not depart from Portsmouth with convoy, then there was to be no contract from Portsmouth to Halifax: why then, the parties have said, ' We make a contract from London to Halifax, but, on a certain contingency, it shall only be a contract from London to Portsmouth.' That contingency not happening, reduced it in fact to a contract from London to Portsmouth only." All the judges, in delivering their opinion, laid the stress upon the contract comprising two distinct conditions, and considering the voyage as being in fact two voyages. And in *Bermon* v. *Woodbridge*, Doug. 790, the same learned judge observed, that in *Stevenson* v. *Snow* there was a contingency specified in the policy, upon the not happening of which the insurance would cease. It depended on the contingency of the ship sailing with convoy from Portsmouth, whether there should be an insurance from that place. This necessarily divided the risk, and made two voyages. And in *Loraine* v. *Thomlinson*, Doug. 587, Lord *Mansfield* again remarked, that *Stevenson* v. *Snow* was decided on the ground of there being two voyages. The next case in which an apportionment has been allowed, is that of *Long* v. *Allan*, B. R. E. 25 Geo. III., 4 Doug. 276; Park, 589; Marsh, 570, *S. C.* There the terms of the policy were, "at and from Jamaica to London, warranted to depart with convoy." The ship sailed without any convoy. An express usage was found, that on insurances couched in the same terms with the policy in question, the premium had been returned, deducting one half per cent. if the ship departed without convoy. The court decided in favour of the return of premium, on the ground of the usage. In *Rothwell* v. *Cook*, 1 Bos. & Bul. 172, the policy was on ship,

" at and from Hull to Bilboa, warranted to depart from England with convoy;" the ship sailed from Hull to Portsmouth, and thence departed with convoy, which not being direct for Bilboa, she afterwards left, and was captured: the warranty not having been complied with, the plaintiff would have been nonsuited, but it was insisted that he was entitled to a verdict for the premium, which was found accordingly. On motion to set aside this verdict, *Eyre*, C. J., said, "The verdict now stands for the return of the whole premium, and the question is, whether it should stand for the whole, for none, or for a part? If for a part, I do not know how we are to settle it; it must depend on there being, or not being, some rule to be found to direct us in making the decision. Certain it is, that if the ship had been lost in coming round to Portsmouth, the underwriters would have been liable; it is not therefore reasonable, that they should have been so liable without retaining a proportion of the premium. You should inquire whether there is any rate of premium among the underwriters from Hull to Portsmouth, and whether the premium has ever been apportioned where there has been only one insurance, without distinguishing the different risks in the policy. If you can find any rule, I recommend you to adopt it. But if you cannot agree, we think the whole premium ought not to be returned; and, therefore, the present verdict must be set aside, and the case go to a new trial." Rule absolute. Where there is an agreement to return part of the premium, "if the ship *arrived*," the assured will be entitled to a return, in the event of an arrival of the ship at the port of destination, although it should appear, that the ship has sustained a loss occasioned by a sea risk (*q*), or that the ship has been captured and recaptured, and the assured has been obliged to pay the salvage (*r*). But every arrival of the ship at the port of her destination is not an arrival within the fair construction of the agreement; such, for instance, as an arrival in possession of an enemy at a neutral port, to which she was insured, or an arrival at her port in England as the property of other persons after her capture. In short, it must be an arrival at the destined port in the course of her voyage (*s*). The captors of a ship and cargo effected an insurance: restitution was afterwards awarded to the owners (with the exception of a small part of the cargo); it was holden, that the captors were not entitled to a return of premium: for they had possession of the property insured; and if it were a legal capture, they were entitled; if it were not, the Court of Admiralty might amerce them in the damages and costs (*t*). Policy at and from Gottenburgh to Riga upon goods and ship, beginning the adventure upon the goods from the loading thereof aboard the ship at Gottenburgh; it appeared that there were not any goods laden at Gottenburgh, but only at London: it was holden (*u*), that as the

---

(*q*) *Simond* v. *Boydell*, Doug. 268.
(*r*) *Aguilar* v. *Rodgers*, 7 T. R. 421.
(*s*) Adm. by *Kenyon*, C. J., *S. C.*

(*t*) *Boehm* v. *Bell*, 8 T. R. 154.
(*u*) *Horneyer* v. *Lushington*, 15 East, 46.

risk upon the goods never commenced, the plaintiff was entitled to a proportiona lreturn of premium. In the preceding case, the adventure upon the goods is expressly mentioned to begin from the loading at Gottenburgh; but if the place had been omitted, the court would have intended a loading at the place whence the voyage commenced (x). The formal receipt in the policy is conclusive evidence of the receipt of the premium as between the assured and underwriter in an action for the return of the premium (y). Where the assured or his agent (z) had been guilty of fraud, as where the assured knew that the ship (a) was lost, at the time of effecting the policy, the premium cannot be recovered; and the same rule holds, where the contract of insurance is illegal (b), unless the assured was ignorant of the illegality at the time of effecting the insurance (c); or unless every thing has been done by the assured which lay in his power to legalize the voyage (d); though the endeavour has failed; and although the adventure is never entered upon, yet there ought at least to be some formal renunciation of the contract before the bringing the action (e). If the language of the policy be large enough to comprise an illegal adventure, and the assured contemplated an illegal adventure, the underwriter is not entitled (f) to sue for the premium. A policy broker is the agent of both the assured and underwriter, and is the trustee for the assured as long as the policy remains in his hands, to adjust and receive returns of premium for him when the events have happened on which they are to be made. Hence the broker, having notice that the events have happened which entitled the assured to such returns, is authorized to deduct so much from the gross amount of the premiums, and to pay over the difference only to the underwriter (g). In assumpsit, on a policy of insurance (h), with a count for money had and received, the defendant had not paid any money into court. The defence was, that the ship was not seaworthy; on which point, without any direct evidence of fraud, the case was submitted to the jury. General verdict for defendant. N. It was not intimated to the jury, that the plaintiff was entitled to a verdict for a return of premium; on an application to the court, it was holden, that the plaintiff was entitled to a verdict for the premium on the count for money had and received; but the court hoped, that in future the counsel would in his opening demand the premium, in every case where it was intended to insist upon it on failure of his claim for the loss. Where a total loss is recovered, there cannot

(x) *Spitta* v. *Woodman*, 2 Taunt. 416.

(y) *Dalzell* v. *Mair*, 1 Campb. 532.

(z) *Chapman* v. *Fraser*, B. R. T. 33 Geo. III., Park, 329.

(a) *Tyler* v. *Horne*, London Sittings after H. T. 25 Geo. III., Lord *Mansfield*, C. J., Park, 329.

(b) *Lowry* v. *Bourdieu*, and other cases, *ante*, vol. i. p. 93.

(c) *Oom* v. *Bruce*, 12 East, 225.

(d) *Hentig* v. *Staniforth*, 5 M. & S. 122.

(e) *Palyart* v. *Leckie*, 6 M. & S. 290.

(f) *Jenkins* v. *Power*, 6 M. & S. 282.

(g) *Shee* v. *Clarkson*, 12 East, 507.

(h) *Penson* v. *Lee*, C. B. M. 41 Geo. III., 2 Bos. & Pul. 330.

be a return of premium for convoy, because the total loss includes the entire premium added to the invoice price (*i*). Upon a mere misrepresentation without fraud, where the risk never attached, the assured is entitled to a return of the premium (*k*).

XII. *Of Bottomry and Respondentia.*

Bottomry.—An agreement entered into by the owner, or, under certain circumstances, by the master of a ship (56), whereby, in consideration of a sum of money advanced, (for the purpose of enabling the borrower to fit out the ship, or purchase a cargo for an intended voyage,) the borrower undertakes to repay the same with a stipulated interest, if the voyage shall terminate successfully, and binds himself and the ship and tackle for the due performance of the agreement, is termed *bottomry.* The term " *bottomry*" is derived from the original language of the agreement, which merely spoke of the keel or bottom of the ship ; but the expression was always considered as being used figuratively, *viz. pars pro toto.* This agreement is sometimes made in the form of a deed-poll, called a bill of bottomry, executed by the borrower, and sometimes in the form of a bond with a penalty. " Instruments of bottomry are in use in all countries wherein maritime commerce is carried on. The lender of the money is entitled to receive a recompense far beyond the rate of legal interest ; this recompense is very properly called in the civil law ' periculi pretium,' and no person can be entitled to it who does not take upon himself the peril of the voyage ; but it is not neces-

(*i*) Per jury, in *Langhorn* v. *Allnutt,*   (*k*) *Feise* v. *Parkinson*, 4 Taunt. 640.
4 Taunt. 511.

(56) In a foreign country, in the absence of the owners, and in cases of necessity, the master may take up money on bottomry for the use of the ship, as where a ship, being on a voyage from Bengal to London, was obliged to put back to Bombay to repair. See the form of bottomry-bond in this case, in Abbott on Shipping, p. 601, 6th ed. by Shee; and see also *The Exeter, Whitford,* 1 Rob. A. R. 176. The master may hypothecate his cargo on freight for repairs in a foreign port, such repairs being necessary for the prosecution of his voyage. *The Gratitudine,* 18th December, 1801, Sir *W. Scott.* The master of a ship has authority by law to pledge the credit of his owner, resident in England, for *money* advanced to the master in an English port where the owner has no agent, if such advance of money was necessary for the prosecution of the voyage ; and whether it was so or not is a question for the jury. *Arthur* v. *Barton,* 6 M. & W. 138 ; as to the power of the master to sell the ship, see *Hunter* v. *Parker,* 7 M. & W. 322.

sary that his doing so shall be declared expressly, and in terms; it is sufficient that the fact can be collected from the language of the instrument considered in all its parts. It has been said, that such instruments, being the language of commercial men, and not of lawyers, should receive a liberal construction, to give effect to the intention of the parties "(l). An assured on bottomry cannot recover against the underwriter, unless there has been an actual total loss of the ship (m); for if the ship exist in specie, in the hands of the owners, though under circumstances that would entitle the assured on the ship to abandon, it will prevent its being an utter loss within the meaning of the bottomry bond.

Respondentia.—If the loan is not upon the vessel, but upon the goods and merchandize, which must necessarily be sold or exchanged in the course of the voyage, then by the terms of the agreement the borrower only personally is bound to answer the contract, who, therefore, in this case, is said to take up money at respondentia. Bottomry and respondentia differ very materially from a simple loan (n). 1. In the case of a loan, the money is at the risk of the borrower, and must be repaid at all events. But where money is lent on bottomry or respondentia, the money is at the risk of the lender during the voyage. 2. Upon a loan, legal interest only can be reserved. But upon bottomry or respondentia, any interest upon which the parties agree may be reserved. By stat. 7 Geo. I. c. 21, s. 2, " all contracts and agreements made or entered into by any of his Majesty's subjects, or any person or persons in trust for them, for the loan of any money by way of bottomry on any ship or ships in the service of foreigners, and bound to or designed to trade in the East Indies, are void." By stat. 19 Geo. II. c. 37, s. 5, "all money lent on bottomry, or at respondentia, upon ships belonging to any of his Majesty's subjects bound to or from the East Indies, must be lent only on the ship, or upon the merchandize on board, and shall be so expressed in the condition of the bond; and the benefit of salvage shall be allowed to the lender, who alone shall have a right to make insurance on the money so lent; and no borrower of money shall recover more than the value of his interest in the ship, or in the effects laden on board, exclusive of the money so borrowed; and in case it shall appear that the value of his share in the ship, or the effects on board, does not amount to the full sum or sums he has borrowed as aforesaid, such borrower shall be responsible to the lender for so much of the money borrowed as he has not laid out on the ship or merchandize laden thereon, with lawful interest for the same, in the proportion the money laid out shall bear to the whole money lent, notwithstanding the ship or merchandize shall be totally lost."

(l) Per Lord *Tenterden*, C. J., delivering judgment, *Simonds* v. *Hodgson*, 3 B. & Ad. 50, on error from C. B.

(m) *Thompson* v. *The Roy. Exch. Ass. Comp.*, 1 M. & S. 30.

(n) Marsh. 634.

XIII. *Insurance upon Lives.*

THE insurance of life is a contract whereby the insurer (o), in consideration of a certain premium, either in a gross sum or by annual payments, undertakes to pay to the person for whose benefit the insurance is made, a stipulated sum of money, or an annuity equivalent, upon the death of the person whose life is insured, *whenever this shall happen*, if the insurance be for the whole life; or *in case it shall happen within a certain period*, if the insurance be for a lesser term than for life. The utility of this species of insurance is obvious. Persons possessed of life incomes are hereby enabled to secure, after their death, a competent provision for their families; and they are also enabled, even in their lifetime, in cases of urgent necessity, to raise money by way of loan, (which they could not do on mere personal security); for, by insuring their lives to the amount of the sum borrowed, the lender may be certain of having repaid the money lent in the event of their death. By these insurances also, the fines to be paid upon the renewal of leases, or on the descent of copyhold estates, may be provided for (p). The making insurances on lives, or other events, wherein the insured had no interest, having introduced a mischievous kind of gaming, it was enacted, by stat. 14 Geo. III. c. 48, first, " That no insurance should be made by any person, body politic or corporate, on lives, *or any other event*, wherein the person for whose benefit or on whose account the policy is made, has no interest, or by way of gaming or wagering. 2dly, That in every policy on lives, or other events, the name of the person interested, or on whose account it is made, must be inserted. 3dly, That no greater sum should be recovered or received from the insurer, than the amount of the interest of the insured (57). Whether the insured has an interest within the meaning of the preceding statute, is sometimes the subject of litigation; as to which, it has been holden, that a creditor has an insurable interest in the life of his debtor, at least where he has only the personal security of the debtor (q) (58). But although a creditor may insure the life of his debtor to the extent of his debt, yet such a contract is substan-

---

(o) Marsh. 664.
(p) Ib.

(q) *Anderson* v. *Edie*, Hil. 1795, per Lord *Kenyon*, C. J., at N. P., Park, 640.

---

(57) Marine insurances are expressly exempted from the operation of this statute. See the proviso in the 4th section.

(58) See the remark of Serjeant *Marshall* on this point in p. 673, 4, 5. In *Read* v. *R. E. A. C.*, Lord *Kenyon* was of opinion, that a wife making an insurance on her husband's life need not prove that she was interested therein, for it must be presumed. See Peake's Additional Cases, p. 70.

tially a contract of indemnity against the loss of the debt (r), and, therefore, if, after the death of the debtor, his executors pay the debt to the creditor, the latter cannot afterwards recover upon the policy, although the debtor died insolvent, and the executors were furnished with the means of payment by a third party, it being immaterial from what fund the debt has been discharged, so as the creditor has received satisfaction. The general principle, however, that the insured shall, in case of a loss, recover no more than an indemnity, may be controlled by mercantile usage (s). The word "interest," in the foregoing statute, means pecuniary interest in the life or event insured; hence a policy effected by a father in his own name, on the life of his son, the father not having any pecuniary interest therein, is void (t). Where the debt accrues by virtue of an illegal security, as a note for money won at play, such interest is not insurable (u). In an action on an insurance on the life of J. S. (x), for one year, and during the life of the plaintiff, but in case the plaintiff should die before J. S., the policy to be void; it appeared that J. S. had granted an annuity to the plaintiff's late brother, which annuity he had bequeathed to persons not parties to this insurance, having appointed the plaintiff executor of his will, and directed him to make assurance. It having been objected, that the insurance was made by a person not having any beneficial interest, Lord *Kenyon*, C. J., held this to be a sufficient interest to support the action; observing, that the plaintiff could not assent to the legacy before the testator's debts were paid, without being guilty of a devastavit; and, being executor, all the interest of the testator vested in him. The cause proceeded; but it appearing that J. S. was in a dying state when the policy was effected, the defendant had a verdict. Before a policy of insurance upon a life is effected, it is usual for the party (whose life is the object of the insurance) to subscribe a written declaration, touching his age, state of health, (e. g. whether he has ever had the small-pox, gout, &c.,) and other circumstances. The substance of this declaration is recited, and the whole is incorporated by reference in the policy: at the end of which a proviso is usually inserted, declaring the policy to be void in case the insured should die upon the seas, or go beyond the limits of Europe, without leave obtained from the directors, or commit suicide, or die by the hands of justice, or if the age of the assured exceed ___ years, or if the assured be afflicted with any disorder which tends to the shortening of life (59); or in case the declaration should contain

(r) *Godsall* v. *Boldero*, 9 East, 72.
(s) See *Palmer* v. *Blackburn*, 1 Bingh. 61.
(t) *Halford* v. *Kymer*, 10 B. & C. 724.
(u) *Dwyer* v. *Edie*, London Sittings after H. 1788, *Buller*, J., Park, 639.
(x) *Tidswell* v. *Ankerstein*, Peake's N. P. C. 151.

(59) It is not to be concluded *, that a disorder with which a person is
* *Watson* v. *Mainwaring*, 4 Taunt. 763.

any averment which is not true. This last stipulation is not restricted (y) to the meaning of being "true" within the knowledge
of the party making the statement; such knowledge is immaterial.
Such are the conditions which are usually required, varied, however,
according to the regulations of the different insurance companies.
The policy of imposing these terms is obvious; for if there be not
any warranty or condition on the part of the insured, the insurer
is subject to all risks, unless he can show that there has been a
fraudulent concealment or suppression of the truth (z).   It is,
however, the duty of the assured to disclose all material facts
within their knowledge (a); and the proper question for the jury
is, whether in their opinion, the facts be material, and not whether
the party believed them to be so.   In an assurance, upon the life
of another, the life insured, if applied to for information, is, in
giving such information, impliedly the agent of the party insuring,
who is bound (b) by his statements, and must suffer if they are
false, although he is not acquainted with the life insured, and
although the agent of the insurance office undertakes to do all that
is required by his office.   In a case where the conditions required a
declaration of the state of the health of the assured, and the policy
was to be valid only if the statements were free from all misrepresentation and reservation: and the declaration described the

(y) Duckett v. Williams, 2 Cr. & M.
348, Hope Assurance Company.
(z) Stackpole v. Simon, per Lord Mansfield, C. J., H. T. 1779, Park, 648.
(a) Lindenau v. Desborough, 8 B. &

C. 586, cited by Parke, B., in Wainwright v. Bland, 1 Tyr. & Gr. 420. See
also Morrison v. Muspratt, 4 Bingh. 60.
(b) Everett v. Desborough, 5 Bingh.
503.

afflicted before he effects an assurance on his life, is a disorder tending to
shorten life within the meaning of the declaration, from the mere circumstance that he afterwards dies of it, if it be not a disorder which generally
has that tendency. In this case of Watson v. Mainwairing, the disorder was
dyspepsy. J. S. was warranted in good health at the time of making the
policy.   In an action on the policy, it appeared, that in consequence of a
wound which J. S. had received in battle many years before, and which
had occasioned a partial relaxation or palsy, he could not retain his urine or
fæces. This had not been mentioned to the insurer.   J. S. died of a fever.
It was proved by several physicians and surgeons, that the wound had not
any connexion with the fever, that the want of retention was not a disorder that shortened life, and that the party might, notwithstanding, have
lived to the common age of man.   Lord Mansfield told the jury, that the
only question was, whether the party was in a reasonable good state of
health, and such a life as ought to be insured on common terms.   The
jury, upon this direction, found a verdict for the plaintiff. Ross v. Bradshaw, 1 Bl. R. 312. A warranty that the party is in a good state of
health will not be falsified by showing that he was troubled with spasms
and cramps, and violent fits of the gout. Willis v. Poole, at N. P., 1780,
Marsh. 669.

assured as resident at Fisherton Anger; whereas, the assured was then a prisoner in the county gaol for Wilts, there. It was holden (c), that it was a question for the jury, whether the imprisonment were a material fact, and ought to have been communicated. False representation in answer to parol questions not comprised in list of printed questions, will avoid (d) the policy. If the contract of insurance be contrary to public policy, e. g., by taking away the restraint of public crimes, it cannot be enforced. The late Mr. Fauntleroy insured his life for a certain sum at the Amicable Assurance Office in 1815. In the same year he committed a forgery. He continued to pay the annual premium on the amount insured, up to 1824, when he was apprehended on the charge of forgery. On the 29th of October, in the same year, he was declared a bankrupt, and an assignment of his property was made to the defendants. In November following, Mr. Fauntleroy was executed. It was adjudged (e), that the assignees were not entitled to recover; Lord *Lyndhurst*, C., observing, that if a party effected an insurance for life, on condition that the sum insured shall be *paid*, in case of suicide, or death by sentence of the law, such contract would be void, as being contrary to public policy, by taking away the restraint of public crimes; then if such condition were void, when expressed, on what principle could it be sustained if it had no other foundation than a mere inference?

XIV. *Insurance against Fire.*

BY this contract (f), the insurer, in consideration of a certain premium received by him, either in a gross sum, or by annual payments, undertakes to indemnify the insured against any loss or damage which he may sustain in his houses, or other buildings, goods, and merchandize, by fire, during a limited period of time. A policy of insurance against fire is a contract which is not in its nature assignable (g): it is merely a special agreement with the person insuring, that the insurer will indemnify him against such loss or damage as he may sustain. The policy, however, may, and frequently is, assigned with the consent of the insurer. In order to entitle the plaintiff to recover on a policy of insurance against

(c) *Huguenin* v. *Rayley*, 6 Taunt. 186.
(d) *Wainwright* v. *Bland*, 1 Tyrw. & Gr. 417.
(e) *Amicable Assurance Society* v. *Bolland and others*, D. P. July 9, 1830, re- versing judgment of M. R.
(f) Marsh. 681.
(g) Per Lord *King*, Ch., in *Lynch* v. *Dalzell*, 3 Bro. P. C. 497, but in Tomlin's ed. 4 Bro. P. C. 431.

fire, it must appear that the policy was duly stamped (60). The amount of the stamp duty on insurances against fire is fixed by stat. 55 Geo. III. c. 184, Schedule, Part I. By stat. 9 Geo. IV. c. 13, s. 1, that the stamp duty may not be evaded, detached buildings, or goods contained in such buildings, occasioning a plurality of risks, are to be valued and insured separately. It is necessary that the insured should have an interest or property at the time of insuring (h), and at the time the fire happens: and in case of loss, the insured can only recover to the extent of his interest, insurances against fire being within the stat. 14 Geo. III. c. 48.

The stat. 14 Geo. III. c. 78, s. 83, (Party Wall Act,) where house insured, situate within the limits of the act, is burnt down, gives any person interested a right to insist upon the insurance money being laid out in rebuilding. A. bought a house on a bad title and insured; B. recovered in ejectment, but before possession delivered, house was burnt down; B. has a right to insist on the money being laid out in rebuilding (i). The form of the policy used by the different companies is nearly the same. The principal difference consists in the articles of the printed proposals, which are incorporated by reference with the policy, and are to be considered as part of the contract (k). By the printed proposals of a fire insurance company (l), it was stipulated, "that the insured should procure a certificate of the minister, &c. of the parish, importing that they knew the character of the insured, &c.;" it was holden, that the procuring such certificate was a condition precedent to the right of the insured to recover; and that supposing the minister, &c. had wrongfully refused to grant such certificate, it would not vary the case,—the rule being, that if a person undertake for the act of a stranger, that act must be done. The policy usually provides, that "no loss or damage by fire, happening by any invasion, foreign enemy, or any military or usurped power whatsoever, will be made good by the insurer." The words "usurped power," in the proviso (m), mean an invasion from abroad, or an internal rebellion, not the power of a common mob. The Sun Fire Office, in the year 1727, introduced into the preceding exception the words

(h) Per Lord *Hardwicke*, in *The Sadlers' Company* v. *Badcock*, 2 Atk. 555. See the statute in the preceding section, p. 1030.

(i) *Pearce* v. *Watts*, B. R. Trin. 20 Geo. III., B. P. B. 97; Dampier MSS. Lincoln's Inn Library.

(k) See *Routledge* v. *Burrell*, 1 H. Bl. 254.

(l) *Worsley* v. *Wood*, 6 T. R. 710. See also *Oldman* v *Bewicke*, 2 H. Bl. 577, n. to the same effect.

(m) *Drinkwater* v. *London Assurance*, 2 Wils. 363; Wilmot, 282, *S. C.*

(60) By stat. 3 & 4 Will. IV. c. 23, insurances on farming stock were exempted from stamp duties, and the duties on certain sea insurances were reduced.

"*civil commotion*," by reason of which it was holden (n), that the office was not liable for a loss sustained by the plaintiff, whose house and distillery were set on fire by the mob during the riots in the year 1780 (61). If a person who is not a linen-draper, insures "his stock in trade, household furniture, *linen*, wearing apparel, and plate," by a policy against fire, this will not protect linen-drapery goods subsequently purchased on speculation; and the word *linen* in the policy must be confined to household linen, or linen used by way of apparel (o). A., abroad, having two warehouses, writes to this country to effect an insurance upon one of them *only*, without stating, as was the fact, that a house nearly adjoining to it had been on fire that evening, and that there was danger of the fire again breaking out; and sends his letter after the regular post time. The fire having broken out again on the day next but one following, and consumed A.'s warehouse; it was holden (p), that this was a material concealment, although A.'s letter was written without any fraudulent intention. A policy of insurance (against fire) is effected on the stock and utensils of a sugar-house, the different stories of which were heated by a chimney running up to the top. By the negligence of the plaintiff's servants, in omitting to open the register, the heat was considerably increased, by means of which large quantities of the sugar were spoiled; but no damage was occasioned to any thing but the sugar, and no greater fire existed than on ordinary occasions: it was holden (q), that this was not a loss *by fire* within the policy. In a policy of insurance against loss by fire, from half a year to half a year, the insured agreed to pay the premium half yearly, "as long as the insurers should agree to accept the same," within fifteen days after the expiration of the former half year; and it was also stipulated, that no insurance should take place until the premium was actually paid: a loss hap-

(n) *Langdale* v. *Mason*, Park, 657; Marsh. 689.

(o) *Watchorn* v. *Langford*, 3 Campb. 422.

(p) *Bufe* v. *Turner*, 6 Taunt. 338; 2

Marsh. Rep. 46, *S. C.*

(q) *Austin and another* v. *Drewe*, Holt's N. P. C. 126, C. B., *Gibbs*, C. J., and afterwards confirmed by the court, 6 Taunt. 436; 4 Campb. 360, S. P.

---

(61) The plaintiff afterwards brought his action against the hundred upon the Riot Act, 1 Geo. I. c. 5, s. 6 *, and recovered. Marsh. 791; 2nd ed, 794; *S. C.*, more fully reported, 3 Doug. 61; *S. C.*, B. P. B. 203; Dampier, MSS. L. I. L. An assurance company having paid a loss occasioned by riots, may recover back such loss in an action against the hundred, on the above act, suing in the name and with the consent of the insured. *Mason* v. *Sainsbury*, E. 22 Geo. III. B. R., Marsh. 794. Recognized in *Clarke* v. *The Inhabitants of Blithing*, 2 B. & C. 254, and in *Yates* v. *Whyte*, 4 Bingh. N. C. 272.

* Repealed by stat. 7 & 8 Geo. IV. c. 27. The present law on the subject is contained in stat. 7 & 8 Geo. IV. c. 31.

pened within fifteen days after the end of one half year, but before the premium for the next was paid : it was holden (r), that the insurers were not liable, though the insured tendered the premium before the end of the fifteen days, but after the loss. By a policy under seal, referring to certain printed proposals, a fire-office insured the defendant's premises from 11th of November, 1802, to 25th of December, 1803, for a certain premium, which was to be paid yearly on each 25th of December, and the insurance was to continue so long as the insured should pay the premium at the said times, and the office should agree to accept it. By the printed proposals it was stipulated, that the insured should make all future payments annually, at the office, within fifteen days after the day limited by the policy, upon forfeiture of the benefit thereof, and that no insurance was to take place till the premiums were paid; and by a subsequent advertisement (agreed to be taken as part of the policy), the office engaged that all persons insured there, by policies for a year or more, had been and should be considered as insured for fifteen days beyond the time of the expiration of their policies : it was holden (s), notwithstanding this latter clause, (the insured having, before the expiration of the year, had notice from the office to pay an increased premium for the year ensuing, or otherwise they would not continue the insurance, and the insured having refused to pay such advanced premium,) that the office was not liable for a loss which happened within fifteen days from the expiration of the year for which the insurance was made; though the insured, after the loss, and before the fifteen days expired, tendered the full premium which had been demanded : for the effect of the whole contract, &c. taken together, was only to give the insured an option to continue the insurance or not, during fifteen days after the expiration of the year, by paying the premium for the year ensuing, notwithstanding any intervening loss, provided the office had not, before the end of the year, determined the option, by giving notice that they would not renew the contract. In covenant against the defendants, who were members of the Sun Fire Office, a tender was pleaded and money paid into court, under the 19 Geo. II. c. 37, s. 7. It was objected, that the statute did not extend to insurances against loss by fire; but the court overruled the objection, on the ground that the statute was not necessarily confined to marine insurances ; that it ought to be construed as extensively as the mischief, and there was as much reason to have money paid into court on a fire insurance as on any other (t).

Insurance on a granary with a kiln for drying corn attached. By the 3rd condition of the policy it was stated, that the trades carried on in the insured premises should be accurately described, and if a

(r) *Tarleton* v. *Staniforth*, 5 T. R. 695. Judgment affirmed in Exch. Chr., 1 Bos. & Pul. 471.

(s) *Salvin* v. *James*, 6 East, 571.

(t) *Solomon* v. *Bewicke*, 2 Taunt. 317.

kiln or any process of fire had been used and not noticed in the policy, the policy was to be void; and by another condition, that if the risk to which the insured premises were exposed should be by any means increased, notice was to·be given to the office, and allowed by indorsement on the policy. A cargo of bark having sunk near the premises of plaintiff, who was the insurer, he allowed the bark to be dried at his kiln, *gratis;* and in consequence of the fire at the kiln during this process, which lasted three days, the premises were burnt down. In an action against the insurance office, the jury having found that drying bark was a more dangerous trade than drying corn: it was holden (*u*), first, that a user of the corn kiln for a different purpose from that intended at the time of making the policy, was not a misdescription or omission, within the meaning of the third condition; secondly, that a single user of the corn kiln as a bark kiln, gratis, was not such an alteration or increase of risk as required notice to be given to the office; thirdly, that the two conditions taken together did not amount to a warranty, that the plaintiff would not use the kiln for other purposes than drying corn; fourthly, that although the fire was occasioned by the negligence of the assured himself, he, not being guilty of fraud, might recover.

The profits of a business may be insured, *quâ* profits (*x*), but not under a general description, as "interest in the inn and offices."

(*u*) *Shaw* v. *Robberds and others*, 1 Nev. & P. 279; 6 A. & E. 75.

(*x*) *In re Wright and Pole*, 1 A. & E. 621; 3 Nev. & M. 819.

I. *Of the Nature of a Libel, and in what Cases an Action may be maintained for this Injury,* p. 1038.

II. *Of the Declaration and Pleadings,* p. 1043.

III. *Of the Evidence,* p. 1046.

I. *Of the Nature of a Libel, and in what Cases an Action may be maintained for this Injury.*

A LIBEL is a malicious defamation expressed in printing or writing, or by signs, pictures, &c., tending to injure the reputation of another, and thereby exposing such person to public hatred, contempt, or ridicule (*a*) (1). And an action on the case is maintainable against any person who falsely and maliciously publishes any libel against another. Where the natural tendency and import of the language used in the publication, is to defame and injure another, it is a libel, and actionable; for the law will presume, that the defendant, by publishing it, intended to produce that injury which it was calculated to effect. In such case, the judge ought to direct the jury, that it is a libel, and not leave it as a question to the jury to say,

(*a*) *Digby* v. *Thompson,* 4 B. & Ad. 821; 1 Nev. & M. 485.

---

(1) "If any man deliberately or maliciously publishes any thing in writing concerning another, which renders him ridiculous, or tends to hinder mankind from associating or having intercourse with him, an action lies against such publisher." Per *Wilmot,* C. J., 2 Wils. 403. "I have no doubt that the writing and publishing any thing which renders a man ridiculous, is actionable." Per *Bathurst,* J., *S. C.* See also the same opinion expressed by *Gould,* J., *S. C.*

whether the defendant *intended* (*b*) to injure the plaintiff; for every man must be presumed to intend the natural and ordinary consequences of his own act. As there is a difference between the malignity and injurious consequences of slanderous words spoken or written (*c*), the one being sudden and fleeting, the other permanent, deliberate, and disseminated with greater ease; many words, which, if spoken, would not be actionable, are actionable if published in the way of libel (2). Hence the word *swindler*, if *spoken* of another, (unless it be spoken in relation to his trade or business,) is not actionable (*d*); but if it be published in the way of libel, it is actionable (*e*). Hence, also, the publication of a letter containing some verses, in which the plaintiff was called an *itchy old toad*, was deemed a libel (*f*). So the publication of a *letter*, in which the plaintiff was stated to be one of the most infernal villains that ever disgraced human nature, has been holden actionable, without proof of special damage (*g*).

A fair and candid comment on a place of public entertainment, in a newspaper, is not a libel (*h*). So a fair, temperate, and reasonable criticism on the buildings of an architect (*i*), is not libellous, however mistaken in point of taste the opinion may be, or however unfavourable to the merits of the architect. In like manner, a comment upon a literary production, exposing its follies and errors, and holding up the author to ridicule, will not be deemed a libel, provided such comment does not exceed the limits of fair and candid

(*b*) *Haire* v. *Wilson*, 9 B. & C. 643; *Fisher* v. *Clement*, 10 B. & C. 472.
(*c*) *Austin* v. *Culpepper*, 2 Show. 314; *King* v. *Lake*, Hardr. 470. Per *Hale*, C. B.
(*d*) *Savile* v. *Jardine*, 2 H. Bl. 531.

(*e*) *J'Anson* v. *Stuart*, 1 T. R. 748.
(*f*) *Villers* v. *Monsley*, 2 Wils. 403.
(*g*) *Bell* v. *Stone*, 1 Bos. & Pul. 331.
(*h*) *Dibdin* v. *Swan*, 1 Esp. N. P. C. 28, *Kenyon*, C. J.
(*i*) *Soane* v. *Knight*, 1 M. & Malk. 74.

(2) In *Bradley* v. *Methwyn*, B. R. M. 10 G. II, MSS., which was an action on the case for a libel, Lord *Hardwicke*, C. J., observed, that "the present case is not for words, but for a libel, in which the rule is different; for some words may be actionable, or prosecuted by way of indictment, if reduced into writing, which would not be so, if spoken only. For the crime in a libel does not arise merely from the scandal, but from the tendency which it has to occasion a breach of the peace, by making the scandal more public and lasting, and spreading it abroad; which was so determined in this court, in the case of *King* v. *Griffin*, Hil. 7 Geo. II." This subject was much discussed in *Thorley* v. *E. of Kerry*, on error in Exch. Chr., 4 Taunt. 355, where a defamatory writing, imputing hypocrisy to the earl, and that he used religion as a cloak for unworthy purposes, was holden to be actionable; Sir *James Mansfield*, who delivered the judgment, observing, that he was bound by the later authorities, although the distinction between speaking and writing was not to be found in Rolle's Abridgement, or the earlier editions of Comyn's Digest: The action was a common action on the case, and not an action for scandalum magnatum.

criticism, by attacking the character of the writer, unconnected
with his publication: and a comment of this description every one
has a right to publish, although the author may suffer a loss from
it. Such a loss the law does not consider as an injury; it is a loss
which the party ought to sustain, inasmuch as it is the loss of fame
and profits to which he was not fairly entitled (*k*). But if a person,
under the pretence of criticising a literary work, defames the
private character of the author, and instead of writing in the spirit,
and for the purpose, of fair and candid discussion, travels into collateral matter, and introduces facts not stated in the work, accompanied with injurious comments upon them, such person is a libeller,
and liable to an action (*l*). So where defendant published of a
painting, publicly exhibited, that it was a mere daub, with other
strong terms of censure; it was holden (*m*), that it was a question
for the jury, whether it was a fair and temperate criticism, or only
a vehicle of personal malignity towards the plaintiff. An advertisement in a public paper, strongly reflecting upon the character
of an individual who has been declared bankrupt, is libellous (*n*),
although published with the avowed intention of convening a
meeting of the creditors for the purpose of consulting upon the
measures proper to be adopted for their own security, if the legal
object might have been attained by means less injurious.

In the celebrated case of *Stockdale* v. *Hansard* (*o*), it was holden,
that it is no defence in law to an action for publishing a libel, that
the defamatory matter is part of a document, which was, by order
of the House of Commons, laid before the House, and thereupon
became part of the proceedings of the House, and which was afterwards, by order of the House, printed and published by defendant;
and that the House of Commons heretofore resolved, declared, and
adjudged, "that the power of publishing such of its reports, votes,
and proceedings, as it shall deem necessary or conducive to the
public interest, is an essential incident to the constitutional functions of parliament, more especially to the Commons House of Parliament as the representative portion of it."   On demurrer, to a
plea suggesting such a defence, a court of law is competent to determine whether or not the House of Commons has such privilege
as will support the plea. *S. C.*

The consequences resulting from the foregoing decision belong
rather to history than to a work of this kind: it is sufficient to state,
that (as on all similar occasions) the authority of the law prevailed,
and the legislature having interposed, it was, by stat. 3 & 4 Vict.

(*k*) *Carr* v. *Hood*, 1 Campb. 355, n.,
Ellenborough, C. J.; *M'Leod* v. *Wakley*,
3 C. & P. 311.
(*l*) *Nightingale* v. *Stockdale*, London
Sittings after H. T. 49 Geo. III., *Ellenborough*, C. J.

(*m*) *Thompson* v. *Shackell*, M. & Malk.
187, *Best*, C. J. See *Green* v. *Chapman*,
4 Bingh. N. C. 92.
(*n*) *Browne* v. *Croome*, 2 Stark. N. P.
C. 297.
(*o*) 9 A. & E. 1.

c. 9, enacted, "that all proceedings, criminal or civil, against any person for the publication of any report, paper, votes, or proceedings, under the authority of either House of Parliament, shall be stayed, by bringing before the court or judge a certificate, under the hand of the chancellor, or of the Speaker of the House of Commons, to the effect that such publication is by order of either House of Parliament, together with an affidavit verifying such certificate."

A fair, plain, unvarnished account of the proceedings of a court of justice, is not a libel (p) (3), but a highly coloured account of such proceedings mixed up with insinuations of perjury (q), cannot be justified; nor can a statement of the circumstances, given as from the mouth of counsel (r), instead of being accompanied or corrected by the evidence. Nor is it lawful to publish even a correct account of the proceedings of a court of justice, or of a preliminary inquiry before a magistrate, if such account (s) contain matter of a scandalous, blasphemous, or indecent nature. A false or scandalous matter contained in a petition to a committee of Parliament (t), or in articles of the peace exhibited to justices of the peace, or in

(p) *Curry* v. *Walter*, 1 Bos. & Pul. 525; but see 1 M. & S. 279, 281.
(q) *Stiles* v. *Nokes*, 7 East, 493.
(r) *Saunders* v. *Mills*, 6 Bingh. 213.
(s) *R.* v. *Mary Carlile*, 3 B. & A. 167;

Duncan v. *Thwaites*, 3 B. & C. 556.
(t) 1 Hawk. B. 1, c. 73, s. 8; *Moulton* v. *Clapham*, B. R. E. 15 Car. I., Sir W. Jones, 431; March. 20, *S. C.*

---

(3) "It must not be taken for granted, that the publication of every matter which passes in a court of justice, however truly represented, is, under all circumstances, and with whatever motive published, justifiable; but that doctrine must be taken with grains of allowance." Per Lord *Ellenborough*, C. J., and *Grose*, J., in *Stiles* v. *Nokes*, 7 East, 503. "It often happens that circumstances necessary for the sake of public justice to be disclosed by a witness in a judicial inquiry, are very distressing to the feelings of individuals, on whom they reflect; and if such circumstances were afterwards wantonly published, I should hesitate to say, that such unnecessary publication was not libellous, merely because the matter had been given in evidence in a court of justice." Per Lord *Ellenborough*, C. J., *S. C.* "If a member of Parliament publishes in the newspapers his speech, as delivered in Parliament, and it contains charges of a slanderous nature against an individual, an information will lie for a libel; though, had the words been merely delivered in Parliament, they would be dispunishable in the courts at Westminster." *The King* v. *Ld. Abingdon*, 1 Esp. N. P. C. 226; *The King* v. *Creevey*, 1 M. & S. 273, S. P., and that the circumstance of the speech being published for the purpose of correcting a misrepresentation, will not render the author less amenable to the common law in respect of the publication. "It does not follow, that because a counsel is privileged as to what he delivers in a court of justice, a publisher may circulate his expressions in a printed paper." Per *Park*, J., *Roberts* v. *Brown*, 10 Bingh. 525; 4 M. & Sc. 407, *S. C.*

any other proceeding in a regular court of justice, will not make the complaint amount to a libel. So, fairly to comment on a petition, which has been presented to the House of Commons, is not libellous (u). Although that which is written may be injurious to the character of another (x), yet, if done *bonâ fide*, or with a view of investigating a fact, in which the party making it is interested, it is not libellous. Hence, where an advertisement was published by the defendant, at the instigation of A., the plaintiff's wife, for the purpose of ascertaining whether the plaintiff had another wife living when he married A.; it was holden, that although the advertisement might impute bigamy to the plaintiff, yet having been published under such authority, and with such a view, it was not libellous. A letter written confidentially to persons who employed A., as their solicitor (y), conveying charges injurious to his professional character in the management of certain concerns which they entrusted to him, and in which B., the writer of the letter, was likewise interested, was holden not to be a libel. So where the defendant had, *on application* for a character, stated in a written answer, that the plaintiff had, whilst in her service, conducted herself disgracefully, and that she had since been a prostitute; and a similar statement had been made by the defendant to persons who had recommended the plaintiff to her: it was holden (z), that they were privileged communications, and that the plaintiff was properly nonsuited for want of proof of malice. But where the master wrote a first letter, without a previous application, and then a second in answer to inquiries made of him as to plaintiff's character, Lord *Tenterden*, C. J., left it to the jury to say, whether the communication contained in that letter was made by the master *bonâ fide*, acting under a belief that he was discharging a duty which he owed to the party who was about to take the plaintiff into his service, or whether it was made maliciously, with an intention of doing an injury to the plaintiff; and the jury having found that the communication was maliciously made, the court (a) refused to disturb the verdict.

There is a difference between publications relating to public and private individuals. Every subject has a right to comment on those acts of public men which concern him as a subject of the realm, if he do not make his commentary a cloak for malice or slander (b).

A petition addressed by a creditor of an officer in the army to the secretary at war (c), *bonâ fide*, and with a view of obtaining, through his interference, the payment of a debt due; and contain-

---

(u) *Dunne* v. *Anderson*, Ry. & M. 287. See also 3 Bingh. 88.

(x) *Delany* v. *Jones*, 4 Esp. N. P. C. 191.

(y) *M'Dougall* v. *Claridge*, 1 Campb. 267, Lord *Ellenborough*, C. J.

(z) *Child* v. *Affleck*, 9 B. & C. 403.

(a) *Pattison* v. *Jones*, 8 B. & C. 578.

(b) Per *Parke*, B., *Parmiter* v. *Coupland*, 6 M. & W. 108.

(c) *Fairman* v. *Ives*, 5 B. & A. 642.

ing a statement of facts which, though derogatory to the officer's character, the creditor believed to be true, is not a malicious libel for which an action is maintainable. A defamatory writing (d), expressing only one or two letters of a name, in such a manner, that, from what goes before and follows after, it must necessarily be understood to signify such a particular person, in the plain, obvious, and natural construction of the whole, and would be nonsense if strained to any other meaning, is as properly a libel, as if it had expressed the whole name at large; for it brings the utmost contempt upon the law, to suffer its justice to be eluded by such trifling evasions. A justice of the peace has authority (e) to issue his warrant for the arrest of a party charged with having published a libel; and upon the neglect of the party so arrested to find sureties, may commit him to prison, there to remain until he be delivered by due course of law. Persons in partnership, as bankers, may, without showing (f) the proportion of their respective shares, join in an action for a libel against them in respect of their business. An alien friend (g), though resident abroad, is entitled to sue in the courts at Westminster, for a libel published in England.

II. *Of the Declaration and Pleadings.*

Venue.—This is a transitory action, and consequently the venue may be laid in any county. It may be stated, as a general rule, that the venue cannot be changed in this action; to this rule, however, there are the two following exceptions. 1st, Where the writing and publication are confined to the same county (h). In this case the venue may be changed into such county (i). 2d, If the libel be sent out of England in a letter, the venue may be changed into that county in which the letter was written (k).

According to the usual form of the declaration in this action, after the prefatory averments which the circumstances of the case may render necessary as inducement to the action, the plaintiff

---

(d) *Hurt's case*, Trin. 12 Ann., Hawk. Book 1, c. 73, s. 5.

(e) *Butt* v. *Conant*, 1 Brod. & Bingh. 548.

(f) *Forster and two others* v. *Lawson*, 3 Bingh. 452.

(g) *Pisani* v. *Lawson*, 6 Bingh. N. C.

90.

(h) *Pinkney* v. *Collins*, 1 T. R. 571.

(i) *Freeman* v. *Norris*, 3 T. R. 306; *Earl of Kerry* v. *Thorley*, B. R. M. 49 Geo. III., MS., S. P.

(k) *Metcalf* v. *Markham*, 3 T. R. 652.

states, " that the defendant falsely and maliciously wrote and *published* (4) of and concerning (5) the plaintiff a false, &c. libel, which libel is according to the tenor and effect following:" the libel is then set forth *in hæc verba*, accompanied, however, with the necessary innuendos, in order to illustrate and explain the tendency and bearing of the libel, and to give it its force and application ; and in this part of the declaration care must be taken, that the libel be so set forth as to agree with that produced in evidence. Where the libellous meaning is apparent on the face of the libel, innuendoes are unnecessary ; but though they be unnecessarily introduced, and be unsupported by prefatory averments, they do not vitiate the declaration (*l*). The words of the libel ought to be stated on the record, in order that the defendant may, if he thinks fit, demur, and bring before the court the question whether they amount to a libel. Hence it is not sufficient to declare that the defendant published a libel concerning the plaintiff in his trade, purporting that his beer was of bad quality, and sold by deficient measure ; the libel itself ought to be set out. And such declaration is bad on general demurrer (*m*). Neither is it sufficient to state that the libel contains in *substance* (*n*) the matters following. If the libel be written in a foreign language, the original should first be set forth in the declaration, and then the translation (*o*). The declaration concludes with the damage, either general, which the law supposes to have been sustained, or special, which the party has actually sustained, in consequence of the publication of the libel.

Of the Pleadings.

Money cannot be paid into court in an action for libel. See stat. 3 & 4 Will. IV. c. 42, s. 21. The defendant may plead the gene-

(*l*) 2 Starkie on Libel, Appendix, cites *Archbishop of Tuam* v. *Robeson*, 5 Bingh. 17.

(*m*) *Wood* v. *Brown*, 6 Taunt. 169.

(*n*) *Wright* v. *Clements*. In arrest of judgment, 3 B. & A. 503.

(*o*) *Zenobio* v. *Axtell*, 6 T. R. 162.

(4) Although the *publication* of the libel must be stated in the declaration, yet it will be sufficient to state such matter as amounts to a publication, without using the formal word *published*. *Baldwin* v. *Elphinston*, 2 Bl. R. 1037. See a comment on this case in *Watts* v. *Fraser*, 7 A. & E. 233.

(5) Judgment was arrested after verdict, because it was not laid that the libel was " of or concerning plaintiff," in *Lowfield* v. *Bancroft and another*, Str. 934, and in *R.* v. *Marsden*, 4 M. & S. 164. See also *Clement* v. *Fisher*, 7 B. & C. 459.

ral issue, not guilty, which under the new rule H. T. 4 Will. IV. operates as a denial only of the breach of duty or wrongful act alleged to have been committed by the defendant, and not of the facts stated in the inducement, and no other defence than such denial is admissible under that plea : all other pleas in denial must take issue on some particular matter of fact alleged in the declaration. If the supposed libel amounts only to what is termed a privileged communication, this is a defence which may be set up under the plea of not guilty (p), notwithstanding the foregoing rule. The proper meaning of a privileged communication is this,—that the occasion on which the communication was made, rebuts the inference *primâ facie* arising from a statement prejudicial to the character of the plaintiff, and puts it upon him to prove that there was malice in fact ; that the defendant was actuated by motives of personal spite or ill will, independent of the occasion on which the communication was made (q).

If the matter of the libel be true, the defendant may plead it in justification ; but in such justification, if there be any thing specific in the subject, issuable facts ought to be stated, and not general charges of misconduct ; for where a libel charged an attorney with gross negligence, falsehood, prevarication, and excessive bills of costs in the business which he had conducted for the defendant ; it was holden (r), that a plea in justification repeating the same general charges, without specifying the particular acts of misconduct, was bad, upon demurrer ; and that it was incumbent on the defendant, who must be taken to know the particular acts of misconduct, to disclose them. And if the plea professes to justify the whole libel, but in effect justifies a part only, it will be bad : as where the libel charged the defendant with having stolen cloth and velvet, and the plea justified the accusation only as to taking the velvet, it was holden (s) ill ; so where the libel charged that plaintiff, a proctor, had been suspended three times, twice by Sir John Nicholl, and once by Lord Stowell, whereby his neighbours had been led to think he was guilty of extortion ; and the plea, professing to answer the whole, justified only one of the suspensions, *viz.* one by Sir John Nicholl, and omitted the other two specific charges, it was holden (t) bad. It is sufficient, however, if the charge on the plaintiff's conduct in the libel is substantially met and answered in the justification (u). It is unnecessary to repeat every word which might have been the subject of the original comment. So much must be justified as meets the sting of the charge ; but if any thing be contained in a charge, which does not add to the sting of it (x),

(p) *Lillie* v. *Price*, 1 Nev. & P. 16 ; 5 A. & E. 645.

(q) Per *Parke*, B., *Wright* v. *Woodgate*, 2 Cr. M. & R. 577 ; 1 Tyr. & Gr. 12, *S. C.*

(r) *Holmes, Gent. one, &c.* v. *Catesby*,

1 Taunt. 543.

(s) *Johns* v. *Gittings*, Cro. Eliz. 239.
(t) *Clarkson* v. *Lawson*, 6 Bingh. 266.
(u) *Edwards* v. *Bell*, 1 Bingh. 403.
(x) *Ib.*

that need not be justified. It is not any bar to the action, that the plaintiff has been in the habit of libelling the defendant (*y*); although it may operate in mitigation of the damages. It is not sufficient to plead that the defendant received the libellous statement from another, and that, upon publication, he disclosed the author's name (*z*). Where the libel tended to make a man ridiculous, it was holden to be no defence (*a*), that he himself told the same story to a party of friends.

Where the defendant pleaded a justification only, without the general issue, he was formerly (*b*) entitled to begin. But, according to *Tindal*, C. J., in *Carter* v *Jones*, Sittings after Trin. T. 3 Will. IV., 1 Moody & Rob. 281, " a resolution has recently been come to by all the judges, that in cases of slander, libel, and other actions, where the plaintiff seeks to recover actual damages, of an unascertained amount, he is entitled to begin, although the affirmative of the issue may, in point of form, be with the defendant."

It seems, that where the allegations in a libel are divisible, one part may be justified separately from the rest, if a proper justification can be made out (*c*). But where the declaration stated, that the defendant published a libel with intent to cause it to be believed, that the plaintiff had been guilty of feloniously stealing a horse ; and the justification only stated, that the plaintiff was on certain grounds suspected of stealing it; it was holden (*d*), on demurrer, to be insufficient.

To this action the defendant may plead the statute of limitations (*e*), that is, " that the cause of action did not accrue at any time within six years next before the commencement of the plaintiff's action."

III. *Of the Evidence.*

The libel must be produced, and before it is read, it must be proved that it was *published* by the defendant. The mode of publication may be proved, in order to enhance the damages. The mere parting with a libel, with such an intent, whereby a defendant loses all power of future control over it, is an uttering, which seems to be the meaning of the word *publishing*, without an actual com-

(*y*) *Finnerty* v. *Tipper*, 2 Campb. 76.
(*z*) *De Crespigny* v. *Wellesley*, 5 Bingh. 392.
(*a*) *Cook* v. *Ward*, 6 Bingh. 409.
(*b*) *Cooper* v. *Wakley*, Moody & M. 248, *Tenterden*, C. J.; *Scarth* v. *Gardiner*, R. R., Middlesex Sittings after M.

T. 2 Will. IV., *Tenterden*, C. J., MSS., S. P.
(*c*) See opinion of *Tenterden*, C. J., in following case.
(*d*) *Mountney* v. *Watton*, 2 B. & Ad. 673.
(*e*) 21 Jac. I. c. 16.

munication of the contents of the paper (*f*). If it be proved, that the libel was bought in the shop of a bookseller (*g*), of a person acting in the shop as the servant of the bookseller, this will be *primâ facie* evidence of a publication by the bookseller, inasmuch as he has the profits of the shop, and is therefore answerable for the consequences. Where a publication is defamatory, the law infers malice (*h*), unless any thing can be drawn from the circumstances attending the publication to rebut that inference. If the libel be in a foreign language, in which case, as it has already been observed, the libel must be set forth in the declaration, both in the original language and in the English translation, further proof will be necessary (6).

Where a libellous paragraph, as proved, contained two references, by which it appeared to be in fact the language of a third person speaking of the plaintiff's conduct, and the declaration in setting it out had omitted those references; it was holden (*i*), that these omissions altered the sense of the remainder, and the variance was fatal. In an action for a libel (*k*), after the libel, on which the action was brought, had been read, the plaintiff's counsel offered in evidence other libels written by the defendant. This having been objected to, on the ground that the plaintiff could not give in evidence any thing which would of itself constitute a ground for a distinct action; Lord *Kenyon*, C. J., said, he thought that the evidence was admissible, and compared it to actions for slander, in which, evidence of other words, besides those stated in the declaration, was usually received [to show the malice of the defendant] (7).

(*f*) *R.* v. *Burdett*, 4 B. & A. 135.
(*g*) *R.* v. *Almon*, 5 Burr. 2686.
(*h*) Per *Le Blanc*, J., in *R.* v. *Creevey*, 1 M. & S. 273.
(*i*) *Cartwright* v. *Wright*, 5 B. & A. 615.
(*k*) *Lee* v. *Huson*, Peake's N. P. C. 166.

---

(6) In the case of *R.* v. *Peltier*, which was an information against defendant for a libel on Napoleon Bonaparte, the evidence on the part of the prosecution was as follows:—A witness proved, that he had purchased several copies of the book, containing the libel in question, of a certain bookseller, which copies he had marked at the time. 2. The bookseller proved that defendant was the publisher of the book, and employed him to dispose of the copies on his account, and that he had accounted for them. 3. *An interpreter was then called, who swore that he understood the French language, and that the translation was correct. The interpreter then read the whole of that which was charged to be a libel in the original, and then the translation was read by the clerk at Nisi Prius.*

(7) *Charlter* v. *Barret*, Peake's N. P. C. 22. So in *Rustel* v. *Macquister*, Middlesex Sittings after H. T. 1807, 1 Campb. 49, n., the plaintiff, having proved the words laid in the declaration, offered evidence of other actionable words spoken by the defendant afterwards; this being

In an action on the case for publishing a libel against the defendant in a paper entitled the "Weekly Political Register" (*l*), a witness was called, who proved that he had purchased one of the papers containing the libel in question *before* the action was brought; he was then proceeding to prove that he had purchased another copy of the same paper *after* the action was brought. This was objected to, on the part of the defendant, on the ground that the publication of the last-mentioned copy might become the subject of a future action, and, therefore, that it ought not to be given in evidence to increase the damages in this action. But Lord *Ellenborough*, C. J., was of opinion, that although it was not admissible for the purpose of aggravating the damages, yet it was evidence to show that the paper was circulated deliberately. But in *Finnerty* v. *Tipper* (*m*), Sir *J. Mansfield* ruled, that the plaintiff could not give in evidence other subsequent libels published concerning him by the defendant, unless they directly referred to the libel set forth in the declaration. And in *Stuart* v. *Lovell*, 2 Stark. 93, Lord *Ellenborough*, C. J., held, that the plaintiff could not give in evidence subsequent publications by the defendant, where the intention of the publication in question was not equivocal.

Under the plea of not guilty, the plaintiff cannot adduce evidence to show that the allegations in the libel are false (*n*). But in an action for a libel purporting to be a report of a coroner's inquest, evidence of the correctness of the report is admissible under the

---

(*l*) *Plunkett* v. *Cobbett*, before Lord *Ellenborough*, Middlesex Sittings, 26th May, 1804, MSS.

(*m*) 2 Campb. 72, confirmed in *Wak-ley* v. *Johnson*, Ry. & M. 422. See also *May* v. *Brown*, 3 B. & C. 113 ; and *Tarpley* v. *Blabey*, 2 Bingh. N. C. 437.

(*n*) *Stuart* v. *Lovell*, 2 Stark. 93.

---

objected to on the ground that these latter words might become the subject of a future action, Lord *Ellenborough* overruled the objection, observing, that evidence might be given of any words as well as any act of the defendants to show *quo animo* he spoke the words which were the subject of the action. Still, however, it would be the duty of the judge to tell the jury, that they must give damages for those words only, which were the subject of the action. So per Sir *J. Mansfield*, in *Finnerty* v. *Tipper*, 2 Campb. 76. " In actions for words, it has been allowed to give evidence of words subsequently spoken, for the purpose of showing that the original words were spoken maliciously and to injure:" but see *Mead* v. *Daubigny*, Peake's N. P. C. 125, where, in an action for slander, Lord *Kenyon*, C. J., confined this doctrine to words not actionable in themselves; admitting, however, that such words might be given in evidence, although it appeared they were not spoken to the same person, to whom the slander was alleged in the declaration to have been spoken. N. This distinction was exploded by Lord *Ellenborough*, in the preceding case of *Rustel* v. *Macquister*, who observed, that it was not founded upon any principle.

general issue in mitigation of damages (o); but evidence of the truth or falsehood of the facts stated at the inquest is not admissible on either side.

Where a libel contains matters imputing to another a crime capable of being tried, evidence cannot be received at the trial of the truth of those imputations. Where, therefore, the libel contained imputations that certain persons at M. had been guilty of murder; the court held (p), that the judge, at the trial, properly refused evidence of the truth of the transactions stated in the libel to have taken place at M.

General evidence, that the plaintiff has been in the habit of libelling the defendant (q), is inadmissible. The defendant cannot be allowed (r) to do more than prove the publication, by the plaintiff, of libels which are connected with the libel which is the subject of the action; and clearly applicable to the defendant's (s) libel. Where the object of the evidence is to show that the defendant was provoked by libels published against him, it is essential that some proof should be given of the libels having come to the defendant's knowledge (t).

It is not competent to a defendant charged with having published a libel, to prove that a paper similar to that for the publication of which he is prosecuted, was published on a former occasion by other persons, who have never been prosecuted for it (u). Proof that the libel was contained in a letter (x) directed to the plaintiff, and delivered into the plaintiff's hands, is not sufficient proof of publication to maintain *an action* (8). The writing and publication (y) must be proved. Proof that the defendant accounted (z) for the

---

(o) *East* v. *Chapman*, 1 M. & Malk. 46, *Tenterden*, C. J.

(p) *R.* v. *Burdett*, 4 B. & A. 145.

(q) *Wakley* v. *Johnson*, Ry. & Moo. 422, *Best*, C. J.

(r) 2 Stark. on Libel, p. 100, cites *May* v. *Brown*, 3 B. & C. 113.

(s) *Tarpley* v. *Blabey*, 2 Bingh. N. C. 437. See *Watts* v. *Fraser*, 1 M. & Rob. 449.

(t) By the court, *Watts* v. *Fraser*, 7 A. & E. 232.

(u) *R.* v. *Holt*, 5 T. R. 436.

(x) *Phillips* v. *Jansen*, 2 Esp. N. P. C. 625, per *Kenyon*, C. J., S. P., admitted by *Chambre*, J., in *R.* v. *Hornbrook*, Devon Summ. Ass. 1812, MS.

(y) 1 Moore, (C. P.) 477.

(z) *Cook* v. *Ward*, 6 Bingh. 409.

---

(8) The same point was admitted in *Hicks's* case, in the Star Chamber, Hob. 215. But an indictment or information may be sustained in this case, because such letter, being a provocation to a challenge and breach of peace, is considered as a misdemeanour. Per *Chambre*, J., in *R.* v. *Hornbrook*, Devon Summer Assizes, 1812, who there said, " It is not necessary to constitute a publication in a criminal prosecution, to show that it has been published to the world. It is sufficient if it is sent to the party libelled, its criminality depending upon its tendency to provoke the party libelled to a breach of the peace."

stamp duties of the newspaper in which the libel was contained, has been holden to be proof of publication. But see new statute, *infra*. In an action for a libel, contained in a letter written by the defendant's daughter, who usually wrote his letters of business, but there not being any evidence given to show that she was authorized or instructed by him to write the letter in question, or that he had recognized it; it was holden (a), that there was not any evidence to go to a jury against the defendant, inasmuch as it was not an act within the scope of the daughter's authority. There having been in a libellous letter a reference to a newspaper (b), as the authority upon which the libel was founded; it was holden, that the newspaper referred to might be given in evidence on the general issue, in mitigation of damages. Defendant may have the whole of the publication read from which the passages charged are extracts (c); so the defendant has a right to have read, *as part of the plaintiff's case* (d), another part of the same newspaper referred to in the libel complained of. Plaintiff declared as proprietor and editor of a newspaper (e); it was proved, that plaintiff was proprietor, but that his *servant* was editor; this was holden to be a fatal variance.

The proceedings against the printers, publishers, and proprietors of newspapers, either civilly or criminally (9), for any libel contained in such paper, are much facilitated by stat. 6 & 7 Will. IV. c. 76, by which it is enacted (f), that no person shall print or publish any newspaper before there shall be delivered at the Stamp Office, or to proper officers, a declaration in writing, containing, 1. The correct title of the newspaper. 2. A true description of the houses or buildings wherein such newspaper is intended to be printed and published. 3. The true name, addition, and place of abode of the printer and publisher, and of every person resident out of the United Kingdom who shall be proprietor thereof; and also, of every proprietor resident in the United Kingdom, if not exceeding two, exclusive of printer and publisher; if they do, then of such two proprietors, the amount of whose respective proportional shares in the property shall not be less than the proportional share of any other proprietor resident in the United Kingdom, exclusive of printer and publisher, specifying the amount of their shares. This declaration is to be signed by printer, publisher, and the named proprietors resident in

(a) *Harding* v. *Greening*, 1 Moore, (C. P.) 477; 8 Taunt. 42, *S. C.*

(b) *Mullett* v. *Hulton*, 4 Esp. N. P. C. 248, *Ellenborough*, C. J.

(c) *Cooke* v. *Hughes*, Ry. & Moo. 112.

(d) *Thornton* v. *Stephen*, 2 Moody &

Rob. 45, *Denman*, C. J., on reference to *R.* v. *Lambert and Perry*, 2 Campb. 398.

(e) *Heriot* v. *Stuart*, 1 Esp. N. P. C. 437.

(f) Sect. 6.

(9) The proprietor of a newspaper is answerable criminally, as well as civilly, for the acts of his servants, in the publication of a libel, although it can be shown, that such publication was without the privity of the proprietor. *R.* v. *Walter*, 3 Esp. N. P. C. 21.

the United Kingdom. The act then directs when fresh declarations shall be made, and before whom the declarations are to be made, and imposes a penalty if the declaration be false or defective. By sect. 8, such declarations are to be filed, and certified copies thereof shall be admitted in all proceedings civil and criminal (*g*), and upon every occasion, touching any newspaper mentioned in such declaration, or touching any publication, matter, or thing contained in such newspaper, as conclusive evidence of the truth of all such matters set forth in such declaration, as are required by the act to be therein set forth, &c.; and after production of the declaration, and of a newspaper corresponding in every respect with the description of it in the declaration, it will not be necessary to prove the purchase of the newspaper.

In an action against the publisher of a newspaper, one of the proprietors not sued is a competent witness for the defendant, as he is not liable to contribution (*h*) : this being an action of tort.

It was observed in the preceding section, that where the defendant contends that the libel is true, he must justify on record; but in one case (*i*), where the *facts* to be proved on the part of the defendant did not constitute a complete justification; as where they showed a ground of suspicion not amounting to actual proof of the plaintiff's guilt; it was holden by *Eyre*, C. J., that such *facts* might be given in evidence, on the general issue, in mitigation of damages. This doctrine, however, to the extent here laid down, seems questionable (10). Where the justification avers the truth of the facts,

(*g*) See *R*. v. *Woolmer*, 4 P. & D. 137. (*i*) *Knobel* v. *Fuller*, Peake's Ev. 287,
(*h*) *Moscati* v. *Lawson*, 7 C. & P. 35, ed. 2 ; Peake's Add. Cases, 139, *S. C.*
Alderson, B.

(10) In *Sir John Eamer* v. *Merle*, before Lord *Ellenborough*, which was an action for words of insolvency, the defendant was permitted to prove that at the time there were *rumours* in circulation that the plaintiff's acceptances were dishonoured. And in a case before *Le Blanc*, J., at Worcester, that learned judge received evidence under the general issue, that the plaintiff had been guilty of attempts to commit the crime, which the defendant had imputed to him. 2 Campb. 253, 254. So in the case of the *E. of Leicester* v. *Walter*, 2 Campb. 251, the defendant was permitted to prove, under the general issue, in mitigation of damages, that before and at the time of the publication of the libel, the plaintiff was generally suspected to be guilty of the crime thereby imputed to him, and that on account of this suspicion, his relations and acquaintances had ceased to associate with him. And in *Wyatt* v. *Gore*, Holt's N. P. C. 299, *Gibbs*, C. J., permitted the defendant, under the general issue, to prove that the substance of the libel charged in the declaration had been previously published in a newspaper; and held, that it was not necessary to lay a basis for this evidence by producing the newspaper. In ——— v. *Moor*, in an action of slander imputing a specific charge of unna-

which form the ingredients of the libel, each and every of the facts
so alleged to be true, must be distinctly proved (*k*), in order to entitle the defendant to a verdict on the justification.

An executor (*l*) may, under the stat. 17 Car. II. c. 8. s. 1, enter
up judgment on a verdict obtained by his testator in an action for a
libel.

Doubts having arisen, whether, on the trial of an indictment or
information for a libel, upon the plea of not guilty, it was competent
to the jury to give their verdict upon the whole matter in issue, it
was by stat. 32 Geo. III. c. 60, enacted and *declared*, that the jury
may give a general verdict of guilty or not guilty upon the whole
matter put in issue, and shall not be required or directed by the
court to find the defendant guilty, merely on the proof of the publication, and of the sense ascribed to the same in the indictment or
information: provided (*m*), that the court shall give their opinion
and direction to the jury on the matter in issue, as in other criminal
cases; and provided also (*n*), that the jury may, in their discretion,
find a special verdict, and also (*o*), that the defendants, if found
guilty, may move in arrest of judgment as before the passing this
act. The foregoing statute does not affect civil cases, but is confined to criminal (*p*).

It has been the course for a long time for a judge, in cases of libel,
as in other cases of a criminal nature, first to give a legal definition
of the offence, and then to leave it to the jury to say, whether the
facts necessary to constitute that offence are proved to their satisfaction; and that, whether the libel is the subject of a criminal

(*k*) *Weaver* v. *Lloyd*, 2 B. & C. 678.   (*n*) Sect. 3.
(*l*) *Palmer* v. *Cohen*, 2 B. & Ad. 966.   (*o*) Sect. 4.
(*m*) Sect. 2.   (*p*) *Levi* v. *Milne*, 4 Bingh. 195.

---

tural practices to plaintiff, where the declaration contained the usual allegation of good fame, &c., it was holden, that the witness who proved
the words might be asked, upon cross-examination, whether he had not
heard reports in the neighbourhood, that the plaintiff had been guilty of
similar practices, in order to diminish the damages. See 1 M. & S.
284. But although general reports have been admitted in mitigation of
damages, under the general issue, specific facts are not so admissible. *Mills*
v. *Spencer*, Holt's N. P. C. 535, *Gibbs*, C. J. See also *Waithman* v.
Weaver, 1 D. & R. 10, and Starkie's Law of Slander and Libel, vol. ii.
p. 80, n., 2nd edition, where this subject is fully discussed. In *Saunders*
v. *Mills*, 6 Bingh. 213, the defendant, (the editor of a newspaper,) was
permitted, under the general issue, in mitigation of damages, to show that
he copied the libellous paragraph from another newspaper, but was not
allowed to show that it had appeared concurrently in several other newspapers. See *East* v. *Chapman*, *ante*, p. 1049; *May* v. *Brown*, 3 B. &
C. 113; *Watts* v. *Fraser*, 7 C. & P. 369.

prosecution, or civil action. The judge is not bound to state to the jury, as matter of law, whether the publication complained of, be a libel or not. Mr. Fox's Libel Bill was a declaratory act, and put prosecutions for libel on the same footing as other criminal cases (*q*).

The reader who is desirous of investigating the law of libel and slander as applied in Scotland, is referred to a very learned and ingenious work published at Edinburgh, by John Borthwick, Esq., advocate. It is worthy of consideration, whether a portion of that law might not be introduced with effect into our system.

(*q*) Per *Parke*, B., *Parmiter* v. *Coup-land*, 6 M. & W. 108, recognized in *Baylis* v. *Lawrence*, 3 P. & D. 526.

CHAPTER XXVII.

MALICIOUS PROSECUTION.

I. *Of the Action on the Case for a Malicious Prosecution, and in what Cases such Action may be maintained,* p. 1054.

II. *Of the Declaration,* p. 1062; *Defence,* p. 1063; *Evidence,* p. 1064.

I. *Of the Action on the Case for a Malicious Prosecution, and in what Cases such Action may be maintained.*

AN action on the case lies against any person who maliciously, and without probable cause, prosecutes another, whereby the party prosecuted sustains an injury, either in person, property, or reputation. The action on the case for a malicious prosecution bears a strong analogy to the old, and now obsolete, action for a conspiracy; hence, it is frequently termed an action on the case in the nature of a conspiracy (a). But the grounds of the old action for conspiracy are narrow and confined, when compared with those on which the action on the case for a malicious prosecution is founded. The action for a conspiracy, having been framed according to the precise terms of a writ in the register, whose limits it does not presume to transgress, lies only in cases where two or more persons maliciously conspire to indict any person falsely of treason or felony (b), who is afterwards *lawfully* acquitted. The action on the case for a malicious prosecution varies its form as the circumstances of each particular grievance may require. Whatever engines of the law malice may employ to compass its evil designs against innocent and unoffending persons, whether in the shape of indictment or informa-

---

(a) *Marsh* v. *Vauhan and another,* Cro. Eliz. 701; *Mills* v. *Mills,* Cro. Car. 239.

(b) See the opinions of *Holt,* C. J., and *Treby,* C. J., that a conspiracy lies only for procuring another to be indicted for *treason* or *felony,* where life was in danger. Ld. Raym. 379.

tion (c), which charge a party with crimes injurious to his fame and reputation, and tend to deprive him of his liberty; or whether such malice is evinced by malicious arrests, or by exhibiting groundless accusations, merely with a view to occasion expense (d) to the party, who is under the necessity of defending himself against them, this action on the case affords an adequate remedy to the party injured. It may be brought against one only (e); and where it is brought against two or more defendants, although a conspiracy be alleged in the declaration, and a verdict be found for all the defendants except one, yet the plaintiff will be entitled to judgment (f). On the contrary, the action for a conspiracy must be brought against two persons at the least (g), because the gist of the action is the conspiracy; and if one only be found guilty (h), or if all except one are discharged by matter of law (i), the action fails. And to maintain an action for a conspiracy, the party indicted must have been acquitted upon a good indictment (k), by verdict, for such is the language of the writ, " *legitimo modo acquietatus,*" or "lawfully acquitted;" which imports such an acquittal of the crime charged as will entitle the party to plead *auter foits acquit*, in case he be afterwards prosecuted for the same crime (l). But in an action on the case for a malicious prosecution, it is not necessary that the plaintiff should allege or prove such an acquittal; for it may be brought under circumstances which preclude the possibility of such an acquittal: as, 1st, where a bill of indictment has been preferred, and returned ignoramus (m). 2ndly, where the indictment has been preferred *coram non judice* (n). And lastly, where a party has been acquitted on a defect in the indictment (o). Formerly, indeed, it was supposed, that an acquittal on the ground of the insufficiency of the indictment was a material objection, where the subject matter of the indictment did not affect the reputation of the party accused, and he had not been imprisoned, because scandal and imprisonment were at that time considered as the only kinds of damage for which this action would lie. But it having been decided, in the case of *Savile* v. *Roberts* (p), that the *expense* incurred by a groundless prosecution, without scandal or imprisonment of the party accused, was sufficient to support this action where the indictment was good, *quoad* the damage; it was shortly afterwards holden, in a case (q) where the subject matter of

(c) *Moore* v. *Shutter*, 2 Show. 295.
(d) *Jones* v. *Gwynn*, Gilb. R. 185; 10 Mod. 148, 214.
(e) *Mills* v. *Mills*, Cro. Car. 239.
(f) *Price* v. *Crofts*, Sir T. Raym. 180; *Pollard* v. *Evans and others*, 2 Show. 50. See also *Subley* v. *Mott*, 1 Wils. 210.
(g) F. N. B. 260, 4to ed. 1755.
(h) 28 Ass. 12, cited in F. N. B. 260.
(i) *Ib. in nota.*
(k) Bro. Conspiracie, pl. 23.

(l) Gilb. 199.
(m) *Payn* v. *Porter*, Cro. Jac. 490; Agr. 2 Roll. R. 188.
(n) 1 Roll. Abr. 112, pl. 9.
(o) *Jones* v. *Gwynn*, Gilb. 185; *Wicks* v. *Fentham*, 4 T. R. 247.
(p) Salk. 13; Carth. 416; Ld. Raym. 374, *S. C.*
(q) *Jones* v. *Gwynn*, Gilb. 185; 10 Mod. 148, 214.

the indictment did not affect the reputation of the plaintiff, and where the only damage which the plaintiff had sustained, was the expense attending the prosecution, that this action might be maintained, although the plaintiff had been prosecuted on an insufficient indictment. The decision of *Savile* v. *Roberts* has been confirmed by the case of *Smith* v. *Hixon*, Str. 977, more fully reported in Ca. Temp. Hardw. 54, where it was adjudged, that a husband alone might maintain an action for the malicious prosecution of his wife, the *expenses* of which had been defrayed by the husband. The case of *Jones* v. *Gwynn* was recognized in *Chambers* v. *Robinson*, Str. 691, and in *Wicks* v. *Fentham*, 4 T. R. 247, where it was holden, that this action would lie, although plaintiff had been acquitted on a defect in the indictment, the subject matter of which did not affect his reputation. See also *Pippett* v. *Hearn*, 5 B. & A. 634, where it was holden, that an action would lie for the malicious prosecution of a bad indictment for perjury.

The grounds of the action for a malicious prosecution are, the malice of the defendant, either express (1) or implied (r) ; want of

(r) *Purcell* v. *Macnamara*, 9 East, 361.

---

(1) If the indictment be found by the grand jury, the plaintiff must prove express malice, per *Holt*, C. J., Lord Raym. 381, unless the facts lie within the knowledge of the defendant. *Parroll* v. *Fishwick*, Bull. N. P. 14, cited by *Park*, J., in *Willans* v. *Taylor*, 6 Bingh. 189 ; but in a fuller note of this case, 9 East, 362, n. (b), it appears that this position is hardly warranted. The case was this: in an action for maliciously indicting the plaintiff for perjury, where the indictment was found, and the plaintiff acquitted by verdict, Lord *Mansfield*, in summing up, said it was not necessary to prove express malice, for *if it appeared* that there was *no probable cause*, that was sufficient to prove an *implied* malice, which was all that was necessary to be proved to support this action. For in this case all the facts lay in the defendant's own knowledge, and if there were the least foundation for the prosecution, it was in his power, and incumbent on him, to prove it. Verdict for plaintiff, £50 damages. N. The indictment was for perjury committed on the trial of an action for use and occupation, brought by the defendant against the plaintiff's master. "Where a person is acquitted by a jury, malice need not be proved at first, on the part of the plaintiff, but it is incumbent on the defendant to show, on the other side, that there was a probable cause; but where the indictment is quashed, it is necessary for the plaintiff to prove express malice." Per *Burnett*, J., in *Hunter* v. *French*, Willes, 520. In *Lilwal* v. *Smallman*, Hereford Summer Assizes, 1753, MSS., which was an action for maliciously indicting plaintiff for stealing a shovel, value 11d.; it was objected, that express malice had not been proved. *Foster*, J., overruled the objection, observing, that where the indictment is for felony, there the evidence of malice shall be left to the jury, and the defendant shall not object that express malice is not proved. But in

probable cause (s); and an injury sustained by the plaintiff, by reason of the malicious prosecution, either in his person by imprisonment, his reputation by the scandal, or in his property by the expense. If the plaintiff cannot prove any such injury, he cannot maintain the action (t). It lies on the plaintiff to give *primâ facie* evidence (u) of want of probable cause; but slight evidence (x) is sufficient to throw the onus on the defendant of showing that there was probable cause.

In *Incledon* v. *Berry*, Devonshire Summer Ass. 1805, 1 Campb. 203, n. (a), recognized by *Dallas*, C. J., in *Turner* v. *Turner*, Gow's N. P. C. 20, in an action for maliciously indicting plaintiff for perjury, Lens, Serjt., for the plaintiff, having proved express malice, contended, that it was not necessary for him to proceed any further, and that it lay on the defendant to show probable cause for having instituted the prosecution; but *Le Blanc*, J., ruled, that some evidence (though slight evidence would be sufficient) must be given *on the part of the plaintiff* of want of probable cause, before the defendant could be called upon for his defence. In *Wallis* v. *Alpine*, 1 Campb. 204, n., Lord *Ellenborough*, C. J., held, that plaintiff was not excused from giving evidence of want of probable cause, from the circumstance of defendant, who had commenced a prosecution, having neglected to prefer a bill of indictment.

" The *essential* ground of this action is, that a legal prosecution was carried on *without probable cause*. We say this emphatically, because every other allegation may be implied from this; but this must be substantively proved, and cannot be implied. From the want of probable cause, malice may be, and most commonly is, implied. The knowledge of the defendant is also implied. A man, from a malicious motive, may take up a prosecution for real guilt, or he may, from circumstances which he really believes, proceed

---

(s) *Farmer* v. *Darling*, 4 Burr. 1971. affirmed on error, B. R., 2 B. & Ad. 845.
(t) *Byne* v. *Moore*, 5 Taunt. 187. (x) *Cotton* v. *James*, 1 B. & Ad. 128.
(u) *Willans* v. *Taylor*, 6 Bingh. 183;

---

indictments for misdemeanours, it was for some time a question whether an action would lie; but it was determined, at last, an action would lie, but in such action evidence of express malice must be given. In action for malicious prosecution, if the indictment was not found, that circumstance shows *primâ facie* that there was no probable cause, and consequently that there was malice, until it be disproved. If the indictment was found, it throws the proof of want of probable cause and of malice on plaintiff; but in that case, if want of probable cause be fully proved, that is evidence to a jury of malice, without showing express declarations, or other circumstances of malice. *Hilditch* v. *Eyles*, C. B., London Sittings, H. 29 Geo. III., coram *Wilson*, J., confirmed by the court, on motion for new trial. Holroyd's MSS. See *Dubois* v. *Keats*, 11 A. & E. 329.

from apparent guilt; and in neither case is he liable to this kind of action (y). "The question of probable cause is a mixed proposition of law and fact. Whether the circumstances alleged to show it probable or not probable are true, and existed, is a matter of fact: but whether, supposing them true, they amount to a probable cause, is a question of law" (z). "The question of probable cause, arising upon the facts proved or admitted, is a question for the court, and in general the plaintiff must give some evidence showing the absence of probable cause. But such evidence is, in effect, the evidence of a negative; and very slight evidence of a negative is sufficient to call upon the other party to prove the affirmative, especially where the nature of the affirmation is such as to admit of proof by witnesses, and cannot depend upon matters lying exclusively within the party's own knowledge, as in some cases of criminal prosecution it may do" (a). "It is difficult to lay down any general rule as to the cases where the opinion of a jury should or should not be taken. I have considered the correct rule to be this: if there be any fact in dispute between the parties, the judge should leave that to the jury, telling them, if they should find in one way as to that fact, then, in his opinion, there was no probable cause, and their verdict should be for the plaintiff; if they should find in the other, then there was, and their verdict should be for the defendant" (b).

By analogy to the action for a malicious prosecution (c), the law in modern times has permitted an action to be maintained for maliciously arresting or holding a party to bail, either where there is not any debt due, or where the party is held to bail for a larger sum than is really due. As in the analogous action for a malicious prosecution, it must appear that the prosecution is determined (d); so in the action for a malicious arrest, it must be stated in the declaration, that the first action has been determined. This allegation must also be proved (e); and it is not sufficient for this purpose to put in a judge's order to stay proceedings on payment of costs, and to prove that the costs were paid accordingly (f). But proof that no declaration was filed or delivered within a year after the return of the writ is sufficient (g) to show a determination of the suit.

(y) *Johnstone* v. *Sutton*, 1 T. R. 544, 5.

(z) Per Lord *Mansfield*, C. J., and Lord *Loughborough*, C. J., in *Sutton* v. *Johnstone*, 1 T. R. 545, and per *Tindal*, C. J., delivering judgment, *Willans* v. *Taylor*, 6 Bingh. 186. See also *Golding* v. *Crowle*, Bull. N. P. 14; Say. R. 1, *S. C.*, *Davis* v. *Hardy*, 6 B. & C. 225; *Musgrove* v. *Newell*, 1 M. & W. 582; 1 Tyrw. & Gr. 957.

(a) Per Ld. *Tenterden*, C. J., delivering judgment of the court in *Cotton* v. *James*, 1 B. & Ad. 133.

(b) Per Ld. *Tenterden*, C. J., *Blachford* v. *Dod*, 2 B. & Ad. 184, cited arg.

James v. *Phelps*, 3 P. & D. 233. See further on this subject, *M'Donald* v. *Rooke*, 2 Bingh. N. C. 217; *Panton* v. *Williams*, Ex. Chr., on error from Q. B., June 15, 1841; *Broad* v. *Ham*, 5 Bingh. N. C. 722.

(c) Admitted in *Goslin* v. *Wilcock*, 2 Wils. 305, per Ld. *Camden*, C. J.

(d) *Parker* v. *Langley*, Gilb. R. 163, adjudged on special demurrer.

(e) *Norrish* v. *Richards*, 3 A. & E. 733; 5 Nev. & M. 268, *S. C.*; *Combe* v. *Capron*, 1 M. & Rob. 398.

(f) 1 Esp. N. P. C. 80.

(g) *Pierce* v. *Street*, 3 B. & Ad. 397.

The termination must be such as to furnish *primâ facie* evidence, that the action was without foundation. Termination of cause by *stet processus*, by consent of parties, is not sufficient (*h*). So in an action for a malicious presentment in the Ecclesiastical Court, it must appear that the presentment (*i*) has been determined. To support an action for a malicious arrest, malice, and that the arrest was without probable cause, must be alleged and proved. The mere not proceeding in an action is not evidence of itself alone sufficient to support this action (*k*). But where there are mutual dealings between two parties, and items known to be due on each side of the account, an arrest for the amount of one side of the account, without deducting what is due on the other, is malicious, and without probable cause (*l*). So where A. arrested B. on an affidavit of debt for money paid to his use, but did not declare until ruled to do so, and afterwards discontinued the action, and paid the costs; it was holden (*m*), that this was sufficient *primâ facie* evidence of malice, and of the absence of probable cause. A., to whom a sum of money was owing from B. (*n*), sued out a writ against B., · for the purpose of holding him to bail ; before the writ was served, B. went to the house of A. and paid the debt, but A. did not immediately after such payment countermand the writ, in consequence of which B. was arrested and kept in prison for several hours ; B. thereupon brought an action against A., alleging, that after payment of the debt, it became the duty of A. to have countermanded the writ, and that he had wrongfully neglected so to do, by reason whereof he was arrested : it was holden, that the action would not lie ; *Eyre*, C. J., observing, that the plaintiff ought to have inquired, at the time when he paid the debt, whether any writ had been sued out, and offering to pay whatever costs were incurred thereby, to have requested a countermand, which he might take to the sheriff. And *Heath*, J., said, " This action is founded on mere nonfeasance, and no case or precedent has been cited to show that such an action was ever maintained. All the cases of arrest, and holding to bail without cause, are founded on malice." In like manner it has been holden (*o*), that evidence of suing out a writ and arresting a party thereon, after the debt has been discharged and a receipt given, will not be sufficient to maintain an action of this kind in a case where actual malice was not proved, and the facts of the case precluded any inference of malice. Malice is a question of fact for the jury, and the jury *may* (*p*), but are not *bound* to, imply malice from

(*h*) *Wilkinson* v. *Howel*, M. & Malk. 495, *Tenterden*, C. J., confirmed by court.

(*i*) *Fisher* v. *Bristow*, 1 Doug. 215.

(*k*) *Sinclair* v. *Eldred*, 4 Taunt. 7.

(*l*) *Austin* v. *Debnam*, 3 B. & C. 139.

(*m*) *Nicholson* v. *Coghill*, 4 B. & C. 21.

(*n*) *Scheibel* v. *Fairbairn*, 1 Bos. &

Pul. 388, recognized in *Page* v. *Wiple*, 3 East, 317, and *Lewis* v. *Morris*, 4 Tyr. 914. See also *Saxon* v. *Browne*, 1 Nev. & P. 661 ; 6 A. & E. 652 ; *Heywood* v. *Collinge*, 9 A. & E. 268.

(*o*) *Gibson* v. *Chaters*, 2 Bos. & Pul. 129.

(*p*) *Mitchell* v. *Jenkins*, 5 B. & Ad. 588 ; 2 Nev. & Man. 301.

want of probable cause. An action on the case may be maintained for maliciously impleading and causing the plaintiff to be excommunicated in the Ecclesiastical Court (q), whereby he was taken upon an *excom. cap.* and imprisoned, until he procured himself to be absolved. The plaintiff declared (r), that the defendant had sued out a *fi. fa.* upon a judgment given against the plaintiff for the defendant in an action of trespass, under which the sheriff took goods of the plaintiff to the value of the damage, and returned that the goods remained in his hands for want of purchasers, and that the defendant, *well knowing this*, to the intent to vex the plaintiff, sued out another *fi. fa.*, under which the sheriff levied the money on other goods of the plaintiff, and paid it over to the defendant. After not guilty pleaded, and verdict for plaintiff, it was holden, on motion in arrest of judgment, that the action was maintainable; *Hobart*, C. J., (who delivered the opinion of the court,) observing, that the plaintiff was twice vexed *wilfully* by the defendant, who had first one execution inchoate, which he ought to have completed, *knowing it*, and not to have taken another; for else he might take twenty executions. An action on the case will lie against a governor for maliciously, and without probable cause, suspending plaintiff from a civil office (s). So an action will lie for falsely and maliciously suing out a commission of bankruptcy against the plaintiff (t), which was afterwards superseded (2); and in such action it cannot be objected, at least after verdict, that it is not averred in the declaration, that the plaintiff had not at any time committed an act of bankruptcy. Formerly, to prove that the commission had been superseded, it was necessary to produce (u) the writ of supersedeas under the great seal; but now the chancellor's order has the effect (x) of a supersedeas. It seems, that the mere order for annulling the fiat is not evidence of want of probable cause, as that may have proceeded on strict legal grounds (y). An action will not lie against a person (z) exhibiting an information for intention to land goods without paying duty, if the goods are condemned by the sub-commissioners, though the commissioners of appeal reverse the condemnation; for the judgment of the sub-commissioners shows that there was a foundation for the infor-

(q) *Hocking* v. *Matthews*, 1 Ventr. 86.
(r) *Waterer* v. *Freeman*, Hob. 205, 266; 1 Brownl. 12.
(s) *Sutherland* v. *General Murray*, 1 T. R. 538.
(t) *Chapman* v. *Pickersgill*, 2 Wils. 145.

(u) *Poynton* v. *Forster*, 3 Campb. 58.
(x) See *ante*, p. 266.
(y) See the opinion of *Tindal*, C. J., as to the effect of a mere supersedeas, *Hay* v. *Weakley*, 5 C. & P. 361.
(z) *Reynolds* v. *Kennedy*, 1 Wils. 232, on error from Ireland.

(2) See *Whitworth* v. *Hall*, 2 B. & Ad. 695. For another remedy in this case, see *ante*, p. 246, and *Smith* v. *Broomhead*, 7 T. R. 300.

mation. Where a justice of the peace maliciously grants a warrant against another (a), without any information, upon a supposed charge of felony, the remedy against the justice is by an action of trespass *vi et armis*, and not by action on the case (3). But a magistrate is not liable for a mere error in judgment, if, when a charge is before him, he does not exceed his jurisdiction. Magistrates ought not to frame depositions in the words of acts of parliament, but that alone will not make their conduct malicious. Hence, where a magistrate committed to prison as a felon the plaintiff, against whom a charge had been made of maliciously cutting down a tree, which grew on land in his own occupation, the property of A.; it was holden (b), that defendant was not liable. A., a captain in the navy, was accused, by his commander-in-chief, of neglect of duty, disobedience of orders, &c. A., having been tried by a court martial, was honourably acquitted, after which he brought an action in the Court of Exchequer, against his commander, for a malicious prosecution. A verdict having been found for the plaintiff, a motion was made in arrest of judgment, which, after a very elaborate discussion, was refused (c); but the defendant afterwards brought a writ of error in the Exchequer Chamber, where the judgment of the Court of Exchequer was reversed (d). This reversal was afterwards affirmed in the House of Lords (e). An action will not lie to recover damages (f) sustained by the plaintiff in defending a vexatious ejectment brought against him by the defendant, in which the nominal plaintiff has been non-prossed (4).

(a) *Morgan* v. *Hughes*, 2 T. R. 225.
(b) *Mills* v. *Collett*, 6 Bingh. 85.
(c) *Sutton* v. *Johnstone*, 1 T. R. 501.
(d) *Ib.* 550.

(e) 1 Bro. P. C. 76, Tomlin's ed.
(f) *Purton* v. *Honnor*, 1 Bos. & Pul. 205.

---

(3) "Where the immediate act of imprisonment proceeds from the defendant, the action must be trespass, and trespass only; but where the act of imprisonment by one person is in consequence of information from another, there an action upon the case is the proper remedy, because the injury is sustained in consequence of the wrongful act of that other." Per *Ashhurst*, J., *S. C.*

(4) Under what circumstances an action will lie for a malicious and vexatious *suit*, see notes on Co. Litt. 161, a. (4) IV., and *Martin* v. *Lincoln*, M. 27 Car. II. C. B., Bull. N. P. 13.

II. *Of the Declaration, p.* 1062; *Defence, p.* 1063; *Evidence, p.* 1064.

THE declaration must state all the material circumstances attending the malicious prosecution, and how it was disposed of (*g*); because, until that be determined, it cannot be known whether the prosecution were malicious or not (*h*), and this absurdity might follow, that plaintiff might recover in the action, and yet be afterwards convicted on the original prosecution (5). Care must be taken in framing the declaration so as to avoid any objection being raised on the ground of a variance. For where in the declaration it was stated, that the trial and the acquittal both took place " in the court of our lord the king, before the king himself;" and upon the production of the record in evidence, it appeared, that the trial was before the chief justice, at nisi prius, and that the acquittal was by the judgment of the court in bank, the variance was holden to be fatal (*i*). But where the allegation was, " that the plaintiff, by ʼa jury of the county of   , was duly and in a lawful manner acquitted ;" and by the record it appeared, " that the *jury* found the plaintiff *not guilty*, and upon that verdict the *judgment* of the *court* was, that the plaintiff should go thereof acquitted:" it was holden sufficient, by construing the words reddendo singula singulis, that the plaintiff was *duly acquitted by the jury*, that is, found not guilty of the facts, and *in a lawful manner acquitted ;* that is, by the judgment of acquittal pronounced by the court (*k*). If it appear on the face of the declaration, that the court in which the indictment was tried had authority to hear and determine upon it, it is sufficient; and there is not any necessity for copying exactly the style of the record; but if the declaration describe a court of incompetent authority, it is bad. This distinction may be illustrated by the following case : The declaration stated plaintiff to have been indicted at the general *quarter* sessions (*l*), and by the record it appeared that he had been indicted at the general sessions ; the word quarter was rejected as surplusage, because plaintiff had been indicted for an offence cognizable at the general sessions ; but if the offence had been cognizable only at the *quarter* sessions, the declara-

---

(*g*) *Arundell* v. *Tregono*, Yelv. 116.
(*h*) *Lewis* v. *Farrel*, Str. 114 ; *Parker* v. *Langley*, Gilb. R. 163.

(*i*) *Woodford* v. *Ashley*, 11 East, 508.
(*k*) *Hunter* v. *French*, Willes, 517.
(*l*) *Busby* v. *Watson*, 2 Bl. 1050.

---

(5) The want of this averment is cured by verdict. *Skinner* v. *Gunton*, 1 Saund. 228, because it will be presumed that it has been proved at the trial. Per *Denison*, J., in *Panton* v. *Marshall*, B. R. M. 28 Geo. II., MSS.

tion would have been bad. So where it was stated in the declaration (*m*), that the plaintiff had been indicted as a common barrator before certain justices, ad felonias, &c., nec non ad pacem conservandam assignat., and defendant having demanded oyer of the indictment, it was certified to have been taken before certain justices ad pacem conservandam assignat.; it was holden, that the action lay, on the ground that the justices mentioned in the indictment were not justices of another nature or power than those which were mentioned in the declaration; both were justices of the peace, and such as had power to receive such manner of indictment. It was admitted, however, if the declaration had mentioned justices of assize, and the certificate had been of a thing taken before justices of gaol delivery, the variance would have been fatal, for they are distinct in power. See stat. 3 & 4 Will. IV. c. 42, s. 23, *ante*, p. 519.

Defence.

Money cannot be paid into court (*n*). The usual defence to this action is, that the defendant had reasonable or probable grounds of suspicion against the plaintiff. It is not necessary that these grounds should be legal grounds; for if it can be inferred, from the circumstances of the case, that the defendant was not actuated by any improper motive, but an honest desire to bring a supposed offender to justice, it will be a sufficient answer to this action (*o*); because such circumstances tend to disprove that which is of the essence of the action, *viz.* the malice of the defendant in preferring the charge. This defence of probable cause ought not (*p*) to be pleaded specially by the defendant, inasmuch as it may be given in evidence under the general issue, not guilty. In case for a malicious arrest, the plea of not guilty puts in issue merely the malicious arrest without probable cause; the averment of the discontinuance of the suit is a material allegation, which should be denied specially (*q*). In case for maliciously and without probable cause laying an information on the game laws, it appeared that there had been a conviction and no appeal. The court held (*r*), that as the defendant had acquiesced in the conviction, this was evidence of probable cause, and so the action could not be maintained.

To a declaration for procuring a false and malicious charge to be made against the plaintiff before a magistrate, and proceedings to be taken thereon without any reasonable or probable cause; the

(*m*) *Barnes* v. *Constantine*, Yelv. 46.
(*n*) See stat. 3 & 4 Will. IV. c. 42, s. 21.
(*o*) *Case* v. *Wirrall*, Cro. Jac. 193, cited by *Tindal*, C. J., in delivering judgment in *Panton* v. *Williams*, on error from Q. B., Exch. Chr., June 15, 1841.

(*p*) *Cotton* v. *Browne*, 3 A. & E. 312; 4 Nev. & M. 831; *Houndsfield* v. *Drury*, 3 P. & D. 127, S. P.
(*q*) *Watkins* v. *Lee*, 5 M. & W. 270.
(*r*) *Mellor* v. *Baddeley*, 2 Cr. & M. 675.

defendant pleaded, that the defendant procured the charge to be made " upon and with a reasonable and probable cause ;" and then proceeded to state what that reasonable and probable cause was, and in so doing alleged the several circumstances attending the transaction out of which the charge before the magistrate arose. Special demurrer, alleging, that the plea did not contain any allegation, that the defendant, at the time he caused the charge to be made, had been informed of, or knew, or in any manner acted on, those circumstances.   The court held (s) the plea bad, not in form only, but in substance, on this ground of objection.   The defendant had indicted the plaintiff for felony, for maliciously obstructing the air-way of a mine; it appeared, that the plaintiff had committed the act in question under a claim of right, and *bonâ fide*.   In an action by the plaintiff for a malicious prosecution; it was holden(t), that the judge ought to have left it to the jury to say, whether the defendant knew, at the time of preferring the indictment, that the plaintiff had done the act under a claim of right, and *bonâ fide ;* for then there was not any probable cause for a charge of felony.

The debtor's going abroad after an arrest for debt is probable cause (u) for the creditor's proceeding to outlawry, notwithstanding the creditor may know that the debtor has an agent in England. In an action for maliciously and without probable cause proceeding to outlawry, which was afterwards reversed, the general issue, not guilty, puts in issue the existence of probable cause only (x), and not the reversal of the outlawry.

This is an action on the case, and consequently, if it be not brought within six years next after the cause of action, the statute of limitations (y) may be pleaded in bar.

Evidence.

The plaintiff must produce an examined copy of the record of the indictment, and, where there has been a verdict of not guilty, of the acquittal.   Among the orders and directions to be observed by justices of the peace at the sessions in the Old Bailey, 26 Car. II., prefixed to Kelyng's Report of Crown Cases, ed. 1708, is the following order, *viz.* " That no copies of any indictment for *felony* be given without special order, upon motion made in open court at the general gaol delivery; for that the late frequency of actions against prosecutors, which cannot be without copies of the indictments, deterreth people from prosecuting for the king upon just occa-

---

(s) *Delegal* v. *Highley*, 3 Bingh. N. C. 950.

(t) *James* v. *Phelps*, 3 P. & D. 231 ; 11 A. & E. 483.

(u) *Drummond* v. *Pigou*, 2 Bingh. N. C. 114.

(x) *S. C.*

(y) 21 Jac. I. c. 16.

sions (6)." In *Evans* v. *Phillips*, Monmouth Sum. Ass. 1763, MSS., *Adams*, Baron, (who had been recorder of London for several years,) said, that in all cases of indictments for misdemeanour, the party is entitled to a copy of the record; but in cases of indictment for *felony*, he should look upon the copy as a surreptitious record, and not pay any regard to it, unless the judge had been applied to, and had ordered a copy. This case, however, was overruled in *Legatt* v. *Tollervey*, 14 East, 302, where it was holden, that the record of the indictment for felony, or a true copy, must be received in evidence, although it does not appear that the officer producing the record, or giving the copy, had any authority from the court, or any fiat from the attorney-general for that purpose. The distinction between felony and misdemeanour was taken by Lord *Mansfield*, C. J., in *Morrison* v. *Kelly*, B. R. Middx. Sittings, 1 Bl. R. 385. That was an action for a malicious prosecution, in indicting plaintiff for keeping a disorderly house. To prove the fact, the clerk of the peace for the Westminster sessions attended with the original record of the acquittal. It was objected, that there ought to be a copy of the record granted by the court before which the acquittal is had, in order to ground an action for a malicious prosecution. But per Lord *Mansfield*, although this is necessary, where the party is indicted for *felony*, yet the practice is otherwise in cases of misdemeanour. There is a short note in Strange's Reports, from which it appears to have been the opinion of *Lee*, C. J., that if the copy of the indictment has been granted by order of court, it is sufficient, although it was not granted to the plaintiff in the action for malicious prosecution, or at his instance. The plaintiff and another were indicted at the Old Bailey sessions for forgery (*z*), and acquitted, and a copy of the indictment granted to the other only. In this action, which was for a malicious prosecution, the plaintiff offered the copy in evidence, and the order at the Old Bailey was read by way of objection. But the Chief Justice (*Lee*) said, he would not refuse to let the plaintiff read it (the copy of the indictment); *for an order was not necessary to make it evidence (a), nor is it ever produced in order to introduce it.* So the copy of the indictment was read, and a verdict obtained for the plaintiff, which the court refused to set aside.

(*z*) *Jordan* v. *Lewis*, Str. 1122; 14 East, 305, n., *S. C.*, from Mr. Ford's MS. See also Str. 856, and *Caddy* v. *Barlow*, 1 Man. & Ry. 275.

(*a*) *Legatt* v. *Tollervey*, 14 East, 302, S. P. See also *Stockfleth* v. *De Tastet*, 4 Campb. 10.

---

(6) " If A. be indicted for felony and acquitted, and he is desirous of bringing an action, the judge will not permit him to have a copy of the record, if there was probable cause for the indictment; and he cannot have a copy without leave." Per *Holt*, C. J., Ld. Raym. 253. But see *Browne* v. *Cumming and others*, 10 B. & C. 70, 73, n. (c).

If the proceeding was by preferring a charge before a magistrate, the magistrate or his clerk should be served with a *subpœna duces tecum*, to produce the proceedings (*b*). If the information was laid by the defendant, his taking the oath and handwriting should be proved, as also the issuing the warrant to the constable, &c.; the warrant must also be produced and proved, and evidence must be given of the apprehension and detention of the plaintiff under the warrant; and his ultimate discharge must also be shown (*c*).

An averment, that the suit is wholly ended and determined, is evidenced by proof of the rule to discontinue upon payment of costs, and that the costs were taxed and paid (*d*). So where a suit was determined by a rule of court, it was holden (*e*), that the production of the rule of court was sufficient evidence of that fact. This action cannot be maintained without proof of malice, either express or implied. Malice may be implied from the want of probable cause, but that must be shown by the plaintiff. Proving an acquittal for want of prosecution is not *primâ facie* evidence of malice to support this action. In an action for a malicious prosecution against the defendant (*f*) for having indicted the plaintiff for perjury, the proof on the part of the plaintiff (in addition to the formal proof of the record of acquittal) was, that after the indictment found was ready for trial, the prosecutor (the present defendant) was called, and did not appear; on which the verdict of acquittal passed. Lord *Ellenborough*, C. J., thought that this was not sufficient to support the action, without evidence of express malice, or at least of circumstances evincing such entire want of probable cause, whence malice was to be presumed, and therefore he nonsuited the plaintiff. The court of B. R. afterwards concurred in opinion with the C. J. N. The indictment assigned the perjury on an affidavit made by the plaintiff swearing to words uttered by the defendant. In an action for a malicious prosecution of indictment for perjury, the chief justice allowed the plaintiff to give in evidence an advertisement put into the papers by the defendant of the finding of the indictment, with other scandalous matter, although an information had been granted for it as a libel; not, as he said, that the jury were to consider it in damages, but only as a circumstance of malice (*g*). In an action for a malicious prosecution for forging a note of hand, four witnesses proving that the handwriting was not the plaintiff's, the judge directed the jury in his favour (*h*). Where a person prosecutes on the representations of others, he should show that he did all he could, or used proper and reasonable means and precau-

(*b*) 2 Stark. Law of Slander and Libel, 70, 71, 2nd edit.

(*c*) *Ib.*

(*d*) *Bristow* v. *Heywood*, 1 Stark. N. P. C. 48; 4 Campb. 214, *S. C.* But see *Watkins* v. *Lee*, 5 M. & W. 270.

(*e*) *Brook* v. *Carpenter*, 3 Bingh. 297.

(*f*) *Purcell* v. *Macnamara*, 9 East, 361.

(*g*) *Chambers* v. *Robinson*, Str. 691.

(*h*) *Norris* v. *Tyler*, Cowp. 37.

tion, to discover the truth, and that he acted on a belief that he was right; otherwise the want of probable cause will subject him to the imputation of malice, and consequently to this action. MSS. It must appear that the plaintiff was acquitted upon the prosecution (*i*), *before* the action was brought; but the day of the acquittal is not material. Hence, where it was stated in the declaration, under a scilicet, that the acquittal took place on the morrow of the Holy Trinity, (which allegation was not accompanied with a prout patet per recordum,) and by the record, when produced in evidence, it appeared that it took place on Tuesday next after Easter Term; the latter day having been before action brought, the variance was holden to be immaterial, on the ground that the day mentioned in the declaration was not alleged as part of the description of the record of acquittal (7). So where, in an action for a false return to a fieri facias, the declaration stated, that the plaintiff in Trinity Term, 2 Geo. IV., recovered, &c., " *as it appears by record,*" and the proof was of a judgment in Easter Term, 3 Geo. IV.; it was holden (*k*), that this was not any variance; for that the averment " as appears by the record," was surplusage, and might be rejected, inasmuch as the judgment was not the foundation of, but inducement to, the action. But where a declaration against the marshal for an escape alleged that S. S. was arrested and gave bail, that afterwards bail above was put in before a judge at chambers, " as appears by the record of the recognizance;" that S. S. surrendered in discharge of the bail and afterwards escaped: it was holden (*l*), that the averment was not made out by the production of the filazer's book, the entry therein importing that the recognizance was taken before a single judge, an examined copy of the entry of the recognizance of bail, stating that the recognizance was taken before the court at Westminster, having also been given in evidence. In an action on the case for a malicious prosecution (*m*), where there

(*i*) *Purcell* v. *Macnamara*, 9 East, 157, in which *Pope* v. *Foster*, 4 T. R. 590, was overruled. See also *Woodford* v. *Ashley*, 2 Campb. 194; *Phillips* v. *Shaw*, 4 B. & A. 435; and *Stoddart* v. *Palmer*, 3 B. & C. 2.

(*k*) *Stoddart* v. *Palmer*, 3 B. & C. 2.
(*l*) *Bevan* v. *Jones*, 4 B. & C. 403.
(*m*) *Johnson* v. *Browning*, 6 Mod. 216.

---

(7) " There are two sorts of allegations; the one of matter of substance, which must be substantially proved; the other of description, which must be literally proved." Per Lord *Ellenborough*, C. J., *S. C.* " Where the day laid is made part of the description of the instrument referred to, which instrument is necessary to be proved, the day laid must be proved as part of that instrument. But where the day laid is not material in itself, and need not have been proved as laid; supposing the proof to have been by parol, if the fact proved will support the declaration, I see no ground for any distinction between making such proof by matter of record or by parol." Per *Lawrence*, J., *S. C.*, 9 East, 162.

was not any person present at the time when the supposed felony was committed, except defendant's wife; *Holt*, C. J., allowed the evidence of the wife, given at the trial of the indictment, as good evidence to prove a felony having been committed. In an action on the case for maliciously indicting plaintiff and others for a conspiracy (n), the counsel for the plaintiff called one of the grand jury, before whom the bill of indictment had been preferred, and found a true bill, to prove that the defendant was the prosecutor of the indictment. *Garrow*, for the defendant, objected to his being examined, observing, that the grand juryman could collect this circumstance of defendant's having been the prosecutor, from the testimony only which had been produced before him in his character of grand juryman, and which by his oath he was bound not to disclose; but *Kenyon*, C. J., thought that the question of "who was the prosecutor of the indictment?" was a question of fact, the disclosure of which did not infringe upon the grand juryman's oath, and therefore permitted him to be examined as to that point. Case for a malicious prosecution of an indictment (o), whereof (as was alleged) plaintiff was *legitimo modo acquietatus;* upon the trial it appeared, that he was acquitted no otherwise than by an entry of a *nolle prosequi. Per Cur.* "This evidence does not support the declaration; for the *nolle prosequi* is a discharge as to the indictment, but it is not an acquittal of the crime." In an action for a malicious arrest, the plaintiff cannot recover (p) damages for the extra costs. If two are found guilty, it must be of joint acts (q), and the damages must be joint. Action for malicious prosecution for perjury, where there had been thirty-three assignments, the defendant proved, that he had probable cause for many of the charges; but knowing one of them to be false, Lord *Mansfield*, C. J., held, that the plaintiff should recover for that one, though there was probable cause for the others. Jury found £100 damages for the plaintiff (r).

(n) *Sykes, Gent., one, &c.* v. *Dunbar*, Middlesex Sittings after M. T. 40 Geo. III., *Kenyon*, C. J., MSS. See the remarks of Mr. Starkie on this case in vol. 2, p. 70, n. (p), of the second edition of his valuable treatise on Slander and Libel.

(o) *Goddard* v. *Smith*, Salk. 21; 6 Mod. 261, *S. C.*

(p) *Sinclair* v. *Eldred*, 4 Taunt. 7,

recognized by *Best*, C. J., in *Webber* v. *Nicholas*, Ry. & Moo. 419. *Contra*, per Ld. *Ellenborough*, C. J., in *Sandback* v. *Thomas*, 1 Stark. N. P. C. 306.

(q) *Hilditch* v. *Eyles*, H., 29 Geo. III., coram *Wilson*, J., Guildhall, MSS.

(r) *Prosser* v. *Nixon*, cited in *Sutton* v. *Johnstone*, 1 T. R. 533.

CHAPTER XXVIII.

MANDAMUS.

I. *Nature of the Writ of Mandamus, p.* 1069; *Mandamus to restore or admit Persons to Corporate Offices, p.* 1070.

II. *In what other Cases the Court will grant a Mandamus, p.* 1075.

III. *Where not, p.* 1078.

IV. *Form of the Writ, p.* 1081.

V. *Of the Return, p.* 1083.

VI. *Of the Remedy, where the Party to whom the Writ of Mandamus is directed, does not make any Return, or where he makes an insufficient, or false Return, p.* 1086.

I. *Nature of the Writ of Mandamus, p.* 1069 ; *Mandamus to restore or admit Persons to Corporate Offices, p.* 1070.

THE writ of mandamus is a prerogative writ, containing a command, in the king's name, and issuing from the Court of King's Bench, directed to persons, corporations, or inferior courts of judicature within the king's dominions, requiring them to do a certain specific act, as being the duty of their office, character, or situation, agreeably to right and justice. This writ affords a proper remedy, in cases where the party has not any other means of compelling a specific performance. The object of the writ is not to supersede legal remedies, but only to supply the defect of them. The only proper ground of the writ is a defect of justice. It is, however, a prerogative writ, and not a writ of right (a), and it is the absence or want of a specific *legal* remedy, which gives the court jurisdiction (b). There must be a specific legal right (c), as well as the

(a) Per *Ashhurst*, J., in *R.* v. *Commissioners of Excise*, 2 T. R. 385.

(b) Per Ld. *Ellenborough*, C. J., *Bristol Dock Company*, M. 52 Geo. III., MS. See also the opinion of *Buller*, J., in *R.* v. *Marquis of Stafford*, 3 T. R. 652.

(c) Per Lord *Ellenborough*, C. J., in *R.* v. *Archbishop of Canterbury*, 8 East, 219. See also *Coleridge*, J., in *R.* v. *Nottingham Old Water Works Company*, 6 A. & E. 372.

2 c 2

want of a specific legal remedy, in order to found an application for a mandamus. And there must have been a direct refusal (d) to do that, which it is the object of the mandamus to enforce, either in terms, or by circumstances, which distinctly show an intention in the party not to do the act required. It is no objection, however, to the granting a mandamus to do a particular act, that an indictment will also lie (e) for the omission to do that act. But the court will not carry the remedy by mandamus so far as to issue the writ, wherever any officer (f) has neglected his duty. "There is considerable doubt (g), whether, when an inferior officer refuses to do his duty, he being amenable to other persons, this court will, under any circumstances, interfere by mandamus." The power to issue this writ belongs exclusively to the Court of King's Bench, and is considered as one of the flowers (h) of that court; but this power ought to be exercised with great caution, as a writ of error does not lie on this proceeding. A mandamus lies either to restore a person wrongfully ousted, or to admit a person wrongfully refused. A mandamus lies to restore a person who has been removed from his office without cause; as a mayor, bailiff (i), alderman (k), burgess (l), jurat (m), common council-man (n), recorder (o), town-clerk (p), or serjeant (q). Formerly, in these cases, the writ was termed "a writ of restitution," and appears to have been confined exclusively to offices of a public nature. The title "mandamus" is not found in the old abridgments. By an extension of the ancient writ of restitution, a remedy has been provided for persons who have been duly elected to offices, although they never had possession. Hence a mandamus lies to *admit*, as well as to restore, a person to his office, as a mayor, alderman (r), town-clerk (s), &c. The admission under the mandamus gives no right, but only a legal possession, to enable the party to assert his right, if he has any. Hence, *non fuit electus* has been holden not to be a good return to a mandamus, to swear in a churchwarden (t), because it is directed only to a ministerial officer, who is to do his duty, and no inconvenience can follow; for if the party has a right, he ought to be

(d) R. v. Brecknock and Abergavenny Canal Company, 3 A. & E. 217; 4 Nev. & M. 871; S. C., R. v. Ford. See also R. v. Wilts and Berks Canal Navigation, 3 A. & E. 477; 5 Nev. & M. 344, S. C.

(e) R. v. The Severn and Wye Railway Company, 2 B. & A. 646. See also R. v. Commissioners of Dean Inclosure, 2 M. & S. 80, cited and commented on by Denman, C. J., 3 A. & E. 422, R. v. Jeyes.

(f) R. v. Jeyes, 3 A. & E. 416; 5 Nev. & M. 101, S. C.

(g) Per Denman, C. J., S. C.

(h) Poph. 176.

(i) 2 Rol. Abr. tit. Restitution, pl. 4.

(k) Shuttleworth v. Corporation of Lincoln, 2 Bulstr. 122; Taylor's case, Poph. 133, S. P.

(l) Clerk's case, Cro. Jac. 506. See also 5 Mod. 257.

(m) Anon., 1 Lev. 148.

(n) 2 Rol. Abr. tit. Restitution, pl. 8.

(o) Ib. pl. 6.

(p) Pasch. 2 Car. said to have been adjudged. See Sty. 457.

(q) 2 Rol. Abr. tit. Restitution, pl. 7.

(r) Com. Dig. Mandamus (A).

(s) Awdeley v. Joye, Poph. 176.

(t) R. v. White, M. 11 Geo. I. (cited by Strange, arg., Str. 894, 5).

admitted; if he has not, the admission will do him no good. Wherever the officer is but ministerial, he is to execute his part, let the
consequence be what it will. *R.* v. *Simpson*, M. 11 Geo. I., Str. 895.
That was a mandamus to the Archdeacon of Colchester, to swear
Rodney Fane into the office of churchwarden. The archdeacon
returned, that before the coming of the writ, he received an inhi-
bition from the bishop; but the court held, that was no excuse, and
that a ministerial officer is to do his duty, whether the act would be
of any validity or not. Where there are two sets of parties, who
have each a colourable title to the office of churchwarden, both sets
must be sworn in (*u*).

By the common law, upon the death of a mayor, or other chief
magistrate of boroughs or corporations within the year, the Court
of King's Bench was authorized to grant a mandamus immediately
to fill up the vacancy thus occasioned by the act of God and an
ordinary contingency (*x*); but, upon an omission to elect at the
charter-day (1), or to do such acts as were by the charter required
to be done at certain times, in order to complete the election, or
upon the removal of an officer unduly chosen, the court had not any
power to compel an election, or the performance of such acts as
were necessary to complete an election, before the day came round
again; for, to compel the corporation to proceed to an election at
another day, would not be enforcing obedience to the king's charter,
but to authorize them to act in opposition to it. The omission to
elect might be owing to the contrivance of the person who ought
to hold the court, or to preside in the assembly where the election
was to be made; or it might be the effect of pure accident: in
either case, the inconvenience was the same: a forfeiture of the
charter might be incurred, and the corporation dissolved, in con-

---

(*u*) *R.* v. *Archdeacon of Middlesex*, 5   *Duffield and another*, 3 A. & E. 617.
Nev. & M. 497; 3 A. & E. 615; *Exp.*   (*x*) See 8 Mod. 129.

---

(1) By stat. 5 & 6 Will. IV. c. 76, for the regulation of municipal corporations in England and Wales, sect. 1, all charters, grants, and letters
patent, relating to the several boroughs named in the Schedules (A) and
(B), inconsistent with that act, are repealed. By sect. 49, the council in
every year are to elect the mayor on the 9th of November, and in case of
vacancy within the year, then another election is to be made within ten
days after the vacancy. In *Reg.* v. *Macgowan*, 3 P. & D. 557, it was
holden, that the election of mayor on the 9th of November, in each year,
must be the first business done by the town council, and that an election
of aldermen on that day previous to the election of mayor is void. By
stat. 6 & 7 Will. IV. c. 105, s. 4, the mayor shall continue in office one
whole year, and until his successor shall have accepted the office of mayor,
and shall have made and subscribed the declaration required in that behalf.

sequence of such omission (y). To remedy the mischiefs which might thus arise, it was enacted, by stat. 11 Geo. I. c. 4, s. 1 (2), That if in any city, borough, or town corporate, in England, Wales, and Berwick-upon-Tweed, no election shall be made of the mayor, bailiff, or other chief officer, upon the day or within the time appointed by the charter or usage, or, such election being made, shall afterwards become void, whether such omission or avoidance shall happen through the default of the officer who ought to hold the court or preside, or by any accident, or other means, the corporation shall not thereby be dissolved or disabled from electing such officers; but *in any case where no election shall be made as aforesaid*, the members of the corporation may meet at the town-hall or other usual place of meeting for making such election, upon the next day after the expiration of the time within which such election ought to have been made, unless such day shall be Sunday, and then on the Monday following, between the hours of ten in the morning and two in the afternoon (3), and proceed to an election; and in case the mayor, or other person who ought to hold the court or preside, shall be absent, the nearest in place or office having a right to vote shall hold the court or preside. And by sect. 2, If in any city, borough, or town corporate, in England, Wales, and Berwick-upon-Tweed, no election shall be made of the mayor, bailiff, or other chief officer, upon the day or within the time appointed by charter or usage for that purpose, and no election of such officer shall be made, pursuant to the directions herein

---

(y) See the case of *The Corporation of Banbury*, 10 Mod. 346, cited from a MS. note by Lord *Hardwicke*, C. J., in *R*. v. *Pasmore*, 3 T. R. 221; *R*. v. *Tregony*, 8 Mod. 127. See also the report of the attorney and solicitor general in 1724, in the *Tiverton* case, 2 Doug. Contro- verted Elections, p. 63, edit. 1775. N. The cases of *Banbury* and *Tiverton* gave rise to the stat. 11 Geo. I. c. 4, founded on a constitutional jealousy, lest the crown should have it in their power to model all corporations upon the death of mayors, &c.

---

(2) By stat. 7 Will. IV. & 1 Vict. c. 78, s. 26, all the powers of this act of 11 Geo. IV., given to the Court of King's Bench, are extended to elections under the 5 & 6 Will. IV. c. 76, and this act of 7 Will. IV. & 1 Vict. c. 78.

(3) "I think the time is not essential; but only directory. It was appointed to prevent surprise; and if the election be *fairly* carried on, though at a different hour, yet such election is good." Per Lord *Hardwicke*, C. J., in *R*. v. *Pole*, B. R. Trin. 7 & 8 Geo. II., MS. The language of Lord *Hardwicke*, in another note, is thus: "As to the hours, they are merely directory to prevent surprise; and so resolved in the case of *the Corporation of Launceston*, 1 R. A. 513, 4, pl. 5." The distinction between matters directory and obligatory is well known and established. Per Lord *Tenterden*, C. J., delivering judgment of court, in *R*. v. *Mayor of London*, 9 B. & C. 31; *R*. v. *Mayor of Norwich*, 1 B. & Ad. 310, S. P.

before prescribed, or such election being made shall afterwards become void as aforesaid, in every such case his Majesty's Court of King's Bench may, upon motion, award a writ of mandamus requiring the members or persons having a right to vote at, or to do any act necessary to be done in order to such election, respectively to assemble themselves at the time prefixed in the writ, and to proceed to the election of a mayor, bailiff, or other chief officer, as the case shall require, and to do every act necessary to be done in order to such election: or to signify to the court good cause to the contrary, and thereupon to cause such proceedings to be had as in any other cases of mandamus for election of officers of corporations; and of the time appointed by such writ of mandamus, for holding such assembly, public notice in writing shall, by such person as the court shall appoint, be affixed in the market-place, or some other public place within such city, &c., six days before the day so appointed: and such officer, or other person respectively, shall preside in such assembly as ought to have presided in case the same had been made upon the day hereinbefore prescribed for that purpose.

Lastly, the persons (z) to whom the mandamus is directed, are to make their return to the first writ. Such are the enactments and provisions of the stat. 11 Geo. I. c. 4, which, as it is a remedial law, is to be expounded in the most liberal sense that the words are capable of (4). Hence the court will grant a mandamus under this statute, to compel the members of a corporation to proceed to the election of a mayor, although more than one year, *e. g.*, three or four years, have elapsed, since a regular election (*a*).

The statute is not confined to annual officers (*b*). The words in the first section of the statute, " no election," are to be construed " no legal election;" and consequently, although there has been an election, *de facto*, the court has a discretionary power, upon considering all the circumstances of the election, to award or not to award a mandamus, as the justice of the case may require (*c*). If the legality of the election, *de facto*, be doubtful, and fit to be tried

(*z*) Sect. 9.

(*a*) R. v. *Burgesses of the Borough of Orford*, M. 9 Geo. II., MS., Bull. N. P. 201; 34 MS. Serjeant Hill, p. 263, *S. C.*, there said by the court, that the *Corporation of Macclesfield*, T. R. 11 Geo. I.,

was an authority in point.

(*b*) R. v. *The Mayor and Burgesses of Thetford*, 8 East, 270.

(*c*) R. v. *Newsham*, Say. R. 211, Borough of Carmarthen.

(4) " This being a remedial law to prevent the inconveniences that may arise, by any accident, from non-elections, if the parliament uses such words in an act that will take in other cases within the same mischief, the court ought to construe such kind of acts as liberally as possible." Per Lord *Hardwicke*, C. J., in R. v. *Pole, ubi sup.*

by information in nature of *quo warranto*, the court will not award a mandamus (*d*) ; but if it appear clearly that the election was illegal, or a merely colourable and void (*e*) election, the court will grant a mandamus (*f*) ; for in such case it would be nugatory to try the legality of the election in an information in the nature of *quo warranto*. And the court will grant a mandamus, not only for the head officer (*g*), but also for others who are necessary constituent parts of the corporation (*h*).

An election completed after the departure of the presiding officer, who forms an integral part in the elective assembly, is void (*i*). An assembly was regularly convened for the purpose of nominating and electing a new mayor, over which the then mayor presided. He declared that the persons with whom the nomination rested were equally divided, and consequently that no election could be made ; and thereupon he directed proclamation to be made for dissolving the assembly. No objection was made to this, nor did any persons give notice that they meant to proceed to make an election. But when the mayor was gone away, and a number of the burgesses also departed, considering the assembly as dissolved, the rest proceeded to make an election. It was holden (*k*), that this election could not be supported ; for assuming it to be clear (though the point has never been judicially decided) that an election begun by one presiding officer, could be completed under another, yet this was not a continuation of the business begun before the mayor, but an attempt to continue that which had been concluded. Considering, also, the case upon the statute, and that if the mayor absent himself, the next in place and order present may preside : yet here the mayor did not absent himself, but did preside, and as presiding officer determined upon the validity of the votes, that they were equal, and that no election could be had, and then dissolved the assembly ; and all this without any objection made at the time ; and in consequence of such dissolution of the assembly, unobjected to, as it appeared, many of the freemen went away, and then the rest of them made the election in question ; this was not an election within the aid of the statute, which never meant to protect elections made by surprise and fraud. Words of permission, when tending to promote the public benefit,

(*d*) *R.* v. *Bankes*, H. 4 Geo. III., 3 Burr. 1452, Borough of Corfe Castle ; *R.* v. *Mayor of Colchester*, 2 T. R. 259 ; *R.* v. *Mayor, &c. of Oxford*, 6 A. & E. 349.

(*e*) As where the person elected mayor was at the time a captain of foot on a voyage to America with his regiment, and likely to continue abroad for six years. *R.* v. *Corporation of Cambridge*, Newland's MS. 4to, 109.

(*f*) *R.* v. *Mayor of Bossiney*, alias *Tintagel*, H. 8 Geo. II., MS. ; *S. C.*, shortly reported, Str. 1003 ; Bull. N. P.

201, cited in *R.* v. *Bankes*, 3 Burr. 1454 ; case of *Aberystwith*, Trin. 14 Geo. II., Str. 1157 ; *Corporation of Scarborough*, Hil. 16 Geo. II., Str. 1180 ; *R.* v. *Newsham*, Borough of Carmarthen, E. 28 Geo. II., Say. 211 ; *R.* v. *Mayor of Cambridge*, H. 7 Geo. III., 4 Burr. 2008.

(*g*) *R.* v. *Corporation of Bridgewater*, 3 Doug. 379.

(*h*) *Corporation of Scarborough*, Str. 1180.

(*i*) *R.* v. *Buller*, 8 East, 389.

(*k*) *R.* v. *Gaborian*, 11 East, 77.

are always held to be compulsory; hence, where the words of the charter were, that the mayor and jurats "*might have power*" to hold a court of record for the recovery of debts, a mandamus was granted (*l*) to compel them to hold it; although it appeared that no such court had been holden for above thirty years.

II. *In what other Cases the Court will grant a Mandamus.*

THE circumstance of the office being subject to the Ecclesiastical Court, affords no objection. Hence, writs of mandamus have been granted to admit or restore prebendaries(*m*), an apparitor-general(*n*), parish clerks (*o*), and sextons (*p*). So to admit scavengers (*q*), &c.; to restore a schoolmaster of a grammar-school founded by the crown (*r*); so to restore a member of an university who had been improperly suspended from his degrees (*s*). In like manner a mandamus will lie to compel a dean and chapter to fill up a vacancy among canons residentiary (*t*); so to the Ecclesiastical Court (*u*), to swear churchwardens elected by the parish; so to grant the probate of a will to an executor (*x*). So a mandamus lies to the judge of the Prerogative Court of Canterbury to grant administration to the husband of the wife's estate, when the husband has done nothing to depart from his right (*y*). In the case of *R.* v. *Windham* (*z*), the court granted a mandamus to compel the warden of Wadham College to affix the common seal of the college to an answer of the fellows, &c., in chancery, although the warden disapproved of the answer of the fellows, and had put in a separate answer. So a mandamus lies to compel a bishop (*a*) to grant inspection of his register of presentations and institutions to a living within his diocese, to a person claiming the right of patronage, although the bishop himself

(*l*) *R.* v. *The Mayor and Jurats of Hastings*, B. R. Hil. 2 & 3 Geo. IV., 5 B. & A. 692, n. See also *R.* v. *Steward, &c. of Havering Atte Bower*, 5 B. & A. 691.

(*m*) *R.* v. *Dean of Norwich*, Str. 159.
(*n*) *Folkes's* case, cited per *Cur.*, in *R.* v. *Ward*, Str. 897.
(*o*) *R.* v. *Ashton*, Say. R. 159; *R.* v. *Warren*, Cowp. 371.
(*p*) *R.* v. *Churchwardens of King's Clere*, 2 Lev. 18; 1 Vent. 143, *S. C.* N. It appeared, by the certificate of the minister and several parishioners, that the sexton was an officer for life, and received twopence from every house, yearly, as wages. But in the same term it was granted for another sexton without such certificate.

(*q*) Said per *Cur.*, in *Ile's* case, 1 Ventr. 143, to have been granted. See also 2 T. R. 181.
(*r*) *R.* v. *Bailiffs of Morpeth*, Str. 58.
(*s*) *R.* v. *U. of Cambridge*, T. 19 Geo. III., *Dr. Ewin's* case.
(*t*) *Bishop of Chichester* v. *Harward*, 1 T. R. 652.
(*u*) *Anon.*, 1 Ventr. 115.
(*x*) 1 Ventr. 335.
(*y*) *R.* v. *Betterworth*, Str. 857, 1118.
(*z*) Cowp. 377.
(*a*) *R.* v. *The Bishop of Ely*, 8 B. & C. 112.

claimed that right; for such register is of a public nature. So to admit a clerk (b) of trustees under the General Turnpike Act.

A mandamus will lie to J. P. to nominate overseers of the poor, although the time mentioned in the stat. 43 Eliz. has expired: because the statutes for the relief of the poor are to be construed liberally (c). So to appoint a surveyor of the highways (d), where the J. P. had not appointed at the time mentioned in the stat. 13 Geo. III. c. 78. s. 1 (e). So to sign and allow a poor's rate; and in this case they will grant the mandamus in the first instance, and not a rule to show cause; for otherwise the poor might starve (f). So to the justices of the peace of a county or borough, to permit an individual (g) on behalf of several persons who contribute to the county rate, to inspect and take copies of the last two rates made by the justices, and all orders for the expenditure thereof, and other proceedings relating thereto. But an application for such inspection must be previously made to the justices assembled at quarter sessions. The court will not grant a mandamus (h) to justices in sessions to do that which may occasion costs, for which they have no means of reimbursing themselves. Neither will the court grant a mandamus to a J. P. to do an act, when there is a legal probability than an action (i) will be brought against him for doing it. A party applying for a mandamus to compel churchwardens to allow him to inspect their accounts, according to the directions of the 17 Geo. II. c. 38, must state some special reasons (k) for which he wishes to see the accounts. It is no answer to the application, that the statute imposes a penalty upon a churchwarden improperly refusing inspection (l). Although it was formerly doubted whether a mandamus would lie to a lord of a manor to admit a copyholder, yet in R. v. Rennett (m), where application was made for a mandamus to the steward of a manor to admit a person who claimed as heir at law to a customary estate within the manor, the court said, they had no doubt but that a mandamus ought to be granted, to compel a lord of a manor to admit a copyholder, if a proper case were laid before them; but as the party making this application claimed by descent, it would not answer any purpose to grant the mandamus, since he had as complete a title without admittance as with it, against all the world but the lord. See also R.

(b) R. v. Trustees of Cheshunt Turnpike, 5 B. & Ad. 438.

(c) R. v. Sparrow, Str. 1123.

(d) R. v. Justices of Denbighshire, 4 East, 142.

(e) Repealed by stat. 5 & 6 Will. IV. c. 50.

(f) R. v. Fisher, Say. R. 160.

(g) R. v. Justices of Leicester, 4 B. & C. 891.

(h) In re Lodge, 2 A. & E. 123; 4 Nev. & M. 312, S. C.

(i) R. v. Greame, 2 A. & E. 615. See also R. v. The Justices of Bucks, 3 Nev. & M. 68.

(k) R. v. Clear, 4 B. & C. 899.

(l) S. C.

(m) 2 T. R. 197; but this case was overruled in R. v. The Brewers' Company, 3 B. & C. 172, recognized by Bayley, J., in R. v. Wilson, 10 B. & C. 87; and see R. v. Lord of the Manor of Bonsall, 3 B. & C. 173.

v. *Lord of the Manor of Hendon* (n), where a mandamus was granted
to the lord, who had refused to admit the surrenderee of a copyhold
estate on account of a disagreement respecting the fine to be paid ;
the court observing, that they would not give an opinion respecting
the lord's fine on an application by a tenant for a mandamus to be
admitted, because the lord had not any right to the fine until admittance. See also *R.* v. *Coggan*, where a mandamus was granted to
the lord and steward of a manor to admit a person to a copyhold
tenement, who had a *prima facie* legal title, in order to enable him
to try his right, though a court of equity had before refused to compel the lord to admit him for want of his showing an equitable right
to the property (o) : Lord *Ellenborough*, C. J., observing, that he
was aware that the power of the Court of King's Bench to grant a
mandamus to admit to a copyhold, had been questioned on the other
side of the Hall, yet the court having, for many years past, been in
the constant habit of granting such writs, upon a sufficient *prima facie*
title made out on the part of the person applying, he could not doubt
their power in this respect. N. There being a claim of a previous
fine due to the lord in respect of the ancestor from whom the party
claimed, the rule for a mandamus was granted, upon the party's undertaking to pay such fine or fines as should be due to the lord.
The court will not grant a mandamus to admit cestui que trust, although he has a clear equity, the legal estate appearing on the court
rolls to be in the trustees. No instance is to be found of the court
granting a mandamus to the lord to *license* (p) under any circumstances. It makes no difference by what mode the party becomes
entitled to the franchise, whether by charter, prescription, or tenure ;
therefore, where, by the custom of the borough of Midhurst, the
jury at a court baron is to present the alienation of every burgage
tenement, and upon such presentment the steward is to admit the
tenant, who then becomes entitled to the franchises of the borough,
the jury, at a court baron in 1749, having refused to present several
conveyances of burgage tenements, the court granted (q) a mandamus to the lord to hold a court, and to the burgesses to attend at
such court, and to present the conveyances. And though one mandamus will not lie to restore several persons, yet the court held it
would lie in this case to the jury to do an act to perfect the rights of
several. So where, by the custom, the court-leet was to present to
the steward the person whom the commonalty of the borough had
chosen to be mayor, the court granted (r) a mandamus to the steward
to hold a court-leet, and to the in-burgesses to attend at such court,
and to present J. D., who had been chosen by the commonalty.
And it is the same where no particular person is interested ; as

(n) 2 T. R. 484.
(o) 6 East, 431.
(p) R. v. Hale, 9 A. & E. 342.
(q) R. v. Midhurst, 1 Wils. 283 ; 1 Bl. R. 60 ; Bull. N. P. 200, S. C., by the

name of R. v. Ld. Montague.
(r) Borough of Christchurch, 12 Geo. II., Bull. N. P. 200 ; S. C., cited in 1 Bl. R. 62.

where by charter or prescription the corporate body ought to consist of a definite number (s), and they neglect to fill up the vacancies as they happen, the court will grant a mandamus. Where a defendant is ousted on quo warranto, the prosecutor (t) is entitled to the writ of mandamus for a new election, if he applies in a reasonable time; if not, the defendant (u).

In cases of actions or suits commenced here, for which cause hath arisen in India, the king's courts at Westminster may award writs of mandamus to the C. J., and judges of the supreme court of judicature, or judges of the mayor's court at Madras, Bombay, or Bencoolen, for the examination of witnesses. The plaintiff obtaining the verdict is entitled (x) to the costs of cross-examining witnesses under a mandamus obtained by the defendant.

In *R.* v. *The Lords Commissioners of the Treasury* (y), the court granted a mandamus on the application of W. C. Smyth, to the lords commissioners to make and issue a Treasury minute or authority for the payment to S. of the arrears of a pension admitted to be held by them for his benefit; inasmuch as the claimant had a legal right and no other remedy, and as the writ was demanded not against the king, but against officers to whom the money had been paid for the claimant's use. A par found guilty by a jury at a session irregularly holden, is entitled to have the record of the proceedings correctly made up according to the fact, and the court will grant a mandamus to the justices to make up such record (z).

III. *Where not.*

It is a general rule that a mandamus does not lie unless the party making the application has not any other specific legal remedy (a). On this ground the court refused to grant a mandamus to a bishop, to license a curate of a curacy, which had been twice augmented by Queen Anne's bounty, where the right of appointing was claimed by two several parties, and there had been cross nominations; because the part had another specific remedy by *quare impedit* (b). So a mandamus does not lie to the governor

---

(s) Case of The *Town of Nottingham*, 23 Geo. II., Bull. N. P. 201.

(t) *R.* v. *M'Kay*, 4 B. & C. 658.

(u) *R.* v. *Mears*, 4 B. & C. 659.

(x) *Whytt* v. *M'Intosh and others*, 8 B. & C. 317.

(y) 4 A. & E. 286; 5 Nev. & M. 589. See 4 A. & E. 976.

(z) *R.* v. *The Justices of Middlesex*,

5 B. & Ad. 1113.

(a) Per *Buller*, J., in *R.* v. *Bishop of Chester*, 1 T. R. 404; in *R.* v. *M. of Stafford*, 3 T. R. 652; *R.* v. *The Bristol Dock Company*, M. 52 Geo. III., S. P. See also 2 Doug. 526.

(b) *R.* v. *Bishop of Chester*, 1 T. R. 396.

and company of the Bank of England to transfer stock, because the party has his remedy by assumpsit (c). The court will not interpose where the subject is purely of ecclesiastical jurisdiction. Hence, it will not grant a mandamus to churchwardens to make a church rate (d). But it will put in motion their functions in *ordine ad.*; *i. e.*, to assemble in order to inquire and agree, whether it be fit that a rate (e) should be made.

Although the court will grant a mandamus in order to enforce the making a poor's rate, they will not grant it with a direction, that certain persons shall be inserted in the rate; although an affidavit be made of the sufficiency of such persons, and that the omission had for its object the preventing their having votes for members of parliament (f). The power of licensing public houses being absolutely in the discretion of the justices of the peace, the court will not award a mandamus for the licensing a public house (g). A mandamus will not lie to compel admission to the degree of barrister (h) (5). Nor to compel the benchers of an inn of court to admit an individual as a member of the society, with a view to his qualifying himself to be called (i) to the bar. Nor to the principal and ancients of Barnard's Inn to admit an attorney (k) into the society. Nor for a fellow of a college, when there is a visitor (6). Nor to the judge of the ecclesiastical court to grant a probate of a will, *lite pendente* (l). Nor to the master and wardens of the company of gun-makers, to cause them to give a proof-mark to a freeman of their company; because they are no legal establishment (m). Nor to the mayor and aldermen of London to admit a person to the office of auditor of the chamberlain's and bridge-master's accounts, who had served it three years successively; because contrary to the custom of the city (n). Nor to compel the repair of a turnpike road (o). Nor to the College of Physicians, commanding them to

(c) *R.* v. *Bank of England*, 2 Doug. 524.

(d) *R.* v. *Churchwardens of St. Peter's, Thetford*, 5 T. R. 364.

(e) *R.* v. *Churchwardens and Overseers of St. John and St. Margaret, Westminster*, 4 M. & S. 250.

(f) *R.* v. *Weobly*, Str. 1259.

(g) *Giles's* case, Str. 881, per *Ryder, C. J.*; *R.* v. *Nottingham*, Say. R. 217.

(h) *R.* v. *Gray's Inn*, Doug. 353.

(i) *R.* v. *The Benchers of Lincoln's Inn, Wooller's* case, 4 B. & C. 855.

(k) *R.* v. *P.* and *A. of Barnard's Inn*, 5 A. & E. 17.

(l) 1 Bl. R. 668.

(m) Ray. 989.

(n) 1 T. R. 423.

(o) *Reg.* v. *Trustees of Oxford and Witney Roads*, 4 P. & D. 154.

(5) The only mode of relief is by appeal to the judges.

(6) Wherever there appears to be a general visitor, the common law courts will not interpose; yet as this is in the nature of a plea to the jurisdiction, it must appear on the return. The court will not supersede the writ of mandamus on an affidavit of the fact; it must appear by matter of record, which the party may contest. *R.* v. *Dr. Whaley, Master of Peterhouse College, Cambridge*, E. 13 Geo. II., 34 MS. Serjt. Hill, p. 325.

examine a doctor of physic, who has been licensed, in order to his being admitted a fellow of the college (p). Nor to a visitor where he is clearly acting under a visitatorial authority (q). In *R.* v. *Jotham* (r), the court refused a mandamus to *restore* a minister of an endowed dissenting meeting-house; because it did not appear, that he had complied with the requisites necessary to give him a *primâ facie* title; adding, that a mandamus to *admit* was granted merely to enable the party to try his right; but the court had always looked much more strictly to the right of the party applying for a mandamus to be *restored;* for if he had been before regularly admitted, he may try his right by action for money had and received. A mandamus will not lie to the Archbishop of Canterbury to issue his fiat to the proper officer for the admission of a doctor of civil law, a graduate of Cambridge, as an advocate of the Court of Arches (s). An authority was given by patent to registrars to exercise the office by themselves or by a sufficient deputy, to be appointed by the registrars, and allowed by the bishop. The registrars appointed a deputy, but the bishop disapproved of the appointment, stating that he had good and sufficient reasons for so doing, but did not allege any reasons. An application for a mandamus to the bishop to admit the party disapproved of was refused, the court being of opinion (t), that as the bishop had the power of approving or disapproving, they could not call upon him to exercise his discretion in a particular manner. A mandamus is granted only for public persons, and to compel the performance of public duties. Hence, the court will not grant it to a trading corporation at the instance of one of its members, to compel them to produce their accounts, for the purpose (u) of declaring a dividend of the profits. The mode of burying the dead is a matter of ecclesiastical cognizance; and therefore, where the question was, whether a parishioner had a right to be buried in a churchyard in an iron coffin, which was a new and unusual mode, the court refused (x) a mandamus. So the court refused a mandamus to a rector (y) to bury a corpse in a vault, or in any particular part of the churchyard, he having a right to exercise a discretion on the subject. The court have no power (z) to grant a mandamus to justices to compel them to come to a particular decision, as, to make an order of maintenance on a particular parish. Although the court will not grant a mandamus which will expose justices to danger, yet it will put them in motion (a) in a case where they clearly ought to proceed. Where

(p) *R.* v. *College of Physicians,* 7 T. R. 282.

(q) Adm. *R.* v. *Bishop of Ely,* 2 T. R. 345.

(r) 3 T. R. 575.

(s) *R.* v. *Archbishop of Canterbury,* 8 East, 213.

(t) *R.* v. *Bishop of Gloucester,* 2 B. & Ad. 158.

(u) *R.* v. *The Governor and Company of the Bank of England,* 2 B. & A. 620. See also *R.* v. *London Ass. Comp.,* 5 B. & A. 899.

(x) *R.* v. *Coleridge,* 2 B. & A. 806.

(y) *Blackmore, Exp.,* 1 B. & Ad. 122.

(z) *R.* v. *Justices of Middlesex,* 4 B. & A. 298.

(a) *R.* v. *Barker,* 6 A. & E. 388.

the certiorari is taken away, the court will not (b) indirectly bring proceedings under review by a mandamus.

IV. *Form of the Writ.*

HAVING endeavoured in the foregoing sections to explain the nature of a mandamus, and having briefly stated those cases in which this remedy may be adopted, I shall proceed to consider the form of the writ; as to which the following rules may be useful:—

1. Care must be taken that the mandamus is properly directed, that is, to the persons who are to obey the writ (c) (7). And this duty is cast upon the person who applies for the writ; for the court, when they grant the writ, will not specify the person to whom it is to be directed (d). If the writ be improperly directed, *e. g.*, if the right of election be in the mayor and aldermen, and the mandamus is directed to the mayor, aldermen, and *common council*, the court will grant a supersedeas, *quia improvide emanavit* (e). If a writ be directed to a corporation by a wrong name, they may return this special matter, and rely upon it; but if they answer the exigency of the writ, they admit themselves to be the corporation to whom the writ is directed; and cannot take advantage of the misnomer (f).

2. The writ must contain convenient certainty, in setting forth the duty to be performed; but it need not particularly set forth by what authority the duty exists. Therefore where a mandamus to the commissary of the Archbishop of York (g), to admit a deputy register, stated *quod minus rite recusavit* to admit, it was holden sufficient; though it was objected, it was the constant form to allege, that the party to whom the writ is directed, is the person to whom it appertains to swear and admit; for if the defendant was not the person to whom the executing this writ belonged, he should have returned so, but instead of that, the return consisted merely of matter of excuse; besides it was laid that *minus rite* he refused, which was an averment that in justice *he ought* to do it. So a

---

(b) *R.* v. *Justices of the West Riding of Yorkshire*, 1 A. & E. 563; 3 Nev. & M. 802.

(c) *R.* v. *Mayor of Hereford*, Salk. 701; *R.* v. *Mayor of Rippon*, Salk. 433.

(d) *R.* v. *Wigan*, 2 Burr. 782.

(e) *R.* v. *Mayor of Norwich*, Str. 55.

(f) *R.* v. *Bailiffs of Ipswich*, Salk. 434, 5.

(g) *R.* v. *Ward*, Str. 897.

---

(7) If the writ is directed to the corporation, it has been held good. But if it be directed to those, who by the constitution of the corporation ought to do the act, without doubt it is good also. Per *Holt*, C. J., *R.* v. *Mayor of Abingdon*, Ld. Raym. 560.

mandamus to the Dean of the Arches to grant probate to Lord Londonderry's executors (*h*), setting out that the dean *juxta juris exigentiam recusavit*, was holden sufficient, though it was objected, that it did not show the dean's title to grant probate; not having set out that there were *bona notabilia;* for the·court will not presume an inferior jurisdiction, and it appeared that he had already done some acts of office as the prerogative judge, and he shall not be received now to say it does not appear he has any jurisdiction. The ground of the application for a mandamus is, that there is no other remedy. Where, therefore, a mandamus directed to a corporation, and commanding them to pay a poor's rate, omitted to state that the defendants had no effects upon which a distress could be levied, it was holden (*i*) bad.

3. If several persons have been removed, there must be a distinct writ for each person: for they cannot join (*k*); for the interest is several, and the amotion of one is not the amotion of the others.

4. Every circumstance that is requisite to show that the party is entitled to be admitted, must be suggested in the writ (*l*); therefore, where in a mandamus to the ordinary to license a curate, it was stated that he had been *duly nominated and appointed by the inhabitants* of a township to be curate of the church of P., but neither the consent of the rector nor any endowment or custom for the inhabitants to make such nomination and appointment was stated, the court quashed the writ (*m*). But although it is essential such facts should be alleged as are necessary to show that the party applying for the writ is entitled to the relief prayed, no precise form is required (*n*).

5. The writ must be granted to proceed to an election to the office, and not to elect a particular person (*o*).

Lastly, the writ must be tested; and there must be fourteen days between the teste and the return, if it goes above forty miles; otherwise only eight days, and one day is to be taken inclusive, the other exclusive (*p*). Upon discovering any informality in the writ, the party may apply to amend at any time before the return (*q*); but after the return has been made and traversed, the court will not permit an amendment in the mandamus (*r*). A motion cannot be made to supersede the writ after the return is out (*s*). Although

(*h*) *R.* v. *Bettesworth*, Str. 857.

(*i*) *R.* v. *Margate Pier Company*, 3 B. & A. 220. Q. Whether in such a case a mandamus will lie.

(*k*) *R.* v. *City of Chester*, 5 Mod. 11; the case of *Andover*, Salk. 433; *Anon.*, Salk. 436, S. P.

(*l*) 6 Mod. 310, per *Holt*, C. J.

(*m*) *R.* v. *Bishop of Oxford*, 7 East, 345.

(*n*) Per *Lee*, C. J., in *R.* v. *M. and B.*

of Nottingham, Say. R. 37.

(*o*) 2 Bulst. 122; 2 Rol. Abr. 456, pl. 5.

(*p*) *R.* v. *Mayor of Dover*, Str. 407.

(*q*) 6 Mod. 133, per *Holt*, C. J.

(*r*) *R.* v. *Mayor of Stafford*, 4 T. R. 690.

(*s*) Said per *Lee*, J., in *Whitwood q. t.* v. *Jocam*, B. R. M. 7 Geo. II., MS., to have been so determined in Lord *Raymond's* time.

it has been said (t) that the defendant will not be permitted to avail himself of any objection to the writ after the return; yet it has since been adjudged that an exception may be taken to the writ even after the return (u), and at any time before a peremptory mandamus issues. Where the court grants a rule to show cause, though upon showing cause it appear doubtful, whether the party have a right or not, yet the court will issue a mandamus, in order that the right may be tried upon the return (x). But the court will not grant a mandamus to a person to exercise a jurisdiction, when it is doubtful whether he has the power to exercise it or not (y). Upon a motion for a mandamus (z) to the warden of the Vintners' Company to swear J. S. one of the court of assistants, the affidavit being only that he was informed by some of the court of assistants that he was elected, and no positive affidavit of an election, the court would only grant a rule to show cause, but said, if there had been a positive affidavit of his election, they would have granted the writ in the first instance.

V. *Of the Return.*

THE next object of consideration is the return.

1. The return must be made by the person to whom the writ is directed.

2. It must be positive and certain (a). The same certainty is required in a return to a mandamus as in indictments or returns to writs of habeas corpus (b). But if the return be certain on the face of it, that is sufficient, and the court cannot intend facts inconsistent with it, for the purpose of making it bad (c). The return must not be argumentative (d). To a mandamus to elect, it is a good return, that a person has been duly elected, and sworn into the office (e). To a mandamus to a commissary to admit A. B. into the office of churchwarden, reciting that he had been duly elected, a return (f) that A. B. was not duly elected is good.

3. Where the mandamus is to *restore* a person who has been removed from an office, the return must be very accurate in stating, first, the power of the corporation to remove (g). Secondly, the

(t) Per *Kenyon*, C. J., and *Buller*, J., in *R.* v. *Mayor of York*, 5 T. R. 74, 5.
(u) *R.* v. *Margate Pier Company*, 3 B. & A. 220.
(x) *R.* v. *Dr. Bland*, Bull. N. P. 200.
(y) *R.* v. *Bishop of Ely*, 1 Wils. 266.
(z) Bull. N. P. 200.
(a) 11 Rep. 99 b. See also *R.* v. *Marquis of Abingdon*, Salk. 432.

(b) Per *Buller*, J., Doug. 158.
(c) Doug. 159.
(d) *R.* v. *Lyme Regis*, Doug. 158.
(e) *R.* v. *Williams*, Say. R. 140.
(f) *R.* v. *Williams*, 8 B. & C. 681.
(g) *R.* v. *Mayor, &c. of Doncaster*, Trin. 25 & 26 Geo. 11., 34 MS. Serjt. Hill, p. 210.

return must set forth a sufficient and reasonable cause of removal. There are three kinds of offences (h) for which a corporator may be removed :—

First,—For any offence committed against his duty as a corporator (8).

Secondly,—For any offence which is in itself of so infamous a nature as to render the offender unfit to execute any public franchise, e. g., forgery, perjury, &c., although such offence has not any immediate relation to his office (9).

Thirdly,—For any offence of a mixed nature, as being an offence not only against the duty of his office, but also a matter indictable at common law (10). Misemploying the corporation money is not a sufficient cause of disfranchisement, because the corporation may have their action for it (i).

Although the return be insufficient, yet if it appear to the court, that the party has no ground for being restored, the court will not restore him (k).

The due execution of the power of amoval must be set forth in the return. In a return to a mandamus to a corporation to restore a member who has been removed, it should appear that the body removing had proved the charge for which the member was removed.

(h) *R.* v. *Mayor of Derby*, 9 Geo. II., Bull. N. P. 206; *R.* v. *Richardson*, 1 Burr. 538 ; *R.* v. *Liverpool*, 2 Burr. 732.

(i) *R.* v. *Chalke*, Lord Raym. 226.
(k) Per *Cur.*, in *R.* v. *Tidderly*, 1 Siderf. 14.

---

(8) In this case the corporator is removable without any previous conviction by a jury. Bull. N. P. 206, cites *R.* v. *Derby*, 9 Geo. II., which case was first brought before the court in E. T. 8 Geo. II. See Session Cases, vol. ii. p. 343. The power of trial, as well as amotion, for an offence of this kind, is incident to *every* corporation. See Lord *Mansfield's* opinion, 1 Burr. 538.

(9) An offence of this kind ought to be established by a previous conviction by a jury, according to the law of the land. Per Lord *Mansfield*, C. J., in *R.* v. *Richardson*, 1 Burr. 539. It is the infamy which renders the corporator an improper person to be continued in an office of trust; therefore, if the crime for which he is convicted be such as does not carry such infamy with it, it will be no cause of disfranchisement; as if he were convicted of a simple assault. Bull. N. P. 206, cites *R.* v. *Derby*, 9 Geo. II.

(10) Where the offence is criminal in both respects, the difference seems to be, that if it consists of one single fact, as burning the charters of the corporation, bribery, &c., there must be a conviction; but not where it may be considered as abstracted, the one from the other, as riot and assault upon any other member, so as to obstruct the business of the corporation. *Ib.*

It is not sufficient to state merely, that he was present when the charge was made, and did not deny it (*l*).

It is not a good return to state, that the party was incapable of being elected; for the proper way of trying whether he was capable of being elected, is by an information in nature of quo warranto (*m*). So, where all the proceedings of the election were set forth in the writ, concluding, " by reason whereof A. was elected," a return, stating A. was not elected, was holden to be bad (*n*). Where, upon a mandamus commanding defendant to take upon himself the office of common council-man of the borough of Leicester, the return was, that, by a by-law, persons refusing to fill the office were subject to a certain fine, and that defendant had paid the fine; it was holden (*o*), that the return was insufficient, as it did not state that the fine was to be in lieu of service.

4. The same certainty is required in the return, as before the stat. of Queen Anne (*p*).

5. The rule is, not to presume every thing against the return, but not to presume any thing either one way or the other (*q*).

6. The return must not contain two inconsistent causes (*r*), otherwise the court will quash the whole return (*s*). But several consistent causes may be returned (*t*); and where the causes are not inconsistent, although some are bad, yet the court may admit the good and reject the bad. It is not necessary that every part of the return should be good; the court will not quash it, if on the whole it state a sufficient reason to justify the party making it (*u*). Masters of grammar schools must be licensed by the ordinary, who may examine the party applying for a license as to his learning, morality, and religion; and it is a good return (*x*) to a mandamus to the ordinary to grant such a license, that the party applying refused to be examined as to his sufficiency in learning. To a mandamus to restore J. S. to the office of sexton, the defendant returned, that J. S. was not duly elected according to the ancient custom of the parish, and further, there was a custom for the inhabitants in vestry to remove the sexton from his office, and that J. S. was removed pursuant to such custom; it was holden (*y*), that there was not any repugnancy in saying, that J. S. was not *duly* elected; but that being in *fact* elected, they had, according to an ancient custom, removed him. In either case, they were equally entitled to exercise that right. The return, therefore, was allowed.

(*l*) *R.* v. *Faversham*, 8 T. R. 352.
(*m*) *R.* v. *Doncaster*, Say. R. 40.
(*n*) *R.* v. *Mayor of York*, 5 T. R. 66.
(*o*) *R.* v. *S. Bower, the younger*, 1 B. & C. 585.
(*p*) Per Lord *Mansfield*, C. J., in *R.* v. *Lyme Regis*, Doug. 157.
(*q*) *R.* v. *Lyme Regis*, E. 19 Geo. III.
(*r*) See 2 T. R. 456.

(*s*) Adm. *R.* v. *Mayor of Cambridge*, 2 T. R. 456. See also *R.* v. *Mayor of York*, 5 T. R. 66.
(*t*) *Wright* v. *Fawcett*, 4 Burr. 2041.
(*u*) *R.* v. *Archbishop of York*, 6 T. R. 490.
(*x*) S. C.
(*y*) *R.* v. *Taunton St. James*, Cowp. 413.

The return need not be under the seal of the corporation, nor need it be signed by the mayor; for the return of a mandamus is matter of record, and acts done by a corporation upon record, are not required to be under hand or seal; for in such case an action lies against a body politic, or the persons who procure the false return (*z*). Where a return of a mandamus to restore a party to a corporate office is defective in form, but, on the whole, it appears that there is good ground for amotion, the court will not award a peremptory mandamus; the only effect of which would be to compel the corporation to restore an officer whom they would be bound immediately to remove in a more formal manner (*a*). Clerical mistakes in the return may be amended, even after it is filed (*b*). The prosecutor of a mandamus (*c*), to which a return has been made, having moved for a concilium, and the court having, upon argument, adjudged that the return is sufficient in law, cannot afterwards traverse the facts contained in the return.

VI. *Of the Remedy, where the Party, to whom the Writ of Mandamus is directed, does not make any Return, or where he makes an insufficient, or false Return.*

THE first writ of mandamus always concludes with commanding obedience, or cause to be shown to the contrary (*d*); but if a return be made to it, which upon the face of it is insufficient, the court will grant a peremptory mandamus, and if that be not obeyed, an attachment will issue against the persons disobeying it. If no return be made, the court will grant an attachment against the persons to whom the mandamus was directed; with this difference, however, that where a mandamus is directed to a corporation to do a corporate act, and no return is made, the attachment is granted only against those particular persons who refuse to pay obedience to the mandamus; but where it is directed to several persons in their natural capacity, the attachment for disobedience must issue against all (*e*), though when they are before the court, the punishment will be proportioned to their offence.

If the return upon the face of it be good, but the matter of it false, an action upon the case lies for the party injured, against the

(*z*) *R.* v. *Mayor of Exeter*, Lord Raym. 223. See also *R.* v. *Chalice*, Lord Raym. 848, S. P.
   (*a*) *R.* v. *Griffiths*, 5 B. & A. 731.
   (*b*) *R.* v. *Lyme Regis*, E. 19 Geo. III., Doug. 157.
   (*c*) *R. on Prosecution of M. Scales* v.

Mayor and Aldermen of London, 3 B. & Ad. 255.
   (*d*) Bull. N. P. 201.
   (*e*) *R.* v. *Overseers of St. Chad's, Salop*, H. 8 Geo. II., MS. Bull. N. P. 201, S. C.

persons making such false return. And where the return is made by several, the action may be either joint or several, it being founded upon a tort: but if it appear upon evidence that the defendant voted against the return, but was overruled by a majority, the plaintiff will be nonsuited (*f*); and though the return be made in the name of the corporation, yet an action will lie against the particular persons who caused the return to be made (*g*); or if the matter concern the public government, and no particular person be so interested as to maintain an action, the court will grant an information against the persons making the return (*h*). The return must be filed and allowed before the information can be moved for. A mandamus was directed to the mayor, bailiff, and burgesses of A. The mayor made a return (*i*); a motion was made to stay the filing of it, upon a suggestion, that the return was made against the votes of the majority, who would have obeyed the writ. But the court resolved, that they could not refuse the mayor's return, because he was the principal officer to whom the writ was directed, and actually delivered; and, as he had returned and brought in the writ, it was not fit that the court should examine upon affidavits, whether the majority consented. But if the mayor had made any return, contrary to the votes of the majority, it was at his peril, and the way to punish him was by information.

Note. Where several join in an application for a mandamus, they may all join in the action for a false return (*k*). And if in such action or information the return be falsified, the court will grant a peremptory mandamus; however, it cannot be moved for until four days after the return of the postea, because the defendants have that time to move in arrest of judgment (*l*): and the court will not award a peremptory mandamus until the proceedings on the original mandamus are complete (*m*). In an action for a false return (*n*), the plaintiff set out, that he was chosen upon the 1st of October, according to the custom. Upon evidence it appeared, that the custom was to choose on the 29th of September, and that the plaintiff was then chosen; and this was holden sufficient to support the declaration, for the day in the declaration is but form. If the mayor of a corporation procure a false return to be made, it will be sufficient evidence against him, that the mandamus was delivered to him, and that the mandamus has such a return made; and that will be presumptive against him, that he made that return, unless he shows the contrary; for the mayor or any other member of the corporation, or others, who shall procure a false return to be made,

(*f*) Carth. 172.
(*g*) Per *Holt*, C. J., Lord Raym. 564.
(*h*) *Surgeons' Comp.*, Salk. 374; *R.* v. *Mayor of Nottingham*, H. 25 Geo. II., Bull. N. P. 203, S. P.
(*i*) *R.* v. *Mayor of Abingdon*, Salk. 431; Carth. 499, *S. C.*

(*k*) *Green* v. *Pope*, Lord Raym. 125.
(*l*) Per *Holt*, C. J., *Buckly* v. *Palmer*, Salk. 430, 1.
(*m*) *Reg.* v. *Baldwin*, 8 A. & E. 947; 3 P. & D. 124.
(*n*) *Vaughan* v. *Lewis*, Carth. 228.

are liable in their private capacity (*o*). In an action brought in C.
B. for a false return, the plaintiff obtained judgment; the Court of
B. R. refused to grant a peremptory mandamus: *Holt*, C. J.,
observing, that every mandamus recites the fact *prout patet nobis
per recordum*, and that they could not take notice of the records of
the Common Pleas (*p*) (11). Before the stat. 9 Ann. c. 20 (*q*),
except in extraordinary cases (*r*), an attachment did not issue for
want of a return, until after the return of an *alias* and *pluries* writ
of mandamus, and disobedience of a peremptory rule to return (*s*).
But by that statute, reciting that persons who had a right to the
office of mayors, or other offices within cities, towns corporate,
boroughs, and places, or to be burgesses or freemen thereof, had
either been illegally turned out, or had been refused to be admitted
thereto, and had no other remedy to procure themselves to be
admitted or restored, than by writs of mandamus, the proceedings
on which were very dilatory and expensive, it was enacted,

1. That a return should be made to the first writ of mandamus (*t*).

2. That the persons prosecuting such writ might plead to (*u*), or
traverse all or any the material facts contained in the return, to
which the persons making such return should reply, take issue, or
demur; and such further proceedings should be had therein, as
might have been had if the persons suing such writ had brought
their action on the case for a false return; and in case a verdict
should be found, or judgment given for them upon a demurrer, or
by *nihil dicit*, or for want of a replication or other pleading, they
should recover damages and costs, and a peremptory writ of mandamus should be granted without delay for them for whom judgment
shall be given, as might have been if such return had been adjudged
insufficient; and in case judgment shall be given for the persons
making such return, they shall recover costs.

3. The stat. for the amendment of the law (4 Ann. c. 16,) and all
the statutes of jeofail shall be extended to writs of mandamus, and
the proceedings thereupon (*x*). The power of traversing the return,

---

(*o*) Per *Cur.*, *R.* v. *Chalice*, Lord Raym.
848.

(*p*) *Anon.*, Salk. 428, probably the *S. C.*
as is reported by the name of *Green* v.
Pope, 1 Lord Raym. 128, where S. P. is
said to have been ruled.

(*q*) Repealed as to so much as prevents

the re-election of mayors and other annual
returning officers, by stat. 3 & 4 Vict. c. 47.

(*r*) See Skinn. 669.
(*s*) Bull. N. P. 203.
(*t*) Sect. 1.
(*u*) Sect. 2.
(*x*) Sect. 7.

---

(11) Yet where, in an action for a false return, judgment was given for
the defendant, and upon a writ of error judgment was reversed in the Exchequer Chamber, the Court of K. B. granted a peremptory mandamus
before judgment entered, saying, it was a mandatory writ, and not a judicial writ founded upon the record. Bull. N. P. 202.

which is given by the second section of the preceding statute, is given in the room of an action for a false return; and as in such action it cannot be said that the damages are collateral, so neither can it be said that they are collateral in a proceeding under the statute, for they are consequent or dependent upon the issue, and the jury are to inquire of the damages as parcel of the charge; and consequently, if, in a proceeding under the statute, the jury omit to find damages and costs for the plaintiff, whether the verdict be general or special, this defect cannot be supplied by a writ of inquiry (y): but in such case the party may bring an action for a false return, for the act does not take away the party's right to bring such action, but only provides, that in case damages are recovered by virtue of that act, against the persons making the return, they shall not be liable to be sued in any other action for making such return (z). Where issue is joined upon the traverse of the return, and the prosecutor does not proceed to trial according to the practice of the court, judgment as in case of a nonsuit may be given (a). Since the preceding statute, a mandamus, in cases to which the statute applies, is in the nature of an action, pleadings therein being admitted, and it seems that in such cases a writ of error lies upon the judgment (b); but upon the award of a peremptory mandamus, in a case to which the stat. of Anne does not apply, a writ of error will not lie (c). It appears from the wording of the statute, that there are many cases to which it does not extend; therefore in all those cases the proceedings must have been according to the course of the common law (d). But now, by stat. 1 Will. IV. c. 21, [30th March, 1831,] s. 2, after reciting that the provisions contained in the 9th Ann. c. 20, had been found useful and convenient, and that the same ought to be extended to the proceedings on other such writs, it is enacted, that the several enactments, contained in the said statute relating to the return to writs of mandamus and the proceedings on such returns, and to the recovery of damages and costs, shall be and are extended and made applicable to all other writs of mandamus and the proceedings thereon, except so far only as the same may be altered by this act. These alterations are as follow:—The 4th section, reciting, that writs of mandamus, other than such as relate to the offices and franchises provided for by the 9th of Anne, are sometimes issued to officers and other persons, commanding them to admit to offices, or to perform other matters, in respect whereof the persons to whom such writs are directed claim no right or interest, or whose functions are merely ministerial in relation to such offices or matters;

(y) *Kynaston* v. *Mayor of Shrewsbury*, T. 9 & 10 Geo. II., MS., and Str. 1052, S. C.

(z) Bull. N. P. 203. See Str. 1053.

(a) *Wigan* v. *Holmes*, Say. R. 110; *R.* v. *Mayor of Stafford*, 4 T. R. 689.

(b) 1 P. Wms. 351; Str. 1052.

(c) *Dean of Dublin* v. *The King*, in error, D. P., 21st April, 1724, 1 Bro. P. C. 73, Tomlins' ed.

(d) Bull. N. P. 204.

and that it may be proper such officers and persons should, in certain cases, be protected against the payment of damages or costs, to which they might otherwise become liable; enacts, that the court, if it shall see fit, may make rules and orders, calling not only on the person to whom such writ may be required to issue, but also every other person having or claiming any right or interest in or to the matter of such writ, to show cause against the issuing of such writ and payment of costs of the application; and upon the appearance of such other person, or in default after service, to exercise all such powers and authorities, and make all such rules and orders, applicable to the case, as are or may be given or mentioned by or in any act passed during this session, for giving relief against adverse claims made upon persons having no interest in the subject of such claims, [see the provisions of 1 & 2 Will. IV. c. 58,] provided, that the return and issues in fact or in law, shall be made and joined in the name of the person to whom the writ is directed; but the court may direct the same to be made and joined on the behalf of such other person as may be mentioned in such rules, and in that case such other person shall be permitted to frame the return, and to conduct the subsequent proceedings at his own expense; and in such case, if any judgment shall be given for or against the party suing such writ, such judgment shall be given against or for the person on whose behalf the return shall be expressed to be made, and who shall have the like remedy for recovery of costs and enforcing judgment, as the person to whom the writ shall have been directed, might and would otherwise have had. The proceedings are, by the 5th section, not to abate by the death, resignation, or removal from office, of the person making the return under the authority of this act, and peremptory writ may be directed to the successor. The 6th section is general, and enacts, that in all cases of application for any writ of mandamus, the costs of such application, whether the writ be granted or refused, and also the costs of writ, issued and obeyed, shall be in the discretion of the court, who is to order by whom, and to whom, the same shall be paid (e). In a case where the proceedings had commenced before this act came into force, the court refused the application (f) for costs. Under this statute, the costs may be obtained (g) by a distinct motion after issuing of the writ.

(e) See *Reg.* v. *Fall*, 1 G. & D. 117; *Reg.* v. *Kelk*, 1 G. & D. 127.

(f) *R.* v. *Wix*, 2 B. & Ad. 203.

(g) *R.* v. *Kirke*, 5 B. & Ad. 1089.

CHAPTER XXIX.

MASTER AND SERVANT.

I. *Of Actions by Servants against their Masters, for the Recovery of their Wages, p.* 1091.

II. *Of the Liability of the Master in respect of a Contract made by the Servant, p.* 1094.

III. *Of the Liability of the Master in respect of a tortious Act done by the Servant, p.* 1097.

IV. *Of Actions brought by Masters for enticing away Apprentices and Servants, and for Injuries done to their Servants, p.* 1102; *and herein of the Action for Seduction, p.* 1103; *Witness, p.* 1104; *Damages, p.* 1106.

I. *Of Actions by Servants against their Masters, for the Recovery of their Wages.*

IF a person retain a servant under an agreement to pay him so much by the day, month, or year, in consideration of the service to be performed, the servant, having fulfilled his part of the contract, may maintain an action against the master, or, in case of his death, against his personal representative, for a breach of the contract on the part of the master. The form of action will depend upon the nature of the contract; if the contract be by deed, an action of debt or covenant must be brought (1); if by parol, (*i. e.* in writing, but not a specialty, or verbal,) an action of debt or assumpsit.

---

(1) If a feme covert, without any authority from her husband, contract with a servant by deed, the servant, having performed the service stipulated, may maintain an action of assumpsit. *White* v. *Cuyler*, 6 T. R. 176.

If a servant be hired in the general way, without mentioning the time, that is a general hiring, and, in point of law (a), a hiring for a year.

If a clerk or servant (b), engaged at a fixed salary, payable quarterly or yearly, resign his employment in the middle of a quarter, he is not entitled to a proportionate part of his salary. But where there has been no misconduct on either side, it may be left as a question for the jury, whether the facts of the case raise a presumption that at the time of the resignation there was an understanding that a payment *pro ratâ* should be made.

In a case (c) where the plaintiff, commencing his service in March, 1793, served the defendant, an army agent, in the capacity of his clerk for several years, until December 23, 1826, at which time the defendant, without assigning any reason, dismissed the plaintiff, who was willing to have continued: it appeared that, in one year, the salary had been paid quarterly, but for the last six years, before 1826, it was paid monthly: it was holden, that there was an implied yearly hiring, and that defendant was bound to pay the salary up to the end of the year, and that a contract in writing was not necessary. So where the contract was to serve as reporter to a newspaper for one whole year from a certain day, and so from year to year to the end of each year commenced, so long as the parties should respectively please; it was holden, that this contract could only be terminated at the end of a current year (d). A commission of bankrupt does not operate (e) as a dissolution of the contract of hiring between the bankrupt and his clerk. In the case of domestic servants, the rule is well established, that the contract may be determined by a month's notice or a month's wages (f). A master may discharge his servant at a moment's warning for misconduct (g), e. g., for being absent when wanted, sleeping from home at night without his master's leave; or in the case of a mercantile clerk (h), for asserting that he is a partner in the business, &c. But if the servant has not been guilty of misconduct, and the master discharges him without warning, the servant in that case will be entitled to a month's wages beyond the wages due for the period of actual service (i). Where a servant under a general hiring at the rate of so much per annum, is dismissed for misconduct, he cannot

(a) *Fawcett* v. *Cash*, 5 B. & Ad. 904; 3 Nev. & Man. 177.

(b) *Lamburn* v. *Cruden*, C. B. Jan. 21, 1841, Law Jour. N. S. vol. x. p. 121. See *Huttman* v. *Boulnois*, 2 C. & P. 512; *Bayley* v. *Rimmell*, 1 M. & W. 506.

(c) *Beeston* v. *Collyer*, 4 Bingh. 309; 12 Moore, 552.

(d) *Williams* v. *Byrne*, 2 Nev. & P. 139; 7 A. & E. 177.

(e) *Thomas* v. *Williams*, 1 A. & E.

685; 3 Nev. & Man. 545.

(f) Per *Littledale*, J., *Fawcett* v. *Cash*, 5 B. & Ad. 908; 3 Nev. & M. 177. See *Nowlan* v. *Ablett*, 2 Cr. M. & R. 54.

(g) *Robinson* v. *Hindman*, B. R. London Sittings after M. T. 41 Geo. III., *Kenyon*, C. J., 3 Esp. N. P. C. 235.

(h) *Amor* v. *Fearon*, 9 A. & E. 548.

(i) Per *Kenyon*, C. J., in *Robinson* v. *Hindman*, *ubi sup.*

recover (k) any of the salary of the current year, even for the time during which he has served. Nor is it necessary that a master, having a good cause of dismissal, should either state it to the servant or act upon it; it is sufficient if the cause exist, and the servant is not entitled to object that it is not the cause for which he was dismissed (l). A servant who comes over from the West Indies (m), where he has been a slave, and who continues in the service of his master, in England, without any agreement for wages, is not entitled to any wages, unless there has been an express promise on the part of the master.

Where a person performed work for a committee, under a resolution entered into by them, "That any service to be rendered by him should, at a certain time, be taken into consideration, and such remuneration be made as should be deemed right; it was holden (n), that an action would not lie to recover a compensation for such work, the resolution importing that the committee were to judge whether any compensation was due. However, in a case where A. agreed to enter into the service of B., and wrote to him a letter as follows: "I hereby agree to enter your service as weekly manager, commencing next Monday; and the amount of payment I am to receive I leave entirely to you." A. served B. in that capacity six weeks. It was holden (o), (Parke, B., dissentiente) that the contract implied that A. was to be paid something at all events for the services performed; and that the jury, in an action on a quantum meruit, might ascertain what B., acting bonâ fide, ought to have awarded.

Where the declaration stated a contract for service for certain wages per annum, subject to be determined at a month's notice, and alleged that the defendant dismissed the plaintiff without a month's notice, by means whereof plaintiff lost all the wages, &c. he might have acquired from being continued in the service; it was holden (p), that the plaintiff was only entitled to recover, as damages, wages for one month; and that the arrears of salary, due to him at the time of dismissal, could only be recovered in indebitatus assumpsit for work and labour. But a servant (q), under a quarterly hiring, improperly dismissed in the middle of a quarter, and who tendered himself, but was not allowed to serve through the remaining part of the quarter, cannot recover wages for such part in an action of indebitatus assumpsit for work and labour commenced before the quarter ended. If the contract be the usual one for a year, determinable at a month's notice, the servant, if improperly

(k) Turner v. Robinson, 5 B. & Ad. 789; 2 Nev. & M. 829.
(l) Ridgway v. Hungerford Market Company, 3 A. & E. 171; 4 Nev. & M. 97.
(m) Alfred v. M. of Fitzjames, 3 Esp.

N. P. C. 3.
(n) Taylor v. Brewer, 1 M. & S. 290.
(o) Bryant v. Flight, 5 M. & W. 114.
(p) Hartley v. Harman, 3 P. & D. 567.
(q) Smith v. Hayward, 7 A. & E. 544; 2 Nev. & P. 432.

turned away, cannot recover on a count stating the contract to be for an entire year; and he cannot recover on a common count for wages for any further period than that during which he served (r). However, where the plaintiff, a domestic servant, entered into the defendant's service on the 19th November, and on the 15th January her mistress caused her to be taken, on a charge of stealing, before a magistrate, who remanded her till the 20th, when she was discharged. On the 22nd, the plaintiff went to demand her clothes and wages, including £1 1s. in lieu of a month's warning. The defendant tendered her £2 2s. for the two months' actual service, but refused to pay the additional guinea. It was holden (s), that, inasmuch as such placing the plaintiff in custody was no dissolution of the contract, the plaintiff was, under the circumstances, entitled to wages for the third month, which had been entered upon; and that the whole might be recovered under the common count for work and labour. Where to an action (t) for wrongfully discharging the plaintiff, the defendant pleads only payment of money into court, he cannot prove in mitigation of damages, that he discharged the plaintiff for misconduct, for evidence of such facts would be a bar to the right to recover, which was admitted by the plea.

A master (u) is not liable to his servant for injuries received by him in consequence of the breaking down of an overloaded van, (conducted by another servant,) in which the servant is travelling on his master's business.

The statutes 20 Geo. II. c. 19, 6 Geo. III. c. 25, and 4 Geo. IV. c. 34, give powers to justices to determine complaints between masters and servants, and between masters, apprentices, artificers, and others.

II. *Of the Liability of the Master in respect of Contracts made by the Servant.*

A CONTRACT made by a servant acting under the express (x) authority of the master, is binding on the master. And the same rule holds, where the servant acts under an implied authority. The defendant (y), who was a dealer in iron, sent a waterman to the plaintiff for iron on trust, and paid for it afterwards. He sent the same waterman a second time, with ready money, who received the goods, but did not pay for them. *Pratt*, C. J., ruled, that the

(r) Per Lord *Tenterden*, C. J., in *Archard* v. *Hornor*, 3 C. & P. 349. A decision approved of and preferred to that of Lord *Ellenborough*, in *Gandell* v. *Pontigny*, 4 Campb. 375, by Court of Q. B.; *Smith* v. *Hayward*, 2 Nev. & P. 432; 7

A. & E. 544.
(s) *Smith* v. *Kingsford*, 3 Scott, 279.
(t) *Speck* v. *Phillips*, 5 M. & W. 279.
(u) *Priestley* v. *Fowler*, 3 M. & W. 1.
(x) F. N. B. 120, G.
(y) *Hazard* v. *Treadwell*, Str. 506.

sending the waterman on trust the first time, and the defendant
paying for the goods, was giving the waterman a credit so as to
make the defendant liable upon the second contract. In an action
by a publican (z), for beer sold, it appeared that the defendant had
dealt with the plaintiff on credit, and paid him several sums for
beer; at length the defendant gave notice to plaintiff's servant, who
brought the beer, that he would pay for the beer as it came in.
The defence to the present action was, that the defendant had paid
the servant. Lord *Eldon*, C. J., thought the defendant was liable;
for, as the change in the usual mode of dealing had been suggested
by the defendant himself, and as he had personal dealings with the
master, in a particular mode, notice to the servant alone of a change
in that mode would not be sufficient; the defendant must show
that the master himself had notice of it, or he could have no defence
to the action. In an action on a farrier's bill (a), it appeared that
the defendant, by an agreement with the groom, allowed him five
guineas a-year, for which he was to keep the horses properly shod,
and furnish them with proper medicines when necessary. Lord
Kenyon said, that it was no defence to the action, unless the plaintiff
knew of this agreement, and expressly trusted the groom. That
if the servant buys things which come to his master's use, the
master should take care to see them paid for; for a tradesman has
nothing to do with any private agreement between the master and
servant. But where an express authority is not given by the
master, and from the nature of the case an authority cannot be
implied, the master is not liable. Hence, where the chaise of the
master had been broken by the negligence of his servant (b), and
the servant desired a coachmaker, *who had never been employed by
the master*, to repair it, which was accordingly done, and the master
refusing to pay the amount of the bill sent in by the coachmaker,
he insisted on retaining the chaise as a lien; Lord *Ellenborough*,
C. J., was of opinion, that the coachmaker was not entitled so to
retain it; for whatever claim of that sort he might have, he must
derive it from legitimate authority; that unless the master had been
in the habit of employing the tradesman in the way of his trade, it
should not be in the power of the servant to bind him to contracts
of which the master had not any knowledge, and to which he had
not given any assent. It was the duty of the tradesman, when he
was employed, to have inquired of the principal, whether the order
was given by his authority; but having neglected to do so, the
master was not liable to the demand, and the detainer of the chaise
was unlawful. When the master is in the habit of paying ready
money for articles furnished in certain quantities to his family (c),
if the tradesman delivers other goods of the same sort to the

(z) *Gratland* v. *Freeman*, 3 Esp. N.
P. C. 85.
(a) *Precious* v. *Abel*, 1 Esp. N. P. C.
350.
(b) *Hiscox* v. *Greenwood*, 4 Esp. N.

P. C. 174. See *Maunder* v. *Conyers*, 2
Stark. N. P. C. 281.
(c) *Pearce* v. *Rogers*, 3 Esp. N. P. C.
214. See also 1 Show. 95.

servant, upon credit, without informing the master of it, and the latter goods do not come to the master's use, the master is not liable. A master contracted with a tradesman to serve him with articles for ready money (d), and the master gave his servant money to pay for the articles, which was done accordingly; after some time, the master turned away his servant and took another, to whom he gave money as before; the second servant did not pay the tradesman, and afterwards ran away: an action having been brought by the tradesman against the master; it was holden, that the master was not liable to pay the money again (2). If a person (e) keeping livery stables, and having a horse to sell, direct his servant not to warrant him, and the servant does nevertheless warrant him, still the master is liable on the warranty, because the servant was acting within the general scope of his authority, and the public cannot be supposed to be cognizant of any private conversation between the master and servant: but if the owner of a horse were to send a stranger to a fair, with express directions not to warrant the horse, and the latter acted contrary to the orders, the purchaser could only have recourse to the person who actually sold the horse, and the owner would not be liable on the warranty, because the servant was not acting within the scope of his employment. A horse-dealer's servant (f), sent to deliver a horse to a purchaser, was held not to have rendered his master liable by warranting the horse on delivery; for a warranty by a person entrusted merely to deliver is not *primâ facie* binding on the principal, but an express authority must be shown. A journeyman to a baker was holden a good witness to prove the delivery of bread to the defendant (g), without a release, in a case where there was not any evidence of an usage for the journeyman to receive the money for the bread delivered. A clerk who receives money for his master is a good witness to prove that he has paid it over to his master *ex necessitate rei*, without a release (h).

(d) *Stubbing* v. *Heintz*, Peake's N. P. C. 47.

(e) Per *Ashhurst*, J., in *Fenn* v. *Harrison*, 3 T. R. 760.

(f) *Woodin* v. *Burford*, 2 Cr. & M.

391, per *Bayley*, B. See *ante*, p. 649.

(g) *Adams* v. *Davis*, 3 Esp. N. P. C. 43, *Eldon*, C. J.

(h) *Matthews* v. *Haydon*, 2 Esp. N. P. C. 509.

---

(2) It was said by Lord *Kenyon*, in this case, that if the master employs the servant to buy things on credit, he will be liable to whatever extent the servant shall pledge his credit.

III. *Of the Liability of the Master in respect of a tortious Act done by the Servant.*

An action on the case will lie against a master for an injury done through the negligence or unskilfulness of the servant acting in his master's employ. As where the servants of a carman ran over a boy in the streets (*i*), and maimed him by negligence, an action was brought against the master, and the plaintiff recovered. So where the servant of A. (*k*), with his cart, ran against the cart of B., which contained a pipe of wine, whereby the wine was spilled; an action was brought against A., the master, and holden to be maintainable. An action on the case is the proper remedy for an injury of this kind, and not an action of trespass (*l*). In these cases, if the declaration state that the defendant (the master) negligently drove his cart (*m*), &c., it will be supported by evidence that the defendant's *servant* drove the cart. In case for negligently driving against the plaintiff's horse, the plaintiff's servant, in whose charge the horse was, is not a competent witness for the plaintiff without a release (*n*). Plaintiffs employed B., a broker, to sell goods for them, and to deliver such goods in the port of London, according to the contracts of sale. C., a lighterman, acted in the delivery of the goods, under B.'s direction, and was employed by the plaintiffs so to do, and was paid by them. Plaintiffs, through B., contracted with a purchaser for the sale to him of a parcel of goods, to be paid for on delivery. The goods were delivered without payment; and the price was in consequence lost. In an action by plaintiffs against B. for the breach of duty, they called C. to prove that, while he was waiting for B.'s orders as to the delivery, a person, whom C. supposed to have proper authority, but who really had not, desired C. to carry them alongside a certain vessel, which he did without orders from B., and the goods were taken away, as on behalf of the purchaser; that C. informed B. of what had happened, and, upon hearing B. had given no orders, said it was not too late to stop the goods, and he would do so; but that B. prevented him, and did not, himself, take proper measures to stop them. It was holden (*o*), that C. was incompetent by reason of his liability to the plaintiffs as their servant. It would seem to be the better opinion, that in an action for a similar injury, the defendant's servant may (*p*) be a witness for him without a release, the objec-

(*i*) 1 Raym. 739, *ex. rel.* M'ri Place.
(*k*) *Id.*
(*l*) *Morley* v. *Gaisford,* 2 H. Bl. 443.
(*m*) *Brucker* v. *Fromont,* 6 T. R. 659.
(*n*) *Morish* v. *Foote,* 8 Taunt. 454; *Sherman* v. *Barnes,* 1 M. & Rob. 69, S. P. These cases were before stat. 3 & 4 Will. IV. c. 42, s. 26, 27; *Harding* v. *Cobley,* 6 C. & P. 664, S. P., per *Denman,* C. J.,

since the statute.
(*o*) *Boorman* v. *Brown,* 9 A. & E. 487.
(*p*) *Pickles* v. *Hollings,* 1 M. & Rob. 468, *Parke,* B.; *Creevy* v. *Bowman,* 1 M. & Rob. 496; *Faith* v. *M'Intyre,* 7 C. & P. 44, by the same learned judge. And see Phillips on Evidence, p. 110, 8th edit.

tion to the witness being removed under the stat. 3 & 4 Will. IV.
c. 42, ss. 26, 27, by making an indorsement on the record, according to the directions of the statute.   To an action on the case
against several partners (q), for negligence in their servant, whereby
the plaintiff's goods were lost, it cannot be pleaded in abatement
that there are other partners not named.   Having stated the cases
in which the law considers the master as responsible for the injurious act of his servant, it may be proper to observe, that where the
servant commits a *wilful* trespass, without the direction or assent
of the master, an action of trespass will not lie against the master:
in such case (r) the servant only is liable.   As if a servant (s),
authorized merely to distrain cattle damage feasant, drives a horse
from the highway into his master's close, and there distrains it.
So where a servant of the defendant wilfully drove the defendant's
chariot against the plaintiff's chaise (t); an action of trespass having
been brought against the defendant, it appeared in evidence, that
the defendant was neither present at the time when the injury was
committed, nor had he in any manner directed or assented to the
act of his servant; it was holden, that the action could not be
maintained.   If a servant driving a carriage, in order to effect some
purpose of his own, wantonly strike the horses of another person,
and produce the accident, the master will not be liable.   But if, in
order to perform his master's orders, he strikes, but injudiciously,
and in order to extricate himself from a difficulty, that will be negligent and careless conduct, for which the master will be liable (u),
being an act done in pursuance of the master's employment.
Where an injury happens through the misconduct of a servant in
driving his master's carriage; it was holden (x), that the master
was liable, if the servant be guilty of negligence whilst on his
master's business, though he may be going out of the way; but not
if the servant uses the carriage for his own purpose, and without
his master's consent.   Where one of a ship's crew wilfully injured
another ship, without any direction from or privity of the master,
it was holden, that trespass could not be maintained against
the master, although he was on board at the time (y).   If a
master command his servant to do an *illegal* act (z), the servant, as well as the master, will be liable to the party injured; for
the servant cannot plead the command of the master in bar of a
trespass.   An action on the case was brought against a master and
his servant (a), for breaking a pair of horses in Lincoln's Inn Fields,

(q) *Mitchell* v. *Turbutt and others*, 5
T. R. 649. See 2 Bos. & Pul. N. R. 365.
(r) See judgment of *Patteson*, J., in
Lyons v. *Martin*, 8 A. & E. 512.
(s) *Lyons* v. *Martin*, 8 A. & E. 512.
(t) *M'Manus* v. *Crickett*, 1 East, 106.
(u) Per *Cur.*, *Croft* v. *Alison*, 4 B. &
A. 592.

(x) *Joel* v. *Morison*, 6 C. & P. 501,
Parke, B.
(y) *Bowcher* v. *Noidstrom*, 1 Taunt.
568. See *Nicholson* v. *Mounsey*, *infra*,
p. 1101.
(z) *Sands* v. *Child*, 3 Lev. 352.
(a) *Michael* v. *Alestree and another*,
2 Lev. 172. See *ante*, p. 434.

where, being unmanageable, they ran against and hurt the plaintiff;
it appeared that the master was absent; but it was holden, on
motion in arrest of judgment, that the action would lie; for it should
be intended that the master sent the servant to train the horses
there. In an action on the case (b) against the defendant for
causing a quantity of lime to be placed on the high road, by means
of which the plaintiff and his wife were overturned and much hurt,
and the chaise in which they then were was considerably damaged;
it appeared that the defendant having purchased a house by the road
side, (but which he had never occupied,) contracted with a surveyor
to put it in repair for a stipulated sum; a carpenter having a contract under the surveyor to do the whole business, employed a
bricklayer under him, and he again contracted for a quantity of
lime with a lime-burner, by whose servant the lime in question was
laid in the road. In support of the action, it was contended, that
the act which caused the injury complained of, was an act done for
the benefit of the defendant, and in consequence of his having
authorized others to work for him; and although the person by
whose neglect the accident happened was the immediate servant of
another, yet, for the benefit of the public, he must be considered as
the servant of the defendant. If the defendant was not liable, the
plaintiff might be obliged to sue all the parties who had sub-contracts
before he could obtain redress. On the part of the defendant, it
was urged, first, that the cause of action did not arise on the defendant's premises, the complaint being, that a quantity of lime, which
should have been placed there, was actually laid on the high road:
that being the case, there was no authority to show that the defendant was liable, merely because the act from which the injury arose
was done for his benefit. If that general proposition were true, it
might be contended, that the defendant must have answered for any
accident which might have happened during the preparation of the
lime in the lime-burner's yard. Secondly, that the liability of the
principal to answer for his agents, is founded in the superintendence
and control which he is supposed to have over them. 1 Bl. Com.
431. In the civil law, that liability was confined to the person
standing in the relation of *pater familias* to the person doing the
injury. Inst. lib. 4. tit. 5, s. 1; Dig. lib. 9, tit. 3. And though in
our law it has been extended to cases where the agent is not a mere
domestic, yet the principle continues the same. Now clearly it was
not in the power of this defendant to control the agent by whom the
injury to this plaintiff was effected. He was not employed by the
defendant, but by the lime-burner; nor was it in the defendant's
power to prevent him, or any one of the intermediate sub-contracting
parties, from executing the respective parts of that business which

(b) *Bush* v. *Steinman*, 1 Bos. & Pul.
404. See *Matthews* v. *West Mid. Water-
works Company*, 3 Campb. 403, and
Harris v. *Baker*, 4 M. & S. 27, cited by

Denman, C. J., in *Pernaby* v. *Lancaster
Canal Company*, 3 Nev. & P. 530; 11 A.
& E. 223.

each had undertaken to perform. The court, however, were of opinion, that the action would lie; and that it was competent to the plaintiff to bring his action either against the person from whom the authority flowed, or against the person by whom the injury was actually committed.

The defendant, a gentleman usually residing in the country, being in London for a few days with his own carriage, sent in the usual way to a stable-keeper for a pair of horses for a day. The stable-keeper accordingly sent a pair, and a person to drive them. The defendant did not select the driver, nor had he any previous knowledge of him; but the stable-keeper sent such person as he chose for this purpose. The driver had no wages from his master, but depended on receiving a gratuity from the person whose carriage he drove; the defendant in this case gave him five shillings as a gratuity; by reason of his negligent driving, the plaintiff's horse sustained an injury; whereupon an action was brought. The Court of King's Bench were equally divided (c): *Abbott*, C. J., and *Little-dale*, J., holding, that the defendant was not liable; *Bayley*, J., and *Holroyd*, J., contra. The opinion of the two former judges was adhered to in the following case. The owners of a carriage were in the habit of hiring horses from the same person, to draw it for a day or drive, and the owner of the horses provided a driver, through whose negligence an injury was done to a third party: it was holden (d), that the owners of the carriage were not liable to be sued for such injury; and that it made no difference, that the owners of the carriage had always been driven by the same driver, he being the only regular coachman in the employ of the owner of the horses; or that they had always paid him a fixed sum for each drive; or that they had provided him with a livery, which he left at their house at the end of each drive, and that the injury in question was occasioned by his leaving the horses while so depositing the livery in their house. The owner of a carriage hired four post horses and two postilions of A., a livery stable-keeper, for the day, to take him from London to Epsom and back. In returning, the postilions damaged the carriage of B. It was holden (e), that A., as owner of the horses and master of the postilions was liable to B., for such damage. A warehouseman at Liverpool employed a master porter to remove a barrel from his warehouse. The master porter employed his own men and tackle; and through the negligence of the men the tackle failed, the barrel fell and injured the plaintiff; it was holden (f), that the warehouseman was liable in case for the injury. But where a butcher employed a licensed drover to drive

(c) *Laugher* v. *Pointer*, 5 B. & C. 547. 499.
See remarks of Lord *Abinger*, C. B., in　(e) *Smith* v. *Lawrence*, 2 Man. & R. 1.
Brady v. *Giles*, 1 M. & Rob. 495, on this　(f) *Randleson* v. *Murray*, 8 A. & E.
case.　　109.
(d) *Quarman* v. *Burnett*, 6 M. & W.

home some bullocks from Smithfield market, and the drover employed a servant of his own for the purpose, through whose negligence a bullock injured the plaintiff's property; it was holden (g), that the butcher was not liable, for the drover was a person carrying on a distinct and independent business of his own. Case for sinking plaintiff's vessel by a steam-boat, of which defendants were possessed and had the care, management, and direction, by their servants and mariners, through the mismanagement of the said servants and mariners. Plea, that the defendants had not the possession and care, &c., by their servants and mariners or otherwise. Defendants, being owners of the steam-vessel, chartered her to D., for six months, at £20 per week, the owners to keep her in good and sufficient order for the conveyance of goods, &c., to and from Newcastle and Goole, or any other coasting station which D. might employ her in: D. to pay all disbursements, including harbour dues, pilotages, seamen's and captain's wages, and coals, oil, tallow, &c. for engines, and to insure the vessel (h); the policy to be deposited with the owners. It was holden, that the issue ought to be found for plaintiff upon the interpretation of the charterparty alone. A fortiori, upon proof, in addition, that D. had no power to appoint or dismiss the officers and crew, and did not interfere in the arrangements of the ship. A. and B. were partners in the business of public carriers; by agreement between them, A. provided horses and drivers for certain stages, and B. for the remainder. It was holden (i), that notwithstanding this division of the concern between them, they were responsible for the misconduct and negligence of their drivers and servants throughout the whole distance. And that it was not any defence to B., that the servant, through whose negligence an injury had been committed, had been hired and was paid by A. alone. The captain of a king's ship of war was holden not to be responsible for the damage done to another vessel, through the negligence of his lieutenant (k), who was upon deck, and had the actual direction and management of the steering and navigating of the ship at the time, and when the captain was not upon deck, nor was called upon by his duty to be there.

(g) *Milligan* v. *Wedge*, Q. B. Nov. 18, 1840, vol. x. Law Journal, N. S. p. 19.

(h) *Fenton* v. *City of Dublin Steam Packet Company*, 8 A. & E. 835.

(i) *Weyland* v. *Elkins*, Holt's N. P. C. 227, *Gibbs*, C. J.

(k) *Nicholson* v. *Mounsey*, 15 East, 384.

IV. *Of Actions brought by Masters for enticing away Apprentices and Servants, and for Injuries done to their Servants, p. 1102; and herein of the Action for Seduction, p. 1103; Witness, p. 1104; Damages, p. 1106.*

An action on the case may be maintained by a master against any person who entices away his apprentice or servant from his service (*l*), or who continues to employ such servant after notice, though the defendant did not procure the servant to leave his master, or know, when he employed him, that he was the servant of another (*m*). But the master may, if he chooses, waive his action for the tort (*n*) ; and bring an action of *indebitatus assumpsit* for work and labour done by his apprentice, against the person who tortiously employed him. So the captain of a ship of war detaining an apprentice who had been impressed, after verbal notice by such apprentice of his condition, is liable in an action by the master for wages for the service of the apprentice (*o*). But the prize money gained by an apprentice serving on board a letter of marque ship, does not belong (*p*) to the master, the usage being proved that such money is the property of the apprentice.

It is not material whether the apprentice be legally apprenticed or not ; it is sufficient if he be so *de facto* (*q*).

It has been holden (*r*), that a master cannot maintain an action for seducing his servant, after his servant has paid him the penalty stipulated by his articles for leaving him. Neither can an action be maintained for harbouring an apprentice, as such, if the master to whom he was bound was then not a housekeeper, and of the age of twenty-four years (*s*).

A master may maintain an action for an injury done to his servant, as false imprisonment, battery, &c., which deprives the master of his service. The form of action is an action of trespass, usually termed an action *per quod servitium amisit*, the gist of the action being the loss of service; and hence, the servant may be a witness (*t*), for he is not interested as to the point. In an action of

(*l*) Adm. per *Cur.*, in Q. v. *Daniel*, 6 Mod. 182.

(*m*) *Blake* v. *Lanyon*, 6 T. R. 221.

(*n*) *Lightly* v. *Clouston*, 1 Taunt. 112. See also *Foster* v. *Stewart*, 3 M. & S. 191, S. P.

(*o*) *Eades* v. *Vandeput*, M. 25 Geo. III., B. R., 5 East, 39, n. ; 4 Doug. 1, S. C.

(*p*) *Carsan* v. *Watts*, 3 Doug. 350.

(*q*) *Barber* v. *Dennis*, Salk. 68 ; 6 Mod.

69, S. C., recognized by Lord *Hardwicke*, C. J., in *R.* v. *St. Nicholas*, 1 Burr. S. C. 94, 95.

(*r*) *Bird* v. *Randall*, 3 Burr. 1345 ; 1 Bl. R. 387.

(*s*) *Gye* v. *Felton*, 4 Taunt. 876.

(*t*) *Jewell* v. *Harding*, T. 10 Geo. I., Gilb. Evid. 94, ed. 1761 ; 1 Str. 595, S. C., by the name of *Duel* v. *Harding*, *Lewis* v. *Fog*, 2 Str. 944, S. P.

tort (*u*) for wounding plaintiff's servant, whereby he was disabled
from serving, the jury may give damages for the loss of service, not
only before action brought, but afterwards, down to the time when
the disability may be expected to cease.

Of the Action for Seduction.

This form of action is frequently adopted by a parent for the
purpose of obtaining a compensation in damages for debauching his
daughter, and getting her with child, and the expenses attending the
lying-in (3). As to the nature of the action, it has been decided (*x*),
that it may be brought either in trespass for the direct injury, or
in case for the consequential damage. It has been holden, that
this action may be maintained, although the daughter was of age
at the time of the seduction (*y*). But as the action is founded on
the loss of service, that must be alleged in the declaration (*z*) (4);
and it must be proved that the relation of master and servant,
(which in these cases the law implies from very slight circumstances) (5), subsisted at the time when the injury was committed (*a*); and the circumstance of the daughter having been under

(*u*) *Hodsoll* v. *Stallebrass*, 11 A. & E.
301; 3 P. & D. 200.

(*x*) *Chamberlain* v. *Hazlewood*, 5 M.
& W. 515; *ante*, p. 8; and see *Woodward* v. *Walton*, 2 Bos. & Pul. N. R. 476,
recognized in *Ditcham* v. *Bond*, 2 M. &
S. 436.

(*y*) *Bennett* v. *Allcott*, 2 T. R. 166.

(*x*) *Satterthwaite* v. *Dewhurst*, B. R.
E. 25 Geo. III., cited in 5 East, 47, n.,
and MSS., and *S. C.*, A. P. B., No. 85,
Dampier MSS., L. I. L.; 4 Doug. 315,
S. C.

(*a*) *Postlethwaite* v. *Parkes*, 3 Burr.
1878, recognized by *Buller*, J., in 2 T.
R. 166.

---

(3) A *master*, not standing in the relation of a parent, may maintain
this action for debauching his servant. *Fores* v. *Wilson*, Peake's N. P.
C. 55. In like manner it may be maintained, for the seduction of an
adopted child. *Irwin* v. *Dearman*, 11 East, 23.

(4) " Although the daughter cannot have an action, yet the father
may, not for assaulting his daughter, and getting her with child, because
this is a wrong particularly done to her, yet *for the loss of her service
caused by this.*" Per *Rolle*, C. J., *Norton* v. *Jason*, Sty. 398.

(5) In one case, *Littledale*, J., expressed an opinion that it was not
necessary to show any acts of service done by the daughter; it was sufficient that she lived in the father's family under such circumstances that
he had a right to her services. *Maunder* v. *Venn*, M. & Malk. 323. In
Holloway v. *Abell*, 7 C. & P. 528, it appeared that A. occupied two
farms seven miles distant from each other; A. resided at one, and his son
and his daughter at the other, where she acted as mistress, and had the
poultry for her benefit. This was holden sufficient to prove her the servant of A., per *Littledale*, J., who thought that it was not necessary for
defendant to plead specially that daughter was not servant of plaintiff.

age at that time, will not dispense with the necessity of this proof (b). It is not necessary, however, to prove a *contract* for service, if the daughter was in fact a servant, nor that she slept in the house (c). But evidence must be given of *acts* of service; the slightest, however, will be sufficient, as milking cows (d) and the like. An action cannot be maintained by a father (e) for the seduction of his daughter, though a minor, while she was in the service of another person; although it be alleged in the declaration, that she was there with the intention, on the part of her father and herself, that she should return to her father's when she quitted her service, unless she should immediately go into another service. In a case where it appeared that the plaintiff's daughter had been married eight years before, had two children, and was then separated from her husband for five years, during which the husband had not any access, the wife having returned to her father's house, and lived with him, and acted as his servant. During this residence with her father she was debauched by the defendant, and had a child by him. It was holden (f), that the relation of master and servant might and did exist in this case, and that in the absence of any interference by the husband, it was not competent to the defendant, a wrongdoer, to set up the rights of the husband as an answer to the action.

Witness.—The daughter or servant is a competent witness to prove the case.

Plaintiff brought trespass against the defendant for breaking and entering his house (g), and debauching his daughter, by which he lost her service for a long space of time. Upon the trial it appeared, that the defendant was admitted in the way of courtship to visit the young woman: that proposals had been made on both sides: that one night she went to bed, and left her chamber window open, and the defendant, by setting a ladder to her window, got into her chamber, and having lain with her, she became pregnant, and afterwards had a child, whereby the father was put to a great expense. These facts the judge at Nisi Prius admitted the daughter to prove, upon which the jury gave £150 damages. A motion for a new trial was made on the following grounds; 1st, Because the verdict was against evidence, there being no proof of any trespass committed in breaking the house, but on the contrary, that the window having been left open by the plaintiff's daughter, the defendant entered by virtue of a license from her, and so could not be a trespasser. *Norton* v. *Jason*, Styl. 398; *Hunt* v. *Wotton*, T. Raym. 260.

(b) *Dean* v. *Peel*, 5 East, 45, but see remarks of *Parke*, B., in *Harris* v. *Butler*, 2 M. & W. 542.

(c) *Mann* v. *Barrett*, 6 Esp. N. P. C. 23.

(d) Per *Buller*, J., in *Bennett* v. *Allcott*, 2 T. R. 168; per *Abbott*, C. J., *Manvell*

v. *Thomson*, 2 C. & P. 304.

(e) *Blaymire* v. *Haley*, 6 M. & W. 55.

(f) *Harper* v. *Luffkin*, 7 B. & C. 387.

(g) *Cock* v. *Wortham*, B. R. M. 10 Geo. II., MSS., S. C. Shortly reported in Str. 1054.

2dly, That the daughter, who was *particeps criminis*, and swearing for her father, and in consequence of that, swearing for herself, was not a competent witness. 3dly, That the damages were excessive, no loss of service having been proved, and the jury mistaken in their assessment of the damages, the girl having since the trial brought another action for breach of the promise of marriage. *Sed per Curiam*, as to the first ground, the defendant's entrance into the house without the privity of the father or mother, is plainly a trespass; as to the 2d, the daughter was a competent witness, and no more interested in the question than servants in actions brought by their masters for beating them, *per quod* their masters lost their service, in which cases the servants are constantly admitted. 3rdly, The damages in this case are far from being excessive: the defendant being admitted in an honourable way, made a very ungenerous use of the acquaintance with the daughter, which is a great aggravation of his offence, and it is hardly possible to estimate the damage of a father under such circumstances; aud as to a loss of service not having been proved, that was quite immaterial, the rule being, that where the loss of service is the gist of the action, there it must be proved; as in trespass by a master for beating his servant; but where laid only in aggravation of damages, loss of service need not be proved; and here the action is founded on the trespass in breaking the house, and the loss of service is only consequential to it. As to the new action that has been brought, we cannot take any notice of it.

Witnesses cannot be examined, on the part of the plaintiff, as to the daughter's general character for chastity, except in answer to evidence adduced by the defendant of *general bad character* (h). A specific breach of chastity alleged on the part of the defendant will not afford ground for such examination (i). Nor does the mere cross-examination of the daughter to show th*a*t she had been guilty of improper conduct, entitle the plaintiff to call other witnesses to her character (k). The daughter is not bound to answer, in cross-examination, whether she had not previously been criminal with other men (l). Neither can evidence be admitted that the defendant accomplished the seduction by means of a promise of marriage (m). The defendant may give evidence not only of the general bad character of the plaintiff's daughter, but he may also examine witnesses to prove particular acts of sexual intercourse (n) between them and the daughter; this evidence, however, does not go to the verdict, but only in mitigation of damages, if the jury are satisfied that the defendant had such intercourse with plaintiff's daughter as caused him to be the father of the child alleged to have been gotten by him.

(h) *Bamfield* v. *Massey*, 1 Campb. 460.   100, *Park*, J.
(i) *S. C.*   (m) *Dodd* v. *Norris*, 3 Campb. 519.
(k) *Dodd* v. *Norris*, 3 Campb. 519.   (n) *Verry* v. *Watkins*, 7 C. & P. 308,
(l) *Ib.;* but see *Bate* v. *Hill*, 1 C. & P.   *Alderson*, B.

Money cannot be paid into court, stat. 3 & 4 Will. IV. c. 42, s. 21.

Of the Damages.

Liberal damages are usually given in an action for seduction, and the courts are disinclined to grant new trials merely on the ground of excess in that respect (o). From a laudable desire, as I conceive, to suppress the vice of seduction, against which our criminal code has not provided any punishment, many eminent judges have thought it proper to direct juries, in ascertaining the amount of the damages in this action, to have regard not merely to the injury sustained by the loss of service, a proper compensation for which might amount to a few pounds only, but also to the wounded feelings of the parent or party standing *in loco parentis*. In *Southernwood* v. *Ramsden*, Middx. Sittings after H. T., 19th Feb. 1805, which was an action by a custom-house officer against a cowkeeper for the seduction of the plaintiff's daughter, *per quod servitium amisit*, Lord *Ellenborough*, C. J., in explaining the nature of this action, said that it was laid as a trespass, and was founded on the injury done to the father by the loss of the service of the child; this was necessary to let in the case, but when this was established, *further damages might be conceded for the loss which the father sustained by being deprived of the society and comfort of his child, and by the dishonour which he receives.* The jury gave £300 damages. Lord *Eldon*, C. J., had expressed a similar opinion at Bristol Summer Assizes, 1800, in the case of *Chambers* v. *Irwin*, where the action was brought by an aunt, for the seduction of her niece, against the defendant, a lieutenant in the navy. The chief justice told the jury, that in calculating the quantum of damages, they were not to look merely to the loss of service, which might amount only to a few pounds, but also to *the wounded feelings* of the party. The jury gave £200 damages. From the amount of the damages in the preceding cases, it will be observed that due respect was paid by the jury to the direction of the judge. It may be remarked, that although this practice of giving damages for the *wounded feelings* of the party can scarcely be reconciled with the strict rule of law, which entitles a person to recover only *secundum allegata et probata;* yet when the nature of the vice of seduction, and the pernicious consequences which result from it, are duly considered, few persons, (however anxious they may be that the boundaries between civil injuries and criminal offences should be preserved as distinct as possible,) will regret that such a practice has been adopted. Since the first publication of the preceding remarks, an application was made to the court of B. R. to set aside an inquisition on the ground

(o) *Tullidge* v. *Wade*, 3 Wils. 18; v. *Allcott*, 2 T. R. 166. *Edmonson* v. *Machell*, 2 T. R. 4; *Bennett*

of excessive damages (p), where the plaintiff had declared against the defendant for the seduction of his adopted daughter and servant, and the jury had given £100 damages, although it appeared that the only pecuniary damage which the party had sustained, was the being obliged to hire another servant for five weeks during the lying-in. The plaintiff had been a serjeant in a regiment of the line, and the servant was the daughter of a deceased comrade, whom the plaintiff had adopted and maintained. It was urged, that she could only be considered as a servant; and a case was cited as having been tried before *Chambre*, J., at Worcester, where, upon an action brought by a father for the seduction of his natural daughter, that learned judge told the jury they must consider her merely in the character of a servant, and award the plaintiff a compensation for the loss of service only. The court, however, in the present instance, refused the application, Lord *Ellenborough*, C. J., observing, that the courts had uniformly expressed their reluctance to disturb the verdict in this action merely on the ground of excessive damages, and referred to *Edmonson* v. *Machell*, 2 T. R. 4,— that it was a case *sui generis*, where, in estimating the damages, the parental damages, and the feelings of those who stood in *loco parentis*, had always been taken into consideration; and although it was difficult to conceive upon what legal principles the damages could be extended *ultra* the injury arising from the loss of service, yet the practice was now inveterate, and could not be shaken. He added (q), that the action having been considered in *Edmonson* v. *Machell* to extend to an aunt, as one standing in *loco parentis*, he thought that the present plaintiff, who had adopted and bred up the daughter of a friend and comrade from her infancy, seemed to be equally entitled to maintain the action on account of the loss of service to him, aggravated by the injury done to the object on whom he had thus placed his affection.

(p) *Irwin* v. *Dearman*, B. R. E. 49   (q) 11 East, 24, 5.
Geo. III., MS., and 11 East, 23.

NUSANCE.

I. *In what Cases an Action for a Nusance may be maintained,* p. 1108 ; *and herein of the Right to Use of Light,* p. 1109 ; *Water,* p. 1110 ; *Way,* p. 1112 ; *and Pew,* p. 1113.

II. *By whom and against whom an Action for a Nusance may be maintained,* p. 1117.

III. *Pleadings,* p. 1119.

IV. *Evidence, &c.,* p. 1120.

V. *Costs,* p. 1121.

I. *In what Cases an Action for a Nusance may be maintained.*

AN action on the case lies for a nusance to the habitation or land of another ; as, if A. build a house so as to hang over the land of B., whereby the rain falls upon B.'s land, and injures it, B. may maintain an action against A. for this nusance (a). So if the owner of the adjacent land erects a building so near the house of the plaintiff as to prevent the air and light from entering and coming through the plaintiff's windows, an action will lie. Formerly it was holden, that a party could not maintain an action for an obstruction of lights, unless he had gained a right in the lights by prescription (b) ; and in conformity with this rule, it was usual to state in the declaration that the house was an ancient house, wherein were ancient windows, through which the light had entered, and had been used to enter from time immemorial (c) (1). But afterwards

(a) *Penruddock's* case, 5 Rep. 100, b. ; 1 Rol. Abr. 107, pl. 18 ; 2 Rol. Abr. 140, pl. 11.
(b) *Bowry* v. *Pope,* 1 Leon. 168 ; Cro.

Eliz. 118, *S. C.*
(c) See Co. Ent. tit. Action sur le Case, pl. 17.

---

(1) Against this prescription a contrary prescription to obstruct the lights could not be alleged. 9 Rep. 85, b.

it was holden (*d*), that upon evidence of an adverse enjoyment of lights for twenty years or upwards, unexplained, a jury might be directed to *presume* a right by grant or otherwise, even though no lights had existed there before the commencement of the twenty years. But if the period of enjoyment fell short of twenty years, then, formerly, other circumstances than the mere length of time must have been brought in aid, in order to raise the presumption of the plaintiff's right. Now, by stat. 2 & 3 Will. IV. c. 71, s. 6, no presumption shall be allowed or made in support of any claim, upon proof of the exercise of enjoyment of the right or matter claimed for less than twenty years. It is well established (*e*) by the decided cases, that where the same person possesses a house having the actual use and enjoyment of certain lights, and also possesses the adjoining land, and sells the house to another person, although the lights be new, he cannot, nor can any one who claims under him, build upon the adjoining land, so as to obstruct or interrupt the enjoyment of those lights. Total privation of light is not necessary to sustain the action. If the plaintiff can prove that, by reason of the obstruction, he cannot enjoy the light in so free and ample a manner as he did before, it will be sufficient (*f*). If an ancient window be enlarged, the owner of the adjoining land cannot lawfully obstruct the passage of light to any part of the space occupied by the ancient window, although a greater portion of light be admitted through the unobstructed part of the enlarged window, than was anciently enjoyed (*g*). A party, however, may (*h*) so alter the mode in which he has been permitted to enjoy this kind of easement as to lose the right altogether.

By stat. 2 & 3 Will. IV. c. 71, s. 3, "When the access and use of light to and for any dwelling house, workshop, or other building, shall have been actually enjoyed therewith for the full period of twenty years without *interruption*, the right thereto shall be deemed absolute and indefeasible, any local usage or custom to the contrary notwithstanding, unless it shall appear that the same was enjoyed by some consent or agreement expressly made or given for that purpose by deed or writing." The foregoing statute took effect on the first day of Michaelmas Term, 1832. By s. 4, "The period of

---

(*d*) *Lewis* v. *Price*, Worcester Summer Ass. 1761, coram *Wilmot*, J.; *Dougal* v. *Wilson*, C. B. T. 9 Geo. III.; *Darwin* v. *Upton*, B. R. M. 26 Geo. III. These cases are reported in 2 Wms. Saund. 175, a.; *Darwin* v. *Upton* will also be found in B. P. B. 397, Dampier MSS. L. I. L. See also *Hubert* v. *Groves*, 1 Esp. N. P. C. 148.

(*e*) Per *Tindal*, C. J., *Swansborough* v. *Coventry*, 9 Bingh. 309, citing *Palmer* v. *Fletcher*, 1 Lev. 122, "that no man shall derogate from his own grant;" *Cox*

v. *Matthews*, 1 Ventr. 237; *Holt*, C. J., in *Rosewell* v. *Pryor*, 6 Mod. 116; *Compton* v. *Richards*, 1 Price, 27. See also *Blanchard* v. *Bridges*, 4 A. & E. 192.

(*f*) *Cotterell* v. *Griffiths*, 4 Esp. N. P. C. 69.

(*g*) *Chandler* v. *Thompson*, 3 Campb. 80, per *Le Blanc*, J., cited by *Patteson* J., delivering judgment, *Blanchard* v. *Bridges*, 4 A. & E. 192.

(*h*) Per *Denman*, C.J., delivering judgment, *Garritt* v. *Sharp*, 3 A. & E. 330.

twenty years shall be taken to be the period next before some suit or action wherein the claim shall have been brought into question, and no act or other matter shall be deemed to be an *interruption* within the meaning of this statute, unless the same shall have been submitted to, or acquiesced in, for one year after the party interrupted shall have had notice thereof, and of the person making or authorizing the same to be made." N. Light (*i*) is not included in the 8th section of this statute, which see *post*, p. 1111.

"The right to the use of water rests on clear and settled principles. *Primâ facie*, the proprietor of each bank of a stream is the proprietor of half the land covered by the stream, but there is no property in the water. Every proprietor has an equal right to use the water which flows in the stream, and consequently no proprietor can have the right to use the water to the prejudice of any other proprietor. Without the consent of the other proprietors, who may be affected by his operations, no proprietor can either diminish the quantity of water which would otherwise descend to the proprietors below, nor throw the water back upon the proprietors above. Every proprietor who claims a right either to throw the water back above, or to diminish the quantity of water which is to descend below, must, in order to maintain his claim, either prove an actual grant or license from the proprietors affected by his operations, or must prove an uninterrupted enjoyment of twenty years. An action will lie at any time within twenty years, when injury happens to arise in consequence of a new purpose of the party to avail himself of his common right." The foregoing remarks of Sir *J. Leach*, V. C., in the case of *Wright* v. *Howard* (*k*), were adopted and recognized by Lord *Tenterden*, C. J., delivering the judgment of the court in *Mason* v. *Hill* (*l*), where it was holden, that the proprietor of land contiguous to a stream may, as soon as he is injured by the diversion of the water from its natural course, maintain an action against the party so diverting it; and it is no answer to the action, that the defendant first appropriated the water to his own use, unless he has had twenty years' undisturbed enjoyment of it in the altered course. A right (*m*) to a watercourse is not destroyed by the owner altering the course of the stream, and the owner may establish his claim, notwithstanding an interruption within twenty years of action brought. A right to the use of water flowing in a stream, and *publici juris*, becomes private by appropriation, but may become (*n*) again *publici juris* by relinquishment.

When a mill has been erected on a stream for a long period of time, it gives to the owner a right that the water shall continue to flow to

(*i*) See Woolrych's Law of Lights.
(*k*) 1 Sim. & Stu. 190.
(*l*) 3 B. & Ad. 304; 2 Nev. & M. 747. See 5 B. & Ad. 1.

(*m*) *Hall* v. *Swift*, 4 Bingh. N. C. 381.
(*n*) *Liggins* v. *Inge*, 7 Bingh. 682.

and from the mill in the manner in which it has been accustomed to flow during all that time. The owner is not bound to use the water exactly in the same manner or to apply it to the same mill; if he were, that would stop all improvements in machinery. Hence the occupier of a mill built on the site of an old mill, which had existed for forty years, may maintain an action for forcing back water, and injuring his mill, although he has not enjoyed the mill precisely in the same state for twenty years; and therefore it was holden to be no defence to such an action, that the occupier had within a few years erected in his mill a wheel of different dimensions, but requiring less water than the old one (o).

In the absence of a special custom, artificial watercourses are not distinguished in law from natural ones; and a title may be gained by twenty years' user, as well to the former as the latter. Therefore where mine owners made an adit through their lands to drain the mine, which they afterwards ceased to work, and the owner of a brewery, through whose premises the water flowed for twenty years after the working had ceased, had during that time used it for brewing; it was holden (p), that he thereby gained a right to the undisturbed enjoyment of the water, and that mines could not afterwards be so worked as to pollute it.

By stat. 2 & 3 Will. IV. c. 71, s. 2, no claim which may be lawfully made at the common law, by custom, prescription, or grant, to any way or other easement, or to any watercourse (q), or the use of any water to be enjoyed or derived upon, over, or from any land or water of our lord the king, his heirs, or successors, or being parcel of the duchy of Lancaster or of the duchy of Cornwall, or being the property of any ecclesiastical or lay person or body corporate, when such way, &c. shall have been actually enjoyed by any person claiming right thereto without interruption for the full period of twenty years, shall be defeated or destroyed by showing only that such way, &c. was first enjoyed at any time prior to such period of twenty years; but nevertheless such claim may be defeated in any other way by which the same is now liable to be defeated; and where such way, &c. shall have been so enjoyed as aforesaid for the full period of forty years, the right thereto shall be deemed absolute and indefeasible, unless it shall appear that the same was enjoyed by some consent or agreement expressly given or made for that purpose, by deed or writing. But by sect. 8, when any land or water, upon, over, or from which any way or other convenient watercourse or use of water shall have been or shall be enjoyed or derived, hath been or shall be held under or by virtue of any term of life, or any term of years, exceeding three years, from the granting thereof, the time of the enjoyment of any such way or other matter as herein

(o) *Saunders* v. *Newman*, 1 B. & A. 258.

(p) *Magor* v. *Chadwick*, 11 A. & E.

571; 3 P. & D. 367.

(q) See *Wright* v. *Williams*, 1 M. & W. 77.

last before mentioned, during the continuance of such term, shall be excluded in the computation of the said period of forty years, in case the claim shall within three years next after the end or sooner determination of such term be resisted by any person entitled to any reversion expectant on the determination thereof. The 6th section disallows any presumption (s) in favour of a claim upon proof of enjoyment for any less period of time than may be applicable under the act to the nature of the right claimed. The statute substitutes positive proof of enjoyment during a limited number of years, for the immemorial enjoyment formerly alleged, and in aid of which, as it never could be proved throughout, presumption was admitted.

Enjoyment " as of right " (t), means an enjoyment had, not secretly or by stealth, or by tacit sufferance, or by permission asked from time to time, on each occasion or even on many occasions of using it; but an enjoyment had openly, notoriously, without particular leave at the time, by a person claiming to use without danger of being treated as a trespasser, as a matter of right, whether strictly legal by prescription and adverse user, or by deed conferring the right, or, though not strictly legal, yet lawful to the extent of excusing a trespass (u).

The enjoyment of an easement, as of right, for twenty years next before the commencement of the suit under the foregoing act, means a *continuous* enjoyment as of right, for the twenty years next before the commencement of the suit, of the easement, as an easement, without interruption acquiesced in for a year. It is therefore defeated by unity of possession during all or part of the twenty years (x).

Unity of possession merely *suspends* a prescriptive easement; there must be an unity of ownership to destroy it (y). Where a party became seised in fee of one set of premises, and possessed of a chattel interest in another, the owner of which latter had previously enjoyed an easement in the former, it was holden (z), that such unity of possession of the land a quâ and in quâ the easement existed, would operate only to suspend, and not to extinguish the easement.

Where a way had been used adversely and under a claim of right, for more than twenty years, over land in possession of a lessee who held under a lease for lives granted by the bishop of Worcester, it was holden (a), that under the foregoing act, this user gave no right as against the bishop, and did not affect the see ; and that, as the

(s) Per *Coleridge*, J., *Bailey* v. *Appleyard*, 3 Nev. & P. 261; 8 A. & E, 161 ; *ante*, p. 425.

(f) See statutes 2 & 3 Will. IV. c. 71, ss. 2 and 5.

(u) Per Lord *Denman*, C. J., delivering judgment of court in *Tickle* v. *Brown*, 4 A. & E. 369 ; 6 Nev. & M. 230.

(x) *Onley* v. *Gardiner*, 4 M. & W. 496.

(y) Per *Bayley*, B., in *Canham* v. *Fisk*, 2 Tyr. 155.

(z) *Thomas* v. *Thomas*, 5 Tyr. 804 ; 2 Cr. M. & R. 34.

(a) *Bright* v. *Walker*, 1 Cr. M. & R. 211.

user could not give a title as against all persons having estate in the locus in quo, it gave no title as against the lessee and the persons claiming under him, and that no title was gained by an user which did not give a valid title as against the bishop, and permanently affect the see. In a plea (b) under this statute, it is sufficient to allege that the user had existed for forty years before the commencement of the suit, and it need not be alleged to have existed for forty years before the act complained of in the declaration. The plea (c) must be supported by user down to the commencement of the action. Proof of user commencing forty years ago, but discontinued four or five years before the commencement of the action, is insufficient. Evidence of user of a way with horses, carts, and carriages, for certain purposes, does not necessarily prove a right of way for all purposes, but the extent of the right is a question for the jury in each particular case (d).

A seat in a church may be annexed to a house, either by a faculty or prescription (e). Extra-parochial persons cannot establish a claim to seats in the body of a parish church without proof of prescription at least, if indeed they can do so by prescription (f). Nor in the case of a pew in the body of a church, can an action at common law be maintained for a disturbance, unless the pew be annexed to a house in the parish. It is only on account of the pew being annexed to a house, that the temporal court can take cognizance of any intrusion into it (g). Where a party claims a right against the ordinary, he ought to show a title by repairing, &c., but not in an action on the case against a trespasser or tort-feasor. In such case it is neither necessary to allege or prove repairs (h). An old entry on the vestry book, signed by the churchwardens, stating that the pew had been repaired by the then owner of the messuage, (under whom plaintiff claimed,) in consideration of his using it, is admissible evidence (i), being made by the churchwardens within the scope of their official authority, and as showing the reputation of the parish upon the right. The right to sit in a pew may be apportioned in consequence of the messuage, to the owners and occupiers of which it was originally granted, becoming subdivided. Thus three or four families may become entitled to use a pew (k), and a question may arise, how many persons are entitled to use the pew in respect of each of the subdivisions. That is, however, a matter to be settled among the respective owners. The churchwardens have no right to interfere.

(b) *Wright* v. *Williams*, 1 M. & W. 77.

(c) *Parker* v. *Mitchell*, 3 P. & D. 655.

(d) *Cowling* v. *Higginson*, 4 M. & W. 245.

(e) Per *Buller*, J., in *Griffith* v. *Matthews*, 5 T. R. 296.

(f) *Byerley* v. *Windus*, 5 B. & C. 1; 2 D. & Ry. 23. See *Hallack* v. *University of Cambridge*, 1 G. & D. 100.

(g) *Mainwaring* v. *Giles*, 5 B. & A. 356.

(h) *Bunton* v. *Bateman*, 1 Lev. 71; *Ashley* v. *Freckleton*, 3 Lev. 73; *Kenrick* v. *Taylor*, 1 Wils. 326; *Sayer's* R. 31; Bull. N. P. 76, *S. C.*

(i) *Price* v. *Littlewood*, 3 Campb. 288.

(k) *Harris* v. *Drewe*, 2 B. & Ad. 164.

It would be an endless task to enumerate all the instances of nusance, for which an action may be maintained. It may be sufficient to observe, that the erection of any thing offensive so near the house of another, as to render it useless and unfit for habitation, *e. g.*, the erection of a swine stye (*l*), lime-kiln (*m*), privy (*n*), smith's forge (*o*), tobacco mill (*p*), tallow furnace near a common inn (*q*), or the like, is actionable. The principle on which the rule of law proceeds, is, *sic utere tuo, ut non lædas alienum* (*r*), "enjoy your own property in such a manner, as not to injure that of another person." According to this rule, a party is liable for the consequence of his own neglect. Hence it has been holden (*s*), that an action lies against a party for so negligently constructing a hay-rick on the extremity of his land, that in consequence of its spontaneous ignition his neighbour's house was burnt down. To an action (*t*) of nusance for carrying on the business of a tallow chandler in a messuage adjoining the messuage of the plaintiff, it is no plea that the defendant was possessed of his messuage, and the business was carried on, before the plaintiff became possessed of the adjoining messuage ; and in a similar case (*u*), the court said that the defendant should at least have alleged a holding of twenty years' duration. It must not, however, be inferred, from the preceding remarks, that an action can be maintained for a *thing* done merely to the *inconvenience* of another. The building a wall which merely intercepts the prospect of ano er, without obstructing the light, is not actionable (*x*). So the opening a window, whereby the privacy of a neighbour is disturbed, is not actionable (*y*). The only remedy in this case is to build on the adjoining land, opposite to the offensive window.

In an action on the case against defendant, for keeping dogs so near plaintiff's dwelling-house (*z*), that he was disturbed in the enjoyment thereof, it appeared in evidence, that defendant kept six or seven pointers so near plaintiff's dwelling-house, that his family were prevented from sleeping during the night, and were very much disturbed in the day-time. There was not any evidence given on the part of the defendant, notwithstanding which the jury found a verdict for defendant. On a motion for a new trial, Lord *Kenyon*, C. J., said, " I know it is very disagreeable to have such neighbours, but we cannot grant a new trial. Cases certainly of this nature have been made the subject of investigation in courts of justice ; I

(*l*) *Aldred's* case, 9 Rep. 59, a.
(*m*) Per *Wray*, C. J., S. C.
(*n*) *Jones* v. *Powell*, Hutt. 136.
(*o*) *Bradley* v. *Gill*, Lutw. 69.
(*p*) *Styan* v. *Hutchinson*, London Sittings after M. T. 40 Geo. III. B. R., *Kenyon*, C. J., MSS.
(*q*) *Morley* v. *Pragnell*, Cro. Car. 510.
(*r*) 9 Rep. 59.
(*s*) *Vaughan* v. *Menlove*, 3 Bingh. N. C. 468 ; 4 Sc. 244, recognizing *Turbervil*

v. *Stamp*, Salk. 13.
(*t*) *Bliss* v. *Hall*, 4 Bingh. N. C. 183.
(*u*) *Elliotson* v. *Feetham*, 2 Bingh. N. C. 137. See *Flight* v. *Thomas*, 10 A. & E. 590 ; 3 P. & D. 442.
(*x*) Per *Wray*, C. J., 9 Rep. 58, b. ; *Knowles* v. *Richardson*, 1 Mod. 55.
(*y*) Per *Eyre*, C. J., *ex relatione Le Blanc*, J., 3 Campb. 82.
(*z*) *Street, Clerk*, v. *Tugwell*, B. R. M. T. 41 Geo. III., MSS.

remember a case in Peere Williams (a), ' where the plaintiff's house being so near the church, that the five o'clock morning bell disturbed her; the plaintiff came to an agreement with the churchwardens, that she should erect a cupola and a clock, and in consideration thereof the five o'clock bell should not be rung. This was considered as a good agreement, and the chancellor decreed an injunction to stay the ringing the bell.' If the defendant continues the nusance, and you think it advisable, you may bring a new action." Rule refused.

An action cannot be maintained for a reasonable use of a person's right, although it may be to the annoyance of another: as if a butcher, brewer, &c., use his trade in a convenient place (b). For a nusance in a public highway, an *action* cannot be maintained, unless there be special damage (c) : and mere obstruction of the plaintiff's business (d), or delaying him a little while in a journey (e), is not such special damage as will sustain an action ; for the damage ought to be direct (f), and not consequential; e. g., the loss of a horse, or some corporal hurt, as falling into a trench, &c. (2) : and the plaintiff must have used common and ordinary caution (g). But in some cases there may have been negligence in both parties, and yet the plaintiff may be entitled to recover; for the rule is, that although there may have been negligence on the part of the plaintiff, yet, unless he might by the exercise of ordinary care have avoided the consequences of the defendant's negligence, he is entitled to recover : if by ordinary care he might have avoided them, he is the author of his own wrong (h). " If I am guilty of negligence in leaving a dangerous thing in a place, where accidents are likely to happen from it, can I, should an accident happen from it, charge another person, the person injured, with negligence, and thus defeat his claim to compensation? Or am I not answerable for my own, which was the first, act of negligence" (i)? *Illidge* v. *Goodwin* (k) is an authority on this point. There it was holden, that if a horse and cart are left standing in the street without any person to watch

(a) *Martin* v. *Nutkin*, 2 P. Wms. 268.
(b) Com. Dig. Action upon the Case for Nusance (C).
(c) 1 Inst. 56, a.
(d) *Hubert* v. *Groves*, 1 Esp. N. P. C. 148, cited in *Rose* v. *Miles*, 4 M. & S. 103. But see *Wilkes* v. *Hungerford Market Company*, 2 Bingh. N. C. 281.
(e) Per *Cur.*, Carth. 191.
(f) Per *Cur.*, in *Paine* v. *Partrich*, Carth. 191.

(g) *Butterfield* v. *Forrester*, 11 East, 60, cited per *Cur.*, in *Lynch* v. *Nurden*, *post*, p. 1116.
(h) Per *Parke*, B., in *Bridge* v. *Grand Junction Railway Comp.*, 3 M. & W. 248.
(i) Per *Denman*, C. J., delivering judgment in *Lynch* v. *Nurden*, *post*, p. 1116. See also *Marriott* v. *Stanley*, 1 M. & Gr, 568 ; 2 Scott, N. R. 60.
(k) 5 C. & P. 190, *Tindal*, C. J.

(2) The grantee of an occupation-way may maintain an action against the owner of the land over which the way leads for obstructing it, without proving special damage, although it appears that such way has been used by the public for twelve years and upwards. *Allen* v. *Ormond*, 8 East, 4.

them, the owner, whose servant had so negligently left the cart, was liable for damage done by them; although there was evidence to show that the damage was directly occasioned by the act of a person striking the horse. So where the plaintiff, a child, with other children, got up and down, into and from a cart, and so frightened the horse, which was not under the control of any person, having been left by the defendant at a door unattended, in a public street; the jury having found for the plaintiff, the court sustained the verdict (k); observing, that there was, on the part of the defendant, a blameable carelessness, which had tempted the children into the commission of the misconduct which had been set up as a defence; but which did not relieve the defendant in the least from his liability for his want of prudence and forethought in leaving his horse unattended in a public street. If the immediate and proximate cause of damage be the unskilfulness of the plaintiff, he cannot recover. As where it appeared (l) that some bricklayers employed by the defendant had laid several barrows full of lime rubbish before the defendant's door; the plaintiff was passing in a single-horse chaise; the wind raised a whirlwind of the lime rubbish, and that frightened the horse, which usually was very quiet; he started on one side, and would have run against a waggon which was meeting them, but the plaintiff hastily pulled him round, and the horse then ran over a lime heap lying before another man's door; by the shock the shaft was broken; and the horse being still more alarmed by it, ran away, and overset the chaise, and the plaintiff was thrown out and hurt. It was holden, that as the immediate and proximate cause of the injury was the unskilfulness of the driver, the action could not be maintained.

Whether the damage stated be sufficient to maintain the action, is frequently the subject of controversy (3). The plaintiff declared (m), that he was entitled to certain tithes, and that his direct way to carry them to his barn was through a certain highway; that the defendant had stopped up the highway by a ditch and gate erected *ex transverso viæ;* and that by reason of such obstruction, he (the plaintiff) was forced to carry his tithes by a longer and more difficult way; verdict for the plaintiff, and £5 damages. It was moved, in arrest of judgment, that this being laid in a common highway, the obstruction was a common nusance, and that, therefore, the action would not lie; and 1 Inst. 56, was cited; but it was resolved by the court, that the action was maintainable; for they said, that this rule, " that the action will not lie for that which every one suffers," ought not to be taken too

(k) *Lynch* v. *Nurden*, Q. B. H. 1840, Law Journal, N. S. vol. x. p. 73.

(l) *Flower* v. *Adam*, 2 Taunt. 314.
(m) *Hart* v. *Basset*, T. Jones, 156.

(3) See an useful note on this subject by Durnford, Willes, 74.

largely; in this case the plaintiff had sustained a particular damage; for the labour and pains which he was forced to take with his cattle and servants, by reason of the obstruction, might be of more value than the loss of a horse, which had been holden to be sufficient damage to maintain such action. This case was recognized in *Chichester* v. *Lethbridge*, Willes, 73, where the declaration was similar to the foregoing, with this addition only, that defendant opposed the plaintiff in attempting to remove the nusance. Where plaintiff declared that before, and at the time of, committing the grievance, he was navigating his barges laden with goods, along a public navigable creek, and that defendant wrongfully moored a barge across, and kept the same so moored, from thence hitherto, and thereby obstructed the public navigable creek, and prevented the plaintiff from navigating his barges so laden, *per quod* plaintiff was obliged to convey his goods a great distance overland, and was put to trouble and expense in the carriage of his goods overland: held (*n*), that this was sufficient special damage, for which an action upon the case would lie. Where there is direct special damage, an action on the case lies for not repairing (*o*), as well as for a nusance in a highway, if an individual is liable to repair; but otherwise, where the county or parish is to repair the highway (*p*).

II. *By whom and against whom an Action for a Nusance may be maintained.*

If the nusance be to the damage of the reversionary as well as the possessory interest, an action may be brought as well by the reversioner (*q*) as by the tenant in possession, and each will be entitled to recover damages commensurate with the injuries, which their respective interests may have sustained. If any thing be done to destroy the evidence of title, an action is maintainable (*r*) by the reversioner. Reversioner may maintain an action for the obstruction of an ancient light, and, in the event of its not being removed, for the continuance (*s*). But where the acts of trespass did not amount to any permanent injury to the land, but only tended to establish a right of way; it was holden (*t*), that the reversioner could not maintain an action on the case in respect thereof.

(n) *Rose* v. *Miles*, 4 M. & S. 101,

(o) 1 Inst. 56, a. n. (2), Hargrave's ed.

(p) *Russell* v. *Men of Devon*, 2 T. R. 671.

(q) *Bedingfield* v. *Onslow*, 3 Lev. 209; *Leader* v. *Moxon*, 3 Wils. 461; 2 Bl. R. 924, S. C.

(r) *Young* v. *Spencer*, 10 B. & C. 152. See also *Alston* v. *Scales*, 9 Bingh. 3.

(s) *Shadwell* v. *Hutchinson*, 2 B. & Ad. 97.

(t) *Baxter* v. *Taylor*, 4 B. & Ad. 72; 1 Nev. & M. 13. N. This action was brought before the stat. 2 & 3 Will. IV. c. 71. See sect. 8. See *Tucker* v. *Newman*, 11 A. & E. 40; 3 P. & D. 14, *ante*, p. 435.

If the house, &c. affected by the nusance be aliened, the alienee, *after request made* to remove or abate the nusance, may maintain an action for the nusance (u). Tenants in common *may* join in an action to recover damages for a nusance, which concerns the tenements which they hold in common. The action may be maintained against the person who erects the nusance, or his alienee (x), who permits the nusance to be continued. If the party, against whom a verdict in an action of this kind has been recovered, does not abate the nusance, another action may be brought for continuing the nusance, in which the jury will be directed to give large damages. N. It is usual, in the first action, to give nominal damages only. Trespass is the proper remedy for wrongfully continuing a building on plaintiff's land, for the erection of which plaintiff has already recovered compensation; and a recovery, with satisfaction, for erecting it, does not operate as a purchase of the right to continue such erection. Therefore, where the trustees of a turnpike road built buttresses to support it on the land of A., and A. thereupon sued them and their workmen in trespass for such erection, and accepted money paid into court in full satisfaction of the trespass; it was holden (y), that after notice to defendants to remove the buttresses, and a refusal to do so, A. might bring another action of trespass against them for keeping and continuing the buttresses on the land, to which the former recovery was no bar.

Tenant for years erected a nusance (z), and afterwards made an underlease to I. S. The question was, whether, after a recovery against the first tenant for years for the erection, an action would lie against him for the continuance, after he had made an underlease? *Et per Cur.* it lies; for he transferred it with the original wrong, and his demise affirms the continuance of it; he hath also rent as a consideration for the continuance, and, therefore, ought to answer the damage it occasions. *Vide* Wm. Jones, 272. Receipt of rent is upholding. Cro. Jac. 373, 555. The action lies against either at the plaintiff's election. Case lies against the landlord of a house demised by lease, who, under his contract with his tenants, employs workmen to repair the house, for a nusance in the house occasioned by the negligence of his workmen (a).

The trustees of a turnpike road, empowered by stat. to make watercourses, to prevent the road from being overflowed, directed their surveyor to present a plan for carrying off the water of an adjacent brook: he recommended, and on that recommendation they adopted, and caused him to make, a wide channel from the road, gradually narrowing, and conducting the water into the ordinary fence-ditches of the plaintiff's land, which were insufficient to discharge it, and his land was consequently overflowed. It was

(u) *Penruddock's* case, 5 Rep. 101, a.   (x) *Rosewell* v. *Prior*, Salk. 460.
(x) 5 Rep. 100, b.   (a) *Leslie* v. *Pounds*, 4 Taunt. 649.
(y) *Holmes* v. *Wilson*, 10 A. & E. 503.

holden (*b*), that the action did not lie against the defendant, who was one of the trustees, and the chairman, who had signed the order for cutting this trench; for the defendant was not a volunteer: he executed a duty imposed on him by the legislature, which he was bound to execute; and he had exercised his best skill, diligence, and caution in the execution of it. But a surveyor of highway, who had subtracted a portion of a bank by the road-side, was holden (*c*) liable in an action on the case at the suit of the reversioner; for it was a permanent injury to the land, and had a tendency to alter the evidence of title.

III. *Pleadings.*

By stat. 2 & 3 Will. IV. c. 71, s. 5, in all actions upon the case and other pleadings, wherein the party claiming may now by law allege his right generally, without averring the existence of such right from time immemorial, such general allegation shall still be deemed sufficient (*d*).

By R. G. H. T. 4 Will. IV., in actions on the case, the plea of not guilty shall operate as a denial only of the breach of duty or wrongful act alleged to have been committed by the defendant, and not of the facts stated in the inducement, and no other defence than such denial shall be admissible under that plea; all other pleas in denial shall take issue on some particular matter of fact alleged in the declaration. *Ex. gr.* In an action on the case for a nusance to the occupation of a house by carrying on an offensive trade, the plea of not guilty will operate as a denial only that the defendant carried on the alleged trade in such a way as to be a nusance to the occupation of the house, and will not operate as a denial of the plaintiff's occupation of the house. In an action on the case, for obstructing a right of way, such plea [not guilty] will operate as a denial of the obstruction only, and not of the plaintiff's right of way; and all matters in confession and avoidance shall be pleaded specially as in actions of assumpsit.

Under the operation of the foregoing rules, "Not guilty," pleaded to a declaration (*e*) in *case* for the wrongful diversion of water from the plaintiff's mill, puts in issue the mere *fact* of the diversion, and not its *wrongful* character. But in an action (*f*) on the case for keeping dogs, *well knowing* them to be accustomed to

---

(*b*) *Sutton* v. *Clarke*, 6 Taunt. 29.
(*c*) *Alston* v. *Scales*, 9 Bingh. 3.
(*d*) See *Tickle* v. *Brown*, 4 A. & E. 369; 6 Nev. & M. 230; and *post,* tit. "Trespass."

(*e*) *Frankum* v. *Earl of Falmouth*, 2 A. & E. 452; 4 Nev. & Man. 330; after a conference with all the judges.
(*f*) *Thomas* v. *Morgan*, 2 Cr. M. & R. 496; 5 Tyr. 1085.

bite cattle, &c., and which bit and worried the plaintiff's cattle; it was holden, that the plea of not guilty put in issue the *scienter*,— that not being inducement, but an essential part, indeed the substance, of the issue.

In case against the defendant for negligently driving his cart and horse against the plaintiff's horse, it was holden (*g*), that under the plea of not guilty, the defendant could not show that he was not the person driving, and that the cart did not belong to him, those being facts stated in the inducement of which the plea could not operate as a denial, and the misconduct in driving being the only wrongful act put in issue thereby.

IV. *Evidence, &c.*

THE plaintiff must be prepared to prove his possession of the land, house, &c. affected by the nusance, and the continuance or erection of the nusance by the defendant, as the circumstances of the case may require, and also the injury thereby sustained. Where the plaintiff complains of an injury to an easement (*h*), it will be incumbent on him (unless he can show an express grant) to carry his evidence of the condition of the land, &c., and the enjoyment of the right, as far back as possible, in order to raise a presumption of right by grant or prescription. This action being local in its nature, the nusance must be proved to have been committed in the *county* where the venue is laid (*i*). But it is not necessary that the gravamen should be described with any local certainty (*k*). It is sufficient if the declaration point out the gravamen with certainty enough to enable the defendant to have notice of it. Notice to remove nusance left at premises is evidence (*l*) against subsequent occupier. The defendant may prove that the plaintiff gave him leave by parol to do the act which occasioned the nusance (*m*), and that it was done under that permission; for a license executed is not countermandable (*n*). Secus, while it remains executory (*o*). "A parol executory license is countermandable at any time" (*p*). Hence a parol license from A. to B. to enjoy an easement over A.'s land, was holden (*q*) to be countermandable at any time whilst it

(*g*) *Taverner* v. *Little*, 5 Bingh. N. C. 678.

(*h*) Peake's Evid. 294. See stat. 3 & 4 Will. IV. c. 71.

(*i*) *Warren* v. *Webb*, 1 Taunt. 379. But see 3 & 4 Will. IV. c. 42, s. 22, *ante*, p. 494.

(*k*) *Mersey and Irwell Navigation* v. *Douglas*, 2 East, 497. See also *Jefferies*

v. *Duncombe*, 11 East, 226.

(*l*) *Salmon* v. *Bensley*, Ry. & M. 189.

(*m*) *Winter* v. *Brockwell*, 8 East, 308.

(*n*) See *Liggins* v. *Inge*, 7 Bingh. 682.

(*o*) Per *Haughton*, J., *Webb* v. *Paternoster*, Poph. 151.

(*p*) Per *Parke*, B., *Wallis* v. *Harrison*, 4 M. & W. 544.

(*q*) S. C.

remained executory; and that if A. conveyed the land to another, the license was determined at once without notice to B. of the transfer. But an authority coupled with an interest cannot be revoked (*r*). The license must be established by clear and satisfactory proof (*s*). Goods which were upon plaintiff's land were sold to defendant; by the conditions of sale, to which plaintiff was a party, the buyer was to be allowed to enter and take the goods; it was holden, that after the sale the plaintiff could not countermand the license (*t*). Although a parol license may be an excuse for a trespass, until such license is countermanded, yet a right (*u*) and title to have a passage for water over another's land, being a freehold interest, requires a deed to create it.

V. *Costs.*

ACTIONS of trespass on the case, under which this action is classed, are within the statute 3 & 4 Vict. c. 24 (*x*), which see, *ante*, p. 37. The operation of this statute is not limited to cases in which the judge has power to certify. Hence in an action on the case for negligently exposing ploughshares on a highway, whereby the plaintiff sustained severe injury; the jury having given a verdict for 1*s*. damages, and the judge having refused to certify, thinking the case not to be within the statute; it was holden (*y*), that the plaintiff was not entitled to costs. An action on the case for the infringement of a patent, is within the operation of this act; and notwithstanding the provisions of the stat. 5 & 6 Will. IV. c. 83, s. 3, the plaintiff recovering only nominal damages, cannot have his full costs or treble costs, without a certificate under the 3 & 4 Vict. c. 24 (*z*).

(*r*) *Gaussen* v. *Morton*, 10 B. & C. 731.

(*s*) Per *Patteson*, J., *Blanchard* v. *Bridges*, 4 A. & E. 195.

(*t*) *Wood* v. *Manley*, 11 A. & E. 34; 3 P. & D. 5.

(*u*) *Hewlins* v. *Shippam*, 5 B. & C. 221.

(*x*) Explained as to actions in which verdicts had been returned before its passing, by stat. 4 & 5 Vict. c. 28.

(*y*) *Marriott* v. *Stanley*, 2 Scott, N. R. 60.

(*z*) *Gillett* v. *Green*, 7 M. & W. 347.

CHAPTER XXXI.

PARTNERS.

I. *What is necessary to constitute a Partnership*, p. 1122.

II. *How far the Acts of one Partner are binding on his Co-partners*, p. 1128.

III. *Of Actions by and against Partners*, p. 1134; *What Remedy one Partner has against another*, p. 1137.

IV. *Evidence*, p. 1140.

I. *What is necessary to constitute a Partnership.*

IN order to constitute a complete partnership, as well between the parties as in respect to strangers who may deal with them, a communion of participation of profits and loss is essential. The shares of the parties must be joint, though it is not necessary that they should be equal. If the parties be jointly concerned in the purchase, they must also be jointly concerned in the future sale, otherwise they are not partners. A., for himself and his two partners (a) (who were general merchants), B., for himself and partner (who were oil merchants), C., for himself and son (who were also oil merchants), agreed to purchase jointly as much oil as they could procure, on a prospect that the price of that commodity would rise. A. was to be the ostensible buyer, and the others were to share in his purchase, at the same price which he might give. A. and Co. were to have a half, B. and Co. a quarter, and C. and Co. the remaining quarter. In pursuance of this agreement, A. and Co. ordered a broker to buy quantities of oil. The broker accordingly bought several ship-loads, and among the rest a ship-load from the plaintiffs. To some of the vendors, (not plaintiffs in this action,) B. and Co. and C. and Co., during the treaty, declared it to be a

(a) *Coope and others v. Eyre and others*, 1 H. Bl. 37.

common concern between them and A. and Co.; but, with respect
to the plaintiffs, the purchase was made in the name of A. and Co.
only, without any notice that the other defendants had any concern in it. The majority of the court, *viz. Heath*, J., *Gould*, J.,
and Lord *Loughborough*, C. J., were of opinion that B. and Co.
and C. and Co. were not to be considered as partners with A. and
Co., on the ground that there was no communion of profit and loss.
Each party was to have a distinct share of the whole; the one to
have no interference with the share of the other, but each to
manage his share as he judged best. The profit or loss of the one
might be more or less than that of the other. This was a sub-
contract, by which was to be understood a contract subordinate to
another contract, made or intended to be made, between the contracting parties on one part, or some of them, and a stranger. A.
and Co. were the only purchasers known to the plaintiffs; entire
credit was given to them alone. The contracts made with the
other merchants were not admissible evidence in this cause, except
to prove a fraud, if the facts had gone that length; namely, that
the house of A. and Co., as a failing house, was to stand forward in
order to protect the other defendants, who by such means might
have the benefit of the speculation, if it proved fortunate, without
sustaining any loss in the event of its failing. No such evidence
had been adduced; on the contrary, it appeared that the objection
made by the other vendors to the firm of A. and Co. was, "*that they
were unknown and new in the trade*." *Wilson*, J., differed in
opinion from the rest of the court; observing, that although the
contract was actually made between the plaintiffs and A. and Co.,
yet if the other defendants were jointly concerned in it, they ought
to be responsible, as much as if they had personally contracted;
that they were so concerned, sufficiently appeared from the contracts with the other merchants, and their own declarations; these
he thought were proper to be given in evidence, being against
themselves.

Where the executors of a deceased partner continued his share
of the partnership property in trade for the benefit of his infant
daughter; it was holden (*b*), that they were liable upon a bill
drawn for the accommodation of the partnership, and paid in discharge of a partnership debt; although their names were not added
to the firm, but the trade was carried on by the other partners
under the same firm as before, and the executors, when they divided
the profits and loss of the trade, carried the same to the account
of the infant, and took no part of the profits themselves.

A father established in business (*c*), on his son's coming of age,
told him, he should have a *share* in it, and held him out to the
world as his partner: the son acted as such for several years, but

(*b*) *Wightman* v. *Townroe*, 1 M. & S.   (*c*) *Peacock* v. *Peacock*, 2 Campb. 45.
412.

the particular share, which the son was to have, was not settled; it was holden, that as there was a partnership as between the parties and the rest of the world, the presumption of law was, that they were partners *inter se*. That this presumption not having been repelled, the son, though not entitled to a moiety, was entitled to a *share* of profits; but it was left to the jury to consider what was a fair and just proportion for the father to give, and the son to expect; the jury found that the son was entitled to a fourth part of the profits. Where an infant held himself out as in partnership with I. S., and continued to act as such till within a short period of his coming of age, but there was no proof of his doing any act as a partner after twenty-one; it was holden (*d*), that it was his duty to notify his disaffirmance of the partnership on arriving at twenty-one; and, as he had neglected to do so, that he was responsible to persons who had trusted I. S. with goods, subsequently to the infant's attaining twenty-one, on the credit of the partnership. In respect of creditors, he who takes a moiety of all the profits indefinitely, shall, by operation of law, be made liable to losses, if losses arise; upon the principle, that by taking a part of the profits, he takes from the creditors a part of that fund which is the proper security to them for the payment of their debts. A. and B., ship-agents at different ports (*e*), entered into an agreement to share, in certain proportions, the profits of their respective commissions, and the discount on tradesmen's bills employed by them in repairing the ships consigned to them, &c. It was, however, expressly stipulated between A. and B., that they were not to be answerable for each other's losses. It was holden, that although, with respect to each other, these persons were not to be considered as partners under this agreement, yet they had made themselves such with regard to all persons with whom either contracted as ship-agent. The distinction taken in the preceding case as to an agreement not constituting a partnership as between the parties themselves, though it may have that effect, *quoad* third parties, was recognized in the following case: A., having neither money nor credit (*f*), offered to B., that if he would order with him certain goods to be shipped upon an adventure, if *any profit should arise from them, B. should have half for his trouble:* B. having lent his credit on this contract, and ordered the goods on their joint account, which were furnished accordingly, and afterwards paid for by B. alone; it was holden, that B. was entitled to recover back such payment in assumpsit against A., who had not accounted to him for the profits; such contract not constituting a partnership as between themselves, but only an agreement for a compensation for trouble and credit, though B. was liable as a partner to third

---

(*d*) *Goode and Bennion* v. *Harrison*, 5 B. & A. 147.

(*e*) *Waugh* v. *Carver*, 2 H. Bl. 235;

recognized by *Bolland*, B., in *Bond* v. *Pittard*, 3 M. & W. 361.

(*f*) *Hesketh* v. *Blanchard*, 4 East, 144.

persons, creditors. But where two persons, who were never in partnership as general partners, concur in giving an order for an undivided parcel of goods, they are not, therefore, liable jointly (g) to the seller, if, upon the whole of the transaction, the intention of the parties appears to have been that the buyers should be severally responsible for the amount of their respective interests in the goods. A party paying a deposit on shares in a trading company, and afterwards signing the deed of partnership, is to be considered (h) as a partner from the time of his paying the deposit. But in an action for goods and work applied *in equipping a mine*, (the defendant being charged as one of the company *concerned in working it;*) it was holden (i), that the mere payment of deposits without any signature of a deed, or interference in management, was not enough to make the defendant liable, unless the jury believed, from the evidence, that an actual conveyance of an interest in the mine had been made to her. Where a mining company was formed, the capital to be £30,000, in 3,000 shares of £10 each, and 2,000 shares only were actually subscribed for, of which the defendant took 100; it was holden, that letters subsequently written by the defendant to the directors, requiring them to call a meeting for the purpose of changing a director, were evidence to go to the jury to show that he authorized the directors to proceed with the smaller amount of capital, so as to render him liable for the price of articles supplied for the use of the mines, on the order of the directors (k). A project having been formed for the establishment of a company for the manufacturing of sugar from beet-root, a prospectus was issued, stating the proposed capital to consist of 10,000 shares of £25 each. The directors began their works and entered into contracts respecting them, and manufactured and sold some sugar; but only a small portion of the proposed capital was raised, and only 1,400 out of the 10,000 shares were taken; it was holden (l), that a subscriber, who had taken shares, and paid a deposit on them, was not liable upon such contracts of the directors, without proof that he knew and assented to their proceeding on the smaller capital, or expressly authorized the making of the contract. Where, however, it was proved, that A. had contributed to the funds of a building society, and had been present at a meeting of the society, and party to a resolution that certain houses should be built; it was holden (m), that he was liable in an action for work done in building those houses, without proof that he had any actual interest in them, or in the land on which they were built. A merchant

(b) Gibson v. Lupton and Wood, 9 Bingh. 297; 2 M. & Sc. 371.

(h) Lawler v. Kershaw, 1 M. & Malk. 93.

(i) Vice v. Lady Anson, 1 M. & Malk. 96; 7 B. & C. 409.

(k) Tredwen v. Bourne, 6 M. & W.

461. See Dickinson v. Valpy, 10 B. & C. 128; 5 M. & Ry. 126; and *ante*, p. 331.

(l) Pitchford v. Davis, 5 M. & W. 2.
(m) Braithwaite v. Skofield, 9 B. & C. 401.

in London recommended consignments to a merchant abroad, and it was agreed that the commission on all sales of goods recommended by one house to the other should be equally divided, without allowing any deduction for expenses; it was holden (n), that this was a participation in profit, and constituted a partnership between the parties *quoad hoc*.　In 1820, W. advanced to A. and B., then carrying on business in partnership as brewers, the sum of 24,000*l*., and the three executed a deed, by the terms of which a partnership stock was created, in which they all had a joint property: W., however, was not to have any definite aliquot proportion of the profits, but was to have an account of the profits as between themselves, so as to get £2,000 or £2,400 a year, as the case might be, out of the clear profits: W.'s name never appeared to the world as a partner: it was holden (o), that W. was a partner; and the new firm having become bankrupt in 1826, that the creditors of the old firm and the creditors of the new firm were both entitled to prove against the property of the new firm.　A., B., and C., the proprietors of a stage coach, dividing the general profits of the concern (p), agreed that they should each work the coach a stage with horses, their separate property, and maintained respectively at their separate expense; it was holden, that B. and C. were not jointly liable as co-partners with A. for the price of hay furnished at A.'s request for the use of the horses which were his separate property, but were kept by him for the purpose of working the coach the stage allotted to him under the agreement.　N. It did not appear in what manner, upon an adjustment of the accounts, the hay furnished to the different horses was paid for; whether as part of the general outgoings, or separately by each party.　Where A., the keeper of a coach-office, and a part owner in several coaches, made a contract with B. for the carriage of parcels which he was in the habit of sending from that office to various places; it was holden (q), that this bound the owners of all the coaches, in which A. was part owner, and as well those who became part owners after making the contract, as those who were so before.　A. was employed by B. (r) to sell goods, and was to receive for his trouble whatever money he could procure for them beyond a stated sum; this was holden not to constitute a partnership between A. and B. as to these goods.　So where A., having purchased two bullocks (s), put them to depasture upon the lands of B., under an agreement that, after they had been fatted, the profit to be made upon the resale, above a certain sum (at which A. then valued the bullocks), should be equally divided between A.

(n) *Cheap* v. *Barclay*, 4 B. & A. 663.
(o) *Exp. Chuck*, 8 Bingh. 469; coram Lord Chancellor, assisted by *Tindal*, C. J., and *Littledale*, J.
(p) *Barton* v. *Hanson and others*, 2 Taunt. 49. See *Weyland* v. *Elkins*, Holt's N. P. C. 227; and *ante*, p. 1101. See

Fromont v. *Coupland*, *post*, 1138.
(q) *Helsby* v. *Mears*, 5 B. & C. 504.
(r) *Benjamin* v. *Porteus*, 2 H. Bl. 590.
(s) *Wish* v. *Small*, Devon Spring Assizes, 1808, coram *Thomson*, B., 1 Campb. 331.

and B. It was holden, that A. and B. were merely partners in the profits, and that this was a mode of paying B. for the pasture ; consequently A. might maintain an action in his own name, without joining B., to recover the price of the bullocks from a person to whom he had sold them. So where there was an agreement between A., the sole owner of a lighter, and B., a lighterman (t), that B., in consideration of working the lighter, should have half her *gross earnings*, Lord *Ellenborough* was of opinion, that as this was only a mode of paying B. wages for his labour, and differed from a participation of profits and loss, it did not constitute a partnership. So an agent, who is paid by a proportion of the profits of the adventure, is not therefore a partner in the goods (u). A partnership cannot acquire property in goods obtained (x) by the fraud of one of the partners, to which the rest are not privy. An agreement to carry on a partnership in violation of an act of parliament is void (y), and will confer no rights on either party against the other.

By stat. 7 Will. IV. & 1 Vict. c. 73, the Queen is enabled to confer certain powers and immunities on trading and other companies by patent ; *inter alia*, 1. The same powers (z) may be granted to companies not incorporated, as if they were so. 2. That suits may be carried on in the name of one of the officers (a). 3. The individual liability of members may be limited (b). 4. The evidence of any officer or member of such company is made admissible (c).

Spiritual Persons (d).—By stat. 4 & 5 Vict. c. 14, after reciting, that " divers associations and copartnerships consisting of more than six members or shareholders have been formed, for the purpose of carrying on the business of banking, and other trades and dealings, for gain and profit, and were then engaged in carrying on the same, by means of boards of directors or managers, committees, or other officers acting on behalf of all the members or shareholders of or persons otherwise interested in such associations or copartnerships; and that divers spiritual persons holding dignities, prebends, canonries, benefices, stipendiary curacies, or lectureships, have been members or shareholders of or otherwise interested in divers of such associations or copartnerships ; and that it was expedient to render legal all contracts entered into by such associations or copartnerships, although the same may now be void by reason of such spiritual persons being or having been such members or shareholders ; it was enacted, that no such association or copartnership already formed, or which may be hereafter formed, nor any contract either as between the members, partners, or shareholders composing such

(t) *Dry* v. *Boswell*, 1 Campb. 329.
(u) *Meyer* v. *Sharpe*, 5 Taunt. 74.
(x) *Kilby* v. *Wilson*, Ry. & Moo. 178.
(y) *Armstrong* v. *Lewis*, 2 Cr. & M. 298.
(z) Sect. 2.

(a) Sect. 3. See *Galloway* v. *Bleaden*, 1 M. & Gr. 247.
(b) Sect. 4.
(c) Sect. 23.
(d) See *ante*, p. 308.

association or copartnership for the purposes thereof, or as between such association or copartnership and other persons, heretofore entered into or which shall be entered into by any such association or copartnership already formed or hereafter to be formed, shall be deemed to be illegal or void, or to occasion any forfeiture whatsoever, by reason only of any such spiritual person as aforesaid being or having been a member, partner, or shareholder of or otherwise interested in the same; but all such associations and copartnerships shall have the same validity, and all such contracts shall be enforced in the same manner, to all intents and purposes, as if no such spiritual person had been or was a member, partner, or shareholder of or interested in such association or copartnership: Provided always, that it shall not be lawful for any spiritual person holding any cathedral preferment, benefice, curacy, or lectureship, or who shall be licensed or allowed to perform the duties of any ecclesiastical office, to act as a director or managing partner, or to carry on such trade or dealing as aforesaid in person."

II. *How far the Acts of one Partner are binding on his Co-Partners.*

A GENERAL partnership agreement (e), though under seal, does not authorize the partners to execute deeds for each other, unless a particular power be given for that purpose; and the power must be given by deed, for one man cannot authorize another to execute a deed for him but by deed; and no subsequent acknowledgment will suffice (f). But although one partner cannot bind the other partners *by deed*, without an authority by deed, yet in mercantile transactions, in drawing and accepting bills of exchange, it never was doubted, but that one partner might bind the rest (g), even without their knowledge or assent. A new partner, however, cannot be bound in this manner for an old debt incurred by the other partners, before the new partner was taken into the firm: this was established in the case of *Sheriff* v. *Wilks*, 1 East, 48. There the plaintiffs had sold a quantity of porter to A. and B., who were then partners, which porter was entered in the plaintiffs' books in the names of A. and B.; and the same was afterwards shipped for the West Indies, and the defendant B. paid the shipping charges. Six months afterwards C. became a partner with A. and B., and continued so for a few months, when their partnership was

(e) *Harrison* v. *Jackson and others*, 7 T. R. 207.

(f) *Steiglitz* v. *Egginton*, Holt, N. P.

C. 141.

(g) See *ante*, tit. "Bills of Exchange," p. 307.

dissolved. The defendant B., previously to the dissolution of the partnership, sent to the plaintiffs a memorandum of calculation, in his own handwriting, of certain deductions claimed by him in respect of the porter. The plaintiffs drew a bill upon the defendants for the balance. This bill was accepted by A. in the partnership firm of all the defendants, by his subscribing thereon, "Accepted, A. & Co." An action having been brought by the plaintiffs, against A., B., and C., upon the acceptance; and A. and C. having been out-lawed, B. pleaded the general issue: it was holden, that the plaintiffs could not recover; *Le Blanc*, J., observing, that this case must be determined in the same manner as if C. had pleaded to the action. It seemed admitted, that if one of several partners pledge the part-nership fund for his individual debt, that would not bind the rest. And he saw no difference between the case of one, and the case of two, of several partners pledging the joint fund for their individual debt, which was the case before the court. The point above alluded to by *Le Blanc*, J., *viz.* that one partner cannot pledge the security of another for his own private debt, appears to have been expressly decided in two cases referred to by Mr. East, in a note to the fore-going decision, *viz.* in *Gregson and others* v. *Hutton and another*, B. R. E. 22 Geo. III., and in *Marsh* v. *Vansommer and another*, London Sittings after Mich. T. 1786, cor. *Buller*, J. See also *Swan* v. *Steele*, *ante*, p. 307, and *Green* v. *Deakin*, 2 Stark. N. P. C. 347.

Where an agreement for a partnership was entered into on the 24th of June, 1824, and such agreement was intended by the parties to have a by-gone operation, *viz.* from the 18th of May preceding: A bill had been discounted for the firm by the plaintiffs in the interval between the 18th of May and the 24th of June; and other bills were discounted subsequently to the latter day; it was holden (h), that the liability of the defendant did not attach upon the bill dis-counted before the 24th of June, until which day he was not in fact a member of the firm. But where A. and B. agreed to become partners from the 1st of January next following, upon certain terms, which were to be embodied in a deed to be executed on that day; and the deed was executed on the 18th of January, but the parties considered themselves as partners from the 1st of January. It was holden (i), that B. was bound by the contracts of A. entered into in the name of the firm between the 1st and 18th of January; for if no deed had ever been executed, each partner would have been liable for the engagements of the firm entered into whilst the business was carrying on for their mutual benefit. To a count in assumpsit on a bill of exchange against three partners, one of them pleaded that the bill was accepted by the other two in the name of the firm without his knowledge, privity, or consent, for a debt due

(h) *Vere* v. *Ashby*, 10 B. & C. 288.　　1 Scott, N. R. 143.
(i) *Battley* v. *Lewis*, 1 M. & Gr. 155;

from them before he became a member of the firm; it was holden (*k*), that this plea was not supported by evidence that the bill was accepted in discharge of a debt which arose partly before and partly after the third partner joined the firm; but that such partner was liable only for so much of the debt for which the bill was accepted as accrued subsequently to his becoming a partner.

One partner may, by procuration, indorse bills for the firm (*l*). A retired partner may give authority by parol to a continuing partner to indorse bills in the partnership name, after the dissolution of the partnership (*m*).

One of several partners cannot bind the others by a submission to arbitration, even of matters arising out of the business of the firm (*n*), and in this respect there is not any distinction between a general partnership, and a partnership in a particular transaction (*o*).

Where one of several partners (*p*) commits an act of bankruptcy, which is afterwards followed up by a commission and assignment, he has no longer any property in the partnership effects; but the property is, from the time of such act of bankruptcy, in his assignees by relation, and in the solvent partners. It may be observed, that the general authority of one partner to draw bills or promissory notes to charge another, is only an implied authority (*q*); and consequently that implication may be rebutted: for it is not essential to a partnership, that one partner should have power to draw bills and notes in the partnership firm to charge the others; they may stipulate between themselves that it shall not be done; and if a third person, having notice of this, will take such a security from one of the partners, he shall not·sue the others upon it, in breach of such stipulation, nor in defiance of a notice previously given to him by one of them, that he will not be liable for any bill or note signed by the others. If one of two partners commit a secret act of bankruptcy (*r*), the other party may, for a valuable consideration, and without fraud, dispose of the partnership effects; and though he himself afterwards become bankrupt, the assignees, under a joint commission, cannot maintain trover against the *bonâ fide* vendee of such partnership effects; and the same rule holds, although the solvent partner knew of the bankruptcy. Hence, where one of two partners, who were country bankers, became bankrupt; and the defendants, being holders of their notes, obtained payment of part of them from the London banker, at whose house they were payable out of the funds in their hands belonging to the country bank; and

(*k*) *Wilson* v. *Lewis*, 2 Scott, N. R. 115.

(*l*) *Williamson* v. *Johnson*, 1 B. & C. 146.

(*m*) *Smith* v. *Winter*, 4 M. & W. 454.

(*n*) *Steed* v. *Salt*, 3 Bingh. 101.

(*o*) *Adams* v. *Bankart*, 1 Cr. M. & R. 681; 5 Tyr. 425.

(*p*) *Bayley*, J., 10 East, 426.

(*q*) *Galloway* v. *Mathew and another*, 10 East, 264. See *Duncan* v. *Lowndes*, 3 Campb. 478. As to the right of director of joint stock company to draw bills, see *ante*, p. 331.

(*r*) *Fox* v. *Hanbury*, Cowp. 449.

the solvent partner, knowing of the bankruptcy, procured a debtor to the firm to give his bill in part satisfaction of his debt, and indorsed and delivered the same to defendants in payment of the residue of the notes in their hands, and afterwards became bankrupt; it was holden (s), that the assignees, under a joint commission, could not recover from the defendants the monies so paid to them by the London bankers, nor the proceeds of the said bill. If one partner becomes a bankrupt, his assignees cannot obtain (t) any share of the partnership effects, until they first satisfy all that is due from him to the partnership. A solvent partner (u) may sue out a writ in the name of his partner, or of his assignees if he is bankrupt, as well as his own, in order to recover a debt due to the partnership; but the partner who objects has a right to be indemnified against the costs.

Where one partner commits an act of bankruptcy, which is afterwards followed up by a commission and assignment, he has no longer any power over the partnership property. And any disposition of it by him is void as against the other partners, it being vested in *them* and his assignees by relation to his act of bankruptcy (x). Where one of two partners (y), with the intention of cheating the other, goes to a shop and purchases articles such as might be used in the partnership business, which he instantly converts to his own separate use, if there was no collusion between him and the seller, this is to be considered as a partnership transaction, and the innocent partner is liable for the price of the goods, without proof of any previous dealings between the parties.

Where goods are ordered by one member of a club for the benefit of all, every member, who either concurs in the order or subsequently assents to it, is liable (z), although the member who ordered the goods is made the debtor in the plaintiff's books, and the bill is sent to him, unless it clearly appear that the plaintiff meant to give credit to that member only. But in a later case, where a club was formed subject to the following among other rules, *viz.* that the entrance fee should be ten guineas, and the annual subscription five guineas; that if the subscription were not paid within a certain limited period, the defaulter should cease to be a member; that there should be a committee to manage the affairs of the club, to be chosen at a general meeting; and that all members should discharge their club bills daily; the steward being authorized, in default of payment, on request, to refuse to continue to supply them:

(s) *Harvey* v. *Crickett*, 5 M. & S. 336. See *Woodbridge* v. *Swann*, 4 B. & Ad. 636.

(t) Per *Tenterden*, C. J., *Holderness* v. *Shackels*, 8 B. & C. 618.

(u) *Whitehead* v. *Hughes*, 4 Tyr. 92; 2 Cr. & M. 318.

(x) Per *Bayley*, B., in *Burt* v. *Moult*, 3 Tyr. 569, recognizing *Thomason* v. *Frere*, 10 East, 418.

(y) *Bond* v. *Gibson and another*, 1 Campb. 185.

(z) *Delauney* v. *Strickland*, 2 Stark. N. P. C. 416, *Abbott*, C. J.

it was holden (a), that a member of the club, merely as such, was not liable for debts incurred by the committee for work done or goods supplied for the use of the club; for that the committee had no authority to pledge the personal credit of the members.

A judgment taken by one of two joint creditors, does not extinguish the debt, unless it be taken with the concurrence of both (b).

A., B., and C. carried on trade in partnership, and A. was also in partnership with D. A. being indebted to the firm of A., B., and C. before the dissolution of that partnership, unknown to D. indorsed a bill and paid over money (belonging to A. and D.) in discharge of the private debt due from A. to A., B., and C., and immediately afterwards indorsed the same bill to a creditor of the firm of A., B., and C. The partnership between A., B., and C. having been dissolved; it was holden, that A. and D. could not maintain trover against B. and C. for the bill, nor assumpsit for the money paid by A. out of the funds of A. and D. to A., B., and C., in discharge of his private debt: and A. and D. having afterwards become bankrupts; it was holden (c), that their assignees could not maintain such action. The principle of this decision was, that if one of the plaintiffs is barred, he cannot recover by joining other plaintiffs in an action to undo his own act (d). So where, to an action by three plaintiffs for a joint demand, the defendant pleaded an accord and satisfaction with one of the plaintiffs, by a part payment in cash, and a set-off of a debt due from that one to the defendant; it was holden, that the plea was good, without alleging any authority from the other two plaintiffs to make the settlement (e).

One of two partners drew bills of exchange in his own name, which he procured to be discounted with a banker, through the medium of the same agent who had discounted other bills drawn in the partnership firm with the same banker; it was holden, that the banker had not any remedy against the *partnership* upon the bill so drawn by the single partner, because they did not appear to have been drawn for and on account of the partnership. And although the proceeds of these bills had been applied to the use of the partnership, yet the court held (f), that the partners were not liable as for money lent, inasmuch as the transaction was originally mere matter of discount, and not an advance of money to the partnership, taking the bills as a collateral security. But where one of several partners, with the privity of the others, draws bills of exchange in his own name upon the partnership firm, in favour of persons who advanced

(a) *Flemyng* v. *Hector*, 2 M. & W. 172, recognized in *Todd* v. *Emly*, 7 M. & W. 427; and *S. C.*, Exch. E. T. 1841, Law Journal, vol. x. N. S. 262. See also *Tyrrell* v. *Woolley*, 2 Scott, N. R. 171, case of a Benefit Society.

(b) Per *Holroyd*, J., in *Biggs* v. *Fel-lows*, 8 B. & C. 405.

(c) *Jones* v. *Yates*, 9 B. & C. 532; 4 M. & Ry. 206.

(d) Per *Parke*, B., in *Wallace* v. *Kensall*, 7 M. & W. 273.

(e) *Wallace* v. *Kensall*, 7 M. & W. 264.

(f) *Emly* v. *Lye*, 15 East, 7.

him the amount, which he applies to the use of the partnership, although the partners are not jointly liable on the bills, they may be jointly sued (g) by the payees for money lent. Where one of three partners, after a dissolution of partnership, undertook by deed to pay a particular partnership debt on two bills of exchange, and that was communicated to the holder, who consented to take the separate notes of the one partner for the amount, strictly reserving his right against all three, and retained possession of the original bills; it was holden (h), that the separate notes having proved unproductive, he might still resort to his remedy against the other partners, and that the taking under these circumstances the separate notes, and even afterwards renewing them several times successively, did not amount to satisfaction of the joint debt. Payment to one of two partners of a partnership debt, after they had appointed a third person to collect the debts, and with notice of such appointment, is, notwithstanding the notice, good (i). In an action (k) brought by partners to recover a debt, if the defendant, to prove payment, gives in evidence a receipt signed by one of the plaintiffs, they are not concluded, but may show that it was given under circumstances which destroy its effect, as fraud on the partners not signing; for a receipt is evidence, but evidence only, and capable of being explained (l). Where one of two partners makes a contract, as to the terms on which any business is to be transacted by the firm, although such business is not in their usual course of dealing, and even contrary to their arrangement with each other, and the business is afterwards transacted by or with the knowledge of the other partner; it was holden, that he is bound by the contract made by his partner (m). So a pledge by one partner of partnership property will bind (n) his partners, although the pledge is made without their privity and consent; provided there be not any fraud, and provided also the pledgee did not know, nor had means of knowing, that the property was partnership property. Mere knowledge by a creditor (o) of the dissolution of partnership, will not release the old partners from their liability to him, though he continue his account with the new firm, unless he appears expressly or by some act to have accepted the substituted credit of the new partnership, instead of the retiring partners.

(g) Denton v. Rodie, 3 Campb. 493.
(h) Bedford v. Deakin, 2 B. & A. 210.
(i) Porter v. Taylor, 6 M. & S. 156.
(k) Farrar v. Hutchinson, 9 A. & E. 641.
(l) See Graves v. Key, 3 B. & Ad. 318, n.; ante, p. 82.

(m) Sandilands v. Marsh, 2 B. & A. 673.
(n) Raba v. Ryland, per Dallas, C. J., confirmed by court, Gow. N. P. C. 132.
(o) Kirwan v. Kirwan, 4 Tyr. 491; 2 Cr. & M. 617. See Blew v. Wyatt, 5 C. & P. 397.

III. *Of Actions by and against Partners, p.* 1134; *What Remedy one Partner has against another, p.* 1137.

Whenever an express contract is made, an action is maintainable upon it, either in the name of the person with whom it was actually made, or in the name of the person with whom in point of law it was made. Hence where three parties agreed to be jointly interested in goods, but that they should be bought by one of them in his own name only, and he made a contract for the purchase accordingly; it was holden (*p*), that all might join in suing the vendor for a breach of that contract. A contract was made by one of several partners in his individual capacity, he declaring at the time that the subject matter was his property alone; it was holden (*q*), that his declaration was evidence of the fact against all the partners, and therefore that they could not sue jointly upon such a contract. The defendant agreed with Sharpe, a coachmaker, for the hire of a carriage for five years. The defendant did not know that Sharpe had a partner, but in fact Robson was partner with Sharpe at the time of the contract. At the end of three years there was a dissolution of partnership between Sharpe and Robson, and notice of that dissolution and of Sharpe having assigned all his interest in the contract to Robson was given to the defendant, who said he would not continue the contract with Robson. It was holden (*r*), that it was competent to the defendant to consider the agreement as at an end; for he might have been induced to enter into the contract by reason of the confidence he reposed in Sharpe; and at all events was entitled to his services in the execution of it.

If a person colludes with one partner in a firm, in order to enable him to injure the other partners, they can maintain (*s*) a joint action against the person so colluding.

F., a partner in a banking-house, transferred stock out of the name of K. in the books of the Bank of England, under a forged power of attorney and without the authority of K., and caused the produce to be mixed with the money of the firm. F. having been convicted of another forgery committed under similar circumstances, and executed; it was holden (*t*), that K. might recover the amount against the surviving partners in an action for money had and received.

An action of assumpsit may be maintained (*u*) by the several

(*p*) *Cothay* v. *Fennell,* 10 B. & C. 671.

(*q*) *Lucas* v. *De la Cour,* 1 M. & S. 249.

(*r*) *Robson and Sharpe* v. *Drummond,* 2 B. & Ad. 303.

(*s*) Per Lord *Tenterden,* C. J., in *Long-*man v. *Pole,* 1 M. & Malk. 225.

(*t*) *Marsh and others* v. *Keating,* D. P., June 25th, 1834, 1 Sc. 5; 1 Bingh. N. C. 198.

(*u*) *Garrett* v. *Handley,* 4 B. & C. 664.

partners of a firm, upon the guarantee given to one of them, if there be evidence, that it was given for the benefit of all. It will be observed, that in the foregoing case the guarantee was not by deed. Covenant lies (x) on a deed of composition with creditors by one of two partners who signs the deed in the name of the firm and sets his seal thereto, for non-payment of an instalment due on a partnership debt; for the other partner, not being a party to the deed, cannot join in covenant. In an action *by* partners for the non-performance of a contract entered into with the partnership, it is essentially necessary that the action should be brought in the joint names of all the persons of whom the partnership consisted at the time the contract was made (1), otherwise the parties suing will be liable to be nonsuited for the omission of their co-partners. In one case, where an action was brought in the names of two persons, with whom the defendants had dealt as partners, and it appeared that at the time of the contract there was in fact another partner, who had, however, withdrawn his name from his firm, but still continued to receive part of the profits: although it was objected that the dormant partner ought to have been joined, Lord *Kenyon*, C. J., is reported to have refused to nonsuit the plaintiffs (y). So where in an action (z) brought by A. for goods sold and delivered, it appeared that B., who proved the delivery and value of the goods, was the principal manager of A.'s trade; and that he received for his service a certain salary, and besides that, a certain proportion, *per cent.*, on the profits of the plaintiff's whole trade, and inclusively on the profits of the demand in question; it was holden, that A. might sue alone, and that it was not necessary that B. should be joined with the plaintiff. So where an action was brought by Mawman (a), a bookseller, against the printer, for not insuring the "Travels of Anacharsis;" and it appeared that several other booksellers, and amongst them Evans, a witness, had a share in the work; but, inasmuch as Evans had never contracted with Gillett, but Mawman was the only ostensible man, the court held, that he was the only proper plaintiff; and with good reason, for the only acting partner might owe much money to the defendant, which the defendant might set off; but if the plaintiff and the dormant partner had sued, that debt of the acting partner could not be set off. "There is a material distinction between the case

(x) *Metcalfe* v. *Rycroft*, 6 M. & S. 75.
(y) *Leveck and another* v. *Pollard and another*, 2 Esp. N. P. C. 468.
(z) *Lloyd* v. *Archbowle*, 2 Taunt. 324.

(a) *Mawman* v. *Gillett*, cited by Sir James Mansfield, C. J., 2 Taunt. 325. See further on this point, *Robson* v. *Drummond*, 2 B. & Ad. 303.

(1) Subsequently admitted partners, though under an agreement to share in profit and loss, from a time antecedent to the contract, ought not to be joined. *Wilsford* v. *Wood*, 1 Esp. N. P. C. 180, Lord *Kenyon*, C. J.

where partners are defendants, and where partners are plaintiffs; if you can find out a dormant partner defendant, you may make him pay, because he has had the benefit of your work; but a person with whom you have no privity of communication in your contract, shall not sue you." But where a merchant, carrying on trade on his own separate account, introduced into his firm the name of a clerk, who did not partake in the profits of the business, but continued to receive a fixed salary; Lord *Ellenborough* held (b), that in an action on a bill of exchange, payable to the order of this firm, the clerk ought to have been joined as a plaintiff, for he was to be considered, in all respects, as a partner as between himself and the rest of the world; that where the name of the real person is introduced with his own consent, it is immaterial what agreement there may be between him and those who share the profit and loss—they are equally responsible, and the contract of one is the contract of all. An ostensible partner, who makes a contract, may, if he pleases, join dormant partners with himself as plaintiffs (c). But a party with whom the contract is actually made, may sue without joining others with whom it is apparently made (d). Where one of several partners in a banking-house, drew a bill in his own name upon a third par y, who accepted the same, upon condition that the drawer should provide for the same when due; it was holden, that all the partners could not recover on the bill (e).

The rule above alluded to formerly held with respect to actions brought *against* partners, and plaintiffs were frequently nonsuited for not naming *all* the partners as defendants. This rule was considered as oppressive, inasmuch as it was not possible for the plaintiffs in many cases, without the assistance of a bill of discovery, to ascertain the names of all the persons constituting the firm with which they had had dealings. On this ground the rule was departed from in the time of Lord *Mansfield,* and it was then laid down that defendants should be permitted to take advantage of this objection by a plea in abatement (f) only. This plea, however, for the non-joinder of a person as co-defendant will not be allowed (g), unless it be stated in the plea, that such person is resident within the jurisdiction of the court, and unless the place of residence of such person shall be stated with convenient certainty in an affidavit verifying such plea. But plaintiff may reply (h), the discharge of such person by bankruptcy and certificate, or under Insolvent Act. The liability of the parties depends upon their being partners at the time when the contract is made (i), and a dormant partner cannot set up the plaintiff's ignorance of his being a partner, to obviate

(b) *Guidon* v. *Robson*, 2 Campb. 302.
(c) *Skinner* v. *Stocks*, 4 B. & A. 437.
(d) *Kell* v. *Nainby*, 10 B. & C. 20.
(e) *Sparrow and others* v. *Chisman*, 9 B. & C. 241.
(f) *Rice* v. *Shute*, 5 Burr. 2611, and

ante, p. 409, n., 412.
(g) Stat. 3 & 4 Will. IV. c. 42, s. 8.
(h) *Ib.* sect. 9.
(i) See Lord *Kenyon's* opinion in *Saville* v. *Robertson*, 4 T.-R. 725.

such liability. But in a case where there was a stipulation between three persons who appeared to the world as partners (*k*), that one of them should not participate in the profit and loss, and should not be liable as a partner; it was holden, that he was not liable as such to persons who had notice of this stipulation. A. and B. (*l*) had entered into a written engagement to employ plaintiff in their trade for a certain time; it was holden, that plaintiff could not sue C., who was a dormant partner, with A. and B., inasmuch as the agreement was in writing and *inter partes;* and it did not contain any intimation that A. and B. were carrying on business as members of a more extensive firm. " I know of no authority for introducing the name of a dormant partner into such a contract. In implied contracts, where the benefit is equal, and the liability not limited, a dormant partner may be included: but there is no authority which extends the principle to express contracts." The non-joinder of a secret partner cannot be pleaded (*m*) in abatement.

It is a general rule, that, between partners, whether they are so in general or for a particular transaction only, no account can be taken at law. Hence, where A. and B. jointly undertook to procure a cargo for a vessel, for certain commission, which they agreed to divide equally between themselves; and B. made all disbursements and received all the monies for the owners, who objected to money claimed by B. for commission; it was holden (*n*), that A. could not maintain money had and received against B. for his share of the commission, the demand arising out of a partnership transaction, and no account having been settled; and the circumstance of all the monies having been received and paid by one partner made no difference. But where A. and B. had been partners in certain transactions for the sale and purchase of wool, having also had other dealings together; and they settled a general account, in which was an item to B.'s debit " to loss on wool," and which showed a balance against him; and B. signed the account and admitted the balance due; it was holden (*o*), that A. might afterwards maintain an action to recover the amount of the item for the loss on the wool.

One partner cannot maintain an action against his co-partners for work and labour performed or money expended on account of the partnership.

A number of persons associating together and subscribing sums of money for the purpose of obtaining a bill in parliament to make a railway, are partners in the undertaking; and, therefore, a subscriber who acted as their surveyor cannot (*p*) maintain an action

(*k*) *Alderson* v. *Pope*, 1 Campb. 404, n.
(*l*) *Beckham* v. *Knight*, 4 Bingh. N. C. 243; 5 Sc. 619. Judgment affirmed on error, in Exch. Chr., 1 M. & Gr. 738; 1 Sc. N. R. 675.
(*m*) *Mullett* v. *Hook*, 1 M. & Malk.

88, recognized in *De Mautort* v. *Saunders*, 1 B. & Ad. 398. See also *Exp. Chuck*, 8 Bingh. 469.
(*n*) *Bovill* v. *Hammond*, 6 B. & C. 149.
(*o*) *Wray* v. *Milestone*, 5 M. & W. 21.
(*p*) *Holmes* v. *Higgins*, 1 B. & C. 74.

for work done by him in that character on account of the partnership against all or any one of the other subscribers. But where the plaintiff, on the 24th of October, entered into an express contract with a committee of individuals, associated together for the purpose of obtaining an act of parliament for making a turnpike road, to do certain work for a specified sum; and on the 14th of November the plaintiff caused his name to be inserted in the list of subscribers for two shares; it was holden (q), that the circumstance of his becoming a partner did not affect his right to recover in respect of the express contract previously made; but that with respect to a sum which had been allowed by the jury for work contracted for after the 14th of November, the plaintiff, being then a partner, could not recover that, the case falling within the principle of *Holmes* v. *Higgins*. One partner (r) cannot recover a sum of money received by the other; unless, on a balance struck, that sum be found to be due to him alone. Where (s) plaintiff and defendant had been engaged in running a coach from B. to L., plaintiff finding horses for one part of the road, defendant for another, and the profits of each party were calculated according to the number of miles covered by his own horses; the plaintiff received the fares, and rendered an account thereof every week to the defendant; it was holden, that plaintiff and defendant were partners in this concern; and that, in an action by the plaintiff against the defendant upon a separate transaction, the defendant could not set off a balance which had been declared in his favour upon these weekly accounts; inasmuch as this was a balance during the continuance of the concern, and not a final balance upon all the partnership accounts. See further on this point, *Coffee* v. *Brian*, 3 Bingh. 54; 10 Moore, 341; *Brown* v. *Tapscott*, 6 M. & W. 119.

The partners in one house of trade cannot maintain an action against the partners in another house of trade, of which one of the partners in the plaintiff's house is also a member, for transactions which took place while he was partner in both houses; whether the action be brought in the lifetime of the common partner or after his decease. But, after his decease, the surviving partners of the one house may sue the surviving partners of the other house, upon transactions subsequent to the decease of the common partner (t). A., B., and C. were partners; A. retired from the firm, whereof notice was given to D., a creditor of the firm, who at the same time was informed that the business would be continued, as heretofore, by B. and C., the remaining partners, " who assume the funds, and charge themselves with the liquidation of the partnership." The balance due to D. was transferred to his credit by the new firm;

(q) *Lucas* v. *Beach*, 1 M. & Gr. 417; 1 Scott, N. R. 350.

(r) Per *Buller*, J., in *Smith* v. *Barrow*, 2 T. R. 478.

(s) *Fromont* v. *Coupland*, 2 Bingh. 172,

recognized in *Green* v. *Beesley*, 2 Bingh. N. C. 108. See *Barton* v. *Hanson*, *ante*, p. 1126.

(t) *Bosanquet* v. *Wray*, 6 Taunt. 597.

and D. was informed of this transfer and assented to it. D. afterwards drew upon the new firm for a part of this balance, and they accepted and paid his bills. The new firm having become insolvent; it was holden (*u*), that B. continued liable for the debt due to D. from the old firm. But where S. and others carried on business under the name of the "*Plas Madoc Colliery Company*," S. withdrew from the firm, which *afterwards* became indebted to C., no notice having been given to C. or the public of S.'s withdrawing. It was holden (*x*), that S. was not liable for the debt; for the name of the company did not give any information of the parties composing it, and there was not any sufficient evidence that S. had ever, while a partner, represented himself as such to C., or appeared so publicly in that character, that C. must have been presumed to know of it

By stat. 1 & 2 Vict. c. 96, after reciting the stat. 7 Geo. IV. c. 46, (An Act for the better regulating Co-partnerships of certain Bankers in England,) and stat. 6 Geo. IV. c. 42, (Irish Act,) it is enacted, that any person now being, or having been, or who may hereafter be, or have been, a member of any co-partnership, carrying on, or which may hereafter carry on, the business of banking under the provisions of these acts, may, at any time during the continuance of this act, in respect of any demand which such person may have, either solely or jointly with any other person, against the said co-partnership, or the funds or property thereof, commence and prosecute, either solely or jointly with any other person, (as the case may require,) any action, suit, or other proceeding at law or in equity against any public officer appointed or to be appointed under the provisions of the said acts, to sue and be sued on behalf of the said co-partnership; and any such public officer may in his own name commence and prosecute any action, &c. against any person being or having been a member of the said co-partnership, either alone or jointly with any other person, against whom any such co-partnership has or may have any demand; and that every person being or having been a member of any such copartnership shall, either solely or jointly with any other person, (as the case may require,) be capable of proceeding against any such co-partnership by their public officer, and be liable to be proceeded against, by or for the benefit of the said co-partnership, by such public officer, by such proceedings and with the same legal consequences as if such person had not been a member of the said co-partnership; and that no action or suit shall in anywise be affected by reason of the plaintiffs or defendants, or any of them respectively, or any other person in whom any interest may be averred, or who may in anywise be interested or concerned in such action, being or having been a member of the said co-partnership; and that all

(*u*) *David* v. *Ellice and others*, 5 B. & C. 196. But see remark of *Parke*, B., in *Kirwan* v. *Kirwan*, 2 Cr. & M. 621,

and *Hart* v. *Alexander*, 2 M. & W. 492. (*x*) *Carter* v. *Whalley*, 1 B. & Ad. 11.

such actions, &c. shall be conducted and have effect as if the same
had been between strangers. And by sect. 2, in case the merits
of any demand by or against any such co-partnership shall have
been determined in any action or suit, by or against any such public
officer, the proceedings in such action or suit may be pleaded in bar
of any other action or suit, by or against the public officer of the
same co-partnership for the same demand. This act has been continued (y) until the 31st of August, 1842.

IV. *Evidence.*

ACTS subsequent to the time of delivering goods (z) on a contract, may be admitted as evidence to show that the goods were
delivered on a partnership account, if it were doubtful at the time
of the contract; but if it clearly appear that no partnership existed
at the time of the contract, no subsequent act by any person, who
may afterwards become a partner, (not even an acknowledgment
that he is liable, or his accepting a bill of exchange drawn on them
as partners for the very goods,) will make him liable in an action
for goods sold and delivered, though he will be liable in an action on
the bill of exchange. It is incumbent on persons dissolving a partnership (a), to send notice of such dissolution to all the persons with
whom they have had dealings in partnership. The Gazette of itself
is not sufficient notice of such dissolution. It seems, however, that
in respect of persons who had not any previous dealings with the
partnership, an advertisement in the Gazette would be sufficient
notice of the dissolution, so as to prevent such persons from recovering against the parties who constituted the firm originally,
upon a security given by one of the parties in the name of the firm,
after such notice of dissolution (b). Bankers ought, regularly, to
give notice of a change in the firm, by a circular letter; but such
change may also be notified by an alteration of the name in the
printed cheque; and persons who have used the new cheques
cannot take advantage of the want of a more express notice (c).
Assumpsit for goods sold and delivered (d). The plaintiff's witness
swore, that the defendant and I. S. were partners in trade, and
that these goods were sold to them in partnership. The defendant
called I. S. to prove that the goods were sold to him, and that the
defendant had no concern in the purchase of them, otherwise than

---

(y) By stat. 3 & 4 Vict. c. 111.
(z) *Saville* v. *Robertson*, 4 T. R. 720.
(a) *Graham* v. *Hope*, Peake's N. P. C.
154. See also *Gorham* v. *Thompson*,
Peake's N. P. C. 42.

(b) *Godfrey* v. *Turnbull and another*,
1 Esp. N. P. C. 371.
(c) *Barfoot* v. *Goodall*, 3 Campb. 147.
(d) *Goodacre* v. *Breame*, Peake's N. P.
C. 174.

as his servant. Lord *Kenyon*, C. J. "He is not a witness to prove this, for he comes to defeat the action of the plaintiff, against a man who is proved to be his partner; and by discharging the present defendant he benefits himself, as he will be liable to pay a share of the costs to be recovered by the plaintiff in this cause." In an action against one partner (*e*), if the plaintiff gives in a particular of his demand, and the defendant pleads partnership in abatement, if the defendant proves any of the items to have been furnished on the partnership account, he will be entitled to a verdict, although the plaintiff should be prepared to prove that some of the items were furnished on the credit of the defendant only. In an action against the drawers of a bill of exchange (*f*), purporting to be drawn by a firm upon one of the partners constituting the firm, if it be proved that the bill was accepted by such drawee, this will be sufficient evidence of the bill having been regularly drawn : and further, it is not necessary, in such case, to prove that the drawers received express notice of the dishonour of the bill, because this must necessarily have been known to one of them, and the knowledge of one is the knowledge of all (2). To establish a partnership between two defendants (*g*), a verdict on the issue directed out of a court of equity, to try whether the defendants were partners, and for what time, on a bill filed by one of them against the other, is admissible evidence to establish a partnership, the verdict having found them to be so. Where a foundation has been laid by *primâ facie* evidence of a partnership, the declaration of one partner is evidence against another partner (*h*). A person who suffers his name to be used in a firm (*i*), although he thereby makes himself a partner to the world, yet if in fact he is not so, nor has any share in the profits, may be a witness in an action brought by the other parties in the firm, for goods sold and delivered. A father who holds out to the world that his son is his partner, and who sends bills and signs receipts in their joint names, in an action brought in his own name, is not precluded from showing that his son is not a partner (*k*). When a partnership is dissolved (*l*), it is not dissolved with regard to things past, but only with regard to things future. Hence an admission made by one of two partners after the dissolu-

---

(*e*) *Colson et al.* v. *Selby*, 1 Esp. N. P. C. 452.

(*f*) *Porthouse* v. *Parker*, 1 Campb. 82.

(*g*) *Whateley* v. *Menheim and another*, 2 Esp. N. P. C. 608.

(*h*) Per *Ellenborough*, C. J., in *Nicholls* v. *Dowding*, 1 Stark. N. P. C. 81.

(*i*) *Parsons* v. *Crosley*, 5 Esp. N. P. C. 199, Lord *Ellenborough*, C. J.

(*k*) *Glossop* v. *Colman*, 1 Stark. N. P. C. 25 ; recognized in *Barker* v. *Stubbs*, 1 M. & Gr. 44.

(*l*) *Wood* v. *Braddick*, 1 Taunt. 104.

---

(2) See *Alderson* v. *Pope*, 1 Campb. 404, n., where it was holden, by Lord *Ellenborough*, C. J., that notice to one member of a firm, was notice to the whole partnership.

tion of the partnership, concerning joint contracts, that took place *during* the partnership, is competent evidence to charge the other partner. But a declaration by one of two partners is not evidence to charge the other with respect to a transaction with that other partner which occurred *previous* to the partnership, unless a joint responsibility in the subject matter is shown (*m*).

A., being indebted to B. and C., partners, and being informed of the intended dissolution of partnership, gave a warrant of attorney to B. alone, who managed the concerns. A. afterwards committed an act of bankruptcy; and after that, and after a dissolution of partnership, paid the money to B. B. died. The assignees of A. sued C. for the money; and it was holden (*n*), that they were entitled to recover; for the money being paid in respect of a debt due to the partnership, both parties were liable to refund, unless some stipulation could be shown to exonerate C. from his liability. If one of several partners promise individually to pay a debt, without making any mention of his partners, such promise is conclusive evidence that the debt was due from him individually, and not from the partnership, and he will not be permitted to show that it was due jointly from himself and his partners (*o*). In an action on a joint contract against several partners (*p*), one of the defendants having suffered judgment to go by default, is not admissible as a witness to prove the partnership of himself and the other defendants, without their consent, although the proposed witness is released as to all other actions, save that on which he is called to give evidence; for it is a general rule, that a party to the record cannot be called as a witness, but by consent, and all the parties to the record must consent.

But in an action brought to charge A. as a partner in a trading company, it was holden (*q*), that a witness, who, by other evidence than his own, appeared to be a shareholder in the company, was competent to prove that A. was a partner.

(*m*) Per *Abbott*, C. J., in *Catt* v. *Howard*, 3 Stark. N. P. C. 3.

(*n*) *Biggs* v. *Fellows*, 8 B. & C. 402.
(*o*) *Murray* v. *Somerville*, 2 Campb. 99, n.

(*p*) *Mant* v. *Mainwaring*, 8 Taunt. 139.

(*q*) *Hall* v. *Curzon*, 9 B. & C. 646; 4 M. & Ry. 565, recognizing *Blackett* v. *Weir*, 5 B. & C. 385; 8 D. & Ry. 142; and *Lockart* v. *Graham*, 1 Str. 35. See *Fowler* v. *Round*, 5 M. & W. 478.

CHAPTER XXXII.

QUO WARRANTO.

I. *Of the Origin and Nature of Quo Warranto Informations,
and Statutes relating thereto, viz. Stat. 4 & 5 Will. &
Ma. c. 18, and 9 Ann. c. 20, p. 1143; Proceedings
against the City of London in the Time of Charles the
Second, p. 1148.*

II. *In what Cases the Court will grant an Information in
Nature of Quo Warranto, p. 1149; Of the Corporation
Act, Stat. 13 Car. II. Stat. 2, c. 1, p. 1153; Test Act,
25 Car. II. c. 2, p. 1153; Repeal, p. 1154.*

III. *Of the Limitation of Time for granting an Information,
p. 1155.*

IV. *Of the Construction of Charters, and of the Operation and
Effect of a New Charter, p. 1155.*

V. *Bye-Laws, p. 1158.*

VI. *Of the Inspection of the Records of the Corporation, p. 1163.*

VII. *Of the Pleadings, p. 1163.*

VIII. *Evidence, p. 1165.*

IX. *Judgment, p. 1168.*

I. *Of the Origin and Nature of Quo Warranto Informations, and
Statutes relating thereto, viz. Stat. 4 & 5 Will. & Ma.
c. 18, and 9 Ann. c. 20, p. 1143; Proceedings against the
City of London in the Time of Charles the Second, p. 1148.*

THE ancient writ of quo warranto (1), whence the information of
the present day derives its origin, was in the nature of a writ of

---

(1) See the form in Rastal's Entr. 540, b. ed. 1670, where the writ

right for the king, against persons who claimed or usurped any office, franchise, liberty, or privilege belonging to the crown, to inquire by what authority they maintained their claim, in order to have the right determined. The judgment on this writ was, that the franchise *capiatur in manum domini regis* (2). This writ having fallen into disuse, on account of the delay with which it was attended, a more expeditious mode of proceeding has been adopted, *viz.* an information filed by the king's attorney general, in nature of a quo warranto, in which the person usurping is considered as an offender, and consequently punishable by fine. The court, however, will not extend this remedy beyond the limits prescribed to the old writ; and, as that could only be prosecuted for an usurpation on the rights or prerogatives of the crown, so an information in nature of quo warranto can only be granted in such cases (a); and upon this principle the court refused to grant an information to try the validity of an election to the office of churchwarden.

By stat. 4 & 5 Will. & Ma. c. 18, it is enacted, " That the clerk of the crown office shall not, without express order of the court, receive or file any information for trespass, or other misdemeanour, or issue any process thereon, before he shall have taken, &c. a recognizance from the prosecutor to the defendant, in the penalty of £20, to prosecute with effect: and in case the defendant shall appear and plead to issue, and the prosecutor shall not, at his own costs, within one year after issue joined, procure the same to be tried (b), or in case the defendant shall have a verdict, or a *noli prosequi* be entered by the informer, the court may award the defendant costs, &c., unless the judge shall, at the trial, certify that there was a reasonable cause for exhibiting the information; and if the informer does not pay the costs taxed within three months after demand, the defendant shall have the benefit of the recognizance to compel him." Although the words of this statute relate only to informations for trespasses, batteries, and other mis- demeanours, yet it has been holden to extend to informations in nature of quo warranto, to try the right of usurping on public franchises; consequently such informations cannot be filed without leave (c), nor can process be issued thereon without a recogni- zance (d), and the defendant is entitled to costs in the cases pro-

---

(a) *R. v. Shepherd*, 4 T. R. 381; *R. v. Dewbeny*, Str. 1196, S. P.
(b) *R. v. Howell*, Ca. Temp. H. 247.
(c) Per Lord *Hardwicke*, C. J., *R. v.*

Howell, C. T. H. 248.
(d) *R. v. Mayor of Hertford*, Carth. 503; Salk. 376.

---

appears to have been prosecuted by the king's attorney general before the justices in Eyre, who are empowered by stat. 18 Edw. I., stat. 2, s. 2, (A. D. 1290,) to determine pleas of quo warranto. See 2 Inst. 497.

(2) See Rast 540, b.

vided for by the statute, as far as the recognizance extends, that is, to £20, but not further (*e*) (3). The foregoing statute is confined to informations exhibited in the King's Bench (*f*).

The usurpation of offices and franchises in corporations constitutes the principal ground for applications to the court for this kind of information. By the common law, such usurpations could be punished only by a prosecution at the king's suit, though the dispute were really between party and party (4). To remedy this inconvenience, it was enacted, by stat. 9 Ann. c. 20, s. 4, that "in case any person should usurp, intrude into, or unlawfully hold and execute any of the said offices or franchises (5), the proper officer of the court may, with leave of the respective courts, exhibit informations in the nature of quo warranto, at the relation of any person desiring to prosecute the same, (and who shall be mentioned in the information to be the relator,) against the person usurping, and proceed therein as is usual in informations in the nature of a quo warranto; and if it shall appear to the courts, that the several rights of divers persons may properly be determined on one information, the courts may give leave to exhibit one information against several persons; the parties prosecuted are to plead the same term or sessions in which the information is filed, unless further time be allowed by the court, and the prosecutors are to proceed with the most convenient speed. By the 5th section, the courts are authorized to give judgment of ouster against, and to fine the parties, if found guilty of the usurpation, and to award costs to the relator; but if judgment be given for the defendants, then the court may award costs against the relator.

Before the statute of Queen Anne, a private person could not interpose in *quo warranto;* the crown, by the attorney general, could file such informations; but although this statute gives liberty to file such informations at the relation of a particular person, who is made liable to costs if there be judgment for the defendant, yet they

(*e*) *R.* v. *Howell*, C. T. H. 249; *S. C.*, *ut videtur*, under the name of *R.* v. *Morgan*, Str. 1042; *R.* v. *Filewood*, 2 T. R.

145; *R.* v. *Brooke*, 2 T. R. 197.
(*f*) *R.* v. *Roberts*, 2 B. & Ad. 63.

---

(3) The ground of the decision appears to have been that such usurpations are misdemeanours. See C. T. H. 248.

(4) In informations at common law, there is no relator.

(5) *i. e.* the offices of mayors, bailiffs, portreves, and other offices within cities, towns corporate, boroughs, and *places* (that is, places of the same kind with those before enumerated, see 5 T. R. 879,) in England and Wales, and the franchises of being burgesses or freemen. See the preamble. "All corporations consist of officers and freemen. This statute was meant to extend to both." Per Lord *Mansfield*, C. J., in *R.* v. *Williams*, 1 Bl. R. 95.

must be filed with leave of the court (*g*). " There is no (*h*) instance of a quo warranto information having been granted by leave of the court against persons for usurping a franchise of a mere private nature, not connected with public government." "As to the granting of an information in nature of quo warranto, I cannot conceive that it can be done (*i*) against a mere servant of a corporation, one who exercises no franchise or authority of any kind under the crown." A quo warranto information does not (*k*) lie for the office of governor and director, elected annually by rated inhabitants, under a local act, for the government of the poor and maintenance of a nightly watch. But an information in nature of quo warranto has been granted against a party claiming to act as guardian of the poor in Exeter (*l*), under stat. 28 Geo. III. c. 76. An information in nature of a quo warranto against persons for claiming to act as a corporation, must (*m*) be filed by and in the name of the attorney general. The courts will not stay proceedings until the prosecutor gives security for costs, on the ground that the relator is in insolvent circumstances, where it appears that he is a corporator, and no fraud is suggested (*n*). It was observed by *Wilmot*, J., in *R.* v. *Trelawney*, 3 Burr. 1616, that the two acts of parliament (of 4 & 5 Will. & Ma. c. 18, and 9 Ann. c. 20,) relate to quite different objects, and are the reverse of each other. The former *restrains* the clerk of the crown in the Court of King's Bench from exhibiting or filing informations *without leave* of the court, in cases where all the king's subjects might, before the making of that act, have made use of the king's name, *without such leave.* The latter *lets in every person* who desires it, to make use of his name in prosecuting usurpers of franchises ; whereas, before, *no subject* could have done so : but it provides, that *these* informations, (as well as those for misdemeanours) must be under the leave and discretion of the court; and the court ought not to give such leave without sufficient reason. The court will make the rule absolute, although the party after rule obtained resigns the office, and his resignation is accepted (*o*).

The stat. 9 Ann. c. 20, only regulates the proceedings on informa-

---

(*g*) Per Lord *Mansfield*, C. J., in *R.* v. *Trelawney*, H. 5 Geo. III., MS., and per *Wilmot*, J., in *S. C.*, 3 Burr. 1615. But see the remarks of Mr. Tancred in his valuable treatise on Informations in Nature of Quo Warranto, p. 14.

(*h*) Per *Bayley*, J., in *R.* v. *Ogden*, 10 B. & C. 233.

(*i*) Per *Lawrence*, J., *R.* v. *The Corporation of Bedford Level*, 6 East, 367.

(*k*) *R.* v. *Ramsden*, 3 A. & E. 456, per *Littledale* and *Patteson*, Js., recognized and adopted by Lord *Denman*, C. J., in

the matter of *The Aston Union*, 6 A. & E. 785 ; *R.* v. *Hanley*, 3 A. & E. 463, per *Tenterden*, C. J., *Taunton* and *Patteson*, Js. ; *Parke*, J., diss. See *Reg.* v. *Stoke Damerel*, case of Sexton.

(*l*) H. T. 1816, *ex relatione magri. Dealtry*, 3 A. & E. 476, in *R.* v. *Beedle*, S. P. where local act created a corporation, cited by *Coleridge*, J., in *R.* v. *M. &c. of Oxford*, 1 Nev. & P. 479.

(*m*) *R.* v. *Ogden*, 10 B. & C. 230.

(*n*) *R.* v. *Wynne*, 2 M. & S. 346.

(*o*) *R.* v. *Warlow*, 2 M. & S. 75.

tions against individuals (p) usurping corporate offices or franchises in corporate places; it does not extend to a private company (q); and consequently, in other cases where the information at common law is exhibited, advantage cannot be taken of the foregoing provisions. If any number of individuals claim to be a corporation without any right so to be, that is an usurpation of a franchise; and an information against the whole corporation, as a body, can be brought only by and in the name of the attorney general (r). In the information at common law there is not any relator; but the addition of a relator to an information at common law may be rejected as surplusage (s). Doubts appear to have been entertained, whether in the common law information a judgment of ouster could be given. In *R.* v. *Mayor of Hertford,* Lord Raym. 426, *Holt,* C. J., speaks of this as the proper form of judgment. In *R.* v. *Bennet* (t), Trin. 4 Geo. I., the judges were equally divided on the question; but in *R.* v. *Ponsonby,* M. 29 Geo. II., Say. R. 245, it was solemnly determined, that, unless the case of the person found guilty be within the statute, judgment of ouster ought not to be given (u). It has also been expressly decided, that, unless the case be within the statute, judgment for costs (x) ought not to be given.

The preceding remarks will be found material, inasmuch as there are many cases not mentioned in the statute, in which informations in nature of *quo warranto* will lie; e. g., it will lie against a private person or against a corporation, for holding a market, a court leet, or other court, or for exercising any other franchise; that is, the king's attorney general may exhibit informations for the usurpation of these franchises upon the crown; but whether informations for such usurpations can be granted upon the application of a private person, is a question which has not hitherto received a solemn determination. The point underwent considerable discussion in the case of *R.* v. *Marsden,* 8 Burr. 1812; 1 Bl. R. 579. *Yates,* J., thought, that as every usurpation of a franchise was a misdemeanour, a private person *might* apply as for the misdemeanour; but he, together with the other judges, declined giving any fixed opinion: in the case then before the court, it was not sufficiently shown, that there had been an usurpation; the court therefore refused to grant the in-

---

(p) *R.* v. *Corporation of Carmarthen,* 2 Burr. 869.

(q) *Horn* v. *Cutlers' Company,* B. R. E. 9 Geo. II., MS. But see *R.* v. *Highmore,* 5 B. & A. 771, where it was holden, that an information may be granted within the 9 Ann. against a party for exercising the office of bailiff in the borough of M., although it was not a corporate office. See, however, this case explained by *Bayley,* J., delivering judgment of court, in *R.* v. *M'Kay,* 5 B. & C. 645, where it was holden, that the provisions of the statute, as to writs of mandamus and quo

warranto informations, apply wholly to *corporate offices in corporate places.* See also *R.* v. *Attwood,* 4 B. & Ad. 481; 1 Nev. & M. 286.

(r) Per Lord *Tenterden,* C. J., *R.* v. *Ogden,* 10 B. & C. 233, recognizing *R.* v. *Corporation of Carmarthen,* 3 Burr. 869.

(s) Per *Denison,* J., 1 Burr. 403.

(t) Cited in Say. R. 247.

(u) See, however, 1 Burr. 402.

(x) *R.* v. *Williams,* B. R. M. 31 Geo. II., 1 Burr. 402; 1 Bl. R. 93, *S. C.*; *R.* v. *Wallis,* 5 T. R. 375; *R.* v. *Hall,* 1 B. & C. 237; *R.* v. *M'Kay,* 5 B. & C. 640.

formation on that ground. There must be an information against each person to enable each to disclaim, for distinct offices; and the court will not consolidate them (y).

By the suggestion of evil counsellors, and in order to increase the power and influence of the crown, it was deemed expedient, in the latter end of King Charles the Second's reign, to new model the corporate cities and boroughs. Against many corporations, (who declined surrendering their charters voluntarily,) informations, in nature of *quo warranto*, were filed, grounded upon the notion that such corporations had forfeited their franchises through neglect or by abuse of them. An information of this kind was filed against the corporation of the city of London. The charge against them was, that they had forfeited the liberty of being a corporation,—first, by making a bye-law for the levying several sums of money of the king's subjects coming to the public markets within the city to sell their provisions. Secondly, by having in common council voted a petition to the king, stating that by the prorogation of the parliament on the 10th of Jan. 32 Car. II., the prosecution of the public justice of the kingdom had received interruption, and by ordering the said petition to be printed, with intention that it should be dispersed among the king's subjects, to induce an opinion that the king, by proroguing the parliament, had obstructed the public justice, and to incite the king's subjects to a hatred of his person and government, and to disturb the peace of the kingdom. The case came before the court upon demurrer, which was joined in M. T. 34 Car. II., at which time *Pemberton* was C. J. of the King's Bench; but before H. T., when it came to be argued, Sir *E. Saunders*, who had been counsel for the crown in drawing and advising upon the pleadings, was appointed C. J. of the King's Bench, in the room of *Pemberton* (z), who entertained doubts. It was argued twice: the first time in H. T. 35 Car. II., 1682-3, by *Finch*, solicitor general, for the crown, and Sir *G. Treby*, recorder of London, for the corporation; the second time in E. T. 35 Car. II., 1683, by Sir *R. Sawyer*, attorney general, for the crown, and *Pollexfen* for the corporation. It was contended, on the part of the crown, that a corporation may be forfeited; that corporations have the same creation as other franchises, and subsist upon the same terms; that there is a trust annexed to all franchises, that they be not abused, and the breach of them is a forfeiture. It was then insisted, that any act of the mayor, aldermen, and common council, in common council assembled, was so much an act of the corporation as would make a forfeiture; and lastly, it was urged, that the acts in question were such acts as, being done by the corporation, worked a forfeiture. It was argued, on the part of the corporation, that no corporation, since the foundation of the monarchy, had ever

(y) *R.* v. *Warlow*, 2 M. & S. 75.
(z) See Burnet's History of his Own

Time, vol. ii. p. 925, ed. 12mo. 1725.

yet been exposed to forfeiture, and the thing itself implied an absurdity; that a corporation, as such, was incapable of all crime and offence, and none were answerable for any iniquity, but the persons themselves who committed it. That the members, in choosing magistrates, had entrusted them with legal powers only; and where the magistrates exceeded those powers, their acts were void, but could never involve the body itself in criminal imputation: that such had ever been the practice of England, except at the Reformation, when the monasteries were abolished; but this was an extraordinary case, which it was afterwards thought necessary to ratify by an act of parliament: that corporate bodies, framed for public good, and calculated for perpetual duration, ought not to be annihilated for the temporary faults of their members, who might themselves, without injuring the community, be questioned for their offences. Judgment was given in Trin. T. 35 Car. II., that the liberty, privilege, and franchise of the mayor, commonalty, and citizens, being a body politic and corporate, should be seized into the king's hands as forfeited. This was a great extension of the prerogative; but it was conceived by the king's advisers, that the example of this proceeding against the metropolis might have an effect (as in fact it had) upon other corporations; and that the crown would be enabled, upon granting new charters, to name the magistrates. This violent exercise of the prerogative, as far as it respected the city of London, was strongly marked by stat. 2 Will. & Ma. sess. 1, c. 8, which reversed the judgment, and declared that the mayor, commonalty, and citizens of the city of London, should for ever continue a body corporate and politic *in re, facto, et nomine,* without any seizure or forejudger of the said franchise, liberty, and privilege, or being thereof excluded or ousted, upon any pretence of any forfeiture or misdemeanour any time theretofore, or thereafter to be done, committed, or suffered.

II. *In what Cases the Court will grant an Information in Nature of Quo Warranto, p.* 1149; *Of the Corporation Act, Stat. 13 Car. II. Stat.* 2, *c.* 1, *p.* 1153; *Test Act,* 25 *Car. II. c.* 2, *p.* 1153; *Repeal, p.* 1154.

HAVING thus endeavoured to explain the general nature of the quo warranto information, and having set forth the alterations made by the statute of Queen Anne, in cases relating to corporate offices and franchises in corporate places, I shall proceed to inquire, what the nature of the office must be for the usurpation of which the court will grant this information. In the case of *R.* v. *Boyles,*

Str. 836, 2 Lord Raymond, 1559, it was holden, that it is not necessary to set forth in the information the whole constitution of the place; or to show, whether the office is by charter or prescription. If it be alleged to be an office, which appears upon the face of the information to concern the public, this is sufficient against the person who usurps it. Hence, the court permitted an information to be exhibited against the defendant, who exercised the office of bailiff of a ville; because it appeared, that it was a public office, and concerned the government of the ville, and the administration of public justice. So¹ the court will grant an information in the nature of quo warranto against the portreve of a borough and manor, who, as portreve, is returning officer of the borough (a). So, against a person claiming to have a right of voting by virtue of a burgage tenement (b). So, against the bailiff of a borough and manor, who, being a prescriptive officer and member of the court leet, had power to summon and select the jury (c); for such discretionary power is a material and important function in the administration of justice (6). So, against the steward of a court leet (d). So, against the constable of a parish (e). There must be an user as well as a claim of a franchise, before the court can entertain an application for an information (f). As to what shall amount to an user, see R. v. Tate (g). Under the stat. 5 & 6 Will. IV. c. 76, (Municipal Corporation Act,) the court will not grant a quo warranto information, unless it be shown that the party is in office *de facto*; and for this purpose it is not enough if the affidavit states simply that he has "accepted the office," without specifying the mode of acceptance; although it be sworn that the presiding alderman has declared the party duly elected (h). But where the affidavit stated that the party had taken upon himself the office, and *acted* in that capacity, and had been seen present at meetings of the council acting as a councillor, though the nature of the acceptance or acting was not further specified, and though it was not stated that he had made the declaration under the 50th section of the 5 & 6 Will. IV. c. 76, the court held the affidavit sufficient (i). Where, in an application for a quo warranto against a constable, the affidavits in support of

(a) *R.* v. *Mein*, 3 T. R. 596, Borough of Fowey.
(b) *Horsham* case, H. 30 Geo. III., 3 T. R. 599, n.
(c) *R.* v. *Bingham*, 2 East, 308, Borough of Gosport.
(d) *R.* v. *Hulston*, Str. 621.

(e) *R.* v. *Goudge*, Str. 1213.
(f) *R.* v. *Whitwell*, 5 T. R. 85, recognized in *Reg.* v. *Pepper*, 7 A. & E. 745.
(g) 4 East, 337.
(h) *Reg.* v. *Slatter*, 11 A. & E. 505; 3 P. & D. 263.
(i) *Reg.* v. *Quayle*, 11 A. & E. 508.

(6) It appeared in this case, that the bailiff was not entitled to any fees, so that an action for money had and received could not have been brought to try the defendant's title; a circumstance which seems to have influenced the decision of the court.

the rule stated that, for fifty years back and as long as deponents could recollect, there had been a custom to elect a constable in a particular mode, but did not state that they believed such custom to be immemorial; it was holden (*k*), that it was not sufficient. If a party (*l*) has been ousted of an office by the election of another party to that office, (the election not being merely colourable,) his remedy is not by mandamus, but by an information in the nature of a quo warranto.

By rule of court, (H. T. 7 & 8 Geo. IV., 1827,) reciting that vexation and expense had been occasioned to defendants, by the practice of raising issues upon various matters distinct from the ground on which the information was granted by the court; it was ordered, that henceforth the objections intended to be made to the title of the defendant shall be specified in the rule to show cause; and no objection, not so specified, shall be raised by the prosecutor on the pleadings without the special leave of the court or some judge thereof. See 6 B. & C. 267. And by another rule of court, (Nov. 8, 1839, M. 3 Vict., 11 A. & E. 2; 3 P. & D. 1,) it is ordered, that no rule be granted for filing an information in nature of a quo warranto, unless at the time of moving, an affidavit shall be produced, by which some person shall depose, upon oath, that such motion is made at his instance as relator, and that such person shall be deemed to be the relator in case such rule shall be made absolute, and shall be named as such relator in such information in case the same shall be filed, unless the court shall otherwise order. Under the foregoing rule the affidavit must state *at whose instance* the application is made; it is not sufficient for a party to depose, that if the court grant the information, it is his intention to become really and *bonâ fide* the relator (*m*).

If the motion for a quo warranto be made on the affidavits of three persons, two of whom are not qualified to be relators, the information may nevertheless be granted, if the third party be unobjectionable as a relator, though his affidavit does not show sufficient ground for the information (*n*). Any inhabitant of a borough may be a relator, although he is not a burgess (*o*).

The court have established a general rule to guide them in exercising their discretionary power of permitting informations in nature of quo warranto to be filed, that they will not permit one corporator to object to the title of another, if he has concurred in the election of that other, or acknowledged his title by acting with him; or if the objection that he makes to the title of that other be equally applicable to his own, or to the title of those under whom he

(*k*) *R.* v. *Lane*, 5 B. & A. 488.
(*l*) *R.* v. *Mayor, &c. of Oxford*, 1 Nev. & P. 474.
(*m*) *R.* v. *Hedges*, 11 A. & E. 163.
(*n*) *R.* v. *Parry*, 6 A. & E. 810.
(*o*) *Reg.* v. *Quayle*, 11 A. & E. 508.

claims (*p*).   It is a valid objection (*q*) to a relator applying for a quo warranto information for usurping the office of burgess, that he was formerly present at, and concurred in, the election of another burgess, when the objection he sought by the application to avail himself of was taken and overruled, and he voted for the party then elected.   But, on motion for a quo warranto against a capital burgess, on the ground of irregularity in his election, it is no answer (*r*) that the relator frequently acted with the party against whom he applies, in corporation business, during the two years following such party's election, the relator not being shown to have concurred in that election ; nor is the relator disqualified by the mere circumstance of having formerly taken part in other elections, where the same irregularity as now complained of existed, but *was not noticed*.   It is not competent to a stranger to the corporation, although an inhabitant of the town, to impeach the title of a corporator (*s*), unless he can show that, as an inhabitant, he is subject to the local jurisdiction of the body corporate.   And it is a valid objection to a relator, that he was present and concurred *at the time* of the objectionable election, even although he was then ignorant of the objection : for a corporator must be taken to be cognizant of the contents of his own charter, and of the law arising therefrom.   The court will not make such a rule absolute, where a relator appeared to be a man in low and indigent circumstances, and there were strong grounds of suspicion that he was applying, not on his own account, or at his own expense, but in collusion with a stranger (*t*).   It is in the discretion of the court to grant the information or not ; and under circumstances tending to throw suspicions on the motives of the relator, they will not grant it, where the consequence will be to dissolve a corporation (*u*).   It has been generally considered as a rule of corporation law, that a person is not to be permitted to impeach a title conferred by an election in which he has concurred, or the titles of those mediately or immediately derived from that election (*x*).   Formerly, elections under the presidency of a bad mayor or other person were void.   Hence where the mayor, who presided at the election of a new mayor, was only mayor *de facto*, and not *de jure*, and was subsequently removed by judgment of ouster ; it was holden (*y*), that the election of the new mayor was void.   But now, by stat. 7 Will. IV. & 1 Vict. c. 78, s. 1, no election of any person into any corporate office, which shall take place after the passing of this act, (17th July, 1837,)

(*p*) *R.* v. *Cudlipp*, 6 T. R. 503, Borough of Launceston.

(*q*) *R.* v. *Parkyn*, 1 B. & Ad. 690, recognizing *R.* v. *Symmons*, 4 T. R. 223.

(*r*) *R.* v. *Benney*, 1 B. & Ad. 684.

(*s*) *R.* v. *St. John*, E. T. 52 Geo. III., MS., Borough of Wotton Bassett ; *R.* v. *Hodge*, 2 B. & A. 344, n.

(*t*) *R.* v. *Trevenen*, 2 B. & A. 339, Borough of Helleston, cited and distinguished in *R.* v. *Wakelin*, 1 B. & Ad. 50.

(*u*) *S. C.*

(*x*) Per *Abbott*, C. J., in *R.* v. *Slythe*, 6 B. & C. 242.

(*y*) *R.* v. *Corporation of Bridgwater*, 3 Doug. 379.

shall be liable to be questioned by reason of any defect in the title or want of title of the person before whom such election may have been had, provided that the person before whom such election shall be had, shall be then in the actual possession of or acting in the office giving the right to preside at such election. Every corporator must be presumed to be conusant of that which has recently taken place in the corporation of which he is a member, unless he shows the contrary (z). But if a person should concur in an election in ignorance of some fact making it invalid, and should afterwards come before the court, and show the objection, and that it has come to his knowledge since the election, and that it is a matter which ought to be inquired into, the application might be heard (a). Where a rule is obtained upon the ground (b), that a party has vacated a corporate office by having accepted a second incompatible office, the affidavits must show a valid appointment to the second office, and that the offices are incompatible. Where different persons filling two offices would be in the relation of master and servant to each other, those offices cannot be held by the same person. But there is nothing inconsistent in one member of a body noting down the acts of the body. Thus, in the borough of Carmarthen (c), the offices of common councilman and town clerk are not incompatible.

By the Corporation Act, 13 Car. II. stat. 2, c. 1, the election of corporate officers who had not taken the sacrament within one year next before their election, was declared to be void. By the Test Act (d), every person admitted, &c. into an office, civil or military, or receiving any pay, &c., by reason of any patent or grant of his Majesty, or admitted into the family of his Majesty, was required to take the oaths of supremacy and allegiance the next term, and subscribe the declaration against transubstantiation; and also receive the sacrament of the Lord's Supper, according to the usage of the Church of England, within three months (7) after their admittance into office, in some public church, upon Sunday, immediately after divine service and sermon. Persons neglecting or refusing to take the oaths and sacrament, and being convicted of executing their offices after such neglect or refusal, were disabled (e) from suing either at law or in equity; from being a guardian, executor, or administrator; from being capable of any legacy, or deed of gift, or to bear any office; and forfeited £500. Several attempts were

---

(z) R. v. Slythe, 6 B. & C. 243.
(a) Per Abbott, C. J., in R. v. Slythe, 6 B. & C. 243.
(b) R. v. Day, 9 B. & C. 702.

(c) R. v. Jones, 1 B. & Ad. 677.
(d) 25 Car. II. c. 2, s. 2, A. D. 1672.
(e) 25 Car. II. c. 2, s. 5.

---

(7) Enlarged to six months by stat. 16 Geo. II. c. 30, s. 3.

made to obtain a repeal of the Corporation and Test Acts, but they were ineffectual until the year 1828, when, by stat. 9 Geo. IV. c. 17, such parts of the stats. 13 and 25 Car. II. and 16 Geo. II. as required the taking the sacrament, were repealed, and a declaration was substituted by the second section of that statute (9 Geo. IV. c. 17), in lieu of the sacramental test, which must, within one calendar month (8) next before or upon admission, be made and subscribed in the presence of the proper officer (sect. 3), otherwise the election is void (sect. 4). And by stat. 10 Geo. IV. c. 7, s. 14, any subject professing the Roman Catholic religion may be a member of any lay corporation, and hold any civil office or place of trust or profit therein, and do any corporate act, or vote in any corporate election, upon taking and subscribing the oath appointed by that act, instead of the oaths of allegiance, supremacy, and abjuration. The inconveniences arising from the Corporation and Test Acts have been greatly mitigated by annual acts of parliament, which since the year 1743 (*f*) have been constantly passed for the indemnity of persons who have omitted to qualify themselves within the time limited, and for allowing further time for that purpose. The annual Indemnity Act is prospective as well as retrospective, and extends to those who may be in default during the time for which it is made, and is not limited to those who had incurred penalties or disabilities before it passed (*g*).

Votes given for a candidate, after notice of his being ineligible, are to be considered as thrown away, that is, as if the persons so voting had not voted at all (*h*). In such case, if there are other candidates, who are duly qualified, he who has the greatest number of legal votes will be duly elected: but until he be sworn in, the office is not legally filled up and enjoyed by him, within the exception in the annual Indemnity Act. And, therefore, if the disqualified person who had the greatest number of votes be sworn into office,

---

(*f*) See 16 Geo. II. c. 30.
(*g*) *In re Steavenson*, 2 B. & C. 34.

(*h*) *R.* v. *Hawkins*, 10 East, 211; *R.* v. *Parry*, 14 East, 549.

. (8) The statute does not give the party elected a month, at all events, for deciding whether he will make the declaration or not, but only excuses him from making it at the time of his admission, if he has made it within a month before. The words "upon admission" mean at the time, and not within a reasonable time after; and the authorities who admit, may prescribe the order in which the ceremonies forming parts of the admission shall take place. Hence, if a party offers himself to the proper court to be admitted, not having made the declaration within a month before, and being asked whether he will make it or not, declines to say, but requires the court to admit him, which they refuse, the election is thereupon void, and a precept may issue for a new election. *The Queen* v. *Humphery*, 10 A. & E. 335.

and afterwards qualify himself by making the declaration, &c. within the time allowed by the Indemnity Act, he is hereby recapacitated, and his title to the office protected; such office not having been then vacated by judgment, or legally filled up and enjoyed by another person (i). Votes given before notice of the ineligibility are not to be considered as thrown away (k).

III. *Of the Limitation of Time for granting an Information.*

IN the year 1767, in the *Winchelsea* cases, the Court of King's Bench determined that the period of possession after which a corporator ought not to be disturbed, by any information in the nature of a quo warranto granted under the discretion of the court, should be twenty years: this limitation was, in the year 1791, by rule of court, narrowed to six years, and that rule was afterwards confirmed by stat. 32 Geo. III. c. 58. Where a rule nisi for a quo warranto information for exercise of a franchise was obtained within six years after the earliest time at which the defendant appeared to have exercised it, but the motion for a rule absolute was not made till the six years had expired, the court discharged the rule; holding, that it was too late, by stat 32 Geo. III. c. 58, s. 1, to file the information (l). By stat. 7 Will. IV. & 1 Vict. c. 78, s. 23, (17th July, 1837,) every application to the Court of King's Bench, for the purpose of calling upon any person to show by what warrant he claims to exercise the office of mayor, alderman, councillor, or burgess, in any borough, shall be made before the end of twelve calendar months after the election, or the time when the person against whom such application shall be directed shall have been disqualified, and not at any subsequent time.

IV. *Of the Construction of Charters, and of the Operation and Effect of a New Charter.*

CONTEMPORANEOUS usage has always been considered as of great importance in the construction of charters (m): not that usage can overturn the clear words of a charter; but if they are doubtful, the

----

(i) *R.* v. *Parry*, 14 East, 549.
(k) *R.* v. *Bridge*, 1 M. & S. 76.
(l) *Reg.* v. *Harris*, 11 A. & E. 518; 3 P. & D. 266.

(m) Per Lord *Kenyon*, C. J., delivering opinion of court, *R.* v. *Bellringer*, 4 T. R. 821.

usage under the charter will tend to explain the meaning of them (*n*). If a corporation has franchises and privileges by grant or prescription, and afterwards they are incorporated by another name, as if they were "the bailiffs and burgesses" before, and afterwards they are to be styled "the mayor and commonalty;" yet the newly-named body shall enjoy all the franchises, privileges, and hereditaments, which the old corporation had either by grant or prescription (*o*). Where the king grants a charter to a corporation, there being a prior charter existing at the time, the new charter is void *ab initio;* because two corporations, for the same purposes of government, cannot exist within one and the same place, and at one and the same time (*p*). Where a corporation takes its rise from the king's charter, the king by granting, and the corporation by accepting, another charter, may alter it; because it is done with the consent of all the parties who are competent to consent to the alteration. But the constitution of a corporation, as settled by act of parliament, cannot be varied by the acceptance of any charter inconsistent (*q*) with it. A corporation cannot accept a part of the charter and not the whole." Per *Yates*, J., in *R.* v. *Spencer*, Hil. 6 Geo. III. B. R. "An acceptance of a charter is like an attornment to a grant, which cannot be limited or qualified." Per *Powell*, J., in case of *Malmsbury Corporation*, Serjt. Hill's MSS. vol. 22, p. 271.

By the Municipal Corporation Act, 5 & 6 Will. IV. c. 76, s. 1, so much of all laws, statutes, and usages, and of all charters, grants, and letters patent, relating to the several boroughs named in the schedules A. and B., as are inconsistent with that act, are repealed. This statute has been amended by a subsequent act, 7 Will. IV. & 1 Vict. c. 78, which enacts (*r*), that after the passing of this act, (17th July, 1837,) in case no election shall be made of any mayor, or any of the aldermen, councillors, or other corporate officers in any borough in the said schedules, upon the day or within the time appointed by the Municipal Corporation Act, or by this act, for any such election, or such election being made, shall afterwards become void, whether such omission or avoidance shall happen through the default of the officer who ought to preside at such election, or by any accident or other means, the corporation shall not thereby be deemed to be dissolved or disabled from electing such mayor, alderman, or councillor, or other corporate officer, for the future; but in any case where no such election shall be made, the election for any such mayor, &c., may be had and proceeded with upon the day next after the day on which such election ought to

(*n*) Per Lord *Mansfield*, C. J., in *R.* v. *Varlo*, Cowp. 250.

(*o*) 4 Rep. 77, b.; per *Cur.*, *Haddock's* case, 1 Ventr. 355.

(*p*) *R.* v. *Amery*, D. P. 20 April, 1790, 2 Bro. P. C. 366, Tomlins' ed.

(*q*) *R.* v. *Miller*, 6 T. R. 268.

(*r*) Sect. 25.

have been made, unless such day shall happen to be on a Sunday, and then on the Monday following.

While a corporation exists capable of discharging its functions, .the crown cannot obtrude another charter upon them (s). It is competent to them, either to accept or reject the proffered charter. A charter cannot be partially accepted, whether it be a charter of creation, or granted to a pre-existing corporation (t). If there be an old charter surrendered, but the surrender is not inrolled, and a new charter, in consideration of the surrender, granted, the second charter is void (u). And if there be any other persons named in the new charter who were not in the old, any law made by them is void; because they act under a void charter; but otherwise if the members nominated are the same as in the old charter, because then they act by their first charter, which still remains good (x). Upon a quo warranto against the town of Liskeard, in the reign of Charles the Second, they surrendered their charter, which was not inrolled until the reign of King James the Second, who, in conside-. ration of the surrender, granted a new charter to them. It was holden, that the second charter, being in consideration of a void surrender, was also void (y).

Where an application is made to the court for a mandamus, to direct the filling up of any vacancies in a definite integral part of a corporation, the court will require strong grounds to induce them to refuse the writ, on account of the great inconvenience which may follow from the not filling up such vacancies, and the risk of dissolving the corporation (z). The court will grant a rule for an information in nature of quo warranto (a), at the suit of a private relator, against an individual member of a corporation, on grounds affecting his individual title, although the affidavits on which the rule is moved disclose matter tending to dissolve the corporation. When a corporation is reduced to such a state as to be incapable of continuing its existence, and of doing any corporate act, it is extinct as a body corporate. In such case, it is competent to the crown to renovate it, by granting a new charter to the remaining members of the old corporation, in conjunction with others, or to others alone (b). It is not necessary that this charter should be accepted by a majority of the remaining members of the old corporation: it is sufficient if it be accepted by a majority of the grantees. Where a charter is silent as to the mode of continuing the succession, a corporation has a right *of necessity,*

(s) Lord *Kenyon*, C. J., *R.* v. *Pasmore*, 3 T. R. 240.

(t) *R.* v. *Westwood*, 4 B. & C. 781. Judgment affirmed on error, D. P., July 21st, 1830, 7 Bingh. 1, Borough of Chepping Wycomb.

(u) *R.* v. *Osbourne*, 4 East, 335.

(x) *Bully* v. *Palmer*, 12 Mod. 247;

Salk. 190, *S. C.*

(y) *Piper* v. *Dennis*, 12 Mod. 253.

(z) *R.* v. *Mayor of Grampond*, 6 T. R. 301.

(a) *R.* v. *White*, 1 Nev. & P. 84; 5 A. & E. 613, recognized in *R.* v. *Parry*, 6 A. & E. 820.

(b) *R.* v. *Pasmore*, 3 T. R. 199.

or an incidental power, to continue itself, and to make reasonable bye-laws for that purpose ; as by election. Where, however, there is a provision of such a nature as is calculated *at all times* to continue the succession, without ever proceeding by way of voluntary election, that may afford a ground for presuming that voluntary elections were meant to be excluded; but where there is no provision affording a supply of burgesses *to that extent*, the corporation has the right of proceeding by election.

By the Municipal Corporation Act (c), after the passing of this act, 9th September, 1835, no person shall be enrolled a burgess of any borough for the purpose of enjoying the rights conferred for the first time by this act, in respect of any title other than by occupancy and payment of rates within such borough, according to the meaning and provisions of this act. The rate must be paid by the party's own act ; it is not sufficient that another person, without his authority, pays the rates for him (d). A municipal corporation cannot enter into a contract to pay a sum of money out of the corporate funds, for the making of improvements within the borough, except under the common seal (e).

V. *Bye-Laws.*

EVERY corporation has power to make bye-laws. This power, like the power of suing, or the capacity of being sued, is included in the very act of incorporation ; and it is not necessary, although usual, for the crown to confer this power in express terms (f). It is incident to the whole body of every corporation ; and, therefore, if a charter give to a select body power to make bye-laws touching certain matters therein specified, that does not take away from the body at large their incidental power to make bye-laws touching other matters not specified in the charter (g). Where the corporation is by charter, such bye-laws may be made as will enforce the end of the charter in a way more convenient, and tending more to the care and good governmen of the society, than what the charter has prescribed. Hence, where it is directed by the charter, that

(c) 5 & 6 Will. IV. c. 76, s. 13.

(d) *R.* v. *M. of Bridgnorth,* 10 A. & E. 66.

(e) *Mayor, &c. of Ludlow* v. *Charlton,* 6 M. & W. 815. See *ante,* p. 66, as to cases of exception to the rule of law requiring contracts entered into by corporations to be entered into under seal; such as retainer by parol of an inferior servant, the doing of acts very frequently recurring, or too insignificant to be worth the

trouble of affixing the common seal; and on the same principle, the power of accepting bills of exchange and issuing promissory notes by companies incorporated for the purposes of trade, *ante,* p. 303.

(f) Hob. 211.

(g) *R.* v. *Westwood,* 4 B. & C. 781. Judgment affirmed on error, D. P., 21st July, 1830, 7 Bingh. 1, Borough of Chepping Wycomb.

the mayor, or aldermen, or other principal officers shall be chosen by the burgesses or commonalty at large, the corporation may, by common assent, for the purpose of avoiding popular confusion, make a bye-law, restraining the power of election to a select number of burgesses or commonalty (h); that is, where the right of election is given to a whole class of men, they may restrain it to a part of themselves; but where a corporation consists of several integral parts, as, 1st, the mayor; 2ndly, the aldermen; 3rdly, the commonalty; and the right of election is given to the three parts conjointly, a bye-law excluding one integral part from the right of election, e. g., the commonalty, is void (i).

By the Municipal Corporation Act (k), the council of any of the boroughs mentioned in the schedules of that act, are empowered to make such bye-laws as to them shall seem meet for the good rule and government of the borough, and for suppression of all such nuisances as are not already punishable in a summary manner, by virtue of any act in force throughout such borough, and to appoint such fines as they shall deem necessary for the prevention of such offences, under certain limitations.

In order to give validity to corporate acts, it is essentially necessary in all cases where by the constitution of the corporation there is a definite body, who form an integral part of the corporation, 1st, that a majority of that definite body should exist (l) at the time when any corporate act is to be done. Hence if an integral part of a corporation is reduced by the death of its members, so that there does not any longer remain a majority of such integral part, there is an end of the corporation (m). 2ndly, That a majority of that body must attend the assembly, where such act is to be done (9). It is not, however, necessary, when met, that there should be a majority of each of the integral parts, to give validity to the corporate act; it is sufficient if it be done by a majority of the whole when so properly assembled (n). " It has now been for many years an established principle in corporation law, that if an election is to be made by a definite body alone, or by a definite together with an indefinite body, a majority of the definite body must

(h) Case of Corporations, 4 Rep. 77, b. See also *Bather* v. *Boulton*, 1 Str. 314; *R.* v. *Bird*, 13 East, 375.
(i) *R.* v. *Head*, 4 Burr. 2515, Borough of Helston.
(k) 5 & 6 Will. IV. c. 76, s. 90.

(l) *R.* v. *Morris*, 4 East, 17.
(m) Lord *Kenyon*, C. J., *R.* v. *Grampound*, 6 T. R. 302.
(n) *R.* v. *Bellringer*, 4 T. R. 819; *R.* v. *Miller*, 6 T. R. 268.

(9) By stat. 5 & 6 Will. IV. c. 76, s. 69, all acts required by virtue of this act to be done by the council of any borough, shall be done and decided by a majority of the councillors present; the whole number present not being less than one third part of the number of the whole council.

be present. The general rule, however, that a majority of each definite part of the elective body shall be present at the election, does not apply to all corporations : *e.g.*, it does not apply to Queenborough, for, from the peculiar constitution of that corporation (*o*), the application of the rule would lead to an absurdity or impossibility." In the case of an election to an office by a select body, it is not necessary in the notice (*p*) to them to state the purpose of the meeting. " If corporate acts are to be done by a select number of members upon a particular day, all who have a right to be present in that assembly ought to be summoned, and to have notice that they are to meet on the business (it is not necessary to specify what business) of the corporation (10). This rule admits of no exception, unless in the case where a member has absolutely deserted the town, by absenting himself and removing his family out of the town. It must be an entire departure from the place ; for if the person has a house and family in a corporate town, though he be abroad at the time of holding the assembly, whether for his health, his diversion, or upon business, he ought to be summoned (11). When the notice is regularly given, a majority have power to do any corporate act—but if the whole assembly meet by accident, they may proceed on business, provided they are unanimous ; but otherwise it is, if any one member of the corporation dissents, he has an absolute negative (*q*). But where the charter is silent on the subject, previous summons is only necessary for the purpose of preventing an election from taking place by surprise, *i. e.* by some of the electors, without due means of attendance upon that occasion being equally afforded to all the others. Hence, where the whole corporation are summoned for a particular purpose, (*e. g.*, to

(*o*) *R.* v. *Greet*, 8 B. & C. 369.

(*p*) *R.* v. *Pulsford*, 8 B. & C. 350.

(*q*) Per Lord *Hardwicke*, C. J., in *R.* v. *Kynaston*, B. R. T. 8 & 9 Geo. II., MS.

---

(10) See the notice of meetings of the council required by the Municipal Corporation Act, 5 & 6 Will. IV. c. 76, s. 69.

(11) By the Municipal Corporation Act, 5 & 6 Will. IV. c. 76, s. 52, if any person holding the office of mayor, alderman, or councillor, shall be declared bankrupt, or shall apply to take the benefit of any insolvent act, or shall compound by deed with his creditors, or, being mayor, shall be absent for more than two calendar months, or, being an alderman or councillor, for more than six months at one and the same time, unless in the case of illness, from the borough, such person shall thereupon immediately become disqualified and shall cease to hold the office, and in case of such absence, shall be liable to the same fine as if he had refused to accept the office, and the council thereupon shall declare the office to be void. A bankrupt uncertificated at the time of election is not disqualified from being elected a councillor under this act. The disqualification exists only where the bankruptcy occurs during the holding of the office. *R.* v. *Chitty*, 1 Nev. & P. 78 ; 5 A. & E. 609.

receive the resignation of a common councilman,) a *select body* who are *all present and consenting*, may (r), at the same meeting, without any particular summons to them for that purpose in their select capacity, proceed to an election of a common councilman, in the place of the other resigned; the power of election being in such select body, and the charter not requiring any previous summons. When a meeting for election or amotion takes place on a day not appropriated to that purpose by the constitution of the borough, notice must be given to all the members. Where the custom was to serve a personal notice on all the resident burgesses; it was holden (s), that a qualification of the custom, that an accidental omission to serve a burgess was not a violation of it, was bad in law. It is essential to the validity of a bye-law, that it should be consistent with, and that it should not be repugnant to, or contradict, the charter; for in a case where the charter directed that the mayor and aldermen, or the major part of them, should yearly nominate four of the burgesses, or inhabitants, to the commonalty at large, out of whom they were to elect one to be mayor, and who, at the end of his year, was to be an alderman; it was holden, that a bye-law, providing that an *alderman,* who was an inhabitant, might be elected mayor, was bad, inasmuch as it was inconsistent with the charter; because it was not intended, that aldermen who were to nominate the candidates for the mayoralty, and who were to commence aldermen by serving the office of mayor, should be chosen mayors, because they happened to be inhabitants (t). A bye-law, though made by the whole body, if it narrow the number of those out of whom the election is to be made, is void. Hence, where the power of electing the mayor was given by the charter, to the mayor, burgesses, and commonalty, who were to choose the mayor *out of the burgesses,* and a bye-law directed, that the mayor and common council (12), or the major part of them, of which the mayor was to be one, should elect *one of the common council* to be mayor; it was holden, that such bye-law was bad; because it was competent to a corporation to make such ordinances only as are for the better government of the corporation; and the present bye-law was prejudicial, inasmuch as it confined their choice; for, on the terms of the charter, they were at liberty to choose out of the burgesses at large. And *Lee,* C. J., observed, that *a corporation could not alter the charter as to the persons eligible,* neither could they set up another government than the charter had prescribed (u). So

(r) *R.* v. *Theodorick,* 8 East, 543.
(s) *R.* v. *Langhorn,* 4 A. & E. 538.
(t) *R.* v. *Tucker,* E. 14 Geo. II., MS.

Serjt. Hill, vol. 27, p. 184, Borough of Weymouth. Affirmed D. P. 1742.
(u) *R.* v. *Phillips, Mayor of Carmar-*

(12) N. The charter contained a provision, that the corporation might elect out of the burgesses twenty to be common council. MS.

a bye-law *extending* the number of persons eligible, if it varies the constitution of the corporation as prescribed by the charter, is bad (*x*). And upon the same principle, a bye-law directing that no person shall be elected mayor a second time within six years, has been holden to be void (*y*). A bye-law made by a part of the corporation to deprive the rest of the right of electing, without their assent, is bad. Hence, where by the charter the power of electing common councilmen was given to the mayor, jurats, and commonalty, and a bye-law was made by the *mayor, jurats, and common council*, restraining the election of common councilmen to the mayor, jurats, such of the commonalty as were of the common council, and sixty others, who were senior common freemen; the bye-law was holden to be bad (*z*). A bye-law cannot explain a doubtful charter; if there be any ambiguity on the face of the charter, it is the province of the court to expound it (*a*). A bye-law which gives a voice in the election to any person to whom it was not given by the constitution of the borough, is bad (*b*). It remains only to observe that a bye-law may be good in part, and bad in part, provided the two parts are entire and distinct from each other (*c*). Although there do not remain any traces of a bye-law in the corporation books, and although there cannot be any proof given of the loss of it, yet, upon evidence of constant usage, a jury may be directed to presume its existence (*d*). See *R.* v. *Head*, 4 Burr. 2518, and *R.* v. *Bird*, 13 East, 368, where defendants pleaded a bye-law not now extant in writing. Sixty years' usage has been considered as evidence of a bye-law (*e*).

---

then, H. 22 Geo. II.; Trin. 22 & 23 Geo. II., MS.; and Bull. N. P. 211, *S. C.*, cited in 3 Burr. 1836, 1838, 1839 (13).

(*x*) *R.* v. *Bumstead*, 2 B. & Ad. 699. See *R.* v. *Attwood*, 4 B. & Ad. 481; 1 Nev. & M. 286.

(*y*) *R.* v. *Mayor of Cambridge*, H. 23 Geo. III., MS.

(*z*) *R.* v. *Cutbush, Common Councilman of Maidstone*, E. T. 8 Geo. III., 4 Burr. 2204 (14).

(*a*) *R.* v. *Tucker*, E. 14 Geo. II., B. R., MS.

(*b*) *R.* v. *Bird*, 13 East, 387.

(*c*) Adm. per Lord *Kenyon*, C. J., in *R.* v. *Fishermen of Faversham*, 8 T. R. 365.

(*d*) See 2 Vez. 330.

(*e*) Per Lord *Mansfield*, C. J., in *Perkin* v. *Master, Warden, &c. of the Company of Cutlers in Hallamshire, in the County of York*, 21 MS. Serjeant Hill, p. 65.

---

(13) "This case was argued several times, and settled the point, that the number of the *eligible* cannot be narrowed, although on the authority of the case in 4 Rep. 78, the number of *electors* may." Per *Buller*, J., in *R.* v. *Mayor of Cambridge, ubi sup.*

(14) See also *R.* v. *Spencer*, 3 Burr. 1827, (the same corporation,) where a bye-law excluding all the commonalty, except such as had served the office of churchwarden and overseer for one year, was holden void; inasmuch as it superadded a qualification not required by the charter, and which had no relation to, or connection with, their corporate character or capacity.

VI. *Of the Inspection of the Records of the Corporation.*

EVERY member of the corporation has, as such, the right to inspect the books belonging to the corporation for any matter that concerns himself, although the corporation are not parties to the dispute which renders the inspection necessary; but the court will not grant the rule generally, but only to inspect the particular book in which the information sought for is to be found (*f*). The 35th section of the Municipal Corporation Act (*g*) directs that, when councillors are elected, "the mayor shall cause the voting papers to be kept in the office of town clerk during six calendar months at the least after every such election; and the town clerk shall permit any burgess to inspect the voting papers, on payment of 1*s.* for every search." Under the foregoing clause, the town clerk is not compellable to allow two persons at once to inspect the voting-papers, or to give two of them to one person at the same time. But he is bound (*h*) to allow any voter who brings a list of his own to compare it with the papers produced by the town clerk, and mark it according to what he finds there. In an action for the breach of a bye-law restraining persons from exercising trades within the limits of a corporate city, unless they become freemen, the court will compel the corporation (*i*) to allow the defendant to inspect the bye-law in the corporation books. But now, by the Municipal Corporation Act (*g*), notwithstanding any custom or bye-law, every person in any borough may keep any shop for the sale of all lawful wares and merchandizes by wholesale or retail, and use every lawful trade, &c. for hire, gain, sale, or otherwise within any borough.

VII. *Of the Pleadings.*

A QUO WARRANTO being in the nature of a writ of right, the defendant cannot plead any plea, except to justify or disclaim (*k*). Hence he cannot plead not guilty (*l*). In like manner he cannot plead *non usurpavit* (*m*), or that he did not usurp the office in question. This appears from the nature of the charge, which calls on the defendant to show by what authority he exercises the office

(*f*) *R.* v. *Hostmen*, in N. upon T. Str. 1223.

(*g*) 5 & 6 Will. IV. c. 76, s. 14.

(*h*) Per *Cur.*, *R.* v. *Arnold*, 4 A. & E. 663.

(*i*) *Harrison* v. *Williams*, 3 B. & C. 162.

(*k*) Per *Holt*, C. J., 12 Mod. 225.

(*l*) Ib.

(*m*) *Queen* v. *Blagden*, 10 Mod. 296.

in question, to which charge the pleas of not guilty and *non usurpavit* do not afford an answer. By stat. 32 Geo. III. c. 58, s. 1, " the defendants to any information in the nature of a *quo warranto*, for the exercise of any office or franchise in any city, borough, or town corporate, whether exhibited with leave of the court, or by his Majesty's attorney general, or other officer of the crown on behalf of his Majesty, and each and every of them, severally and respectively, may plead, that he or they had first actually taken upon themselves, or held or executed, the office or franchise which is the subject of such information, six years (15) or more before the exhibiting of such information, such six years to be computed from the day on which such defendant *was actually admitted and sworn into* (n) such office or franchise ; which plea may be pleaded either singly, or together with such plea as they might have lawfully pleaded before the passing of this act, or such several pleas as the court, on motion, shall allow ; and if, upon the trial of such information, the issue joined upon the plea aforesaid shall be found for the defendants, or any of them, he or they shall be entitled to judgment, and to such costs as they would by law have been entitled to, if a verdict and judgment had been given for them upon the merits of their title. The second section provides, that the prosecutor may reply a forfeiture, surrender, or avoidance, by the defendant, of the office or franchise happening within six years before exhibiting of the information, whereon the defendant may take issue, and shall be entitled to costs in manner aforesaid. The preceding statute having been made *in pari materiâ* with stat. 9 Ann. c. 20, is confined to corporate officers (o). But the defendant is entitled, by this act, to plead several pleas, although the limitation of time does not form the subject of one of his pleas (p). Where the plea consists of several facts, from which the defendant infers that he is entitled to the office, the replication may contain a denial of any of the facts stated in the plea ; but if it contain merely a denial of the inference drawn by the defendant from those facts, it will be bad ; for that amounts merely to a denial of the law ; for the judges are to determine whether the inference drawn by the defendant is fairly drawn. In an information against the defendant for usurping the office of portreve, defendant showed a title, and concluded his plea, " and so he says that he did not usurp in manner and form as in the said information is alleged ; " the coroner replied that he did usurp

---

(n) See *R.* v. *Brooks,* 8 B. & C. 323.

(o) *R.* v. *Richardson,* 9 East, 469, re-

cognised in *R.* v. *M'Kay,* 5 B. & C. 645, 6.

(p) *R.* v. *Autridge,* 8 T. R. 467.

---

(15) By 7 Will. IV. & 1 Vict. c. 78, s. 23, proceedings by quo warranto against mayor, &c. must be commenced within twelve months. See *ante,* s. III. p. 1155.

in manner and form, &c. The replication was adjudged to be bad(r).

VIII. *Evidence.*

CORPORATION books are generally allowed to be given in evidence, when they have been publicly kept·as such, and the entries made by the proper officers (*s*) ; not but that entries made by other persons may be good, as if the town clerk be sick, or refuse to attend; but then the circumstances under which the entries have been made must be proved. Corporation books being of a public nature, examined copies of the entries therein may also be given in evidence : and consequently the court will not enforce the production of the original books (*t*), unless it appear to be necessary that they should be inspected on account of a rasure, new entry, or the like, which must be verified by affidavit. An entry in the public books of a corporation, is not evidence for them (*u*), unless it be an entry of a public nature. The deed of a corporation cannot be given in evidence, without some evidence that the seal affixed to it is the seal of the corporation. It is not necessary to prove the seal of a corporation in the same manner as the seal of an individual, by producing the witness who saw the seal affixed; but when an instrument having a seal affixed to it, purporting to be a corporate seal, is produced in evidence, it is necessary to prove that the seal is the seal of the corporation, if there be any doubt about it, otherwise any instrument with a seal to it might be produced in court as an instrument sealed by the corporation (*x*).

In a case (*y*), where it was insisted, that by the constitution of a corporation by prescription, no person was capable of being elected a common councilman, who did not inhabit within the borough, and also hold a burgage tenure ; to prove that such was the constitution, a witness was called, who was an inhabitant of the borough, but had no burgage tenure. The court were of opinion, that he was a good witness, observing that there was a necessity of allowing such people in a question of this nature, since they must best know the right; besides, he was in effect a witness against himself, by saying, " though I am an inhabitant, yet I have no right to be chosen, because I have not a burgage tenure." In quo warranto for exercising the office of mayor, upon issue joined, that H., the presiding officer at defendant's election, was not then mayor ; the title of H.

(*r*) *R.* v. *Portreve of Honiton in De-vonshire*, E. 1 Geo., MS.

(*s*) Per *Cur.*, *R.* v. *Mothersell*, 1 Str. 93.

(*t*) *Brocas* v. *Mayor, &c. of London*, 1 Str. 307.

(*u*) *Marriage* v. *Lawrence*, 3 B. & A. 142.

(*x*) Per *Lawrence, J., Moises* v. *Thornton*, 8 T. R. 307.

(*y*) *Stevenson* v. *Nevinson*, Str. 583 ; Lord Raym. 1353.

2 I 2

to be mayor, and not merely whether he was mayor *de facto*, is put in issue (*z*) ; and evidence was holden to be admissible, to show, that H. had not been lawfully elected; H. being then dead, but, before his death, an information having been filed against him for usurping the office. A regular usage for twenty years, unexplained and uncontradicted, is sufficient to warrant a jury in finding an immemorial custom (*a*). A custom for the steward of a court-leet to nominate certain persons to the bailiff, to be summoned on the jury, is a good custom (*b*). A person having a bare authority, and not being a party to the record, is not prevented from being a witness (*c*). And so a bailiff who executes a writ may be a witness if he is not a party in the cause, but an office is always an interest. See, however, the statute 3 & 4 Will. IV. c. 42, ss. 26, 27, *ante*, page 825, n., by which an objection to a witness solely on the ground of the verdict or judgment being produced for or against him, is removed.

A judgment of ouster may be given in evidence to prove the ouster of a third person, by whom the defendant was admitted. In a quo warranto to try defendant's right to be a bailiff of Scarborough (*d*) ; in setting out his right, he showed his own election under Batty and Armstrong, two former bailiffs, alleging, that at the time of his election they were bailiffs. Among many other issues the coroner took this, that Batty and Armstrong were not bailiffs, as alleged in the plea. The proof of this issue lying upon the defendant, he gave general evidence of the election and right of Batty and Armstrong. And to encounter that, the prosecutor gave evidence of the custom of the borough of electing bailiffs, and produced a record whereby judgment of ouster was given against Batty and Armstrong, to remove them from the office, as not being duly elected to it. And it being objected on the trial, that this record ought not to be read against the defendant, and the judge having allowed it to be read, and left the whole evidence on both sides to the jury, to consider whether these persons were bailiffs or not, and the issue being found for the king, defendant moved for a new trial ; 1st, because this record was *res inter alios acta*, to which the defendant was neither party nor privy, and so *illi nocere non debuit :* although the judgment should have been obtained by default, mispleading, ignorance of their case, or even by collusion, as the defendant was a stranger to it, he by law could not be let in to prevent any of those inconveniences, and therefore it ought not to have been admitted as any evidence against him, but, in the trial of his right, should have been totally rejected. 2ndly, that the instances where records between other parties have been read, are,

(*z*) *R.* v. *W. Smith,* 5 M. & S. 271. But see 7 Will. IV. & 1 Vict. c. 78, s. 1, *ante,* p. 1152, 3.

(*a*) *R.* v. *Joliffe,* 2 B. & C. 54.

(*b*) *Ib.*

(*c*) *R.* v. *Gray, Mayor of Tintagel,* B. R. Hil. 10 Geo. II., MS. ; *S. C.,* by the name of *R.* v. *Bray,* C. T. H. 358.

(*d*) *R.* v. *Hebden,* E. 12 Geo. II., MSS.

in cases of general customs, as in the *City of London* v. *Clerke*, Carth. 181, where, in a demand of toll, verdicts against other persons were read against the defendant, and were undoubtedly good evidence, amounting to no more than payment of the toll by strangers, which is always allowed as evidence to prove a custom. But, in this instance, the record was read to a single fact, *viz.* the election, which the law does not allow. *Lock* v. *Norborne*, 3 Mod. 141, where it is expressly laid down, that none can be bound by a verdict against another that is not party or privy to it, as the heir of the ancestor, or the like. 2ndly, That this record, as read, must necessarily be conclusive evidence, and could not by law be left to the jury, as a matter that they could find against. Records are of so high a nature, that there can be no averment, much less parol proof admitted against them: and, therefore, to say that the whole evidence was left to the jury, was impossible; and the rather, because the credit of a record ought not, in any case, to be submitted to them. On the other side were cited Trials per Pais, 206; Skin. 15, *Brounker* v. *Sir Robert Atkins*, where a nonsuit against a predecessor in the same office was read against a successor, because he came in privity, as an heir under an ancestor. So *Rumball* v. *Norton*, upon a traverse to the return of a mandamus, to swear plaintiff a burgess of Calne, on *non fuit electus*, a judgment of ouster against one of the plaintiff's electors was given in evidence against the plaintiff. So Mich. 13 Geo. I., the *King* v. *Bulcock*, on a trial of quo warranto to try defendant's right to be a mayor of Southampton, a judgment of ouster against his predecessor was read against him. Besides, it was objected, that several other material issues were found against the defendant; and, therefore, though this evidence ought not to have been given, yet the party ought not to have a new trial. *Per Cur.* This evidence seems to have been rightly admitted. The defendant has made the title of Batty and Armstrong part of his right; and if he gives evidence of the right of their election, can that be better disproved than by a judgment of ouster, wherein such election is declared to be void? Indeed, this evidence was not of itself conclusive, but might have been repelled by proving fraud, neglect, or any other circumstance which would have abated the weight of the judgment. And if any thing of that kind had appeared, the force of it, as to the defendant, would have been greatly lessened. But what makes this case still plainer is, that defendant, by his plea, makes title under, and takes upon himself to justify, their election; and therefore ought to be bound by what has been transacted by them. And if this evidence had been erroneously admitted, yet here are many more issues found against him, to which no objection is made; and being any of them sufficient to entitle the crown to a judgment of ouster against defendant, there is no colour to grant a new trial on this point. And for these reasons it was denied. But although a judgment of ouster against one corporator is admissible against another, deriving title through him, it is not conclusive (e). The insertion of the name of a town in schedule A. of the Municipal Corporation Act, is *primâ facie* evidence of the existence of a municipal corporation there, but may be rebutted by evidence, that the name had been inserted in the act by mistake; as in the case of Gateshead (f).

IX. *Judgment.*

BY stat. 9 Ann. c. 20, s. 5, it is enacted and *declared*, " That in case any person, against whom any information, in the nature of a quo warranto, shall be exhibited in any of the said courts (16), shall be found or adjudged guilty of an usurpation, or intrusion into, or unlawfully holding and executing any of the said offices or franchises, it shall be lawful for the said courts respectively, as well to give judgment of *ouster* against such person from any of the said offices or franchises, as to fine such person for his usurping, &c. any of the said offices or franchises; and the said courts, respectively, may give judgment, that the relator shall recover his costs of such prosecution: and if judgment shall be given for the defendant, in such information, he shall recover his costs against such relator; such costs to be levied in manner aforesaid. In an information against defendant for exercising the office of mayor of Penryn, it appeared, that by the letters patent of incorporation it was directed, that the mayor elect, before he should be admitted to execute his office, should take a corporal oath, before the last mayor, for the faithful execution of his office. The defendant pleaded, that he was elected and duly sworn mayor; and issue being taken in the replication, both as to his being elected and sworn, upon the trial, the jury found that he was elected, but that he was not sworn; and thereupon judgment of ouster was given (g) in B. R. Upon writ of error (h) brought in D. P., it was insisted, that the judgment was erroneous; for it appeared upon the record, that his right to the office was established by the verdict, which found that he was elected; and yet, whilst this judgment of ouster stood, the plaintiff could not have the effect of a mandamus to be sworn in, though the legality of his election was not disputed, and though no time was limited by the charter for his being sworn in, nor was he by law

---

(e) *R.* v. *Grimes*, 5 Burr. 2598.   cited per *Cur.*, Str. 582, *S. C.*, case of the
(f) *R.* v. *Greene*, 1 Nev. & P. 631.   *Mayor of Penryn.*
(g) *R.* v. *Pinder*, Lord Raym. 1447,   (h) 2 Bro. P. C. 294, Tomlins' ed.

---

(16) Court of King's Bench, courts of sessions of counties palatine, or courts of grand sessions in Wales.

debarred from having such mandamus, although he acted before
he was sworn in. For the defendant, in error, it was contended,
that it being expressly required by the charter of incorporation,
that the mayor elect should take the oath of office, before he should
be admitted to execute such office, it became necessary for the
plaintiff, in order to make his justification complete, to allege, that
he did accordingly take such oath ; and this allegation having been
falsified by the verdict, the justification, being entire, was destroyed, and he was found to be an usurper, and consequently
subject to the judgment of ouster, as being the only legal judgment
in this case. The judgment of the Court of King's Bench was
affirmed (17). In a subsequent term, *viz.* E. 11 Geo., Str. 625,
Pindar having applied for a mandamus to swear him into the office
to which he had been elected, the court refused to grant it, in consequence of the judgment of ouster, which, according to the opinion
of *Raymond*, C. J., did away the election ; and he thought, that
without a new election, since the judgment, the party was not
entitled to a mandamus. In this case, Lord *Raymond*, *Powys*,
and *Fortescue*, Js., concurred in the propriety of the absolute judgment of ouster, which had been given in the former case ; *Raymond*,
C. J., observing, that he believed no precedent could be shown,
where the judgment was ever entered in any other manner. And
Fortescue, J., added, that a quo warranto was the king's writ of
right, and as against the crown want of swearing in was as much as
want of an election ; the jury, therefore, having found in effect,
that he had no title to the office, it was of course, that he should
be excluded from it by the judgment of the court. He remarked,
also, that he had never heard of any other judgment, and that it
was reasonable to exclude a person who appeared to have no title.
Reynolds, J., however, expressed an opinion, that there ought properly to have been a judgment of ouster, *quousque*, only, upon the
finding of the jury, in *R.* v. *Pindar*. And in the case of *R.* v.
Clarke, (2 East, 75,) who, having been ill sworn in, had afterwards
disclaimed upon an information filed against him for usurping the
office, and though having submitted to a judgment of complete
ouster, he was held to be concluded from setting up again his original right, yet Lord *Kenyon* intimated, that there might have been
a judgment *quousque* only against him. The same point was
again agitated in *R.* v. *Courtenay*, 9 East, 246 ; the court, however, being of opinion, that the defendant had been well elected
and sworn in, were not required to pronounce any opinion as to the
nature of the judgment ; but they said that, after diligen search,
they could not find, upon the files of the court, any precedent of a
judgment of ouster *quousque*. In the case of the *King* v. *Biddle*,

---

(17) The judgment was affirmed *without costs ;* the judges having
delivered it as their opinion, that costs were not recoverable in this case.

Str. 952, the defendant confessed an usurpation during part of the time charged in the information, and from that time insisted on an election. The prosecutor having entered up judgment of ouster, the court ordered, that all the judgment, except that of *capiatur pro fine*, might be expunged, observing, that it would be hard that a subsequent good election should be done away, as it would be by the judgment of ouster. And they distinguished it from *Pindar's* case, where the party had been guilty of an usurpation during all the time charged in the information. A quo warranto information has, of late years, been considered merely in the nature of a civil proceeding; and consequently the court will grant a new trial (*i*). The office of register and clerk of the Court of Requests, at Bristol, which was created by statute, is not an office within the meaning of the stat. 9 Ann. c. 20; and, therefore, although judgmen had been given for the defendant upon a quo warranto for usingt that office, yet it was holden (*k*), that he was not entitled to costs. So the office of bailiff (the returning officer), in a borough sending burgesses to parliament (*l*), but not a town corporate.

(*i*) *R.* v. *Francis*, 2 T. R. 484.
(*k*) *R.* v. *Hall*, 1 B. & C. 237.

(*l*) *Borough of Stockbridge, R.* v. *M'Kay*, 5 B. & C. 640.

CHAPTER XXXIII.

REPLEVIN.

I. *In what Cases a Replevin may be maintained, p. 1172.*

II. *Of the Proceedings in Replevin at Common Law, and the Alterations made therein by Statute, p. 1174.*

III. *Of the Duty of the Sheriff in the Execution of the Replevin, p. 1176; Of the Pledges, p. 1176; Bond from the Party Replevying, p. 1176; Sureties under Stat. 11 Geo. II. c. 19, s. 23, p. 1177.*

IV. *Of claiming Property, and of the Writ de Proprietate probandâ, p. 1182.*

V. *Of the Process for removing the Cause out of the Inferior Court, p. 1183; and herein of the Writs of Pone, Recordari facias loquelam, and Accedas ad Curiam, p. 1183, 4.*

VI. *By whom a Replevin may be maintained, p. 1185.*

VII. *Of the Declaration, p. 1186.*

VIII. *Of the Pleadings:*

    1. *Of Pleas in Abatement, and herein of the Plea of Cepit in alio loco, p. 1188.*

    2. *General Issue, p. 1190.*

    3. *Of the Avowry and Cognizance:*

        1. *General Rules, &c. relating to the Avowry, and herein of the New Rules, p. 1190.*

        2. *Of the Avowry for Damage feasant, p. 1192; Pleas in Bar, p. 1193; Escape through Defect of Fences, p. 1193; Right of Common, p. 1194; Tender of Amends, p. 1196.*

        3. *Of the Avowry for Rent Arrear, p. 1197; Pleas in Bar, p. 1198; Eviction, p. 1198; Non Dimisit, Non Tenuit, p. 1199; Riens in Arrear, p. 1200; Tender of Arrears, p. 1201.*

    4. *Property*, p. 1201.

    5. *Statutes*:

        1. *Of Limitations*, p. 1201.

        2. *Of Set-off*, p. 1202.

IX. *Of the Judgment*:

    1. *For the Plaintiff*, p. 1203.

    2. *For the Defendant*, p. 1203.

X. *Of the Costs*, p. 1207.

I. *In what Cases a Replevin may be maintained.*

IT is said, in 3 Bl. Com. 147, that a replevin is founded on a distress taken wrongfully and without sufficient cause (1); whence it may be inferred that the learned commentator supposed that this remedy was *confined* to a taking *by distress*. But, (as it was justly remarked by Lord *Redesdale*, Ch., in *Shannon* v. *Shannon*, 1 Sch. & Lef. 327,) this definition of replevin is too narrow, and many old authorities will be found in the books, of a replevin having been brought where there was not any distress (2). The

---

(1) Although, generally speaking, wherever there is a distress, replevin may be maintained, yet this rule is not universally true; for it appears from *R.* v. *Monkhouse*, Str. 1184, that the court directed an attachment to be issued against an under-sheriff, for granting a replevin of goods distrained on a conviction for deer-stealing. So a replevin will not lie upon a distress made for a duty to the crown. *R.* v. *Oliver*, Bunb. 14. See note by editor of Willes, in *Pearson* v. *Roberts*, Willes, 672. But where the plaintiff brought replevin for goods levied under a warrant of distress, for an assessment made by a special sessions under the Highway Act, 13 Geo. III. c. 78, s. 47, on the ground of the premises, for which he was assessed, being situated without the township which was liable to repair the road; the court refused to set aside the proceedings. *Fenton* v. *Boyle*, 2 Bos. & Pul. N. R. 399. Where a party having no stock in trade, is rated as an inhabitant of a parish, his remedy is by appeal to the quarter sessions. Replevin does not lie for a distress under such a rate; for, being an inhabitant, he is within the jurisdiction of the justices, and the rate is a question of amount for the sessions. *Marshall* v. *Pitman*, 9 Bingh. 595, distinguishing *Milward* v. *Caffin*, 2 Bl. R. 1330, where there was an entire want of jurisdiction. See *post, Sibbald* v. *Roderick*, p. 1173.

(2) *Replegiare est, rem apud alium detentam, cautione legitimâ interpositâ, redimere.* Spelm. Gloss. 485. *Quant les biens ou chattels*

writ, as was further remarked by Lord *Redesdale*, is founded on a taking, and the right which the party from whom the goods are taken, has to have them restored to him, until the question of title to the goods is determined. The person who takes them may claim property in them; and if he does, the sheriff cannot deliver the goods until the question is tried; but this claim of property can be made only where there has been a taking; and it appeared to him that the writ of replevin was calculated in such cases to supply the place of detinue or trover, and to prevent the party from whom the goods were taken being put to those actions, except in cases where the other could show property. A replevin lies for goods and chattels only (a); hence it cannot be maintained for things affixed to the freehold. In a replevin for taking goods and chattels (b), to wit, one kiln, &c. of the plaintiff, to which there was an avowry for rent in arrear, the plaintiff, in his plea in bar, said, that the lime kiln, before and at the said time, when, &c., was affixed to the freehold of the piece or parcel of ground on which, &c., and as such was by law exempt from any distress for the arrears of rent in the avowry mentioned, and ought not to have been distrained for the same, &c. To this plea, the defendant demurred generally. After argument, the court were of opinion, that the plea in bar could not be supported, because it was a departure from the declaration. That the declaration, treating the lime kiln as a chattel, might possibly be true; because lime may be burnt in a portable oven, and the kiln need not therefore necessarily be affixed to the freehold; but as the plea in bar stated it to be affixed to the freehold, it was inconsistent with the declaration.

Where some poor-rates had not been duly published on the Sunday following the allowance, according to stat. 17 Geo. II. c. 3, s. 1, and a warrant of distress issued for a single sum made up of these rates and of others which were regular; it was holden (c), that the warrant did not justify the distress; and the replevin which had been brought for taking cattle under the warrant was

(a) 1 Inst. 145, b.
(b) *Niblet* v. *Smith*, 4 T. R. 504.
(c) *Sibbald* v. *Roderick*, 11 A. & E. 38.

---

d'aucun sont prises, il avera per common ley un breve hors de Chancery commandant, &c. Doct. Plac. Replevin, 313. Replevin lies of all goods and chattels unlawfully taken. Comyn's Dig. Replevin (A). A replevin is a judicial writ to the sheriff, complaining of an unjust taking and detention of goods and chattels. Gilb. Repl. 58. Note, by the learned reporters of the Irish Chancery Cases, temp. Lord Redesdale. See also Bull. N. P. B. 9, c. 4.—" Replevin may be brought *in any case* where a man has had his goods taken from him by another." See also 1 Inst. 145, b.

sustained, although it was objected, that the plaintiff should have appealed.

II. *Of the Proceedings in Replevin at Common Law, and the Alterations made therein by Statute.*

AT the common law (*d*), the proceedings in replevin commenced with suing out of the Court of Chancery a writ of replevin, directed to the sheriff of the county where the distress was taken. Generally, writs directed to the sheriff gave him a ministerial power only; but the writ of replevin was in the nature of a justicies, not returnable, and gave the sheriff a judicial authority to determine, in the county court, the matter in question between the parties. Thus distinguished from other writs, it was called *festinum remedium*, a speedy remedy; but, notwithstanding the advantage accruing to the subject, from the circumstance of its being a justicial writ, it was frequently attended with so much delay as to require the interposition of the legislature. This delay arose from several causes: 1. From the necessity of an application to Chancery, when the distress was taken in a distant part of the kingdom. To obviate this inconvenience, it is provided by stat. 52 Hen. III. (commonly called the statute of Marlebridge,) c. 21, that if the beasts (3) of any person are taken and unjustly detained, the sheriff, after complaint made to him, may deliver them without the hindrance or refusal of the person who shall have taken the beasts. This statute extends to goods distrained for a poor-rate, and the sheriff must replevy such goods (*e*) upon being required; and an action may be maintained against him for refusing to do so. To make this remedy more effectual, and to render the delivery of distresses more expeditious, it is enacted by stat. 1 & 2 Ph. & Ma. c. 12, s. 3, that "Every sheriff of shires, not being cities, or towns made shires, shall, at his first county day, or within two months next after he has received his patent of office, appoint and proclaim, in the shire-town, four deputies at the least, dwelling not above twelve miles one from the other, who shall have authority, in the sheriff's name, to make replevins and delivery of distresses, in such manner and form as the sheriffs may and ought to do. By force of the statute of

(*d*) 2 Inst. 140.
(*e*) *Sabourin* v. *Marshall*, 3 B. & Ad. 440.

---

(3) The word in the statute is " averia," " beasts; " but it is usual for the sheriff to hold plea of replevin by *plaint* of other goods and chattels as well as cattle.

Marlebridge (*f*), (52 Hen. III. c. 21,) the sheriff may hold plea in replevin by plaint of any value, and this plaint may be taken out of the county court (*g*), and replevin made immediately (*h*) (4). But it is incumbent on the sheriff to enter the plaint at the next county court, in order that it may appear on the rules of the court. This statute does not extend to hundred courts. The hundred court, which derives its authority from the county court (*i*), cannot prescribe to grant replevins by plaint by its steward out of court; for, at common law, the sheriff could only replevy by writ *in* his county court. But this decision is to be confined to replevins in hundred courts, which courts are all *ejusdem generis*, and owe their jurisdiction to the common law, and does not furnish a rule for replevins in other courts which owe their origin and jurisdiction to charters from the crown, and in which, pleas of replevin upon plaint, and without writ, may be maintained (*k*). The proceeding by replevin by plaint under the statute has superseded the replevin by writ. The observations, therefore, made in this chapter, with respect to the method of prosecuting replevin, must be understood with reference to the replevin by *plaint*, except where the proceeding by *writ* is expressly mentioned.

2. Another cause of delay at common law proceeded from the sheriffs not being able to enter a liberty without a *non omittas*, where the distress was taken and impounded within any liberty which had return of writs, and the bailiff of such liberty did not pay any regard to the warrant of the sheriff. The statute of Marlebridge has removed the necessity of suing out the *non omittas*, but still the sheriff must make a warrant to the bailiff of the liberty before he can enter.

3. The same cause of delay as that last mentioned was experienced in cases where the distress, though not taken within a liberty, yet. was impounded within it. By force of the statute of Marlebridge, the sheriff may in this case enter the liberty immediately, even without previously issuing a warrant.

(*f*) 2 Inst. 139.
(*g*) Id.
(*h*) 1 Inst. 145, b.; 2 Inst. 139.
(*i*) *Hallet* v. *Byrt*, 5 Mod. 248; Lord

Raym. 218; Carth.382; Salk. 580; Skinner, 674, *S. C.*
(*k*) *Wilson* v. *Hobday*, 4 M. & S. 120.

---

(4) This position, which is to be found in 2 Inst. 139, is not warranted by 21 Edw. IV. 66, there referred to. But it is said in Broke, Repl. pl. 46, to be the best opinion. The reason assigned for it by Sir *Edw. Coke*, is, "that it would militate against the scope of the statute, that the owner of the beasts should be deprived of the use of them, until the day on which the county court is holden." The same doctrine is laid down in 1 Inst. 145, b.

III. *Of the Duty of the Sheriff in the Execution of the Replevin,
p. 1176; Of the Pledges, p. 1176; Bond from the Party
replevying, p. 1176; Sureties under the Stat. 11 Geo. II.
c. 19, s. 23, p. 1177.*

AT the commencement of a suit, it was the duty of the sheriff at
the common law, in all actions, to take from the plaintiff pledges for
the prosecution of his suit.   This duty was the same in replevin;
but as these pledges were only answerable for the amerciament to
the king, *pro falso clamore*, if the plaintiff did not prevail in the
suit, they were found insufficient for the security of the defendant
in replevin, inasmuch as if the party distrained upon, either sold or
eloigned the distress after the replevy, the defendant was wholly
prevented from reaping any advantage from an award of a return.
To remedy this mischief, the stat. Westm. 2 (13 Edw. I.), c. 2, requires the sheriff, before he makes deliverance of the distress, to
take from the plaintiff not only pledges for the prosecution of the
suit, but also for the return of the beasts, if a return be awarded.
And if the sheriff take pledges in any other manner, he is to answer
for the price of the cattle to the distrainors; and if the bailiff has
not wherewith to make restitution, it is to be made by his superior.
The course pursued by sheriffs, or other officers making replevins, in
carrying into effect the provisions of this statute, does not appear to
have been uniform.   Two different methods have been adopted by
them for the protection of the defendant.   The first method has
been to take a bond from *the pledges* conditioned for the appearance
of the party replevying at the next county court (*l*), for his prosecuting his suit with effect, and making return of the distress, if the
return should be adjudged.   In taking this security (*m*), the sheriff
has been considered as pursuing the directions of the statute; for
the word pledges has been holden to be synonymous with sureties.
The other method has been to take a bond from *the party replevying* (5); the condition of which is similar to the former, *viz.* that the
obligor will appear at the next county court, and then and there
prosecute his suit with effect, and also that he will make return of

(*l*) Dalton's Shff. 439.
(*m*) Lord Raym. 278; Lutw. 687; Dalton's Shff. 438.

(5) I have not been able to discover the origin or first introduction of
these securities, and, consequently, I cannot ascertain which is the most
ancient. The usage has been not to take both securities at the same
time, but the sheriff has exercised his discretion in taking either one or
the other, as seemed most convenient. The bond from the party replevying has, I believe, been most generally adopted.

the beasts, if return thereof be adjudged by law (6). Although the statute of Westm. 2d, c. 2, is entirely silent as to a bond from the party replevying, yet it has been decided that bonds of this kind are lawful (n), and if the condition be not performed, an action may be brought on them.   It does not appear that the sum in which these securities, *viz.* the bond from the pledges, or the bond from the party replevying, should be taken, has ever been ascertained.   To provide, therefore, a more effectual security for defendants, by fixing the responsibility of the sureties, and to prevent vexatious replevins in cases of distress for *rent arrear*, it is enacted by stat. 11 Geo. II. c. 19, s. 23, " that sheriffs, and other officers having authority to grant replevins, *shall* (7), in every replevin of distress for *rent*, before any deliverance of the distress, take *in their own names* from the plaintiff and two responsible persons, as sureties, a bond in double the value of the goods, conditioned for prosecuting the suit with effect, and without delay, and for duly returning the distress in case a return shall be awarded."   The statute then proceeds to authorize the sheriff or other officer to assign such bond to the avowant, or person making cognizance, who may maintain an action upon it in the superior courts (o), in the event of its being forfeited.   A replevin bond may be taken and assigned by any officer who has power to grant replevins ; and it has been holden (p), that one of the sheriffs of London has such power, without his companion, and may therefore take and assign replevin bonds.   Replevin bond may be assigned to avowant only (q), without cognizors, by this statute.   The avowants are the parties interested, and person making cognizance merely a man of straw.   Both avowant and person making cognizance may make an assignment of the bond,

(n) *Blackett* v. *Crissop*, 1 Lord Raym. 278.

(o) *Dias* v. *Freeman*, 5 T. R. 195.

(p) *Thompson* v. *Farden*, 1 M. & Gr. 535.

(q) *Archer and others, Assignees, &c.* v. *Dudley and others*, B. R. E. 22 Geo. III., B. P. B. 186, Dampier MSS., L. I. L.

---

(6) " In all replevin bonds there are several *independent* conditions ; one to prosecute, another to return the goods replevied, and a third to indemnify the sheriff ; and a breach may be assigned upon any of these distinct conditions."   Per *Lee*, C. J., delivering the opinion of the court in *Morgan* v. *Griffith*, M. 14 Geo. II. B. R., 7 Mod. 380, Leach's ed., cited by *Holroyd*, J., delivering judgment in *Perreau* v. *Bevan*, 5 B. & C. 302.   Or the breach may be assigned thus : " that defendant did not prosecute his suit with effect, and hath not made return."   *Phillips* v. *Price*, 3 M. & S. 180.

(7) If the sheriff or other officer neglect to take a bond, according to the directions of this statute, the courts will not grant an attachment against him, such negligence not being an abuse of any process of the courts.   *Twells* v. *Colville*, Willes, 375 ; *R.* v. *Lewis*, 2 T. R. 617.

and sue jointly on it (r). In this action, if the declaration state that the plaintiff, as bailiff of one J. S., distrained, &c., it is sufficient, without stating that the plaintiff, at the time of the assignment of the bond, was either avowant or person making cognizance in the suit in replevin (s). Although the bond be executed by one of the sureties only, it is still available by the sheriff against such surety (t). In *Chapman* v. *Butcher*, Carth. 248, the plaintiff in replevin had given a bond to the bailiffs of the borough of New Windsor, conditioned to prosecute his suit with effect in the court of record of that borough, and to make return, if return should be adjudged by law. A replevin was brought in the borough court, and judgment given for the defendant, which was afterwards reversed in the Court of King's Bench, on error, and a new judgment was given that the plaint should abate, and that the defendant should have a return. An action was brought on the bond, *and it was holden a lawful bond* (u), *and the court said, that it was the common course to take such bonds.* With respect to the condition, it was determined, that it was not confined to a prosecution in the court of Windsor, but extended to the prosecution of a writ of error in the King's Bench, for that was part of the suit commenced below : and by the words, "if a return should be adjudged by law," the condition was not confined to the judgment of any particular court (8), for which reasons the court gave judgment for the bailiffs, the obligees. So where the condition of the replevin bond was to appear in the county court (x) and *then and there* to prosecute with effect ; it was holden, that the word *then* and *there* related to so much of the prosecution as should be in the county court, but that they did not restrain it, and that the bond was forfeited, the plaintiff having been nonsuited in the superior court, to which the cause had been removed. Where the defendant had permitted two years to elapse without taking any steps in the

(r) *Phillips* v. *Price*, 3 M. & S. 180.
(s) *Dias* v. *Freeman*, 5 T. R. 195.
(t) *Austen* v. *Hayward*, 2 Marsh. 352; 7 Taunt. 28; *S. C.*, by the name of *Aus-* ten v. *Howard*.
(u) See also Fortesc. 210, 11.
(x) *Vaughan* v. *Norris*, Ca. Temp. Hardw. 137.

(8) " To prosecute with effect, the plaintiff must not only proceed to a decision of the suit, but must have success in it, or he does nothing; and it is not a completion of the condition to have levied a plaint in the county court: for the words extend to all the proceedings, from the original to the conclusion of the action, as well in the court below as in the superior court, by *re. fa. lo.*, which is the case in Carth. 249." Per *Lee*, C. J., delivering the opinion of the court in *Morgan* v. *Griffith*, 7 Mod. 380, Leach's ed. See a copy of Mr. Ford's note of this case, in Serjt. Hill's MS., vol. 27, p. 178. " The failure of prosecuting the suit with success is, we think, a failure of prosecuting the same with effect." Per *Holroyd*, J., delivering judgment of court in *Perreau* v. *Bevan*, 5 B. & C. 300.

replevin cause; it was holden (y), that the bond was forfeited, and that the obligee might recover, although he had not signed any judgment of non pros in the county courts. A plaintiff in replevin (z), who does not use due diligence in prosecuting the suit, is guilty of a breach of that part of the condition of the bond which requires him to prosecute without delay, even though it may not appear that the suit is determined. Plaintiff in replevin having given a bond to prosecute his suit with effect (a), levied a plaint against the defendant, who obtained an injunction to stay proceedings until a certain day, on which the plaintiff in replevin died; it was adjudged, that the plaintiff had prosecuted his suit with effect, there not having been either a nonsuit or a verdict against him; and *Holt*, C. J., compared it to the case of a recognizance on a writ of error, which was to prosecute with effect; there, if the plaintiff was not nonsuit, nor the judgment affirmed, the recognizance was not forfeited.

It is sufficient to plead that the party did appear at the next county court, and there prosecuted the suit according to the form and effect of the condition, and that the suit is still depending and undetermined (b). A declaration on a replevin bond, after alleging that the plaint was removed into the court above, that the defendant avowed, and that, the plaintiff in replevin having omitted to plead to the avowry, a judgment for a return was awarded, averred, that the plaintiff in replevin did not prosecute his suit with effect. A plea that, after the judgment for a return, a writ to inquire of the arrear of the rent and the value of the cattle, goods, &c. distrained, was prayed by the avowant, granted, and executed, and that thereupon avowant had judgment to recover the arrear of rent found, together with a sum for his costs and damages, was holden (c) ill on demurrer. In an action brought by the assignee of a replevin bond (d), where it did not appear on the face of the declaration, that the plaintiff was avowant, or person making cognizance, the court referred to the replevin suit, which was of record in the same court, for the purpose of ascertaining the fact, the declaration concluding *prout patet per recordum*. The breach assigned in the declaration ought to pursue the condition of the bond; but it is not necessary that it should extend any further (e). The sureties are liable only to the amount of the penalty in the bond, and costs of suit on the bond (f). They will not be discharged by time being given to the plaintiff in replevin (g), nor by

(y) *Axford* v. *Perrett*, 4 Bingh. 586.
(z) *Harrison* v. *Wardle*, 5 B. & Ad. 146; 2 Nev. & M. 703.
(a) *Duke of Ormond* v. *Bierly*, Carth. 519, and 12 Mod. 380.
(b) *Brackenbury* v. *Pell*, 12 East, 585.
(c) *Turnor* v. *Turner*, 2 Brod. & Bingh. 107.
(d) *Barker* v. *Horton*, C. B. 17 Geo. II., Willes, 460.
(e) 5 T. R. 195.
(f) *Hefford* v. *Alger*, 1 Taunt. 218.
(g) *Moore* v. *Bowmaker*, 2 Marsh. 81; 6 Taunt. 379, S. C.

the execution of a writ of inquiry (h) under the stat. 17 Car. II. c. 19, s. 23. But where the suit was referred, and it was agreed between the plaintiff and defendant, without the privity of the sureties, that the bond should stand as a security for the award, it was holden (i), that the sureties were discharged. The avowant, by having elected to proceed under the stat. 17 Car. II. c. 7, is not confined to his execution under the statute, but may proceed upon the replevin bond, if it has been assigned, or against the sheriff for his 'negligence for the loss of it, notwithstanding what is stated to have been said by *Bathurst*, J., in *Cooper* v. *Sherbrooke*, 2 Wils. 117, that "by stat. 17 Car. II. c. 7, the legislature intended that the proceedings upon that statute by writ of inquiry, fieri facias, and elegit, should be final for the avowant to recover his damages, and that the plaintiff should keep his cattle, notwithstanding the course of awarding a writ de retorno habendo, which is a right judgment: for the statute has not altered the judgment at common law, but only gives a further remedy to the avowant." The Court of Common Pleas, in *Turnor* v. *Turner*, decided contrary to that doctrine of *Bathurst*, J. See 5 B. & C. 303, 4, per *Holroyd*, J., delivering judgment of court in *Perreau* v. *Bevan*. When the defendant has obtained judgment for a return, if the sheriff return to the writ *de retorno habendo*, that the cattle are eloigned, the defendant may, if the sheriff has not taken any pledges (k), or, what amounts to the same thing, has taken such as are insufficient (l), immediately, without any previous proceedings (9), commence an action on the case (m) (10) against the sheriff; in which action, (since the 11

(h) *Turnor* v. *Turner*, 2 Brod. & Bingh. 107.

(i) *Archer* v. *Hale*, 4 Bingh. 464.

(k) *Moyser* v. *Gray*, Cro. Car. 446; *Anon.*, Sir W. Jones, 278.

(l) *Rouse* v. *Patterson*, 16 Vin. 399,

400; 7 Mod. 387, Leach's ed.; Bull. N. P. 60, *S. C.*

(m) This method of proceeding against the sheriff was settled, after much debate, in *Rouse* v. *Patterson*.

---

(9) Formerly, where the sheriff had taken insufficient pledges, it was the practice to proceed in the first instance by *scire facias*, against the pledges. A detailed account of this method is given in the 1st vol. of Serjt. Wms. ed. of Saunders, p. 195, a. n. (3), and Gilb. Repl. cap. 2, s. VII. 4.

(10) In this action, some evidence must be given by the plaintiff of the insufficiency of the pledges, but very slight evidence is sufficient to throw the burthen of proof on the sheriff. *Saunders* v. *Darling*, Bull. N. P. 60. The sheriff is to exercise a reasonable discretion in deciding upon the sufficiency of the sureties. He is not bound to go out of the office to make inquiries; but if the parties are unknown to him, he ought to require information beyond their own statement, as to their sufficiency. It is for the jury to decide whether he has exercised a reasonable discretion.

Geo. II. c. 19, s. 23,) in cases of a distress for rent arrear, three
different resolutions have taken place with respect to the extent of
the sheriff's liability.   The first case (n) decided, that the statute
11 Geo. II. c. 19, s. 23, had not enlarged the responsibility of the
sheriff, and that the value of the goods distrained ought to be the
measure of the damages against him, as it was under the stat.
Westm. 2 (13 Edw. I. c. 2).   In the second case (o), it was resolved, that as the proceeding against the sheriff was an action on
the case for a culpable neglect of duty, the plaintiff was entitled to
recover a full compensation for the injury sustained by him in consequence of that neglect, although such compensation exceeded
double the value of the goods distrained (11); but in the third
determination (p), it was holden, that the sheriff should not be
liable any further than the sureties would have been, if he had
done his duty, and taken a bond, and they had been sufficient ; and
that, as the responsibility of the sureties was limited by the statute
to double the value of the goods distrained, that sum ought to be
the measure of the damages; and this decision has since been recognized in *Paul* v. *Goodluck*, 2 Bingh. N. C. 220, where it was
holden, that inasmuch as the two sureties together are liable only
to the amount of the penalty of the bond, in case against the sheriff
for taking insufficient sureties, he is liable to the extent only of the
penalty of the bond given by the sureties.   The sheriff is not bound
to warrant the sufficiency of the pledges; if they are apparently
responsible (q), it is enough.   The expenses of a fruitless action
against the pledges cannot be recovered as special damages (r)

(n) *Yea* v. *Lethbridge*, 4 T. R. 433.
(o) *Concanen* v. *Lethbridge*, 2 H. Bl.
36.
(p) *Evans* v. *Brander*, 2 H. Bl. 547.
(q) *Hindle* v. *Blades*, 5 Taunt. 225 ;

1 Marsh. 27, *S. C.*   But see *Jeffery* v.
Bastard, 4 A. & E. 823 ; *ante*, p. 1180, 1,
n. (10).
(r) *Baker* v. *Garrat*, 3 Bingh. 56.

Jeffery v. *Bastard*, 4 Ad. & Ell. 823.   If the sheriff has assigned the
bond to the plaintiff, it is unnecessary to prove the execution of the
sureties.   *Barnes* v. *Lucas*, Ry. & Moo. 264.

(11) The damages given by the jury in this case were £100.

The rent in arrear was	-	-	10 10	0
The costs of the replevin suit	-	-	84 0	0
Expenses of *de retorno habendo*			5 0	0

£99 10   0

The value of the goods was £22 14s. ; and the penalty of the bond was
£50.   The court permitted the verdict to be entered for the whole sum
(£100) found by the jury.   In *Pattison* v. *Prowse*, the damages given
by the jury, for which judgment was entered, were made up of the costs
of the replevin suit, and the rent in arrear, but there the value of the goods
was more than the sum for which the judgment was entered.

beyond the penalty of the bond, unless notice be given to the sheriff of the intention to sue them. In *Richards* v. *Acton*, 2 Bl. Rep. 1220, the Court of Common Pleas, on a summary application, made a rule on the sheriff, under-sheriff, and the replevin clerk, who had refused to discover the names of the pledges taken on granting the replevin, to pay to the defendant in replevin the damages (12) and costs recovered by him. On an application to the Court of C. B. (*s*), for a rule to show cause why the officer of the court below should not pay the costs recovered by the defendant in replevin, on account of the insufficiency of the pledges taken by him *de retorno habendo*, the court refused to grant the rule ; observing, that the defendant's remedy was by action, there not having been any cause in the court at the time when the replevin bond was taken.

IV. *Of claiming Property, and of the Writ de Proprietate probandâ.*

IF the defendant claims property (*t*), the sheriff's power to re-deliver the beasts is suspended, and the plaintiff must sue out a writ *de proprietate probandâ*, or of proving property, because questions of property cannot be determined in the county court without the king's writ. On the purchasing the writ *de proprietate probandâ*, an inquest of office is holden ; and if on such inquest the property be found for the plaintiff, the sheriff is to make deliverance ; but if it be found for the defendant, the replevin by *plaint* is determined, and the sheriff cannot proceed any further ; yet the plaintiff may bring a new replevin *by writ;* for what is done on the plaint will not operate as a bar, because it is not connected with the proceeding by writ. Property must be claimed by the defendant in person (*u*) ; it cannot be claimed by his bailiff or servant. A bailiff cannot claim property below, because being only servant to another, in whose right he has taken the goods, he cannot say that they are his own ; but the bailiff above may *plead* property in a stranger, for this is a sufficient reason to

---

(*s*) *Tesseyman* v. *Gildart*, 1 Bos. &   (*t*) 1 Inst. 145, b.
Pul. N. R. 292.   (*u*) *Ib.*

---

(12) Nothing was said in this case respecting the quantum of damages; but it is conceived, that since the case of *Evans* v. *Brander*, if a similar application should be made, the court will not compel the sheriff, or other officer granting replevin, to pay more than double the value of the goods distrained.

excuse him from damages, since he has not taken the plaintiff's goods from him.

V. *Of the Process for removing the Cause out of the Inferior Courts, p.* 1183; *and herein of the Writs of Pone, Recordari facias loquelam, and accedas ad Curiam, p.* 1183, 4.

FOUR different forms of writs are prescribed by law for the removal of the proceedings in replevin out of an inferior into a superior court: 1. The writ of pone at common law. 2. The writ of pone under the statute of Westminster the 2nd (13 Edw. I.), c. 2. 3. The writ of recordari facias loquelam. 4. The writ of accedas ad curiam.

1. *Of the Writ of Pone at Common Law.*

When the proceedings in the county court were instituted by writ out of chancery, and the plaintiff was desirous of removing them, this was the proper form of writ for that purpose; but the proceeding in replevin *by writ* having fallen into disuse, the writ of pone has consequently shared the same fate: it will not be necessary, therefore, to trouble the reader with an explanation of it. The different forms of this writ, as adapted to a removal into the Court of King's Bench and Common Pleas, will be found in F. N. B. 69, M.

2. *Of the Writ of Pone under the Stat. Westm. 2.*

At the common law, where the lord avowed taking the distress for services or customs, if the plaintiff disavowed the tenure, and disclaimed holding of the avowant, the inferior court had not any further cognizance of the suit, and the proceeding there was stayed; because the disclaimer brought the freehold in question, which the county court, not being a court of record, had not any authority to try. This inconvenience was remedied by the stat. Westm. 2, (13 Ed. I. c. 2,) which gave the avowant in this case the writ of pone to remove the proceedings into the king's courts. It appears from the preamble, that the avowant is entitled to this writ of pone, as well where the proceedings are instituted in the inferior court by *plaint*, as where they are commenced by *writ* out of Chancery. There is one passage in this statute which is worthy of remark, because it may be inferred from it, that before this statute the *defendant* in replevin could not remove the proceedings out of the inferior court (13). The words are these : *Nec per istud statutum derogatur legi communi usitatæ, quod non permisit aliquod placitum poni coram justiciariis ad petitionem defendentis ; quia licet primâ facie videatur tenens actor, et dominus defendens, habito tamen respectu ad hoc quod dominus distrinxit, et sequitur pro servitiis et consuetudinibus sibi aretro existentibus, realiter apparebit potius actor, sive querens, quam defendens.*

3. Of the Writ of Recordari facias loquelam.

This form of writ is adapted to the removal of the proceedings in replevin (*x*), when they have been instituted in the county court by plaint, and not by writ; and as the method of suing by plaint has superseded the ancient method of proceeding by writ, the *recordari facias loquelam* is the writ now in general use. By this writ the sheriff is commanded to record the plaint, and when recorded, to return it into the King's Bench or Common Pleas, at a fixed day, on which the parties are to attend in court. This being done, the superior courts have authority to proceed. When the record is removed (*y*), and the party declares *in banco*, the plaint is determined. Hence advantage cannot be taken of a variance between the plaint and the declaration in the superior court. By virtue of the writ of *re. fa. lo.* the plaint may be removed either by the plaintiff or defendant ; but the defendant must allege in the writ some cause of removal : this allegation (*z*), however, is not a material point in the writ ; it is a mere form, not traversable (*a*) by the sheriff, and the defendant may avow or justify the taking and detention on other grounds. The delivery of the *re. fa. lo.* to the clerk of a county court, after interlocutory and before final judgment, is a bar to any further proceeding in that court. The officer of the inferior court cannot refuse paying obedience to the writ (*b*), under pretence of his fee not having been paid ; because he may bring an action for such fees.

4. Of the Writ of Accedas ad Curiam.

This writ is only a species of *re. fa. lo.* adapted to the removal of replevins, sued by plaint *in the Lord's Court*. It derives its name

(*x*) F. N. B. 70, B.
(*y*) *Hargreave* v. *Arden*, Cro. Eliz. 543.
(*z*) 10 Edw. II., Avowry, 213 ; 20

Edw. III., Avowry, 130.
(*a*) *Parkes* v. *Renton*, 3 B. & Ad. 105.
(*b*) *Bevan* v. *Prothesk*, 2 Burr. 1151.

---

(13) I am aware that Sir Edw. Coke has given a different explanation of this passage in the 2nd Inst. p. 339, but his explanation seems to be at variance with the context.

from the language of the writ, " *accedas ad curiam W. de C. et in illâ plenâ curiâ recordari facias loquelam, quæ est in eâdem curiâ sine brevi nostro, &c.* See the form of this writ in Gilb. Repl. 145, ed. 1757. N. If the writ of removal was made returnable on the first return of the term (c), it was incumbent on the plaintiff to declare in the superior court within four days before the end of that term; otherwise the defendant, (although he had not appeared,) was entitled to an imparlance; but see R. G. T. 1 Will. IV. No. 7.

VI. *By whom a Replevin may be maintained.*

To maintain replevin, the plaintiff ought to have either an absolute or special property (d) in the goods in question vested in him at the time of the taking (14): A mere possessory right is not sufficient (e). If the goods of a feme sole are taken, and she marries, the husband alone may (15) sue the replevin; because the property is transferred by the marriage, and vested absolutely in the husband, so that he may release it; and, consequently, he may have an action in his own name to bring back the property (f). If the goods are taken *after* marriage, husband and wife ought not to join in the replevin; but if they do join in the action, and after verdict a motion is made on this ground in arrest of judgment, it will be presumed that the husband and wife were jointly possessed of the goods before marriage, and that the goods were taken before marriage, in which case the husband and wife might join (g). Executors may maintain replevin for the goods of the testator taken in his lifetime (h). Parties who have a joint interest in the distress may join in the replevin (i), but where the interest in the goods taken is several (k), there ought to be several replevins.

(c) *Thompson* v. *Jordan*, 2 Bos. & Pul. 137.

(d) Bro. Repl. pl. 8, 20.

(e) Per *Cur.*, in *Templeman* v. *Case*, 10 Mod. 25.

(f) F. N. B. 69, K.

(g) *Bern et Ux.* v. *Mattaire*, Ca. Temp. Hardw. 119.

(h) Bro. Repl. pl. 59.

(i) 3 Hen. IV. 16, a.; 1 Inst. 145, b.

(k) Bro. Abr. Repl. pl. 12.

---

(14) There are two kinds of property,—a general property which every absolute owner has, and a special property, as goods pledged or taken to manure his lands, or the like,—and of both these a replevin lies. 1 Inst. 145, b.

(15) Or the husband and wife may join. Agreed by Lord *Hardwicke*, C. J., in *Bern* v. *Mattaire*, Ca. Temp. Hardw. 119. See *ante*, p. 295.

VII. *Of the Declaration.*

Venue.—The venue must be laid in the county in which the distress was taken. By R. G. H. T. 4 Will. IV. the name of a county shall in all cases be stated in the margin of a declaration, and shall be taken to be the venue intended by the plaintiff, and no venue shall be stated in the body of the declaration, or in any subsequent pleading. Provided, that, in cases where local description is now required, such local description shall be given. See further, on this point, stat. 3 & 4 Will. IV. c. 42, s. 22, *ante*, p. 494.

Locus in quo.—The place in which the distress was taken, technically termed the *locus in quo*, as well as the vill or parish, must be named in the declaration; because the right of caption may turn on the place, and the freehold may come in question (*l*). If the *locus in quo* be not named, the defendant may take advantage of the omission by special demurrer (*m*); but if he plead over, the defect is cured (*n*). This obligation on the defendant to name the *locus in quo*, has, from the supposed difficulty of ascertaining it in *all* cases, been frequently considered as a great hardship. It must be admitted, that if the law required the plaintiff to name the place where the distress was *first* taken, such a rule might deserve censure; but the law does not require such strictness; it being sufficient for the plaintiff to name that place in which he finds the defendant in *possession* of the distress (*o*); for the law considers the distress as wrongfully taken in every place in which the defendant may have it in his custody (16). Hence where the plaintiff declared of a taking in A. (*p*), and the defendant pleaded *non cepit modo et formâ*, the plaintiff having proved that he found the cattle in the possession of the defendant in A., it was adjudged sufficient, although the defendant proved, that he first took them in B., and was only driving them through A. to the pound (17). If the replevin be

(*l*) 2 Hen. VI. 14, a.

(*m*) *Ward* v. *Lavile*, Cro. Eliz. 896; Moor, 678, *S. C.*, under the name of *Ward* v. *Lakin*. See also *Read* and *Hawke's* case, the arguments in which are reported in Godb. 186, and the judgment of the court in Hob. 16, and 1

Brownl. 176.

(*n*) *Bullythorpe* v. *Turner*, Willes, 476; and per *Bridgman*, C. J., 1 Sidf. 10.

(*o*) Per *Chambre*, J., 2 Bos. & Pul. 481.

(*p*) *Walton* v. *Kersop*, 2 Wils. 354.

---

(16) If the distress be taken in one county, and carried into another, the plaintiff may have replevin in either county, because it is a caption in every county into which the distress is taken by the defendant. F. N. B. 69; 1 Doct. Pla. 315. See also Bro. Repl. pl. 63.

(17) If the defendant never had the goods in the place named in the declaration, *non cepit modo et formâ* seems a proper plea, where the de-

brought in an inferior court, the *locus in quo* must be alleged to be within the jurisdiction of the court (*q*). Where the close has not any name, it should be described by abuttals, or as in the occupation of (*r*) I. S. With respect to the description of the goods taken (*s*), it is stated in some of the books as a rule, that the goods must be described in the declaration with such certainty, that the sheriff may make a re-deliverance of them. The following cases contain all the learning on this subject: Replevin for taking *bona et catalla sua* (*t*), *viz. quandam parcell' lintei et quandam parcell' papyri ipsius querentis;* the defendant avowed the taking as a distress for rent arrear. Verdict for the plaintiff, with entire damages. It was objected, in arrest of judgment, that " *quandam parcell' papyri et lintei* " was too general and uncertain a description; and although it might be well enough in trover and trespass, yet it was ill in replevin; because it was not a sufficient direction to the jury in assessing the damages, nor to the sheriff in re-delivering the goods: but *Parker*, C. J., observed, that although the declaration would have been ill on demurrer, yet the pleadings had supplied the defect; because the defendant having avowed the taking, he had thereby admitted that he knew what the goods were, and, consequently, both parties agreeing on this point, the only question was, who should have them. He added, that it would not be of any advantage to the defendant to have the goods particularized; because, if the plaintiff should demand 500 reams of paper, and prove that the defendant had wrongfully taken one only, yet he would be entitled to recover, agreeably to the rule, that in actions of tort, it is sufficient for the plaintiff to prove part only of his declaration; and as to the necessity of an exact description of the goods on account of the re-delivery by the sheriff upon the *retorn' habend'*, he observed, that the sheriff might require the defendant to show him the goods (18), and that it was a good return for the sheriff to make,

(*q*) *Quarles* v. *Searle*, Cro. Jac. 95.
(*r*) *Potten* v. *Bradley*, 2 M. & P. (C. P.) 78.
(*s*) See Bull. N. P. p. 53.

(*t*) *Kempster* v. *Nelson*, Pasch. 13 Ann., 4 Bac. Abr. 387, cited and recognized in *Bern* v. *Mattaire*, Ca. Temp. Hardw. 121.

---

fendant does not seek a return. The plaintiff declared for taking guns *in quodam loco vocat.* the Minories; the defendant pleaded *non cepit modo et formâ*. At the trial, the plaintiff proved the taking at a place in Surrey, upon which it was objected, that he had failed in proving his issue; to which *Pratt*, C. J., assented, observing, that where the defendant does not insist on a return, he may plead *non cepit modo et formâ*, and prove the taking to be at another place; the plaintiff was nonsuited. *Johnson* v. *Wollyer*, Str. 507.

(18) This argument has frequently been urged, when exceptions in arrest of judgment have been made in actions of ejectment, for uncertainty of description in the declaration. See *Portman* v. *Morgan*, Cro. Eliz. 465.

" that no person came on the part of the defendant to show him the goods," and that such a return might be found in Rastall's Entries, and Dalton's Sheriff, c. 73. So where in replevin for taking fourteen skimmers and ladles (*u*), and three pots and covers, an exception was taken, after verdict, in arrest of judgment, to the declaration, for uncertainty in the description, in not expressing how many of each sort were taken; the court, adopting the reasons of *Parker*, C. J., in the preceding case, were of opinion, that the declaration was sufficient, and gave judgment for the plaintiff. But a declaration in replevin for taking " divers goods and chattels," was holden insufficient (*x*).

VIII. *Of the Pleadings:*

1. *Of Pleas in Abatement, p.* 1188; *and herein of the Plea of Cepit in alio Loco, p.* 1189.

2. *General Issue, p.* 1190.

3. *Of the Avowry and Cognizance:*

   1. *General Rules, &c. relating to the Avowry, and herein of the New Rules, p.* 1190.

   2. *Of the Avowry for Damage feasant, p.* 1192; *Pleas in Bar, p.* 1193; *Escape through Defect of Fences, p.* 1193; *Right of Common, p.* 1194; *Tender of Amends, p.* 1196.

   3. *Of the Avowry for Rent Arrear, p.* 1197; *Pleas in Bar, p.* 1198; *Eviction, p.* 1198; *Non Dimisit, Non Tenuit, p.* 1199; *Riens in Arrear, p.* 1200; *Tender of Arrears, p.* 1201.

4. *Property, p.* 1201.

5. *Statutes:*

   1. *Of Limitations, p.* 1201.

   2. *Of Set-off, p.* 1202.

---

1. *Of Pleas in Abatement, and herein of the Plea of Cepit in alio Loco.*

THERE is a difference between pleas in abatement in replevin, and in other actions, arising from the peculiar nature of the pro-

---

(*u*) *Bern* v. *Mattaire*, Ca. Temp. Hardw. 124.

(*x*) *Pope* v. *Tillman*, 1 Moore, (C. P.) 386; 7 Taunt. 642, *S. C.*

ceedings in replevin. In other actions, as actions of assumpsit, debt, or trespass, the plaintiff is not put in possession of any thing until after judgment and execution thereon: as soon, therefore, as the writ or count is quashed, by a judgment for the defendant, on a plea in abatement, the defendant is thereby restored to the same situation in which he was before the action was brought: but in replevin the mere quashing the writ or count does not afford the defendant complete redress, the plaintiff being in possession of the defendant's goods by previous delivery from the sheriff. To remedy this inconvenience, and to entitle himself to a return of the distress, the defendant must, to a plea of abatement in replevin, subjoin a suggestion in the nature of an avowry or cognizance. As this suggestion, however, is merely for the purpose of a return, the matter of it is not traversable (y). To the plea of *cepit in alio loco* (z), the defendant must add a suggestion of this kind, if he seeks a return.

Of the Plea of Cepit in alio Loco.

The defendant pleaded *cepit in alio loco* (a), and prayed judgment of the court, and that the count be quashed. On demurrer, the question was, whether the plea ought not to have prayed judgment of the writ; but it was insisted, that the place being mentioned in the count only, and not in the writ, the exception was properly taken to the count where the fault was. The court gave judgment for the plaintiff, being of opinion that the conclusion was good. But though this plea properly concludes with a prayer of judgment of the count or declaration, yet in a case (b) where to replevin for taking the plaintiff's goods, at the parish of St. Mary-le-Bow, in the ward of Cheap, in London, the defendant in his plea prayed judgment of the declaration, because he took the goods in the parish of St. Martin, Ludgate Without, in the ward of Farringdon Without, in London, in a certain dwelling-house there, called the White Swan, without this, that he took them at the parish of St. Mary-le-Bow, in the ward of Cheap, and this he is ready to verify; wherefore he prays judgment of the declaration, and added a suggestion in the nature of an avowry for a return; it was holden, that the plea of the defendant was a plea in bar, and not a plea in abatement, for the following reasons: 1st, because the place in replevin is of the essence of the action, otherwise the defendant in replevin could not demur for want of a certain place in the declaration; 2ndly, because in a plea in abatement, an objection cannot

(y) *Foot's* case, Salk. 93; Willes, 475. II., MSS.
(z) Bro. Repl. 45; *Anon.*, Salk. 94. (b) *Bullythorpe* v. *Turner*, Willes, 475.
(a) *Dockett* v. *Booth*, B. R. E. 1 Geo.

be made for any defect in the declaration; in support of this reason, *Hastrop* v. *Hastings*, Salk. 212, was cited; 3rdly, because, upon inquiring of the officers in the Court of Common Pleas and in the King's Bench, it was not found that an affidavit had ever been made of the truth of this plea, as is required in pleas in abatement by stat. 4 & 5 Ann. c. 16; nor were defendants obliged to put in such pleas within the first four days of the term, as pleas in abatement must be by the course of the court; 4thly, because it appeared by the manner of pleading these pleas and the judgment given upon them, that they had always been considered as pleas in bar (c); lastly, because whoever pleads a plea in abatement must show that the plaintiff can have a better writ, whereas he cannot have a better writ in the present case; for it is in the usual form, as appears by the register, fo. 81, and Glanville, l. 12, c. 12.

2. *The General Issue.*

The general issue in replevin is "*non cepit,*" by which the property is admitted to be in the plaintiff, and the caption only put in issue. If the plaintiff take husband after suing out the writ, and before the declaration, the defendant cannot give the coverture in evidence under the general issue, but must plead it in abatement (d).

3. *Of the Avowry and Cognizance:*

1. *General Rules, &c. relating to the Avowry, and herein of the New Rules,* p. 1190.

2. *Of the Avowry for Damage feasant,* p. 1192; *Pleas in Bar,* p. 1193; *Escape through Defect of Fences,* p. 1193; *Right of Common,* p. 1194; *Tender of Amends,* p. 1196.

3. *Of the Avowry for Rent Arrear,* p. 1197; *Pleas in Bar,* p. 1198; *Eviction,* p. 1198; *Non Dimisit, Non Tenuit,* p. 1199; *Riens in Arrear,* p. 1200; *Tender of Arrears,* p. 1201.

1. *General Rules, &c. relating to the Avowry, and herein of the New Rules.*—The avowry or cognizance, which is in the nature of a declaration, ought to contain sufficient matter, upon which the avowant, or person making cognizance, may have judgment for a

---

(c) 1 Rast. Entr. 555, pl. 4, 5; 556, pl. 7; Thomps. Ent. 274, pl. 11; Clift's Entr. 644.

(d) *Hollis* v. *Freer,* 2 Bingh. N. C. 719, recognizing *Morgan* v. *Painter,* 6 T. R. 265.

return (19). But if the avowry, &c. be defective in form; or if circumstance of time, place, &c. should be omitted, such omission may be helped by the plea of the adverse party; otherwise it is of a defect in substance (e). The avowry (f), &c. must answer every material part of the declaration; hence, if the plaintiff alleges a taking in two places, and the defendant avows as to one only, it is a discontinuance. So if the declaration be for taking goods (g), chattels, and beasts, and the avowry is confined to the taking the beasts only, it will be bad on demurrer. By stat. 4 Ann. c. 16, s. 4, any defendant in any action, or any plaintiff in replevin, in any court of record, may, with leave of the court, plead as many several matters thereto as he shall think necessary for his defence. An avowant is a defendant within the meaning of this section, and may plead several avowries with leave of the court (20). But now, by R. G. H. T. 4 Will. IV. No. 5, avowries and cognizances founded on one and the same principal matter, but varied in statement, description, or circumstance only, (and pleas in bar in replevin are within the rule,) are not to be allowed. Avowries for distress for rent, and for distress for damage feasant, are to be allowed; but avowries for distress for rent, varying the amount of rent reserved, or the times at which the rent is payable, are not to be allowed. Since these rules, in a case (h) where D. and L. were defendants in replevin, the court allowed D. to avow for a distress damage feasant, in his own right as tenant from year to year, to W., tenant in fee, and also to make cognizance as bailiff of C., tenant in fee; and L. to make cognizance as bailiff of D., tenant to W., as above; and also as bailiff of C., tenant in fee. In replevin for taking cattle (i), the defendant made cognizance as bailiff to J. S.; the plaintiff traversed the defendant being bailiff to J. S.; on demurrer, after argument, it was holden, that the traverse was well taken; for although J. S. had a right to take the cattle, yet a stranger, without his authority, could not; and that, as both parts of the cognizance must be true, an answer to either part was sufficient (21).

(e) *Butt's case*, C. B., 7 Rep. 25, a.
(f) *Weeks* v. *Speed*, Salk. 94.
(g) *Hunt* v. *Braines*, 4 Mod. 402.
(h) *Evans* v. *Davies*, 8 A. & E. 362; 3 Nev. & P. 464.
(i) *Trevilian* v. *Pyne*, Salk. 107.

(19) "In replevin, because the avowant is to have a return, he ought to make a good title *in omnibus*." Per *Cur.*, *Goodman* v. *Aylin*, Yelv. 148.

(20) I am not aware of any authority for this position, but it has been so considered in practice, and it is confirmed by the case of *Stone* v. *Forsyth*, Doug. 708, n. 2, where an avowant was considered as a defendant within the 5th sect. of the same statute, and holden to be liable to pay costs on the avowries found against him.

(21) Prior decisions on this point are very contradictory. I have

2. *Of the Avowry for Damage feasant.*—The defendant may
state in his avowry, that the *locus in quo* was his *soil and freehold*,
(without specifying whether he had an estate in fee, fee-tail, or for
life,) and that he took the plaintiff's cattle because they were doing
damage there.   From this plea it will be intended, that it is the
avowant's sole freehold, and in his own right; consequently, if the
avowant be seised merely in right of his wife, that ought to be
specially stated (*k*); and although this general form of pleading
soil and freehold be allowed, yet if the defendant does not pursue
this form, but merely alleges that he is *seised*, without showing of
what estate, the avowry will be bad on special demurrer (*l*) for
uncertainty.   So it seems, if defendant plead by way of justification of the taking, that he was possessed (22) of a messuage, with

(*k*) *Bonner* v. *Walker*, Cro. Eliz. 524.
(*l*) *Saunders* v. *Hussey*, Carth. 9; 1 Lord Raym. 332; 2 Lutw. 1231.

---

abridged the last determination, which has, I believe, been considered as
law ever since.   It was recognized by *Burnett*, J., in *George* v. *Kinch*, T.
17 & 18 Geo. II., C. B., 7 Mod. 481, Leach's ed., where he says, " This
distinction as to traversing of commands is laid down in *Trevilian* v. *Pyne*,
namely, that in *clausum fregit*, the command is not traversable; but it is
otherwise in replevin, or trespass laid transitorily, as for taking cattle or •
goods.   In trespass *quare clausum fregit*, which is a local trespass, if
defendant justify an entry into the close by the command of, or as bailiff
to A., in whom he alleges the freehold to be, the plaintiff cannot in his
replication traverse such command, because it would admit the freehold to
be in A., and not in himself, which would be sufficient to bar his action,
although the defendant had no such command •; for it is not material that
the defendant has done wrong to a stranger, if it be not any to the plaintiff.   But in replevin or trespass for taking goods or cattle, if the defendant
justify by a command from, or as bailiff to A., in whom he states a title to
take them as for distress or other cause, there it may be material to traverse the command or authority; for though A. has a right to take the
goods or cattle, yet a stranger who had not any authority from him, will
be liable; so that both parts of the defendant's plea must be true, and
therefore an answer to any part is sufficient."   In *Robson* v. *Douglas*,
Trin. 1681, C. B., Freem. 535, it was admitted by the court, that the
plaintiff in replevin might traverse the defendant's being bailiff.   If the
reader wishes to pursue this subject, he will find the authorities bearing
upon this point collected in Serjeant Williams's Saunders, vol. i. p. 347,
c. note (4).

(22) There is a difference in this respect between replevin and trespass
for taking cattle or goods; for to trespass for taking cattle or goods, the
defendant may plead generally that he was *possessed* of a close, and that
he took the cattle or goods damage feasant therein.   *Anon.*, Salk. 643;
11 Mod. 219, *S. C., ut videtur*, under the name of *Harrington* v. *Bush;*
Searl v. *Bunion*, 2 Mod. 70; *Langford* v. *Webber*, Carth. 9; 3 Mod. 132,

• This distinction is now exploded, and the plaintiff may traverse the command in
trespass *qu. cl. fr.* as well as in replevin.   *Chambers* v. *Donaldson*, 11 East, 65.

common appurtenant, and that the plaintiff's cattle were doing damage on the common, and conclude in bar *without praying a return*, such plea is bad (*m*). As tenants in common must join in actions concerning the personalty (*n*), one tenant in common cannot avow alone for taking cattle damage feasant; because it is an injury to the possession, and an avowry of this kind is in the nature of a declaration in trespass for an injury done to the possession. An avowry for damage feasant in a place where the avowant had a right of common (*o*), must allege special damage, *viz.* that the avowant could not enjoy his common in so ample and beneficial a manner. The declarations of the person under whom a defendant makes cognizance are not evidence for the plaintiff (*p*).

Pleas in Bar.   Escape through Defect of Fences.—In a plea in bar of an avowry for taking cattle damage feasant, *viz.* that the cattle escaped from a public highway into the *locus in quo*, through defect of fences, it must be shown, that they were *passing* on the highway when they escaped; it is not sufficient to state, that *being* in the highway they escaped; for that word is equivocal, and does not show whether the cattle were passing and repassing, or whether they were trespassing on the highway (*q*) (23). The general rule of law is, that a person is only bound to take care that his cattle do not wander from his own land and trespass upon the land of others. He is under no legal obligation, therefore, to keep up fences between adjoining closes, of which he is owner; and even where adjoining lands, which have once belonged to different persons, one of whom was bound to repair the fences between the two, afterwards become the property of the same person, the pre-existing obligation

(*m*) *Hawkins* v. *Eckles*, 2 Bos. & Pul. 359.
(*n*) *Cully* v. *Spearman*, 2 H. Bl. 386.
(*o*) *Woolton* v. *Salter*, 3 Lev. 104.
(*p*) *Hart* v. *Horn*, 2 Campb. 92.
(*q*) *Dovaston* v. *Payne*, 2 H. Bl. 527.

S. C. The reason of this distinction appears to be this,—that where the interest of the land is not in question, the defendant may justify upon his own possession against a wrong doer. But such a justification will not be good as against the person who has the title to the land, and who makes an entry in, and puts the cattle or goods there in pursuance of that title. *Taylor* v. *Eastwood*, 1 East, 212.

(23) " If the cattle of one person escape into the land of another, it is not any excuse that the fences were out of repair, if the cattle were trespassers in the close whence they came." Per *Heath*, J., in *Dovaston* v. *Payne*, 2 H. Bl. 527. See also a similar opinion expressed by *Wilmot*, C. J., in 3 Wils. 126.

So in an action for digging a pit in a common, into which the plaintiff's mare fell and was killed; it was holden, that the declaration ought to have stated, that the mare was *lawfully* on the common, otherwise the digging the pit, as against the plaintiff, was justifiable, and although the plaintiff's mare fell in, yet it was *damnum absque injurid*. *Blyth* v. *Topham*, Cro. Jac. 158.

to repair the fences is destroyed by the unity of ownership. And where the person, who has so become the owner of the entirety afterwards parts with one of the two closes, the obligation to repair the fences will not revive, unless express words be introduced into the deed of conveyance for that purpose (r).

Right of Common.—To an avowry for damage feasant, a right of common may be pleaded in bar (24). In a prescription for a right of common during a certain portion of the year only (s), it must appear on the face of the plea, that the right was exercised during the time allowed. In an avowry, the defendant stated (t), that he was seised in fee of a messuage, with the appurtenances situate, &c., "and that he and all those whose estate he had *from time whereof, &c.* have, and of right, *during all the time aforesaid,* ought to have had, and still of right ought to have, common of pasture in the place in question for a certain number of cattle as appurtenant to the messuage." On special demurrer, assigning for cause, that it was not stated in the avowry at what time, or for what period of time, the avowant had common of pasture in the place in question, nor whether he had common every year, or in what part or period of the year; the avowry was holden to be bad. According to a case in Coke's Reports, a copyholder claiming common in the soil of other persons than the lord (u), cannot prescribe *in his own name* on account of the weakness of his estate; he ought to prescribe in the name of the lord, *viz.* "that the lord of the manor and all his ancestors, and all those whose estate he has, had common in such place for himself and his tenants at will," &c. But where a copyholder claims common in the soil *of the lord,* then he cannot prescribe in the name of the lord; for the lord cannot prescribe to have common in his own soil, and as the copyholder cannot prescribe in his own name, he must allege (x), that "within the manor there is a custom from time immemorial, that all customary tenants of certain messuages have common in such a place," &c. "If the issue be on a right of common, which depends on a custom pervading the whole manor, the evidence of a commoner is not admissible, because, as it depends upon a custom, the record in that action would be evidence in a subsequent action brought by that very witness to try the same right; therefore there is a good reason for not receiving his testimony in such case. But the same reason does not hold where common is claimed by prescription in right of a particular estate;

(r) Per *Bayley,* J., in *Boyle* v. *Tomlyn,* 6 B. & C. 337.

(s) Cro. Jac. 637.

(t) *Hawkins* v. *Eckles,* 2 Bos. & Pul. 359.

(u) 4 Rep. 31, b. But see stat. 2 & 3

Will. IV. c. 71, for shortening the time of prescription in certain cases, and particularly sect. 5, *ante,* p. 428, and Mr. Shelford's work on the Real Property Statutes, p. 38.

(x) *Gateward's* case, 6 Rep. 60, b.

(24) For the nature of this right, see *ante,* tit. "Common."

because it does not follow, if A. has a prescriptive right of common belonging to his estate, that B., who has another estate in the same manor, must have the same right; neither would the judgment for A. be evidence for B.; and yet there are cases, which lay it down as a general rule, that one commoner is in no case a witness for another" (y). The plaintiff prescribed (z) for common of pasture, upon Hampton Common, for all cattle, *levant* and *couchant* upon his ancient messuage, &c. as appurtenant thereto, and declared that the defendant was bound, by reason of his occupation, to repair the fence of his close contiguous to the common, and permitted it to be ruinous, whereby the plaintiff's cattle escaped, and plaintiff lost the use of them. At the trial, the plaintiff called several witnesses, inhabitants of Hampton, who deposed, that all inhabitants of Hampton, paying church and poor, had a right to turn their cattle upon the common. The court held, that the question to be considered was, whether commoners, having a common interest in the preservation of this hedge, could be competent witnesses for each other ? It might be, that no one was bound to repair it. It might be, that a hayward was usually paid to the commoners to keep their cattle on the common. But the production of this record would be evidence for another commoner, that the occupier of the adjacent land was bound to repair this fence. The commoner, therefore, would derive an advantage, by exonerating himself from the charge of maintaining a hayward, if he could throw on this defendant the charge of repairing the hedge, and consequently, he was interested in the event of the suit. But now, by stat. 3 & 4 Will. IV. c. 42, ss. 26, 27, witnesses interested solely on account of the verdict or judgment are admissible. See *ante*, p. 825, n. There may, however, be cases in which the witness has a direct interest independent of the verdict and judgment. Thus, a tenant, who is called in ejectment for the purpose of establishing his lessor's title, has a direct interest to secure his own possession under the lease; such witness, therefore, is still incompetent. But, where there is not any immediate benefit resulting to the witness from the termination of the suit one way or the other, and his interest arises solely on the supposition that if a subsequent action were brought, his defence to that action would be the recovery in this action, then the statute applies (a). If a right of way be pleaded for the inhabitant householders of M. to fetch water, an inhabitant householder of M. may be examined as a witness (b) in support of this plea, under the statute. The lord of a manor may, in respect of common land in his own manor, have a

---

(y) Per *Buller*, J., in *Walton* v. *Shelley*, 1 T. R. 302; *Harvey* v. *Collison*, *ante*, p. 426, S. P.

(z) *Anscomb* v. *Shore*, 1 Taunt. 261.

(a) *Bowman* v. *Willis*, 3 Bingh. N. C. 669, cited by *Parke*, B., as in point in *Yeomans* v. *Legh*, 2 Mee. & Wels. 421.

See also *Stewart* v. *Barnes*, 1 M. & Rob. 472, where *Alderson*, B., taking the same view, decided that the statute did not apply. See the other cases in this statute collected, *ante*, p. 375, 650.

(b) *Knight* v. *Woore*, 7 C. & P. 258, *Williams*, J.

right to turn his own sheep on the common of an adjoining manor (c). A custom that every inhabitant within any ancient messuage in an ancient vill (d), by reason of his commorancy therein, has had common in the place in question, is bad ; for inhabitants, unless they are incorporated, cannot prescribe to have profit in another's soil, but only in matters of easement, as in a way to a church, or in matters of discharge, as to be discharged of toll or of tithes. But although *inhabitants*, on account of the vagueness of the description, cannot claim a right *in alieno solo*, yet the occupiers of houses may set up a custom to cut turves, and occupiers of lands may, by custom, claim a right *in alieno solo* (e). Where a prescriptive right of common is pleaded (f), and issue is joined on the prescription, and there is a verdict in favour of the right, the want of averring that the plaintiff's cattle were in that part of the land in which the common is claimed, or that the cattle were levant and couchant upon the land of the plaintiff, is aided by the statute of jeofail. See new rule as to pleas of common of pasture for divers kinds of cattle and similar rights, under title " Common," *ante*, p. 428.

Tender of Amends.—Tender of amends *before* the taking of a distress makes the distress unlawful, and in such case an action of trespass may be maintained for taking the cattle (g). Tender of amends *after* distress, and before impounding, makes the *detainer* unlawful, and gives the plaintiff a right of action for detaining his cattle. In a case where the sheep damage feasant had been distrained by the avowant, and having been placed in an outhouse, about 200 yards from the place where they were taken, the plaintiff's son applied to the avowant's wife for the sheep, no one else being on the premises. The plaintiff's son had done business before with the avowant's wife on the subject of impounding the same sheep. Upon being asked what amends she required, she said 23s. if they did not impound the sheep, and 25s. if they took them to the public pound at Leominster. On the part of the avowant, it was contended, that the tender came too late, the sheep being already impounded; but the court ruled otherwise, observing, that the pound which will exclude a tender, must be a pound in which the cattle are no longer in the custody of the party, but in the custody of the law ; here the agent of the distrainor (for the wife must be so considered,) admitted that the sheep were destined for another pound, and consequently the tender was good. The stat. 21 Jac. I. c. 16, s. 5, by which it is enacted, " that in all actions of trespass *quare clausum fregit*, wherein the defendants shall disclaim in their plea to make any title or claim to the land in which the trespass is by declaration supposed to be done, and the trespass be by negligence, or involuntary, the defend-

. (c) *Earl of Sefton* v. *Court*, 5 B. & C. 917.

(d) *Smith* v. *Gatewood*, Cro. Jac. 152 ; 6 Rep. 59, b.

(e) Adm. per *Cur.*, in *Bean* v. *Bloom*, 2 Bl. R. 928.

(f) *Stennel* v. *Hogg*, 1 Saund. 225.

(g) 2 Inst. 107.

ants shall be admitted to plead a disclaimer, and that the trespass was by negligence or involuntary, and a tender or offer of sufficient amends for such trespass before action brought," is confined to actions of trespass, and does not extend to replevin (*h*).

Avowry, &c. for Rent Arrear.—At the common law, it was necessary for a termor, in an avowry for rent due from his tenant, to show out of what estate and in what manner the term was derived, because particular estates being created by agreement of the parties out of the primitive estate, it was the office of the court to judge, whether the primitive estate and agreement were sufficient to produce the particular estate (*i*). To obviate the difficulties which the avowant for rent arrear had to encounter, in setting forth long and intricate titles, it was enacted by stat. 11 Geo. II. c. 19, s. 22, that defendants in replevin might avow or make cognizance *generally*, that the plaintiff in replevin, or other tenant of the lands, whereon the distress was made, enjoyed the same under a grant or demise at such a certain rent during the time wherein the rent distrained for incurred, which rent was then and still remains due; or that the place, where the distress was taken, was parcel of such certain tenements holden of such honour, lordship, or manor, for which tenements the rent, relief, heriot, or other service distrained for, was at the time of such distress, and still remains due (25), without further setting forth the grant, tenure, demise, or title : and if the plaintiff shall become nonsuit, discontinue, or have judgment against him, defendant shall recover double costs. It is not necessary in an avowry for rent under this statute, to aver that the rent continued in arrear (*k*), at the time of making the avowry. Avowries for distress for rent, varying the amount of rent reserved, or the time at which rent is payable, are not allowed under the new rules (*l*). The statute does not extend to a rent charge (*m*). Proof of payment of rent to the avowant is *primâ facie* evidence (*n*), that he is owner of the land. Evidence that plaintiff held under an agreement for a lease, (where rent has not been paid,) will not support an avowry or cognizance under this statute, *viz.* that plaintiff held by virtue of a demise; for there is not any demise either expressed or implied (*o*). Secus, where rent has been paid (*p*).

(*h*) *Allen* v. *Bayley*, Lutw. 1596.
(*i*) *Scilly* v. *Dally*, Salk. 562 ; Carth. 445 ; Lord Raym. 331, *S. C.* ; *Reynolds* v. *Thorpe*, Str. 796.
(*k*) *Clarke* v. *Davies*, 7 Taunt. 72.
(*l*) See *ante*, p. 1191.

(*m*) *Bulpit* v. *Clarke*, 1 Bos. & Pul. N. R. 56.
(*n*) *Rogers* v. *Pitcher*, 6 Taunt. 202.
(*o*) *Hegan* v. *Johnson*, 2 Taunt. 148.
(*p*) *Knight* v. *Benett*, 3 Bingh. 361.

(25) *Nil habuit in tenementis* cannot be pleaded in bar to an avowry for rent arrear under this statute. *Syllivan* v. *Stradling*, 2 Wils. 208. Nor a plea which amounts to *nil habuit*. *Alchorne* v. *Gomme*, 2 Bingh. 54. See also *Parry* v. *House*, Holt's N. P. C. 489. But see *post*, p. 1202, *Taylor* v. *Zamira*.

Tenant from year to year, during a current year, entered into an agreement for a lease to be granted to him and A. B.; and from that time A. B. entered and occupied jointly with him. It was holden (q), that by this agreement, and the joint occupation under it, the former tenancy was determined, although the lease contracted for was never granted. The sum stated in the avowry or cognizance to be due for rent is not material; for if it appears that less rent is due than defendant has avowed or made cognizance for, yet is he entitled to recover for so much as is due (r). Where the avowry is for parcel of a rent (s), or penalty (t) only, it ought to show that the residue has been satisfied or discharged, otherwise it will be bad on demurrer (u). If the defendant avow for so much rent arrear (x), part whereof is not due at the time of the distress, and enters judgment for the whole, it will be error: but it may be cured before judgment, by abating the avowry as to the part not as yet due (y). Money may be paid into court on an avowry for rent arrear (z). A rent is granted to A. for a term of years, with a clause in the deed, that A. and his heirs may distrain for the rent during the term; A. dies; the executor shall have the rent and distrain for it, and not the heir (a). One joint tenant may distrain for the whole rent (b), but he ought to avow for part only in his own right, and for the residue he ought to make cognizance as bailiff to his companion. Parceners must join in an avowry for rent arrear (c). A. and B. were tenants in common in fee of land (d); A. granted a lease for years of his moiety to C., reserving a rent; C. assigned the lease to B.; it was holden, that A. might distrain upon B. for rent arrear, and avow for taking the distress in any part of the land. An avowry, justifying the taking a distress for rent arrear for ready furnished lodging, is good; it having been holden, that a landlord is entitled to distrain for the rent of ready furnished lodgings (e).

Pleas in bar. Eviction.—To an avowry for rent arrear, the plaintiff may plead in bar an eviction or expulsion; for that occasions a suspension of the rent. But care must be taken, that an absolute eviction is stated in the plea, or at least such facts as amount in law to an eviction; for where, to an avowry for rent arrear for a dwelling house (f), the plaintiff pleaded, that the defendant pulled down a summer house, part of the premises, whereby the plaintiff was deprived of the use thereof; it was holden, that the plea was insufficient, because it stated merely a

(q) *Hamerton* v. *Stead*, 3 B. & C. 478.
(r) Said by Lord *Ellenborough*, C. J., in *Forty* v. *Imber*, 6 East, 437, to be the constant practice.
(s) *Hunt* v. *Braines*, 4 Mod. 402.
(t) *Holt* v. *Sambach*, Cro. Car. 104.
(u) *Johnson* v. *Baynes*, 12 Mod. 84.
(x) *Richards* v. *Cornforth*, Salk. 580.
(y) See 1 Williams's Saunders, 285, n. 6, 8, and *Harrison* v. *Barnby*, 5 T. R.

248.
(z) *Vernon* v. *Wynne*, 1 H. Bl. 24.
(a) *Darrel* v. *Wilson*, Cro. Eliz. 644.
(b) 5 Mod. 73; 12 Mod. 96.
(c) *Stedman* v. *Bates*, Lord Raym. 64.
(d) *Snelgar* v. *Henston*, Cro. Jac. 611.
(e) *Newman* v. *Anderton*, 2 Bos. & Pul. N. R. 224.
(f) *Hunt* v. *Cope*, Cowp. 242.

trespass, and not an eviction. See *Neale* v. *Mackenzie*, 2 Cr. M. & R. 84; 5 Tyrw. 1106.

Non dimisit. Non tenuit.—The most usual pleas in bar to an avowry for rent arrear are, 1. Non dimisit, that is, that the avowant did not demise; 2. Non tenuit modo et formâ, or that the plaintiff did not hold the land in manner and form, &c. When issue is joined on the non tenuit modo et formâ, the defendant is not holden to strict proof as to the identical time during which he alleges the tenant to have holden and enjoyed the land, &c. demised. Hence, where the defendant made cognizance for two years and a quarter's rent in arrear (g), and alleged, that for a long time, to wit, for two years and a quarter, ending on the 25th December, 1803, the plaintiff held and enjoyed the property demised, to which the plaintiff pleaded *non tenuit modo et formâ*, and issue was joined thereon; proof that the plaintiff held and enjoyed from the 23d of December, 1801, was adjudged sufficient to entitle defendant to a verdict for two years' rent. Where the plaintiff came into possession under one who had paid rent upon distress by defendant: it was holden (h), that after proof of that fact, the plaintiff was estopped to dispute the defendant's title to the rent. Where the plaintiff did not originally *receive the possession of the land from the avowant*, it is competent to the plaintiff, although he has paid rent to the avowant, or otherwise acknowledged the avowant as landlord, to rebut the supposed title of the avowant, by showing that he paid rent under circumstances which did not entitle the avowant to the rent. And such evidence may be given on the issue non tenuit modo et formâ (i). Declaration for taking plaintiff's corn in four closes, naming them. Avowry, that plaintiff held the closes in which, &c., under a certain rent, &c. Plea, non tenuit. The evidence was, that the plaintiff held the four closes mentioned in the declaration, and two others also, at the rent mentioned in the avowry; it was

(g) *Forty* v. *Imber*, 6 East, 434.

(h) *Cooper* v. *Blundy*, 1 Bingh. N. C. 45, recognizing *Panton* v. *Jones*, 3 Campb. 372.

(i) *Rogers* v. *Pitcher*, 6 Taunt. 202. See also *Williams* v. *Bartholomew*, 1 Bos. & Pul. 326; *Gravenor* v. *Woodhouse*, 1 Bingh. 38; *Fenner* v. *Duplock*, 2 Bingh. 10; *Gregory* v. *Doidge*, 3 Bingh. 474, S. P.; *Brook* v. *Biggs*, 2 Bingh. N. C. 572. In *Rogers* v. *Pitcher*, and *Gravenor* v. *Woodhouse*, the distinction is pointed out between the case where a person has actually received possession from one who has no title, and the case where he has merely attorned, by mistake, to one who has no title. In the former case, the tenant cannot (except under very special circumstances), dispute the title; in the

latter he may. Per *Bayley*, J., in *Cornish* v. *Searell*, 8 B. & C. 475; *Hall* v. *Butler*, 10 A. & E. 204. See also another distinction in *Hoperaft* v. *Keys*, 9 Bingh. 613, where defendant having only a defeasible title, demised to plaintiff for years; before the first quarter's rent was due, plaintiff was evicted by title paramount to defendant's, and remained out of possession for some weeks; he then entered again under a new agreement with the person who had so evicted him: it was holden, that a distress which had been taken by the defendant, could not be sustained; and that the eviction might in this case be given in evidence on the issue of non tenuit. See also *Doe d. Bullen* v. *Mills*, 2 A. & E. 17, and *ante*, under title "Ejectment," p. 689.

holden (*k*), that the proof supported the avowry; for each part of the land was liable to the whole rent; the tenant, therefore, held the portion of the land mentioned in the declaration at the whole rent, and a distress for the whole might have been taken on that or any part. But the contract on which the rent becomes due must be truly stated; hence where avowry alleged that the plaintiff held at a yearly rent of £170, as tenant to A.: On *non tenuit modo et formâ*, it was holden (*l*), that proof that plaintiff held as tenant to defendant of two thirds only, at a rent of £170 for the whole, was a variance. So where defendant avowed on a contract for £100, and proved a demise at 15*s*. an acre, amounting to £111, it was holden (*m*) a variance. Cognizance by defendant as bailiff to R. W. for rent arrear on a demise from R. W. Plea, non tenuit. It appeared by the lease, that R. W. was a receiver appointed by Chancery, in a cause wherein A. was plaintiff and B. defendant; the reddendum was to R. W., or any future receiver. Verdict for defendant, which the court refused to set aside (*n*), observing, that plaintiff could not take a lease from R. W., and then turn round and say that he did not demise. The defendant made cognizance, 1st, under a demise by A. to B.; 2ndly, under a demise from B. to the plaintiff. Plea in bar to each cognizance. The defendant may at the trial abandon the second cognizance and examine (*o*) B. in support of the first issue, B. stating on the voir dire, that he did not employ the attorney.

Riens in Arrear.—Riens in arrear, or no rent in arrear, may be pleaded in bar to this avowry; but such plea ought to conclude to the country; for where *de injuriâ suâ propriâ absque hoc quod redditus fuit in aretro* was pleaded to a cognizance for rent arrear; it was holden (*p*) ill, on special demurrer, as putting the defendant to an unnecessary replication. This plea admits the holding to be as stated in the avowry; hence if the avowry state that the plaintiff held the premises under a rent reserved quarterly, under the issue riens in arrear, the plaintiff will not be permi ed to show that he held (*q*) under a rent reserved half-yearly. Attgeneral plea of *de injuriâ suâ propriâ absque tali causâ* to an avowry or a cognizance for rent arrear will be bad (*r*), on special demurrer; for this general plea can be pleaded only "where the defendant's plea rests merely upon matter of excuse, and not upon any matter of interest or authority, mediately or immediately derived from the plaintiff, or any commandment" (*s*).

(*k*) *Hargrave* v. *Shewin*, 6 B. & C. 34.

(*l*) *Philpott* v. *Dobbinson*, 6 Bingh. 104.

(*m*) *Brown* v. *Sayce*, 4 Taunt. 320.

(*n*) *Dancer* v. *Hastings*, 4 Bingh. 2.

(*o*) *King* v. *Baker*, 4 Nev. & M. 228, in which the accuracy of the report in *Upton* v. *Curtis*, 1 Bingh. 210, was questioned.

(*p*) *Horn* v. *Lewin*, Salk. 583.

(*q*) *Hill* v. *Wright*, 2 Esp. N. P. C. 670.

(*r*) *Jones* v. *Kitchen*, 1 Bos. & Pul. 76.

(*s*) *Crogate's* case, 8 Rep. 66, b. See the learned comments on this case in *Selby* v. *Bardons*, 3 B. & Ad. 2; Doct. pl. 114, 115.

Tender of Arrears.—The same rule holds in this case as in the case of tender of amends for damage feasant (*t*); for if the tenant, before distress, tender on the land the arrears of rent, the taking of the distress becomes wrongful, and the tenant may maintain trespass for the caption; but if the distress has been made, and before impounding the arrears are tendered, then the *detainer* only is unlawful, and the tenant may bring detinue or replevin. Replevin for taking and detaining, &c. Avowry for rent arrear; plea, that after the taking and before the impounding, plaintiff tendered the rent and expenses. On special demurrer that the plea was an answer only to part, the avowry justifying the taking *and detaining*, it was argued that there was not any instance of a replevin for a mere detention; but the court held (*u*) the plea good; for the detention after the tender satisfied the allegation; every unlawful detention was a new taking. After the distress has been impounded, a tender of the rent and charges is too late (*x*). And it is incumbent on a party pleading a tender to be accurate in his plea, and to prove a tender to the full amount stated (*y*). Hence where defendant pleaded nothing in arrear beyond £16, and pleaded a tender of that sum; proof of a tender of £15 16s. was holden (*z*) insufficient, although the latter sum only was proved to be due for rent.

4. *Property.*

The defendant may plead property in himself, in bar of the action (*a*), and this plea may conclude with a prayer for a return and damages (*b*). So property in a stranger may be pleaded in bar (*c*), and the conclusion of this plea, praying a return, is good (*d*). So it is a good plea to say, that the property is to the plaintiff and to a stranger; and where there are two plaintiffs, that the property is to one of them (*e*).

5. *Statutes :*

1. *Of Limitations.*
2. *Of Set-off.*

1. *Stat. of Limitations.*—By stat. 21 Jac. I. c. 16, s. 3, actions of replevin shall be commenced and sued within six years after the cause of action. Hence *actio non accrevit infra sex annos* is a good plea in bar in replevin.

(*t*) 2 Inst. 107.
(*u*) *Evans* v. *Elliott*, 5 A. & E. 142.
(*x*) *Ladd* v. *Thomas*, 4 P. & D. 9.
(*y*) *John* v. *Jenkins*, 1 Cr. & M. 227; 3 Tyr. 170.
(*z*) *Ib.*

(*a*) *Wildman* v. *Norton*, 1 Ventr. 249.
(*b*) *Presgrave* v. *Saunders*, 1 Salk. 5.
(*c*) *Butcher* v. *Porter*, Carth. 243.
(*d*) *Parker* v. *Mellor*, Ld. Raym. 217, and Carth. 398.
(*e*) 1 Inst. 145. b.

2. *Set-off.*—There cannot be a set-off in replevin. Avowry for rent arrear [*plea, riens in arrear,*] *and issue thereon.* Plaintiff had given a notice of set-off (*f*), and offered to support it by evidence at the trial; but *Denison*, J., rejected it. The court of C. B. were of opinion, that the evidence was properly rejected, observing, that this case was neither within the letter nor the intention of the statute (*g*). The issue was special, and not general. It was not an action upon a personal contract. The rent savoured of the realty, and the remedy was by distress; replevin, they added, was a mixed action. The judgment, if for the avowant, must be for a return of the cattle. To take the benefit of the statute, plaintiff and defendant must plead properly. In debt on bond, defendant cannot set-off under *non est factum* or *solvit ad diem*, but must plead specially. *Perhaps by way of special plea to the avowry, plaintiff might have pleaded a mutual debt of more than the rent.* There could not have been a set-off by defendant under *non cepit*, nor could there be for plaintiff under riens in arrear. To an avowry for rent arrear (*h*), the tenant pleaded that a certain sum (equal in amount to the rent arrear) was due for ground rent from the avowant to the original landlord; that payment of that sum was demanded of the avowant, who refused to pay the same, whereupon the original landlord demanded payment of the tenant, and threatened to distrain, and that tenant, in order to avoid a distress, paid the ground rent: on demurrer, the plea was holden to be good; *Buller*, J., observing, that there was a difference between a payment and a set-off; the former might be pleaded to an avowry, though the latter could not. So the tenant may plead (*i*) payment of an annuity secured out of the demised lands previously to the demise to him, for the arrears of which the grantee had threatened to distrain. So to an avowry for rent (*k*), the tenant may plead payment of it to a mortgagee, to whom the premises had been mortgaged in fee before the demise to the plaintiff, and who had demanded payment from the plaintiff, and threatened "to put the law in force" in case of refusal; for such a plea is, in substance, a plea of payment, and not of nil habuit in tenementis (*l*), nor of eviction.

(*f*) *Absalom* v. *Knight*, C. B. E. 16 Geo. II., Barnes, 450, 4to, ed.; Bull. N. P. 181, *S. C.*; *Graham* v. *Fraine*, B. R. H. 24 Geo. II.; *Laycock* v. *Tuffnell*, B. R. E. 27 Geo. III., B. P. B. 499, S. P.

(*g*) 2 Geo. II. c. 22, s. 13.

(*h*) *Sapsford* v. *Fletcher*, 4 T. R. 511.
(*i*) *Taylor* v. *Zamira*, 2 Marsh. R. 220; 6 Taunt. 524, *S. C.*
(*k*) *Johnson* v. *Jones*, 9 A. & E. 809; 1 P. & D. 651.
(*l*) See *ante*, p. 1197, n.

IX. *Of the Judgment:*

1. *For the Plaintiff.*
2. *For the Defendant.*

1. *For the Plaintiff.*—As, by the nature of the proceedings in replevin, the goods distrained are delivered by the sheriff to the plaintiff; if he recovers, he can have judgment for damages only. If the plaintiff has judgment on a demurrer, the form of entry is, "that the plaintiff do recover his damages, by reason of the premises" (*m*); whereupon a writ of inquiry is awarded to ascertain the damages, and on return of the inquisition, final judgment is entered for the damages found by the inquisition, and costs *de incremento*. If the plaintiff obtains a verdict (*n*), then the jury, on that verdict, ascertains the damages and costs, and the judgment is, "that the plaintiff do recover against the defendant, the damages assessed by the jurors, and costs *de incremento*."

2. *For the Defendant.*—At the common law, when the merits of a suit in replevin were decided by a verdict for the defendant, or judgment for him on demurrer, or confession by the plaintiff, the judgment for the defendant awarded him a return of the distress irreplevisable. A different rule obtained in the case of a nonsuit, for in that case the defendant was not entitled to this judgment. To remedy the inconvenience which proceeded from the plaintiff, in the case of nonsuits, having several replevins for one and the same cause, it was enacted, by stat. 13 Edw. I. c. 2, that as soon as the return of the beasts should be adjudged to the distrainor, the sheriff should be commanded by a judicial writ to return the beasts to the distrainor, in which writ is to be inserted a direction to the sheriff not to deliver the beasts without a writ making mention of the judgment given *by the justices* (26). By this statute, if the plaintiff in replevin be once nonsuited, he cannot have a new replevin, but must sue out a writ according to the directions of the statute. This writ is termed a writ of second deliverance. It is a judicial

(*m*) 2nd Book of Judgm. 20.   (*n*) *Ib.*

---

(26) It appears from the words printed in italics, and those which follow them in the statute, *viz.* "*quod fieri non poterit nisi per breve quod exeat de rotulis justic' coram quibus deducta fuerit loquela,*" that the provisions of this statute are confined to those cases where the cause has been removed into the superior court, and the plaintiff has been nonsuited there. If this be the true construction, it will follow that, so long as the cause remains in the county court, the plaintiff may replevy the distress after nonsuit there, and return made *in infinitum*, as he might before this statute.

writ, issuing out of the court of record in which the nonsuit was had (27). The writ of second deliverance (*o*), is a supersedeas in law to the sheriff to forbear to execute the writ *de retorno habendo* (28) obtained on the nonsuit of the plaintiff, if delivered to the sheriff before return is made. If upon the writ of second deliverance, the party replevying makes default a second time for any other cause, the statute has provided, that the distress shall remain irreplevisable for ever.

In the case of a distress for rent arrear, the stat. 17 Car. II. c. 7, has prescribed to the defendant the mode of proceeding in the four following cases :—

I. If the plaintiff shall be nonsuit, *before issue joined*, in any suit of replevin by plaint or writ lawfully removed: The defendant must make a suggestion in nature of an avowry or cognizance for the rent arrear, whereupon the court, upon prayer of the defendant, will award a writ of inquiry touching the sum in arrear at the time of the distress, and the value of the distress. On the return of the inquisition, the defendant will have judgment to recover the rent arrear, if the distress amounts to the value of it; if not, then to recover the value of the distress, with full costs (29).

II. If the plaintiff shall be nonsuit, after cognizance or avowry made, and issue joined : In this case the jurors that are impanelled to inquire of such issue, shall, at the prayer of the defendant, inquire concerning the sum of the arrears and the value of the distress, and thereupon the defendant is entitled to the same judgment as in case I.

III. If, after cognizance or avowry made, and issue joined, the verdict shall be given against the plaintiff: As in the last case, the jurors that are impanelled to inquire of such issue shall, at the prayer of the defendant, inquire concerning the sum of the arrears, and the value of the distress, and thereupon the defendant is entitled to the same judgment as in case I.

(o) 2 Inst. 341.

---

(27) See the form of this writ, Gilb. Repl. Cap. II. S. VII. 4.

(28) But not to the writ of inquiry of damages on stat. 21 Hen. VIII. c. 19, Salk. 95, or on stat. 17 Car. II. c. 7, Ventr. 64 ; 2 Wils. 117.

(29) For the form of prayer, writ of inquiry, and judgment, where the distress amounts to the value of the rent, see Lilly's Entries, 3d edition, 1758, p. 610. For the form of the judgment where the distress is of less value than the rent, see Tidd's Practical Forms, 1st ed. p. 292. If the plaintiff be nonprossed after defendant has avowed, for want of a plea in bar, it seems unnecessary to add a suggestion, the cause of the distress being sufficiently ascertained by the avowry. See the form of the writ of inquiry in this case, in Tidd's Prac. Forms, 1st ed. p. 163, 164.

It must be observed, that if the jurors give a defective verdict, *e. g.*, if they find the value of the distress, but omit to find the sum of the arrears, this omission cannot be supplied by a writ of inquiry; because the statute directs that the jurors, who are impanelled to try the issue, shall inquire concerning the sum of the arrears (*p*). The case of *Sheape* v. *Culpeper* was recognized by Lord *Hardwicke*, C. J., in *R.* v. *Kynaston*, B. R. T. 10 Geo. II., MS.; where it was holden, that the court could not supply a defective verdict, where several traverses had been taken on a return to a mandamus, under the statute 9 Ann. c. 20, and the jury had omitted to find damages and costs for the plaintiff. See also Ca. Temp. Hardw. 297. This point was again moved in *Freeman* v. *Lady Archer*, 2 Bl. 763; and *Gould*, J., then expressed a doubt, whether a writ of inquiry could be granted to supply a defective verdict for the defendant in the case of an avowry for rent arrear. It appears clearly, from the case of *Sheape* v. *Culpeper*, that it cannot. And in a subsequent case, where the jury found a verdict for the avowant, and damages to the amount of the rent claimed in the avowry, but did not find either the amount of the rent in arrear, or the value of the distress, and judgment was entered for the damages assessed; it was holden, that this judgment was erroneous, and could not be amended into a judgment under the statute, *because the neglect of such inquiry by the jury could not be in any manner supplied* (*q*). But in cases where the court is not restrained by the express words of the stat. 17 Car. II. c. 7, s. 2, (which relates to rent arrear only,) an inquiry may be granted to supply omissions on the part of the jury at the trial of the replevin. Hence, where the defendant avowed, as overseer of the poor, for a distress for a rate under stat. 43 Eliz. c. 2, and at the trial, the plaintiff was nonsuit, and the jury was discharged without any inquiry of the treble damages given by the 19th section of that statute to defendants in case of a nonsuit after appearance; an application was made to the court that the avowants might have a writ of inquiry awarded to supply this defect, which application, after much debate, was granted (*r*). A similar application was made in the case of *Valentine* v. *Fawcett*, 2 Str. 1021; Ca. Temp. Hard. 138, where a *verdict* had been given for the defendant, who had avowed under the same statute, 43 Eliz. c. 2. Lord *Hardwicke*, C. J., (with whom the rest of the court concurred,) was of opinion, that a writ of inquiry ought to be granted, upon the ground, that the words of this section of the statute were sufficient to take in this case, *viz.* "that defendant shall recover treble damages, to be assessed by the same jury, *or writ to inquire of the damages*, as the same shall require." The case of *Valentine* v. *Fawcett* was recog-

(*p*) *Sheape* v. *Culpeper*, 1 Lev. 255.
(*q*) *Rees* v. *Morgan*, 3 T. R. 349. But the court in this case permitted the defendant to amend his judgment by entering a common law judgment.
(*r*) *Herbert* v. *Walters*, Ld. Raym. 59; Salk. 205; Carth. 362, *S. C.*

nized in *Dewell* v. *Marshall*, 2 Bl. R. 921, and 3 Wils. 442, in which the court awarded a supplemental writ of inquiry, after verdict found for the defendant, who had avowed under the statute 43 Eliz. c. 2.

IV. If judgment be given upon *demurrer* for the avowant or person making the cognizance : In this case the court, at the prayer of the defendant, will award a writ to inquire of the value of the distress (30), and upon return thereof the like judgment shall be given as in case I., that is to say, to recover the rent alleged to be in arrear in the avowry or cognizance, if the distress shall amount to the value of it ; if not, then to recover the value of the distress, with full costs (31). That there may not be any failure of justice, the fourth and last section of the statute directs, that in all the preceding cases, where the value of the cattle (32) distrained shall not be found to be to the full value of the arrears, the party to whom such arrears are due, his executors, or administrators, may, from time to time, distrain again for the residue. It is worthy of remark, that this statute, which defines with so much accuracy the mode of proceeding to be adopted by a defendant who succeeds in a replevin suit, has not superseded the judgment at common law, which may still be entered, if the defendant shall be so advised ; for the statute is considered as giving a further remedy, and not as extinguishing the remedy to which the defendant was entitled at common law. Under this view of the statute, it has been holden (r), that an avowant may enter a common law judgment, and also pray a writ of inquiry under the statute. It ought, however, to be observed, that the remedy provided by the statute is attended with this advantage, that the writ of inquiry awarded under it may be executed, notwithstanding the plaintiff has sued out a writ of second deliverance (s) (33) ; whereas the writ of second deliverance, if deli-

---

(r) *Baker* v. *Lade*, Carth. 254.   (s) *Cooper* v. *Sherbrooke*, 2 Wils. 116.

---

(30) The amount of the rent alleged to be due in the avowry or cognizance being admitted by the demurrer, it is not necessary in this case, as it is in the three preceding cases, that the inquiry should extend to the amount of the rent in arrear.

(31) See the form of a judgment on demurrer for an avowant, prayer of writ of inquiry, award thereof, writ, return of the value of the distress, amounting to less than the rent alleged to be due, and final judgment thereupon, in *Mounson* v. *Redshaw*, 1 Saund. 195.

(32) The preceding clauses of this statute mention *goods* and cattle distrained, but this speaks of cattle only. The omission of the word "goods" in this clause appears to be casual.

(33) The same rule holds with respect to the writ of inquiry of damages under the 21 Hen. VIII. c. 19, which may be executed after a writ of second deliverance has been served. *Pratt* v. *Rutlidge*, Salk. 95.

vered to the sheriff before return made, operates as a supersedeas to the writ of *retorno habendo*, issuing on the common law judgment (*t*).

X. *Of the Costs, and herein of the Costs in Error.*

1. *As to the Plaintiff.*—At the common law, the plaintiff obtaining judgment in replevin was not entitled to costs (*u*); but now, by the stat. of Gloucester, 6 Edw. I. c. 1, s. 2, the plaintiff is entitled to costs in all cases where he was entitled to *damages* antecedently to the statute of Gloucester; of course, therefore, the plaintiff is entitled to costs in replevin.

2. *As to the Defendant.*—At the common law, if an avowry, or cognizance, or justification, was found for the defendant in replevin, or if the plaintiff was otherwise barred, the defendant was not entitled to costs; but now, by stat. 7 Hen. VIII. c. 4, s. 3, persons making avowry, cognizance, or justification in replevin, or second deliverance, for any *rent, custom,* or *service,* if their avowry, &c. be found for them, or if the plaintiff be otherwise barred, shall recover their damages or costs, as the plaintiff should have done if he had recovered. And by stat. 21 Hen. VIII. c. 19, (which permits avowries, &c. in replevin, and second deliverance to be made by the lord, &c., alleging the land to be holden of him, without naming the tenant,) damages and costs are given to the defendants in replevin, not only in the cases provided for by the preceding stat. of 7 Hen. VIII. c. 4, but also in the cases of avowries, &c., for damage feasant, or for other rents, if such avowries, &c. be found for them, or if the plaintiff be otherwise barred. See stat. 11 Geo. II. c. 19, s. 22, as to double costs, *ante,* p. 1197. Under this statute it has been holden (*x*), that defendants were entitled to double costs upon a judgment in their favour, where they had avowed generally under the statute, although they pleaded many other avowries in various rights, from which it was suggested, that they did not distrain as landlords, but with a view merely to try a title. Upon a distress for an heriot, the defendant will be entitled to costs, but not upon a distress for an amerciament, in a leet, for not doing suit, because the statute extends only to customs and services (*y*). A replevin is not within the meaning of the statute 8 & 9 Will. III. c. 11, s. 1 (*z*), which gives costs to persons who are improperly made defendants in actions or plaint of trespass, assault, false imprisonment, or *ejectio firmæ.*

(*t*) 2 Inst. 341, and S. P. per *Holt,* C. J., in *Pratt* v. *Rutleis,* 12 Mod. 547.

(*u*) Tidd's Pr. 956, ed. 7th.

(*x*) *Johnson* v. *Lawson,* 2 Bingh. 341.

(*y*) *Porter* v. *Gray,* Cro. Eliz. 300. See *Gotobed* v. *Wool,* 6 M. & S. 128.

(*z*) *Ingle* v. *Wordsworth,* 3 Burr. 1285.

Costs in Error.—By stat. 3 Hen. VII. c. 10, reciting that writs of error were often brought for delay, it is enacted, " That if any *defendant* or *tenant*, against whom judgment is given, sue any writ of error to reverse it, in delay of execution, if judgment be affirmed, &c., the person against whom the writ of error is issued shall recover his *costs*, and *damages* for the delay and vexation." This statute applies only to cases where the judgment below is for the *plaintiff;* and subsequent statutes, *viz.* 3 Jac. I. c. 8, and 16 & 17 Car. II. c. 8, have not extended the description of persons to whom relief was meant to be given by the stat. 3 Hen. VII. c. 10. Hence, where in replevin in C. B. (*a*), the defendant made cognizance for rent in arrear, and had a verdict and judgment pursuant to the stat. 17 Car. II. c. 7, which judgment was affirmed in B. R. on a writ of error brought by the plaintiff. On application to the court of B. R. that the defendant in error might be allowed interest on the sum recovered by the judgment below, by force of the stat. 3 Hen. VII. c. 10, the court refused to grant relief, observing, that the case of *Cone* v. *Bowles*, 4 Mod. 7, 8, had settled the question, that an avowant in replevin, for whom judgment below was given, which was afterwards affirmed in error, was not within the statute. By stat. 8 & 9 Will. III. c. 11, s. 2, " Costs in error are given to the defendant, where the judgment below is for him and is affirmed on error." This statute applies only to those cases (*b*) where judgment is given on *demurrer* for defendants below; consequently, where an avowant in replevin for rent arrear had a *verdict* and judgment below, which judgment was afterwards affirmed on error; it was holden, that such defendant was not entitled to his costs under the preceding statute.

(*a*) *Golding* v. *Dias*, 10 East, 2. (*b*) *Golding* v. *Dias*, 10 East, 4.

CHAPTER XXXIV.

RESCOUS.

THE term rescous, as far as relates to the subject of this chapter (1), means the setting at liberty, against law, a person arrested by process or course of law (a). To recover a compensation for this injury, the plaintiff may bring an action of rescous, or an action on the case, against the party guilty of the rescous. The action of rescous having fallen into disuse, the usual mode of proceeding is by an action on the case, to support which, it is necessary for the plaintiff to prove;

1. The original cause of action.

2. The writ and warrant, by the production of copies of them, sworn to be true copies by a witness who has compared and examined them with the originals.

3. The manner of the arrest, in order that it may appear to the court whether the arrest was legal or not; for without a legal arrest there cannot be a rescue.

Mere words only, as if the officer says to the defendant, " that he has a warrant against him, and that he arrests him," will not constitute an arrest (b), if the defendant afterwards escapes from the officer; but if the defendant acquiesces, and goes along with the officer, this will be considered as submitting himself to the process, and as complete an arrest as if the officer had touched the

---

(a) 1 Inst. 160, b.   (b) *Genner* v. *Sparks*, Salk. 79.

---

(1) For rescous of distress, see *ante*, tit. " Distress," sect. VIII. p. 678. Where cattle of defendant's, taken as a distress *damage feasant*, in the absence of the distrainor, escaped back into the defendant's grounds, and remained for half an hour, whence they were again driven by the plaintiff, and were retaken by defendant; it was holden not to amount to a rescue, there being an abandonment of the right of freshly following. *Knowles* v. *Blake*, 5 Bingh. 499. In case of distress for rent arrear, if the distress escapes, the party may distrain de novo. *Vasper* v. *Eddows*, Ca. Temp. Holt, 257.

person of the defendant (c). An officer having two warrants *in his pocket* against the defendant (d), at the several suits of A. and B., laid his hands on the defendant, and said to him, "I arrest you by virtue of a warrant that I have;" but he did not show the defendant the warrant, *nor had it in his hand,* nor told the defendant at whose suit he arrested him, neither did the defendant demand to see the warrant, or to be informed at whose suit he was arrested. It was holden, 1st, that this arrest, without showing the warrant, and without mentioning at whose suit the defendant was arrested, was legal, and that it was not incumbent on the officer to show the warrant to the defendant until he obeyed and demanded it. 2ndly, That this arrest was legal, although the officer had not the warrant in his hand, and although he had two warrants in his pocket for the defendant; for, being under the bailiff's arrest, he was in custody for all causes for which the sheriff had made his warrant against him, although the sheriff or bailiff did not mention any specially.

By stat. 29 Car. II. c. 7, s. 6, "No person upon the Lord's day shall serve or execute any writ, process, warrant, order, judgment, or decree, (except in cases of felony or breach of the peace,) but the service of every such writ, &c. shall be void to all intents and purposes." As it is matter of public policy (e), that proceedings of the nature described in the statute should not be executed on a Sunday, the regularity or irregularity of them cannot depend on the assent of the party afterwards to waive an objection to such proceedings, because they are in themselves absolutely void by the statute. In the construction of this statute (f), it has been holden, that an arrest cannot be made on a Sunday for non-payment of a penalty by a defendant who has been convicted on a penal statute. The statute prohibits original arrests only on Sundays. Hence a defendant, who wrongfully escapes from the custody of the law, may be retaken upon a Sunday, on fresh pursuit (g), or by virtue of an escape warrant (h), which is in the nature of fresh pursuit, for it is not original process, and a commitment upon it is only the old commitment continued down. But after a voluntary escape, defendant cannot be retaken on a Sunday (i). So where A. was arrested at the suit of B., and discharged, the sheriff not knowing that there was also a detainer in his office against A. at the suit of C., and on the Sunday following the sheriff arrested A. at the suit of C., the court discharged him out of custody, considering the arrest on the Sunday, either as an original taking, which was prohibited by the statute, or as a retaking after a voluntary escape,

(c) *Horner* v. *Battyn*, B. R. H. 12 Geo. II., Bull. N. P. 62.
(d) *Hodges* v. *Marks*, Cro. Jac. 485.
(e) *Taylor* v. *Phillips*, 3 East, 155.
(f) *R.* v. *Myers*, 1 T. R. 265.
(g) Admitted in *Parker* v. *Moor*, Salk.

626.
(h) Adjudged in *Parker* v. *Moor*, Lord Raym. 1028; Salk. 626; 6 Mod. 95.
(i) *Featherstonehaugh* v. *Atkinson*, — Barnes, 373.

which was bad under the authority of the preceding case (k), where the distinction between a voluntary and a negligent escape was recognized. A person may be arrested on a Sunday on an attachment for a rescue (l). But a rule nisi for an attachment for non-payment of a sum of money, pursuant to the master's allocatur, cannot be served on a Sunday (m). If a defendant (n), after an arrest on mesne process, is rescued on his way to gaol, the only remedy which the plaintiff has, is by an action against the rescuers, since the sheriff is excusable by reason of the rescue; for on mesne process the sheriff is not bound to take the posse comitatus with him, and therefore upon such process it is a good return to return the rescous (2). In an action against the sheriff for an escape on mesne process, if he pleads a rescue, it is not incumbent on him to show that the rescue was returned (o).

4. The plaintiff must prove the damage sustained by the rescue, viz. the loss of the debt by reason of the escape of the defendant (3).

By a contract of sale, the property sold was to be paid for in ready money. The vendee induced the servant of the vendor to deliver it for a check upon a banker, by representing it to be as good as ready money; in fact, he had overdrawn his account for many months. The vendor, after keeping the check for two days, presented it at the bankers, when payment was refused. On the same day that the goods were purchased, the vendee gave a warrant

<hr/>

(k) *Atkinson* v. *Jameson*, 5 T. R. 25.
(l) Willes, 459.
(m) *M'Ilcham* v. *Smith*, 8 T. R. 86.

(n) *May* v. *Proby*, Cro. Jac. 419.
(o) *Gorges* v. *Gore*, 3 Lev. 46.

<hr/>

(2) If the party is once within the walls of the prison*, though the custody is on mesne process only, yet a rescue thence by any persons, (except the king's enemies)†, will not excuse the sheriff. So on writs of execution the sheriff cannot return a rescue; for the law supposes that the sheriff is attended with his *posse comitatus*‡. So if the defendant is brought out of prison after judgment, and before any charge in execution on a habeas corpus, and is rescued on his way to the judge's chambers, the sheriff will be answerable in an action for an escape; for it is his duty, and so he is directed by the writ, to provide for the sure and safe conduct of the party§.

(3) With respect to damages, *Holt*, C. J., in *Wilson* v. *Gary*, 6 Mod. 211, said, that the defendants were not entitled to any favour because they were guilty of a violence against the process of the law, and, therefore, this case was not to be compared to the case of a negligent escape.

* *May* v. *Proby*, 1 Roll. Rep. 441. Resolved, per *tot. Cur.*, recognized in 1 Str. 435.
† Per *Coke*, in his report of *Southcote's* case, 4 Co. 84, a.
‡ *May* v. *Proby*, 1 Roll. Rep. 441. Resolved per *tot. Cur.*
§ *Crompton* v. *Ward*, Str. 429.

of attorney to a creditor, under which judgment was immediately entered up and execution issued, and the property in question seized by the bailiff of a liberty; while it was in his custody, the vendor rescued it; it was holden (p), in an action brought against the latter by the bailiff of the liberty, for the rescue, that the question whether the contract of sale was so vitiated by fraud, as to prevent the property in the goods passing to the vendee, depended upon a question of fact which ought to have been submitted to the jury, *viz.* whether the vendee had obtained possession of the goods with a preconceived design not to pay for them! for if he had, that would be such a fraud as would vitiate the sale, and prevent the property from passing to him.

Where a draft for money was intrusted to a broker to buy exchequer bills for his principal, and the broker received the money and misapplied it by purchasing American stock and bullion, intending to abscond with it and go to America, and did accordingly abscond, but was taken before he quitted England, and thereupon surrendered to the principal the securities for the American stock and the bullion, who sold the whole and received the proceeds: it was holden (q), that the principal was entitled to withhold the proceeds from the assignees of the broker, who became bankrupt on the day on which he so received and misapplied the money.

(p) *Earl of Bristol* v. *Wilsmore*, 1 B. & C. 514.

(q) *Taylor* v. *Plumer*, 3 M. & S. 562. See *Gladstone* v. *Hadwen*, 1 M. & S. 517.

CHAPTER XXXV.

SHIPPING.

I. *Of the Ship Registry Statute,* 3 & 4 *Will. IV. c.* 55, *p.* 1213.

II. *Of Seamen's Wages and the Statutes relating thereto, viz.*
5 & 6 *Will. IV. c.* 19, *p.* 1231 ; 8 *Geo. I. c.* 24, *p.* 1234.

III. *Of the Liability of Ship-owner for Repairs, &c., p.* 1239.

I. *Of the Ship Registry Statute,* 3 & 4 *Will. IV. c.* 55 (1).

THE registering of ships appears to have been first introduced (*a*) into practice in this country by the Navigation Act, 12 Car. II. c. 18, s. 10, A. D. 1660 (*b*), but that statute only required foreign ships British owned to be registered. The stat. 7 & 8 Will. III. c. 22, s. 17, required British or plantation built ships, British owned, if intended to be employed in the plantation trade, and also prize ships, to be registered. All former laws relating to the registering of British vessels, having been repealed by the stat. 6 Geo. IV. c. 105, an act was passed, 6 Geo. IV. c. 110, which came into operation on the 5th of January, 1826.—This act has also been since repealed by stat. 3 & 4 Will. IV. c. 50, and new provisions for registering British vessels have been made by stat. 3 & 4 Will. IV. c. 55.

(*a*) See Abbott on Shipping, p. 246, n. c., 5th edit.
(*b*) The present Navigation Act is the

3 & 4 Will. IV. c. 54, amended by stat. 4 & 5 Will. IV. c. 89, s. 11.

---

(1) So much of this act as establishes rules for ascertaining the tonnage of ships has been repealed, so far as respects the merchant shipping of the United Kingdom, by stat. 5 & 6 Will. IV. c. 56. As to ships built and trading within the limits of the East India Company's charter, see stat. 3 & 4 Vict. c. 56.

The important points of difference (*b*) between the regulations now in force, and those which were in force before the stat. 6 Geo. IV. c. 110, are these: 1st, It is no longer necessary to recite the certificate of registry in a contract for the sale of a ship (*c*). 2ndly, In a bill of sale or other instrument intended to operate as a transfer of the property, it is sufficient to recite the principal contents of the certificate, and a provision is introduced with a view to prevent the effect of certain errors in the recital—see sect. 31 (2). 3dly, The indorsement on the certificate is to be made by the public officers, instead of the party transferring—sect. 34. 4thly, A mortgagee or trustee for the payment of debts, is not to be deemed an owner, (see sect. 42,) nor is his interest to be affected by the subsequent bankruptcy of the mortgagor or assignor, on the ground of reputed ownership, (see sect. 43, *Robinson* v. *M'Donnell*, 5 M. & S. 228, and *ante*, vol. 1, p. 217, n.). 5thly, The specific share of every part owner must be mentioned in the registry, except in the case of partners in trade, whose interest is to be considered as partnership property—see sect. 32. Before the statute 6 Geo. IV. c. 110, it was not necessary that the proportions in which the several owners were interested should appear on the registry (*d*). 6thly, Only thirty-two persons shall be entitled to be legal owners as tenants in common, or to be registered as such, with a provision for the equitable title of minors, legatees, creditors, &c., and also for joint stock companies—see sect. 33. Lastly, Copies of declarations and entries in the books of the Custom House are made evidence, in order to prevent the necessity of the attendance of the public officers to produce the originals. Having premised that it does not appear (*e*) that any ship is absolutely required to be registered, and that the register is necessary only for the purpose of conferring the privileges of a British ship ; I shall proceed to arrange the several enactments of the last Register (*f*) Act, as far as they fall within the limits of this work, under the following heads, suggested by the learned author of the Treatise on Shipping :—

I. *What Ships are entitled to become and continue registered Ships*, p. 1215. II. *Who may be registered as Owners*, p. 1217.

(*b*) See Abbott on Shipping, p. 26. & C. 327.
(*c*) This had been holden to be necessary under the 34 Geo. III. c. 68, s. 14. See *Biddell* v. *Leeder and Pulham*, 1 B.
(*d*) See *Exp. Jones*, 4 M. & S. 450.
(*e*) Abbott, 28.
(*f*) See 3 & 4 Will. IV. c. 55, s. 2.

---

(2) It had been holden, under the former statutes, that a mere clerical mistake would not vitiate the bill of sale, where the certificate was in effect the same with the recital, and the error was apparent on the face of the instrument. *Rolleston* v. *Smith*, 4 T. R. 161 ; but that a substantial variance between the certificate and the recital was fatal. *Westerdell v. Dale*, 7 T. R. 306.

III. *At what Place Ships shall be registered*, p. 1218. IV. *Of the Requisites of the Certificate*, p. 1218. V. *What is required on the Part of the Owners to obtain Registry*, p. 1219. VI. *Of the Transfer*, p. 1221. VII. *When and how Registry de novo is to be made, and herein in what Cases a temporary Certificate or License may be granted*, p. 1226. VIII. *What is required upon the Change of a Master*, p. 1229. IX. *Penalty for Detention of Certificate*, p. 1229. X. *What shall be sufficient Evidence of Affidavits and Books of Registry*, p. 1230.

I. *What Ships are entitled to become and continue registered, and herein of the three Instances in which Ships once registered lose their Privileges.*

No ship (*g*) shall be registered, or, having been registered, shall be deemed to be duly registered, by virtue of this act, except such as are wholly of the built of the United Kingdom (3), or of the Isle of Man, or Guernsey or Jersey; or of some of the colonies, plantations, islands, or territories in Asia, Africa, or America; or of Malta, Gibraltar, or Heligoland, which belong to his Majesty at the time of the building of such vessels; or such vessels as shall have been condemned, in any court of admiralty, as prize, or in any competent court, as forfeited for the breach of the laws made for the prevention of the slave trade, and which shall belong wholly to his Majesty's subjects duly entitled to be owners of vessels registered by virtue of this act.

(*g*) Sect. 5.

---

(3) By stat. 3 & 4 Will. IV. c. 54, s. 12, no ship shall be admitted to be a British ship unless duly registered and navigated as such; and every British registered ship shall be navigated during the whole of every voyage, (whether with a cargo or in ballast,) in every part of the world, by a master who is a British subject, and by a crew whereof three fourths at least are British seamen; and if such ship be employed in a coasting voyage from one part of the United Kingdom to another, or in a voyage between the United Kingdom and the islands of Guernsey, Jersey, Alderney, Sark, or Man, or from one of the said islands to another of them, or be employed in fishing on the coasts of the United Kingdom, or of the said islands, then the whole of the crew shall be British seamen.

*In what Cases a Ship shall cease to enjoy the Privileges of a British
Ship; 1st, In the Case of Repair in a Foreign Country.*

If a ship has been repaired (*h*) in a foreign country, and the
repairs exceed 20*s*. for every ton, unless such repairs shall have been
necessary, by reason of extraordinary damage sustained by the
vessel, during her absence from his Majesty's dominions, to enable
her to perform the voyage in which she shall have been engaged,
and to return to some place in his Majesty's dominions. In this
case, upon arrival at a port in his Majesty's dominions, the master,
upon the first entry, is to report to the collector and comptroller, that the vessel has been so repaired, under penalty of 20*s*.
per ton, and in the event of its being proved, to the satisfaction
of the commissioners, that the vessel was seaworthy when she last
departed from his Majesty's dominions, and that no greater quantity of repairs had been done than was necessary, the commissioners
may direct the collector and comptroller to certify, on the certificate
of registry, that it has been proved that the privileges of the vessel
have not been forfeited.

2. If Ship be Stranded or not Seaworthy.

If any ship (*i*) registered under the authority of this or any other
act, shall be deemed or declared to be stranded or unseaworthy, and
incapable of being recovered or repaired to the advantage of the
owners, and shall for such reasons be sold, by order or decree of any
competent court, for the benefit of the owners or other persons
interested therein, the same shall be deemed to be a ship lost or
broken up to all intents and purposes within the meaning of this
act, and shall never again be entitled to the privileges of a British
built ship for any purposes of trade or navigation.

3. In the Case of Capture.

No British ship (*k*) which has been or shall hereafter be captured
by and become prize to an enemy, or sold to foreigners, shall again
be entitled to the privileges of a British ship ; provided that nothing
contained in this act shall extend to prevent the registering of any
ship which shall be condemned in any court of admiralty as prize of
war, or in any competent court, for breach of laws made for the
prevention of the slave trade.

(*h*) Sect. 7.   (*i*) Sect. 8.   (*k*) Sect. 9.

II. *Who may be registered as Owners.*

The owners must be subjects of Great Britain (*l*). No foreigners may, directly or indirectly, have any part or share in the ship (*m*). No person may be an owner of any ship authorized to be registered, who has taken the oath of allegiance to any foreign state except under the terms of some capitulation, unless he shall afterwards become a denizen or naturalized subject of the United Kingdom; nor any person usually residing in any country not under the dominion of his Majesty, unless he be a member of some British factory, or agent for or partner in a house or partnership actually carrying on trade, in Great Britain or Ireland (*n*). The statute (*o*) considers the property in every vessel, of which there are more owners than one, as divided into sixty-four parts, and requires the number of sixty-fourth parts held by each owner, and his name, to be mentioned; and no person is entitled to be registered as an owner in respect of any proportion which is not an integral sixty-fourth part : and upon the first registry, the owners who take (*p*) and subscribe the declaration are to declare (*q*) the number of parts held by each owner, which are to be registered accordingly. Where the property cannot, by division, be reduced into any number of integral sixty-fourth parts, the owners of the fractional parts above such number of integral sixty-fourth parts as the property can be reduced into, may transfer the same, one to another, or jointly to any new owner, by memorandum upon their bills of sale, or by fresh bill of sale, without a stamp; and the right of the owners of such fractional part will not be affected by not having been registered. The foregoing regulation does not bind the partners (*r*) in any house carrying on trade in any part of his Majesty's dominions; for they may hold any vessel or any share, in the name of such house, as joint owners, without distinguishing the proportionate interest of each, which is to be taken to be partnership property, and governed by the same rules, both in law and equity, as govern partnership property in all other goods and chattels; (but the names of all the partners must appear on the ship's register) (*s*). No greater number than thirty-two persons (*t*) can be legal owners at one and the same time as tenants in common, or be registered as such; but this enactment does not affect the equitable title of minors, legatees, or creditors exceeding that number, represented by or holding from persons within that number registered as legal owners. And in the

(*l*) See the end of sect. 5.
(*m*) See the form of the declaration in sect. 13.
(*n*) See sect. 12.
(*o*) See the form in sect. 2, and see sect. 32.

(*p*) Sic.
(*q*) Sect. 32.
(*r*) Sect. 32, in fine.
(*s*) *Slater* v. *Willis*, 1 Beavan, 354.
(*t*) Sect. 33.

case of a joint stock company, for the purpose of owning a vessel, where such company have elected any number, not less than three, of their members to be trustees, they or any three of them may, with the permission of the commissioners of customs, make and subscribe the declaration; but in this case the name and description of the company must be stated in the register, instead of the names and description of the owners.

III. *At what Place Ships shall be registered.*

The statute (*u*) requires the registry to be made, and certificate granted, at the port or place to which the ship belongs, (with the exception of ships condemned as prizes in Guernsey, Jersey, or Man, as to which a special provision is made in the thirtieth section of the act;) and every registry and certificate not so granted is declared void, unless authorized by an order in writing under the hands of the commissioners of customs. Ships shall be deemed to belong to some port (*x*) at or near which some or one of the owners, who shall make and subscribe the declaration required before registry, shall reside. No ship (*y*) which shall be taken and condemned as prize or forfeiture shall be registered in the islands of Guernsey, Jersey, or the Isle of Man, although belonging to his Majesty's subjects residing in those islands, or in some one or other of them; but the same shall be registered either at Southampton, Weymouth, Exeter, Plymouth, Falmouth, Liverpool, or Whitehaven, by the collector and comptroller at such ports respectively, who are hereby authorized and required to register such ship, and to gran a certificate thereof, in the form and under the regulations and restrictions in this act contained.

IV. *Of the Requisites of the Certificate—s. 2.*

The act requires that the following particulars should be enumerated in the certificate: 1st, the title of the act; 2ndly, the names, occupation, and residence of the subscribing owners, and that they have made and subscribed the declaration required; that they have declared that they, together with the non-subscribing owners, (setting forth their names, &c.) are owners of the ship in the proportions specified; 3dly, the name of the ship, place to which she belongs, burthen, master's name, when and where built, or whether she has

(*u*) Sect. 10.　　　(*x*) Sect. 11.　　　(*y*) Sect. 30.

been condemned as prize, referring to the certificate of builder or judge, or of last registry then delivered up to be cancelled. It must then state, that the surveying officer (naming him) has certified the number of decks, &c.; that the subscribing owners having agreed to the description and given security, the vessel has been registered at the port of   on such a day. It is then signed by the proper officers, and on the back an account of the parts held by each owner must be given in the form prescribed, and must also be signed by the proper officers.

V. *What is required on the Part of the Owners to obtain Registry.*

No registry (z) shall henceforth be made, or certificate granted, until the following declaration be made and subscribed, before the persons authorized to make registry and grant certificate respectively, by the owner of such ship, if such ship belongs to one person only, or in case there shall be two joint owners, then by both, if both shall be resident within twenty miles of the port or place where such register is required; or by one, if one or both shall be resident at a greater distance from such port or place; or if the number of owners exceed two, then by the greater part; if the greater number of them shall be resident within twenty miles of such port or place as aforesaid, not in any case exceeding three of such owners; unless a greater number shall be desirous to join in making and subscribing the declaration; or, by one of such owners, if all or all except one shall be resident at a greater distance: then follows the form of declaration, and lastly a provision as to the person, by whom the declaration is to be made, and the form of such declaration, where the ship belongs to any corporate body in the United Kingdom. In case (a) the required number of joint owners of any ship shall not personally attend to make and subscribe the declaration (b), then such owner, as shall personally attend and make and subscribe the declaration, shall further declare that the part owners, then absent, are not resident within twenty miles of such port or place, and have not, to the best of his knowledge or belief, wilfully absented themselves, in order to avoid making the declaration, or are prevented by illness from attending. At the time (c) of obtaining the certificate of registry, sufficient security shall be given by bond to his Majesty, by the master and such of the owners as shall personally attend, such security to be approved of and taken by the persons authorized to make registry and grant certificate, at the port or place in which such certificate shall be granted, in penalties varying

(z) Sect. 13.
(a) Sect. 14.

(b) See the form in sect. 13.
(c) Sect. 20.

from £100 to £1000, according to the tonnage, with a condition, that such certificate shall not be sold, lent, or otherwise disposed of, to any other person, and that the same shall be solely made use of for the service of the ship for which it is granted; and that in case such ship shall be lost or taken by the enemy, burnt, or broken up, or otherwise prevented from returning to the port to which she belongs, or shall, on any account, have lost or forfeited the privileges of a British ship, or shall have been seized and legally condemned for illicit trading, or shall have been taken in execution for debt and sold by due process of law, or shall have been sold to the crown; or shall, under any circumstances, have been registered de novo, the certificate, if preserved, shall be delivered up, within one month after the arrival of the master in any port or place in his Majesty's dominions, to the collector and comptroller of some port in Great Britain, or the Isle of Man, or the British plantations, or to the governor, or lieutenant-governor, or commander-in-chief for the time being, of the islands of Guernsey or Jersey; and if any foreigner, or any person for his use and benefit, shall purchase, or otherwise become entitled to, the whole or any part of or any interest in such ship, and the same shall be within the limits of any port of Great Britain, Guernsey, Jersey, Man, or the British colonies, plantations, islands, or territories, then the certificate of registry shall, within seven days after such purchase or transfer of property in such ship, be delivered up to the persons authorized to make registry and grant certificate at such port or place respectively; and if such ship shall be in any foreign port, when such purchase or transfer of interest or property shall take place, then the same shall be delivered up to the British consul, or other chief British officer, resident at or nearest to such foreign port: or if such ship shall be at sea, when such purchase or transfer of interest or property shall take place, then the same shall be delivered up to the British consul, or other chief British officer, at the foreign port or place in or at which the master or other person having or taking the charge or command of such ship shall first arrive after such purchase or transfer of property at sea, immediately after his arrival in such foreign port; but if such master, or other person who had the command thereof at the time of such purchase or transfer of property at sea, shall not arrive at a foreign port, but shall arrive at some port of Great Britain, Guernsey, Jersey, Man, or his Majesty's colonies, plantations, islands, or territories, then the same shall be delivered up, in manner aforesaid, within fourteen days after the arrival of such ship, or of the persons who had the command thereof, in any port of Great Britain, Guernsey, Jersey, Man, or any of his Majesty's colonies, plantations, islands, or territories; provided, that if it shall happen that at the time of registry, the same shall be at any other port than the port to which the ship belongs, so that the master of such ship cannot attend at the port of registry to join with the owners in such bond, it shall be lawful for him to give a separate bond, to the like effect, at the port where the ship may then be, and the collector and comptroller of such other port shall transmit such bond to the collector and comptroller of the port where such ship is to be registered, and such bond and the bond also given by the owners shall together be of the same effect against the master and owners, or either of them, as if they had bound themselves jointly and severally in one bond. Every person (d) who shall apply for a certificate, is required to produce, to the persons authorized to grant such certificate, a true and full account, under the hand of the builder of such ship, of the proper denomination, and of the time when and the place where such ship was built; and also an exact account of the tonnage of such ship, together with the name of the first purchasers thereof, (which account such builder is hereby directed and required to give under his hand, on the same being demanded by such persons so applying for a certificate,) and shall also make and subscribe a declaration before the persons authorized to grant such certificate, that the ship, for which such certificate is required, is the same with that which is so described by the builder.

VI. *Of the Transfer; ss.* 31, 34, 35, 36, 37, 41, 42, 43.

When and so often as the property (e) in any ship or any part thereof belonging to any of his Majesty's subjects shall after registry thereof be sold to any other of his Majesty's subjects, the same shall be transferred by bill of sale or other instrument in writing, containing a recital of the certificate of registry, or the principal contents thereof; otherwise such transfer shall not be valid for any purpose, either in law or equity: provided that no bill of sale shall be deemed void by reason of any error in such recital, or by the recital of any former certificate of registry instead of the existing certificate: provided the identity of the ship therein intended be effectually proved thereby.

The statute does not necessarily require a bill of sale; an instrument in writing, reciting the certificate of registry, is enough; nor does it require such instrument to bear the signature of the party conveying. Hence, where, in consequence of injury received by a ship during the voyage, she was sold by auction, under the authority of a letter from the master, and transferred by an instrument, executed by the auctioneer, *under seal*, but in other respects complying with the requisites of the statute, the proceeds of the sale having been received by the owner, that

(d) Sect. 25.   (e) Sect. 31.

was holden (*f*) to be a sufficient ratification by him of the act of the master in selling her, and such ratification was holden to be sufficient to give validity to the transfer; for although the instrument was the deed of the auctioneer, and not of the principal, it was still a writing, and might have the effect of a written transfer by the principal, as well as that of the deed of the agent.

No bill of sale (*g*), or other instrument in writing, shall be valid to pass property in any ship, or in any share thereof, or for any other purpose, until such bill of sale or instrument in writing shall have been produced to the collector and comptroller of the port at which such ship is registered, or to the collector and comptroller of any other port at which she is about to be registered de novo, as the case may be; nor until such collector and comptroller respectively shall have entered in the book of registry, or in the book of intended registry, of such ship, as the case may be (and which they are respectively hereby required to do upon the production of the bill of sale or other instrument for that purpose); the name, residence, and description of the vendor or mortgagor, or of each vendor or mortgagor, if more than one; the number of shares transferred; the name, residence, and description of the purchaser or mortgagee, or of each purchaser or mortgagee, if more than one; and the date of the bill of sale, or other instrument, and of the production of it: and if such ship is not about to be registered de novo, the collector and comptroller of the port where such ship is registered, shall, and they are hereby required to indorse the particulars of such bill of sale, or other instrument, on the certificate of registry of the ship, when the same shall be produced to them for the purpose in manner following; *viz.*

Custom-house, [*port and date, name, residence, and description of vendor or mortgagor*] has transferred by [*bill of sale or other instrument*] dated [*date, number of shares*] to [*name, residence, and description of purchaser or mortgagee*].

A. B., Collector.
C. D., Comptroller.

And forthwith to give notice thereof to the commissioners of customs; and in case the collector and comptroller shall be desired so to do, and the bill of sale or other instrument shall be produced to them for that purpose, then the collector and comptroller are hereby required to certify, by indorsement upon the bill of sale, or other instrument, that the particulars before mentioned have been so entered in the book of registry, and indorsed upon the certificate of registry. When the particulars of any bill of sale (*h*), or other instrument, by which any ship or any share thereof shall be transferred, shall have been so entered in the book of registry, the bill of

(*f*) *Hunter v. Parker*, 7 M. & W. 322.   (*g*) Sect. 34.   (*h*) Sect. 35.

sale or other instrument shall be valid and effectual to pass the property thereby intended to be transferred as against all and every
person and to all intents and purposes, except as against such subsequent purchasers and mortgagees who shall first procure the indorsement to be made upon the certificate of registry of such ship,
in manner hereinafter mentioned.   When and after the particulars
of any bill of sale (i) or other instrument, by which any ship or any
share thereof shall be transferred, shall have been so entered in the
book of registry, as aforesaid, the collector and comptroller shall not
enter in the book of registry the particulars of any other bill of sale,
or instrument purporting to be a transfer by the same vendor or
mortgagor of the same ship, or share thereof, to any other person,
unless thirty days shall elapse from the day on which the particulars
of the former bill of sale, or other instrument, were entered in the
book of registry; or in case the ship was absent from the port to
which she belonged, at the time when the particulars of such
former bill of sale, or other instrument, were entered in the book
of registry, then unless thirty days shall have elapsed from the
day on which the ship arrived at the port, to which the same belonged ; and in case the particulars of two or more such bills of sale,
or other instruments, as aforesaid, shall at any time have been
entered in the book of registry of the said ship, the collector and
comptroller shall not enter in the book of registry the particulars
of any other bill of sale, or other instrument, as aforesaid, unless
thirty days shall in like manner have elapsed from the day on which
the particulars of the last of such bills of sale, or other instrument,
were entered in the books of registry, or from the day on which the
ship or vessel arrived at the port to which she belonged, in case of
her absence as aforesaid ; and in every case where there shall at any
time happen to be two or more transfers by the same owner, of the
same property, in any ship entered in the book of registry, the
collector and comptroller are hereby required to indorse upon the
certificate of registry of such ship, the particulars of that bill of
sale, or other instrument, under which the person claims property,
who shall produce the certificate of registry for that purpose, within
thirty days next after the entry of his bill of sale, or other instrument, in the book of registry, as aforesaid, or within thirty days
next after the return of the said ship to the port to which she
belongs, in case of her absence at the time of such entry ; and in
case no person shall produce the certificate of registry, within either
of the said spaces of thirty days, then it shall be lawful for the collector and comptroller, and they are hereby required to indorse upon
the certificate of registry, the particulars of the bill of sale, or
other instrument, to such person as shall first produce the certificate of registry, for that purpose; it being the true intent and
meaning of this act, that the several purchasers and mortgagees

(i) Sect. 36.

of such ship, or share thereof, when more than one appear to claim
the same property, shall have priority one over the other, not according to the respective times when the particulars of the bill of
sale, or other instrument, by which such property was transferred to
them, were entered in the book of registry, but according to the
time when the indorsement is made upon the certificate of registry:
provided, that if the certificate of registry shall be lost or mislaid,
or shall be detained by any person, so that the indorsement cannot
in due time be made thereon, and proof thereof shall be made by
the purchaser or mortgagee, or his known agent, to the satisfaction
of the commissioners, the commissioners may grant such further
time as to them shall appear necessary, for the recovery of the certificate of registry, or for the registry de novo of the said ship or
vessel, under the provisions of this act; and thereupon the collector
and comptroller shall make a memorandum in the book of registers,
of the further time so granted, and during such time no other bill
of sale shall be entered for the transfer of the same ship, or the
share thereof.

If the certificate of registry (k) of such ship shall be produced to
the collector and comptroller of any port where she may then be
after any such bill of sale shall have been recorded at the port to
which she belongs, together with such bill of sale containing a
notification of such record, signed by the collector and comptroller
of such port, as before directed; the collector and comptroller of
such other port may indorse on such certificate of registry (being
required so to do,) the transfer mentioned in such bill of sale, and
such collector and comptroller shall give notice thereof to the collector and comptroller of the port to which such ship belongs, who
shall record the same in like manner as if they had made such
indorsement themselves, but inserting the name of the port at which
such indorsement was made; provided, that the collector and
comptroller of such other port shall first give notice to the collector
and comptroller of the port to which such ship belongs, of such
requisitions made to them to indorse the certificate of registry;
and the collector and comptroller of the port, to which such ship
belongs, shall thereupon send information to the collector and
comptroller of such other port, whether any and what other bill
or bills of sale have been recorded in the book of registry of such
ship, and the collector and comptroller of such other port, having
such information, shall proceed in manner directed by this act in all
respects to the indorsing of the certificate of registry, as they would
do if such port were the port to which such vessel belonged. If the
ship (l), or the share of any owner who may be out of the kingdom,
shall be sold in his absence by his known agent, under his directions,
express or implied, and acting for his interest, and such agent, who
shall have executed a bill of sale to the purchaser of the whole or

(k) Sect. 37.   (l) Sect. 41.

any share, shall not have received a legal power to execute the same, the commissioners of customs, upon proof to their satisfaction of the fair dealings of the parties, may permit such transfer to be registered, if registry de novo be necessary, or recorded and indorsed, as if such legal power had been produced : and if any bill of sale cannot be produced, or if by time, absence, or death of parties, it cannot be proved that a bill of sale for any shares had been executed, and registry de novo shall have become necessary, the commissioners, upon proof of fair dealing, may permit a registry de novo, as if such bill of sale had been produced, *provided* that good security shall be given to produce a legal power or bill of sale within a reasonable time, or to abide the future claims of the absent owner, and such bond shall be available for the protection of the interest of the party whose property has been so transferred, until he shall receive full indemnity for any loss.

When any transfer of any ship or share is made as a *security* (m) for the payment of a debt, either by mortgage or assignment to a trustee for sale, the collector or comptroller of the port, where the vessel is registered, shall, in the entry of the book of registry, and also in the indorsement on the certificate, express that such transfer was made only as a security for the payment of debts, or by way of mortgage, or to that effect; and the person to whom the transfer is made, or any other person claiming under him as mortgagee or trustee only, shall *not*, by reason thereof, *be deemed the owner* of such vessel or share; nor shall the person making the transfer *be deemed*, by reason thereof, *to have ceased to be an owner*, any more than if no such transfer had been made, except so far as may be necessary for the purpose of rendering the vessel or share so transferred available, by sale or otherwise, for the payment of the debt (4). The mortgagor does not cease to be owner, and the

(m) Sect. 42.

---

(4) Before the statute 6 Geo. IV. c. 110, a difference in opinion had existed on the question, whether the mortgagee of a ship was to be deemed in law the owner of it, entitled to the benefits, and liable to the burdens which belong to that character, before he took possession. See Abbott, 17, and the following cases there referred to : *Chinnery* v. *Blackburne*, 1 H. Bl. 117, n.; *S. C.* by the name of *Chinnery* v. *Blackman*, 3 Doug. 391; *Jackson* v. *Vernon*, 1 H. Bl. 114; *Westerdell* v. *Dale*, 7 T. R. 306; *Twentyman* v. *Hart*, 1 Stark. 366; *Annett* v. *Carstairs and another*, 3 Campb. 354. In *Young* v. *Brander*, 8 East, 10, and *M'Iver* v. *Humble*, 16 East, 169, the party had made a transfer of his interest, but, for want of compliance with certain forms, the legal ownership remained with him ; that, however, was not deemed sufficient to make him liable for the ship's debts. See also *Briggs* v. *Wilkinson*, 7 B. & C. 30,

mortgagee has a distinct interest to the extent, *primá facie*, of the value mortgaged (*n*). When any transfer (*o*) of any ship or share shall have been made as a security for the payment of any debt, either by mortgage or assignment, as aforesaid, and such transfer shall have been duly registered, the interest of the mortgagee or other assignee shall not be affected by any act of bankruptcy committed by such mortgagor or assignor, after the time of the registering the mortgage or assignment, notwithstanding such mortgagor or assignor, at the time he shall become bankrupt, shall have in his possession, order, and disposition, and shall be the reputed owner of the ship or share, but that such mortgage or assignment shall be preferred to any right, claim, or interest, which may belong to the assignee of such bankrupt.

VII. *When and how Registry de novo is to be made; sects.* 11, 26, 28, 38, 39; *and herein, in what Cases a temporary Certificate or License may be granted.*

Every ship (*p*) shall be deemed to belong to some port at or near to which some or one of the owners, who shall make and subscribe the declaration required by this act before registry be made, shall reside; and whenever such owner shall have transferred all his share in such ship, the same shall be registered *de novo* before such ship shall depart from the port to which she shall then belong, or from any other port which shall be in the same part of the United Kingdom, or the same colony, plantation, island, or territory as the said port shall be in; provided, that if the owner cannot, in sufficient time, comply with the requisites of this act, so that registry may be made before it shall be necessary for such ship to depart upon another voyage, the collector and comptroller of the port where such ship may then be, may certify, upon the back of the existing certificate of registry, that the same is to remain in force for the voyage upon which the ship is then about to sail; provided also, that if any ship shall be built in any of the colonies, plantations, islands, or territories in Asia, Africa, or America, to his Majesty

---

(*n*) *Irving* v. *Richardson*, 2 B. & Ad.   (*o*) Sect. 43.
193.   (*p*) Sect. 11.

---

and *Reeve* v. *Davis*, 1 Ad. & Ell. 312; 3 Nev. & M. 873, and *post*, p. 1239, to the same effect. By the mortgage of a ship, accruing freight was holden to pass to the mortgagee, notwithstanding 6 Geo. IV. c. 110, s. 45. *Dean* v. *M'Ghie*, 4 Bingh. 45.

belonging, for owners residing in the United Kingdom, and the master, or the agent for the owner, shall have produced to the collector and comptroller of the port, at or near to which such ship was built, the certificate of the builder required by this act, and shall have made and subscribed a declaration before such collector and comptroller of the names and descriptions of the principal owners, and that she is the identical ship mentioned in such certificate of the builder, and that no foreigner, to the best of his knowledge and belief, has any interest therein, the collector and comptroller of such port shall cause such ship to be surveyed and measured in like manner as is directed for the purpose of registering any ship, and shall give the master a certificate under their hands and seals purporting to be under the authority of this act, and stating when and where and by whom such ship was built, the description, tonnage, and other particulars required on registry of any ship, and such certificate shall have all the force of a certificate of registry, under this act, during the term of two years, unless such ship shall sooner arrive at some place in the United Kingdom, and such collector and comptroller shall transmit a copy of such certificate to the commissioners of his Majesty's customs.

If the certificate of registry (*q*) of any ship *shall be lost or mislaid,* so that the same cannot be found for the use of such ship when needful, and proof thereof shall be made to the satisfaction of the commissioners of his Majesty's customs, such commissioners shall and may permit such ship to be registered de novo, and a certificate thereof to be granted ; provided, that if such ship be absent and far distant from the port to which she belongs, or by reason of the absence of the owner, or of any impediment, registry of the same cannot then be made in sufficient time, such commissioners shall and may grant a license for the present use of such ship, which license shall, for the time and to the extent specified therein, and no longer, be of the same force and virtue as a certificate of registry granted under this act ; provided, that before such registry de novo be made, the owners and masters shall give bond to the commissioners in such sum as to them shall seem fit, with a condition, that if the certificate of registry shall at any time afterwards be found, the same shall be forthwith delivered to the proper officers of his Majesty's customs to be cancelled, and that no illegal use has been or shall be made thereof with his privity or knowledge ; and further, that before any such license shall be granted as aforesaid, the master of such ship shall also make and subscribe a declaration that the same has been registered as a British ship, naming the port where and the time when such registry was made, and all the particulars contained in the certificate thereof, to the best of his knowledge and belief ; and shall also give such bond and with the

(*q*) Sect. 26.

same condition as is before mentioned; provided, that before any such license shall be granted, such ship shall be surveyed in like manner as if a registry de novo were about to be made thereof, and the certificate of such survey shall be preserved by the collector and comptroller of the port to which such ship shall belong : and, in virtue thereof, it shall be lawful for the said commissioners, and they are hereby required, to permit such ship to be registered after her departure, whenever the owner shall personally attend to take (r) and subscribe the declaration required by this act before registry be made, and shall also comply with all other requisites of this act, except so far as relates to the bond to be given by the master of such ship ; which certificate of registry the said commissioners shall and may transmit to the collector and comptroller of any other port, to be by them given to the master of such ship upon his giving such bond and delivering up the license which had been granted for the then present use of such ship. The 27th section authorizes a registry de novo in the case of a wilful detention of the certificate, by the master or other person, and conviction on absconding. See *post*, p. 1229, 1230.

If any ship (s), after she shall have been registered pursuant to the directions of this act, shall in any manner be altered so as not to correspond with all the particulars contained in the certificate of her registry, in such case such ship shall be registered de novo in manner hereinbefore required, as soon as she returns to the port to which she belongs, or to any other port which shall be in the same part of the United Kingdom, or in the colony, plantation, island, or territory, as the said port shall be in, on failure whereof such ship shall be, to all intents and purposes, considered a ship not duly registered. If it become necessary to register (t) any ship de novo, and any share of such ship shall have been sold, since she was last registered, and the transfer of such share shall not have been recorded and indorsed in manner hereinbefore directed, the bill of sale thereof shall be produced to the collector and comptroller, who are to make registry of such ship: otherwise such sale shall not be noticed in such registry de novo, except as hereinafter excepted ; provided, that upon the future production of such bill of sale and of the existing certificate of registry, such transfer shall and may be recorded and indorsed as well after such registry de novo as before. If upon any change of property (u) in any ship, the owner shall desire to have the same registered de novo, although not required by this act, and the owner or proper number of owners shall attend at the custom-house at the port to which such ship belongs for that purpose, it shall be lawful for the collector and comptroller at such port to make registry de novo of such ship at

(r) Sic.
(s) Sect. 28.

(t) Sect. 38.
(u) Sect. 39.

the same port, and to gran a certificate thereof, the several requisites of this act being first duly complied with.

VIII. *What is required upon the Change of a Master.*

When the master (x) or other person having or taking the charge or command of a ship registered, shall be changed, the master or owner shall deliver to the person authorized to make registry and grant certificates at the port where the change shall take place, the certificate of registry belonging to the ship, who shall thereupon indorse and subscribe a memorandum of such change, and shall forthwith give notice of the same to the proper officer of the port or place where such ship was last registered, who shall likewise make a memorandum of the same in the book of registers, and shall forthwith give notice thereof to the commissioners of customs; provided that before the name of such new master shall be indorsed on the certificate of registry, he shall give a bond in the like penalties and under the same conditions as are contained in the bond required to be given at the time of registry.

IX. *Penalty for Detention of Certificate—s. 27.*

In case any person (y), who shall have received or obtained, by any means or for any purpose, the certificate of registry, (whether such person shall claim to be the master or owner or one of the owners or not,) shall *wilfully* (z) detain and refuse to deliver up the same to the *proper* (a) officers of the customs for the *purposes* of the ship, as occasion shall require, or to the person having the actual command, possession, and management of such ship as ostensible and reputed master or owner, such last mentioned person may complain on oath of such detainer and refusal, to any justice of the peace residing near to the place where such detainer and refusal shall be in Great Britain or Ireland, or to any member of the supreme court of justice, or any justice of the peace in the islands of Jersey, Guernsey, or Man, or in any colony, plantation, island, or territory to his Majesty belonging, in Asia, Africa, or America, or in Malta, Gibraltar, or Heligoland, where such detainer and re-

---

(x) Sect. 21.
(y) Sect. 27.
(z) See *Bowen* v. *Fox*, 10 B. & C. 41.

(a) See *R.* v. *Walsh*, 1 A. & E. 481; 3 Nev. & M. 632.

fusal shall be in any of the places last mentioned; and on such complaint the justice or other magistrate is required, by warrant under his hand and seal, to cause the person so complained against to be brought before him to be examined, touching such detainer and refusal; and if it shall appear, on examination of such person, or otherwise, that the certificate of registry is not lost or mislaid, but is wilfully detained by the said person, such person shall be thereof convicted, and shall forfeit and pay the sum of £100; and, on failure of payment, he shall be committed to the common gaol, there to remain, without bail or mainprize, for such time as the said justice or other magistrate shall in his discretion deem proper, not being less than three months, nor more than twelve months; and the justice or other magistrate is required to certify the detainer, refusal, and conviction, to the person who granted such certificate of registry, who shall, on the terms and conditions of law being complied with, make *registry* de novo, and grant a certificate, notifying on the back of such certificate, the ground upon which the ship was so registered de novo: and if the person who shall have detained and refused to deliver up such certificate of registry as aforesaid, or shall be verily believed to have detained the same, shall have absconded, so that the said warrant of the justice or other magistrate cannot be executed upon him, and proof thereof shall be made to the satisfaction of the commissioners of his Majesty's customs, they may permit such ship to be registered de novo, or otherwise, in their discretion, grant a license for the present use of such ship in like manner as is hereinbefore provided in the case wherein the certificate of registry is lost or mislaid.

A conviction under the foregoing section must state for what purpose the certificate was required (*b*).

X. *Evidence—what shall be sufficient Evidence of Affidavits and Books of Registry.*

Great inconvenience having arisen from registering officers being served with subpoenas requiring them to produce the oaths, or declarations and books of registry, the legislature has deemed it expedient to dispense with their attendance, and for that purpose has enacted (*c*), that the collector and comptroller of his Majesty's customs, at any port or place, and persons acting for them respectively, shall, upon every reasonable request by any persons, produce and exhibit for inspection and examination, any oath or declaration

(*b*) Per *Denman*, C. J., and *Williams*, J., in *R.* v. *Walsh*, 1 A. & E. 481; 3 Nev. & M. 632.

(*c*) Sect. 40.

sworn or made by any owner or proprietor, and also any register or entry in any book of registry required by this act to be made or kept relative to any ship, and shall, upon every reasonable request by any persons, permit them to take a copy or an extract thereof respectively, and that the copy of such oath or declaration, register or entry, shall, upon being proved to be a true copy, be received as evidence, upon every trial at law, without the production of the original, and without the testimony or attendance of any collector or comptroller, or other persons acting for them respectively, in all cases, as fully and to all intents and purposes *as such original* if produced by any collector and comptroller, or other persons acting for them.

For regulations as to the carriage of passengers from the United Kingdom, see stat. 5 & 6 Will. IV. c. 53. See also stat. 7 Will. IV. & 1 Vict. c. 89, intituled, "An Act to amend the Laws relating to burning or destroying Buildings and Ships."

II. *Of Seamen's Wages, and the Statutes relating thereto, viz.* *5 & 6 Will. IV. c. 19, 8 Geo. I. c. 24.*

THE legislature, in its wisdom, has thought fit to make several provisions relating to seamen employed in merchant ships, for the better securing the wages of the seamen, and to guard against desertion. Seamen employed in merchant ships are usually hired at a certain sum, either by the month or for the voyage (*d*). By stat. 5 & 6 Will. IV. c. 19, intituled, An "Act to amend and consolidate the Laws relating to the Merchant Seamen of the United Kingdom, and for forming and maintaining a Register of all the Men engaged in that Service," masters of ships, trading to parts beyond the seas, or of any British registered ship of the burden of 80 tons or upwards, employed in any of the fisheries of the United Kingdom, or in trading coastwise or otherwise, are prohibited (*e*) from carrying any seaman or other person as one of their crew (apprentices excepted) to sea upon any voyage, without first agreeing with them for their wages ; and this agreement must, 1st, be in writing (5) ; 2dly, it

(*d*) Abbott, 432, ed. 5th, 1827.   (*e*) Sect. 2.

---

(5) The statutes relating to seamen's wages do not declare that a verbal agreement shall be void, but impose a penalty on the master, if there be not a written agreement. When a written agreement is made, it becomes the only evidence of the contract between the parties, and a mariner cannot recover any money agreed to be given in reward for his

must declare the monthly or other wages which each seaman is to have; 3dly, the capacity in which the seaman is to act; 4thly, the nature of the voyage in which the ship is intended to be employed; 5thly, the day and month of the year in which the agreement shall be made; 6thly, it must be signed by the master in the first instance, and by the seamen respectively at the port or place where such seamen shall be respectively shipped; 7thly, the agreement must be read over in the presence of the attesting witness before the seaman is required to sign the same. Masters offending against these provisions, are made liable (*f*) to a penalty of £10 for every seaman carried out, without having entered into the requisite agreement; the penalty to be recoverable (*g*) by information before J. P., and to be paid, one moiety to the informer, and the residue divided between Greenwich Hospital and the Merchant Seamen's Hospital, at the port to which the ship belongs. The 11th section of the act regulates the periods within which the wages are to be paid. The penalty imposed on masters for disobedience to this regulation, is recoverable by the same method as the wages (*h*). Seamen, by entering into or signing the agreement, are not to be deprived of using any lawful means for the recovery of wages against the ship, master, or owners (*i*). The 15th section gives the seaman a summary remedy by complaint upon oath to a J. P. for wages not exceeding £20; and the 16th section deprives the seaman of costs in cases where he proceeds for wages recoverable before a J. P. in any court of admiralty or court of record. In all cases where it may be necessary to produce the written agreement in court, no obligation shall lie on the mariner to produce the same, but on the master or owner;

(*f*) Sect. 4.   (*h*) Sect. 11.
(*g*) Sect. 53.   (*i*) Sect. 5.

---

service, which is not specified in the articles. Abbott, 440. A sailor brought an action against the master of a ship, and declared on an agreement, whereby it was stipulated, that the sailor should have a certain sum per month during a voyage from London to Africa, and thence to the West Indies, *and also so much money as should be the average price of a negro slave in the West Indies.* In the ship's articles no mention was made of the money to be paid to the plaintiff as the average price of the negro slave. It was holden, that the additional perquisites of the average price of a negro slave could only be considered as wages, and, therefore, ought to been inserted in the written agreement. *White* v. *Wilson,* 2 Bos. & Pul. 116. In like manner it has been holden, that a sail-maker, serving in a ship belonging to the East India Company, cannot recover upon a promise to pay him a monthly sum beyond the wages mentioned in the ship's articles, which had been signed by him as a sail-maker. *Elsworth and Wife* v. *Woolmore,* London Sittings, December, 1803, before Lord *Alvanley,* C. J. C. B., Abbott, 440. See a note of this case, 2 Esp. N. P. C. 84.

and no mariner shall fail in any action, &c. for the recovery of
wages, for want of such agreement being produced (k). It is not
necessary for the seaman to give the captain notice to produce this
agreement (l).

The penalties imposed on seamen for refusing to join the ship, or
absenting themselves without leave, or desertion, are as follow :—

1. A seaman (m) refusing to join the ship or absenting himself
therefrom, may be committed to gaol by a J. P.; provided, that in
case such seaman shall consent to join the ship he may at the
master's request be conveyed on board the ship.

2. Any mariner (n) absenting himself from his ship, without
leave from the master, &c., shall, for every such day's absence,
forfeit two days' pay.

3. Any seaman (n) who, after having signed such agreement, or
after the ship's arrival at her port of delivery, and before her cargo
is discharged, quits the ship without a previous discharge or leave
from the master, forfeits *one month's pay.*

4. Any seaman absolutely (o) deserting after having signed the
agreement, forfeits *to the owner or master* the clothes left on board,
and all wages due at the time of his deserting.

"Entering or being entered into the service of his Majesty, on
board any of his Majesty's ships, will not occasion a forfeiture of
clothes or wages, nor is it to be deemed a desertion."—Sect. 45.
Being compelled to quit the ship through the inhuman treatment
of the master (p), or being dismissed without any lawful cause, will
not be deemed desertion (q). So where the seaman is impressed
into the royal service, he will be entitled to receive a proportion of
his wages up to the time of impressing (r).

The 9th section applies to the case of the desertion of a ship
whilst in foreign parts, and before her arrival at her port of delivery; and the 7th section to the quitting of a ship after her
arrival in her port of delivery, but before the discharge of her
cargo : hence, where a seaman who had signed the articles required by this statute, absolutely quitted the ship without any
animus revertendi after her arrival, and being moored at her port
of delivery, but before her cargo had been discharged; it was
holden (s), that he did not thereby incur a total forfeiture of his

(k) Sect. 5.

(l) *Bowman* v. *Manselman*, 2 Campb.
315.

(m) Sect. 6.

(n) Sect. 7.

(o) Sect. 9.

(p) *Limland* v. *Stephens*, 3 Esp. N. P.
C. 269, *Kenyon*, C. J.

(q) *Sigard* v. *Roberts*, 3 Esp. N. P. C.
72, *Eldon*, C. J. See *Sherman* v. *Ben-*

nett, M. & Malk. 489.

(r) *Wiggins* v. *Ingleton*, 2 Lord Raym.
1211, per *Holt*, C. J., but nothing further.
Clements v. *Mayborn*, B. R. T. 24 Geo.
III., Abbott, 444 ; *S. C.*, nom. *Clements*
v. *Mavor*, B. P. B., Dampier MSS., L.
I. L., No. 333 ; and the voyage must be
completed, 2 Campb. 320, n.

(s) *M'Donald* v. *Jopling*, 4 M. & W.
285.

wages, under the 9th section, but only of a month's wages, under the 7th section.

By sect. 10, no debt exceeding 5s. incurred by any seaman after he has signed the agreement, shall be recoverable until the voyage shall have been concluded; and the effects of seamen are not to be detained by keepers of lodging houses for any pretended debt.

By sect. 13, masters are liable to a penalty of £5 for not giving seamen their certificates of service on their discharge; and in certain cases, where seamen are desirous of proceeding on another voyage, they may obtain (u) immediate payment of their wages by application to a J. P.

When a ship (x) is sold at a foreign port, the crew are to be sent home at the expense of the master or owners.

Sect. 19 enacts, that there shall be a general register office of merchant seamen.

Sect. 25 contains regulations for the disposal of the effects of seamen dying abroad.

By the 31st section, the master of every ship belonging to any subject of the United Kingdom, and of the burden of eighty tons and upwards, is obliged under a penalty to have on board his ship a number of apprentices according to her tonnage.

By the 41st and 42nd sections, no master shall discharge or leave any of his crew at any port or place abroad, without the sanction of one of the functionaries mentioned in the act; and if any seamen (y) shall be so left on shore at any place abroad, they shall be paid their wages.

By sect. 49, no seaman is to be shipped at any foreign port without the privity of the consul.

The 53rd section gives directions how the penalties imposed by this act shall be recovered and applied.

This act does not extend (z) to any ship registered in or belonging to any British colony having a legislative assembly.

By stat. 8 Geo. I. c. 24, s. 7, (made perpetual by stat. 2 Geo. II. c. 28, s. 7,) masters or owners of any merchant ship or vessel are prohibited from paying or advancing to any seaman or mariner, while he is in parts beyond the seas, any money or effects upon account of wages, exceeding one moiety of the wages due at the time of such payment, until the return of the ship to Great Britain or Ireland, or the plantations, or to some other of his Majesty's dominions whereto they belong, under a penalty double the money so paid or advanced, recoverable by common informer in the High Court of Admiralty.

(u) Sect. 14.　　　　　　　(y) Sect. 44.
(x) Sect. 17.　　　　　　　(z) Sect. 54.

Having detailed the most material legislative provisions on this subject, it will be proper to take notice of the rules of law and judicial decisions, as far as they affect the contract under consideration. The most important rule on this head is, "that freight is the mother of wages" (a); i. e., if the ship has earned its freight, and the seaman has performed his stipulated duty, he becomes entitled to his wages (6). But it is not part of the proof incumbent on the plaintiff, to show that the ship has earned freight (b); it lies on the defendant, who disaffirms the right to wages, to prove that the ship has not earned freight. If the ship be captured (c), or lost in the voyage, the seamen lose their wages. In an action for seaman's wages (d), it appeared that the seaman had entered into the usual articles, "to serve as a mariner on board a West India ship bound for the ports of Madeira, any of the West India Islands, and Jamaica, and to return to London," and in consideration of the monthly wages therein mentioned, to perform the above mentioned voyage; but it was expressly stipulated, that he was not to demand or be entitled to his wages, *or any part thereof*, until the arrival of the ship at the above mentioned *port of discharge*. The ship sailed, delivered her cargo at Madeira, and took in wine, part of which she delivered at Dominica, other part at Kingston in Jamaica, there took in government stores, delivered them at Port Antonio, in Jamaica, and the remainder of the wine at Martha Bray, in the same island. She was then freighted with a cargo of sugars for London, for which she sailed, but was lost at sea in the course of her passage home. It was contended, on the part of the plaintiff, that the voyage being, by the terms of it, divided into three parts; 1st, to Madeira, next to the West Indies, and lastly home; and freight having been earned in the two first stages of the voyage, the plaintiff was entitled to recover his wages *pro ratâ*, for

---

(a) *Anon.*, 2 Show. 283; Abbott, 447.
(b) *Brown* v. *Milner*, 7 Taunt. 319, C. B., after consulting with Lord *Ellenborough* and judges of B. R.
(c) *Abernethy* v. *Landale*, Doug. 539.

Per *Buller*, J., 1 T. R. 79.
(d) *Appleby* v. *Dods*, 8 East, 300, recognized in *Jesse* v. *Roy*, 1 Cr. M. & R. 316; 4 Tyr. 626.

---

(6) If the ship be lost before the first port of delivery, the seamen lose all their wages; but if lost after she has been at the first port of delivery, then they lose only those accrued due from the last port of delivery; but if the seamen run away, although they have been at a port of delivery, yet they lose all their wages. Per *Holt*, C. J., ex relatione M'ri Jacob, 1 Ld. Raym. 639. If a ship be bound for the East Indies, and thence to England, and the ship unlades at a port in the East Indies, and takes freight for England, and in her return she is taken by enemies, the mariners shall have their wages for the voyage to the East Indies, and for half the time that they stayed there to unlade, and no more. Per *Holt*, C. J., London Sittings, 1 Ld. Raym. 739; 12 Mod. 409, *S. C.* See also *Appleby* v. *Dods*, 8 East, 300.

so many entire months as had been spent in the voyage. But Lord
Ellenborough, C. J., being of opinion, that, according to the true
construction of the articles, the port of London was to be considered
as the port of discharge, and consequently, as the ship had not
arrived there, the plaintiff was precluded by the express stipulation
from recovering any part of his wages, nonsuited the plaintiff. On
motion to set aside the nonsuit, the Court of King's Bench concurred in opinion with the C. J. There has not been any case
wherein it has been decided, that a ship seized by way of retaliation,
and afterwards restored, has been considered as captured; or in
which the consequences of capture, as dissolving a contract for
wages, have been considered as attaching. Seizure, even hostile
seizure (e), is not necessarily capture, though such is its usual and
probable result. The ultimate act or adjudication of the state, by
which the seizure has been made, assigns its proper and conclusive
quality and denomination to its own original proceeding. If it
condemn in such case, it is a capture *ab initio;* if it award restitution as an act of justice, it pronounces on its own act, as not being
a valid act of capture, but as an act of temporary seizure and detention upon grounds not warranting the condemnation of the property,
or the dealing with it as captured (7). Hence, in the case of the
seamen (*f*) who were forcibly taken out of British merchant ships
at Petersburgh, by order of the Russian government, and marched
into the interior of the country, after which hostilities between
Great Britain and Russia took place, but on the re-establishment
of peace, the ships of both countries were restored, and the seamen
were permitted to return with their vessels, which brought home
their cargoes and earned their freight; it was holden, that this
seizure, however hostile in the manner, so far partook of the nature
of an embargo in its result, and not of a capture, that it did not put
an end to the contract of the seamen for wages, even during the
time of the detention and imprisonment; but even considering it as
a temporary capture, yet, like the case of a capture and recapture,
the seamen were still entitled to their wages; their being so entitled depended on the ship earning her freight for the voyage, and
the performance of their stipulated duty; and here freight for the
voyage was ultimately earned, and the seamen were not guilty of any

---

(e) Per *Ellenborough*, C. J., delivering
the opinion of the court in *Beale* v.
Thompson, 4 East, 561.

(*f*) *Beale* v. *Thompson*, in error, 4
East, 546.

---

(7) " It seems to be immaterial for this purpose, whether the restitution
be awarded by the government of the country, as an act of state, or by
any of the ordinary courts of civil judicature to which the administration
of justice on these subjects is usually delegated." Per Lord *Ellenborough*, C. J., 4 East, 561.

breach of duty; for the stipulation in the articles (8) not to be on shore under any pretence, without leave, before the voyage was ended, must be understood of a being on shore · by the party's own unauthorized act; and even if such imprisonment on shore could be so considered, yet the master having afterwards received them again on board, without objection, amounted to a dispensation of the service in the interval, and entitled them to wages according to the original contract. This case was afterwards brought by writ of error before the House of Lords, when the opinion of the judges was taken on the question, whether, on the whole of the facts found on the special verdict, the original plaintiff was entitled to recover wages during the time he was kept out of the ship, as found in the special verdict. The judges were unanimously of opinion (g), that he was so entitled to recover, and the Lord Chancellor concurred in their opinion. In the foregoing case the plaintiff was an Englishman; but in a similar case, where the plaintiff was a foreigner, the decision (h) was the same. If a seaman can prove that he was disabled from performing his duty by an accident (i), e. g., by receiving a blow from a piece of timber accidentally falling on him, he will be entitled to recover his wages for the whole voyage, in like manner as if he had actually served. A seaman, who is impressed before a ship returns to a port of delivery, is entitled to his wages pro tanto (k), if the ship complete her voyage; but not if she is captured on her return (l). But in a case where the defendant (m) gave a written promise to pay the plaintiff's intestate, a gross sum, (thirty guineas,) provided he proceeded, continued, and did his duty as second mate in a certain ship, from Jamaica to Liverpool, and the intestate, who had regularly performed his duty, died about a month after the ship had sailed, and before her arrival at Liverpool; and it appeared, that the common rate of wages was £4 per month, when the party was paid in proportion to the time he served, and that the voyage was generally performed in two months; it was holden, that the representative of the intestate was not entitled to recover any wages on the express contract, because it was an entire contract and not divisible; nor on an implied contract, by reason of the axiom of law, that where the parties have entered into an express contract, no other can be implied. During a voyage the ship was wrecked, and the captain gave the mariners an order upon the owners for the amount of their wages to the date of the wreck, acknowledging at the same time

(g) Thompson v. Beale, D. P. 1st, Dow. 299.
(h) Johnson v. Broderick, 4 East, 566.
(i) Chandler v. Grieves, 2 H. Bl. 606, n. But see the remarks of Grose, J., 6
T. R. 325.
(k) Per Holt, C. J., in Wiggins v. Ingleton, 2 Lord Raym. 1211.
(l) Anon., 2 Campb. 320, n.
(m) Cutter v. Powell, 6 T. R. 320.

(8) The seamen had signed the articles in the usual form.

that he had hired them by the month. It was holden (n), that under these circumstances no action for wages could be maintained by the mariners against the captain, at least without proving that they had first made a demand upon the owners. It only remains to state the remedies which the law has provided for the recovery of seamen's wages. If the hiring be on the usual terms (o), and made by word or by writing only, and not by deed, the seamen, or any one or more of them, and every officer, except the master, may sue in the Court of Admiralty, and may, by the process of that court, arrest the ship as a security for their demand (9), or cite the master or owner personally to answer to them. But if the agreement be by deed, and the terms of such agreement are not the usual terms, then the only remedy is in the common law courts (10). But whether the party sue in the Court of Admiralty (p), or bring an action in the courts of common law (q); in both cases the suit or action must be commenced within six years next after the cause thereof has accrued, unless the party suing should have been under any of the disabilities mentioned in the statute of limitations, as infancy, absence beyond the seas, &c. If foreign sailors stipulate in their own country before the commencement of a voyage that they will not sue the captain for any money abroad, but be satisfied with what he may advance them abroad in deduction of their wages, such stipulation is binding, and an action cannot be maintained by the seaman for his wages in the courts of this country (r).

In an action (s) against the defendants, as part owners, for seamen's wages, the question arose whether A. and B., being partners, and also part owners of a vessel, the admission of A., as to a subject of co-part ownership, but not of co-partnership, was binding on B.; and Lord *Ellenborough* held, that it was not.

(n) *Forsboom* v. *Kruger*, 3 Campb. 197.
(o) Abbott, 476, cites Winch. 8; 2 Vent. 181; 8 Mod. 379; 2 Lord Raym. 1206; 1 Str. 707; Say. 136; 1 Lord Raym. 632; Salk. 33; 2 Str. 858; 1 Barnard. 297; Str. 937.
(p)·Stat. 4 Ann. c. 16, s. 17, 18, 19.
(q) 21 Jac. I. c. 16, s. 3, 7. See *ante*, p. 135.
(r) *Johnson* v. *Machielsne*, 3 Campb. 44.
(s) *Jaggers* v. *Binnings*, 1 Stark. N. P. C. 64.

(9) In proceedings against the ship in specie, if the value thereof be insufficient to discharge all the claims upon it, the seaman's claim for his wages is preferred before all other charges; for the labour of the seamen, having brought the ship to the destined port, has furnished to all other persons the means of asserting their claims upon it, which otherwise they could not have had. Abbott, 484.

(10) In the courts of common law the seamen may sue either the master, as the person immediately contracting with them, and answerable to them, or the owners, as the persons virtually contracting with them through the agency of the master, and answerable for the performance of his engagement. Abbott, 485.

See stat. 5 & 6 Will. IV. c. 19, s. 15, (*ante*, p. 1232,) empowering justices, on complaint of seamen, to hear and settle disputes about wages not exceeding £20.

III. *Of the Liability of Ship Owners for the Repairs, &c.*

Upon a general order (*t*) for repairs given by the captain, the party executing them has the security of the ship, of the captain, and of the owners; but in an action against parties as owners, the question is, who are so for this purpose? the persons registered are not necessarily so; the Register Acts were not passed for this purpose; and the question of ownership, as it regards the liability for repairs, must be considered as it would have been before those acts were passed.

The registered owner of a ship is not liable for repairs, unless actually done upon his credit. Legal ownership is *primâ facie* evidence of liability, which may be rebutted by proof of the beneficial interest having been parted with, and of the legal owners having ceased to interfere with the management of the ship (*u*). As where A., the managing owner of a ship, mortgaged his share to B., who procured the transfer to be duly indorsed on the certificate of registry, but A. continued in the management as before, and gave orders for repairs and stores, and B. did not take possession or interfere in the concerns of the ship; it was holden (*x*), that B. was not liable for such repairs and stores so ordered by A. So where a steam vessel was let by charter-party for twelve months, the registered owners engaging to keep the engine in repair, but the charterer binding himself to do all other repairs, to pay all wages and charges of navigating, &c., and to indemnify the owners against all debts, costs, damages, expenses, &c. incurred in respect of the charter-party and employment of the vessel. The owners were to appoint the engineers. The charterer, who acted as captain, had repairs done to the vessel by persons unacquainted with the contract: it was holden (*y*), that no action lay, in respect of those repairs, against the registered owners. A party who takes a share in a ship, under a conveyance, void for want of conformity with the provisions of the Registry Acts, is not (*z*) liable for articles furnished to the ship, unless credit be given to him individually, or he holds himself out as owner. The master of a ship has authority by law

---

(*t*) Per *Littledale*, J., in *Reeve* v. *Davis*, 1 A. & E. 315, 6.

(*u*) *Jennings* v. *Griffiths*, 1 Ry. & M. 42.

(*x*) *Briggs* v. *Wilkinson*, 7 B. & C. 30.

(*y*) *Reeve* v. *Davis*, 1 A. & E. 312; 3 Nev. & M. 873, recognising *Briggs* v. *Wilkinson*.

(*z*) *Harrington* v. *Fry*, 2 Bingh. 179.

to pledge the credit of his owner, resident in England, for *money* advanced to the master in an English port where the owner has no agent, if such advance of money was necessary for the prosecution of the voyage; and whether it was so or not is a question for the jury (*a*); but the owner of a ship is not (*b*) liable for money advanced to the master, although it has been properly expended by the master for the purpose of the ship, unless the money was borrowed by the master expressly for that purpose.

(*a*) *Arthur* v. *Barton*, 6 M. & W. 138, *ante*, p. 1028, n., recognized in *Weston* v. *Wright*, 7 M. & W. 396.

(*b*) *Thacker* v. *Moates*, 1 M. & Rob. 79.

SLANDER.

I. *Scandalum Magnatum, p.* 1241.

II. *Of the Action for Slander, and in what Cases it may be maintained, p.* 1243.

III. *Of the Declaration, and herein of the Nature and Office of the Innuendo, p.* 1250.

IV. *Of the Pleadings, p.* 1254; *Evidence, p.* 1256; *Costs, p.* 1258.

I. *Scandalum Magnatum.*

SLANDER spoken and published of a peer is termed scandalum magnatum. The stat. 3 Edw. I. Westm. 1, c. 34, commands, " That none be so hardy to tell or publish any false news or tales, whereby discord, or occasion of discord, or slander, may grow between the king and his people, or the great men of the realm; and he that doth so, shall be taken and kept in prison, until he hath brought *him* into the court *which was the first author of the tale*" (1). And by stat. 2 Ric. II. c. 5, " None shall devise or speak false news, lies, or other such false things of the prelates, dukes, earls, barons, and other noble and great men of the realm, and of the chancellor, treasurer, clerk of the privy seal, steward of the king's house, justices of the one bench or the other, and other great officers of the realm, and he that doth shall incur the pain of the stat. Westm. 1, c. 34." And by stat. 12 Ric. II. c. 11, " When any such [person, as is described in the foregoing statutes,] is taken and imprisoned, and cannot find him by whom the speech be moved, he may be punished by the advice of the council, notwithstanding the

---

(1) See Sir Edw. Coke's exposition of this statute, 2 Inst. 225.

statute of Westm. 1, c. 34, and 2 Ric. II. c. 5." The foregoing
statutes do not expressly give an action, yet it has been holden, that
the party injured may maintain an action on the stat. 2 Ric. II. c. 5,
upon the principle of law (a), that an action lies on a statute, which
prohibits the doing an act to the prejudice of another. Though the
dignity of viscount was not created at the time when this statute
was made, yet it has been holden, that such dignity is within the
statute (b); and a peer of Scotland, since the union, may also take
advantage of the statute (c) (2). The form of declaration is, *tam
pro domino rege quam pro seipso* (3), concluding *contra formam
statuti* (d). The stat. 2 Ric. II. c. 5, is a general law (e), and
consequently need not be pleaded (f), but if the party undertake
to recite it, and fail in a material part, it will be fatal (g). It must
appear on the face of the declaration, that the party injured was
unus magnatum at the time when the words were spoken (h). Special bail is not required in this action (i), and the venue cannot be
changed upon the common affidavit (k). Neither can a writ of
error be brought upon it in the Exchequer Chamber (l), for it has
been holden, that this action is not an action on the case within the
meaning of the stat. 27 Eliz. c. 8, which gives the writ of error in
Exchequer Chamber in certain actions. There is a dictum in 2
Show. 506, that in a scand. mag. the plaintiff obtaining a verdict
will not be entitled to costs. It has been holden, that certain
words are actionable in the case of a peer, which would not have
been deemed so in the case of a common person; as in *Lord
Townshend* v. *Hughes* (m), where the defendant said of the plaintiff,
" he is an unworthy man, and acts against law and reason."

(a) 2 Inst. 118; 10 Rep. 75, b.
(b) *Visc. Say and Seale* v. *Stephens*,
Cro. Car. 135.
(c) *Visc. Falkland* v. *Phipps*, Comyns
R. 439.
(d) Vid. Entr. 74.
(e) Doct. Plac. 339; 4 Rep. 13, a.
(f) *Lord Shaftesbury* v. *Lord Digby*,
2 Mod. 98.
(g) 4 Rep. 12, b., for instances of mis-
recital, what fatal, and what not, see 1

Com. Dig. 188, (B.) 3.
(h) Adm. Cro. Jac. 136.
(i) 12 Mod. 420; 2 Mod. 215, S. P.
(k) *Duke of Norfolk* v. *Alderton*, Carth.
400; *Duke of Richmond* v. *Costelow*, 11
Mod. 234; 2 Salk. 668; 1 Lev. 56; 1
Bac. Abr. 36.
(l) *Lord Say and Seale* v. *Stephens*,
Cro. Car. 142; Ley, 82, *S. C.*; Sir W.
Jones, 194, *S. C.*
(m) 1 Mod. 232; 2 Mod. 150, *S. C.*

(2) Some of the old precedents state the plaintiff to have *vocem et locum
in parliamento*. See Vid. Ent. 74, and Bohun, 319, 320; but these
words are unnecessary, and they are omitted in two precedents in
Herne, 200, 201. Vid. 61, 3.

(3) An action upon a statute which prohibits a thing, but does not
give any penalty, must be brought *tam pro rege quam pro seipso*, because
in such case the king is to have a fine. *Waterhouse* v. *Bawde*, Cro. Jac.
134. See the precedents cited in n. (2).

II. *Of the Action for Slander, and in what Case it may be maintained.*

In former times, the action for slander was very rare; the first action for words to be found in the books was in the 30th year of Edw. III. Lib. Ass. fo. 177, pl. 19; and from that time to the reign of Queen Elizabeth, these actions were few in number, and not brought on frivolous causes; during the reign of Queen Elizabeth and King James, they began to increase, and in modern times the action has been more frequent. Actions for words should not be brought upon slight and trivial occasions; and where the words are merely words of heat, anger, or passion, spoken suddenly or without deliberation, such actions should be discountenanced; at the same time it has been truly said (by *Wray*, C. J.), that unless the party injured by false and malicious scandal had a remedy at law, it would be *à verbis ad verbera*, and the consequences might be fatal.

It would exceed the limits prescribed to this work to enumerate with particularity all the cases which have been adjudged, as to what words are actionable, and what are not so. It may be sufficient for the present purpose to observe, that an action on the case lies against any person for falsely and maliciously speaking and publishing of another, words which directly (4) charge him with any crime, for the commission of which the offender is punishable by law (*n*) (5), as treason (*o*), murder (*p*), larceny (*q*), perjury (*r*), keeping a bawdy-house (*s*), or with *having* (6) any contagious dis-

(*n*) Finch, B. 3, C. 2.
(*o*) *Lewis* v. *Roberts*, Hard. 203.
(*p*) 1 Roll. Abr. 72, pl. 4.
(*q*) Aleyn, 31.
(*r*) 1 Rol. Abr. 39, l. 25.
(*s*) 1 Rol. Abr. 44, l. 15.

---

(4) " The words must contain an express imputation of some crime, &c., and the charge upon the person spoken of must be precise. Per *De Grey*, C. J., in *Onslow* v. *Horne*, 3 Wils. 187 " Words to be actionable must be unequivocally so. Imputing to a person an evil inclination, which is not carried into effect, is not actionable." Per *Ellenborough*, C. J., in *Harrison* v. *Stratton*, M. T. 1803. 4 Esp. N. P. C. 218. The charging another with a crime of which he cannot by any possibility be guilty, as killing a person who is then living, is not actionable, because the plaintiff cannot be in any jeopardy from such a charge. *Snag* v. *Gee*, 4 Rep. 16, a.

(5) That is, by common law or statute; for charging a man with an offence examinable only in the spiritual court, unless special damage ensues, is not actionable. *Parrat* v. *Carpenter*, Cro. Eliz. 502; *Graves* v. *Blanchet*, Salk. 696.

(6) But charging a person with *having had* a contagious disorder, is not

order, the imputation of which may exclude him from society, as leprosy (*t*), plague, French pox (*u*), &c. There are two sorts of malice (*x*); one denoting an act done from ill will towards an individual, the other a wrongful act, intentionally done, without just cause or excuse. In ordinary actions for slander, malice in law may be inferred from the publishing the slanderous matter, the act itself being wrong and intentional, and without just cause or excuse; but in actions for slander, *primâ facie* excusable on account of the cause of publishing the slanderous matter, malice in fact must be proved. When the defendant, in the presence of a third person, not an officer of justice, charged the plaintiff with having stolen his property, and afterwards repeated the charge to another person, also not an officer of justice, who was called in to search the plaintiff with the consent of the latter; it was holden, that the charge was privileged if the defendant believed in its truth, acted *bonâ fide*, and did not make the charge before more persons, or in stronger language, than was necessary; and that it was a question for the jury, and not the judge, whether the facts brought the case within this rule (*y*).

In order to sustain this action, it is essentially necessary that *the words should contain an express imputation of some crime liable to punishment, some capital offence, or other infamous crime or misdemeanour.* An imputation of the mere defect or want of moral virtue, moral duties, or obligations, is not sufficient (*z*). To call a man a swindler is not actionable (*a*); so to call a man a thief is not actionable, unless it be intended to impute felony to him. Hence, where that expression is accompanied with other words, which clearly denote that the speaker did not intend to impute felony to the party charged, no action can be maintained. No action lies for these words (*b*): " I will take him to Bow Street on a charge of forgery." In an action for words, the words proved were (*c*), " He is a thief, for he has stolen my beer." It appeared in evidence, that the defendant was a brewer, and that the plaintiff had lived

(*t*) *Taylor* v. *Perkins*, Cro. Jac. 144.
(*u*) 1 Rol. Abr. 66, l. 38.
(*x*) *Bromage* v. *Prosser*, 4 B. & C. 247.
(*y*) *Padmore* v. *Lawrence*, 11 A. & E. 380; 3 P. & D. 209, recognizing *Toogood* v. *Spyring*, 1 Cr. M. & R. 181; 4 Tyrw. 582. See *Kine* v. *Sewell*, 3 M. & W. 297; *Martin* v. *Strong*, 5 A. & E. 535. On the subject of privileged communications, see

post, p. 1255.
(*z*) Per *De Grey*, C. J., delivering judgment in *Onslow* v. *Horne*, 3 Wils. 177, recognized by *Lawrence*, J., in *Holt* v. *Scholefield*, 6 T. R. 694.
(*a*) *Savile* v. *Jardine*, 2 H. Bl. 531.
(*b*) *Harrison* v. *King*, in error, 7 Taunt. 431; *post*, 1253.
(*c*) *Christie* v. *Cowell*, Peake, N. P. C. 4.

actionable; for unless the words spoken impute a continuance of the disorder at the time of speaking them, the ground of the action fails; for such a charge cannot produce the effect which makes it the subject of an action, namely, his being avoided by society. Per *Ashhurst*, J., in *Carslake* v. *Mapledoram*, 2 T. R. 475; 2 Str. 1189, S. P.

with him as servant; in the course of which service he had sold beer to different customers of the defendant, and received money for the same, which he had not duly accounted for. Lord *Kenyon*, C. J., directed the jury to consider whether these words were spoken in reference to the money received, and unaccounted for, by the plaintiff, or whether the defendant meant that the plaintiff had actually *stolen* beer; for if they referred to the money not accounted for, that being a mere breach of contract, so far explained the words "thief," as to make it not actionable. Thus, if a man says to another, "You are a thief, for you stole my tree," it is not actionable (*d*), for it shows he had a trespass,' and not a felony, in his contemplation. V. for defendant: See also *Thompson* v. *Bernard*, 1 Camph. 48, to the same effect. The rule which at one time prevailed (*e*), that words are to be understood *in mitiori sensu*, has been long ago superseded, and words are now construed by courts, as they always ought to have been, in the plain and popular sense in which the rest of the world naturally understand them. In an action for words, it was stated in the declaration (*f*), that the plaintiff had lived among the neighbours with credit and reputation, and without being suspected of felony, and that the defendant, in order to charge him with the crime of felony, falsely and maliciously spoke of the plaintiff these false, malicious, and scandalous words, *viz.* "that the plaintiff was in Winchester gaol, and was tried for his life, and would have been hanged, if it had not been for Abraham Legat, for breaking farmer Atkin's granary and stealing his sacks." Plea, N. G. After verdict for plaintiff, it was moved, in arrest of judgment, that the words did not import any guilt in the plaintiff, being only a narrative of what passed on the trial, and rather tended to show the plaintiff was cleared by the evidence of Legat, than that he was guilty of any crime for which he deserved to be hanged. But per Lord *Hardwicke*, C. J. "The construction now made upon actions for words is very different from what it was formerly. Judges, anciently, to discourage little frivolous actions, used their utmost endeavour to explain away the most opprobrious words: but this was certainly wrong; and as the character and reputation of mankind is under the protection of the law, as well as their estates, we ought to do equal justice to both, and take care that neither the one nor the other are injured. The question then is, whether the words spoken do import any slander or reproach, for which an action lies. To say a man has been in gaol and tried for his life, is certainly scandalous: and that he would have been hanged but for such a one, does naturally import, that he was saved by some indirect means. (And he cited the case of *Halley* v.

(*d*) Cro. Jac. 114; Bull. N. P. 5.
(*e*) 9 East, 96.
(*f*) *Carpenter* v. *Tarrant*, M. T. 10 Geo. II., B. R., MSS.; Ca. Temp.

Hardw. 339, *S. C.*, cited by Lord *Ellenborough*, C. J., delivering the opinion of the court in *Roberts* v. *Camden*, 9 East, 97.

Stanton, Cro. Car. 268, as a very strong authority in point.) As to the 2d question, whether the plaintiff ought not to have averred, that he was not in gaol, &c., it was anciently held, that such averments were necessary : but in later times, it has been holden, that the alleging the words to have been spoken falsely amounted to such an averment; and, if so, the court must now take it, that all the imputation cast on the plaintiff was false. If the words had been true, the defendant should have pleaded that specially." So where the defendant said of the plaintiff (g), that " he was under a charge of a prosecution for perjury, and that G. W., an attorney, had the attorney general's directions to prosecute the plaintiff *for perjury;*" the defendant pleaded N. G. After verdict for plaintiff, it was objected, in arrest of judgment, that the words were not actionable, as not conveying any opinion of the speaker upon the truth of the charge. But the court overruled the objection; Lord *Ellenborough*, C. J., (who delivered judgment,) observing, that the words must mean, that the plaintiff was ordered by the attorney general to be prosecuted, either for a perjury which he had committed, or which he had not committed, or which he was supposed only to have committed. In the first sense they were clearly actionable. In the second, they could not possibly be understood consistently with the context. And if the defendant had used the words in the last sense, the jury might have acquitted him, according to the doctrine in the case of *Oldham* v. *Peake*, both in the Court of Common Pleas (h), and in this court (i). And certainly, if the sense of the defendant, in speaking these words, had varied from that ascribed to them by the plaintiff, he might by specially pleading have shown them not actionable, had he not chosen to have rested the defence merely on the general issue. It appeared, therefore, that these words must fairly be understood in the first of these three senses, namely, that he was ordered to be prosecuted for a perjury, *which he had committed;* and, so understood, they were unquestionably actionable. There are in the books various authorities to show, that the understanding of the hearers is the rule to go by. In a MS. case, 1 Viner, 507, it is laid down that the question is only what is understood by the hearers. In *Fleetwood* v. *Curly*, Hob. 268, Lord *Hobart* says, the slander and damage consist in the apprehension of the hearers; and in Gilbert's Cases in Law and Equity, 117, the rule laid down is, that the words shall be taken in the sense in which the hearers understood them (k).

In addition to the preceding instances, it may be observed, that it is actionable, falsely and maliciously to speak and publish of another words which tend to disinherit him (l), or to deprive him

(g) *Roberts* v. *Camden*, 9 East, 93.   (k) See also *Read* v. *Ambridge*, 6 C. &
(h) 2 Bl. 961, 2.   P. 308.
(i) Cowp. 278.   (l) 1 Rol. Abr. 37, l. 27.

of his estate (m), or which slander him in his office (n), profession (o), or trade (p); e. g., in speaking of a justice of the peace in the execution of his office, to say that "He is a rascal, a villain, and a liar," is actionable; for the words import a charge of acting corruptly and partially (q). Saying of a churchwarden, "He is a cheat (r), and cheated the parish of £4, and notwithstanding I have given him a receipt upon his bill of £9 1s. expended, it was a false thing, and I never received more than £5 of the £9 1s." But words imputing to a churchwarden that he stole the parish bell ropes (s), are not actionable; the possession of the bell ropes being in him. Words of an innkeeper, imputing insolvency, were holden to be actionable; although, at the time they were spoken (t), an innkeeper was not subject to the bankrupt laws. For slander of this kind an action may be brought before any injury has been sustained, in consequence of the words having been spoken. From the nature of the words, the law implies the injury; hence such words are said to be actionable in themselves.

To maintain an action for slander of title, there must be malice either express or implied (u). Hence where a person, thinking he had a right to recover possession of a term for some misconduct of his tenant, and hearing that the term was to be sold, went to the auction and said, the vendor could not make a title; it was holden, that an action could not be maintained, there being no proof of malice (x). So the attorney (y) of a party claiming title to premises put up for sale, is not liable to an action for slander of title, if he, bonâ fide, though without authority, makes such objections to the seller's title, as his principal would have been authorized in making. Malice and special damage must be alleged and proved. See post, p. 1249, Malachy v. Soper.

In Harwood v. Sir J. Astley, in error, 1 Bos. & Pul. N. R. 47, it was contended, that an action could not be maintained, because the words were alleged to have been spoken of the plaintiff, (below,) as a candidate to serve in parliament; but it was holden, that the words being actionable in themselves (7), it is quite immaterial

(m) Bois v. Bois, 1 Lev. 134.
(n) How v. Prinn, Salk. 694; Lord Raym. 812, S. C.
(o) Hardwick v. Chandler, Str. 1138.
(p) Upsheer v. Betts, Cro. Jac. 578, 9; Jones v. Littler, 7 M. & W. 423.
(q) Aston v. Blagrave, Str. 617; Lord Raym. 1369, S. C.
(r) Philips v. Harrison, C. B. Hil. Geo. II., on motion in arrest of judg-

ment, Lord King's MSS. p. 44.
(s) Jackson v. Adams, 2 Bingh. N. C. 402; 2 Sc. 599.
(t) Whittington v. Gladwin, 5 B. & C. 180.
(u) Hargrave v. Le Breton, 4 Burr. 2422.
(x) Smith v. Spooner, 3 Taunt. 246. See also Pitt v. Donovan, 1 M. & S. 639.
(y) Watson v. Reynolds, M. & Malk. 1.

(7) The words charged the plaintiff (below) with having murdered his father. "Words are actionable when spoken of one in an office of profit,

whether they were spoken of the plaintiff as candidate or not. If the plaintiff has sustained any special damage in consequence of words actionable in themselves having been spoken (z), and seeks to recover a compensation for it, such special damage must be stated in the declaration, with as much certainty as the subject matter is capable of, in order that the defendant may be sufficiently apprized of the nature of the case which is intended to be proved against him, and consequently be prepared to meet it. Where the words charged the plaintiff, a horse-dealer, "with privately stealing certain horses sold by him," and consequently were actionable; after proving the words, the plaintiff's counsel applied to be admitted to give general evidence of loss of customers, but was denied (a).

By the stat. 21 Jac. I. c. 16, s. 3, "Actions on the case for *words* must be commenced and sued within two years next after the words spoken." But by sect. 7, " Infant, feme covert, non compos mentis, person imprisoned or beyond sea, may sue within two years after the removal of their respective disabilities."

Of Words not actionable in themselves.—Words not actionable in themselves may become so, by reason of some special damage arising from them, *e. g.*, if a person say to a woman, " You are a whore," whereby she loses her marriage (b), or a substantial benefit arising from the hospitality of friends (c) (8). So if a person slander

---

(z) *Geare* v. *Britton*, Bull. N. P. 7; *Hatheway* v. *Newman*, B. R. Middlesex Sittings, Feb. 17, 1804, S. P., per Lord *Ellenborough*, C. J.

(a) *Waterhouse* v. *Gill*, coram *Buller*,

J., Lancaster Lent Ass. 1790, Holroyd, MSS.

(b) 1 Rol. Abr. 35, l. 15.

(c) *Moore* v. *Meagher*, in error, Exch. Chr., 1 Taunt. 39.

---

which may probably occasion the loss of his office, or when spoken of persons touching their respective professions, trades, and business, and do or may probably lead to their damage." Per *De Grey*, C. J., in *Onslow* v. *Horne*, 3 Wils. 186.

(8) Calling a married woman or a single one a whore is not actionable, because fornication and adultery are subjects of spiritual not temporal censures. Lord Raym. 1004; except in the city of London, by reason of the custom there to cart whores, 1 Viner, S. 13. But there the words must charge that she was a whore in London; it is not sufficient if the declaration merely allege that she resided in London. *Robertson* v. *Powell*, B. R. Sittings at Serjeant's Inn, before M. T. 57 Geo. III. Action for calling plaintiff's wife a whore in London, suggesting the custom of London to cart whores, plaintiffs were nonsuited for want of proving the custom. Lord *Mansfield* said, he could not take notice of such custom, unless proved. No proof of it could be got from the town clerk's office; and it was then said that no proof of it had ever been given so as to maintain such actions out of the city courts, but that in the city courts they would take notice of their own custom. *Stainton et Ux.* v. *Jones*, Sittings after Mich. Term, at Guildhall, coram Lord *Mansfield*, 1782, MS.

the title of another, whereby he is prevented from selling his estate (d): but in these cases, it is incumbent on the party injured, not only to state and prove the speaking of the words, but also the particular injury which he has sustained; because, the words not being actionable in themselves, the special damage is considered as the gist of the action (e). It must also appear (f), that the special damage was the *legal* and natural consequence of the words spoken; for an illegal consequence, *viz.* a tortious act, will not be sufficient. In slander for words uttered of the plaintiff to her employer, who stated that she dismissed the plaintiff from her service, not because she believed the words, but because she was afraid she should offend her landlord, by keeping her; it was holden (g), being the consequence of the words used, the action was maintainable; the court could not speculate on the motives of witnesses. And per *Patteson*, J., it is not like *Vicars* v. *Wilcocks*, because here the whole cause of the special damage proceeds from the defendant himself; nothing is done by any other person. Two persons cannot join in an action for slanderous words spoken of them (h), for the injury which the one sustains by the slander is not an injury done to the other. But if defamatory words be spoken of partners in trade (i), *whereby they are injured in their trade*, a joint action will lie at the suit of the partners, although the words be actionable of themselves. It is actionable to republish any slander invented by another (k), unless the republication be accompanied by a disclosure of the author's name, and a precise statement of the author's words, so as to enable the party injured to maintain an action against the author. This disclosure and statement must be made *at the time* of republishing the slander; for it will not avail the defendant to make it for the first time in pleading to an action brought by the party injured; and according to *Holroyd*, J., in *Lewis* v. *Walter*, 4 B. & A. 914, the republication must be on a fair and justifiable occasion; and, according to *Bayley*, J., in *M'Pherson* v. *Daniels* (l), the defendant must show also, that he believed it to be true. In that case, which was an action for words spoken by the plaintiff in his trade, importing a direct assertion made by defendant, that the plaintiff was insolvent; the defendant pleaded that one T. W. spoke and published to the defendant the same words, and that the defendant, at

(d) *Lowe* v. *Harewood*, Sir W. Jones, 196; Cro. Car. 140, recognized in *Malachy* v. *Soper*, 3 Bingh. N. C. 383; 3 Scott, 736.

(e) *Browne* v. *Gibbons*, Salk. 206.

(f) *Vicars* v. *Wilcocks*, 8 East, 1. See *Kelly* v. *Partington*, 5 B. & Ad. 645; 3 Nev. & M. 117.

(g) *Caroline Knight* v. *Gibbs*, 1 A. & E. 43; 3 Nev. & M. 467.

(h) Dyer, 19, a, pl. 112.

(i) *Cook and another* v. *Batchellor*, 3 Bos. & Pul. 150.

(k) *Davis* v. *Lewis*, 7 T. R. 17; *Maitland* v. *Goldney*, 2 East, 426. These cases were recognized in *Woolnoth* v. *Meadows*, 5 East, 463. Semble that this defence is not applicable to written slander. See *Lewis* v. *Walter*, 4 B. & A. 605.

(l) 10 B. & C. 271; 5 M. & R. 251. See also *Ward* v. *Weeks*, 7 Bingh. 211, and *Bennett* v. *Bennett*, 6 C. & P. 588, *Alderson*, B. And the remarks of *Best*, C. J., in *De Crespigny* v. *Wellesley*, 5 Bingh. 401.

the time of speaking and publishing them, declared that he had heard and been told the same from and by the said T. W.; it was holden, upon demurrer, that the plea was bad; first, because it did not confess and avoid the charge made in the declaration, the words in the declaration importing an unqualified assertion made by defendant, and the words in the plea importing that the defendant mentioned the fact on the authority of T. W. Secondly, because the plea did not give the plaintiff any cause of action against T. W.; inasmuch as it did not allege that T. W. spoke the words falsely and maliciously. Thirdly, because it is no answer to an action for oral slander, for a defendant merely to show that he heard it from another, and named the person at the time, without showing also that he believed it to be true, and that he spoke the words on a justifiable occasion.

From the preceding remarks it appears, that the falsehood and malice, either express or implied, are of the essence of the action for slander and special damage, where the words are not actionable in themselves. Where words, falsely and maliciously spoken, are actionable in themselves, the law *primâ facie* presumes a consequent damage, without proof.

III. *Of the Declaration, and herein of the Nature and Office of the Innuendo.*

In the declaration, after such prefatory averments as the circumstances of the case may render necessary (9), it must be alleged expressly what words were spoken (10), and that they were spoken and *published* of the plaintiff (*m*) falsely and maliciously. If the

(*m*) *Johnson* v. *Aylmer*, Cro. Jac. 126.

---

(9) By rule of court, B. R. M. 1654, it is ordered, " That in actions of slander, long preambles be forborne : and no more inducement than what is necessary for the maintenance of the action, except where it requires a special inducement or colloquium."

(10) " That the defendant spake of the plaintiff, quædam falsa et scandalosa verba, *quorum tenor* sequitur in hæc verba," &c., was holden insufficient, because it was not an express allegation, that the defendant spake the same identical words. *Garford* v. *Clerk*, Cro. Eliz. 857. This rule, that the words spoken should be set forth precisely, is not confined to those cases only in which the action is, properly speaking, for slander, but extends also to cases where special damage is the ground of the action. *Gutsole* v. *Mathers*, 1 M. & W. 495, recognizing *Cook* v. *Cox*, 3 M. & S. 110, and *post*, p. 1253.

words were spoken in a foreign language, it must be averred in the declaration, that the hearers understood such language (n). Where the charge alleged against the plaintiff relates to his office, profession, or trade, there it ought to appear on the face of the declaration, that plaintiff was in office (o), or exercising his profession or trade (p), at the time when the words were spoken, and that they were spoken in relation to his office, profession, or trade (q). In an action for slander, imputing adultery to plaintiff, a physician, where no special damage was laid, it was holden (r) not sufficient to state the words to have been spoken of him "in his profession;" but that it ought to have been set forth in the declaration in what manner the scandalous conduct was connected by the speaker with that profession.

In an action of slander, imputing incontinence to one, who was a preacher at a dissenting meeting-house, by reason of which he was dismissed from his employment, it is not (s) necessary to state that he was legally in the exercise of the employment, nor is it necessary to state the names of the persons who dismissed him; but it is sufficient to say, that the persons who frequented the chapel refused to permit him to preach, by reason whereof he had lost the emoluments he would otherwise have acquired.

In an action for words spoken of a person who was a candidate to serve in parliament, it is not necessary to set forth the writ in the declaration (t). It is sufficient for the plaintiff to state that he was a candidate to serve in the (present) parliament, which cannot exist without a writ to call the parliament together. In that part of the declaration which states the slander, the words ought to be explained in such manner as they may require. Whilst the pleadings were in Latin, this explanation was introduced by the word "innuendo:" e. g., "Thou (eundem quer' *innuendo*) art a thief;" which in a modern declaration would stand thus: "Thou (*meaning* the said plaintiff) art a thief." The term *innuendo* is still retained, whenever this part of the declaration is mentioned. In the foregoing instance, it may be observed, that the innuendo is the same in effect as "that is to say." Its office is merely to explain and designate, that the person intended by the word "thou" is the plaintiff. But that the plaintiff was the person intended, must appear from the manner in which the words were spoken, which must be stated in the declaration, namely, that they were spoken of the plaintiff, or to the plaintiff, or in a conversation with the plain-

(n) *Price* v. *Jenkings*, Cro. Eliz. 865.
(o) Yelv. 158.
(p) *Collis* v. *Malin*, Cro. Car. 282.
(q) *Todd* v. *Hastings*, 2 Saund. 307; *Savage* v. *Robery*, Salk. 694.
(r) *Ayre* v. *Craven*, 2 A. & E. 2; 4 Nev. & M. 220, recognized in *Doyley* v. *Roberts*, 3 Bingh. N. C. 840, cited by

Parke, B., in *Jones* v. *Littler*, 7 M. & W. 423.
(s) *Hartley* v. *Herring*, Jan. 31, 1799, B. R., L. P. B. 258; Dampier MSS., L. I. L.
(t) *Harwood* v. *Sir J. Astley*, 1 Bos. & Pul. N. R. 47, on error, in Exch. Chr.

tiff, and not from the *innuendo* only (*u*); for if the person of whom the words were spoken be uncertain, an action will not lie; and a plaintiff cannot merely, by the force of an innuendo, apply the words to himself (*x*). When the innuendo is annexed to the charge preferred against the plaintiff, then its office is to give the words spoken their proper signification, but not to extend the sense of them beyond their natural import. Therefore, where a declaration stated that defendant said of the plaintiff, "He has forsworn himself, (*meaning* that the plaintiff had committed wilful and corrupt perjury,)" it was holden, that the words not being actionable in themselves, because they did not necessarily imply that the plaintiff had forsworn himself *in a judicial proceeding*, their meaning could not be extended by the innuendo (*y*). But if the defendant had spoken the words concerning some judicial proceeding that had before taken place, in which the plaintiff had given testimony, and these facts had been averred in the declaration, then such an innuendo would have been good; because the words, coupled with the preceding facts, would have shown, that the defendant meant to charge the plaintiff with perjury punishable by law. So where the slander was, "He has burnt my barn," the plaintiff cannot say (*z*), by way of innuendo, "my barn *full of corn;*" because that is not an explanation of the words, but an addition to them. But if, in the introductory part of the declaration, it is averred, *that the defendant had a barn full of corn*, and also, *that in a discourse about that barn*, the defendant had spoken the words, an innuendo, that he meant by those words the barn full of corn, would have been good. This distinction was recognized in a later case (*a*): it was stated in the declaration, that the plaintiff had, in due manner, put in his answer upon oath to a bill filed against him in the Court of Exchequer by the defendant, (but it was not averred that the words were spoken in a discourse about that answer;) it was then alleged, that defendant said of the plaintiff that he had forsworn himself, (*meaning that the plaintiff had perjured himself in his aforesaid answer to the bill so filed against him;*) it was holden, on motion in arrest of judgment after verdict, that the declaration was bad, for want of an averment of colloquium respecting the answer in the Exchequer, which was not supplied by the innuendo, and further, that the defect was not cured by verdict. In all cases, therefore, where the words can be understood in an actionable sense only by reference to certain facts, such facts must be distinctly stated in the body of the declaration: for the mere introduction of those facts, under an innuendo, will not be deemed a sufficient averment

---

(*u*) 4 Rep. 17 b.; 3 Bulstr. 227.

(*x*) *Johnson* v. *Aylmer*, Cro. Jac. 126.

(*y*) *Holt* v. *Scholefield*, 6 T. R. 691. See also *Core* v. *Morton*, Yelv. 27.

(*z*) Per *De Grey*, C.J., in *R.* v. *Horne*, Cowp. 684.

(*a*) *Hawkes* v. *Hawkey*, 8 East, 427, recognized by *Bayley*, J., in *Goldstein* v. *Foss*, 6 B. & C. 160, and by *Tindal*, C. J., delivering judgment in *Alexander* v. *Angle*, on error in Exch. Chr., 1 Cr. & J. 146.

of them (b); that which comes after the innuendo not being issuable (c); and further, it must be averred, that the words were spoken in a conversation about those facts. In short, the words must be sufficient to maintain the action without the innuendo (d). And the meaning given by the innuendo must be such as may fairly be collected, either from the words alone or from the words coupled with facts, which were the subject of the conversation, previously averred in the declaration; for an innuendo cannot be used to enlarge the meaning of words without prefatory averments (e). It is to be observed, however, that although new (f) matter cannot be introduced by an innuendo, but must be brought upon the record in another way, yet, where such new matter is not necessary to support the action, an innuendo, without any colloquium, may be rejected as surplusage (g).

An action will not lie for these words, " I will take him to Bow Street on a charge of forgery," without an innuendo (h). In a declaration for slander of plaintiff in his trade, a count alleging that the defendant, in a certain discourse in the presence and hearing of divers subjects, falsely and maliciously charged and asserted and accused plaintiff of being in insolvent circumstances, and stating special damage, but without setting out the words, is ill; and if it be joined with other counts, which set out the words, and a general verdict given, the court will arrest the judgment (i). It is the province of the jury to decide, whether the defendant's meaning was such as is imputed to him by the innuendo (k). In an action for calling the plaintiff a thief, it was proved, that the defendant said of the plaintiff, " Why don't you come out, you blackguard, rascal, scoundrel. Penfold, you are a thief"(l); but the witness who proved the words was not asked, whether by the word "thief" he understood, that the defendant meant to charge the plaintiff with felony. *Chambre*, J., in his direction to the jury, said, that it lay on the defendant to show, that felony was not imputed by the word "thief;" and a verdict was found for the plaintiff. On a motion to set aside the verdict, on the ground, that it appeared from the expressions which accompanied the word "thief," that the defendant did not intend to impute felony, but merely used that word, together with the others, in the heat of passion; that no evidence was given to show that the word "thief" was understood by those who heard it, to charge the plaintiff with any crime, the court refused the application; Sir *J. Mansfield*, C. J., observing,

(b) 1 Rol. Abr. 83, l. 10.
(c) *Slocomb's* case, Cro. Car. 443.
(d) *Lovet* v. *Hawthorn*, Cro. Eliz. 834.
(e) Per *Patteson*, J., *Gompertz* v. *Levy*, 9 A. & E. 285, citing *Goldstein* v. *Foss*.
(f) *Day* v. *Robinson*, in error, 1 Ad. & Ell. 554.
(g) *Roberts* v. *Camden*, 9 East, 95.

(h) *Harrison* v. *King*, in error, 7 Taunt. 431.
(i) *Cook* v. *Cox*, 3 M. & S. 110.
(k) Per *Gould* and *Blackstone*, Js., 2 Bl. R. 961, 2, cited by Lord *Ellenborough*, C. J., in *Roberts* v. *Camden*, ubi sup.
(l) *Penfold* v. *Westcote*, 2 Bos. & Pul. N. R. 335.

that the jury ought not to have found a verdict for the plaintiff,
unless they understood the defendant to impute theft to the plaintiff. The manner in which the words were pronounced, and various
other circumstances, might explain the meaning of the word ; and
if the jury had thought, that the word was only used by the defendant as a word of general abuse, they ought to have found a
verdict for the defendant. Supposing that the general words which
accompany the word " thief" might have warranted the jury in
finding for the defendant, yet, as they have not done so, the court
cannot say that the word did not impute theft to the plaintiff. A
count, charging that defendant had imposed (*m*) upon the plaintiff
the crime of felony, is good after verdict. Where the words were,
" You have committed a crime for which I can transport you," they
were holden (*n*), (on motion in arrest of judgment,) to be actionable
without any colloquium or innuendo.

IV. *Of the Pleadings, p.* 1254 ; *Evidence, p.* 1256 ; *Costs,
p.* 1258.

Of the Pleadings.

MONEY cannot be paid into court (*o*). The general issue in this
action is, Not guilty. But now (*p*), in actions on the case, the plea
of not guilty shall operate as a denial only of the breach of duty or
wrongful act alleged to have been committed by the defendant, and
not of the facts stated in the inducement, and no other defence
than such denial shall be admissible under that plea : all other pleas
in denial shall take issue on some particular matter of fact alleged
in the declaration. In an action of slander of the plaintiff in his
office, profession, or trade, the plea of not guilty will operate to the
same extent precisely as at present in denial of speaking the words,
of speaking them maliciously, and in the sense imputed, and with
reference to the plaintiff's office, profession, or trade ; but it will
not operate as a denial of the fact of the plaintiff holding the office
or being of the profession or trade alleged (*q*). On the general issue,
the defendant will not be allowed to give the truth of the fact
imputed to the plaintiff in evidence, even in mitigation of damages ;
and this rule holds in all cases, whether the words do or do not
import a charge of felony (*r*), or whether a charge of felony be

(*m*) *Blizard* v. *Kelly*, 2 B. & C. 283.
(*n*) *Curtis* v. *Curtis*, 10 Bingh. 477 ; 4
M. & Sc. 337. See *Francis* v. *Roose*, 3
M. & W. 191.
(*o*) Stat. 3 & 4 Will. IV. c. 42, s. 21.

(*p*) R. G. H. T. 4 Will. IV.
(*q*) *Ibid.*
(*r*) *Underwood* v. *Parkes*, Str. 1200,
S. P., per Lord *Mansfield*, C. J., Middlesex Sittings, 1767, MS. *Chambre*, J.

particular (*s*), or general (*t*). If, however, the charge be true, the
defendant may *plead* it in justification. If the words were spoken
by the defendant as counsel, and were pertinent to the matter in
issue (*u*): or in confidence; as by a master, upon being applied
to for the character of a servant (*x*) (11): in these, and similar
cases (*y*), an action will not lie, because malice, (one of the essential
grounds in an action for slander,) is wanting; but, " if without
ground (*z*), and purely to defame, a false character should be given,
it would be proper ground for an action." The plea of privileged
communication must allege that the defendant made the communication on a lawful occasion, believing it to be true and without
malice, or at least *bonâ fide* (*a*). A plea negativing the special
damage in slander for words actionable in themselves is bad on
demurrer (*b*).

The defendant may plead that the *words* were not spoken within
two years before the commencement of the action (*c*).

(*s*) *Smith* v. *Richardson*, Willes, 24,
per eight judges.
(*t*) Per twelve judges, *S. C.*
(*u*) *S. C.; Hodgson* v. *Scarlett*, Holt's
N. P. C. 621; 1 B. & A. 232.
(*x*) *Edmondson* v. *Stephenson and another*, Bull. N. P. 8; *Weatherston* v.
Hawkins, 1 T. R. 110. See also *Hargrave* v. *Le Breton*, 4 Burr. 2425.
(*y*) *Warr* v. *Jolly*, 6 C. & P. 497;

Woodward v. *Lander*, 6 C. & P. 548.
(*z*) Per Lord *Mansfield*, C. J., in *Edmondson* v. *Stephenson*, Bull. N. P. 8,
cited by *Park*, J., in *Blackburn* v. *Blackburn*, 4 Bingh. 408.
(*a*) *Smith* v. *Thomas*, 2 Bingh. N. C.
372; 2 Scott, 546.
(*b*) *S. C.*
(*c*) Stat. 21 Jac. I. c. 16, s. 3.

(11) Where a person intending to hire a servant applies to the former
master for a character, the master (except where express malice is proved)
shall not be obliged to prove the truth of the character he gives, for in
such case the disclosure is not made officiously, but in confidence, and the
facts may happen to rest only in the knowledge of master and servant.
But where the master voluntarily, and without being applied to, speaks
defamatory words of his servant, it will be incumbent on him to plead and
prove the truth of the words. Said by Lord *Mansfield*, C. J., to be so
settled, and that he had often ruled it so at Nisi Prius. *Lawry* v. *Acken-
head and Ux.*, B. R. Sittings M. 8 Geo. III., Chambre, MSS.; *Kelly* v.
Partington, 4 B. & Ad. 700; 2 Nev. & M. 460. " I take the law to be
well settled, that where a master is applied to for a character of a servant,
the former is not called upon in an action to prove the truth of any aspersions thrown out by him against the latter, but that it lies upon the
servant to prove the falsehood of such aspersions. In such case the master
is justified, unless the servant prove express malice." Per *Chambre*, J.,
in *Rogers* v. *Clifton*, M. 44 Geo. III., C. B., 3 Bos. & Pul. 594. The
case itself is well worthy of attention on this subject, but the circumstances
of it are too special for insertion in this work. N. A servant cannot bring
an action against his master for not giving him a character. Per *Kenyon*,
C. J., in *Carrol* v. *Bird*, 3 Esp. N. P. C. 201.

Evidence.

The words must be proved as laid in the declaration (d); that is, such of them as will support the action; for it is not necessary for the plaintiff to prove *all* the words stated in the declaration; only what is (e) material. Formerly, indeed, it was holden, that the plaintiff must prove the words precisely as laid (f); but now it is sufficient to prove the substance of them. However, if the words be laid in the third person, *e. g.*, *he* is a thief, proof of words spoken in the second person, *e. g.*, *you* are a thief, will not support the declaration (g); for there is a great difference between words spoken in a passion to a man's face, and words spoken deliberately behind his back (h). Nor will proof of words spoken *to* a person support an *indictment* (i) charging that the defendant spoke them *of* such person. So an averment that slanderous words spoken concerning the (three) plaintiffs in their joint trade, was holden (k) not to be supported by evidence of words addressed by the defendant personally to one only of the partners. In like manner a count for slanderous words spoken affirmatively, cannot be supported by proof that they were spoken by way of interrogatory: as where the declaration stated (l), that the defendant *spoke* these words, " he, the plaintiff, cannot pay his labourers," and the evidence was, that the defendant had asked a witness " if he had heard that plaintiff could not pay his labourers." Where the declaration alleged that the plaintiff was of two trades, although the plaintiff failed to prove that he was of both; it was holden (m), that he might recover upon proof that he was of that trade concerning which the defendant was charged to have spoken the words; for the allegation was partible. The plaintiff, after proving the words as laid in the declaration, may prove that the defendant spoke other (n) words on the same subject or referring to it, either before

(d) *Barnes* v. *Holloway*, 8 T. R. 150. Per *Lawrence*, J., in *Maitland* v. *Goldney*, 2 East, 430; *Walters* v. *Mace*, 2 B. & A. 756; *Hancock* v. *Winter*, 7 Taunt. 205.

(e) Per *Bayley*, B., *Cox* v. *Thomason*, 2 Cr. & J. 364.

(f) Bull. N. P., cites 2 Rol. Abr. 718.

(g) See *Stannard* v. *Harper*, 5 M. & R. 295.

(h) *Avarillo* v. *Rogers*, London Sittings, Trin. 1773, B. R., Lord *Mansfield*, C. J., cited by *Buller*, J., in *R.* v. *Berry*, 4 T. R. 217, where the same doctrine was applied, and *Buller*, J., said he had known

a variety of nonsuits on the same objection; although there was a case in *Strange* e contra, and also a dictum of Lord *Hardwicke*, C. J., in *Nelson* v. *Dixie*, C. Temp. Hardw. 306.

(i) *R.* v. *Berry*, 4 T. R. 217.

(k) *Solomons and two others* v. *Medex*, 1 Stark. N. P. C. 191.

(l) *Barnes* v. *Holloway*, 8 T. R. 150.

(m) *Figgins* v. *Cogswell*, 3 M. & S. 369.

(n) See 2 Phillips, c. 9, and *ante*, tit. "Libel," p. 1047, n., 1048, n. (7). See also *Defries* v. *Davis*, 7 C. & P. 112, *Tindal*, C. J.

or afterwards, although such words may be actionable; for this evidence is admissible, not in aggravation of damages, but for the purpose of proving the malice of the defendant in deliberately speaking the words which are the subject of the action.

In an action for words of perjury, the plaintiff offered in evidence a bill of indictment, which had been preferred against him by the defendant, and which the grand jury returned ignoramus. This was holden to be admissible evidence to show the malicious intent with which the words were spoken (o). If the declaration contain several actionable words, it is sufficient for plaintiff to prove some of them (p). Express malice need not be proved; if the charge be false, malice will be implied. The existence of express malice is only a matter of inquiry (q), where the injurious expressions, which are the subject of complaint, are uttered upon a lawful occasion. In an action for slander of title, it must appear that the words were spoken maliciously : it is not necessary for the defendant to plead specially; but the plaintiff must prove malice, which is the gist of the action (r). Where in the declaration it was alleged, that the plaintiff was a physician, and exercised that profession in England, and on that account was called doctor, meaning doctor of medicine, and that defendant slandered plaintiff in his character of a physician, and denied his right to be called a doctor of medicine; it was holden (s), that the plaintiff must prove that he was entitled to practise as a physician in England; it was not sufficient to show that he had in fact so practised; nor that he had received the degree of doctor of medicine at the University of St. Andrew's in Scotland. It is not competent for the defendant, under the general issue, to offer, in mitigation of damages, evidence that the specific facts in which the slander consists, and for which the action is brought, were communicated to him by a third person (t). In an action for words imputing felony, with a count for maliciously charging the plaintiff with theft before a justice, to which the defendant pleaded the general issue, and also pleas of justification, evidence of general good character (u) is not admissible for the plaintiff. Where words are given in evidence in order to prove malice, which are not stated in the declaration, the defendant may prove (x) the truth of such words; as, not being on the record, the defendant has had no opportunity of justifying them. Where the words are not actionable

(o) *Tate* v. *Humphrey*, 2 Campb. 73, n. See also *Rustell* v. *M'Quister*, ante, p. 1047, n.

(p) *Compagnon and Wife* v. *Martin*, Bl. R. 790.

(q) Per *Tindal*, C. J., *Hooper* v. *Truscott*, 2 Bingh. N. C. 464. See *Padmore* v. *Lawrence*, and the other cases cited, ante, p. 1244.

(r) *Smith* v. *Spooner*, 3 Taunt. 246.

(s) *Collins* v. *Carnegie*, 1 A. & E. 695, 3 Nev. & M. 703.

(t) *Mills* v. *Spencer*, Holt's N. P. C. 533.

(u) *Cornwall* v. *Richardson*, Ry. & M. 305, *Abbott*, C. J.

(x) *Warne* v. *Chadwell*, 2 Stark. N. P. C. 457.

in themselves, and the only ground of action is the special damage, such special damage must be proved (y) as alleged. Where the words are actionable without the inducement, the insertion of what is not material and not proved, does not occasion a variance (z) of which advantage can be taken.

Costs.

By stat. 21 Jac. I. c. 16, s. 6, " In all actions upon the case for slanderous words, if the jury upon the trial of the issue, or the jury *that shall inquire of the damages*, assess the damages *under forty shillings*, then the plaintiff shall recover only so much costs as the damages so assessed amount unto." This statute does not extend to actions founded on special damage only, because, properly speaking, they are not actions for *words*, but for the special damage (a). But where words are actionable in themselves (b), and special damage is laid in the declaration only by way of aggravation, although the special damage be proved, yet if the damages recovered are under 40s. there shall be no more costs than damages. In *Baker* v. *Hearne* (c), B. R. H. 1767, argued by Dunning for plaintiff, and Ashhurst for defendant, the distinction was not controverted by plaintiff's counsel ; the court being of opinion that the words were actionable as relating to plaintiff in his way of trade, they allowed no more costs than damages, the damages being under 40s., notwithstanding the special damages laid in the declaration. If some of the counts in the declaration be for words that are actionable (d), and others for words not actionable, and special damage be laid referring to all the counts, and there be a general verdict for plaintiff, he is entitled to full costs, though he recover less than 40s. damages. In a case where the declaration embraced two distinct objects (e), viz. a charge for speaking words actionable in themselves, and a charge that defendant procured plaintiff to be indicted, without probable cause, for felony ; it was holden, that such an action, not being merely an action for words, but also an action on the case for a malicious prosecution, was not within the statute ; and, therefore, although plaintiff recovered damages under 40s. yet he should be entitled to full costs. In cases within the statute, if damages are under 40s. plaintiff cannot have more costs taxed than

(y) *Ward* v. *Weeks*, 7 Bingh. 211.
(z) *Cox* v. *Thomason*, 2 Cr. & J. 361 ; 2 Tyrw. 411.
(a) *Lowe* v. *Harewood*, Sir William Jones, 196 ; *Collier* v. *Gaillard*, 2 Bl. Rep. 1062.
(b) Lord Raym. 1583; *Burry* v. *Perry*,

2 Str. 936, *S. C.* ; *Turner* v. *Horton*, Willes, 438, S. P.
(c) MSS., *Chambre*, J.
(d) *Savile* v. *Jardine*, 2 H. Bl. 531.
(e) *Topsall* v. *Edwards*, Cro. Car. 163 ; *Blizard* v. *Barnes*, Cro. Car. 307, S. P.

the damages, *notwithstanding defendant has justified* (*f*). By stat. 58 Geo. III. c. 30, s. 2, in actions or suits for slanderous words, in courts not holding plea to the amount of 40*s.*, if the jury assess the damages under 30*s.*, the plaintiff shall recover costs only to the amount of the damages.

See the new statute relating to costs, 3 & 4 Vict. c. 24, *ante,* p. 37.

(*f*) *Halford* v. *Smith*, 4 East, 567, S. P. said, per *Clive,* J., in *Bartlett* v.   *Robbins,* to have been determined in the court of B. R. 2 Wils. 258, E. 5 Geo. I.

CHAPTER XXXVII.

STOPPAGE IN TRANSITU.

Nature of this Right, p. 1260; *Who shall be considered as capable of exercising it*, p. 1261; *Where the Transitus may be said to be continuing*, p. 1263; *Where determined*, p. 1272; *How far the Negociation of the Bill of Lading may tend to defeat the Right*, p. 1278.

NATURE of the Right of Stopping in Transitu.—When goods are consigned upon credit by one merchant to another, it frequently happens that the consignee becomes a bankrupt or insolvent, before the goods are delivered. In such case the law, deeming it unreasonable that the goods of one person should be applied to the payment of the debts of another, permits the consignor to resume the possession of his goods. This right which the consignor has of resuming the possession of his goods, if the full price has not been paid, in the event of the insolvency of the consignee, is technically termed the right of stopping in transitu. The doctrine of stopping in transitu owes its origin to courts of equity (*a*), but it has since been adopted and established by a variety of decisions in courts of law, and is now regarded with favour as a right which those courts are always disposed to assist. This right is paramount to any lien against the purchaser (*b*). The following cases will illustrate the nature of this right. B. at London, gave an order to A. at Liverpool, to send him a quantity of goods (*c*). A. accordingly shipped the goods on board a ship there, whereof the defendant was master, who signed a bill of lading to deliver them in good condition to B. in London. The ship arrived in the Thames, but B. having become a bankrupt, the defendant was ordered, on behalf of A., not to deliver the goods, and accordingly refused, though the freight was tendered. It appeared, by the plaintiffs' witnesses, that no particular ship was mentioned, whereby the goods should be sent, in

---

(*a*) See *D'Aguila* v. *Lambert*, 9th June, 1761; 2 Eden, 75, and Amb. 399, *S. C.,* where the doctrine was first recognized.

(*b*) *Morley* v. *Hay*, 3 Man. & Ry. 396.

(*c*) *Assignees of Burghall, Bankrupt,* v. *Howard*, London Sittings after Hil. T. 32 Geo. II., coram Lord *Mansfield*, C. J., 1 H. Bl. 366, n.

which case the shipper is to be at the risk of the perils of the seas. An action on the case upon the custom of the realm having been brought against the defendant as a carrier, Lord *Mansfield* was of opinion that the plaintiffs were not entitled to recover, and said, he had known it several times ruled in Chancery, that where the consignee becomes a bankrupt, and no part of the price has been paid, it was lawful for the consignor to seize the goods before they come to the hands of the consignee or his assignees; and that this was ruled, not upon principles of equity only, but the laws of property. The plaintiffs were nonsuited. The right of stopping in transitu does not proceed on the ground of rescinding the contract, but, in the language of Lord *Kenyon*, it is an equitable lien adopted by the law, for the purposes of substantial justice. Hence the circumstance of the vendee having paid in part for the goods (d) will not defeat the vendor's right of stopping them in transitu; the vendor has a right to retake them, unless the full price of the goods has been paid; and the only operation of a partial payment is to diminish the lien, pro tanto. The unpaid vendor may stop in transitu before the goods come to the hands of the vendee's factor, although the factor has the bill of lading, indorsed to order, in his hands, and is under acceptance to the vendee on a general account; wherefore, in such case, where the vendee became bankrupt, and the factor also became bankrupt, and the messenger under the factor's commission, upon the arrival of the ship, went on board and seized the cargo, the agent of the vendor having previously given notice to the captain to deliver the cargo to him, and the captain having agreed thereto; it was holden (e), that trover would lie by the vendor against the assignee of the bankrupt factor. The cases which have been decided on this subject may be arranged under the following divisions: 1st, Who shall be considered as capable of exercising the right of stopping in transitu; 2ndly, Under what circumstances the transitus shall be considered as continuing; 3rdly, When the transitus shall be considered as determined; and lastly, Where the right of the vendor has been defeated by the negotiation of the bill of lading.

1. *Who shall be considered as capable of exercising the Right of Stopping in Transitu.*—As to the first division, I am aware of two cases only, in which the subject has been brought under the consideration of the court, viz. *Feise* v. *Wray*, 3 East, 93, and *Siffken* v. *Wray*, 6 East, 371. From these cases it may be collected, that if the party exercising the right stand in the relation of vendor, quoad the bankrupt or insolvent, it is sufficient; but that a mere surety, for the price of the goods, is not entitled to stop them in

---

(d) *Hodgson* v. *Loy*, 7 T. R. 440, recognized in *Feise* v. *Wray*, 3 East, 93, and *post*, p. 1262, cited and distinguished in *Nicholls* v. *Hart*, 5 C. & P. 179, *Tin-*

dal, C. J.
  (e) *Patten* v. *Thompson*, 5 M. & S 350.

transitu. The case of *Feise* v. *Wray* was shortly this. B., a trader in England, gave an order to C., his correspondent abroad, to purchase a quantity of goods for him (*f*). C. bought the goods accordingly of another merchant, (who was a stranger to B. and had not any account or correspondence with him,) and shipped them on board a general ship, on the account and risk of B.; the bill of lading was filled up to the order of B.; C. drew bills of exchange on B. for the price of the goods, including also a charge for commission. These bills were accepted, but not paid; for, before the goods arrived, B. became a bankrupt; whereupon C. authorized his agent in England to obtain possession of the goods on their arrival, which he did accordingly. An action of trover having been brought by the assignees of B. against the agent of C., to recover the value of the goods; it was contended, on the part of the plaintiffs, that the right of stopping in transitu did not attach between B. and C.; that B. must be considered as the principal for whom the goods were originally purchased, and that C. was only his factor or agent, purchasing them on his account; and that the right of stopping in transitu did in point of law apply solely to the case of vendor and vendee; but, per *Lawrence, J.*, "If that were so, it would nearly put an end to the application of that law in this country; for I believe it happens, for the most part, that orders come to the merchants here, from their correspondents abroad, to purchase and ship certain merchandize to them; the merchants here, upon the authority of those orders, obtain the goods from those whom they deal with; and they charge a commission to their correspondents abroad, upon the price of the commodity thus obtained. It never was doubted but that the merchant here, if he heard of the failure of his correspondent abroad, might stop the goods in transitu. But, at any rate, *this is a case between vendor and vendee; for there was no privity between the original owner of the goods and the bankrupt;* but the property may be considered as having been first purchased by C., and again sold to B. at the first price, with the addition of his commission upon it. He then became the vendor as to B., and consequently had a right to stop the goods in transitu, unless he is estopped by the circumstance of B. having accepted bills for the amount, which bills, it is contended, may be proved under B.'s commission, and are equivalent at least to part payment of the goods; but it was decided, in *Hodgson* v. *Loy*, 7 T. R. 440, that part payment for the goods does not conclude the right to stop in transitu; it only diminishes the vendor's *lien*, pro tanto, on the goods detained. Then, having lawfully possessed himself of them, he has a lien on them till the whole price be paid, which cannot therefore be satisfied by showing a part payment only. It is possible that part payment may be obtained by proving the bills under B.'s commission; but if the loss must fall on one side or the

---

(*f*) *Feise* v. *Wray*, 3 East, 93.

other, the maxim applies, " Qui prior est tempore potior est jure."
The court were of opinion, that the assignees were not entitled to
recover. Since this case it has been holden (g), that a consignor of
goods, who has received the acceptance of the consignee for part of
the goods, may stop them in transitu on the consignee's insolvency,
and retain possession of them without tendering back the bill.

The facts of the case in *Siffken* v. *Wray* were as follow:—B., a
trader in London, ordered goods to be shipped to him by C. (h) his
correspondent at Dantzic, with directions to C. to draw for the
amount on D. at Hamburgh (who had agreed to accept the bills,
upon receiving a commission on the amount), and to transmit the
bills of lading and invoices to D., who was to forward them to B. in
London. The goods were shipped, D. accepted the bills, and on
the receipt of the bills of lading, transmitted the same, (which were
made out to the orders of the shippers and not indorsed,) to B. in
London, who received them, together with the invoices and letter
of advice, five days after he had committed an act of bankruptcy.
D.'s acceptances were afterwards dishonoured, whereby C. was
obliged to take up the bills of exchange. J. S., the agent of D. in
England, procured from B. the bills of lading, upon an undertaking
that he would dispose of the goods, on their arrival, to the best
advantage, and apply the proceeds to the discharge of the bills
drawn against them. J. S., having obtained possession of the
goods, sold them, and paid the proceeds into the Court of Chancery,
to abide the verdict in an action directed by that court to be
brought by the assignees of B. against J. S. C., having been
apprized of what had been done by J. S., wrote a letter, signifying
his approbation of J. S.'s conduct, and therein claimed the proceeds.
The action directed by the Court of Chancery having been brought,
the Court of B. R. were of opinion, that the assignees of B. were
entitled to the proceeds: for, 1st, D. did not stand in the relation
of vendor of these goods quoad the bankrupt, but was a mere
surety for the price of the goods, and consequently he was not
entitled to stop them in transitu; 2ndly, although C. was the
vendor of the goods, yet J. S. could not be considered as his agent
in this transaction, not having received any authority from C. until
after he had obtained possession of the goods; but, supposing him
to have been the agent of C. before, yet there was not any adverse
taking possession of the goods, inasmuch as they had been taken
under an amicable agreement with B. after his bankruptcy.

2. *Under what Circumstances the Transitus shall be considered
as continuing.*—As to the second division, under what circumstances
the transitus shall be considered as continuing, the cases are more
numerous than in the last division; and as they depend in great
measure on their own special circumstances, it will be necessary to

---

(g) *Edwards* v. *Brewer*, 2 M. & W.
375, recognizing *False* v. *Wray*.

(h) *Siffken and another, Assignees of
Browne, Bankrupt*, v. *Wray*, 6 East, 371.

state them at some length. The first in order of time is *Stokes* v. *La Riviere*, cited in 3 T. R. 466, and more correctly by *Lawrence*, J., in *Bothlingk* v. *Inglis*, 3 East, 397. Messrs. Duhem, of Lisle, who had jus arrived in London, applied to the plaintiff (a ribbon-weaver) for a quantity of ribbon. The plaintiff having received a favourable account, by the defendants, of Duhem's circumstances, packed up goods to a large amount, and delivered them to the defendants to be forwarded to Lisle. These goods, with others purchased in like manner of another tradesman of the name of Twigge, were forwarded, on or about the 12th of May, to the defendants' correspondent at Ostend, with directions to send them to the order of Messrs. Duhem. On the receipt of the goods, *viz.* on the 29th of May, the defendants' correspondents at Ostend wrote to the Duhems an acknowledgment, and that they waited their directions. On the 12th June, the Duhems stopped payment; and, by an instrument signed the 13th of August, consented to Twigge's taking back his goods. But Messrs. Duhem not having fulfilled some engagement with the defendants, and being considerably indebted to them, the defendants countermanded the order they had given to their correspondents at Ostend, as to the delivery of the goods, by letter of the 31st May, and directed them to alter the marks and deliver them to their order, which was accordingly done; and they were afterwards disposed of in satisfaction of the defendants' demand upon Messrs. Duhem; they contending that, immediately upon the delivery of the goods by the plaintiff to them, the property vested in Messrs. Duhem, and that they, the defendants, had a right to detain them. Lord *Mansfield* said, " No point is more clear, than if goods are sold, and the price not paid, the seller may stop them in transitu; I mean in every sort of passage to the hands of the buyers. There have been a hundred cases of this sort; ships in harbour, carriers, bills, have been stopped. In short, where the goods are in transitu, the seller has that proprietary lien. *The goods are in the hands of the defendants to be conveyed;* the owner may get them back again."

In *Hunter and another, Assignees of Blanchard and Lewis,* v. *Beal,* cited 3 T. R. 466, an action of trover was brought for a bale of cloth, which was sent by Messrs. Steers and Co. of Wakefield, to the defendant, who was an innkeeper, directed for the bankrupts, to whom the defendant's book-keeper gave notice that a bale was arrived for them: and Steers and Co. at the same time sent them a bill of parcels by the post, the receipt of which they acknowledged, and wrote word that they had placed the amount to the credit of Steers and Co. The bankrupts gave orders to the defendant's book-keeper to send the bale down to the Galley Quay, in order to ship it on board the Union, to be carried to Boston. The defendant accordingly sent the bale to the Quay; but, arriving too late to be shipped, it was sent back to him. Within ten days afterwards, a clerk of the bankrupts went to the defendant's warehouse, when the defendant asked him what was to be done with the bale in question, and was ordered to keep it in his custody till another ship sailed, which would happen in a few days. The bankruptcy happened soon afterwards; and Messrs. Steers and Co. sent word to the defendant not to let the bale out of his hands: accordingly, when the bankrupts applied for it, he refused to deliver it up. Lord *Mansfield* was clearly of opinion, that though the goods might be legally delivered to the vendees for many purposes, yet as for this purpose there must be an absolute and actual possession by the bankrupts, or (as his lordship expressed it,) they must have come to the *corporal touch* of the vendees; otherwise they may be stopped in transitu; a delivery to the third person, to convey them, is not sufficient. The preceding case of *Hunter* v. *Beal* was much commented upon by Lord *Ellenborough*, in *Dixon* v. *Baldwen*, 5 East, 184. The impression on his lordship's mind appears to have been against the determination. His words are these: " As to *Hunter* v. *Beal*, in which it is said, that the goods must come to the *corporal touch of the vendees*, in order to oust the right of stopping *in transitu*, it is a *figurative* expression, rarely, if ever, strictly true. If it be predicated of the vendee's own actual *touch*, or of the touch of any other person, it comes in each instance to a question, whether the party to whose touch it actually comes, be an agent so far representing the principal, as to make the delivery to him a full, effectual, and final delivery to the principal, as contradistinguished from a delivery to a person virtually acting as a carrier, or mean of conveyance to or on the account of the principal, in a mere course of transit towards him. I cannot but consider the transit as having been once completely at an end in the direct course of the goods to the vendee; *i. e.* when they had arrived at the innkeeper's, and were afterwards, under the immediate orders of the vendee, thence actually launched again in a course of conveyance from him, in their way to Boston; being in a new direction prescribed and communicated by himself. And if the transit be once at an end, the delivery is complete, and the transitus for this purpose cannot commence de novo, merely because the goods are again sent upon their travels towards a new and ulterior destination." In *Hunt and others, Assignees of Bennet and Heaven*, v. *Ward*, cited in 3 T. R. 467, where goods had been sent by orders from the vendee to a packer; the packer was considered as a middle man between the vendor and vendee: and, therefore, the court held they might be stopped *in transitu*, on the bankruptcy of the vendee. So where A. sold goods to B., and, according to B.'s directions, sent them to C., a wharfinger (*i*), to be by him forwarded to B.; it was holden, that while they were in C.'s hands, they might be stopped by A., because they were merely at a stage upon their transit, and could not be considered as having arrived at their final destination.

(*i*) *Smith and another* v. *Goss*, 1 Campb. 282.

The plaintiff, living at Leghorn, consigned goods to B. at Liverpool, by a ship chartered on account of B. (*k*). The captain signed three bills of lading, as usual, one of which was sent to B. Before the ship arrived at L., B. became a bankrupt. On the ship's arrival at L., she was ordered to perform quarantine. Pending the quarantine, one of the assignees of B. went on board the vessel, claimed the cargo as belonging to the bankrupt, and put two persons on board with a view of keeping possession. A few days after, but before the expiration of the quarantine, the plaintiff's agent served a notice of the bankruptcy on the captain of the vessel, and claimed the goods on behalf of the plaintiff; a similar notice was served on the assignees, the defendants. It was contended, that the principal's right to stop *in transitu* was completely at an end when the consignee had got possession, by any means, of the goods consigned: that the consignee might have met the vessel at sea on her voyage, and have taken possession by virtue of the first bill of lading; which possession, they contended, would be complete to divest any right the consignor might have to stop the goods in transitu: but Lord *Kenyon* was of opinion, that this was a stopping in transitu sufficient to maintain the action: his lordship said, that in order to give the consignee a right to claim by virtue of possession, it should be a possession obtained by the consignee, on the completion of the voyage; that the case put, that the consignee had a right to go out to sea to meet the ship, could not be supported, as it might go the length of saying that the consignee might meet the vessel coming out of the port, from whence she had been consigned, and that that should divest the property out of the consignor and vest it in himself, which was a position not to be supported (*l*), as there would be then no possibility of any stoppage *in transitu* at all. That in the present case the voyage was not completed, till she had performed quarantine, till which time she was *in transitu;* and as the plaintiff's agent had given notice, and claimed the cargo before the completion of the voyage, he was of opinion that the plaintiff had stopped the goods time enough to prevent the property from vesting in the assignees. The Court of B. R., on a motion for a new trial, confirmed the opinion given by Lord *Kenyon.* The like judgment was given in the case of *Northey and another, Assignees of Leyland and another,* v. *Field,* 2 Esp. N. P. C. 613. There a quantity of wine was consigned to B. After the arrival of the vessel, aboard which the wine in question had been shipped, but pending the twenty days allowed for payment of the duty, B. became a bankrupt. After the expiration of the twenty days the wine was removed into the king's cellar, where by the excise law it is allowed to remain three months: during which time the owner may have the wine on paying the duty, warehouse-room, &c.: but if not

---

(*k*) *Holst* v. *Pownal and another,* 1 Esp. N. P. C. 240.

(*l*) But see 2 Bos. & Pul. 461.

paid at the end of the three months, the wine is sold. The day before the expiration of the three months, the agents of the consignors applied for, and endeavoured to obtain, possession of the wine, but in vain. The wine was sold, and the produce paid into the hands of a broker. An action having been brought by the assignees of the bankrupt, who claimed the produce, Lord *Kenyon* was of opinion, that they were not entitled to recover; observing, that the courts of late years had inclined much in favour of the power of the consignor to stop his goods *in transitu*, it was a leaning to the furtherance of justice. Lord *Hardwicke* had been of opinion, that in order to stop goods *in transitu*, there must be an actual possession of them obtained by the consignor, before they come to the hands of the consignee; but that rule has since been relaxed; and it was now held, that an actual possession was not necessary, that a claim was sufficient, and to that rule he subscribed. In the present case, the bankrupt had no title to the actual possession, until the duties were paid—until then they were *quasi in custodiâ legis;* before the sale, the agent for the consignors claimed, and endeavoured to get possession; that was a sufficient stopping *in transitu*, in his opinion, to secure the rights of the consignor.

B., resident in Cumberland, purchased a quantity of butter from A. (*m*), who agreed to deliver it to D., a carrier. B. desired that it might be marked with the initials of C., his brother's name, to whom he usually sent his butter consigned for sale on his own account, and which initials B. had constantly used for some years upon such consignments. The butter was delivered by the vendors to D., the carrier agreed on, who was desired by B. to forward it as usual to a wharfinger usually employed by B., at Stockton, to be by him shipped for London. It was stated in the case, that D., entered the butter in his way-bill in the name of B., and carried it on his account, the vendor telling him that B. was to pay the carriage. He carried the firkins as far as Bowes, where he delivered them to E., another carrier, who received no other instructions but from the way-bill; E. proceeded with them to Stockton, and there delivered them to the wharfinger, who had general directions from B. to send to C., his brother in London. The wharfinger immediately wrote to B. acknowledging the receipt of the butter, and also to C., and acquainted the latter with the name of the ship by which the butter was to be forwarded to London. Before the butter reached London, B. and C. became bankrupts, and the defendant, as agent of the seller, got possession of the butter on its arrival in the river. In an action brought by the assignees of B., one of the questions was, whether there was any such delivery to the bankrupt as was sufficient to divest the vendor's right to stop *in transitu*. It was contended on the part of the defendant, that there was not; that the delivery to D., in the first instance, and

(*m*) *Hodgson v. Loy,* 7 T. R. 440.

afterwards that by him to E., and by E. to the wharfinger, were all deliveries made to them in the capacity of common carriers, and not as private agents of the bankrupt. The circumstance of the bankrupt desiring D. to carry the goods to the wharfinger as usual could not vary the nature of the agency. But supposing it did, and that it amounted to the appointment of the wharfinger as a special carrier named by the vendee, that would not alter the vendor's right to stop *in transitu* (1); that *Buller*, J., had expressly said in *Ellis* v. *Hunt*, 3 T. R. 469, that that would make no difference, and that the case of *Stokes* v. *La Riviere*, where the right was allowed, was a case of delivery to a particular carrier; and as to the mark on the goods, that was not for the purpose of taking possession of them, as in *Ellis* v. *Hunt*, but merely as a direction to whom they were to be sent. The court were of opinion, that the defendant was entitled to stop the goods *in transitu*. Lord *Ellenborough*, adverting to the preceding case, in *Dixon* v. *Baldwen*, 5 East, 185, observed, " that it was a clear case of transit uncompleted; for the butter purchased in Cumberland was proceeding through different stages of country conveyance to the purchaser in London, but before it reached the place of its destination, it was stopped."

B., being in trade at North Tawton, in Devonshire, gave orders to the plaintiffs to send the goods in question to him from London, but did not direct that they should be sent by any particular ship (*n*); his orders were, that they should be sent to him at Exeter, to be forwarded to N. T. They were accordingly shipped, arrived at Exeter, and were put into the hands of the wharfinger to be forwarded to their journey's end. In the books of the wharfinger they were put to the account of B. as the person to whom they were directed, and he was considered as the wharfinger's paymaster. In this state of things a letter was received by the plaintiffs, in which the vendee said, that his situation was such that he should not receive the goods, and that they might take them back again, if they thought proper. The plaintiffs, immediately on the receipt of this letter, sent to the wharfinger, and forbade him to deliver them according to the direction. The wharfinger promised

(*n*) *Mills* v. *Ball*, 2 Bos. & Pul. 457.

---

(1) It seems, however, that, if a person be in the habit of using the warehouse of a wharfinger as his own, and make that the repository of his goods, and dispose of them there, the journey would be considered as at an end when the goods arrived at such warehouse. Per *Chambre*, J., *Richardson* v. *Goss*, 3 Bos. & Pul. 127. And Lord *Alvanley* expressed his concurrence in that opinion in *Scott* v. *Petit*, 3 Bos. & Pul. 469, cited by *Bayley*, J., in *Foster* v. *Frampton*, 6 B. & C. 109, and *post*, p. 1276.

not to deliver them until he could do so with safety, notwithstanding which he afterwards delivered them to the assignees of B. The question was, whether the goods, in the hands of the wharfinger, were in such a situation that the vendors could stop them. The court were of opinion that they were, and that in point of fact the goods had been stopped in transitu; for, although there had not been any corporal touch, yet that took place which was equivalent to it. The plaintiffs gave notice to the wharfinger and demanded the goods as their property; and the wharfinger undertook not to deliver them until he was certain of a safe delivery. *Chambre*, J., added, that there was another point, however, upon which he had entertained some doubt. The vendor did not get possession of these goods by his own diligence and care, or in consequence of casual information, but through the intervention of the bankrupt himself, eight days after the act of bankruptcy committed. That circumstance raised some doubt in his mind; since it appeared that the bankrupt had thereby given a preference to the plaintiffs over the rest of his creditors. But still, upon the whole, he was inclined to agree with the rest of the court: that he was not fond of multiplying small distinctions; and thought that too many had been already taken, and the general inconvenience would not be very great, since many cases of this kind were not likely to arise. It seemed, indeed, that there would be a certain degree of discretion vested in the bankrupt, since he would be empowered to accept goods which were coming to him from one consignor, and to give notice to another consignor, to stop them in transitu. But, as no fraud appeared to have been committed on the part of the plaintiffs in this case, he was inclined, on this point, as well as the others, though not without some doubt, to concur with the rest of the court. It only remains to observe, that where the right of stopping *in transitu* vests in the consignor, it cannot be divested by any claim made upon the goods in their *transit* by a creditor of the consignee, as, *e. g.*, by process of foreign attachment at the suit of such creditor (o); or by a common carrier, claiming to retain the goods as a lien for his general balance due from the consignee (p); for the vendor's right of stopping *in transitu* is the elder and preferable lien.

If a carrier, after notice from the vendor of goods to stop them *in transitu*, by mistake delivers them to the vendee, the sale is nevertheless rescinded, and the vendor may bring trover (q) for them against the vendee; and although the vendee having become a bankrupt, the goods have passed into the hands of his assignees, yet, inasmuch as they did not come to the possession of the bankrupt, with the consent of the true owner, they are not in the order and

(o) *Smith* v. *Goss*, 1 Campb. 282.
(p) *Butler* v. *Woolcott*, 2 Bos. & Pul. N. R. 64.

(q) *Litt* v. *Cowley*, 7 Taunt. 169. See *Clay* v. *Harrison*, 10 B. & C. 106.

disposition of the bankrupt within the statute. Although goods have been delivered at the packers of the purchaser, he having no warehouse of his own, if they were to be paid for in ready money, and this was intimated to the packer when he received them, they may still be stopped *in transitu* (r). A resale of goods by a vendee, and payment to him, does not destroy (s) the vendor's right of stoppage *in transitu*. An order sent by the vendor to the wharfinger to deliver the goods to the vendee, is sufficient to pass the property to the vendee, provided nothing remains to be done but to make the delivery; but if any thing remains to be done, *e. g.*, weighing, &c., the property does not pass (t), and the right of stoppage *in transitu* is not defeated until that be done. Where goods were sold, free on board, and upon their shipment the agent of the vendors tendered to the mate, (the captain being absent,) a receipt by which the goods were acknowledged to be shipped on account of the vendors, which the mate kept, but refused to sign, and on the following day signed bills of lading to the orders of the vendees; it was holden (u), that the transitus was not at an end, but that on the insolvency of the vendees, the vendors were entitled to stop the goods. So where A. delivered a quantity of iron to a carrier to be conveyed to B., the vendee in the country, and the carrier, on his arrival at B.'s premises, landed a part of the iron on his wharf, and then, finding that B. had stopped payment, reloaded the same on board his barge, and took the whole of the iron to his own premises; it was holden (x), that there was not a delivery of any part of the iron, so as to divest the consignor of his right to stop in transitu, the special property remaining in the carrier, until the freight for the whole cargo was either tendered or paid, or until he had done some act showing that he assented to part with the possession of the goods, without receiving his freight.

The transitus is not at an end until the goods have reached the place named by the buyer to the seller, as the place of their destination. Goods were purchased by a commission agent, at Manchester, for A., *to be sent to Lisbon.* A. had no warehouse at Manchester, and the vendor delivered the goods to the agent, who was to forward them to Lisbon: it was holden (y), that the transitus continued until the goods reached Lisbon; and that, the vendee having become insolvent, the vendor might stop the goods in the hands of the agent. So where the shippers acting for G. purchased and paid for, with their own money, flour at Stockton, which was sent by a vessel to London, and the invoice forwarded to G. A manifest of the flour was also forwarded by the shippers to a wharfinger in

(r) *Loeschman* v. *Williams*, 4 Campb. 181.

(s) *Craven* v. *Ryder*, 6 Taunt. 433, recognised in *Dixon* v. *Yates*, 5 B. & Ad. 343.

(t) *Withers* v. *Lys*, Holt's N. P. C. 18;

4 Campb. 237, S. C.

(u) *Ruck* v. *Hatfield*, 5 B. & A. 632.

(x) *Crawshay* v. *Eades*, 1 B. & C. 181.

(y) *Coates* v. *Railton*, 6 B. & C. 422.

See also *Nicholls* v. *Le Feuvre*, 2 Bingh. N. C. 81.

London, whose practice it was to deliver goods to the consignee named in the manifest, upon application, and till application to keep them on board the vessel; if not applied for before the vessel returned, he landed them, and kept them in his warehouse to the order of the shipper; if the goods were to be delivered to order, he delivered them to persons producing either bills of lading or the shipper's invoice. G. was in the habit of having flour consigned to him at the wharf, and sometimes sold it on board, sometimes when it was landed, and kept for him in the wharfinger's warehouses. The flour in question arrived at the wharf on the 12th of April, but was not landed until the 23rd; on the 17th of April, and before any application by G., who had become bankrupt, the flour was claimed under an order from the shippers, it was holden (z), that the shippers might stop it in transitu; for no act of ownership had been exercised over it by G., no invoice or bill of lading had been produced by him or any agent; so that the very first act done upon the flour, after the ship's arrival at the wharf, was done by the shipper, before the transit to the hand or possession of the vendee was complete. The transitus continues (a) until the goods have reached their ultimate destination under the contract of sale, or the vendee has given the direction to the goods. Goods were consigned to A., to be delivered in the river Thames; on the arrival of the vessel in the river, the captain pressed A. to have them landed immediately; A., in consequence, sent B. his son with directions to land them at a wharf where he was accustomed to have goods landed for him and kept until he carted them away to customers in his own carts; but A. (being then insolvent) at the same time told B. he would not meddle with the goods, that he did not intend to take them, and that the vendor ought to have them. The goods were, by B.'s direction, landed at the wharf, and there stopped in transitu by the vendor: in trover for the goods, by the assignees of A. against the wharfinger; it was holden (b), that the declarations so made by A. to B. were admissible in evidence, although they were not communicated to the vendor or to the wharfinger, and that they showed that A. had not taken possession of the goods as owner; and, therefore, that the transitus was not determined.

The general rule is, that the transitus is not at an end until the goods arrive at the actual or constructive possession of the consignee; and a mere demand by the consignee, without any delivery, before the voyage has completely terminated, does not deprive the consignor of his right of stoppage. Hence, where M. purchased lead of the plaintiff at Newcastle, without specifying any place of delivery; after a time M. desired that it should be forwarded to him in London, and plaintiff gave M.'s agent at Newcastle an order on plaintiff's

(z) *Tucker* v. *Humphrey*, 4 Bingh. 516. See also *Bartram* v. *Farebrother*, 4 Bingh. 579.

(a) *Morley* v. *Hay*, 3 Man. & Ry. 396.
(b) *James* v. *Griffin*, 2 M. & W. 623, per three Barons, *Abinger*, C. B. diss.

servant for its delivery; the agent indorsed the order to a keelman, who received the lead and put it on board a vessel for London; the vessel arrived on the 21st of June, and defendants, as wharfingers, undertook the delivery of the lead; M. failed on that day; on the 23d and 24th, M. demanded the lead of the captain of the vessel, who refused to deliver it, though the freight was tendered, alleging that defendants had stopped it on account of the failure of M. On the 28th, a letter arrived from plaintiff, ordering the lead to be stopped in transitu; it was then on board a lighter belonging to defendants; it was holden (c), that the transitus was not at an end, and that plaintiff was in time to stop the lead.

3. *When the Transitus may be considered as determined.*—We now proceed to the third division, under which it is proposed to arrange those cases in which it has been decided that the transitus was complete, and the delivery of such a nature as to divest the vendor's right of stopping *in transitu.*

The first case, on this branch of the subject, is that of *Ellis* v. *Hunt*, 3 T. R. 464, the facts of which were shortly these: B. ordered a quantity of files from the plaintiff, a manufacturer at Sheffield; the files were packed in a cask, and sent by a waggon, directed to B. in London. Before their arrival in London, B. became a bankrupt. On their arrival there, the goods, while they remained at the inn, were attached by a creditor of the bankrupt by process of foreign attachment; afterwards, the provisional assignee under B.'s commission demanded the goods from the carrier, and put his mark upon the cask, but did not take them away. A few days afterwards, the plaintiff, who had not been paid for his goods, wrote a letter to the carrier, directing him, in case the goods were not delivered, to keep them in his warehouse, as he had been informed that B. had become a bankrupt. The court were of opinion, that the goods were not in transitu at the time when the plaintiff wrote to countermand the delivery of them; before that, the provisional assignee, who stood in the place of the bankrupt, had put his mark on the cask (d): when the goods were marked, they were delivered to the commissioners as far as the circumstances of the case would permit, for, being under an attachment, the assignee could not then take them away. Where a part of the goods sold by an entire contract, has been taken possession of by the vendee, that shall be deemed taking possession of the whole. A., at a foreign port (e), shipped goods by order and on account of B., to be paid for on a future day, and bills of lading were accordingly signed by the master of the ship; one of the bills was immediately transmitted to B., who, before the arrival of the ship at the place of destination, sold the goods and indorsed the bill of lading to C.; after the arrival of

(c) *Jackson* v. *Nichol*, 5 Bingh. N. C. 508.

(d) See *Stoveld* v. *Hughes*, 14 East,

308, and *post*, p. 1278.

(e) *Slubey and another* v. *Heyward and others*, 2 H. Bl. 504.

the ship, and delivery of part of the goods to the agent of C., B. became bankrupt, without having paid A. the price of the goods. It was holden, that the transitus was ended by the part delivery, which must be taken to be a delivery of the whole, there appearing no intention, either previous to, or at the time of the delivery, to separate part of the cargo from the rest. So where a number of bales of bacon, then lying at a wharf (*f*), having been sold for an *entire* sum, to be paid for by a bill at two months, an order was given to the wharfinger to deliver them to the vendee, who went to the wharf, weighed the *whole*, and took away several bales, and then became bankrupt: whereupon the vendor, within ten days from the time of the sale, ordered the wharfinger not to deliver the remainder. By the custom of the trade, the charges of warehousing were to be paid, by the vendor, fourteen days after the sale. It was holden, that the contract being entire, and part having been taken away, the delivery to the vendee was complete, and consequently, the privilege of stopping in transitu could not attach: *Chambre*, J., observing, that the payment of the warehouse room, by the vendor, could not make any difference. The vendor, of course, charged just so much more as would pay the expense of warehouse room: that if the expense had been paid by the vendee, it would not make a delivery at the wharf a delivery to him; nor could the vendor avail himself of the circumstance of the expenses being paid by him to prevent a delivery to the vendee from operating as such. This was a much stronger case than the preceding one of *Slubey* v. *Heyward*: that proceeded upon the principle that a delivery of part, where the contract was entire, was a delivery of the whole; here there was an actual delivery of the whole. The bankrupt had actual manual possession of every article, and having weighed them all, he took upon himself to separate them. N. The two last cases of *Slubey* v. *Heyward*, and *Hammond* v. *Anderson*, underwent some discussion in *Hanson* v. *Meyer*, 6 East, 614, (which see under tit. " Trover," sect. 1,) but their authority does not appear to have been shaken in the slightest degree.

On a contract for the sale of goods lying in a warehouse, the handing of a delivery order to the vendee, and transfer of the goods to him in the warehouseman's book, will not vest the property in him, if something remains to be done for the purpose of ascertaining the identity or quantity of the goods; as the weighing of an article forming part of a bulk, and sold by weight. But if the identity and quantity are ascertained, as where the oats in a particular bin, which contains nothing else, are sold, and a bill accepted at the same time for the price, the property vests, and the vendor cannot afterwards stop in transitu (*g*).

(*f*) *Hammond and others* v. *Anderson*,
1 Bos. & Pul. N. R. 69.

(*g*) *Swanwick* v. *Sothern*, 9 A. & E.
895; 1 P. & D. 648.

If a person purchase goods here to be sent abroad, and they are delivered in a port of this kingdom, on board a ship chartered by and under the complete control of the vendee, such delivery is in effect a delivery to the vendee.

Trover by the assignees of bankrupts (h), to recover the value of a quantity of tobacco shipped by the defendants, by order of the bankrupts, on board a ship bound from London for Alexandria, which ship was chartered to the bankrupts for three years, from July, 1792, and which was paid for by a bill at three months, drawn by the defendants, on the bankrupts, and accepted by them. The goods were shipped on the 4th of February, 1793, for which the mate's receipt was given, and an invoice thereof made out by the defendants in the names of the bankrupts; the bankrupts were to find stock and provisions, and to pay the master. The vessel was detained by contrary winds at Portsmouth: during which time, the bankrupts having stopped payment about the 11th of March, 1793, the defendants procured bills of lading to be signed by the captain to them, and obtained possession of the tobacco in September, 1794, and procured it to be relanded, and afterwards disposed of for their benefit. It was holden, that the delivery was complete, by putting the goods on board the ship, and consequently, that the assignees were entitled to recover. It will be observed, that, in the preceding case, the bankrupts were to have the entire disposition of the ship (i), and the complete control over her during the three years. The ship had been one voyage to Alexandria, and had the goods put on board her, to carry them on another voyage to the same place; not for the purpose of conveying them *from* the vendors to the bankrupts, but that they might be sent *by the bankrupts* upon a mercantile adventure, for which they had bought them. From not adverting to these material circumstances, an inference was drawn from the preceding decision, which the case did not warrant, namely, that the right of stopping in transitu could not exist after a delivery of goods on board a chartered ship. This opinion, however, was exploded in the case of *Bothlingk* v. *Inglis*, 3 East, 381. There a trader who resided in England, chartered a ship, on certain conditions, for a voyage to Russia, and to bring goods home from his correspondent there, who accordingly shipped the goods on account, and at the risk of the freighter, and sent him the invoices and bills of lading of the cargo. It was holden, that the delivery of the goods on board such chartered ship, did not preclude the right of the consignor to stop the goods while in transitu on board the same to the vendee, in case of his insolvency, in the mean time, before actual delivery, any more than if they had been delivered on board a general ship for the same purpose. The plaintiff (k), a

(h) *Fowler and another, Assignees of Hunter and Co.*, v. *M'Taggart and Co.*, cited in 7 T. R. 442; 1 East, 522, and 3 East, 388.

(i) Per *Lawrence*, J., 3 East, 396, 7.
(k) *Wright* v. *Lawes*, 4 Esp. N. P. C. 82.

manufacturer at Norwich, agreed with I. S. for the purchase of some pipes of wine, one of which was to be paid for in money, and for the remainder I. S. was to take goods. I. S. wrote to C., his correspondent in London, to send the wines; C. accordingly purchased the wines of D., shipped them, and, by the bill of lading, consigned them to the plaintiff by a vessel employed in the course of trade between Yarmouth and London. On the arrival of the wine at Yarmouth, an agent for the plaintiff received it on his account, and deposited it in the cellar of the defendant, who was to be paid for the cellar room by the plaintiff. A few days after, the plaintiff arrived at Yarmouth, tasted the wines and took samples of them. Shortly afterwards, D., discovering that C., to whom he had sold the wines, was a man of no property, desired the defendant to keep possession of the wine, giving him an indemnity. The plaintiff having brought this action for the recovery, the payment for one pipe, and the agreement as to the remainder, was proved. This, in Lord *Kenyon's* opinion, gave the plaintiff a title to the whole. It was then contended, that, as the plaintiff lived at Norwich, the goods must be deemed to be *in transitu* until they arrived there; whereas here, they had arrived only at Yarmouth, and had never been delivered at Norwich; that the usual course was, to put them into lighters, at Yarmouth, and forward them to Norwich; so that, until their arrival there, they were *in transitu*, and could be stopped by the owners. But per Lord *Kenyon*, "There is no colour for saying that these goods were *in transitu*. I once said, that to confer a property on the consignee, a corporal touch was necessary. I wish the expression had never been used, as it says too much : but here, if a corporal touch was necessary to confer a property on the consignee, it had taken place : but all that is necessary is, that the consignee exercise some act of ownership on the property consigned to him, and he has done so here; he has paid for the warehouse room; he has tasted and taken samples of the wines; but it is said, they have not reached the plaintiff's place of abode, where they were to be ultimately delivered; but I think there was a complete delivery at Yarmouth."

The reader will have collected from the cases in the preceding section, *viz. Hunt* v. *Ward*, and *Mills* v. *Ball*, that where goods have been delivered to a packer or wharfinger, for the purpose of being forwarded to an ulterior destination, and the packer or wharfinger may be considered merely as a middle man, in such cases the right of stopping in transitu remains. It now becomes necessary to remark, that, where the insolvent has no warehouse, or no other place of delivery than the warehouse of the packer, &c., and there is no place of ulterior delivery in view, the transitus will be considered as at an end when the goods have arrived at such warehouse, that being their last place of delivery. The following cases will illustrate this rule :—

Trover for goods. The goods in question had been ordered by the bankrupt (*l*), who was a merchant in London, of Messrs. Wallers, of Manchester, and were forwarded by them, directed to the bankrupt, at the Bull and Mouth Inn, on the 16th of March, 1802. On the 23d of March, the goods were sent from the Bull and Mouth Inn to the defendant's house, who was a packer, not in consequence of any orders respecting those particular goods, but in consequence of a general order from the bankrupt to send all goods directed to him to the defendant's house. On the 11th of March, the bankrupt, who lived in lodgings, and *had no warehouse of his own*, absconded, leaving no clerk to accept goods or orders for him. On the arrival of the goods at the defendant's house, they were booked for the account of the bankrupt; and the defendant, not knowing that the bankrupt had then absconded, and not having any directions from him respecting the goods, caused them to be unpacked with a view to ascertain of what they consisted. On the 31st of March, Messrs. Wallers, having learned the situation of the bankrupt's affairs, claimed the goods from the defendant; and on the day after, they were demanded by the assignees. The defendant, being indemnified by Messrs. Wallers, refused to deliver the goods to the plaintiffs. It was holden, that the transitus was at an end, inasmuch as there was not any other place of delivery than the warehouse of the packer; the goods, when arrived there, had come to their last place of delivery, and consequently were no longer liable to the right of stoppage *in transitu.* So where goods are to be delivered to the vendee at a particular place, the transitus in general continues until they are delivered to him at that place; but if he by his own act prevent the delivery, which otherwise in the ordinary course would take place, and does any act equivalent to taking possession, the transitus is thereby determined; and, therefore, where the vendee of several hogsheads of sugar, upon receiving from the carrier notice of their arrival, took samples from them, and, for his own convenience, desired the carrier to let them remain in his warehouse, until he should receive further directions; and before they were removed became bankrupt; it was holden (*m*), that the transitus was at an end, and that the vendor was not entitled to stop them. So where goods were sent by water-carriage and deposited in the carrier's warehouse at the end of the voyage, in the usual course of business between him and the consignee, *viz.* to be delivered out to him or to his customers as they should be wanted, without being sent to his residence elsewhere; it was holden (*n*), that the transitus was determined, and that the vendor's right to stop the goods was gone, though the carrier claimed as such a lien on the goods against the consignee. So where the goods have so far gotten to the end of their journey, that they wait for

(*l*) *Scott and others, Assignees of Berkley, a Bankrupt,* v. *Pettit,* 3 Bos. & Pul. 469. See also *Leeds* v. *Wright,* 3 Bos. & Pul. 320.

(*m*) *Foster* v. *Frampton,* 6 B. & C. 107.

(*n*) *Allen* v. *Gripper,* 2 Tyrw. 217; 2 Cr. & J. 218.

new orders from the purchaser to put them again in motion, to communicate to them another substantive destination, and if, without such orders, they would continue stationary, the right of stopping in transitu is gone. A. and B. (o), traders living in London, were in the course of ordering goods of the defendants, cotton manufacturers at Manchester, to be sent to M. and Co. at Hull, for the purpose of being afterwards sent to the correspondents of A. and B. at Hamburgh; and on the 31st of March, A. and B. sent orders to the defendants for certain goods, to be sent to M. and Co. at Hull, to be shipped for Hamburgh as usual. It was holden, that, as between buyer and seller, the right of the defendants to stop, as in transitu, was at an end when the goods came to the possession of M. & Co. at Hull, for they were for this purpose the appointed agents of the vendees, and received orders from them as to the ulterior destination of the goods; and the goods, after their arrival at Hull, were to receive a new direction from the vendees.

A trader in London was in the habit of purchasing goods at Manchester, and exporting them to the Continent soon after their arrival in London. The goods so consigned to him remained in the waggon-office of the defendants, who were carriers, until they were removed by his agent, for the purpose of being shipped. A consignment of goods for the trader was delivered to the defendants on the 9th and 12th of August: on the 14th and 17th the goods arrived at the waggon-office of the defendants; on the 16th or 17th the trader became bankrupt; and, on the 19th, notice of nondelivery to the bankrupt was given by the consignor to the defendants, who, according to order, on the 21st delivered the goods to a third house: it was holden (p), that the assignees of the bankrupts were entitled to recover the goods deposited with the defendants; and that the right of the consignor to stoppage in transitu ceased on the arrival of the goods at the waggon-office of the defendants in London. So if, after goods are sold (q), they remain in the warehouse of the vendor, and he receives warehouse-rent for them, this amounts to a delivery of the goods to the purchaser, so as to put an end to the vendor's right of stopping them in transitu. So where the purchaser of goods received from the seller an order to the wharfinger in whose warehouse the goods were deposited, to deliver them; and the purchaser, having lodged the order with the wharfinger, he transferred the goods into the name of the purchaser; it was holden (r), that by such transfer the wharfinger became a trustee for the purchaser, and there was an executed delivery as much as if the goods had been delivered into the hands

(o) *Dixon and others, Assignees of Battier, a Bankrupt*, v. *Baldwen*, 5 East, 175.
(p) *Rowe* v. *Pickford and another*, 8 Taunt. 83.

(q) *Hurry* v. *Mangles*, 1 Campb. 452.
(r) *Harman* v. *Anderson*, 2 Campb. 243. See *Whitehouse* v. *Frost*, 12 East, 614.

of the purchaser. So where goods being entered in the books of
the W. I. Dock Company in the name of A., he received the usual
check for them, which, having sold the goods for money to B., he
indorsed and delivered to him, and B. afterwards sold the goods on
credit and delivered the check to C.; it was holden (s), that on C.'s
insolvency, A. could not (for the benefit of B.) stop the goods,
although they continued to stand in his name, and he paid rent for
them, and although the check had not been lodged with the Dock
Company. So where the defendants sold to I. S. a quantity of
timber, then lying at their wharf, for the price of which I. S. gave
the defendants bills payable at a future day; I. S., having marked
the timber with his own mark, afterwards sold it to the plaintiff,
who paid him for the same. The plaintiff went to the wharf,
apprized the defendants of his purchase, received for answer *that it
was very well*, and that they would go with him and show him the
timber, which they accordingly did, and thereupon the plaintiff put
his own mark on the timber. The bills given by I. S. to the
defendants having been dishonoured, they claimed to stop in transitu; but it was holden (t), that there was an executed delivery, and
that the plaintiff having given notice to the defendants that I. S.
had sold the property to him, and his then marking it as his own,
made an end of the transit, and the defendants could no longer
detain or stop the timber. Lord *Ellenborough*, C. J., observed in
this case, that the change of mark from A. to B. on bales of goods
in a warehouse, had been holden by the House of Lords, in a late
case, to operate as an actual delivery of the goods. Where goods
are delivered to a vendee at a wharf, who afterwards ships them
there, no subsequent stoppage (u) of the goods in transitu can take
place.

  4. *How far the Negotiation of the Bill of Lading may tend
to defeat the Right of stopping in Transitu.*—Where the property
in goods has passed to a vendee, subject only to be divested by the
vendor's right to stop them while in transitu, such right must be
exercised, if at all, before the vendee has parted with the property
to another for a valuable consideration, *bonâ fide*, and by indorsement of the bill of lading, (without notice of such circumstances as
render the bill of lading not fairly and honestly assignable,) has
given him a right to recover them (x); for the indorsement of a
bill of lading for a valuable consideration, and without notice to the
indorsee of a better title, passes the property. The legal title,
however, of the indorsee of a bill of lading, may be impeached on
the ground of fraud (y); but the mere circumstance of the indorsee
knowing at the time when the bill of lading was indorsed and

  (s) *Spear* v. *Travers*, 4 Campb. 251.   See the argument of *Buller*, J., 6 East,
  (t) *Stoveld* v. *Hughes*, 14 East, 308.   21, n.
  (u) *Noble* v. *Adams*, 7 Taunt. 59.   (y) *Wright* v. *Campbell*, 4 Burr. 2046;
  (x) *Lickbarrow* v. *Mason*, 2 T. R. 63.   *Salomons* v. *Nissen*, 2 T. R. 674.

delivered to him, that the consignor had not received money payment for his goods, but had only taken the consignee's acceptances, payable at a future day not then arrived, is not sufficient to invalidate the title of the indorsee, in a case where the absence of fraud and mala fides is found (z). Where the vendor's legal right of stopping in transitu had been determined by the indorsement of the bill of lading, but such transfer had been made only as a security for advances made by the indorsee; it was holden (a), upon reference to an arbitrator, that in a court of equity, such transfer would be treated as a pledge or mortgage only, and that the vendor had an equitable quasi right of stoppage in transitu, subject to the previous right of the indorsee to be repaid his advances. A. being indebted to B. on the balance of accounts, including bills of exchange still running, accepted by B. for A., consigned goods to B. on account of this balance. It was holden, that A. was not entitled to stop the goods in transitu, upon B. becoming insolvent before the bills were paid; because, the goods being consigned to B. on account of the balance which then existed in B.'s favour, the property vested in B. absolutely (b). So if the purchaser of goods to be paid by bill, after giving his acceptance, during the time of credit, and while the goods are in transitu, sells them to a third person for a valuable consideration, without transferring any bill of lading to him, the right of the original vendor to stop the goods in transitu is taken away (c). By the usage of trade, West India Dock warrants (d) indorsed, bonâ fide, and for good consideration, transfer the property in the goods, like a bill of lading, and prevent the exercise of the right of stopping in transitu (2). A., by contract, sold to B. a quantity of tallow then lying at a wharf, at so much per cwt.; and on the same day gave a written order upon the wharfinger to weigh, deliver, transfer, and re-house the same. B., having entered into a contract to sell tallow to C., obtained from the wharfingers, and gave to C., a written acknowledgment that they had transferred the tallow to the account of C., and that C. was to be liable to charges from a given date. B. having stopped payment, A. gave notice to the wharfingers not to deliver the tallow to B.'s order: it was holden (e),

---

(z) *Cuming* v. *Brown*, 9 East, 506. See further on this subject, *Coxe* v. *Harden*, 4 East, 211; *Waring* v. *Cox*, 1 Campb. 369, and *Barrow* v. *Coles*, 3 Campb. 92.

(a) *In re Westzinthus*, 5 B. & Ad. 817; 2 Nev. & M. 644.

(b) *Vertue* v. *Jewel*, 4 Campb. 31.

(c) *Davis* v. *Reynolds*, 4 Campb. 267.

(d) *Zwinger* v. *Samuda*, Holt, N. P. C. 395, per *Park*, J.; but see the case in banc, 7 Taunt. 265, and *Lucas* v. *Dorrien*, 7 Taunt. 278.

(e) *Hawes* v. *Watson*, 2 B. & C. 540.

---

(2) Quære; whether a document, similar in form to a bill of lading, but given by the master of a boat navigating an inland canal, has the effect of such an instrument in transferring the property in the goods. See *Bryans* v. *Nix*, 4 M. & W. 775; *post*, tit. "Trover."

in an action of trover by C. against the wharfingers, that after their acknowledgment, they held the tallow as agents of C., and that they could not therefore set up as a defence a right in A. to stop it in transitu. But the delivery of a shipping note by the consignee of goods to a third person, with an order to the wharfinger to deliver the goods to such third person, does not pass the property in them so as to prevent a stoppage in transitu by the consignor (*f*). The unpaid vendor (*g*) of goods remaining in his own warehouse rent-free, may stop them in transitu, although he has given the vendee a delivery order, under which part of the goods have been removed. This was the case of pipes of wine at Liverpool.

(*f*) *Akerman* v. *Humphrey*, 1 C. & P. 53, recognized by *Park*, J., delivering judgment in *Tucker* v. *Humphrey*, 4 Bingh. 522, 3.

(*g*) *Townley* v. *Crump*, 5 Nev. & M. 606; 4 A. & E. 58.

CHAPTER XXXVIII.

TITHES.

I. *Definition, p.* 1281; *Of the Remedies in the Common Law Courts for the Recovery of Tithes, or the Value thereof, p.* 1282.

II. *Debt on Stat.* 2 & 3 *Edw. VI. c.* 13, *for not setting out Tithes, p.* 1284; *Of the Provisions of the Statute, and the Construction thereof, p.* 1284; *Of the Persons to whom Tithes are due, p.* 1300; *Of the Persons by whom and against whom an Action on the Statute may be brought, p.* 1301; *Of the Declaration, p.* 1302; *Pleadings, and herein of the Statutes of Limitation, p.* 1303; *Evidence, p.* 1304; *Verdict, p.* 1307; *Costs, p.* 1308; *Judgment, p.* 1308.

III. *Of the Stat.* 6 & 7 *Will. IV. c.* 71, *for the Commutation of Tithes in England and Wales, amended by Stat.* 7 *Will. IV.* & 1 *Vict. c.* 69, *p.* 1309; *Stat.* 1 & 2 *Vict. c.* 64, *for facilitating Merger of Tithes, Stat.* 2 & 3 *Vict. c.* 62, *for explaining the Acts for the Commutation of Tithes, p.* 1311.

I. *Definition, p.* 1281; *Of the Remedies in the Common Law Courts for the Recovery of Tithes, or the Value thereof, p.* 1282.

DEFINITION.—TITHES are a tenth part of the annual increase of land, or of beasts, &c. on the land, and of the labour and industry of the occupier, payable to the parson of the parish for his maintenance. They are an incorporeal ecclesiastical inheritance, collateral to the estate of the land (a). For small quantities involuntarily left in the process of raking, tithe is not payable; otherwise, if there be any particular fraud, or intention to deprive the parson of his full right. The parson's right is to a tenth of the corn, to be taken generally, when it comes to such a state or stage as that the parson may see he has his fair tenth (b). As to the time of the introduction of tithes into England, and their being claimed as a civil right, with the history of them before their legal establishment, see Selden's History of Tithes. Before the stat. 32 Hen. VIII. c. 7, an action for tithes could not have been maintained in the temporal courts; but by the 7th section of that statute it is enacted, " That any person having an estate of inheritance, freehold, term, or interest in tithes, and being disseised, or otherwise kept or put out of possession thereof, shall have such remedy in the temporal courts for recovering the same as the case may require, in like manner as they may for lands, tenements, and other hereditaments." By force of this statute, tithes have at this day all the incidents belonging to temporal inheritances. Hence an ejectment may be maintained for tithes (c). Where the person entitled to tithes agrees by parol with the occupiers of the land that they shall hold the lands discharged of tithes for a certain time, or during the life of the tithe-owner, in consideration of the payment of a certain sum annually, an action of indebitatus assumpsit may be maintained by the tithe-owner, against the occupier, for the non-payment of the sum agreed on. In order to support this action, the plaintiff must prove the occupation of the defendant, the agreement, and the retainer of the tithes under that agreement (d). To this action the defendant cannot set up as a defence, that the plaintiff was simoniacally presented (e). Tithes, being an incorporeal hereditament, cannot pass by parol, but by deed only. Hence where, by an instrument, not under seal, A. agreed to let to B., on lease, the rectory of L., and the tithes arising from the lands in the parish of L., and also a messuage used as a homestead for collecting the tithes, at the yearly rent of £200; and the rent being in arrear, A. distrained, whereupon B. brought trespass; it was holden (f), that the distress was altogether unlawful, because the agreement not being under seal, it did not operate as a demise of the tithes, and consequently there was no valid demise of the whole subject matter, nor was there any distinct rent reserved for that part of the subject matter, viz. the homestead, for which there might have been a legal distress.

By stat. 7 & 8 Will. III. c. 6, (made perpetual by stat. 3 & 4 Ann. c. 18, s. 1, and amended by stat. 7 Geo. IV. c. 15,) a sum-

(a) 11 Rep. 13, b.
(b) Per Cur., Glanvill v. Stacey, 6 B. & C. 543.
(c) Priest v. Wood, Cro. Car. 301.
(d) Peake's Evid. 411, ed. 2nd.

(e) Brooksby v. Watts, 2 Marsh. 38; 6 Taunt. 333, S. C.
(f) Gardiner v. Williamson, 2 B. & Ad. 336.

mary method of proceeding before two J. P. is prescribed for recovering small tithes under the value of 40s. (1). But this statute contains a proviso (g), that if the party complained of shall insist before the J. P. upon any prescription, composition, modus, agreement, or title, and deliver the same in writing to the J. P. subscribed by him or her, and shall give security to the complainant to pay such costs as, upon a trial at law, shall be given against him, in case the prescription, &c. be not allowed, then the J. P. shall forbear to give judgment, and the complainant may prosecute the adverse party for the subtraction of tithe in any court, as before this act. The 9th section directs the judgment given by virtue of this statute to be enrolled at the next general quarter sessions; and after enrolment, and satisfaction made, the judgment shall be a bar to conclude the party entitled to the tithes from any other remedy. And by stat. 53 Geo. III. c. 127, s. 4, the jurisdiction of the said justices was extended to *all* tithes, oblations, and compositions subtracted or withheld, where the same should not exceed £10 from any one person; and by stat. 5 & 6 Will. IV. c. 74 (*h*), "for the more easy Recovery of Tithes," sect. 1, it is enacted, that proceedings for the recovery of any tithes, &c. under the yearly value of £10, (except in the case of Quakers,) shall be had only under the powers of the two foregoing acts; with a proviso, that nothing in this act contained shall extend to any case in which actual title to any tithe, &c. shall be *bonâ fide* in question. And by stat. 7 & 8 Will. III. c. 34, (made perpetual and extended to all customary payments belonging to any church or chapel by 1 Geo. I. stat. 2, c. 6,) the like remedy is extended to *all* tithes due from Quakers; and two J. P. are empowered to ascertain what is due, and to order payment, so as the sum ordered does not exceed £10, extended to £50 by stat. 53 Geo. III. c. 127, s. 6. These statutes were made in favour (*i*) to, and for the ease and benefit of, Quakers, and to save them from troublesome and expensive prosecutions. But it was never meant that a mere scruple of theirs, or an obstinate withholding of the tithes, should be any hindrance to the matter's being determined by the J. P. This would have frustrated the very intention of the legislature, which meant to give this jurisdiction to

(g) Sect. 8.
(h) Amended by stat. 4 & 5 Vict. c. 36.

(i) See *R.* v. *Wakefield*, 1 Burr. 487; Burn's Justice, tit. Tithes, *S. C.*

(1) As to the principle of the stat. 7 & 8 Will. III. c. 6, it is clear that this act was intended to apply only to those cases in which the tithes are actually due, independently of any dispute upon matters of law, either with regard to the person receiving them, or the manner of receiving them. The object of it was to give to the owner of tithes an expeditious mode of recovering them, &c. &c. By *Abbott*, C. J., in *R.* v. *Jeffery*, 2 Dow. & Ry. 860.

the justices in that very case; where the *real right and title* to the tithes should not be in dispute. By stat. 5 & 6 Will. IV. c. 74, s. 2, in the case of Quakers, no execution, or decree, or order, shall be made against the person, but against the goods or other property of the defendant. Another remedy for the subtraction of tithe is, the action of debt on the stat. 2 Edw. VI., which will be the subject of the following section.

II. *Debt on Stat. 2 & 3 Edw. VI. c. 13, for not setting out Tithes,* p. 1284; *Of the Provisions of the Statute, and the Construction thereof,* p. 1284; *Of the Persons to whom Tithes are due,* p. 1300; *Of the Persons by whom and against whom an Action on the Statute may be brought,* p. 1301; *Of the Declaration,* p. 1302; *Pleadings, and herein of the Statutes of Limitation,* p. 1303; *Evidence,* p. 1304; *Verdict,* p. 1307; *Costs,* p. 1308; *Judgment,* p. 1308.

Of the Provisions of the Statute, and the Construction thereof (2).

By the first section of this statute it is enacted, " That every of the king's subjects shall truly and justly, without fraud or guile, divide, set out, and pay all manner of their *predial tithes* (3) in their proper kind, as they arise, *in such manner and form as hath been of right yielded and paid within forty years next before the making this act, or of right or custom ought to have been paid.* And no person shall carry away such or like tithes which have been yielded or paid within the said forty years, or of right ought to have been paid in the places titheable, before he has *justly divided or set forth,* for the tithe thereof, the tenth part of the same, or otherwise *agreed for the tithes with the parson,* vicar, or other owner or farmer of the same tithes, under the pain of forfeiture of treble value of the tithes so carried away."

This statute was made soon after the dissolution of the monasteries, before which time the tithes were in the hands of religious persons, and the usual remedy for the subtraction of them was in the ecclesiastical courts. But, when tithes became lay fees, it was thought necessary to provide a remedy for these injuries in the

---

(2) See Sir Edward Coke's exposition of this statute, 2 Inst. 648.

(3) Remarks will be found in the subsequent pages on those parts of the statute which are printed in italics.

temporal courts, and this statute was made for that purpose. It is worthy of remark, however, that several years (nearly forty) elapsed before any proceeding was instituted on this statute in the temporal courts. An opinion at first prevailed, that as the person to whom the treble value was given was not specified, such value belonged of right to the king. But in E. T. 29 Eliz., upon an information filed by the Queen's Attorney General against one Wood, for not setting out his tithe, whereon the defendant was found guilty, it was solemnly adjudged by the Court of Exchequer, (upon motion in arrest of judgment,) that the treble value did not belong to the king, but to the party interested, who might maintain an action of debt for recovering the same. In conformity with this opinion, an action of debt at the suit of the party interested, (more frequently termed the part grieved,) has ever since been considered as the proper remedy; and in *Beadils* v. *Sherman*, E. T. 40 Eliz., B. R., (see the record, Co. Ent. p. 161, 2nd ed.,) where this form of action was adopted, the plaintiff obtained judgment; although, on motion in arrest of judgment, it was urged, that as the statute had not mentioned the court in which the treble value was to be recovered, the only remedy was in the spiritual court. This judgment was afterwards affirmed on error in the Exchequer Chamber. "And now, (adds Sir *E. Coke*, at the conclusion of the record, Co. Ent. p. 162,) actions of debt on this statute are frequent and usual."

Predial Tithes.]—This clause is expressly confined to predial tithes, and does not extend to mixed or personal tithes. Hence, when in an action on this statute for not setting out the tithes of *cheese, calves, lambs,* &c., the plaintiff obtained a verdict; on motion in arrest of judgment (k), it was objected, that the tithes in question were not *predial* tithes, and consequently not within this statute, which, being penal, ought not to be extended by equity: and of this opinion was the whole court. So where the plaintiff declared for not setting out predial tithes (l), *and other tithes,* as the tithes of lambs, wool, &c., and the jury found a general verdict, judgment was arrested upon the like objection.

Description of predial Tithes.—In general, under the term of *predial* tithes, are comprehended the tithes of such products of the earth as are renewed yearly, either spontaneously or by culture: as the tithes of corn, flax, hay, hops, saffron, wood (m), &c.; and the fruit of trees, as apples, cherries, pears, &c.

Tithe of wood also, as coppice-wood, &c. (4), is predial, and must

(k) *Booth* v. *Southraie*, 2 Inst. 649.
(l) *Pain* v. *Nichols*, 1 Brownl. 65.
(m) *Norton* v. *Clarke*, 1 Gwill. 428.

---

(4) "All coppice woods are liable to tithes; and although *non annuatim renovantur*, yet, in a certain course of time after they are cut, they

be set out on the spot at the time of falling; but timber trees (gros-boys,) of the age of twenty years or more, are exempted from paying tithe by stat. 45 Edw. III. c. 3. That statute, which is declaratory of the common law (*n*), has been construed to comprehend all timber trees, (of twenty years' growth or upwards,) whether timber by law, as oak, elm, or ash; or by custom, as beech in Buckinghamshire and other places (*o*); and the exemption from tithe, by operation of this statute, extends not to the body of such trees only, but also the bark (*p*), lop, and top (*q*). The subsequent use and application of the wood will not determine the right to tithes (5). Hence it has been resolved, that the tops and lops of pollard oaks, ashes, and elms, (such oaks, &c. being above twenty years' growth,) although cut for the purpose of being used as fuel, are not titheable (*r*); and further, that the age of the tops and lops is immaterial, the trees whence they were taken having been once privileged (*s*). In like manner (*t*), faggot-wood, and billets made of top-wood, cut from timber trees of above twenty years' growth, before they were made pollards, are not titheable. It is laid down in 2 Inst. 643, that if a person cut down timber trees, tithes shall not be paid for the germins which grow out of the roots, of what age soever, for the root is parcel of the inheritance. But this position is said by Lord *Hardwicke*, Ambl. 133, to have been contradicted, and for good reason; because a great part of coppices grow from germins of old timber trees, and it would deprive the clergy of great part of their tithes. And it was afterwards decided, that oak wood of more than twenty years' standing, growing not from acorns, but from old stools, which stools belonged originally to trees which had stood more than twenty years, was not so clearly and universally entitled to exemption by this statute, as to make a verdict (*u*) which subjects them to tithe necessarily a wrong verdict. And in *Evans* v. *George and Rowe*, 12 Price, 76, and M. & Y. 577, it was holden, that germins, or trees of more than twenty years' growth, which had grown from old stools of timber trees felled upwards of eighty years ago, were titheable. Per *Alexander*,

(*n*) Per Lord *Hardwicke*, Ch., in *Walton* v. *Tryon*, Ambl. 132, 3.
(*o*) *Abbott* v. *Hicks*, 1 H. Wood, 320; *Layfield* v. *Cowper*, 1 H. Wood, 330.
(*p*) 2 Inst. 643.
(*q*) Ambl. 132.

(*r*) *Walton* v. *Tryon*, Ambl. 130.
(*s*) See *Ram* v. *Patenson*, Cro. Eliz. 477.
(*t*) *Morden* v. *Knight*, 2 Gwill. 841.
(*u*) *Ford* v. *Racster*, 4 M. & S. 130.

grow up again, like saffron, which in some places is not gathered oftener than once in three years: but as to timber trees, from the ordinary use of them, the law is otherwise: they are not cut at a certain stated time." Per Ld. *Hardwicke*, Ch., in *Walton* v. *Tryon and others*, Ambl. 131.

(5) But it seems that wood, applied to special purposes, may be exempted from tithes by special custom, but not otherwise.

C. B., *Garrow*, B., and *Hullock*, B.; *Graham*, B., dissentiente. But in a recent case in Chancery (x), in which all these authorities were reviewed; it was holden, that wood of the growth of twenty years or upwards, springing from the roots or stools of trees which have formerly been felled, are exempt from tithe; Lord *Cottenham*, C., observing, that, although he was very reluctant to alter what had been considered by many, and particularly by *Alexander*, C. B., in *Evans* v. *Rowe*, to be a rule of law, still he thought the interpretation which had been put upon the statute of Edw. III. for 400 years was the correct one, namely, that this wood was exempt from the payment of tithes. Wood growing in hedge-rows, not being timber, is titheable (y). Birch is not such wood as the statute intends by gros-boys (z). The parson *de mero jure* is entitled to tithe-wood, if the vicar be neither endowed of the same, nor claims to have it by prescription (a). It seems, that an action of debt may be maintained on this statute for not setting out small tithes, as well as great tithes, provided they are predial tithes. Whether a tithe be great or small is determined by the nature of it, and not by the mode or place of its cultivation.

" I have never been able to discover any intelligible principle upon which to decide what is a great and what is a small tithe. For a long time it was considered as a question of fact depending upon the quantity of the article cultivated in the particular parish. It is now settled that the question depends upon the nature of the thing, and not upon the quantity of it which may happen to be produced. It would be satisfactory if any precise authority could be found as to what things are to be considered great, and what small tithes. In the absence of any authority, all that we can do is to determine the nature of any tithe by its resemblance to some other article, with respect to which a decision has already taken place. That is the only safe rule upon which we can proceed" (b).

On the dissolution of a religious house, the rectory of H. became vested in the crown. Queen Eliz., by letters patent, granted to A. and B. " omnes decimas nostras garbarum et granorum in H." On an issue between the grantees and the vicar to try the right to the tithe of seed tares, it was proved that the former had always received it, and that the vicar had received all that were considered small tithe, and the tithes of tares cut green and of hay; no endowment was produced. It appeared in evidence that the tithe in question was claimed and paid as a great or rector's tithe. It was holden (c), first, that under the grant of Queen Eliz., every thing

---

(x) *Loxon* v. *Pryse*, Law Journ. vol. x., N. S., p. 103.
  (y) *Biggs* v. *Martin and another*, 1 H. Wood, 321; *Mantell* v. *Paine*, 4 Gwill. 1504.
  (z) *Foster* v. *Lennard*, Cro. Eliz. 1.

(a) Per Cur., in *Renoulde* v. *Green*, 2 Bulst. 27. See *Norton* v. *Clarke*, 1 Gwill. 428.
  (b) Per *Best*, J., in *Dawe* v. *Benn*, 1 B. & C. 768, 9.
  (c) *Dawe* v. *Benn*, 1 B. & C. 751.

passed that was before vested in the crown, and that the grantee stood in the situation of rector. Secondly, that the tithe in question was a tithe garbarum. Thirdly, that it was a great tithe. Fourthly, that the presumed endowment of the vicar must be limited by prescription, and that never having received this tithe, he could not establish a right to it, whether it was great or small.

[*In such manner and form as hath been of right yielded and paid within forty years next before this act, or of right and custom ought to have been paid.*]

In debt on this statute by a rector (d), it was stated, in the declaration, that the plaintiff was the rector of the parish, the defendant occupier of lands within the same; that the tithes were within forty years next before the statute of right yielded and *payable* and yielded and paid; that defendant, in November, 1791, ploughed and sowed the land with corn, which he afterwards carried away, without setting out the tithe: on *nil debet* pleaded, it appeared at the trial, that the land in question, as far back as any witness knew, had been in grass, and had been ploughed for the first time in 1791, and no evidence was given of its ever having paid tithe. *Chambre*, J., for the defendant, contended, that the jury were bound to find for the defendant, unless they found that tithes had actually been paid in respect of this land within forty years before the statute, of which there was not any evidence; on the contrary, the evidence given rather went to rebut such a presumption, and was sufficient to warrant the jury in presuming a grant in favour of the defendant. Verdict for plaintiff. On a motion to enter a nonsuit, Lord *Kenyon*, C. J., said, that the usage had constantly been against the necessity of the proof contended for by the defendant; that he remembered many actions having been tried, where the lands, in respect of which the tithes were claimed were lately inclosed, and where the same objection, had it been available, must have prevailed; but the plaintiff recovered in all: that the non-payment of tithe of itself signified nothing: and that there was not any ground for saying, that tithe ought not to have been paid here. *Buller*, J., observed, that with respect to the presumption of a grant in favour of the defendant, he thought he could not leave that question to the jury without some evidence to support it, and here was none: *if indeed it appeared that this land had been ploughed before, and yet no tithes had been exacted for it, that might have afforded some ground for such a presumption* (e), but he thought that the onus of proving the exemption lay with the defendant. Rule discharged. But in a case where the declaration merely stated (f), that the tithe had been yielded and paid forty

(d) *Mitchell* v. *Walker*, 5 T. R. 260. See *post*, p. 1305, under tit. "Evidence," *Hallewell* v. *Trappes*.

(e) See the same opinion expressed by

Wilmot, C. J., in *Mansfield* v. *Clarke*, 5 T. R. 265, n.

(f) *Mansfield* v. *Clarke*, 5 T. R. 264, n.; 3 Gwill. 950, n. (9); *S. C.*

years before making the act, without averring that tithes *were payable, and of right ought to be paid,* and there was not any evidence of tithe ever having been paid; it was holden, that the plaintiff could not recover. The court, however, granted a new trial, ordering the declaration to be amended by the introduction of the necessary averment. It was admitted by *Wilmot,* C. J., (delivering the opinion of the court in the preceding case,) that if it appeared that the land had never paid tithe, *and had been constantly ploughed,* it would be open to presumption of a grant; but the onus of proving the exemption lay on the defendant. In a subsequent case, where the defendant omitted to state that the tithes had been paid within forty years before the passing of the act, the declaration was holden *(g)* to be bad after verdict. For the stat. 2 & 3 Will. IV. c. 100, for shortening the time required in claims of modus decimandi, or exemption from or discharge of tithes, see *post,* p. 1296.

Justly divided or set forth.]—If the owner justly divide the tithe from the nine parts (*h*), and sets it out, but immediately afterwards carries the same away, this will be considered as fraud and guile within the statute.

Agreed for the Tithes with the Parson, &c.]—Although a lease of tithes cannot be without deed (*i*), yet a parol agreement for retaining tithes will be sufficient to bar the parson, &c. of his action of debt on this statute. An agreement for the retaining of tithes is frequently termed a composition; but in the adoption of this term, care must be taken not to confound it with a composition real, which is an agreement of a different nature, and upon which some remarks will be made, when that term occurs in the subsequent provisions of this statute.

It is clear, that where a parson, &c. has entered into an agreement with the occupiers of the land for the retaining of their tithes, an action cannot be maintained for not setting out the tithe, until such agreement or composition is determined, and that such composition cannot be determined, by the parson, &c., without giving a reasonable notice to the occupiers of the land. There have been several cases in which it has been discussed, what is reasonable notice for the determination of such composition. In *Wyburd* v. *Tuck,* 1 Bos. & Pul. 465, *Buller,* J., considered this point as quite determined, observing, that in the case of *Hewitt* v. *Adams,* D. P., April 19th, 1782, where the notice had been given only one month before Michaelmas Day, at which time the composition was payable; upon a question put to the judges, whether such notice was sufficient, they were unanimously of opinion, it was not; and said expressly, that *a notice to determine a composition ought to be given with analogy to*

(g) *Butt* v. *Howard,* 4 B. & A. 655.
(h) *Heale* v. *Sprat,* 2 Inst. 649; *Anderson's* case, Clayton, 20, S. P.

(i) *Bernard* v. *Evens,* 1 Lev. 24; T. Raym. 14, *S. C.*

the notice given in a holding of land. So in *Bishop* v. *Chichester*, E. 27 Geo. III., in Canc., 4 Gwill. 1316; 2 Bro. Ch. C. 161, *S. C.*, Lord *Thurlow*, Ch., said, that he thought the rules of notice for determining compositions for tithes were exactly the same as those between landlord and tenant from year to year. In *Wyburd* v. *Tuck*, 1 Bos. & Pul. 458, the principle of the above mentioned decision in the House of Lords was adopted by *Buller*, *Heath*, and *Rooke*, Js. (6). And in *Goode* v. *Howells*, 4 M. & W. 202, Lord *Abinger*, C. B., and *Parke*, B., said, that it is now to be taken as established law that a composition for tithes from year to year must be determined by a notice analogous to a notice to quit lands. Agreeably to these opinions, reasonable notice for the determination of a composition is *half a year's* notice, ending at the expiration of the year. But this notice is not required to be given to an occupier who disclaims the tithe-owner's title to the tithes in kind; as where the occupier, who had been under a composition, refused to pay it or to set out the tithe (*k*), alleging that he was exempted by a modus. The general doctrine laid down in *Hewitt* v. *Adams*, as to the necessity of a notice to determine a composition, was recognized in *Fell* v. *Wilson*, 12 East, 83, where it was holden, that a mere general demand of tithe and a refusal to take the sum tendered, could not be considered as a determination of a subsisting composition. A composition between the incumbent and the occupiers of land within the parish, determines on the death of the incumbent (*l*), and his successor is not obliged to give notice of his intention to take the tithes in kind; but if the successor, after induction into the benefice, accept the composition, such acceptance will be deemed a confirmation, and in such case the regular notice must be given (7). If a

---

(*k*) *Bower* v. *Major*, C. B., 1 Brod. & Bingh. 4.

(*l*) Agreed in *Brown* v. *Barlow*, H. 3 Geo. II., Scacc., 3 Gwill. 1001.

---

(6) *Eyre*, C. J., expressed a different opinion, observing, " that the analogy between land and tithe did not appear satisfactory to him; land was either taken on a holding from Lady-day, or from Michaelmas, or from some other time, and then notice to quit must be given accordingly. But if a composition is to be determined on any just principles, the notice must be given from a period suitable to the nature of the tithes, and with relation to the manner and cultivation of the land. There must be such a rule as will enable the tenant to cultivate his land in the manner most beneficial to himself, according as he is to pay a composition or in kind." It has always been the received opinion of the Court of Exchequer, that such a reasonable notice should be given as might determine the farmer in what manner to cultivate his land. See *Hulme* v. *Pardoe*, M'Leland's R. Exch. 39.

(7) A rector agreed with an occupier of land for a certain sum of money, in lieu of tithes, payable yearly at Michaelmas*. The rector

* M. T. 1730, Bunb. 294.

rector, &c. having made a composition (*m*), lease tithes, and the lessee makes no alteration in the composition, when the tithes revert to the rector, &c., the occupier of land will continue to hold under the composition originally made by the rector, &c. and consequently will be entitled to notice, before the rector, &c,. can take the tithes in kind. Compositions were not apportionable under the stat. 11 Geo. II. c. 19 ; and therefore the occupier was not accountable (*n*) for any proportion, and executor had not any remedy, unless the new incumbent adopted the same composition.

Second Section of Stat. 2 & 3 Edw. VI.]—The second section "empowers the rector, &c. or his servant, to see that the tithe is justly set forth, and to carry away the same, and gives a remedy in the ecclesiastical court for the recovery of the *double value* of tithe subtracted, with *costs.*"

As to the first part of this branch, it is merely declaratory of the common law, because, for stopping the way of the party to whom the tithes ought to be paid, an action on the case might have been maintained at common law. Although the tithe owner is entitled to use the way by which the farmer carries his nine tenths, yet, where the farmer *bonâ fide* stopped up the old way, it was holden (*o*), that the rector could not claim the old road as a permanent way, although the new one was more circuitous and inconvenient. As to the second part, it is to be observed, that the parson, &c. was entitled in the ecclesiastical court to recover the tithes themselves, and therefore the double value in addition made the recovery in the ecclesiastical court equivalent to the treble forfeiture under the former clause ; but costs being given by this action, rendered the suit in the ecclesiastical court more advantageous ; for, at the common law, the plaintiff was not entitled to costs (*p*) ; but now, by stat. 8 & 9 Will. III. c. 11, s. 3, "in actions of debt upon the statute for not setting forth tithes, wherein the single value or damage found by the jury shall not exceed the sum of twenty nobles (£6 13*s.* 4*d.*), the plaintiff obtaining judgment, or any award of execution after plea pleaded or demurrer joined, shall recover his costs." In like manner, if the plaintiff was nonsuit, or the defendant obtained a verdict, the defendant was not entitled to costs under the stat. 23 Hen. VIII. c.

(*m*) *Wyburd* v. *Tuck*, 1 Bos. & Pul. 458.

(*n*) *Aynsley* v. *Wordsworth*, 2 Ves. & B. 331, impeaching *Williams* v. *Powell*,

10 East, 270, as to the proportions of the composition.

(*o*) *James* v. *Dods*, 2 Cr. & M. 266.
(*p*) 2 Inst. 651.

---

died about a month before Michaelmas. It was decreed, that, the agreement having been determined by the death of the rector, the successor should be entitled to tithes in kind from such death, and the executor of the last incumbent to a proportion, according to the agreement, until the death of the testator.

15; for an action on this stat. 2 Edw. VI. was not an action upon a specialty or contract, nor for a wrong personal immediately done to the plaintiff, but for a non-feasance (*q*); but now, by the same stat. 8 & 9 Will. III. c. 11, s. 3, "If the plaintiff shall become nonsuit, or suffer a discontinuance, or a verdict shall pass against him, the defendant shall recover his costs."

Third Section of Stat. 2 & 3 Edw. VI.—The third section provides, "that tithe of cattle, feeding in any waste whereof the parish is not known, shall be paid to the parson, &c. of the parish in which the owner of the cattle dwells."

Fourth Section.—By the fourth section it is enacted, "that no person shall be sued or otherwise compelled to yield or pay tithes for any manors, lands, &c. which either by the *laws* and *statutes of the realm*, or by any *privilege or prescription* (*r*), are not chargeable with the payment of tithes, or are discharged by any *composition real*."

Laws of the Realm.]—That is, by the common law and customs of the realm. Of common right, no tithes are to be paid of quarries of stone or slate, because they are parcel of the freehold (*s*), and the parson hath tithe of the grass or corn which grows upon the surface of the land in which the quarry is; so also not for coal, turf, flags, tin, lead, brick, tile, earthen pots, lime, marle, chalk, and such like, because they are not the increase, but of the substance of the earth. And the like has been resolved of houses considered separately from the soil, as having no annual increase; but, by particular custom, tithes of any of these may be payable. See Bunb. 102.

Statutes.]—See stat. 27 Hen. VIII. c. 20; 31 Hen. VIII. c. 13; 32 Hen. VIII. c. 7; 37 Hen. VIII. c. 12.

Privilege or Prescription.]—At the common law (*t*), spiritual persons, that is, bishops, abbots, &c., were capable of a discharge of tithes: 1, By bull of the pope; 2ndly, By composition; 3dly, By prescription; and these were absolute; 4thly, By order, as the Cistertians, Templars, and Hospitallers of Jerusalem (8). This

---

(*q*) *Downton* v. *Finch*, 2 Inst. 651.
(*r*) See stat. 2 & 3 Will. IV. c. 100, *post*, p. 1296.

(*s*) 2 Inst. 651.
(*t*) Hob. 296, 7.

---

(8) The Italian merchants founded the convent and hospital of St. John of Jerusalem, the cradle of the monastic and military order which has since reigned in the isles of Rhodes and Malta. See "Gibbon's Decline and Fall." Pope Innocent the Third, A. D. 1197, by bull or decretal epistle, discharged the order of Præmonstratenses from the payment of tithes for lands of their own culture; but this bull not having been received and allowed in England, it has been holden, that lands, formerly parcel of a greater abbey of this order, are not, by virtue of this bull,

privilege was granted to these orders, by an ancient council explained by the council of Lateran, A. D. 1215, and allowed by the general consent of the realm (u); but it is extended to such lands only as they had before the council, A. D. 1215, and could be enjoyed only by the religious persons themselves, while those lands remained in their manurance. The greater part of these exemptions would have fallen with the spiritual persons, to whom they were annexed, upon the dissolution of the abbeys by Henry VIII., had they not been supported and upholden by the 21st section of the stat. 31 Hen. VIII. c. 13, (by which all the religious houses above the value of £200 per annum, were dissolved,) whereby it is enacted, " that the king, and every person having hereditaments belonging to monasteries, or other religious houses, shall enjoy the same, discharged of *payment* of tithes, in as large and ample a manner as the abbots, &c. enjoyed the same, at the time of their dissolution." By virtue of this clause, laymen holding abbey lands enjoy the several exemptions from tithe before mentioned, as derivatives from the religious persons who were entitled to them previously to the dissolution. These exemptions extend to monasteries which were dissolved and came to the crown after the 4th of February, 27 Hen. VIII., and before the 31 Hen. VIII., although they were not in possession (x) of the crown at the time when the stat. 31 Hen. VIII. c. 13, passed. And not only tenants in fee of such lands enjoy these exemptions, but also, where the estate is divided into portions, as under a marriage settlement, the several parties, whether tenants for life (y), or in tail (z), as they successively come into possession, are entitled to hold the lands tithe free. But where an abbot enjoying a privilege of discharge of tithe while the land was in his own manurance, made a gift in tail; and afterwards, by the 31 Hen. VIII., the abbey was dissolved; it was holden, that the donee in tail was not entitled to the exemption from tithe (a). Secus, if a common recovery had been suffered. Exemptions of this kind are usually supported by documentary evidence, contemporary, or about the period of the dissolution, detailing the lands being the possessions of the abbey or religious house, which, coupled with proof of non-payment, affords strong ground for presuming them discharged. See *Earl of Carysfort* v. *Wells and others*, 1 M. & Y. 600. By virtue of this clause, also, the owner of abbey lands is entitled to a discharge of the payment

(u) See *Stavely* v. *Ullithorn*, Hardr. 101.

(x) *Tate* v. *Skelton*, 4 Gwm. 1503.

(y) *Hett* v. *Meeds*, T. 39 Geo. III.,

Scacc., 4 Gwm. 1515.

(z) *Wilson* v. *Redman*, Hardr. 174.

(a) *Farmer* v. *Sheeman*, Hetl. 133.

exempt from payment of tithes. *Townley* v. *Tomlinson*, T. 2 Geo. III., Scacc., 3 Gwm. 1004; *Same* v. *Same*, E. 11 Geo. III., Scacc., 3 Gwm. 1017.

of tithes, if he can show that *at the time of the dissolution* there had been an unity of possession of the rectory and land titheable from time immemorial, and there be not any evidence that tithes have ever been paid: for, although a perpetual unity, in the prior of the monastery, or religious house, before the statute, operated not as a discharge, but only as a suspension of payment, because he could not pay tithes to himself; yet, inasmuch as the greater part of the monasteries were discharged from tithe, by bull or prescription, the courts, after a lapse of years, will presume that such discharge existed at the time of the dissolution, but that the records, or proofs of those discharges, cannot be produced after so long a unity of possession. A discharge of unity therefore is, as Pollexfen terms it, a discharge by bull, or by prescription *presumed*, but not proved. And the mere circumstance of the lands titheable being under lease at the time of the dissolution, will not destroy this presumption (b); but if it appear that the lessee paid tithe, that will destroy the presumption (c). The discharge by unity must be pleaded as a discharge of the *payment* of tithe, and not as a discharge generally. Lands formerly belonging to a Cistertian abbey are discharged of tithes (d) whilst in the manurance of the owner, although such lands were under lease for years (9) at the time of the dissolution of the abbey; for the privilege, though personal, existed at the time of the dissolution, though not *in esse*, yet in right; and the reversioners were entitled to the discharge, as soon as the lands reverted into their own hands. In *Fosset* v. *Francklin*, T. Raym. 225; and *Star* v. *Ellyot*, Freem. 299; it was holden, that lands formerly parcel of the possession of the prior of St. John of Jerusalem, and which came to the crown by 32 Hen. VIII. c. 24, were discharged from payment of tithes. Lands belonging to those abbeys which came to the crown by stat. 27 Hen. VIII. c. 24, (that is the lesser abbeys,) are not entitled (e) to these exemptions, although such lands were discharged in the hands of the religious houses; for that statute does not contain any clause similar to the 21st section of 31 Hen. VIII. c. 13. Having enumerated the several discharges from tithe, which were enjoyed by religious persons at the common law and before the dissolution of monasteries, and by laymen, as derivatives from those religious persons since that period, it remains only to add a few observations relative to the exemption from tithes, which might be claimed by

---

(b) *Wildman* v. *Oades*, Pollexfen, 1.
(c) *Benton* v. *Trot*, Moor, 528.
(d) *Cowley* v. *Keys*, Scacc. 1788, 4 Gwm. 1308, per *Eyre*, C. B., recognizing *Porter* v. *Bathurst*, Cro. Jac. 559; 2 Roll.

Rep. 148; Palm. 111; Dyer, 277, b., S. C., in margin.
(e) See Clayt. 41, pl. 70; Hob. 307; Cro. Jac. 607; Cro. Car. 422; Sir W. Jones, 3.

---

(9) Or for life, or in tail, per *Cur.*, in *Wilson* v. *Redman*, Hardr. 190; *Hett* v. *Meeds*, Trin. T. 1799, Excheq., 4 Gwm. 1515, 16.

laymen at the common law; and these were two only—1st, by composition real; and 2nd, by prescription de modo decimandi; for it is clearly established (*f*), that by the common law a layman could not prescribe in a non decimando (10), or set up as a defence to a claim of tithe, the mere non-payment of tithe from time immemorial, whether the party claiming the tithe be lay impropriator (*g*), or ecclesiastical rector, and whether the non-payment extend to all, or a portion (*h*) only, of the tithes.

Composition real.]—A composition real, according to Gibson (*i*), is, " where the incumbent, *together with the patron and ordinary*, make agreement, by deed executed under their hands and seals, that certain lands shall be discharged from the payment of tithe in specie, in consideration of a recompense to the incumbent, either in money or in lands, to him and his successors for ever, or in some other thing for their benefit and advantage. So Sir Simon Degge (*k*) observes, " That which we call a real composition is where the present incumbent of any church, together with the patron and ordinary, do agree, under their hands and seals, or by fine in the king's courts, that such lands shall be freed and discharged of payment of all manner of tithe for ever, paying some annual payment, or doing some other thing to the ease, profit, or advantage of the parson or vicar, to whom the tithe did belong." From the preceding definitions, it appears that there must be the following requisites to constitute a real composition :—1. That the tithe be discharged; 2. That a composition be given in lieu of such discharge; 3. That the composition must be made with the consent of the patron and ordinary; 4. To these it may be added, that a composition must have been made before the stat. 13 Eliz. c. 10; for, by the third section of that statute, " masters and fellows of colleges, deans and chapters, masters of hospitals, parsons, vicars, or other persons having ecclesiastical living or tithe, are restrained

(*f*) *Breary* v. *Manby*, 3 Wood's Dec. 43; 3 Burn's Ecc. L. 438; 3 Gwm. 904.
(*g*) *Burg. of Bury St. Edmund's* v. *Evans*, Com. Rep. 643; 2 Gwm. 757, *S. C.; Jennings* v. *Lettis*, 3 Gwm. 952, S. P. See also *Andrews* v. *Drever*, 2 Bingh. N. C. 1; 2 Sc. 1.
(*h*) *Nagle* v. *Edwards*, 4 Gwm. 1442.

But see the remarks of Lord *Loughborough*, Ch., on this case, in *Rose* v. *Calland*, 5 Ves. jun. 186, and of *Wood*, B., in *Mead* v. *Norbury*, 2 Price, 347.
(*i*) Gibson's Codex, tit. 30, c. 5, p. 705, in notis, ed. 1713. See also Sir W. Jones, 368.
(*k*) Degge, pt. 2, c. 20.

(10) Neither could a hundred or a county prescribe in a non decimando, for a thing that is in its nature *de jure* titheable; but of things which in their nature are not titheable *de jure*, a hundred or county might prescribe in a non decimando; because, in such case, they were discharged without a custom to the contrary, and they did but insist on their ancient right, and that the custom had not prevailed against it. *Hicks* v. *Woodson*, Lord Raym. 137; Salk. 655, *S. C.* But see stat. 2 & 3 Will. IV. c. 100, *post*, p. 1296.

from making any conveyance of the same, other than by lease for 21 years, or three lives, from the time when such lease shall be made, and reserving thereupon the accustomed yearly rent." And it has been holden (*l*), that a decree in equity, confirming an agreement for the acceptance of land, in lieu of tithe, made since the stat. 13 Eliz. c. 10, is not binding on a succeeding incumbent, although such agreement was sanctioned by the concurrence of all the parties, and although it had been acquiesced under for 130 years.

But now, by stat. 2 & 3 Will. IV. c. 100 (*m*), intituled, " An Act for shortening the Time required in Claims of Modus Decimandi, or Exemption from or Discharge of Tithes;" all prescriptions and claims of or for any modus decimandi, or of or to any exemption from or discharge of tithes, by composition, real or otherwise, shall, in cases where the render of tithes in kind shall be hereafter demanded by the King, Duke of Cornwall, or by any lay person not being a corporation sole, or by any body corporate of many, be sustained upon evidence, showing, in cases of claim of a modus decimandi, the payment or render of such modus; and in cases of claim to exemption or discharge, showing the enjoyment of the land without payment or render of tithes, money, or other matter, in lieu thereof, for the full period of thirty years next before the time of such demand, unless, in the case of a claim of a modus decimandi, the actual payment or render of tithes in kind, or of money or other thing differing in amount, quality, or quantity from the modus claimed, or, in case of claim to exemption or discharge, the render or payment of tithes, or of money or other matter in lieu thereof, shall be shown to have taken place at some time prior to such thirty years, or it shall be proved that such payment or render of modus was made, or enjoyment had, by some consent or agreement expressly made or given for that purpose by deed or writing; and if such proof in support of the claim shall be extended to the full period of sixty years next before the time of such demand, in such cases the claim shall be deemed absolute and indefeasible, unless it shall be proved that such payment or render of modus was made or enjoyment had by some consent or agreement by deed or writing; and where the render of tithes in kind shall be demanded by any archbishop, bishop, dean, prebendary, parson, vicar, master of hospital, or other corporation sole, whether spiritual or temporal, then every such prescription or claim shall be valid and indefeasible, upon evidence showing such payment or render of modus made, or enjoyment had, as is hereinbefore mentioned, applicable to the nature of the claim, for and during the whole time that two persons in succession shall have held the office or benefice, in respect whereof

(*l*) *Jones* v. *Snow*, 3 Gwm. 1199, See also *Cartwright* v. *Colton*, E. T. 19 Geo. III., 4 H. Wood's D. 88 ; *Attorney General* v. *Cholmley*, Amb. 510, S. P.; 7 Bro. P. C. 34, Tomlins' ed., *S. C.*, D. P.

(*m*) Amended by stat. 4 & 5 Will. IV. c. 83.

such render of tithes in kind shall be claimed, and for not less than three years after the appointment and institution or induction of a third person thereto; provided, that if the whole time of the holding of such two persons shall be less than sixty years, then it shall be necessary to show such payment or render of modus made or enjoyment had, (as the case may be,) not only during the whole of such time, but also during such further number of years, either before or after such time, or partly before and partly after, as shall with such time be sufficient to make up the full period of sixty years, and also for and during the further period of three years after the appointment and institution or induction of a third person to the same office or benefice, unless it shall be proved that such payment or render of modus was made or enjoyment had by some consent or agreement by deed or writing.

By sect. 2, compositions for tithes confirmed by decrees of courts of equity, and which have not since been set aside, abandoned, or departed from, are made valid in law (*n*); and no modus, exemption, or discharge shall be deemed to be within the provisions of this act, unless such modus, &c. shall be proved to have existed and been acted upon within one year next before the passing of this act.

By sect. 4, this act shall not extend to any case where the tithes of any lands, tenements, or hereditaments shall have been demised by deed for life or years, or where any composition for tithes shall have been made by deed or writing, by the person entitled to such tithes, with the owner or occupier of the land, for any such term of years, and such demise or composition shall be subsisting at the time of the passing of this act, and where any action or suit shall be instituted for the recovery or enforcing the payment of tithes in kind within three years next after the expiration, surrender, or other determination of such demise or composition.

By sect. 5, it is provided that the time during which lands shall be held by persons entitled to the tithes thereof shall be excluded in the computation under this act; as also (*o*) the time during which any person capable of resisting any claim shall be an infant, &c.

By sect. 7, in all actions and suits it shall be sufficient to allege that the modus or exemption or discharge claimed was actually exercised and enjoyed for such of the periods mentioned in this act as may be applicable to the case; and if the other party shall intend to rely on any proviso, exception, incapacity, disability, contract, agreement, deed, or writing herein mentioned, or any other matter of fact or of law not inconsistent with the simple fact of the exercise and enjoyment of the matter claimed, the same shall be specially alleged and set forth in answer to the allegation of the

(*n*) See *Thorpe* v. *Mallingley*, 5 M. & W. 302.   (*o*) Sect. 6.

party claiming, and shall not be received in evidence on any general traverse or denial of the matter claimed.

By sect. 8, in the several cases provided for by this act, no presumption shall be allowed in support of any claim upon proof of the exercise or enjoyment of the right or matter claimed for any less period of time than for such period mentioned in this act as may be applicable to the case and to the nature of the claim. This act does not extend to Scotland or Ireland (*p*).

5th Section of Stat. 2 & 3 Edw. VI.—By the 5th section, it is enacted, " that if *barren heath or waste ground*, (other than such as is discharged from the payment of tithes, by act of parliament,) which has laid barren and paid no tithes, by reason of the same barrenness, be improved and converted into arable ground or meadow, it shall, after the end of seven years next after such improvements, pay tithe of corn and hay growing upon the same." But (*q*) if any such barren waste or heath ground has been charged with the payment of any tithes, and the same be improved or converted into arable ground or meadow, the owner shall, during the seven years next following after the improvement, pay such kind of tithes as was paid for the same before the improvement.

Barren Heath or Waste Ground.]—*Barren ground* (*r*) is understood, by the opinion and judgment of the common law, to be ground whereof no profit arises or grows : but ground which has been stubbed, and afterwards bears corn or grass, is not barren. By *waste ground* is understood such ground as no man challenges as his own, or no man can tell to whom it certainly belongs, and which lies uninclosed and unbounded with hedge and ditch; but the ground which is inclosed and hedged and ditched in, and the land known, is not waste ground. By *heath ground* is to be understood, ground which is dispersed and lies as common. The fifth clause was designed for the advancement of tillage, and consequently, although the land yield some fruit, yet if it be barren land, *quoad agriculturam*, it is within this statute (*s*). On the other hand, if the land be not *suâpte naturâ sterilis*, but is capable of producing a crop of corn, without extraordinary expense in the tillage, it is not protected by the statute. Such lands only are within this clause, as, over and above the necessary expense of inclosing and clearing, require also expense in manuring before they can be made proper for agriculture (11). In a case where it appeared (*t*) that the land had been

(*p*) Sect. 9.
(*q*) Sect. 6.
(*r*) Per *Cur.*, Dyer, 170, b. in margin. See *Warwick* v. *Collins, post,* p. 1299.
(*s*) 2 Inst. 656.

(*t*) *Witt* v. *Buck,* 3 Bulst. 165 ; 1 Roll. Rep. 354, *S. C.* See also *Jones* v. *Le David,* 4 Gwm. 1336; and *Byron* v. *Lamb,* 4 Gwm. 1594.

(11) Barren ground is such ground as will not bear corn of itself, without very great cost in the extraordinary manuring of it. Agreed per *Cur.*,

marsh and sandy land, and covered with salt water; that from time immemorial no grass had been known to grow thereon, and no profit had been made of it, until the tenant, at a great expense, by the erection of banks and sea-walls, prevented the sea from overflowing the land, and thereby was enabled to convert it into arable land, which produced corn: it was holden, that this land was not protected by the statute; *Coke*, C. J., *Dodderidge*, and *Haughton*, Js., observing, that land was not barren which could bear corn without cost, as this did, and therefore tithes ought to be paid for it; and that the circumstance of the party having been at great costs in raising a mound to make this good land, by the exclusion of the sea, would not alter the case (12).

The rule of law for determining what is barren ground is, whether the land is of such nature as to require an *extraordinary* expense in manuring or tilling, to bring it into a proper state of cultivation (*u*), and not whether it is or is not in its own nature so fertile as after being ploughed and sown to produce of itself, without manuring or tillage, a crop worth more than the expense of ploughing, sowing, and reaping. Where upon an inclosure of barren lands, the defendant put in cattle on his land, but did no other act of improvement; it was holden (*x*), that the seven years only began to run from the first act of ploughing to render the land productive. It seems, the act is to be so construed, as to apply to such improvement as would make the land produce more corn or hay for tithe.

(*u*) *Warwick* v. *Collins*, 2 M. & S. 349;   (*x*) *Ross* v. *Smith*, 1 B. & Ad. 907.
Lord Selsea v. *Powell*, 6 Taunt. 297, S. P.

---

3 Bulstr. 166. Barren inclosed, within the meaning of the stat. Edw. VI., must be such land as is barren *sudpte naturâ*, and not land upon which wood or the like grew before, which is afterwards burnt, and the lands converted into tillage. Per *Powell*, J., Lord Raym. 991. See also *Horner* v. *Bonner*, 6 Mod. 96.

(12) This case is alluded to by Lord *Hardwicke*, Ch., in *Stockwell* v. *Terry*, 1 Ves. 117. "There is an expense in gaining land from the sea, yet the seven years are not allowed*, though overflown time out of mind, because the benefit is lasting; but if an additional expense is necessary to make it produce the first crop, seven years shall be allowed." "As to the case of land newly gained from the sea, if that determination can be supported at all, it must be by other reasons than those assigned in the book. If such land is not protected, it must be because it is not within the description in the statute; because it is neither barren, nor waste, nor heath ground, but from the moment of its existence as land, is fertile, enclosed, and capable of tillage, and, therefore, of a description which the statute cannot attach upon." Per *Eyre*, C. B., in *Jones* v. *Le David*, 4 Gwm. 1338, 9.

* See *Sherington* v. *Fleewood*, Cro. Eliz. 475.

Land which is of a good natural quality shall pay tithe immediately, although the expense attending the breaking it up and liming it exceeds the return made to the farmer in the several first years of cultivating it (*y*). The onus of proving that the land is barren lies on the defendant (*z*).

Of the Persons to whom Tithes are due.

Primâ facie all tithes not appropriated belong to and are due to the rector of the church of that parish wherein they arise. But the parson of one parish may claim by prescription a portion (13) of tithes in the parish of another (*a*). Extra-parochial tithes belong to the king (*b*), who is a mixed person (*c*), and capable of tithes at the common law in pernancy (*d*). This right extends to all extra-parochial lands (*e*), and is not confined to such as are strictly speaking forests. Antecedently to the statutes for the dissolution of monasteries, spiritual persons only, or a mixed person, had capacity to take tithes: mere laymen were incapable of them (*f*), except in special cases (*g*). Since the statutes for the dissolution of monasteries (*h*), the tithes which were appropriated to the monasteries so dissolved, are become lay fee, and laymen are capable of them in pernancy, not quâ laymen, but as the derivatives of the ecclesiastical persons to whom they formerly belonged. As laymen were incapable of having any tithes until the dissolution of the monasteries, there cannot be any ancient descent with respect to tithes. A rectory in Kent (*i*), formerly belonging to one of the dissolved monasteries, having been granted by Henry VIII. to a layman, to be holden in fee by knight's service in capite; it was adjudged, that although the lands were descendible according to the custom of gavelkind, yet the tithes must descend to the

(*y*) *Warwick* v. *Collins*, 5 M. & S. 166.
(*z*) Agreed per *Cur.*, in *Lord Selses* v. *Powell*, 6 Taunt. 299.
(*a*) 14 Hen. IV. 17, a; 44 Ass. pl. 25; 1 Roll. Abr. 657.
(*b*) 22 Ass. pl. 75; 2 Inst. 647; 1 Roll. Abr. 657.
(*c*) 10 Hen. VII. 18, a.
(*d*) 2 Rep. 44, a; Cro. Eliz. 512, per *Cur.*, in *Bannister* v. *Wright*, Sty. Rep. 137.

(*e*) *Attorney General* v. *Lord Eardley*, 8 Pri. 53.
(*f*) Adm. in *Doe* v. *Landaff*, 2 Bos. & Pul. N. R. 508.
(*g*) *Pigot* v. *Hearn*, Cro. Eliz. 599, 785, cited in 2 Rep. 45, a.
(*h*) Cro. Eliz. 512.
(*i*) *Doe* d. *Lushington* v. *Bishop of Landaff and others*, 2 Bos. & Pul. N. R. 491.

(13) Portions are the remains of those arbitrary consecrations of tithes which took place before the settlement of the parochial right of tithes. The precise time at which the parochial right of tithes was settled cannot be ascertained; according to Sir Simon Degge, it was settled by a perpetual constitution early in the thirteenth century.

eldest son, according to the rules of descent at the common law. A parson shall not pay tithe for his glebe to the vicar : for ecclesia decimas solvere ecclesiæ non debet (*k*). But if the parson lets his glebe for years (*l*), reserving a rent, the lessee shall pay him tithes. A rector is of common right entitled to all kinds of tithes ; the vicar can claim against the rector, by endowment only, or prescription and usage, as evidence of endowment. Where there is not any written endowment (*m*), and the vicar has been in the perception of all the small tithes, the court will presume him entitled to all small tithes of modern introduction. Where an estate had been purchased free from rectorial tithe, with a right of common thereto annexed, and the common was afterwards inclosed under an act of parliament, and certain land was allotted to the owner of the estate in lieu of the right of common; it was holden, that tithe was not (*n*) payable in respect of the allotted land.

By whom and against whom an Action on the Statute may be brought.

This action may be brought by the rector (*o*), or by one or more (*p*) farmers of the rectory. If the rector be entitled to two parts, and the vicar to a third part of the tithe, and the parson and vicar, by several leases, demise their respective shares to a third person, such lessee may maintain an action for not setting forth all the tithes (*q*). The right to tithes accrues immediately on the severance, consequently this action must be brought by the person entitled to the tithes at the time of severance; hence, where A. executed a lease of tithes to B. on a day subsequent to their severance, but before the tithes were carried away by the occupiers of the land, it was adjudged that B. could not maintain an action on this statute (*r*). The action can be brought by the party grieved only : hence where this action was brought by the plaintiff for himself *and the queen*, judgment was arrested (*s*). A man being possessed of a lease of tithes in right of his wife, as executrix to her former husband (*t*), grants " all his right, title, and interest" in the aforesaid tithes to A. B. : it was holden, that the grant was good, and that A. B. might maintain an action on this statute for not setting out tithes. If executrix of lessee for years of a rectory take husband, the husband and wife may join in an action on this

(*k*) *Blunco* v. *Marston*, Cro. Eliz. 479. See also Cro. Eliz. 578.

(*l*) Owen, 39.

(*m*) *Payne* v. *Powlett*, 3 Gwm. 1247.

(*n*) *Steele* v. *Manns*, 5 B. & A. 22.

(*o*) *Day* v. *Peckvell*, Moor. 915.

(*p*) *Kent* v. *Penkevon*, Cro. Jac. 70.

(*q*) *Champernon* v. *Hill*, Yelv. 63; Cro. Jac. 68.

(*r*) *Wyburd* v. *Tuck*, 1 Bos. & Pul. 458.

(*s*) *Johns* v. *Carne*, Moor, 911 ; Cro. Eliz. 621, *S. C.*

(*t*) *Arnold* v. *Bidgood*, Cro. Jac. 318, recognized by *De Grey*, C. J., in *Thrustout* v. *Coppin*, 3 Wils. 278.

statute (*u*). As the action on this statute is a personal action, tenants in common of tithe ought to join as plaintiffs (*x*); and if they do not join, advantage may be taken of it by plea in abatement, but not in arrest of judgment (*y*). This action may be maintained by and against executors (*z*). Generally (*a*), the person entitled to the nine parts at the time of severance, ought to set forth the tithe; and if he fails in so doing, the owner of the tithe may sue him, although his interest in the *land* be determined before the tithes were carried away, provided he remain owner of the *corn*. If there be two joint-tenants (*b*), and one only enter and occupy, this action is maintainable against the joint tenant, who occupied alone. So if there be two tenants in common (*c*), and one of them sets out his tithe, and the other carries it all away, the action shall be brought against that tenant in common alone who carried the whole tithe away. If a person buy corn, standing, of the proprietor of a rectory (*d*), he must pay tithe, unless he has special words in the contract to discharge him from payment of tithe; and the carrying away such corn, without setting out the tithe, will render him liable to an action on this statute.

Of the Declaration.

It is not necessary for the plaintiff to set forth his title specially; because it is but inducement to the action; it is sufficient for him to allege, generally, that he is rector, proprietor, or farmer, without showing by what title (*e*); for this is a personal action, grounded merely upon a contempt against the statute, in not setting forth the tithes, and not for the recovery of the tithes, although the title to the tithes may come in question. In an action by two farmers upon this statute, who claimed under a lease from a patentee for life of the king, an exception was taken, because they did not show the patent (*f*), but the objection was overruled—1st, because the letters patent did not belong to the plaintiffs; 2dly, because the plaintiffs did not demand the tithes themselves, but damages for a tort; and the title shown in the declaration is only conveyance to the action. Plaintiff declared (*g*), that he was rector of A., and entitled to the tithes of certain lands, in the parish of A., and the tithes of certain lands in the parish of B., without showing how he became entitled to

(*u*) *Beadles and Wife* v. *Sherman*, Cro. Eliz. 613, judgment affirmed on error.

(*x*) *Greenwood's* case, Clayt. 28.

(*y*) *Cole* v. *Banbery*, 1 Sidf. 49.

(*z*) *Mr. J. Moreton's* case, 1 Ventr. 30; 1 Sidf. 407; 2 Keb. 502, S. C.; 1 Sidf. 88. See also stat. 3 & 4 Will. IV. c. 42, s. 2, *ante*, p. 792, 8.

(*a*) *Kipping* v. *Swayn*, Cro. Jac. 324.

(*b*) *Cole* v. *Wilkes*, Hutt. 121.

(*c*) *Gerard's* case, cited and said to have been adjudged, Hutt. 122.

(*d*) *Moyle* v. *Ewer*, Cro. Jac. 361.

(*e*) *Babington* v. *Matthews*, Bulst. 228; 1 Brownl. 86, 7; *Moyle* v. *Ewer*, Cro. Jac. 362; *Champernon* v. *Hill*, Yelv. 63, S. P.

(*f*) *Dagg and Kent* v. *Penketon*, Exch. Chr., Cro. Jac. 70.

(*g*) *Phillips* v. *Kettle*, Hard. 173.

the tithes of land out of his parish; after verdict this was holden sufficient. So where plaintiff declared (h), that he was rector of D. and S. and that defendant, being occupier of lands in D. and S., carried off the corn untithed, without showing which part of the lands lay in D. and which in S. After verdict for plaintiff, on motion in arrest of judgment, the declaration was holden sufficient, for this action is in the nature of a trespass founded in a tort. So if the plaintiff declare (i), that he was seised in fee of a portion of tithes of corn growing upon such a grange, this will be sufficient. Neither is it necessary to specify the kinds of grain (k), or by whom sown, or the number of loads of corn (l) or hay carried away. It is sufficient for the plaintiff to state in his declaration the single value of the tithes (m), without adding the treble value; and where the treble value is set forth, a mistake in computing it will not vitiate. Where the severance was alleged to have been before the sowing (n), and exception taken on this ground, after verdict it was disallowed, because the allegation of the sowing was superfluous, and so aided by verdict. Regularly, the declaration, pursuing the words of the statute, ought to allege, that the defendant is *subditus domini regis;* but to allege defendant to be *occupator terræ,* has been holden to be equivalent, for that implies that he is *subditus* (o). It is not necessary for the plaintiff to set forth the title of the defendant (p); alleging generally, that he was occupier, without showing how or what interest he had, will be sufficient. A count for treble value of tithes not set out, and also a count for the same tithes bargained and sold will not be allowed (q), under R. G. H. T. 4 Will. IV. Reg. 1, s. 5.

Pleadings, and herein of the Statutes of Limitation.

Nil debet is the general issue usually pleaded to this action (r), and notwithstanding the new rules is still a good plea; for the judges have not (by reason of the proviso in sect. 1 of 3 & 4 Will. IV. c. 42 (s),) any power to deprive the defendant of the plea given by the stat. 21 Jac. I. c. 4, s. 4 (t), this being a penal action. Plea that the plaintiff sowed the corn, and sold it to the defendant, is not a good plea, because such sale will not excuse the payment of tithes (u). The statute of limitations (21 Jac. I. c. 16,) cannot be pleaded to this action (x); for that statute—sect. 3, is confined to actions of

(h) *Fellows* v. *Kingston,* 2 Lev. 1.
(i) *Sanders* v. *Sandford,* Cro. Jac. 437.
(k) *Bedell and Wife* v. *Sherman,* 2 Inst. 650; 13 Rep. 47, *S. C.*
(l) 1 Brownl. 71.
(m) *Coke* v. *Smith,* H. 7 Car. I., B. R.
(n) *Pellett* v. *Henworth,* Degge, 395, 6th ed.
(o) *Phillips* v. *Kettle,* Hardr. 173.
(p) March, 21, pl. 49.
(q) *Lawrence* v. *Stephens,* 3 Dowl. P.

C. 777.
(r) *Bawtrey* v. *Isted,* Hob. 218.
(s) See *ante,* p. 148.
(t) *Earl Spencer* v. *Swannell,* 3 M. & W. 154; 6 Dowl. (P. C.) 326.
(u) *Moyle* v. *Ewer,* 2 Bulst. 183; Cro. Jac. 361, *S. C.*
(x) *Talory* v. *Jackson,* Cro. Car. 513, recognized in *Cockram* v. *Welby,* 1 Mod. 246.

debt grounded upon a lending or contract, *without specialty*, and to debt for arrears of rent. But by stat. 53 Geo. III. c. 127, s. 5, " No action shall be brought for the recovery of any penalty for not setting out tithes, nor any suit instituted in any court of equity, or in any ecclesiastical court, to recover the value of any tithes, unless such action shall be brought or such suit commenced within six years from the time when such tithes became due."

The stat. 3 & 4 Will. IV. c. 27 (*y*), for the limitation of actions and suits relating to real property, extends to tithes, (except tithes belonging to a spiritual or eleemosynary corporation sole,) and by sect. 43, no person claiming *any tithes*, for the recovery of which he might bring an action or suit at law or in equity, shall bring a suit or other proceeding in any spiritual court to recover the same, but within the period during which he might bring such action or suit at law or in equity.

Evidence.

Long possession, acquiesced in by the defendant (*z*), is *primâ facie* evidence of the rector's title against defendant, and supersedes the necessity of proving institution, induction, or reading Thirty-nine Articles (14). The plaintiff declared as farmer of the rectory of Friston, in Sussex (*a*), and proved himself lessee of J. S., who was lessee to the dean and chapter of Chichester, to whom the rectory belonged, and produced the lease from J. S., but did not produce the lease from the dean and chapter to J. S.; however, upon proving that he received tithe of others, as farmer, it was holden sufficient. So where the plaintiff (*b*), being farmer under the dean and chapter

---

(*y*) See *ante*, p. 733.
(*z*) Clayt. 48, pl. 83. See also *Chapman* v. *Beard*, 4 Gwm. 1482, and *Harris* v. *Adge*, 2 Gwm. 560. See also *Ganson*

v. *Wells*, 8 Taunt. 542.
(*a*) *Selwyn* v. *Baldy*, Bull. N. P. 188, per *Pemberton*, C. J., Sussex Ass. 1682.
(*b*) *Hartridge* v. *Gibbs*, Bull. N. P. 188.

---

(14) " In penal actions on stat. 2 & 3 Edw. VI., it has always been holden sufficient proof against the defendant, that the party suing is in the act of receiving the tithes from defendant." Per Lord *Kenyon*, C. J., in *Radford, q. t.* v. *M'Intosh*, 3 T. R. 632, where it was holden, that in an action for penalties on this statute, laying a tax on post-horses, brought by the farmer of the tax, it is not necessary for the plaintiff to give in evidence his appointment by the lords commissioners of the treasury, or the commissioners of the stamp duties authorized by them. Proof that the defendant has accounted with him, as farmer, for the duties, is sufficient. A lay impropriator is entitled to all the favourable presumptions, to which a rector is entitled, both with respect to time and exemptions; and, consequently, if he prove himself impropriator, it will be sufficient without proving the receipt of tithes within time of memory. *Whieldon* v. *Harvey*, 3 Gwm. 951.

of Canterbury, proved that he had received tithes for some years as such, it was holden sufficient, without producing any lease. The plaintiff declared on a lease made to him for six years by the parson (c), if the parson should so long live and *continue parson there.* The jury found the lease for six years, if the parson should so long live, but the words "if he continue parson" were not in the lease. The variance was holden to be immaterial; 1st, for the additional words in the declaration, "*if he should so long continue parson,*" are only what the law implies; 2dly, because the lease is not the ground of the action, nor is the declaration founded upon the lease, but upon the carrying away the tithes. The declaration stated (d), that " *the tithes of turnips were yielded and paid, and were of right due and payable within forty years next before the making the stat. Edw. VI.*" The second count contained a similar averment, as to the tithes of potatoes. After verdict for the plaintiff, it was moved to set it aside, on the ground that the averments were not, and could not be, proved, inasmuch as turnips and potatoes were not cultivated before the statute of Edw. VI. But the court said, that the true construction of the stat. Edw. VI. was, that if the lands charged were subject to the payment of tithe within the period mentioned in the statute, that was sufficient to prove the allegation in declarations of this kind, and to support the plaintiff's action; that if it were clear that nothing but wheat had ever been sown upon this land, still that would not preclude the tithe of other tithable produce from being taken, and that as no evidence had been offered at the trial to prove that turnips and potatoes were not cultivated previously to the stat. Edw. VI., they could make no such presumption against the justice of the case, even though such a fact might be asserted by persons who had written upon the subject. They added, that whatever might be the case with respect to potatoes, their own information led them to believe that turnips were in cultivation, in this country, before the stat. of Edw. VI. By stat. 5 & 6 Will. IV. c. 75, intituled "An Act for the Amendment of the Law as to the Tithing of Turnips in certain Cases," turnips severed from the land, for the purpose of being consumed by sheep or cattle thereon, are made subject to tithe as if not so severed.

The defendant (e) under nil debet may give in evidence a modus, or customary payment, and thereby defeat the plaintiff's action. " All moduses were at first upon an agreement (f) between the parson, patron, and ordinary, by some instrument in writing in the nature of a contract or composition, which, though decayed by time, or lost by accident, yet being run out into a prescription remained

(c) *Wheeler* v. *Heydon*, Cro. Jac. 328.
(d) *Hallewell* v. *Trappes*, 2 Bos. & Pul. N. R. 173.
(e) *Charry* v. *Garland*, Dorset Lent Ass. 1699, coram *Ward*, C. B., 3 Gwm.

951.
(f) Per Lord *Hardwicke*, Ch., *Hardcastle* v. *Smithson*, MSS. Serjt. Hill, vol. 7, p. 63, and 3 Atk. 245.

good, and the court would not break in upon such ancient usages upon slight reasons, for fear of introducing general inconvenience." A modus must have been immemorial, that is, it must have existed before the time of Richard the First's return from the Holy Land : but as this could not be proved by living witnesses, and in many cases not by written evidence, it was sufficient to prove that such a sum had been paid as far back as living memory extended ; and that being established, it lay on the other side to prove the negative. But see stat. 2 & 3 Will. IV. c. 100, *ante*, p. 1296. A modus ought to be equally certain to the parson or lay impropriator, as the tithe in lieu of which it comes (*g*), or, as it is expressed in Salk. 657, a modus ought to be as certain as the duty which is destroyed by it. A modus is sometimes payable in respect of a particular farm, and then it is called a farm modus. A modus may also be payable for part of a farm ; as where a farm lay in three different parishes, and a general modus was set up for all tithes for that part of the farm which lay in one of the parishes, such modus was holden to be good (*h*) ; for the minister of one parish and the land-owner might have thought proper to contract for a money payment for so much of the farm as lay in one parish, although the ministers of the other two parishes might not have thought proper so to contract. A pension is a sum of money paid in respect of lands which are tithe free, and is quite a different thing from a composition either temporary or real. Where a modus has covered a farm and common, or right in nature of right of common and all tithes arising therefrom, and then by an Inclosure Act an allotment is made, on which new crops of a different nature from those raised before are raised, the modus will cover such new crops (*i*). A modus will cover the tithe of a common, if that common be inclosed (*k*). Where, in a declaration in debt for not setting out tithe of hay, it was averred, that there was an immemorial custom as to the setting out the tithe within the parish, and the limits, bounds, and titheable places thereof ; it was holden (*l*), that this averment was proved by evidence that the custom prevailed in all parts of the parish where tithe of hay was set out, and that proof of a modus for hay in one township made no difference. Evidence (*m*) of a right to all kinds of tithes, in a lay impropriator, up to a given time, and of the receipt of the corn tithe since that time by another party, is evidence from which a jury may, if they think fit, infer a grant of all the tithes by the first mentioned impropriator to such latter party ; and, therefore, the latter, in support of a claim for hay tithe, may give documentary or other evidence of hay tithe having

(*g*) Per Lord *Hardwicke*, 3 Atk. 246.

(*h*) Per Lord *Eldon*, Ch., in *White* v. *Lisle*, July, 1819.

(*i*) *Stockwell* v. *Terry*, 1 Ves. 117, 118, per Lord *Hardwicke*, Ch.

(*k*) *Steele* v. *Mann*, 5 B. & A. 22,;

Askew v. *Wilkinson*, 3 B. & Ad. 152.

(*l*) *Pigott* v. *Bayley*, 6 B. & C. 16, *Littledale*, J., dissent.

(*m*) *Bayley* v. *Drever*, 1 A. & E. 449 ; 3 Nev. & M. 885, *S. C.*

been taken by the presumed grantor. A terrier cannot be received in evidence, unless it comes from the proper repository (*m*), that is, the registry of the bishop of the diocese; but if the original cannot be found there, it seems (*n*) that a copy from the parish chest would be admissible. An ancient document, in the nature of a terrier, produced from the proper custody, and under the proper authority, although without date, and signed by various persons, without designating their character, has been holden (*o*), to be admissible. An ancient statement concerning the payment of tithes of a parish by a modus, signed by the rector for the time being, was holden (*p*) to be evidence against a succeeding rector as an admission by his predecessor, although it was found among the title deeds of a land owner in the parish, and although a terrier was produced from the bishop's registry, which was silent as to the modus.

The word tithes (*q*) in ancient documents does not necessarily import tithes in kind; but may mean, according to circumstances, either tithes in kind or a money payment in lieu thereof.

Verdict.

If the verdict be given for the plaintiff (*r*), it is incumbent on the jury to find how much of the debt demanded by the declaration is due to the plaintiff, which is to be done by trebling the value of the tithe subtracted. The plaintiff shall recover according to the verdict (*s*); hence, where, in the statement of the treble value of the tithe, there was error in the calculation, and the plaintiff demanded less than he was entitled to; on motion in arrest of judgment after verdict, an exception was taken on the ground that the plaintiff, having demanded less than was due, ought to have acknowledged satisfaction for the residue; but the court overruled the objection, observing, that the demand in this case was not for any sum certain, as in an action grounded on a specialty, but only for so much as should be given by the jury, the plaintiff being entitled to recover, not according to his demand, but according to the verdict. Where it was found, by a special verdict (*t*), that the abbot of A. was seised in fee of certain land, and that he and his predecessors held the land discharged of tithe, and that he had granted the land to All Souls' College; it was holden, that the prescription was personal to the abbot, and did not run with the land, and that it could not be intended to be a discharge by a real composition, it not being so pleaded, nor found by the jury to be so. An action on this statute being brought by the party grieved, for the purpose of trying a

(*m*) *Atkins* v. *Hatton*, Gwill. 140.
(*n*) *S. C.*
(*o*) *Hall* v. *Farmer*, 2 Younge & Coll. 145.
(*p*) *Maddison* v. *Nuttall*, 6 Bingh. 226.

(*q*) *Beck* v. *Bree*, 1 Cr. & J. 246.
(*r*) Degge, 6th ed. 404.
(*s*) *Pemberton* v. *Shelton*, Cro. Jac. 498; 2 Rol. R. 54, *S. C.*
(*t*) *Bolls* v. *Atkinson*, 1 Lev. 185.

right, and being more beneficial to the defendant, than to be carried into the spiritual court, is not considered as a penal action brought by a common informer (*u*). Consequently a new trial will be granted, where it is clear that the verdict has been given for the defendant against the weight of evidence (*x*), although, in penal actions, the courts will not permit a verdict for the defendant to be disturbed on this ground (*y*).

Costs.

As to the costs, see the remarks on the second section, *ante*, p. 1291, and *post*, under tit. *Judgment*, and stat. 3 & 4 Will. IV. c. 42, s. 32, *ante*, p. 38.

Judgment.

This being an action for the recovery of the treble value of the tithes, in a case where the single value was not recoverable at common law, did not fall within the stat. of Gloucester (15) ; the plaintiff, therefore, was not entitled to recover costs under that statute, consequently the judgment formerly was only for the debt (*z*) found by the jury ; and if the jury upon the trial had given costs and damages, it was incumbent on the plaintiff to enter a remittitur, and take judgment for the debt only (*a*) ; but an alteration has been made in this respect by stat. 8 & 9 Will. III. c. 11, which see, *ante*, p. 1291. If judgment be for the plaintiff by *nil dicit*, *non sum informatus*, or upon demurrer (*b*), the judgment may be entered for the whole debt demanded by the declaration. So if the issue be on a collateral matter (*c*), as on the custom of tithing or discharge by statute (*d*), which is found against the defendant, and the defendant hath not taken the value by protestation, he shall pay the value expressed by the plaintiff in his declaration ;

(*u*) See *Earl Spencer* v. *Swannell*, 3 M. & W. 154.

(*x*) *Holloway* v. *Hewitt*, Trin. 13 Geo. III. 10 MSS., Serjt. Hill, p. 339 ; *Lord Selsea* v. *Powell*, 6 Taunt. 297, S. P.

(*y*) *Brook q. t.* v. *Middleton*, 10 East, 268.

(*z*) Co. Ent. 162, a, 2nd ed.

(*a*) See *Dagg* v. *Penkevon*, Cro. Jac. 70, where this mode was adopted.

(*b*) Degge, 404.

(*c*) *Costerdam's* case, cited in Yelv. 127.

(*d*) *Bowles* v. *Broadhead*, Aleyn, 88.

---

(15) "Where a statute gives damages by creation, there the plaintiff shall recover no costs ; the reason is, because damages being given out of course, and where the common law does not give them, and the statute being therefore introductive of a new law, the plaintiff shall recover what the statute appoints him to recover, and no more." Arg. Hardr. 152.

for by the collateral matter pleaded in bar, the declaration is confessed in the whole. If the action be brought against two or more defendants (e), and a verdict is given against one or two only of the defendants, plaintiff is entitled to judgment against those, although there be a verdict for the other defendants. It is expressly provided, that the statute of jeofails, 16 & 17 Car. II. c. 8, shall extend to this action.

III. *Of the Stat. 6 & 7 Will. IV. c. 71, for the Commutation of Tithes in England and Wales, amended by Stat. 7 Will. IV. & 1 Vict. c. 69, p. 1309; Stat. 1 & 2 Vict. c. 64, for facilitating Merger of Tithes, Stat. 2 & 3 Vict. c. 62, for explaining the Acts for the Commutation of Tithes, p. 1311.*

THE object of the statute 6 & 7 Will. IV. c. 71, as it may be gathered from the preamble, is to amend the laws relating to tithes in England and Wales, and to provide the means for an adequate compensation for tithes, and for the commutation thereof. The plan pursued for effecting this object, is to convert all the uncommuted tithes into a corn rent-charge, payable in money, according to the value of fixed quantities of wheat, barley, and oats, as ascertained from year to year by the average price for the seven years ending at the preceding Christmas.

Sections 1 to 11 contain regulations relating to the appointment and general power of commissioners and assistant commissioners for the execution of the act; and by s. 2, all agreements and awards, and other instruments, or copies thereof, under their seal, are to be received in evidence without further proof; and no agreement or award is to be of any force, unless sealed or stamped as the act directs. Sections 12 to 16 relate to the interpretation of the act. Sections 17 to 31 provide for voluntary agreements for a rent-charge in lieu of tithes between land-owners and tithe-owners. The act treats the commutation as consisting of two separate processes: 1st, The determination of the total sum to be paid for the tithes of any parish; 2ndly, The apportionment of the total sum among the different lands on which it is to be charged. The first of these processes may be effected, 1st, voluntarily; 2ndly, after the 1st of October, 1838, compulsorily (f). Sections 32 to 35 regulate the mode in which the second of these processes is to be carried into effect. Sections 36 to 52 provide for the commutation on the supposition that no

(e) Styles, 317, 318. See also *ante*, under *Verdict*, p. 1307.

(f) See a correct Analysis of this Act, by J. M. White, p. xvi.

voluntary agreement has been made.   By the 49th section, nothing
in this act shall revive any right to tithes, which now is, or hereafter
shall be, barred by any law (*g*) in force for shortening the time
required in claims of *modus decimandi*, or exemption from or discharge from tithes, or for the limitation of actions and suits relating to real property.   Sections 53 to 55, and 58 to 68, contain
further provisions applicable to apportionment.   The 56th and
57th sections, which, according to Mr. White, appear to have been
misplaced, and also the 67th section, relate to the conversion of
the money rent-charge into a corn rent-charge.   By sect. 67, lands
are to be discharged from tithes from the 1st of January next
following the confirmation of the apportionment, and the rent-
charge paid in lieu thereof on the 1st of July and the 1st of
January in every year (*h*) ; and by 7 Will. IV. & 1 Vict. c. 69,
s. 10, it is enacted, that, with the first payment of rent-charge
under any agreement, shall also be paid any sum which shall be
agreed to be paid in consideration of the time (if any) which may
intervene between the termination of any previous agreement or
composition, and the time at which, by the agreement for commutation, the lands shall be discharged ; and by sect. 11, the parties to
a parochial agreement are empowered to agree that the lands shall
be discharged from the 1st day of January next preceding, or the
1st day of April, July, or October preceding or following the confirmation of the apportionment, instead of the 1st day of January
next following the confirmation.   And by stat. 3 & 4 Vict. c. 15, s. 1,
in every case where an annual sum by way of rent-charge shall have
been fixed in any parish instead of the tithes, the commissioners are
empowered to declare lands discharged from tithes at any period
after the confirmation of the agreement or award, and before the
confirmation of the apportionment, upon security being given for
the payment of the rent-charge.   By stat. 6 & 7 Will. IV. c. 71,
ss. 69 to 71, the rent-charge is made liable to parochial and county
rates, and subject to the same incumbrances and incidents as tithe
before the act : these rates and charges were, by the 70th section,
to be assessed on the occupier, who was entitled to deduct the
amount thereof from his rent ; but now, by stat. 7 Will. IV. &
1 Vict. c. 69, s. 8, the assessment may at once be made on the
owner of the rent-charge.   Section 71 of the stat. 6 & 7 Will. IV.
c. 71 contains a provision, that any person seised in possession of
an estate in fee simple or fee tail of any tithes, or rent-charge in
lieu of tithes, may by deed or declaration, under hand and seal, in
such form as the commissioners shall approve and confirm under
their seal, release, assign, or otherwise dispose of the same, so as
the same may be absolutely merged in the freehold and inheritance
of the lands on which the same shall have been charged.   This

(*g*) See stat. 2 & 3 Will. IV. c. 100,   (*h*) See also stat. 3 & 4 Vict. c. 15, s.
ante, p. 1296.   13.

provision is extended by stat. 1 & 2 Vict. c. 64, s. 1, to any person
or persons who either alone or together are seised of or have the
power of acquiring or disposing of the fee simple in possession of
any tithes or rent-charge; and by s. 3, where tithes and the lands
charged therewith are settled to the same uses, the tenant for life
may cause them to merge in the land. These statutes (*i*) extend to
land of copyhold or any other tenure. A further extension of the
merger of tithes will be found in the stat. 2 & 3 Vict. c. 62. Section 72 of the stat. 6 & 7 Will. IV. c. 71, contains a provision for
future alteration of the apportionment; by virtue of this provision,
any land-owner may discharge such portion as he may wish to sell,
provided the residue of his land left charged with the rent-charge
be of the value required by sect. 58, that is, three times the value of
the rent-charge (*k*). By sects. 79 and 80, if any tenant of lands
at rack-rent dissent from paying the rent-charge, the landlord may
take the tithes during the tenancy; and any tenant paying the
rent-charge, is to be allowed the same in account with his landlord.
By sect. 81, when the rent-charge is in arrear for twenty-one days,
the person entitled thereto may distrain, after ten days' notice;
but only two years' arrears can be recovered: and by sects. 82, 83,
if rent-charge be in arrear for forty days, and there is no sufficient
distress, a judge may order a writ to issue to sheriff to summon a
jury to inquire and assess arrears; on the return of the inquisition,
a writ of habere facias possessionem may issue, under which the
land may be held by the owner of the rent-charge, till the arrears
and costs, including the costs of cultivation, be satisfied; but not
more than two years' arrears can be recovered. Section 84 provides for the case of Quakers. By sect. 86, the provisions of stat.
4 & 5 Will. IV. c. 22, and 11 Geo. II. c. 19, (for which, see *ante*,
p. 602, 3,) shall extend to all rent-charges payable under this act.
By sect. 89, this act shall not affect any right to any tithes which
shall have become due before the commutation. By sect. 90, this
act is not to extend to any of the following matters, except by
special agreement: 1. Easter offerings, mortuaries, and surplice
fees (*l*). 2. Tithes of fish or of fishing. 3. Personal tithes, except
mills. 4. Mineral tithes. 5. Tithes in the city of London.
6. Permanent rent-charge or payment in lieu of tithes on houses
or lands in any city or town, under any custom or private act.
7. Lands, of which the tithes are already perpetually commuted or
extinguished by act of parliament.

(*i*) 1 & 2 Vict. c. 64. s. 4.   (*l*) See stat. 2 & 3 Vict. c. 62, s. 9.
(*k*) See stat. 2 & 3 Vict. c. 62, s. 2.

CHAPTER XXXIX.

TRESPASS.

I. *In what Cases an Action of Trespass may be maintained, p. 1312.*

II. *Where Trespass cannot be maintained, p. 1318.*

III. *Of the Declaration, p. 1321.*

IV. *Of the Pleadings, and herein of the new Rules, p. 1325.*

    1. *Of the Plea of Not Guilty, p. 1325.*

    2. *Accord and Satisfaction, p. 1326.*

    3. *Liberum Tenementum, p. 1327.*

    4. *Estoppel, p. 1328.*

    5. *License, p. 1329.*

    6. *Process, p. 1332.*

    7. *Right of Common, p. 1333.*

    8. *Right of Way, p. 1334.*

    9. *Tender of Amends, p. 1340.*

V. *Evidence, p. 1340.*

VI. *Damages, p. 1342; Costs, p. 1342.*

I. *In what Cases an Action of Trespass may be maintained.*

THE land of every owner or occupier is inclosed and set apart from that of his neighbour, either by a visible or tangible fence, as one field is separated from another by a hedge, wall, &c., or by an ideal invisible boundary, existing only in the contemplation of law, as when the land of one man adjoins to that of another in the same open or common field. Hence every unwarrantable entry upon the land of another is termed a trespass by breaking his close. The form of action which the law has prescribed for this injury is an áction of trespass *vi et armis quare clausum fregit*, in which the plaintiff may recover a compensation in damages for the injury sustained. Although the words of the writ are quare *clausum fregit*, yet it has been adjudged, in many instances where the plaintiff had not an interest in the soil, but an interest in the profits only, that trespass may be maintained, and this form pursued. Hence, it was holden (a), that the grantee or patentee of the king de herbagio forestæ, might maintain trespass against any person who consumed or destroyed the grass, and that the writ should be quare clausum fregit. So where plaintiff is entitled to the vesture of land (b), that is, corn, grass, underwood (c), and the like. So where plaintiff had an exclusive (1) right of cutting turves in a moss: although the manor in which the moss was situate belonged to another (d). So if it is agreed between J. S. (e), and the owner of the soil, that J. S. shall plough and sow the ground, and that in consideration thereof, J. S. shall give the owner of the soil half the crop, J. S. may maintain trespass for treading down the corn (2). So if a meadow be divided annually among certain persons by lot, then after the several portion of each person is allotted, each is capable of maintaining an action of trespass *quare clausum fregit;* for each has an exclusive interest for the time (f). The plaintiff, on the 6th of June, 1804 (g), agreed with the defendant for the purchase of a standing crop of mowing grass, then growing in a close of defendant's. The grass was to be mowed, and made into hay, by the plaintiff; but the time at which the mowing was to begin was not fixed. Possession of the close was retained by the defendant. Before the plaintiff had done any act towards carrying the agreement into effect, the defendant refused to complete the

---

(a) Dyer, 285, b. pl. 40.
(b) 1 Inst. 4 b.
(c) Moor, 355, pl. 483.
(d) *Wilson* v. *Mackreth*, 3 Burr. 1824.

(e) *Welsh* v. *Hall*, per *Powell*, J., at Wells, 1700, Salk. MSS.; Bull. N. P. 85.
(f) See Cro. Eliz. 421.
(g) *Crosby* v. *Wadsworth*, 6 East, 602.

---

(1) "To maintain trespass, it is essential that the plaintiff should have exclusive possession at the time of the injury committed. Hence *trespass* will not lie for entering into a pew or seat in a church, because the plaintiff has not the exclusive possession, the possession of the church being in the parson." Per *Buller*, J., 1 T. R. 430. The proper form of action for this injury is an action of trespass on the case; to support which, the plaintiff must prove a right, either by a faculty or by prescription, which supposes a faculty having been formerly granted. For the law on this subject, see *ante*, p. 1113.

(2) In such case the owner is not jointly concerned in the growing corn, but is to have half after it is reaped, by way of rent, which may be of other things than money; although, in 1 Inst. 142, it is said, it cannot be of the profits themselves. But that, as it seems, must be understood of the natural profits. Bull. N. P. 85.

agreement, and sold the grass to another person, whom he directed to cut and carry away the same. Trespass *quare clausum fregit* was brought, stating in the declaration that the close was in the possession of the plaintiff. Lord *Ellenborough*, C. J., said, that as the plaintiff appeared to have been entitled, (if entitled at all under the agreement stated,) to the exclusive enjoyment of the crop growing on the land, during the proper period of its full growth, and until it was cut and carried away, he might, in respect of such exclusive right, maintain trespass against any person doing the acts complained of, according to the authority of 1 Inst. 4 b.; Fitz. Abr. Tres. 149, and Bro. Abr. Tres. 273, and *Wilson* v. *Mackreth*, 3 Burr. 1826. But the court were of opinion, that as the agreement was by parol, it was competently discharged by parol while it remained executory, and that on this ground the plaintiff was not entitled to recover. Where trees are excepted in a lease, the land on which they grow is necessarily excepted also; consequently, if the tenant cut down the trees, the landlord may maintain trespass for *breaking his close* and cutting down the trees (h). The property in bushes (i) is in the tenant, even where they are cut down by a stranger. If a tree grows near the confines of the land of two parties, so that the roots extend into the soil of each, the property (k) in the tree belongs to the owner of that land in which the tree was first sown or planted. Where two adjacent fields are separated by a hedge and ditch, the hedge *primâ facie* belongs to the owner of the field in which the ditch is not. If there are two ditches, one on each side of the hedge, then the ownership of the hedge must be ascertained by proving acts of ownership (l). The rule about ditching is this (m): a person, making a ditch, cannot cut into his neighbour's soil, but usually he cuts it to the very extremity of his own land; he is of course bound to throw the soil which he digs out, upon his own land, and often, if he likes it, he plants a hedge on the top of it; therefore, if he afterwards cut beyond the edge of the ditch, which is the extremity of his land, he cuts into his neighbour's land, and is a trespasser: no rule about four feet and eight feet has any thing to do with it (3). He may cut the thing as much wider as he will, if he enlarges it into his own land.

The rule, that waste land near a highway is to be presumed

(h) *Rolls* v. *Rock*, Somerset Summ. Ass., 2 Geo. II., per *Probyn*, J., MSS.
   (i) *Berriman* v. *Peacock*, 9 Bingh. 384.
   (k) *Holder* v. *Coates*, 1 M. & Malk. 112, per *Littledale*, J.

(l) Per *Bayley*, J., in *Guy* v. *West*, Somerset Summ. Ass. 1808.
   (m) Per *Lawrence*, J., in *Vowles* v. *Miller*, 3 Taunt. 138.

---

(3) It had been contended, that the party to whom the hedge and ditch belonged, was entitled at common law to have a width of eight feet, as the reasonable width for the base of his bank and the area of his ditch together.

primâ facie to belong to the owner of the land next adjoining, is not confined to a case where the owner of that land is a freeholder, but extends equally to cases where the owner is a copyholder (*n*): but in either case evidence may be given to rebut the presumption. The common user of a wall separating adjoining lands, belonging to different owners, is *primâ facie* evidence that the wall and the land on which it stands belong (*o*) to the owners of adjoining lands in equal moieties as tenants in common. Secus, where the quantity of land, which each party contributes (*p*) is known, and the wall built at the joint expense of the two.

The action of trespass (*q*) *quare clausum fregit* is a local action (*r*). Hence, where trespass was brought for entering the plaintiff's house in Canada, it was holden, that the action could not be maintained; *Buller*, J., observing, "It is now too late for us to inquire whether it were wise or politic to make a distinction between transitory and local actions; it is sufficient for the courts, that the law has settled the distinction, and that an action *quare clausum fregit* is local. We may try actions here, which are in their nature transitory, though arising out of a transaction abroad, but not such as are in their nature local." The action of trespass *vi et armis* is termed a possessory action, to distinguish it from those actions in which the plaintiff must show a title. Being founded on an injury to the possession, it is essential that the plaintiff should be in the actual possession of the close at the time when the injury is committed; but, as against a stranger or wrong-doer, it is immaterial whether such possession be founded on a good title or not (*s*). Even a tortious possession will support trespass against a wrong-doer. The plaintiff declared in trespass upon his possession (*t*); defendant made title, and gave colour to the plaintiff; plaintiff replied *de injuriâ suâ propriâ*, and traversed the title set out by the defendant; and upon demurrer, on the authority of *Goslin* v. *Williams*, P. 5 Geo. I., the court held this a good replication; for it lays the defendant's title out of the case, and then it stands upon the plaintiff's possession, *which is enough against a wrong-doer* (*u*), and the plaintiff need not reply a title. In like manner it was holden (*x*), that plaintiff in possession of glebe land under a lease, void by stat. 13 Eliz. c. 20, by reason of the rector's non-residence, might maintain trespass against a wrong-doer. By induction the parson is put into possession of a part for the whole, and may maintain an action for a trespass on the glebe land (*y*), although he has not

(*n*) *Doe d. Pring* v. *Pearsey*, 7 B. & C. 304. See *Doe d. Barrett* v. *Kemp*, 2 Bingh. N. C. 102, *ante*, p. 748.
(*o*) *Cubitt* v. *Porter*, 8 B. & C. 257; *Wiltshire* v. *Sidford*, ib. 259, n.
(*p*) *Matts* v. *Hawkins*, 5 Taunt. 20.
(*q*) *Doulson* v. *Matthews and another*, 4 T. R. 503.
(*r*) But see stat. 3 & 4 Will. IV. c. 42,

s. 22, *ante*, p. 494.
(*s*) See *Dent* v. *Oliver*, Cro. Jac. 123.
(*t*) *Cary* v. *Holt*, Str. 1238; 11 East, 70, n.
(*u*) *Holmes* v. *Newlands*, 11 A. & E. 52.
(*x*) *Graham* v. *Peat*, 1 East, 244.
(*y*) *Bulwer* v. *Bulwer*, 2 B. & A. 470.

taken actual possession of it. The contractors for making a navigable canal having, with the permission of the owner of the soil, erected a dam of earth and wood upon his close, across a stream there, for the purpose of completing their work, have a possession sufficient to entitle them (z) to maintain trespass against a wrong-doer. Where wood-lands, and the timber thereon, belonged to the crown, and the plaintiff (a) paid a nominal rent to the crown for the privilege of shooting the game, and it appeared that a person, by leave from him, cut and took away the grass from the sides; it was holden, that although he took no legal estate from the crown for non-compliance with the stat. 1 Ann. c. 7, s. 5, and could not therefore have maintained ejectment, nor even have retained possession as against the crown, yet that he might maintain trespass against a party having no title, and a wrong-doer; held also, that payment of the rent, the exercise of the privilege of shooting over the land, and the cutting of the grass by the plaintiff's permission, was sufficient evidence to go to a jury, and for them to find that he was in the actual possession of all but the trees. It seems that the plaintiff could not have been treated by the crown as an intruder. If a man be disseised, after his re-entry he may have an action of trespass against the disseisor for any trespass done by him after the disseisin (b); for by his re-entry his possession is restored ab initio. If he who has the right to land enters, he thereby acquires the lawful possession, and may maintain (c) trespass against any person who being in possession at the time of his entry, wrongfully continues upon the land; and a lessor, having entered at the expiration of the term, may sue in trespass persons claiming under the late tenant as well as the late tenant himself (d); but where a tenant remains in possession after the expiration of his term, the landlord is not justified in expelling him by force, in order to regain possession (e). It is not necessary that the party who makes the entry should declare that he enters to take possession: it is sufficient, if he does any act to show his intention.

By the common law, he that agrees to a trespass after it is done, is no trespasser, unless the trespass is done to his use (f) or for his benefit, and then his agreement subsequent amounts to a command; for, in this case, *omnis ratihabitio retrotrahitur et mandato æquiparatur.* But it is otherwise, if the trespass be not done to his use. A. having knowingly received from B. a chattel, (which B. has wrongfully seized,) upon demand refused to give it back to the owner; there was not any proof that the seizure was to A.'s use;

(z) *Dyson* v. *Collick*, 5 B. & A. 600.

(a) *Harper* v. *Charlesworth*, 4 B. & C. 574.

(b) 2 Rol. Abr. 554, pl. 5.

(c) *Butcher* v. *Butcher*, 7 B. & C. 399, recognizing *Taunton* v. *Costar*, 7 T. R. 432; *ante*, p. 670.

(d) *Hey* v. *Moorhouse*, 6 Bingh. N. C. 52, recognizing *Butcher* v. *Butcher*.

(e) *Newton* v. *Harland*, 1 M. & Gr. 644.

(f) 4 Inst. 317, cited by *Parke*, J., 4 B. & Ad. 616.

it was holden (g), that A. was not a joint trespasser with B. Although every person has of common right a liberty of coming into a public market for the purpose of buying and selling (h), yet he has not of common right a liberty of placing a stall there, but he must acquire such liberty by a compensation, which is called stallage. Hence trespass may be maintained by the owner of the soil against a person who unlawfully places a stall in the market. The authority of the preceding case was recognized in the *Mayor, &c. of Norwich,* v. *Swann,* 2 Bl. R. 1117, where it was holden, that trespass would lie for setting tables in a market-place for the sale of goods without leave of the owner of the soil. The lord or owner of the soil may maintain trespass against a commoner (i), who is guilty of an entry on the common, for the purpose of chasing the conies there: for the commoner can justify an entry merely for the purpose of using his common.

Tenants in common ought to join in trespass *quare clausum fregit;* for if one tenant in common bring trespass *qu. cl. fr.* without his companion, it may be pleaded in abatement (k). In trespass *vi et armis* for taking and carrying away goods, it is not essentially necessary that the plaintiff should, at the time when the act was done which constitutes the trespass, have the actual possession of the thing which is the subject matter of the trespass: it is sufficient, if he has a constructive possession in respect of the right being actually vested in him. Hence (l), if a lord be entitled to a waif and estray, within his manor, he may, before seizure, maintain trespass against a stranger who shall take away the waif or estray; for the right is in the lord, and a constructive possession, in respect of the thing being within the manor of which he is lord. So an executor (m) has a right immediately on the death of the testator, and this right draws after it a constructive possession from the time of the death of the testator. If a man gives me goods (n), which are at York, and before I have possession a stranger take them, yet I shall have trespass; because by the gift the property is in me, to which the law annexes possession. But semble that the gift must be by deed or instrument of gift (o). The owner of a piece of land granted liberty to A. (p) and his heirs to build a bridge on his land, and A. covenanted to build a bridge for public use, to keep it in repair, and not to demand toll. The bridge was built by A. of materials purchased at his expense: part of the materials of the bridge having been taken away by a wrong-doer; it was holden, that the public had only a license to make use of the materials while

(g) *Wilson* v. *Barker and Mitchell,* 4 B. & Ad. 614.

(h) *Mayor, &c. of Northampton* v. *Ward,* 2 Str. 1238; 1 Wils. 107.

(i) *Hadesden* v. *Gryssell,* Cro. Jac. 195.

(k) Comyns' Dig. Abatement (E. 10).

(l) F. N. B. 91, b.

(m) *Fisher* v. *Young,* 2 Bulstr. 268.

(n) Bro. Abr. Trespass, pl. 303.

(o) *Irons* v. *Smallpiece,* 2 B. & A. 551; post, p. 1347, and see *Reeves* v. *Capper,* 5 Bingh. N. C. 136; 6 Scott, 877.

(p) *Harrison* v. *Parker,* 6 East, 154.

they formed part of the bridge for the purpose of passage; and when they ceased to be part of the bridge, A.'s original property in them reverted to him, discharged of the right of user by the public, and consequently that A. might maintain trespass for the *asportavit* against the wrong-doer. In like manner, if the owner of land builds houses (q), and marks out a street, and assigns part of the land as a public highway; this will not be considered as a transfer of the absolute property in the soil, so as to prevent the owner from maintaining trespass for an injury to the soil, *e. g.*, for placing the end of a bridge thereon.

An action of trespass lies against any person who gleans on another's ground after harvest (r); for a right to glean cannot be claimed by any person at common law. Neither have the *poor* of a parish *legally settled* such right. Trespass will lie (s) against a peace officer who seizes goods under a search-warrant not specified therein. Though the freehold of the churchyard is the parson's, trespass lies at the suit of a person at whose expense a tomb-stone has been erected, against a person who wrongfully removes it from the churchyard and erases the inscription (t). It is a direct trespass to injure the person of another, by driving a carriage against the carriage wherein such person is sitting, although the last mentioned carriage be not the property nor in the possession of the person injured (u). And although if a person does an injury by an unavoidable accident, an action does not lie, yet if any blame attaches to him, although he be innocent of any intention to injure, as if he drive a horse too spirited, or pull the wrong rein (x), or use imperfect harness, and the horse taking fright kills another horse, then trespass may be maintained.

By stat. 21 Jac. I. c. 16, s. 3, all actions of trespass *quare clausum fregit* shall be commenced and sued within six years next after the cause of such actions.

II. *Where Trespass cannot be maintained.*

IF the entry be warranted by law, it is not a trespass. Such is an entry to demand rent due for the enjoyment of the land, to take and carry off tithes after they have been set forth, or to distrain for rent arrear or damage feasant. It had been holden, that a person might justify the following a fox with hounds over the grounds of

---

(q) *Lade* v. *Shepherd*, Str. 1004.

(r) *Steel* v. *Houghton and Wife*, per Lord *Loughborough*, C. J., *Heath*, J., and *Wilson*, J.; dissentiente *Gould*, J., 1 H. Bl. 51.

(s) *Crozier* v. *Cundey*, 6 B. & C. 232.

(t) *Spooner* v. *Brewster*, 3 Bingh. 136.

(u) *Hopper and Wife* v. *Reeve*, 7 Taunt. 698.

(x) *Wakeman* v. *Robinson*, 1 Bingh. 213.

another, if there were not any further damage committed than was absolutely necessary for the killing the fox (y); but the law now is, that a person may not enter the grounds of another merely for the sport and diversion of the chase (z). Where a person goes out sporting with his friends, and purposely leads them on to another's land, he is equally guilty of a trespass (a), although he may remain off the land whilst his friends go on it. But in *Mason* v. *Keeling*, Lord Raym. 608, *Holt*, C. J., said, that if a dog breaks a neighbour's close, the owner will not be subject to an action. One tenant in common cannot bring an action of trespass against his co-tenant, because each of them may enter and occupy in common, &c. *per my et per tout*, the lands and tenements which they hold in common (b). So if from the finding of the jury it appears to be a tenancy in common (c); judgment shall be given for defendant, although the issue be found against him. Bargainee for years cannot maintain trespass before entry and actual possession (d). If A. make a lease for years (e), excepting the trees, and had afterwards an intention to sell them, the law gives the lessor, and those who would buy, power as incident to the exception to enter and show the trees to those who would buy them, for without sight none would buy, and without entry none could see. A lessor, during the term, cut down some oak pollards growing upon the demised premises which were unfit for timber; it was holden (f), that as tenant for life or years would have been entitled to them, if they had been blown down, and was entitled to the usufruct of them during the term, the lessor could not, by wrongfully severing them, acquire any right to them; and, consequently, that he or his vendee could not maintain trespass against the tenant for taking them. The plaintiff was the landlord of a house (g), which he let to A., ready furnished, and the lease contained a schedule of the furniture. An execution issued against A., under which defendant, as sheriff, seized part of the furniture, although notice was given to the officer that it was the property of plaintiff: plaintiff brought trespass. Adjudged per. *Cur.*, that it would not lie. *Trespass* will not lie by the assignees of a bankrupt against a sheriff (h) for taking the goods of a bankrupt in execution, after an act of bankruptcy, and before the issuing of the commission, notwithstanding he sells them after the issuing of the commission, and after the provisional assignment, and notice from the provisional assignee

(y) *Gundry* v. *Feltham*, 1 T. R. 334.

(z) *Earl of Essex* v. *Capel*, Hertford Sum. Ass. 1809, Lord *Ellenborough*, C. J., 2 Chitty, Game, 1381. And see the remarks there of the C. J. on *Gundry* v. *Feltham*.

(a) *Hill* v. *Walker*, Peake's Addl. Cases, 234.

(b) Littl. Sec. 323.

(c) *Benington* v. *Benington*, Cro. Eliz.

157.

(d) Admitted, *Lutwich* v. *Mitton*, Cro. Jac. 604.

(e) *Liford's* case, last resolution, 11 Rep. 52, a.

(f) *Channon* v. *Patch*, 5 B. & C. 897.

(g) *Ward* v. *Macauley and another*, 4 T. R. 489.

(h) *Smith* v. *Milles*, 1 T. R. 475. See *ante*, p. 241.

not to sell. Condemnation of goods in the Exchequer is so conclusive and so alters the property (i), that trespass will not lie against the officer for seizing the goods condemned; for the condemnation has relation to the time of seizure, at which time the goods were the goods of the king, and not of the plaintiff. So where a ship was seized as forfeited under the Navigation Act, 12 Car. II. c. 18 (k), by a governor of a foreign country belonging to Great Britain; it was holden (l), that the owner cannot maintain trespass against the party seizing, although the latter do not proceed to condemnation; for by the forfeiture the property is divested out of the owner. So where a ship is *bonâ fide* seized as a prize, the owner cannot (m) sustain an action in a court of common law for the seizure, though she be released without any suit being instituted against her; his remedy, if any, being in the court of admiralty. Trespass cannot be maintained for taking an excessive distress, where the distress is lawful, the whole being one entire act (n). Neither will trespass lie for an irregular distress, where the irregularity complained of is not in itself an act of trespass (o), but consists merely in the omission of some of the forms required in conducting the distress, such as not procuring goods to be appraised before they are sold. The true construction of the provision in 11 Geo. II. c. 19, s. 19, that the party may recover a compensation for the special damage which he sustains by an irregular distress, "*in an action of trespass, or on the case,*" (see *ante,* p. 680,) is, that he must bring *trespass,* if the injury be a trespass; and *case,* if it be the subject matter of an action on the case. The nature of the irregularity must determine the form of action. Hence for an irregularity consisting in the omission to appraise the goods before they were sold, the action ought to be an action on the case. But where the party remained in possession of the goods in the plaintiff's house beyond the five days, and then removed the goods, it was holden, that trespass was maintainable; Lord *Ellenborough* being of opinion, that the removal of goods was a distinct, subsequent, and substantive act of trespass; and *Bayley,* J., conceiving, that although the party was warranted in removing the goods, yet the action would lie for remaining in possession beyond the five days, that being a new act of trespass; and that damages might be given for such continuance, although the party was not a trespasser - during the five days. Lord *Ellenborough* observed, that he could not understand the statute as giving an option to maintain trespass, where trespass would not lie by the rules of the common law; but as giving an election to bring trespass, where trespass was the proper remedy,

(i) *Scott* v. *Shearman and another,* 2 Bl. R. 977.
(k) Repealed. See *ante,* p. 93.
(l) *Wilkins and others* v. *Despard,* 5 T. R. 112.

(m) *Faith* v. *Pearson,* 4 Campb. 357; 2 Marsh. 133.
(n) *Lynne* v. *Moody,* 2 Str. 851.
(o) *Messing* v. *Kemble,* 3 Campb. 115.

and case where case (*q*). If a sheriff continues in possession after the return day of the writ, that irregularity makes him a trespasser *ab initio*, but will not support the allegation of a new trespass committed by him after the acts which he justifies under the execution (*r*).

Trespass will not lie against an officer for taking goods or cattle by virtue of a replevin (*s*), unless a claim of property be made at the time when the officer comes to demand them. Trespass will not lie against a coroner for causing a person to be put out of the room where an inquest was about to be holden, after his refusal to depart. It did not appear that the plaintiff had any interest in the matter of the inquest which the coroner was about to take, or any information to offer, which might further the object of the inquiry (*t*). If a person rated to the poor, object to the rate (*u*), *e. g.*, because it is a prospective rate, he ought to appeal to the next sessions; and if he do not, he cannot maintain trespass against the overseers of the poor, who distrain on him for non-payment of the rate. The house of the plaintiff, an uncertificated bankrupt, was broken open, and effects acquired by him, subsequently to his bankruptcy, were taken by the defendants, who had become his creditors since the bankruptcy, and did not know who were the assignees under the bankruptcy. The bankrupt having sued the defendants in trespass, they obtained, after a rule for plea, a surrender of the assignees' interest in the effects seized: it was holden (*x*), that this was a ratification of the seizure, and that the plaintiff could not recover. So where the assignees of an uncertificated bankrupt, by agreement, for a valuable consideration paid to them by a third party, had left the bankrupt's furniture, &c. in his possession, and afterwards, notwithstanding such agreement, seized the same, it was holden (*y*), that they were justified in so doing, an uncertificated bankrupt not being entitled to retain any property against his assignees.

III. *Of the Declaration.*

Venue.—The action of trespass *quare clausum fregit* is a local action, and consequently the venue must be laid in the county where the land lies; for otherwise the plaintiff, on the general issue, may

(*q*) *Winterbourne* v. *Morgan*, 11 East, 395. See *Etherton* v. *Popplewell*, *ante*, p. 681.

(*r*) *Aitkenhead* v. *Blades*, 5 Taunt. 198.

(*s*) Per *Holt*, C. J., in *Hallett* v. *Byrt*, Carth. 381.

(*t*) *Garnett* v. *Ferrand and another*, 6 B. & C. 611.

(*u*) *Durrant* v. *Boys*, 6 T. R. 580. Secus, if he has no land in the parish in which the rate is made. *Weaver* v. *Price*, 3 B. & Ad. 409. See *ante*, p. 1173.

(*x*) *Hull* v. *Pickersgill*, 1 Brod. & Bingh. 282.

(*y*) *Nias* v. *Adamson*, 3 B. & A. 225.

be nonsuited at the trial, unless advantage be taken of the stat. 3 &
4 Will. IV. c. 42, s. 22, (see *ante*, p. 494,) under which local actions
may be tried and writs of inquiry executed in any county, if court or
judge shall so order; but trespass for taking goods is transitory, and
the venue may be laid in any county; subject, however, to its being
changed upon an application to the court, supported by the usual
affidavit, if not laid in the county where the action arose. The
declaration ought to allege the commission of the fact directly and
positively, and not by way of recital, *e. g.*, for *that* on such a day the
defendant broke and entered the plaintiff's close, and not for that,
whereas, &c.

By R. G. H. T. 4 Will. IV. several counts in trespass for acts
committed at the same time and place are not to be allowed.

Day.—It is not necessary to state the precise day on which the
trespass was committed; it will be sufficient to insert any day before
the commencement of the action. Formerly, in order to avoid the
necessity of bringing several actions, it was usual for the plaintiff, in
cases where the nature of the trespass permitted it (4), to declare
with a *continuando*, as it was termed, that is, that defendant on such
a day committed certain trespasses (specifying them), *continuing
the same trespasses* from such day to such a day, *at divers days and
times;* and if, as was generally the case, the declaration contained
a charge for some acts which did not lie in continuance, as well as
for some which did, then the continuing was expressly confined to
those trespasses which did lie in continuance (5). This was the
regular mode of declaring, but it frequently happened through in-
advertence, that the *continuando* was not so restrained, but was
applied to all the trespasses by the general words *transgressiones
prædictas continuando*, in which case objections used to be made;
but the courts, in order to prevent judgments being arrested on this
ground, laid down a rule (z), that where several trespasses were laid
in one declaration, some of which might be laid with a continuando,
and some not, and the continuando, instead of being confined to such

---

(z) *Gillam* v. *Clayton*, 3 Lev. 93;
Brook v. *Bishopp*, Salk. 639. See also
Butler v. *Hedges*, 1 Lev. 210, and *Font-
leroy* v. *Aylmer*, Lord Raym. 239.

---

(4) Treading down and consuming grass, &c. with cattle, was considered as a trespass which lay in continuance; but taking a horse, killing
a dog, cutting down a tree, and the like, being acts, which, when executed, could not be repeated, as they terminated upon the commission of
them, were holden not to lie in continuance.

(5) See Co. Ent. tit. Trespass, p. 4, where the declaration stated,
that the defendant, on such a day, broke the close of the plaintiff, and eat
up, trod down, and consumed the grass there growing, with cattle, and
continuing the said trespass as to the eating up, treading down, and consuming the said grass from the day aforesaid until such a day, &c.

as lay in continuance, went to all, the court, after verdict, would restrain the continuando by intendment to those trespasses which might be laid with a continuando. The form of declaring with a continuando has fallen into disuse, the language of the modern declarations being, "that defendant, on such a day, in such a year, and on divers other days and times, between that day and the day of the commencement of the suit, committed several trespasses." It will be perceived, that the principal object of the ancient and modern form is the same, *viz.* to comprehend several trespasses under one declaration. In substance, also, both forms are the same: but the modern form is more concise, and it is attended with this further advantage, that it does not afford any scope for those nice and subtle objections, which used to be raised on the difference between acts which lay in continuance and acts which did not (6). Still, however, care must be taken not to allege that defendant committed a single act, or an act which terminated in itself, on divers days and times, for that would be absurd (*a*), and afford just cause for special demurrer.

Formerly, in trespass *quare clausum fregit,* the plaintiff might have declared generally without naming the close (*b*); but now, by R. G. H. T. 4 Will. IV., the close or place in which, &c. must be designated in the declaration by name or abuttals, or other description, in failure whereof the defendant may demur specially. A party is not to be turned round on account of some minute variance in one of several particulars, but there must be a general accurate correspondence, faithfully describing the close in substance, and conveying full information to the defendant of the place in which he is alleged to have committed the trespass (*c*).

The close (*d*) in which, &c. does not mean the whole close referred to in the declaration, but the place in which the trespass is proved to have happened, and the defendant may so apply it. Where the plaintiff had named the close in his declaration, and the defendant pleaded *liberum tenementum* generally, without giving any further description of the close; it was holden (*e*), that the plaintiff was not

---

(*a*) See *English* v. *Purser*, 6 East, 395.
(*b*) 2 Bl. 1069.
(*c*) Per Lord *Denman*, C. J., delivering judgment of the court in *Webber* v. *Richards*, 1 G. & D. 114.
(*d*) *Richards* v. *Peake*, 2 B. &. C. 918,

recognized in *Bassett* v. *Mitchell*, 2 B. & Ad. 99.
(*e*) *Cocker* v. *Crompton*, 1 B. & C. 489, recognized since the new rules in *Lempriere* v. *Humphrey*, 3 A. & E. 181; 4 Nev. & M. 638.

---

(6) If by continuance, as applied to this subject, trespasses without any intermission were to be understood, it is scarcely possible to conceive many acts of which continuance, in this strict sense, could justly be predicated. Consuming and spoiling grass, &c., with cattle, which may be presumed to be levant and couchant on the land, day and night, is one instance, but it would be difficult to enumerate many more.

driven to a new assignment, but was entitled to recover upon proving a trespass done in a close bearing the name given in the declaration, although the defendant might have a close in the same parish known by the same name.

In trespass for taking goods, the goods must be specified (*f*), and an omission in this respect will not be aided even by verdict (*g*). The declaration must also state, that the land or goods were the plaintiff's land or goods; hence, if the words " of the plaintiff," or " his," be omitted, the declaration will be bad; but this omission may be aided by pleading over (*h*). In declarations for taking animals *feræ naturæ*, it must be stated that the animals were either dead, tame, or confined; otherwise property in the plaintiff cannot be alleged; at least such allegations will be bad on demurrer. In trespass for taking *duas damas ipsius* plaintiff, in a certain close of the plaintiff, called the park (*i*); on general demurrer, the declaration was holden to be bad, because a person cannot have property in deer unless they are tame and reclaimed (7). The value of fixtures may be recovered under the terms, "goods, chattels, and effects," in a declaration in trespass (*k*). As to the necessity of alleging the trespass *vi et armis* and *contra pacem*, see *ante*, p. 28.

(*f*) 5 Rep. 34, b.
(*g*) *Wyat* v. *Essington*, Str. 637; *Bertie* v. *Pickering*, 4 Burr. 2455.
(*h*) See an instance of this kind in

Brooke v. *Brooke*, 1 Sidf. 184.
(*i*) *Mallocke* v. *Eastly*, 3 Lev. 227.
(*k*) *Pitt* v. *Shew*, 4 B. & A. 206.

---

(7) John Rough being convicted on an indictment for stealing a pheasant *, value 40*s*., of the goods and chattels of H. S., all the judges, on a second conference, in Easter Term, 1779, after much debate and difference of opinion, agreed that the conviction was bad; for in cases of larceny of animals *feræ naturæ*, the indictment must show that they were either dead, tame, or confined; otherwise they must be presumed to be in their original state; and that it is not sufficient to add " of the goods and chattels" of such an one.

* *Rough's* case, 2 East, P. C. 607.

IV. *Of the Pleadings; and herein of the New Rules;*

1. *Of the Plea of Not Guilty,* p. 1325.
2. *Accord and Satisfaction,* p. 1326.
3. *Liberum Tenementum,* p. 1327.
4. *Estoppel,* p. 1328.
5. *License,* p. 1329.
6. *Process,* p. 1332.
7. *Right of Common,* p. 1333.
8. *Right of Way,* p. 1334.
9. *Tender of Amends,* p. 1340.

1. *Of the Plea of Not Guilty.*

THE general issue in this action is, *not guilty.* Under stat. 3 & 4 Will. IV. c. 42, s. 1 (*l*), (which provides that the contemplated rules of pleading shall not disable any person from pleading the general issue, and giving the *special matter* in evidence, where by statute he may now do so,) an overseer sued in trespass for taking A.'s goods, may still prove, on plea of not guilty, that he, as overseer, distrained the goods for a poor's rate due from B., and that the goods were the goods of B., and not of A. (*m*). Wherever a statute says that a party may prove his defence under the general issue, it means that he may prove the whole matter of defence (*n*). By R. G. H. T. 4 Will. IV., in actions of trespass *quare clausum fregit,* the plea of *not guilty* shall operate as a denial that the defendant committed the trespass alleged in the place mentioned, but not as a denial of the plaintiff's possession or right of possession of that place, which, if intended to be denied, must be traversed specially. In actions of trespass *de bonis asportatis,* the plea of not guilty shall operate as a denial of the defendant having committed the trespass alleged by taking or damaging the goods mentioned, but not of the plaintiff's property therein. To a declaration for breaking and entering plaintiff's close, the defendant pleaded—1st, not guilty; 2ndly, that the close was not the close of the plaintiff; 3rdly, that the close was the soil and freehold of the defendant: it was holden (*o*), that evidence of possession was sufficient to entitle the plaintiff to a verdict on the second plea. By stat. 11 Geo. II. c. 19, s. 21, "In actions of trespass brought against any person

---

(*l*) See *ante,* p. 148.
(*m*) See stat. 43 Eliz. c. 2, s. 19; *Haine* v. *Davey,* 4 A. & E. 892; 6 Nev. & M. 356.

(*n*) Per *Patteson,* J., *S. C.*
(*o*) *Heath* v. *Milward,* 2 Bingh. N. C. 98, recognized by *Patteson,* J., in *Carnaby* v. *Welby,* 8 A. & E. 878.

2 T 2

entitled to rents or services of any kind, their bailiff or receiver, or other person, relating to an *entry* by virtue of this act, or otherwise, *upon the premises*, chargeable with such rents or services, or to *any distress*, or seizure, sale, or disposal of any goods or chattels *thereupon*, the defendants may plead the general issue, and give the special matter in evidence." In a case where rent being in arrear (*p*), the tenant had removed his goods clandestinely from the demised premises, but the landlord had seized them as a distress within thirty days, as allowed by the preceding stat. 11 Geo. II. c. 19, s. 21; it was holden, that to an action of trespass brought by the tenant against the landlord for such seizure, the defendant could not give the special matter in evidence upon the general issue by virtue of the preceding clause (sect. 21); for that clause is confined to those cases where the distress is made *upon* the premises demised. In this case, the defence must be pleaded specially (*q*).

Where a person is arbitrarily made defendant to exclude his testimony, he may, if nothing is proved against him, be acquitted, and sworn as a witness for the other defendants (*r*). But if there be the slightest evidence against one of the defendants, he cannot be acquitted so as to make him a witness (*s*). With regard to defendants, against whom there is not any evidence, the rule is, that the verdict in their favour is to be taken at the end of the plaintiff's case (*t*); but where defendants against whom the counsel abandons the case have pleaded special pleas of justification, they have an interest in the record, by reason of their liability to the costs of those pleas, and ought not to be acquitted till the special pleas in which they have joined are disposed of (*u*).

2. *Accord and Satisfaction.*

Accord *and* satisfaction, being a good plea in all actions where damages only are to be recovered, is consequently a good plea in trespass (*x*); but a plea of accord, without satisfaction, cannot be supported. Hence, in trespass for taking cattle, it cannot be pleaded, that it was agreed " *that plaintiff should have his cattle again*" (*y*); for this is no satisfaction for the injury done. So where to trespass for breaking and entering the plaintiff's close, the defendant pleaded " that in Easter Term (*z*), in the thirty-first year of the present reign, the plaintiff declared against the defendant in this cause for the several trespasses above supposed by the defendant

(*p*) *Vaughan* v. *Davis*, 1 Esp. N. P. C. 257, *Rooke*, J.

(*q*) *Furneaux* v. *Fotherby*, 4 Campb. 136, Lord *Ellenborough*, C. J.

(*r*) B. N. P. 285.

(*s*) Peake's Evid. 168.

(*t*) *Child* v. *Chamberlain*, 1 M. & Rob.

318; 6 C. & P. 212.

(*u*) *Hitchen* v. *Teale*, 2 M. & Rob. 30, *Patteson*, J.

(*x*) 9 Rep. 78, a.

(*y*) 1 Roll. Abr. 128, Accord, (A.) pl. 7.

(*z*) *James* v. *David*, 5 T. R. 141.

to have been done; and that afterwards, and before plea pleaded in this cause, to wit, on such a day, it was agreed between the plaintiff and defendant, in respect to an action then lately commenced between them, which was that day settled, as follows: that the defendant was to pay £1 1s. on account of the matter in dispute, and the plaintiff was to pay the law charges; and further, that whatsoever disputes then were, or had been, or might be in being, touching suits or actions, to the day of the date of the said agreement, should cease and terminate for ever; and they further agreed to bind themselves in the sum of £100, whoever should commence an action or suit, in respect to anything in being to the then present day." It was then averred, that the present action, and the action in the agreement mentioned, were the same. On demurrer to this plea, it was contended, in support of the plea, on the authority of an admission in *Reniger* v. *Fogassa* (z), that the agreement, which is an effectual plea in bar, is either such an agreement, as is executed and satisfied with a recompense in fact, *or with an action or other remedy to execute it, and to recover a recompense;* that here the parties agreed to bind themselves in the penalty of £100 to abide by their accord; that, therefore, was a new remedy, which fell directly within the authority cited. But the court were of opinion that the plea was bad; *Ashhurst,* J., observing, that, "supposing the proposition were true, that whenever the agreement is such, for the breach of which an action might be maintained, [it may be pleaded in bar,] yet it is incumbent on the party pleading it, to show that an action could have been supported on it. In order to found an action on this agreement, the plaintiff must have stated not only the agreement, but also that he tendered an obligation in £100, ready executed to the defendant, and that the defendant refused to execute, &c.; but no action could have been sustained on this contract, without that previous step, which is not pleaded here."

3. *Liberum Tenementum.*

In trespass to real property, the defendant may plead that the close in which, &c. is the freehold (liberum tenementum) or customary tenement of the defendant, or of a third person under whom he acted.

To a plea of liberum tenementum (a), where the plaintiff replied, that the place in question was the soil and freehold of the plaintiff, and not the soil and freehold of the defendant; it was holden, on special demurrer, that the replication was good; for the words, "that it is the freehold of the plaintiff," were either to be rejected as surplusage, or to be considered only as inducement; that if the plaintiff had said, that it was his freehold, absque hoc that it was

(z) Plowd. 5, 11, b.   (a) *Lambert* v. *Stroother,* Willes, 218.

the freehold of the defendant, it would have been plainly an inducement only : and yet that was exactly the same case as the present,
for there is not any distinction between traverses and denials.
Where the defendant pleads liberum tenementum in I. S., and
that the defendant entered by his command, the plaintiff, in his
replication, may traverse the command. This point was solemnly
adjudged in *Chambers* v. *Donaldson*, 11 East, 65, (notwithstanding
the case of *Witham* v. *Barker*, Yelv. 147, and the dicta in *Trevilian*
v. *Pyne*, Salk. 107, and *ante*, tit. "Replevin," n. (21), p. 1191 ;) the
court observing, that it had become a settled rule, that possession
was sufficient to maintain trespass against a wrong-doer, but that
this rule would be of no avail if the command were not traversable ;
for in that case the wrong-doer might shelter himself under a plea
of an outstanding freehold in a stranger, from whom he derived no
authority to commit the trespass : and *Bayley*, J., added, that it
was not competent to a wrong-doer to call on a person in actual possession to set out his title. The plaintiff had lands abutting on one
side of a public highway, called Shepherd's Lane (b), (which was
primâ facie evidence that half of the lane was his soil and freehold ;)
it was holden, that he might declare generally for a trespass in his
close, called Shepherd's Lane, and that it was incumbent on the
defendant to plead soil and freehold in another, in order to drive the
plaintiff to new assign the trespass complained of in the part of the
lane which was his exclusive property. Where the plaintiff, in his
declaration, avers a single act of trespass, *e. g.*, that on such a day
the defendant stopped the plaintiff's cattle and cart, and the defendant justifies the act, there cannot be a new assignment (c).

4. *Estoppel.*

If, in an action of trespass, a verdict be found on any fact or
title distinctly put in issue, such verdict may be pleaded by way of
estoppel in another action between the same parties, or their
privies, in respect of the same fact or title. To an action of
trespass for digging and getting coals out of a coal-mine (d), alleged
by the plaintiff to be within and under his close called the Cow
Close ; the defendants pleaded, and showed title regularly brought
down to them in right of the wife, by fine, recovery, &c., from one
Sir John Zouch, who in the 39th year of Elizabeth was seised in
fee of the manor of Alfreton, and of certain messuages and lands
within the manor, by virtue of which title they claimed all the coals
under those lands, except such as were within and under any of the
messuages, buildings, orchards, and grounds, which, at the time of
a recovery suffered in the reign of Queen Elizabeth, were standing

(b) *Stevens* v. *Whistler*, 11 East, 51.   (d) *Outram* v. *Morewood*, 3 East, 346.
(c) *Taylor* v. *Smith*, 7 Taunt. 156.

and being upon the said lands and tenements, and which coal mines, with the exception aforesaid, passed under a bargain and sale from Sir John Zouch to certain bargainees; and the defendants averred, that the coals in question were under the lands of that former owner, Sir J. Zouch, and were derived by bargain and sale to certain immediate bargainees, and from them to the defendant, the wife, and were not within or under any of the messuages, buildings, orchards, and gardens, which were the subject of the exception. To this plea the plaintiff replied, and relied, by way of estoppel, upon a former verdict obtained by him in an action of trespass, brought by him against one of the defendants, Ellen, the wife of the other defendant, she being then sole, in which he declared for the same trespass as now; to which the wife pleaded, and derived title in the same manner as now done by her and her husband, and alleged, that the coal mines in question, in the declaration mentioned, were, at the time of making the before-mentioned bargain and sale, by Sir John Zouch, parcel of the coal mines by that indenture bargained and sold: upon which point, *viz.* whether the coal mines claimed by the plaintiff, and mentioned in his declaration, were parcel of what passed under Zouch's bargain and sale to the persons under whom the wife claimed, an issue was taken, and found for the plaintiff, and against the wife. The question was, whether the defendants, the husband and wife, were estopped by this verdict, and judgment thereupon, from averring in the present action, (contrary to the title so there found against the wife,) that the coal mines now in question were parcel of the coal mines bargained and sold by the before-mentioned indenture. It was holden, that the husband and wife were so estopped, and consequently, that the plaintiff ought to recover. But since the case of *Vooght* v. *Winch*, 2 B. & A. 662, recognized in *Doe* v. *Huddart*, 2 Cr. M. & R. 323 (e), the judgment will not be conclusive, unless it is pleaded as an estoppel.

5. License.

To an action of trespass, the defendant may *plead*, that he committed the supposed trespass by leave of the plaintiff. Where a person is licensed to do an act, it is necessarily implied, that he may do every thing without which that act cannot be done. Hence, where to trespass against A., B., and C. (f), for breaking and entering plaintiff's house, and continuing there ten days, and selling divers goods; the defendants pleaded, that before the time, when, &c., the plaintiff licensed A. to enter the house, and to continue therein for the sale of his goods; by virtue of which license, A. in his own right, and B. and C. as his servants, peaceably entered the

(e) *Ante*, p. 767.
(f) *Dennett* v. *Grover and others*, Willes, 195.

house by the door, then open, to sell the said goods, and in and about the sale of goods, *necessarily continued in the house for ten days*, &c., concluding with a verification. On demurrer, it was objected, that the license was personal to A., and, consequently, it could not justify the entry of any other person; and at least it ought to have appeared on the face of the plea, that the entry of the other defendants was necessary for the purposes mentioned in the license. But the court overruled the objection, *Willes*, C. J., observing, that unless a man could sell goods to himself, it was absurd to contend that this was a license to A. only to go into the house; besides, it was highly probable, that he might want to take several persons with him, in order to assist in the sale; and this is sufficiently set forth in the plea; for it is alleged, that all three *necessarily continued* in the house for ten days, to sell the goods; and if their continuance therein were necessary, their entrance must certainly be so too, and was therefore sufficiently alleged (8). Where the plaintiff complains of several trespasses committed on several days (*g*), and the defendant pleads a license to which the plaintiff replies *de injuriâ suâ propriâ absque tali causâ;* it is incumbent on the defendant to show a license for each act of trespass proved by the plaintiff. In such case it is not necessary for the plaintiff to new assign; for the meaning of the replication is, that the defendant committed the several trespasses without a license for each. Where a defendant justified the stopping the plaintiff's cart, on the ground that he was loading his cart with turf wrongfully cut from the waste of the manor, and that defendant, as bailiff of the lord, stopped the cart. Plaintiff having replied de injuriâ suâ propriâ; it was holden (*h*), that in order to rebut the justification, he could not give in evidence a license from the lord to cut the turf, that not having been pleaded by way of replication. License to enter and occupy land for a certain time amounts to a lease, and ought to be pleaded as such (*i*).

The defendant may also justify an entry into the house or land of another under a license in law. Such is the entry into an inn or tavern at seasonable times, an entry to demand rent due for the enjoyment of the land, or to distrain for the rent in arrear,

---

(*g*) *Barnes* v. *Hunt*, 11 East, 451.
(*h*) *Taylor* v. *Smith*, 7 Taunt. 156.

(*i*) Adm. per *Cur.*, 5 Hen. VII. 1, a., cited in Plowd. 542, a.

---

(8) In Hil. 13 Hen. VII. 13, b., the distinction is taken between those licenses that are given for pleasure, and those for profit; that the former are merely personal, but that in the latter case, the person to whom the license is given may take others with him: "Et issint si home me license a avoir un arbre in son bois, mes servants justifieront le sier del arbre et l'entrer." The former branch of this distinction is also supported by a passage in Finch's Law, 16 and 17, and the latter by a case in M. 13 Hen. VII. 10; Durnford's note, Willes, 197.

or to distrain cattle damage feasant. Such also is an entry for the purpose of executing (in a legal manner) the process of the law ; the entry of a remainder-man or reversioner to view the state of repair, and see whether any waste has been committed on the estate ; the entry of a landlord (k) in the absence of a tenant, who had omitted to deliver up possession when his term had expired ; the entry of a commoner to view his cattle, and the like. Having stated several instances in which the law permits a person to enter the house or land of another, we proceed to inquire in what cases a party shall be deemed a trespasser *ab initio ;* as to which the following distinctions must be observed :—

1. Where an entry, authority, or license, is given to any person *by law,* and he abuses it by the commission of some act, there he shall be considered as a trespasser *ab initio; i. e.,* from the first entry ; for the law determines from the subsequent act, *quo animo,* or to what intent, the original entry was made ; as, if a person enters an inn or tavern, and afterwards commits a trespass, by carrying away any thing, the law adjudges that he entered for that purpose ; and because the act which demonstrates it is a trespass, he shall be a trespasser *ab initio ;* but, in such case, if the party is guilty of a mere non-feasance, as in the case of an entry into an inn, and refusing to pay for the liquor which he has consumed (l), there he cannot be considered as a trespasser *ab initio,* because a mere non-feasance does not amount to a trespass. So where one who has distrained a beast damage feasant, or taken an estray, kills or works it (m), he shall be deemed a trespasser *ab initio ;* but a refusal to deliver the beast, on tender of amends, being a mere non-feasance, will not be considered as a trespass with force *ab initio.* It is clear, therefore, that in order to constitute a person a trespasser *ab initio,* the party must have been guilty of a subsequent act of trespass.

2. Where the entry, authority, or license, to do any thing is given *by the party,* there although the person to whom the authority is given may, by the commission of subsequent acts, be a trespasser, yet such subsequent acts will not affect the original entry, so as to make that which was sanctioned by the authority of the party complaining a trespass. In this case, therefore, the subsequent acts only will amount to trespasses. A person cannot justify (n) entering the close of another to take his own property *without showing* the circumstances under which it came there; even though he alleges he did not do any unnecessary damage ; but all the old authorities say, that where a party places upon his own close the goods of another, he gives to the owner of them an implied license to enter for the

(k) *Turner* v. *Meymott,* 1 Bingh. 158.
(l) *Six Carpenters'* case, 8 Rep. 146, a, cited by *Littledale,* J., in *Smith* v. *Eg-*
gington, 7 A. & E. 176.
(m) *Oxley* v. *Watts,* 1 T. R. 12.
(n) *Anthony* v. *Haneys,* 8 Bingh. 186.

purpose of recaption (o). Hence a plea to a declaration in trespass for breaking and entering the plaintiff's close, that the defendant being possessed of certain goods, the plaintiff without his leave and against his will, took the goods and placed them on the close, in the declaration mentioned, wherefore the defendant made fresh pursuit and entered to retake the goods, is a good plea, and a good justification of the entry on the plaintiff's close (q). If A. wrongfully place goods in B.'s building, B. may lawfully go upon A.'s close adjoining the building, for the purpose of removing and depositing the goods there for A.'s use (r). On the subject of revoking a license, see *ante*, p. 1120.

6. *Process* (9).

It is a general rule (10), that an officer cannot justify the breaking open an outward door or window (s) in order to execute process in a civil suit (t) ; but if he finds the outward door open and enters that way, or if the door be opened to him from within, and he enters, he may break open inward doors, if he finds that necessary, in order to execute his process. And, as it seems (u), this rule holds, although the defendant be not in the house at the time ; but in such case the officer must first demand admittance, and this demand must be pleaded. In the execution of criminal process against any person in the case of a misdemeanour, it is necessary to demand admittance, before the breaking the outer door can be justified (x). And the officer cannot justify breaking the inner doors of the house of a stranger, upon suspicion that a defendant is there, to search for him in order to arrest him on mesne process (y). A., an excise officer (z), applied to the commissioners of excise for a warrant to search the house of B. The commissioners, being satisfied with the reasonableness of his suspicion, granted a warrant, empowering A. to enter the

(p) Per *Parke*, B., in *Patrick* v. *Colerick*, 3 M. & W. 483.

(q) S. C.

(r) *Rea* v. *Sheward*, 2 M. & W. 424.

(s) Foster's Discourse of Homicide, chap. 8, sect. 19.

(t) But see *Burdett* v. *Abbot*, 14 East, 1.

(u) *Ratcliffe* v. *Burton*, 3 Bos. & Pul. 223.

(x) *Launock* v. *Brown*, 2 B. & A. 592.

(y) *Johnson* v. *Leigh*, 6 Taunt. 246.

(z) *Cooper* v. *Booth*, on error from C. B., 3 Esp. N. P. C. 135, in which *Bostock* v. *Saunders*, 2 Bl. R. 912; 3 Wils. 434, was overruled.

(9) For justifications under process of superior and inferior court, see *ante*, tit. " Imprisonment," p. 922.

(10) There may, however, be circumstances of necessity or constraint which may justify the officer in breaking the outer door. See *White* v. *Wiltsheire*, 2 Roll. Rep. 137; Cro. Jac. 555; Palm. 52; *Pugh* v. *Griffith*, 7 A. & E. 827 ; 3 Nev. & P. 187.

house of B., and seize all run tea which should be there found fraudulently concealed. A. accordingly entered B.'s house, in the daytime, and broke open a lock which B. had refused to open, and rummaged his goods, but did not find any tea. In an action of trespass brought by B. against the officer; it was holden, that upon the true construction of the stat. 10 Geo. I. c. 10, s. 13, the officer was justified, although there was not any tea found, or any evidence given of the grounds of his suspicion. In an action against a sheriff for breaking and entering plaintiff's house, and staying therein three weeks, the defendant pleaded a justification under process as to breaking and entering, and staying in the house twenty-four hours (a). The plaintiff, admitting the writ, replied *de injuriâ suâ propria absque residuo causæ.* The defendants proved their justification; but it appeared that the officer continued in the plaintiff's house beyond twenty-four hours. Lord *Ellenborough* was of opinion, that the plea applied to the whole declaration, and that if the plaintiff meant to rely upon the excess beyond the twenty-four hours, he ought to have said so by a new assignment. *The residue of the cause* mentioned in the plea was alone put in issue, and the length of time, during which the officers remained in the house, was rendered immaterial. For the powers given to commissioners of bankrupt to break open houses, &c., see stat. 6 Geo. IV. c. 16, ss. 27, 29, 31.

7. *Right of Common (b).*

The defendant may justify under a right of common of pasture, of estovers, or of turbary. See *ante*, p. 414, and stat. 2 & 3 Will. IV. c. 71, s. 5, (for shortening the time of prescription,) *ante*, p. 428. Under this statute a plea of enjoyment of right of common for thirty years before the commencement of the suit, is sufficient (c), without saying thirty years *next* before. By R. G. H. T. 4 Will. IV., in trespass quare clausum fregit, pleas of soil and freehold of the defendant in the locus in quo, and of the defendant's right to an easement there; pleas of right of way, of common of pasture, of common of turbary, and of common of estovers, are distinct, and are to be allowed. But, pleas of right of common at all times of the year, and of such right at particular times, or in a qualified manner, are not to be allowed.

(a) *Monprivatt* v. *Smith*, 2 Campb. 175.

(b) For right of common, see *ante*, p. 414, tit. "Common," and tit. "Replevin," Pleas in Bar to an Avowry for Damage feasant, p. 1194. For right of fishery, see *ante*, tit. "Fishery," p. 827.

(c) *Jones* v. *Price*, 3 Bingh. N. C. 52; 3 Sc. 376. See further on this subject, *ante*, p. 425.

8. *Right of Way* (*d*).

To trespass *qu. cl. fr.* the defendant may plead a right of way over the *locus in quo*, and that in the exercise of such right he committed the trespasses complained of. There are four kinds of ways (*e*): 1, a footway; 2, a horseway, which includes a footway; 3, a carriageway, which includes both horseway and footway; 4, a driftway. Although a carriageway comprehends a horseway, yet it does not necessarily include a driftway (*f*). It is said (*g*), however, that evidence of a carriageway is strong presumptive evidence of the grant of a driftway. These ways are either public or highways for all persons, or private ways (11). An highway (termed in law French *chimin*) is a way for all the king's subjects to pass and repass (*h*). It is called *regia via*, or the king's highway, although the king can only claim a passage for himself and his subjects; for the freehold and the profits growing there, as trees and other things, are in the lord of the soil. Where there has been a public king's highway, no length of time, during which it may not have been used, will prevent the public from resuming the right (*i*), if they think proper. The public have not any common law right (*k*) of bathing in the sea; and as incident thereto, of crossing the sea-shore on foot, or with bathing machines for that purpose. Where the owner of land builds houses upon it (*l*), forming a street, which he permits to be used as a highway, although an absolute transfer of the property in the soil cannot be presumed, yet a dedication of the way to the public will be presumed, so far as the public have occasion for it, for the purpose of passing and repassing along the same. But proof of a bar having been placed across the street (*m*), at the time when the street was made, even although such bar may have been subsequently destroyed, will rebut the presumption of a dedication to the public: for it must

(*d*) See further on this subject, under tit. "Nusance," *ante*, p. 1112.

(*e*) 1 Inst. 56, a.

(*f*) *Ballard* v. *Dyson*, 1 Taunt. 279.

(*g*) Per *Chambre*, J., *S. C.*

(*h*) Terms de la Ley, Chimin; Bro. Abr. Chimin, pl. 9, 10, 11.

(*i*) Per *Gibbs*, J., in *R.* v. *The Inhabitants of St. James*, *Taunton*, MS. See

also *Vooght* v. *Winch*, 2 B. & A. 662.

(*k*) *Blundell* v. *Catterall*, 5 B. & A. 268. See *Benest* v. *Pipon*, Lord *Wynford's* judgment, Cases before the Privy Council, by J. W. Knapp, vol. 1. p. 67.

(*l*) *Lade* v. *Shepherd*, Str. 1004.

(*m*) *Roberts* v. *Karr*, Surrey Lent Ass. 1808, coram *Heath*, J., 1 Campb. 262.

---

(11) "If a way lead to a market, and is a common way for all travellers, and communicates with a great road, it is an highway; but if it leads only to a church, to a private house, or village, or to fields, it is a private way. But this is matter of fact, and much depends on reputation. Per *Hale*, C. J., *Austin's* case, Vent. 189.

appear that the dedication was made openly, and with a deliberate purpose. N. There cannot be a partial dedication to the public (*n*), although there may be a grant of footway only. Permitting the public to have the free use of a way in a street in London for six years, has been holden sufficient evidence of a dereliction, where no bar has been put up (*o*). To give the public a right, however, the dedication must be with the consent of the owner of the fee; for where it is given by an individual having only a limited right, it continues for a limited period only. In trespass and justification under a public right of way, it appeared that the *locus in quo* had been under lease from 1719 to 1818, but as far back as living memory could go it had been used by the public, though not a thoroughfare, and lighted, paved, and watched under an act of parliament, in which it was enumerated as one of the streets in Westminster. After 1818, the plaintiff, who had previously lived for 24 years in the neighbourhood, inclosed it. It was holden (*p*), that, under these circumstances, the jury were well justified in finding that there was no public right of way, inasmuch as there could not be any dedication to the public by the tenants for 99 years, nor by any one except the owner of the fee (*q*). To constitute a dedication (*r*), there must be a clear intention to dedicate. Trespass for entering plaintiff's close (*s*) and pulling down a gate. Plea, that there was a public footway over the *locus in quo*, and because the gate was wrongfully erected across the same, defendant pulled it down. It appeared in evidence, that the gate in question had been recently put up in a place where a similar gate had formerly stood, but where, for the last twelve years, there had been none. It was thereupon contended, for the defendant, that, from suffering the gate to be down so long, and permitting the public to use the way, without obstruction, for so many years, the plaintiff, and those under whom he claimed, must be considered as having completely dedicated the way to the public, and that the gate could not be replaced. The plaintiff, however, had a verdict, which the Court of King's Bench, the following term, refused to set aside.

(*n*) *S. C.* See also *Marquis of Stafford* v. *Coyney*, 7 B. & C. 257.

(*o*) Per Lord *Kenyon*, C. J., *Trustees of Rugby Charity* v. *Merryweather*, 11 East, 376, n. N. This was the case of a thoroughfare. But where the plaintiff made a street, leading out of a highway, across his own close, and terminating at the edge of the defendant's adjoining close, which was separated from the end of the street for twenty-one years, (during ten of which the houses were completed, and the street publicly watched, cleansed, and lighted, and both footways, and half the horseway thereof, paved at the expense of the inhabitants,) by the defendant's fence; it was holden, that this street was not so dedicated to the public, that the defendant pulling down his fence might enter it at the end adjoining to his land, and use it as a highway. *Woodyer* v. *Hadden*, 5 Taunt. 125. See *R.* v. *Barr*, 4 Campb. 16. See also *Wood* v. *Veal*, 5 B. & A. 454, and *Jarvis* v. *Dean*, 3 Bingh. 447.

(*p*) *Wood* v. *Veal*, in the case of *Little Abingdon Street, Westminster*, 5 B. & A. 454.

(*q*) See stat. 2 & 3 Will. IV. c. 71, s. 8, *ante*, p. 1111.

(*r*) *Barraclough* v. *Johnson*, 3 Nev. & P. 233; 8 A. & E. 99. See *Grand Surrey Canal Company* v. *Hall*, 1 M. & Gr. 392.

(*s*) *Lethbridge* v. *Winter*, 1 Campb. 263.

A private way is a right which one or more persons have of going over the land of another. This may be claimed either by grant, prescription, custom, by express reservation, or as necessarily incident to a grant of land, or by virtue of an Inclosure Act.

1. *By Grant.*—A private way may be claimed by grant : as if A. grant that B. shall have a way from C. through such a close (belonging to A.) to M. So if A. covenants that B. shall enjoy such a way, it amounts to a gran (*t*). Under the grant (*u*) "*of a free and convenient way* in, through, and over a slip of land, leading from ————— to —————, with liberty to make and lay causeways, &c.," and " to use the same with carriages, and to carry coals, &c.," the grantee has a right to make any such way as is necessary for the carrying that commodity, *e. g.*, a framed waggon way. Under the grant of a way from A. to B. (*x*) in, through, and along a particular way, the grantee is not justified in making a transverse road *across* the same. If a person has a way through a close (*y*), in a particular direction, and he afterwards purchases other closes adjoining, he cannot extend the way to those closes. In pleading a right of way under a grant, regularly there ought to be a profert of the deed; but if the deed has been lost (*z*) "by time or accident," it may be so stated in the plea, and that will dispense with the necessity of a profert. A lease was granted, in 1814, to take effect from 1820, of certain houses, together with a piece of ground which was part of an adjoining yard, and all ways with the said premises, or *any part thereof, used or enjoyed.* At the time of granting the lease, the whole yard was in the occupation of one person, who had always used and enjoyed a certain right of way to every part of that yard. It was holden (*a*), that the lessee was entitled to such right of way to the part of the yard demised to him. At common law, the right to repair is incident to the grant of way (*b*). A. granted to B. (*c*), his heirs, and assigns, occupiers of certain houses abutting on a piece of land about eleven feet wide (which divided those houses from a house then belonging to A.), the right of using the piece of land as a foot or carriageway, and gave him "all other powers, &c. incident or necessary to the enjoyment of the way;" it was holden, that under the terms of this grant, the grantee was entitled to put down a flagstone upon a piece of land in front of a door opened by him out of his house into this piece of land ; *Chambre*, J., observing, that the nature of the thing was material in considering the effect of the words. The way was granted for the occupation of a dwelling house, and the grantee ought to have every thing needful for the

(*t*) 3 Lev. 305.
(*u*) *Senhouse* v. *Christian*, 1 T. R. 560. See *Dand* v. *Kingscote*, 6 M. & W. 174, case of a railroad.
(*x*) *Senhouse* v. *Christian*, 1 T. R. 560.
(*y*) 1 Rol. 391, 1. 50 ; 1 Mod. 190.
(*z*) *Read* v. *Brookman*, 3 T. R. 151.
(*a*) *Kooystra* v. *Lucas*, 5 B. & A. 830.

See *Oakley* v. *Adamson*, 8 Bingh. 356 ; and *James* v. *Plant*, 4 A. & E. 761, *post*, 1337.
(*b*) Sembl. 1 Saund. 323. Admitted per *Heath* and *Chambre*, Js., in 2 Bos. & Pul. N. R. 109.
(*c*) *Gerrard* v. *Cooke*, 2 Bos. & Pul. N. R. 109.

occupation of his dwelling-house; he ought, therefore, to have the opportunity of repairing the way in such a manner, that it should not be wet or dirty, when he, or his family, or his visitors enter. If any inconvenience had been occasioned to the grantor, it might make a difference; but that was not the case here, nor was it to be feared that any right could hereafter be set up in respect of the soil, in consequence of this stone having been put down; for the precise extent of the road was pointed out. A person having a *private* way over the land of another (*d*), cannot, when the way is become impassable by the overflowing of a river, justify going on the adjoining land, although such land, together with the land over which the way is, both belong to the grantor of the way. Highways are governed by a different principle. They are for the public service, and if the usual track is impassable, it is for the general good that people should be entitled to pass in another line (*e*).

2. *By Prescription.*—A private way may also be claimed by prescription (*f*), *e. g.*, that defendant is seised in fee of a certain messuage, and that he, and all those *whose estate he has* in the said messuage, have, from time immemorial, had a footway, &c. (as the case may be) from —— to ——. From the words in italics, this plea is termed prescribing in a que estate. By stat. 2 & 3 Will. IV. c. 71, s. 5, (*ante*, p. 428,) where a party used to allege his claim from time immemorial, the period mentioned in the act may be alleged, and the party need not claim, as heretofore, in the name or right of the owner of the fee. In pleading a prescriptive private way, it is not necessary (*g*) to describe all the closes intervening between the two termini. A right of way being an easement merely, and not an interest, it is not proper to lay the way as appendant or appurtenant (*h*). Unity of possession of the land to which a way is appurtenant by prescription, and of the land over which the way is, will extinguish the way; for the prescription is gone, and the way is against common right (*i*).

Where there is a unity of seisin (*k*) of the land, and of the way over the land, in one and the same person, the right of way is either extinguished or suspended, according to the duration of the respective estates in the land and the way; and, after such extinguishment, or during such suspension of the right, the way cannot pass as an appurtenant under the ordinary legal sense of the word. In the case of a unity of seisin, in order to pass a way existing in point of user, but extinguished or suspended in point of law, the grantor must either employ words of express grant, or must describe the

(*d*) *Taylor* v. *Whitehead*, Doug. 744. See also *Bullard* v. *Harrison*, 4 M. & S. 387, and *post*, p. 1338.
(*e*) Per Lord *Mansfield*, C. J., in *Taylor* v. *Whitehead*, *ubi sup.*
(*f*) Rastall's Entr. 617, pl. 5, ed. 2.
(*g*) *Simpson* v. *Lewthwaite*, 3 B. & Ad.

226.
(*h*) *Godley* v. *Frith*, Yelv. 159.
(*i*) 1 Roll. Abr. 935, (C.) pl. 8.
(*k*) Per *Tindal*, C. J., delivering judgment in error, in Exch. Chr., *James* v. *Plant*, 4 A. & E. 761. See *ante*, p. 1112, as to unity of possession.

way in question as one "used and enjoyed with the land," which forms the subject matter of the conveyance.

3. *By Custom.*—A custom that every inhabitant of such a vill shall have a way over such land, either to church or to market, is good, because it is but an easement, and not a profit. A tithe-owner is entitled to make use of the road ordinarily used for the ordinary occupation of the close in which the tithe is taken (*l*); but he cannot justify carrying his tithes home by any other road, although the farmer himself may have used it for the occupation of his farm (*m*).

4. *By express Reservation.*—A right of way may be claimed by express reservation; as where A. grants land to another, reserving to himself a way over such land.

5. *For Necessity.*—If a person having a close, bounded on every side by his own land, grants the close to another, the grantee shall have a way to the close, as incident to the grant, or, as it is some-times termed, a way of necessity; for otherwise he cannot derive any benefit from the grant (*n*); but this kind of way cannot be pleaded generally without showing the manner in which the land over which the way is claimed is charged with it (*o*). If A. has four closes lying together, and sells three of them to B., reserving the middle close, to which A. has not any way except through one of those closes which he sold, although he reserved not any way, yet A. shall have a way to the middle close, as reserved to him by ope-ration of law (*p*); and unity of possession will not extinguish this species of way (*q*). J. S., as a trustee, conveyed land to another, to which there was not any way, except over the trustee's land; it was holden, that a right of way passed of necessity, as incidental to the grant (*r*). If A., the owner of a close over which there is a right of way (*s*), plough up the way, and assign a new way, any person may justify using the new way as long as it lies open: but if A. afterwards stops up the new way, the removal of the obstruction to the new way cannot be justified (*t*). A way of necessity exists after unity of possession of the close to which, and the close over which, and after a subsequent severance. If a person purchases close A., with a way of necessity thereto over close B., a stranger's land, and afterwards purchases close B., and then purchases close C., adjoining to close A., and through which he may enter close A., and then sells close B. without reservation of any way, and then

(*l*) Admitted in *Cobb* v. *Selby*, 2 Bos. & Pul. N. R. 466. See also 1 Bulstr. 108, and *ante*, p. 1291, tit. "Tithes."
(*m*) Adjudged, *S. C.*
(*n*) 2 Rol. Abr. 60, pl. 17.
(*o*) *Bullard* v. *Harrison*, 4 M. & S 387.

(*p*) Per *Cur.*, in *Clark* v. *Cogge*, Cro. Jac. 170.
(*q*) *Ib.*, and *Beaudeley* v. *Brook*, Cro. Jac. 190.
(*r*) *Howton* v. *Frearson*, 8 T. R. 50.
(*s*) *Horne* v. *Widlake*, Yelv. 141.
(*t*) *Reignolds* v. *Edwards*, Willes, 282.

sells closes A. and C., the purchaser of close A. shall nevertheless
have the ancient way of necessity to close A. over close B. (*u*).
Having detailed the several methods by which a party may entitle
himself to a way over the land of another, it may not be improper to
subjoin a few remarks relative to the form of pleading a right of
way, and of replying thereto.

Pleading Right of Way.—In pleading a right of way, the defendant ought to show the nature of the way, *i. e.* whether it be a
footway, horseway, or carriageway; otherwise the plea will be bad,
on demurrer (*x*), for uncertainty: this rule applies both to public
and private ways; but in other respects the form of pleading a
public highway is more general than that of pleading a private way.
Hence, it has been holden, that in a plea of a public highway, it is
not necessary to state either the places from which and to which it
leads (*y*), or that such way has existed from time immemorial (*z*).
It is sufficient to state compendiously, that it is a public highway;
but wherever the precise locality becomes material to the defence,
the defendant is bound to fix it in his pleadings (*a*). In pleading a
private way, the *terminus a quo*, and *terminus ad quem*, ought to
be set forth (*b*). By R. G. H. T. 4 Will. IV., pleas of a right of
way over the locus in quo varying the termini or the purposes, are
not to be allowed; and where the defendant pleads a right of way
with carriages and cattle and on foot in the same plea, and issue is
taken thereon, the plea shall be taken distributively; and if a right
of way with cattle or on foot only shall be found by the jury, a
verdict shall pass for the defendant in respect of such of the trespasses proved as shall be justified by the right of way so found;
and for the plaintiff in respect of such of the trespasses as shall not
be so justified. And in all actions in which such right of way or
other similar right is so pleaded, that the allegations as to the
extent of the right are capable of being construed distributively,
they shall be taken distributively. In replying to a plea of right of
way, the plaintiff either admits the right, and new assigns, *e. g.*, *extra
viam*, or that the plaintiff has used the way in a different manner
than that to which he was entitled; or he denies the right; and
here it is to be observed, that in denying the right the plaintiff ought
to deny or traverse it specially, in conformity to the rules of pleading, which do not allow the general traverse *de injuriâ suâ propriâ
absque tali causâ* to be pleaded in cases where the defendant insists
on a right (*c*); and which rule holds as well where the defendant

(*u*) *Buckby* v. *Coles*, 5 Taunt. 311.
(*x*) *Alban* v. *Brownsall*, Yelv. 163.
(*y*) *Rouse* v. *Bardin*, 1 H. Bl. 351.
(*z*) *Aspindall* v. *Brown*, 3 T. R. 265.
(*a*) *Ellison* v. *Iles*, 3 P. & D. 391; 11
A. & E. 665.
(*b*) 2 Leon. 10.
(*c*) *Ruishbrook* v. *Pusanie*, 4 Leon. 16;

Crogate's case, 8 Rep. 66, b.; *Cooper* v.
Monke, Willes, 54. See the learned comments on *Crogate's* case in *Selby* v. *Bardons*, 3 B. & Ad. 2, affirmed on error in
the Exchequer Chamber, 9 Bingh. 756.
See also *Hooker* v. *Nye*, 1 Cr. M. & R.
258; 4 Tyr. 777; *Bowler* v. *Nicholson*, 4
P. & D. 16.

justifies by command of another claiming the right, as where he insists on the right in himself (*d*). To a plea claiming a right of way, the plaintiff may traverse the right, and give in evidence that the way had been stopped up by an order of justices (*e*).

8. *Tender of Amends.*

If a person brings an action of trespass for taking away his beasts, or other goods, tender of sufficient amends before action brought is not a bar; because the party making the tender is not the owner of the goods, as in the case of a distress (12), but a trespasser to whom the law does not show any favour (*f*).

By stat. 21 Jac. I. c. 16, s. 5, "in all actions of trespass *quare clausum fregit*, wherein the defendant shall disclaim in his plea, to make any title or claim to the land, and the trespass be by negligence or involuntary, defendant may plead a disclaimer, and that the trespass was by negligence or involuntary, and a tender of sufficient amends before action brought."

V. *Evidence.*

THE plaintiff may prove the trespass to have been committed at any time before action brought, though it be before or after the day laid in the declaration. But in trespass with a continuando, the plaintiff ought to confine himself to the time in the declaration; yet he may waive the continuando, and prove a trespass on any day before action brought, or he may give in evidence only part of the

(*d*) *Cockerill* v. *Armstrong*, Willes, 99.
(*e*) See 5 & 6 Will. IV. c. 50, ss. 84 to 92, (repealing 13 Geo. III. c. 78, and 55 Geo. III. c. 68,) amended by stat. 2 & 3 Vict. c. 45, and 4 & 5 Vict. c. 51. For cases on the repealed statutes, see 8th edition of this work, p. 1359, tit. "Trespass."

(*f*) 2 Inst. 107.

(12) With respect to distresses, either for rent arrear or damage feasant, the law is*, that if a tender is made before the taking the distress, the taking is wrongful; if after the taking, and before impounding, the detainer is wrongful. But a tender, after impounding, comes too late. Hence, in pleading a tender of amends to an avowry for damage feasant, it ought to appear on the face of the plea, that the tender was before impounding. The clause in stat. 21 Jac. I. c. 16, s. 5, hath not made any alteration in this respect, for that clause is confined to actions of trespass†.

* 2 Inst. 107. † *Allen* v. *Bayley*, Lutw. 1596.

time in the continuando. Bull. N. P. 86. So where trespasses are alleged to have been committed on a particular day, and on divers other days and times between that day and the commencement of the action, the plaintiff may prove either one trespass before the day specified, or as many trespasses as he can within the space of time mentioned in the declaration, but he cannot do both, and must waive the one or the other. Per *Gould*, J., Northumberland Summ. Ass. 1775, MSS., *Chambre*, J. In trespass (h) against several, the plaintiff having proved a joint trespass by all, cannot waive that, and give evidence of another trespass committed by one defendant only. Declarations respecting the subject matter of a cause, by a person who at the time of making them had the same interest in such matter as the plaintiff, were holden (i) to be admissible in evidence against him, although the maker of them was alive, and might have been called as a witness. Where the declaration charges the commission of trespasses in a close of the plaintiff, which it describes by abuttals, the plaintiff, in support of the declaration, is not obliged to prove trespasses committed in every part of the close. And if the defendant pleads that the "close in which, &c." is part of certain ground once waste, but which was set out under an award for particular purposes, and that he (defendant) is entitled to use it for those purposes; and if it appears that the whole extent of ground mentioned in the plea was not set out under the award, but if part of it was so set out, and the place where the trespasses proved were committed was within that part, then the defendant has proved his justification; for as the plaintiff is not bound to carry his proof of trespasses to every part of the close mentioned in the declaration, so the defendant is not bound to support his justification as to all parts. The "close in which, &c." does not mean the whole close referred to in the declaration, but the place in which the trespass is proved to have been committed, and the defendant may so apply it (k). To support a plea (framed on stat. 2 & 3 Will. IV. c. 71, s. 2, which see *ante*, p. 1111) of a right of way enjoyed for forty years, evidence (l) may be given of user more than forty years back. Under a plea (m) denying that the defendant had used the way for forty years, as of right and without interruption, the plaintiff is at liberty to show the character and description of the user and enjoyment of the way during any part of the time; as that it was used by stealth, or in the absence of the occupier of the close and without his knowledge, or that it was merely a precarious enjoyment by leave and license, or any other

(h) *Tait* v. *Harris*, 1 M. & Rob. 282; 6 C. & P. 73; but see the remarks of *Patteson*, J., on this case, in *Hitchen* v. *Teale*, 2 M. & Rob. 31.

(i) *Woolway* v. *Rowe*, 1 A. & E. 114; 3 Nev. & M. 849.

(k) *Bassett* v. *Mitchell*, 2 B. & Ad. 99,

recognizing *Richards* v. *Peake*, 2 B. & C. 918.

(l) *Lawson* v. *Langley*, 4 A. & E. 890.

(m) *Beasley* v. *Clarke*, 2 Bingh. N. C. 709, recognizing *Tickle* v. *Brown*, 4 A. & E. 369; 6 Nev. & M. 230.

circumstances which negative that it is an user or enjoyment under a claim of right; the words of the 5th section (*n*), "not inconsistent with the simple fact of enjoyment," being referable to the fact of enjoyment as before stated in the act, *viz.* an enjoyment claimed and exercised "as of right."

VI. *Damages; Costs.*

Damages.—By stat. 3 & 4 Will. IV. c. 42, s. 29, the jury, on the trial of any issue, or on any inquisition of damages, may, if they shall think fit, give damages in the nature of interest over and above the value of the goods at the time of the seizure, in actions of trespass de bonis asportatis.

In trespass for cutting into the plaintiff's close, and carrying away the soil, the proper measure of damages is the value to the plaintiff of the land removed, not the expense of restoring it to its original condition (*o*).

Costs.—On the subject of costs in actions of trespass, see the stat. 3 & 4 Vict. c. 24, (*ante*, p. 37,) explained as to actions in which verdicts had been returned before the passing of that act, by stat. 4 & 5 Vict. c. 28.

By R. G. H. T. 4 Will. IV. 7, upon the trial, where there is more than one count, plea, avowry, or cognizance upon the record, and the party pleading fails to establish a distinct subject matter of complaint in respect of each count, or some distinct ground of answer or defence in respect of each plea, avowry, or cognizance, a verdict and judgment shall pass against him upon each count, plea, avowry, or cognizance which he shall have so failed to establish, and he shall be liable to the other party for all the costs occasioned by such count, &c., including those of the evidence as well as those of the pleadings. Upon a plea (*p*) of a right of way to fetch water and goods from a river, the jury having found the right to fetch water, and negatived the right to fetch goods, the court ordered judgment to be entered for the defendant as to the right to fetch water, and for the plaintiff as to the right to fetch goods. But where to an action of trespass, the defendant pleaded a right of way on foot and with horses, cattle, carts, waggons, and other carriages, for the convenient occupation of his close, K.: the jury having found that he had a right of carting timber and wood only from K.; it was holden (*q*), that plaintiff was entitled to the entire verdict, and that defendant could not enter it distributively for such right as the jury found.

(*n*) For which see *ante*, p. 428.

(*o*) *Jones* v. *Gooday*, 8 M. & W. 146.

(*p*) *Knight* v. *Woore*, 3 Bingh. N. C. 3;

3 Scott, 326.

(*q*) *Higham* v. *Rabett*, 5 Bingh. N. C. 622; 7 Scott, 827.

CHAPTER XL.

TROVER.

I. *Of the Nature and Foundation of the Action of Trover, and in what Cases such Action may be maintained,* p. 1343.

II. *By whom and against whom Trover may be maintained,* p. 1364.

III. *The Declaration,* p. 1366; *Plea, and herein of the New Rules,* p. 1368; *Defence, and herein of the Doctrine of Liens,* p. 1370; *Evidence,* p. 1378; *Of staying the Proceedings,* p. 1383; *Damages,* p. 1383; *Costs,* p. 1384; *Judgment,* p. 1384.

I. *Of the Nature and Foundation of the Action of Trover, and in what Cases such Action may be maintained.*

DEFINITION.—The action of trover is a special action upon the case, which may be maintained by any person who has either an absolute or special property in goods, for recovering the value of such goods, against another, who having, or being supposed to have, obtained possession of such goods by lawful means, has wrongfully converted them to his own use.

In order to maintain an action of trover, it is necessary that it should appear,

1. That the plaintiff had either an absolute or a special property in the goods which are the subject of the action :

2. That the plaintiff had also the right of possession in the goods :

3. That *personal* goods constitute the subject matter of the action :

4. That the defendant has been guilty of a wrongful conversion.

1. *Absolute Property.*—It must appear, that the plaintiff had a property, either absolute or special (*a*), in the goods which are the

---

(*a*) Per Lord *Mansfield*, C. J., 1 T. R. 56.

subject of the action; but it is not necessary to show that the plaintiff had both an absolute and special property (b); either the one or the other is sufficient. Absolute property is where one (c), having the possession of goods, has also the exclusive right to enjoy them, and which can only be defeated by his own act. Timber (d) while standing is part of the inheritance; but when severed, either by the act of God, as by tempest, or by a trespasser and by wrong, it belongs to him who has the first estate of inheritance, whether in fee or in tail, who may bring trover for it. Trover was brought by a tenant in tail, expectant on the determination of an estate for life (e), without impeachment of waste, for timber which grew upon, and had been severed from, the estate, and was in the possession of the defendant. It was holden, that the plaintiff could not recover; because an action of trover must be founded on the property of the plaintiff, and in this case the plaintiff had not any property in the timber; for a tenant for life, without impeachment of waste, has a right to the trees at the moment when they are cut down. In like manner tenant in tail, after possibility of issue extinct, is entitled to timber when cut (f). Trustees of an estate *pur autre vie* cannot maintain trover for trees felled upon the estate (g); for although they have a special property in the trees while standing, yet that property ceases when they are cut down, and the trees then belong to the owner of the inheritance. It was for a long time in great doubt whether the landlord had such a possession of timber cut down during the continuance of a lease, on which he could maintain trover; but it was finally determined (h) that he had; because the interest of the lessee in the timber remained no longer than while it was growing on the land demised, and determined instantly upon the severance. The defendant, a wharfinger, having acknowledged timber on his wharf to be the property of the plaintiff; it was holden (i), that he could not afterwards dispute it, and set up the title of a third person. The owner of goods stolen, prosecuting the felon to conviction, cannot recover the value of them in trover from a person (k) who has purchased the goods *in market overt* (l), and sold them again before the conviction, notwithstanding the owner gave the purchaser notice of the robbery, while the goods were in his possession; for, in order to maintain trover, the plaintiff must prove that the goods were his property, and that *while they were so* they came into the possession of the defendant, who converted them to his own use. But where property feloniously taken from the plaintiff was sold by the felon to defendant, who purchased *bonâ fide,*

(b) Per *Lawrence*, J., 7 T. R. 398.
(c) Ib.
(d) Per Lord *Talbot*, C., in *Bewick* v. *Whitfield*, 3 P. Wms. 268.
(e) *Pyne* v. *Dor*, 1 T. R. 55.
(f) *Williams* v. *Williams*, 12 East, 209.
(g) *Blaker* v. *Anscombe*, 1 Bos. & Pul.

N. R. 25.
(h) *Berry* v. *Herd*, Palm. 327, and Cro. Car. 242, cited by *Lawrence*, J., in *Gordon* v. *Harper*, 7 T. R. 13.
(i) *Gosling* v. *Birnie*, 7 Bingh. 339.
(k) *Horwood* v. *Smith*, 2 T. R. 750.
(l) See as to sales in shops, *Lyons* v. *De Pass*, 3 P. & D. 177; 11 A. & E. 326.

but not in market overt; the plaintiff gave notice of the felony to the defendant, who afterwards sold the property in market overt, after which the plaintiff prosecuted the felon to conviction; it was holden (*m*), that the plaintiff might recover from the defendant the value of the property. An arbitrator, to whom all matters in difference between a landlord and tenant had been referred, awarded that a stack of hay should be delivered up by the tenant to the landlord, upon being paid a certain sum for it. The landlord tendered the money, *but the tenant refused to receive it*, or to deliver up the hay: whereupon the landlord brought trover against the tenant for the hay. It was holden (*n*), that this action could not be maintained; for the property was not transferred by the mere force of the award; and that the landlord's only remedy was to proceed against the tenant upon the award; but Lord *Ellenborough* observed, that the case might have been different if the tenant had accepted the money tendered, for that would have been a ratification of the award, and an assent on the part of the tenant to the transfer of the property. If a tradesman order goods to be sent by a carrier (*o*), though he does not name any particular carrier, the moment the goods are delivered to the carrier, such delivery operates as a delivery to the purchaser, and the whole property is immediately vested in him; and if any accident should happen to the goods, it will be at the risk of the purchaser (1). So if A. order goods to be transmitted to him by a particular carrier (*p*), though upon condition to return them again, if he dislike them; yet upon delivery to the carrier the property is vested in A., and he will be bound to pay the price to the vendor, and consequently the vendor cannot bring trover against the carrier, if the carrier convert the goods to his own use (2). If A. order a tradesman to send him goods by a hoyman (*q*), and the tradesman send the goods by a porter, to the house where the hoyman resides, when in town, and the porter, not finding him, leave the goods with the landlord, A. cannot maintain trover against the landlord, for the property never vested in A., but remained in the tradesman; but if the person to whom the goods were delivered

---

(*m*) *Peer* v. *Humphrey*, 2 A. & E. 495; 4 Nev. & M. 430.

(*n*) *Hunter* v. *Rice*, 15 East, 100.

(*o*) Said to have been determined by *Eyre*, C. J., at Shrewsbury Assizes, 3 P. Wms. 186; *Dutton* v. *Solomonson*, 3 Bos.

& Pul. 582, S. P.

(*p*) *Haynes* v. *Wood*, per *Herbert*, J., Surrey Ass. 1686, Bull. N. P. 36.

(*q*) *Colston* v. *Woolston*, T. 1 Ann., London Sittings, per *Holt*, C. J., Salk. MSS.; Bull. N. P. 35, 6.

---

(1) The only exception to the purchaser's right over the goods is, that the vendor, in the case of the purchaser becoming insolvent, may stop them *in transitu*. See *ante*, Chap. XXXVII. p. 1260.

(2) Trover will not lie against a carrier for the *mere non-delivery* of goods. See *ante*, p. 411.

had been a servant to the hoyman, and entrusted by him to receive
the goods, A. might have maintained trover (r); for, by such delivery, the property would have vested in him, and therefore in such
case the tradesman could not have brought trover against the
hoyman. The property of goods passes by the indorsement and
delivery of the bill of lading, by the consignee, to another, bonâ fide,
for a valuable consideration, and without collusion with the consignee (s), although the indorsee knew at the time that the consignor had not received payment in money for his goods, but had
taken the consignee's acceptances payable at a future day not
then arrived. Tempany, a corn-merchant at Longford, who employed the plaintiffs as his factors at Liverpool, shipped on board
the boat, No. 604, a full cargo of oats, and took a bill of lading or
boat receipt for them, signed by the master, bearing date the 31st
of January, 1837, whereby he acknowledged the receipt of the oats
on board, deliverable in Dublin to John and T. Delany, in care for
and to be shipped to the plaintiffs in Liverpool; on the same day he
procured from the master of another boat, No. 54, a like bill of
lading or receipt, for 530 barrels, but no oats were then on board
that boat, although a cargo was prepared for that purpose. On the
2nd of February, Tempany wrote to the plaintiffs a letter inclosing
both these instruments, and stating that he had valued on the plaintiffs for £730 against those oats; on the 7th, the plaintiffs received
this letter, and accepted the bill of exchange, and returned it to
Tempany, who received it on the 9th. In the mean time, the
defendant, who was a creditor of Tempany to a considerable amount,
sent over Mr. Walker, an agent, to Longford. Walker arrived on
the 6th, and pressed him for security; Tempany consented on that
day to give him an order, addressed to Tempany's brother, his agent
in Dublin, desiring him to deliver to Walker, for the defendant, the
cargo of boat 604, which had then sailed for Dublin, and four other
cargoes, including that of boat 54, (which was stated to be 560
barrels,) and also all that was in Tempany's store in Dublin. The
boat 54 was then partially loaded, and Tempany promised to send
the boat receipt for it to Walker; the loading was completed on
the 9th; the boat receipt or bill of lading for 550 barrels, which
were on board, signed by the master and transmitted to Walker, to
whom the cargo was made deliverable, and he received it the next
day; the boats were both hired by Tempany, and the men paid by
him. Walker, on the 8th, procured an agreement from J. Tempany,
in Dublin, to hold the oats for him, when they arrived: and he
afterwards got possession of the whole by legal process. It was
contended, that under these circumstances, the property in neither
cargo vested in the plaintiffs; first, because the instruments were
not regular bills of lading, and could give no title; and secondly, if

(r) See *Staples* v. *Alden*, 2 Mod. 309,   (s) *Cuming* v. *Brown*, 9 East, 506.
per *Holt*, C. J.; Salk. 18, S. P.

·they were, they could not operate to give the plaintiffs a title, because they, being factors, could acquire no lien without actual possession. The court thought it unnecessary to decide whether the instruments were regular bills of lading, so as to have all the properties which the custom of merchants has attached to those documents: but they held (*t*), that the property in the cargo of boat 604 vested in the plaintiffs on their acceptance of the bill, and that they were entitled to maintain trover for it; but they could not maintain trover for the cargo of boat 54, since none of it was on board, or otherwise specifically appropriated to the plaintiffs, when the receipt for that boat was given by the master; *Parke*, B., (who delivered the judgment of the court,) observed, that if the intention of the parties to pass the property, whether absolute or special, in *certain ascertained chattels*, is established, and they are placed in the hands of a depositary, no matter whether such depositary be a common carrier, or ship-master, employed by the consignor, or a third person, and the chattels are so placed on account of the person who is to have that property; and the depositary assents; it is enough: and it matters not by what documents this is effected; nor is it material whether the person who is to have the property be a factor or not; for such an agreement may be made with a factor, as well as any other individual. With respect to the cargo of boat 54, at the time of the agreement, proved by the boat receipt of the 31st of January, to hold the 530 barrels therein mentioned for the plaintiffs, there were no such oats on board, and consequently no *specific chattels* which were held for them.

A verbal gift of a chattel, without actual delivery, does not (*u*) pass the property to the donee. Donatio mortis causâ is a gift by a person *believing* himself to be at the point of death, upon the condition, that if the donor die, the donee is to keep the thing given in preference of any other. It is not necessary that the donor should be actually dying: but it is essential that the donee should have immediate actual possession of the gift, and uncontrolled dominion over it, subject, however, to the express condition of the gift not passing while the donor lives (*x*).

If goods are sold to be paid for within a limited time (*y*), and, if not removed at the end of that time, that warehouse rent shall be paid for them, the property in the goods vests absolutely in the purchaser, from the moment of the sale.

The sale of a specific chattel on credit, though that credit may be · limited to a definite period, transfers the property in the goods to the vendee, giving the vendor a right of action for the price, and a lien upon the goods, if they remain in his possession, until that price

(*t*) *Bryans* v. *Nix*, 4 M. & W. 775. See *ante*, p. 1279.
(*u*) *Irons* v. *Smallpiece*, 2 B. & A. 551. See *Reeves* v. *Capper*, 5 Bingh. N. C.

136; 6 Scott, 877.
(*x*) Holt, N. P. C. 12.
(*y*) *Phillimore* v. *Barry*, 1 Campb. 513.

be paid; but default of payment does not rescind the contract; and the vendee, on tender of the price, though after the expiration of the period of credit, may maintain trover against the vendor to recover such chattel; for in sales of chattels, time is not of the essence of the contract, unless it is made so by express agreement (z).

If a person contracts with another for the purchase of a chattel, e. g., a barge, which is not in existence at the time of the contract, although the full value of the article contracted for is paid in advance, and the order is proceeded on, yet the purchaser does not acquire any property in the article until it is finished and delivered to him (a); but it is otherwise where the bargain stipulates for advances, which are to be regulated by the progress of the work (b). After earnest given, the vendor cannot sell the goods to another, without a default in the vendee; and, therefore, if the vendee do not come and pay for and take away the goods, the vendor ought to go and request him; and then, if he do not come and pay for and take away the goods in a convenient time, *the agreement is dissolved*, and the vendor is at liberty to sell them to any other person (c). " If I sell my horse for money, I may keep him until I am paid; but I cannot have an action of debt until he be delivered; yet the *property* of the horse is *by the bargain* in the buyer. But if he do presently tender me my money, and I do refuse it, he may take the horse, or have an action of detainment. *And if the horse die in my stable, between the bargain and the delivery*, I may have an action of debt for my money, *because by the bargain the property was in the buyer*" (d). With respect to stolen horses, the property is not altered by a sale in market overt, unless the provisions of 2 Phil. & Ma. c. 7, and 31 Eliz. c. 12, are complied with. The regulations are in substance as follows: First, the horse must be exposed openly in the place used for sales for one whole hour, between ten in the morning and sunset, and afterwards brought both by vendor and vendee to the book-keeper of the fair or market: secondly, toll must be paid, if any due, and if not, one penny to the book-keeper, who shall enter the price, colour, and marks of the horse, with the names, additions, and abode of the vendor and vendee; and if the vendor is not known to the book-keeper, the vendor shall bring one credible witness to avouch his knowledge of the vendor, whose name in like manner is to be entered. The property of the owner is not to be taken away by such sale, if, within six months after the horse is stolen, he put in his claim before some magistrate where the horse is found, and within forty days more proves such property by the

(z) *Martindale* v. *Smith*, 1 G. & D. 1.
(a) *Mucklow* v. *Mangles*, 1 Taunt. 318. See also *Atkinson* v. *Bell*, 8 B. & C. 277; *Laidler* v. *Burlinson*, 2 M. & W. 602.
(b) See *Woods* v. *Russell*, 5 B. & A. 947, and the comments on that case in *Clarke* v. *Spence*, 4 A. & E. 448; 6 Nev.

& M. 399.
(c) Per *Holt*, C. J., in *Langford* v. *Administratrix of Tiler*, Salk. 113.
(d) Noy's Maxims, 88, recognized by Lord *Ellenborough*, C. J., in *Hinde* v. *Whitehouse*, 7 East, 571.

óath of two witnesses, and tenders to the person in possession of the horse such price as he *bond fide* paid for it in market overt.

The goods of a debtor are bound from the delivery of a writ of execution to the sheriff, and the execution creditor cannot be defeated by a vesting order subsequently made by the Insolvent Debtors Court, under the stat 1 & 2 Vict. c. 110, s. 37, although the provisional assignee seize before the sheriff, for such vesting order is not equivalent to sale in market overt (e) : but the property in the goods is not changed by the delivery of the writ, and is still in the debtor, and he may sell them, subject to the rights of the execution creditor, to which they will be liable, unless the sale took place in market overt (f). But after condemnation of goods in the Exchequer, the property is altered (g), so as that neither trespass nor trover will lie for the proprietor against the person who seized them.

The action of trover cannot be supported, unless there is a perfect and complete right of property in the plaintiff. Hence, when goods are sold, if any thing remain to be done on the part of the seller, *as between him and the buyer* (h), to ascertain the price, quantity (i), or individuality (k) of the goods, before the commodity purchased is to be delivered, a complete present right of property does not attach in the buyer, and consequently, trover is not maintainable. The plaintiff purchased of the defendant a quantity of starch (l), which was lying at the warehouse of a third person, at so much per cwt., by bill at two months, for the delivery of which, fourteen days were to be allowed; the weight not having been ascertained at the time of purchase, the defendant gave, according to the usual mode, a note to the warehouse-keeper to *weigh and deliver* all his (the defendant's) starch. By virtue of this order, a partial weighing and delivery of several quantities of the starch took place. Trover having been brought for the remainder, which was unweighed and not delivered; it was holden, that the action could not be supported; although it was contended, on the part of the plaintiff, that a delivery of part of an entire quantity of goods contracted for was a virtual delivery of the whole, so as to vest in the vendee the entire property in the whole, although the price for the same should not have been paid. *Per Cur.* Without deciding what might be the legal effect of such part delivery, in a case where

(e) *Woodland* v. *Fuller*, 3 P. & D. 570.

(f) *Samuel* v. *Duke*, 3 M. & W. 622, recognizing *Payne* v. *Drew*, 4 East, 523.

(g) *Ekins* v. *Smith*, T. Raym. 336, cited per *Cur.*, Carth. 327, and per Sir *W. Blackstone*, in *Scott* v. *Shearman*, 2 Bl. R. 981.

(k) See *Whitehouse* v. *Frost*, 12 East, 614.

(i) *Wallace* v. *Breeds*, 13 East, 522.

(k) *Busk* v. *Davis*, 2 M. & S. 397. See also *White* v. *Wilks*, 5 Taunt. 176 ; *Shepley* v. *Davis*, 5 Taunt. 617 ; 1 Marsh. 252, S. C.; and *Withers* v. *Lyss*, 4 Campb. 237 ; 1 Holt's N. P. C. 18, S. C.

(l) *Hanson* v. *Meyer*, 6 East, 614. See also *Zagury* v. *Furnell*, 2 Campb. 240.

the payment of price was the only act necessary to be performed,
in order to vest the property; in this case, another act was necessary to precede both payment of price and delivery of the goods
bargained for, *viz.* weighing. Until the starch was weighed, the
warehouse-keeper, as agent of the defendant, was not authorized
to deliver it; still less was the buyer authorized to take it by his
own act from the warehouse: and if he could not so take it, neither
can he maintain an action of trover founded on such a supposed
right to take, or in other words, founded on such supposed right of
property in the subject matter of his action. But where every
thing has been done by the sellers which they contracted to do,
the proper will in many cases pass to the buyers, although the
goods still continue in the possession of the sellers. As where tur-
pentine in casks was sold by auction (*m*) at so much per cwt., and
the casks were to be taken at a certain marked quantity, except the
two last, out of which the seller was to fill up the rest, before they
were delivered to the purchasers, on which account the two last
casks were to be sold at uncertain quantities; and a deposit was to
be paid by the buyers, at the time of the sale, and the remainder
within thirty days on the goods being delivered; and the buyers
had the option of keeping the goods in the warehouse, at the charge
of the seller, for those thirty days, after which they were to pay the
rent; and the buyers having employed the warehouseman of the
seller as their agent, he filled up some of the casks out of the two
last, but left the bungs out, in order to enable the custom-house
officer to gauge them; but before he could fill up the rest, a fire
consumed the whole in the warehouse within the thirty days. It
was holden, that the property passed to the buyers in all the casks
which were filled up, because nothing further remained to be done
to them by the seller; for it was the business of the buyers to get
them gauged, without which they could not have been removed; and
the act of the warehouseman in leaving them unbunged after filling
them up, which was for the purpose of the gauging, must be taken
to have been done as agent for the buyers, whose concern the
gauging was. But the property in the casks not filled up remained
in the seller, at whose risk they continued. So where the oats in a
particular bin, which contained nothing else, were sold, and a bill
accepted at the same time for the price; it was holden (*n*), that the
property vested in the buyer, for nothing remained to be done
for the purpose of ascertaining the identity or quantity of the
goods.

Special Property.—A special property is, where he who has the
possession of goods, holds them subject to the claims of other

---

(*m*) *Rugg* v. *Minett*, 11 East, 210. See   (*n*) *Swanwick* v. *Sothern*, 9 A. & E.
also *Tarling* v. *Baxter*, 6 B. & C. 360.   895; 1 P. & D. 648; *ante*, p. 1273.

persons (o) (3). This is sufficient to enable him to maintain trover against a stranger. Hence this action may be brought:—By a bailee (p): By a carrier (q): By lessee for life against a stranger, who takes away the timber of a house which has been blown down; for the lessee for life has a special property to make use of the timber (as if he would rebuild), though the general property be in the reversioner (r): By a lord who seizes an estray or wreck, against a stranger, before the year and day are expired (s): By a sheriff against a person who takes away goods (which have been seized by the sheriff in execution,) before they are sold (t). But a landlord who has distrained goods, cannot maintain trover for them (u); for he had at common law a power to detain the goods as a pledge only, and although by statute he is authorized to sell, yet he has not any property. The party, however, purchasing the goods distrained, may maintain trover (x), though the distress be irregular. In addition to these instances of special property, it is to be observed, that there may be special property without possession, or there may be special property arising simply out of a lawful possession, and which ceases when the true owner appears: as where a chimney-sweeper's boy having found a jewel (y), carried it to a goldsmith, to be informed what it was, who refused to return it; it was holden, that though the boy, who was the plaintiff, did not by such finding acquire an absolute property in the jewel, yet he had such a property as would enable him to keep it against all persons except the rightful owner, and consequently that he might maintain trover for it against the goldsmith, who was a wrong-doer. So a possession under the rightful owner is sufficient against a person having no colour of right. As where the plaintiff bought and paid for a ship stranded on the coast, but did not comply with the regulations of the Register Acts; he endeavoured for several days to get the ship off, but without success; at length she went to pieces. The defendant having possessed

(o) Per *Lawrence*, J., in *Webb* v. *Fox*, 7 T. R. 398.
(p) Bro. Trespass, 92; *Arnold* v. *Jefferson*, Lord Raym. 275.
(q) *Goodwin* v. *Richardson*, 1 Rol. Abr. 4, (I) pl. 1.
(r) Per *Powell*, J., Midland Circuit, Salk. MSS.; Bull. N. P. 33.
(s) *Sir W. Courtenay's* case, C. B.,

Salk. MSS.; *Pye* v. *Pleydell*, Berks, 1750, per *Clarke*, B., S. P., Bull. N. P. 33.
(t) *Wilbraham* v. *Snow*, 2 Saund. 47.
(u) *Moneux* v. *Goreham*, per *Probyn*, C. B., at Huntingdon, 29 MSS., Serjt. Hill, 279.
(x) *Lyon* v. *Weldon*, 2 Bingh. 334.
(y) *Armory* v. *Delamirie*, 1 Str. 505, Middlesex Sittings, coram *Pratt*, C. J.

---

(3) "The immediate right to real property must be vested in one person only, [or in several persons in the same right;] whereas a special property, in the case of personalty, may be in one, as in the instance of carriers, while the absolute right to it may exist in another. When a competition arises between those two persons, the right of the latter must prevail; but as against all other persons a special property is sufficient." Per Lord *Kenyon*, C. J., 7 T. R. 396.

himself of parts of the wreck which had drifted on his farm; it was
holden (z), that the plaintiff had sufficient property in him to enable
him to maintain trover against a wrong-doer; for as far as regarded
the possession of the plaintiff, it was good as against all except the
vendor; and although the plaintiff had no absolute property as
against the vendor, yet he claimed under him, and had the possession
against those who tortiously took the goods without colour of right.
So where K., the owner of furniture, lent it to plaintiff under the
terms of a written agreement; plaintiff placed it in a house occupied
by the wife of C., a bankrupt; C.'s assignees having seized the furniture; it was holden (a), that plaintiff might maintain trover
without producing the agreement. In the case (b) of a simple
bailment of a chattel without reward, it may be recovered either by
the bailor or the bailee, if taken wrongfully out of the bailee's possession. There is one case in which a temporary property (c) merely
has been holden sufficient to maintain trover : as where defendant,
having agreed to sell the plaintiff an estate, with the usual proviso,
that in case the vendor could not make a title, the contract should
be void, delivered to the plaintiff an abstract of the title. The
plaintiff laid this abstract before counsel, and having received it back
with an opinion written at the foot, and several queries in the
margin, he left it with the defendant, requesting him to copy the
opinion and marginal observations, and return the abstract as soon
as he had copied them. After the plaintiff had several times in vain
applied to have the abstract returned, at length he made a formal
demand of it, when the defendant refused to re-deliver it, observing
that as he had been unable to clear up the objections of the plaintiff's
counsel, the abstract would be useless to the plaintiff. The plaintiff
having brought an action of trover for the abstract; it was holden,
that he was entitled to recover; *Chambre*, J., observing, that as to
the general property in the abstract, while the contract is open, it
is neither in the vendor nor in the vendee absolutely, but if the sale
goes on, it is the property of the vendee; if the sale is broken off, it
is the property of the vendor. In the mean time the vendee has a
temporary property, and a right to keep it, even if the title be
rejected, until the dispute be finally settled, for his own justification,
in order to show on what ground he did reject the title. Trover
will lie for bills of exchange indorsed to an agent of the plaintiff's (d)
or order, for their account, and deposited with the defendants, by
such agent, as a security for past and future advances by the
defendants to him.

2. *Right of Possession.*—The plaintiff must not only have a right
of property but a right of possession also, and unless both these

(z) *Sutton* v. *Buck*, 2 Taunt. 302.
(a) *Burton* v. *Hughes and others*, 2
Bingh. 173.
(b) *Nicolls* v. *Bastard*, 2 Cr. M. & R.
659; 1 Tyr. & Gr. 156.

(c) *Roberts* v. *Wyatt*, 2 Taunt. 268.
(d) *Treuttel and Wurts* v. *Barandon*,
8 Taunt. 100, recognized in *Evans* v. *Kymer*, 1 B. & Ad. 535.

rights concur, the action will not lie. Hence where a person leased
a house with the furniture therein (e), to another for a certain time,
and during the term the furniture was taken in execution by the
sheriff, at the suit of J. S., against the person to whom the furniture formerly belonged ; it was holden, that the landlord could not
maintain trover against the sheriff for the value of the furniture,
because the landlord had not the right of possession during the
demise ; the tenant's property and interest did not determine by the
sheriff's trespass ; the tenant might have maintained trespass
against the wrong-doer, and recovered damages. It is to be remarked, that in the foregoing case, the goods removed were personal
chattels, and at the time of the seizure continued to be in the qualified possession of the tenant, which the lessor agreed he should
have. But where certain mill-machinery, together with a mill, had
been demised for a term to a tenant, and he without permission of
his landlord severed the machinery from the mill ; and it was afterwards seized under a fi. fa. by the sheriff, and sold by him (f) ; it
was holden, that no property passed to the vendee, and that the
landlord was entitled to bring trover for the machinery, even during
the continuance of the term. A., a hop-merchant, on several days
in August, sold to B., by contract, various parcels of hops ; part of
them were weighed, and an account of the weights together with
samples delivered to the vendee. The usual time of payment in the
trade was the second Saturday subsequent to the purchase. B. did
not pay for the hops at the usual time ; whereupon A. gave notice,
that unless they were paid for by a certain day, they would be resold.
The hops were not paid for, and A. resold a part with the consent
of B., who afterwards became a bankrupt, and then A. sold the
residue of the hops, without the assent of B. or his assignees.
Account sales of the hops so sold, were delivered to B., in which he
was charged warehouse-rent from the 30th of August. The assignees of B. demanded the hops of A., and tendered the warehouse-
rent, charges, &c., and A. having refused to deliver to them, brought
trover. The jury found that defendant had not rescinded the
contract of sale : it was holden (g), that the assignees were not
entitled to maintain trover to recover the value of the hops ; inasmuch, as the party must have not only a right of property, but a
right of possession ; and that although a vendee of goods acquires a
right of property by the contract of sale (h), yet he does not acquire
a right of possession to the goods, until he pays or tenders the price.
So where the defendants sold to the plaintiffs wheat, for which the
plaintiffs were to pay by a draft on a London banker : the defendants
delivered the wheat to a carrier, and sent the bill of lading to the

(e) *Gordon* v. *Harper*, 7 T. R. 9 ; *Pain*
v. *Whittaker*, 1 Ry. & M. 99, S. P., per
Abbott, C. J. ; *Fraser* v. *Swansea Canal*,
1 A. & E. 354 ; 3 Nev. & M. 391 ; *Owen*
v. *Knight*, 4 Bingh. N. C. 54 ; 5 Sc. 307.

(f) *Farrant* v. *Thompson*, 5 B. & A.
826.
(g) *Bloxam* v. *Sanders*, 4 B. & C. 941.
See *Winks* v. *Hassall*, 9 B. & C. 372.
(h) See *ante*, p. 1347, 8.

plaintiffs, but took the wheat again, and sold it before it came to the plaintiffs' possession, because the plaintiffs failed to send a draft on a London banker ; it was holden, that the plaintiffs could not sue the defendants in trover for the wheat (i).

The right of possession is sufficient without having had actual possession (4). Hence (k), where in trover the plaintiff, as executor, declared upon the possession of his testator, it was holden to be sufficient ; because the personal property of the testator was vested in the executor ; and no other person having a right to the possession, the property drew after it the possession in law. So if A. be indebted (l) to C., and B. indebted to A., and it is agreed between them that B. shall deliver goods to C., in satisfaction of the debt due from A. to C., and B. afterwards converts the goods to his own use, C. may maintain trover against B., though C. never had possession ; for by the agreement the right was in C., and the conversion a wrong done to him.

3. *Personal Goods.*—The subject matter of this action is confined to *personal* goods. Hence trover will not lie for things fixed to the freehold. Questions respecting the right of what are ordinarily called *fixtures* principally arise between three classes of persons (m) ;

1st. Between different descriptions of representatives of the same owner of the inheritance, *viz.* between the heir and executor. In the first case, *i. e.* as between heir and executor, the rule obtains with the utmost rigour in favour of the inheritance, and against the right to disannex therefrom, and to consider as a personal chattel any thing which has been affixed to the freehold or inheritance.

2dly. Between the executor of tenant for life, or in tail, and the remainder-man or reversioner ; in which case the right to fixtures is considered more favourably for executors than in the preceding case between heir and executor.

In deciding whether a particular fixed instrument, machine, or even building, should be considered as removable by the executor as between the executor and the heir, or between the executor and the person in remainder, the court, in the three principal cases on this

(i) *Wilmshurst* v. *Bowker*, 5 Bingh. N. C. 541.

(k) *Hudson* v. *Hudson*, Latch. 214, cited by *Lawrence*, J., 7 T. R. 13.

(l) *Flewellin* v. *Rave*, 1 Buls. 68, cited in Bull. N. P. 35.

(m) Per Lord *Ellenborough*, C. J., delivering the judgment of the court in *Elwes* v. *Maw*, 3 East, 51.

(4) Hence, on the trial of an ejectment for a mine, it was holden, that a recovery in trover for a parcel of lead dug out of the mine was not evidence of the plaintiff's possession. *Lord Cullen's* case at bar, B. R., Bull. N. P. 33.

subject, viz. *Lawton* v. *Lawton*, 3 Atk. 13, which was the case of a fire-engine to work a colliery, erected by tenant for life; *Lord Dudley* v. *Lord Warde*, Ambler, 113, which was also the case of a fire-engine to work a colliery, erected by tenant for life; (these two cases before Lord *Hardwicke;*) and *Lawton, Executor*, v. *Salmon*, E. 22 Geo. III., B. P. B. 188; Dampier MSS., L. I. L.; 1 H. Blac. 259, in notis, before Lord *Mansfield*, which was the case of salt-pans (n), and which came on in the shape of an action of trover, brought for the salt-pans, by the executor against the tenant of the heir at law, the court may be considered as having decided mainly on this ground, that *where the fixed instrument, engine, or utensil (and the building covering the same falls within the same principle,) was an accessory to a matter of a personal nature, that it should be itself considered as personalty.* The fire-engine, in the cases in 3 Atk. and Ambler, was an accessory to the carrying on the trade of getting and vending coals, a matter of a personal nature. Lord *Hardwicke* says, in the case in Ambler, " A colliery is not only an enjoyment of the estate, but in part carrying on a trade." And in the case in 3 Atk. he says, " One reason that weighs with me is, its being a mixed case, between enjoying the profits of the land, and carrying on a species of trade; and considering it in this light, it comes very near the instances in brewhouses, &c. of furnaces and coppers." Upon the same principle, Lord C. B. *Comyns* may be considered as having decided (o), that a cider-mill should go to the executor and not to the heir, *i. e.* as a mixed case between enjoying the profits of the land, and carrying on a species of trade, and as considering the cider-mill as properly an accessory to the trade of making cider. In the case of the salt-pans, Lord *Mansfield* does not seem to have considered them as accessory to the carrying on a trade, but as merely the means of enjoying the benefit of the inheritance. He says, " *The salt-spring is a valuable inheritance*, but no profit arises from it, unless there be a salt-work, which consists of a building, &c. for the purpose of containing the pans, &c., which are fixed to the ground. *The inheritance cannot be enjoyed without them. They are accessories necessary to the enjoyment of the principal. The owner erected them for the benefit of the inheritance.*" Upon this principle he considered them as belonging to the heir, as parcel of the inheritance, for the enjoyment of which they were made, and not as belonging to the executor, as the means or instrument of carrying on a trade." Per Lord *Ellenborough*, C. J., delivering the opinion of the court in *Elwes* v. *Maw*, 3 East, 53, 54. In trover, by the executor against the heir, *Lee*, C. J., held, that hangings, tapestry, and iron backs to chimnies, belonged to the executor, who recovered accordingly against the heir (p). Standing

(n) See *Earl of Mansfield* v. *Blackburne*,   3 Atk. 13, 16.
6 Bingh. N. C. 426.   (p) *Harvey* v. *Harvey*, Str. 1141.
(o) In a case cited in *Lawton* v. *Lawton*,

corn belongs to a devisee of land, and not to the executor (*q*), but a legatee of goods and stock on the farm (*r*), shall take it from both. It is agreed, however, that as between the executor and the heir, if there be not any devisee of the land, the executor is entitled to standing corn (*s*).

The 3rd case, and that in which the greatest latitude and indulgence has always been allowed in favour of the claim to having any particular articles considered as personal chattels, as against the claim in respect of freehold or inheritance, is the case between landlord and tenant. It is a general rule, that where a lessee having annexed any personal chattel to the freehold during his term, afterwards takes it away, it is waste. Some exceptions have been engrafted on this rule: 1st, In favour of utensils set up in relation to trade (*t*); 2nd, Of matters of ornament, as *pier glasses, hangings* (*u*), cornices (*x*), wainscot fixed only by screws, pump erected by tenant, and slightly affixed, so as to be capable of being removed entire (*y*) (5). These the tenant may remove during the original term, and during such further period of possession by him, as he holds the premises under a right still to consider himself as tenant (*z*). But if he does not remove them during that time, they become the property (*a*) of the landlord. A lessee cannot (*b*), even during his term, maintain *trover* for fixtures *remaining affixed* to the freehold, for the principle of law is, that whatsoever is planted in the soil belongs to the soil; and though the tenant has a right to remove fixtures of this nature during his term, or during what may, for this purpose, be considered as an excrescence on his term, they are not goods and chattels at all, but parcel of the freehold, and as such not

---

(*q*) *Spencer's* case, Winch, 51; Harg. Co. Litt. 55, b. n. (2).

(*r*) *Cox* v. *Godsalve*, 6 East, 604, n.; *West* v. *Moore*, 8 East, 339.

(*s*) See the authorities cited in Harg. Co. Litt. 55, b. n. (2).

(*t*) *Penton* v. *Robart*, 2 East, 88.

(*u*) *Beck* v. *Rebow*, 1 P. Wms. 94.

(*x*) See *Avery* v. *Cheslyn*, 3 A. & E. 75; 5 Nev. & M. 372.

(*y*) *Grymes* v. *Boweren*, 6 Bingh. 437.

(*z*) Agreed in *Minshall* v. *Lloyd*, 2 M. & W. 450; *Weeton* v. *Woodcock*, 7 M. & W. 14.

(*a*) *Lyde* v. *Russell*, case of Bells, 1 B. & Ad. 394.

(*b*) *Mackintosh* v. *Trotter*, 3 M. & W. 184, recognizing *Minshall* v. *Lloyd*, 2 M. & W. 450.

---

(5) " During the term the tenant may take away chimney-pieces, and even wainscot, which is a very strong case, but not after the term; if he did, he would be a trespasser." Per *Hardwicke*, Ch., 1 Atk. 477. See also Ambl. 113. But tenant remaining in possession, after the expiration of the term, may remove fixtures annexed to the freehold, for the purpose of carrying on trade. *Penton* v. *Robart*, 2 East, 88. " What would have been held to be waste in the time of Henry the 7th*, as removing wainscot fixed only by screws, and marble chimney-pieces, is now allowed to be done." Per Lord *Hardwicke*, Ch., in *Lawton* v. *Lawton*, 3 Atk. 15.

* See also *Herlakenden's* case, 31 Eliz., 4 Rep. 64.

recoverable in trover. A covenant by a tenant, to yield up in repair, at the expiration of his lease, all buildings which should be erected, during the term, upon the demised premises, includes buildings erected and used by the tenant for the purpose of trade and manufacture, if such buildings be let into the soil, or otherwise fixed to the freehold (c), but not where they merely rest upon blocks or pattens. A barn erected by the tenant upon pattens and blocks of timber lying upon the ground, but not fixed in or to the ground, may be removed (d). So where certain parts of a machine had been put up by the tenant during his term, and were capable of being removed without either injuring the other parts of the machine or the building, and had been usually valued between the outgoing and incoming tenant; it was holden (e), that these were the goods and chattels of the outgoing tenant, for which he might maintain trover. In *R.* v. *Otley* (f), a wooden mill, resting by mere weight upon a foundation of brick, was holden not to be part of the freehold, so as to contribute to the value of a tenement on a question of settlement. And so a tenant, who had erected on a foundation of brick and stone let into the ground, a wooden barn, which rested upon the foundation by weight alone, was holden (g) to be entitled to remove it at the expiration of his term. But a tenant for mere agricultural purposes cannot remove buildings fixed to the freehold, which have been constructed by such tenant for the ordinary purposes of husbandry, and are not connected with any description of trade (h). Things of an ornamental nature may be in a degree affixed, and yet, *during the term*, may be removed : on the other hand, there may be that sort of fixing or annexation, which, though the thing annexed may have been merely for ornament, will yet make the removal of it waste. Hence a conservatory erected by tenant for years, (who had a remainder for life after the death of his lessor,) on a brick foundation attached to a dwelling house, and communicating with it by windows opening into the conservatory, and a flue passing into the parlour chimney, was considered (i) as part of the freehold, and not removable by the tenant or his assignees.

There is no doubt that by a conveyance, whether to a purchaser or a mortgagee, fixtures annexed to the freehold will pass, unless there be some words in the deed to exclude them (k). The owner of a freehold house, in which there were various fixtures, sold it by auction. Nothing was said about the fixtures. A conveyance of the house was executed, and possession given to the purchaser, the fixtures still remaining in the house; it was holden (l), that they

---

(c) *Naylor* v. *Collinge*, 1 Taunt. 19.
(d) *Culling* v. *Tufnel*, per *Treby*, C. J., at Hereford, 1694, Bull. N. P. 34.
(e) *Davis* v. *Jones*, 2 B. & A. 165.
(f) 1 B. & Ad. 161.
(g) *Wansbrough* v. *Maton*, 4 A. & E. 884.

(h) *Elwes* v. *Maw*, 3 East; 38.
(i) *Buckland* v. *Butterfield*, 2 B. & B. 54.
(k) Per *Parke*, B., in *Hitchman* v. *Walton*, 4 M. & W. 416.
(l) *Colegrave* v. *Dias Santos*, 2 B. & C. 76. See also *Longstaff* v. *Meagoe*, 2 A. & E. 170; 4 Nev. & M. 211.

passed by the conveyance of the freehold; and that even if they did not, the vendor, after giving up the possession, could not maintain trover for them. A few articles which were not fixtures, were also left in the house : the demand described them, together with the other articles, as fixtures, and the refusal was of the *fixtures demanded;* it was holden (*m*), that upon this evidence, the plaintiff could not recover them in this action. Where a lessee for years mortgaged his lease and all his estate and interest in the premises, and afterwards became bankrupt; it was holden (*n*), that the mortgagee might declare in case as reversioner against the assignee of the tenant for the removal of the fixtures from the premises, whereby they were injured; and that he was also entitled to recover in trover against such assignee the value of all the fixtures, whether landlord's or tenant's, which were affixed to the premises before the execution of the mortgage; although there was a covenant in the original lease to the mortgagor to deliver up to the lessor at the determination of the term all fixtures and things to the premises belonging and to belong. This action may be maintained for an undivided part of a chattel, *e. g.*, three fourths of a ship (*o*).

4. *Conversion.*—It must appear that the defendant has been guilty of a wrongful conversion. The wrongful conversion by the defendant is considered as the gist of the action. If A. take the horse of B. (*p*), and ride him, and after deliver him to B., yet B. may maintain trover against A., for the riding was a conversion, and the re-delivery will not bar the action, although it will go in mitigation of damages. Drawing out part of the liquor in a vessel, and filling it up with water, is a conversion of the liquor (*q*). But the mere taking away or destroying a part of the property which remains in the hands of a bailee, is not such a conversion (*r*) that the owner may sue in trover for the whole. If A. find the goods of B., and, upon the demand of the goods, answer that he knows not whether B. is the true owner, and therefore refuses to deliver them; this is not evidence of a conversion, if A. keep them for the true owner (*s*). A person is guilty of a conversion who takes the property of one person by assignment from another, who has not any authority to dispose of it (6). A. (*t*), a tobacco broker, purchased in his own

(*m*) *Colegrave* v. *Dias Santos*, 2 B. & C. 76.

(*n*) *Hitchman* v. *Walton*, 4 M. & W. 409.

(*o*) *Watson* v. *King*, 4 Campb. 272.

(*p*) *Countess of Rutland's* case, T. 38 Eliz. B. R., 1 Rol. Abr. 5, (L.) pl. 1.

(*q*) *Richardson* v. *Atkinson*, Middlesex Sittings, coram *Eyre* and *Fortescue*, (ab-

sente, C. J.) 1 Str. 576.

(*r*) Per *Patteson* and *Coleridge*, Js., in *Philpott* v. *Kelley*, 3 A. & E. 116, 7; 4 Nev. & M. 611.

(*s*) Per *Coke*, C. J., 2 Bulst. 312.

(*t*) *M'Combie* v. *Davies*, 6 East, 538, cited by *Denman*, C. J., in *Weeding* v. *Aldrich*, 9 A. & E. 865.

(6) " Assuming to oneself the property and right of disposing of another man's goods is a conversion." Per *Holt*, C. J., in *Baldwin* v. *Cole*, 6 Mod. 221, recognized by Lord *Ellenborough*, C. J., in 6 East, 540.

name, for the plaintiff, some tobacco, which was then in the king's warehouse, and afterwards pledged the same, in his own name, with the defendant, for a sum of money, and transferred it into the defendant's name in the king's warehouse. The defendant was informed of the plaintiff's right to the tobacco, and was applied to, both by the plaintiff and the broker, to deliver the same to the plaintiff, but the defendant refused to make the transfer, or to give an order for the delivery. It was holden, that the acts of the defendant amounted to a conversion. So a servant may be guilty of a conversion, although the act be done by him for the benefit of his master (u); "for a person is guilty of a conversion who intermeddles with my (x) property and disposes of it, and it is no answer that he acted under authority from another, who had himself no authority to dispose of it." But it is to be observed that this was the case of an actual conversion by the servant. For where goods, the property of the plaintiff, had been, by the servants of an insurance company, carried to a warehouse, of which the defendant, a servant of the company, kept the key, and the defendant, on being applied to by the plaintiff to deliver them up, refused to do so without an order from the company; it was holden (y), that this was not such a refusal as amounted to a conversion of the goods by the defendant. In a case where the defendant had taken the plaintiff's boat for the purpose of assisting the plaintiff (z), and from a motive of kindness to the plaintiff, and the boat was sunk in the endeavour, Lord *Ellenborough*, C. J., was of opinion, that the act of the defendant could not be deemed an illegal conversion. Trover will lie for the misdelivery of goods by a warehouseman, although such misdelivery has occurred (a) by mistake only. With respect to negotiable instruments, *e. g.*, bank notes, possession is *primâ facie* evidence of property; and persons holding them cannot, without strong evidence of fraud, be compelled by any prior holder, who may have been robbed, to disclose the manner in which they received them (b). "For the purpose of rendering bills of exchange negotiable, the right of property in them passes with the bills. Every holder, with the bills, takes the property, and his title is stamped upon the bills themselves. The property and the possession are inseparable. This was

(u) *Stephens* v. *Elwall*, 4 M. & S. 259; *Cranch* v. *White*, 1 Scott, 314; 1 Bingh. N. C. 414.
(x) Per Lord *Ellenborough*, C. J., in *Stephens* v. *Elwall*.
(y) *Alexander* v. *Southey*, 5 B. & A. 247.
(z) *Drake* v. *Shorter*, 4 Esp. N. P. C. 165.
(a) *Devereux* v. *Barclay*, 2 B. & A. 702.
(b) *King* v. *Milsom*, 2 Campb. 5.

The very taking of goods from one who has no right to dispose of them is a conversion. *Hurst* v. *Gwennap*, 2 Stark. N. P. C. 306. See also *Carlisle* v. *Garland*, 7 Bingh. 298; *Robson* v. *Rolls*, 1 M. & Rob. 239.

necessary to make them negotiable, and in this respect they differ essentially from goods of which the property and possession may be in different persons " (c). An exchequer bill, the blank in which was not filled up, having been placed for sale in the hands of A., he, instead of selling it, deposited it at his banker's, who made him advances to the amount of the value. A. afterwards becoming bankrupt, it was holden (d), that the owner of the exchequer bill could not maintain trover against the bankers, the property in such an exchequer bill, like bank-notes and bills of exchange indorsed in blank, passing by delivery. A banker discounts a bill drawn on a customer, and, by acceptance, made payable at his bank, after notice that it has been lost by the holder, and afterwards debits his customer with the amount of the bill, and writes a discharge on it, and delivers it up to the customer as the banker's voucher of his account; it was holden (e), that the banker is thereby guilty of a conversion, and the loser of the bill may recover in trover without previous demand of the bill. Although it appears formerly to have been doubted whether in the case of a tortious taking, the plaintiff was not confined to an action of trespass, yet it is now agreed, in such case, that the plaintiff has his election to bring either trespass or trover; for a tort may be qualified, though it cannot be increased (f). If A. lodges jewels, sealed up, at a banker's, for safe custody only (g), and the banker breaks open the box, and *pawns* the jewels to another, A. may maintain trover against the pawnee for the conversion of the jewels to his own use. In an action of trover for plate (h), it appeared that the plaintiff claimed under a remainder-man, against the defendant, to whom it was pawned by the tenant for life. That I. S., by will, gave his plate to trustees for the use of his wife, *durante viduitate*, requiring her to sign an inventory, which she did at the time the plate was delivered into her possession. She afterwards pawned it with the defendant for a valuable consideration, who had no notice of the settlement, and before the commencement of this action she died. A demand and refusal was proved. After verdict for plaintiff, the court were of opinion, on a case reserved, that the defendant was bound to deliver up the plate, without being paid the money he had advanced on it, observing, that the point was clearly established, and the law must remain as it is, until the legislature thought fit to provide, that the possession of such chattels shall be a proof of ownership. By stat. 1 Jac. I. c. 21, the sale of any goods wrongfully taken to any *pawnbroker* in London, or within two miles thereof, shall not alter the property. If goods stolen are pawned, the owner may maintain trover against the pawnbroker (i).

(c) Per *Eyre*, C. J., delivering the opinion of the court in *Collins* v. *Martin*, 1 Bos. & Pul. 651.

(d) *Wookey* v. *Pole*, 4 B. & A. 1, per three justices, *Bayley*, J., dissentient.

(e) *Lovell* v. *Martin*, 4 Taunt. 799.

(f) *Bishop* v. *Montague*, Cro. Eliz. 824;

Cro. Jac. 50, S. C.

(g) *Hartop* v. *Hoare*, Str. 1187, more fully reported in 3 Atk. 44, and 1 Wils. 8.

(h) *Hoare* v. *Parker*, 2 T..R. 376.

(i) *Packer* v. *Gillies*, 2 Campb. 336, n., Lord *Ellenborough*, C. J.

N. In this case the goods had been stolen from the plaintiff's house and pawned with defendant by a person who had been tried for the felony, and acquitted on the absence of a material witness. A pawnbroker has no right to sell unredeemed pledges (*k*) after the expiration of a year from the time the goods were pledged, if the original owner tender him the principal and interest due. A pawnbroker, who, in taking pledges, omits to pursue the course required by stat. 40 Geo. III. c. 99, s. 6, acquires no property in the pledges, and cannot maintain a lien on them against the assignees of a pawner who afterwards becomes bankrupt (*l*). A wharf, even in London, is not a market overt (*m*) for the articles bought there. A person having three bills of exchange, applied to a country banker, with whom he had not had any previous dealings, to give for them a bill on London of the same amount; this bill was afterwards dishonoured: it was holden (*n*), that as there was a complete exchange of securities, trover would not lie for the three bills of exchange. If a tradesman sell goods to be paid for on delivery, and his servant by mistake delivers them without receiving the money, he may, after demand and refusal to deliver or pay, bring trover (*o*) for the goods against the purchaser. So where iron was to be delivered under a contract that certain bills outstanding against the plaintiff should be taken out of circulation, and after part of the iron had been delivered, and no bills had been taken out of circulation, the plaintiff stopped the further delivery, and brought trover for what had been delivered; it was holden (*p*), that the action would lie. If, upon an information of seizure, the goods be condemned, no action will lie for them. But if there be no condemnation, and the goods were not liable to be seized, trespass or trover will lie against the officer for them (*q*). But by stat. 3 & 4 Will. IV. c. 53, s. 102, if the judge certify on the record, that there was a probable cause for such seizure, then the plaintiff, beside his ship or goods so seized, or the value thereof, shall not be entitled to above twopence damages, nor to any costs of suit.

Formerly, if goods had been obtained from A. by fraud (*r*), and pawned to B. without notice, and A. prosecuted the offender to conviction, and got possession of his goods, B. might maintain trover for them, for this was distinguishable from the case of felony, where the owner's right of restitution was given by positive statute (21 Hen. VIII. c. 11); but this statute has been repealed by 7 & 8 Geo. IV. c. 27, s. 1; and the stat. 7 & 8 Geo. IV. c. 29, s. 57, substitutes other enactments as to restitution, and extends them

(*k*) *Walter* v. *Smith*, 5 B. & A. 439.
(*l*) *Fergusson* v. *Norman*, 5 Bingh. N. C. 76.
(*m*) *Wilkinson* v. *King*, 2 Campb. 335.
(*n*) *Hornblower* v. *Proud*, 2 B. & A. 327.
(*o*) Per *Bayley*, J., 2 B. & A. 329, n.

(*p*) *Bishop* v. *Shillito*, 2 B. & A. 329, n.
(*q*) *Tinkler* v. *Poole*, 3 Wils. 146; 5 Burr. 2657.
(*r*) *Parker* v. *Patrick*, 5 T. R. 175. See *Irving* v. *Motly*, 7 Bingh. 549, and *Peer* v. *Humphrey*, 2 A. & E. 495; *ante*, p. 1345.

to the case of goods obtained by fraud, as well as by felony. In the foregoing case the absolute property in the goods was obtained by fraud; but if the vendor (s) of a leasehold estate delivers the conveyance as an escrow to take effect on payment of the residue of the purchase money, the property in the title deeds is so vested in the vendee, that the vendor obtaining possession of them and pawning them, confers on the pawnee no right to detain them after tender of the residue of the purchase money. When property in land passes by a deed, the property in the deed passes with it (t). An estate was conveyed in 1803 by J. B. to W. H., who in 1812 conveyed it to A. H., and he sold it in 1826 to the plaintiff. The first vendor did not deliver up the title deeds. In 1824 he was sued by A. H., the then owner of the estate, for the deeds, and a verdict was recovered against him, but the judgment was not docquetted. The first vendor absconded, and in 1825 obtained a sum of money as on a mortgage of the estate from one of the defendants, with whom he deposited the deeds. On trover brought in 1829, after demand and refusal; it was holden (u), that the plaintiff, being the legal owner of the estate, might recover the deeds without tendering the mortgage-money. By a postnuptial contract, B. conveyed to plaintiffs, as trustees for his wife, property, the title deeds of which he obtained from the trustees, and deposited with the defendants as a security for money advanced; it was holden (x), that the plaintiffs were entitled to maintain trover for the deeds; for upon the deposit the defendant acquired no more than a right to go into a court of equity to compel a legal conveyance, and such right did not constitute the defendants purchasers within the stat. 27 Eliz. c. 4, s. 2, which enacts, " that every conveyance of land made for the intent to defraud such persons as have purchased in fee simple, fee tail, for lives or years, the same land so formerly conveyed, shall be deemed to be utterly void." As the master (y) of a ship has no general authority by law, in the absence of his employers, to *sell* the ship intrusted to his care, but only an implied authority to act for the benefit of the concern, exercising a sound discretion, such as the owner himself would exercise if he were upon the spot, it follows, that the owner of a ship may recover in an action of trover the value of the same from a vendee claiming by purchase from the master, unless the vendee can show that the ship was sold by the master under such an urgent necessity as would have induced the owner to have sold the ship if he had been present. So although the captain of a ship find it impossible to reach his port of destination, he has not any implied

(s) *Hooper* v. *Ramsbottom*, 6 Taunt. 12.
(t) *Lord* v. *Wardle*, 3 Bingh. N. C. 680.
(u) *Harrington* v. *Price and another*, 3 B. & Ad. 170..
(x) *Kerrison* v. *Dorrien*, 9 Bingh. 76.

(y) *Hayman* v. *Moulton*, Abbott, p. 8, ed. 5th; and 5 Esp. N. P. C. 65, *S. C.*; *Reid* v. *Darby*, 10 East, 143, cited by *Parke*, B., in *Hunter* v. *Parker*, 7 M. & W. 342; *ante*, p. 1222.

authority, as the agent of the shippers, to sell the cargo for their benefit in a foreign port into which he is driven; and if he does so, although it should appear that he acted *bonâ fide* for the interest of all persons concerned in the adventure, yet such sale will be considered as a tortious conversion, for which the ship-owner is liable (*z*). The captain of a ship has no authority to sell the cargo, except in cases of absolute necessity; and therefore where, in the course of a voyage from India, the ship was wrecked off the Cape of Good Hope, and some indigo, which was part of the cargo, was saved, and the same was there sold by public auction, by the authority of the captain, acting *bonâ fide* according to the best of his judgment, for the benefit of all persons concerned, but the jury found that there was no absolute necessity for the sale; it was holden (*a*), that the purchaser at such sale acquired no title, and the indigo having been sent to this country, the original owners were held entitled to recover its value. As to the master's power to *hypothecate* his cargo, see *ante*, p. 1028, n. A. entrusted B. with goods to sell in India (*b*), agreeing to take back from B. what he should not be able to sell, and allowing him what he should obtain beyond a certain price, with liberty to sell them for what he could get, if he could not obtain that price. B., not having been able to sell the goods in India himself, left them with an agent to be disposed of by him, directing the agent to remit the money to him (B.) in England. It was holden, that A. could not maintain trover against B. for the goods. Where goods were placed in the hands of a factor for sale, and he indorsed the bills of lading to the defendants, who thereupon accepted a bill for him, and he, at the same time, directed the defendants to sell the goods and reimburse themselves the amount of the bill out of the proceeds: it was holden (*c*), that the defendants, having sold the goods, could not be sued for them in trover by the original owner. It seems, that the original owner might have maintained an action for money had and received for the proceeds, and that the defendants could not have retained the amount of the money advanced to the factor. Trover will not lie for goods irregularly sold under a distress (*d*); the statute 11 Geo. II. c. 19, s. 19, having declared that the party selling should not be deemed a trespasser *ab initio*, and having given an action on the case to the party grieved by such sale. But if a party pay money in order to redeem his goods from a wrongful distress for rent (*e*), he may maintain trover against the wrong-doer. So trover will lie by the assignees of a bankrupt against a sheriff (*f*), who sells goods to satisfy an invalid as well as a valid execution against a bankrupt in order to recover the surplus.

(*z*) *Van Omeron* v. *Dowick*, 2 Campb. 42.

(*a*) *Freeman and another* v. *The East India Company*, 5 B. & A. 617.

(*b*) *Bromley* v. *Coxwell*, 2 Bos. & Pul. 438.

(*c*) *Stierneld* v. *Holden and others*, 4 B. & C. 5.

(*d*) *Wallace* v. *King*, 1 H. Bl. 13.

(*e*) *Shipwick* v. *Blanchard*, 6 T. R. 298.

(*f*) *Stead* v. *Gascoigne*, 8 Taunt. 527.

II. *By whom and against whom Trover may be maintained.*

ONE joint tenant, or tenant in common, or parcener, cannot bring trover against his companion for goods remaining in his possession, because the possession of one is the possession of both ; if trover be brought, the joint tenancy, &c. is good evidence upon the plea of not guilty (*g*). Upon this principle it was holden (*h*), that A., a member of an amicable society, who had been entrusted with a box, containing the sums of money subscribed, and was bound by bond to keep it safely, could not maintain trover against B., another member of the same society, and a stranger, in a case where B. had got possession of the box, carried it away, and delivered it to the stranger; *Buller*, J., observing, that it was admitted, that one of the defendants was a member of the society, and, consequently, had a general property in the box ; that a special property could not give a right in this action against a general property. The *custody* only was committed to the plaintiff, the *property* remained in the society. If, after an act of bankruptcy, but before commission, a person sue out execution against the goods of the bankrupt, under which the sheriff, without notice of the act of bankruptcy, makes a seizure, and then, within two months, a commission issues, and afterwards the sheriff sells the goods, the assignees may (*i*) maintain *trover* against the sheriff. After an act of bankruptcy committed by one of two partners (*k*), joint effects were sent away, which came to the defendant's hands ; then the solvent partner died, leaving the defendant his executor, and afterwards a commission of bankrupt was taken out against the surviving partner, and his estate assigned to the plaintiffs ; it was holden, that they were tenants in common with the solvent partner, and after his decease with his representatives, by relation from the act of bankruptcy; and, consequently, could not maintain trover against the defendant, claiming under such solvent partner. After an act of bankruptcy, committed by one of two partners (*l*), the other delivered goods, part of their joint property, to *a creditor*, for a joint debt, and died, and afterwards a commission issued against the surviving partner; it was holden, that this was in substance the same with the preceding case; that the creditor, by virtue of such delivery by the solvent partner, became tenant in common of the goods with the assignees of the bankrupt by relation from the act of bankruptcy, which was in the lifetime of the solvent partner,

(*g*) 2 Leon. 220, case 278. See *Stancliffe* v. *Hardwicke*, 2 Cr. M. & R. 1 ; 5 Tyrw. 551, *post*, under tit. " Plea," p. 1369, since the new rules.

(*h*) *Holliday* v. *Camsell and White*, 1 T. R. 658.

(*i*) *Garland* v. *Carlisle*, 2 Cr. & M. 31, in error; diss. four justices. Affirmed on error in D. P., 4 Bingh. N. C. 7 ; 3 M. & W. 152 ; but see *ante*, p. 241.

(*k*) *Smith and others, Assignees, &c.*, v. *Stokes*, 1 East, 363. See *Hogg* v. *Bridges*, 2 Moore, (C. P.) 122.

(*l*) *Smith and others, Assignees, &c.*, v. *Oriell*, 1 East, 368. See *Harvey* v. *Crickett*, *ante*, tit. " Partners," p. 1131.

and, consequently, that the assignees could not maintain trover against such creditor. If one tenant in common merely takes the thing in common out of the possession of his companion, and carries it away, there no action lies by the other tenant in common (m), but if he destroy the thing in common, the other may bring trespass or trover. As (n) where it appeared that one tenant in common of a ship had forcibly taken it out of the possession of his companion, and secreted it from him, so that he knew not where it was carried, and changed the name of it, and it afterwards got into the hands of a third person, who sent it on a foreign voyage, where it was lost, Lord *King*, C. J., left it to the jury, whether, under the circumstances, the destruction was not by the defendant's (the tenant in common) means; and the jury finding in the affirmative, the court, on motion for a new trial, approving of the chief justice's direction, refused to set aside the verdict (7). The preceding case proceeded upon the principle that there was a destruction of the subject matter; and it is now established, that one tenant in common cannot recover for a chattel in trover against his companion, without first proving a destruction of the chattel, or something that is equivalent to it. Hence, where one of two tenants in common of a whale, cut it up and expressed the oil; it was holden (o), that such alteration in the form of the property did not amount to a tortious conversion, so as to enable the companion to maintain trover; for the act done was an application of the whale to the only purpose which could make it profitable to the owners, and tended to preserve it instead of destroying it, which one tenant in common was clearly entitled to do; and as the parties were clearly tenants in common of the whale, they became tenants in common of the produce, after it was converted into oil. N. It was admitted in this case, that the taking by the defendant, and the refusal to deliver on demand made, was not any misfeasance in a tenant in common, and did not give a right of action. See *Cubitt* v. *Porter*, 8 B. & C. 257, where it was holden, that where an ancient wall was pulled down by one of two tenants in common with the intention of rebuilding it, and a new wall was built of a greater height than the old one, this was not such a total

---

(m) *Brammel* v. *Jones*, B. R. T. 22 Geo. III., MS.

(n) *Barnardiston* v. *Chapman*, C. B. Hil. T. 1 Geo. I., cited from Ld. C. J. King's MS., in *Heath* v. *Hubbard*, 4 East, 121.

See *Barton* v. *Williams*, 5 B. & A. 395, and *Farrar* v. *Beswick*, 1 M. & W. 688.

(o) *Fennings* v. *Lord Grenville*, 1 Taunt. 241.

---

(7) It seems that the sale of the whole of a ship by one who is only a part owner, in exclusion of the right of another, who is tenant in common with him, is not equivalent to the destruction of the subject matter, mediately or immediately, so as to enable his co-tenant to maintain trover against him for it. 4 East, 110. See also *Graves* v. *Sawyer*, T. Raym. 15.

destruction of the wall as to enable one of the tenants in common to maintain trespass against the other. The rule that one tenant in common cannot bring trover against his companion, holds only in those cases where the law considers the possession of one to be the possession of both. Hence (*p*), where A. is tenant in fee of one fourth part of an estate, and B. tenant in common with him, of the other three parts, *for a term of years*, without impeachment of waste, if A. cut down any trees, and B. take them away, A. may maintain trover; for though B., being dispunishable of waste, might cut down what trees he would, yet trees having an inheritable quality, and B. not having any interest in the inheritance, he cannot take the trees when felled by him who has the inheritance, and, consequently, his possession, being tortious, cannot be said to be the possession of the other. It is to be observed also, that if one joint-tenant, &c. bring trover, without his companion, against a *stranger*, the defendant cannot give the joint-tenancy, &c. in evidence *on the general issue*, so as to bar the plaintiff of his action, but only to prevent him from recovering any more than his own share in the value of the property in question (*q*); for it is a general rule, that the defendant can avail himself of an objection of this sort, *viz. that all the part owners in a chattel have not joined in an action of trespass or tort, brought in respect of such chattel, by a plea in abatement only* (*r*); and if one of two part owners of a chattel sue alone for a tort, and the defendant do not plead in abatement, the other part owner may afterwards sue alone, and the defendant cannot plead in abatement of such action (*s*). Trover will lie against a corporation (*t*).

III. *The Declaration, p.* 1366; *Plea, and herein of the New Rules, p.* 1368; *Defence, and herein of the Doctrine of Liens, p.* 1370; *Evidence, p.* 1378; *Of staying the Proceedings, p.* 1383; *Damages, p.* 1383; *Costs, p.* 1384; *Judgment, p.* 1384.

Venue.—This is a transitory action, and the venue may be laid in any county (*u*). The declaration states, that the plaintiff was lawfully possessed of the goods in question, as of his proper goods and chat-

(*p*) *West* v. *Parmore*, at Exeter, per *Turton*, J., Salk. MS.; Bull. N. P. 35.

(*q*) *Neithorpe* v. *Farrington*, 2 Lev. 113; adm. in *Barnardiston* v. *Chapman*, C. B. H. T. 1 Geo. I., cited in 4 East, 121.

(*r*) *Bloxam* v. *Hubbard*, 5 East, 420.
(*s*) *Sedgworth* v. *Overend*, 7 T. R. 279.
(*t*) *Yarborough* v. *The Bank of England*, 16 East, 6.
(*u*) *Brown* v. *Hedges*, Salk. 290.

tels (8), and that, being so possessed, he casually lost them, and that they came to the hands and possession of the defendant, by finding, who afterwards (9) converted (10) them to his own use.

The goods in question should be described with such convenient certainty, that the jury may know what is meant; but in this action the same accuracy and precision are not required as in the action of detinue, which is for the recovery of the things themselves in specie, if to be had. Hence, a declaration in trover for twenty ounces of cloves and mace (*x*), ten pair of curtains and valance (*y*); for a parcel of diamonds (*z*); for the furniture, apparel, &c. belonging to such a ship (*a*); has been holden good.

The conversion is the gist of the action, and the manner in which the goods came to the hands of the defendant is only inducement (*b*), and therefore, the plaintiff may declare that the goods came to the possession of the defendant generally or specially, by finding, (though the defendant came to the goods by delivery) (*c*), or that the defendant fraudulently, at cards, won money of the plaintiff from the wife of the plaintiff (*d*).

This is the substance of the declaration in common cases. Where the action is brought by an executor, administrator, or the assignees of a bankrupt, the character in which the parties sue must of course appear on the face of the declaration. Care must be taken to state the possession to be in the person to whom the property belongs. In an action of trover by the assignee of bankrupt partners (*e*), the declaration consisted of one count only, in which the possession was

(*x*) *Hartford* v. *Jones*, Salk. 654.
(*y*) *Taylor* v. *Wells*, 2 Saund. 74.
(*z*) *White* v. *Graham*, Str. 827; Lord Raym. 1530.
(*a*) *Nightingale* v. *Bridges*, Carth. 131.
(*b*) *Issack* v. *Clark*, 2 Bulstr. 306.

(*c*) 2 Bulstr. 313, per *Coke*, C. J.
(*d*) *Vid.* Ent. 265.
(*e*) *Cock, Assignee of Kent and Pemberton*, v. *Tunno*, London Sittings after H. T. 41 Geo. III., B. R.; *Kenyon*, C. J., MSS.

---

(8) The omission of the words " as of his proper goods," is cured by verdict, *Jones* v. *Winkworth*, Hardr. 111; but fatal after a judgment by default. *Swallow* v. *Ayncliff*, B. R. M. 2 Geo. II., MSS.

(9) In the declaration the conversion was laid, under a scilicet, to be on a day before the trover*. Upon motion in arrest of judgment, the declaration was holden to be good, for the *postea convertit* is sufficient, and the scilicet is void.

(10) Though it be necessary to allege a day and place of conversion †, (or of a request and refusal, which is tantamount‡,) yet as it is a transitory action, the conversion may be laid here, and proved in Ireland§.

* *Tesmond* v. *Johnson*, Cro. Jac. 428.
† *Hubbard's* case, Cro. Eliz. 78.
‡ *Wilson* v. *Chambers*, Cro. Car. 262.
§ *Brown* v. *Hedges*, Salk. 290.

stated to be in the partners. It appeared in evidence, that the greater part of the goods in question belonged to one of the partners only, before the commencement of the partnership, and had never been brought into the partnership fund. It was proved, that the residue of the goods was part of the joint estate. Per *Kenyon*, C. J. The plaintiff under this declaration is entitled to recover the value of such goods only as have been proved to belong to both the partners as partners. Had there been a count in the declaration, stating the possession of the assignee, as this was a joint commission, and the assignment under such commission passes both separate and joint effects (*f*), the whole might have been recovered; as it is, the verdict must be for that part only which has been proved to be the property of the partners. The jury found a verdict accordingly. In trover *by* husband and wife, the declaration ought not to allege the possession in them both (*g*), nor state the damage to have accrued to them both (*h*); for the law transfers, in point of ownership, the whole interest to the husband. If trover be brought *against* husband and wife, and it is alleged in the declaration that they converted the goods to their own use, formerly the judgment might have been arrested (*i*) or reversed (*k*) on writ of error, but the law is otherwise now (*l*). So in *trespass* (*m*) against baron and feme for entering a house, and taking goods, the declaration stated, that they converted the goods to their own use; on motion in arrest of judgment, the declaration was holden good; for the conversion in this case is not the gist of the action; and the action being maintainable for entering the house and taking the goods, the court will intend that the damages were given for those trespasses only. It seems (*n*), as the conversion is a tort, that the wife may be charged with it in the same manner as with a trespass; that is, the declaration may state, that the husband and wife converted the goods, omitting the words, to their own use.

Plea, and herein of the New Rules.

The general issue in this action is not guilty. By R. G. H. T. 4 Will. IV. 4, 1, in an action for converting the plaintiff's goods, the plea of not guilty shall operate as a denial of the conversion only, and not of the plaintiff's title to the goods; and by 4, 2, all matters in confession and avoidance shall be pleaded

(*f*) *Exp. Cook,* 2 P. Wms. 500. See also 4 Burr. 2176, S. P., per Lord *Mansfield,* C. J.

(*g*) Per *Yelverton,* J., Yelv. 165.

(*h*) Salk. 114.

(*i*) *Rhemes* v. *Humphrys,* Cro. Car. 254.

(*k*) *Berry* v. *Nevys,* Cro. Jac. 661; *Perry* v. *Diggs,* Cro. Car. 494, S. P.

(*l*) *Keyworth* v. *Hill,* 3 B. & A. 685, recognized in *Vine* v. *Saunders,* 4 Bingh. N. C. 101; 5 Sc. 359.

(*m*) *Smalley* v. *Kerfoot,* Str. 1094; Andr. 242, *S. C.; Pullen* v. *Palmer,* Bull. N. P. 46, S. P.

(*n*) *Draper* v. *Fulkes,* Yelv. 165; *Anon.,* 1 Vent. 24.

specially as in actions of assumpsit. Evidence of lien is not admissible under the general issue (o); for that plea, by the new rules, denies the conversion only, and admits the title of the plaintiff, which consists of the right of property and right of possession, at the time of conversion; whereas a lien is inconsistent with and negatives the plaintiff's right of possession. Since the new rules, a defendant who pleads not guilty alone in an action of trover (p), admits thereby that the plaintiff has some property in the goods, in respect of which he would be entitled to recover against the defendant; but such admission does not preclude the defendant from showing that he is tenant in common with the plaintiff; if, however, there has been a conversion in fact, as by seizure and sale, he must justify such conversion specially by way of confession and avoidance, and he cannot, under the plea of not guilty, show that he was justified, as tenant in common with the plaintiff, in committing the conversion in fact. The conversion (q) which is put in issue by the plea of not guilty, since the new rules, is a conversion in fact, and not merely a wrongful conversion; and wherever there has been a conversion in fact, and the defendant insists that such conversion was lawful, he must confess and avoid it, by pleading specially the right or title by which he was justified in the conversion; for the plea (r) of not guilty puts in issue the conversion in fact only, and not the legality of the conversion. Under the plea of not guilty, the defendant cannot set up an absolute property in himself in the chattel by sale from the plaintiff (s), although the only evidence of a conversion is a demand and refusal.

Where the plaintiff in trover (t) claims under a sale, the defendant, under a plea that the goods are not the plaintiff's property, cannot show the sale to have been fraudulent; the fraud must be pleaded specially. A party who negligently or culpably stands by and allows another to contract on the faith and understanding of a fact which he can contradict, cannot afterwards dispute that fact in an action against the person whom he has himself assisted in deceiving; and this defence is admissible on the plea of not possessed as of his own property (u). The plea (x) of no property in the plaintiff, means no property as against the defendant, and puts in issue the right of the plaintiff to the possession of the goods as against the defendant at the time of the conversion; therefore, in an action (y) of trover against assignees of a bankrupt, this plea lets in evi-

(o) *White* v. *Teale*, 4 P. & D. 43.

(p) *Stancliffe* v. *Hardwick*, 2 Cr. M. & R. 1; 5 Tyr. 551. And see *Farrar* v. *Beswick*, 1 M. & W. 682; *Vernon* v. *Shipton*, 2 M. & W. 13.

(q) *Stancliffe* v. *Hardwick, ubi sup.*

(r) Per *Coleridge*, J., in *Weeding* v. *Aldrich*, 9 A. & E. 866, on the authority of *Stancliffe* v. *Hardwick*.

(s) *Barton* v. *Brown*, 5 M. & W. 298.

(t) *Howell* v. *White*, 1 M. & Rob. 400.

(u) *Gregg* v. *Wells*, 10 A. & E. 90; 2 P. & D. 296, recognizing *Pickard* v. *Sears*, 6 A. & E. 469; 2 Nev. & P. 488.

(x) *Nicolls* v. *Bastard*, 2 Cr. M. & R. 659; 1 Tyr. & G. 156.

(y) *Isaac* v. *Belcher*, 5 M. & W. 139, recognizing *Owen* v. *Knight*, 4 Bingh. N. C. 54; 5 Scott, 307.

dence that the goods were, at the time of the bankruptcy, within
the order and disposition of the bankrupt as reputed owner, and
that the defendants as assignees sold the goods. A lien may be
given in evidence under the plea that the plaintiff was not lawfully
possessed (z).

The defendant may plead the statute of limitations (a), viz. that
the cause of action did not accrue at any time within six years
next before the commencement of the plaintiff's action. Where
the plea was, that the cause of action did not accrue within six
years next before the exhibiting of the plaintiff's bill, and the declaration was filed generally as of Michaelmas Term, it was holden (b),
that defendant might give evidence of the time when it was actually
filed, in order to support the allegation in his plea. The statute is
a bar to an action commenced more than six years after the conversion (c), although the plaintiff did not know of the conversion
until within that period, the defendant not having practised any
fraud to prevent the plaintiff from obtaining that knowledge at an
earlier period. Where an executor, several years before, had left
some goods in the house, by the consent of the heir (d), who used
them afterwards, and within six years of the action brought, the
executor demanded the goods, and the heir refused to deliver them,
whereupon trover was brought and the statute of limitations
pleaded; it was holden, that the user *before* the demand was neither
a conversion, nor any evidence of it; for it was with the consent of
the executor until that time: and the demand being within six
years, the refusal, which ensued it, and which was the only evidence
of a conversion in the case, was within the six years; and if a trover
be before the six years, and a conversion after, the statute cannot be
pleaded. Bankruptcy of the defendant, after the cause of action
accrued, cannot be pleaded, because the damages in trover are
uncertain (e).

Defence, and herein of the Doctrine of Liens.

The most usual defence to this action is, that the defendant has
a lien (f) on the goods, or a right to detain them. It will be
proper, therefore, to inquire under what circumstances a party may
insist on this defence. There are two species of liens known to the
law, namely, *particular* liens and *general* liens (g). *Particular*

(z) *Owen* v. *Knight*, 4 Bingh. N. C. 54;
5 Sc. 307; *Brandao* v. *Barnett*, 2 Scott,
N. R. 96.

(a) 21 Jac. I. c. 16.
(b) *Granger* v. *George*, 5 B. & C. 149.
(c) *Ib.*
(d) *Wortley Montague* v. *Lord Sand-
wich*, 7 Mod. 99, cited by *Lawrence*, J.,
in *Topham* v. *Braddick*, 1 Taunt. 577.

See *Philpott* v. *Kelley*, 3 A. & E. 106;
4 Nev. & M. 611.
(e) *Parker* v. *Norton*, 6 T. R. 695.
(f) As to what plea a lien may be given
in evidence under, see *ante*, p. 1369, 1370.
(g) Per *Heath*, J., 3 Bos. & Pul. 494;
and per *Kenyon*, C. J., 1 Esp. N. P. C.
109; per Lord *Mansfield*, C. J., 4 Burr.
2221.

liens are, where persons claim a right to retain goods, in respect of labour or money expended on such goods, and these liens are favoured in law. *General* liens are claimed in respect of a general balance of account; and these are founded on express agreement, or are raised by implication of law, from the usage of trade, or from the course of dealing between the parties, whence it may be inferred, that the contract in question was made with reference to their usual course of dealing. By the common law, where a party is obliged to receive goods, he is also entitled to retain them for his indemnity (11). Upon this principle, it has been holden, that common carriers (*h*) (12) and innkeepers (13) have a particular lien on the *goods* intrusted to their care. In like manner, millers have a particular lien on the produce of corn, which they have ground, for the price of grinding (*i*). So a shipwright (*k*) has a lien upon a ship for repairs. A person (*l*), who by his own labour preserves goods, which the owner, or those entrusted with the care of them, have either abandoned in distress *at sea*, or are unable to protect and secure, is entitled by the common law of England to retain the possession of the goods saved, until a proper compensation is made to him for his trouble (14). The reason of this rule is obvious;

(*h*) *Skinner* v. *Upshaw*, Ld. Raym. 752.
(*i*) *Exp. Ockenden*, 1 Atk. 235.
(*k*) *Franklin* v. *Hosier*, 4 B. & A. 341.

(*l*) Per *Holt*, C. J., in *Hartfort* v. *Jones*, Lord Raym. 393; Salk. 654; Abbott, 398, 5th ed.

---

(11) It was said by *Ryder*, C. J., delivering the opinion of the court in *Brenan* v. *Currint*, T. 28 & 29 Geo. II., B. R., MSS., that he had not found it laid down as a general rule, that the remedy by retainer was co-extensive with the obligation to receive goods. But see Lord Raym. 867.

(12) See further as to the lien of carriers, *ante*, tit. " Carriers," Sect. III. p. 404, and *Rushforth* v. *Hadfield*, 7 East, 224.

(13) An innkeeper cannot detain the person* of his guest, or take off his clothes to secure payment of his bill.

(14) By stat. 26 Geo. II. c. 19, s. 5, it is enacted, " That in case any person not employed by the master, mariners, or owners, or other persons lawfully authorized, in the salvage of any ship, or the cargo or provision thereof, shall, in the absence of persons so employed or authorized, save any such ship or goods, and cause the same to be carried for the benefit of the proprietors, into port, or to any adjoining custom-house or 'place of safe custody, immediately giving notice thereof to some justice, magistrate, custom-house or excise officer, or shall discover to any such magistrate or officer, where any such effects are wrongfully bought, sold, or concealed, such persons shall be entitled to a reasonable reward to be paid by the master or owner of the vessel or goods, and to be adjusted in case of disagreement about the *quantum*, in the same manner as salvage is to be adjusted or paid by stat. 12 Ann. st. 2, c. 18, or by stat. 26 Geo. II. c. 19."

* *Sunbolf* v. *Alford*, 3 M. & W. 248.

goods carried by sea are necessarily and unavoidably exposed to the
perils which storms, tempests, and accidents (m), (far beyond the
reach of human foresight to prevent,) are hourly creating, and
against which it too often happens, that the greatest diligence, and
the most strenuous exertions of them ariner, cannot protect them.
When goods are thus in imminent danger of being lost, it is most
frequently at the hazard of the lives of those who save them, that
they are saved.   Principles of public policy dictate to civilized and
commercial countries, not only the propriety, but even the absolute
necessity, of establishing a liberal recompense for the encouragement
of those who engage in so dangerous a service.

There cannot be any lien, unless there is possession.   The defendant was the owner of a ship, B. was the charterer, and for one
sum of £2100, to be paid by bills at different periods, B. was to
have the use of the ship for the voyage out to the Cape of Good
Hope and home to London.   A quantity of goods belonging to B.
formed part of the homeward cargo.   B. having become a bankrupt
shortly before the vessel left the Cape on her homeward voyage, the
defendant, on her arrival at the port of London, seized B.'s goods.
The plain iffs, the assignees of B., demanded the goods, and tendered a sum of money, but not equal in amount to that in respect
of which the defendant claimed a lien on the goods.   But the court
were of opinion (n), that the defendant was not entitled to any lien;
for B., the bankrupt, was the owner of the ship for the voyage;
that having put his own goods on board his own ship, the master
and crew ought to have obeyed him until the voyage was ended,
which was not until a full delivery was made of the goods; and until
that time possession of the ship did not revert to the defendant.
But a master of a vessel (o) being turned out of possession, upon
the vessel's being captured, does not deprive him of his lien for the
freight, in case of her recapture.

As to general liens, it has been determined, that the attornies
and solicitors of the different courts have a lien on all papers
remaining in their hands, and judgments recovered, for their
costs (p) (15).   An attorney has a lien for his general balance on

(m) *Nicholson* v. *Chapman,* 2 H. Bl.
254.

(n) *Hutton* v. *Bragg,* 7 Taunt. 14.

(o) *Exp. Cheesman, re Welfitt,* 2 Eden,
C. T. N. 181.

(p) *Mitchell* v. *Oldfield,* 4 T. R. 123.

(15) But in one case, where A. purchased the interest of a lease for
years, and the writings were left in the hands of B., an attorney, to draw
an assignment of the lease; B. drew the assignment, and it was sealed,
but B. refused to deliver it, until A. paid for the drawing, &c.; upon
which A. brought trover against B. for the deed: *Holt,* C. J., held, that
the action would lie; because B. might have an action for what he deserved, but that he could not detain for it. *Anon.,* Pasch. 6 Will. & Ma.

papers of his clients, which come to his hands in the course of his professional employment; therefore, where C. gave his attorney a specific sum for the purpose of satisfying a debt for which an execution had issued against his goods at the suit of B., and the attorney paid the money to B., who thereupon delivered to him a lease which had been deposited by C. with B. as a security for the debt; it was holden (q), that the attorney had a lien on it for his general balance due from C.; and that such lien was not extinguished by his having taken acceptances from C. for the amount of that balance before the lease came into his hands; some of those acceptances, when the lease did come to his hands, having been dishonoured, and one of them taken up by the attorney. The lien which an attorney has on the papers in his hands, is only commensurate with the right which the party delivering the papers to him has therein. Every one, whether attorney or not, has, by the common law, a lien on the specific deed or paper delivered to him to do any work or business thereon, but not on other muniments of the same party, unless the person claiming the lien be an attorney or solicitor (r). So where a banker has advanced money to a customer (s), he has a lien upon all the securities which come into his hands belonging to that person, for the amount of his general balance: unless there be evidence to show that he received any particular security, under special circumstances, which would take it out of the general rule. But a banker has no lien (t) on muniments casually left in his shop after he has refused to advance money on them as a security. Where a mortgage deed was delivered to an appraiser to obtain the money, which after several applications, he failed in doing; it was holden (u), that he could not retain the deed as a lien for the compensation for his trouble, there being no work done on the subject

(q) *Stevenson* v. *Blakelock*, 1 M. & S. 535.
(r) *Hollis* v. *Claridge*, 4 Taunt. 807.
(s) *Davis* v. *Bowsher*, 5 T. R. 488.
(t) *Lucas* v. *Dorrien*, 7 Taunt. 278.
(u) *Sanderson* v. *Bell*, 2 Cr. & M. 304.

at Nisi Prius, ex. rel. Mr. Place, 1 Ld. Raym. 738. Plaintiff having contracted to purchase an estate of B., had the deeds of conveyance prepared at his own expense and sent them to B. for execution. B. executed and gave them to a servant to be sent back. The servant delivered them to defendant, an attorney, who had a demand upon B. for business done in his profession. No directions were given to the defendant to retain the deeds, until the purchase money should be paid. Some necessary parties refused to execute the deeds, and plaintiff having abandoned the contract, demanded the deeds from defendant, who refused to deliver them up, claiming to have a lien for his demand against B. In trover for deeds and stamped pieces of parchment, it was holden*, that the plaintiff was entitled to recover the deeds at all events in a cancelled, if not in an uncancelled, state. *Littledale*, J., dubitante.

* *Esdaile* v. *Oxenham*, 3 B. & C. 225.

2 Y 2

matter in dispute. A calico printer has a lien upon the linen in his possession (x), for the general balance of his account, for work done in the course of that business. So a printer employed to print certain numbers, but not all consecutive numbers, of an entire work, has a lien upon the copies not delivered, for his general balance due for printing the whole of the numbers (y). In like manner it has been determined, that dyers (z), factors (a) (16), and wharfingers (b), have liens for their general balance; but not a fuller (c), or a public warehouse-keeper in London (d).

Where the defendants, as brokers, contracted for a quantity of staves to remain on the premises of the vendor rent-free, for one month, and after that, at a certain rent to be paid by their principal, who subsequently gave orders for a removal of part, and directed that the residue should not be removed until further orders from him; it was holden (e), that never having, in fact, been in the possession or control of the brokers, they had not a lien on the goods for their general balance. The master of a vessel has a lien on the trunk of a person whom he has conveyed in his vessel, until a reasonable sum has been tendered for the passage (f). N. It did not appear in this case, what were the terms of the contract: but it was proved, that the defendant had brought the plaintiff, and his trunk containing his wearing apparel, home in his vessel from the Brazils to London; £15 had been paid by the plaintiff, but the defendant claimed £15 more, and insisted on detaining the trunk until the rest was paid. It was proved, that £50 was a reasonable sum for the conveyance of the plaintiff. But the master of a ship has not a lien on the ship (g) for money expended or debts incurred by him for repairs done to it on the voyage. Nor has he a lien on the freight (h) for his wages, or for his disbursements on account of the ship during the voyage, or for the premiums paid by him abroad for the purpose of procuring the cargo. A house of public entertainment in London, where beds, provisions, &c. are furnished for all persons paying for the same, but which was merely called a

(x) Exp. Andrews, 21 June, 1764, per Lord Northington, Ch., Co. B. L. 429, 5th edit.; Weldon v. Gould, 3 Esp. N. P. C. 268, Kenyon, C. J.

(y) Blake v. Nicholson, 3 M. & S. 167.

(z) Saville v. Barchard, 4 Esp. N. P. C. 53, Kenyon, C. J.; evidence having been given of the usage of the trade; but, according to Bennett v. Johnson, 3 Doug. 387, dyers have not a general lien independent of this usage. In Stainton v. Lane, Sittings after Trin. 1773, a custom to retain as lien for the whole due for dyeing was holden good. See further on this point, Close v. Waterhouse, 6 East, 523, (n).

(a) Kruger v. Wilcox, Ambl. 252; Gardener v. Coleman, cited 1 Burr. 494, and 6 East, 28, per Buller, J., S. P.

(b) Naylor v. Mangles, 1 Esp. N. P. C. 109.

(c) Rose v. Hart, 8 Taunt. 499; 2 Moore, 547.

(d) Leuckhart v. Cooper, 3 Bingh. N. C. 103.

(e) Taylor v. Robinson, 2 Moore, (C. P.) 730.

(f) Wolf v. Summers, 2 Campb. 631, Lawrence, J.

(g) Hussey v. Christie, 9 East, 426.

(h) Smith v. Plummer, 1 B. & A. 575.

(16) See further as to the lien of factors, ante, tit. " Factors," p. 817.

tavern and coffee-house, and was not frequented by stage coaches and waggons from the country, and which had no stables belonging to it, is to be considered as an inn (i), and the owner is subject to the liabilities of innkeepers, and has a lien on the *goods* (k) of his guest for the payment of his bill; and that, even where the guest did not appear to have been a traveller, but one who had previously resided in furnished lodgings in London. Policy brokers have a lien for their general balance (l), even as against agents who do not disclose their principals (m); but not where they have notice, that the person who employs them acts merely as an agent (n); and it has been holden, that where an English subject, in time of war, informed the broker, that the property insured was neutral, that was a sufficient indication to the broker, that the party acted as agent (o). If the broker (p) has lost by his own act the right to retain as a lien, upon which he relies in his plea under a particular custom of the city of London, he will not be allowed to desert his plea of lien and rest his defence upon another and totally distinct ground (e. g., a right to retain the property for a balance due to him on mutual credit), without specially pleading it. A stereotype printer has no general lien (q) on stereotype plates not manufactured by himself, but put into his hands to print from. If a broker having a lien on a policy part with it, his lien (r) revives on repossession. But if a party having a lien on goods causes them to be taken in execution at his own suit, and purchases them, he thereby loses his lien (s), although the goods are never removed off the premises. If a person (t) having a lien, abuses it by pledging the goods, the owner's right to the possession revives, and he may maintain trover.

A. commissioned B. to sell a ship, and having deposited her register with him for that purpose, became bankrupt: it was holden, that the Register Acts did not prevent B. having a lien on the register deposited with him (u). So where certificate of registry (x) had been deposited as a security for advances made for the use of the ship. A general right of detaining a thing until the money due for the work done upon it be paid, may be waived by a special agreement, as to the time or mode of payment; but not merely by an agreement for the payment of a fixed sum (y), although a con-

(i) *Thompson* v. *Lacy*, 3 B. & A. 283.

(k) See *ante*, p. 1371, n. (13).

(l) *Whitehead* v. *Vaughan*, B. R. T. 25 Geo. III., Co. B. L. 566, 5th ed.

(m) *Mann* v. *Forrester*, 4 Campb. 60; *Westwood* v. *Bell*, *ib.* 349.

(n) *Maanss* v. *Henderson*, 1 East, 335; *Snook* v. *Davidson*, 2 Campb. 218. See also 2 Campb. 597.

(o) *Snook* v. *Davidson*, *ubi sup.*

(p) *Hewison* v. *Guthrie*, 2 Bingh. N. C. 760.

(q) *Bleaden* v. *Hancock*, 1 M. & Malk. 465.

(r) *Levy* v. *Barnard*, 8 Taunt. 149.

(s) *Jacobs* v. *Latour*, 5 Bingh. 130.

(t) *Scott* v. *Newington*, 1 M. & Rob. 252.

(u) *Mestaer* v. *Atkins*, 1 Marsh. 76; 5 Taunt. 381, *S. C.*

(x) *Bowen* v. *Fox*, 10 B. & C. 41.

(y) *Chase* v. *Westmore*, 5 M. & S. 180, cited and distinguished by *Bayley*, B., in *Sanderson* v. *Bell*, 2 Cr. & M. 311. See also the opinion of *Gibbs*, C. J., to the same effect, in *Hutton* v. *Bragg*, 2 Marsh. 345 and 349, and 7 Taunt. 25. But see *Tate* v. *Meek*, 8 Taunt. 280.

trary doctrine is laid down in several cases (z). The principle appears to be this—that a special agreement does not of itself destroy the right to detain; but if it contain some term inconsistent with that right, it will. A set-off cannot be considered as destroying a lien, unless it be so agreed upon between the parties (a). If a security is taken (b) for the debt for which the party has a lien upon property of the debtor, such security being payable at a distant day, the lien is gone. A quantity of iron was imported by A., and landed on the 14th October at defendant's wharf. On the 15th October, the plaintiffs purchased the iron of A., paid for it, and obtained an order for the delivery, under which, part was delivered at different times, until the March following, when A., the importer, becoming bankrupt, the remainder of the iron was detained by the defendants claiming a lien on it in respect of their charges for wharfage. The course of dealing proved was, that these charges were usually paid by the merchant importer, at the Christmas following the importation, whether the iron had, in the mean time, been removed or not. *Abbott*, C. J., was of opinion, that the defendants were not entitled to a lien ; for, at the time the iron was purchased by the plaintiffs, the defendants had not any lien upon it for their charges ; and in this opinion the court afterwards concurred (c). *Holroyd*, J., observing, that the wharfage was not payable till Christmas, and by the sale the plaintiff had a right to an immediate delivery ; and the subsequent default of the importers to pay the debt due from them would not alter the case. A trainer has a lien (d) on a race-horse for the expenses and skill bestowed in the keeping and training him ; on the principle, that, where a bailee bestows labour and skill in the improvement of the subject delivered to him, he has a lien for the charge. So where S. sent a mare to M., to be covered by a stallion belonging to him, which was done accordingly ; it was holden (e), that M. was entitled to a specific lien on the mare for the charge of covering her. But the case of agistment does not fall within this principle, as the agister does not confer any additional value on the article, either by the exertion of any skill of his own, or indirectly by means of any instrument in his possession, but simply takes in an animal to feed it. Hence an agister of milch cows has no lien (f) ; and a person to whom a horse is delivered to be stabled, taken care of, fed, and kept (g), has not any lien for the charge.

(z) *Brenan* v. *Currint*, Say. R. 224, shortly stated in Bull. N. P. 45, and MSS. See also *Collins* v. *Ongley*, *post*, p. 1377. But these authorities were overruled in *Chase* v. *Westmore*.

(a) *Pinnock* v. *Harrison*, 3 M. & W. 532.

(b) *Cowell* v. *Simpson*, 16 Ves. 275, recognized by *Tindal*, C. J., in *Hewison* v. *Guthrie*, 2 Bingh. N. C. 759.

(c) *Crawshay* v. *Homfray*, 4 B. & A. 50.
(d) *Bevan* v. *Waters*, 1 M. & Malk. 236, *Best*, C. J. But see the remarks on this case in *Jackson* v. *Cummins*, 5 M. & W. 350.

(e) *Scarfe* v. *Morgan*, 4 M. & W. 270.
(f) *Jackson* v. *Cummins*, 5 M. & W. 342.

(g) *Judson* v. *Etheridge*, 3 Tyr. 954; 1 Cr. & M. 743.

In trover, by an assignee of a bankrupt (*h*), it appeared that the goods had been attached in the hands of J. S. (to whom they had been delivered by the bankrupt) (17), in a plaint at the suit of the defendant. Afterwards, and before condemnation, an act of bankruptcy was committed: then the goods were condemned, and satisfaction entered on the record by the defendant; it was holden, that this evidence was sufficient to charge the defendant, the property not being altered until condemnation; and that the person who delivered the goods by compulsion of law was discharged. The C. J. added, that if goods were delivered to a manufacturer, he might detain them for what he deserved for his labour; but if there was an agreement for the price he could not; in that case he must rely on the contract, and be in the same condition with other creditors. If a person having a lien upon goods, *e. g.*, for warehouse rent, when they are demanded of him, claims to retain them upon a different ground, *viz.* that the goods are his own property, and does not make any mention of the lien, trover may be maintained against him, without evidence of a tender having been made to him in respect of his lien (*i*). A lord of a manor seized a beast as an estray (*k*), and kept it for some time after having proclaimed it; the owner afterwards, and within the year, claimed it, and brought trover, without having first tendered a satisfaction for the keeping of it; and for the want of this it was holden, that the action would not lie. But if a horse be distrained in order to compel an appearance in a hundred court (*l*), after appearance the plaintiff cannot justify detaining the horse, until his keep is paid for. Where a person has a simple lien on goods, he cannot sell and dispose of them; but if he has a special property in those goods in trust for another, subject to a claim of his own, in such case, the party may sell in order to repay himself (*m*). A party cannot acquire a lien by his wrongful act (*n*). If the defendant is to be considered as a mere wrong-doer (*o*), it is not necessary for the plaintiff to tender him an indemnification for expenses which have been incurred by him in order to obtain a wrongful possession; so no formal tender is neces-

---

(*h*) *Colline* v. *Ongley*, B. R. E. 9 Will. III., per *Holt*, C. J., cited by *Ryder*, C. J., in *Brenan* v. *Currint*, MSS.; but *Brenan* v. *Currint* was overruled in *Chase* v. *Westmore*.

(*i*) *Boardman* v. *Sill*, 1 Campb. 410, n., Lord *Ellenborough*, C. J.

(*k*) *Taylor* v. *James*, 2 Rol. Abr. 92,

(M.) pl. 3.

(*l*) *Lenton* v. *Cook*, H. 9 Geo. II., Bull. N. P. 45.

(*m*) Per *Holroyd*, J., *Cazenove* v. *Prevost*, 5 B. & A. 78.

(*n*) *Griffiths* v. *Hyde*, Dorset Sum. Ass. 1809, *Lawrence*, J.

(*o*) *Lempriere* v. *Pasley*, 2 T. R. 485.

---

(17) It is not stated for what purpose the goods had been delivered to J. S., but it seems, from the subsequent part of the case, that J. S. was a manufacturer to whom the goods had been delivered by the bankrupt, in order to have some work done to them, under an agreement to pay a certain sum of money for such work.

sary (*p*) where the defendant is not in a situation to deliver up the goods (18).

Property held by a party in right of a lien cannot be taken in execution; for a lien is a personal right, and continues only so long as the possessor holds the goods; and the sheriff cannot sell an interest of this description, which is a mere personal interest in the goods (*q*).

Evidence.

In order to maintain this action, the plaintiff must prove,

1. Property and right of possession in himself in the goods in question.

2. The nature and value of the goods.

3. A conversion.

In general this is the only proof requisite (*r*); for it is not necessary to prove the manner in which the goods came to the hands of the defendant, that being matter of inducement only. In trover for a debenture (*s*), the plaintiff must prove the number of the debenture as laid in the declaration, and the exact sum to a farthing, or he will be nonsuited, but he need not set out the number (any more than the date of a bond (*t*), for which trover is brought); for the plaintiff, not being possessed of the debenture, may not know the number, and if he should mistake in the number, he must fail in the action. In trover for a bond (*u*), the plaintiff will be permitted to give parol evidence of the contents, although he has not given the defendant notice to produce the instrument itself; and although defendant offers to produce the instrument, plaintiff is not bound to put it in. So in trover for the certificate of a ship's registry (*x*), the certificate may be proved to have been granted to the plaintiff by the production of the registry, from which it was copied, though notice has not

---

(*p*) *Jones* v. *Cliff*, 1 Cr. & M. 540; 3 Tyr. 576.
(*q*) *Legg* v. *Evans*, 6 M. & W. 36.
(*r*) Bull. N. P. 33.
(*s*) Per *Holt*, C. J., London Sitt. A. D. 1707; Bull. N. P. 37.

(*t*) *Wilson* v. *Chambers*, Cro. Car. 262.
(*u*) *How* v. *Hall*, 14 East, 274; and see 1 Campb. 144, and *Whitehead* v. *Scott*, 1 M. & Rob. 2.
(*x*) *Bucher* v. *Jarrat*, 3 Bos. & Pul. 143.

---

(18) It seems, that the same rule holds where the defendant has incurred an expense in respect of the plaintiff's goods, without an authority from the plaintiff. *Stone* v. *Lingwood*, Str. 651; which case, however, was denied to be law by Lord *Mansfield*, C. J., 4 Burr. 2218. Where possession has been obtained by a misrepresentation on the part of the defendant, he cannot set up a lien, to which he might otherwise have been entitled. *Madden* v. *Kempster*, 1 Campb. 12.

been given to the defendant to produce the certificate itself (19). In these cases the nature of the action is sufficient notice to the defendant of the subject of inquiry. In trover for a ship (*y*), the mere fact of possession as owner is sufficient *primâ facie* evidence of ownership, without the aid of any documentary proof of title, as the bill of sale or ship's register, until such further evidence is rendered necessary in consequence of the adduction of some contrary proof on the other side (20). To determine what evidence will be sufficient to prove a conversion in the defendant, it must be known in what manner the goods came to his hands (*z*); for if they came to his hands by delivery, finding, or bailment, an actual demand and refusal ought to be proved; but proof of a tortious taking will supersede the necessity of proving a demand and refusal; for where the taking is unlawful, it is of itself a conversion; so likewise, if an actual conversion be proved, it is not necessary to prove a demand and refusal (*a*). A mere non-delivery of goods, which have been placed in the defendant's hands for a specific purpose, will not amount to a tortious conversion. Hence (*b*), where goods have been delivered to a manufacturer, in order that he may do something to the goods in the course of his business, and then return them; if the manufacturer, upon being applied to for the goods, merely makes excuses for not having returned them, and does not absolutely refuse to deliver them, *trover* cannot be maintained: the proper remedy is an action of assumpsit for non-performance of the contract. Where plaintiffs sold goods to T., who paid for them, and was to take them away, but defendant becoming possessed of the place in which the goods

(*y*) *Robertson* v. *French*, 4 East, 130. See also *Sutton* v. *Buck*, 2 Taunt. 302.
(*z*) Per *Cur.* in *Bruen* v. *Roe*, 1 Sidf. 264.

(*a*) *Forsdick* v. *Collins*, 1 Stark. N. P. C. 173, Lord *Ellenborough*, C. J.
(*b*) *Severin* v. *Keppel*, 4 Esp. N. P. C. 157, Lord *Ellenborough*, C. J.

---

(19) " Where a written instrument is to be used as a medium of proof, by which a claim to a demand arising out of the instrument is to be supported, there I admit the instrument itself must be produced, or notice to produce it must have been given to the defendant, before any evidence of its contents can be received; but this being an action of trover for the certificate of registry itself, I can see no sound reason why evidence should not be admitted of the existence of the certificate, in the same manner as evidence of a picture, or other specific thing, is constantly admitted where it is sought to be recovered in the same form of action." Per *Rooke*, J., 3 Bos. & Pul. 146.

(20) Entries in the custom-house books of the port of London, and of the out-port to which a ship belongs, stating that she was transferred to A. by B., the original owner, was holden not sufficient evidence to prove that A. was liable as registered owner, there not being any proof to connect A. with the entries. *Fraser* v. *Hopkins and another*, 2 Campb. 170. See also *Tinkler* v. *Walpole*, 14 East, 226; *Smith* v. *Fuge*, 3 Campb. 456; *Strother* v. *Willan*, 4 Campb. 24.

were deposited, plaintiffs' attorney, accompanied by T., demanded them of defendant, telling him that they belonged to plaintiffs and that they had sold them to T.; to which defendant answered that he would not deliver them to any person whatsoever; and afterwards plaintiff repaid the money to T. and brought trover against defendant: it was holden (c), that this demand and refusal were sufficient evidence of a conversion to support the action, and that a new demand by the plaintiffs, after they had repaid the money to T., was not necessary. A bailee can never be in a better situation than the bailor. If the bailor has no title, the bailee can have none. Hence, where the captain of a ship, who had taken goods on freight and claimed to have a lien upon them, delivered them to a bailee; and the real owner demanded them of the bailee, who refused to deliver them without the directions of the bailor: it was holden (d), that the bailor not having any lien, the refusal by the bailee was sufficient evidence of a conversion. Goods consigned to A., upon their arrival are landed on the defendant's wharf; the plaintiff in an action of trover, may prove his title by parol, although the bill of lading which has been indorsed to him cannot be received in evidence for want of a stamp (e). A trader, on the eve of bankruptcy, made a collusive sale of his goods to A. It was holden, that the assignees could not maintain trover for the goods against A., without proving a demand and refusal (f). But the sale of a ship, which was afterwards lost at sea, made by the defendant, who claimed under a defective conveyance from a trader before his bankruptcy, has been holden to be a sufficient conversion so as to enable the assignees to maintain trover, without proving a demand and refusal (g). N. The defendant sold the ship by public auction, and afterwards assigned it to the vendees, who sent her to sea. A demand and refusal is only evidence to induce a jury to presume a conversion (h); and, therefore, if the jury find a special verdict, that there was a demand and refusal, the court cannot adjudge it to be a conversion. A demand and refusal is not evidence of a conversion (i), where it is apparent that the defendant has not been guilty of a conversion: as in the case of the defendant having cut down the trees of the plaintiff, and left them lying in the plaintiff's ground; for in such case it is clear that there has not been any conversion, if they continue there. If A., into whose possession goods happen to come, being ignorant that B. is the real owner, refuses to deliver them to B., until he proves that he is the real owner; such qualified refusal is not evidence of a conversion (k).

(c) *Pattison* v. *Robinson*, 5 M. & S. 105.

(d) *Wilson* v. *Anderton*, 1 B. & Ad. 450.

(e) *Davis* v. *Reynolds*, 1 Stark. N. P. C. 115.

(f) *Nixon* v. *Jenkins*, 2 H. Bl. 135.

(g) *Bloxam* v. *Hubbard*, 5 East, 407.

(h) Per Sir *E. Coke*, C. J., 10 Rep. 56, b. 57.

(i) Per *Cur.*, 2 Mod. 245.

(k) *Green* v. *Dunn*, 3 Campb. 215, n., Lord *Ellenborough*, C. J. See also to the same effect, dict. per *Coke*, C. J., 2 Bulst. 312, *ante*, p. 1358, and Lord *Kenyon*, C. J., in *Solomon* v. *Dawes*, 1 Esp. N. P. C. 83.

In order to make a demand and refusal sufficient evidence of a conversion, the party, when he refuses, must have it in his power to deliver up or to detain the article demanded. Hence, where in trover for a deed (*l*), the evidence was, that when the deed was demanded from the defendant, he said he would not deliver it up, but that it was in the hands of his attorney, who had a lien upon it. This was holden insufficient. In trover against a carrier, a refusal to deliver is not evidence of a conversion, if it appears (*m*) clearly that the goods have been lost through negligence; but if that does not appear, or if the carrier had the goods in his custody when he refused to deliver them, it is good evidence of a conversion (*n*) (21). But he may give in evidence the detaining of the goods for his hire (*o*). So he may give in evidence, that the goods were stolen (*p*); for then he is not guilty of a conversion, though he will be liable in an action on the case to make compensation for the loss of the goods. If A. sends goods by B. (*q*), a common carrier, to be delivered to C., proof that B. asserted he had delivered the goods to C., whereas in truth C. had never received them, is not sufficient evidence of a conversion to support trover against B. So in trover for a horse in an innkeeper's possession, refusal is not a conversion, or evidence of a conversion, unless the plaintiff tender a sum sufficient for the keep of the horse, and the jury is to judge of the sufficiency of the tender (*r*) (22). But if A. put a horse to pasture with B.,

(*l*) *Smith* v. *Young*, 1 Campb. 439.

(*m*) *Anon.*, Salk. 655; *Ross* v. *Johnson*, 5 Burr. 2825; *Kirkman* v. *Hargreaves*, *ante*, p. 411.

(*n*) Salk. 655; *Dewell* v. *Moxon*, 1 Taunt. 391, S. P.

(*o*) *Skinner* v. *Upshaw*, 2 Lord Raym. 752. The case of the *Exeter Carrier*, cited by *Holt*, C. J., in *Yorke* v. *Grenaugh*, Lord Raym. 867.

(*p*) *George* v. *Wyburn*, 1 Rol. Abr. 6, (L.) pl. 4.

(*q*) *Attersol* v. *Briant*, 1 Campb. 409, *Ellenborough*, C. J.

(*r*) *Anon.*, 2 Show. 161, per *North*, C. J.

---

(21) " If a carrier. says he has the goods in his warehouse, and refuses to deliver them, that will be evidence of a conversion, and trover may be maintained, but not for a bare non-delivery, without any such refusal." Per Lord *Ellenborough*, C. J., in *Severin* v. *Keppel*, 4 Esp. N. P. C. 157.

(22) " If a man bring his horse to an inn, and leave him there in the stable without any special agreement as to what he is to pay, the innkeeper is not bound to deliver the horse until the owner has defrayed his charge for the horse; but he may justify the detainer of the horse for his food and keeping; and after the horse has eat as much as he is worth, the innkeeper, upon a reasonable appraisement, may sell him, and it is a good sale in law. But if there be a special agreement, that the owner of the horse shall pay a certain sum for the keep, in that case, although the horse eat out double his price, the innkeeper cannot sell him." Per *Popham*, C. J., Yelv. 67. But see *Chase* v. *Westmore*, *ubi sup.*, *ante*, p. 1375, and *Judson* v. *Etheridge*, *ante*, p. 1376; and see also *Jones* v. *Pearle*, Str. 556, where it was holden, that an innkeeper cannot sell the horse of his guest, except in the city of London. See *Thompson* v. *Lacy*,

and agree to pay him a certain sum per week as long as he remains at pasture, and afterwards sell him to C., who brings trover against B., B. cannot detain the horse against C., the purchaser, until he be paid, but must have recourse to his action against A. (s). Where bills of exchange were delivered by a trader, in contemplation of bankruptcy, to a creditor, with a view of giving him a preference, and the amount due on the bills was received by him after the bankruptcy; it was holden (t), that the receipt of the money did not amount to a conversion, and consequently that it was necessary to prove a demand of the bills and a refusal. The vendor of a quantity of tin, shipped the same on board a ship to Leghorn, by the orders of the vendee; and the captain, by his bill of lading, undertook to deliver the tin to an individual at Leghorn; the tin, being heavy, was placed at the bottom of the hold, with other goods over it; the vendee having become bankrupt, the vendor required the captain to deliver the tin, but did not tender the freight, or offer to make any compensation to him for the trouble of unloading the vessel. The captain refused, alleging, that he signed a bill of lading to deliver the tin to another person; and that he would not deliver to plaintiff; it was holden (u), that this was presumptive evidence of a conversion; for the captain had dispensed with the tender.

In trover against several defendants, all cannot be found guilty on the same count, without proof of a joint conversion by all (x). Possession ought to be proved in the *defendant himself* (y), for delivery to a servant is not sufficient, if the goods do not come to the hands of the defendant, unless the servant be employed by his master to receive goods for him, and the goods are delivered in the way of his trade; as if a pawn be delivered to a pawnbroker's servant (z). In trover against defendant for not delivering some wine deposited with her as a security for an advance of money; it was holden (a), that it

(s) *Chapman* v. *Allen*, Cro. Car. 271, recognized in *Jackson* v. *Cummins*, 5 M. & W. 342, *ante*, p. 1376. But see *Chase* v. *Westmore*, 5 M. & S. 180.
(t) *Jones* v. *Fort*, 9 B. & C. 764.
(u) *Thompson* v. *Trail*, 6 B. & C. 36.

(x) *Nicoll* v. *Glennie and others*, 1 M. & S. 588.
(y) Bull. N. P. 44.
(z) *Jones* v. *Hart*, Salk. 441.
(a) *Pothonier* v. *Dawson*, Holt's N. P. C. 383.

ante, p. 1375. In *Johnson* v. *Hill*, 3 Stark. N. P. C. 172, where A., under the colour of a legal proceeding, having wrongfully seized the horse of B., took it to an inn, where it was kept for several days. The landlord refused to deliver up the horse to B., upon a demand made soon after the delivery to him; but a few days afterwards offered to give up the horse to B. on being paid ten shillings for the keep. The chief justice was of opinion, that if the landlord knew, at the time the horse was delivered in his custody, that A. was not the owner of the property, but a mere wrong-doer, he made himself a party to the wrongful act of A., and could not insist on any recompense for keeping the horse; and this being left to the jury, they found for B., the plaintiff.

was not sufficient evidence of a conversion, to show that her son, who acted as her *general* agent, refused to give it up; and that it was necessary to prove that such agent acted under a special direction, in order to make the defendant liable as a wrong-doer. In trover for a bill of exchange, the damages are to be calculated according to the amount of the principal and interest due upon the bill at the time of the conversion (*b*).

Of Staying the Proceedings.

Formerly, if the defendant was desirous of staying the proceedings against him, by bringing the subject matter of the action into court, and undertaking to pay the costs incurred, the court refused to listen to the application (*c*), unless the action was brought for money (*d*), observing, that they had not any warehouse for the purpose. But of late years it has been usual to grant applications of this kind, when a proper case has been brought before the court (*e*) (23). But not where it appears that the goods are altered, and of less value than they were when taken (*f*). Where the goods are ponderous, the court will grant a rule to show cause, why, on the delivery of the goods to the plaintiff, and on payment of costs, the proceedings should not be stayed (*g*).

Damages.

By stat. 3 & 4 Will. IV. c. 42, [14th August, 1833,] s. 29, the jury, on the trial of any issue, or on any inquisition of damages, may, if they shall think fit, give damages in the nature of interest over and above the value of the goods at the time of the conversion, in all actions of trover. Where (*h*), after an act of bankruptcy, a sheriff seizes and sells goods, in trover by the assignees, the jury may deduct, in their estimate of damages, the expenses of the sale. Where the owner of adjoining land had worked coal-mines within the land of the plaintiff; it was holden (*i*), that the plaintiff being entitled to the coals as chattels, the proper estimate of damages was

---

(*b*) *Mercer* v. *Jones*, 3 Campb. 477.
(*c*) Salk. 597; *Bowington* v. *Parry*, Str. 822; *Olivant* v. *Perineau*, Str. 1191; 1 Wils. 23, *S. C.*; *Harding* v. *Wilkin*, Say. 120.
(*d*) *Anon.*, Str. 142.
(*e*) Per Lord *Kenyon*, C. J., 7 T. R. 54; *Everard* v. *Lathbury*, Bull. N. P. 49.

(*f*) *Royden* v. *Batty*, Barnes, 284; *Fisher* v. *Prince*, 3 Burr. 1363.
(*g*) *Cooke* v. *Holgate*, C. B., Barnes, 281, ed. 4to; *Watts* v. *Phipps*, B. R. E. 7 Geo. III., Bull. N. P. 49.
(*h*) *Clarke* v. *Nicholson*, 1 Cr. M. & R. 724; 5 Tyr. 233.
(*i*) *Martin* v. *Porter*, 5 M. & W. 351.

---

(23) See *Pickering* v. *Truste*, 7 T. R. 53, where this doctrine was extended to trespass for taking goods.

the value of the coals when gotten, without deducting the expense of getting them. Defendant (*k*), a sheriff, who held goods taken in execution, delivered them to the plaintiffs, assignees of a bankrupt, after an action of trover had been commenced by them : the plaintiffs accepted the goods without condition : it was holden, that they could not recover in the action more than nominal damages ; at all events, not without alleging special matter in the declaration.

Costs.

On the subject of costs, see stat. 3 & 4 Vict. c. 24, *ante*, p. 37, explained as to actions in which verdicts had been returned before the passing of that act, by stat. 4 & 5 Vict. c. 28.

Judgment.

The judgment in this action is for the recovery of damages only (*l*), and in this respect it differs from the judgment in the analogous action of detinue, which is for the recovery of the *goods in question*, or the value thereof, if the plaintiff cannot have the goods.

(*k*) *Moon* v. *Raphael*, 2 Bingh. N. C. 310.
(*l*) *Knight* v. *Bourne*, Cro. Eliz. 116.

CHAPTER XLI.

USE AND OCCUPATION.

FORMERLY an action of assumpsit (a) for rent arrear upon a parol lease for years could not have been maintained, either pending (b), or after the expiration of the term (c), because it was considered as a real contract: the only remedies were by distress or action of debt. But on a mere promise to pay a sum of money (d), or so much as the plaintiff deserved to have (e), in consideration of the plaintiff's permitting the defendant to occupy lands, &c., an action of assumpsit might have been maintained by the common law. In this case the objection as to the contract being *real*, was removed by considering the permission to occupy as not amounting to a lease, and the mere promise to pay a sum of money in consideration of such permission, as not amounting to a reservation of rent. In order, however, more effectually to obviate the difficulties which occurred in the recovery of rent, where the demise was not by deed, it was enacted, by stat. 11 Geo. II. c. 19, s, 14, "that landlords, *where the agreement is not by deed,* may recover a reasonable satisfaction for the lands, tenements, or hereditaments, held *or* occupied by the defendant, in an action on the case, for the use and occupation of what was so held or enjoyed ; and if in evidence on the trial of such action, any parol demise, or any agreement (not being by deed) whereon a certain rent was reserved, shall appear, the plaintiff in such action shall not therefore be nonsuited, but may make use thereof as an evidence of the quantum of the damages to be recovered." Under this statute (f), a landlord who has rent owing to him is allowed to recover, not the rent, but an equivalent for the rent, a reasonable satisfaction for the use and occupation of the premises, which have been holden and enjoyed under the demise,

---

(a) *Brett* v. *Read*, Sir W. Jones, 329 ; Cro. Car. 343.

(b) 1 Rol. Abr. 7, (O.) pl. 1.

(c) *Ib.*, pl. 2. See also *Green* v. *Harrington*, Hob. 284 ; Hutt. 34, *S. C.*

(d) *Dartnal* v. *Morgan*, Cro. Jac. 598 ; *Chapman* v. *Southwicke*, 1 Lev. 204 ;

Johnson v. *May*, 3 Lev. 150. Adjudged on demurrer.

(e) *How* v. *Norton*, 1 Lev. 179 ; *Mason* v. *Welland*, Skin. 238, 242.

(f) Per *Eyre*, C. J., delivering the opinion of the court in *Naish* v. *Tatlock*, 2 H. Bl. 323.

by action for the use and occupation : and it is provided on his behalf, that, if the demise be produced against him, it shall not defeat his action, as it would have done before the statute ; but the fixed rent shall be only used as a medium, by which the uncertain damages to be recovered in this form of action shall be liquidated. A reasonable satisfaction for the use and occupation is the thing intended to be given ; the form of action marked out (being enlarged by a necessary construction, so as to be allowed to be maintained without an express promise), is the proper form in which such reasonable satisfaction is to be recovered ; but the reasonable satisfaction which in its own nature must apply to something specific by which it can be estimated, being here given for use and occupation, and for nothing else, it is a remedy which, in its own nature, is not co-extensive with a contract for rent, nor does it seem to have been within the scope and purview of the statute to make this remedy co-extensive with all the remedies for the recovery of rents claimed to be due by the mere force of the contract for rent. The statute meant to provide an easy remedy in the simple cases of actual occupation, leaving other more complicated cases to their ordinary remedy.

Since this statute, the action for use and occupation has been resorted to as one of the most convenient remedies for the recovery of rent arrear, in cases to which the statute applies. The plaintiff usually declares in the form of a general indebitatus assumpsit (1). Hence the declaration is very concise. The statute provides a remedy, in such cases only, where the agreement is not by deed ; but it has been holden (*g*), where the defendant held under a mere agreement for a lease, which did not amount to an actual demise, that the plaintiff might maintain an action for the use and occupation, although such agreement was by deed. A corporation aggregate may sue in assumpsit for use and occupation (*h*), where tenant has held premises under them without deed, and previously paid rent. In an action for use and occupation of apartments in the plaintiff's house during half a year (*i*), it appeared that the rent was claimed in consequence of the defendant having neglected to give a notice to quit : the defence set up was, that the plaintiff, after the defendant had quitted, had put up a bill at the window ; but Lord *Kenyon*, C. J., expressed an opinion, that the defence insisted on

(*g*) *Elliot* v. *Rogers*, 4 Esp. N. P. C. 59, *Kenyon*, C. J.; *Banister* v. *Usborne*, Peake's Addl. Cases, 76.

(*h*) *Mayor and B. of Stafford* v. *Till*, 4 Bingh. 75, recognizing *Dean and Chap-*

ter of Rochester v. *Pierce*, 1 Campb. 466, adopted in *Beverley* v. *The Lincoln Gas Light Comp.*, 6 A. & E. 843, *ante*, p. 66.

(*i*) *Redpath* v. *Roberts*, 3 Esp. N. P. C. 285.

(1) As to the action of debt for use and occupation, see *ante*, tit. " Debt," p. 601.

would afford no answer to the plaintiff's action. It was for the benefit of the defendant that the apartments should be let; nor would he infer from the circumstance of the party's endeavouring to let them, that the contract was put an end to; that there must be other circumstances to show it, and not merely an act of so equivocal a kind (*k*). That as the plaintiff had proved the taking the premises, and the payment of the rent, it was incumbent on the defendant to prove that the tenancy was determined, by express evidence. The defendant thereupon proved, that a notice to quit had been given, in which the plaintiff had acquiesced, and obtained a verdict. The delivery of the keys of the house by an agent of the tenant to a female servant at the house of the landlord, was held (*l*) by Lord *Ellenborough*, C. J., not sufficient to prove a determination of the tenancy, the female servant not having been called, and it not appearing that the keys had ever reached the plaintiff and been accepted by him. A tenancy from year to year (*m*), created by parol, is not determined by a parol license from the landlord to the tenant to quit in the middle of a quarter, and the tenant's quitting the premises accordingly. The statute of frauds (*n*) requires a deed or note in writing, or a surrender (*o*) by operation of law. But the necessity of a written surrender may be dispensed with by the admission of another tenant; and where a lessee quitted, in the middle of his term, apartments which he had taken for a year, and the lessor let them to another tenant, who occupied a short time; it was holden (*p*), that the lessor could not recover in an action for use and occupation against the lessee for a subsequent portion of the year, during which the apartments had been unoccupied; for the lessor, having precluded the defendant from occupying the apartments by letting them to another, must be taken to have rescinded the agreement, and to have dispensed with the necessity of a surrender. So where A. demised to B. part of a house for a year, at a rent payable quarterly, B. entered at Christmas and paid a quarter's rent at Lady-day. In April, a dispute having arisen between A. and B., B. said she would quit, A. told her she might go when she pleased, and he should be glad to get rid of her. B. accordingly quitted and delivered the keys of the rooms to A. on the 19th of April, who accepted them. It was holden (*q*), that A. could not recover rent *pro ratâ* for so long a time as B. had occupied; for

(*k*) This doctrine was recognized by Lord *Ellenborough*, C. J., in *Mills* v. *Bottomly*, Middlesex Sittings after M. T. 58 Geo. III., B. R.

(*l*) *Harland* v. *Bromley*, 1 Stark. 455.

(*m*) *Mollett* v. *Brayne*, 2 Campb. 104. See remark of *Gibbs*, C. J., on this case, in *Whitehead* v. *Clifford*, 5 Taunt. 519. In *Walls* v. *Atcheson*, 2 C. & P. 268, *Park*, J., says, that he should like to have this case of *Mollett* v. *Brayne* reconsidered.

(*n*) See section 3, and cases thereon, *ante*, p. 838.

(*o*) *Thomas* v. *Cook*, 2 B. & A. 119, cited by *Patteson*, J., in *Gore* v. *Wright*, 8 A. & E. 121.

(*p*) *Walls* v. *Atcheson*, 3 Bingh. 462.

(*q*) *Grimman* v. *Legge*, 8 B. & C. 324, cited by *Williams*, J., in *Slack* v. *Sharpe*, 8 A. & E. 374; 3 Nev. & P. 390; *ante*, p. 254.

where there is an express contract, none can be implied; and A., having destroyed his right to recover the rent, according to the contract, had destroyed it altogether. The defendant was tenant from year to year of a house and premises, at a rent payable half-yearly, on the 1st of April and 1st of October. The premises being required for the purposes of a railway, the Railway Company, in pursuance of a power given by their act of parliament, gave the defendant six months' notice to quit, which expired on the 28th of July. The defendant gave up possession to the company accordingly on that day, without obtaining or requiring compensation for his interest in the premises which he was entitled to under the act; it was holden (r), that he was liable for the rent of the half-year ending on the following 1st of October. Although an agreement may be void by the statute of frauds, as where a lease is granted in reversion for three years; yet if tenant take possession under it, he becomes tenant at will (s), and recourse may be had to the original agreement to calculate the amount of the rent. But where a lessee took a farm under an agreement, which he never signed, and the terms of which his lessor in a material point failed to fulfil; in an action for use and occupation of the farm, it was holden (t), that the jury might ascertain the value of the land, without regarding the amount of rent reserved by the agreement. When premises have been let to B. for a term determinable by a notice to quit, and pending such term, C. applies to A., the landlord, for leave to become the tenant instead of B., and upon A. consenting, agrees to stand in B.'s place and offers to pay rent; it was holden (u), that (although B.'s term had not been determined either by notice to quit or a surrender in writing,) A might maintain an action for use and occupation against C., and that C. could not set up B.'s title as a defence to that action. But where the defendant, in 1799, agreed by writing to take certain premises for 17 years, at a yearly rent, and entered: in 1813, the plaintiffs contracted to sell the fee to A., who thereupon bought from the defendant the residue of his term, and, without the assent of the plaintiffs, put in a new tenant who occupied for two years; the contract for sale was then rescinded; it was holden (x), that the plaintiffs were entitled to recover from the defendant, in an action for use and occupation, the rent from 1813 to the end of the original term, as there had not been any surrender in writing of his interest, and as the plaintiffs had not assented to the change of tenancy. " When a lease is expired, the tenant's responsibility is not at an end; for if the premises are in possession of an under-tenant, the landlord may refuse to accept the

(r) *Wainwright* v. *Ramsden*, 5 M. & W. 602.

(s) *De Medina* v. *Polson*, Holt's N. P. C. 47.

(t) *Tomlinson* v. *Day*, 2 Brod. & Bingh. 680.

(u) *Phipps* v. *Sculthorpe*, 1 B. & A. 50. See *Hyde* v. *Moakes*, 5 C. & P. 42.

(x) *Matthews and another* v. *Sawell*, 8 Taunt. 270; *Ibbs* v. *Richardson*, 9 A. & E. 849.

possession, and hold the original lessee liable; for the lessor is entitled to receive the absolute possession at the end of the term." Tenants are bound to give up (y) possession of the premises at the expiration of their terms: if they omit to do so, and retain possession, either by themselves or their under-tenants, they are liable to pay rent to their landlord, unless, indeed, he has consented to accept other parties as his tenants instead of them (z).

The words of the statute are, that the plaintiff may "recover a reasonable satisfaction for the lands, &c. held *or* occupied by the defendant in an action for use and occupation." Hence use and occupation lies for a constructive (a) as well as an actual occupation. An occupation by the tenant of the defendant is, as far as respects the plaintiff, an occupation by the defendant himself: hence (b), if A. agree to let his lands to B., who permits C. to occupy them, A. may recover the rent in an action against B. for the use and occupation. So rent accruing after premises are burnt down, may be recovered (c), although no longer inhabited by the tenant, inasmuch as he must be taken still to *hold* the land, and that is sufficient to satisfy the words of the statute. So where defendants, as tenants from year to year, occupied a second floor, which during their occupation was consumed by an accidental fire; it was holden (d), that notwithstanding the destruction of the premises, they were liable to an action for use and occupation for the period which elapsed between the fire and the regular determination of the tenancy; *Tindal,* C. J., observing, that if there had been an agreement in writing between the parties for a term of years, no question could have been made; but that the term of years still existed, and a tenancy from year to year, until it is determined by a notice to quit, is as to its legal character and consequences the same as a term for years. If the landlord rebuilds, and the tenant chooses to re-enter and to continue his occupation of the new building, there seems nothing to prevent him, as no notice to quit has been given on either side; and if so, the obligation of each of the parties must be reciprocal, and the tenant must make satisfaction for the rent. So where a second floor of a house was occupied at a rent payable quarterly, and during the currency of a quarter the house was burnt; it was holden (e), that as, in the action for use and occupation, the rent is considered as accruing de die in diem, the plaintiff was entitled to recover for the occupation at least up to the time of the fire taking place; *Patteson,* J., observed, that the defendant is in this dilemma,—that if there is an express demise, he is liable for the rent, notwithstanding the fire;

(y) Per *Kenyon*, C. J., in *Harding* v. *Crulhorne,* 1 Esp. N. P. C. 56, recognized in *Christy* v. *Tancred*, 7 M. & W. 127.

(z) Per *Parke*, B., *Christy* v. *Tancred,* ubi sup.

(a) *Pinero* v. *Judson*, 6 Bingh. 206.
(b) *Bull* v. *Sibbs*, 8 T. R. 327.
(c) *Baker* v. *Holtzaffell*, 4 Taunt. 45.
(d) *Ison* v. *Gorton*, 5 Bingh. N. C. 501.
(e) *Packer* v. *Gibbins*, 1 G. & D. 10.

if there is not, he is liable for the period during which the premises were actually occupied. Where the defendant has not obtained possession under the plaintiff, the plaintiff can only recover rent from the time he has had the legal estate in him, although he may have had the equitable estate long before. The defendant entered upon a leasehold cottage under J. S., who soon after mortgaged it to W. S., and in 1806 assigned the equity of redemption to the plaintiff (*f*). On the 18th of July, 1808, W. S. assigned the legal estate in the premises to the plaintiff. The defendant continued in possession till the Michaelmas following, and had paid no rent for the last two years. It was contended, that although a person having the equitable estate only, perhaps could not maintain use and occupation without privity of contract, yet the plaintiff being now clothed with the legal estate, his title would have reference to the time when the equity of redemption was assigned to him, so as to entitle him to two years' rent. But Lord *Ellenborough* clearly held, that he could only recover rent for the period between the 18th of July and Michaelmas-day, 1808. His Lordship likewise ruled, in the same cause, that the defendant, who just before he quitted had been distrained upon by the ground landlord for several years' ground rent, amounting to a much larger sum than was due to the plaintiff, could only set off a part of the sum proportioned to the period during which the plaintiff had the legal estate ; and that the fact of the plaintiff having brought an ejectment for the same premises, laying a demise on the 18th of July, 1808, was no bar to the present action, but was only matter of special application to the court. Where defendant (*g*), in expectation of a lease by indenture, which he had agreed to take from the plaintiff, procured attornments from some of the tenants, and received rent from others; it was holden, that the occupation by the tenants was an occupation by the defendant, as much as if the defendant were in the actual possession himself; and it being one entire holding, under the expectation of a demise of the whole, the defendant was liable for the whole amount. In an action against the assignees of B. (*h*), a bankrupt, the declaration stated, that the defendants, on such a day, were indebted to the plaintiff in £— for the use and occupation of two houses, &c., before that time occupied, *as well by the bankrupt, whose estate therein the defendants afterwards had, as by the defendants, at their special instance and request*, for one year then elapsed, and as tenants thereof respectively, to the plaintiff, and by his permission. The facts were, that after B. had occupied the premises during part of the year, under an agreement to pay £— a year for them, he became a bankrupt, whereupon the defendants, his assignees, entered into

(*f*) *Cobb* v. *Carpenter*, 2 Campb. 13, n.
(*g*) *Neal* v. *Swind*, 2 Cr. & J. 377; 2 Tyr. 464.

(*h*) *Naish* v. *Tatlock and others, Assignees of Lediard, a Bankrupt*, 2 H. Bl. 319.

possession and continued in the possession for the remainder of the year. A proportion of the annual rent for that part of the year during which the defendants were in possession, was paid into court. It was holden, that if the plaintiff could recover at all in this form of action against one person for the use and occupation of another, (as to which the court would not give any opinion,) it must be on the ground of that occupation having been permitted at the defendant's request, and that request must be proved; that the words "at the special instance and request of the defendants," were in this case words of substance, and operative, connecting the occupation of the defendants, for which they were bound to make a satisfaction, with the occupation of B., a stranger, for whose occupation, *primâ facie* at least, the defendants were not liable; that in point of fact it was not at the request of the defendants that B. had been permitted to occupy; the defendants had no relation to B., but as his assignees, and that relation did not commence until the close of B.'s occupation; that relation, therefore, alone could not have the effect of making them personally liable to answer for his occupation before his bankruptcy. The averment, that he had been permitted to occupy "at the request" of the defendants, was therefore substance, and not mere form, and as the plaintiff had failed in the proof of it, he was not entitled to recover from the defendants the rent due for B.'s occupation.

The defendant contracted to purchase of the plaintiff the lease of a house (*i*),, and on payment of the purchase money, was permitted to take possession. A few months afterwards, the plaintiff not having made out a good title, defendant declared his intention to rescind the contract; he accordingly quitted possession of the house, and brought an action for money had and received against the plaintiff, and recovered the whole of the purchase money and the expenses of investigating the title. The plaintiff then brought an action for use and occupation against the defendant; but it was holden, that it would not lie; *Mansfield*, C. J., observing, that a contract could not arise by implication of law under circumstances, the occurrence of which neither of the parties ever had in their contemplation; that if no money had been paid, perhaps it might be a different question; but if a person paid his money, and was so unwise as to take possession without a title, justice required that the one party should take back his money and the other his house. In this case, the fact of the defendant having paid the whole purchase money at the time of the contract was relied on, and it was considered that the interest was a sufficient compensation for the use which defendant had of the premises. But in *Hall v. Vaughan*, Peake's N. P. C. 254, 2nd edition, n. (*a*), the court held, that the vendor might, in cases where the contract went off without

(*i*) *Kirtland* v. *Pounsett*, 2 Taunt. 145, cited in *Keating* v. *Bulkely*, 2 Stark. N. P. C. 421. But see *Hearn* v. *Tomlin*, Peake's N. P. C. 253, 2nd edition.

fault on his part, and the occupation had been beneficial to the vendee, recover a compensation for such occupation in this form of action. So in *Howard* v. *Shaw*, 8 M. & W. 118, where a party was let into possession of land under a contract of purchase, which afterwards went off; it was holden, that he was liable in this form of action at the suit of the vendor, for the period during which he continued in possession after the contract went off. Before the stat. 6 Geo. IV. c. 16, s. 75, (*ante*, p. 254, 473,) an action for use and occupation might have been maintained against a tenant from year to year, upon an agreement by him to pay rent during the tenancy, notwithstanding his bankruptcy and the occupation of his assignees during part of that time for which the rent accrued (*k*).

Debt for Use and Occupation.—At the trial, it appeared that plaintiff had recovered a judgment against A., upon which, in E. T. 1826, an elegit was issued. The sheriff returned an inquisition, by which it was found that A., at the time of the judgment, was seised, for life, of land in the occupation of defendant, (being the land in respect of the rent of which the present action was brought,) and in September, plaintiff served defendant with notice of the inquisition, and with a demand of the rent then due. A large sum was then due, and defendant, upon being served, said that A. was his land-lord, and that he paid his rent to him. On the part of the defendant, it was proved, that A. had not any legal interest in the land; that it was vested in trustees for a long term of years, in order, among other purposes, to raise a large sum of money for the aunt of A., which money had not been raised; in the meantime, A. was per-mitted to receive the rents and profits. The plaintiff was non-suited; and the court confirmed (*l*) the opinion of the C. J., on the ground that the plaintiff could not recover in ejectment; nor in an action for the rent, because he could not claim the rent, unless he had a right to enter; that although the inquisition found that A. was seised, yet a stranger to the inquisition was not bound to traverse it; he might dispute its correctness in any other way. A., however, had nothing in the premises but a joint equitable interest, of which a court of equity alone could take cognizance.

By R. G. H. T. 4 Will. IV. No. 5, counts upon a demise, and for use and occupation of the same land for the same time, are not to be allowed. But where the first count of a declaration was framed on the stat. 11 Geo. II. c. 19, s. 18, (see *ante*, p. 599,) for the recovery of double rent, and the second count was for use and occupation, the court rejected an application to strike out one of the two counts (*m*).

Bringing an ejectment will not be a bar to an action for use and occupation for rent due before the day of the demise laid in the

---

(*k*) *Boot* v. *Wilson*, 8 East, 311.
(*l*) *Harris* v. *Booker*, 4 Bingh. 96.

(*m*) *Thornton* v. *Whitehead*, 1 Tyr. & Gr. 313; 1 M. & W. 14.

declaration in ejectment (*n*), but rent due subsequent to that day cannot be recovered in an action for use and occupation (*o*).

The defendant in this action will not be allowed to impeach the title of the plaintiff, by whose permission he entered upon and occupied the tenement demised. Hence a plea of *nil habuit in tenementis* cannot be pleaded (*p*); and this rule holds, even where the declaration does not state the tenement demised to belong to the plaintiff, provided it is stated, that defendant occupied by the permission of the plaintiff (*q*). A. hired apartments by the year of B.; B. afterwards let the entire house to C., who sued A. in an action for the use and occupation, for the hire of the apartments. It was holden (*r*), that A. could not impeach C.'s title. So where the occupier of a house had submitted to a distress for rent, stated in the notice of distress to be due from him as tenant to the distrainor; it was holden (*s*), that this was an acknowledgment of the tenancy. So where A. had come into occupation under J. S., who had paid rent upon a distress by B.; it was holden (*t*), that after proof of the fact, A. was estopped to dispute B.'s title to the rent. So a person who has occupied premises and paid rent to the apparent proprietor as his landlord, and who, when sued by him for the use and occupation, has paid money into court, cannot allege that he has only the equitable estate, or that he is entitled only as

(*n*) *Birch* v. *Wright*, 1 T. R. 378.
(*o*) Per *Buller*, J., *S. C.*, 1 T. R. 388.
(*p*) *Richards* v. *Holditch* (2), H. 13 Geo. II., cited in *Lewis* v. *Wallis*, Say. R. 13; *Curtis* v. *Spitty*, 1 Bingh. N. C. 15; 4 M. & Sc. 554, S. P., action of debt for use and occupation.
(*q*) *Richards* v. *Holditch*, H. 13 Geo.

II., cited in *Lewis* v. *Wallis*, Say. R. 13; 1 Wils. 314, *S. C.*
(*r*) *Rennie* v. *Robinson*, 1 Bingh. 147.
(*s*) *Panton* v. *Jones*, 3 Campb. 372, Bayley, J.
(*t*) *Cooper* v. *Blandy*, 1 Bingh. N. C. 45; in which *Park*, J., recognized *Panton* v. *Jones*.

(2) The case of *Richards* v. *Holditch*, was this:—Error to reverse a judgment in action on the case upon several promises, in Stepney Court, because the plaintiff declared, that in consideration he permitted the defendant to enjoy several houses, without showing what title he had. Yelv. 227, 8, *Glasses's* case, and *Aylet* v. *Williams*, 3 Lev. 193, were cited. E contra it was said, that permission to enjoy without showing any title, was a sufficient consideration. 1 Leon. 43; Cro. Jac. 498; 1 Lev. 304; 3 Lev. 150. An objection was made to the plea, that this action being founded on a collateral promise, and not on a contract for the rent, nil habuit in tenementis, as was pleaded in this case, was not a good plea, and of that opinion was the whole court; for if any one enjoys a benefit at his request, and by permission of another, that is a sufficient consideration for an assumpsit. N. Chapple cited a case, as ruled by Lord *Hardwicke*, where A., without title, gave possession of a house to B.; C., the owner, brought assumpsit for the use and enjoyment; but because B. did not receive his possession from C., nor any wise occupied under him, Lord *Hardwicke* held the action not maintainable by him.

co-executor with others who do not join in the action; although the plaintiff, at the trial, discloses that fact in proving his own case (*u*).

Under the new rules, the plea of non-assumpsit operates only as a denial in fact of the express contract alleged, or of the matters of fact from which the contract or promise alleged may be implied by law. This action is brought for a reasonable satisfaction given by the statute for the occupation of land held and enjoyed by the defendant by the permission of plaintiff. It is, therefore, a matter of fact stated in the declaration, from which the promise arises by operation of law, " that the defendant held and enjoyed by the permission of the plaintiff." Where the plaintiff had mortgaged the premises before the defendant came into possession, and the mortgagee had given notice to the defendant not to pay the plaintiff any rent becoming due after such notice; it was holden (*x*), that under non-assumpsit, the defendant might give these facts in evidence; for the notice was evidence that the subsequent holding was not by permission of plaintiff, as alleged in the declaration, but by permission of the mortgagee. Obedience to the mortgagee's notice as to rent due before the notice must be specially pleaded.

In an action for use and occupation of glebe lands (*y*), it appeared, that the former incumbent had let the lands in question to the defendant, who had continued tenant to the present incumbent, the plaintiff, who had paid him half a year's rent for the same. The action being brought for some arrears of rent, the defendant offered to give evidence of the plaintiff's having been simoniacally presented, of which, as it was stated, the defendant was ignorant, when he paid the former rent; but Lord *Kenyon*, C. J., refused to receive this evidence, being of opinion that the case fell within the common rule, that a tenant should not be permitted to impeach the title of his landlord in an action for use and occupation. There was a verdict accordingly for the plaintiff. The court of B. R., on motion for a new trial, concurred in opinion with the C. J. Neither will a defendant (*z*), who has obtained possession under the plaintiff, be permitted to show that the plaintiff's title had expired, unless he solemnly renounced the plaintiff's title at the time, and commenced a fresh holding under another person. Proof of payment of rent to a third person claiming title is not sufficient, without a formal renunciation of the plaintiff's title at the time, and commencing a fresh holding under another person. Where premises are let at an entire rent, an eviction from part, if the tenant thereupon gives up possession of the residue, is a complete defence to this

---

(*u*) *Dolby* v. *Iles*, 11 A. & E. 335 ; 3 P. & D. 287.

(*x*) *Waddilove* v. *Barnett*, 2 Bingh. N. C. 538 ; 2 Sc. 763. See *Brown* v. *Storey*, 1 M. & Gr. 117 ; 1 Scott, N. C. 9, and the other cases cited, *ante*, p. 669.

(*y*) *Cooke, Clerk*, v. *Loxley*, 5 T. R. 4, recognized in *Brooksby* v. *Watts*, 1 Marsh. 38 ; 6 Taunt. 333, *S. C.* See *Cripps* v. *Blank*, 9 D. & R. 480.

(*z*) *Balls* v. *Westwood*, 2 Campb. 11.

action (a). If there be a lawful eviction (b) from part by an elder title, the rent is apportioned only, and not suspended. A tenant from year to year (c), not under any agreement to repair, may quit without previous notice to his landlord, on the premises becoming unsafe and useless from want of repairs. A tenant (d) of a house bound by agreement to keep it in tenantable repair, may quit without notice in the course of his term, if the premises become unwholesome to reside in, not from any default or neglect of his own, but from something over which he had no control, or none except at an extravagant or unreasonable expense. A. being in possession under a lease for years, underlet the premises, from year to year, to the defendants, who knew the extent of A.'s interest. The plaintiff, afterwards, took a lease of the same premises expectant on the determination of A.'s term; and the defendants, after the determination of A.'s term, continued in possession for a quarter of a year, when they paid rent for that period to the plaintiff, at the same rate they had previously paid to A., and claimed to give up possession. This was refused, and the premises remained unoccupied for some time. The plaintiff brought an action for use and occupation, but the C. J. held (e), that the old tenancy having been determined, there was not any evidence of a new continuing tenancy, for the fact relied on admitted equally well of a different construction. So where defendant, who had occupied under a lease, which expired at Lady-day, 1829, paid a quarter's rent on Midsummer-day, 1829, deducting something for repairs; he was not afterwards seen on the premises, but the rent was paid, at irregular intervals, by L., who had occupied the premises. In an action for use and occupation against the defendant, claiming two quarter's rent due at Lady-day, 1831; the judge left it to the jury to find whether the landlord had not accepted L. as the tenant; and the jury having found for the defendant, the court refused (f) to disturb the verdict. A. lets lands to B., who underlets to C. and others; during these tenancies, A. gives notice to C. and the other under-tenants to quit, and C. does quit, and the lands before occupied by him remain unoccupied for a year, and are then again let by B.; A. cannot recover against B. for the use and occupation of this land for the year. And semble, under these circumstances, an eviction might be pleaded to the whole demand (g). The husband is not liable in an action for use and occupation (h), upon an occupation by the wife dum sola, not at the request of the husband.

(a) Smith v. Raleigh, 3 Campb. 513.
(b) Neale v. Mackenzie, 2 Cr. M. & R. 84; 5 Tyr. 1106.
(c) Edwards v. Etherington, Ry. & M. 268; Salisbury v. Marshall, 4 C. & P. 65, S. P., Tindal, C. J.
(d) Per Bayley, B., in Collins v. Barrow, 1 M. & Rob. 112.
(e) Freeman v. Jury and another, 1 M. & Malk. 19.
(f) Woodcock v. Nuth, 8 Bingh. 170; 1 M. & Sc. 317.
(g) Burn v. Phelps, 1 Stark. N. P. C. 94.
(h) Richardson v. Hall, 1 Brod. & Bingh. 50.

In an action for use and occupation (i); if it appear that the premises were let to the defendant for the purposes of prostitution, the action cannot be sustained, the contract being *contra bonos mores* (3); but where the premises are not let to the defendant for the purposes of prostitution, the defendant cannot evade the payment of a fair rent (k), although she prove that she has used them for those purposes. In an action for use and occupation of a lodging under a weekly tenancy, where it did not appear that the lodging was originally let for the purposes of prostitution; it was holden (l), that the plaintiff could not recover the weekly rent which had accrued after he was fully informed that the defendant occupied the lodging for the purposes of prostitution. See further on this subject, *ante*, p. 63.

Assumpsit for use and occupation (m); on examination of a witness who proved the occupation by defendant, it appeared, that there had been an agreement in writing, but not stamped. It was contended, by plaintiff's counsel, that the agreement, not having been stamped, was not binding on the parties, and that therefore the plaintiff might waive this, and go into evidence generally for use and occupation. It was insisted for defendant, that it appeared that defendant held under a written contract, and therefore the plaintiff was bound to give it in evidence. *Eldon*, C. J., was of this opinion; observing, that this being a specific contract between plaintiff and defendant, the plaintiff is bound to show what that contract was: it may contain clauses which may prevent plaintiff from recovering; others for the benefit of defendant, which he had a right to have produced: but the contract not being stamped, it could not be given in evidence (4), therefore the plaintiff must be nonsuited. An action

(i) *Girarday* v. *Richardson*, 1 Esp. N. P. C. 13.

(k) *Wiggins* v. *George*, per *Abbott*, C. J., Middx. Sittings after E. T. 5 Geo. IV.

(l) *Jennings* v. *Throgmorton*, Ry. & M. 251.

(m) *Brewer* v. *Palmer*, 3 Esp. N. P. C. 213.

---

(3) So the first publisher of a libellous and immoral work, *e. g.*, the Memoirs of Harriette Wilson, cannot maintain an action against any person for publishing a pirated edition. *Stockdale* v. *Onwhyn*, 5 B. & C. 173. In *Poplett* v. *Stockdale*, 2 C. & P. 198, it was holden, that the printer could not recover against the publisher.

(4) *R.* v. *The Inhabitants of St. Paul's, Bedford*, 6 T. R. 452, S. P. But see *R.* v. *Pendleton*, 15 East, 449, 455, where a question had been agitated at the sessions upon the settlement of a person who had served first under unstamped articles of agreement, and afterwards for four years; *Bayley*, J., said, " It has been argued, that inasmuch as a pauper served for some part of the time at least under a written instrument, unstamped, we cannot look at the instrument, even to see for what time it enured, and that no parol evidence could be given of any contract with reference to the subject matter of it. But though we cannot look at the unstamped

for use and occupation (n) is maintainable without attornment upon the stat. 4 & 5 Ann. c. 16, ss. 9 and 10, by the trustees of one whose title the tenant (defendant) had notice of before he paid over his rent to his original landlord; although the tenant had no notice of the legal title being in the plaintiffs on the record.

(n) *Lumley* v. *Hodgson*, 16 East, 99.

---

instrument for the purpose of proving by it any agreement between the parties, for such is the general import of the Stamp Acts, yet the court may look at it to see whether it applies to other evidence of a contract between them. As if a contract in writing be made, not stamped, for the sale and delivery of certain goods on certain terms, the court, in an action for non-delivery of goods, upon a contract proved by parol evidence only, may look at the instrument to see whether it applies to the goods then sought to be recovered for: and if those goods were not included in the contract, parol evidence may be received of the contract sought to be recovered upon. So here, the court might look at the instrument to see the duration of the first contract under it, in order to guide them in receiving parol evidence of the subsequent service, to which it did not apply." An unstamped instrument may be looked at *by the court* for the purpose of seeing whether it requires a stamp, or is properly stamped, that being a part of the duty of the judges, with which the jury have nothing to do, and of which they are supposed not to take any cognizance. It may be looked at *by the jury* also for a collateral object, as was done in *Gregory* v. *Fraser*, 3 Campb. 454, [to prove or disprove the fraud of the plaintiff, in having made the defendant drunk;] but such an instrument cannot be read in evidence as *a security*; per Lord *Tenterden*, C. J., delivering judgment in *Jardine* v. *Payne*, 1 B. & Ad. 670.

CHAPTER XLII.

WAGER.

I. *Introduction, p.* 1398; *Of Legal Wagers, p.* 1398; *Form of Action, p.* 1400.

II. *Of Illegal Wagers, p.* 1400.

I. *Introduction, p.* 1398; *Of Legal Wagers, p.* 1398; *Form of Action, p.* 1400.

INTRODUCTION.—It has frequently been lamented, that idle and impertinent wagers between persons not interested in the subject or event were ever considered as valid contracts. Grave and learned judges have thought that it would have been more beneficial for the public, if it had been originally determined, that an action would not lie for the enforcing the payment of any wager (1). Actions, however, on wagers relating to a variety of subjects, having been entertained under certain restrictions, and the legislature not having as yet interposed to prohibit them entirely, it may be proper to state in what cases an action will lie for enforcing the payment of a wager, and in what such action cannot be maintained.

Of Legal Wagers.—In *Andrews* v. *Herne* (a), where a wager was laid, that Charles Stuart would be King of England within twelve months next following, he then being in exile, it was holden good (2). So in the *Earl of March* v. *Pigot* (b), where two heirs

---

(a) 1 Lev. 33.
(b) 5 Burr. 2802, recognised in *Mead* v. *Davison*, 3 A. & E. 307. But see the observation of *Heath*, J., on this case, in 3 Campb. 172, *viz.* that it was a case not to be cited, being of very doubtful authority. See also *Bland* v. *Collett*, 4 Campb. 157.

---

(1) " I think it would have been better if wagers had originally been left to the decision of the Jockey Club." *Maule*, B., 5 M. & W. 82.

(2) But as it was justl observed, by Lord *Ellenborough*, C. J., in *Gilbert* v. *Sykes*, 16 East, 150, the illegality of this wager, on the ground to its being against public policy, does not appear to have been brought

apparent betted on the lives of their respective fathers, no objection was made to the subject of the wager ; and it was further holden, that the circumstance of one of the fathers being dead at the time when the wager was made, but of which circumstance the parties were ignorant, did not affect the validity of the wager. In *Murray* v. *Kelly*, B. R. M. 25 Geo. III., on a rule to show cause why the defendant should not be discharged on filing common bail, on the ground that the action was on a wager, whether A. kept a military academy at such a place, or not ; Lord *Mansfield* said, that as it was merely a wager on a private event, he saw no reason why it should not be considered as a legal debt; and the rule was discharged. A wager (c) on the event of an appeal to the House of Lords from the Court of Chancery, was holden good ; the wager having been made between parties who could not in any degree bias the judgment of the House, and there not being any fraud or colour in the case. So where (d) the subject of the wager was, whether one S. T. had or had not, before a certain day, bought a waggon, lately belonging to D. C. ; it was holden good, per three justices ; but *Buller*, J., was of a different opinion—1st, on the ground that two persons shall not be permitted, by means of a voluntary wager, to try any question upon the right or interest of a third person ; and 2dly, that all wagers, whether in the shape of a policy or not, between parties not having any interest, were prohibited by stat. 14 Geo. III. c. 48. So a wager (e) of a *rump and dozen*, whether the defendant was older than the plaintiff, was holden to be legal. A wager on the future price of foreign funds is not void or illegal, either by the 7 Geo. II. c. 8, or at common law (f). With respect

(c) *Jones* v. *Randall*, Cowp. 37.
(d) *Good* v. *Elliott*, 3 T. R. 693.
(e) *Hussey* v. *Crickitt*, 3 Campb. 168.

(f) *Morgan* v. *Pebrer*, 3 Bingh. N. C. 457 ; 4 Sc. 230, recognizing *Good* v. *Elliott*.

under the consideration of the court. In *Gilbert* v. *Sykes*, the defendant, in the year 1802, in consideration of one hundred guineas, agreed to pay the plaintiff a guinea a day during the life of Buonaparte. The defendant paid the guinea a day for some years; but then desisted. The action was brought to recover the arrears. The jury having found a verdict for the defendant ; on motion for a new trial, it was contended, in support of the verdict, that the wager was illegal, inasmuch as it had a tendency to create an interest in the plaintiff in the life of a foreign enemy, and which, in the case of invasion, might induce him to act contrary to hi allegiance. The court, being of opinion that the justice of the case had been satisfied, refused to disturb the verdict ; and Lord *Ellenborough*, C. J., expressed a strong opinion against the legality of the wager, as well on the ground before mentioned, as also on the ground that the party suffering under such a contract, might be induced to compass and encourage the horrid practice of assassination, in order to get rid of a life so burdensome to him. This decision was recognized in *Evans* v. *Jones*, 5 M. & W. 77, *post*, p. 1405.

to the form of declaring on a wager, it may be observed, that before
the time of *Holt*, C. J., it was a question, whether a general indebitatus assumpsit would not lie for a wager; it was, however, finally
agreed, that it would not (*g*); but although an action does not lie in
that particular form, yet a special assumpsit on the wager itself,
laid by way of mutual promises, may be maintained.

II. *Of Illegal Wagers.*

1. WAGERS are illegal which are specially prohibited by positive
statute. A policy of insurance is, in the nature of it, a contract of
indemnity, and of great benefit to trade. But the use of it was
perverted by its being turned into a wager. To remedy this evil,
the stat. 19 Geo. II. c. 37 (*h*) was made, which, after enumerating
in the preamble the various frauds and pernicious practices introduced by the perversion of this species of contract, and, among
others, that of gaming or wagering, under pretence of insuring
vessels, &c., proceeds under general words to prohibit all contracts
of assurance by way of gaming or wagering. An agreement, in
writing, was made (*i*), that plaintiff should pay the defendant £20,
at the next port a ship should reach; in consideration whereof, the
defendant undertook that the ship should save her passage to China
that season, and if she did not, then he would pay the plaintiff
£1,000, at the end of one month after she arrived in the Thames.
It was holden, that this agreement being made without reference to any property on board, although it appeared that the
plaintiff had some little interest in the cargo, was a wagering policy
within the meaning of the preceding statute. A similar provision
has been made with respect to insurances on lives, or any other
event, in consequence of a mischievous kind of gaming, which had
been introduced by such insurances, wherein the assured had no
interest. To remedy this evil it was enacted, by stat. 14 Geo. III.
c. 48, s. 1, " That insurances made on the life of any person, or *any
other event*, wherein the person for whose use such policy shall be
made, shall have no interest, or by way of gaming or wagering, shall
be void." The second section directs, that in all policies on lives or
other events, the names of the persons interested shall be inserted.
A wager in the form of a policy, between two uninterested persons
upon the sex of a third (*k*), is within the meaning of the preceding
statute, and consequently illegal. In *Mollison* v. *Staples*, Park,
Ins. 640, n., where a policy was made on the event of there being an

(*g*) *Jackson* v. *Colegrave*, in error,
Exch. Chr. H. 6 Will. III., Carth. 338;
Bovey v. *Castleman*, 1 Ld. Raym. 69.

(*h*) See *ante*, p. 1014.

(*i*) *Kent* v. *Bird*, Cowp. 583.
(*k*) *Roebuck and another* v. *Hammer-
ton*, Cowp. 737.

open trade between Great Britain and the province of Maryland, on or before the 6th July, 1778, Lord *Mansfield* said, "that it was clear the plaintiff could not recover." The authority of the two foregoing cases was recognized in *Paterson* v. *Powell*, 9 Bingh. 320; 2 M. & Sc. 399; in which it was holden, that an engagement in consideration of forty guineas, to pay £100, in case Brazilian shares should be done at a certain sum on a certain day, subscribed by several persons, each for themselves, was holden to be a policy of insurance, and void within the foregoing statute of 14 Geo. III. c. 48. In *Good* v. *Elliott*, 3 T. R. 693, *Kenyon*, C. J., *Grose* and *Ashhurst*, Js., were of opinion, that the preceding statute was confined to *policies* of insurance, and that from the words used in the second clause, it was apparent, that the legislature had *written* instruments only in contemplation. But the construction which was put by *Buller*, J., on this statute, was, that it had nothing to do with what, in the true sense and meaning of the word, is a policy, that is, a mercantile policy made on interest, but that it prohibited *all wagers* made on any event in which the parties had not any interest. By stat. 16 Car. II. c. 7, s. 2, "The winner of any money, or other valuable thing, *by deceit*, in playing at cards, dice, tables, tennis, bowls, skittles, shovel-board, or in cock-fighting, horse-races, dog-matches, foot-races, or other games; or by bearing a part in the stakes, or by betting on the sides of such as play, ride, or run; shall forfeit treble the value." By the third section, all securities and promises given or made for the payment of sums exceeding £100, which have been lost at one time, by playing at any one of the said games, or by betting on the players, are declared void, and the winner shall forfeit treble the value of the money or other thing won, above £100. By 9 Ann. c. 14, s. 1 *(l)*, "All notes, bills, bonds, judgments, mortgages, or other securities, given by any person where the whole or any part of the consideration of such securities shall be for money, or other valuable thing, won by gaming, or playing at cards, dice, tables, tennis, bowls, or other game, or by betting on the sides of such as game at any of the aforesaid games, or for repaying any money knowingly lent for such gaming or betting, or lent at the time and place of such play, to any person that shall play or bet, shall be void"*(m)*. But now, by stat. 5 & 6 Will. IV. c. 41, (see *ante*, p. 322,) notes, bills, or mortgages, which under the foregoing acts would have been absolutely void, shall be deemed to have been made for an illegal consideration.

The construction which has been put on the 3rd section of the 16th Car. II. c. 7, may be gathered from the following case:—In debt for £100, the plaintiff declared upon articles *(n)* of agreement, purporting that the plaintiff and defendant should run a horse for

---

(*l*) See *ante*, p. 321, 548.
(*m*) See *Sigel* v. *Jebb*, 3 Stark. N. P.C.1.

(*n*) *Hedgeborrow* v. *Rosenden*, 1 Ventr. 253.

£100, and if the defendant lost, he should pay the £100, &c. The defendant pleaded the 3rd section of stat. 16 Car. II. *Holt*, for the plaintiff, insisted, that the statute intended to avoid securities given for money lost at play, but not where the contract was precedent; but the court were of a different opinion: observing, that such construction would wholly elude the statute, and let men loose to play for any great sum, provided they secured it beforehand, and added, that this statute, being to suppress the practice of excessive gaming (*o*), should be construed in the most extensive manner that could be to answer that end. A. lost at play to the plaintiff (*p*), and gave him a bill for the amount of the sum lost, on the defendant, who accepted the bill, and afterwards refused payment; to an action brought on the bill, the defendant pleaded, that after the 29th day of September, 1664 (*q*), and before the making the said bill, A. and the plaintiff were playing together at hazard, and that A. then, at one time and meeting, lost to the plaintiff above £100, and that, for securing the payment thereof, A. drew the bill in question on the defendant, who accepted the same, and that by force of the statute (*r*), that acceptance was void in law. On demurrer to this plea, it was insisted, in support of the demurrer, that this case was not within the statute; because the nature of the duty was altered, and a new contract created by the acceptance, which was the ground of the action. But the court overruled the objection; for although this was a kind of new contract, yet all was founded on the illegal and tortious winning, and it only secured the payment of that money, and, therefore, it was within the statute, the plaintiff being privy to the first wrong. Another objection was made (*s*), that if this case should be taken to be within the statute, it would very much endanger the credit of English bills of exchange, if they might be defeated by such collateral matter; for it would be injurious to the public trade of England, both foreign and domestic. To this it was answered, by the court, that as to inconvenience concerning trade, there could not be any in this particular case, because the bill had gone no further than to the first hands, *viz.* to the hands of the plaintiff, who won the money, and so no damage could accrue to any person but to him, who was certainly a person within the statute.

It appears, from the cases of *Goodburn* v. *Marley*, Str. 1159, *Blaxton* v. *Pye*, 2 Wils. 309, and *Clayton* v. *Jennings*, 2 Bl. R. 706, that wagers on horse-races are within the statutes 16 Car. II. c. 7, and 9 Ann. c. 14. In the case of *Blaxton* v. *Pye*, the court said, that though horse-racing was not mentioned in the statute

---

(*o*) 2 Lev. 94.
(*p*) *Hussey* v. *Jacob*, Salk. 344; Carth. 356; and see the pleadings, 5 Mod. 176.
(*q*) The day from which the 16 Car. II.

c. 7, s. 3, was to take effect.
(*r*) 16 Car. II. c. 7, s. 3.
(*s*) Carth. 357.

9 Ann., yet it was within the words "other game" (3). So in *Lynall* v. *Longbothom*, 2 Wils. 36, the Court of C. B. were of opinion, that a foot-race was within the 9 Ann., for foot-race was mentioned in the 16 Car., to which the 9 Ann. must relate. And this opinion was recognized and adopted by the court in *Brown* v. *Berkeley*, Cowp. 281. It is clear, that if these statutes had not been affected by any subsequent provisions of the legislature, every species of wagers at horse-races would have been illegal; but now, by stat. 13 Geo. II. c. 19 (*t*), *matches* (4) for £50 (5) and upwards, are legalized, provided they are run at certain places, and the horses carry certain weights; and by the stat. 18 Geo. II. c. 34, s. 11, the restrictions as to running at particular places, and with certain weights, are taken away (6). But horse-races for a less sum than £50 are expressly prohibited by the second section of

(*t*) So much of this act as relates to horse-racing was repealed by stat. 3 & 4 Vict. c. 5.

---

(3) In *Jeffreys* v. *Walter*, 1 Wils. 220, the court inclined to think, that cricket was a game within the meaning of the stat. 9 Ann.; and in *Hodson* v. *Terrill*, 3 Tyr. 929; 1 Cr. & M. 797; it was holden, that a match at cricket for £20 was within the meaning of the 2d section of this statute, and therefore illegal.

(4) In *Connor* v. *Quick*, cited by *Aston*, J., in 2 Bl. R. 708, the court took a distinction between running a horse for £50, which was lawful, and betting on the side of a horse, which was not so; but if neither of the sums betted by the parties amount to £10, on a horse-race for £50 or upwards, such bet is legal, not being contrary to 9 Ann. c. 14. *M'Allester* v. *Haden*, 2 Campb. 438. But a bet above £100, even on a legal horse-race, cannot be sustained. *Shillito* v. *Theed*, 7 Bingh. 405.

(5) It was agreed between plaintiff and defendant, that each should start his mare, and that if either should refuse, he should forfeit £25 to the other, but the plaintiff was to pay the defendant £5 beforehand, as a consideration to induce him to make the match. The defendant afterwards refusing to run the match, the plaintiff brought an action against him for the £25. *Perrott*, Baron, before whom the cause was tried, considered this as a match for £50, and, on a motion in arrest of judgment, the Court of K. B. were of the same opinion. *Bidmead* v. *Gale*, 4 Burr. 2432; 1 Bl. R. 671, *S. C.*

(6) "There seems to be much ground for arguing, from the nature of 16 Car. II. and 9 Ann., that these statutes ought to be construed strictly, in order to enforce the principle on which they are founded, *viz.* to prohibit all horse-racing; and that the 13 & 18 Geo. II. are from their nature to be so construed as to encourage the breed of horses, and to permit that species of horse-racing only called running on the turf. It is to be observed, that stat. 13 Geo. II. speaks of entering, placing, starting, &c.; and that the expression, "any place or places whatsoever," used in 18 Geo. II., can hardly mean "all England." Per Lord *Eldon*, C. J., in *Whaley* v. *Pajot*, 2 Bos. & Pul. 54.

13 Geo. II.; and, consequently, wagers on such horse-races are illegal (*u*). These statutes, *viz*. 13 & 18 Geo. II., are confined to *bonâ fide* horse-racing only ; for in *Ximenes* v. *Jaques*, 6 T. R. 499, where the plaintiff obtained a verdict on a wager for 100 guineas, that he could perform a certain journey, in a post-chaise and pair, within a given time, the court arrested the judgment (7). So where A. betted with B. " 500 guineas and a dinner," that A.'s horse should go from London to Sittingbourne (*x*), sooner than B.'s two horses should go the same distance, B.'s horses to be placed at any distance from each other that B. should think proper : the wager having been won by B., and an action brought to recover the amount of the wager, and verdict for plaintiff, the court arrested the judgment, on the ground that the subject of the wager was not that species of horse-race or match which was legalized by stat. 13 and 18 Geo. II. An agreement, by which defendant sold plaintiff a horse for £200 if he trotted 18 miles within the hour, but for 1*s*. if he failed, was holden (*y*) to be illegal, as amounting to a wager on an illegal game in the way of a trotting race, in which more than £10 was at stake, and therefore within the statute 9 Ann. c. 14. A wager of £50 to £1 that a certain horse had not won a *bygone* horse-race is lawful; for such a wager neither accompanies anything then in a course of being done, nor contemplates anything then remaining to be done ; and therefore is not within the stat. 9 Ann. c. 14 (*z*). Semble, that a wager between the proprietors of two carriages for the conveyance of passengers for hire, that a given person should go by one of these carriages, and no other, is illegal (*a*). The plaintiff laid an illegal wager with B.; the defendant took a part in the bet. The plaintiff won : it was expected that B. would pay on a certain day, before which the plaintiff, at the defendant's request, because he was going to a distance, advanced to the defendant his share of the winnings. B. died insolvent before the day, and the bet never was paid. It was holden (*b*), inasmuch as the plaintiff could not establish his case without the aid of the illegal wager in his proof, in which all were concerned, he could not recover.

(*u*) *Johnson* v. *Bann*, 4 T. R. 1.
(*x*) *Whaley* v. *Pajot*, 2 Bos. & Pul. 51.
(*y*) *Brogden* v. *Marriott*, 3 Bingh. N. C. 88.

(*z*) *Pugh* v. *Jenkins*, 1 G. & D. 40.
(*a*) *Eltham* v. *Kingsman*, 1 B. & A. 683.
(*b*) *Simpson* v. *Bloss*, 7 Taunt. 246.

---

(7) The reason of this decision is not stated in the report of the case; but in *Whaley* v. *Pajot*, 2 Bos. & Pul. 54, Lord *Eldon*, C. J., said, " Upon inquiry of the judges of the Court of King's Bench, we find, that the judgment of the court in *Ximenes* v. *Jaques* proceeded on an opinion, that the stat. 13 and 18 Geo. II. related to *bonâ fide* horse-racing only."

2. An action cannot be maintained upon such wagers as in the event may have an influence on the public policy of the kingdom. On this principle it was holden (c), that a wager between two electors, on the event of the election of members to serve in parliament, was void; because it raised an improper bias in the minds of the parties to vote for one or other of the candidates, which bias would be subversive of the freedom of elections, and detrimental to the constitution. So it is a reasonable objection to a wager, that it has a tendency to influence and pervert the course of criminal justice. Hence, a wager as to the conviction or acquittal of a prisoner on trial, on a criminal charge, is illegal (d), as being against public policy. Every contract in restraint of marriage is illegal, as being against the sound policy of the law. Hence, a wager that the plaintiff would not marry within six years, was holden to be void (e); for although the restraint was partial, yet the immediate tendency of such contract, as far as it went, was to discourage marriage, and no circumstance appeared to show that the restraint, in the particular instance, was prudent and proper. Any wager which leads to a public inquiry into the mode of playing an illegal game (f), e. g., hazard, by which the by-standers may acquire a knowledge of it, is contrary to good morals and the policy of the law, and, therefore, not a ground on which an action can be maintained. In like manner, the court will not entertain an action on a wager upon an abstract question of law or judicial practice, not arising out of pre-existing circumstances, in which the parties have an interest (g). And in another case (h), Gibbs, C. J., following the example of Lord Loughborough and Lord Ellenborough, in the foregoing cases of Brown v. Leeson, and Henkin v. Guerss, refused to try an action upon a wager, whether an unmarried woman had had a child. An action cannot be maintained upon a wager on a cock-fight (i), because it is a barbarous diversion, which ought not to be encouraged or sanctioned in a court of justice; and further, because it would tend to the degradation of the court to entertain such inquiries.

3. So if the subject of the wager lead to improper inquiries, which respect the interest and general importance of the country, they are illegal, as being contrary to sound policy; as wagers on the amount of the hop duties (k), or the receipt tax, or any other branch of the public revenue. And this rule holds, although the actual discussion may be excluded by the special circumstances of the case : as where the wager being on the amount of the hop duties, the defendant had

(c) Allen v. Hearn, 1 T. R. 56.
(d) Evans v. Jones, 5 M. & W. 77.
See ante, n. (2), p. 1399.
(e) Hartley v. Rice, 10 East, 22.
(f) Brown v. Leeson, 2 H. Bl. 43.
(g) Henkin v. Guerss, 12 East, 247.

(h) Ditchburn v. Goldsmith, 4 Campb. 152.
(i) Squires v. Whisken, 3 Campb. 140 Lord Ellenborough, C. J.
(k) Atherfold v. Beard, 2 T. R. 610.

admitted that he had lost his wager (*l*); so where defendant had given a promissory note for the amount of the wager (*m*).

4. Where the discussion of the subject of the wager will be attended with injury to a third person, and lead to indecent evidence. On this principle (*n*), a wager between two indifferent persons on the sex of the Chevalier D'Eon, who had appeared to the world as a man, and acted in that character in a variety of capacities, was holden illegal.

(*l*) *Atherfold* v. *Beard*, 2 T. R. 610.   130.
(*m*) *Shirley* v. *Sankey*, 2 Bos. & Pul.   (*n*) *Dacosta* v. *Jones*, Cowp. 729.

AN INDEX

TO

THE PRINCIPAL MATTERS.

ABANDONMENT:
    of contract, 867.
    assured may *elect* to abandon, 965.
    what loss is necessary to justify, 966, 9.
    notice of, must be given in reasonable time, 967.
    one jointly interested with others may give notice for all, 969.
    not necessary in case of total loss, 967, 8, 9.

ABATEMENT:
    for nonjoinder, stat. 3 & 4 Will. IV. c. 42, s. 8, 115.
    of coverture, not within stat., *ib.*
    of nuisance, by commoner, 422.
    plea in, in assumpsit, 115.
        covenant, 458, n.
        debt on bond, 541.
        non joinder of partner, 1136.

ABBIES:
    dissolution of, 1293, 4.

ABSENTING:
    otherwise absenting himself, when an act of bankruptcy, 192.

ABSTRACT:
    property in, 1352.
    vendor must be prepared to verify, 179.

ABUTTALS:
    R. G. H. 4 Will. IV. respecting, 1323.
    proof of, 1341.

ACCEDAS AD CURIAM:
    nature of this writ, 1184, 5.

ACCEPTANCE OF BILLS OF EXCHANGE:
    nature of, 301, 327, 8.
    presentment for, 327.
    qualified, conditional, 328, 9.
    absolute, 330.
    special, 329.
    of inland bill, must be in writing, 328.
    of foreign bill, may be by parol, *ib.*
        or by collateral writing, *ib.*
        but not, of non-existing bill, *ib.*

ACCEPTANCE OF BILLS OF EXCHANGE—*continued*.

non-acceptance, notice, protest, 332, 3.
cancellation of, 329.

ACCEPTANCE OF CHARTER:

cannot be partial, 1156, 7.

ACCEPTANCE OF GOODS:

what sufficient, within stat. of frauds, 858.

ACCEPTOR OF BILL OF EXCHANGE:

liability of, 330.
is considered as principal debtor, *ib.*
effect of entering into composition with, 362.
when competent witness, 375.
evidence in action against, 371.
accommodation acceptor, where not discharged, 331.

ACCESS:

what is considered as such, 749.

ACCIDENT:

where no excuse for trespass, 26.
coach owner not liable for inevitable, 399.
from negligence, 1115.

ACCOMMODATION BILL:

where no effects, notice to drawer of dishonour unnecessary, 333.

ACCORD AND SATISFACTION:

plea of, in assumpsit, 118.
     covenant, 510.
     debt on bond, 541.
     trespass, 1326.

ACCOUNT:

action of, 1.
how to declare on the stat. 4 Ann. c. 16, 2.
lies not against infant, 3.
nor by executor against co-executor, *ib.*
plea in, 4.
evidence on ne unques receiver, *ib.*
judgment quod computet, form of, 4, 5.
proceedings thereon, 5.
auditors, their power, *ib.*
bail, proceeding in default of bail, *ib.*
rules for pleading before auditors, 5, 6.
final judgment, form of, 6.
execution, *ib.*

ACCOUNT STATED:

assumpsit on, 65.
evidence upon count on, 65 n. (21).
infant not liable on, 129.

ACKNOWLEDGMENT:

of debt, what sufficient to take case out of statute of limitations, 137.
stat. relating to, 139.

ACQUITTAL:

of co-defendant for purpose of making him a witness, 1326.

ACT OF BANKRUPTCY:

proof of, when required, 263.
of the several acts of bankruptcy by statute, 190—211.

ACT BOOK:

when proof of persons being executors, 807.

ACTION:

commencement of, now by writ of summons, 152 n.
on penal statutes, 621.

ACTION ON THE CASE:

where case or trespass is the proper remedy, 430—438, 681.
what is the true criterion, 430.
trespass or case for false imprisonment, 1061 n.
case or trespass for irregular distress, 1320.

ADJUDICATION:

of bankruptcy, to be entered of record, 186, 7.

ADJUSTMENT:

nature and effect of, 979.

ADMINISTRATION:

by whom to be granted, 770.
where void, 771, n.
where administration de bonis non is necessary, 778.
during minority of executor, 779.
during absence of executor beyond sea, ib.
pending litigation, 781.
during lunacy, ib.
evidence of, 806.
effect of statute of limitations as to, 809.

ADMINISTRATOR:

interest of, in property of intestate, 774.
actions by, 791.
against, 796.
plea by, 801.
how he may lay demise, in ejectment, 716.

ADMIRALTY:

effect of sentences in a court of, 1001, 2.

ADMISSION:

of assets, 788.

ADMITTANCE:

surrender of copyhold before, 689 n.

ADULTERY:

action for, 7.
form of action, 8.
what will bar the action, 8, 9.
correct statement of *Cibber* v. *Sloper*, 8 n. (3).
what circumstances will go in mitigation of damages, 10, 23.
of circumstances operating in aggravation, 23.
when husband and wife live apart, whether action is maintainable, 10.

ADULTERY—*continued*.

how statute of limitations is to be pleaded, 12.
actual marriage must be proved, *ib.*
new trial, in what cases granted, 24.

ADVERSE POSSESSION:

for 20 years, 733, 8.

ADVOWSON:

in fee, purchase of, when not simony, 554.
ejectment will not lie for, 696.

AGENT:

where action must be brought against, and where against principal, 84 n.
obtaining money illegally, cannot discharge himself by paying it over, 85 n., 86 n.
tender to, where good, 151.
notice to principal, notice to agent, 235, 820.
principal is *civilly* responsible for acts of, 820.
authorized to act in usual way of business only, 813.
acceptance of bills by, 305, 306.
attorney's agent, taxing bill of, 158 n.
who is deemed such within statute of frauds, 863.
See FACTOR.

AGISTER:

has not any lien, 1376.

AGREEMENT:

nature of, 40.
    parol, *ib.*
    illegal, 53.
    contrary to public policy, 56.
    fraudulent, 60.
    immoral, 63.
void by statute of frauds, 838.
parol evidence of, cannot be given, in what case, 1396.
——————, variation or waiver of written, 867.

ALIEN:

wife of, when chargeable as a feme sole, 285.
enemy cannot sue on a policy of insurance, 985.

ALIMONY:

what debts husband liable for, after decree for alimony, to wife, 276.

ALLEGATION:

of substance, requires substantial proof only, 1067 n.

ALLOWANCE:

separate, 276.

ALTERATION:

of bills of exchange, 317.

ALTERNATIVE:

in contract, how stated, 559.

AMBASSADOR:

marriage in chapel of English ambassador, valid, 21.
no distress of goods of, 666.

AMENDMENT:
    during the trial, 9 Geo. IV. c. 15, 518.
                  3 & 4 Will. IV. c. 42, s. 23, 24, 519.

AMENDS:
    tender of, in case of irregular distress, 680, 1196.
        by justice, 915, 6.

AMERCIAMENT:
    in court leet, debt lies for, 529.
    what must be averred in the declaration, *ib.*

ANCESTOR:
    debt on bond of, 585.

ANCIENT DEMESNE:
    how proved, 757.

ANNUITY:
    debt for arrears of, 595.

APOTHECARY:
    must prove his qualification, 118.

APPEARANCE:
    in ejectment, 721.

APPOINTEE:
    where he cannot be sued as assignee, 487, 8.

APPORTIONMENT:
    statutes concerning, 603, 793, 1311.

APPRAISEMENT:
    of distress, when and how to be made, 676.

APPRENTICE:
    may plead infancy to covenant upon an indenture of apprenticeship, 513, 4.
    of actions by masters for seducing and harbouring, 1102.
    master entitled to wages earned by impressed apprentice, *ib.*
    promissory note given as an apprentice fee, is void, for want of considera-
        tion, if indentures are void, 386.

APPROPRIATION:
    of payments, 130, 1.
    how made, *ib.*

APPROVEMENT:
    of commons, 420.

APPURTENANT:
    common, 417.

ARREST:
    what acts the officer may justify in making an arrest, 32.
    may be made without touching the person, *ib.*
    evidence of, in action against sheriff for escape, 617.
    words merely will not make an arrest, 1209.
    trespass for false imprisonment will lie for an unlawful arrest, as on mesne
        process not returned, 907.
        or not being the person named in the writ, *ib.*
        or if the arrest be made on a Sunday, 910.
        or after return day of writ, 911.

ARREST—*continued*.
>original arrests only prohibited on a Sunday, 911, 1210.
>action for malicious arrest, 1058.
>in bankruptcy, 196.

ARRESTS: *See* INSURANCE.
>loss by, 957.

ARTIFICIAL WATERCOURSES:
>law as to, 1111.

ASSAULT AND BATTERY:
>what acts amount to an assault, 25.
>>the remedy, 26.
>>battery defined, remedy, *ib*.
>>where it lies, *ib*.
>*See* PLEADINGS—COSTS.

ASSETS:
>all separate debts deemed assets, 788 n.
>assets quando acciderint, 808.
>wife's choses in action, where, 271.
>of the replication of assets to a plea of riens per descent, and by what proof
>>it may be supported, 587.
>admission of, by executor, 788.

ASSIGN:
>covenant not to, 470.
>>by bankrupt, 254.

ASSIGNEE:
>of reversion, 479.
>assignee by parol, 482.
>where the heir may be charged as, 483.
>where liable, though not named, 485.
>where, if named, 485, 6.
>of parcel of estate, liable on covenant to repair, 488.
>liable to pay rent for a moiety though the other moiety be evicted, *ib*.
>not liable for breaches incurred before or after assignment, *ib*.
>what will be a sufficient conveyance in order to exonerate, 489.
>of term, by way of mortgage, liable to covenants in the lease, 489 n.
>of the averment of entry and possession of, 490.
>the whole estate must be conveyed to make assignee chargeable, 491.
>but devisee of equitable estate is not liable as, 492.
>under-lessee not liable as, *ib*.
>but reserving the rent to the lessee will not exonerate assignee, *ib*.
>how to declare against, *ib*.
>actions by and against assignee of reversion are transitory, 493.

ASSIGNEES OF BANKRUPTS:
>actions by, 238. *See tit.* BANKRUPT.

ASSIGNMENT:
>voluntary, by insolvent, 197, 8.
>property of bankrupt vested in assignees, without, 185.
>of bond by chancellor, after fraudulent commission, 246.
>where lessee may plead, in bar to debt for rent, though he has assigned
>>over the premises, 602.
>of the covenant not to assign without license, 470.
>>what is a breach, *ib*.
>>assignment by operation of law, no breach, 472.
>>condition discharged by leave once granted, *ib*.

ASSIGNMENT—*continued*.

equity will not relieve against forfeiture occasioned by breach, 474.
for assignment of bail-bond, *see tit.* BAIL.

ASSUMPSIT:

nature of action, 39.
of the indebitatus assumpsit, 64.
will not lie on special agreement to be paid in money until terms are performed, 68.
nor where remedy of higher nature, 40, 441 n.
of the declaration, 101.
venue, *ib.*
as to the day, 102.
how the contract ought to be stated, 103.
what variance will be fatal, *ib.*
of stating the consideration, 104.
assigning breach, 105.
averring notice, *ib.*
or request, 106.
See Money paid, and Money had and received—PLEADINGS.

ATTESTATION:

of will, 873, 891.

ATTESTING WITNESS:

must be called, 537.
exceptions to this rule, 538.

ATTORNEY:

examination of, before admission, 157 n.
must declare employer, 166.
actions by, for recovery of fees, 157.
statute of limitations may be pleaded to action brought by attorney for his fees, 157.
of giving bills to their clients under stat. 3 Jac. I. c. 7, s. 1, and cases thereon, 158.
of the stat. 2 Geo. II. c. 23, s. 23, relating to delivery of bills, 159.
where necessary to deliver a bill, 159, 160.
bill must be left with party to be charged, 161.
conveyancing business not within this statute, *ib.*
amount of bill may be set off, though it has not been delivered, 163.
copy of a bill, in what cases sufficient evidence, 164.
of the stat. 12 Geo. II. c. 13, s. 6, and construction thereof, *ib.*
taxation of bill, 165.
costs of taxation, *ib.*
negligence cannot be set up as defence to action on attorney's bill, 166.
but client may sue attorney for negligence or unskilfulness, 169.
what proof will be sufficient for this purpose, 170, 1.

AUCTION:

sale of lands and goods by auction, within the statute of frauds, 172, 863.
assent of seller signified by fall of hammer, 173.
verbal declaration of auctioneers, in what case not evidence, *ib.*
puffing vitiates contract, 174.
of the recovery of deposit and interest, on defect of title, and how to declare for interest, 176, 7.
at what time vendor must be ready with title deeds—must verify abstract at the day fixed—making out good title afterwards will not avail him at law, 178, 9.
good title, what is, 180.

AUCTION—*continued*.

    particulars and conditions of sale, 181.
    duty, bankrupts' estates and effects not liable to, 175.
    duty on sale of mortgaged estates, *ib*.

AUCTIONEER:

    agent of both parties within the statute of frauds, 172.
    has special property in goods, which he is employed to sell, 174.
    where he may sue for goods sold, 174.
    when liable for deposit, 176.
    not liable for interest, 178.

AUDITORS:

    in account, 5, 6.

AUTHORITY:

    money paid under a void authority may be recovered in action for money
        had and received, 76.
    party justifying under an authority must set it forth in his plea, 33, 921.

AUTRE DROIT:

    property which bankrupt has in, will not pass to assignees, 224.

AVERAGE:

    general, 940.

AVERMENT:

    where necessary in declaration in assumpsit, 106.

AVOWRY AND COGNIZANCE:

    requisites of, 1190.
    several avowries may be pleaded, 1191; new rule, *ib*.
    plaintiff may traverse defendant's being bailiff, *ib*.
    defendant may avow that locus is his freehold, 1192.
    how tenant in common must avow, 1193.
    what avowry for damage feasant must allege, 1192.
        plea in bar,
            that cattle escaped through defect of fences, what it must state, 1193.
            right of common, how pleaded by copyholder, 1194.
            tender of amends, 1196.
    for rent arrear,
        how pleaded at common law, 1197.
        under stat. 11 Geo. II. c. 19, *ib*.
        this statute does not extend to rent-charges, *ib*.
        sum stated in avowry to be due for rent not material, 1198.
    for rent, where part is not due, *ib*.
    money may be paid into court, *ib*.
    of avowries for rent arrear by joint tenant, *ib*.
        parceners, *ib*.
        tenants in common, *ib*.
        eviction may be pleaded in bar, *ib*.
        what proof will be sufficient on non tenuit, 1199.
        nothing in arrear, how it ought to conclude, 1200.
        tender of arrears, when it may be pleaded, 1201.

AWARD:

    upon an award to pay money at several days, assumpsit will lie for each
        sum, as it becomes due, 535 n.
    in what cases submission to an award, by an executor, shall be deemed an
        admission of assets, 790.
    on money awarded to be paid on a particular day, interest is recoverable,
        378.

B.

BAIL:

of the obligation on sheriff to take bail on arrests on mesne process by common law and by statute, 570.

of the bail bond—form—condition, 571.

of immaterial variances between the writ and condition, 572.

bonds given to plaintiff or his attorney not within the statute, 574 n.

of the assignment of bail-bond, 575.

sheriff not compellable to assign at common law, *ib.*

provisions by stat. 4 Ann. c. 16, to remedy the inconveniences at common law, *ib.*

in what court action on bail-bond must be brought, 576.

not necessary to aver that the assignment was under hand and seal of sheriff, 577.

nor to set forth names of witnesses, nor that indorsement was attested by them, *ib.*

profert of assignment not necessary, *ib.*

how far the bail are liable, 578.

sheriff must consent to surrender ; otherwise the party will not be considered as in his custody, *ib.*

of the plea of comperuit ad diem, 578.

of the replication, nul tiel record—how it ought to conclude, 579.

BAILEE :

answerable for misfeasance, although there was not any consideration, 398, 9.

may maintain trover, 1351.

See CARRIER.

BAILIFF :

account against, 2.

the being bailiff is traversable,

in replevin, 1191.

and now in trespass qu. cl. fr., 1192 n.

BANK :

shares in joint stock, not within 17th sect. of stat. of frauds, 857.

BANKER :

bill accepted payable at house of, 329, 354.

statutes relating to banking copartnerships, 1139.

BANKING HOUSE :

presentment of bill at, 329, 355.

BANK OF ENGLAND :

exclusive privileges of, 303.

BANK NOTES :

tender of, 152.

property in, 1359.

BANKRUPT :

of the alterations in bankrupt laws, 183.

the stat. 1 & 2 Will. IV. c. 56, establishing a court of bankruptcy, 184.

persons liable to be, 187 ; persons not liable, 189.

estate of, vested in assignees without deed, 185.

conveyance of bankrupts' estates, 185, 6.

of the several acts of bankruptcy, 189—210.

BANKRUPT—*continued*.

> *petitioning creditor's debt*, 212.
> *property in possession of bankrupt as reputed owner*, 217.
> *warrants of attorney, conveyances, and payments made by and to bankrupts*, 231.
>
> *actions by assignees*, 238; *against assignees*, 244.
>> by bankrupt, 245.
>> uncertificated bankrupt, *ib*.
>> of the general plea of bankruptcy, 246.
>> cannot be pleaded to actions for uncertain damages, 253.
>> will not avail under second commission, unless fifteen shillings in the pound have been paid, 255.
>> three cases in which bankrupt cannot avail himself of his certificate, 256.
>> effect of certificate obtained by assignees debtors to estate of bankrupt, 257.
>> discharge of debt in the country where it is contracted, is a discharge everywhere, 259.
>> set-off—cases thereon, 260.
>> what must be proved by assignees, 262.
>> in what cases bankrupt may be a witness, what he may prove, 266.
>> what a certificated bankrupt may prove, 268.
>> where an uncertificated bankrupt may be a witness, *ib*.
>> in what cases a creditor may be a witness, 269.
>> uncertificated, not disqualified from being elected councillor, 1160 n.

BANKRUPTCY:

> notice of disputing, 263.

BANNS:

> marriage without due publication of, void, 17, 18.

BAPTISM:

> register of, how proved, 752.

BARGE:

> owner of, liable as common carrier, 395.

BARON AND FEME:

> justification by husband in respect of wife, 30.
> husband must be sued in lifetime of wife, on contracts made by wife before coverture, 270.
> wife is liable to such debt if she survive husband, 271.
> cohabitation, presumptive evidence of assent in respect of contracts made by wife during coverture, 272.
> presumption of husband's assent, destroyed by elopement and adultery of wife, 273.
> husband not liable for debts of wife turned out of doors for having committed adultery under his roof, 274.
> husband *paying* wife separate allowance, is not liable; but otherwise, if he does not pay such allowance, 275, 6.
> husband causelessly turning away wife, sends credit with her for necessaries, 277.
> person permitting woman to pass as his wife is liable for necessaries, 282.
> feme covert may be considered as feme sole, by custom of city of London, or civil death of husband, but not on the ground of temporary absence of husband, 283.
> where husband is an alien, having deserted this kingdom, whether wife may be considered as feme sole, 285.

BARON AND FEME—*continued*.

in what cases action must be brought in joint names of husband and wife, 288.

where husband must sue alone, 290.

where husband and wife may join, or husband may sue alone, 292.

how actions must be brought against husband and wife, 296.

for slander spoken by husband and wife, there must be separate actions, 298.

BARRATRY:

the meaning of, as applied to subjects of British marine insurance, 959.

how it may be committed, 960.

not necessary that the master should derive any benefit from the act done, in order to constitute barratry, *ib*.

but there must be fraud, 961.

by whom and against whom barratry may be committed, *ib*.

no barratry where ship-owner consents to acts done, 962.

not necessary that loss should happen in the act of committing barratry, *ib*.

allegation that ship was lost by fraud and neglect of master, equivalent to alleging a loss by barratry, 963.

master *having been released*, may prove barratry to have been committed with consent of owner, 1020.

BARREN LAND:

what such, and exempt from tithe, 1298, 9.

BARRISTER:

words spoken by, where justifiable, 1255.

BASTARDY:

what proof sufficient, 749.

BATTERY:

action for, 26.

BELLS:

removable only during term, 1356.

BILL:

attorney's, action on, 157.

in equity, where not evidence, 756.

BILL OF EXCHANGE:

definition of, 301.

peculiar properties of, *ib*.

of the parties, their names, *ib*.

a bill is a simple contract, and must be postponed to specialties in a course of administration, 302.

of the capacity of contracting parties, 303; corporation, 303; infant, 304; feme covert, 304; agents, 305; partners, 307; spiritual person, 308.

interest in bill given to feme covert vests in her husband, and he must indorse it, 304.

agents should not accept in their own names, 305.

partners, when bound, 307.

forms of foreign and inland bill, 309.

bill must not purport to be payable out of a particular fund, or upon a contingency, 310.

table of stamp duties, 311, 2, 3.

stamp must be of proper denomination, 314, 5.

if material alteration is made in bill, new stamp is necessary, 315, 6.

omission of date not material, 316.

BILLS OF EXCHANGE—*continued.*

alteration of date avoids the bill, 317.
but immaterial alteration of bill will not avoid it, 318.
words "or order," effect of, 320.
"value received" not essential, *ib.*
consideration, presumed to be good, *ib.*
bills given for gaming or usury, statutes concerning, 321, 2, 3.
a bill may be negotiated after it is due, unless there be an agreement for the purpose of restraining it, 325.
where it is necessary to present bills for acceptance, 327.
acceptance, how made—parol—by collateral writing, as by letter—after bill becomes due, binding, 327, 8.
qualified acceptance, explained and illustrated, 328.
partial acceptance—instance of, holden good, 329.
liability of acceptor, 330.
    may be sued by drawer, *ib.*
upon what terms court will stay proceedings, when acceptor is sued by several parties, 330, 1.
acceptor can be discharged by express agreement only, 330.
notice of non-acceptance must be given within a reasonable time, 332.
reasonable time, question of law, dependent on facts, *ib.*
notice to drawer ought to be given by holder, 333.
in what case notice may be dispensed with, as where drawer has not effects, *ib.*
knowledge by drawer of the insolvency of acceptor is not equivalent to notice of dishonour, 335.
notice to indorser necessary in all cases except where the transaction is unfair, *ib.*
need not be given by holder, 334, 6.
subsequent promise to pay is a waiver of want of notice, 336.
not necessary to demand payment of *drawer*, 337.
how to declare on a bill, 366.
where several actions are commenced by holder, upon what terms court will stay proceedings, 369.
of the reference to the Master to compute principal and interest, after interlocutory judgment, 369.
at what time application may be made for this rule, *ib.*
how to proceed after interlocutory judgment, on bill for foreign money, 369, 370.
what must be proved on executing writs of inquiry, 370.
pleading under the new rules, *ib.*
evidence—proof against acceptor, 371.
against indorser, 373.
foreign bill, in case of, protest must be proved, 374.
and on inland bills, if stated, 374 n.
acceptor, in what case a witness, 375.
where payee may prove bill void for want of stamp, *ib.*
in what cases interest is recoverable, 376.
how computed, 377.
demand, of principal in particular, sufficient, 378.
property in, passes with the bill, 1359.
See INDORSEMENT—PROTEST.

BILL OF LADING:

when evidence of property, 407, 8.
where property passes by indorsement of, 1279, 1346.

BILL OF PARTICULARS, 66, 533.

BILL OF SALE:

of ship, what valid, 1221.

BIRTH:

evidence of, 749, 750, 754.

BISHOP:

ejectment by, for forfeiture during vacancy of see, 689 n.

BLINDNESS:

of attesting witness, lets in proof of handwriting; 538.

BODY CORPORATE:

when extinct, 1157.

BONA NOTABILIA, 770.

BOND:

when a bond is payable, if a day is not mentioned in the condition, 534.

of bonds, covenants, or promises to pay money at several days—when action may be brought, *ib.*

place of date must be set forth in declaration, 535.

of the pleadings to debt on bond, *ib.*

non est factum, *ib.*

how to prove execution, 536.

proof of delivery, *ib.*

of the general rule that subscribing witness must be called to prove the execution, 537.

of the exceptions to this rule, 538.

how to prove deed executed in the East Indies, 540.

bond thirty years old may be given in evidence without proof of execution, *ib.*

exception to this rule, 541.

what evidence will avoid the bond, 542, 3.

of avoiding bonds on the ground of immoral consideration, 543.

of bonds made in restraint of trade, *ib.*

what restraint the law permits, 543, 4.

bond given for the purpose of suppressing a prosecution for perjury is illegal, 545.

obligor may plead matter whether consistent or not with the condition, 546 n.

of considerations illegal by statute, 548; gaming, 548; sale of offices, 548; simony, 551; usury, 558.

bond originally good, cannot be avoided in the hands of a bonâ fide holder, on the ground of subsequent usury, 559.

bond conditioned to perform covenants, 581.

how the obligee used to proceed at common law, *ib.*

inconveniences of this mode, *ib.*

of the remedy provided by stat. 8 & 9 Will. III. c. 11, *ib.*

construction of this statute, 581 n.

bond debts, where bona notabilia, 771.

 how paid in a course of administration, 784.

replevin bond,

 condition of, 1176.

 how construed, 1178.

 how the breach may be assigned, 1179.

 penalty of, fixed by stat. 11 Geo. II. c. 19, s. 23, 1177.

in trover for a bond, not necessary to set forth date, 1378.

for debt on bond of ancestor against heir, *see* HEIR.

BOROUGH:

exclusive right of trading in, abolished, 1163.

BOTTOMRY:

    definition of, 1028.
    difference between bottomry and a mere loan, 1029.
    statutes relating to, *ib.*

BOUGHT AND SOLD NOTES, 173 n., 863 n.

BOUNDARY:

    evidence of, 744.
    rule as to, 1323.

BREACH:

    of close, 1312.
    of pound, 678.
    of assigning the breach in assumpsit, 105.
            covenant, 496.
            debt on bond conditioned to perform co
               at common law and under stat. 8 & 9 W
               III. c. 11, 581, 2, 3.
            on replevin bond, 1179.

BREWERS' DRUGS:

    action on sale of, not maintainable, 59, 60.

BRIBERY:

    debt on stat. against, 624.

BRICKS:

    under statutable size, price of, cannot be recovered, 56.

BROKER:

    where agent of both parties, 863.
    stock, cannot sell on credit, 813.
    bought and sold notes by, 173 n., 863 n.
    book of, where evidence, 863 n.
    insurance, how to receive payment, 980.
    authority of, when revocable, 991 n.

BULL, PAPAL:

    exemption of tithe by, 1294.

BULLION:

    action for loss of, 408.

BURGESS:

    enrolment of, by occupancy and payment of rates only, 1158.

BURIALS:

    register of, 752.

BURNING:

    of will, 882, 892.

BUTTER:

    price of firkins, if not marked as statute directs, cannot be recovered, 56.

BUYING AND SELLING:

    persons, liable to become bankrupt, 189.

BYE-LAWS:

    Where good, 1158.
        void, 1162.
        evidence of, *ib.*

C.

CANCELLING:

wills, what an effectual cancelling, 882, 892.
acceptances of bills of exchange, 319.

CANONRY:

ejectment will not lie for a, 695.

CANONS:

of 1603 not binding on laity proprio vigore, 769 n.

CAPTURE:

definition of, 955.
of losses by, *ib.*
insurance against all captures does not include British capture, 957.

CARRIER:

of common carriers and their responsibility, 395.
who are common carriers, *ib.*
how far their liability extends, 396, 7.
    as to losses by fire, 397.
    by robbery, 398.
coach-owners not liable for inevitable accident, 399.
stat. 11 Geo. IV. & 1 Will. IV., limiting the responsibility of carriers by land, 400.
lien of, 404.
of actions against common carriers—must be brought by the owner of the goods, 406.
same rule holds, in the case of carrier by water, 407.
of the declaration, on the custom of the realm, breach of duty, assumpsit, 409.
trover will not lie against carrier for mere loss, ib.
where trover will lie, 411 n.
pleading under new rules, 412.
ship-owners liable in respect of freight, 411.
    of declaring against partners, 412.
owners of chartered ship liable, though king's pilot on board, 412.
in what cases money may be paid into court, 133, 412.
master good witness in action against ship-owner, 412.
book-keeper a good witness, 413.

CASE:

where case or trespass is the proper remedy, 430.
where case lies, though remedy of a higher nature, 441 n.
where special action on the case or trover, 1379.
case lies against sheriff for taking insufficient pledges in replevin, 1180.
case lies for preventing a party from distraining, 679.
so for rescuing a distress, *ib.*
against a sheriff for an escape on mesne process, or in execution, 607 n.
for a nuisance.
        disturbance of common, 422.
        how to declare, *ib.*
        disturbance of seat in a pew, 1113.
        darkening windows, 1109.
        malicious prosecution, 1054.
        ———— arrest, 1058.
for a rescous of person arrested, 1209.

CASE—*continued.*

for shooting off a gun to the injury of plaintiff's decoy, 437.
use and occupation, 1385.

CASUAL EJECTOR:

judgment against, 720.

CAVEAT EMPTOR:

where this rule applies, 82, 637 n.

CERTIFICATE;

of the judge under stat. 3 & 4 Vict. c. 24, to entitle plaintiff to full costs, 37, 1121.
        under stat. 8 & 9 Will. III., that there was a reasonable cause for making a person defendant in trespass, 38.
bankrupt's certificate, 246.
where necessary to render bankrupt competent witness, 266.
game certificate, 898, 904.

CHANCERY:

bill in, when evidence, 756.
decree of court of, equal to a judgment, 786 n.

CHAPEL:

as to marriage in, 19.

CHARACTER:

of servants, 1255.
evidence of good, of plaintiff, where inadmissible in slander, 1257.
evidence of good, of daughter, where inadmissible, in case for seduction, 1105.

CHARTER:

construction of, 1155.
cannot be partial acceptance of, 1156, 7.

CHATTEL:

effect of verbal gift of, 1347.
assumpsit lies for, 67.

CHECK:

on banker, when payable, 349.
holder of, how to present it, 361.
forged in part, where banker liable, *ib.*
forged, where banker not liable, 362.
where exempt from stamp duty, 314.

CHIROGRAPH:

proof of fine, but not of proclamations, 732.

CHOSES IN ACTION:

goods and chattels within 6 Geo. IV. c. 16, s. 72, 218.
wife's, where assets, in case of her death, 271.
        husband's interest in, 272.

CHRISTMAS DAY:

bill due on, to be presented on previous day, 351.
notice of dishonour good on day after, 353.

CHURCH SEAT:

action on the case for disturbance of, 1113.

CHURCHWARDEN:
is within the meaning of the words " other officer," in stat. 24 Geo. II. c. 44, 916 n.

CLOSE, BREACH OF:
where action lies for, 1312.
in which, &c., meaning of, 1341.

CLERGYMAN:
trading, prohibited, 187, 308.
to what extent legalized, 308, 1127.

CLUB:
liability of members of, 1131, 2.

COCKFIGHT:
wager on, 1405.

CO-CONTRACTOR:
where not a witness, 1140, 1.

CODICIL:
in writing, necessary to effectual revocation of will, 881.
how it must be signed, *ib.*
how it must be executed under new act, 892.

COGNIZANCE:
in replevin, nature of, 1190, 1.

COGNOVIT:
taken from drawer of accommodation bill, effect of, 364.

COHABITATION:
where proof of marriage, 12.
where not, *ib.*
where proof of husband's assent to wife's contract, 272, 3.

COLLOQUIUM:
where necessary, in slander, 1252, 3.
use of, *ib.*

COMMAND:
traversable in replevin or trespass laid transitorily, and now in trespass quare clausum fregit, 1192 n.

COMMENCEMENT OF SUIT:
what now is, 366.

COMMERCE:
illegal, 985.

COMMISSION:
of bankrupt, fiat substituted for, 187 n.
maliciously suing out, 246, 438 n.
supersedeas of—evidence of, 266.

COMMISSIONERS OF BANKRUPT:
commitment by, 913.

COMMITTEE OF LUNATIC:
cannot bring ejectment, 692.
administration granted to, 781.

COMMON:

    right of, defined, 414.
        of pasture, 415.
        its kinds, 416.
        appendant, *ib.*
        sans nombre, *ib.*
        appurtenant, 417.
        because of vicinage, 416.
        in gross, 419.
        disturbance of, remedy, 422.
        of fishery, 832.
    of the interest of the owner of the soil, 419.
    of the statute of Merton, and other statutes relating to improvement, 420.
    what right the lord may inclose against, 421.
    right of common, plea of, 424.

COMMONER:

    in what case may abate nusance, 422.
    of action on the case by, *ib.*
    how to declare, *ib.*
    what injury sufficient to maintain action, *ib.*
    how to plead license from lord to dig turves, 423.
    of the ancient remedy for surcharge, *ib.*
    of the modern remedy by action on the case, *ib.*
    how to declare, *ib.*
    where person claiming common in the same place may be a witness, 426, 1194, 5.
    of pleading a prescription for common during part of the year, 1194.
    how a copyholder ought to plead when claiming common, either in the lord's soil, or in the soil of other persons, *ib.*
    inhabitants of a vill, unless incorporated, cannot *prescribe* for common, 1196.

COMMUTATION:

    of tithes, statutes relating thereto, 1309.

COMPETENCY OF WITNESSES:

    stat. 3 & 4 Will. IV. c. 42, ss. 26, 27; 650, 825 n., 1097, 8, 1195.
    to a will, 876, 891, 2.

COMPOSITION:

    with creditors, 60.
    for tithes, 1289.
    real for tithes, 1295.
    stat. 2 & 3 Will. IV. c. 100, s. 2, relating to compositions for tithes, 1297.

CONCEALMENT:

    where it vacates contract of insurance, 989.

CONDEMNATION:

    effect of, as to property, 1320.
    where trover will not lie after, 1349.

CONDITION:

    of the nature of conditions precedent in assumpsit, 107.
                      in covenant, 498.

CONDITIONAL ACCEPTANCE:

    how declared on, 367.

CONFIDENTIAL COMMUNICATION, 1255.

CONSENT:

rule, in ejectment, 721.

CONSEQUENTIAL DAMAGES:

action for, 430.

CONSIDERATION:

of the consideration required to support an assumpsit, 40.
must be of some value in contemplation of law, 41.
where forbearance of suit is a sufficient consideration, 43.
where not, 45.
must move from plaintiff, 46.
party undertaking must have power to perform it, 48.
past, or executed, not sufficient, *ib.*
moral obligation, when a sufficient, 50.
how the consideration ought to be stated in the declaration, 104.
of insufficient consideration, *ib.*
executory and executed, 105.
illegality of, must be specially pleaded, 117.
where matter dehors the deed may be averred, in order to show illegal consideration, 546, and n.
consideration of bill of exchange, 320, 2, 4, 5,
of promissory note, 386.
for a deed presumed, where, 459.
of bond, 543.
immoral, *ib.*
in restraint of trade, *ib.*

CONSIGNOR:

where he may stop in transitu, 1262, 3.

CONSOLIDATION:

rule, explanation of, 984.

CONSPIRACY:

how the modern action on the case for malicious prosecution differs from the old action for a conspiracy, 1054.

CONSTABLE:

action against, must be laid in proper county, 913.
    must be commenced within six months, 918, 9.
may plead general issue, 920.
entitled to double costs, 918.
but must procure certificate, *ib.*
no action will lie against, until demand made of the perusal and copy of warrant, 916.
in what cases constable may justify in arrest, 926.

CONSTRUCTION:

of covenants, 442.
of policy, 947.
of charters, 1155.

CONTINGENT DEBT:

proof of, 249, 258.

CONTINUANDO:

in trespass, 1322.

CONTRACT:

open and rescinded, 648.

CONTRACT—*continued.*

when entire, cannot be split, 70.
executory, within 17th section of statute of frauds, 857.
made here to pay in France, Add.
parol evidence of alteration or waiver of written, 867.

CONTRIBUTION, 75.

CONVERSION :

what shall be, 1358.
evidence of, 1379.
of bill, how damages computed, 1383.

CONVOY :

warranty to depart with, meaning of, 997.

COPARCENERS :

Ejectment by, 714.

COPY OF INDICTMENT :

in felony, only granted by leave, 1064.

COPYHOLD :

heir at law may devise before admittance, 689 n.
grantee of the reversion of copyhold lands is within the intention of the stat. 32 Hen. VIII. c. 34, and may maintain covenant against lessee, &c., 481, 2.
ejectment may be brought by a bishop for a forfeiture of copyhold committed during the vacancy of the see, 689 n.
heir may maintain ejectment for copyhold before admittance, 689 n.
but until admittance of surrenderee, surrenderor remains seised, and if he die his heir may bring ejectment, 690 n.
how surrenderee, after admittance, may lay the demise, 690 n., 716.
devisee of devisee, who died before admittance, cannot maintain ejectment, 690 n.
within the stat. against fraudulent conveyances, *ib.*
not within the stat. of frauds, relating to devises of lands, 871.

COPYRIGHT :

not assigned by writing, must be specially pleaded, 118.

CORN :

standing, to whom it belongs on death of testator, 1355, 6.

CORPORATION :

See BILL OF EXCHANGE.
Municipal Corporation Act, 5 & 6 Will. IV. c. 76, amended by 7 Will. IV. & 1 Vict. c. 78, 1071 n., 1156, 8, 9, 1163.
aggregate, where it may sue and be sued in indebitatus assumpsit, 66.
where it may contract without common seal, *ib.*
trover lies against, 1366.
may maintain use and occupation, 1386.
aggregate, may maintain ejectment, 691.
ought to state that the demise was by deed, 716.
must execute a letter of attorney to some person, empowering him to enter on the land, 697.
incidents and powers of, 1156, 8.
when extinct, 1159.

CORRECTION:

of children, 33.
scholars, *ib.*
servants, *ib.*

COSTS:

new statute, 3 & 4 Vict. c. 24, as to costs where damages under 40*s.*, 37.
in assault and battery, *ib.*
stat. 8 & 9 Will. III. c. 11, giving costs to defendants in trespass who are acquitted, unless judge certify that there was reasonable cause for making them defendants, 38.
in covenant, 525.
in replevin,
   plaintiff entitled to costs, by virtue of the stat. of Gloucester, 1207.
   defendant avowing the rent, custom, or service entitled to costs by stat. 7 Hen. VIII. c. 4, *ib.*
   this stat. extends to avowries for heriots, but not to an amerciament, *ib.*
in slander,
   plaintiff recovering under 40*s.* is only entitled to so much costs as damages amount to, 1258.
in debt on stat. 2 & 3 Edw. VI., for not setting forth tithes, 1308.
in trespass, 1342.
in trover, 1384.

COUCHANCY:

meaning of, 417 n., 426.

COUNTERMAND:

a license executed is not countermandable, but otherwise when it is executory, 1120.

COUNTERPART:

where evidence, 746.

COURT:

sentence of a council of war, conclusive in an action of battery, 33.

COVENANT:

express and implied covenants defined, 440.
   damages only recoverable in actions of covenant, *ib.*
   on promises by deed, covenant or debt the only remedy, 441.
   exceptions to this rule, 441 n.
   how covenants are to be construed, 442.
   express, nature of, 445.
   running with the land, 450.
usual, 470 n.
   for act of stranger, binding, 500.
implied covenants explained, 453.
   follow the nature of the interest granted, 454.
   restrained and qualified by express covenants, *ib.*
joint and several covenants, 455.
   action follows the nature of interest, *ib.*
   where the interest is joint, action must be brought by survivors, and death of companion must be averred, 456.
void and illegal covenants, 459, 513.
covenants for title, 462.
not to assign without license, 470.
to repair, 474.
ejectment for breach of, 709.

COVENANT—*continued.*

to insure, 476.
    relative, in void lease, 460.
    of independent covenants, 504.
    requisites of declaration in, 493.
    of assigning the breach, 496.

COVERTURE:

in abatement, 115.
of defendant, at time of contract, 116.
defence in assumpsit, 116.
must be pleaded specially, *ib.*
so in debt on bond, 536.
wife of foreigner living abroad chargeable here as feme sole, 285, 6.
wife living apart and having separate maintenance, not liable as feme sole,
    283.

CREDIT:

mutual, 260.
to wife, what act of husband gives, 279, 280.
    where it exempts husband, 281.
not expired, defence in action for goods sold, 69.
    under the general issue, 117.
    though fraudulently bought, 70.
    sale of chattel on, when it passes the property, 1347.

CREDITOR:

composition with, 60—63.
where witness, 269.

CREW:

of competent skill required to render ship seaworthy, 1011, 2.

CRICKET:

a game within the stat. of 9 Ann., 1403 n.

CRIMINAL CONVERSATION: See ADULTERY.

CRITICISM:

fair, of literary production, defence in libel, 1039.

CROPS:

growing, when sale of, is sale of interest in land, 850, 1.
    where trespass q. c. f. will lie for, 1313.
to whom belonging on death of testator, 1535, 6.

CUSTODY:

deeds and writings, if found in proper custody, 30 years old, admissible
    without proof of execution, 540.
what is such custody, 541.

CUSTOM:

in manors, 757.
See PRESCRIPTION.
as to common rights, 1194.

D.

DAMAGE FEASANT:
avowry for, 1192.

DAMAGE, SPECIAL:
where it must be stated, and how, in slander, 1248.

DAMAGES:
where jury may give damages in the nature of interest, 1022, 1342, 1383.
in assumpsit, how computed, 154, 5.
of liquidated, 155.
unliquidated, cannot be set off, 524.
what circumstances will operate in increase, and what in mitigation, of damages in an action for adultery, 10, 23.
how the damages are to be assessed upon a verdict against joint trespassers, 36.
of stating special damage, in consequence of words actionable and not actionable in themselves, 1248, 9.
for conversion of bill of exchange, how calculated, 1383.
liberal, in action for seduction, 1106.

DATE:
of bill of exchange, 316.
alteration of, 317.
of bond, 534, 5.
of policy, 944.

DAY:
when inclusive, 206, 7, 210 n., 1082.
exclusive, 70, 159 n., 914 n., 1082.
fraction of, when allowed, 207, 611.
priority of facts on same day, 207, 611.
what shall be deemed day-time in Game Act, 900, 901.

DAYS OF GRACE:
what allowed on bills, in England, 350, 1.
none in France, Add.

DEATH:
presumption of, time of, proof necessary, 753.
of attesting witness, effect of, 538.

DEBT:
for what it lies, 528.
in the debet and detinet, or detinet only, 586, 600.
what must be alleged in debt on an amerciament, 529.
debt lies on promissory note, ib.
foreign judgment, 530.
not necessary that plaintiff should recover exact sum demanded, 531.

DEBTEE EXECUTOR:
where debt is released by making, 564.

DECEIT:
action on the case lies for, 637.
on implied warranty, ib.

DECEIT—*continued*.

on express warranty, 639.

action lies for deceit against any person who deceives, by a false assertion, another who has placed a reasonable confidence in him, 639, 652.

fraudulent misrepresentations by persons not parties to the contract, 650.

DECLARATION :

in action for adultery, 11.

of assault and battery, 27.

assumpsit, 101.

on bills of exchange, 366.

against carriers, 409.

in covenant, 493.

on bail-bond, 576.

of debt for rent, 600.

debt for use and occupation, 601.

of debt against sheriff for escape of prisoner in execution, 615.

on stat. against bribery, 628.

in detinue, 657.

ejectment, 714.

insurance, 980.

libel, 1043.

malicious prosecution, 1062.

replevin, 1186.

slander, 1250.

tithes, 1302.

trespass, 1321.

trover, 1366.

of what persons, are admissible in cases of pedigree, 753.

of trader, as to being absent, 267.

of wife, in action for adultery, 23.

of persons speaking against their own interest, 743, 754.

subscription of, in policy on life, 1031.

DECOY :

action for injury to, 437.

DEDICATION :

of way to the public, 1334, 5.

DEED :

custody of, 541.

how avoided by rasure, or alteration, *ib.*

where profert is necessary, 494 n.

case will not lie where there is a deed, 441.

exceptions to this rule, 441 n.

where counterpart is evidence, 746.

where a deed from its antiquity may be given in evidence without proof of execution, 540.

trover for, 1378.

See TITLE DEEDS.

DEER :

property in, 1324.

DEFAMATION : *See* LIBEL—SCAN. MAG.—SLANDER.

DE INJURIA SUA PROPRIA :

meaning of, 1330.

DE INJURIA SUA PROPRIA—*continued.*

absque tali causâ, where a good replication, 35.
where not, 1330.

DEL CREDERE:

commission, nature of, 810 n.

DELIVERY:

of attorney's bill, 159, 161.
of deed, what sufficient, 537.
of goods, what sufficient to satisfy stat. of frauds, 858 n.
to carrier, vests property in vendee, 406, 7.

DEMAND AND REFUSAL:

evidence only of a conversion, 1380.

DEMESNE LAND:

meaning of term, 897.

DEMISE:

how laid in ejectment, 714, 5, 6.
from year to year, 698.

DENOMINATION:

of stamp, 311.

DEPARTING:

the realm, act of bankruptcy, 190.

DEPARTURE:

of vessel, on a particular day, 994.
with convoy, 997.
what shall be, in replevin, 1173.

DEPOSIT:

at sale by auction, when recoverable, 176.

DEPOSITION:

where not evidence, 756, 7.
of Gentoo, 876.

DEPUTATION:

to gamekeeper, 902.

DESCENT:

liability of heir having assets by, 585.
stat. 3 & 4 Will. IV. c. 106, concerning, 741, 2.

DESCRIPTION:

allegation of, must be literally proved, 1067 n.
matter of, must be proved, as laid, *ib.*

DETAINMENTS:

of kings and people, insurers liable for, 957.

DETENTION:

unlawful, how declared on, 907.
unlawful, new taking, 1201.

DETERMINATION:

of suit, proof of, necessary, in action for malicious prosecution, 1058, 1066.

DETINUE:

where this action will lie, 655.
the goods or value may be recovered, *ib.*
property must be in plaintiff, at the time of the action brought, 656.
the property, without having had possession is sufficient, *ib.*
detinue will lie for specific goods only, *ib.*
defendant must be in possession, 657.
grounds of the action, *ib.*
bailment not traversable, *ib.*
judgment in, 658.

DEVASTAVIT:

what is such, 790.

DEVIATION:

nature and effect of, on contracts of insurance, 1004.
must be voluntary act of persons having management of ship, 1006.
unreasonable delay equivalent to, 1007.
intention to deviate not a deviation, 1008.
to succour vessel in distress, whether justifiable, 1009.
what will justify a deviation, 1005.
grounds of necessity, 1007.

DEVISE: *See* WILL.

DEVISEES:

liability of, upon bond made by testator, 590.

DEVISEE OF TERM:

what he must prove, 743.

DIRECTORS:

of joint stock company, drawing and acceptance of bills by, 331.

DISCLAIMER:

dispenses with notice to quit, 710.

DISCONTINUANCE:

in pleading, 4 n.

DISHONOUR:

of bill, notice of, 352.

DISSEISOR:

account does not lie against, 1.

DISTRESS:

distress formerly considered as a pledge only, 659.
for what a distress may be taken at common law, by prescription, by statute, 660.
of the general rule, that all moveable chattels may be distrained for rent arrear, 662.
what things are privileged absolutely, 663.
　　　what conditionally, 665.
what may be distrained damage feasant, 666.
who may distrain,
　　　recoverors of manors, &c., 667.
　　　personal representatives of tenants of freehold rents, *ib.*
　　　husbands seised in right of their wives, 667.
　　　tenants pur auter vie, *ib.*

DISTRESS—*continued*.

person entitled to separate herbage, 669.
tenant in common, *ib*.
executor, *ib*.
mortgagee, *ib*.
commoner, *ib*.
lessee for years having assigned, cannot distrain, 670.
of the time at which a distress may be taken,
at common law, 670.
by stat. 8 Ann. c. 14, 671.
distress for *rent* must be taken in the day-time, *ib*.
of the place where a distress may be taken,
distress for rent service must be taken on the land, 672.
of distraining in houses, 672 n.
if separate demises, distress must be on the several premises, 673.
of fresh suit, *ib*.
how to proceed when goods are clandestinely removed, 673, 4.
of driving the distress out of the hundred, 674.
remedy for the same, *ib*.
where growing crops may be laid up, 675.
of the sale of distresses for rent arrear under stat. 2 Will. & Ma. c. 5, *ib*.
of abusing the distress, and thereby becoming a trespasser ab initio, 680.
trespass will not lie for excessive distress merely, 681.
nor for irregular distress, where irregularity is not an act of trespass, 1320.
action on the case for excessive distress, 681.

DISTURBANCE :

of common, 422.
of seat in pew, 1113.

DITCHES :

rule concerning, 1314.

DIVIDENDS :

no action to be brought for bankrupts', 244, 5.
apportionable, 603.

DIVORCE :

by Jewish law, proof of, 19.

DOCK WARRANT :

where transfer of property, 1279.

DOGGET :

of judgment, when necessary, 785, n.

DOMESDAY :

book, evidence as to ancient demesne, 757.

DOMICILE :

personal property distributed according to law of, 751.

DONATIO MORTIS CAUSA :

nature of, 1347.

DOOR :

breaking open, rule as to, 1332.

DORMANT PARTNER:
  liability of, 1137.

DOUBLE RENT:
  stat. 11 Geo. II. c. 19, s. 18, tenants holding over after notice given by themselves liable to, 599.

DOUBLE YEARLY VALUE:
  tenants wilfully holding over after determination of term, 596.

DRAFTS:
  on bankers, where exempt from stamp duty, 314.

DRAWEE:
  of bill, 301.
  presentment to, 327.
  competency of, 375.

DRAWER:
  of bill, 301.
  where he may sue acceptor, 330.
  competency of, 375.

DRUGS:
  sale of, to brewer, illegal, 59, 60.

DRUNKENNESS:
  where ground of avoiding deed, 536.

DURANTE ABSENTIA:
  administration, 779.

DURATION OF LIFE:
  presumption of, 753.

DURESS:
  plea of, to debt on bond, 542.
  must be of the person, ib.
  replication to plea, ib.
  of goods, does not avoid agreement. 84.

DUTY: See AUCTION.

DYERS:
  lien of, 1374.
    for general balance by usage only, 1374, (z).

E.

EARNEST:
  what amounts to, 858.

EASEMENT:
  enjoyment of, under 2 & 3 Will. IV. c. 71, 1111, 2.
  unity of possession suspends prescriptive, 1112.
  evidence of right to, 435.
  injury to, how proved, 1120.

EAST INDIES:
how to prove deed executed there, 540.

ECCLESIASTICAL COURTS:
probate granted by, conclusive, while unrepealed, 776.

EFFECTS:
when want of, will excuse notice of dishonour, 333.
specific, of testator, not seizable by assignees of bankrupt executor, 775 n., 776 n.

EJECTMENT:
nature of the action, 684.
party who has the legal estate must prevail, 685.
plaintiff must recover on the strength of his own title, 687.
for breach of covenant to repair, 709.
by whom ejectment may be brought, 689.
what description will be sufficient of the thing for which ejectment is brought, 694.
instances of insufficient description, 695.
of entries before ejectment brought, 696.
of the declaration, 714.
    of the notice subscribed to the declaration, 717.
of the pleadings, 728.
    evidence, 743.
    verdict, 759.
    judgment, 760.
execution, 761.
costs, 762.
See ERROR—NOTICE TO QUIT—MESNE PROFITS.

ELEGIT:
tenant by, what he must prove, 745.

ELOPEMENT:
of wife, liability of husband for debts after, 273.

EMBARGO:
nature of, 959.
effect of, on contract of insurance, *ib.*

ENLARGEMENT:
of demise in ejectment, 716 n.

ENTRY:
actual entry, where necessary to avoid fine, 696, 7.
        where not, 697.
entry into part is a suspension of rent, but not of a covenant to repair, 512, 3.
what is a waiver of a right of entry for a forfeiture, 707.
by auctioneer binds parties as to sale of land as well as goods, 853.

EQUITY OF REDEMPTION:
release of, good consideration, 42 n.

ERROR:
writ of error, in account, can be brought after second judgment only, 6.
no writ of error allowed after *verdict* in ejectment, unless plaintiff in error finds bail, 763.
of the costs of error in replevin, 1208.

ESCAPE:

    of the remedy for, at common law, 605.

                by statutes, *ib.*

    debt for escape, more eligible proceeding than action on the case, 607.

    sheriff liable for escape after recaption on escape warrant, *ib.*

    of voluntary and negligent escapes, *ib.*

    of escapes upon habeas corpus, 608.

    sheriff liable for escape, though judgment on process be erroneous, 608, 9.

    so where court has not jurisdiction, 609.

    by whom and against whom an action for escape may be brought, 613.

    of the declaration, 615.

    pleadings, 616.

    proof necessary to support the action for escape, 617.

ESCROW:

    what is an, 537.

ESTATE:

    pur autre vie, where assets by descent, 792.

ESTOPPEL:

    of replying the estoppel to nil habuit in tenementis,

        in covenant, 516.

        in debt, 604.

    assignee of reversion may take advantage of estoppel running with the land, 515.

    what is necessary in order to give a party the benefit of an estoppel, 515, 6.

    where the estoppel will not operate, 516, 7.

    a verdict found in trespass on any fact or title, distinctly put in issue, may be pleaded as an estoppel in another action between the same parties, 1328.

    where judgment not conclusive, unless pleaded as an estoppel, 1329.

ESTOVERS:

    common of, 414, 421.

EVICTION:

    lessee may plead eviction, but not a mere trespass, in bar to covenant for rent arrear, 512.

    plea of, in debt, 602.

    plea of, in bar to avowry for rent, 1198.

    by eviction from part by elder title, rent is apportioned only, 611 n.

    eviction by stranger, what necessary to be shown on, 513.

EVIDENCE:

    in action for adultery, 12.

    in actions by assignees of bankrupts, 262.

        on bills of exchange, 371.

        on executing writ of inquiry, 370.

        on promissory notes, 391.

        against carriers, 412.

        by and against commoners, 426—429.

        of covenant, 524.

    in debt,

        on foreign judgment, 530.

        on bond, 535, 7, 8.

        against sheriff for escape, 617.

        on statute against bribery at elections of members of parliament, 630.

    in actions for deceit, 642, 654.

EVIDENCE—*continued.*

in detinue, 657.
in ejectment,
 on the part of lessor of plaintiff, 743.
 on the part of defendant, 758.
in trespass for mesne profits, 766.
in actions by and against executors, 806.
factor, 825.
effect of parol, of a variation or waiver of written contract, 867.
in actions on policies of insurance, 1016.
 for libel, 1046.
 for malicious prosecution, 1064.
 for a nusance, 1120.
 relating to partners, 1140.
in quo warranto informations, 1165.
in actions for rescous, 1211.
 under Shipping Act, 1230.
 for slander, 1256.
 on stat. 2 & 3 Edw. VI. *c.* 13, for not setting out tithes, 1304.
 for trespass, what may be given in evidence under the general issue, 1325.
 of trespass, 1340.
 of trover, 1378.

EXAMINATION:
of attornies, 157 n.

EXCESSIVE DISTRESS:
action for, 681.

EXCHEQUER:
condemnation in, effect of, 1320, 1349.

EXCHEQUER BILL:
property in, passes by delivery, 1360.

EXECUTION:
when execution and act of bankruptcy on same day, priority may be inquired into, 207.
taking prisoner in execution, satisfaction of judgment, 612.
goods of debtor bound by delivery of writ of, 1349.

EXECUTOR:
in action *by* executors, all must join, 794, 5.
not so *against* executors, 800.
how to sue, when any of executors die, 801.
order of payment by, 784.
nature of interest of, 774.
testator's property does not pass to assignee of, 224.
when debt against, must be in debet and detinet, or in detinet only, 600.
of executor de son tort, 781.
admission of assets by, 788.
may distrain, 668.
promise by, to pay testator's debts, must be in writing, 840.
when entitled to standing corn, 1356.
account by and against, 3.
where executor may sue in covenant, 477.
when chargeable in covenant, 484.
See ADMINISTRATION.

EXECUTOR DE SON TORT:
>description of, 781.
>retainer by, 805.

EXEMPLIFICATION:
>of probate, where evidence, 806.

EXPRESS:
>malice, where not necessary to prove, 1056 n.
>where necessary, 1066.
>warranty,
>>action lies on, 639.
>>breach of, in insurance, 994.

EXTENT:
>in chief, or in aid, priority of, 660.

EXTRA PAROCHIAL:
>persons cannot claim pew, 1113.
>tithes, to whom due, 1300.

F.

FACTOR:
>nature of his employment, 810.
>pledge by factor, effect of, 811.
>sale by, how it operates, 814.
>where debt due from, may be set off in action by principal, ib.
>lien of, 817.
>principal responsible for, 820.
>alterations in law of, by statute, 820—825.
>factors good witnesses from necessity, 825.
>goods in possession of, do not pass to assignees, 225.

FALSE IMPRISONMENT:
>what is such, 907.
>actions against justices for, 913.
>where it lies against sheriff, 907.
>justification,
>>by party and officer, 921.
>>under process issuing out of superior and inferior courts, 922.
>>>out of foreign court, 923.
>>money not to be paid into court, in action for, 920.

FALSE REPRESENTATION:
>action for, 650.

FAST DAY:
>bill due on, payable on day preceding, 351.
>notice of dishonour, where good on following day, 353.

FEES:
>action for, 67, 77.

FEE-FARM RENT:
>import of, 661 n.

FEME-COVERT:

where considered as feme sole, 283.
suing with or without her husband, 288.
separate estate of, 271 n.

FENCES:

escape of cattle, through defect of, 1193.
obligation to repair, 1193, 4.

FIAT:

substituted for commission of bankrupt, 187 n.
evidence of, 265.

FINE:

actual entry necessary to avoid fine levied with proclamations, but not a
fine at common law, 696, 7.
in what cases an entry is barred by fine and non-claim, 728, 9.
how proved, 732.
fines and recoveries abolished by stat. 3 & 4 Will. IV. c. 74, 696 n.

FIRE:

rent of premises destroyed by, 447, 474 n., 1389.
insurance against, 1033.
loss by, in marine insurance, 963.

FISHERY:

several, 829.
free, 830.
common of, 832.
ejectment will not lie for, 696.

FIXTURES:

law concerning what are, and what are not, 1354—1358.
not removed during term become the property of landlord, 1356.

FLEET BOOKS:

not evidence of marriage, 13.
new statute concerning, *ib.*

FORBEARANCE:

of suit, where a consideration, 43.
where not, 45.

FOREIGN BILL OF EXCHANGE:

form of, 309.
stamp, 315.
presentment of, 327.
protest, 359.

FOREIGN JUDGMENT:

action on, 65, 6, 7, 8, 530.
proof, 530.

FOREIGN LAW: see 142.

when it regulates contract made here, Add.

FOREIGN MARRIAGE:

proof of, 20, 1.

FOREIGNER:

liability of, as feme sole, 285, 6.

FORFEITURE:

what shall be a waiver of, 707.

FORGERY:

where party paying money on forged instrument may recover it, 98, 9.
payment under probate of forged will, good, 776.

FRACTION:

of a day, when allowed, 207, 611.

FRAUD:

defence on ground of, must be specially pleaded, 117. ·

FRAUDS, STATUTE OF:

of the persons who are supposed to have drawn this statute, 833.
first, second, and third sections, relating to parol demises, assignments, and
　　surrenders, 834—838.
　　　　what effect they have, if not, in writing, 837.
fourth section,
　　　　as to charging executor upon special promise, 838, 9, 40.
　　　　leading case thereon, 840.
　　　　as to charging defendant on special promise to answer for another
　　　　　person, 841.
　　　　cases within this clause, 841—843.
　　　　cases not within, 845—850.
　　　　as to charging any person, upon agreement made in consideration
　　　　　of marriage, 850.
　　　　　　upon contract or sale of land, 850—854.
　　　　　　upon agreement not to be performed within the year, 854.
　　　　agreement must be in writing, 856.
seventeenth section,
　　　　as to contract for sale of goods, wares, and merchandizes, 857.
　　　　executory contracts within this clause, ib.
　　　　stat. 9 Geo. IV. c. 14, s. 7, on this subject, ib.
　　　　shares, not wares, 857, 8.
　　　　what shall be considered as acceptance, 858.
　　　　note in writing of bargain by party or agent, 861.
　　　　signature, what sufficient, 862.
　　　　agent, who is deemed such, 863.
fifth section, relating to execution of wills, 870.
　　　　devises of lands, what such within this clause, 871.
　　　　must be in writing, ib.
　　　　signature, what sufficient, 872.
　　　　attestation and subscription, what required, 873.
　　　　in the presence of devisor, what deemed sufficient, 874, 5.
　　　　by three or more witnesses, who are sufficient, 876, 7, 8, 9.
　　　　of the evidence by, 879.
sixth section, relating to revocation of wills, 881.
　　　　what required to make a valid revocation, 881.
　　　　　　by other will, ib.
　　　　　　　　or codicil, ib.
　　　　　　　　or other writing, 882.
　　　　　　　　burning, tearing, or obliterating, ib.
　　　　implied revocations, 885.
　　　　　　what are such, 885, 6, 7, 8.
　　　　how wills may be annulled, 888.
　　　　See NEW STAT. OF WILLS, 1 VICT. c. 26, 890—894.

FRAUDULENT AGREEMENTS, 60.
considered in same light as illegal, *ib*.

FRAUDULENT CONVEYANCE:
where act of bankruptcy, 197.

FRAUDULENT PREFERENCE:
what amounts to, 202.

FRAUDULENT MISREPRESENTATION:
action for, 650.
as to credit of another, where action lies for, 651.
not necessary that defendant should have derived advantage from the
deceit, 651.
statute relating to, 653.

FREE FISHERY:
meaning of the term, 830.
remarks of Mr. J. Blackstone thereon, 830, 1.
and of Mr. Hargrave, *ib*.

FREE WARREN:
franchise of, explained, 896.

FREIGHT:
insurance of, 950, 1.
cases relating to, 509.
mother of wages, 1235.

FRESH RIVERS:
soil of, to whom it belongs, 828.

FUNERAL EXPENSES:
limit of, 784 n.

G.

GAME:
what the term includes, 898.
opinion of Blackstone as to the property of the game being vested in the
king alone, 895.
stat. 1 & 2 Will. IV. c. 32, concerning, 898, 9.
penalties for killing game at improper seasons, 904.
penalties imposed by Certificate Act, 904, 5.
See WAGER.

GAMEKEEPERS:
appointment and authority of, 902.

GAMING:
statutes against, concerning bonds, bills, notes, &c., 321, 548, 1401.
See WAGER.

GENERAL AVERAGE:
meaning of, 940.

GENERAL ISSUE:

by statute, plea of, 29.
magistrates not deprived of, 920.
effect of, entitling party to begin, 1046.
what may be given in evidence under, in assumpsit, since new rules, 116.
in case against carrier, 412.
no general issue in covenant, 517.
in debt on bond, 535.
in case, for malicious prosecution, 1063.
   replevin, 1190.
   slander, 1254.
   trespass for assault, 29.
   in actions against justices, &c., 29, 920.
   in trespass q. c. f., 1325.
   in trover, 1368.

GENTOO:

deposition of, where admissible, 876.

GIFT:

verbal, effect of, 1347.

GLEANING:

illegal, 1318.

GLEBE:

neglect to cultivate, not actionable, 46.

GOOD FRIDAY:

bill due on, to be presented on previous day, 351.
   notice of dishonour, good by statute on following day, 353.

GOODS:

what deemed acceptance of, 858.

GOODS SOLD AND DELIVERED:

indebitatus assumpsit for, 66.
fraudulently on credit, trover lies for, before credit expires, 70.
where *bond fide* on credit, action cannot be maintained until after expiration
   of credit, 69.

GRANT:

of right of way, 1336.

GROSS:

common in, nature of, 419.

GUARDIAN:

in socage, account against, 2, and n.
ejectment by, 691.
testamentary, how appointed, 691 n.

GUEST:

goods and money of, where innkeeper liable for, Add.
goods of, where innkeeper may detain, 1375; but not person, 1371 n.

H.

HABEAS CORPUS:
of escapes upon, 608.

HABERE FACIAS POSSESSIONEM:
writ of, 762.

HAND-WRITING:
of witnesses to instruments,
bond, 537.
will, 879.

HEARSAY:
general rule, 753.
admissible on questions as to pedigree, under what limitations, 753, 4.
declaration of parent as to *time* of child's birth, admissible, 754.
aliter, as to place, 755.
declarations of surgeon as to time of child's birth, 754.
of members of family, 753.
post litem motam not admissible, 755.
evidence, when admissible, 753, 4.
husband within exception, 755.

HEDGE:
presumption as to ownership of, 1314.

HEIR:
account by, 1.
covenant by and against, 477, 483.
debt on bond of ancestor against, 585.
not bound unless named, 585 n.
rules as to the heir taking by purchase or descent, 588.
statute relating to descent, 741.
plea by, 587.
judgment against, 592.
where witness, 879.

HEIRLOOM:
detinue lies for, 656.

HERALD:
books of, where evidence, 753.

HIGHWAY:
of pleading, 1339.
waste land near, property in, 748, 1314, 5.

HOLDING OVER:
penalty on, 596—599.

HOP DUTY:
wager on amount of, illegal, 1405.

HORSE-RACES:
law relating to wager on, 1402, 3, 4.

HORSES:
detainer and sale of, by innkeeper, 1381 n.

HORSES—*continued.*

doctrine relating to warranty of, 642.
sale of, when stolen, 1348.

HOTEL KEEPER:

who is, within bankrupt law, 188, 9 n.

HOYMAN:

liable as common carrier, 395.

HUSBAND:

how husband, seised in right of wife, must declare in covenant, 496.
husband, member of wife's family, as to hearsay declarations in pedigree,
755.
See BARON AND FEME.

I.

ILLEGAL:

agreements, 53, 4.
consideration must be specially pleaded, 117.
covenants, 459.
consideration, plea of, in debt on bond, 543.
by common law, *ib.*
by statute, 548.
plea of illegal purpose, 513.

IMPLIED:

covenant, 453.
malice, 1056, 1247, 1257.
warranty, 637.
in insurance, 1004.

IMPRISONMENT: *See* FALSE.

INDEBITATUS ASSUMPSIT:

nature of, 64.
where it may be brought by, or maintained against, corporation aggregate, 66.
lies for fees, tolls, &c., 67.

INDORSEMENT:

of the different kinds of, 342, 3.

INFANCY:

plea of, in assumpsit, 122.
            covenant, 513.

INFANT:

account does not lie against, 3.
cannot be guardian in socage, 3 n.
marriage of, 17.
not liable as acceptor of a bill of exchange, though drawn for necessaries,
304.
for what necessaries chargeable, 122—129.
commission of bankruptcy against, void, 188.
where not liable on covenant, 513.
where liable, having confirmed the contract at full age, 123, 4, 561 n.
whether bond of infant be void or voidable, 560 n.

INFERIOR COURTS:

of the allegations necessary in a declaration on promises in an inferior court, 102.
how officer or party must justify under process of, 922.

INFORMATION:

in nature of quo warranto, 1143.
limitation of time for granting, 1155.

INHERITANCE:

stat. 3 & 4 Will. IV. c. 106, rules of, 741, 2.

INJUNCTION:

perpetual after several verdicts in ejectment, 763.

INNKEEPER:

demand for spirituous liquors, 55. *See Hughes v. Doane*, Add.
has lien on *goods* of guest, 1375.
but cannot detain person, or take off clothes, 1371 n.
may be bankrupt, 188.
liability of, as to guest's goods, Add.

INNUENDO:

nature of, 1251, 2.

INQUIRY:

if jurors give a defective verdict under stat. 17 Car. II. c. 7, omission cannot be supplied by a writ of inquiry, 1205.

INSOLVENT:

voluntary assignment by, 199.
filing petition for discharge, effect of, by trader, 210.

INSOLVENT DEBTORS COURT:

vesting order of, 1349.

INSPECTION:

of records of corporation, 1163.

INSTALMENTS:

how to sue for money due by, 534, 5 n.

INSURANCE:

definition of, 929.
of the policy, 930.
who and what may be insured, 948, 950.
of the several grounds of defence, 985.
re-assurance, nature of, 1013.
    illegal by statute, except in three cases, *ib.*
wager policy, ib.
insurance upon lives, 1030.
    party insuring life must be interested, *ib.*
    name of person interested must be inserted in policy, *ib.*
    creditor is interested in life of his debtor, *ib.*
    insured must subscribe a declaration touching his age, state of health, &c., 1031.
insurance against fire, 1033.
    covenant to keep premises insured, construction of, 447, 476.
See ABANDONMENT—ADJUSTMENT.

INTEREST:
  where recoverable, 376.
  by 3 & 4 Will. IV. c. 42, s. 28, jury may allow interest, 377.
  in policies: *see* INSURANCE—WAGER—POLICY—and INSURANCE ON
    LIVES AND FIRE.
  of witnesses, 825.
  statute relating thereto, 825 n., 1097, 8, 1195.

INTRODUCTORY AVERMENT:
  when necessary, slander, 1251, 2.

I. O. U.
  effect of, 100.

IRELAND:
  a place beyond seas within stat. 4 Ann. c. 16, s. 19, 144, 5, 738 n.
  marriage in, 20.
  going to, when act of bankruptcy, 191.
  bill drawn in, does not require English stamp, 315.

IRISH:
  judgment, since Union, indebitatus assumpsit lies on, 66 n.

ISSUE:
  on count for voluntary, plaintiff may prove negligent escape, 618.

J.

JERSEY:
  when considered beyond the seas, 59 n., 144.
  not part of United Kingdom, 59 n.

JETTISON:
  loss by, contribution, 75 n.

JEW:
  marriage of, 19.
  divorce, proof of, *ib.*

JEWISH FESTIVAL:
  respect paid to, by law, 353.

JOINT AND SEVERAL:
  of joint and several promissory notes, 385, 393.
  of joint and several covenants, 455.

JOINT STOCK COMPANY:
  right of director to draw and accept bills, 331.
  where, cannot accept customer's bill, 304.
  spiritual persons, partners in, 308.
    how far legalized, 1127.
  shares in, not wares within 17th sect. of stat. of frauds, 857, 8.
  directors proceeding with less than proposed capital, 1125.

JOINT TENANTS:
  account by, 2.
  laying the demise in ejectment by joint tenants, 714, 5.
  joint tenancy, where it may be given in evidence, under not guilty in
    trover, 1364.

JUDGE:

order of, to stay proceedings, not evidence of termination of suit, 1058.

JUDGMENT:

where a party must show it in a justification in trespass, 921.
foreign, indebitatus assumpsit lies on, 65, 6, 7, 8.
Irish, 66 n.
debt lies on foreign, 530.
how proved, *ib.*
of confessing, by executor, 803.
debt on, 593.
Irish judgment, how proved, 594.
form of,

    in account, 4, 5.
    assault and battery, 36.
    covenant, 525, 6.
    debt on bond against heir, 592.
    detinue, 658.
    ejectment, 760, 1.
    executor, 808.
    heir, 592.
    quo warranto, 1168.
    replevin, 1203.
    tithes, 1308.
    trover, 1384.
where not conclusive, unless pleaded as an estoppel, 1329.
warrant of attorney to confess, attestation of, 231 n.

JUS TERTII:

where it cannot be set up, 87 n., 1344.

JUSTICES OF THE PEACE:

statutes relating to action against, 913, 4, 5, 6, 9, 20.
actions against, shall be laid in proper county, 913.
may plead general issue, *ib.*
how pleaded, under new rule, 29, 920, 1.
notice of suit must be delivered to J. P. one calendar month before action,
    914.
how month is computed, 159 n., 914 n.
form of notice required, 914 n., 915.
Secretary of State not J. P., 914 n.
J. P. may tender amends, 915.
within what time actions against J. P. must be brought, 918, 9.

JUSTIFICATION:

in defence of person, 30.
              possession, 30, 1.
by officers executing process, 32, 3.
on other grounds, 33.
local and transitory, 34.
replication to, 35.
how to plead, 921.

L.

LADING:

bill of, when evidence of property, 407, 8.
when property passes by indorsement of, 1279, 1346.

LAND:
sale of, within the 4th clause of stat. of frauds, 850.

LANDLORD AND TENANT:
action by landlord against tenant for misusing farm, 46.
where landlord may justify an entry on land demised, 1318, 9, 1330, 1.
where landlord may re-enter, 711.
of evidence by landlord to support ejectment, 746.
where tenant shall pay double the *yearly value* for wilfully holding over, 596, 7.
where tenant shall pay *double rent* for not quitting, 599.
tenants must give notice to landlords of ejectments, 722.
duty of tenant on expiration of term, 1388, 9.
See EJECTMENT—NOTICE TO QUIT—RENT.

LAW:
wager of, abolished, 64 (*l*).

LEASE:
vendor of, bound to produce his landlord's title, 181.
bankrupt entitled to, statute relating to, 254.
mere cancelling not a deed or note in writing, 838.
parol, when good, *ib.*
made by attorney, where void, 461, 2.
modern doctrine relating to leases from year to year, 698.
where a license to occupy amounts to a lease, 1330.

LEGACY:
where an action will not lie for, 797.
in what order to be paid, 788.

LEGAL EFFECT:
contract may be stated according to, 103.

LEGAL TENDER:
bank notes, where, 152.

LEGATEE:
witness to will, 878, 891.

LEGITIMACY:
child may be illegitimate, though husband is within the kingdom, 749.
where husband, by course of nature, cannot have been the father, child is illegitimate, *ib.*
wife is witness of necessity to prove adulterous intercourse, *ib.*
but non-access must be proved by other witnesses, *ib.*
even though husband be dead, *ib.*

LETTERS OF ADMINISTRATION:
where an administration de bonis non is necessary, 778.
of limited, 779.

LEVANT AND COUCHANT:
meaning of these terms, 417 n., 427.

LEX LOCI:
real property follows the, 751.
contract made here governed by law of country, where party agrees to pay, Add.

LIBEL:

    remedy for, by action on the case, 1038.
    where it lies, *ib.*
    where not, 1039.
    how the declaration ought to be framed, 1043.
    what may be pleaded, 1044.
    if libel be true, defendant may justify, 1045.
    evidence :
        what admissible, 1046.
        what not, 1048.
        what necessary, where libel is in foreign language, 1047.
    jury may give a general verdict, 1052.
    course adopted by judges, in criminal and civil cases, 1052, 3.

LIBERTY:

    personal, injury to, 907.

LIBERUM TENEMENTUM

    plea of, 1327.

LICENSE:

    to alien, effect of, 472.
    to trade with enemy, 986.
    executory, countermandable, 1120.
    executed, cannot be countermanded, *ib.*
    evidence, to establish, 1121.
    plea of, to action for trespass, 1329.
    evidence in support of plea of, where plaintiff replies de inj., 1330.

LIEN:

    cannot exist, without possession, 1372.
    reviver of, where it takes place, 1375.
    cannot be acquired by wrongful act, 1377.
    a personal right, 1378.
    of carriers :
        how it arises, 404.
    of factors, 817.
    nature of liens, 1370, 1.
    foundation of general liens, 1371.
    nature and extent of innkeeper's, 1371 n.
    how a right of detainer may be waived, 1375.

LIFE ?

    insurance on, 1030.

LIGHT:

    action for obstruction of, 1108, 9.

LIGHTER:

    where insurer liable for loss on board of, 955.
    where not, *ib.*

IMITATION:

    of actions on penal statutes, 622.
    stat. 3 & 4 Will. IV. c. 27, for limitation of actions and suits relating to real property, 732.
    in quo warranto, 1155.

LIMITATION OF ACTIONS:
>   in adultery, 12.
>   assault and battery, 27.
>   assumpsit, 135.
>   of replication of process sued out to plea of statute of limitations, 142.
>   of executors renewing suits commenced by testator, 143, 4.
>   of the stat. 4 Ann. c. 16, s. 19, permitting defendants to be sued within a
>   limited time after returning from beyond seas, 146.
>   in covenant, 514.
>   in debt for rent arrear, 604, 5.
>   for not setting forth tithe, 1303, 4.
>   ejectment, 732, 3.
>   imprisonment, 926.
>   libel, 1046.
>   malicious prosecution, 1064.
>   replevin, 1201.
>   slander, 1255.
>   trespass, 1318.

LIQUIDATED DAMAGES, 155.

LIVES:
>   insurance on, 1030.

LLOYD'S:
>   usage at, where not binding, 955, 980.

LOCAL AND TRANSITORY:
>   actions now triable in any county, 494.
>   where covenant on lease is local, and where transitory, 493.
>   of local and transitory justification, 34.

LONDON:
>   custom of, as to femes covert sole traders, 283.
>   as to apprentices, 514.

LORD OF MANOR:
>   mandamus lies to, to admit copyholder, 1076, 7.
>   lien of, on estray, 1377.

LOSS: See INSURANCE.

LOST BILL OF EXCHANGE OR NOTE:
>   when plaintiff can recover, 341.

LOST BYE-LAW:
>   proof of, 1162.

LOST REGISTRY OF SHIP:
>   certificate of, 1224, 1227.

LUNATIC:
>   asylum, keeping, not a trade, 444.
>   committee of, cannot bring ejectment, 692.
>   limited administration during lunacy, 781.

M.

MAGISTRATES:
  action against, statute relating to, 913.
                notice of, 914, 5.
  liability of, 1061.
  form of action against, *ib.*

MAIHEM:
  may be justified by an officer in the army, 33.

MAINTENANCE:
  separate, of wife, 460.

MAKER OF NOTE:
  evidence in action by payee against, 391.
          by first indorsee against, *ib.*
  competency of, as witness, 393.

MALICIOUS ARREST:
  where action lies for, 1058.
  must appear, that action is determined, *ib.*
  proof of determination of suit, 1058, 9.
  stet processus insufficient, 1059.
  plea of not guilty, what it puts in issue, 1063.

MALICIOUS PROSECUTION:
  remedy for, 1054.
  of the grounds of this action, 1056, 7.
  what declaration must state, 1062.
  what will be a sufficient defence, 1063.

MANDAMUS:
  nature and object of the writ of, 1069.
  in what cases court will grant it, 1075.
  where not, 1078.
  form of the writ, 1081.
  of the return to the writ, 1083.
  peremptory, where grantable, 1086.

MANOR:
  of the appointment of gamekeepers by lords of manors, 902.
  See LORD OF.

MARKET OVERT, 1344, 1348.

MARRIAGE:
  what good at common law, 13, 14.
  of the alterations and provisions made by several statutes, 14—22.
  evidence as to, in action for adultery, 12.
  provisions of statute of frauds relating to, 850.
  revocation of will by marriage and birth of child, 886.
  clause in new act, 892.
  contract in restraint of, illegal, 56, 459, 1405.

MARKSMAN:
  signing will by, 872.

MASTER AND SERVANT:

of actions by servants against their masters for wages, 1091.
where master may discharge servant, 1092.
of master's liability in respect of contracts made by his servants, 1094,
    1095, 6.
cases on this point, *ib.*
in what cases the servant is a witness for the master, without a release,
    1096.
where master is liable for negligence or unskilfulness, 1097—1101.
where the master may maintain an action:
    for enticing away his apprentice or servant, 1102.
    for beating or imprisoning him, *ib.*
    for debauching his servant or daughter, 1103.
in what case the action for seduction may be maintained, and what are
    the requisites to support it, *ib.*
daughter or servant is a competent witness, 1104.
courts unwilling to disturb the verdict on the ground of excessive
    damages, 1106.
of slander spoken by master of servant, 1255 and n.
of ship, what authority he has, 1362.

MAYOR:

mandamus lies to admit and to restore, 1070.
statute relating to the election of, 1072.
cases on it, 1073, 4.

MEMBERS OF PARLIAMENT:

privilege of, in *speaking* defamatory words, 1041 n.
bankruptcy of, 211.
wager on election of, illegal, 1405.
See BRIBERY.

MEMORANDUM:

where memorandum indorsed on bond taken as part of condition, 566.
memorandum in policy, 939, 940.

MERCHANT:

clause relating to merchant's accounts in statute of limitations, 141 n.
See FACTOR.

MESNE PROFITS:

action for, in whose name it may be brought, 765.
of the evidence after judgment upon verdict in ejectment, 766.
of the evidence after judgment by default, *ib.*
how far judgment in ejectment is conclusive evidence of plaintiff's title, *ib.*
of pleading the statute of limitations, 767.

MINES:

liability of partners in, 1125.
damages for working coal mines, 1383.

MINORITY:

See INFANCY.

MISREPRESENTATION:

insurance, 989.
action for fraudulent, 650.

MISTAKE:
of fact, money paid under, 77, 79, 80.
of law, 77.

MIXED TITHES:
not within stat. 2 & 3 Edw. VI., 1285.

MODUS:
statute 2 & 3 Will. IV. c. 100, for shortening time in claims of modus, 1296.
requisites of, 1306.
for part of a farm, good, *ib.*

MONASTERIES:
dissolution of, 1293, 4.

MONEY HAD AND RECEIVED:
action for, where it lies, 76—100.
See BANKRUPT.

MONEY PAID:
where action for, lies, 71—76.

MORAL OBLIGATION, 50 n.

MORE OR LESS:
meaning of, 155, 6.

MORTGAGE:
mortgagee may maintain ejectment, 691.
    what proof necessary to support the action, 751.
    where court will stay proceedings on payment of principal and costs, 691 n.
    where mortgagee may distrain, 669.
    cannot defend as landlord, not having taken possession, 722.
    where statute of limitations will not bar, 1 Vict. c. 28, 740, 1.
    suable as assignee, 489 n.
mortgagor: where he may be sued on his personal covenant, though bill of sale void, 461.
    mortgage of trader continuing in possession void as against creditors, 218.
    mortgagor in possession is not entitled to notice to quit, 711.
    sale by, auction duty, 175.

MUTUAL ACCOUNTS:
effect of, in taking a case out of statute of limitations, 141.

MUTUAL CREDIT:
in bankruptcy, 260.

MUTUAL DEBTS:
may be set off, 147.

N.

NAME:
true, as to marriage, 18.

NECESSARIES:
> what are deemed such in case of infant, 122.
>> in case of wife, 272.

NEGLIGENCE:
> of attornies, 169.
> of carriers, 402.
> of servants, 1097.

NEGLIGENT ESCAPE:
> what is considered as such, 607.

NE UNQUES:
> accouple, 297.
> bailiff, 4.
> receiver, *ib.*

NEUTRALITY:
> evidence to disprove, 1001.

NEW ASSIGNMENT:
> where necessary, 35 n.
> where not, 1328.

NEW RULES: *See* TABLE in Vol. I. lxxxix. after Table of Statutes.

NEWSPAPERS:
> statute (6 & 7 Will. IV. c. 76,) relating to printers of, 1050.
> proprietor of, not sued, may be a witness, 1051.

NIL DEBET:
> plea of, not allowed in any action, 46 (y).
> but see exception, where it is given by statute, 1303.

NIL HABUIT IN TENEMENTIS:
> plea of, in covenant, 514.
> where lease is by indenture, plaintiff may demur to this plea, unless want of title appear on declaration, 514, 5.
> cannot be pleaded to action for use and occupation, 1393.

NON-ACCESS:
> neither husband or wife competent to prove, 749.

NON-ASSUMPSIT:
> limitation of, under new rules, 116.
> infra sex annos, 135.

NON CEPIT:
> plea of, in replevin, 1190.

NON-CLAIM:
> in what cases a bar, 728, 730.

NON DIMISIT:
> good plea in replevin, 1199.

NON EST FACTUM:
> plea of, in covenant, 517.
> what it puts in issue, 518.
> what may be given in evidence under it, when pleaded to debt on bond, 535.

NONJOINDER:

plea in abatement for, 115.

NONSUIT:

of judgment of nonsuit before and after issue joined in replevin, 1204.

NOTE:

of bargain, in writing, where necessary, 861.

NOTES:

brokers', bought and sold, 173 n., 863 n.

NOTES, PROMISSORY:

definition, 379.

common law doctrine respecting actions on promissory notes, how altered by stat. 3 & 4 Ann. c. 9, *ib.*

what notes are within this stat., 380.

what not, 381.

banker's cash notes, 385.

of the consideration, 386.

in what case want or illegality of consideration may be insisted on, 387.

stamp, *ib.*

payment of note, when due, must be demanded within a reasonable time, 388.

days of grace, *ib.*

mode of computation, *ib.*

notice of default of payment by maker must be given by indorsee to prior indorsers, 388, 9.

of the remedy on a note by action of assumpsit, 390.

what may be pleaded, *ib.*

of the evidence necessary to support action on note, 391.

by payee, *ib.*

indorsee, *ib.*

in what cases an indorser may be a witness, 393.

of the analogy between an indorsed note and a bill, *ib.*

NOT GUILTY:

"by statute," plea of, 29, 920.

NOTICE:

to principal, notice to agents, 235, 820.

of action against officers, 96 n., 915.

of non-acceptance of bill, 332.

of non-payment, 352, 3.

where notice may be presumed, 358.

waiver of objection for want of, what is, 336, 358.

of auctioneers' conditions, 646 n.

to tenant of distress, 676 n.

subscribed to declaration in ejectment, 717.

by tenant to landlord of delivery of declaration in ejectment, 722.

of the notice required by stat. 24 Geo. II. c. 44, to be delivered to J. P. before action brought, 915.

requisites of this notice, *ib.*

what notice of dissolution of partnership is required, 1140.

notice to determine composition, 1289.

NOTICE TO QUIT:

on tenancies from year to year, half a year's notice to quit must be given, 698.

NOTICE TO QUIT—*continued.*

no distinction between land and houses, 699.
how the notice must be given where tenant holds over, 700.
where tenant holds under a void agreement, *ib.*
where tenant enters upon the different parts at different times, 701.
requisites of notice, *ib.*
insufficient notice will not amount to surrender, 699.
forms of notices which have been holden good, 701, 2.
need not be directed, 703.
what shall be considered as evidence of tenant's receiving it, 704.
waiver of, 705.
cases where notice to quit is not necessary, 710.
    in the case of mortgages, 711.

NUDUM PACTUM:

assumpsit will not lie on, 40, 1.

NUL TIEL RECORD, 594.

new rule concerning, *ib.*

NUNQUAM INDEBITATUS:

plea of, its operation, 532.

NUSANCE:

case lies for nusance to habitation or land, 1108.
    e. g. for darkening windows, *ib.*
twenty years' enjoyment of lights, sufficient to maintain action for obstructing them, 1109.
not necessary to show total privation of them, *ib.*
instances of nusance for which an action may be maintained, 1114.
to support an *action* for nusance in public highway, plaintiff must show special damage, 1115.
and that he was using ordinary caution, 1116.
what shall be deemed such special damage as will maintain an action, 1115.
case lies for not repairing highway, where special damage, 1117.
action for nusance may be brought by reversioner or tenant in possession *ib.*
or alienee, 1118.
tenants in common may join, *ib.*
person erecting nusance, or his alienee, is liable, *ib.*
of the general issue, and what may be given in evidence under it, 1119.
effect of new rules, *ib.*
of the evidence necessary to support an action for a nusance, 1120.

O.

OBLIGATION ON BOND:

debt on, 534.
bond from party replevying, 1176.

OBLIGEE:

release by, 563, 4.

OBLIGOR:

how one of two obligors sued must plead, 541.
release to, 564.

OCCUPIER:

deceased, declarations of, admissible, 743.

OFFICE:

stat. against sale of offices, 548.

what offices are within this statute, 548, 9.

excise, though no part of the revenue at the time of making this statute, yet within the mischief, 550, 1.

bond given by officer for securing all the profits to person appointing, is void, 550.

so bond to surrender when person appointing chooses, *ib.*

OFFICER:

officer in the army may justify even maihem for disobeying orders, flagrante bello, 33.

assumpsit does not lie against officer for recovery of duties which he has paid over, but otherwise if not paid over, 85 n.

whether excise officer is entitled to a month's notice before action brought, 96 n.

where peace officer may justify an arrest, 925.

of justifications by officers, how pleaded, 29, 920.

OPTION:

of determining lease, who has, 442 n.

ORDER AND DISPOSITION:

effect of bankrupt having, 217.

OUSTER IN QUO WARRANTO:

where judgment of, admissible, 1166.

OVERSEER:

whether promise made by overseer to pay for cure of pauper is binding, 51, 2.

liable to refund money illegally received for maintenance of bastard child, though he has paid it over to successor, 86 n.

entitled to demand copy of warrant, 916.

where trespass will not lie against, for distress for poor rate, 1321.

OWNER:

reputed, in bankruptcy, 217.

OWNERSHIP:

of soil of river, 828.

of waste adjoining highway, 748, 1314, 5.

OYSTERS:

dredging for, where illegal, 828.

P.

PARCELS:

exceeding the value of £10, see stat. 11 Geo. IV. & 1 Will. IV. c. 68, 400, 1.

PARCENERS:

ejectment by, 714, 5.
must join in an avowry for rent arrear, 1198.
one parcener cannot maintain trover against comparison, 1364.

PARENT:

may justify assault in defence of child, 30.
may chastise his child moderately, 33.
may maintain action for seduction of daughter, 1103.

PARISH:

officers, liability for accident to casual poor, 51, 2.
what overseer may give in evidence since new rules under general issue,
1325.

PARISH REGISTERS:

proof of baptism, &c., 752.

PARLIAMENT:

trader having privilege of, bankruptcy, 211.
parliamentary papers, publication of, 1040.
See BRIBERY.

PARSON:

trading by, 187.
members of trading company, 308, 1127.
See TITHES.

PARTIAL LOSS:

nature of, 976.
evidence of, will sustain allegation of total loss, 1017, 8.

PARTICULARS:

of demand, 66, 368, 378.
must now be annexed to record, 66.
of payment, 130.
of set off, 149.
of sale, auction, 181.

PART PAYMENT:

effect of, as to statute of limitations, 140, 1.
verbal acknowledgment of, not sufficient, *ib.*

PARTNER:

commission of bankrupt against, 212.
may accept bill drawn on firm if on joint account, 307.
may pass the partnership interest in bill by indorsement, *ib.*
but secus, if creditor knows that it is without consent of the other partners, *ib.*
after bankruptcy of one partner, bill must be indorsed by solvent partner
and assignees of bankrupt, 308.
assumpsit lies on express promise to pay balance struck after dissolution,
441 n.
covenant not to sue entered into by one partner, where it will not operate
as a release, 566 n.
participation of profits and loss is necessary to constitute a partnership, 1122.
where there is a partnership, as between the parties and strangers, the law
will presume that they are partners, inter se, 1123, 4.
in respect of creditors, he who takes a moiety of profits shall be liable to
losses, 1124.
although an agreement may constitute a partnership as between the parties

PARTNER—*continued.*

and strangers, yet it may not have that effect as between the parties themselves, 1124.

one partner cannot execute a deed for another, without a particular power, 1128.

nor bind another by a submission to arbitration, 1130.

but one partner may bind another by the acceptance of a bill, 1128.

a new partner, however, cannot be bound in this manner for debt of old partner, 1129.

one partner cannot pledge the security of another for his own private debt, *ib.*

in whom the property in partnership effects is, when one partner becomes a bankrupt, 1130.

authority of one partner to draw bills to charge another is only an implied authority, *ib.*

solvent partner, what he may do, 1131.

how partners ought to sue, 1134.

where really interested, action by may be brought in name of all, though contract made by one, 1135.

dormant partner, liability of, 1136.

what remedy one partner has against another, 1137.

what notice ought to be given of a dissolution of partnership, 1140.

a person who suffers his name to be used in a firm, if no partner, may be a witness for the firm, 1141.

effect of act of bankruptcy by one partner, 1364.

PARTY :

assumpsit cannot be maintained by person who is a stranger to consideration, 47.

bringing covenant on deed-poll must be named therein, 440.

PASTURE :

common of, 415.

converting into tillage, where additional rent recoverable for, 444.

PATRON :

of bonds given by clerks to patrons, 554.

history of the law of, *ib.*

statutes concerning, 556, 7.

PAWN :

where trover lies by and against pawnee, 1360, 1.

PAWNBROKER :

trover lies against for goods stolen, 1361.

PAYMENT :

by bill, 69 n.

good plea in assumpsit, 129.

where several demands, party paying may apply it as he pleases *at time of payment,* 130.

particulars of, *ib.*

appropriation of, 130, 1.

payment of money into court, statute concerning, 133.

in covenant, 522.

where payment may be pleaded to debt on bond, 561.

of plea of payment at the day, and after the day, 562.

part payment, effect of as to statute of limitations, 140, 1.

PEACE OFFICER :

where he may justify arrest, 925.

PEDIGREE:

hearsay evidence admissible as to pedigree, 753, 4.
hence declarations of members of family are evidence as to pedigree, *ib.*
See HEARSAY.
husband to be considered as member of wife's family, 755.
but declarations must not be post litem motam, *ib.*

PENAL STATUTES:

rules relating to actions on, 621.
limitation of actions on, 622.

PENALTY:

on bonds with penalty conditioned for payment of money only; principal, interest, and costs only are recoverable by statute 4 Ann. c. 16, s. 13, 582 n.
where court will stay proceedings thereon, 534.
infancy may be pleaded to bond with penalty, 560.
so to bond with penalty conditioned for payment of interest, 561.

PENDENTE LITE:

administration, 781.

PENSION:

definition of, 1306.

PEREMPTORY MANDAMUS:

where grantable, 1086.

PERFORMANCE:

how pleaded where covenants in the affirmative, 522.
negative, *ib.*
must be pleaded in terms of covenant, 523.

PERILS:

insured against, 939.
of the sea, 953.

PERJURY:

persons convicted of, incompetent witnesses, 877.
but may be restored to their competency by pardon, if indicted at common law; but otherwise, if indicted on statute, 634, 877, 8.
copy of judgment, entered upon a verdict of conviction, must be produced, 878.

PERMISSION:

occupation by, where no defence, 748.

PETITIONING CREDITOR'S DEBT, 212.

PEW:

annexed to house by faculty or prescription, 1113.
how presumption of prescriptive right to pew may be rebutted, *ib.*
extra-parochial persons cannot claim, *ib.*
right to sit in may be apportioned, *ib.*

PICTURES:

warranty of, 642.
libel by, 1038.

PILOT:

necessity of having, 1011.
statutes relating to, 1011 n., 1012 n.

PISCARY:

See FISHERY—COMMON.

PLAINT:

proceeding in replevin by, 1175.

PLEADINGS:

in account, 4.
before auditors, 6.
in adultery, 11, 12.
assault and battery, 29.
in assumpsit, 115—154.
in bankruptcy, 246.
in covenant, 510—523.
in debt on bond, 535—566.
    on bail bond, 578.
    on bond of ancestor against heir, 587.
      riens per descent, *ib.*
    for rent, 601.
against sheriff for escape, 616.
in actions founded on penal statutes, 623.
in detinue:
    non detinet, 657.
in ejectment, 728.
by executors:
    executors may plead same plea that testator might, 801.
    plene administravit, outstanding judgment, or bond—how pleaded, 801, 802.
    executor may plead outstanding judgment, recovered in debt on simple contract, 802.
    several administrators may plead outstanding judgment recovered against one, 802, 3.
    of the replication to plea on outstanding judgment, how pleaded, 803.
    in the case of the statute of limitations, as against executor, the six years are computed from the time when action first accrued to testator, 803, 4.
    how computed in case of administration, *ib.*
    difference between executor and administrator in setting forth a right of retainer, 805.
in quo warranto:
    statute of limitations, 1155.
in replevin:
    in abatement—cepit in alio loco, may conclude with prayer of judgment that count may be quashed, 1189.
    of the general issue, non cepit, 1190.
    of avowries for damage feasant, 1192.
    pleas in bar, 1193, 9.
    for rent arrear, 1197.
    property, 1201.
    statute of limitations, *ib.*
    set-off, 1202.

PLEADINGS—*continued.*

in slander :
   general issue, 1254.
   statute of limitations, 1255

in action on stat. for not setting forth tithes :
   nil debet, statute of limitations, 1303, 4.

in trespass :
   general issue, 1325.
   accord and satisfaction, 1326.
   liberum tenementum, 1327.
   estoppel, 1328.
   license, 1329.
   process, 1332.
   right of common, 1333.
   right of way, 1334—1340.
   tender of amends, 1340.

in trover :
   general issue (new rules) and statute of limitations, 1368, 9.

in action for use and occupation :
   defendant cannot plead nil habuit in tenementis, 1393.

PLEDGES :
   at common law and by statute in replevin, 1176, 7.

PLENE ADMINISTRAVIT :
   plea of, 801.

POLICY :
   actions cannot be maintained on contracts which violate public policy, 56, 7, 1405.
   of insurance, nature of, 929.
   is a simple contract, 931.
   may be altered by consent, 931 n.
   how to be construed, 947.
   of the different kinds of policies, 931.
   of the essential parts of a policy, 932.
   See INSURANCE.

POLL :
   copy of poll, admissible, 632.

PONE :
   writ of, 1183.

POOR RATE :
   replevin does not lie for distress under, where matter of appeal, 1172 n.
   but does, where rate has not been duly published, 1173.
   by stat. 17 Geo. II. c. 38, party distraining for poor rate is not to be deemed a trespasser, ab initio, for any irregularity in warrant of appointment, of distress, or in the rate, 680, 1.
   beasts of the plough are distrainable for, 665 n.

POSSESSION :
   justification in defence of, 30.
   tortious possession sufficient to maintain trespass, 1315.
   right of possession must concur with right of property, in order to maintain trover, 1352, 3.

POSSESSION—*continued.*

but right of possession is sufficient, without having had actual possession, 1354.

party cannot maintain ejectment without having been in possession, or clothed with right of possession, at time of ouster, 685.

how to proceed in ejectment, upon a vacant possession, 725.

what shall be deemed vacant, 726.

uninterrupted adverse possession for twenty years will bar ejectment, 732.

under lease, for one year, sufficient, 748.

permissive occupation, no bar, *ib.*

necessary, to give validity to lien, 1372.

unity of, 415, 1112.

of chattels, where not proof of ownership, 1360.

POUND-BREACH:

action lies for, 678.

POWER:

execution of, by assignees of bankrupt, 186.

appointment by will, in exercise of, 891.

PRECEPT:

not necessary to show return, 630, 1.

immaterial variance between precept alleged and proved, 631.

PREDIAL TITHES:

description of, 1285.

PREFERENCE:

voluntary, 202.

fraudulent, what amounts to, *ib.*

PREMIUM:

where assured is entitled to a return of, 1022.

PRESCRIPTION:

2 & 3 Will. IV. c. 71, for shortening time of, 424, 1109, 1111.

prescriptive right of common is suspended only, by taking a lease of the land for years, 415: *see* 1112.

common appendant ought not to be claimed by prescription, 416 n.

prescription for common for cattle levant and couchant on messuage, cum pertinentiis, is good, 418.

but not if messuage has not land or curtilage belonging to it, 418.

party prescribing for common, in right of a particular estate, may call, as a witness, a person who claims common in the same place, 426, 1195.

inhabitants, as such, cannot prescribe for profit in another's soil, 1196.

of claiming a right of way by prescription, how pleaded, 1337.

PRESUMPTION:

of payment, as to bond, 563.

statutes relating thereto, *ib.*

of surrender of satisfied terms, 685, 6, and n.

of death, where, 753.

of loss of ship, 953.

when not allowed, stat. 2 & 3 Will. IV. c. 71, s. 6, 1109.

PRINCIPAL:

notice to, notice to agents, 235, 820.

where action must be brought against, and where against agent, 84 n.

PRIORITY:
    of facts on same day, when it may be inquired into, 207, 611.

PRISON:
    keepers of prisons shall give to persons desirous of charging a person in execution a note, in writing, of persons in their custody, by stat. 8 & 9 Will. III. c. 27, s. 9, 610.
    such note is evidence of persons being in custody at that time, *ib.*

PRIVILEGED COMMUNICATIONS, 1244, 1255.

PRIVITY:
    between plaintiff and defendant, necessary to sustain assumpsit, 99.
    between parties to bill of exchange, 530.

PRIZE:
    action will not lie where imprisonment is merely in consequence of taking a ship as prize, 910.

PRIZE COURTS:
    effect of sentence of foreign, 1001.

PROBATE:
    what executor may do before probate, 774.
    probate unrepealed cannot be impeached in temporal courts, 776.
    legal evidence of will of personalty, 806.
    exemplification of, when allowed, *ib.*
    where not produced, what evidence held sufficient, 744.

PROCESS:
    justification under, 32.
    of the difference between justification under process by party to the cause, or stranger, and officer executing process, 921.
    final, not necessary to allege it returned, but secus as to mesne, 921 n.
    of inferior courts, justification under, 922.
    of foreign court, 923.
    ought to describe party against whom it is issued, 924.
    where officer may justify breaking open doors for execution of process, 1332.

PROCLAMATIONS:
    of fine, how proved, 732.

PROFERT:
    plaintiff, in covenant, must make profert, 494 n.
    profert is dispensed with, where deed is lost by time or accident, 494 n., 1336.
    so where deed has been destroyed by fire, 494 n.
    where profert is made in declaration, deed must be produced, *ib.*
    of deed, where necessary, 1336.
            where not necessary, 577.

PROMISE:
    of wife void, 297.
    See ASSUMPSIT.

PROMISSORY NOTE: *See* NOTES, PROMISSORY.

PROOF OF DEBTS:
    in bankruptcy, 249.

PROPERTY:

in bills of exchange passes with the bills, 1359.
in exchequer bill, passes by delivery, 1360.
where not altered, by sale of goods, *ib*.
in title deeds, in whom vested, 1362.
no property, plea of, its meaning, 1369.
absolute or special, necessary to maintain replevin, 1185.
so to maintain trover, 1343.
nature of absolute, 1185 n., 1344.
right of, must be complete to maintain trover, 1349.
special, defined, 1185 n., 1350, 1.
cases illustrating the nature of, 1351.
where vests in purchaser, 406, 7.
where vested by delivery, 656.
where divested by illegal importation, 656.
temporary, where sufficient to maintain trover, 1352.

PROTEST:

statutes relating to, 360, 1.
evidence of, where required, 374, 5.
where copy of protest of foreign bill need not be sent, 360.

PROVISO:

defendant must set forth proviso in deed operating in his favour, 495.
saving proviso may be given in evidence on general issue in action on penal
    statutes, 623.
what will amount to a forfeiture of a lease containing proviso against
    alienation, 470, 1.

PURCHASE:

deposit paid on, where interest recoverable, 177.
                    where not, 178.

Q.

QUAKERS:
marriage, 22.
of recovering tithe against, 1283, 4.

QUANTUM MERUIT:
where this count may be rendered available, 68 n., 9 n.

QUIET ENJOYMENT:
covenant for quiet enjoyment does not extend to entries by strangers, 465.
how the declaration must be framed for breach of such covenant, 466.
in what manner the averment of title in party evicting ought to be made,
    466, 7.

QUOD COMPUTET:
judgment of, 4, 5.

QUO WARRANTO:
information in nature of, 1143.

R.

REAL ACTIONS:

abolished, with exceptions, 684 n.

RE-ASSURANCE, 1013.

REASONABLE TIME:

as to notice of dishonour of bill or note, 336, 352.
     abandonment, 967, 8.

RECAPTION:

after escape, by negligence, 611.
plea of, 616.

RECEIPT:

legal effect of, 82, 1133.
not conclusive evidence, that party signing it has actually received the
 money, 82.
receipt of rent is evidence of subsisting tenancy, 700.

RECEIVER:

how chargeable in account, 2.
plea by, 4.
receiver, appointed by Court of Chancery, is an agent within stat. 4 Geo. II.
 c. 28, and may give tenant notice to deliver up possession, 597 n.
where land is in possession of receiver, ejectment must be brought with
 leave of the Court of Chancery, 697.

RECOGNIZANCE:

in what order debts due on recognizances ought to be paid by executor,
 786, and 786 n.
recognizance not enrolled is considered as a bond, 787 n.

RECORD:

debt lies upon record, 528.
of the plea of nul tiel record, 594.
how tried, *ib.*
of the replication of nul tiel record, 579.
how it must conclude, *ib.*
of judgment thereon, *ib.*
where record inter alios is evidence, 1166, 7.

RECTORY:

in ejectment for rectory, what must be proved, 751, 2.

RE-ENTRY:

provisions of statute relating to, for non-payment of rent, 723, 4.

REGISTER:

register evidence of a marriage, 12, 13.
omission in entry will not affect validity of marriage, 13.
non-parochial registers, when evidence, 13.
register, or examined copy, is evidence to prove christenings, marriages, or
 burials, 752.
registration of marriage, statutes concerning, 22.
register of merchant seamen, statute concerning, 1231, 2.

REGISTRY:

what proof necessary in trover for certificate of ship's registry, 1378.
what ships are entitled to be registered, 1215.

REGISTRY—*continued*.

where ship ceases to enjoy privileges of British ship, 1216.
who may be registered as owners, 1217.
at what place ships shall be registered, 1218.
of the requisites of the certificate, 1218, 9.
what is required on the part of the owners to obtain registry, 1219.
of the transfer by bill of sale, 1221, 2.
when and how registry de novo is to be made, 1226.
what is required upon change of master, 1229.
penalty for detention of certificate, *ib*.
evidence, 1230.
lien by reason of deposit of, 1375.

RELATOR:

who may be, 1151.
new rule concerning, *ib*.

RELEASE:

plea of release puis darrein continuance, 134.
of the plea of release to debt on bond, 563, 4.
fraud may be replied, 563 n.
release *by* one of several obligees will bind all, 563, 4.
so a release *to* one of several obligors may be pleaded by the others, 564.
whether such release be by deed or operation of law, *ib*.
if feme obligee take obligor to husband, this is a release in law, 565.
covenant not to sue will operate as a release by construction only, *ib*.
covenant not to sue must be perpetual, in order to enure as a release, 566.
covenant not to sue by one of plaintiff's partners, effect of, 566 n.
release of all actions will not discharge covenant before breach, 523.
in what cases the servant is a witness, for a master, without a release, 1096.

RELIGION:
of witness, 876.

REMAINDER-MAN:
where incompetent witness, 879.

RENT:

of premises destroyed by fire, 447, 1389.
debt for rent arrear,
    lies at common law on lease for years or at will, 595.
    lies by statute on lease for life, though life is continuing, *ib*.
    lies by statute, by executor of person seized of rent-service, &c., in fee tail or for life, *ib*.
    against whom the action must be brought, 596.
    lessee for years, having assigned term, may sue for rent reserved, *ib*.
    tenant wilfully holding over, after notice by landlord, forfeits *double the yearly value* of the land, by stat. 4 Geo. II. c. 28, *ib*.
    construction of this statute, 596 n.
    action on this statute may be brought by one tenant in common without companion, 597.
    action on this statute may be brought after a recovery in ejectment, *ib*.
    tenant not delivering up possession after he has given notice to quit, forfeits double rent by stat. 11 Geo. II. c. 19, 599.
    tenant for a year within this statute, 599 n.
    of declaring in debt for use and occupation, 600.
of the pleadings in debt for rent arrear, 601—605.

RENT—*continued*.

rent reserved by parol is in equal degree with bond debt in the administration of estates by executors, 787 D.

See DISTRESS—LANDLORD AND TENANT—NOTICE TO QUIT.

REPAIRS:

covenant to repair, 474.
old premises, 475.
heir, though not named, may sue on a covenant for not repairing, 477.
heir may recover damages for not repairing in time of ancestor, *ib.*
plea by heir claiming to retain money laid out in repairs, where bad, 590.

REPLEVIN:

lies on any tortious taking of goods, as well as a taking by distress, 1172.
but not taking things affixed to the freehold, 1173.
of the inconveniences attending the proceedings in replevin at common law, 1174.
how remedied by stat. of Marlebridge, 1174, 5.
how to proceed, where defendant claims property, 1182.
of the different forms of writs for the removal of proceedings out of inferior into superior courts, 1183, 4.
what property the plaintiff ought to have to maintain replevin, 1185.
where husband may sue alone, 294, 1185.
of the declaration, 1186.
of pleas in abatement, 1188, 9.
See JUDGMENT—PLEADINGS—COSTS.

REPLICATION:

of replying de injuriâ suâ propriâ absque tali causâ to son assault demesne, 35.
of the meaning of this replication, when pleaded to a plea of license, 1330.
where defendant insists on a matter of interest, de injuriâ suâ propriâ cannot be pleaded or replied, 1200, 1330.
of replying to the plea of liberum tenementum, 1327.
plaintiff may traverse the command, 1328.

REPRESENTATION:

to *first* underwriter, effect of, 990 n.
distinction between representation and warranty, 991.
action for fraudulent misrepresentation, 650.

REPUTED OWNER, 217.

See BANKRUPT.

REQUEST:

where it must be made before action brought, 106.
where not necessary, *ib.*
where proof of, is required, 1391.

RESCUE:

definition, 1209.
remedy, *ib.*
evidence:
1. the original cause of action, *ib.*
2. writ and warrant, *ib.*
3. manner of arrest, *ib.*
what constitutes an arrest, 1209, 1210.
of executing process on Sunday, 1210.
4. damage sustained, 1211.
for rescue of distresses, *see* DISTRESS.

RESIGNATION:
bond, 554.
history of law relating to, general, *ib.*
statutes relating to special, 556, 7.

RESPONDENTIA:
nature of the contract, 1029.
difference between bottomry and respondentia and a loan, *ib.*
statutes relating to money lent upon respondentia, *ib.*

RESTRAINT:
of marriage, illegal, 56, 459, 1405.
of trade, where illegal, 56, 543.

RETAINER:
may be given in evidence on plene administravit, 807.
of the right of retainer by an executor, 805.
executor de son tort cannot retain, *ib.*
See LIEN.

RETURN:
of premium, 1022.
of process, 921 n.
requisites of, to a mandamus, 1083, 4.

REVERSION:
assignee of reversion may enter for non-payment of rent, &c., or bring covenant by stat. 32 Hen. VIII. c. 34, 479, 480.
assignee of part of, may sue in covenant, 480 n.
assignee of, may take advantage of estoppel, 515.

REVOCATION:
of will, 881, 892.

RIBBONS:
giving, prohibited at elections, 635.

RIENS IN ARREAR:
of pleading riens in arrear to an avowry for rent arrear, 1200.

RIGHT TO BEGIN:
resolution of judges as to, 1046.

RIGHT OF SHOOTING:
what gives, 898.

RISK:
inception of, delay in, where it discharges policy, 1007.

ROOKS:
feræ naturæ, 896.

RULES: *See* TABLE OF NEW RULES in Vol. I. lxxxix. after Table of Statutes.

S.

SAILING:
time of, 994.
with convoy, 997.

SALE:

of office, illegal, 548, 9.

action cannot be maintained for price of goods sold upon credit, until the time for credit is expired, 69.

doctrine relating to the sale and warranty of horses, 642.

in whom the property is upon the sale of goods, 1345.

under what circumstances vendor may resell his goods, 1348.

sale is complete by delivery of goods to carrier, 406, 7.

under what circumstances innkeeper may sell horse left in his stable, 1381 n.

bill of, requisites of, to transfer ship, 1221, 2.

SALVAGE:

persons preserving goods which have been abandoned at sea are entitled to a compensation, 1371, 2.

SATISFIED TERM:

presumption as to, 685, 6, and n.

SCANDALUM MAGNATUM:

of the remedy for this injury, 1241.

how to declare, 1242.

words actionable in the case of a peer, which would not be in the case of a commoner, ib.

SCHOOL:

keeping, when breach of covenant, 444.

SCIENTER:

must be averred and proved, 638.

SCOTLAND:

where party seeking to avail himself of law of England, cannot claim the benefit of law of Scotland, 142.

SEA:

of plaintiffs beyond sea, at time of cause of action, within what time they may sue, 144.

defendants beyond sea, at time of cause of action, may be sued on their return, 146.

perils of, 953.

SEAMEN:

register of, statute concerning, 1231,2.

of their wages :

agreement relating to, must be in writing, 1231.

must specify the wages and voyage, 1232.

mariner not obliged to produce the written agreement in court, 1233.

of the penalties imposed upon seamen for desertion, ib.

what shall be deemed desertion, ib.

of the regulations :

ship-owners must not advance to seamen, beyond sea, more than a moiety of wages due, 1234.

freight the mother of wages, 1235.

if ship be captured, or ost in the voyage, seamen lose their wages, ib.

SEAMEN—*continued.*

    ship seized by way of retaliation, and afterwards restored, cannot be considered as captured, 1236.

    where impressed seaman is entitled to wages pro tanto, 1237.

    of the remedies for the recovery of seamen's wages:
        in the Court of Admiralty, 1238.
        and at common law, *ib.*

SEA-WORTHINESS:

    implied warranty, 1010.

SECOND COMMISSION:

    of bankrupt, 265, 6.

SECOND DELIVERANCE:

    writ of, when it must be sued, 1203, 4.
    in what case it operates as supersedeas to the retorno habendo, 1204.

SEDUCTION:

    action for, 1103.

SEISIN:

    unity of, of land and way over land, 1112, 1337.

SEIZURE:

    owner of ship, seized as forfeited, cannot maintain trespass, 656 n.
    hostile seisure is not necessarily capture, so as to defeat seaman's claim for wages, 1236.

SENTENCE:

    of council at war, where evidence, 33.
    sentences of foreign courts of admiralty are conclusive evidence, in actions on policies, upon all subjects within their jurisdiction, 1001.
    where a warranty of neutrality shall be falsified by foreign sentence, 1000, 1.
    but these sentences must be legal sentences, 1003.

SEPARATE MAINTENANCE, 460.

SEPARATE USE:

    of wife, property settled to, 271 n., 2 n.

SEPARATION:

    effect of, between husband and wife, in case of adultery, 10, 11.
    covenant by husband in case of, 459, 460.

SERVANT:

    See MASTER AND SERVANT.
    carrier not protected from loss or injury arising from felonious act of, 401.

SERVICE:

    of declaration in ejectment, 718, 9.
    of notice to quit, 702, 4.

SET-OFF:

    at common law, 146, 566.
    by statutes, *ib.*
    particulars of, 149.
    debts must be mutual and due in same right, 147, 569.
    in cases of executors, 147.
    cannot be of debt barred by statute of limitations, 148, 569.
    cannot be of a penalty, *ib.*

SET-OFF—*continued.*
reducing demand under 40*s.* does not affect jurisdiction of superior court, 149.
cannot be given in evidence under notice, 148.
to debt on bond, 566—570.
cannot be, in replevin, 1202.

SHARES:
in joint stock bank not within 17th sect. of stat. of frauds, 857.

SHERIFF:
remedy against, for escape,
        at common law, 605.
        by statute, *ib.*
liable for escape after recaption on escape warrant, 607.
where action lies against, for false imprisonment, 907.
must appoint deputies to make replevins, 1174.
one sheriff of London may take replevin bond, 1177.
liable for taking insufficient pledges, 1180.
extent of liability, 1181, 2.
cannot be made a trespasser by relation, 241, 1319, 1320.
cannot justify breaking open outward door to execute process in civil suit, 1332.
trover lies by sheriff against person taking away goods seized in execution, 1351.
seizure by, after bankruptcy, what remedy for, 241.

SHIP:
presumption of loss of, 953.
ship-owners not liable for embezzlement by mariners, 403.
nor for any loss exceeding value of vessel and freight, *ib.*
nor for any loss by fire, 404.
nor for jewels, &c., unless the value is specified, *ib.*
action against ship-owner must be brought by consignee of goods, 407.
liability of ship-owner for seamen's wages, 1238.
        for repairs, 1239.
master of ship has no lien on ship for money expended in repairs, nor in freight for wages, 1374.
sale of the whole of a ship by part-owner is not equivalent to destruction, so that co-tenant may maintain trover, 1365 n.
master of ship has no general authority, by law, to sell ship or cargo, 1362, 3.
See INSURANCE—REGISTRY.

SIMONY:
statutes relating to, 552.
resignation bonds, when simoniacal, 554.
history of the law on this subject, *ib.*
how far special bonds of resignation are legalized, 556, 7.

SLANDER:
scandalum magnatum, 1241.
of the action for slander, 1243.
    what special damage sufficient to support action, 1249.
    in what case two persons may join for slander, *ib.*
    where the republication of slander is actionable, *ib.*
    of the declaration, 1250.
    meaning of the term innuendo, 1251, 2.
    office of the innuendo, *ib.*
    in what case averment of colloquium is necessary, 1252.
    jury to decide whether meaning is such as is imputed by the innuendo, 1253.

SLANDER—*continued.*
> pleadings, 1254.
> evidence, 1256.
> costs, 1258.
> *See* LIBEL.

SOCIETY:
> one member of amicable society cannot maintain trover against another for taking away a chattel belonging to the society, 1364.

SOLD:
> bought and, notes, 863 n., 4 n.

SOLVIT AD DIEM, AND SOLVIT POST DIEM:
> of pleading payment at common law and by statute, 562, 3.

SPECIAL CASES:
> how construed, 974.

SPECIAL DAMAGE:
> in nusance, 1115.
> > slander, 1249.

SPECIALTY:
> assumpsit will not lie on, 441.
> exceptions to this rule, 441 n.

SPIRITUAL PERSON:
> as to trading by, 187, 308, 1127.

SPIRITUOUS LIQUORS:
> restraint of actions for debt due for, 54, 5.   See *Hughes* v. *Doane*, Add. xci.

SPLINT:
> where unsoundness, 643.

STABLE-KEEPER:
> liable for the negligence of his servants, 400.

STAGE-COACH:
> proprietor of, how far liable as common carrier, 399, 400.
> *See* CARRIER.

STAKE-HOLDER:
> where liable, 90 n.
> mere, not liable for interest, 178.

STAMP:
> amount of stamp duties on bills and notes, 311, 2, 3.
> not necessary on illegal agreement, 58.
> where unstamped instrument may be looked at by court, 1397 n.
> stamp must be of proper denomination, 315.
> where new stamp is required on bill of exchange, *ib.*
> > on policy of insurance, 944, 5, 6.

STANDING CORN:
> where it goes to devisee of land, 1356.

STATUTE MERCHANT OR STAPLE:
> in what order to be paid by executors, 786.

STATUTES: *See* TABLE OF STATUTES in Vol. I., after Names of Cases.

STATUTORY PROTECTION:
who entitled to, 912.

STOCK:
whether bond for securing money paid for stock-jobbing differences be good, 89 n.

STOLEN HORSES:
statute regulations as to, 1348, 9.

STOPPAGE IN TRANSITU:
nature of this right, 1260.
who may exercise it, 1261.
See TRANSITUS.

STRANDING:
loss by, what constitutes, 942.
what not, 943.

STRANGER:
covenant for act of, binding, 500, 1.

STREET:
dedication of way in, 1334, 5.

SUBSCRIBING:
witness, must be called, 537.
to will, 879.
or other instruments, 1020, and n.
exceptions to this rule, 538.

SUBSCRIPTION:
proof of will by, 879.

SUIT:
commencement of, what now is, 152 (m), 366.

SUNDAY:
date of bill on, 317.
sale of horse on, 647.
execution of writ on, 1210.

SUMMONS:
writ of, now commencement of action, 152 (m), 366.

SUPERSEDEAS:
evidence that commission or fiat issued on a particular day, 266.

SUPPRESSION:
in insurance, 989.
defence on this ground must be specially pleaded, 117, 1010.

SURCHARGE:
of common, 423.

SURETY:
when action will lie against, 72.
when not, 81.
when discharged, 364.
principal cannot be released without its operating for the benefit of the surety, 386.

SURRENDER:

defendant discharged out of custody on giving bail-bond, cannot surrender himself without assent of sheriff, 578, and n.

presumption of surrender of satisfied terms, 685, 6, and n.

by stat. of frauds, leases, &c. cannot be surrendered without deed or note in writing, 838, 1387.

heir of copyhold estate may surrender before admittance, 689 n.

until admittance of surrenderee, copyhold remains in the surrenderor, 690 n.

SWEAR IN:

mandamus to, where colourable title in two sets, 1071.

T.

TAX:

a wager on the amount of, illegal, 1405.

TAXABLE ITEMS:

in bill of attorney, 160, 1.

TENANCY:

at will, not favoured, 698.

from year to year, 698, 9.

TENANT:

is not permitted to object to title of landlord, 515, 688, 1199.

qualifications of this rule,

where attornment by mistake, 688, 1199.

where lease has expired, 688.

or in case of defeasible title, 1199 n.

when liable in use and occupation, 1385.

duty of, on expiration of term, 1388, 9.

wilfully holding over, penalty for, 596, 9.

what are fixtures as between landlord and tenant, 1356.

See NOTICE TO QUIT.

TENANT IN COMMON:

of account by, against his companion, 2.

how he must declare in ejectment, 715.

of trespass by, against his companion, for mesne profits, 765.

may join in action for nuisance, 1118.

must join in trespass q. c. f., 1317.

of trover by, against his companion, 1364.

of joining in actions by, 1118, 1193.

TENDER:

bank-notes, legal, where, 152.

plea of, in assumpsit, 150.

form of, 152.

what good, 150.

at what time must be made, 152.

tender and refusal equivalent to performance, 114.

by magistrates, 915, 6.

in case of irregular distress, 680.

for damage done, 1196, 1340.

TENDER—*continued*.
    of arrears of rent, 1201.
    effect of, before and after impounding, *ib*.
    cannot be pleaded in replevin under stat. 21 Jac. 1, c. 16, 1196, 7.
    but may in trespass, 1340.

TERM :
    outstanding, where it bars an ejectment, 685, 6.
    satisfied, presumption of surrender of, 686, and n.
    enlargement of, 716 n.

TERMINI :
    how pleaded, 1339.
    new rule as to, *ib*.

TERRIER :
    when evidence, 1307.

THEATRES :
    unlicensed, 60, 552.

TIMBER :
    where exempt from tithe, 1286, 7.
    late decision of Ld. Cottenham thereon, 1287.
    trees growing in hedge-rows tithable, *ib*.
    who may maintain trover for timber cut down, 1344.

TIME :
    computation of, 206, 7, 919.
    not essence of contract in sale of chattels, 1348.

TIME BARGAIN :
    where not illegal, 58, 9.

TITHES :
    definition, 1281.
    remedy for, by stat. 32 Hen. VIII. c. 7, 1282.
    remedy for recovering small tithes under 40*s*., by application to two J. P., 1283.
    extended to all tithes under £10, *ib*.
    provisions of stat. 2 & 3 Edw. VI. c. 13, for not setting out tithes, 1284.
    predial tithes, 1285.
    of wood, 1285, 6, 7.
    small tithe, 1287.
    parol agreement for retaining tithes is good, 1289.
    second section of stat. 2 & 3 Edw. VI. relating to the remedy in Ecclesiastical Court and costs, 1291.
    third section, as to the tithe of cattle feeding on waste, 1292.
    fourth section as to exemptions, ib.
    of exemption of laymen at common law :
        1. by composition real, 1295.
        2. de modo decimandi, 1305, 6.
        stat. 2 & 3 Will. IV. c. 100, shortening time required in claims of modus or exemption, 1296, 7.
    of the person to whom tithes are due, 1300.
        party bringing action must be entitled to tithes at time of severance, 1301.
        action must be brought by party grieved only, *ib*.
            may be maintained by and against executors, 1302.
        against whom the action may be brought, *ib*.

TITHES—*continued.*

declaration:
> not necessary to set forth title, 1302.

evidence:
> possession primâ facie evidence of title, 1304.
> what may be given in evidence on general issue, 1305.
> new statutes for the commutation of tithes, 1309—1311.
> See JUDGMENT—PLEADINGS—VERDICT.

TITLE:
> covenants for, 462.
> vendor of lease, bound to produce landlord's, 181.
> slander of, 1247.
> time for making out, 179.

TITLE DEEDS:
> property in, in whom vested, 1362.

TOLLS:
> assumpsit for, 67.
> thorough, 67 n.
> traverse, *ib.*

TRADE:
> covenant not to carry on particular, 444.
> infant cannot trade, 125, 6.
> of bonds in restraint of, 543.
> exclusive rights of trading in boroughs abolished, 1163.

TRANSITUS:
> doctrine of stoppage in transitu, 1260.
> who shall be considered as capable of exercising this right, 1261.
> under what circumstances the transitus shall be considered as continuing, 1263.
> where the transitus is determined, 1272.
> how far the negociation of the bill of lading may tend to defeat the right of stopping in transitu, 1278.

TREATING:
> at elections, 634.

TREES:
> trespass for cutting down, 1314.
> property in, 1314, 1344.
> See TIMBER.

TRESPASS:
> for crim. con.: See ADULTERY.
> where case, or trespass, is the proper remedy, 430, 680.
> where it does not lie against sheriff, 241.
> evidence, 1340.
> damages, 1342.
> of trespass quare clausum fregit, 1312, 3.
>> where it may be maintained, 1312—1318.
>> where trespass will not lie, 1318—1321.
> *of the declaration,* 1321.
> *of the general issue,* 1325.

TRESPASS—*continued*.
    of the plea of liberum tenementum, 1327.
     of the new assignment, 1328.
    See VENUE—ACCORD AND SATISFACTION—ESTOPPEL—LICENSE—
      PROCESS—WAY—TENDER—COSTS.

TROVER:
    requisites to maintain the action :
      1. absolute or special property, 1343.
        nature of absolute property, 1344.
        the right of property must be complete, 1349.
        special property defined, 1350, 1.
      2. right of possession, 1352, 3.
      3. personal goods—trover will not lie for things fixed to the free-
        hold, 1354.
      4. wrongful conversion, 1358, 9.
        what shall be considered as a conversion, *ib.* 1367, 1379.
    by whom trover cannot be maintained :.
      by one tenant in common, &c. against another, 1364.
      but if tenant in common *destroy* the thing in common, trover will lie,
        1365.
      rule that tenant in common cannot maintain trover against his com-
        panion, holds only where the law considers the possession of one to
        be the possession of both, 1366.
    declaration, ib.
    plea :
      not guilty, 1368, 9.
      what may be given in evidence under it, 1369.
      statute of limitations, 1370.
    evidence :
      what necessary to support the action, 1378.
      what necessary to prove conversion, 1379.
      See COSTS—JUDGMENT—LIEN—VENUE.

TRUST :—
    under what circumstances court will presume an outstanding term surren-
      dered, 685, 6, and n.
    if it appear that legal estate is outstanding in another person, cestui que
      trust cannot recover in ejectment, *ib.*
    devisee or executor in trust may be a witness in support of will, 880.

TURBARY :
    common of, 414.

TURNIPS :
    tithe of, new statute concerning, 1305.

U.

UNCERTIFICATED BANKRUPT :
    where he may sue, 245.
    cannot retain property against assignees, 1321.

UNDERLEASE :
    no breach of covenant not to assign, 471.

UNITY OF POSSESSION:

    where suspension only of right, and not an extinguishment, 415, 1112, 1337.

UNSOUNDNESS:

    • in horses, what constitutes, 643.
    where splint is, *ib.*

UNSTAMPED INSTRUMENT:

    not admissible in evidence, 747 n.
    for what purpose it may be looked at, 1396 n., 7 n.

USE AND OCCUPATION:

    where assumpsit for rent arrear might have been maintained at common law, 1385.
    of stat. 11 Geo. II. c. 19, s, 14, which gives the action for use and occupation, *ib.*
    form of declaration, 1386.
    where use and occupation lies, 1386, 7.
    occupation of tenant of defendant is occupation of defendant, 1389.
    lies for constructive occupation, *ib.*
    defendant cannot plead nil habuit in tenementis, or impeach the plaintiff's title, 1393.

USURY:

    statutes concerning, 322, 3.
    how the plea of usury must be framed to debt on bond, 563, 4.
    bills payable at or within twelve months not subject to usury laws, 324.
    this provision to remain in force until 1st Jan. 1844, by 4 & 5 Vict. c. 54, Add. xcii.
    bond originally good cannot be avoided in the hands of a bonâ fide holder, on the ground of subsequent usury, 559.
    where substituted security, given for security tainted by usury, is void, *ib.*

V.

VACANT POSSESSION:

    how to proceed in case of, 725, 6, 7.

VALUE RECEIVED:

    not essentially necessary to insert in bill of exchange, 320.
    though omitted, debt will lie, 530.

VARIANCE:

    what will be fatal in assumpsit, 103.
            in an action on a bill of exchange, 366.
    immaterial, between writ and condition of bail-bond, 572.
    where, on the face of a receipt, it appears that money was paid for a horse, defendant cannot prove a different consideration, in order to take advantage of a variance, 649.
    objection on ground of, much obviated by statutes, 518.

VAULT:

    mandamus to bury in *particular*, will not lie, 1080.

VENUE:

new rule, 1186.

of laying the venue in actions:
 for adultery, 11.
  assault and battery, 27.
  assumpsit, 101.
  covenant, 493.
  debt on bond, dated abroad, 535.
  debt on judgment, 594.
  debt by executor of one seised of rent service, &c., 595 n.
  debt for rent arrear, 600.
  debt for escape, 615.
  on penal statutes, 621.
  ejectment, 714.
  false imprisonment, 909.
  nusance, 1120.
  replevin, 1186.
  trespass, 1315, 1321, 2.
  trover, 1366.

VERBAL:

gift of chattel, 1347.

VERDICT:

in actions against joint trespassers, 36.
in ejectment, 759, 760.
in libel may be general, 1052.
in debt on stat. 2 & 3 Edw. VI. for not setting out tithes, 1307.
for defendant against the weight of evidence in *penal* actions, 1308.
on any fact distinctly put in issue, effect of, 1328.

VESTING ORDER:

by Insolvent Debtors Court, 1349.

VESTURA TERRÆ:

person entitled to, may maintain trespass, 1313.

VICAR:

claim of tithes by, by endowment or prescription, 1287, 1301.

VOID AND VOIDABLE:

whether bond of infant be void or voidable, 560 n.
what covenants are void, 459.

VOLUNTARY PREFERENCE:

in contemplation of bankruptcy, 202.
history of this doctrine, *ib.*

VOTE:

when thrown away, 1155.

VOYAGE:

illegal, 985.

W.

WAGER:

of law, abolished, 64 (*l*).
policy, 1013.

WAGER—*continued.*

impolicy of considering wagers as valid contracts, 1398.
cases where the wagers have been holden to be legal, 1398, 9.
form of action for recovery of a wager, 1400.

of illegal wagers, ib.
    1. prohibited by statute, 1400, 1.
    2. contrary to public policy, 1405.
    3. leading to improper inquiries, *ib.*
    4. injurious to third persons, and leading to indecent evidence, 1406.

WAIVER:

of notice to quit, 705.
of forfeiture, 707, 8.
parol evidence of, of written contracts, 867.

WALL:

property in, 1315.

WARRANT:

party, justifying under warrant, must set it forth in his plea, 33, 921.
no action shall be brought against constable for an act done under a jus-
    tice's warrant, until demand of copy of such warrant, 916, 7, 8.

WARRANT OF ATTORNEY:

given by infant is void, 129.
to confess judgment, must be attested by an attorney, 231 n.

WARRANTY:

of the sale and warranty of horses, 642.
purchaser of horse ought to procure a warranty, otherwise seller is not
    liable, except on the ground of fraud, *ib.*
doctrine of sound price being equivalent to warranty is now overturned, *ib.*
roaring, unsoundness, 643.
crib-biting is not, *ib.*
how party may proceed where warranty is false, 644.
form of declaring on a warranty, 646.
trial of horse means a reasonable trial, *ib.*
condition of sale that purchaser of horse, warranted sound, shall return it
    within two days, does not extend to age of horse, 646, 7.
how to declare where contract of warranty is open, 648.
receipt, containing warranty, if stamped with receipt stamp, will be good
    evidence, 649.
for warranty in policies, *see* INSURANCE.

WARREN:

free, franchise of, 896.
whether grouse be bird of, *ib.*
Manwood's description of birds of, *ib.*

WASTE:

breach assigned, that defendant had committed waste, is not supported by
    evidence that he had not used the premises in a husbandlike manner,
    524, 5.

WATERCOURSE:

what enjoyment of water, in any particular manner, gives a right to party
    so enjoying it, 1110, 1.
artificial, law as to, 1111.
See FISHERY.

WAY:

of the different kinds of ways, 1334.
how a private way may be claimed:
    by grant, 1336.
        prescription, 1337.
        effect of unity of possession, 415 n., 1337.
        where it extinguishes, 1112, 1337.
        where it suspends only, 1112.
        custom, 1338.
        express reservation, *ib.*
        necessity, *ib.*
how to plead a right of way, 1339.
replication thereto, *ib.*
enjoyment "as of right," meaning of, 1112.
extent of right, question for jury, 1113.
adverse user, what not sufficient, 1112.
    effect of, for twenty years, *ib.*
where a dedication of way to the public may be presumed, 1334, 5.
permitting the public to have the free use of a way for six years is sufficient
    evidence of a dereliction, where no bar has been put up, 1335.
but dedication must be with deliberate purpose, *ib.*
dedication of way to the public is not a transfer of the absolute property
    of the soil, 1334.

WHARFINGER:

lien of, 405 n., 1374.

WIFE:

letters of, when evidence, 22, 3.
confession of, not evidence, where, *ib.*
where witness of necessity, 749.
where payment by, does not take case out of statute of limitations, 296.
coverture: *See* BARON AND FEME.
separate property of, 271 n., 2 n.

WILL:

of personal estate, how proved, 806.
of the execution of a will of land, under the old law, 870.
of real and personal estate under new, 891.
will of copyhold land is not within the statute of frauds, 871.
surrender to the use of, not necessary, 871.
sixth section of the statute of frauds relating to the revocation of wills,
    881.
of the different acts of revocation, 882—889.
of implied revocations, 885.
stat. 7 Will. IV. & 1 Vict. c. 26, amending the law relating to wills, 889
    —894.—*See* TABLE OF STATUTES in Vol. I.

WINDOWS:

action for darkening, 1108, 9.

WITNESS:

competency of, under stat. 3 & 4 Will. IV. c. 42, s. 26, 27, 825 n., 1097, 8,
    1195.

of the necessary qualifications of witnesses:
    1. use of reason, 876.
    2. such religious belief as to be sensible of the obligation of an
       oath, *ib.*

WITNESS—*continued.*

    3. not convicted of any infamous crime, 877.

    4. not influenced by interest, 878.

to disqualify a witness on the ground of his having been convicted of an infamous offence, a copy of the judgment entered on the record of conviction must be produced, *ib.*

certificated bankrupt having released assignees, may prove property in himself, but cannot prove his own act of bankruptcy, 266, 7.

and this rule holds on cross-examination, 267.

where certificated bankrupt is not a witness, 393.

where bankrupt's declarations, in explanation of his own act, are admissible, 267, 8.

where an uncertificated bankrupt may be a witness, 268.

where a creditor may be a witness, 269.

where assignee may be a witness, *ib.*

husband and wife cannot give evidence either for or against each other, 299.

acceptor of bill of exchange may prove that drawer had no effects in his hands, 375.

payee and indorser may prove bill void for want of stamp, *ib.*

    or for usury, *ib.*

in an action by indorsee against drawer, payee may prove consideration for indorsement, 375, 6.

indorser of note who has received money from the maker to take it up, may prove the note satisfied in an action by indorsee against maker, 393.

book-keeper to carrier is a good witness, without release, 413.

so a journeyman to a baker, 1096.

    or a clerk, *ib.*

so are factors and brokers, 825, 6.

where a person prescribes for common by virtue of a custom within a manor, another commoner is not a good witness, 426, 1194.

but where a person prescribes for common in respect of a messuage, another commoner, claiming common in respect of another messuage, may be a witness to support the right, 426.

secus, if called by plaintiff to negative defendant's right, *ib.*

execution of instrument must be proved by subscribing witness, 537, 879, 880.

exceptions to this rule where subscribing witness becomes interested, 538.

    or dead, *ib.*

    or insane, *ib.*

    or infamous, *ib.*

    or is absent in a foreign country, *ib.*

    or intelligence cannot be obtained of him, upon fair, serious, and diligent inquiry, *ib.*

generally, production of instrument, in pursuance of a notice, does not supersede the necessity of proving it by subscribing witness, 879, 880, 1020 n.

party escaping may be a witness to prove a voluntary escape, 618.

in action for bribery, party giving or receiving bribe may prove the fact, 633.

so person claiming to be first discoverer may be a witness, *ib.*

person who has been convicted of perjury at common law and pardoned, is a competent witness, 634, 877.

tenant in possession cannot be a witness to support his own possession, 752.

a person who is employed to sell goods, and is to receive for his trouble whatever money he can procure for them beyond a stated sum, is a competent witness to prove the contract between buyer and seller, 826.

4 379

WITNESS—*continued.*

servant is a good witness in an action by master for battery of servant, 1102.

so the daughter is a good witness in an action brought by the father for seduction, 1104.

where one of several partners may be a witness, 1141.

where a partner cannot be a witness, 1142.

declarations of persons under whom defendant makes cognizance are not evidence for the plaintiff, 1193.

See EVIDENCE.

WORDS:

actionable in themselves, 1243.

how to be construed, 1246.

words not actionable in themselves, 1248, 9.

subsequently spoken may be given in evidence, 1047 n.

See LIBEL—SLANDER.

WORK AND LABOUR:

new rule containing count for, 66.

uncertificated bankrupt may maintain action for, 245.

WRIT:

of inquiry, under stat. 8 & 9 Will. III. c. 11, may, by 3 & 4 Will. IV. c. 42, s. 16, be executed before sheriff, unless otherwise ordered, 584 n.

THE END.

William Stevens, Printer, Bell Yard, Temple Bar.